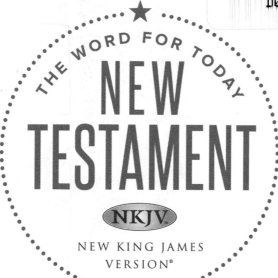

THE WORD FOR TODAY

NEW TESTAMENT

NKJV

NEW KING JAMES
VERSION®

PRESENTED TO:

_____

GIVEN BY:

_____

DATE AND OCCASION:

_____

THE WORD FOR TODAY

NEW TESTAMENT

NKJV.

NEW KING JAMES
VERSION®

WITH COMMENTARY AND STUDY HELPS BY

CHUCK
SMITH

THE WORD
FOR TODAY

P.O. Box 8000 • Costa Mesa, CA 92628 • (800) 272-WORD (9673) • www.twft.com

THE WORD FOR TODAY
NEW TESTAMENT

Copyright © 2015 The Word For Today

ISBN: 978-1-59751-073-8

Sixth Printing, 2023

The Holy Bible, New King James Version
Copyright © 1982 by Thomas Nelson, Inc.

"365 Days Through the Whole Bible"
Copyright © 1996 by The Livingstone Corporation
All Rights Reserved

Printed in the United States of America

TABLE OF CONTENTS

THE NEW TESTAMENT

A WORD FROM
PASTOR
CHUCK

DEAR READER,

You are holding in your hands the most powerful book in the world. This New Testament is a message directly from God to you. Breathed from the Holy Spirit of God, it has the power to change your life. As you prayerfully read it on a daily basis, you will find that it will do more for you than any other undertaking or activity.

Paul told Timothy, "From childhood you have known the Holy Scriptures, which are able to make you wise for salvation through faith which is in Christ Jesus. All Scripture is given by inspiration of God [literally, God-breathed], and is profitable for doctrine, for reproof, for correction, for instruction in righteousness, that the man of God may be complete, thoroughly equipped for every good work" (2 Timothy 3:15–17). As you read this New Testament may you come to salvation, if you haven't already, and may you grow to know God in a more personal way. God will complete anything that is lacking in your life. He promises that He will.

Like Timothy, I was blessed to have a mother who taught me the Word of God from my childhood. I learned to love the Bible from a young age and to live my life by it. It never failed to lead me into the truth. As I continued to read, it spoke more than when I first began to read it. Truly, it is our daily bread.

I believe God has a marvelous work that He wants to do in and through your life as well. And it all starts with reading the Bible. Devote your life to studying it and applying it to your life, and you will see God do things beyond anything you could ever ask or imagine.

May God bless you as you read His Word!

PASTOR CHUCK SMITH

FREQUENTLY ASKED QUESTIONS

HOW DO I KNOW GOD LOVES ME?

In John 3:16 Jesus says, "For God so loved the world that He gave His only begotten Son, that whoever believes in Him should not perish but have everlasting life."

God's love for you is unique for a couple of reasons. Primarily, it is unconditional. Unconditional love means God loves you without you earning it. First John 4:10 says, "In this is love, not that we loved God, but that He loved us and sent His Son to be the propitiation (sacrifice) for our sins."

Secondly, His love is sacrificial. He sent His own Son, Jesus, to die so you would not be condemned as a sinner. Because of His amazing love, Jesus was willing to give the greatest sacrifice in order to have a personal relationship with you forever. Romans 5:8 declares, "But God demonstrates His own love toward us, in that while we were still sinners, Christ died for us."

WHO IS JESUS?

Jesus is God incarnate. He is God in the flesh. John tells us, "And the Word (Jesus) became flesh and dwelt among us, and we beheld His glory, the glory as of the only begotten of the Father, full of grace and truth" (John 1:14). The Bible teaches that God was manifested in His Son; that Jesus was God manifested in the flesh. Jesus was able to say, "He who has seen Me has seen the Father" (John 14:9)—so that when we see God the Father laying upon Jesus the sin of us all, we see Jesus, the Son of God, taking the responsibility for our sin and guilt. When Jesus suffered the cruel death on the cross, we see God dying for our sins.

Don't ever think that Jesus died on the cross in order to persuade God to love you. God so loved you that He sent His only begotten Son that we would not have to perish but have everlasting life. As I look at the life of Jesus, I see the perfection of God. I see righteousness, a life that was totally pure and holy.

Jesus was 100% God, but also 100% man. Many times as we emphasize the divinity of Jesus, we are prone to forget His humanity. The purpose of Jesus taking on a body of flesh was to give us His sympathetic understanding of the weaknesses we experience in our bodies. Paul the apostle encourages us to have the same mind in us that was in Christ Jesus. "Who, being in the form of God, did not consider it robbery to be equal with God, but made Himself of no reputation, taking the form of a bondservant, and coming in the likeness of men" (Philippians 2:6-7). Yes, Jesus was God, but He became man and experienced humanity and the weaknesses that we experience in our flesh.

WHY DID JESUS DIE ON THE CROSS?

The cross has always signified death. In ancient times, the cross was used as a means of execution for criminals. It was a way of torturing a person by inflicting the severest pain and causing them to feel the deepest shame. The convicted person was first physically punished by being beaten and whipped. He was then nailed to a cross where he was left to die a slow and painful death, usually from suffocation.

It is amazing that Jesus offered Himself to die by crucifixion—in the place of every sinner in the whole world. Being born into sin, already guilty, it should have been us up there on the cross. It was an unfair exchange: our guilty lives for His guiltless one. Yet God did it because He loves us and He did not want to be separated from us. (See 1 Peter 3:18). Jesus said, "Greater love has no one than this, than to lay down one's life for his friends" (John 15:13). Now we are made free from spiritual death having "no condemnation to those who are in Christ" (Romans 8:1).

IS THERE ANY EVIDENCE OF THE RESURRECTION OF CHRIST?

Jesus of Nazareth was the only person to ever die and come back to life (resurrection) by His own power. There are documented eyewitness accounts of Jesus' resurrection. In these appearances, the witnesses saw, heard, or touched a fully alive Jesus after He had died and been buried. The witnesses also bore evidence of the empty tomb, linen clothes, and the scars.

Jesus was seen by:

1. Mary and Mary Magdalene (Matthew 28:1-10; Luke 24:10)

2. Two men on the road to Emmaus (Luke 24:13-16)

3. The apostles (Matthew 28:16-17; John 20:19-31)

4. Five hundred people (1 Corinthians 15:6)

5. Paul (formerly known as Saul) (Acts 9:1-9)

There were physical proofs of the resurrection:

1. His empty tomb (Matthew 28:6-15)

2. His linen clothes (Luke 24:12; John 20:6-10)

3. He ate food (Luke 24:30; 41-43; John 21:12-13)

4. He bore scars from the nails (Luke 24:39-40; John 20:27)

5. He was touched by people (Matthew 28:9; Luke 24:39; 1 John 1:1)

6. He was flesh and bones (Luke 24:39)

WHAT IS THE BIBLE?

The Bible is the Word of God. As a new Christian, you will need to use the Bible to grow in your new relationship with God. Jesus Himself said, "Man shall not live by bread alone, but by every word that proceeds from the mouth of God" (Matthew 4:4).

The Bible is composed of many different accounts, letters, and writings that are called the books of the Bible. The sixty-six books are divided into two major sections, the Old Testament and the New Testament. The books themselves are divided into sections called chapters, and the chapters are divided into verses. This makes it easier to locate specific Scriptures. Special notation is used to indicate exactly where you can find a verse in the Bible. For example: John 20:30-31 means the book of John, chapter 20, verses 30 and 31.

The men who wrote these books lived during different periods of history and in different places, writing as they were led by the Spirit of God. Inspired by the Holy Spirit, they wrote God's commands and eternal plans for man. What the Bible contains is God's truth that came from God Himself. Second Peter 1:19-21 reads, "And so we have the prophetic word confirmed, which you do well to heed as a light that shines in a dark place, until the day dawns and the morning star rises in your hearts; knowing this first, that no prophecy of Scripture is of any private interpretation, for prophecy never came by the will of man, but holy men of God spoke as they were moved by the Holy Spirit."

HOW DO I USE THE BIBLE?

1. Pray for understanding before and while you read the Bible.

2. Use the Table of Contents to find the various books of the Bible.

3. Locate a specific chapter and verse by looking at the top of the left and right-hand pages in your Bible.

4. Think about what you read, especially the thoughts that touched your heart. God will use His Word to speak to you.

5. Ask yourself questions. *Is there a promise for me, an action I should take, a truth I must learn, an example I should follow, or something I should pray about?*

6. Highlight and date important places so that you can find them easily again.

7. Believe, memorize, and obey what God says to you!

WHAT DOES THE BIBLE TEACH?

1. The Bible teaches that it is the inspired, infallible (without error), authoritative Word of God. It is important never to accept another book as the Word of God (2 Timothy 3:16; 2 Peter 1:21).

2. The Bible teaches that there is one God, eternally existent in three persons called the Trinity: Father, Son, and Holy Spirit. (Deuteronomy 6:4; Matthew 3:16; 28:19).

3. The Bible teaches that Jesus Christ was born of a virgin (Matthew 1:23), lived a sinless life (Hebrews 4:15, 7:26), performed many miracles (John 2:11), died a violent death and paid the price for our sins through His blood (1 Corinthians 15:3; Hebrews 2:9), was resurrected in body (John 11:25; 1 Corinthians 15:4), ascended to heaven (Mark 16:19), and will return in power and glory (Acts 1:11). Remember, for Jesus to have done this, He had to be God (John 20:28).

4. The Bible teaches that lost and sinful people must be saved and that mankind's only hope of redemption is through the shed blood of Jesus Christ, the Son of God. Only God can save man. Man cannot save himself no matter what he does (Romans 3:23; Ephesians 2:8-10; Titus 3:4-5).

5. The Bible teaches that the present ministry of the Holy Spirit, by His indwelling, enables the Christian to live a godly life (Romans 6:8).

6. The Bible teaches the resurrection of both the saved and the unsaved; the saved unto the resurrection of life and the unsaved unto the resurrection of damnation (John 5:28-29).

7. The Bible teaches that the spiritual unity of believers is in our Lord Jesus Christ and is not limited to any one particular congregation (Romans 8:14-15; 1 Corinthians 12:12-13; Galatians 3:26-28).

WHAT ARE THE BIBLE FACTS?

1. The Bible was written over a period of approximately 4,000 years.

2. It contains 66 books written by 40 different authors.

3. It contains two Testaments, the Old and the New.

4. The Old Testament is comprised of 39 books while the New Testament contains 27.

5. Each Testament can be broken up into four subdivisions:

OLD TESTAMENT
Law: Genesis-Deuteronomy (5 books)
History: Joshua-Esther (12 books)
Poetic: Job-Song of Solomon (5 books)
Prophetic: Isaiah-Malachi (17 books)

NEW TESTAMENT

Gospels: Matthew-John (4 books)
History: Acts (1 book)
Epistles (letters): Romans-Jude (21 books)
Prophetic: Revelation (1 book)

The Old Testament is written in anticipation of the Messiah: Jesus, the Son of God. The New Testament is written from the perspective that the Messiah has come. Although the 66 different books cover a variety of subjects, a common theme runs throughout the whole Bible: Man is a sinner in need of a Savior and that Savior is Jesus Christ.

Therefore, the expectations and prophecies of Jesus' coming are in the Old Testament, and the record and results of Jesus' coming are in the New Testament.

WHAT ARE GOD'S PROMISES?

There are many promises given throughout the Bible that will help you become steadfast and immovable in your walk with the Lord. These promises include assurances of peace, hope, and comfort. Two of the greatest promises God gives you are eternal life (1 John 2:25) and His omnipresence, "I will never leave you nor forsake you" (Hebrews 13:5). These verses alone give you the confidence you need in this life to face trials, as well as the expectation that you will be in heaven with Jesus when you pass from this life to the next.

HOW CAN I BECOME A CHRISTIAN?

If you believe in Jesus as the Son of God and accept Him as your Savior, the guilt of your sin is immediately gone. You no longer stand before God as a sinner but as righteous. You are declared righteous because of your faith in Christ. You are called "born again" because your spirit has just come to life and you are now pure. You are justified.

Justification means that though you were a sinner (guilty), you are pure (not guilty) because Jesus took the consequences of your sins on Himself. This doesn't mean that you won't sin anymore, but it does mean that you are forgiven and sinless in God's eyes. The term "justification" means you are in right standing before God. It's like a trial in which the accused person is acquitted and pronounced "not guilty." To be justified means "just as if I had never sinned."

"For all have sinned and fall short of the glory of God, being justified freely by His grace through the redemption that is in Christ Jesus, whom God set forth as a propitiation by His blood, through faith, to demonstrate His righteousness, because in His forbearance God had passed over the sins that were previously committed, to demonstrate at the present time His righteousness, that He might be just and the justifier of the one who has faith in Jesus" (Romans 3:23-26).

WHY BE HOLY?

The term "sanctification" means "to be made holy" and "to be set apart." This is both a position and a process in the Christian life (see Hebrews 10:10 and 1 Peter 1:2). The moment we are born again we are sanctified, made holy, and set apart for God's purposes. A good example is the life of Jeremiah: "Before I formed you in the womb I knew you; before you were born I sanctified you; I ordained you a prophet to the nations" (Jeremiah 1:5).

Jeremiah the prophet, though he was born into sin, was called to walk holy before God and to be set apart, or sanctified, for the service of God. As you behold the Lord through His Word and through intimate communion with Him, you become more like Him (2 Corinthians 3:18). You don't

become sinless, but reading the Bible in faith actually transforms or changes you and you live a holy life. In Galatians 5:16 the Bible says, "Walk in the Spirit, and you shall not fulfill the lust of the flesh."

WHAT IS GOD'S WILL FOR MY LIFE?

In the simplest sense, God's will is that you serve Him. God wants you to make Him top priority in your life. Jesus said, "But seek first the kingdom of God and His righteousness, and all these things shall be added to you" (Matthew 6:33).

Most people want to know God's personal will for their lives. This can be difficult to figure out since God's personal will is specific to each individual. There are four criteria that you can use to test whether or not something is God's will. Ask yourself:

1. Does this agree with the Word of God?

2. Do I have peace in my heart and sense the Lord confirming it in my heart when I pray?

3. Do the circumstances seem to be lining up—are doors opening?

4. Has God confirmed this through other Christians?

The first two questions should always be answered yes if it is God's will. The second two may be less certain, but all four questions will help you assess whether or not God is guiding you in a certain direction. Keep in mind, even when you are sure God is speaking to you, stepping out takes faith. "For we walk by faith, not by sight" (2 Corinthians 5:7).

WHAT ARE THE THREE ENEMIES OF MY SOUL?

The World, the Flesh, and the Devil. You will always battle these three forces in this life. The first force is the world (your physical environment and its attractions). Concerning the world the apostle John states, "Do not love the world or the things in the world. If anyone loves the world, the love of the Father is not in him. For all that is in the world—the lust of the flesh, the lust of the eyes, and the pride of life—is not of the Father but is of the world. And the world is passing away, and the lust of it; but he who does the will of God abides forever" (1 John 2:15-17).

The second force is your own fleshly desires. "Now the works of the flesh are evident, which are: adultery, fornication, uncleanness, lewdness, idolatry, sorcery, hatred, contentions, jealousies, outbursts of wrath, selfish ambitions, dissensions, heresies, envy, murders, drunkenness, revelries, and the like; of which I tell you beforehand, just as I also told you in time past, that those who practice such things will not inherit the kingdom of God. But the fruit of the Spirit is love, joy, peace, longsuffering, kindness, goodness, faithfulness, gentleness, self-control. Against such there is no law. And those who are Christ's have crucified the flesh with its passions and desires (Galatians 5:19-24).

The third force is the Devil, also called Satan. The Bible says, "Be sober, be vigilant; because your adversary the devil walks about like a roaring lion, seeking whom he may devour" (1 Peter 5:8). "Therefore submit to God. Resist the devil and he will flee from you" (James 4:7).

WHO IS SATAN?

Some say Satan isn't real, but just a figure of speech or a metaphor. His existence is usually challenged by those who deny the supernatural or spiritual realm. However, the Bible emphatically demonstrates that Satan is a real person who should be viewed in a literal sense.

1. The Bible speaks of a spiritual realm in which both angels and demons exist. "For we do not wrestle against flesh and blood, but against principalities, against powers, against the rulers of the darkness of this age, against spiritual hosts of wickedness in the heavenly places" (Ephesians 6:12). The good news is that when Christ was crucified on the cross for our sins, He won the victory over our foes. "Having disarmed principalities and powers, He made a public spectacle of them, triumphing over them in it" (Colossians 2:15).

2. Satan is mentioned throughout the Old and New Testaments, and is referred to more than any other person outside of God the Father, Jesus Christ, and the Holy Spirit.

3. The Bible also attributes a personality to Satan by referring to him with personal pronouns such as "he" and "him." Nearly twenty different names are attributed to Satan throughout the Bible, including: Lucifer, Devil, serpent, dragon, prince of this world, god of this world, angel of light, murderer, father of lies, accuser, and deceiver. It also describes him as having a will, an intellect, knowledge, as well as the emotions of anger, jealousy, and hatred.

4. There are numerous warnings throughout the Bible concerning Satan's attempts to deceive believers. Referring to Satan, Jesus said, "The thief does not come except to steal, and to kill, and to destroy" (John 10:10). He is real and the Word of God warns us strongly about him.

5. Matthew 4:1-11 describes the encounter of Jesus with Satan in the wilderness. This passage describes Satan's attempt to tempt Jesus into not offering His life for the salvation of mankind. It was there Satan took Jesus up on a high mountain and demanded the Son of God to worship him! Satan is not a mere figure of speech, but a real person and our deadliest foe.

HOW CAN I BE VICTORIOUS?

You can draw strength from God and be victorious over the temptations of the world, the desires of your flesh, and attacks of the Devil. To do this, you must immerse yourself in the things of God. In Philippians 4:13, Paul says, "I can do all things through Christ who strengthens me." Paul also exhorts you to set your heart on seeking Jesus so you don't give in to the temptations you face. "I say then: Walk in the Spirit, and you shall not fulfill the lust of the flesh. For the flesh lusts against the Spirit, and the Spirit against the flesh; and these are contrary to one another, so that you do not do the things that you wish" (Galatians 5:16-17).

Scripture also talks about putting on the full spiritual armor of God which is vital to victory (Ephesians 6:11-18). Remember that the victory has already been won, and you are on the winning team through Jesus Christ. Jesus said, "I have overcome the world" (John 16:33); through Him you can overcome and be called more than a conqueror (Romans 8:37).

HOW AND WHY SHOULD I WORSHIP ONLY GOD?

Worship is essential for Christians. The only way to truly worship God is to accept and appreciate His love for you. When you do, worship is a natural response to please God because it results from your personal relationship with Him and love for Him.

If you don't understand who He is, what He has done, and what He wants for you, it will be hard to worship. Ultimately, true worship isn't because of what you can get, but because of who He is. "Behold, God is my salvation, I will trust and not be afraid; 'for YAH, the LORD, is my strength and song; He also has become my salvation'" (Isaiah 12:2).

Worship involves your whole being: your emotional, intellectual, physical, and spiritual self. This is why Jesus said the Father was looking for those that would worship Him in spirit and in truth. "But the hour is coming, and now is, when the true worshipers will worship the Father in spirit and truth; for the Father is seeking such to worship Him. God is Spirit, and those who worship Him must worship in spirit and truth" (John 4:23-24).

WHAT IS WATER BAPTISM?

As Christians, you are commanded to be baptized as a declaration of your faith in Christ. "Go therefore and make disciples of all the nations, baptizing them in the name of the Father and of the Son and of the Holy Spirit" (Matthew 28:19). Jesus also said, "Go into all the world and preach the gospel to every creature. He who believes and is baptized will be saved; but he who does not believe will be condemned" (Mark 16:15-16).

The word "baptize" literally means "to dip" or "immerse." The act of going under water during baptism symbolizes being buried in death. It means you die to your old life and come back to life (resurrect) a changed person (Romans 6:1-4). It is also the appropriate public expression of inward change. Baptism is a testimony of your faith in Jesus Christ.

Some say water baptism is necessary for salvation, but that's not really true. In Scripture, those who were baptized were already believers. Remember, salvation is based upon what Jesus did, not on what you've earned (Ephesians 2:8-9). And since it is only for believers who profess faith in Christ, infants are excluded because they can't make their own profession of faith.

WHAT IS THE BAPTISM OF THE HOLY SPIRIT?

The Holy Spirit is your Helper, and there are three ways you experience Him. The first is called the "with" experience. The Holy Spirit comes alongside you to guide you, convicts you of sin, and helps you come to Jesus. The Holy Spirit is always with you, even before you become a Christian.

The second is the "in" experience. The Holy Spirit lives inside you when you accept Jesus as Lord and Savior. These first two experiences are mentioned in John 14:16-17. The third experience is the "upon" experience. This means the Holy Spirit empowers you for Christian service. The power of God's Spirit will flow through you to touch the lives of those around you. Jesus describes this in John 7:38: "He who believes in Me, as the Scripture has said, out of his heart will flow rivers of living water."

The "upon" experience is also found in Acts 1:8, where Jesus says, "But you shall receive power when the Holy Spirit has come upon you; and you shall be witnesses to Me in Jerusalem, and in all Judea and Samaria, and to the end of the earth." This is what is known as the baptism of the Holy Spirit.

WHAT HAPPENS WHEN I DIE?

When a person's physical body dies, their soul continues to live spiritually, either in heaven or hell. A person is still conscious. Paul states that to be absent from the body is to be present with the Lord (2 Corinthians 5:8). For the believer, death leads to a glorious thing. "Glorification" refers to the final, eternal state of the believer. It means the believer has received a new, transformed heavenly (or glorified) body at the resurrection (2 Corinthians 5:1-4; Philippians 3:21).

IS HEAVEN FOR REAL?

Jesus described heaven as paradise (a place of future happiness) to the repentant thief crucified beside Him. "Assuredly, I say to you, today you will be with Me in Paradise" (Luke 23:43). He also assures you in this verse you will be immediately in the presence of God upon your death.

The original word for "heaven" means "high or lofty" or "that which is above." In heaven there is no sickness, temptation, sorrow, or death. There will be no more pain, suffering, or tears, because God will make all things new. "And God will wipe away every tear from their eyes; there shall be no more death, nor sorrow, nor crying. There shall be no more pain, for the former things have passed away" (Revelation 21:4).

The book of Revelation has many descriptions of heaven including the throne room. "Behold, a throne set in heaven, and One sat on the throne. And He who sat there was like a jasper and a sardius stone in appearance; and there was a rainbow around the throne, in appearance like an emerald" (Revelation 4:2-3). Revelation 5:1-7 describes Jesus sitting on the throne, and the angels worshiping God in verses 8-14. Ultimately, heaven is where we will live in the immediate presence of God and have a personal intimate fellowship with Him throughout eternity (1 Thessalonians 4:17; Revelation 21:1-4).

WHAT IS HELL?

The Bible is very clear about hell. First, it describes hell as a place prepared for the Devil and his angels (who became evil when they turned away from God). People who have died rejecting Jesus as their Lord and Savior are also there (2 Thess. 1:9). Jesus tells us that God the Father "will also say to those on the left hand, 'Depart from Me, you cursed, into the everlasting fire prepared for the devil and his angels'" (Matt. 25:41).

Secondly, Scripture says there is a temporary dwelling place for the wicked who await the final judgment, a place of torment (see Luke 16:22-24). After the final judgment, they will be cast into the lake of fire. "The sea gave up the dead who were in it, and Death and Hades delivered up the dead who were with them. And they were judged, each one according to his works. Then Death and Hades were cast into the lake of fire. This is the second death" (Revelation 20:13-14).

Lastly, whoever goes to hell will never die, but live in torment forever and ever, eternally separated from God. Jesus describes hell as a place where "their worm does not die, and the fire is not quenched" (Mark 9:44, 46, 48).

HOW CAN GOD SEND SOMEONE TO HELL?

God the Father sent His Son to die on the cross so a person wouldn't have to go to hell. Jesus came "to seek and to save that which was lost" (Luke 19:10). So man, by his own choice, chooses hell. He is never sent there by God.

I believe that one day Satan will be cast into this burning lake of fire that God has prepared for him, including all of those who have chosen to rebel. I believe this because the Bible says it. I believe this because Jesus affirms it (see Matthew 25:41; Mark 9:42-48; Revelation 20:13-14). I believe this since God was willing to pay such an awesome price in order to keep men from going to this place.

So rather than foolishly asking, "How can a God of love send a man to hell?" one should truthfully inquire, "How can a man choose to go to hell when God has made all of the provisions to keep him from it?" But rather than ask about hell, perhaps one should ask, "How can I go to heaven?"

HOW CAN A MAN BE
BORN AGAIN?

By Chuck Smith

Jesus said, "Most assuredly, I say to you,
unless one is born again, he cannot see the kingdom of God".

JOHN 3:3

WHAT DOES BORN AGAIN MEAN?

When God originally created man, He created him as a trinity of spirit, mind, and body. With the mind governed by the Spirit, the spirit rules and man lives in communion and fellowship with God.

Plant life is one-dimensional. Having a physical body, it feeds on nutrients from the soil and atmosphere. Animal life, being two-dimensional, possesses a physical body, as well as a consciousness or "mind." But because man has three dimensions—spirit, body, and mind—the added dimension of the spirit puts man a quantum leap above the plant and animal kingdoms, putting him in touch with God.

Jesus said, "God is Spirit, and those who worship Him must worship in spirit and truth" (John 4:24). God designed man for fellowship. However, when a man's spirit is dead, he is reduced to living in the "animal" plane of existence. His thoughts are primarily concerned with his physical needs and appetites.

WHAT CAUSES SPIRITUAL DEATH?

In the beginning, man lived in an ideal, pure environment. He possessed a strong, healthy body with no genetic defects, and since his spirit was alive, he had fellowship and communion with God. But there was a dilemma.

Did man live in fellowship with God because he loved Him? Or did he live in fellowship because there was no other alternative? To reveal man's true heart, God placed an extremely attractive tree in the midst of the garden of Eden: a tree with forbidden fruit, fruit that carried the threat of spiritual death. Man now needed to make a choice. Did he want to continue in fellowship with God, or did he want to satisfy his own fleshly desires at the cost of alienation from God?

Unfortunately, Adam chose to live after the lust of his flesh and he ate of the forbidden fruit. And in so doing, his spirit died. At that moment, man became a two-dimensional being: body (physical) and soul (mind). As a consequence, every person born after Adam was born as a two-dimensional being.

In John 3:7 Jesus told Nicodemus that he had to be born again. Like Nicodemus, we all need to have a spiritual birth. We were born once of the flesh and alienated from God, but if we want to know the blessing and joy that comes from living in fellowship with God, we must be born again of the Spirit. Adam, having killed the spirit, found that there was no way he could resuscitate it by being good, by being religious, or by keeping rules or regulations. We may try to be good, but we can never be good enough.

A natural man can't understand this spiritual dimension. He is without comprehension. Paul wrote to the Corinthians, "For what man knows the things of a man except the spirit of the man which is in him? Even so no one knows the things of God except the Spirit of God. But the natural man does not receive the things of the Spirit of God, for they are foolishness to him; nor can he know them, because they are spiritually discerned" (1 Corinthians 2:11, 14). A natural man cannot know or understand the things of the Spirit. It's foolishness to him. This makes it hard to communicate because a gulf exists between a spirit-governed man and a flesh-governed man.

Have you ever noticed how difficult it is to explain things to a child? It can be frustrating because you think, *Why can't he understand? It's so clear. It's so obvious and rational. Why can't he see?* In spiritual things, a natural man is like a child. If you're going to see this dimension of God's kingdom, it requires a spiritual birth. Therefore, you must be born again.

Without a spiritual birth, at best you're only two-thirds of the person God created you to be. The natural man is somehow subtly conscious of the fact that there's something missing in his life, and he constantly seeks to fill that void. The problem is that he usually seeks to fill that void through a physical or emotional experience. But ultimately, even though a man may gorge himself with physical pleasures or emotional experiences, he still comes up with a sense that something is missing. For nothing can fill that void of the Spirit, except by being born again.

WHAT AM I LIVING FOR?

Worship is an innate part of our existence as humans. If you don't worship the true and living God, then you'll find a substitute. It may be your car or your home or your boat. The list can go on and on forever.

God doesn't want you to live the life of the flesh. He wants you to live the life of the Spirit, and enjoy the blessings and benefits that come from fellowship with Him.

Right now you may be on a dangerous path that leads to destruction. You need to turn to God before you're destroyed. The wonderful promise of God is that if you will just believe in His Son, you will not perish but have everlasting life. Everlasting life is not just quantity; it's quality. You see, quantity without quality is hell. But life in the Spirit possesses a quality of life that is far above the animal (or physical) plane of existence, far above our imagination.

That's the life that God is calling you to, the life of the Spirit, the life of fellowship with Him. God desires for you to experience eternal life, peace, and joy; joy that comes from living in fellowship with God, knowing that He is there with you, guiding you, knowing that God is in control.

HOW CAN I BECOME BORN AGAIN?

A man becomes born again by believing in the loving provision that God made for the forgiveness of your sins, sins that Jesus took upon Himself. Thus, when you receive Jesus as your Savior and believe that He died for your sins, there is a marvelous, mysterious transformation that takes place as your spirit is born. And suddenly, you're living a fuller life with a new dimension of the Spirit that you never knew existed. It is so glorious and wonderful and so far beyond anything that you've ever experienced before. Ask Jesus to become Lord and ruler of your life.

Today you're in one of two camps; it all depends on your relationship to Jesus Christ. You can either believe and look in faith to Jesus, who died for you on the cross; or you can continue going on as you are. It's an amazing thing—to be lost, you don't have to do anything. Just keep on doing what you're doing now and you will perish.

But if you look to the cross and believe in the One who died for your sins, then the free gift of God is yours...the gift of eternal life.

HOW DO I RECEIVE CHRIST?

If you want a personal relationship with God and the assurance that your sins have been forgiven, here is a suggested prayer:

Father, I come to You, confessing my sin and asking for Your forgiveness. I thank You, Lord, for You have promised that if I will confess my sins, You will be faithful to forgive me and cleanse me from all unrighteousness. I want to turn from my sins and live in a way that pleases You. And so I ask for Your help, Lord. I pray for You to give me the power through Your Holy Spirit to live the right way.

I thank You that Jesus Christ died on the cross, paying the price for my sins, and then rose from the dead. I accept Him now as my Savior, my Lord, and my friend. I also thank You, because You've said that whoever comes to You, You will in no way cast out. Thank You for giving me a new life in Christ. I surrender myself to You. Make me what You want me to be. In Jesus' name, amen.

WHAT NEXT?

If you prayed to accept Jesus Christ as your Savior, you have just become born again. Here are four things that will help you to grow as a Christian:

PRAY—prayer is like a telephone line that goes directly to God. It's important to spend time talking to Him every day, the more, the better (see Philippians 4:6).

READ THE BIBLE—the Bible is like a love letter from God. The more you read it, the more you'll fall in love with Him (see 1 Peter 2:2).

FELLOWSHIP—you need friends who share your beliefs and who can encourage you. This is why it's so important to find a good Bible-believing church where you can meet other Christians (see Hebrews 10:24-25). To find a Bible-teaching church in your area, we suggest that you visit **www.calvarychapel.com**

WITNESS TO OTHERS—share your faith in Jesus Christ with others. Pray that the Lord will reveal how you should witness and when (see Mark 16:15).

30-DAY
READING PLAN

DAY 1
Matthew 1-9

DAY 2
Matthew 10-15

DAY 3
Matthew 16-22

DAY 4
Matthew 23-28

DAY 5
Mark 1-8

DAY 6
Mark 9-16

DAY 7
Luke 1-6

DAY 8
Luke 7-11

DAY 9
Luke 12-18

DAY 10
Luke 19-24

DAY 11
John 1-7

DAY 12
John 8-13

DAY 13
John 14-21

DAY 14
Acts 1-7

DAY 15
Acts 8-14

DAY 16
Acts 15-21

DAY 17
Acts 22-28

DAY 18
Romans 1-8

DAY 19
Romans 9-16

DAY 20
1 Corinthians 1-9

DAY 21
1 Corinthians 10-16

DAY 22
2 Corinthians 1-13

DAY 23
Galatians - Ephesians

DAY 24
Philippians - 2 Thessalonians

DAY 25
1 Timothy - Philemon

DAY 26
Hebrews

DAY 27
James - 2 Peter

DAY 28
1 John - Jude

DAY 29
Revelation 1-11

DAY 30
Revelation 12-22

THE GOSPEL ACCORDING TO
MATTHEW

The book of Matthew is the first of the four Gospels, or accounts of the life of Jesus.

Between the conclusion of the book of Malachi and the beginning of the book of Matthew there were four hundred years of silence. During this inter-testamental period there was a lot going on with the nation of Israel, but God was silent.

It was during this time that the Apocryphal Books were written. These are books that are not considered to be canonical by the Protestant church, or by the Jewish scholars, but the Roman Catholic Church has included them in their Scriptures, as has the Eastern Orthodox Church. We reject them on the basis of the fact that the early church rejected them as canonical and because they are never quoted by Jesus or the other authors of the New Testament. So the book of Matthew begins again the revelation of the words of God, following four hundred years of silence.

The book doesn't reveal its author internally, but it was considered to be the work of Matthew, the disciple of Jesus, from a very early date. Matthew, as a tax collector, would certainly have had the ability to write such a book, and many have suggested that since it contains more references to money than any of the other Gospels, a tax collector would be a likely candidate.

This book was obviously written by a Jew and was intended for a Jewish readership. Tradition says that it was originally written in Hebrew and later translated into Greek. We don't know exactly when it was written, but it was clearly completed before AD 70, when the temple was destroyed.

The purpose of the book of Matthew was to present Jesus Christ as Messiah and King. It opens with the genealogy demonstrating that Jesus had the right to reign on the throne of David through the line of His adoptive father Joseph. (Later, in Luke 3, it was established that Jesus was also biologically a descendant of David through His mother Mary.) Throughout Matthew's gospel the evidence is presented to identify Jesus as the fulfillment of the messianic prophecies. Numerous quotes are given from the Old Testament to connect Jesus with prophecy. His miracles and teachings are also presented as further evidence. The Sermon on the Mount, His various kingdom parables, and the Olivet Discourse all point to the kingdom of heaven. It was the clear intention of Matthew that the Jewish people would recognize Jesus as their King and Messiah.

THE GENEALOGY OF JESUS CHRIST

1 The book of the ᵃgenealogy¹of Jesus Christ, ᵇthe Son of David, ᶜthe Son of Abraham:

2 ᵃAbraham begot Isaac, ᵇIsaac begot Jacob, and Jacob begot ᶜJudah and his brothers. 3 ᵃJudah begot Perez and Zerah by Tamar, ᵇPerez begot Hezron, and Hezron begot Ram. 4 Ram begot Amminadab, Amminadab begot Nahshon, and Nahshon begot Salmon. 5 Salmon begot ᵃBoaz by Rahab, Boaz begot Obed by Ruth, Obed begot Jesse, 6 and ᵃJesse begot David the king.

ᵇDavid the king begot Solomon by her ¹who had been the wife of Uriah. 7 ᵃSolomon begot Rehoboam, Rehoboam begot ᵇAbijah, and Abijah begot ¹Asa. 8 Asa begot ᵃJehoshaphat, Jehoshaphat begot Joram, and Joram begot ᵇUzziah. 9 Uzziah begot Jotham, Jotham begot ᵃAhaz, and Ahaz begot Hezekiah. 10 ᵃHezekiah begot Manasseh, Manasseh begot ¹Amon, and Amon begot ᵇJosiah. 11 ᵃJosiah begot ¹Jeconiah and his brothers about the time they were ᵇcarried away to Babylon.

12 And after they were brought to Babylon, ᵃJeconiah begot Shealtiel, and Shealtiel begot ᵇZerubbabel. 13 Zerubbabel begot Abiud, Abiud begot Eliakim, and Eliakim begot Azor. 14 Azor begot Zadok, Zadok begot Achim, and Achim begot Eliud. 15 Eliud begot Eleazar, Eleazar begot Matthan, and Matthan begot Jacob. 16 And Jacob begot Joseph

CHAPTER 1

1 ᵃLuke 3:23
ᵇJohn 7:42
ᶜGen. 12:3; 22:18
¹Lit. generation
2 ᵃGen. 21:2, 12
ᵇGen. 25:26; 28:14
ᶜGen. 29:35
3 ᵃGen. 38:27; 49:10
ᵇRuth 4:18–22
5 ᵃRuth 2:1; 4:1–13
6 ᵃ1Sam. 16:1
ᵇ2Sam. 7:12; 12:24
¹Words in italic type have been added for clarity. They are not found in the original Greek.
7 ᵃ1Chr. 3:10
ᵇ2Chr. 11:20
¹NU Asaph
8 ᵃ1Chr. 3:10
ᵇ2Kin. 15:13
9 ᵃ2Kin. 15:38
10 ᵃ2Kin. 20:21
ᵇ1Kin. 13:2
¹NU Amos
11 ᵃ1Chr. 3:15, 16
ᵇ2Kin. 24:14–16
¹Or Coniah or Jehoiachin
12 ᵃ1Chr. 3:17
ᵇEzra 3:2
16 ᵃMatt. 13:55

Matt. 1:3–6

SHADY RELATIVES

Women were not usually mentioned in genealogies, but this one contains the names of four women, and they weren't the most distinguished of women either. Tamar was a woman who had been disgraced and posed as a prostitute in order to deceive Judah. Rahab was a prostitute in Jericho. Ruth was a Moabitess, and the Moabites were under a curse. And Bathsheba (who was listed but not named) was the woman who had an illicit affair with David, which led to the murder of her husband. What a collection of relatives!

These women were all damaged and tainted, and yet they all appear in the adoptive heritage of Jesus, as they were ancestors of His adoptive father Joseph. And they remind us that the Lord adopts us as well, though we are tainted and damaged. He isn't ashamed of us, His shady relatives.

THE GENEALOGY OF JOSEPH　Matt. 1:1–16

This genealogy is the legal genealogy of Jesus Christ, but it is not the biological genealogy. This traces the lineage of Joseph, the stepfather of Jesus. There is a genealogy in Luke chapter 3 that is the biological genealogy of Jesus through His mother Mary.

This genealogy here in Matthew is important because it demonstrates that Jesus has the legal right to sit on the throne of David. That right would be passed down through the father. This record goes back to David, then to Judah, then to Abraham. This shows Jesus inheriting the right to serve as a Jew, from the tribe of Judah, from the lineage of David.

By contrast, Luke goes through Mary all the way back to Adam, to show that Jesus was biologically human. Both Mary and Joseph were from the lineage of David, but Joseph came through Solomon, while Mary came through Nathan. There were important differences. In verse 11, you see that one of Joseph's ancestors was Jeconiah. But in Jeremiah 22:30, there was a curse put on the house of Jeconiah, saying that none of his descendants would sit on the throne.

If Jesus had been Joseph's son, He couldn't have become king because of this curse. But He was the son of Mary, not Joseph. He inherited the right to rule through Joseph and had the required genetics through Mary.

the husband of ªMary, of whom was born Jesus who is called Christ.

17So all the generations from Abraham to David are fourteen generations, from David until the captivity in Babylon are fourteen generations, and from the captivity in Babylon until the Christ are fourteen generations.

CHRIST BORN OF MARY

18Now the ªbirth of Jesus Christ was as follows: After His mother Mary was betrothed to Joseph, before they came together, she was found with child bof the Holy Spirit. 19Then Joseph her husband, being 1a just man, and not wanting ªto make her a public example, was minded to put her away secretly. 20But while he thought about these things, behold, an angel of the Lord appeared to him in a dream, saying, "Joseph, son of David, do not be afraid to take to you Mary your wife, ªfor that which is 1conceived in her is of the Holy Spirit. 21ªAnd she will bring forth a Son, and you shall call His name 1JESUS, bfor He will save His people from their sins."

Matt. 1:21

Call Him Jesus. Joseph was told, "You shall call His name JESUS, for He will save His people from their sins." The name "Jesus" is a Greek version of the Hebrew name "Joshua," which is a contraction of *Yahweh*, the name for God, and *Shua*, which means "salvation." It is shortened to "Joshua" and describes His mission. Jesus was God, and He came to save. His name describes His nature and His reason for coming.

22So all this was done that it might be fulfilled which was spoken by the Lord through the prophet, saying: 23ª"Behold,1 the virgin shall be with child, and bear a Son, and they shall call His name Immanuel," which is translated, "God with us."

24Then Joseph, being aroused from sleep, did as the angel of the Lord commanded him and took to him his wife, 25and 1did not know her till she had brought forth ªher 2firstborn Son. And he called His name JESUS.

---

18 ª Luke 1:27
b Luke 1:35

19 ª Deut. 24:1
1 *an upright*

20 ª Luke 1:35
1 Lit. *begotten*

21 ª Luke 1:31; 2:21
b John 1:29
1 Lit. *Savior*

23 ª Is. 7:14
1 Words in oblique type in the New Testament are quoted from the Old Testament.

25 ª Luke 2:7, 21
1 Kept her a virgin
2 NU *a Son*

CHAPTER 2

1 ª Luke 2:4–7
b Gen. 25:6
1 Gr. *magoi*

2 ª Luke 2:11
b [Num. 24:17]

4 ª 2 Chr. 36:14
b 2 Chr. 34:13
c Mal. 2:7

6 ª Mic. 5:2
b [Rev. 2:27]

7 ª Num. 24:17
1 Gr. *magoi*

WISE MEN FROM THE EAST

2 Now after ªJesus was born in Bethlehem of Judea in the days of Herod the king, behold, 1wise men bfrom the East came to Jerusalem, 2saying, ª"Where is He who has been born King of the Jews? For we have seen bHis star in the East and have come to worship Him."

Matt. 2:2

The Star of Bethlehem. This star that guided the magi to Bethlehem has been the subject of much speculation. Some suggest that it might have been the conjunction of the planets Jupiter and Saturn that took place in 6 BC. Others have suggested that it was a supernova. But when we find out that it stood over Bethlehem, it is clear that it was a supernatural phenomenon and not anything ordinary. It was a guiding star that was prepared by God. It is as simple as that.

3When Herod the king heard this, he was troubled, and all Jerusalem with him. 4And when he had gathered all ªthe chief priests and bscribes of the people together, che inquired of them where the Christ was to be born. 5So they said to him, "In Bethlehem of Judea, for thus it is written by the prophet:

6   'But ª you, Bethlehem, in the land of Judah,
       Are not the least among the rulers of Judah;
       For out of you shall come a Ruler
     b Who will shepherd My people Israel.'"

7Then Herod, when he had secretly called the 1wise men, determined from them what time the ªstar appeared. 8And he sent them to Bethlehem and said, "Go and search carefully for the young Child, and when you have found Him, bring back word to me, that I may come and worship Him also." 9When they heard the king, they departed; and behold, the star which they had seen in the East went before them, till it came and stood over where the young Child was. 10When they saw the star, they rejoiced with exceedingly

Matt. 2

A MAD GENIUS

If you look at all the structures that were built by Herod the Great, you realize what a genius he was. He built the Herodian Fortress, Masada, the Alexandrian Fortress, the city of Caesarea, and the great wall of Jerusalem in the temple mount area. All these and more testify to the genius of this man.

But he was also paranoid and insane. He was insecure and threatened by everyone. So when he heard from the magi that there was supposed to be a Child born who would be the King of the Jews, he went nuts and tried to destroy all the male children born in the area, thus eliminating any perceived competition.

Selfishness destroys clear thinking, even in a genius. And pride and insecurity will always end in disgrace for the one who gives his life over to it.

great joy. ¹¹And when they had come into the house, they saw the young Child with Mary His mother, and fell down and worshiped Him. And when they had opened their treasures, ᵃthey presented gifts to Him: gold, frankincense, and myrrh.

¹²Then, being divinely warned ᵃin a dream that they should not return to Herod, they departed for their own country another way.

THE FLIGHT INTO EGYPT

¹³Now when they had departed, behold, an angel of the Lord appeared to Joseph in a dream, saying, "Arise, take the young Child and His mother, flee to Egypt, and stay there until I bring you word; for Herod will seek the young Child to destroy Him."

¹⁴When he arose, he took the young Child and His mother by night and departed for Egypt, ¹⁵and was there until the death of Herod, that it might be fulfilled which was spoken by the

11 ᵃ Is. 60:6

12 ᵃ Matt. 1:20

15 ᵃ Hos. 11:1

18 ᵃ Jer. 31:15

20 ᵃ Luke 2:39
ᵇ Matt. 2:16

22 ᵃ Matt. 2:12, 13, 19
ᵇ Luke 2:39

23 ᵃ John 1:45, 46
ᵇ Judg. 13:5

Lord through the prophet, saying, ᵃ"Out of Egypt I called My Son."

MASSACRE OF THE INNOCENTS

¹⁶Then Herod, when he saw that he was deceived by the wise men, was exceedingly angry; and he sent forth and put to death all the male children who were in Bethlehem and in all its districts, from two years old and under, according to the time which he had determined from the wise men. ¹⁷Then was fulfilled what was spoken by Jeremiah the prophet, saying:

18   "Aᵃvoice was heard in Ramah,
      Lamentation, weeping, and great
        mourning,
      Rachel weeping for her children,
      Refusing to be comforted,
      Because they are no more."

THE HOME IN NAZARETH

¹⁹Now when Herod was dead, behold, an angel of the Lord appeared in a dream to Joseph in Egypt, ²⁰ᵃsaying, "Arise, take the young Child and His mother, and go to the land of Israel, for those who ᵇsought the young Child's life are dead." ²¹Then he arose, took the young Child and His mother, and came into the land of Israel.

²²But when he heard that Archelaus was reigning over Judea instead of his father Herod, he was afraid to go there. And being warned by God in a ᵃdream, he turned aside ᵇinto the region of Galilee. ²³And he came and dwelt in a city called ᵃNazareth, that it might be fulfilled ᵇwhich was spoken by the prophets, "He shall be called a Nazarene."

Matt. 2:13–23

Bethlehem, Egypt, & Nazareth.
We see in this chapter that Jesus fulfilled the prophecies that the Messiah would be born in Bethlehem, would come out of Egypt, and would be called a Nazarene. What are the chances that one person could fulfill all these prophecies? But Mary and Joseph were away from home, so He would be born in Bethlehem. Herod went crazy, so they would flee to Egypt. And Jerusalem wasn't safe, so they moved to Nazareth. Amazing details, all predicted ahead of time.

JOHN THE BAPTIST PREPARES THE WAY

3 In those days ᵃJohn the Baptist came preaching ᵇin the wilderness of Judea, ²and saying, "Repent, for ᵃthe kingdom of heaven is at hand!" ³For this is he who was spoken of by the prophet Isaiah, saying:

> ᵃ"The voice of one crying in the wilderness:
> ᵇ'Prepare the way of the LORD;
> Make His paths straight.'"

⁴Now ᵃJohn himself was clothed in camel's hair, with a leather belt around his waist; and his food was ᵇlocusts and ᶜwild honey. ⁵ᵃThen Jerusalem, all Judea, and all the region around the Jordan went out to him ⁶ᵃand were baptized by him in the Jordan, confessing their sins.

⁷But when he saw many of the Pharisees and Sadducees coming to his baptism, he said to them, ᵃ"Brood of vipers! Who warned you to flee from ᵇthe wrath to come? ⁸Therefore bear fruits worthy of repentance, ⁹and do not think to say to yourselves, ᵃ'We have Abraham as our father.' For I say

CHAPTER 3

1 ᵃ Mark 1:3–8
ᵇ Josh. 14:10

2 ᵃ Dan. 2:44

3 ᵃ Is. 40:3
ᵇ Luke 1:76

4 ᵃ Mark 1:6
ᵇ Lev. 11:22
ᶜ 1 Sam. 14:25, 26

5 ᵃ Mark 1:5

6 ᵃ Acts 19:4, 18

7 ᵃ Matt. 12:34
ᵇ [1 Thess. 1:10]

9 ᵃ John 8:33

10 ᵃ Matt. 7:19

11 ᵃ Luke 3:16
ᵇ [Acts 2:3, 4]
1 M omits and fire

12 ᵃ Mal. 3:3

Matt. 3:2

A WORD FROM THE LORD

The people of God hadn't heard anything from Him for four hundred years. Now God broke the silence, and the first word He said was "Repent." The word "repent" means "to turn around" and when you are headed in the wrong direction, that is precisely what you need to do.

John said, "Repent, for the kingdom of heaven is at hand!" The kingdom of heaven is God ruling. He will rule one day on the earth, but the kingdom of heaven can come to us here and now if we allow Him to rule and reign in our lives and hearts. If He is reigning in your heart right now, then you are now in the kingdom of heaven. It just takes repentance.

Matt. 3:7–9

PHARISEES AND SADDUCEES

The Pharisees and Sadducees were two groups of religious leaders with whom Jesus had problems throughout His ministry. At this point, they came out to see John the Baptist in the wilderness.

The Pharisees, who were the legalists of the day, tried to keep the Mosaic Law meticulously. They are the ones who wrote the Talmud. They were self-righteous religionists.

The Sadducees were the materialists of the day. They wore religious garb but they didn't believe in angels, spirits, or the resurrection. They were purely materialists. They were basically the liberals of the day, while the Pharisees were the conservatives.

Both groups came out to see John the Baptist, and he called them both out to repent of their hypocrisy. He said, "Your lives haven't really changed. Show some fruits of repentance." He warned them of a coming fire that would destroy those who weren't fruitful.

John wasn't impressed with outward religion, and neither is God. Dressing religiously, talking religiously, and even acting religiously, just doesn't cut it. God looks for a change of heart, and He desires a real relationship.

to you that God is able to raise up children to Abraham from these stones. ¹⁰And even now the ax is laid to the root of the trees. ᵃTherefore every tree which does not bear good fruit is cut down and thrown into the fire. ¹¹I indeed baptize you with water unto repentance, but He who is coming after me is mightier than I, whose sandals I am not worthy to carry. ᵇHe will baptize you with the Holy Spirit ¹and fire. ¹²ᵃHis winnowing fan is in His hand,

and He will thoroughly clean out His threshing floor, and gather His wheat into the barn; but He will b burn up the chaff with unquenchable fire."

Matt. 3:16–17

The Trinity in Action. At the baptism of Jesus, we see the three persons of the Godhead. Jesus is seen coming out of the water. The Holy Spirit descends upon Jesus. Then God the Father speaks from heaven, "This is My beloved Son, in whom I am well pleased."

Among other doctrinal errors, the error of modalism is certainly refuted by this scene. Modalism teaches that there is one God who sometimes appears as the Father, sometimes as the Son, and sometimes as the Holy Spirit. But here they are, all three together at once.

12 b Matt. 13:30

13 a Mark 1:9–11
b Matt. 2:22

16 a Mark 1:10
b John 1:32
1 Or he

17 a John 12:28
b Ps. 2:7

CHAPTER 4

1 a Mark 1:12
b Ezek. 3:14

JOHN BAPTIZES JESUS

13 a Then Jesus came b from Galilee to John at the Jordan to be baptized by him. 14 And John tried to prevent Him, saying, "I need to be baptized by You, and are You coming to me?" 15 But Jesus answered and said to him, "Permit it to be so now, for thus it is fitting for us to fulfill all righteousness." Then he allowed Him.

16 a When He had been baptized, Jesus came up immediately from the water; and behold, the heavens were opened to Him, and 1 He saw b the Spirit of God descending like a dove and alighting upon Him. 17 a And suddenly a voice came from heaven, saying, b "This is My beloved Son, in whom I am well pleased."

SATAN TEMPTS JESUS

4 Then a Jesus was led up by b the Spirit into the wilderness to be tempted by the devil. 2 And when He had fasted forty days and forty nights, afterward He was hungry. 3 Now when the tempter came to Him, he said, "If You are the Son of God, command that these stones become bread."

THE TEMPTATION OF JESUS   Matt. 4:1–11

Jesus came to the earth to bridge the gap between God and man. The gap was so vast, it could never have been bridged by man reaching out to God. It required God reaching out to man. Paul has told us in 1 Timothy 2:5 that "there is one God and one Mediator between God and men, the Man Christ Jesus." Hebrews 2:14–18 explains that in order to be our High Priest, He had to suffer as we do. And in Hebrews 4:15 we are told, "For we do not have a High Priest who cannot sympathize with our weaknesses, but was in all points tempted as we are, yet without sin."

Here in Matthew 4, we see the account of Jesus being tempted by Satan. This temptation was necessary to qualify Jesus as our High Priest. The first temptation from Satan suggested that since Jesus is the Son of God, and since He was hungry, that He should turn stones into bread. This was the temptation to allow the flesh to rule over the Spirit. The second temptation, as Satan took Him up to the pinnacle of the temple, was to throw Himself down from the pinnacle, and to let the angels save Him. Here Satan took a verse out of context and tried to get Jesus to presumptuously test God. The third temptation Satan offered was that he would give to Jesus all the kingdoms of the world if He would just bow down to him. Jesus had come to save the world, and to buy it back from the grip and control of Satan. But it would take a horrible death on the cross to accomplish that. Satan was essentially offering Jesus a shortcut. "You don't have to suffer and go to the cross. Just compromise and I'll give You what You want." Jesus responded in each case by quoting Scripture and by resisting the temptation.

We are often tempted by Satan as well and often in these three areas. We are tempted to put our flesh over the Spirit. We are tempted to test God by misusing His Word and by finding loopholes to do what we want to do. And we are tempted to take shortcuts, to find ways of getting satisfaction and fulfillment without going the way of the cross, taking it up daily to follow Jesus. We need to resist Satan's lies with the truth.

4But He answered and said, "It is written, a'*Man shall not live by bread alone, but by every word that proceeds from the mouth of God.*'"

5Then the devil took Him up ainto the holy city, set Him on the pinnacle of the temple, 6and said to Him, "If You are the Son of God, throw Yourself down. For it is written:

a'*He shall give His angels charge over you,*'

and,

'b*In their hands they shall bear you up,
Lest you dash your foot against a stone.*'"

7Jesus said to him, "It is written again, a'*You shall not 1tempt the LORD your God.*'"

8Again, the devil took Him up on an exceedingly high mountain, and ashowed Him all the kingdoms of the world and their glory. 9And he said to Him, "All these things I will give You if You will fall down and worship me."

10Then Jesus said to him, 1"Away with you, Satan! For it is written, a'*You shall worship the LORD your God, and Him only you shall serve.*'"

11Then the devil aleft Him, and behold, bangels came and ministered to Him.

Matt. 4:10–11

He Who Is in You Is Greater.
After being tempted by Satan, Jesus told him, "Away with you, Satan!" After this word from Jesus, we are told, "Then the devil left Him." Satan had to go. He is under the authority of Jesus. He did come back to attack many other times, but each time Jesus overcame him. "He who is in you is greater than he who is in the world" (1 John 4:4).

JESUS BEGINS HIS GALILEAN MINISTRY

12aNow when Jesus heard that John had been put in prison, He departed to Galilee. 13And leaving Nazareth, He came and dwelt in Capernaum, which is by the sea, in the regions of Zebulun and Naphtali, 14that it might be fulfilled which was spoken by Isaiah the prophet, saying:

Cross references (center column):
4 a Deut. 8:3
5 a Neh. 11:1, 18
6 a Ps. 91:11 b Ps. 91:12
7 a Deut. 6:16 1 test
8 a [1 John 2:15–17]
10 a Deut. 6:13; 10:20 1 M Get behind Me
11 a [James 4:7] b [Heb. 1:14]
12 a John 4:43
15 a Is. 9:1, 2
16 a Luke 2:32
17 a Mark 1:14, 15 b Matt. 3:2; 10:7 1 has drawn near
18 a Mark 1:16–20 b John 1:40–42

---

15 "The aland of Zebulun and the land of Naphtali,
By the way of the sea, beyond the Jordan,
Galilee of the Gentiles:
16 a The people who sat in darkness have seen a great light,
And upon those who sat in the region and shadow of death Light has dawned."

17aFrom that time Jesus began to preach and to say, b"Repent, for the kingdom of heaven 1is at hand."

FOUR FISHERMEN CALLED AS DISCIPLES

18aAnd Jesus, walking by the Sea of Galilee, saw two brothers, Simon bcalled

---

Matt. 4:23

PREACHING, TEACHING, HEALING

Notice the three aspects of the ministry of Jesus. He was preaching (which is proclaiming the gospel to the lost), He was teaching (instructing the believers from the Scriptures), and He was healing (meeting the personal needs of the people). These three areas represent a balance of what the church should be doing today.

There are some churches where there is a lot of preaching but no teaching. Other churches are proud of their teaching, but they don't reach out to the lost. Still other churches emphasize healing and meeting the material and emotional needs of the people, but they neglect to give them the gospel, or to teach them the Word so they can grow.

We need to balance these three elements in our ministries. We share the gospel with the lost through preaching and teaching the Word, while at the same time reaching them in practical ways to receive God's healing in their lives.

Peter, and Andrew his brother, casting a net into the sea; for they were fishermen. ¹⁹Then He said to them, "Follow Me, and ªI will make you fishers of men." ²⁰ªThey immediately left their nets and followed Him.

²¹ªGoing on from there, He saw two other brothers, James the son of Zebedee, and John his brother, in the boat with Zebedee their father, mending their nets. He called them, ²²and immediately they left the boat and their father, and followed Him.

JESUS HEALS A GREAT MULTITUDE

²³And Jesus went about all Galilee, ªteaching in their synagogues, preaching ᵇthe gospel of the kingdom, ᶜand healing all kinds of sickness and all kinds of disease among the people. ²⁴Then ¹His fame went throughout all Syria; and they ªbrought to Him all sick people who were afflicted with various diseases and torments, and those who were demon-possessed, epileptics, and paralytics; and He healed them. ²⁵ªGreat multitudes followed Him—from Galilee, and from ¹Decapolis, Jerusalem, Judea, and beyond the Jordan.

THE BEATITUDES

5 And seeing the multitudes, ªHe went up on a mountain, and when He was seated His disciples came to

19 ªLuke 5:10
20 ªMark 10:28
21 ªMark 1:19
23 ªMatt. 9:35
ᵇ[Matt. 24:14]
ᶜMark 1:34
24 ªLuke 4:40
¹Lit. the report of Him
25 ªMark 3:7, 8
¹Lit. Ten Cities

CHAPTER 5

1 ªMark 3:13
2 ª[Matt. 7:29]
3 ªLuke 6:20–23
4 ªRev. 21:4
5 ªPs. 37:11
ᵇ[Rom. 4:13]
¹Or land
6 ªLuke 1:53
ᵇ[Is. 55:1; 65:13]
7 ªPs. 41:1
8 ªPs. 15:2; 24:4
ᵇ1 Cor. 13:12
10 ª1 Pet. 3:14
11 ªLuke 6:22
ᵇ1 Pet. 4:14
12 ª1 Pet. 4:13, 14
ᵇActs 7:52

Him. ²Then He opened His mouth and ªtaught them, saying:

3 "Blessedª are the poor in spirit,
    For theirs is the kingdom of heaven.
4   ª Blessed are those who mourn,
    For they shall be comforted.
5   ª Blessed are the meek,
    For ᵇthey shall inherit the ¹earth.
6   Blessed are those who ªhunger and thirst for righteousness,
    ᵇ For they shall be filled.
7   Blessed are the merciful,
    ª For they shall obtain mercy.
8   ª Blessed are the pure in heart,
    For ᵇthey shall see God.
9   Blessed are the peacemakers,
    For they shall be called sons of God.
10 ª Blessed are those who are persecuted for righteousness' sake,
    For theirs is the kingdom of heaven.

¹¹ª"Blessed are you when they revile and persecute you, and say all kinds of ᵇevil against you falsely for My sake. ¹²ªRejoice and be exceedingly glad, for great is your reward in heaven, for ᵇso they persecuted the prophets who were before you.

A DIFFERENT WAY OF LIFE   Matt. 5:3–12

The Sermon on the Mount, which is contained here in Matthew 5–7, outlines the way that Jesus expects His people to live. These aren't commandments for the world; they are the standards for His disciples.

The sermon starts with the Beatitudes. These are the character qualities that should exist in the life of His followers. The word "blessed" means "happy," and these are the qualities that will lead to true happiness. And notice, these aren't the qualities that the world will tell you are the most admirable. These aren't rules for how to win friends and influence people. In fact, these qualities may cause those in the world to resent us. It is a backwards way to happiness.

Those who are "poor in spirit" are those who recognize their own poverty, in light of who the Lord is. Poverty of spirit is the opposite of pride. It causes us to mourn and to be meek. When we realize our poverty and weep over it, we begin to hunger and thirst for righteousness. This leads us to be more merciful. As we recognize our own need for mercy, we begin to show more mercy. This has a cleansing effect on our lives, making us more pure. This enables us to be peacemakers, but some will resent and persecute us.

The ultimate result of all this is to "Rejoice and be exceedingly glad." We have given up so much that the world has to offer, but we get the kingdom of heaven. We've been comforted, we've inherited the earth, we've been filled, we've obtained mercy, we see God, and we are called the sons of God. We are truly blessed and happy to be blessed.

BELIEVERS ARE SALT AND LIGHT

13"You are the salt of the earth; ᵃbut if the salt loses its flavor, how shall it be seasoned? It is then good for nothing but to be thrown out and trampled underfoot by men. 14ᵃ"You are the light of the world. A city that is set on a hill cannot be hidden. 15Nor do they ᵃlight a lamp and put it under a basket, but on a lampstand, and it gives light to all who are in the house. 16Let your light so shine before men, ᵃthat they may see your good works and ᵇglorify your Father in heaven.

Matt. 5:16
Let Your Light Shine. As God works in your life, your light shines. But it is possible to let your light shine in such a way that you attract a lot of attention to yourself, bringing a lot of glory to you. That isn't what God wants. Seeing your glory doesn't help anyone.

Seeing God's glory is a life-and-death issue. When others see our good works, we want them to go away saying, "Isn't God wonderful?"

CHRIST FULFILLS THE LAW

17ᵃ"Do not think that I came to destroy the Law or the Prophets. I did not come to destroy but to fulfill. 18For assuredly, I say to you, ᵃtill heaven and earth pass away, one ¹jot or one ²tittle will by no means pass from the law till all is fulfilled. 19ᵃWhoever therefore breaks one of the least of these commandments, and teaches men so, shall be called least in the kingdom of heaven; but whoever does and teaches them, he shall be called great in the kingdom of heaven. 20For I say to you, that unless your righteousness exceeds ᵃthe righteousness of the scribes and Pharisees, you will by no means enter the kingdom of heaven.

MURDER BEGINS IN THE HEART

21"You have heard that it was said to those ¹of old, ᵃ'*You shall not murder*, and whoever murders will be in danger of the judgment.' 22But I say to you that ᵃwhoever is angry with his brother ¹without a cause shall be in danger of the judgment. And whoever says to his

---

Side notes:
13 ᵃLuke 14:34
14 ᵃ[John 8:12]
15 ᵃLuke 8:16
16 ᵃ1 Pet. 2:12 ᵇ[John 15:8]
17 ᵃRom. 10:4
18 ᵃLuke 16:17 ¹Gr. *iota*, Heb. *yod*, the smallest letter ²The smallest stroke in a Heb. letter
19 ᵃ[James 2:10]
20 ᵃ[Rom. 10:3]
21 ᵃEx. 20:13; Deut. 5:17 ¹*in ancient times*
22 ᵃ[1 John 3:15] ᵇ[James 2:20; 3:6] ¹NU omits *without a cause* ²Lit., in Aram., *Empty head* ³Gr. *More* ⁴Gr. *Gehenna*
23 ᵃMatt. 8:4
24 ᵃ[Job 42:8]
25 ᵃLuke 12:58, 59 ᵇ[Is. 55:6]
27 ᵃEx. 20:14; Deut. 5:18 ¹NU, M omit *to those of old*

Matt. 5:21–32

TOUGH STANDARDS

Jesus took some of the commandments, such as, "You shall not murder" and "You shall not commit adultery," and He expounded on them in such a way that a self-righteous person would be disturbed. A person who takes pride in the fact that they haven't murdered or committed adultery would be rattled by what Jesus said. "Whoever is angry with his brother without a cause shall be in danger of the judgment." "Whoever looks at a woman to lust for her has already committed adultery with her in his heart." This sounds so severe, but only if you believe you can be righteous by your own merits.

The purpose of the Law wasn't to save us; it was to show us that we can't save ourselves. The truth is, sin starts in our hearts. Actions follow, but it starts in the heart. By looking at the heart, Jesus has let us know that we are all guilty. It isn't just "those people." It is all of us. We all need help.

---

brother, ᵇ'Raca!'²shall be in danger of the council. But whoever says, ³'You fool!' shall be in danger of ⁴hell fire. 23Therefore ᵃif you bring your gift to the altar, and there remember that your brother has something against you, 24ᵃleave your gift there before the altar, and go your way. First be reconciled to your brother, and then come and offer your gift. 25ᵃAgree with your adversary quickly, ᵇwhile you are on the way with him, lest your adversary deliver you to the judge, the judge hand you over to the officer, and you be thrown into prison. 26Assuredly, I say to you, you will by no means get out of there till you have paid the last penny.

ADULTERY IN THE HEART

27"You have heard that it was said ¹to those of old, ᵃ'*You shall not commit*

adultery.' [28]But I say to you that whoever [a]looks at a woman to lust for her has already committed adultery with her in his heart. [29a]If your right eye causes you to [1]sin, [b]pluck it out and cast it from you; for it is more profitable for you that one of your members perish, than for your whole body to be cast into hell. [30]And if your right hand causes you to [1]sin, cut it off and cast it from you; for it is more profitable for you that one of your members perish, than for your whole body to be cast into hell.

MARRIAGE IS SACRED AND BINDING

[31]"Furthermore it has been said, [a]'Whoever divorces his wife, let him give her a certificate of divorce.' [32]But I say to you that [a]whoever divorces his wife for any reason except [1]sexual immorality causes her to commit adultery; and whoever marries a woman who is divorced commits adultery.

JESUS FORBIDS OATHS

[33]"Again you have heard that [a]it was said to those of [1]old, [b]'You shall not swear falsely, but [c]shall perform your oaths to the Lord.' [34]But I say to you, [a]do not swear at all: neither by heaven, for it is [b]God's throne; [35]nor by the earth, for it is His footstool; nor by Jerusalem, for it is the city of [a]the great King. [36]Nor shall you swear by your head, because you cannot make one hair white or black. [37a]But let [1]your 'Yes' be 'Yes,' and your 'No,' 'No.' For whatever is more than these is from the evil one.

GO THE SECOND MILE

[38]"You have heard that it was said, [a]'An eye for an eye and a tooth for a tooth.' [39a]But I tell you not to resist an evil person. [b]But whoever slaps you on your right cheek, turn the other to him also. [40]If anyone wants to sue you and take away your tunic, let him have your cloak also. [41]And whoever [a]compels you to go one mile, go with him two. [42]Give to him who asks you, and [a]from him who wants to borrow from you do not turn away.

LOVE YOUR ENEMIES

[43]"You have heard that it was said, [a]'You shall love your neighbor [b]and hate your enemy.' [44][1]But I say to you, [a]love your enemies, bless those who curse you, [b]do good to those who hate you, and pray [c]for those who spitefully use you and persecute you, [45]that you

---

28 [a] Prov. 6:25
29 [a] Mark 9:43
[b] [Col. 3:5]
[1] Lit. stumble or offend
30 [1] Lit. stumble or offend
31 [a] Deut. 24:1
32 [a] [Luke 16:18]
[1] Or fornication
33 [a] Matt. 23:16
[b] Lev. 19:12
[c] Deut. 23:23
[1] ancient times
34 [a] James 5:12
[b] Is. 66:1
35 [a] Ps. 48:2
37 [a] [Col. 4:6]
[1] Lit. your word be yes yes
38 [a] Ex. 21:24; Lev. 24:20; Deut. 19:21
39 [a] Luke 6:29
[b] Is. 50:6
41 [a] Matt. 27:32
42 [a] Luke 6:30–34
43 [a] Lev. 19:18
[b] Deut. 23:3–6
44 [a] Luke 6:27
[b] [Rom. 12:20]
[c] Acts 7:60
[1] NU But I say to you, love your enemies and pray for those who persecute you
45 [a] Job 25:3
46 [a] Luke 6:32
47 [1] M friends
[2] NU Gentiles
48 [a] [Col. 1:28; 4:12]
[b] Eph. 5:1

CHAPTER 6
2 [a] Rom. 12:8
4 [a] Luke 14:12–14
[1] NU omits openly
5 [1] pretenders
6 [a] 2 Kin. 4:33
[1] NU omits openly
7 [a] Eccl. 5:2
[b] 1 Kin. 18:26
8 [a] [Rom. 8:26, 27]
9 [a] Luke 11:2–4
[b] [Matt. 5:9, 16]
[c] Mal. 1:11
10 [a] Matt. 26:42
[b] Ps. 103:20
11 [a] Prov. 30:8
12 [a] [Matt. 18:21, 22]
13 [a] [2 Pet. 2:9]
[b] John 17:15
[1] NU omits the rest of v. 13.

---

may be sons of your Father in heaven; for [a]He makes His sun rise on the evil and on the good, and sends rain on the just and on the unjust. [46a]For if you love those who love you, what reward have you? Do not even the tax collectors do the same? [47]And if you greet your [1]brethren only, what do you do more than others? Do not even the [2]tax collectors do so? [48a]Therefore you shall be perfect, just [b]as your Father in heaven is perfect.

DO GOOD TO PLEASE GOD

6 "Take heed that you do not do your charitable deeds before men, to be seen by them. Otherwise you have no reward from your Father in heaven. [2]Therefore, [a]when you do a charitable deed, do not sound a trumpet before you as the hypocrites do in the synagogues and in the streets, that they may have glory from men. Assuredly, I say to you, they have their reward. [3]But when you do a charitable deed, do not let your left hand know what your right hand is doing, [4]that your charitable deed may be in secret; and your Father who sees in secret [a]will Himself reward you [1]openly.

THE MODEL PRAYER

[5]"And when you pray, you shall not be like the [1]hypocrites. For they love to pray standing in the synagogues and on the corners of the streets, that they may be seen by men. Assuredly, I say to you, they have their reward. [6]But you, when you pray, [a]go into your room, and when you have shut your door, pray to your Father who is in the secret place; and your Father who sees in secret will reward you [1]openly. [7]And when you pray, [a]do not use vain repetitions as the heathen do. [b]For they think that they will be heard for their many words. [8]"Therefore do not be like them. For your Father [a]knows the things you have need of before you ask Him. [9]In this [a]manner, therefore, pray:

[b] Our Father in heaven,
Hallowed be Your [c]name.
10   Your kingdom come.
      [a] Your will be done
      On earth [b]as it is in heaven.
11   Give us this day our [a]daily bread.
12   And [a]forgive us our debts,
      As we forgive our debtors.
13   [a] And do not lead us into
      temptation,
      But [b]deliver us from the evil one.
      [1] For Yours is the kingdom and the

PRAYING TO BE SEEN

Prayer and worship should be between you and God. When it becomes a show for people's benefit in order to impress them with your spirituality, it does more harm than good. Jesus warned against those hypocrites who love to be seen by others when they stand and pray.

Today there has developed, in some circles, the practice of having some people standing during worship while most others are seated. I'm sure in many cases the hearts of the people are good, but it draws attention to people rather than God. I can't judge others, but I know how my heart works; and I don't know if I could help but think, *I hope people notice how spiritual I am, standing here and raising my hands to the Lord while everyone else is sitting down.*

There are all sorts of things we can do in prayer that draw attention to us rather than to God. A super spiritual voice, an enraptured facial expression, a particular way of clasping our hands, a way of holding our head, these are all potential ways of drawing attention to ourselves rather than to God. Be careful.

---

power and the glory forever. Amen.

14 a "For if you forgive men their trespasses, your heavenly Father will also forgive you. 15 But a if you do not forgive men their trespasses, neither will your Father forgive your trespasses.

FASTING TO BE SEEN ONLY BY GOD

16 "Moreover, a when you fast, do not be like the 1hypocrites, with a sad countenance. For they disfigure their faces that they may appear to men to be fasting. Assuredly, I say to you, they have their reward. 17 But you, when you fast, a anoint your head and wash your face, 18 so that you do not appear to men to be fasting, but to your Father who is in the secret place; and your Father who sees in secret will reward you 1 openly.

LAY UP TREASURES IN HEAVEN

19 a "Do not lay up for yourselves treasures on earth, where moth and rust destroy and where thieves break in and steal; 20 but lay up for yourselves treasures in heaven, where neither moth nor rust destroys and where thieves do not break in and steal. 21 For where your treasure is, there your heart will be also.

THE LAMP OF THE BODY

22 a "The lamp of the body is the eye. If therefore your eye is 1good, your whole body will be full of light. 23 But if your eye is 1bad, your whole body will be full of darkness. If therefore the light that is in you is darkness, how great is that darkness!

---

14 a Mark 11:25

15 a Matt. 18:35

16 a Is. 58:3–7
1 pretenders

17 a Ruth 3:3

18 1 NU, M omit openly

19 a Prov. 23:4

20 a Matt. 19:21

22 a Luke 11:34, 35
1 Clear, or healthy

23 1 Evil, or unhealthy

24 a Luke 16:9, 11, 13
b [Gal. 1:10]
1 Lit., in Aram., riches

25 a Luke 12:22

26 a Luke 12:24

27 1 About 18 inches
2 height

You Can't Take It with You. Jesus warned against laying up treasures on earth, "where moth and rust destroy and where thieves break in and steal." If we invest in earthly treasure, it will all be worthless someday. As Greg Laurie says, "You never see a hearse pulling a U-Haul trailer."

On the other hand, the investments you make in eternity will pay eternal dividends. The best investment decision we can make is to include the Lord's work as a significant item in our budgets.

YOU CANNOT SERVE GOD AND RICHES

24 a "No one can serve two masters; for either he will hate the one and love the other, or else he will be loyal to the one and despise the other. b You cannot serve God and 1mammon.

DO NOT WORRY

25 "Therefore I say to you, a do not worry about your life, what you will eat or what you will drink; nor about your body, what you will put on. Is not life more than food and the body more than clothing? 26 a Look at the birds of the air, for they neither sow nor reap nor gather into barns; yet your heavenly Father feeds them. Are you not of more value than they? 27 Which of you by worrying can add one 1cubit to his 2stature?

28"So why do you worry about clothing? Consider the lilies of the field, how they grow: they neither toil nor spin; 29and yet I say to you that even Solomon in all his glory was not 1arrayed like one of these. 30Now if God so clothes the grass of the field, which today is, and tomorrow is thrown into the oven, will He not much more clothe you, O you of little faith?

31"Therefore do not worry, saying, 'What shall we eat?' or 'What shall we drink?' or 'What shall we wear?' 32For after all these things the Gentiles seek. For your heavenly Father knows that you need all these things. 33But aseek first the kingdom of God and His righteousness, and all these things shall be added to you. 34Therefore do not worry about tomorrow, for tomorrow will worry about its own things. Sufficient for the day is its own trouble.

Matt. 6:33

God at the Top. We need to put God first, at the top of our list of priorities. If we do that, He will take care of everything else. "But seek first the kingdom of God and His righteousness, and all these things shall be added to you."

God knows what you need, and He'll take care of your needs. But if you allow other things in your life to be the top priorities, your life will be out of balance. Put Him first, and everything will be in a perfect balance.

DO NOT JUDGE

7 "Judge1 anot, that you be not judged. 2For with what 1judgment you judge, you will be judged; aand with the measure you use, it will be measured back to you. 3aAnd why do you look at the speck in your brother's eye, but do not consider the plank in your own eye? 4Or how can you say to your brother, 'Let me remove the speck from your eye'; and look, a plank is in your own eye? 5Hypocrite! First remove the plank from your own eye, and then you will see clearly to remove the speck from your brother's eye.

6a"Do not give what is holy to the dogs; nor cast your pearls before swine,

---

29 1 dressed

33 a [1 Tim. 4:8]

CHAPTER 7

1 a Rom. 14:3
1 Condemn

2 a Luke 6:38
1 Condemnation

3 a Luke 6:41

6 a Prov. 9:7, 8

7 a [Mark 11:24]

8 a Prov. 8:17

9 a Luke 11:11

11 a Gen. 6:5;
8:21

12 a Luke 6:31
b Gal. 5:14

13 a Luke 13:24

Matt. 7:1–2

YOU WILL BE JUDGED

When I judge someone else, I am then setting the standard by which I am to be judged. Let me suggest that you are probably much more lenient with your own faults than you are with the faults of others. You are much more understanding and forgiving of yourself than you are of others.

How horrible our sins look to us when someone else is committing them! Remember how infuriated David was when Nathan told him the story about the man who took another man's pet lamb and killed it? But when Nathan said, "You are the man," it hit David hard (2 Sam. 12:5–7).

As we look on with horror at the sins of others, we are admitting that we know those things are wrong, thus bringing greater condemnation on ourselves when we do the same thing.

---

lest they trample them under their feet, and turn and tear you in pieces.

KEEP ASKING, SEEKING, KNOCKING

7a"Ask, and it will be given to you; seek, and you will find; knock, and it will be opened to you. 8For aeveryone who asks receives, and he who seeks finds, and to him who knocks it will be opened. 9aOr what man is there among you who, if his son asks for bread, will give him a stone? 10Or if he asks for a fish, will he give him a serpent? 11If you then, abeing evil, know how to give good gifts to your children, how much more will your Father who is in heaven give good things to those who ask Him! 12Therefore, awhatever you want men to do to you, do also to them, for bthis is the Law and the Prophets.

THE NARROW WAY

13a"Enter by the narrow gate; for wide is the gate and broad is the way

Matt. 7:12

The Golden Rule. Jesus gave the statement that has come to be known as "The Golden Rule." It had been stated before by Buddha and others in different ways, but Jesus was the first one to state it positively: "Whatever you want men to do to you, do also to them, for this is the Law and the Prophets."

This is the ethic of Jesus, put simply. This is what the Law was about. Just treat people in the way that you would want to be treated. Is that so difficult? Is that so controversial?

that leads to destruction, and there are many who go in by it. [14]1Because narrow is the gate and 2difficult is the way which leads to life, and there are few who find it.

YOU WILL KNOW THEM BY THEIR FRUITS

[15]a"Beware of false prophets, bwho come to you in sheep's clothing, but inwardly they are ravenous wolves. [16]aYou will know them by their fruits. bDo men gather grapes from thornbushes or figs from thistles? [17]Even so, aevery good tree bears good fruit, but a bad tree bears bad fruit. [18]A good tree cannot bear bad fruit, nor can a bad tree bear good fruit. [19]aEvery tree that

Matt. 7:15–20

Known by Fruit. Jesus provided the barometer by which one can judge his own religious system or the system of another. It comes down to fruit. I have to ask myself, "Is my life really fruitful for the Lord? Does my life demonstrate the character described by the fruit of the Spirit? (Gal. 5:22–23). Has my walk with the Lord made me a kinder, more compassionate person? Or am I critical, judgmental, and angry?" As Jesus said here, "By their fruits you will know them." And you will know yourself the same way.

14 1 NU, M *How narrow . . . !*
2 *confined*

15 a Jer. 23:16
b Mic. 3:5

16 a Matt. 7:20; 12:33
b Luke 6:43

17 a Matt. 12:33

19 a [John 15:2, 6]

21 a Luke 6:46
b Rom. 2:13

22 a Num. 24:4

23 a [2 Tim. 2:19]
b Ps. 5:5; 6:8

24 a Luke 6:47–49

28 a Matt. 13:54

29 a [John 7:46]

does not bear good fruit is cut down and thrown into the fire. [20]Therefore by their fruits you will know them.

I NEVER KNEW YOU

[21]"Not everyone who says to Me, a'Lord, Lord,' shall enter the kingdom of heaven, but he who bdoes the will of My Father in heaven. [22]Many will say to Me in that day, 'Lord, Lord, have we anot prophesied in Your name, cast out demons in Your name, and done many wonders in Your name?' [23]And athen I will declare to them, 'I never knew you; bdepart from Me, you who practice lawlessness!'

BUILD ON THE ROCK

[24]"Therefore awhoever hears these sayings of Mine, and does them, I will liken him to a wise man who built his house on the rock: [25]and the rain descended, the floods came, and the winds blew and beat on that house; and it did not fall, for it was founded on the rock.

[26]"But everyone who hears these sayings of Mine, and does not do them, will be like a foolish man who built his house on the sand: [27]and the rain descended, the floods came, and the winds blew and beat on that house; and it fell. And great was its fall."

[28]And so it was, when Jesus had ended these sayings, that athe people were astonished at His teaching, [29]afor He taught them as one having authority, and not as the scribes.

Matt. 7:28–29

One Having Authority. At the end of the Sermon on the Mount, the people were amazed at the teaching of Jesus. They saw that He was different from the scribes.

The scribes weren't sure of anything. They endlessly tossed ideas back and forth, never coming to authoritative conclusions. They were much like the so-called "scholars" and theologians of today, with many questions but no solid answers. But Jesus taught and still teaches with authority because He is the ultimate authority. He is God.

JESUS CLEANSES A LEPER

8 When He had come down from the mountain, great multitudes followed Him. 2 a And behold, a leper came and b worshiped Him, saying, "Lord, if You are willing, You can make me clean."

3 Then Jesus put out His hand and touched him, saying, "I am willing; be cleansed." Immediately his leprosy a was cleansed.

4 And Jesus said to him, a "See that you tell no one; but go your way, show yourself to the priest, and offer the gift that b Moses c commanded, as a testimony to them."

JESUS HEALS A CENTURION'S SERVANT

5 a Now when Jesus had entered Capernaum, a b centurion came to Him, pleading with Him, 6 saying, "Lord, my servant is lying at home paralyzed, dreadfully tormented."

7 And Jesus said to him, "I will come and heal him."

8 The centurion answered and said, "Lord, a I am not worthy that You should come under my roof. But only b speak a word, and my servant will be healed. 9 For I also am a man under authority, having soldiers under me. And I say to this one, 'Go,' and he goes; and to another, 'Come,' and he comes; and to my servant, 'Do this,' and he does it."

10 When Jesus heard it, He marveled, and said to those who followed, "Assuredly, I say to you, I have not found such great faith, not even in Israel! 11 And I say to you that a many will come from east and west, and sit down with Abraham, Isaac, and Jacob in the kingdom of heaven. 12 But a the sons of the kingdom b will be cast out into outer darkness. There will be weeping and gnashing of teeth." 13 Then Jesus said to the centurion, "Go your way; and as you have believed, so let it be done for you." And his servant was healed that same hour.

PETER'S MOTHER-IN-LAW HEALED

14 a Now when Jesus had come into Peter's house, He saw b his wife's mother lying sick with a fever. 15 So He touched her hand, and the fever left her. And she arose and served 1 them.

MANY HEALED IN THE EVENING

16 a When evening had come, they brought to Him many who were demon-possessed. And He cast out the spirits with a word, and healed all who were sick, 17 that it might be fulfilled which was spoken by Isaiah the prophet, saying:

a "He Himself took our infirmities
And bore our sicknesses."

Cross-references

CHAPTER 8

2 a Mark 1:40–45
b John 9:38

3 a Luke 4:27

4 a Mark 5:43
b Luke 5:14
c Deut. 24:8

5 a Luke 7:1–3
b Matt. 27:54

8 a Luke 15:19, 21
b Ps. 107:20

11 a Mal. 1:11

12 a [Matt. 21:43]
b Luke 13:28

14 a Mark 1:29–31
b 1 Cor. 9:5

15 1 NU, M Him

16 a Luke 4:40, 41

17 a Is. 53:4

LEPROSY HEALED

Matt. 8:2–4

L eprosy was a horrible disease. It would attack the nervous system and take away all sensation. Eventually the body would deteriorate, and the person would die. The leper was removed from society, was forced to live away from his family and friends, and was forbidden to have any contact with the world outside the leper colony.

Leprosy was used in the Bible as a type, or picture, of sin. Sin corrupts us by destroying our sensitivity; it alienates us, then rots our lives. Like leprosy, sin is incurable, apart from a miracle.

Interestingly, although leprosy was incurable, the Law gave a procedure for how to be pronounced clean if one ever was cured of it. No one could be cured, apart from a touch of God, and there were very few examples of healings, but the procedure for verifying a cleansed leper would get a real workout once Jesus arrived on the scene.

One of the most amazing statements in this account is: "Then Jesus put out His hand and touched him." No one touched lepers. If a leper came within 150 feet of other people, he was required to cry out, "Unclean!" But Jesus reached out to touch this man with a touch of compassion, love, caring, and concern.

So many times we think we are untouchable. "The Lord wouldn't want to touch me. My life is so rotten, and I have failed Him so often. Surely He's not interested in me." But Jesus was always interested in the people who needed Him the most. He wants to touch you and heal you.

Matt. 8:16–17

A Busy Day. Jesus had quite a day. He preached the Sermon on the Mount in the morning. He then healed a leper, a centurion's servant, Peter's mother-in-law, many demon-possessed people, and a whole lot of other sick people. Matthew pointed out that it was a fulfillment of Isaiah 53:4–5 as Jesus made it clear that He was the Messiah by healing the sicknesses and infirmities of the people. "He Himself took our infirmities and bore our sicknesses."

THE COST OF DISCIPLESHIP

18And when Jesus saw great multitudes about Him, He gave a command to depart to the other side. 19aThen a certain scribe came and said to Him, "Teacher, I will follow You wherever You go."

20And Jesus said to him, "Foxes have holes and birds of the air have nests, but the Son of Man has nowhere to lay His head."

21aThen another of His disciples said to Him, "Lord, blet me first go and bury my father."

22But Jesus said to him, "Follow Me, and let the dead bury their own dead."

WIND AND WAVE OBEY JESUS

23Now when He got into a boat, His disciples followed Him. 24aAnd suddenly a great tempest arose on the sea, so that the boat was covered with the waves. But He was asleep. 25Then His disciples came to Him and awoke Him, saying, "Lord, save us! We are perishing!"

26But He said to them, "Why are you fearful, O you of little faith?" Then aHe arose and rebuked the winds and the sea, and there was a great calm. 27So the men marveled, saying, 1"Who can this be, that even the winds and the sea obey Him?"

TWO DEMON-POSSESSED MEN HEALED

28aWhen He had come to the other side, to the country of the 1Gergesenes, there met Him two demon-possessed men, coming out of the tombs, exceedingly fierce, so that no one could pass that way. 29And suddenly they cried

---

19 aLuke 9:57, 58

21 aLuke 9:59, 60
b 1Kin. 19:20

24 aMark 4:37

26 aPs. 65:7; 89:9; 107:29

27 1 Lit. *What sort of man is this*

28 aMark 5:1–4
1 NU *Gadarenes*

31 1 NU *send us into*

34 aLuke 5:8; Acts 16:39

CHAPTER 9

1 aMatt. 4:13; 11:23

2 aLuke 5:18–26

---

out, saying, "What have we to do with You, Jesus, You Son of God? Have You come here to torment us before the time?"

30Now a good way off from them there was a herd of many swine feeding. 31So the demons begged Him, saying, "If You cast us out, 1permit us to go away into the herd of swine."

32And He said to them, "Go." So when they had come out, they went into the herd of swine. And suddenly the whole herd of swine ran violently down the steep place into the sea, and perished in the water.

33Then those who kept them fled; and they went away into the city and told everything, including what had happened to the demon-possessed men. 34And behold, the whole city came out to meet Jesus. And when they saw Him, athey begged Him to depart from their region.

Matt. 8:23–27

JESUS ON BOARD

The disciples were in this huge storm in a small boat, and they thought they were going to be killed. Jesus was just sleeping in the back of the boat, seemingly oblivious to the desperate circumstances.

So often, as we find ourselves in the middle of danger, it seems like the Lord is sleeping. "God, why don't You help us? We are sinking fast, and You are not doing anything! Don't You care, Lord?"

But God responds, "O you of little faith!" He knows all about our problems, and He plans to deal with them in His way. When Jesus is on board, you can't sink. That is why it is so important to have Jesus on board. "Even the winds and the sea obey Him." Everything else does too.

JESUS FORGIVES AND HEALS A PARALYTIC

9So He got into a boat, crossed over, aand came to His own city. 2aThen behold, they brought to Him a paralytic

lying on a bed. bWhen Jesus saw their faith, He said to the paralytic, "Son, be of good cheer; your sins are forgiven you."

3And at once some of the scribes said within themselves, "This Man blasphemes!"

4But Jesus, aknowing their thoughts, said, "Why do you think evil in your hearts? 5For which is easier, to say, 'Your sins are forgiven you,' or to say, 'Arise and walk'? 6But that you may know that the Son of Man has power on earth to forgive sins"—then He said to the paralytic, "Arise, take up your bed, and go to your house." 7And he arose and departed to his house.

8Now when the multitudes saw it, they amarveled1 and glorified God, who had given such power to men.

Matt. 9:1–8

Healing the Paralytic. Some friends brought this paralyzed man to Jesus. Jesus said, "Son, be of good cheer; your sins are forgiven you."

There were probably three different responses to this announcement. His friends probably thought, "No, Lord. We didn't bring him here to have his sins forgiven. We wanted him to be healed." The scribes were outraged because Jesus was claiming divinity by forgiving sins as only God can do. But the paralyzed man was, no doubt, thrilled to be free of his sins. "I don't care if I walk again; I've been forgiven!" Then Jesus also healed him.

MATTHEW THE TAX COLLECTOR

9aAs Jesus passed on from there, He saw a man named Matthew sitting at the tax office. And He said to him, "Follow Me." So he arose and followed Him.

10aNow it happened, as Jesus sat at the table in the house, that behold, many tax collectors and sinners came and sat down with Him and His disciples. 11And when the Pharisees saw it, they said to His disciples, "Why does your Teacher eat with atax collectors and bsinners?"

12When Jesus heard that, He said to

Cross references (center column):
2 b Matt. 8:10
4 a Matt. 12:25
8 a John 7:15
1 NU were afraid
9 a Luke 5:27
10 a Mark 2:15
11 a Matt. 11:19
b [Gal. 2:15]
13 a Hos. 6:6
b 1 Tim. 1:15
1 NU omits to repentance
14 a Luke 5:33–35; 18:12 1 NU brackets often as disputed.
15 a John 3:29
b Acts 13:2, 3; 14:23
1 Lit. sons of the bridechamber
16 1 Lit. that which is put on
17 1 burst

Matt. 9:9

THE CALL OF MATTHEW

Matthew told of the day when he left his profession to follow the Lord. Matthew was a tax collector; and in those days, the tax collectors were even more unpopular than they are today. They were generally shysters who made their real money from graft and corruption. They were basically allowed to keep all the money they could steal. Jesus called Matthew to leave the life of financial security and to follow Him in full-time ministry.

Jesus could take even a despicable character like a crooked tax collector and use him for the kingdom. All it would take was a positive response to the invitation, "Follow Me." That is still all it takes to turn from a life of meaningless corruption to become a servant of the living God. Just follow Him.

---

them, "Those who are well have no need of a physician, but those who are sick. 13But go and learn what this means: a'I desire mercy and not sacrifice.' For I did not come to call the righteous, bbut sinners, 1to repentance."

JESUS IS QUESTIONED ABOUT FASTING

14Then the disciples of John came to Him, saying, a"Why do we and the Pharisees fast 1often, but Your disciples do not fast?"

15And Jesus said to them, "Can athe 1friends of the bridegroom mourn as long as the bridegroom is with them? But the days will come when the bridegroom will be taken away from them, and bthen they will fast. 16No one puts a piece of unshrunk cloth on an old garment; for 1the patch pulls away from the garment, and the tear is made worse. 17Nor do they put new wine into old wineskins, or else the wineskins 1break, the wine is spilled, and the wineskins are ruined. But they put new wine into new wineskins, and both are preserved."

A GIRL RESTORED TO LIFE AND A WOMAN HEALED

18a While He spoke these things to them, behold, a ruler came and worshiped Him, saying, "My daughter has just died, but come and lay Your hand on her and she will live." 19 So Jesus arose and followed him, and so did His a disciples.

20a And suddenly, a woman who had a flow of blood for twelve years came from behind and b touched the hem of His garment. 21 For she said to herself, "If only I may touch His garment, I shall be made well." 22 But Jesus turned around, and when He saw her He said, "Be of good cheer, daughter; a your faith has made you well." And the woman was made well from that hour.

23a When Jesus came into the ruler's house, and saw b the flute players and the noisy crowd wailing, 24 He said to them, a "Make room, for the girl is not dead, but sleeping." And they ridiculed Him. 25 But when the crowd was put outside, He went in and a took her by the hand, and the girl arose. 26 And the a report of this went out into all that land.

TWO BLIND MEN HEALED

27 When Jesus departed from there, a two blind men followed Him, crying out and saying, b "Son of David, have mercy on us!"

28 And when He had come into the house, the blind men came to Him. And Jesus said to them, "Do you believe that I am able to do this?"

They said to Him, "Yes, Lord."

29 Then He touched their eyes, saying, "According to your faith let it be to you." 30 And their eyes were opened. And Jesus sternly warned them, saying, a "See that no one knows it." 31a But when they had departed, they 1 spread the news about Him in all that 2 country.

A MUTE MAN SPEAKS

32a As they went out, behold, they brought to Him a man, mute and demon-possessed. 33 And when the demon was cast out, the mute spoke. And the multitudes marveled, saying, "It was never seen like this in Israel!"

34 But the Pharisees said, a "He casts out demons by the ruler of the demons."

THE COMPASSION OF JESUS

35 Then Jesus went about all the cities and villages, a teaching in their synagogues, preaching the gospel of the kingdom, and healing every sickness and every disease 1 among the people. 36a But when He saw the multitudes, He was moved with compassion for them, because they were 1 weary and scattered, b like sheep having no shepherd. 37 Then He said to His disciples, a "The harvest truly is plentiful, but the laborers are few. 38a Therefore pray the Lord of the harvest to send out laborers into His harvest."

Matt. 9:36

SHEEP WITHOUT SHEPHERDS

Jesus looked at the people with compassion because they were like sheep without shepherds. Their religious system wasn't giving them what they needed the most, but they were finding it in Jesus.

Deep inside the heart of every man is a search for God. Unfortunately, many religious systems actually keep men from God, instead of leading them to God. So many times you hear people preaching about loyalty to a church or to a denomination, when our loyalty should always be to Him, the Good Shepherd. He has compassion for us and will lead us.

THE TWELVE APOSTLES

10 And a when He had called His twelve disciples to Him, He gave them power over unclean spirits, to cast them out, and to heal all kinds of sickness and all kinds of disease. 2 Now the names of the twelve apostles are these: first, Simon, a who is called Peter, and Andrew his brother; James the son of Zebedee, and John his brother; 3 Philip and Bartholomew; Thomas and Matthew the tax collector; James the son of Alphaeus, and 1 Lebbaeus, whose surname was Thaddaeus; 4a Simon the 1 Cananite, and Judas b Iscariot, who also betrayed Him.

SENDING OUT THE TWELVE

5 These twelve Jesus sent out and commanded them, saying: a "Do not go

Cross-references (center column)

18 a Luke 8:41–56

19 a Matt. 10:2–4

20 a Luke 8:43
b Matt. 14:36; 23:5

22 a Luke 7:50; 8:48; 17:19; 18:42

23 a Mark 5:38
b 2 Chr. 35:25

24 a Acts 20:10

25 a Mark 1:31

26 a Matt. 4:24

27 a Matt. 20:29–34
b Luke 18:38, 39

30 a Matt. 8:4

31 a Mark 7:36
1 Lit. *made Him known*
2 Lit. *land*

32 a Matt. 12:22, 24

34 a Luke 11:15

35 a Matt. 4:23
1 NU omits *among the people*

36 a Mark 6:34
b Num. 27:17
1 NU, M *harassed*

37 a Luke 10:2

38 a 2 Thess. 3:1

CHAPTER 10

1 a Luke 6:13

2 a John 1:42

3 1 NU omits *Lebbaeus, whose surname was*

4 a Acts 1:13
b John 13:2, 26
1 NU *Cananaean*

5 a Matt. 4:15

into the way of the Gentiles, and do not enter a city of ᵇthe Samaritans. ⁶ᵃBut go rather to the ᵇlost sheep of the house of Israel. ⁷ᵃAnd as you go, preach, saying, ᵇ'The kingdom of heaven ¹is at hand.' ⁸Heal the sick, ¹cleanse the lepers, ²raise the dead, cast out demons. ᵃFreely you have received, freely give. ⁹ᵃProvide neither gold nor silver nor ᵇcopper in your money belts, ¹⁰nor bag for your journey, nor two tunics, nor sandals, nor staffs; ᵃfor a worker is worthy of his food.

¹¹ᵃ"Now whatever city or town you enter, inquire who in it is worthy, and stay there till you go out. ¹²And when you go into a household, greet it. ¹³ᵃIf the household is worthy, let your peace come upon it. ᵇBut if it is not worthy, let your peace return to you. ¹⁴ᵃAnd whoever will not receive you nor hear your words, when you depart from that house or city, ᵇshake off the dust from your feet. ¹⁵Assuredly, I say to you, ᵃit will be more tolerable for the land of Sodom and Gomorrah in the day of judgment than for that city!

PERSECUTIONS ARE COMING

¹⁶ᵃ"Behold, I send you out as sheep in the midst of wolves. ᵇTherefore be wise as serpents and ᶜharmless¹ as doves. ¹⁷But beware of men, for ᵃthey will deliver you up to councils and ᵇscourge you in their synagogues. ¹⁸ᵃYou will be brought before governors and kings for My sake, as a testimony to them and to the Gentiles. ¹⁹ᵃBut when they deliver you up, do not worry about how or what you should speak. For ᵇit will be given to you in that hour what you should speak; ²⁰ᵃfor

it is not you who speak, but the Spirit of your Father who speaks in you.

²¹ᵃ"Now brother will deliver up brother to death, and a father his child; and children will rise up against parents and cause them to be put to death. ²²And ᵃyou will be hated by all for My name's sake. ᵇBut he who endures to the end will be saved. ²³ᵃWhen they persecute you in this city, flee to another. For assuredly, I say to you, you will not have ᵇgone through the cities of Israel ᶜbefore the Son of Man comes.

²⁴ᵃ"A disciple is not above his teacher, nor a servant above his master. ²⁵It is enough for a disciple that he be like his teacher, and a servant like his master. If ᵃthey have called the master of the house ¹Beelzebub, how much more will they call those of his household! ²⁶Therefore do not fear them. ᵃFor there is nothing covered that will not

---

5 ᵇ John 4:9
6 ᵃ Matt. 15:24
ᵇ Jer. 50:6
7 ᵃ Luke 9:2
ᵇ Matt. 3:2
1 has drawn near
8 ᵃ [Acts 8:18]
1 NU raise the dead, cleanse the lepers
2 M omits raise the dead
9 ᵃ 1 Sam. 9:7
ᵇ Mark 6:8
10 ᵃ 1 Tim. 5:18
11 ᵃ Luke 10:8
13 ᵃ Luke 10:5
ᵇ Ps. 35:13
14 ᵃ Mark 6:11
ᵇ Acts 13:51
15 ᵃ Matt. 11:22, 24
16 ᵃ Luke 10:3
ᵇ Eph. 5:15
ᶜ [Phil. 2:14–16]
1 innocent
17 ᵃ Mark 13:9
ᵇ Acts 5:40; 22:19; 26:11
18 ᵃ 2 Tim. 4:16
19 ᵃ Luke 12:11, 12; 21:14, 15
ᵇ Ex. 4:12
20 ᵃ 2 Sam. 23:2
21 ᵃ Mic. 7:6
22 ᵃ Luke 21:17
ᵇ Mark 13:13
23 ᵃ Acts 8:1
ᵇ [Mark 13:10]
ᶜ Matt. 16:28
24 ᵃ John 15:20
25 ᵃ John 8:48, 52
1 NU, M Beelzebul; a Philistine deity, 2 Kin. 1:2, 3
26 ᵃ Mark 4:22

Matt. 10:25

To Be Like the Master. The goal and desire of every true believer is to be like Jesus. "It is enough for a disciple that he be like his teacher, and a servant like his master." There is a twofold relationship seen here. Jesus is our Teacher, and we are His disciples, or students. He is also the Master, and we are to serve Him. In both cases, our goal is to be what He wants us to be, and He wants us to be like Him. That is enough.

THE SPIRIT WILL SPEAK
Matt. 10:17–20

Jesus warned His disciples they would face persecution; but He promised that, in those times, they wouldn't need to worry about what they should say. "It will be given to you in that hour what you should speak."

A classic example of this is recorded in Acts 7, when Stephen was brought before the Jewish council to defend his faith. Stephen wasn't a trained preacher or orator. He was hired to help feed the widows. But he gave one of the most masterful sermons in the Bible, outlining the history of Israel and calling the people to repentance. He didn't have time to rehearse or plan. It was too late for him to go get a seminary degree. He just opened his mouth; the Spirit spoke, and it was in power.

God will do the same for us. There are times when we find ourselves in a situation that we couldn't have possibly prepared for, and we open our mouths and God speaks on our behalf. We are almost bystanders as the Spirit works in power. God wants to speak to people, and He doesn't need any special abilities on our part. He just needs a mouth and a willing heart.

be revealed, and hidden that will not be known.

JESUS TEACHES THE FEAR OF GOD

27"Whatever I tell you in the dark, ᵃspeak in the light; and what you hear in the ear, preach on the housetops. 28ᵃAnd do not fear those who kill the body but cannot kill the soul. But rather bfear Him who is able to destroy both soul and body in ¹hell. 29Are not two ᵃsparrows sold for a ¹copper coin? And not one of them falls to the ground apart from your Father's will. 30ᵃBut the very hairs of your head are all numbered. 31Do not fear therefore; you are of more value than many sparrows.

CONFESS CHRIST BEFORE MEN

32ᵃ"Therefore whoever confesses Me before men, bhim I will also confess

Matt. 10:32–33

CONFESSING BEFORE MEN

This is heavy duty! If you want Jesus to confess you before the Father, then you need to be confessing Him before men, and you'd better be careful about denying Him before men. Peter made this mistake, as he denied even knowing Jesus. But Jesus lovingly restored him to fellowship. But if you continue to deny Him, and fail to repent, He will deny you.

There are those who use these verses in connection with an altar call, supporting the need to walk forward publicly to accept Jesus. This isn't really what the passage is talking about. Really, Jesus is talking about living our lives daily in obedience to Him, agreeing with what He says about our sins. The word "confess" means "to say the same thing." Confession isn't something you do once in front of people. Confession is a way of life. It is living our lives before others in a way that shows we agree with Jesus on a day-to-day basis.

Cross-references

27 ᵃActs 5:20

28 ᵃLuke 12:4
bLuke 12:5
1 Gr. Gehenna

29 ᵃLuke 12:6, 7
1 Gr. assarion, a coin worth about 1/16 of a denarius

30 ᵃLuke 21:18

32 ᵃLuke 12:8
b[Rev. 3:5]

33 ᵃ2 Tim. 2:12

34 ᵃ[Luke 12:49]

35 ᵃMic. 7:6
1 alienate a man from

36 ᵃJohn 13:18

37 ᵃLuke 14:26

38 ᵃ[Mark 8:34]

39 ᵃJohn 12:25

40 ᵃLuke 9:48

41 ᵃ1 Kin. 17:10

42 ᵃMark 9:41

CHAPTER 11

1 ᵃLuke 23:5

2 ᵃLuke 7:18–35
bMatt. 4:12; 14:3
1 NU sent by his

3 ᵃJohn 6:14

5 ᵃIs. 29:18; 35:4–6
bIs. 61:1

6 ᵃ[Rom. 9:32]

7 ᵃLuke 7:24
b[Eph. 4:14]

before My Father who is in heaven. 33aBut whoever denies Me before men, him I will also deny before My Father who is in heaven.

CHRIST BRINGS DIVISION

34ᵃ"Do not think that I came to bring peace on earth. I did not come to bring peace but a sword. 35For I have come to ᵃ'set¹ a man against his father, a daughter against her mother, and a daughter-in-law against her mother-in-law'; 36and ᵃ'a man's enemies will be those of his own household.' 37ᵃHe who loves father or mother more than Me is not worthy of Me. And he who loves son or daughter more than Me is not worthy of Me. 38ᵃAnd he who does not take his cross and follow after Me is not worthy of Me. 39ᵃHe who finds his life will lose it, and he who loses his life for My sake will find it.

A CUP OF COLD WATER

40ᵃ"He who receives you receives Me, and he who receives Me receives Him who sent Me. 41ᵃHe who receives a prophet in the name of a prophet shall receive a prophet's reward. And he who receives a righteous man in the name of a righteous man shall receive a righteous man's reward. 42ᵃAnd whoever gives one of these little ones only a cup of cold water in the name of a disciple, assuredly, I say to you, he shall by no means lose his reward."

JOHN THE BAPTIST SENDS MESSENGERS TO JESUS

11 Now it came to pass, when Jesus finished commanding His twelve disciples, that He departed from there to ᵃteach and to preach in their cities.

2ᵃAnd when John had heard bin prison about the works of Christ, he ¹sent two of his disciples 3and said to Him, "Are You ᵃthe Coming One, or do we look for another?"

4Jesus answered and said to them, "Go and tell John the things which you hear and see: 5ᵃThe blind see and the lame walk; the lepers are cleansed and the deaf hear; the dead are raised up and bthe poor have the gospel preached to them. 6And blessed is he who is not ᵃoffended because of Me."

7ᵃAs they departed, Jesus began to say to the multitudes concerning John: "What did you go out into the wilderness to see? bA reed shaken by the wind? 8But what did you go out to see? A man clothed in soft garments? Indeed, those who wear soft clothing

Matt. 11:2–6	9 ªLuke 1:76; 20:6

JOHN WAS WONDERING

10 ªMal. 3:1

John the Baptist had been imprisoned. He knew that Jesus was the Messiah. God had shown him that at the baptism of Jesus. But things weren't progressing the way he had thought they would. Jesus wasn't setting up His kingdom, and John was in jail.

12 ªLuke 16:16

13 ªMal. 4:4–6

It would have been hard for a man like John to be in prison. He didn't even like being in a house. He was an outdoorsman who ate locusts and wild honey. Here he was, confined in a prison, and perhaps wondering if he had been wrong about Jesus. In a sense, he was saying to Jesus, "Come on. Let's get this show on the road! Kick out the Romans and establish Your kingdom." Jesus replied by telling John's disciples of all the healings He was performing and how He was fulfilling the prophecy in Isaiah 35:5.

14 ªLuke 1:17

15 ªLuke 8:8

16 ªLuke 7:31

Often God doesn't act according to our timetable, but it is always according to His eternal plan. He knows what He is doing.

17 ¹Lit. *beat your breast*

GREATER THAN JOHN

Matt. 11:11	

Jesus proclaimed John the Baptist as being the greatest of the prophets, which is pretty amazing when you think of Moses, Daniel, Isaiah, Jeremiah, and so many others. But Jesus then said, "But he who is least in the kingdom of heaven is greater than he." How can that be?

It is because we have a fuller knowledge than John and the other prophets had. They could proclaim judgment and impending doom, while we know fully the love of God as He showed it on the cross. We are the least, but now we know more than they did.

to come. 15 ªHe who has ears to hear, let him hear!

16 ª"But to what shall I liken this generation? It is like children sitting in the marketplaces and calling to their companions, 17and saying:

19 ªMatt. 9:10
b Luke 7:35
1 *wine drinker*
2 NU *works*

> 'We played the flute for you,
>   And you did not dance;
> We mourned to you,
>   And you did not ¹lament.'

18For John came neither eating nor drinking, and they say, 'He has a demon.' 19The Son of Man came eating and drinking, and they say, 'Look, a glutton and a ¹winebibber, ªa friend of tax collectors and sinners!' bBut wisdom is justified by her ²children."

20 ªLuke 10:13–15, 18

WOE TO THE IMPENITENT CITIES

20ªThen He began to rebuke the cities in which most of His mighty works had been done, because they did not repent: 21"Woe to you, Chorazin! Woe to you, Bethsaida! For if the mighty works which were done in you had been done in Tyre and Sidon, they would have repented long ago ªin sackcloth and ashes. 22But I say to you, ªit will be more tolerable for Tyre and Sidon in the day of judgment than for you. 23And you, Capernaum, ªwho¹ are

21 ªJon. 3:6–8

22 ªMatt. 10:15; 11:24

23 ªIs. 14:13
1 NU *will you be exalted to heaven? No, you will be*

are in kings' houses. 9But what did you go out to see? A prophet? Yes, I say to you, ªand more than a prophet. 10For this is he of whom it is written:

> ª'Behold, I send My messenger
>   before Your face,
> Who will prepare Your way
>   before You.'

11"Assuredly, I say to you, among those born of women there has not risen one greater than John the Baptist; but he who is least in the kingdom of heaven is greater than he. 12 ªAnd from the days of John the Baptist until now the kingdom of heaven suffers violence, and the violent take it by force. 13 ªFor all the prophets and the law prophesied until John. 14And if you are willing to receive it, he is ªElijah who is

exalted to heaven, will be brought down to Hades; for if the mighty works which were done in you had been done in Sodom, it would have remained until this day. 24But I say to you ᵃthat it shall be more tolerable for the land of Sodom in the day of judgment than for you."

JESUS GIVES TRUE REST

25ᵃAt that time Jesus answered and said, "I thank You, Father, Lord of heaven and earth, that ᵇYou have hidden these things from the wise and prudent ᶜand have revealed them to babes. 26Even so, Father, for so it seemed good in Your sight. 27ᵃAll things have been delivered to Me by My Father, and no one knows the Son except the Father. ᵇNor does anyone know the Father except the Son, and the one to whom the Son wills to reveal Him. 28Come to ᵃMe, all you who labor and are heavy laden, and I will give you rest. 29Take My yoke upon you ᵃand learn from Me, for I am ¹gentle and ᵇlowly in heart, ᶜand you will find rest for your souls. 30ᵃFor My yoke is easy and My burden is light."

Matt. 11:27–30

COME TO ME

So many of the people thought they knew God, but they really didn't. Jesus pointed out that He is the only One who really knows the Father and that He wants to introduce others to Him. Then He extended the invitation, "Come to Me, all you who labor and are heavy laden, and I will give you rest."

We are carrying many burdens. We have the burden to find pleasure, the burden to succeed, the burden to survive, the burden for meaningful relationships; but most basically, we have the burden to know God. Come to Him.

JESUS IS LORD OF THE SABBATH

12 At that time ᵃJesus went through the grainfields on the Sabbath. And His disciples were hungry, and began to ᵇpluck heads of grain and to eat. 2And when the Pharisees saw it,

24 ᵃMatt. 10:15

25 ᵃLuke 10:21, 22
ᵇPs. 8:2
ᶜMatt. 16:17

27 ᵃMatt. 28:18
ᵇJohn 1:18; 6:46; 10:15

28 ᵃ[John 6:35–37]

29 ᵃ[Phil. 2:5]
ᵇZech. 9:9
ᶜJer. 6:16
¹meek

30 ᵃ[1 John 5:3]

CHAPTER 12

1 ᵃLuke 6:1–5
ᵇDeut. 23:25

3 ᵃ1 Sam. 21:6

4 ᵃLev. 24:5
ᵇEx. 29:32

5 ᵃNum. 28:9
¹desecrate

6 ᵃ[Is. 66:1, 2]

7 ᵃ[Hos. 6:6]

8 ¹NU, M omit even

9 ᵃMark 3:1–6

10 ᵃJohn 9:16

14 ᵃMark 3:6

they said to Him, "Look, Your disciples are doing what is not lawful to do on the Sabbath!" 3But He said to them, "Have you not read ᵃwhat David did when he was hungry, he and those who were with him: 4how he entered the house of God and ate ᵃthe showbread which was not lawful for him to eat, nor for those who were with him, ᵇbut only for the priests? 5Or have you not read in the ᵃlaw that on the Sabbath the priests in the temple ¹profane the Sabbath, and are blameless? 6Yet I say to you that in this place there is ᵃOne greater than the temple. 7But if you had known what this means, ᵃ'I desire mercy and not sacrifice,' you would not have condemned the guiltless. 8For the Son of Man is Lord ¹even of the Sabbath."

Matt. 12:8

The Lord of the Sabbath. The Pharisees were questioning Jesus because His disciples were violating a tradition of the Sabbath by picking heads of grain to eat. He defended His disciples by referring to David and also to the priests who worked on the Sabbath, then got down to the bottom line, which was that Jesus is the One who invented the Sabbath and He can do whatever He wants.

If you stick with Him, you won't need to worry about the rules. He makes the rules.

HEALING ON THE SABBATH

9ᵃNow when He had departed from there, He went into their synagogue. 10And behold, there was a man who had a withered hand. And they asked Him, saying, ᵃ"Is it lawful to heal on the Sabbath?"—that they might accuse Him. 11Then He said to them, "What man is there among you who has one sheep, and if it falls into a pit on the Sabbath, will not lay hold of it and lift it out? 12Of how much more value then is a man than a sheep? Therefore it is lawful to do good on the Sabbath." 13Then He said to the man, "Stretch out your hand." And he stretched it out, and it was restored as whole as the other. 14Then ᵃthe Pharisees went out and

plotted against Him, how they might destroy Him.

BEHOLD, MY SERVANT

15But when Jesus knew it, aHe withdrew from there. bAnd great 1multitudes followed Him, and He healed them all. 16Yet He awarned them not to make Him known, 17that it might be fulfilled which was spoken by Isaiah the prophet, saying:

18 "Behold!a My Servant whom I
      have chosen,
      My Beloved bin whom My soul is
      well pleased!
      I will put My Spirit upon Him,
      And He will declare justice to the
      Gentiles.
19   He will not quarrel nor cry out,
      Nor will anyone hear His voice in
      the streets.
20   A bruised reed He will not
      break,
      And smoking flax He will not
      quench,
      Till He sends forth justice to
      victory;
21   And in His name Gentiles will
      trust."

A HOUSE DIVIDED CANNOT STAND

22aThen one was brought to Him who was demon-possessed, blind and mute; and He healed him, so that the 1blind and mute man both spoke and saw. 23And all the multitudes were amazed and said, "Could this be the aSon of David?"
24aNow when the Pharisees heard it they said, "This fellow does not cast out demons except by 1Beelzebub, the ruler of the demons." 25But Jesus aknew their thoughts, and said to them: "Every kingdom divided against itself is brought to desolation, and every city or house divided against itself will not stand. 26If Satan casts out Satan, he is divided against himself. How then will his kingdom stand? 27And if I cast out demons by Beelzebub, by whom do your sons cast them out? Therefore they shall be your judges. 28But if I cast out demons by the Spirit of God, asurely the kingdom of God has come upon you. 29aOr how can one enter a strong man's house and plunder his goods, unless he first binds the strong man? And then he will plunder his house. 30He who is not with Me is against Me, and he who does not gather with Me scatters abroad.

15 aMark 3:7
b Matt. 19:2
1 NU brackets
multitudes as
disputed.

16 a Matt. 8:4;
9:30; 17:9

18 a Is. 42:1–4;
49:3
b Matt. 3:17;
17:5

22 a Luke 11:14,
15
1 NU omits blind
and

23 a Matt. 9:27;
21:9

24 a Matt. 9:34
1 NU, M
Beelzebul, a
Philistine deity

25 a Matt. 9:4

28 a [Dan. 2:44;
7:14]

29 a Is. 49:24

31 a Mark 3:28–
30
b Acts 7:51

32 a John 7:12,
52
b 1 Tim. 1:13

33 a Matt. 7:16–
18

34 a Matt. 3:7;
23:33
b Luke 6:45
1 Offspring

35 1 NU, M omit
of his heart

38 a Mark 8:11

39 a Matt. 16:4

Matt. 12:30

NO NEUTRALITY

Jesus said, "He who is not with Me is against Me." You can't be neutral concerning Jesus Christ. You are either for Him or against Him, and there is no ground of neutrality. He made such radical statements, it eliminates any thought of Him as just a marvelous teacher, a great philosopher, or a remarkable man. He is either the Son of God, or He is a lunatic and a liar. There is no middle ground.

You may say, "I'm not for or against Him." Yes, you are. According to Him, you are against Him.

THE UNPARDONABLE SIN

31"Therefore I say to you, aevery sin and blasphemy will be forgiven men, bbut the blasphemy against the Spirit will not be forgiven men. 32Anyone who aspeaks a word against the Son of Man, bit will be forgiven him; but whoever speaks against the Holy Spirit, it will not be forgiven him, either in this age or in the age to come.

A TREE KNOWN BY ITS FRUIT

33"Either make the tree good and aits fruit good, or else make the tree bad and its fruit bad; for a tree is known by its fruit. 34aBrood1 of vipers! How can you, being evil, speak good things? bFor out of the abundance of the heart the mouth speaks. 35A good man out of the good treasure 1of his heart brings forth good things, and an evil man out of the evil treasure brings forth evil things. 36But I say to you that for every idle word men may speak, they will give account of it in the day of judgment. 37For by your words you will be justified, and by your words you will be condemned."

THE SCRIBES AND PHARISEES ASK FOR A SIGN

38aThen some of the scribes and Pharisees answered, saying, "Teacher, we want to see a sign from You." 39But He answered and said to them, "An evil and aadulterous generation

seeks after a sign, and no sign will be given to it except the sign of the prophet Jonah. ⁴⁰ᵃFor as Jonah was three days and three nights in the belly of the great fish, so will the Son of Man be three days and three nights in the heart of the earth. ⁴¹ᵃThe men of Nineveh will rise up in the judgment with this generation and ᵇcondemn it, ᶜbecause they repented at the preaching of Jonah; and indeed a greater than Jonah is here. ⁴²ᵃThe queen of the South will rise up in the judgment with this generation and condemn it, for she came from the ends of the earth to hear the wisdom of Solomon; and indeed a greater than Solomon is here.

AN UNCLEAN SPIRIT RETURNS

⁴³ᵃ"When an unclean spirit goes out of a man, ᵇhe goes through dry places,

Matt. 12:31–32

BLASPHEMY AGAINST THE SPIRIT

The Holy Spirit draws people to Jesus Christ. That is His job. He convicts you of sin and points the way to Jesus. But if you reject Jesus and refuse to come to Him, there is no other way to be saved.

The longer you reject Jesus, the easier it is to reject Him. That is the road that leads to the unpardonable sin. Continual rejection of the call of the Spirit will leave you hard and calloused. Eventually, as you continue on the path of rejection, it will be too late. You will die without Jesus, and pardon will be impossible.

There are often people today who are worried that they have blasphemed the Holy Spirit and committed the unpardonable sin. There is a simple way to tell. Do you care? Are you worried about committing this sin? If so, the Holy Spirit is still working on you and you haven't committed the unpardonable sin. If you don't care, who knows?

seeking rest, and finds none. ⁴⁴Then he says, 'I will return to my house from which I came.' And when he comes, he finds it empty, swept, and put in order. ⁴⁵Then he goes and takes with him seven other spirits more wicked than himself, and they enter and dwell there; ᵃand the last state of that man is worse than the first. So shall it also be with this wicked generation."

JESUS' MOTHER AND BROTHERS SEND FOR HIM

⁴⁶While He was still talking to the multitudes, ᵃbehold, His mother and ᵇbrothers stood outside, seeking to speak with Him. ⁴⁷Then one said to Him, "Look, ᵃYour mother and Your brothers are standing outside, seeking to speak with You."

⁴⁸But He answered and said to the one who told Him, "Who is My mother and who are My brothers?" ⁴⁹And He stretched out His hand toward His disciples and said, "Here are My mother and My ᵃbrothers! ⁵⁰For ᵃwhoever does the will of My Father in heaven is My brother and sister and mother."

Matt. 12:47–50

Who Is My Mother? This passage would concern me if I were depending on Mary to intercede for me. I'd be a little worried. Someone told Jesus that His mother and brothers were outside wanting to talk to Him. He replied, "Who is My mother and who are My brothers?"

The glorious truth is that "there is one God and one Mediator between God and men, the Man Christ Jesus" (1 Tim. 2:5). All of us have direct access to Jesus Christ. None of us is worthy to come to Him, but we come because of His worthiness. We can come boldly (Heb. 4:16).

THE PARABLE OF THE SOWER

13 On the same day Jesus went out of the house ᵃand sat by the sea. ²ᵃAnd great multitudes were gathered together to Him, so that ᵇHe got into a boat and sat; and the whole multitude stood on the shore.

³Then He spoke many things to them in parables, saying: ᵃ"Behold, a sower

---

Cross references (center column):

40 ᵃ Jon. 1:17

41 ᵃ Luke 11:32
ᵇ Jer. 3:11
ᶜ Jon. 3:5

42 ᵃ 1 Kin. 10:1–13

43 ᵃ Luke 11:24–26
ᵇ [1 Pet. 5:8]

45 ᵃ [2 Pet. 2:20–22]

46 ᵃ Luke 8:19–21
ᵇ John 2:12; 7:3, 5

47 ᵃ Matt. 13:55, 56

49 ᵃ John 20:17

50 ᵃ John 15:14

CHAPTER 13

1 ᵃ Mark 4:1–12

2 ᵃ Luke 8:4
ᵇ Luke 5:3

3 ᵃ Luke 8:5

went out to sow. [4]And as he sowed, some seed fell by the wayside; and the birds came and devoured them. [5]Some fell on stony places, where they did not have much earth; and they immediately sprang up because they had no depth of earth. [6]But when the sun was up they were scorched, and because they had no root they withered away. [7]And some fell among thorns, and the thorns sprang up and choked them. [8]But others fell on good ground and yielded a crop: some [a]a hundredfold, some sixty, some thirty. [9][a]He who has ears to hear, let him hear!"

THE PURPOSE OF PARABLES

[10]And the disciples came and said to Him, "Why do You speak to them in parables?"

[11]He answered and said to them, "Because [a]it has been given to you to know the [1]mysteries of the kingdom of heaven, but to them it has not been given. [12][a]For whoever has, to him more will be given, and he will have abundance; but whoever does not have, even what he has will be taken away from him. [13]Therefore I speak to them in parables, because seeing they do not see, and hearing they do not hear, nor do they understand. [14]And in them the prophecy of Isaiah is fulfilled, which says:

[a]'Hearing you will hear and shall not understand,
And seeing you will see and not [b]perceive;

[8] [a]Gen. 26:12

[9] [a]Matt. 11:15

[11] [a]Mark 4:10, 11
[1]secret or hidden truths

[12] [a]Matt. 25:29

[14] [a]Is. 6:9, 10
[b][John 3:36]

[15] [a]Heb. 5:11
[b]Luke 19:42
[c]Acts 28:26, 27
[1]NU, M would

[16] [a]Luke 10:23, 24

[17] [a]Heb. 11:13

[18] [a]Mark 4:13–20

[19] [a]Matt. 4:23

[20] [a]Is. 58:2

[21] [a][Acts 14:22]
[b]Matt. 11:6

[22] [a]1 Tim. 6:9
[b]Jer. 4:3

[15] For the hearts of this people have grown dull.
Their ears [a]are hard of hearing,
And their eyes they have [b]closed,
Lest they should see with their eyes and hear with their ears,
Lest they should understand with their hearts and turn,
So that I [1]should [c]heal them.'

[16]But [a]blessed are your eyes for they see, and your ears for they hear; [17]for assuredly, I say to you [a]that many prophets and righteous men desired to see what you see, and did not see it, and to hear what you hear, and did not hear it.

THE PARABLE OF THE SOWER EXPLAINED

[18][a]"Therefore hear the parable of the sower: [19]When anyone hears the word [a]of the kingdom, and does not understand it, then the wicked one comes and snatches away what was sown in his heart. This is he who received seed by the wayside. [20]But he who received the seed on stony places, this is he who hears the word and immediately [a]receives it with joy; [21]yet he has no root in himself, but endures only for a while. For when [a]tribulation or persecution arises because of the word, immediately [b]he stumbles. [22]Now [a]he who received seed [b]among the thorns is he who hears the word, and the cares of this world and the deceitfulness of riches choke the word, and he becomes unfruitful. [23]But he who received seed

---

EARS TO HEAR

Matt. 13:9, 16

After telling the parable of the sower, Jesus said, "He who has ears to hear, let him hear!" Then, in verse 16, He told the disciples that they were blessed because their eyes saw and their ears heard. In the book of Revelation, in the letters to the seven churches in chapters 2 and 3, Jesus repeatedly said, "He who has ears to hear, let him hear." He was not talking about physical hearing, but about real spiritual comprehension.

It is possible to hear something without really understanding it. The natural man, who is devoid of the Spirit of God, lacks the faculties to really comprehend the things of the Spirit. He can't know them because "they are spiritually discerned" (1 Cor. 2:14). There is a danger of people hearing, but not really hearing. Sometimes I hear about a couple who go to Calvary Chapel, and yet they are living together; and I think, *Don't people hear what I'm saying?*

Well, there is a certain kind of hearing that only happens as the Spirit enables a person, allowing them the spiritual capacities to really get it. And in this parable we see that only a fourth of the seed that is sown actually bears fruit. The difference is in the soil. And if a fourth of the people we minister to actually get it, and hear with spiritual ears, then we are within the ratio that Jesus suggests here. But if you want to be one of those who hear, then you need to stay close to Jesus and be filled with the Spirit.

Matt. 13:22
The Cares of This World.

I believe that the seed that is sown among thorns probably represents the largest group of people who are active in churches today. They grow, they develop, but they never bring forth fruit because it is choked out by the cares of the world and the deceitfulness of riches.

How many Christians are just being robbed of fruitfulness because they are too busy trying to get ahead, trying to achieve, caught up in caring about things that don't matter! I think this entails probably the vast majority within the church.

on the good ground is he who hears the word and understands it, who indeed bears [a]fruit and produces: some a hundredfold, some sixty, some thirty."

THE PARABLE OF THE WHEAT AND THE TARES

24Another parable He put forth to them, saying: "The kingdom of heaven is like a man who sowed good seed in his field; 25but while men slept, his enemy came and sowed tares among the wheat and went his way. 26But when the grain had sprouted and produced a crop, then the tares also appeared. 27So the servants of the owner came and said to him, 'Sir, did you not sow good seed in your field? How then does it have tares?' 28He said to them, 'An enemy has done this.' The servants said to him, 'Do you want us then to go and gather them up?' 29But he said, 'No, lest while you gather up the tares you also uproot the wheat with them. 30Let both grow together until the harvest, and at the time of harvest I will say to the reapers, "First gather together the tares and bind them in bundles to burn them, but [a]gather the wheat into my barn."'"

THE PARABLE OF THE MUSTARD SEED

31Another parable He put forth to them, saying: [a]"The kingdom of heaven is like a mustard seed, which a man took and sowed in his field, 32which indeed is the least of all the seeds; but

when it is grown it is greater than the herbs and becomes a [a]tree, so that the birds of the air come and nest in its branches."

THE PARABLE OF THE LEAVEN

33[a]Another parable He spoke to them: "The kingdom of heaven is like leaven, which a woman took and hid in three [1]measures of meal till [b]it was all leavened."

PROPHECY AND THE PARABLES

34[a]All these things Jesus spoke to the multitude in parables; and without a parable He did not speak to them, 35that it might be fulfilled which was spoken by the prophet, saying:

    [a]"I will open My mouth in parables;
    [b]I will utter things kept secret
       from the foundation of the
       world."

THE PARABLE OF THE TARES EXPLAINED

36Then Jesus sent the multitude away and went into the house. And His disciples came to Him, saying, "Explain to us the parable of the tares of the field." 37He answered and said to them: "He who sows the good seed is the Son of Man. 38[a]The field is the world, the good seeds are the sons of the kingdom, but the tares are [b]the sons of the wicked one. 39The enemy who sowed them is the devil, [a]the harvest is the end of the age, and the reapers are the angels. 40Therefore as the tares are gathered and burned in the fire, so it will be at the end of this age. 41The Son of Man will send out His angels, [a]and they will gather out of His kingdom all things that offend, and those who practice lawlessness, 42[a]and will cast them into the furnace of fire. [b]There will be wailing and gnashing of teeth. 43[a]Then the righteous will shine forth as the sun in the kingdom of their Father. [b]He who has ears to hear, let him hear!

THE PARABLE OF THE HIDDEN TREASURE

44"Again, the kingdom of heaven is like treasure hidden in a field, which a man found and hid; and for joy over it he goes and [a]sells all that he has and [b]buys that field.

THE PARABLE OF THE PEARL OF GREAT PRICE

45"Again, the kingdom of heaven is like a merchant seeking beautiful pearls, 46who, when he had found [a]one

---

Center column cross-references:

23 [a]Col. 1:6

30 [a]Matt. 3:12

31 [a]Luke 13:18, 19

32 [a]Ezek. 17:22–24; 31:3–9

33 [a]Luke 13:20, 21
[b][1 Cor. 5:6]
[1]Gr. sata, same as a Heb. seah; approximately 2 pecks in all

34 [a]Mark 4:33, 34

35 [a]Ps. 78:2
[b]Eph. 3:9

38 [a]Rom. 10:18
[b]John 8:44

39 [a]Rev. 14:15

41 [a]Matt. 18:7

42 [a]Rev. 19:20; 20:10
[b]Matt. 8:12; 13:50

43 [a][Dan. 12:3]
[b]Matt. 13:9

44 [a]Phil. 3:7, 8
[b][Is. 55:1]

46 [a]Prov. 2:4; 3:14, 15; 8:10, 19

Matt. 13:44

BURIED TREASURE

Jesus told a parable about a man who found a treasure in a field and sold everything that he had to buy the field in order to get the treasure.

The field is the world. Jesus gave everything to redeem the world to God. Satan offered to give Him the world, but it wasn't really the world that He was after. He purchased the world with His own blood because He wanted a treasure that was hidden in the world. He wanted us. A shortcut would have given Him the world, but we would have been lost, and we are the treasure He was after.

Jesus can make new worlds with just a word, and He will, but He wants us. You are His treasure.

pearl of great price, went and sold all that he had and bought it.

THE PARABLE OF THE DRAGNET

47"Again, the kingdom of heaven is like a dragnet that was cast into the sea and ªgathered some of every kind, 48which, when it was full, they drew to shore; and they sat down and gathered the good into vessels, but threw the bad away. 49So it will be at the end of the age. The angels will come forth, ªseparate the wicked from among the just, 50and cast them into the furnace of fire. There will be wailing and gnashing of teeth."

51 1Jesus said to them, "Have you understood all these things?"

They said to Him, "Yes, 2Lord."

52Then He said to them, "Therefore every 1scribe instructed 2concerning the kingdom of heaven is like a householder who brings out of his treasure ªthings new and old."

JESUS REJECTED AT NAZARETH

53Now it came to pass, when Jesus had finished these parables, that He departed from there. 54ªWhen He had

Cross-references

47 ªMatt. 22:9, 10

49 ªMatt. 25:32

51 1NU omits *Jesus said to them* 2NU omits *Lord*

52 ªSong 7:13 1A scholar of the Old Testament 2Or *for*

54 ªLuke 4:16

55 ªJohn 6:42 bMatt. 12:46 cMark 15:40 1NU *Joseph*

57 ªMatt. 11:6 bLuke 4:24

58 ªMark 6:5, 6

CHAPTER 14

1 ªMark 6:14–29

3 ªLuke 3:19, 20

4 ªLev. 18:16; 20:21

5 ªLuke 20:6

13 ªJohn 6:1, 2

14 ªMark 6:34

15 ªLuke 9:12

come to His own country, He taught them in their synagogue, so that they were astonished and said, "Where did this Man get this wisdom and these mighty works? 55ªIs this not the carpenter's son? Is not His mother called Mary? And bHis brothers cJames, 1Joses, Simon, and Judas? 56And His sisters, are they not all with us? Where then did this Man get all these things?" 57So they ªwere offended at Him.

But Jesus said to them, b"A prophet is not without honor except in his own country and in his own house." 58Now ªHe did not do many mighty works there because of their unbelief.

JOHN THE BAPTIST BEHEADED

14 At that time ªHerod the tetrarch heard the report about Jesus 2and said to his servants, "This is John the Baptist; he is risen from the dead, and therefore these powers are at work in him." 3ªFor Herod had laid hold of John and bound him, and put him in prison for the sake of Herodias, his brother Philip's wife. 4Because John had said to him, ª"It is not lawful for you to have her." 5And although he wanted to put him to death, he feared the multitude, ªbecause they counted him as a prophet.

6But when Herod's birthday was celebrated, the daughter of Herodias danced before them and pleased Herod. 7Therefore he promised with an oath to give her whatever she might ask. 8So she, having been prompted by her mother, said, "Give me John the Baptist's head here on a platter." 9And the king was sorry; nevertheless, because of the oaths and because of those who sat with him, he commanded it to be given to her. 10So he sent and had John beheaded in prison. 11And his head was brought on a platter and given to the girl, and she brought it to her mother. 12Then his disciples came and took away the body and buried it, and went and told Jesus.

FEEDING THE FIVE THOUSAND

13ªWhen Jesus heard it, He departed from there by boat to a deserted place by Himself. But when the multitudes heard it, they followed Him on foot from the cities. 14And when Jesus went out He saw a great multitude; and He ªwas moved with compassion for them, and healed their sick. 15ªWhen it was evening, His disciples came to Him, saying, "This is a deserted place, and the hour is already late. Send the mul-

Matt. 14:13–14

Moved with Compassion. Jesus headed out across the Sea of Galilee to try to get some privacy and rest. But when He got to the other side, thousands of people had followed Him there.

It would've been easy for Him to be irritated or frustrated. He had been working hard and deserved a break. But the people just kept coming with their needs. And Jesus was "moved with compassion for them," and He healed their sick. What an example!

titudes away, that they may go into the villages and buy themselves food."
16But Jesus said to them, "They do not need to go away. You give them something to eat."
17And they said to Him, "We have here only five loaves and two fish."
18He said, "Bring them here to Me."
19Then He commanded the multitudes to sit down on the grass. And He took the five loaves and the two fish, and looking up to heaven, aHe blessed and broke and gave the loaves to the disciples; and the disciples gave to the multitudes. 20So they all ate and were filled, and they took up twelve baskets full of the fragments that remained. 21Now those who had eaten were about five thousand men, besides women and children.

Matt. 14:19

From Jesus to the Disciples to the People. There is an interesting picture here. Jesus gave to the disciples, who in turn gave to the people. This is typical of the way God provides bread for His children.

Paul told the Corinthians, "I received from the Lord that which I also delivered to you" (1 Cor. 11:23). And in my own heart, when I stand up before the congregation, I want to be able to say the same thing. "I am giving to you what I've received from the Lord."

19 a Matt. 15:36; 26:26

22 1 invited, strongly urged

23 a Mark 6:46
b John 6:16

24 1 NU many furlongs away from the land

26 a Job 9:8

27 a Acts 23:11; 27:22, 25, 36
1 Take courage
2 Lit. I am

30 1 NU brackets that and boisterous as disputed.

31 a Matt. 6:30; 8:26

33 a Ps. 2:7
1 NU omits came and

JESUS WALKS ON THE SEA

22Immediately Jesus 1made His disciples get into the boat and go before Him to the other side, while He sent the multitudes away. 23aAnd when He had sent the multitudes away, He went up on the mountain by Himself to pray. bNow when evening came, He was alone there. 24But the boat was now 1in the middle of the sea, tossed by the waves, for the wind was contrary.

Matt. 14:23

Solitude with the Father. Things were beginning to come to a head for Jesus. His fame had now reached Herod, who wanted to see Him. There were crowds who wanted to make Him king prematurely. He had spent a busy day ministering to the needs of the people. He was no doubt exhausted.

So how did He spend the night? In prayer. We would just feel like hitting the sack early. "It's been a tough day. I'm going to bed." But instead Jesus chose to gain strength by communing with the Father, all alone.

25Now in the fourth watch of the night Jesus went to them, walking on the sea. 26And when the disciples saw Him awalking on the sea, they were troubled, saying, "It is a ghost!" And they cried out for fear.
27But immediately Jesus spoke to them, saying, 1"Be of good acheer! 2It is I; do not be afraid."
28And Peter answered Him and said, "Lord, if it is You, command me to come to You on the water."
29So He said, "Come." And when Peter had come down out of the boat, he walked on the water to go to Jesus.
30But when he saw 1that the wind was boisterous, he was afraid; and beginning to sink he cried out, saying, "Lord, save me!"
31And immediately Jesus stretched out His hand and caught him, and said to him, "O you of alittle faith, why did you doubt?" 32And when they got into the boat, the wind ceased.
33Then those who were in the boat 1came and worshiped Him, saying, "Truly aYou are the Son of God."

MANY TOUCH HIM AND ARE MADE WELL

34 aWhen they had crossed over, they came 1to the land of Gennesaret. 35And when the men of that place recognized Him, they sent out into all that surrounding region, brought to Him all who were sick, 36and begged Him that they might only atouch the hem of His garment. And bas many as touched it were made perfectly well.

DEFILEMENT COMES FROM WITHIN

15 Then athe scribes and Pharisees who were from Jerusalem came to Jesus, saying, 2a"Why do Your disciples transgress the tradition of the elders? For they do not wash their hands when they eat bread."

3He answered and said to them, "Why do you also transgress the commandment of God because of your

---

Matt. 15:1–9

TRADITION OVER COMMANDMENT

The scribes and Pharisees were criticizing Jesus because His disciples were not honoring all of their detailed traditions that had developed over the years. Jesus turned it around on them and said that, although they kept all the traditions, they ignored and violated the specific commandments from God. They were "teaching as doctrines the commandments of men." Their traditions were allowing them to circumvent the laws of God.

Tradition is death to a true relationship with God. It allows people to go through the motions without having a heart experience. When the church starts doing things just because "we've always done it that way," it is moving in the direction of a man-made religion. It is just an easy step to go from there to the elevation of tradition to dogma, allowing tradition to crowd out the Word and to excuse violations of the Word.

---

34 a Mark 6:53
1 NU *to land at*

36 a [Mark 5:24–34]
b [Luke 6:19]

CHAPTER 15

1 a Mark 7:1

2 a Mark 7:5

4 a [Deut. 5:16]
b Ex. 21:17

5 a Mark 7:11, 12

6 1 NU omits *or mother*
2 NU *word*

7 a Mark 7:6

8 a Is. 29:13
1 NU omits *draw near to Me with their mouth, And*

9 a [Col. 2:18–22]

10 a Mark 7:14

11 a [Acts 10:15]

13 a [John 15:2]

14 a Luke 6:39

15 a Mark 7:17

16 a Matt. 16:9

17 a [1 Cor. 6:13]

18 a [James 3:6]

---

tradition? 4For God commanded, saying, a'Honor your father and your mother'; and, b'He who curses father or mother, let him be put to death.' 5But you say, 'Whoever says to his father or mother, a"Whatever profit you might have received from me is a gift to God"— 6then he need not honor his father 1or mother.' Thus you have made the 2commandment of God of no effect by your tradition. 7aHypocrites! Well did Isaiah prophesy about you, saying:

8   'These a people 1draw near to Me
        with their mouth,
     And honor Me with their lips,
     But their heart is far from Me.
9   And in vain they worship Me,
     a Teaching as doctrines the
        commandments of men.' "

10aWhen He had called the multitude to Himself, He said to them, "Hear and understand: 11aNot what goes into the mouth defiles a man; but what comes out of the mouth, this defiles a man."

12Then His disciples came and said to Him, "Do You know that the Pharisees were offended when they heard this saying?"

13But He answered and said, a"Every plant which My heavenly Father has not planted will be uprooted. 14Let them alone. aThey are blind leaders of the blind. And if the blind leads the blind, both will fall into a ditch."

15aThen Peter answered and said to Him, "Explain this parable to us."

16So Jesus said, a"Are you also still without understanding? 17Do you not yet understand that awhatever enters the mouth goes into the stomach and is eliminated? 18But athose things which proceed out of the mouth come from

---

Matt. 15:18–20

What Defiles a Man. If you listen to what a person says, it will soon reveal what is in that person's heart. "Evil thoughts, murders, adulteries, fornications, thefts, false witness, blasphemies"— these are the kinds of things that betray a defiled heart.

What do we watch on television? What kind of movies do we enjoy? What do we talk about with others? Be careful. These are indications of our true heart.

the heart, and they defile a man. ¹⁹ᵃFor out of the heart proceed evil thoughts, murders, adulteries, fornications, thefts, false witness, blasphemies. ²⁰These are the things which defile a man, but to eat with unwashed hands does not defile a man."

A GENTILE SHOWS HER FAITH

²¹ᵃThen Jesus went out from there and departed to the region of Tyre and Sidon. ²²And behold, a woman of Canaan came from that region and cried out to Him, saying, "Have mercy on me, O Lord, ᵃSon of David! My daughter is severely demon-possessed."

²³But He answered her not a word. And His disciples came and urged Him, saying, "Send her away, for she cries out after us."

²⁴But He answered and said, ᵃ"I was not sent except to the lost sheep of the house of Israel."

²⁵Then she came and worshiped Him, saying, "Lord, help me!"

²⁶But He answered and said, "It is not good to take the children's bread and throw it to the little ᵃdogs."

²⁷And she said, "Yes, Lord, yet even the little dogs eat the crumbs which fall from their masters' table."

²⁸Then Jesus answered and said to her, "O woman, ᵃgreat is your faith! Let it be to you as you desire." And her daughter was healed from that very hour.

JESUS HEALS GREAT MULTITUDES

²⁹ᵃJesus departed from there, ᵇskirted the Sea of Galilee, and went up on the mountain and sat down there. ³⁰ᵃThen great multitudes came to Him, having with them the lame, blind, mute, ¹maimed, and many others; and they laid them down at Jesus' ᵇfeet, and He healed them. ³¹So the multitude marveled when they saw the mute speaking, the ¹maimed made whole, the lame walking, and the blind seeing; and they ᵃglorified the God of Israel.

FEEDING THE FOUR THOUSAND

³²ᵃNow Jesus called His disciples to Himself and said, "I have compassion on the multitude, because they have now continued with Me three days and have nothing to eat. And I do not want to send them away hungry, lest they faint on the way."

³³ᵃThen His disciples said to Him, "Where could we get enough bread in the wilderness to fill such a great multitude?"

19 ᵃProv. 6:14

21 ᵃMark 7:24–30

22 ᵃMatt. 1:1; 22:41, 42

24 ᵃMatt. 10:5, 6

26 ᵃMatt. 7:6

28 ᵃLuke 7:9

29 ᵃMark 7:31–37
ᵇMatt. 4:18

30 ᵃIs. 35:5, 6
ᵇLuke 7:38; 8:41; 10:39
¹crippled

31 ᵃLuke 5:25, 26; 19:37, 38
¹crippled

32 ᵃMark 8:1–10

33 ᵃ2 Kin. 4:43

36 ᵃMatt. 14:19; 26:27
ᵇLuke 22:19

39 ᵃMark 8:10
¹NU *Magadan*

CHAPTER 16

1 ᵃMark 8:11

Matt. 15:21–28

A GENTILE WITH GREAT FAITH

This Gentile was crying out to the Lord for her daughter to be healed. The response wasn't immediately encouraging. He first just seemed to ignore her. Then He was suggesting that she didn't have a right to come to Him, as she was a Gentile. The disciples were discouraging her as well. But she continued to cry out to Him and to call Him "Lord."

Jesus ultimately healed the woman's daughter and commended her for her faith. "O woman, great is your faith!" Jesus never commended any of His disciples for their great faith, but He commended this Gentile woman for her faithful persistence.

What would He say to us relative to our persistence in prayer? If our prayers are answered partly based on our faith, is it any wonder that we don't see many miracles happening?

³⁴Jesus said to them, "How many loaves do you have?"

And they said, "Seven, and a few little fish."

³⁵So He commanded the multitude to sit down on the ground. ³⁶And ᵃHe took the seven loaves and the fish and ᵇgave thanks, broke them and gave them to His disciples; and the disciples gave to the multitude. ³⁷So they all ate and were filled, and they took up seven large baskets full of the fragments that were left. ³⁸Now those who ate were four thousand men, besides women and children. ³⁹ᵃAnd He sent away the multitude, got into the boat, and came to the region of ¹Magdala.

THE PHARISEES AND SADDUCEES SEEK A SIGN

16 Then the ᵃPharisees and Sadducees came, and testing Him asked that He would show them a sign from heaven. ²He answered and said to

them, "When it is evening you say, 'It will be fair weather, for the sky is red'; [3] and in the morning, 'It will be foul weather today, for the sky is red and threatening.' [1]Hypocrites! You know how to discern the face of the sky, but you cannot discern the signs of the times. [4] [a]A wicked and adulterous generation seeks after a sign, and no sign shall be given to it except the sign of [1]the prophet Jonah." And He left them and departed.

THE LEAVEN OF THE PHARISEES AND SADDUCEES

[5]Now [a]when His disciples had come to the other side, they had forgotten to take bread. [6]Then Jesus said to them, [a]"Take heed and beware of the [1]leaven of the Pharisees and the Sadducees."

Matt. 16:5–12

BEWARE OF HYPOCRISY

Jesus warned His disciples about the danger of becoming hypocrites like the Pharisees and Sadducees, allowing religion to become an outward thing that wasn't real on the inside. For the religious people of the day, it was all an act. Jesus' followers were to be concerned with lasting changes in their hearts.

It is interesting to me that one of the first problems that arose in the early church was the problem of hypocrisy. Ananias and Sapphira had sold a piece of real estate and had given part of the proceeds to the apostles, but pretended like they had given it all. They were lying to God, and God judged them (Acts 5:1–11).

Hypocrisy has probably done more damage to the church throughout history than any other sin. So Jesus was warning His disciples to avoid hypocrisy, to be careful of putting on an act, pretending to be very religious when it isn't there inside.

[7]And they reasoned among themselves, saying, "It is because we have taken no bread." [8]But Jesus, being aware of it, said to them, "O you of little faith, why do you reason among yourselves because you [1]have brought no bread? [9] [a]Do you not yet understand, or remember the five loaves of the five thousand and how many baskets you took up? [10] [a]Nor the seven loaves of the four thousand and how many large baskets you took up? [11]How is it you do not understand that I did not speak to you concerning bread?—but to beware of the [1]leaven of the Pharisees and Sadducees." [12]Then they understood that He did not tell them to beware of the leaven of bread, but of the [1]doctrine of the Pharisees and Sadducees.

PETER CONFESSES JESUS AS THE CHRIST

[13]When Jesus came into the region of Caesarea Philippi, He asked His disciples, saying, [a]"Who do men say that I, the Son of Man, am?" [14]So they said, [a]"Some say John the Baptist, some Elijah, and others Jeremiah or [b]one of the prophets."

Matt. 16:13–16

WHO DO YOU SAY I AM?

In Jesus' day, there were many theories as to who He really was, with some saying John the Baptist, others suggesting Elijah, Jeremiah, or some other prophet. But the crucial question Jesus asked to His disciples was, "But who do you say that I am?"

Peter was commended for his great answer, "You are the Christ, the Son of the living God." He recognized Jesus as the Messiah (the anointed One) and as the Son of God (making Him equal with God).

The most important question you will ever have to answer in your life is this same question: Who is Jesus? Your eternity hangs on the answer to that simple question.

---

3 [1]NU omits *Hypocrites*

4 [a]Matt. 12:39 [1]NU omits *the prophet*

5 [a]Mark 8:14

6 [a]Luke 12:1 [1]*yeast*

8 [1]NU *have no bread*

9 [a]Matt. 14:15–21

10 [a]Matt. 15:32–38

11 [1]*yeast*

12 [1]*teaching*

13 [a]Luke 9:18

14 [a]Matt. 14:2 [b]Matt. 21:11

[15]He said to them, "But who do [a]you say that I am?"

[16]Simon Peter answered and said, [a]"You are the Christ, the Son of the living God."

[17]Jesus answered and said to him, "Blessed are you, Simon Bar-Jonah, [a]for flesh and blood has not revealed this to you, but [b]My Father who is in heaven. [18]And I also say to you that [a]you are Peter, and [b]on this rock I will build My church, and [c]the gates of Hades shall not [1]prevail against it. [19][a]And I will give you the keys of the kingdom of heaven, and whatever you bind on earth [1]will be bound in heaven, and whatever you loose on earth will be loosed in heaven."

[20][a]Then He commanded His disciples that they should tell no one that He was Jesus the Christ.

JESUS PREDICTS HIS DEATH AND RESURRECTION

[21]From that time Jesus began [a]to show to His disciples that He must go to Jerusalem, and suffer many things from the elders and chief priests and scribes, and be killed, and be raised the third day.

[22]Then Peter took Him aside and began to rebuke Him, saying, [1]"Far be it from You, Lord; this shall not happen to You!"

[23]But He turned and said to Peter, "Get behind Me, [a]Satan! [b]You are [1]an offense to Me, for you are not mindful of the things of God, but the things of men."

TAKE UP THE CROSS AND FOLLOW HIM

[24][a]Then Jesus said to His disciples, "If anyone desires to come after Me, let him deny himself, and take up his cross, and [b]follow Me. [25]For [a]whoever desires to save his life will lose it, but whoever loses his life for My sake will find it. [26]For what [a]profit is it to a man if he gains the whole world, and loses his own soul? Or [b]what will a man give in exchange for his soul? [27]For [a]the Son of Man will come in the glory of His Father [b]with His angels, [c]and then He will reward each according to his works.

15 [a] John 6:67
16 [a] Acts 8:37; 9:20
17 [a] [Eph. 2:8] [b] Gal. 1:16
18 [a] John 1:42 [b] [Eph. 2:20] [c] Is. 38:10 [1] be victorious
19 [a] Matt. 18:18 [1] Or will have been bound . . . will have been loosed
20 [a] Luke 9:21
21 [a] Luke 9:22; 18:31; 24:46
22 [1] Lit. Merciful to You, (May God be merciful)
23 [a] Matt. 4:10 [b] [Rom. 8:7] [1] a stumbling block
24 [a] [2 Tim. 3:12] [b] [1 Pet. 2:21]
25 [a] John 12:25
26 [a] Luke 12:20, 21 [b] Ps. 49:7, 8
27 [a] Mark 8:38 [b] [Dan. 7:10] [c] Rom. 2:6

THE CHURCH'S FOUNDATION   Matt. 16:17–19

Much misunderstanding has come from the statements Jesus made to Peter after his confession as to who Jesus was. Jesus talked about this rock being the foundation that His church would be built on. He said that He would give Peter the keys to the kingdom of God, and that whatever he bound on earth would be bound in heaven, and whatever he loosed on earth would be loosed in heaven.

But what we need to understand is that Jesus wasn't saying that Peter was the rock upon which He would build His church. If the church had been built on Peter, it certainly wouldn't have survived. A few verses later Jesus was calling him "Satan." Peter would eventually deny even knowing Jesus.

Rather, Jesus would build His church on the confession of who He is. He was using a play on words, involving Peter's name. The name "Peter" comes from the Greek word for "rock." But the word for Peter is *petros*, which means "little rock," while the word Jesus used for "rock" when He said, "upon this rock I will build My church" is the word *petra*, which means "a great rock." Peter's confession was the great rock upon which the church would be built.

And the keys to the kingdom that Jesus referred to are not some kind of special place that Peter would have in letting people into heaven. The gospel is the key to the kingdom. The declaration of who Jesus is and what He did is what opens the door to heaven, allowing others to make that same declaration that will set them free.

As we introduce people to Jesus and they trust in Him, they are bound to Him on earth and will be bound to Him in heaven. As they are loosed from their sins here on earth, so also will they be loosed forever in heaven, freed from the bondage of sin. It is interesting that Peter was the first one of the disciples to preach the gospel and that he was also the first one to introduce the Gentiles to the gospel. But in doing so he exercised the same privilege that is ours as we take the confession of who Jesus is and share it with the lost and dying world.

JESUS TRANSFIGURED ON THE MOUNT

[28]Assuredly, I say to you, [a]there are some standing here who shall not taste death till they see the Son of Man coming in His kingdom."

17 Now [a]after six days Jesus took Peter, James, and John his brother, led them up on a high mountain by themselves; [2]and He was transfigured before them. His face shone like the sun, and His clothes became as white as the light. [3]And behold, Moses and Elijah appeared to them, talking with Him. [4]Then Peter answered and said to Jesus, "Lord, it is good for us to be here; if You wish, [1]let us make here three tabernacles: one for You, one for Moses, and one for Elijah."

[5][a]While he was still speaking, behold, a bright cloud overshadowed them; and suddenly a voice came out of the cloud, saying, [b]"This is My beloved Son, [c]in whom I am well pleased. [d]Hear Him!" [6][a]And when the disciples heard it, they fell on their faces and were greatly afraid. [7]But Jesus came and [a]touched them and said, "Arise, and do not be afraid." [8]When they had lifted up their eyes, they saw no one but Jesus only.

[9]Now as they came down from the mountain, Jesus commanded them,

---

Matt. 17:1–5

HEAR HIM

Peter, James, and John had gone up into the hills with Jesus; and they saw Him transfigured before their very eyes. Jesus took on the glory of His resurrection body and was standing there talking with Moses and Elijah. Moses represented the Law, and Elijah represented the prophets.

The voice of the Father came from heaven and said, "This is My beloved Son, in whom I am well pleased. Hear Him!" God had spoken through the Law, then through the prophets, but was now speaking through His Son (Heb. 1:1–2). He is the revelation of God.

---

28 [a]Luke 9:27

CHAPTER 17

1 [a]Mark 9:2–8

4 [1]NU *I will make*

5 [a]2 Pet. 1:17
[b]Mark 1:11
[c]Matt. 3:17; 12:18
[d][Deut. 18:15, 19]

6 [a]2 Pet. 1:18

7 [a]Dan. 8:18

10 [a]Mal. 4:5

11 [a][Mal. 4:6]
[1]NU omits *first*

12 [a]Mark 9:12, 13
[b]Matt. 14:3, 10
[c]Matt. 16:21

13 [a]Matt. 11:14

14 [a]Mark 9:14–28

15 [1]Lit. *moonstruck*

17 [a]Phil. 2:15
[1]*unbelieving*

18 [a]Luke 4:41

---

saying, "Tell the vision to no one until the Son of Man is risen from the dead." [10]And His disciples asked Him, saying, [a]"Why then do the scribes say that Elijah must come first?" [11]Jesus answered and said to them, "Indeed, Elijah is coming [1]first and will [a]restore all things. [12][a]But I say to you that Elijah has come already, and they [b]did not know him but did to him whatever they wished. Likewise [c]the Son of Man is also about to suffer at their hands." [13][a]Then the disciples understood that He spoke to them of John the Baptist.

A BOY IS HEALED

[14][a]And when they had come to the multitude, a man came to Him, kneeling down to Him and saying, [15]"Lord, have mercy on my son, for he is [1]an epileptic and suffers severely; for he often falls into the fire and often into the water. [16]So I brought him to Your disciples, but they could not cure him." [17]Then Jesus answered and said, "O [1]faithless and [a]perverse generation, how long shall I be with you? How long shall I bear with you? Bring him here to Me." [18]And Jesus [a]rebuked the demon, and it came out of him; and the child was cured from that very hour.

Matt. 17:14–18

At the Bottom of the Mountain.

After the Mount of Transfiguration, no sooner had Jesus and His followers come down from this incredible mountaintop experience than Satan met them at the bottom of the hill. They encountered a demon-possessed boy who was being tortured by the Enemy, and the other disciples hadn't been able to deliver him.

So often, when God has done a special work in our lives, and we are so excited about what He has done, Satan is waiting for us to destroy what God has done. Satan is waiting at the bottom of every mountaintop experience.

---

[19]Then the disciples came to Jesus privately and said, "Why could we not cast it out?" [20]So Jesus said to them, "Because of

your [1]unbelief; for assuredly, I say to you, [a]if you have faith as a mustard seed, you will say to this mountain, 'Move from here to there,' and it will move; and nothing will be impossible for you. [21][1]However, this kind does not go out except by prayer and fasting."

Matt. 17:21

Prayer and Fasting. When Jesus said, "This kind does not go out except by prayer and fasting," was He referring to the demons or to the faith that is necessary to remove mountains? I don't know. But I do know that in order to do anything for the Lord, whether removing mountains and obstacles or dealing in the spiritual realm, it is important that we fast and pray. I think that we as a church need to spend more time fasting and praying so that God will remove the obstacles that Satan sets in our way.

JESUS AGAIN PREDICTS HIS DEATH AND RESURRECTION

[22][a]Now while they were [1]staying in Galilee, Jesus said to them, "The Son of Man is about to be betrayed into the hands of men, [23]and they will kill Him, and the third day He will be raised up." And they were exceedingly [a]sorrowful.

PETER AND HIS MASTER PAY THEIR TAXES

[24][a]When they had come to [1]Capernaum, those who received the [2]temple tax came to Peter and said, "Does your Teacher not pay the temple tax?"

[25]He said, "Yes."

And when he had come into the house, Jesus anticipated him, saying, "What do you think, Simon? From whom do the kings of the earth take customs or taxes, from their sons or from [a]strangers?"

[26]Peter said to Him, "From strangers."

Jesus said to him, "Then the sons are free. [27]Nevertheless, lest we offend them, go to the sea, cast in a hook, and take the fish that comes up first. And when you have opened its mouth, you will find a [1]piece of money; take that and give it to them for Me and you."

---

20 [a]Luke 17:6
[1]NU *little faith*

21 [1]NU omits v. 21.

22 [a]Mark 8:31
[1]NU *gathering together*

23 [a]John 16:6; 19:30

24 [a]Mark 9:33
[1]NU *Capharnaum*, here and elsewhere
[2]Lit. *double drachma*

25 [a][Is. 60:10–17]

27 [1]Gr. *stater*, the exact temple tax for two

CHAPTER 18

1 [a]Luke 9:46–48; 22:24–27

2 [a]Matt. 19:14

3 [a]Luke 18:16

4 [a][Matt. 20:27; 23:11]

5 [a][Matt. 10:42]

6 [a]Mark 9:42

7 [a][1 Cor. 11:19]
[b]Matt. 26:24; 27:4, 5
[1]*enticements to sin*

8 [a]Matt. 5:29, 30

9 [1]Gr. *Gehenna*

WHO IS THE GREATEST?

18 At [a]that time the disciples came to Jesus, saying, "Who then is greatest in the kingdom of heaven?"

[2]Then Jesus called a little [a]child to Him, set him in the midst of them, [3]and said, "Assuredly, I say to you, [a]unless you are converted and become as little children, you will by no means enter the kingdom of heaven. [4][a]Therefore whoever humbles himself as this little child is the greatest in the kingdom of heaven. [5][a]Whoever receives one little child like this in My name receives Me.

Matt. 18:1–5

Becoming Like a Child. The disciples were arguing about who would be the greatest in the kingdom, when Jesus called a little child over and said that "whoever humbles himself as this little child is the greatest in the kingdom of God."

Jesus taught that the way up was down, and the way down is up. "Whoever exalts himself will be humbled, and he who humbles himself will be exalted" (Luke 14:11). If you want to be great in God's kingdom and if you want to be successful in His eyes, be a "servant of all" (Mark 9:35).

JESUS WARNS OF OFFENSES

[6][a]"Whoever causes one of these little ones who believe in Me to sin, it would be better for him if a millstone were hung around his neck, and he were drowned in the depth of the sea. [7]Woe to the world because of [1]offenses! For [a]offenses must come, but [b]woe to that man by whom the offense comes!

[8][a]"If your hand or foot causes you to sin, cut it off and cast it from you. It is better for you to enter into life lame or maimed, rather than having two hands or two feet, to be cast into the everlasting fire. [9]And if your eye causes you to sin, pluck it out and cast it from you. It is better for you to enter into life with one eye, rather than having two eyes, to be cast into [1]hell fire.

THE PARABLE OF THE LOST SHEEP

[10]"Take heed that you do not despise one of these little ones, for I say to you

that in heaven [a]their angels always [b]see the face of My Father who is in heaven. [11][a]For[1] the Son of Man has come to save that which was lost.

Matt. 18:10

GUARDIAN ANGELS

The Bible does seem to indicate that there are angels who are given the responsibility of watching over and protecting us. Here Jesus warned His hearers to be careful how they treat children because "in heaven their angels always see the face of My Father who is in heaven." Psalm 91:11 tells us "He shall give His angels charge over you, to keep you in all your ways." We are told in Hebrews that the angels are "ministering spirits sent forth to minister for those who will inherit salvation" (Heb. 1:14).

There have been some times when I think my angel was asleep on the job, but many other times when God so miraculously preserved me that I don't have a doubt that His angels were responsible. We probably wouldn't be alive if it were not for our guardian angels.

10 [a][Heb. 1:14]
[b]Luke 1:19

11 [a]Luke 9:56
1 NU omits v. 11.

12 [a]Luke 15:4–7

14 [a][1 Tim. 2:4]

15 [a]Lev. 19:17
[b][James 5:20]

16 [a]Deut. 17:6; 19:15

17 [a][2 Thess. 3:6, 14]

18 [a][John 20:22, 23]

19 [a][1 Cor. 1:10]
[b][1 John 3:22; 5:14]
1 NU, M Again, assuredly, I say

20 [a]Acts 20:7

21 [a]Luke 17:4

12[a]"What do you think? If a man has a hundred sheep, and one of them goes astray, does he not leave the ninety-nine and go to the mountains to seek the one that is straying? [13]And if he should find it, assuredly, I say to you, he rejoices more over that sheep than over the ninety-nine that did not go astray. [14]Even so it is not the [a]will of your Father who is in heaven that one of these little ones should perish.

DEALING WITH A SINNING BROTHER

15"Moreover [a]if your brother sins against you, go and tell him his fault between you and him alone. If he hears you, [b]you have gained your brother. [16]But if he will not hear, take with you one or two more, that [a]'by the mouth of two or three witnesses every word may be established.' [17]And if he refuses to hear them, tell it to the church. But if he refuses even to hear the church, let him be to you like a [a]hea then and a tax collector. [18]"Assuredly, I say to you, [a]whatever you bind on earth will be bound in heaven, and whatever you loose on earth will be loosed in heaven. [19][a]"Again[1] I say to you that if two of you agree on earth concerning anything that they ask, [b]it will be done for them by My Father in heaven. [20]For where two or three are gathered [a]together in My name, I am there in the midst of them."

THE PARABLE OF THE UNFORGIVING SERVANT

21Then Peter came to Him and said, "Lord, how often shall my brother sin against me, and I forgive him? [a]Up to seven times?"

IF YOUR BROTHER SINS   Matt. 18:15–17

Jesus here outlined the process whereby a sinning brother is to be dealt with. First of all, He said to go to him privately and talk about it. If that clears it up, you've saved a lot of trouble and preserved the relationship without involving anyone else. But if that doesn't work, bring along a witness or two. Some people will twist what will be said, and it is a good idea to have a witness in those cases. Where that doesn't work, bring the matter before the church, publicly addressing and exposing the issue. The next step is to realize that such offenders aren't really a part of the fellowship of God's people.

Very few situations will ever need to get to this final point. In fact, most problems would be dealt with if we only took the first step, going to a person privately. This isn't a process for kicking people out of the church, as some would think. This is a process of healing and restoration. And if more people would take the first step, as Jesus commanded, instead of resorting to gossip and backbiting, most church problems would be nonexistent.

22Jesus said to him, "I do not say to you, a up to seven times, but up to seventy times seven. 23Therefore the kingdom of heaven is like a certain king who wanted to settle accounts with his servants. 24And when he had begun to settle accounts, one was brought to him who owed him ten thousand talents. 25But as he was not able to pay, his master commanded a that he be sold, with his wife and children and all that he had, and that payment be made. 26The servant therefore fell down before him, saying, 'Master, have patience with me, and I will pay you all.' 27Then the master of that servant was moved with compassion, released him, and forgave him the debt.

28"But that servant went out and found one of his fellow servants who owed him a hundred denarii; and he laid hands on him and took him by the throat, saying, 'Pay me what you owe!' 29So his fellow servant fell down 1at his feet and begged him, saying, 'Have patience with me, and I will pay you 2all.' 30And he would not, but went and threw him into prison till he should pay the debt. 31So when his fellow servants saw what had been done, they were

very grieved, and came and told their master all that had been done. 32Then his master, after he had called him, said to him, 'You wicked servant! I forgave you a all that debt because you begged me. 33Should you not also have had compassion on your fellow servant, just as I had pity on you?' 34And his master was angry, and delivered him to the torturers until he should pay all that was due to him.

35 a"So My heavenly Father also will do to you if each of you, from his heart, does not forgive his brother 1his trespasses."

MARRIAGE AND DIVORCE

19 Now it came to pass, a when Jesus had finished these sayings, that He departed from Galilee and came to the region of Judea beyond the Jordan. 2 aAnd great multitudes followed Him, and He healed them there.

3The Pharisees also came to Him, testing Him, and saying to Him, "Is it lawful for a man to divorce his wife for just any reason?"

4And He answered and said to them, "Have you not read that He who 1made them at the beginning a'made them

Cross-references
22 a Col. 3:13
25 a 2 Kin. 4:1
29 1 NU omits at his feet
2 NU, M omit all
32 a Luke 7:41–43
35 a James 2:13
1 NU omits his trespasses
CHAPTER 19
1 a Mark 10:1–12
2 a Matt. 12:15
4 1 NU created
a Gen. 1:27; 5:2

WHAT ABOUT DIVORCE?   Matt. 19:3–9

In the Law, Moses gave permission for a man to divorce his wife if "she finds no favor in his eyes because he has found some uncleanness in her" (Deut. 24:1). The passage wasn't very clear as far as what specifically would constitute grounds for divorce, and two basic schools of interpretation developed.

One position, advocated by Rabbi Shimmai, took a very narrow position and said that the only grounds for divorce was adultery. But there was a more liberal school of thought, led by Rabbi Hillel, that interpreted "uncleanness" as anything about the wife that displeased her husband. Thus, according to Hillel, if a woman burned the breakfast or nagged her husband, he could divorce her.

The Pharisees were trying to get Jesus to choose one of these interpretations, either the strict one or the liberal one. They hoped to polarize the people by pinning Jesus down on this controversial question. But Jesus went back before the Law and said that in marriage the two become one and "what God has joined together, let not man separate." He took a stricter position than either popular view. He basically said that divorce shouldn't happen at all.

Now they thought they had Him trapped because He was in seeming conflict with Moses, who permitted divorce. Jesus responded, "Moses, because of the hardness of your hearts, permitted you to divorce your wives, but from the beginning it was not so." Essentially what Jesus was teaching was that God's ideal for marriage is that the two become one, for life. If people's hearts are hard, they will fail to live up to God's ideal, but God made provision for that.

So divorce is always less than the ideal. But God doesn't stop working with you because you come short of the ideal, and it is a good thing that He doesn't. He provides for our failure to live up to His ideal, although it is always a tragedy when we settle for less than His best.

male and female,' 5and said, a*'For this reason a man shall leave his father and mother and be joined to his wife, and* b*the two shall become one flesh'?* 6So then, they are no longer two but one flesh. Therefore what God has joined together, let not man separate."

7They said to Him, a"Why then did Moses command to give a certificate of divorce, and to put her away?"

8He said to them, "Moses, because of the ahardness of your hearts, permitted you to divorce your bwives, but from the beginning it was not so. 9aAnd I say to you, whoever divorces his wife, except for 1sexual immorality, and marries another, commits adultery; and whoever marries her who is divorced commits adultery."

10His disciples said to Him, a"If such is the case of the man with his wife, it is better not to marry."

JESUS TEACHES ON CELIBACY

11But He said to them, a"All cannot accept this saying, but only those to whom it has been given: 12For there are 1eunuchs who were born thus from their mother's womb, and athere are eunuchs who were made eunuchs by men, and there are eunuchs who have made themselves eunuchs for the kingdom of heaven's sake. He who is able to accept it, let him accept it."

JESUS BLESSES LITTLE CHILDREN

13aThen little children were brought to Him that He might put His hands on them and pray, but the disciples rebuked

---

Matt. 19:13-15

Let the Children Come to Me. Many of the mothers were bringing their children to Jesus, wanting Him to bless them. The disciples were concerned that this would take up too much of His time and they thought they were protecting Him by keeping them away. But He said, "Let the little children come to Me, and do not forbid them; for of such is the kingdom of heaven." Then He proceeded to lay hands on them.

I love it that Jesus is always touchable. Never too busy or too pressured to take time, even with children.

---

them. 14But Jesus said, "Let the little children come to Me, and do not forbid them; for aof such is the kingdom of heaven." 15And He laid His hands on them and departed from there.

JESUS COUNSELS THE RICH YOUNG RULER

16aNow behold, one came and said to Him, b"Good1 Teacher, what good thing shall I do that I may have eternal life?"

17So He said to him, 1"Why do you call Me good? 2No one is agood but One, that is, God. But if you want to enter into life, bkeep the commandments."

18He said to Him, "Which ones?"

Jesus said, a"'You shall not murder,' 'You shall not commit adultery,' 'You

---

Matt. 19:16-17

WHY DO YOU CALL ME GOOD?

A young man came to Jesus and asked how he could find eternal life. He knew something was missing in his own life and saw Jesus had something he wanted.

Before Jesus dealt with his question, He went after the more crucial question as to who Jesus was. The young man had called Jesus "Good Teacher"; and Jesus responded by saying, "Why do you call Me good? No one is good but One, that is, God."

Jesus was making one of two possible points. Either He was saying, "I am not good"; or He was saying, "I am God." The fact that He went on to tell him how to find eternal life would certainly eliminate the first possibility, that He was saying He wasn't good. The only option left is that Jesus was claiming to be God. And if He claimed to be God, and He really wasn't, then He couldn't be good. He can't be good and not be God. Which is it?

Cross-references

5 a Gen. 2:24
b [1 Cor. 6:16; 7:2]

7 a Deut. 24:1-4

8 a Heb. 3:15
b Mal. 2:16

9 a [Matt. 5:32]
1 Or fornication

10 a [Prov. 21:19]

11 a [1 Cor. 7:2, 7, 9, 17]

12 a [1 Cor. 7:32]
1 Emasculated men

13 a Luke 18:15

14 a Matt. 18:3, 4

16 a Mark 10:17-30
b Luke 10:25
1 NU omits Good

17 a Nah. 1:7
b Lev. 18:5
1 NU Why do you ask Me about what is good?
2 NU There is One who is good. But

18 a Ex. 20:13-16

shall not steal,' 'You shall not bear false witness,' [19a]'Honor your father and your mother,' and, [b]'You shall love your neighbor as yourself.' "

[20]The young man said to Him, "All these things I have [a]kept [1]from my youth. What do I still lack?"

[21]Jesus said to him, "If you want to be perfect, [a]go, sell what you have and give to the poor, and you will have treasure in heaven; and come, follow Me."

[22]But when the young man heard that saying, he went away sorrowful, for he had great possessions.

WITH GOD ALL THINGS ARE POSSIBLE

[23]Then Jesus said to His disciples, "Assuredly, I say to you that [a]it is hard for a rich man to enter the kingdom of heaven. [24]And again I say to you, it is easier for a camel to go through the eye of a needle than for a rich man to enter the kingdom of God."

[25]When His disciples heard it, they were greatly astonished, saying, "Who then can be saved?"

[26]But Jesus looked at them and said to them, "With men this is impossible, but [a]with God all things are possible."

[27]Then Peter answered and said to Him, "See, [a]we have left all and followed You. Therefore what shall we have?"

[28]So Jesus said to them, "Assuredly I say to you, that in the regeneration, when the Son of Man sits on the throne of His glory, [a]you who have followed Me will also sit on twelve thrones, judging the twelve tribes of Israel. [29a]And everyone who has left houses or brothers or sisters or father or mother [1]or wife or children or [2]lands, for My name's sake, shall receive a hundredfold, and inherit eternal life. [30a]But many

Marginal notes:
19 [a]Ex. 20:12–16; Deut. 5:16–20 [b]Lev. 19:18
20 [a][Phil. 3:6, 7] [1]NU omits *from my youth*
21 [a]Acts 2:45; 4:34, 35
23 [a][1 Tim. 6:9]
26 [a]Jer. 32:17
27 [a]Deut. 33:9
28 [a]Luke 22:28–30
29 [a]Mark 10:29, 30 [1]NU omits *or wife* [2]Lit. *fields*
30 [a]Luke 13:30
CHAPTER 20
6 [1]NU omits *idle*
7 [1]NU omits the rest of v. 7.
11 [1]*grumbled*

who are first will be last, and the last first.

THE PARABLE OF THE WORKERS IN THE VINEYARD

20 "For the kingdom of heaven is like a landowner who went out early in the morning to hire laborers for his vineyard. [2]Now when he had agreed with the laborers for a denarius a day, he sent them into his vineyard. [3]And he went out about the third hour and saw others standing idle in the marketplace, [4]and said to them, 'You also go into the vineyard, and whatever is right I will give you.' So they went. [5]Again he went out about the sixth and the ninth hour, and did likewise. [6]And about the eleventh hour he went out and found others standing [1]idle, and said to them, 'Why have you been standing here idle all day?' [7]They said to him, 'Because no one hired us.' He said to them, 'You also go into the vineyard, [1]and whatever is right you will receive.'

[8]"So when evening had come, the owner of the vineyard said to his steward, 'Call the laborers and give them their wages, beginning with the last to the first.' [9]And when those came who were hired about the eleventh hour, they each received a denarius. [10]But when the first came, they supposed that they would receive more; and they likewise received each a denarius. [11]And when they had received it, they [1]complained against the landowner, [12]saying, 'These last men have worked only one hour, and you made them equal to us who have borne the burden and the heat of the day.' [13]But he answered one of them and said, 'Friend,

---

GOD DOES WHAT HE WANTS   Matt. 20:1–16

Jesus told this parable about a man who owned a vineyard. The man hired workers at the beginning of the day and agreed on their wages. Throughout the day, he continued to hire workers, right up until the last hour. At the end of the day, he paid them all the same amount, which bothered those who had worked all day. The owner's response was that he had kept his word to them, and he could do whatever he wanted with his own things.

In the kingdom of God there are some people who are given huge opportunities to serve the Lord for long periods of time. There are others who have less opportunities. But the point of the parable is that we all need to remain faithful in what God has called us to.

We can't watch other people and grade ourselves on the curve. We can't compare what we are doing or what we are given with what is entrusted to others. We must simply remain faithful in our own situation. And whatever God does is always fair and right.

I am doing you no wrong. Did you not agree with me for a denarius? ¹⁴Take what is yours and go your way. I wish to give to this last man the same as to you. ¹⁵ᵃIs it not lawful for me to do what I wish with my own things? Or ᵇis your eye evil because I am good?' ¹⁶ᵃSo the last will be first, and the first last. ᵇFor¹ many are called, but few chosen."

JESUS A THIRD TIME PREDICTS HIS DEATH AND RESURRECTION

¹⁷ᵃNow Jesus, going up to Jerusalem, took the twelve disciples aside on the road and said to them, ¹⁸ᵃ"Behold, we are going up to Jerusalem, and the Son of Man will be betrayed to the chief priests and to the scribes; and they will condemn Him to death, ¹⁹ᵃand deliver Him to the Gentiles to ᵇmock and to ᶜscourge and to ᵈcrucify. And the third day He will ᵉrise again."

Matt. 20:17–19

Death and Resurrection. Notice how clearly Jesus spelled out what was going to happen to Him. He told His followers about His trial, the mocking and scourging, His crucifixion, and His resurrection after three days. And yet, they really didn't get it; so when it came to pass, they were befuddled about the whole thing.

Sometimes we just hear what we want to hear, and everything else goes in one ear and out the other. But the Lord tells us what will be happening so that it won't be a surprise when it happens. That is the purpose of prophecy.

GREATNESS IS SERVING

²⁰ᵃThen the mother of ᵇZebedee's sons came to Him with her sons, kneeling down and asking something from Him.

²¹And He said to her, "What do you wish?"

She said to Him, "Grant that these two sons of mine ᵃmay sit, one on Your right hand and the other on the left, in Your kingdom."

²²But Jesus answered and said, "You do not know what you ask. Are you able to drink ᵃthe cup that I am about

---

15 ᵃ[Rom. 9:20, 21]
ᵇDeut. 15:9

16 ᵃMatt. 19:30
ᵇMatt. 22:14
1 NU omits the rest of v. 16.

17 ᵃMark 10:32–34

18 ᵃMatt. 16:21; 26:47–57

19 ᵃMatt. 27:2
ᵇMatt. 26:67, 68; 27:29, 41
ᶜMatt. 27:26
ᵈActs 3:13–15
ᵉMatt. 28:5, 6

20 ᵃMark 10:35–45
ᵇMatt. 4:21; 10:2

21 ᵃ[Matt. 19:28]

22 ᵃLuke 22:42
ᵇLuke 12:50
1 NU omits and be baptized with the baptism that I am baptized with

23 ᵃ[Acts 12:2]
1 NU omits and be baptized with the baptism that I am baptized with

24 ᵃMark 10:41

26 ᵃ[1 Pet. 5:3]
ᵇMatt. 23:11

27 ᵃ[Matt. 18:4]

28 ᵃJohn 13:4
ᵇ[Phil. 2:6, 7]
ᶜLuke 22:27
ᵈ[Is. 53:10, 11]
ᵉ[Rom. 5:15, 19]

29 ᵃMark 10:46–52

30 ᵃMatt. 9:27
ᵇ[Ezek. 37:21–25]

31 ᵃMatt. 19:13

---

to drink, ¹and be baptized with ᵇthe baptism that I am baptized with?"

They said to Him, "We are able."

²³So He said to them, ᵃ"You will indeed drink My cup, ¹and be baptized with the baptism that I am baptized with; but to sit on My right hand and on My left is not Mine to give, but it is for those for whom it is prepared by My Father."

²⁴ᵃAnd when the ten heard it, they were greatly displeased with the two brothers. ²⁵But Jesus called them to Himself and said, "You know that the rulers of the Gentiles lord it over them, and those who are great exercise authority over them. ²⁶Yet ᵃit shall not be so among you; but ᵇwhoever desires to become great among you, let him be your servant. ²⁷ᵃAnd whoever desires to be first among you, let him be your slave— ²⁸ᵃjust as the ᵇSon of Man did not come to be served, ᶜbut to serve, and ᵈto give His life a ransom ᵉfor many."

Matt. 20:25–28

To Serve. The disciples always seemed to be jockeying for position in the kingdom. Jesus explained to them that this was how the world worked, but that wasn't how He did things. In the Lord's economy, it is through service that you achieve greatness.

How this is so often lost on those who call themselves "ministers," which means "servants." Often the church more resembles the world than it does the kingdom of God when it comes to service. Ministry isn't about power and position. It is about serving.

TWO BLIND MEN RECEIVE THEIR SIGHT

²⁹ᵃNow as they went out of Jericho, a great multitude followed Him. ³⁰And behold, ᵃtwo blind men sitting by the road, when they heard that Jesus was passing by, cried out, saying, "Have mercy on us, O Lord, ᵇSon of David!"

³¹Then the multitude ᵃwarned them that they should be quiet; but they cried out all the more, saying, "Have mercy on us, O Lord, Son of David!"

³²So Jesus stood still and called them, and said, "What do you want Me to do for you?"

³³They said to Him, "Lord, that our

eyes may be opened." 34So Jesus had acompassion and touched their eyes. And immediately their eyes received sight, and they followed Him.

THE TRIUMPHAL ENTRY

21 Now awhen they drew near Jerusalem, and came to 1Bethphage, at bthe Mount of Olives, then Jesus sent two disciples, 2saying to them, "Go into the village opposite you, and immediately you will find a donkey tied, and a colt with her. Loose them and bring them to Me. 3And if anyone says anything to you, you shall say, 'The Lord has need of them,' and immediately he will send them."

41All this was done that it might be fulfilled which was spoken by the prophet, saying:

5 "Tella the daughter of Zion,
    'Behold, your King is coming to you,
    Lowly, and sitting on a donkey,
    A colt, the foal of a donkey.'"

6aSo the disciples went and did as Jesus commanded them. 7They brought the donkey and the colt, alaid their clothes on them, 1and set Him on them.

8And a very great multitude spread their clothes on the road; aothers cut down branches from the trees and spread them on the road. 9Then the multitudes who went before and those who followed cried out, saying:

    "Hosanna to the Son of David!
    a'Blessed is He who comes in the name of the LORD!'
    Hosanna in the highest!"

10aAnd when He had come into Jerusalem, all the city was moved, saying, "Who is this?"

11So the multitudes said, "This is Jesus, athe prophet from Nazareth of Galilee."

JESUS CLEANSES THE TEMPLE

12aThen Jesus went into the temple 1of God and drove out all those who bought and sold in the temple, and overturned the tables of the bmoney changers and the seats of those who sold doves. 13And He said to them, "It is written, a'My house shall be called a house of prayer,' but you have made it a b'den of thieves.'"

14Then the blind and the lame came to Him in the temple, and He healed

Margin references

34 a Matt. 9:36; 14:14; 15:32; 18:27

CHAPTER 21

1 a Luke 19:29–38
b [Zech. 14:4]
1 M Bethsphage

4 1 NU omits All

5 a Zech. 9:9

6 a Mark 11:4

7 a 2 Kin. 9:13
1 NU and He sat

8 a Lev. 23:40

9 a Ps. 118:26; Matt. 23:39

10 a John 2:13, 15

11 a John 6:14; 7:40; 9:17

12 a Mark 11:15–18
b Deut. 14:25
1 NU omits of God

13 a Is. 56:7
b Jer. 7:11

THE TRIUMPHAL ENTRY

Matt. 21:1–11

As we see the triumphal entry of Jesus, as He rode a donkey into Jerusalem while the people were proclaiming Him to be the Messiah, crying out, "Blessed is He who comes in the name of the LORD," we see a significant fulfillment of at least three prophecies.

In Zechariah 9:9, the coming of Messiah was prophesied: "Rejoice greatly, O daughter of Zion! Shout, O daughter of Jerusalem! Behold, your King is coming to you; He is just and having salvation, lowly and riding on a donkey, a colt, the foal of a donkey."

Then in Psalm 118, the coming of the Messiah was declared; and in verses 25 and 26 we see the words that were said by the people at this entry of our Lord into Jerusalem. In verse 25, "Save now," which is the meaning of the word Hosanna, and in verse 26, "Blessed is He who comes in the name of the LORD."

The third prophecy that was fulfilled on this day is found in Daniel, chapter 9, and it predicted the time this event would occur. In Daniel 9:25, we read that "from the going forth of the command to restore and build Jerusalem until Messiah the Prince, there shall be seven weeks and sixty-two weeks." The word for "weeks" is actually "sevens" and can refer to seven lengths of time, whether days, weeks, or years. Sir Robert Anderson, in his book The Coming Prince, has computed from the command from Artaxerxes to restore and rebuild Jerusalem, which happened on March 14, 445 BC, he has calculated 483 years from that date (69 times 7), using the 360-day Babylonian calendar, which gives you 173,880 days; and when you figure it out, it takes you to April 6, 32 AD, which was precisely the day Jesus came into Jerusalem riding on a donkey.

So Jesus' transportation was predicted, what the crowd said was predicted, and the very day was predicted. Simply amazing, and inexplicable, apart from divine intervention and foreknowledge.

Matt. 21:12–13

A DEN OF THIEVES

The temple had become a place of business and crooked business at that.

Money changers and those who sold sacrificial animals were ripping people off in the name of the Lord. The people had to exchange their Roman money for shekels in order to give an offering, and they were being cheated on the exchange rate. The animals they offered had to be approved, and the temple workers sold approved animals at inflated prices.

What was supposed to be a place of prayer and a place to meet God had just become another crooked business. Jesus put them out of business.

them. 15But when the chief priests and scribes saw the wonderful things that He did, and the children crying out in the temple and saying, "Hosanna to the aSon of David!" they were 1indignant 16and said to Him, "Do You hear what these are saying?"

And Jesus said to them, "Yes. Have you never read,

a'*Out of the mouth of babes and nursing infants
You have perfected praise*'?"

17Then He left them and awent out of the city to Bethany, and He lodged there.

THE FIG TREE WITHERED
18aNow in the morning, as He returned to the city, He was hungry. 19aAnd seeing a fig tree by the road, He came to it and found nothing on it but leaves, and said to it, "Let no fruit grow on you ever again." Immediately the fig tree withered away.

THE LESSON OF THE WITHERED FIG TREE
20aAnd when the disciples saw it, they marveled, saying, "How did the fig tree wither away so soon?"
21So Jesus answered and said to

---

15 a John 7:42
1 angry

16 a Ps. 8:2

17 a John 11:1, 18; 12:1

18 a Mark 11:12–14, 20–24

19 a Mark 11:13

20 a Mark 11:20

21 a Matt. 17:20
b James 1:6
c 1 Cor. 13:2

22 a Matt. 7:7–11

23 a Luke 20:1–8
b Ex. 2:14

25 a [John 1:29–34]
b John 1:15–28

26 a Matt. 14:5; 21:46
b Mark 6:20

---

them, "Assuredly, I say to you, aif you have faith and bdo not doubt, you will not only do what was done to the fig tree, cbut also if you say to this mountain, 'Be removed and be cast into the sea,' it will be done. 22And awhatever things you ask in prayer, believing, you will receive."

JESUS' AUTHORITY QUESTIONED
23aNow when He came into the temple, the chief priests and the elders of the people confronted Him as He was teaching, and bsaid, "By what authority are You doing these things? And who gave You this authority?"
24But Jesus answered and said to them, "I also will ask you one thing, which if you tell Me, I likewise will tell you by what authority I do these things: 25The abaptism of bJohn—where was it from? From heaven or from men?"

And they reasoned among themselves, saying, "If we say, 'From heaven,' He will say to us, 'Why then did you not believe him?' 26But if we say, 'From men,' we afear the multitude, bfor all count John as a prophet." 27So they answered Jesus and said, "We do not know."

Matt. 21:18–19

CURSING THE FIG TREE

Jesus saw this fig tree that had leaves but no figs, and He cursed it so that it would never bear fruit again. That sounds rather cruel, but He was making a point. The fig tree was a picture of Israel. They hadn't borne fruit. There were signs of activity, leaves growing on the tree, but no fruit.

On a fig tree, the best figs show up even before the leaves grow. If the leaves are there and there are no figs, the tree is not producing. Jesus was demonstrating that Israel wasn't producing. They had leaves but no fruit, religion but no relationship. As a result, they had rejected their Messiah and would miss out on the kingdom for a long time.

And He said to them, "Neither will I tell you by what authority I do these things.

THE PARABLE OF THE TWO SONS

28"But what do you think? A man had two sons, and he came to the first and said, 'Son, go, work today in my ªvineyard.' 29He answered and said, 'I will not,' but afterward he regretted it and went. 30Then he came to the second and said likewise. And he answered and said, 'I go, sir,' but he did not go. 31Which of the two did the will of his father?"

They said to Him, "The first."

Jesus said to them, ª"Assuredly, I say to you that tax collectors and harlots enter the kingdom of God before you. 32For ªJohn came to you in the way of righteousness, and you did not believe him; bbut tax collectors and harlots believed him; and when you saw it, you did not afterward 1relent and believe him.

THE PARABLE OF THE WICKED VINEDRESSERS

33"Hear another parable: There was a certain landowner ªwho planted a vineyard and set a hedge around it, dug a winepress in it and built a tower. And he leased it to vinedressers and bwent into a far country. 34Now when vintage-time drew near, he sent his servants to the vinedressers, that they might receive its fruit. 35ªAnd the vinedressers took his servants, beat one, killed one, and stoned another. 36Again he sent other servants, more than the first, and they did likewise to them. 37Then last of all he sent his ªson to them, saying, 'They will respect my son.' 38But when the vinedressers saw the son, they said among themselves, ª'This is the heir. bCome, let us kill him and seize his inheritance.' 39ªSo they took him and cast him out of the vineyard and killed him.

40"Therefore, when the owner of the vineyard comes, what will he do to those vinedressers?"

41ªThey said to Him, b"He will destroy those wicked men miserably, cand lease his vineyard to other vinedressers who will 1render to him the fruits in their seasons."

42Jesus said to them, "Have you never read in the Scriptures:

ª'The stone which the builders rejected
Has become the chief cornerstone.

This was the LORD's doing,
And it is marvelous in our eyes'?

43"Therefore I say to you, ªthe kingdom of God will be taken from you and given to a nation bearing the fruits of it. 44And ªwhoever falls on this stone will be broken; but on whomever it falls, bit will grind him to powder."

45Now when the chief priests and Pharisees heard His parables, they 1perceived that He was speaking of them. 46But when they sought to lay hands on Him, they ªfeared the multitudes, because bthey took Him for a prophet.

THE PARABLE OF THE WEDDING FEAST

22 And Jesus answered ªand spoke to them again by parables and said: 2"The kingdom of heaven is like a certain king who arranged a marriage for his son, 3and sent out his servants to call those who were invited to the wedding; and they were not willing to come. 4Again, he sent out other servants, saying, 'Tell those who are invited, "See, I have prepared my dinner; ªmy oxen and fatted cattle are killed, and all things are ready. Come to the wedding."' 5But they made light of it and went their ways, one to his own farm, another to his business. 6And the rest seized his servants, treated them 1spitefully, and killed them. 7But when the king heard about it, he was furious. And he sent out ªhis armies, destroyed

Cross references

28 ªMatt. 20:1; 21:33

31 ªLuke 7:29, 37–50

32 ªLuke 3:1–12; 7:29 bLuke 3:12, 13 1regret it

33 ªLuke 20:9–19 bMatt. 25:14

35 ª[1 Thess. 2:15]

37 ª[John 3:16]

38 ª[Heb. 1:2] bJohn 11:53

39 ª[Acts 2:23]

41 ªLuke 20:16 b[Luke 21:24] c[Acts 13:46] 1give

42 ªPs. 118:22, 23

43 ª[Matt. 8:12]

44 ªIs. 8:14, 15 b[Dan. 2:44]

45 1knew

46 ªMatt. 21:26 bMatt. 21:11

CHAPTER 22

1 ª[Rev. 19:7–9]

4 ªProv. 9:2

6 1insolently

7 ª[Dan. 9:26]

Matt. 22:1–14

The Right Clothes. In Jesus' day when you invited someone to a wedding, the invitation included a special robe to be worn to the event. In this parable the people who were originally invited to the ceremony turned down the invitation, so the invitations were passed on to other less deserving, but willing, guests.

This passage is a picture of the nation of Israel rejecting their Messiah, and His alternative invitation of Himself to the Gentiles. And you can't come to the party without the right clothes, and the right clothes are the white robes of the righteousness of Jesus Christ.

those murderers, and burned up their city. 8Then he said to his servants, 'The wedding is ready, but those who were invited were not aworthy. 9Therefore go into the highways, and as many as you find, invite to the wedding.' 10So those servants went out into the highways and agathered together all whom they found, both bad and good. And the wedding hall was filled with guests.

11"But when the king came in to see the guests, he saw a man there awho did not have on a wedding garment. 12So he said to him, 'Friend, how did you come in here without a wedding garment?' And he was aspeechless. 13Then the king said to the servants, 'Bind him hand and foot, 1take him away, and cast him ainto outer darkness; there will be weeping and gnashing of teeth.'

14a"For many are called, but few are chosen."

THE PHARISEES: IS IT LAWFUL TO PAY TAXES TO CAESAR?

15aThen the Pharisees went and plotted how they might entangle Him in His talk. 16And they sent to Him their disciples with the aHerodians, saying, "Teacher, we know that You are true, and teach the way of God in truth; nor do You care about anyone, for You do not 1regard the person of men. 17Tell us, therefore, what do You think? Is it lawful to pay taxes to Caesar, or not?"

18But Jesus 1perceived their wickedness, and said, "Why do you test Me, you hypocrites? 19Show Me the tax money."

So they brought Him a denarius. 20And He said to them, "Whose image and inscription is this?"

21They said to Him, "Caesar's."

And He said to them, a"Render1 therefore to Caesar the things that are bCaesar's, and to God the things that are cGod's." 22When they had heard these words, they marveled, and left Him and went their way.

THE SADDUCEES: WHAT ABOUT THE RESURRECTION?

23aThe same day the Sadducees, bwho say there is no resurrection, came to Him and asked Him, 24saying: "Teacher, aMoses said that if a man dies, having no children, his brother shall marry his wife and raise up offspring for his brother. 25Now there were with us seven brothers. The first died after he had married, and having no offspring, left his wife to his brother.

26Likewise the second also, and the third, even to the seventh. 27Last of all the woman died also. 28Therefore, in the resurrection, whose wife of the seven will she be? For they all had her."

29Jesus answered and said to them, "You are 1mistaken, anot knowing the Scriptures nor the power of God. 30For in the resurrection they neither marry nor are given in marriage, but aare like angels 1of God in heaven. 31But concerning the resurrection of the dead, have you not read what was spoken to you by God, saying, 32a'I am the God of Abraham, the God of Isaac, and the God of Jacob'? God is not the God of the dead, but of the living." 33And when the multitudes heard this, athey were astonished at His teaching.

Matt. 22:29

TWO MISTAKES

The Pharisees and Sadducees had been trying to trip Jesus with trick questions. The Sadducees had asked this phony question about a woman who had been widowed seven times, and they wondered who she would be married to in heaven. But Jesus told them that there are two basic reasons why they are wrong. Two mistakes they were making. "You are mistaken, not knowing the Scriptures nor the power of God."

These are the same two errors that mislead people today: ignorance of the Scriptures and ignorance of the power of God. If you want to make less mistakes, study the Word diligently and believe in God's power to do anything.

THE SCRIBES: WHICH IS THE FIRST COMMANDMENT OF ALL?

34aBut when the Pharisees heard that He had silenced the Sadducees, they gathered together. 35Then one of them, aa lawyer, asked Him a question, testing Him, and saying, 36"Teacher, which is the great commandment in the law?"

37Jesus said to him, a"'You shall love

---

8 aMatt. 10:11

10 aMatt. 13:38, 47, 48

11 a[Col. 3:10, 12]

12 a[Rom. 3:19]

13 aMatt. 8:12; 25:30
1NU omits take him away, and

14 aMatt. 20:16

15 aMark 12:13–17

16 aMark 3:6; 8:15; 12:13
1Lit. look at the face of

18 1knew

21 aMatt. 17:25
b[Rom. 13:1–7]
c[1 Cor. 3:23; 6:19, 20; 12:27]
1Pay

23 aLuke 20:27–40
bActs 23:8

24 aDeut. 25:5

29 aJohn 20:9
1deceived

30 a[1 John 3:2]
1NU omits of God

32 aEx. 3:6, 15

33 aMatt. 7:28

34 aMark 12:28–31

35 aLuke 7:30; 10:25; 11:45, 46, 52; 14:3

37 aDeut. 6:5; 10:12; 30:6

the LORD your God with all your heart, with all your soul, and with all your mind.' ³⁸This is the first and great commandment. ³⁹And the second is like it: ᵃ'You shall love your neighbor as yourself.' ⁴⁰ᵃOn these two commandments hang all the Law and the Prophets."

Matt. 22:35–40

THE GREATEST COMMANDMENT

The Pharisees tried to catch Jesus in a trap by asking Him which of the commandments is the greatest. They argued about this all the time, and it was hard to pick just one of the Ten Commandments that was the most important.

Jesus didn't pick one of the ten, but He went to Deuteronomy 6:5 and the commandment to love God. He then picked a second, that was like the first, by quoting Leviticus 19:18, "Love your neighbor as yourself." He then said, "This sums up the entire Old Testament."

The Pharisees had tried to complicate the Law, but it just came down to "love God and love your neighbor." Jesus had a marvelous way of simplifying the complicated.

JESUS: HOW CAN DAVID CALL HIS DESCENDANT LORD?

⁴¹ᵃWhile the Pharisees were gathered together, Jesus asked them, ⁴²saying, "What do you think about the Christ? Whose Son is He?"

They said to Him, "The ᵃSon of David."

⁴³He said to them, "How then does David in the Spirit call Him 'Lord,' saying:

⁴⁴   'The ᵃ LORD said to my Lord,
   "Sit at My right hand,
    Till I make Your enemies Your
    footstool"'?

⁴⁵If David then calls Him 'Lord,' how is He his Son?" ⁴⁶ᵃAnd no one was able to answer Him a word, ᵇnor from that day on did anyone dare question Him anymore.

---

39 ᵃ Lev. 19:18

40 ᵃ [Matt. 7:12]

41 ᵃ Luke 20:41–44

42 ᵃ Matt. 1:1; 21:9

44 ᵃ Ps. 110:1

46 ᵃ Luke 14:6 ᵇ Mark 12:34

CHAPTER 23

2 ᵃ Neh. 8:4, 8

3 ᵃ [Rom. 2:19] ¹ NU omits to observe

4 ᵃ Luke 11:46

5 ᵃ [Matt. 6:1–6, 16–18]

6 ᵃ Luke 11:43; 20:46 ¹ Or place of honor

8 ᵃ [James 3:1] ¹ Leader ² NU omits the Christ

9 ᵃ [Mal. 1:6]

11 ᵃ Matt. 20:26, 27

12 ᵃ Luke 14:11; 18:14 ¹ put down ² lifted up

13 ᵃ Luke 11:52

14 ᵃ Mark 12:40 ¹ NU omits v. 14.

WOE TO THE SCRIBES AND PHARISEES

23 Then Jesus spoke to the multitudes and to His disciples, ²saying: ᵃ"The scribes and the Pharisees sit in Moses' seat. ³Therefore whatever they tell you ¹to observe, that observe and do, but do not do according to their works; for ᵃthey say, and do not do. ⁴ᵃFor they bind heavy burdens, hard to bear, and lay them on men's shoulders; but they themselves will not move them with one of their fingers. ⁵But all their works they do to ᵃbe seen by men. They make their phylacteries broad and enlarge the borders of their garments. ⁶ᵃThey love the ¹best places at feasts, the best seats in the synagogues, ⁷greetings in the marketplaces, and to be called by men, 'Rabbi, Rabbi.' ⁸ᵃBut you, do not be called 'Rabbi'; for One is your ¹Teacher, ²the Christ, and you are all brethren. ⁹Do not call anyone on earth your father; ᵃfor One is your Father, He who is in heaven. ¹⁰And do not be called teachers; for One is your Teacher, the Christ. ¹¹But ᵃhe who is greatest among you shall be your servant. ¹²ᵃAnd whoever exalts himself will be ¹humbled, and he who humbles himself will be ²exalted.

¹³"But ᵃwoe to you, scribes and Pharisees, hypocrites! For you shut up

Matt. 23:8

We Are All Brothers. Jesus was telling the people not to get hung up on titles. There was a major distinction in those days between the clergy and laity, as there sometimes is today. But we are all just brothers in Christ.

No one has the spiritual edge over anyone else. God will listen to your prayers as readily as He will listen to mine. None of us has a position spiritually that is above another. As a pastor/teacher, I have certain responsibilities before God to teach you faithfully, but it doesn't mean I'm closer to God.

the kingdom of heaven against men; for you neither go in yourselves, nor do you allow those who are entering to go in. ¹⁴¹Woe to you, scribes and Pharisees, hypocrites! ᵃFor you devour widows' houses, and for a pretense make

Matt. 23:13

Shutting Up the Kingdom. Jesus pronounced a woe on the scribes and Pharisees because by their rigid rules and regulations they were keeping people from entering the kingdom. Their barriers scared people away from God rather than drawing people to God. They made it so difficult that even they themselves couldn't meet the requirements. It is so sad when man-made traditions of religion obscure the path to God.

long prayers. Therefore you will receive greater condemnation.

15"Woe to you, scribes and Pharisees, hypocrites! For you travel land and sea to win one proselyte, and when he is won, you make him twice as much a son of ¹hell as yourselves.

16"Woe to you, ᵃblind guides, who say, ᵇ'Whoever swears by the temple, it is nothing; but whoever swears by the gold of the temple, he is obliged to perform it.' 17Fools and blind! For which is greater, the gold ᵃor the temple that ¹sanctifies the gold? 18And, 'Whoever swears by the altar, it is nothing; but whoever swears by the gift that is on it, he is obliged to perform it.' 19Fools and blind! For which is greater, the gift ᵃor the altar that sanctifies the gift? 20Therefore he who ¹swears by the altar, swears by it and by all things on it. 21He who swears by the temple, swears by it and by ᵃHim who ¹dwells in it. 22And he who swears by heaven,

Matt. 23:14

Devouring Widows' Houses. God certainly has a woe reserved for those today who through pretense and hypocrisy conduct their ministries in such a way that widows feel compelled to send them their Social Security checks. They even suggest that people should go borrow money to send to their ministry, and they take advantage of the poor and ignorant to build their lavish ministries and so enjoy their obscene lifestyles. Woe!

15 ¹Gr. Gehenna

16 ᵃMatt. 15:14; 23:24
ᵇ[Matt. 5:33, 34]

17 ᵃEx. 30:29
¹NU sanctified

19 ᵃEx. 29:37

20 ¹Swears an oath

21 ᵃ1 Kin. 8:13
¹M dwelt

22 ᵃMatt. 5:34

23 ᵃLuke 11:42; 18:12
ᵇ[Hos. 6:6]

25 ᵃLuke 11:39
¹M unrighteousness

27 ᵃActs 23:3

29 ᵃLuke 11:47, 48
¹decorate

31 ᵃ[Acts 7:51, 52]

swears by ᵃthe throne of God and by Him who sits on it.

23"Woe to you, scribes and Pharisees, hypocrites! ᵃFor you pay tithe of mint and anise and cummin, and ᵇhave neglected the weightier matters of the law: justice and mercy and faith. These you ought to have done, without leaving the others undone. 24Blind guides, who strain out a gnat and swallow a camel!

Matt. 23:24

Gnats and Camels. These hypocrites had no sense of priority. They would make a big deal out of little things, while ignoring the big things and the important things. They would strain their wine to make sure they didn't swallow any gnats or other impurities; but they were figuratively swallowing camels, excusing abuse in major areas of their lives.

Legalism always leads to straining at gnats and swallowing camels. It is only living in the Spirit that allows us to see what is really important.

25"Woe to you, scribes and Pharisees, hypocrites! ᵃFor you cleanse the outside of the cup and dish, but inside they are full of extortion and ¹self-indulgence. 26Blind Pharisee, first cleanse the inside of the cup and dish, that the outside of them may be clean also.

27"Woe to you, scribes and Pharisees, hypocrites! ᵃFor you are like whitewashed tombs which indeed appear beautiful outwardly, but inside are full of dead men's bones and all uncleanness. 28Even so you also outwardly appear righteous to men, but inside you are full of hypocrisy and lawlessness.

29ᵃ"Woe to you, scribes and Pharisees, hypocrites! Because you build the tombs of the prophets and ¹adorn the monuments of the righteous, 30and say, 'If we had lived in the days of our fathers, we would not have been partakers with them in the blood of the prophets.' 31"Therefore you are witnesses against yourselves that ᵃyou are sons of those who murdered the prophets.

Matt. 23:37

THE HEART OF JESUS

I n Jesus' lament over Jerusalem, we hear the heart of God. As wicked as its people were, He still loved them. He still desired to do good for them. He still wanted to protect them, as a mother hen protects her young. He said, "I wanted to protect you; I wanted that closeness with you" but "you were not willing."

Human failure to receive God's love keeps God from being able to do what He wants to do. To a Calvinist this makes no sense, but God wants everyone to come to Him, and the only thing in the way is our will. He gives us a real choice, although He wants us desperately. He's "not willing that any should perish" (2 Pet. 3:9). Our will is the problem.

---

32 ªFill up, then, the measure of your fathers' guilt. 33 Serpents, ªbrood¹ of vipers! How can you escape the condemnation of hell? 34 ªTherefore, indeed, I send you prophets, wise men, and scribes: ᵇsome of them you will kill and crucify, and ᶜsome of them you will scourge in your synagogues and persecute from city to city, 35 ªthat on you may come all the righteous blood shed on the earth, ᵇfrom the blood of righteous Abel to ᶜthe blood of Zechariah, son of Berechiah, whom you murdered between the temple and the altar. 36 Assuredly, I say to you, all these things will come upon this generation.

JESUS LAMENTS OVER JERUSALEM

37 ª"O Jerusalem, Jerusalem, the one who kills the prophets ᵇand stones those who are sent to her! How often ᶜI wanted to gather your children together, as a hen gathers her chicks ᵈunder her wings, but you were not willing! 38 See! Your house is left to you desolate; 39 for I say to you, you shall see Me no more till you say, ª'Blessed is He who comes in the name of the LORD!'"

Cross-references column:

32 ª[1 Thess. 2:16]

33 ª Matt. 3:7; 12:34
1 offspring

34 ª Luke 11:49
ᵇ Acts 7:54–60; 22:19
ᶜ 2 Cor. 11:24, 25

35 ª Rev. 18:24
ᵇ Gen. 4:8
ᶜ 2 Chr. 24:20, 21

37 ª Luke 13:34, 35
ᵇ 2 Chr. 24:20, 21; 36:15, 16
ᶜ Deut. 32:11, 12
ᵈ Ps. 17:8; 91:4

39 ª Ps. 118:26

CHAPTER 24

1 ª Mark 13:1

2 ª Luke 19:44

3 ª Mark 13:3
ᵇ [1 Thess. 5:1–3]

4 ª [Col. 2:8, 18]

5 ª John 5:43
ᵇ Matt. 24:11

6 ª [Rev. 6:2–4]
1 NU omits all

7 ª Hag. 2:22
ᵇ Rev. 6:5, 6
1 NU omits pestilences

JESUS PREDICTS THE DESTRUCTION OF THE TEMPLE

24 Then ªJesus went out and departed from the temple, and His disciples came up to show Him the buildings of the temple. 2 And Jesus said to them, "Do you not see all these things? Assuredly, I say to you, ªnot one stone shall be left here upon another, that shall not be thrown down."

THE SIGNS OF THE TIMES AND THE END OF THE AGE

3 Now as He sat on the Mount of Olives, ªthe disciples came to Him privately, saying, ᵇ"Tell us, when will these things be? And what will be the sign of Your coming, and of the end of the age?"

Matt. 24:3

THE OLIVET QUESTIONS

T he Olivet Discourse, here in Matthew 24, was occasioned by three questions that the disciples asked Jesus. "When will these things be?" (That is, the destruction of the temple that He was just discussing.) "What will be the sign of Your coming?" "What will be the sign of the end of the age?"

The disciples didn't understand that these questions referred to different times in history, but Jesus' answer addressed both the time of the destruction of the temple in AD 70 and the future events of His return to earth. It is sometimes difficult to follow, but we need to keep these questions in mind.

4 And Jesus answered and said to them: ª"Take heed that no one deceives you. 5 For ªmany will come in My name, saying, 'I am the Christ,' ᵇand will deceive many. 6 And you will hear of ªwars and rumors of wars. See that you are not troubled; for ¹all these things must come to pass, but the end is not yet. 7 For ªnation will rise against nation, and kingdom against kingdom. And there will be ᵇfamines, ¹pestilences, and

earthquakes in various places. 8All these are the beginning of sorrows. 9a"Then they will deliver you up to tribulation and kill you, and you will be hated by all nations for My name's sake. 10And then many will be offended, will betray one another, and will hate one another. 11Then amany false prophets will rise up and bdeceive many. 12And because lawlessness will abound, the love of many will grow acold. 13aBut he who endures to the end shall be saved. 14And this agospel of the kingdom bwill be preached in all the world as a witness to all the nations, and then the end will come.

THE GREAT TRIBULATION

15a"Therefore when you see the b'abomination of desolation,' spoken of by Daniel the prophet, standing in the holy place" c(whoever reads, let him understand), 16"then let those who are in Judea flee to the mountains. 17Let him who is on the housetop not go down to take anything out of his house. 18And let him who is in the field not go back to get his clothes. 19But awoe to those who are pregnant and to those who are nursing babies in those days! 20And pray that your flight may not be in winter or on the Sabbath. 21For athen there will be great tribulation, such as has not been since the beginning of the world until this time, no, nor ever shall be. 22And unless those days were shortened, no flesh would be saved; abut for the 1elect's sake those days will be shortened.

9 a Matt. 10:17

11 a 2 Pet. 2:1
b [1 Tim. 4:1]

12 a [2 Thess. 2:3]

13 a Matt. 10:22

14 a Matt. 4:23
b Rom. 10:18

15 a Mark 13:14
b Dan. 9:27; 11:31; 12:11
c Dan. 9:23

19 a Luke 23:29

21 a Dan. 9:26

22 a Is. 65:8, 9
1 chosen ones'

Matt. 24:6

Not Yet. Jesus' disciples would see these wars and rumors of wars as the Roman troops came and besieged and destroyed Jerusalem and the temple. But Jesus was letting them know "the end is not yet."

From the disciples' perspective, they associated all the events as one; when you are in the middle of a great time of trouble, you can't imagine that it could ever get worse, but it will get a lot worse in the future. Jesus was tipping them off to the fact that the end would come much later.

Matt. 24:7–8

Beginning of Sorrows. Jesus gave some of the signs that the end is approaching. There will be major world wars, famine, pestilence, and earthquakes, all in places we've never heard of. "These are the beginning of sorrows."

We are certainly living in a time of great wars. But there has also been horrible famine in many parts of the world, and AIDS and other diseases are spreading at unprecedented rates. We are also having more earthquakes and other natural disasters than ever before. We are at the beginning of the end.

WHO ARE THE ELECT?

Matt. 24:22, 31

There are those who would interpret "the elect" to be the church, and thus they see the church still here during the tribulation, in verse 22, and being gathered to Him in verse 31. This is where they get the idea that the rapture will come at the end of the tribulation.

But this is why you need to compare Scripture with Scripture, and throughout the Old Testament we see this described event as specifically applying to Israel. In Isaiah 11:12, we read: "He will set up a banner for the nations, and will assemble the outcasts of Israel, and gather together the dispersed of Judah from the four corners of the earth." Again and again Israel was referred to as God's elect, as He promised to gather them from all over the world.

The church at this point will already be in heaven, having been raptured at the beginning of the tribulation. We are represented in Revelation by the twenty-four elders who say they have been redeemed to God by the blood of Jesus "out of every tribe and tongue and people and nation" (Rev. 5:9). No one can say that except the church, and the church is in heaven in Revelation 4 and 5.

Matt. 24:15–28

THE GREAT TRIBULATION

The Antichrist will form an alliance with Israel during the first half of the tribulation period, and will allow them to rebuild their temple. But in the middle of the tribulation period he will turn on them and defile the Most Holy Place. Jesus said, "Therefore when you see the abomination of desolation, spoken of by Daniel the prophet, standing in the holy place," then get out of there. Flee to the mountains.

Daniel 9:27 prophesied this event that will take place. This will be the worst time the world has ever seen. "For then there will be great tribulation, such as has not been seen since the beginning of the world until this time, no, nor ever shall be. And unless those days were shortened, no flesh would be saved."

23a"Then if anyone says to you, 'Look, here is the Christ!' or 'There!' do not believe it. 24For afalse christs and false prophets will rise and show great signs and wonders to deceive, bif possible, even the elect. 25See, I have told you beforehand. 26"Therefore if they say to you, 'Look, He is in the desert!' do not go out; or 'Look, He is in the inner rooms!' do not believe it. 27aFor as the lightning comes from the east and flashes to the west, so also will the coming of the Son of Man be. 28aFor wherever the carcass is, there the eagles will be gathered together.

THE COMING OF THE SON OF MAN
29a"Immediately after the tribulation of those days bthe sun will be darkened, and the moon will not give its light; the stars will fall from heaven, and the powers of the heavens will be shaken. 30aThen the sign of the Son of Man will appear in heaven, band then all the tribes of the earth will mourn, and they will see the Son of Man com-

23 a Luke 17:23

24 a [2 Thess. 2:9]
b [2 Tim. 2:19]

27 a Luke 17:24

28 a Luke 17:37

29 a [Dan. 7:11]
b Ezek. 32:7

30 a [Dan. 7:13, 14]
b Zech. 12:12

31 a [1 Cor. 15:52]
1 chosen ones

32 a Luke 21:29

33 a [James 5:9]
1 Or He

34 a [Matt. 10:23; 16:28; 23:36]

35 a Luke 21:33

ing on the clouds of heaven with power and great glory. 31aAnd He will send His angels with a great sound of a trumpet, and they will gather together His 1elect from the four winds, from one end of heaven to the other.

THE PARABLE OF THE FIG TREE
32"Now learn athis parable from the fig tree: When its branch has already become tender and puts forth leaves, you know that summer is near. 33So you also, when you see all these things, know athat 1it is near—at the doors! 34Assuredly, I say to you, athis generation will by no means pass away till all these things take place. 35aHeaven and

Matt. 24:34

THIS GENERATION WON'T PASS AWAY

Jesus cited the budding of the fig tree, or the restoring of Israel as a nation, as a sign that we are getting close. And God has miraculously brought Israel back as a nation, in 1948, and has preserved and protected them.

The word translated "generation" usually refers to a national or ethnic group. There are people who have tried to calculate how many years a generation is, to figure when Jesus would return, counting years from 1948 or 1967. That is probably stretching the meaning of the term "generation."

Jesus was probably referring to the fact that He would preserve the ethnic identity of the Jewish people, even though they would be dispersed all over the earth. This is miraculous, that a people without a homeland for thousands of years could still maintain their national identity. It is unprecedented in history. But God has preserved them and brought them back, and this lets us know that the time of the end is drawing near.

earth will pass away, but My words will by no means pass away.

NO ONE KNOWS THE DAY OR HOUR

36a"But of that day and hour no one knows, not even the angels of [1]heaven, bbut My Father only. 37But as the days of Noah were, so also will the coming of the Son of Man be. 38aFor as in the days before the flood, they were eating and drinking, marrying and giving in marriage, until the day that Noah entered the ark, 39and did not know until the flood came and took them all away, so also will the coming of the Son of Man be. 40aThen two men will be in the field: one will be taken and the other left. 41Two women will be grinding at the mill: one will be taken and the other left. 42aWatch therefore, for you do not know what [1]hour your Lord is coming. 43aBut know this, that if the master of the house had known what [1]hour the thief would come, he would have watched and not allowed his house to be broken into. 44aThere-

Matt. 24:36

NO ONE KNOWS

Everyone should underline this verse in his Bible. No one knows the day or the hour, but people continue to write books trying to predict when Jesus will return. They have always been wrong so far and will continue to be wrong. When Jesus returns for His church and raptures us into heaven, it will come as a complete surprise. This is why Jesus went on here to discuss the unexpected nature of His return, as He talked about one of two workers taken and so forth.

The rapture is the next prophetic event to occur, and it will come as a surprise. After that you can count three and a half years until the abomination of desolation, another three and a half years until the second coming, a thousand years of the kingdom, then eternity. But the rapture is coming when no one expects it.

36 a Acts 1:7
b Zech. 14:7
1 NU adds nor the Son

38 a [Gen. 6:3–5]

40 a Luke 17:34

42 a Matt. 25:13
1 NU day

43 a Luke 12:39
1 Lit. watch of the night

44 a [1 Thess. 5:6]

45 a Luke 12:42–46
1 at the right time

46 a Rev. 16:15

47 a Matt. 25:21, 23

48 a [2 Pet. 3:4–9]
1 NU omits his coming

50 a Mark 13:32

51 a Matt. 8:12; 25:30

CHAPTER 25

1 a [Eph. 5:29, 30]

2 a Matt. 13:47; 22:10

5 a 1 Thess. 5:6

6 a [1 Thess. 4:16]
1 NU omits is coming

7 a Luke 12:35

10 a Luke 13:25

11 a [Matt. 7:21–23]

12 a [Hab. 1:13]

13 a Mark 13:35
b Matt. 24:36, 42
1 NU omits the rest of v. 13.

14 a Luke 19:12–27
b Matt. 21:33

fore you also be ready, for the Son of Man is coming at an hour you do not expect.

THE FAITHFUL SERVANT AND THE EVIL SERVANT

45a"Who then is a faithful and wise servant, whom his master made ruler over his household, to give them food [1]in due season? 46aBlessed is that servant whom his master, when he comes, will find so doing. 47Assuredly, I say to you that ahe will make him ruler over all his goods. 48But if that evil servant says in his heart, 'My master ais delaying [1]his coming,' 49and begins to beat his fellow servants, and to eat and drink with the drunkards, 50the master of that servant will come on a day when he is not looking for him and at an hour that he is anot aware of, 51and will cut him in two and appoint him his portion with the hypocrites. aThere shall be weeping and gnashing of teeth.

THE PARABLE OF THE WISE AND FOOLISH VIRGINS

25 "Then the kingdom of heaven shall be likened to ten virgins who took their lamps and went out to meet athe bridegroom. 2aNow five of them were wise, and five were foolish. 3Those who were foolish took their lamps and took no oil with them, 4but the wise took oil in their vessels with their lamps. 5But while the bridegroom was delayed, athey all slumbered and slept.

6"And at midnight aa cry was heard: 'Behold, the bridegroom [1]is coming; go out to meet him!' 7Then all those virgins arose and atrimmed their lamps. 8And the foolish said to the wise, 'Give us some of your oil, for our lamps are going out.' 9But the wise answered, saying, 'No, lest there should not be enough for us and you; but go rather to those who sell, and buy for yourselves.' 10And while they went to buy, the bridegroom came, and those who were ready went in with him to the wedding; and athe door was shut.

11"Afterward the other virgins came also, saying, a'Lord, Lord, open to us!' 12But he answered and said, 'Assuredly, I say to you, aI do not know you.'

13a"Watch therefore, for you bknow neither the day nor the hour [1]in which the Son of Man is coming.

THE PARABLE OF THE TALENTS

14a"For the kingdom of heaven is blike a man traveling to a far country,

Matt. 25:1–13

Wise and Foolish Virgins. The point of this parable is found in the end, in verse 13. "Watch therefore, for you know neither the day nor the hour in which the Son of Man is coming." No one knew when the bridegroom was coming; but some were prepared, and others weren't. Some had oil in their lamps; some lamps had burned out for lack of oil.

The oil is a symbol of the Holy Spirit. Since we don't know when Jesus will return, we need to be filled with the Spirit at all times, waiting for Him.

who called his own servants and delivered his goods to them. 15And to one he gave five talents, to another two, and to another one, ato each according to his own ability; and immediately he went on a journey. 16Then he who had

Matt. 25:14–30

INVESTING TALENTS

In this parable, Jesus has let us know how important it is that we stay busy while He is gone. We aren't to just sit and wait for His return, but we are to be productive with what He has entrusted to us. The three servants didn't know when he would return, but two of them used what they had, to the best of their abilities, and had fruit to show for it. The evil servant just buried his talent in the ground.

What are you doing with what God has given to you? Are you using your time, money, and talent for His glory, bearing fruit for the kingdom? Don't just sit around. I don't know when He will return; but He will return, and we will answer to Him about our stewardship.

---

15 a [Rom. 12:6]

21 a [1 Cor. 4:2]
b [Luke 12:44; 22:29, 30]
c [Heb. 12:2]

23 a Matt. 24:45, 47; 25:21
b [Ps. 16:11]

26 a Matt. 18:32

29 a Matt. 13:12

30 a Matt. 8:12; 22:13
b Matt. 7:23; 8:12; 24:51
c Ps. 112:10

31 a [1 Thess. 4:16]
1 NU omits holy

32 a [2 Cor. 5:10]
b Ezek. 20:38

---

received the five talents went and traded with them, and made another five talents. 17And likewise he who had received two gained two more also. 18But he who had received one went and dug in the ground, and hid his lord's money. 19After a long time the lord of those servants came and settled accounts with them.

20"So he who had received five talents came and brought five other talents, saying, 'Lord, you delivered to me five talents; look, I have gained five more talents besides them.' 21His lord said to him, 'Well done, good and faithful servant; you were afaithful over a few things, bI will make you ruler over many things. Enter into cthe joy of your lord.' 22He also who had received two talents came and said, 'Lord, you delivered to me two talents; look, I have gained two more talents besides them.' 23His lord said to him, a'Well done, good and faithful servant; you have been faithful over a few things, I will make you ruler over many things. Enter into bthe joy of your lord.'

24"Then he who had received the one talent came and said, 'Lord, I knew you to be a hard man, reaping where you have not sown, and gathering where you have not scattered seed. 25And I was afraid, and went and hid your talent in the ground. Look, there you have what is yours.'

26"But his lord answered and said to him, 'You awicked and lazy servant, you knew that I reap where I have not sown, and gather where I have not scattered seed. 27So you ought to have deposited my money with the bankers, and at my coming I would have received back my own with interest. 28So take the talent from him, and give it to him who has ten talents.

29a'For to everyone who has, more will be given, and he will have abundance; but from him who does not have, even what he has will be taken away. 30And cast the unprofitable servant ainto the outer darkness. bThere will be weeping and cgnashing of teeth.'

THE SON OF MAN WILL JUDGE THE NATIONS

31a"When the Son of Man comes in His glory, and all the 1holy angels with Him, then He will sit on the throne of His glory. 32aAll the nations will be gathered before Him, and bHe will separate them one from another, as a shepherd divides his sheep from the goats.

Matt. 25:31–46

THE COMING JUDGMENT

Everyone will face the Lord one day and will answer for what they have done with Jesus Christ. What He will say to those on His right hand is what He has always wanted to say to everyone: "Come, you blessed of My Father, inherit the kingdom prepared for you from the foundation of the world." But He won't be able to say that to everyone, because not everyone will have personally accepted the sacrifice of Jesus.

There are two kinds of people—those inside the kingdom and those outside the kingdom. In either case, it is your choice that puts you there.

33And He will set the ᵃsheep on His right hand, but the goats on the left. 34Then the King will say to those on His right hand, 'Come, you blessed of My Father, ᵃinherit the kingdom ᵇprepared for you from the foundation of the world: 35ᵃfor I was hungry and you gave Me food; I was thirsty and you gave Me drink; ᵇI was a stranger and you took Me in; 36I was ᵃnaked and you clothed Me; I was sick and you visited Me; ᵇI was in prison and you came to Me.'
37"Then the righteous will answer Him, saying, 'Lord, when did we see You hungry and feed You, or thirsty and give You drink? 38When did we see You a stranger and take You in, or naked and clothe You? 39Or when did we see You sick, or in prison, and come to You?' 40And the King will answer and say to them, 'Assuredly, I say to you, ᵃinasmuch as you did it to one of the least of these My brethren, you did it to Me.'
41"Then He will also say to those on the left hand, ᵃ'Depart from Me, you cursed, ᵇinto the everlasting fire prepared for ᶜthe devil and his angels: 42for I was hungry and you gave Me no food; I was thirsty and you gave Me no drink; 43I was a stranger and you did not take Me in, naked and you did not

Marginal references

33 ᵃ [John 10:11, 27, 28]

34 ᵃ [Rom. 8:17]
  ᵇ Mark 10:40

35 ᵃ Is. 58:7
  ᵇ [Heb. 13:2]

36 ᵃ [James 2:15, 16]
  ᵇ 2 Tim. 1:16

40 ᵃ Mark 9:41

41 ᵃ Matt. 7:23
  ᵇ Matt. 13:40, 42
  ᶜ [2 Pet. 2:4]

44 ¹ NU, M omit Him

45 ᵃ Prov. 14:31

46 ᵃ [Dan. 12:2]

CHAPTER 26

2 ᵃ Luke 22:1, 2

3 ᵃ John 11:47
  ¹ NU omits the scribes

4 ᵃ Acts 4:25–28
  ¹ deception

5 ᵃ Matt. 21:26

6 ᵃ Mark 14:3–9

8 ᵃ John 12:4

clothe Me, sick and in prison and you did not visit Me.'
44"Then they also will answer ¹Him, saying, 'Lord, when did we see You hungry or thirsty or a stranger or naked or sick or in prison, and did not minister to You?' 45Then He will answer them, saying, 'Assuredly, I say to you, ᵃinasmuch as you did not do it to one of the least of these, you did not do it to Me.' 46And ᵃthese will go away into everlasting punishment, but the righteous into eternal life."

THE PLOT TO KILL JESUS

26 Now it came to pass, when Jesus had finished all these sayings, that He said to His disciples, 2ᵃ"You know that after two days is the Passover, and the Son of Man will be delivered up to be crucified."
3ᵃThen the chief priests, ¹the scribes, and the elders of the people assembled at the palace of the high priest, who was called Caiaphas, 4and ᵃplotted to take Jesus by ¹trickery and kill Him. 5But they said, "Not during the feast, lest there be an uproar among the ᵃpeople."

Matt. 26:5

Not on Feast Day. The chief priests, scribes, and elders of the people were plotting to take Jesus and kill Him, but they didn't want to do it on the feast day because they thought the people would get upset. Despite their plans to the contrary, Jesus was killed on the Passover, right on time at 3:00 in the afternoon, which was the time when the Passover lamb was always killed.

The Jewish leaders had their plans, but God had His plans; and His plans always supercede those of others.

THE ANOINTING AT BETHANY

6And when Jesus was in ᵃBethany at the house of Simon the leper, 7a woman came to Him having an alabaster flask of very costly fragrant oil, and she poured it on His head as He sat at the table. 8ᵃBut when His disciples saw it, they were indignant, saying, "Why this waste? 9For this fragrant oil might have been sold for much and given to the poor."
10But when Jesus was aware of it, He said to them, "Why do you trouble the

woman? For she has done a good work for Me. ¹¹ᵃFor you have the poor with you always, but ᵇMe you do not have always. ¹²For in pouring this fragrant oil on My body, she did it for My ᵃburial. ¹³Assuredly, I say to you, wherever this gospel is preached in the whole world, what this woman has done will also be told as a memorial to her."

JUDAS AGREES TO BETRAY JESUS

¹⁴ᵃThen one of the twelve, called ᵇJudas Iscariot, went to the chief priests ¹⁵and said, ᵃ"What are you willing to give me if I deliver Him to you?" And they counted out to him thirty pieces of silver. ¹⁶So from that time he sought opportunity to betray Him.

JESUS CELEBRATES PASSOVER WITH HIS DISCIPLES

¹⁷ᵃNow on the first day of the Feast of the Unleavened Bread the disciples came to Jesus, saying to Him, "Where do You want us to prepare for You to eat the Passover?" ¹⁸And He said, "Go into the city to a certain man, and say to him, 'The Teacher says, ᵃ"My time is at hand; I will keep the Passover at your house with My disciples."'" ¹⁹So the disciples did as Jesus had directed them; and they prepared the Passover.

²⁰ᵃWhen evening had come, He sat down with the twelve. ²¹Now as they were eating, He said, "Assuredly, I say to you, one of you will ᵃbetray Me." ²²And they were exceedingly sorrowful, and each of them began to say to Him, "Lord, is it I?" ²³He answered and said, ᵃ"He who dipped his hand with Me in the dish will betray Me. ²⁴The Son of Man indeed goes just ᵃas it is written of Him, but ᵇwoe to that man by whom the Son of Man is betrayed! ᶜIt would have been good for that man if he had not been born." ²⁵Then Judas, who was betraying Him, answered and said, "Rabbi, is it I?" He said to him, "You have said it."

JESUS INSTITUTES THE LORD'S SUPPER

²⁶ᵃAnd as they were eating, ᵇJesus took bread, ¹blessed and broke it, and gave it to the disciples and said, "Take, eat; ᶜthis is My body." ²⁷Then He took the cup, and gave thanks, and gave it to them, saying, ᵃ"Drink from it, all of you. ²⁸For ᵃthis is My blood ᵇof the ¹new cov-

enant, which is shed ᶜfor many for the ²remission of sins. ²⁹But ᵃI say to you, I will not drink of this fruit of the vine from now on ᵇuntil that day when I drink it new with you in My Father's kingdom."

³⁰ᵃAnd when they had sung a hymn, they went out to the Mount of Olives.

Matt. 26:26–30
The Meaning of the Passover.

Jesus gave His disciples a new understanding of the Passover Feast. They had celebrated the Passover all their lives, but here He told them, "Take, eat; this is My body." He was the Bread of Life. And as He gave them the wine, He said, "This is My blood of the new covenant, which is shed for many for the remission of sins."

The introduction of the new covenant was a whole new way of relating with God. The price would shortly be paid.

JESUS PREDICTS PETER'S DENIAL

³¹Then Jesus said to them, ᵃ"All of you will ᵇbe ¹made to stumble because of Me this night, for it is written:

> ᶜ'I will strike the Shepherd,
>   And the sheep of the flock will be
>   scattered.'

³²But after I have been raised, ᵃI will go before you to Galilee." ³³Peter answered and said to Him, "Even if all are ¹made to stumble because of You, I will never be made to stumble." ³⁴Jesus said to him, ᵃ"Assuredly, I say to you that this night, before the rooster crows, you will deny Me three times." ³⁵Peter said to Him, "Even if I have to die with You, I will not deny You!" And so said all the disciples.

THE PRAYER IN THE GARDEN

³⁶ᵃThen Jesus came with them to a place called Gethsemane, and said to the disciples, "Sit here while I go and pray over there." ³⁷And He took with Him Peter and ᵃthe two sons of Zebedee, and He began to be sorrowful and deeply distressed. ³⁸Then He said to them, ᵃ"My soul is exceedingly sorrowful, even to death. Stay here and watch with Me."

---

11 ᵃ[Deut. 15:11]
ᵇ[John 13:33; 14:19; 16:5, 28; 17:11]

12 ᵃJohn 19:38–42

14 ᵃMark 14:10, 11; Luke 22:3–6
ᵇMatt. 10:4

15 ᵃZech. 11:12

17 ᵃEx. 12:6, 18–20

18 ᵃLuke 9:51

20 ᵃMark 14:17–21

21 ᵃJohn 6:70, 71; 13:21

23 ᵃPs. 41:9

24 ᵃ1 Cor. 15:3
ᵇLuke 17:1
ᶜJohn 17:12

26 ᵃMark 14:22–25
ᵇ1 Cor. 11:23–25
ᶜ[1 Pet. 2:24]
¹M gave thanks for

27 ᵃMark 14:23

28 ᵃ[Ex. 24:8]
ᵇJer. 31:31
ᶜMatt. 20:28
¹NU omits new
²forgiveness

29 ᵃMark 14:25
ᵇActs 10:41

30 ᵃMark 14:26–31

31 ᵃJohn 16:32
ᵇ[Matt. 11:6]
ᶜZech. 13:7
¹caused to take offense at Me

32 ᵃMatt. 28:7, 10, 16

33 ¹caused to take offense at You

34 ᵃJohn 13:38

36 ᵃMark 14:32–35

37 ᵃMatt. 4:21; 17:1

38 ᵃJohn 12:27

Matt. 26:39

LET THIS CUP PASS

Jesus prayed, "O My Father, if it is possible, let this cup pass from Me; nevertheless, not as I will, but as You will." If what is possible? If salvation and redemption can come in any other way. If man can be saved by any other method—by being good, by being religious, by being sincere—then let this cup pass from Me.

If it were possible for man to be saved in any other way, Jesus would not have gone to the cross. People sometimes take offense at the fact that we teach that Jesus is the only way. But His death was the only way; so He prayed, in beautiful submission to the Father, "Not as I will, but as You will."

39 He went a little farther and fell on His face, and ªprayed, ᵇ"O My Father, if it is possible, ᶜlet this cup pass from Me; nevertheless, ᵈnot as I will, but as You will."

40 Then He came to the disciples and found them sleeping, and said to Peter, "What! Could you not watch with Me one hour? 41 ªWatch and pray, lest you enter into temptation. ᵇThe spirit indeed is willing, but the flesh is weak."

42 Again, a second time, He went away and prayed, saying, "O My Father, ¹if this cup cannot pass away from Me unless I drink it, Your will be done." 43 And He came and found them asleep again, for their eyes were heavy.

44 So He left them, went away again, and prayed the third time, saying the same words. 45 Then He came to His disciples and said to them, "Are you still sleeping and resting? Behold, the hour ¹is at hand, and the Son of Man is being ªbetrayed into the hands of sinners. 46 Rise, let us be going. See, My betrayer is at hand."

BETRAYAL AND ARREST IN GETHSEMANE

47 And ªwhile He was still speaking, behold, Judas, one of the twelve, with a

39 ª[Heb. 5:7–9]
ᵇJohn 12:27
ᶜMatt. 20:22
ᵈJohn 5:30; 6:38

41 ªLuke 22:40, 46
ᵇ[Gal. 5:17]

42 ¹NU *if this may not pass away unless*

45 ªMatt. 17:22, 23; 20:18, 19
¹*has drawn near*

47 ªActs 1:16

49 ª2 Sam. 20:9

50 ªPs. 41:9; 55:13

51 ªJohn 18:10

52 ªRev. 13:10
¹M *die*

53 ªDan. 7:10

54 ªIs. 50:6; 53:2–11

56 ªLam. 4:20
ᵇJohn 18:15

57 ªJohn 18:12, 19–24

58 ªJohn 18:15, 16

59 ªPs. 35:11
¹NU omits *the elders*

60 ªMark 14:55
ᵇDeut. 19:15
¹NU *but found none, even though many false witnesses came forward.*
²NU omits *false witnesses*

61 ªJohn 2:19

62 ªMark 14:60

63 ªIs. 53:7
ᵇLev. 5:1

64 ªDan. 7:13

great multitude with swords and clubs, came from the chief priests and elders of the people. 48 Now His betrayer had given them a sign, saying, "Whomever I kiss, He is the One; seize Him." 49 Immediately he went up to Jesus and said, "Greetings, Rabbi!" ªand kissed Him.

50 But Jesus said to him, ª"Friend, why have you come?"

Then they came and laid hands on Jesus and took Him. 51 And suddenly, ªone of those who were with Jesus stretched out his hand and drew his sword, struck the servant of the high priest, and cut off his ear.

52 But Jesus said to him, "Put your sword in its place, ªfor all who take the sword will ¹perish by the sword. 53 Or do you think that I cannot now pray to My Father, and He will provide Me with ªmore than twelve legions of angels? 54 How then could the Scriptures be fulfilled, ªthat it must happen thus?"

55 In that hour Jesus said to the multitudes, "Have you come out, as against a robber, with swords and clubs to take Me? I sat daily with you, teaching in the temple, and you did not seize Me. 56 But all this was done that the ªScriptures of the prophets might be fulfilled."

Then ᵇall the disciples forsook Him and fled.

JESUS FACES THE SANHEDRIN

57 ªAnd those who had laid hold of Jesus led Him away to Caiaphas the high priest, where the scribes and the elders were assembled. 58 But ªPeter followed Him at a distance to the high priest's courtyard. And he went in and sat with the servants to see the end.

59 Now the chief priests, ¹the elders, and all the council sought ªfalse testimony against Jesus to put Him to death, 60 ¹but found none. Even though ªmany false witnesses came forward, they found none. But at last ᵇtwo ²false witnesses came forward 61 and said, "This fellow said, ª'I am able to destroy the temple of God and to build it in three days.'"

62 ªAnd the high priest arose and said to Him, "Do You answer nothing? What is it these men testify against You?" 63 But ªJesus kept silent. And the high priest answered and said to Him, ᵇ"I put You under oath by the living God: Tell us if You are the Christ, the Son of God!"

64 Jesus said to him, "It is as you said. Nevertheless, I say to you, ªhereafter

you will see the Son of Man bsitting at the right hand of the Power, and coming on the clouds of heaven."

65 aThen the high priest tore his clothes, saying, "He has spoken blasphemy! What further need do we have of witnesses? Look, now you have heard His bblasphemy! 66What do you think?" They answered and said, a"He is deserving of death."

67 aThen they spat in His face and beat Him; and bothers struck Him with 1the palms of their hands, 68saying, a"Prophesy to us, Christ! Who is the one who struckYou?"

PETER DENIES JESUS, AND WEEPS BITTERLY

69 aNow Peter sat outside in the courtyard. And a servant girl came to him, saying, "You also were with Jesus of Galilee."

70But he denied it before them all, saying, "I do not know what you are saying."

71And when he had gone out to the gateway, another girl saw him and said to those who were there, "This fellow also was with Jesus of Nazareth."

72But again he denied with an oath, "I do not know the Man!"

73And a little later those who stood by came up and said to Peter, "Surely you also are one of them, for your aspeech betrays you."

74Then ahe began to 1curse and 2swear, saying, "I do not know the Man!"

Immediately a rooster crowed. 75And Peter remembered the word of Jesus who had said to him, a"Before the rooster crows, you will deny Me three times." So he went out and wept bitterly.

JESUS HANDED OVER TO PONTIUS PILATE

27 When morning came, aall the chief priests and elders of the people plotted against Jesus to put Him to death. 2And when they had bound Him, they led Him away and adelivered Him to 1Pontius Pilate the governor.

JUDAS HANGS HIMSELF

3aThen Judas, His betrayer, seeing that He had been condemned, was remorseful and brought back the thirty bpieces of silver to the chief priests and elders, 4saying, "I have sinned by betraying innocent blood."

And they said, "What is that to us? You see to it!"

5Then he threw down the pieces of silver in the temple and adeparted, and went and hanged himself.

6But the chief priests took the silver pieces and said, "It is not lawful to put them into the treasury, because they are the price of blood." 7And they consulted together and bought with them the potter's field, to bury strangers in. 8Therefore that field has been called athe Field of Blood to this day.

9Then was fulfilled what was spoken by Jeremiah the prophet, saying, a"And they took the thirty pieces of silver, the value of Him who was priced, whom they of the children of Israel priced, 10and agave them for the potter's field, as the LORD directed me."

JESUS FACES PILATE

11Now Jesus stood before the governor. aAnd the governor asked Him, saying, "AreYou the King of the Jews?" Jesus said to him, b"It is as you say."

12And while He was being accused by the chief priests and elders, aHe answered nothing. 13Then Pilate said to Him, a"Do You not hear how many things they testify against You?" 14But He answered him not one word, so that the governor marveled greatly.

TAKING THE PLACE OF BARABBAS

15aNow at the feast the governor was accustomed to releasing to the multitude one prisoner whom they wished. 16And at that time they had a notorious

Cross-references

65 a 2 Kin. 18:37
b John 10:30-36

66 a Lev. 24:16

67 a Is. 50:6;
53:3
b Luke 22:63-65
1 Or rods,

68 a Mark 14:65

69 a John
18:16-18,
25-27

73 a Luke 22:59

74 a Mark 14:71
1 call down
curses
2 Swear oaths

75 a Matt. 26:34

CHAPTER 27

1 a John 18:28

2 a Acts 3:13
1 NU omits
Pontius

3 a Matt. 26:14
b Matt. 26:15

5 a Acts 1:18

8 a Acts 1:19

9 a Zech. 11:12

10 a Jer. 32:6-9;
Zech. 11:12, 13

11 a Mark 15:2-
5
b John 18:37

12 a John 19:9

13 a Matt. 26:62

15 a Luke
23:17-25

Matt. 27:12–14

Not a Word. As wild allegations were brought against Jesus, "He answered nothing." In fact, Pilate was amazed that He didn't defend Himself. His accusers were making ridiculous statements, and He said nothing. But that was a fulfillment of Isaiah 53:7, which said, "He was oppressed and He was afflicted, yet He opened not His mouth; He was led as a lamb to the slaughter, and as a sheep before its shearers is silent, so He opened not His mouth."

Jesus didn't need to defend Himself. He was doing the will of the Father.

prisoner called [1]Barabbas. [17]Therefore, when they had gathered together, Pilate said to them, "Whom do you want me to release to you? Barabbas, or Jesus who is called Christ?" [18]For he knew that they had handed Him over because of [a]envy.

[19]While he was sitting on the judgment seat, his wife sent to him, saying, "Have nothing to do with that just Man, for I have suffered many things today in a dream because of Him."

[20a]But the chief priests and elders persuaded the multitudes that they should ask for Barabbas and destroy Jesus. [21]The governor answered and said to them, "Which of the two do you want me to release to you?"

They said, [a]"Barabbas!"

[22]Pilate said to them, "What then shall I do with Jesus who is called Christ?"

They all said to him, "Let Him be crucified!"

[23]Then the governor said, [a]"Why, what evil has He done?"

But they cried out all the more, saying, "Let Him be crucified!"

[24]When Pilate saw that he could not prevail at all, but rather that a [1]tumult was rising, he [a]took water and washed his hands before the multitude, saying, "I am innocent of the blood of this [2]just Person. You see to it."

[25]And all the people answered and said, [a]"His blood be on us and on our children."

[26]Then he released Barabbas to them; and when [a]he had [1]scourged Jesus, he delivered Him to be crucified.

THE SOLDIERS MOCK JESUS

[27a]Then the soldiers of the governor took Jesus into the [1]Praetorium and gathered the whole [2]garrison around Him. [28]And they [a]stripped Him and [b]put a scarlet robe on Him. [29a]When they had [1]twisted a crown of thorns, they put it on His head, and a reed in His right hand. And they bowed the knee before Him and mocked Him, saying, "Hail, King of the Jews!" [30]Then [a]they spat on Him, and took the reed and struck Him on the head. [31]And when they had mocked Him, they took the robe off Him, put His own clothes on Him, [a]and led Him away to be crucified.

THE KING ON A CROSS

[32a]Now as they came out, [b]they found a man of Cyrene, Simon by name. Him they compelled to bear His cross. [33a]And

(Footnotes center column)

16 [1]NU *Jesus Barabbas*
18 [a]Matt. 21:38
20 [a]Acts 3:14
21 [a]Acts 3:14
23 [a]Acts 3:13
24 [a]Deut. 21:6–8
[1]*an uproar*
[2]NU omits *just*
25 [a]Josh. 2:19
26 [a][Is. 50:6; 53:5]
[1]*flogged* with a Roman scourge
27 [a]Mark 15:16–20
[1]*The governor's headquarters*
[2]*cohort*
28 [a]John 19:2
[b]Luke 23:11
29 [a]Is. 53:3
[1]Lit. *woven*
30 [a]Matt. 26:67
31 [a]Is. 53:7
32 [a]Heb. 13:12
[b]Mark 15:21
33 [a]John 19:17
34 [a]Ps. 69:21
[1]NU omits *sour*
35 [a]Luke 23:34
[b]Ps. 22:18
[1]NU, M omit the rest of v. 35.
36 [a]Matt. 27:54
37 [a]John 19:19
38 [a]Is. 53:9, 12
39 [a]Mark 15:29
40 [a]John 2:19
[b]Matt. 26:63
41 [1]M *scribes, the Pharisees, and the elders*
42 [a][John 3:14, 15]
[1]NU omits *If*
[2]NU, M in Him
43 [a]Ps. 22:8

Matt. ch. 27

Prophecy Fulfilled. As you read this account of the death of Jesus, it is helpful to read Isaiah 53 and Psalm 22 along with it.

These passages provide and predict so many details of what happened on the cross. Psalm 22 contains insights and details about crucifixion long before anyone had ever witnessed such a thing. Isaiah predicted Christ's scourging and mocking five hundred years before they occurred.

All the way through this chapter, you see references to these various prophecies. God knew what would happen, and He was in charge.

when they had come to a place called Golgotha, that is to say, Place of a Skull, [34a]they gave Him [1]sour wine mingled with gall to drink. But when He had tasted it, He would not drink.

[35a]Then they crucified Him, and divided His garments, casting lots, [1]that it might be fulfilled which was spoken by the prophet:

[b]"*They divided My garments among them,*
And for My clothing they cast lots."

[36a]Sitting down, they kept watch over Him there. [37]And they [a]put up over His head the accusation written against Him:

THIS IS JESUS THE KING
OF THE JEWS.

[38a]Then two robbers were crucified with Him, one on the right and another on the left.

[39]And [a]those who passed by blasphemed Him, wagging their heads [40]and saying, [a]"You who destroy the temple and build it in three days, save Yourself! [b]If You are the Son of God, come down from the cross."

[41]Likewise the chief priests also, mocking with the [1]scribes and elders, said, [42]"He [a]saved others; Himself He cannot save. [1]If He is the King of Israel, let Him now come down from the cross, and we will believe [2]Him. [43a]He trusted in God; let Him deliver Him now if He will have Him; for He said, 'I am the Son of God.'"

44a Even the robbers who were crucified with Him reviled Him with the same thing.

JESUS DIES ON THE CROSS

45a Now from the sixth hour until the ninth hour there was darkness over all the land. 46And about the ninth hour a Jesus cried out with a loud voice, saying, "Eli, Eli, lama sabachthani?" that is, b"My God, My God, why have You forsaken Me?"

Matt. 27:46

WHY HAVE YOU FORSAKEN ME?

Jesus cried out, in Aramaic, "Eli, Eli, lama sabachthani?" which means, "My God, My God, why have You forsaken Me?" It was at that moment that Jesus took your sins and mine upon Himself, bearing our iniquities as had been prophesied in Isaiah 53:6. God couldn't have fellowship with sin, so the Father had to turn His back on Jesus at that moment, the first time there was a break of fellowship within the Godhead. Our sin separated the Father from the Son.

Jesus quoted from Psalm 22, recognizing the horrible cost of His sacrifice. But He cried "My God, My God, why have You forsaken Me?" so that you would never have to cry it yourself. He bore the rejection so we wouldn't have to. No man would ever need to be forsaken by God again. Anyone forsaken by God from that moment on is that way by choice.

47Some of those who stood there, when they heard that, said, "This Man is calling for Elijah!" 48Immediately one of them ran and took a sponge, a filled it with sour wine and put it on a reed, and offered it to Him to drink. 49The rest said, "Let Him alone; let us see if Elijah will come to save Him." 50And Jesus a cried out again with a loud voice, and b yielded up His spirit. 51Then, behold, a the veil of the tem-

---

44 a Luke 23:39–43

45 a Mark 15:33–41

46 a [Heb. 5:7]
b Ps. 22:1

48 a Ps. 69:21

50 a Luke 23:46
b [John 10:18]

51 a Ex. 26:31

54 a Mark 15:39
b Matt. 14:33

55 a Luke 8:2, 3

56 a Mark 15:40, 47; 16:9
1 NU Joseph

57 a John 19:38–42

60 a Is. 53:9

---

ple was torn in two from top to bottom; and the earth quaked, and the rocks were split, 52and the graves were opened; and many bodies of the saints who had fallen asleep were raised; 53and coming out of the graves after His resurrection, they went into the holy city and appeared to many.

Matt. 27:51

THE RIPPED VEIL

The veil in the temple was an eighteen-inch thick woven cloth curtain. The purpose of the veil was to keep man from coming to God. It blocked the way to the Most Holy Place where only the high priest was permitted to enter, and only once a year. But when the veil was torn, it signaled the fact that through Jesus Christ we now have access to God. We can now come boldly before the throne of God (Heb. 4:16).

It is interesting to note that the veil was torn from top to bottom, not from bottom to top. This was because God tore the veil. He ripped the way open for us to approach Him.

54a So when the centurion and those with him, who were guarding Jesus, saw the earthquake and the things that had happened, they feared greatly, saying, b"Truly this was the Son of God!" 55And many women a who followed Jesus from Galilee, ministering to Him, were there looking on from afar, 56a among whom were Mary Magdalene, Mary the mother of James and 1Joses, and the mother of Zebedee's sons.

JESUS BURIED IN JOSEPH'S TOMB

57Now a when evening had come, there came a rich man from Arimathea, named Joseph, who himself had also become a disciple of Jesus. 58This man went to Pilate and asked for the body of Jesus. Then Pilate commanded the body to be given to him. 59When Joseph had taken the body, he wrapped it in a clean linen cloth, 60and a laid it in his

new tomb which he had hewn out of the rock; and he rolled a large stone against the door of the tomb, and departed. [61]And Mary Magdalene was there, and the other Mary, sitting [1]opposite the tomb.

PILATE SETS A GUARD

[62]On the next day, which followed the Day of Preparation, the chief priests and Pharisees gathered together to Pilate, [63]saying, "Sir, we remember, while He was still alive, how that deceiver said, [a]'After three days I will rise.' [64]Therefore command that the tomb be made secure until the third day, lest His disciples come [1]by night and steal Him away, and say to the people, 'He has risen from the dead.' So the last deception will be worse than the first." [65]Pilate said to them, "You have a guard; go your way, make it as secure as you know how." [66]So they went and made the tomb secure, [a]sealing the stone and setting the guard.

HE IS RISEN

28 Now [a]after the Sabbath, as the first day of the week began to dawn, Mary Magdalene [b]and the other Mary came to see the tomb. [2]And behold, there was a great earthquake; for [a]an angel of the Lord descended

from heaven, and came and rolled back the stone [1]from the door, and sat on it. [3][a]His countenance was like lightning, and his clothing as white as snow. [4]And the guards shook for fear of him, and became like [a]dead men.

[5]But the angel answered and said to the women, "Do not be afraid, for I know that you seek Jesus who was crucified. [6]He is not here; for He is risen, [a]as He said. Come, see the place where the Lord lay. [7]And go quickly and tell His disciples that He is risen from the dead, and indeed [a]He is going before you into Galilee; there you will see Him. Behold, I have told you."

[8]So they went out quickly from the tomb with fear and great joy, and ran to bring His disciples word.

THE WOMEN WORSHIP THE RISEN LORD

[9]And [1]as they went to tell His disciples, behold, [a]Jesus met them, saying, "Rejoice!" So they came and held Him by the feet and worshiped Him. [10]Then Jesus said to them, "Do not be afraid. Go and tell [a]My brethren to go to Galilee, and there they will see Me."

THE SOLDIERS ARE BRIBED

[11]Now while they were going, behold, some of the guard came into the city and reported to the chief priests all the

Cross-references

61 [1]in front of

63 [a]Mark 8:31; 10:34

64 [1]NU omits by night

66 [a]Dan. 6:17

CHAPTER 28

1 [a]Luke 24:1–10 [b]Matt. 27:56, 61

2 [a]Mark 16:5 [1]NU omits from the door

3 [a]Dan. 7:9; 10:6

4 [a]Rev. 1:17

6 [a]Matt. 12:40; 16:21; 17:23; 20:19

7 [a]Mark 16:7

9 [a]John 20:14 [1]NU omits as they went to tell His disciples

10 [a]John 20:17

DIFFERENT RESURRECTION ACCOUNTS

Matt. 28:1–10

Each of the four Gospels gives a different perspective on the events that happened after the resurrection, giving us different information and insights. Matthew was there himself and recorded his personal witness. Mark was just a kid at the time and probably got his information from Peter. Luke came along later and interviewed a lot of eyewitnesses to the event. And John wrote later than the other Gospel writers, filling in some of the gaps. He didn't bother repeating what had already been said, but filled in some of the details that hadn't been recorded.

It is rather confusing when you put the accounts side by side. But let me say, first of all, that if all of their stories had been identical, their witness would be suspect. If four witnesses are all telling an identical story, it is obvious that they are in collusion, comparing their stories and adjusting them to match. Thus, I am glad that their accounts differ. Eyewitness accounts that are credible always do.

It is possible to harmonize all four of the accounts to see that they aren't contradictory. It just involves laying out the four accounts and meshing them together. If you are so inclined, you can do this yourself; or you may consult one of the many Gospel harmonizations that do it for you. *Halley's Bible Handbook* has a good one, and there are other books that harmonize the entire four Gospels, such as *A Harmony of the Gospels* by A. T. Robertson. The important thing to realize is that all these apparent contradictions can easily be dealt with and have been.

things that had happened. ¹²When they had assembled with the elders and consulted together, they gave a large sum of money to the soldiers, ¹³saying, "Tell them, 'His disciples came at night and stole Him away while we slept.' ¹⁴And if this comes to the governor's ears, we will appease him and make you secure." ¹⁵So they took the money and did as they were instructed; and this saying is commonly reported among the Jews until this day.

THE GREAT COMMISSION

¹⁶Then the eleven disciples went away into Galilee, to the mountain ᵃwhich Jesus had appointed for them. ¹⁷When they saw Him, they worshiped Him; but some ᵃdoubted.

Matt. 28:18–20

THE GREAT COMMISSION

Jesus told His disciples that all authority, in heaven and earth, belongs to Him; and on the basis of the power and authority, He commissioned them to ministry. He told them to go, to make disciples, to baptize, and to teach. The mission of the church is to go out and share the message of Jesus—to take His teaching to the world.

It is a great privilege to bear witness to Jesus and to spread His teachings. It may sometimes be intimidating, but we have His promise that "I am with you always, even to the end of the age." And remember, the One who is with you always is the same One who said, "All authority has been given to Me."

16 ᵃ Matt. 26:32; 28:7, 10

17 ᵃ John 20:24–29

18 ᵃ [Dan. 7:13, 14]

19 ᵃ Mark 16:15
ᵇ Luke 24:47
¹ M omits *therefore*

20 ᵃ [Acts 2:42]
ᵇ [Acts 4:31; 18:10; 23:11]
¹ NU omits *Amen.*

¹⁸And Jesus came and spoke to them, saying, ᵃ"All authority has been given to Me in heaven and on earth. ¹⁹ᵃGo ¹therefore and ᵇmake disciples of all the nations, baptizing them in the name of the Father and of the Son and of the Holy Spirit, ²⁰ᵃteaching them to observe all things that I have commanded you; and lo, I am ᵇwith you always, even to the end of the age." ¹Amen.

Matt. 28:19

THE FORMULA FOR BAPTISM

Jesus here told the disciples to baptize people "in the name of the Father and of the Son and of the Holy Spirit." This wording is then used by many for baptism. But in Acts 2:38, Peter referred to being baptized "in the name of Jesus." So there are some who feel that when we baptize we should say "in the name of Jesus." It really doesn't matter; but just to touch all the bases, I usually say, "I baptize you now in the name of Jesus, in the name of the Father, the Son, and the Holy Spirit."

Incidentally, this verse is also a great verse to prove the Trinity. The word "name" is singular. Thus, it isn't "in the names of the Father, Son, and Holy Spirit" but "in the name," singular. There is one God, eternally existent in three persons. This is just one more place in the Bible that makes this clear.

THE GOSPEL ACCORDING TO

MARK

INTRODUCTION The gospel of Mark is thought by many scholars to be the earliest of the gospel accounts. There have been some who dispute this, but people will argue over anything, and it really doesn't matter whether it was written first or not.

It was written by John Mark (his Jewish name was John and his Roman name was Mark). Mark was the nephew of Barnabas and was just a boy when these events took place. He went with Paul and his uncle Barnabas on Paul's first missionary journey. Mark didn't make it through the entire missionary journey, but later he was of value to Paul, and had earned his respect.

It is generally accepted that Mark's account of the life of Jesus is really the recounting of Peter's story and that it was compiled from Peter's sermons, his other writings, and from the personal conversations Mark had with Peter, combined perhaps with the personal experiences of the young Mark. (He is perhaps referring to himself in Mark 14:51–52.)

While the book of Matthew depicts Jesus as the King, the book of Mark presents Jesus as a servant. It tells the story of what Jesus did. It is a book of action, which is to be expected since Peter was always a man of action. It is shorter than the other Gospels because it tells the stories without transcribing the sermons of Jesus. Again, the book is concerned more with what Jesus did than with what He said.

It was probably written by Mark when he and Peter were both in Rome, or perhaps shortly after Peter was killed, and the intended audience was Roman Christians. They were undergoing severe persecution for their faith, and the story of the servanthood of Jesus, and the fact that His followers are called to be servants, too, had personal relevance to them.

In sharp contrast to Matthew, who quoted the Old Testament constantly, Mark contains almost no Old Testament quotes, and he spends a lot of time explaining Jewish traditions that would be foreign to the Roman readers.

The most common word in the book of Mark is the conjunction "and." As a book of action it streams events together in a rapid-fire style, using the word "and" to hold the stories together.

In our busy society today, where everyone is fighting to get ahead, the message of the serving Jesus, who kept constantly on the move, always responding immediately to the instructions of the Father, is a wonderful reminder of how we need to live. May we learn to serve incessantly, and respond immediately, to the call of our Master.

JOHN THE BAPTIST PREPARES THE WAY

1 The ᵃbeginning of the gospel of Jesus Christ, ᵇthe Son of God. 2As it is written in ¹the Prophets:

ᵃ"*Behold, I send My messenger before Your face, Who will prepare Your way before You.*"
3 "*The*ᵃ *voice of one crying in the wilderness: 'Prepare the way of the LORD; Make His paths straight.'*"

Mark 1:3

Preparing the Way. Mark begins by quoting the prophecies from Malachi and Isaiah concerning John the Baptist, the one who would announce the coming of Jesus. John is seen as he preaches, "Prepare the way of the LORD." Whose way was he preparing? Clearly it was the way of Jesus.

The original quotation from Isaiah 40:3 uses the word "Yahweh" or "Jehovah" for "Lord." So according to the prophecy, John would be preparing the way of Yahweh. This clearly identifies Jesus as God. This presents a real problem for anyone who doesn't believe that Jesus was Jehovah God.

4ᵃJohn came baptizing in the wilderness and preaching a baptism of repentance ¹for the remission of sins. 5ᵃThen all the land of Judea, and those from Jerusalem, went out to him and were all baptized by him in the Jordan River, confessing their sins.

6Now John was ᵃclothed with camel's hair and with a leather belt around his waist, and he ate locusts and wild honey. 7And he preached, saying, ᵃ"There comes One after me who is mightier than I, whose sandal strap I am not worthy to stoop down and loose. 8ᵃI indeed baptized you with water, but He will baptize you ᵇwith the Holy Spirit."

JOHN BAPTIZES JESUS

9ᵃIt came to pass in those days *that* Jesus came from Nazareth of Galilee, and was baptized by John in the Jordan.

CHAPTER 1

1 ᵃLuke 3:22
ᵇMatt. 14:33

2 ᵃMal. 3:1
¹NU *Isaiah the prophet*

3 ᵃIs. 40:3

4 ᵃMatt. 3:1
¹Or *because of forgiveness*

5 ᵃMatt. 3:5

6 ᵃMatt. 3:4

7 ᵃJohn 1:27

8 ᵃActs 1:5; 11:16
ᵇIs. 44:3

9 ᵃMatt. 3:13–17

10 ᵃMatt. 3:16
ᵇActs 10:38
¹NU *out of*
²*torn open*

11 ᵃMatt. 3:17; 12:18

12 ᵃMatt. 4:1–11
¹*sent Him out*

13 ᵃMatt. 4:10, 11

14 ᵃMatt. 4:12
ᵇMatt. 4:23
¹NU omits *of the kingdom*

15 ᵃ[Gal. 4:4]
ᵇMatt. 3:2; 4:17
¹*has drawn near*

16 ᵃLuke 5:2–11

17 ᵃMatt. 13:47, 48

18 ᵃ[Luke 14:26]

10ᵃAnd immediately, coming up ¹from the water, He saw the heavens ²parting and the Spirit ᵇdescending upon Him like a dove. 11Then a voice came from heaven, ᵃ"You are My beloved Son, in whom I am well pleased."

SATAN TEMPTS JESUS

12ᵃImmediately the Spirit ¹drove Him into the wilderness. 13And He was there in the wilderness forty days, tempted by Satan, and was with the wild beasts; ᵃand the angels ministered to Him.

Mark 1:12–13

The Spirit Drove Him. It is interesting that as Jesus' ministry was starting, right after the Holy Spirit had descended upon Him, the first thing that happened was that the Spirit drove Him into the wilderness to be tempted. It wasn't Satan who drove Him to the wilderness; it was the Spirit.

Jesus' first item of business was a time of testing and a time of confrontation with the powers of darkness. Many believers have had this same type of experience, immediately after beginning to serve the Lord.

JESUS BEGINS HIS GALILEAN MINISTRY

14ᵃNow after John was put in prison, Jesus came to Galilee, ᵇpreaching the gospel ¹of the kingdom of God, 15and saying, ᵃ"The time is fulfilled, and ᵇthe kingdom of God ¹is at hand. Repent, and believe in the gospel."

FOUR FISHERMEN CALLED AS DISCIPLES

16ᵃAnd as He walked by the Sea of Galilee, He saw Simon and Andrew his brother casting a net into the sea; for they were fishermen. 17Then Jesus said to them, "Follow Me, and I will make you become ᵃfishers of men." 18ᵃThey immediately left their nets and followed Him.

19When He had gone a little farther from there, He saw James the *son of* Zebedee, and John his brother, who also *were* in the boat mending their nets. 20And immediately He called them, and they left their father Zebedee

in the boat with the hired servants, and went after Him.

JESUS CASTS OUT AN UNCLEAN SPIRIT

21aThen they went into Capernaum, and immediately on the Sabbath He entered the bsynagogue and taught. 22aAnd they were astonished at His teaching, for He taught them as one having authority, and not as the scribes. 23Now there was a man in their synagogue with an aunclean spirit. And he cried out, 24saying, "Let us alone! aWhat have we to do with You, Jesus of Nazareth? Did You come to destroy us? I bknow who You are—the cHoly One of God!"

25But Jesus arebuked him, saying, 1"Be quiet, and come out of him!" 26And when the unclean spirit ahad convulsed him and cried out with a loud voice, he came out of him. 27Then

Mark 1:24

LET US ALONE!

As Jesus confronted this man who was possessed by demons, the demons said to Jesus, "Let us alone!" This is so often the cry that comes from those who are doing evil. They want to be left alone. They don't want to hear about their sin. Evil doesn't like to be confronted.

Several years ago some men from our church had been going up to West Hollywood to share the gospel in this predominantly homosexual community. This prompted a large group of radical homosexual activists to come to Calvary Chapel on a Sunday morning to protest. It was a pathetic scene as all these angry men and women were carrying signs and screaming and yelling in front of our church. But the gist of what they were saying and the thrust of most of their rantings was "Leave us alone!"

It is so sad when people are being destroyed by evil and they just want to be left alone.

they were all amazed, so that they questioned among themselves, saying, 1"What is this? What new 2doctrine is this? For with authority He commands even the unclean spirits, and they obey Him." 28And immediately His afame spread throughout all the region around Galilee.

PETER'S MOTHER-IN-LAW HEALED

29aNow as soon as they had come out of the synagogue, they entered the house of Simon and Andrew, with James and John. 30But Simon's wife's mother lay sick with a fever, and they told Him about her at once. 31So He came and took her by the hand and lifted her up, and immediately the fever left her. And she served them.

MANY HEALED AFTER SABBATH SUNSET

32aAt evening, when the sun had set, they brought to Him all who were sick and those who were demon-possessed. 33And the whole city was gathered together at the door. 34Then He healed many who were sick with various diseases, and acast out many demons; and He bdid not allow the demons to speak, because they knew Him.

PREACHING IN GALILEE

35Now ain the morning, having risen a long while before daylight, He went out and departed to a 1solitary place; and there He bprayed. 36And Simon and those who were with Him searched for Him. 37When they found Him, they said to Him, a"Everyone bis looking for You."

38But He said to them, a"Let us go into the next towns, that I may preach there also, because bfor this purpose I have come forth." 39aAnd He was preaching in their synagogues throughout all Galilee, and bcasting out demons.

JESUS CLEANSES A LEPER

40aNow a leper came to Him, imploring Him, kneeling down to Him and saying to Him, "If You are willing, You can make me clean." 41Then Jesus, moved with acompassion, stretched out His hand and touched him, and said to him, "I am willing; be cleansed." 42As soon as He had spoken, aimmediately the leprosy left him, and he was cleansed. 43And He strictly warned him and sent him away at once, 44and said to him, "See that you say nothing to anyone; but go

---

21 aLuke 4:31–37
bMatt. 4:23

22 aMatt. 7:28, 29; 13:54

23 a[Matt. 12:43]

24 aMatt. 8:28, 29
bJames 2:19
cPs. 16:10

25 a[Luke 4:39]
1Lit. Be muzzled

26 aMark 9:20

27 1NU What is this? A new doctrine with authority! He 2teaching

28 aMatt. 4:24; 9:31

29 aLuke 4:38, 39

32 aMatt. 8:16, 17

34 aLuke 13:32
bActs 16:17, 18

35 aLuke 4:42, 43
bLuke 5:16; 6:12; 9:28, 29
1deserted

37 aJohn 3:26; 12:19
b[Heb. 11:6]

38 aLuke 4:43
b[Is. 61:1, 2]

39 aMatt. 4:23; 9:35
bMark 5:8, 13; 7:29, 30

40 aLuke 5:12–14

41 aLuke 7:13

42 aMatt. 15:28

your way, show yourself to the priest, and offer for your cleansing those things ᵃwhich Moses commanded, as a testimony to them."

45 ᵃHowever, he went out and began to proclaim *it* freely, and to spread the matter, so that Jesus could no longer openly enter the city, but was outside in deserted places; ᵇand they came to Him from every direction.

JESUS FORGIVES AND HEALS A PARALYTIC

2 And again ᵃHe entered Capernaum after *some* days, and it was heard that He was in the house. 2 ¹Immediately many gathered together, so that there was no longer room to receive *them*, not even near the door. And He preached the word to them. 3Then they came to Him, bringing a ᵃparalytic who was carried by four *men*. 4And when they could not come near Him because of the crowd, they uncovered the roof where He was. So when they had broken through, they let down the bed on which the paralytic was lying.

5When Jesus saw their faith, He said to the paralytic, "Son, your sins are forgiven you."

6And some of the scribes were sitting there and reasoning in their hearts, 7"Why does this *Man* speak blasphemies like this? ᵃWho can forgive sins but God alone?"

8But immediately, when Jesus perceived in His spirit that they reasoned thus within themselves, He said to them, "Why do you reason about these things in your hearts? 9ᵃWhich is easier, to say to the paralytic, '*Your* sins are forgiven you,' or to say, 'Arise, take up your bed and walk'? 10But that you may know that the Son of Man has ¹power on earth to forgive sins"—He said to the paralytic, 11"I say to you, arise, take up your bed, and go to your house." 12Immediately he arose, took up the bed, and went out in the presence of them all, so that all were amazed and ᵃglorified God, saying, "We never saw *anything* like this!"

MATTHEW THE TAX COLLECTOR

13ᵃThen He went out again by the sea; and all the multitude came to Him, and He taught them. 14ᵃAs He passed by, He saw Levi the *son* of Alphaeus sitting at the tax office. And He said to him, ᵇ"Follow Me." So he arose and ᶜfollowed Him.

15ᵃNow it happened, as He was dining in *Levi's* house, that many tax col-

---

44 ᵃLev. 14:1–32

45 ᵃLuke 5:15
ᵇMark 2:2, 13; 3:7

CHAPTER 2

1 ᵃMatt. 9:1

2 ¹NU omits *Immediately*

3 ᵃMatt. 4:24; 8:6

7 ᵃIs. 43:25

9 ᵃMatt. 9:5

10 ¹*authority*

12 ᵃ[Phil. 2:11]

13 ᵃMatt. 9:9

14 ᵃLuke 5:27–32
ᵇJohn 1:43; 12:26; 21:22
ᶜLuke 18:28

15 ᵃMatt. 9:10

16 ¹NU *of the*

17 ᵃMatt. 9:12, 13; 18:11
¹NU omits *to repentance*

18 ᵃLuke 5:33–38

19 ¹Lit. *sons of the bride-chamber*

Mark 2:10

THE SON OF MAN

This is the first time in the gospel of Mark where Jesus took upon Himself the title "The Son of Man." It is a messianic title that Jesus would use to describe Himself several times.

In Daniel 7:13, Daniel wrote, "I was watching in the night visions, and behold, One like the Son of Man, coming with the clouds of heaven!" He went on to further describe the coming of Messiah, whose kingdom "shall not be destroyed." So, when Jesus said He is the Son of Man, He wasn't just saying He was human. Anyone could say that. He was saying that He was the Messiah.

Other messianic titles emphasize the fact that Messiah would be God, but this title emphasized that He would also be a man.

---

lectors and sinners also sat together with Jesus and His disciples; for there were many, and they followed Him. 16And when the scribes ¹and Pharisees saw Him eating with the tax collectors and sinners, they said to His disciples, "How *is it* that He eats and drinks with tax collectors and sinners?"

17When Jesus heard *it*, He said to them, ᵃ"Those who are well have no need of a physician, but those who are sick. I did not come to call *the* righteous, but sinners, ¹to repentance."

JESUS IS QUESTIONED ABOUT FASTING

18ᵃThe disciples of John and of the Pharisees were fasting. Then they came and said to Him, "Why do the disciples of John and of the Pharisees fast, but Your disciples do not fast?"

19And Jesus said to them, "Can the ¹friends of the bridegroom fast while the bridegroom is with them? As long as they have the bridegroom with them they cannot fast. 20But the days will come when the bridegroom will be

ataken away from them, and then they will fast in those days. ²¹No one sews a piece of unshrunk cloth on an old garment; or else the new piece pulls away from the old, and the tear is made worse. ²²And no one puts new wine into old wineskins; or else the new wine bursts the wineskins, the wine is spilled, and the wineskins are ruined. But new wine must be put into new wineskins."

20 a Acts 1:9; 13:2, 3; 14:23

23 a Luke 6:1–5 b Deut. 23:25

24 a Ex. 20:10; 31:15

25 a 1 Sam. 21:1–6

26 a Lev. 24:5–9

27 a Deut. 5:14

28 a Matt. 12:8

CHAPTER 3

1 a Luke 6:6–11

2 a Luke 14:1; 20:20

Mark 2:14–17

DUBIOUS ASSOCIATIONS

Jesus had just called Levi (also called Matthew) to follow Him. Levi apparently had a party for a bunch of his sinner friends, so they could meet Jesus too. Many of them were converted as well. But the religious leaders were indignant that Jesus would hang out with such a sinful bunch, and they criticized Him.

Jesus' response was, "Those who are well have no need of a physician, but those who are sick. I did not come to call the righteous, but sinners, to repentance." Jesus used associations for the purpose of outreach. We should too.

JESUS IS LORD OF THE SABBATH

²³ªNow it happened that He went through the grainfields on the Sabbath; and as they went His disciples began ᵇto pluck the heads of grain. ²⁴And the Pharisees said to Him, "Look, why do they do what is ªnot lawful on the Sabbath?"

²⁵But He said to them, "Have you never read ªwhat David did when he was in need and hungry, he and those with him: ²⁶how he went into the house of God in the days of Abiathar the high priest, and ate the showbread, ªwhich is not lawful to eat except for the priests, and also gave some to those who were with him?"

²⁷And He said to them, "The Sabbath was made for man, and not man for the ªSabbath. ²⁸Therefore ªthe Son of Man is also Lord of the Sabbath."

HEALING ON THE SABBATH

3 And ªHe entered the synagogue again, and a man was there who had a withered hand. ²So they ªwatched

NEW WINESKINS
Mark 2:22

Old wineskins become hard and crusty, and you wouldn't want to put valuable new wine in them. The new wine would break and tear apart the old wineskins. You put new wine in new wineskins that are soft and pliable.

Jesus used this imagery to explain a basic principle that is true of every new work of God. God will almost always go outside the organized religious systems to begin a new work. The old religious system that the scribes and Pharisees were a part of would not be able to handle the new work that God wanted to do. It was too hard and stiff, and no longer pliable, which is why we always want to avoid the stiffening effect of tradition. This is basically how I came up with one of the few parables I have written, which is: "Blessed are the flexible, for they shall not be broken."

Calvary Chapel started as a movement that was truly a fresh work, outside the scope of most other churches that were around at the time. God wanted to do a fresh work, so He created a new skin to pour His Spirit into, and we got to see His blessings. But if the Lord tarries, and He takes me home before the rapture, I hope no one tries to institutionalize what God has done at Calvary Chapel. I don't want anyone saying, "When Chuck was here" and "This is the way Chuck did it."

May God help us not to get rigid. I want to stay flexible and open. I want to see a continual movement of the Spirit of God; so I need to stay supple, flexible, and pliable. If we create a religious system, with rigid controls and traditions, then God will have to once again go outside of us in order to do a new work of His Spirit.

Him closely, whether He would ᵇheal him on the Sabbath, so that they might ¹accuse Him. ³And He said to the man who had the withered hand, ¹"Step forward." ⁴Then He said to them, "Is it lawful on the Sabbath to do good or to do evil, to save life or to kill?" But they kept silent. ⁵And when He had looked around at them with anger, being grieved by the ᵃhardness of their hearts, He said to the man, "Stretch it out, and his hand was restored ¹as whole as the other. ⁶ᵃThen the Pharisees went out and immediately plotted with ᵇthe Herodians against Him, how they might destroy Him.

Mark 3:5

STRETCH OUT YOUR HAND

Jesus told this man with a withered hand to stretch out his hand. He was telling him to do something that is impossible. The crippled man couldn't stretch out his hand. He had two options. He could argue with Jesus, telling Him about his condition, describing the history of the problem, and telling Him of all the times he'd tried to stretch it out and couldn't. Or he could just stretch it out, as Jesus had commanded. He chose, by faith, to obey Jesus, and he was healed.

Jesus gives us many commands that we are unable to do, in our own flesh. We can either argue with Him, telling Him all the reasons why we are disabled from doing what He wants us to do, or we can obey by faith. If He commands us to do something, we can do it, with His help.

A GREAT MULTITUDE FOLLOWS JESUS

⁷But Jesus withdrew with His disciples to the sea. And a great multitude from Galilee followed Him, ᵃand from Judea ⁸and Jerusalem and Idumea and beyond the Jordan; and those from Tyre and Sidon, a great multitude, when

2 ᵇ Luke 13:14
¹ *bring charges against*

3 ¹ Lit. *Arise into the midst*

5 ᵃ Zech. 7:12
¹ NU omits *as whole as the other*

6 ᵃ Mark 12:13
ᵇ Matt. 22:16

7 ᵃ Luke 6:17

8 ᵃ Mark 5:19

10 ᵃ Luke 7:21
ᵇ Matt. 9:21; 14:36

11 ᵃ Luke 4:41
ᵇ Matt. 8:29; 14:33

12 ᵃ Mark 1:25, 34

13 ᵃ Luke 9:1

14 ¹ NU adds *whom He also named apostles*

15 ¹ *authority*
² NU omits *to heal sicknesses and*

16 ᵃ John 1:42
¹ NU *and He appointed the twelve: Simon . . .*

20 ᵃ Mark 6:31

21 ᵃ Mark 6:3
ᵇ John 7:5; 10:20

they heard how ᵃmany things He was doing, came to Him. ⁹So He told His disciples that a small boat should be kept ready for Him because of the multitude, lest they should crush Him. ¹⁰For He healed ᵃmany, so that as many as had afflictions pressed about Him to ᵇtouch Him. ¹¹ᵃAnd the unclean spirits, whenever they saw Him, fell down before Him and cried out, saying, ᵇ"You are the Son of God." ¹²But ᵃHe sternly warned them that they should not make Him known.

THE TWELVE APOSTLES

¹³ᵃAnd He went up on the mountain and called to *Him* those He Himself wanted. And they came to Him. ¹⁴Then He appointed twelve, ¹that they might be with Him and that He might send them out to preach, ¹⁵and to have ¹power ²to heal sicknesses and to cast out demons: ¹⁶¹Simon, ᵃto whom He gave the name Peter; ¹⁷James the *son* of Zebedee and John the brother of James, to whom He gave the name Boanerges, that is, "Sons of Thunder"; ¹⁸Andrew, Philip, Bartholomew, Matthew, Thomas, James the *son* of Alphaeus, Thaddaeus, Simon the Cananite; ¹⁹and Judas Iscariot, who also betrayed Him. And they went into a house.

Mark 3:13
Those He Himself Wanted.

Many people were following Jesus by now, but here we see He called twelve of them to serve a special role as apostles. These were the ones He would train and then send out to preach. He "called to Him those He Himself wanted." Jesus told His disciples in John 15:16, "You did not choose Me, but I chose you and appointed you that you should go and bear fruit."

God has a special role for each of us to play in His body, and He called you because He wanted you.

A HOUSE DIVIDED CANNOT STAND

²⁰Then the multitude came together again, ᵃso that they could not so much as eat bread. ²¹But when His ᵃown people heard *about this*, they went out to lay hold of Him, ᵇfor they said, "He is out of His mind."

²²And the scribes who came down from Jerusalem said, a"He has Beelzebub," and, "By the bruler of the demons He casts out demons."

²³ aSo He called them to *Himself* and said to them in parables: "How can Satan cast out Satan? ²⁴If a kingdom is divided against itself, that kingdom cannot stand. ²⁵And if a house is divided against itself, that house cannot stand. ²⁶And if Satan has risen up against himself, and is divided, he cannot stand, but has an end. ²⁷aNo one can enter a strong man's house and plunder his goods, unless he first binds the strong man. And then he will plunder his house.

THE UNPARDONABLE SIN

²⁸a"Assuredly, I say to you, all sins will be forgiven the sons of men, and whatever blasphemies they may utter; ²⁹but he who blasphemes against the Holy Spirit never has forgiveness, but is subject to eternal condemnation"— ³⁰because they asaid, "He has an unclean spirit."

JESUS' MOTHER AND BROTHERS SEND FOR HIM

³¹aThen His brothers and His mother came, and standing outside they sent to Him, calling Him. ³²And a multitude was sitting around Him; and they said to Him, "Look, Your mother and Your brothers *I*are outside seeking You." ³³But He answered them, saying, "Who is My mother, or My brothers?" ³⁴And He looked around in a circle at those who sat about Him, and said,

---

Mark 3:35

The Closest Relationship. Jesus taught here that there is a closer bond of relationship than those of blood. The one who does the will of God enters into a relationship that is closer than any other human relationship.

Often, as we grow in the Lord, we find that the relationships we make within the body of Christ are so much closer than what we enjoy with those who are naturally related to us. The family of God becomes closer to you as you do the will of God. It is a beautiful, intimate relationship with the Lord.

"Here are My mother and My brothers! ³⁵For whoever does the awill of God is My brother and My sister and mother."

THE PARABLE OF THE SOWER

4 And aagain He began to teach by the sea. And a great multitude was gathered to Him, so that He got into a boat and sat in *it* on the sea; and the whole multitude was on the land facing the sea. ²Then He taught them many things by parables, aand said to them in His teaching:

³"Listen! Behold, a sower went out to sow. ⁴And it happened, as he sowed, *that* some *seed* fell by the wayside; and the birds *I*of the air came and devoured it. ⁵Some fell on stony ground, where it did not have much earth; and immediately it sprang up because it had no depth of earth. ⁶But when the sun was up it was scorched, and because it had no root it withered away. ⁷And some *seed* fell among thorns; and the thorns grew up and choked it, and it yielded no *I*crop. ⁸But other *seed* fell on good ground and yielded a crop that sprang up, increased and produced: some thirtyfold, some sixty, and some a hundred."

⁹And He said *I*to them, "He who has ears to hear, let him hear!"

THE PURPOSE OF PARABLES

¹⁰aBut when He was alone, those around Him with the twelve asked Him about the parable. ¹¹And He said to them, "To you it has been given to aknow the *I*mystery of the kingdom of God; but to bthose who are outside, all things come in parables, ¹²so that

> a*'Seeing they may see and not perceive,*
> *And hearing they may hear and not understand;*
> *Lest they should turn,*
> *And their sins be forgiven them.'*"

THE PARABLE OF THE SOWER EXPLAINED

¹³And He said to them, "Do you not understand this parable? How then will you understand all the parables? ¹⁴aThe sower sows the word. ¹⁵And these are the ones by the wayside where the word is sown. When they hear, Satan comes immediately and takes away the word that was sown in their hearts. ¹⁶These likewise are the ones sown on stony ground who, when they hear the word, immediately receive it with gladness; ¹⁷and they have no root in themselves,

---

22 aMatt. 9:34; 10:25
b[John 12:31; 14:30; 16:11]

23 aMatt. 12:25–29

27 a[Is. 49:24, 25]

28 aLuke 12:10

30 aMatt. 9:34

31 aMatt. 12:46–50

32 *I*NU, M add *and Your sisters*

35 aEph. 6:6

CHAPTER 4

1 aLuke 8:4–10

2 aMark 12:38

4 *I*NU, M omit *of the air*

7 *I*Lit. *fruit*

9 *I*NU, M omit *to them*

10 aLuke 8:9

11 a[1 Cor. 2:10–16]
b[Col. 4:5]
I secret or hidden truths

12 aIs. 6:9, 10; 43:8

14 aMatt. 13:18–23

and so endure only for a time. Afterward, when tribulation or persecution arises for the word's sake, immediately they stumble. [18]Now these are the ones sown among thorns; *they are* the ones who hear the word, [19]and the [a]cares of this world, [b]the deceitfulness of riches, and the desires for other things entering in choke the word, and it becomes unfruitful. [20]But these are the ones sown on good ground, those who hear the word, [1]accept *it*, and bear [a]fruit: some thirtyfold, some sixty, and some a hundred."

Mark 4:20

Good Ground Bears Fruit. How glorious it is to see a fruitful Christian life! One whose life is just bringing forth fruit, as God's love radiates from their life, with the fruit of the Spirit abounding. Seeing the maturity in a life, as the child of God grows and bears fruit for the kingdom. And so, it might be well for all of us to look at our lives and ask, "Is my life fruitful for Jesus Christ? Is the fruit of the Spirit shining forth from my life?"

LIGHT UNDER A BASKET

[21][a]Also He said to them, "Is a lamp brought to be put under a basket or under a bed? Is it not to be set on a lampstand? [22][a]For there is nothing hidden which will not be revealed, nor has anything been kept secret but that it should come to light. [23][a]If anyone has ears to hear, let him hear."

[24]Then He said to them, "Take heed what you hear. [a]With the same measure you use, it will be measured to you; and to you who hear, more will be given. [25][a]For whoever has, to him more will be given; but whoever does not have, even what he has will be taken away from him."

THE PARABLE OF THE GROWING SEED

[26]And He said, [a]"The kingdom of God is as if a man should [1]scatter seed on the ground, [27]and should sleep by night and rise by day, and the seed should sprout and [a]grow, he himself does not know how. [28]For the earth [a]yields crops by itself: first the blade, then the head, after that the full grain in

---

Reference column:

19 [a] Luke 21:34
[b] 1 Tim. 6:9, 10, 17

20 [a] [Rom. 7:4]
[1] *receive*

21 [a] Matt. 5:15

22 [a] Matt. 10:26, 27

23 [a] Matt. 11:15; 13:9, 43

24 [a] Matt. 7:2

25 [a] Luke 8:18; 19:26

26 [a] [Matt. 13:24–30, 36–43]
[1] *sow*

27 [a] [2 Pet. 3:18]

28 [a] [John 12:24]

29 [a] Rev. 14:15

30 [a] Matt. 13:31, 32

33 [a] Matt. 13:34, 35

34 [a] Luke 24:27, 45

35 [a] Luke 8:22, 25

---

the head. [29]But when the grain ripens, immediately [a]he puts in the sickle, because the harvest has come."

THE PARABLE OF THE MUSTARD SEED

[30]Then He said, [a]"To what shall we liken the kingdom of God? Or with what parable shall we picture it? [31]*It is* like a mustard seed which, when it is sown on the ground, is smaller than all the seeds on earth; [32]but when it is sown, it grows up and becomes greater than all herbs, and shoots out large branches, so that the birds of the air may nest under its shade."

JESUS' USE OF PARABLES

[33][a]And with many such parables He spoke the word to them as they were able to hear *it*. [34]But without a parable He did not speak to them. And when they were alone, [a]He explained all things to His disciples.

WIND AND WAVE OBEY JESUS

[35][a]On the same day, when evening had come, He said to them, "Let us cross over to the other side." [36]Now when they had left the multitude, they took Him along in the boat as He was. And other little boats were also with Him. [37]And a great windstorm arose, and the waves beat into the boat, so

---

Mark 4:21

A LAMP UNDER A BASKET

Jesus said that we are to be "the light of the world" (Matt. 5:14). But here He pointed out that a light that is put under a basket doesn't do any good. The purpose of light is to shine forth and give light to others. So lamps are to be put on lampstands, and we are to shine forth to the world.

God's intention is for us to live on the higher spiritual plane, demonstrating to the world the superiority of the spiritual life over the material life. If we are like the world, they won't see the contrast; and our lights will be hidden.

Mark 4:33

AS THEY WERE ABLE

Jesus taught His listeners the word "as they were able to hear it." There were many things they just couldn't comprehend. He told them, "I still have many things to say to you, but you cannot bear them now" (John 16:12). When He tried to talk to His disciples about His death and resurrection, they couldn't comprehend it.

It is so important that we have ears to hear and that we have hearts ready to comprehend anything He wants to tell us. If we do hear, more will be given. God, make us hearers of the word!

that it was already filling. 38But He was in the stern, asleep on a pillow. And they awoke Him and said to Him, a"Teacher, bdo You not care that we are perishing?" 39Then He arose and arebuked the wind, and said to the sea, b"Peace, 1be still!" And the wind ceased and there was a great calm. 40But He said to them, "Why are you so fearful? aHow 1is it that you have no faith?" 41And they feared exceedingly, and said to one another, "Who can this be, that even the wind and the sea obey Him!"

A DEMON-POSSESSED MAN HEALED

5 Then athey came to the other side of the sea, to the country of the 1Gadarenes. 2And when He had come out of the boat, immediately there met Him out of the tombs a man with an aunclean spirit, 3who had *his* dwelling among the tombs; and no one could bind 1him, not even with chains, 4because he had often been bound with shackles and chains. And the chains had been pulled apart by him, and the shackles broken in pieces; neither could anyone tame him. 5And always, night and day, he was in the mountains and in the tombs, crying out and cutting himself with stones.

---

38 a [Matt. 23:8–10]
b Ps. 44:23

39 a Luke 4:39
b Ps. 65:7; 89:9; 93:4; 104:6, 7
1 Lit. *Be quiet*

40 a Matt. 14:31, 32
1 NU *Have you still no faith?*

CHAPTER 5

1 a Matt. 8:28–34
1 NU *Gerasenes*

2 a Mark 1:23; 7:25

3 1 NU adds *anymore*

7 a Acts 19:13
1 *adjure*

8 a Mark 1:25; 9:25

11 a Deut. 14:8

13 1 NU *He gave*

15 a Matt. 4:24; 8:16

6When he saw Jesus from afar, he ran and worshiped Him. 7And he cried out with a loud voice and said, "What have I to do with You, Jesus, Son of the Most High God? I aimplore1You by God that You do not torment me."

8For He said to him, a"Come out of the man, unclean spirit!" 9Then He asked him, "What *is* your name?"

And he answered, saying, "My name *is* Legion; for we are many." 10Also he begged Him earnestly that He would not send them out of the country.

11Now a large herd of aswine was feeding there near the mountains. 12So all the demons begged Him, saying, "Send us to the swine, that we may enter them." 13And 1at once Jesus gave them permission. Then the unclean spirits went out and entered the swine (there were about two thousand); and the herd ran violently down the steep place into the sea, and drowned in the sea.

Mark 5:1–13

DEMONS IN SWINE

I'm sure there are animal activists who would be horrified that Jesus would cast all these demons into a herd of swine, causing the swine to commit suicide.

It is important to remember that God had forbidden the children of Israel to eat pork. There is a certain worm that is sometimes in pork; and if you don't cook it thoroughly, the worm isn't always destroyed, and you can get trichinosis and die. So these swine farmers were conducting an illegal industry; and Jesus just killed two birds with one stone as He delivered this man from the torment of the demons and, at the same time, shut down an illegal and harmful business.

14So those who fed the swine fled, and they told *it* in the city and in the country. And they went out to see what it was that had happened. 15Then they came to Jesus, and saw the one *who had been* ademon-possessed and had

the legion, bsitting and cclothed and in his right mind. And they were afraid. 16And those who saw it told them how it happened to him who had been demon-possessed, and about the swine. 17Then athey began to plead with Him to depart from their region.

18And when He got into the boat, ahe who had been demon-possessed begged Him that he might be with Him. 19However, Jesus did not permit him, but said to him, "Go home to your friends, and tell them what great things the Lord has done for you, and how He has had compassion on you." 20And he departed and began to aproclaim in lDecapolis all that Jesus had done for him; and all bmarveled.

Mark 5:18–20

TELL YOUR FRIENDS

The man who had been delivered from the demons wanted to go with Jesus and to follow Him. This is understandable. I wouldn't want to live in a place where people cared more about pigs than about me. But Jesus had work for him to do instead. "Go home to your friends, and tell them what great things the Lord has done for you, and how He has had compassion on you."

There are times when we would just rather be with Jesus. But He has a job for us to do. We need to share with the world. Apparently this guy was a pretty good missionary too, because in the next chapter, in verse 53, when Jesus came to the land of the Gadarenes, to Gennesaret, the people came running because they immediately recognized Him.

A GIRL RESTORED TO LIFE AND A WOMAN HEALED

21aNow when Jesus had crossed over again by boat to the other side, a great multitude gathered to Him; and He was by the sea. 22aAnd behold, one of the rulers of the synagogue came, Jairus by name. And when he saw Him, he fell at His feet 23and begged Him earnestly,

15 bLuke 10:39
c[Is. 61:10]

17 a Acts 16:39

18 a Luke 8:38, 39

20 a Ps. 66:16
b Matt. 9:8, 33
1 Lit. Ten Cities

21 a Luke 8:40

22 a Matt. 9:18–26

23 a Acts 9:17; 28:8

25 a Lev. 15:19, 25

27 a Matt. 14:35, 36

29 1 suffering

30 a Luke 6:19; 8:46

33 a [Ps. 89:7]

34 a Matt. 9:22
b Luke 7:50; 8:48

35 a Luke 8:49

36 a [John 11:40]

38 a Acts 9:39
1 an uproar

39 a John 11:4, 11

40 a Acts 9:40

42 a Mark 1:27; 7:37

saying, "My little daughter lies at the point of death. Come and alay Your hands on her, that she may be healed, and she will live." 24So Jesus went with him, and a great multitude followed Him and thronged Him.

25Now a certain woman ahad a flow of blood for twelve years, 26and had suffered many things from many physicians. She had spent all that she had and was no better, but rather grew worse. 27When she heard about Jesus, she came behind Him in the crowd and atouched His garment. 28For she said, "If only I may touch His clothes, I shall be made well."

29Immediately the fountain of her blood was dried up, and she felt in her body that she was healed of the laffliction. 30And Jesus, immediately knowing in Himself that apower had gone out of Him, turned around in the crowd and said, "Who touched My clothes?"

31But His disciples said to Him, "You see the multitude thronging You, and You say, 'Who touched Me?'"

32And He looked around to see her who had done this thing. 33But the woman, afearing and trembling, knowing what had happened to her, came and fell down before Him and told Him the whole truth. 34And He said to her, "Daughter, ayour faith has made you well. bGo in peace, and be healed of your affliction."

35aWhile He was still speaking, some came from the ruler of the synagogue's house who said, "Your daughter is dead. Why trouble the Teacher any further?"

36As soon as Jesus heard the word that was spoken, He said to the ruler of the synagogue, "Do not be afraid; only abelieve." 37And He permitted no one to follow Him except Peter, James, and John the brother of James. 38Then He came to the house of the ruler of the synagogue, and saw la tumult and those who awept and wailed loudly. 39When He came in, He said to them, "Why make this commotion and weep? The child is not dead, but asleeping." 40And they ridiculed Him. aBut when He had put them all outside, He took the father and the mother of the child, and those who were with Him, and entered where the child was lying. 41Then He took the child by the hand, and said to her, "Talitha, cumi," which is translated, "Little girl, I say to you, arise." 42Immediately the girl arose and walked, for she was twelve years of age. And they were aovercome with great

Mark 5:22–43

THE TOUCH OF JESUS

Jairus had a twelve-year-old daughter who was sick and would shortly die. There was a woman, at the same time, who had been hemorrhaging for twelve years. Jairus wanted Jesus to lay hands on his precious daughter. The woman wanted to touch Jesus. They both knew that would make a difference. They were both right, and the touch of Jesus raised the little girl from the dead and healed the hemorrhaging woman.

We see the glorious powers of our Lord Jesus Christ and the difference He makes when He touches a person's life.

amazement. 43But aHe commanded them strictly that no one should know it, and said that *something* should be given her to eat.

JESUS REJECTED AT NAZARETH

6 Then aHe went out from there and came to His own country, and His disciples followed Him. 2And when the Sabbath had come, He began to teach in the synagogue. And many hearing *Him* were aastonished, saying, b"Where

---

Mark 6:3

Brothers and Sisters. Some churches teach a doctrine of the perpetual virginity of Mary, which says that Mary remained a virgin her whole life. This verse, though, makes it clear that Jesus had at least four half-brothers, listed here, as well as some sisters. It would appear that His brothers did not accept Him as the Messiah until after His resurrection. But James became one of the foremost leaders in the church and wrote the book of James.

---

43 a[Matt. 8:4; 12:16–19; 17:9]

CHAPTER 6

1 aMatt. 13:54

2 aMatt. 7:28
b John 6:42

3 aMatt. 12:46
b[Matt. 11:6]

4 a John 4:44

5 aGen. 19:22; 32:25

6 aIs. 59:16
bMatt. 9:35

7 aMark 3:13, 14
b[Eccl. 4:9, 10]

9 a[Eph. 6:15]

10 aMatt. 10:11

11 aMatt. 10:14
bActs 13:51; 18:6
1 NU *whatever place*
2 NU omits the rest of v. 11.

---

did this Man *get* these things? And what wisdom *is* this which is given to Him, that such mighty works are performed by His hands! 3Is this not the carpenter, the Son of Mary, and abrother of James, Joses, Judas, and Simon? And are not His sisters here with us?" So they bwere offended at Him.

4But Jesus said to them, a"A prophet is not without honor except in his own country, among his own relatives, and in his own house." 5aNow He could do no mighty work there, except that He laid His hands on a few sick people and healed *them*. 6And aHe marveled because of their unbelief. bThen He went about the villages in a circuit, teaching.

Mark 6:5–6

NO MIGHTY WORK THERE

Jesus couldn't do many mighty works in His hometown, except for a few healings, "and He marveled because of their unbelief." It wasn't that He needed the people to have more faith so He could perform miracles. He healed plenty of people who didn't have much faith. But their unbelief kept them from coming to Jesus to receive His help.

How many people there in Nazareth could have been helped had they only come to Jesus? Just like today, so many people are in misery and could be delivered by God, but they just won't come.

SENDING OUT THE TWELVE

7aAnd He called the twelve to *Himself*, and began to send them out btwo by two, and gave them power over unclean spirits. 8He commanded them to take nothing for the journey except a staff—no bag, no bread, no copper in *their* money belts— 9but ato wear sandals, and not to put on two tunics. 10aAlso He said to them, "In whatever place you enter a house, stay there till you depart from that place. 11aAnd 1whoever will not receive you nor hear you, when you depart from there, bshake off the dust under your feet as a testimony against them. 2Assuredly,

I say to you, it will be more tolerable for Sodom and Gomorrah in the day of judgment than for that city!" 12So they went out and preached that *people* should repent. 13And they cast out many demons, ªand anointed with oil many who were sick, and healed *them.*

JOHN THE BAPTIST BEHEADED

14aNow King Herod heard *of Him,* for His name had become well known. And he said, "John the Baptist is risen from the dead, and therefore ᵇthese powers are at work in him."

15aOthers said, "It is Elijah."

And others said, "It is ¹the Prophet, ᵇor like one of the prophets."

16aBut when Herod heard, he said, "This is John, whom I beheaded; he has been raised from the dead!" 17For Herod himself had sent and laid hold of John, and bound him in prison for the sake of Herodias, his brother Philip's wife; for he had married her. 18Because John had said to Herod, ª"It is not lawful for you to have your brother's wife."

19Therefore Herodias ¹held it against him and wanted to kill him, but she could not; 20for Herod ªfeared John, knowing that he *was* a just and holy man, and he protected him. And when he heard him, he ¹did many things, and heard him gladly.

21aThen an opportune day came when Herod ᵇon his birthday gave a feast for his nobles, the high officers, and the chief *men* of Galilee. 22And when Herodias' daughter herself came in and danced, and pleased Herod and those who sat with him, the king said to the girl, "Ask me whatever you want, and I will give *it* to you." 23He also swore to her, ª"Whatever you ask me, I will give you, up to half my kingdom."

24So she went out and said to her mother, "What shall I ask?"

And she said, "The head of John the Baptist!"

25Immediately she came in with haste to the king and asked, saying, "I want you to give me at once the head of John the Baptist on a platter."

26aAnd the king was exceedingly sorry; *yet,* because of the oaths and because of those who sat with him, he did not want to refuse her. 27Immediately the king sent an executioner and commanded his head to be brought. And he went and beheaded him in prison, 28brought his head on a platter, and gave it to the girl; and the girl gave it to her mother. 29When his disciples heard

13 ª[James 5:14]

14 ªLuke 9:7–9 ᵇLuke 19:37

15 ªMark 8:28 ᵇMatt. 21:11 1NU, M a prophet, like one

16 ªLuke 3:19

18 ªLev. 18:16; 20:21

19 ¹held a grudge

20 ªMatt. 14:5; 21:26 1NU was very perplexed, yet

21 ªMatt. 14:6 ᵇGen. 40:20

23 ªEsth. 5:3, 6; 7:2

26 ªMatt. 14:9

29 ª1Kin. 13:29, 30

30 ªLuke 9:10

31 ªMatt. 14:13 ᵇMark 3:20

32 ªMatt. 14:13–21

33 ª[Col. 1:6] 1NU, M they

34 ªMatt. 9:36; 14:14 ᵇNum. 27:17 ᶜLuke 9:11

35 ªMatt. 14:15

of it, they came and ªtook away his corpse and laid it in a tomb.

FEEDING THE FIVE THOUSAND

30aThen the apostles gathered to Jesus and told Him all things, both what they had done and what they had taught. 31aAnd He said to them, "Come aside by yourselves to a deserted place and rest a while." For ᵇthere were many coming and going, and they did not even have time to eat. 32aSo they departed to a deserted place in the boat by themselves.

Mark 6:31

A DESERTED PLACE

Jesus and His disciples had been very busy and hadn't even had time to eat. So Jesus said to them, "Come aside by yourselves to a deserted place and rest a while." They got into a boat and headed over to the other side of the Sea of Galilee.

There is something about sailing that is very relaxing, as you are out on the water with the wind blowing gently and the water lapping up on the side of the boat. It is a restful experience. The only rest they got, though, was on the boat because more people were waiting for them when they got to the other side.

We all need times to get away to spend time alone with the Lord. This is why we have our conference centers. Sometimes we just need to get away for a while, to hear God speak.

33But ¹the multitudes saw them departing, and many ªknew Him and ran there on foot from all the cities. They arrived before them and came together to Him. 34aAnd Jesus, when He came out, saw a great multitude and was moved with compassion for them, because they were like ᵇsheep not having a shepherd. So ᶜHe began to teach them many things. 35aWhen the day was now far spent, His disciples came

to Him and said, "This is a deserted place, and already the hour *is* late. [36]Send them away, that they may go into the surrounding country and villages and buy themselves [1]bread; for they have nothing to eat."

[37]But He answered and said to them, "You give them something to eat."

And they said to Him, [a]"Shall we go and buy two hundred denarii worth of bread and give them *something* to eat?"

[38]But He said to them, "How many loaves do you have? Go and see."

And when they found out they said, [a]"Five, and two fish."

[39]Then He [a]commanded them to make them all sit down in groups on the green grass. [40]So they sat down in ranks, in hundreds and in fifties. [41]And when He had taken the five loaves and the two fish, He [a]looked up to heaven, [b]blessed and broke the loaves, and gave *them* to His disciples to set before them; and the two fish He divided among *them* all. [42]So they all ate and were filled. [43]And they took up twelve baskets full of fragments and of the fish. [44]Now those who had eaten the loaves were [1]about five thousand men.

JESUS WALKS ON THE SEA

[45a]Immediately He [1]made His disciples get into the boat and go before Him to the other side, to Bethsaida, while He sent the multitude away. [46]And when He had sent them away, He [a]departed to the mountain to pray. [47]Now when evening came, the boat was in the middle of the sea; and He *was* alone on the land. [48]Then He saw them straining at rowing, for the wind was against them. Now about the fourth watch of the night He came to them, walking on the sea, and [a]would have passed them by. [49]And when they saw Him walking on the sea, they supposed it was a [a]ghost, and cried out; [50]for they all saw Him and were troubled. But immediately He talked with them and said to them, [a]"Be [1]of good cheer! It is I; do not be [b]afraid." [51]Then He went up into the boat to them, and the wind [a]ceased. And they were greatly [b]amazed in themselves beyond measure, and marveled. [52]For [a]they had not understood about the loaves, because their [b]heart was hardened.

MANY TOUCH HIM AND ARE MADE WELL

[53a]When they had crossed over, they came to the land of Gennesaret and

---

36 [1]NU *something to eat and omits the rest of v. 36.*

37 [a] 2 Kin. 4:43

38 [a] John 6:9

39 [a] Matt. 15:35

41 [a] John 11:41, 42
[b] Matt. 15:36; 26:26

44 [1]NU, M omit *about*

45 [a] John 6:15–21
[1] *invited, strongly urged*

46 [a] Luke 5:16

48 [a] Luke 24:28

49 [a] Matt. 14:26

50 [a] Matt. 9:2
[b] Is. 41:10
[1] *Take courage*

51 [a] Ps. 107:29
[b] Mark 1:27; 2:12; 5:42; 7:37

52 [a] Mark 8:17, 18
[b] Mark 3:5; 16:14

53 [a] Matt. 14:34–36

54 [1] Lit. *they*

56 [a] Matt. 9:20
[b] Num. 15:38, 39

CHAPTER 7

1 [a] Matt. 15:1–20

2 [a] Matt. 15:20
[1]NU omits *when*
[2]NU omits *they found fault*

3 [a] Gal. 1:14
[1] Lit. *with the fist*

5 [a] Matt. 15:2

6 [a] Matt. 23:13–29
[b] Is. 29:13

---

anchored there. [54]And when they came out of the boat, immediately [1]the people recognized Him, [55]ran through that whole surrounding region, and began to carry about on beds those who were sick to wherever they heard He was. [56]Wherever He entered, into villages, cities, or the country, they laid the sick in the marketplaces, and begged Him that [a]they might just touch the [b]hem of His garment. And as many as touched Him were made well.

DEFILEMENT COMES FROM WITHIN

7 Then [a]the Pharisees and some of the scribes came together to Him, having come from Jerusalem. [2]Now [1]when they saw some of His disciples eat bread with defiled, that is, with [a]unwashed hands, [2]they found fault. [3]For the Pharisees and all the Jews do not eat unless they wash *their* hands [1]in a special way, holding the [a]tradition of the elders. [4]*When they come* from the marketplace, they do not eat unless they wash. And there are many other things which they have received and hold, *like* the washing of cups, pitchers, copper vessels, and couches.

[5a]Then the Pharisees and scribes asked Him, "Why do Your disciples not walk according to the tradition of the elders, but eat bread with unwashed hands?"

[6]He answered and said to them, "Well did Isaiah prophesy of you [a]hypocrites, as it is written:

> [b]'*This people honors Me with their lips,*
> *But their heart is far from Me.*

Mark 7:1–13

True Righteousness. The Pharisees and scribes had intricate rules for ceremonial washings, and they questioned Jesus as to why His disciples didn't follow these rules and rituals. Jesus took the opportunity to point out that following man-made rules can't make anyone righteous.

Righteousness is a matter of the heart and only Jesus can change your heart. Legalism can only make a person self-righteous, but it can never make you truly righteous.

7 *And in vain they worship Me,*
Teaching as doctrines the
commandments of men.'

8For laying aside the commandment of God, you hold the tradition of men—[1]the washing of pitchers and cups, and many other such things you do."

9He said to them, "*All too well* [a]you [1]reject the commandment of God, that you may keep your tradition. 10For Moses said, [a]'*Honor your father and your mother'*; and, [b]'*He who curses father or mother, let him be put to death.'* 11But you say, 'If a man says to his father or mother, [a]"Whatever profit you might have received from me is Corban"—' (that is, a gift *to God),* 12then you no longer let him do anything for his father or his mother, 13making the word of God of no effect through your tradition which you have handed down. And many such things you do."

14[a]When He had called all the multitude to *Himself,* He said to them, "Hear Me, everyone, and [b]understand: 15There is nothing that enters a man from outside which can defile him; but the things which come out of him, those are the things that [a]defile a man. 16[a]If[1] anyone has ears to hear, let him hear!"

17[a]When He had entered a house away from the crowd, His disciples asked Him concerning the parable. 18So He said to them, [a]"Are you thus without understanding also? Do you not perceive that whatever enters a man from outside cannot defile him, 19because it does not enter his heart but his stomach, and is eliminated, [1]thus purifying all foods?" 20And He said, [a]"What comes out of a man, that defiles a man. 21[a]For from within, out of the heart of men, [b]proceed evil thoughts, [c]adulteries, [d]fornications, murders, 22thefts, [a]covetousness, wickedness, [b]deceit, [c]lewdness, an evil eye, [d]blasphemy, [e]pride, foolishness. 23All these evil things come from within and defile a man."

A GENTILE SHOWS HER FAITH

24[a]From there He arose and went to the region of Tyre [1]and Sidon. And He entered a house and wanted no one to know *it,* but He could not be [b]hidden. 25For a woman whose young daughter had an unclean spirit heard about Him, and she came and [a]fell at His feet. 26The woman was a [1]Greek, a [2]Syro-Phoenician by birth, and she kept [3]asking Him to cast the demon out of her daughter. 27But Jesus said to her, "Let the children be filled first, for it is not good to take the children's bread and throw *it* to the little dogs."

28And she answered and said to Him, "Yes, Lord, yet even the little dogs under the table eat from the children's crumbs."

29Then He said to her, "For this saying go your way; the demon has gone out of your daughter."

30And when she had come to her house, she found the demon gone out, and her daughter lying on the bed.

Footnotes

8 [1]NU omits the rest of v. 8.
9 [a]Prov. 1:25
[1]set aside
10 [a]Ex. 20:12; Deut. 5:16
[b]Ex. 21:17
11 [a]Matt. 15:5; 23:18
14 [a]Matt. 15:10
[b]Matt. 16:9, 11, 12
15 [a]Is. 59:3
16 [a]Matt. 11:15
[1]NU omits v. 16.
17 [a]Matt. 15:15
18 [a][Heb. 5:11–14]
19 [1]NU sets off the final phrase as Mark's comment that Jesus has declared all foods clean.
20 [a]Ps. 39:1
21 [a]Gen. 6:5; 8:21
[b][Gal. 5:19–21]
[c]2 Pet. 2:14
[d]1 Thess. 4:3
22 [a]Luke 12:15
[b]Rom. 1:28, 29
[c]1 Pet. 4:3
[d]Rev. 2:9
[e]1 John 2:16
24 [a]Matt. 15:21
[b]Mark 2:1, 2
[1]NU omits *and Sidon*
25 [a]John 11:32
26 [1]Gentile
[2]A Syrian of Phoenicia
[3]begging

A GENTILE'S FAITH

Mark 7:24–30

As Jesus interacted with this Gentile woman, it sounded almost like He was being mean to her, even calling her a dog. For the Jews, one of the worst things you could call someone is a Gentile dog. They had packs of dogs that roamed around as dirty scavengers, eating out of garbage. That is what they generally thought of Gentiles. In the Greek, Jesus actually used the word "dog" in the diminutive form, which could be translated as "puppy." The people had puppies for pets and thought of puppies in an endearing way. But we still have a hard time understanding why He seemed to give her such a hard time and why He was so discouraging.

It sounds on the surface like she talked Jesus into delivering her daughter from demons. But, remember, Jesus knew her heart; and He knew that she had enough faith to hang in there, despite the discouragement. He wanted to draw out her faith to its full expression so she could serve as an example of faith.

It is only when we are tested and when it is looking like God isn't going to help us that our faith is really tested. It is then that the Lord allows us to see and to show what we are really made of. Don't just pray once for something and then give up. Be faithful and persistent in prayer, no matter how the circumstances look, and you will see some miracles.

JESUS HEALS A DEAF-MUTE

31a Again, departing from the region of Tyre and Sidon, He came through the midst of the region of Decapolis to the Sea of Galilee. 32 Then a they brought to Him one who was deaf and had an impediment in his speech, and they begged Him to put His hand on him. 33 And He took him aside from the multitude, and put His fingers in his ears, and a He spat and touched his tongue. 34 Then, a looking up to heaven, b He sighed, and said to him, "Ephphatha," that is, "Be opened." 35a Immediately his ears were opened, and the 1impediment of his tongue was loosed, and he spoke plainly. 36 Then a He commanded them that they should tell no one; but the more He commanded them, the more widely they proclaimed it. 37 And they were a astonished beyond measure, saying, "He has done all things well. He b makes both the deaf to hear and the mute to speak."

Mark 7:32–35

A FORMULA FOR HEALING

As we see Jesus healing so many people, it seems like He never did it exactly the same way twice. With one blind man, He spit on the ground, made mud, and rubbed it in his eyes. Other times He just spoke to someone, or He laid hands on them. You just can't find a formula for healing in the ministry of Jesus. Here, with this deaf mute, He put His fingers in his ears, spit, and touched his tongue, then looked up into heaven and said, "Be opened."

Why did the Lord use such complicated and varied approaches? Because He didn't want to create a magic ritual and He didn't want to start a new tradition for doing things. It should never be about a formula; it should be about the Lord and relying on Him. He is God, and He does whatever He wants, in whatever way He chooses.

Cross-references:

31 a Matt. 15:29

32 a Luke 11:14

33 a Mark 8:23

34 a Mark 6:41
b John 11:33, 38

35 a Is. 35:5, 6
1 Lit. bond

36 a Mark 5:43

37 a Mark 6:51; 10:26
b Matt. 12:22

CHAPTER 8

1 a Matt. 15:32–39

2 a Mark 1:41; 6:34

5 a Mark 6:38

7 a Matt. 14:19

10 a Matt. 15:39

11 a Matt. 12:38; 16:1

12 a Mark 7:34

FEEDING THE FOUR THOUSAND

8 In those days, a the multitude being very great and having nothing to eat, Jesus called His disciples to Him and said to them, 2 "I have a compassion on the multitude, because they have now continued with Me three days and have nothing to eat. 3 And if I send them away hungry to their own houses, they will faint on the way; for some of them have come from afar." 4 Then His disciples answered Him, "How can one satisfy these people with bread here in the wilderness?" 5a He asked them, "How many loaves do you have?"

And they said, "Seven."

6 So He commanded the multitude to sit down on the ground. And He took the seven loaves and gave thanks, broke them and gave them to His disciples to set before them; and they set them before the multitude. 7 They also had a few small fish; and a having blessed them, He said to set them also before them. 8 So they ate and were filled, and they took up seven large baskets of leftover fragments. 9 Now those who had eaten were about four thousand. And He sent them away, 10a immediately got into the boat with His disciples, and came to the region of Dalmanutha.

THE PHARISEES SEEK A SIGN

11a Then the Pharisees came out and began to dispute with Him, seeking from Him a sign from heaven, testing Him. 12 But He a sighed deeply in His

---

Mark 8:11–12

Seeking a Sign. The Pharisees came to Jesus and asked Him for a sign from heaven. He had just fed four thousand people with seven loaves of bread. They had seen Him heal the blind and deaf, He had raised the dead, and numerous sick people had been restored to health. What did they want? But this is so typical.

Skeptics always want to see a miracle, or they want to hear a problem solved. But they still won't believe. It will never be enough. Jesus just sighed deeply in His Spirit.

spirit, and said, "Why does this generation seek a sign? Assuredly, I say to you, [b]no sign shall be given to this generation."

BEWARE OF THE LEAVEN OF THE PHARISEES AND HEROD

13And He left them, and getting into the boat again, departed to the other side. 14[a]Now [1]the disciples had forgotten to take bread, and they did not have more than one loaf with them in the boat. 15[a]Then He charged them, saying, "Take heed, beware of the [1]leaven of the Pharisees and the leaven of Herod."

16And they reasoned among themselves, saying, "It is because we have no bread."

17But Jesus, being aware of it, said to them, "Why do you reason because you have no bread? [a]Do you not yet perceive nor understand? Is your heart [1]still hardened? 18Having eyes, do you not see? And having ears, do you not hear? And do you not remember? 19[a]When I broke the five loaves for the five thousand, how many baskets full of fragments did you take up?"

They said to Him, "Twelve."

20"Also, [a]when I broke the seven for the four thousand, how many large baskets full of fragments did you take up?"

And they said, "Seven."

21So He said to them, "How is it [a]you do not understand?"

A BLIND MAN HEALED AT BETHSAIDA

22Then He came to Bethsaida; and they brought a [a]blind man to Him, and begged Him to [b]touch him. 23So He took the blind man by the hand and led him out of the town. And when [a]He had spit on his eyes and put His hands on him, He asked him if he saw anything.

24And he looked up and said, "I see men like trees, walking."

25Then He put His hands on his eyes again and made him look up. And he was restored and saw everyone clearly. 26Then He sent him away to his house, saying, [1]"Neither go into the town, [a]nor tell anyone in the town."

PETER CONFESSES JESUS AS THE CHRIST

27[a]Now Jesus and His disciples went out to the towns of Caesarea Philippi; and on the road He asked His disciples, saying to them, "Who do men say that I am?"

12 [b] Matt. 12:39

14 [a] Matt. 16:5
[1] NU, M they

15 [a] Luke 12:1
[1] yeast

17 [a] Mark 6:52; 16:14
[1] NU omits still

19 [a] Matt. 14:20

20 [a] Matt. 15:37

21 [a] [Mark 6:52]

22 [a] John 9:1
[b] Luke 18:15

23 [a] Mark 7:33

26 [a] Mark 5:43; 7:36
[1] NU "Do not even go into the town."

27 [a] Luke 9:18–20

28 [a] Matt. 14:2
[b] Luke 9:7, 8

29 [a] John 1:41; 4:42; 6:69; 11:27

30 [a] Matt. 8:4; 16:20

31 [a] Matt. 16:21; 20:19
[b] Mark 10:33
[c] Mark 9:31; 10:34

33 [a] [Rev. 3:19]
[1] setting your mind on

34 [a] Luke 14:27

35 [a] John 12:25

38 [a] Matt. 10:33
[b] 2 Tim. 1:8, 9; 2:12

Mark 8:22–23

Gently Leading. There is a beautiful picture of Jesus here. A blind man wanted to be healed. "So He took the blind man by the hand and led him out of the town."

Can you see the tenderness and compassion of Jesus? The multitudes were seeking Jesus, and the crowds were closing in on Him. But He took the time for this one blind man, as He held his hand and led him out of town to minister to him.

28So they answered, [a]"John the Baptist; but some say, [b]Elijah; and others, one of the prophets."

29He said to them, "But who do you say that I am?"

Peter answered and said to Him, [a]"You are the Christ."

30[a]Then He strictly warned them that they should tell no one about Him.

JESUS PREDICTS HIS DEATH AND RESURRECTION

31And [a]He began to teach them that the Son of Man must suffer many things, and be [b]rejected by the elders and chief priests and scribes, and be [c]killed, and after three days rise again. 32He spoke this word openly. Then Peter took Him aside and began to rebuke Him. 33But when He had turned around and looked at His disciples, He [a]rebuked Peter, saying, "Get behind Me, Satan! For you are not [1]mindful of the things of God, but the things of men."

TAKE UP THE CROSS AND FOLLOW HIM

34When He had called the people to Himself, with His disciples also, He said to them, [a]"Whoever desires to come after Me, let him deny himself, and take up his cross, and follow Me. 35For [a]whoever desires to save his life will lose it, but whoever loses his life for My sake and the gospel's will save it. 36For what will it profit a man if he gains the whole world, and loses his own soul? 37Or what will a man give in exchange for his soul? 38[a]For whoever [b]is ashamed of Me and My words in this adulterous and sinful generation, of him the Son of Man also will be

THREE STEPS TO DISCIPLESHIP   Mark 8:34

Jesus told His disciples and the people, "Whoever desires to come after Me, let him deny himself, and take up his cross, and follow Me." To deny yourself means to deny the self-life. To give up on selfishness and pride and humble yourself before Him and others.

Jesus demonstrated this so clearly, and Paul described it in Philippians 2. He said, "Let this mind be in you which was also in Christ Jesus." He went on to describe how He "made Himself of no reputation." The word there literally means He "emptied Himself." We need this same spirit of humility and self-denial. To take up your cross means to lay down your own ambitions to do His will. It is a full surrender of your life.

Jesus went to the cross because there was no other way for us to be saved. In the garden of Gethsemane, He prayed, "Not My will but Yours." To follow Jesus means that we see His example and try to imitate it. He was compassionate, loving, and caring; and we need to follow Him in that behavior. Loving, tender, forgiving—these are the characteristics that marked His life and that should mark ours.

---

ashamed when He comes in the glory of His Father with the holy angels."

JESUS TRANSFIGURED ON THE MOUNT

9 And He said to them, a"Assuredly, I say to you that there are some standing here who will not taste death till they see bthe kingdom of God 1present with power."

2 aNow after six days Jesus took Peter, James, and John, and led them up on a high mountain apart by themselves; and He was transfigured before them. 3His clothes became shining, exceedingly awhite, like snow, such as no launderer on earth can whiten them. 4And Elijah appeared to them with Moses, and they were talking with Jesus. 5Then Peter answered and said to Jesus, "Rabbi, it is good for us to be here; and let us make three tabernacles: one for You, one for Moses, and one for Elijah"— 6because he did not know what to say, for they were greatly afraid.

7And a acloud came and overshadowed them; and a voice came out of the cloud, saying, "This is bMy beloved Son. cHear Him!" 8Suddenly, when they had looked around, they saw no one anymore, but only Jesus with themselves.

9aNow as they came down from the mountain, He commanded them that they should tell no one the things they had seen, till the Son of Man had risen from the dead. 10So they kept this word to themselves, questioning awhat the rising from the dead meant.

11And they asked Him, saying, "Why do the scribes say athat Elijah must come first?"

CHAPTER 9

1 a Luke 9:27
b [Matt. 24:30]
1 having come

2 a Matt. 17:1–8

3 a Dan. 7:9

7 a Ex. 40:34
b Mark 1:11
c Acts 3:22

9 a Matt. 17:9–13

10 a John 2:19–22

11 a Mal. 4:5

12 a Is. 53:3
b Phil. 2:7

13 a Luke 1:17

14 a Matt. 17:14–19

Mark 9:5–6

Say Something. Jesus was on the Mount of Transfiguration with Peter, James, John, Moses, and Elijah. It was a sight to behold, as the disciples saw Jesus in His glory, talking with Moses and Elijah.

Peter, being true to form, piped up with a dumb comment. "Let us make three tabernacles: one for You, one for Moses, and one for Elijah." We are told that Peter said this "because he did not know what to say."

When you don't know what to say, don't say anything. Peter always seemed to want to fill the silence. Silence is sometimes most appropriate.

12Then He answered and told them, "Indeed, Elijah is coming first and restores all things. And ahow is it written concerning the Son of Man, that He must suffer many things and bbe treated with contempt? 13But I say to you that aElijah has also come, and they did to him whatever they wished, as it is written of him."

A BOY IS HEALED

14aAnd when He came to the disciples, He saw a great multitude around them, and scribes disputing with them. 15Immediately, when they saw Him, all the people were greatly amazed, and running to Him, greeted Him. 16And He

asked the scribes, "What are you discussing with them?"

17Then ᵃone of the crowd answered and said, "Teacher, I brought You my son, who has a mute spirit. 18And wherever it seizes him, it throws him down; he foams at the mouth, gnashes his teeth, and becomes rigid. So I spoke to Your disciples, that they should cast it out, but they could not."

19He answered him and said, "O ᵃfaithless¹ generation, how long shall I be with you? How long shall I ²bear with you? Bring him to Me." 20Then they brought him to Him. And ᵃwhen he saw Him, immediately the spirit convulsed him, and he fell on the ground and wallowed, foaming at the mouth.

Mark 9:17–20

Destructive Evil. The boy in this passage was being harassed by a demon. The demon would take control of the boy and would try to throw him into the fire or the water "to destroy him."

Sin is always destructive. Jesus said that Satan comes "to steal, and to kill, and to destroy" (John 10:10). And that is exactly what sin does. Sin is sin because it is destructive.

God wants to protect us, so He forbids the kind of behavior that will destroy us. All sin will ultimately kill you. And that is Satan's agenda.

21So He asked his father, "How long has this been happening to him?" And he said, "From childhood. 22And often he has thrown him both into the fire and into the water to destroy him. But if You can do anything, have compassion on us and help us."

23Jesus said to him, ᵃ"If¹ you can believe, all things are possible to him who believes."

24Immediately the father of the child cried out and said with tears, "Lord, I believe; ᵃhelp my unbelief!"

25When Jesus saw that the people came running together, He ᵃrebuked the unclean spirit, saying to it, "Deaf and dumb spirit, I command you, come out of him and enter him no more!" 26Then the spirit cried out, convulsed him greatly, and came out of him. And he became as one dead, so that many said, "He is

---

Cross references (center column):

17 ᵃLuke 9:38

19 ᵃJohn 4:48
¹ unbelieving
² put up with

20 ᵃMark 1:26

23 ᵃJohn 11:40
¹ NU "'If You can!' All things

24 ᵃLuke 17:5

25 ᵃMark 1:25

28 ᵃMatt. 17:19

29 ᵃ[James 5:16]
¹ NU omits and fasting

31 ᵃLuke 9:44
ᵇMatt. 16:21; 27:50
ᶜ1 Cor. 15:4

32 ᵃLuke 2:50; 18:34

33 ᵃMatt. 18:1–5
¹ discussed

34 ᵃ[Prov. 13:10]
ᵇLuke 22:24; 23:46; 24:46

35 ᵃLuke 22:26, 27

36 ᵃMark 10:13–16

37 ᵃMatt. 10:40

38 ᵃNum. 11:27–29

39 ᵃ1 Cor. 12:3

40 ᵃ[Matt. 12:30]
¹M you
²M your

41 ᵃMatt. 10:42

42 ᵃLuke 17:1, 2
¹ To fall into sin

43 ᵃMatt. 5:29, 30; 18:8, 9

---

dead." 27But Jesus took him by the hand and lifted him up, and he arose.

28ᵃAnd when He had come into the house, His disciples asked Him privately, "Why could we not cast it out?"

29So He said to them, "This kind can come out by nothing but ᵃprayer ¹and fasting."

JESUS AGAIN PREDICTS HIS DEATH AND RESURRECTION

30Then they departed from there and passed through Galilee, and He did not want anyone to know it. 31ᵃFor He taught His disciples and said to them, "The Son of Man is being betrayed into the hands of men, and they will ᵇkill Him. And after He is killed, He will ᶜrise the third day." 32But they ᵃdid not understand this saying, and were afraid to ask Him.

WHO IS THE GREATEST?

33ᵃThen He came to Capernaum. And when He was in the house He asked them, "What was it you ¹disputed among yourselves on the road?" 34But they kept silent, for on the road they had ᵃdisputed among themselves who would be the ᵇgreatest. 35And He sat down, called the twelve, and said to them, ᵃ"If anyone desires to be first, he shall be last of all and servant of all." 36Then ᵃHe took a little child and set him in the midst of them. And when He had taken him in His arms, He said to them, 37"Whoever receives one of these little children in My name receives Me; and ᵃwhoever receives Me, receives not Me but Him who sent Me."

JESUS FORBIDS SECTARIANISM

38ᵃNow John answered Him, saying, "Teacher, we saw someone who does not follow us casting out demons in Your name, and we forbade him because he does not follow us." 39But Jesus said, "Do not forbid him, ᵃfor no one who works a miracle in My name can soon afterward speak evil of Me. 40For ᵃhe who is not against ¹us is on ²our side. 41ᵃFor whoever gives you a cup of water to drink in My name, because you belong to Christ, assuredly, I say to you, he will by no means lose his reward.

JESUS WARNS OF OFFENSES

42ᵃ"But whoever causes one of these little ones who believe in Me ¹to stumble, it would be better for him if a millstone were hung around his neck, and he were thrown into the sea. 43ᵃIf

Mark 9:38–41

LET'S START A DENOMINATION

John told Jesus that the disciples had seen someone who was doing miracles in the name of Jesus, but he wasn't a part of their group. So the disciples had told him not to do it anymore. John wanted to start the first denomination to exclude those who aren't with us. Jesus told John to accept anyone who was working in His name and not to stand in their way. "He who is not against us is on our side."

If anyone is ministering in the name of Christ, they should be blessed. They don't need to join us; they just need to join Him. We can become so divisive and suspicious. It comes from our insecurity. There are plenty of ministry opportunities to go around. We don't need to think we have cornered the market.

your hand causes you to sin, cut it off. It is better for you to enter into life [1]maimed, rather than having two hands, to go to [2]hell, into the fire that shall never be quenched— 44 [1]where

　a'*Their worm does not die*
　　And the fire is not quenched.'

45 And if your foot causes you to sin, cut it off. It is better for you to enter life lame, rather than having two feet, to be cast into [1]hell, [2]into the fire that shall never be quenched— 46 where

　a'*Their worm does not die*
　　And the fire is not quenched.'

47 And if your eye causes you to sin, pluck it out. It is better for you to enter the kingdom of God with one eye, rather than having two eyes, to be cast into [1]hell fire— 48 where

　a'*Their worm does not die*
　　And the b fire is not quenched.'

TASTELESS SALT IS WORTHLESS

49 "For everyone will be a seasoned with fire, b and [1]every sacrifice will be

Notes

43 [1]crippled
[2]Gr. *Gehenna*

44 a Is. 66:24
[1]NU omits v. 44.

45 [1]Gr. *Gehenna*
[2]NU omits the rest of v. 45 and all of v. 46.

46 a Is. 66:24

47 [1]Gr. *Gehenna*

48 a Is. 66:24
b Jer. 7:20

49 a [Matt. 3:11]
b Lev. 2:13 [1]NU omits the rest of v. 49.

50 a Matt. 5:13
b Col. 4:6
c Rom. 12:18; 14:19

CHAPTER 10

1 a Matt. 19:1–9

2 a Matt. 19:3

4 a Deut. 24:1–4

5 [1]command

6 a Gen. 1:27; 5:2

7 a Gen. 2:24

11 a [Matt. 5:32; 19:9]

seasoned with salt. 50 a Salt *is* good, but if the salt loses its flavor, how will you season it? b Have salt in yourselves, and c have peace with one another."

MARRIAGE AND DIVORCE

10 Then a He arose from there and came to the region of Judea by the other side of the Jordan. And multitudes gathered to Him again, and as He was accustomed, He taught them again. 2 a The Pharisees came and asked Him, "Is it lawful for a man to divorce *his* wife?" testing Him.

3 And He answered and said to them, "What did Moses command you?"

4 They said, a "Moses permitted *a man* to write a certificate of divorce, and to dismiss *her.*"

5 And Jesus answered and said to them, "Because of the hardness of your heart he wrote you this [1]precept. 6 But from the beginning of the creation, God a '*made them male and female.*' 7 a '*For this reason a man shall leave his father and mother and be joined to his wife,* 8 *and the two shall become one flesh*'; so then they are no longer two, but one flesh. 9 Therefore what God has joined together, let not man separate."

Mark 10:5–9

Hard Hearts. It is so sad when the ideal that God has for marriage as a beautiful union of two becoming one is not realized. When a hardness of the hearts sets in, making it impossible for a couple to stay together. They cannot or will not rise to the ideal that God desires.

Rising to God's ideal is a mutual thing that you have to do together. If two people both love God and are committed to Him, there is no reason why they would ever divorce. Divorce comes when hearts are hard. It is always a tragedy.

10 In the house His disciples also asked Him again about the same *matter.* 11 So He said to them, a "Whoever divorces his wife and marries another commits adultery against her. 12 And if a woman divorces her husband and marries another, she commits adultery."

JESUS BLESSES LITTLE CHILDREN

13 aThen they brought little children to Him, that He might touch them; but the disciples rebuked those who brought *them*. 14But when Jesus saw *it*, He was greatly displeased and said to them, "Let the little children come to Me, and do not forbid them; for aof such is the kingdom of God. 15Assuredly, I say to you, awhoever does not receive the kingdom of God as a little child will bby no means enter it." 16And He took them up in His arms, laid *His* hands on them, and blessed them.

JESUS COUNSELS THE RICH YOUNG RULER

17aNow as He was going out on the road, one came running, knelt before Him, and asked Him, "Good Teacher, what shall I bdo that I may inherit eternal life?"

18So Jesus said to him, "Why do you call Me good? No one *is* good but One, *that is,* aGod. 19You know the commandments: a'*Do not commit adultery,' 'Do not murder,' 'Do not steal,' 'Do not bear false witness,' 'Do not defraud,' 'Honor your father and your mother.' "*

20And he answered and said to Him, "Teacher, all these things I have akept from my youth."

21Then Jesus, looking at him, loved him, and said to him, "One thing you lack: Go your way, asell whatever you have and give to the poor, and you will have btreasure in heaven; and come, ctake up the cross, and follow Me."

22But he was sad at this word, and went away sorrowful, for he had great possessions.

WITH GOD ALL THINGS ARE POSSIBLE

23aThen Jesus looked around and said to His disciples, "How hard it is for those who have riches to enter the kingdom of God!" 24And the disciples were astonished at His words. But Jesus answered again and said to them, "Children, how hard it is 1for those awho trust in riches to enter the kingdom of God! 25It is easier for a camel to go through the eye of a needle than for a arich man to enter the kingdom of God."

26And they were greatly astonished, saying among themselves, "Who then can be saved?"

27But Jesus looked at them and said, "With men *it is* impossible, but not

Cross references (center column)

13 aLuke 18:15–17

14 a[1 Pet. 2:2]

15 aMatt. 18:3, 4; 19:14
bLuke 13:28

17 aMatt. 19:16–30
bJohn 6:28

18 a1 Sam. 2:2

19 aEx. 20:12–16; Deut. 5:16–20

20 aPhil. 3:6

21 a[Luke 12:33; 16:9]
bMatt. 6:19, 20; 19:21
c[Mark 8:34]

23 aMatt. 19:23

24 a[1 Tim. 6:17]
1NU omits *for those who trust in riches*

25 a[Matt. 13:22; 19:24]

27 aJer. 32:17

28 aLuke 18:28

29 1NU omits *or wife*
2Lit. *fields*

30 aLuke 18:29, 30
b[1 Pet. 4:12, 13]

31 aLuke 13:30

32 aMatt. 20:17–19
bMark 8:31; 9:31

34 1*flog Him* with a Roman scourge

Mark 10:26–27

IS SALVATION POSSIBLE?

As Jesus was talking about how difficult it is for someone to be saved, the disciples asked Him, in exasperation, "Who then can be saved?" Jesus told them, "With men it is impossible, but not with God; for with God all things are possible." In other words, it is impossible for a man to get saved, but God is in the business of doing the impossible.

Sometimes there are people we see and we think it would be impossible for them to get saved. But it was impossible for any of us to get saved. God just did it anyway.

awith God; for with God all things are possible."

28aThen Peter began to say to Him, "See, we have left all and followedYou."

29So Jesus answered and said, "Assuredly, I say to you, there is no one who has left house or brothers or sisters or father or mother 1or wife or children or 2lands, for My sake and the gospel's, 30awho shall not receive a hundredfold now in this time—houses and brothers and sisters and mothers and children and lands, with bpersecutions—and in the age to come, eternal life. 31aBut many *who are* first will be last, and the last first."

JESUS A THIRD TIME PREDICTS HIS DEATH AND RESURRECTION

32aNow they were on the road, going up to Jerusalem, and Jesus was going before them; and they were amazed. And as they followed they were afraid. bThen He took the twelve aside again and began to tell them the things that would happen to Him: 33"Behold, we are going up to Jerusalem, and the Son of Man will be betrayed to the chief priests and to the scribes; and they will condemn Him to death and deliver Him to the Gentiles; 34and they will mock Him, and 1scourge Him, and spit on Him, and kill Him. And the third day He will rise again."

GREATNESS IS SERVING

35aThen James and John, the sons of Zebedee, came to Him, saying, "Teacher, we want You to do for us whatever we ask."

36And He said to them, "What do you want Me to do for you?"

37They said to Him, "Grant us that we may sit, one on Your right hand and the other on Your left, in Your glory."

38But Jesus said to them, "You do not know what you ask. Are you able to drink the acup that I drink, and be baptized with the bbaptism that I am baptized with?"

39They said to Him, "We are able."

So Jesus said to them, a"You will indeed drink the cup that I drink, and with the baptism I am baptized with you will be baptized; 40but to sit on My right hand and My left is not Mine to give, but it is for those afor whom it is prepared."

41aAnd when the ten heard it, they began to be greatly displeased with James and John. 42But Jesus called them to Himself and said to them, a"You

---

Mark 10:41–45

POWER CORRUPTS

The disciples were in another squabble over who was the greatest. Jesus pointed out that this was Gentile thinking. It was part of the power-hungry way of the world.

Those who rule end up lording it over the others. The power goes to their heads. And this is the problem with one trying to reign over another. It is extremely difficult to handle power. Very few people are capable of handling leadership over others without abusing it. The world is a testimony of the old adage, "Power tends to corrupt, and absolute power corrupts absolutely."

That is why Jesus doesn't do it this way. He turned the power structure upside down. Real authority comes from service. And He didn't just teach it; He demonstrated it.

---

35 a [James 4:3]

38 a John 18:11
b Luke 12:50

39 a Acts 12:2

40 a [Heb. 11:16]

41 a Matt. 20:24

42 a Luke 22:25

43 a Mark 9:35

45 a [Phil. 2:7, 8]
b [Titus 2:14]

46 a Luke 18:35–43

47 a Rev. 22:16
b Matt. 15:22

51 1 Lit. My Great One

52 a Matt. 9:22
1 Lit. saved you

CHAPTER 11

1 a Matt. 21:1–9
1 M Bethsphage

4 1 NU, M a

---

know that those who are considered rulers over the Gentiles lord it over them, and their great ones exercise authority over them. 43aYet it shall not be so among you; but whoever desires to become great among you shall be your servant. 44And whoever of you desires to be first shall be slave of all. 45For even athe Son of Man did not come to be served, but to serve, and bto give His life a ransom for many."

JESUS HEALS BLIND BARTIMAEUS

46aNow they came to Jericho. As He went out of Jericho with His disciples and a great multitude, blind Bartimaeus, the son of Timaeus, sat by the road begging. 47And when he heard that it was Jesus of Nazareth, he began to cry out and say, "Jesus, aSon of David, bhave mercy on me!"

48Then many warned him to be quiet; but he cried out all the more, "Son of David, have mercy on me!"

49So Jesus stood still and commanded him to be called.

Then they called the blind man, saying to him, "Be of good cheer. Rise, He is calling you."

50And throwing aside his garment, he rose and came to Jesus.

51So Jesus answered and said to him, "What do you want Me to do for you?"

The blind man said to Him, 1"Rabboni, that I may receive my sight."

52Then Jesus said to him, "Go your way; ayour faith has 1made you well." And immediately he received his sight and followed Jesus on the road.

THE TRIUMPHAL ENTRY

11 Now awhen they drew near Jerusalem, to 1Bethphage and Bethany, at the Mount of Olives, He sent two of His disciples; 2and He said to them, "Go into the village opposite you; and as soon as you have entered it you will find a colt tied, on which no one has sat. Loose it and bring it. 3And if anyone says to you, 'Why are you doing this?' say, 'The Lord has need of it,' and immediately he will send it here."

4So they went their way, and found 1the colt tied by the door outside on the street, and they loosed it. 5But some of those who stood there said to them, "What are you doing, loosing the colt?"

6And they spoke to them just as Jesus had commanded. So they let them go. 7Then they brought the colt to Jesus and threw their clothes on it, and

He sat on it. ⁸ᵃAnd many spread their clothes on the road, and others cut down leafy branches from the trees and spread *them* on the road. ⁹Then those who went before and those who followed cried out, saying:

"Hosanna!
ᵃ'*Blessed is He who comes in the name of the LORD!'*
10 Blessed *is* the kingdom of our father David
That comes ¹in the name of the Lord!
ᵃ Hosanna in the highest!"

¹¹ᵃAnd Jesus went into Jerusalem and into the temple. So when He had looked around at all things, as the hour was already late, He went out to Bethany with the twelve.

Mark 11:1–11

THIS IS THE DAY

Up until this point, Jesus was resistant to any outward attempts to pronounce Him as the King. As He healed people, He often told them not to tell anyone. He said that His hour hadn't come. But now His hour had come, and He instructed the disciples where to find a donkey so He could ride into Jerusalem as had been prophesied in Zechariah 9:9.

The day had finally arrived. The day that had been foretold by Daniel, in Daniel 9:24–27. Exactly 173,880 days after the decree to restore and rebuild Jerusalem. This was the day, talked about in Psalm 118:24. It was time.

THE FIG TREE WITHERED

¹²ᵃNow the next day, when they had come out from Bethany, He was hungry. ¹³ᵃAnd seeing from afar a fig tree having leaves, He went to see if perhaps He would find something on it. When He came to it, He found nothing but leaves, for it was not the season for figs. ¹⁴In response Jesus said to it, "Let no one eat fruit from you ever again."
And His disciples heard *it.*

Side notes (center column):

8 ᵃ Matt. 21:8

9 ᵃ Ps. 118:25, 26

10 ᵃ Ps. 148:1
¹ NU omits *in the name of the Lord*

11 ᵃ Matt. 21:12

12 ᵃ Matt. 21:18–22

13 ᵃ Matt. 21:19

15 ᵃ John 2:13–16
ᵇ Lev. 14:22

17 ᵃ Is. 56:7
ᵇ Jer. 7:11

18 ᵃ Matt. 21:45, 46
ᵇ Matt. 7:28

20 ᵃ Matt. 21:19–22

Mark 11:14

FRUITLESS CURSE

The fig tree was cursed because it wasn't bearing fruit. It was a picture of the nation of Israel, who would be scattered and judged because of their lack of fruit.

It is interesting to me that in the book of Revelation, in chapter 2, as Jesus addressed the church in Ephesus, He didn't criticize any of their works. Their works were good. His complaint was their lack of love. Love is the fruit of the Spirit (Gal. 5:22). And the threat of Jesus was that He would remove His presence from their church if they didn't return to their first love. He would not stay around a loveless church. And what a warning and lesson that should be to us.

O God, may Your love ever flow forth from this church. As You come and dwell among Your people, may You find the fruit You are looking for, as You come to Your garden to enjoy us. May our lives be fruitful.

JESUS CLEANSES THE TEMPLE

¹⁵ᵃSo they came to Jerusalem. Then Jesus went into the temple and began to drive out those who bought and sold in the temple, and overturned the tables of the money changers and the seats of those who sold ᵇdoves. ¹⁶And He would not allow anyone to carry wares through the temple. ¹⁷Then He taught, saying to them, "Is it not written, ᵃ'*My house shall be called a house of prayer for all nations'*? But you have made it a ᵇ'den of thieves.' "
¹⁸And ᵃthe scribes and chief priests heard it and sought how they might destroy Him; for they feared Him, because ᵇall the people were astonished at His teaching. ¹⁹When evening had come, He went out of the city.

THE LESSON OF THE WITHERED FIG TREE

²⁰ᵃNow in the morning, as they passed by, they saw the fig tree dried

up from the roots. 21And Peter, remembering, said to Him, "Rabbi, look! The fig tree which You cursed has withered away."

22So Jesus answered and said to them, "Have faith in God. 23For aassuredly, I say to you, whoever says to this mountain, 'Be removed and be cast into the sea,' and does not doubt in his heart, but believes that those things he says will be done, he will have whatever he says. 24Therefore I say to you, awhatever things you ask when you pray, believe that you receive *them,* and you will have *them.*

FORGIVENESS AND PRAYER

25"And whenever you stand praying, aif you have anything against anyone, forgive him, that your Father in heaven may also forgive you your trespasses. 26 IBut aif you do not forgive, neither will your Father in heaven forgive your trespasses."

JESUS' AUTHORITY QUESTIONED

27Then they came again to Jerusalem. aAnd as He was walking in the temple, the chief priests, the scribes, and the

---

Mark 11:25–26

FORGIVE TO BE FORGIVEN

Jesus told His disciples that our forgiveness of others opens the door for us to be forgiven. So, when we pray, if we think of any problem we have with another, we are to forgive them on the spot. This is a very serious thing, and this isn't the only time Jesus said it. In Matthew 6:14–15, Jesus said, "For if you forgive men their trespasses, your heavenly Father will also forgive you. But if you do not forgive men their trespasses, neither will your Father forgive your trespasses."

But how does that line up with salvation by grace? I don't know. But I won't diminish or water down what God has said. The point is, you'd better forgive, just in case Jesus meant what He said.

Marginal references

23 a Matt. 17:20; 21:21

24 a Matt. 7:7

25 a [Col. 3:13]

26 a Matt. 6:15; 18:35
1 NU omits v. 26.

27 a Luke 20:1–8

28 a John 5:27

30 a Luke 7:29, 30

32 a Matt. 3:5; 14:5

CHAPTER 12

1 a Luke 20:9–19
1 tenant farmers

4 1 NU omits *and at him they threw stones*

5 a 2 Chr. 36:16

7 1 tenant farmers

8 a [Acts 2:23]

10 a Ps. 118:22, 23

---

elders came to Him. 28And they said to Him, "By what aauthority are You doing these things? And who gave You this authority to do these things?"

29But Jesus answered and said to them, "I also will ask you one question; then answer Me, and I will tell you by what authority I do these things: 30The abaptism of John—was it from heaven or from men? Answer Me."

31And they reasoned among themselves, saying, "If we say, 'From heaven,' He will say, 'Why then did you not believe him?' 32But if we say, 'From men'"—they feared the people, for aall counted John to have been a prophet indeed. 33So they answered and said to Jesus, "We do not know."

And Jesus answered and said to them, "Neither will I tell you by what authority I do these things."

THE PARABLE OF THE WICKED VINEDRESSERS

12 Then aHe began to speak to them in parables: "A man planted a vineyard and set a hedge around *it,* dug *a place for* the wine vat and built a tower. And he leased it to 1vinedressers and went into a far country. 2Now at vintage-time he sent a servant to the vinedressers, that he might receive some of the fruit of the vineyard from the vinedressers. 3And they took *him* and beat him and sent *him* away empty-handed. 4Again he sent them another servant, 1and at him they threw stones, wounded *him* in the head, and sent *him* away shamefully treated. 5And again he sent another, and him they killed; and many others, abeating some and killing some. 6Therefore still having one son, his beloved, he also sent him to them last, saying, 'They will respect my son.' 7But those 1vinedressers said among themselves, 'This is the heir. Come, let us kill him, and the inheritance will be ours.' 8So they took him and akilled *him* and cast *him* out of the vineyard.

9"Therefore what will the owner of the vineyard do? He will come and destroy the vinedressers, and give the vineyard to others. 10Have you not even read this Scripture:

a'*The stone which the builders rejected*
Has become the chief cornerstone.
11 *This was the Lord's doing,*
And it is marvelous in our eyes'?"

12aAnd they sought to lay hands on Him, but feared the multitude, for they knew He had spoken the parable against them. So they left Him and went away.

THE PHARISEES: IS IT LAWFUL TO PAY TAXES TO CAESAR?

13aThen they sent to Him some of the Pharisees and the Herodians, to catch Him in *His* words. 14When they had come, they said to Him, "Teacher, we know thatYou are true, and 1care about no one; for You do not 2regard the person of men, but teach the away of God in truth. Is it lawful to pay taxes to Caesar, or not? 15Shall we pay, or shall we not pay?"

But He, knowing their ahypocrisy, said to them, "Why do you test Me? Bring Me a denarius that I may see *it*." 16So they brought *it*.

And He said to them, "Whose image and inscription *is* this?" They said to Him, "Caesar's."

17And Jesus answered and said to them, 1"Render to Caesar the things that are Caesar's, and to aGod the things that are God's."

And they marveled at Him.

THE SADDUCEES: WHAT ABOUT THE RESURRECTION?

18aThen *some* Sadducees, bwho say there is no resurrection, came to Him; and they asked Him, saying: 19"Teacher, aMoses wrote to us that if a man's brother dies, and leaves *his* wife behind, and leaves no children, his brother

should take his wife and raise up offspring for his brother. 20Now there were seven brothers. The first took a wife; and dying, he left no offspring. 21And the second took her, and he died; nor did he leave any offspring. And the third likewise. 22So the seven had her and left no offspring. Last of all the woman died also. 23Therefore, in the resurrection, when they rise, whose wife will she be? For all seven had her as wife."

24Jesus answered and said to them, "Are you not therefore 1mistaken, because you do not know the Scriptures nor the power of God? 25For when they rise from the dead, they neither marry nor are given in marriage, but aare like angels in heaven. 26But concerning the dead, that they arise, have you not read in the book of Moses, in the *burning* bush *passage*, how God spoke to him, saying, b'*I am the God of Abraham, the God of Isaac, and the God of Jacob*'? 27He is not the God of the dead, but the God of the living. You are therefore greatly 1mistaken."

THE SCRIBES: WHICH IS THE FIRST COMMANDMENT OF ALL?

28aThen one of the scribes came, and having heard them reasoning together, 1perceiving that He had answered them well, asked Him, "Which is the 2first commandment of all?"

29Jesus answered him, "The 1first of all the commandments *is*: a'*Hear, O Israel, the LORD our God, the LORD is*

Cross references (center column):

12 aJohn 7:25, 30, 44

13 aLuke 20:20–26

14 aActs 18:26
1Court no man's favor
2Lit. *look at the face of men*

15 aLuke 12:1

17 a[Eccl. 5:4, 5]
1*Pay*

18 aLuke 20:27–38
bActs 23:8

19 aDeut. 25:5

24 1Or *deceived*

25 a[1 Cor. 15:42, 49, 52]

26 a[Rev. 20:12, 13]
bEx. 3:6, 15

27 1Or *deceived*

28 aMatt. 22:34–40
1NU *seeing*
2*foremost*

29 aDeut. 6:4, 5 1*foremost*

MARRIAGE IN HEAVEN?

Mark 12:24–25

Marriage is ordained by God as an institution whereby two people enter into the deepest, most intimate, abiding relationship we can experience on the human level. It is a beautiful, close bond that God uses to bring children into the world; and when you have a good marriage, it is probably the closest we can come to heaven on earth. Of course, man has corrupted marriage in so many ways that this beautiful union is not experienced or seen in quite the way it was intended.

But some people who have been blessed with great marriages and loving families get upset with this passage where Jesus says that there won't be marriage in heaven. I have even heard some people say things like, "If he can't be my husband in heaven, then I don't want to go to heaven."

The truth is, the relationships we have in heaven will far exceed the best relationships we have here. Heaven is going to be a glorious place, more blessed than we can imagine. That which we get occasional glimpses of down here will be our everyday existence in heaven. Everything will be infinitely better up there, including our relationships. If we aren't sure of that, it is because we are in error in our knowledge of Scripture and in our understanding of God's power. Don't worry. It is going to be great!

one. ³⁰And you shall ᵃlove the LORD your God with all your heart, with all your soul, with all your mind, and with all your strength.' ¹This is the first commandment. ³¹And the second, like it, is this: ᵃ'You shall love your neighbor as yourself.' There is no other commandment greater than ᵇthese."

³²So the scribe said to Him, "Well said, Teacher. You have spoken the truth, for there is one God, ᵃand there is no other but He. ³³And to love Him with all the heart, with all the understanding, ¹with all the soul, and with all the strength, and to love one's neighbor as oneself, ᵃis more than all the whole burnt offerings and sacrifices."

³⁴Now when Jesus saw that he answered wisely, He said to him, "You are not far from the kingdom of God." ᵃBut after that no one dared question Him.

JESUS: HOW CAN DAVID CALL HIS DESCENDANT LORD?

³⁵ᵃThen Jesus answered and said, while He taught in the temple, "How is it that the scribes say that the Christ is the Son of David? ³⁶For David himself said ᵃby the Holy Spirit:

ᵇ' The LORD said to my Lord,
"Sit at My right hand,
Till I make Your enemies Your
footstool." '

Mark 12:35–37

Son or Lord? After the Pharisees, Sadducees, and scribes were through questioning Jesus, He had a question for them. If the Messiah ("the Christ") was going to be the Son of David, then why did David (Ps. 110:1) refer to Him as "Lord"? In their culture, they had a patriarchal system whereby a father was revered greatly by his offspring. No father would ever refer to his offspring as "Lord." But David called the Messiah, his offspring, "Lord."

Of course, the only explanation is that Jesus was the Son of David, and the Son of Man, but also the Son of God, and therefore David's Son and Lord.

Cross references (center column)

30 ᵃ[Deut. 10:12; 30:6]
¹NU omits the rest of v. 30.

31 ᵃLev. 19:18
ᵇ[Rom. 13:9]

32 ᵃDeut. 4:39

33 ᵃ[Hos. 6:6]
¹NU omits with all the soul

34 ᵃMatt. 22:46

35 ᵃLuke 20:41–44

36 ᵃ2Sam. 23:2
ᵇPs. 110:1

37 ᵃ[Acts 2:29–31]

38 ᵃMark 4:2
ᵇMatt. 23:1–7
ᶜMatt. 23:7

39 ᵃLuke 14:7

40 ᵃMatt. 23:14
¹for appearance' sake

41 ᵃLuke 21:1–4
ᵇ2Kin. 12:9

42 ¹Gr. lepta, very small copper coins
²A Roman coin

43 ᵃ[2Cor. 8:12]

44 ᵃDeut. 24:6

CHAPTER 13

1 ᵃLuke 21:5–36

2 ᵃLuke 19:44

---

³⁷Therefore David himself calls Him 'Lord'; how is He then his ᵃSon?" And the common people heard Him gladly.

BEWARE OF THE SCRIBES

³⁸Then ᵃHe said to them in His teaching, ᵇ"Beware of the scribes, who desire to go around in long robes, ᶜlove greetings in the marketplaces, ³⁹the ᵃbest seats in the synagogues, and the best places at feasts, ⁴⁰ᵃwho devour widows' houses, and ¹for a pretense make long prayers. These will receive greater condemnation."

THE WIDOW'S TWO MITES

⁴¹ᵃNow Jesus sat opposite the treasury and saw how the people put money ᵇinto the treasury. And many who were rich put in much. ⁴²Then one poor widow came and threw in two ¹mites, which make a ²quadrans. ⁴³So He called His disciples to Himself and said to them, "Assuredly, I say to you that ᵃthis poor widow has put in more than all those who have given to the treasury; ⁴⁴for they all put in out of their abundance, but she out of her poverty put in all that she had, ᵃher whole livelihood."

Mark 12:43–44

The Widow's Mites. The poor widow was really putting in more offering than the rich who were contributing huge amounts, according to Jesus. This teaches us that it isn't really the amount you give to the Lord that matters; but, rather, it is the sacrifice involved.

Real giving comes in when the giving is a sacrifice and you are giving from your very livelihood. Giving out of your abundance is fine, but God recognizes sacrificial giving as being of much more significance.

JESUS PREDICTS THE DESTRUCTION OF THE TEMPLE

13 Then ᵃas He went out of the temple, one of His disciples said to Him, "Teacher, see what manner of stones and what buildings are here!" ²And Jesus answered and said to him, "Do you see these great buildings? ᵃNot one stone shall be left upon another, that shall not be thrown down."

GREAT BUILDINGS

Mark 13:1–2

The temple complex that was built by Herod the Great was one of the most impressive buildings ever built. He intended it to be the crowning glory of all he built, and he had built many impressive projects. It wasn't just a temple, but it included many other buildings, a massive retaining wall around the whole thing, and a 300-foot bridge leading up to it.

According to Josephus, the temple itself was 180 feet high, which would be equivalent to an eighteen-story building. There were stones in its construction that would have weighed 180 tons. It was a massive edifice and an impressive accomplishment. But Jesus predicted that the day would come when not one stone would be left on another. He predicted complete demolition.

When someone makes a radical prediction like that, it is fairly easy to verify their credibility. Did it happen? As unlikely as it was, it happened. Jesus can be trusted.

THE SIGNS OF THE TIMES AND THE END OF THE AGE

3Now as He sat on the Mount of Olives opposite the temple, aPeter, bJames, cJohn, and dAndrew asked Him privately, 4a"Tell us, when will these things be? And what will be the sign when all these things will be fulfilled?"

5And Jesus, answering them, began to say: a"Take heed that no one deceives you. 6For many will come in My name, saying, 'I am He,' and will deceive many. 7But when you hear of wars and rumors of wars, do not be troubled; for such things must happen, but the end is not yet. 8For nation will rise against nation, and akingdom against kingdom. And there will be earthquakes in various

3 a Matt. 16:18
b Mark 1:19
c Mark 1:19
d John 1:40

4 a Matt. 24:3

5 a Eph. 5:6

8 a Hag. 2:22
b Matt. 24:8
1 NU omits and troubles
2 Lit. birth pangs

9 a Matt. 10:17, 18; 24:9
1 NU, M stand

10 a Matt. 24:14

11 a Luke 12:11; 21:12–17
b Acts 2:4; 4:8, 31
1 NU omits or premeditate

12 a Mic. 7:6

13 a Luke 21:17
b Matt. 10:22; 24:13
1 bears patiently

14 a Matt. 24:15
b Dan. 9:27; 11:31; 12:11
c Luke 21:21
1 NU omits spoken of by Daniel the prophet

17 a Luke 21:23

19 a Dan. 9:26; 12:1

places, and there will be famines 1and troubles. bThese are the beginnings of 2sorrows.

9"But awatch out for yourselves, for they will deliver you up to councils, and you will be beaten in the synagogues. You will 1be brought before rulers and kings for My sake, for a testimony to them. 10And athe gospel must first be preached to all the nations. 11aBut when they arrest you and deliver you up, do not worry beforehand, 1or premeditate what you will speak. But whatever is given you in that hour, speak that; for it is not you who speak, bbut the Holy Spirit. 12Now abrother will betray brother to death, and a father his child; and children will rise up against parents and cause them to be put to death. 13aAnd you will be hated by all for My name's sake. But bhe who 1endures to the end shall be saved.

Mark 13:10

All the Nations. This verse has inspired many missions organizations to do what they can to preach the gospel to the whole world. "The gospel must first be preached to all the nations." Jesus told His disciples, "Go therefore and make disciples of all the nations" (Matt. 28:19).

God never just wanted to bless a select few people from one continent or one racial background. His love has always been for the world (John 3:16). And we are fulfilling His desires and heart as we preach to all the nations.

THE GREAT TRIBULATION

14a"So when you see the b'abomination of desolation,' 1spoken of by Daniel the prophet, standing where it ought not" (let the reader understand), "then clet those who are in Judea flee to the mountains. 15Let him who is on the housetop not go down into the house, nor enter to take anything out of his house. 16And let him who is in the field not go back to get his clothes. 17aBut woe to those who are pregnant and to those who are nursing babies in those days! 18And pray that your flight may not be in winter. 19aFor in those days

there will be tribulation, such as has not been since the beginning of the creation which God created until this time, nor ever shall be. [20]And unless the Lord had shortened those days, no flesh would be saved; but for the elect's sake, whom He chose, He shortened the days. [21a]"Then if anyone says to you, 'Look, here *is* the Christ!' or, 'Look, *He is* there!' do not believe it. [22]For false christs and false prophets will rise and show signs and [a]wonders to deceive, if possible, even the [1]elect. [23]But [a]take heed; see, I have told you all things beforehand.

THE COMING OF THE SON OF MAN

[24a]"But in those days, after that tribulation, the sun will be darkened, and the moon will not give its light; [25]the stars of heaven will fall, and the powers in the heavens will be [a]shaken. [26a]Then they will see the Son of Man coming in the clouds with great power and glory. [27]And then He will send His angels, and gather together His [1]elect from the four winds, from the farthest part of earth to the farthest part of heaven.

THE PARABLE OF THE FIG TREE

[28a]"Now learn this parable from the fig tree: When its branch has already become tender, and puts forth leaves, you know that summer is near. [29]So you also, when you see these things happening, know that [1]it is near—at the doors! [30]Assuredly, I say to you, this generation will by no means pass away till all these things take place.

Mark 13:31

My Words Will Not Pass Away. Heaven and earth are in a slow process of decay, and they will one day pass away. But the Word of God will never pass away. When we are in the new heaven and earth, the words of Jesus will still be with us.

Can you imagine a Man making a statement like this in a little village to a handful of followers? "My words will by no means pass away." You'd think He was a nut. But here we are, two thousand years later, reading His words.

---

[31]Heaven and earth will pass away, but [a]My words will by no means pass away.

NO ONE KNOWS THE DAY OR HOUR

[32]"But of that day and hour [a]no one knows, not even the angels in heaven, nor the Son, but only the [b]Father. [33a]Take heed, watch and pray; for you do not know when the time is. [34a]*It is* like a man going to a far country, who left his house and gave [b]authority to his servants, and to each his work, and commanded the doorkeeper to watch. [35a]Watch therefore, for you do not know when the master of the house is coming—in the evening, at midnight, at the crowing of the rooster, or in the morning— [36]lest, coming suddenly, he find you sleeping. [37]And what I say to you, I say to all: Watch!"

THE PLOT TO KILL JESUS

14 After [a]two days it was the Passover and [b]*the Feast* of Unleavened Bread. And the chief priests and the scribes sought how they might take Him by [1]trickery and put *Him* to death. [2]But they said, "Not during the feast, lest there be an uproar of the people."

THE ANOINTING AT BETHANY

[3a]And being in Bethany at the house of Simon the leper, as He sat at the table, a woman came having an alabaster flask of very costly [1]oil of spikenard. Then she broke the flask and poured *it* on His head. [4]But there were some who were indignant among

---

Mark 14:4

Why This Waste? The disciples felt that the woman's pouring out this expensive ointment on Jesus was a waste of money. Jesus corrected them sharply and let them know that her act would be long remembered.

There are those today who would suggest that certain acts of devotion to the Lord are a waste. Many gifted young people who desire to go into the ministry are told by guidance counselors, teachers, friends, and family members that they are wasting their potential. But know this: Nothing that is given to Jesus is wasted.

Cross references (center column):

21 [a] Luke 17:23; 21:8

22 [a] Rev. 13:13, 14
[1] chosen ones

23 [a] [2 Pet. 3:17]

24 [a] Zeph. 1:15

25 [a] Is. 13:10; 34:4

26 [a] [Dan. 7:13, 14]

27 [1] chosen ones

28 [a] Luke 21:29

29 [1] Or He

31 [a] Is. 40:8

32 [a] Matt. 25:13
[b] Acts 1:7

33 [a] 1 Thess. 5:6

34 [a] Matt. 24:45; 25:14
[b] [Matt. 16:19]

35 [a] Matt. 24:42, 44

CHAPTER 14

1 [a] Luke 22:1, 2
[b] Ex. 12:1–27
[1] deception

3 [a] Luke 7:37
[1] Perfume of pure nard

themselves, and said, "Why was this fragrant oil wasted? [5]For it might have been sold for more than three hundred [a]denarii and given to the poor." And they [b]criticized[1]her sharply.

[6]But Jesus said, "Let her alone. Why do you trouble her? She has done a good work for Me. [7][a]For you have the poor with you always, and whenever you wish you may do them good; [b]but Me you do not have always. [8]She has done what she could. She has come beforehand to anoint My body for burial. [9]Assuredly, I say to you, wherever this gospel is [a]preached in the whole world, what this woman has done will also be told as a memorial to her."

JUDAS AGREES TO BETRAY JESUS

[10][a]Then Judas Iscariot, one of the twelve, went to the chief priests to betray Him to them. [11]And when they heard it, they were glad, and promised to give him money. So he sought how he might conveniently betray Him.

JESUS CELEBRATES THE PASSOVER WITH HIS DISCIPLES

[12][a]Now on the first day of Unleavened Bread, when they [1]killed the Passover lamb, His disciples said to Him, "Where do You want us to go and prepare, that You may eat the Passover?"

[13]And He sent out two of His disciples and said to them, "Go into the city, and a man will meet you carrying a pitcher of water; follow him. [14]Wherever he goes in, say to the master of the house, 'The Teacher says, "Where is the guest room in which I may eat the Passover with My disciples?"' [15]Then he will show you a large upper room, furnished and prepared; there make ready for us."

[16]So His disciples went out, and came into the city, and found it just as He had said to them; and they prepared the Passover.

[17][a]In the evening He came with the twelve. [18]Now as they sat and ate, Jesus said, "Assuredly, I say to you, [a]one of you who eats with Me will betray Me."

[19]And they began to be sorrowful, and to say to Him one by one, "Is it I?" [1]And another said, "Is it I?"

[20]He answered and said to them, "It is one of the twelve, who dips with Me in the dish. [21][a]The Son of Man indeed goes just as it is written of Him, but woe to that man by whom the Son of Man is betrayed! It would have been

good for that man if he had never been born."

JESUS INSTITUTES THE LORD'S SUPPER

[22][a]And as they were eating, Jesus took bread, blessed and broke it, and gave it to them and said, "Take, [1]eat; this is My [b]body."

[23]Then He took the cup, and when He had given thanks He gave it to them, and they all drank from it. [24]And He said to them, "This is My blood of the [1]new covenant, which is shed for many. [25]Assuredly, I say to you, I will no longer drink of the fruit of the vine until that day when I drink it new in the kingdom of God."

[26][a]And when they had sung [1]a hymn, they went out to the Mount of Olives.

Mark 14:26

The Apostles' Choir. At the end of the Passover, Jesus and His disciples sang a hymn and then headed out to the Mount of Olives. Don't you wish they had recordings in those days? Don't you wish we had a recording of Jesus and the disciples singing a hymn? I would love to have heard that.

The song they probably sang was Psalm 136. This was the final hymn they would have sung at the end of Passover. The psalm keeps repeating, "His mercy endures forever."

JESUS PREDICTS PETER'S DENIAL

[27][a]Then Jesus said to them, "All of you will be made to stumble [1]because of Me this night, for it is written:

[b]'I will strike the Shepherd,
And the sheep will be scattered.'

[28]"But [a]after I have been raised, I will go before you to Galilee." [29][a]Peter said to Him, "Even if all are made to [1]stumble, yet I will not be." [30]Jesus said to him, "Assuredly, I say to you that today, even this night, before the rooster crows twice, you will deny Me three times." [31]But he spoke more vehemently, "If I have to die with You, I will not deny You!" And they all said likewise.

Center column references

5 [a]Matt. 18:28
[b]John 6:61
[1]scolded

7 [a]Deut. 15:11
[b][John 7:33; 8:21; 14:2, 12; 16:10, 17, 28]

9 [a]Luke 24:47

10 [a]Matt. 10:2–4

12 [a]Matt. 26:17–19
[1]sacrificed

17 [a]Matt. 26:20–24

18 [a]John 6:70, 71; 13:18

19 [1]NU omits the rest of v. 19.

21 [a]Luke 22:22

22 [a]1 Cor. 11:23–25
[b][1 Pet. 2:24]
[1]NU omits eat

24 [1]NU omits new

26 [a]Matt. 26:30
[1]Or hymns

27 [a]Matt. 26:31–35
[b]Zech. 13:7
[1]NU omits because of Me this night

28 [a]Mark 16:7

29 [a]John 13:37, 38
[1]fall away

Mark 14:29–31

NOT ME!

Jesus had told the disciples that they would all stumble. But Peter elevated himself above the others by saying, "Even if all are made to stumble, yet I will not be." Peter could imagine all the other disciples falling away, but he didn't think he ever could.

So often we give ourselves more credit than we really deserve. In this case, Jesus specifically told Peter that he personally would deny Jesus three times before the cock crowed twice, and Peter still wouldn't accept it. He argued with Jesus. God knows us better than we know ourselves. Before the end of this chapter, Peter denied Jesus three times and was devastated.

Why was he so devastated? Because he had an unrealistic view of himself. Jesus sees us as we really are and loves us anyway. We see ourselves as we wish we were, and we constantly disappoint ourselves. But it's impossible to disappoint God. He already knows.

THE PRAYER IN THE GARDEN

32 aThen they came to a place which was named Gethsemane; and He said to His disciples, "Sit here while I pray." 33And He atook Peter, James, and John with Him, and He began to be troubled and deeply distressed. 34Then He said to them, a"My soul is exceedingly sorrowful, *even* to death. Stay here and watch." 35He went a little farther, and fell on the ground, and prayed that if it were possible, the hour might pass from Him. 36And He said, a"Abba, Father, ball things *are* possible for You. Take this cup away from Me; cnevertheless, not what I will, but what You *will*." 37Then He came and found them sleeping, and said to Peter, "Simon, are you sleeping? Could you not watch one hour? 38aWatch and pray, lest you enter into temptation. bThe spirit indeed *is* willing, but the flesh *is* weak."

39Again He went away and prayed, and spoke the same words. 40And when He returned, He found them asleep again, for their eyes were heavy; and they did not know what to answer Him. 41Then He came the third time and said to them, "Are you still sleeping and resting? It is enough! aThe hour has come; behold, the Son of Man is being betrayed into the hands of sinners. 42aRise, let us be going. See, My betrayer is at hand."

BETRAYAL AND ARREST IN GETHSEMANE

43aAnd immediately, while He was still speaking, Judas, one of the twelve, with a great multitude with swords and clubs, came from the chief priests and the scribes and the elders. 44Now His betrayer had given them a signal, saying, "Whomever I akiss, He is the One; seize Him and lead *Him* away safely." 45As soon as he had come, immediately he went up to Him and said to Him, "Rabbi, Rabbi!" and kissed Him. 46Then they laid their hands on Him and took Him. 47And one of those who stood by drew his sword and struck the servant of the high priest, and cut off his ear. 48aThen Jesus answered and said to them, "Have you come out, as against a robber, with swords and clubs to take Me? 49I was daily with you in the temple ateaching, and you did not seize Me. But bthe Scriptures must be fulfilled." 50aThen they all forsook Him and fled.

A YOUNG MAN FLEES NAKED

51Now a certain young man followed Him, having a linen cloth thrown around *his* naked *body*. And the young men laid hold of him, 52and he left the linen cloth and fled from them naked.

JESUS FACES THE SANHEDRIN

53aAnd they led Jesus away to the high priest; and with him were bassembled all the cchief priests, the elders, and the scribes. 54But aPeter followed Him at a distance, right into the courtyard of the high priest. And he sat with the servants and warmed himself at the fire. 55aNow the chief priests and all the council sought testimony against Jesus to put Him to death, but found none. 56For many bore afalse witness against Him, but their testimonies ldid not agree.

Cross references (center column):

32 a Luke 22:40–46

33 a Mark 5:37; 9:2; 13:3

34 a John 12:27

36 a Gal. 4:6
b [Heb. 5:7]
c John 5:30; 6:38

38 a Luke 21:36
b [Rom. 7:18, 21–24]

41 a John 13:1; 17:1

42 a John 13:21; 18:1, 2

43 a Luke 22:47–53

44 a [Prov. 27:6]

48 a Matt. 26:55

49 a Matt. 21:23
b Is. 53:7

50 a Ps. 88:8

53 a Matt. 26:57–68
b Mark 15:1
c John 7:32; 18:3; 19:6

54 a John 18:15

55 a Matt. 26:59

56 a Ex. 20:16
1 *were not consistent*

Mark 14:51–52

A Certain Young Man. There is speculation, and it is probably correct, that Mark inserted this little story because it was about him personally. Mark was about twelve or thirteen years old at the time Jesus died; but several of his older family members were involved with Jesus, and he was probably hanging around as young boys often do.

Mark's gospel is thought to have been relayed to Mark primarily by Peter, but this little story was perhaps Mark's own personal recollection of Jesus.

⁵⁷Then some rose up and bore false witness against Him, saying, ⁵⁸"We heard Him say, ᵃ'I will destroy this temple made with hands, and within three days I will build another made without hands.'" ⁵⁹But not even then did their testimony agree.

⁶⁰ᵃAnd the high priest stood up in the midst and asked Jesus, saying, "Do You answer nothing? What *is it* these men testify against You?" ⁶¹But ᵃHe kept silent and answered nothing.

ᵇAgain the high priest asked Him, saying to Him, "Are You the Christ, the Son of the Blessed?"

⁶²Jesus said, "I am. ᵃAnd you will see the Son of Man sitting at the right hand of the Power, and coming with the clouds of heaven."

⁶³Then the high priest tore his clothes and said, "What further need do we have of witnesses? ⁶⁴You have heard the ᵃblasphemy! What do you think?"

And they all condemned Him to be deserving of ᵇdeath.

⁶⁵Then some began to ᵃspit on Him, and to blindfold Him, and to beat Him, and to say to Him, "Prophesy!" And the officers ¹struck Him with the palms of their hands.

PETER DENIES JESUS, AND WEEPS

⁶⁶ᵃNow as Peter was below in the courtyard, one of the servant girls of the high priest came. ⁶⁷And when she saw Peter warming himself, she looked at him and said, "You also were with ᵃJesus of Nazareth."

⁶⁸But he denied it, saying, "I neither know nor understand what you are

saying." And he went out on the porch, and a rooster crowed.

⁶⁹ᵃAnd the servant girl saw him again, and began to say to those who stood by, "This is *one* of them." ⁷⁰But he denied it again.

ᵃAnd a little later those who stood by said to Peter again, "Surely you are *one* of them; ᵇfor you are a Galilean, ¹and your ²speech shows *it*."

⁷¹Then he began to curse and swear, "I do not know this Man of whom you speak!"

⁷²ᵃA second time *the* rooster crowed. Then Peter called to mind the word that Jesus had said to him, "Before the rooster crows twice, you will deny Me three times." And when he thought about it, he wept.

JESUS FACES PILATE

15 Immediately, ᵃin the morning, the chief priests held a consultation with the elders and scribes and the whole council; and they bound Jesus, led *Him* away, and ᵇdelivered *Him* to

Mark 15:1

DEATH PENALTY

The Jews took Jesus off to Pilate because they no longer had the ability to give out the death penalty. The Romans had taken that right away from the Jews during the time of the childhood of Jesus. In fact, when Jesus was a young boy and the Romans took away the power of capital punishment from the Jews, some of the Jews were mourning in sackcloth and ashes because they felt this meant the end of their reign.

This was a big deal to them because of the prophecy from Jacob: "The scepter shall not depart from Judah, nor a lawgiver from between his feet, until Shiloh [Messiah] comes" (Gen. 49:10). They felt that since Messiah hadn't come yet, the prophecy had failed. Little did they know that a little Boy, growing up in Nazareth, was the Messiah, and that God had kept His word.

Cross-references (center column):

58 ᵃJohn 2:19

60 ᵃMatt. 26:62

61 ᵃIs. 53:7
ᵇLuke 22:67–71

62 ᵃLuke 22:69

64 ᵃJohn 10:33, 36 ᵇJohn 19:7

65 ᵃIs. 50:6; 52:14
¹NU received Him with slaps

66 ᵃJohn 18:16–18, 25–27

67 ᵃJohn 1:45

69 ᵃMatt. 26:71

70 ᵃLuke 22:59
ᵇActs 2:7
¹NU omits the rest of v. 70.
²accent

72 ᵃMatt. 26:75

CHAPTER 15

1 ᵃPs. 2:2
ᵇActs 3:13

Pilate. [2][a]Then Pilate asked Him, "Are You the King of the Jews?"

He answered and said to him, "*It is as you say.*"

[3]And the chief priests accused Him of many things, but He [a]answered nothing. [4][a]Then Pilate asked Him again, saying, "Do You answer nothing? See how many things [1]they testify against You!" [5][a]But Jesus still answered nothing, so that Pilate marveled.

TAKING THE PLACE OF BARABBAS

[6]Now [a]at the feast he was accustomed to releasing one prisoner to them, whomever they requested. [7]And there was one named Barabbas, *who was* chained with his fellow rebels; they had committed murder in the rebellion. [8]Then the multitude, [1]crying aloud, began to ask *him to do* just as he had always done for them. [9]But Pilate answered them, saying, "Do you want me to release to you the King of the Jews?" [10]For he knew that the chief priests had handed Him over because of envy.

[11]But [a]the chief priests stirred up the crowd, so that he should rather release Barabbas to them. [12]Pilate answered and said to them again, "What then do you want me to do *with Him* whom you call the [a]King of the Jews?"

[13]So they cried out again, "Crucify Him!"

[14]Then Pilate said to them, "Why, [a]what evil has He done?"

But they cried out all the more, "Crucify Him!"

[15][a]So Pilate, wanting to gratify the crowd, released Barabbas to them; and he delivered Jesus, after he had scourged *Him,* to be [b]crucified.

THE SOLDIERS MOCK JESUS

[16][a]Then the soldiers led Him away into the hall called [1]Praetorium, and they called together the whole garrison. [17]And they clothed Him with purple; and they twisted a crown of thorns, put it on His *head,* [18]and began to salute Him, "Hail, King of the Jews!" [19]Then they [a]struck Him on the head with a reed and spat on Him; and bowing the knee, they worshiped Him. [20]And when they had [a]mocked Him, they took the purple off Him, put His own clothes on Him, and led Him out to crucify Him.

THE KING ON A CROSS

[21][a]Then they compelled a certain man, Simon a Cyrenian, the father of Alexander and Rufus, as he was coming out of the country and passing by, to bear His cross. [22][a]And they brought Him to the place Golgotha, which is translated, Place of a Skull. [23][a]Then they gave Him wine mingled with myrrh to drink, but He did not take *it.* [24]And when they crucified Him, [a]they divided His garments, casting lots for them *to determine* what every man should take.

[25]Now [a]it was the third hour, and they crucified Him. [26]And [a]the inscription of His [1]accusation was written above:

THE KING OF THE JEWS.

[27][a]With Him they also crucified two robbers, one on His right and the other on His left. [28][1]So the Scripture was fulfilled which says, [a]"*And He was numbered with the transgressors.*"

Center column cross-references

[2][a]Matt. 27:11–14

[3][a]John 19:9

[4][a]Matt. 27:13
[1]NU *of which they accuse You*

[5][a]Is. 53:7

[6][a]Matt. 27:15–26

[8][1]NU *going up*

[11][a]Acts 3:14

[12][a]Mic. 5:2

[14][a]1 Pet. 2:21–23

[15][a]Matt. 27:26
[b][Is. 53:8]

[16][a]Matt. 27:27–31
[1]The governor's headquarters

[19][a][Is. 50:6; 52:14; 53:5]

[20][a]Luke 22:63; 23:11

[21][a]Matt. 27:32

[22][a]John 19:17–24

[23][a]Matt. 27:34

[24][a]Ps. 22:18

[25][a]John 19:14

[26][a]Matt. 27:37
[1]*crime*

[27][a]Luke 22:37

[28][a]Is. 53:12
[1]NU omits v. 28.

Mark 15:6–15

THE CHOICE

Pilate knew that Jesus hadn't done anything wrong, so he suggested that He be released. But he gave the people the choice of either releasing Jesus or Barabbas, who was a murderer. The people chose to release Barabbas and to crucify Jesus. Jesus represented the Law of God, while Barabbas represented lawlessness. The people chose lawlessness over the Law, and people really haven't changed much over the years.

Today every person must also answer the question that Pilate asked the crowd, "What then do you want me to do with Him whom you call the King of the Jews?" This is the universal question that every person must face. This question is as relevant for you as it was for Pilate. What will you do with Jesus? You have to make the decision. Will you confess Him or deny Him? Will you receive Him or reject Him? Will you submit to Him or rebel against Him? It is the ultimate question.

Mark 15:23

No Anesthesia. A drink of wine mixed with myrrh was offered to Jesus. This was intended as an anesthesia to deaden some of the pain He was experiencing. There was a group of women in those days who would make up this concoction and offer it to those who were being crucified, feeling sorry for them.

Jesus refused to drink it. He wasn't going to go through this in an altered state of consciousness. He was taking the punishment for our sin full force.

29 And ᵃthose who passed by blasphemed Him, ᵇwagging their heads and saying, "Aha! ᶜYou who destroy the temple and build it in three days, 30 save Yourself, and come down from the cross!"

31 Likewise the chief priests also, ᵃmocking among themselves with the scribes, said, "He saved ᵇothers; Himself He cannot save. 32 Let the Christ, the King of Israel, descend now from the cross, that we may see and ¹believe."

Even ᵃthose who were crucified with Him reviled Him.

JESUS DIES ON THE CROSS

33 Now ᵃwhen the sixth hour had come, there was darkness over the

Mark 15:31

He Can't Save Himself. As the chief priests and scribes were mocking Jesus, right before He died, they said, "He saved others; Himself He cannot save." There was more truth in that statement than they could have comprehended.

Jesus could not save Himself if He was going to save others. If He had saved Himself, He couldn't have saved others. It certainly was possible for Him to save Himself, but it would have been at the expense of losing you and me, and He chose to love us to death.

---

29 ᵃPs. 22:6, 7; 69:7
ᵇPs. 109:25
ᶜJohn 2:19–21

31 ᵃLuke 18:32
ᵇJohn 11:43, 44

32 ᵃMatt. 27:44
¹M believe Him

33 ᵃLuke 23:44–49

34 ᵃPs. 22:1

36 ᵃJohn 19:29
ᵇPs. 69:21

37 ᵃMatt. 27:50

38 ᵃEx. 26:31–33

39 ᵃLuke 23:47
¹NU He thus breathed His last

40 ᵃMatt. 27:55
ᵇPs. 38:11

41 ᵃLuke 8:2, 3

42 ᵃJohn 19:38–42

43 ᵃLuke 2:25, 38; 23:51

46 ᵃMatt. 27:59, 60

CHAPTER 16

1 ᵃJohn 20:1–8
ᵇLuke 23:56

2 ᵃLuke 24:1

---

whole land until the ninth hour. 34 And at the ninth hour Jesus cried out with a loud voice, saying, "Eloi, Eloi, lama sabachthani?" which is translated, ᵃ*"My God, My God, why have You forsaken Me?"*

35 Some of those who stood by, when they heard *that*, said, "Look, He is calling for Elijah!" 36 Then ᵃsomeone ran and filled a sponge full of sour wine, put *it* on a reed, and ᵇoffered *it* to Him to drink, saying, "Let Him alone; let us see if Elijah will come to take Him down."

37 ᵃAnd Jesus cried out with a loud voice, and breathed His last.

38 Then ᵃthe veil of the temple was torn in two from top to bottom. 39 So ᵃwhen the centurion, who stood opposite Him, saw that ¹He cried out like this and breathed His last, he said, "Truly this Man was the Son of God!"

40 ᵃThere were also women looking on ᵇfrom afar, among whom were Mary Magdalene, Mary the mother of James the Less and of Joses, and Salome, 41 who also ᵃfollowed Him and ministered to Him when He was in Galilee, and many other women who came up with Him to Jerusalem.

JESUS BURIED IN JOSEPH'S TOMB

42 ᵃNow when evening had come, because it was the Preparation Day, that is, the day before the Sabbath, 43 Joseph of Arimathea, a prominent council member, who ᵃwas himself waiting for the kingdom of God, coming and taking courage, went in to Pilate and asked for the body of Jesus. 44 Pilate marveled that He was already dead; and summoning the centurion, he asked him if He had been dead for some time. 45 So when he found out from the centurion, he granted the body to Joseph. 46 ᵃThen he bought fine linen, took Him down, and wrapped Him in the linen. And he laid Him in a tomb which had been hewn out of the rock, and rolled a stone against the door of the tomb. 47 And Mary Magdalene and Mary *the mother* of Joses observed where He was laid.

HE IS RISEN

16 Now ᵃwhen the Sabbath was past, Mary Magdalene, Mary *the mother* of James, and Salome ᵇbought spices, that they might come and anoint Him. 2 ᵃVery early in the morning, on the first *day* of the week, they came to the tomb when the sun had risen. 3 And they said among themselves, "Who will

roll away the stone from the door of the tomb for us?" 4But when they looked up, they saw that the stone had been rolled away—for it was very large. 5aAnd entering the tomb, they saw a young man clothed in a long white robe sitting on the right side; and they were alarmed.

6aBut he said to them, "Do not be alarmed. You seek Jesus of Nazareth, who was crucified. He is risen! He is not here. See the place where they laid

---

Mark 16:9

Appearing to Mary Magdalene.
Jesus had cast seven demons out of Mary Magdalene. Can you imagine what her life was like before she met Jesus? Her life must have been a living hell, filled with torment and bondage. But Jesus set her free. She must have had a love for Jesus that was incomparable. Jesus said that the one who is forgiven much loves much (Luke 7:47).

Mary followed closely after Jesus. She was there at the cross, and now she was probably the first to arrive at the tomb and the first to see the risen Lord.

---

5 a John 20:11, 12

6 a Matt. 28:6

7 a Matt. 26:32; 28:16, 17
1 ahead of

8 a Matt. 28:8
1 NU, M omit quickly

9 a Luke 8:2
1 Vv. 9–20 are bracketed in NU as not in the original text. They are lacking in Codex Sinaiticus and Codex Vaticanus, although nearly all other mss. of Mark contain them.

10 a Luke 24:10

11 a Luke 24:11, 41

12 a Luke 24:13–35

14 a 1 Cor. 15:5

15 a Matt. 28:19

Him. 7But go, tell His disciples—and Peter—that He is going 1before you into Galilee; there you will see Him, aas He said to you."

8So they went out 1quickly and fled from the tomb, for they trembled and were amazed. aAnd they said nothing to anyone, for they were afraid.

MARY MAGDALENE SEES THE RISEN LORD

9 1Now when He rose early on the first day of the week, He appeared first to Mary Magdalene, aout of whom He had cast seven demons. 10aShe went and told those who had been with Him, as they mourned and wept. 11aAnd when they heard that He was alive and had been seen by her, they did not believe.

JESUS APPEARS TO TWO DISCIPLES

12After that, He appeared in another form ato two of them as they walked and went into the country. 13And they went and told it to the rest, but they did not believe them either.

THE GREAT COMMISSION

14aLater He appeared to the eleven as they sat at the table; and He rebuked their unbelief and hardness of heart, because they did not believe those who had seen Him after He had risen. 15aAnd He said to them, "Go into all the

---

IS THIS IN THE ORIGINAL?   Mark 16:9–20

There has been some question raised among scholars as to whether or not the last half of Mark 16 (from verse 9 to the end) was in the original text as written by Mark. Many of the newer versions of the Bible either omit it or suggest that some of the "older manuscripts" or "best manuscripts" don't contain these verses. We believe this to be wrong, and we are convinced that this whole chapter was in the original and is inspired by God.

When scholars say that this does not appear in "some of the better manuscripts," they are talking about just two manuscripts, the Codex Sinaiticus and the Codex Vaticanus. These were two New Testament manuscripts that were discovered in the nineteenth century that date back to the fifth century. They are older than the other manuscripts we have, but we have thousands of manuscripts and other writings that don't agree with them. It is only these two manuscripts that delete the last part of Mark 16, while all other manuscripts include it. Not only that, we have record of ministers in the second century, such as Irenaeus, who quote from this disputed section of Mark. Additionally, if you scratch the last half of Mark 16, the book doesn't make sense. The fullness of the resurrection doesn't even take place.

We are convinced that it is preferable to go with the vast majority of New Testament manuscripts and include all of Mark 16 than to agree with these two aberrant manuscripts and exclude it. This is why we prefer versions of the Bible such as the King James Version and the New King James Version, as they are based on the Majority Text.

world band preach the gospel to every creature. 16aHe who believes and is baptized will be saved; bbut he who does not believe will be condemned. 17And these asigns will follow those who 1believe: bIn My name they will cast out demons; cthey will speak with new tongues; 18athey1 will take up serpents; and if they drink anything deadly, it will by no means hurt them; bthey will lay hands on the sick, and they will recover."

CHRIST ASCENDS TO GOD'S RIGHT HAND

19So then, aafter the Lord had spoken to them, He was breceived up into heaven, and csat down at the right hand of God. 20And they went out and

15 b [Col. 1:23]

16 a [John 3:18, 36]
b [John 12:48]

17 a Acts 5:12
b Luke 10:17
c [Acts 2:4]
1 have believed

18 a Acts 28:3–6
b James 5:14
1 NU and in their hands they will

19 a Acts 1:2, 3
b Luke 9:51; 24:51
c [Ps. 110:1]

20 a [Heb. 2:4]

preached everywhere, the Lord working with them aand confirming the word through the accompanying signs. Amen.

Mark 16:19

At the Right Hand of God. After Jesus ascended, He "sat down at the right hand of God." And that is where He is today. He is there interceding for us. "Therefore He is also able to save to the uttermost those who come to God through Him, since He always lives to make intercession for them" (Heb. 7:25).

THE GOSPEL ACCORDING TO
LUKE

The gospel of Luke is the only book of the New Testament that was written by a Gentile. Luke was a physician who never met Jesus, and was not an eyewitness of the events of the gospel account. He was a dear friend of the apostle Paul and probably traveled with him on his last two missionary journeys.

Luke was writing as a historian who had compiled the accounts of others in a carefully researched way. He addressed this book and its sequel, the book of Acts, to Theophilus, who was probably a Greek believer. Luke's intent was to confirm to Theophilus that the events he was recording were absolutely true. It was an apologetic for an early Greek Christian.

While Matthew presented Jesus as the Jewish Messiah and King, and Mark painted the picture of Jesus as a servant, Luke emphasized the humanity of Jesus, and presented Him as the perfect Man. And who would be better qualified to bear witness to the humanity of Jesus than a physician?

Luke wrote in a very high form of Greek, with a very sophisticated vocabulary. He used numerous medical terms, as one might expect. The Greeks were obsessed with humanity, and the quest for perfect humanity, and Luke wanted to show them Jesus, the perfect Man.

It is quite likely that Luke interviewed Mary, the mother of Jesus. He included details of her story that no one else would be privy to. While Matthew's gospel gives the legal genealogy of Jesus (Matt. 1:1–16), through His stepfather Joseph, Luke gives the actual biological genealogy of Jesus through His mother Mary (Luke 3:23–38). Many heresies would arise in the early church concerning the biology of Jesus, including the gnostics who denied the humanity of Jesus. Luke clearly demonstrated to a Greek audience that these philosophical heresies were unfounded and that Jesus was in fact a man, fully God and fully man.

We don't know exactly when the gospel of Luke was written. It is generally thought to have been written at a later date than Mark and Matthew, but that isn't necessarily true. Some liberal scholars have dated it much later, after the fall of Jerusalem in AD 70. Their reasoning is based on the fact that Luke quotes Jesus as giving such detailed and accurate predictions of the destruction of Jerusalem that it must have been written after the events. Of course, if you believe in prophecy, and you believe that Jesus could foretell the future, you come to a different conclusion.

The gospel of Luke provides a unique perspective of the life of Christ, and along with the other three Gospels helps us to see who Jesus really is, and what He said and did.

DEDICATION TO THEOPHILUS

1 Inasmuch as many have taken in hand to set in order a narrative of those [a]things which [1]have been fulfilled among us, [2]just as those who [a]from the beginning were [b]eyewitnesses and ministers of the word [c]delivered them to us, [3]it seemed good to me also, having [1]had perfect understanding of all things from the very first, to write to you an orderly account, [a]most excellent Theophilus, [4][a]that you may know the certainty of those things in which you were instructed.

JOHN'S BIRTH ANNOUNCED TO ZACHARIAS

[5]There was [a]in the days of Herod, the king of Judea, a certain priest named Zacharias, [b]of the division of [c]Abijah. His [d]wife *was* of the daughters of Aaron, and her name *was* Elizabeth. [6]And they were both righteous before God, walking in all the commandments and ordinances of the Lord blameless. [7]But they had no child, because Elizabeth was barren, and they were both well advanced in years.

[8]So it was, that while he was serving as priest before God in the order of his division, [9]according to the custom of the priesthood, [1]his lot fell [a]to burn incense when he went into the temple of the Lord. [10][a]And the whole multitude of the people was praying outside at the hour of incense. [11]Then an angel of the Lord appeared to him, standing

CHAPTER 1

1 [a] John 20:31
[1] Or *are most surely believed*

2 [a] Acts 1:21, 22
[b] Acts 1:2
[c] Heb. 2:3

3 [a] Acts 1:1
[1] Lit. *accurately followed*

4 [a] [John 20:31]

5 [a] Matt. 2:1
[b] 1 Chr. 24:1, 10
[c] Neh. 12:4
[d] Lev. 21:13, 14

9 [a] Ex. 30:7, 8
[1] *he was chosen by lot*

10 [a] Lev. 16:17

11 [a] Ex. 30:1

12 [a] Luke 2:9

13 [a] Luke 1:57, 60, 63

14 [a] Luke 1:58

15 [a] [Luke 7:24–28]
[b] Num. 6:3
[c] Jer. 1:5

17 [a] Mal. 4:5, 6; Matt. 3:2; 11:14

18 [a] Gen. 17:17

Luke 1:13

A Message from God. Four hundred years had passed since God had spoken. God had been silent ever since the last words He spoke to the prophet Malachi. Now God broke the silence; and His first word after four hundred years of silence was, "Do not be afraid."

on the right side of [a]the altar of incense. [12]And when Zacharias saw *him*, [a]he was troubled, and fear fell upon him. [13]But the angel said to him, "Do not be afraid, Zacharias, for your prayer is heard; and your wife Elizabeth will bear you a son, and [a]you shall call his name John. [14]And you will have joy and gladness, and [a]many will rejoice at his birth. [15]For he will be [a]great in the sight of the Lord, and [b]shall drink neither wine nor strong drink. He will also be filled with the Holy Spirit, [c]even from his mother's womb. [16]And he will turn many of the children of Israel to the Lord their God. [17][a]He will also go before Him in the spirit and power of Elijah, '*to turn the hearts of the fathers to the children*,' and the disobedient to the wisdom of the just, to make ready a people prepared for the Lord."

[18]And Zacharias said to the angel, [a]"How shall I know this? For I am an old man, and my wife is well advanced in years."

SPIRIT AND POWER OF ELIJAH   Luke 1:17

The last time God spoke to man, before this revelation to Zacharias, was when He told Malachi that Elijah would be returning before the coming of Messiah. Now John the Baptist would come in "the spirit and power of Elijah." John would have a similar role to Elijah's, as John would introduce Jesus as the Messiah.

Jesus, however, was rejected by the people of Israel, which led to this period of the church age in which we live; and this will culminate in the second coming of Jesus Christ. Before that second coming, there will be a time of tribulation on the earth; and during that time, Elijah and another witness (probably Moses) will testify of Jesus (Rev. 11:3).

The question has been asked, "What would have happened if Israel had accepted Jesus as their Messiah the first time?" We don't really know. Jesus certainly still had to die for our sins. Perhaps, if they had accepted Him as Messiah, then John the Baptist would have fulfilled the prophecy in Malachi. Jesus said, concerning John the Baptist, "If you are willing to receive it, he is Elijah who is to come" (Matt. 11:14). Later in Matthew, however, Jesus made it clear that the coming of Elijah is still future (Matt. 17:11).

At any rate, John the Baptist had the same basic function in announcing the first coming of Jesus that Elijah will have at the second. And John came in the spirit and power of Elijah with a similar anointing and calling.

¹⁹And the angel answered and said to him, "I am ªGabriel, who stands in the presence of God, and was sent to speak to you and bring you ¹these glad ᵇtidings. ²⁰But behold, ªyou will be mute and not able to speak until the day these things take place, because you did not believe my words which will be fulfilled in their own time."

²¹And the people waited for Zacharias, and marveled that he lingered so long in the temple. ²²But when he came out, he could not speak to them; and they perceived that he had seen a vision in the temple, for he beckoned to them and remained speechless.

²³So it was, as soon as ªthe days of his service were completed, that he departed to his own house. ²⁴Now after those days his wife Elizabeth conceived; and she hid herself five months, saying, ²⁵"Thus the Lord has dealt with me, in the days when He looked on *me*, to ªtake away my reproach among people."

CHRIST'S BIRTH ANNOUNCED TO MARY

²⁶Now in the sixth month the angel Gabriel was sent by God to a city of Galilee named Nazareth, ²⁷to a virgin ªbetrothed to a man whose name was Joseph, of the house of David. The virgin's name *was* Mary. ²⁸And having come in, the angel said to her, ª"Rejoice, highly favored *one*, ᵇthe Lord *is* with you; ¹blessed *are* you among women!"

²⁹But ¹when she saw *him*, ªshe was troubled at his saying, and considered what manner of greeting this was. ³⁰Then the angel said to her, "Do not be afraid, Mary, for you have found ªfavor with God. ³¹ªAnd behold, you will conceive in your womb and bring forth a Son, and ᵇshall call His name JESUS. ³²He will be great, ªand will be called the Son of the Highest; and ᵇthe Lord God will give Him the ᶜthrone of His ᵈfather David. ³³ªAnd He will reign over the house of Jacob forever, and of His kingdom there will be no end."

³⁴Then Mary said to the angel, "How can this be, since I ¹do not know a man?"

³⁵And the angel answered and said to her, ª"*The* Holy Spirit will come upon you, and the power of the Highest will overshadow you; therefore, also, that Holy One who is to be born will be called ᵇthe Son of God. ³⁶Now indeed, Elizabeth your relative has also conceived a son in her old age; and this is

Marginal references:

19 ª Dan. 8:16
ᵇ Luke 2:10
¹ *this good news*

20 ª Ezek. 3:26; 24:27

23 ª 2 Kin. 11:5

25 ª Gen. 30:23

27 ª Matt. 1:18

28 ª Dan. 9:23
ᵇ Judg. 6:12
¹ NU omits *blessed are you among women*

29 ª Luke 1:12
¹ NU omits *when she saw him*

30 ª Luke 2:52

31 ª Is. 7:14
ᵇ Luke 2:21

32 ª Mark 5:7
ᵇ 2 Sam. 7:12, 13, 16
ᶜ 2 Sam. 7:14–17
ᵈ Matt. 1:1

33 ª [Dan. 2:44]

34 ¹ Am a virgin

35 ª Matt. 1:20
ᵇ [Heb. 1:2, 8]

37 ª Jer. 32:17

39 ª Josh. 21:9

41 ª Acts 6:3

42 ª Judg. 5:24

45 ª John 20:29
¹ Or *believed that there*

Luke 1:28

Blessed among Women. The angel greeted Mary, saying, "Rejoice, highly favored one, the Lord is with you; blessed are you among women!" God chose her, probably at the age of fifteen or sixteen, for the highest honor of any woman ever born, to bear the Messiah. We see her level of spirituality and dedication to the Lord, expressed in the song she sang later in this chapter.

I think there is, among Protestants, a real backlash against Mary. Because Catholics have elevated her to a level almost equal with Jesus, many Protestants have reacted to this excess by denigrating Mary. Protestants do not believe that she was perfect, nor that she was taken up into heaven without tasting death, nor is she our co-redemptrix. But she was a very special and blessed woman, and we should appreciate that.

---

now the sixth month for her who was called barren. ³⁷For ªwith God nothing will be impossible."

³⁸Then Mary said, "Behold the maidservant of the Lord! Let it be to me according to your word." And the angel departed from her.

MARY VISITS ELIZABETH

³⁹Now Mary arose in those days and went into the hill country with haste, ªto a city of Judah, ⁴⁰and entered the house of Zacharias and greeted Elizabeth. ⁴¹And it happened, when Elizabeth heard the greeting of Mary, that the babe leaped in her womb; and Elizabeth was ªfilled with the Holy Spirit. ⁴²Then she spoke out with a loud voice and said, ª"Blessed *are* you among women, and blessed *is* the fruit of your womb! ⁴³But why *is* this granted to me, that the mother of my Lord should come to me? ⁴⁴For indeed, as soon as the voice of your greeting sounded in my ears, the babe leaped in my womb for joy. ⁴⁵ªBlessed *is* she who ¹believed, for there will be a fulfillment of those things which were told her from the Lord."

THE SONG OF MARY

46And Mary said:

a"My soul *1*magnifies the Lord,
47   And my spirit has arejoiced in
      bGod my Savior.
48   For aHe has regarded the lowly
      state of His maidservant;
      For behold, henceforth ball
      generations will call me blessed.
49   For He who is mighty ahas done
      great things for me,
      And bholy *is* His name.
50   And aHis mercy *is* on those who
      fear Him
      From generation to generation.
51 a He has shown strength with His
      arm;
    b He has scattered *the* proud in the
      imagination of their hearts.
52 a He has put down the mighty from
      their thrones,
      And exalted *the* lowly.
53   He has afilled *the* hungry with
      good things,
      And *the* rich He has sent away
      empty.
54   He has helped His aservant Israel,
    b In remembrance of *His* mercy,
55 a As He spoke to our bfathers,
      To Abraham and to his cseed
      forever."

56And Mary remained with her about three months, and returned to her house.

BIRTH OF JOHN THE BAPTIST

57Now Elizabeth's full time came for her to be delivered, and she brought forth a son. 58When her neighbors and relatives heard how the Lord had shown great mercy to her, they arejoiced with her.

CIRCUMCISION OF JOHN THE BAPTIST

59So it was, aon the eighth day, that they came to circumcise the child; and they would have called him by the name of his father, Zacharias. 60His mother answered and said, a"No; he shall be called John."

61But they said to her, "There is no one among your relatives who is called by this name." 62So they made signs to his father—what he would have him called.

63And he asked for a writing tablet, and wrote, saying, "His name is John." So they all marveled. 64Immediately his mouth was opened and his tongue *loosed*, and he spoke, praising God.

65Then fear came on all who dwelt around them; and all these sayings were discussed throughout all the hill country of Judea. 66And all those who heard *them* akept *them* in their hearts, saying, "What kind of child will this be?" And bthe hand of the Lord was with him.

ZACHARIAS' PROPHECY

67Now his father Zacharias awas filled with the Holy Spirit, and prophesied, saying:

68   "Blesseda *is* the Lord God of Israel,
      For bHe has visited and redeemed
      His people,
69 a And has raised up a horn of
      salvation for us
      In the house of His servant David,
70 a As He spoke by the mouth of His
      holy prophets,
      Who *have been* bsince the world
      began,
71   That we should be saved from our
      enemies
      And from the hand of all who
      hate us,
72 a To perform the mercy *promised* to
      our fathers
      And to remember His holy
      covenant,
73 a The oath which He swore to our
      father Abraham:
74   To grant us that we,
      Being delivered from the hand of
      our enemies,
      Might aserve Him without fear,
75 a In holiness and righteousness
      before Him all the days of our
      life.
76   "And you, child, will be called the
      aprophet of the Highest;
      For byou will go before the face of
      the Lord to prepare His ways,
77   To give aknowledge of salvation
      to His people
      By the remission of their sins,
78   Through the tender mercy of our
      God,
      With which the *1*Dayspring from
      on high *2*has visited us;
79 a To give light to those who sit in
      darkness and the shadow of
      death,
      To bguide our feet into the way of
      peace."

80So athe child grew and became strong in spirit, and bwas in the deserts till the day of his manifestation to Israel.

Cross references

46 a 1 Sam. 2:1–10
1 Declares the greatness of
47 a Hab. 3:18
b 1 Tim. 1:1; 2:3
48 a Ps. 138:6
b Luke 11:27
49 a Ps. 71:19; 126:2, 3
b Ps. 111:9
50 a Ps. 103:17
51 a Ps. 98:1; 118:15
b [1 Pet. 5:5]
52 a 1 Sam. 2:7, 8
53 a [Matt. 5:6]
54 a Is. 41:8
b [Jer. 31:3]
55 a Gen. 17:19
b [Rom. 11:28]
c Gen. 17:7
58 a [Rom. 12:15]
59 a Gen. 17:12
60 a Luke 1:13, 63
66 a Luke 2:19
b Acts 11:21
67 a Joel 2:28
68 a 1 Kin. 1:48
b Ex. 3:16
69 a Ps. 132:17
70 a Rom. 1:2
b Acts 3:21
72 a Lev. 26:42
73 a Gen. 12:3; 22:16–18
74 a [Heb. 9:14]
75 a [Eph. 4:24]
76 a Matt. 3:3; 11:9
b Is. 40:3
77 a [Mark 1:4]
78 1 Lit. *Dawn*; the Messiah
2 NU *shall visit*
79 a Is. 9:2
b [John 10:4; 14:27; 16:33]
80 a Luke 2:40
b Matt. 3:1

Luke 1:78–79

The Dayspring. Zacharias prophesied that John the Baptist would prepare the way for "the Dayspring from on high," who would "give light to those who sit in darkness." The Greek word for "Dayspring" literally means "dawn." The prophecy of Malachi 4:2 says, "But to you who fear My name the Sun of Righteousness shall arise with healing in His wings." So the coming of Jesus was like a sunrise. The night was over; the day was dawning.

CHRIST BORN OF MARY

2 And it came to pass in those days *that* a decree went out from Caesar Augustus that all the world should be registered. 2ªThis census first took place while Quirinius was governing Syria. 3So all went to be registered, everyone to his own city.

4Joseph also went up from Galilee, out of the city of Nazareth, into Judea, to ªthe city of David, which is called Bethlehem, bbecause he was of the house and lineage of David, 5to be registered with Mary, ªhis betrothed *1*wife, who was with child. 6So it was, that while they were there, the days were completed for her to be delivered. 7And ªshe brought forth her firstborn Son, and wrapped Him in swaddling cloths, and laid Him in a *1*manger, because there was no room for them in the inn.

GLORY IN THE HIGHEST

8Now there were in the same country shepherds living out in the fields, keeping watch over their flock by night. 9And *1*behold, an angel of the Lord stood before them, and the glory of the Lord shone around them, ªand they were greatly afraid. 10Then the angel said to them, ª"Do not be afraid, for behold, I bring you good tidings of great joy bwhich will be to all people. 11aFor there is born to you this day in the city of David ba Savior, cwho is Christ the Lord. 12And this *will be* the sign to you: You will find a Babe wrapped in swaddling cloths, lying in a *1*manger."

13ªAnd suddenly there was with the angel a multitude of the heavenly host praising God and saying:

14 "Glorya to God in the highest,
And on earth bpeace,
cgoodwill *1*toward men!"

15So it was, when the angels had gone away from them into heaven, that the shepherds said to one another, "Let us now go to Bethlehem and see this thing that has come to pass, which the Lord has made known to us." 16And they came with haste and found Mary and Joseph, and the Babe lying in a manger. 17Now when they had seen *Him,* they made *1*widely known the saying which was told them concerning this Child. 18And all those who heard *it* marveled at those things which were told them by the shepherds. 19aBut Mary kept all these things and pondered *them* in her heart. 20Then the shepherds returned, glorifying and apraising God for all the things that they had heard and seen, as it was told them.

Cross-references

2 a Acts 5:37

4 a 1 Sam. 16:1
b Matt. 1:16

5 a [Matt. 1:18]
1 NU omits *wife*

7 a Matt. 1:25
1 *feed trough*

9 a Luke 1:12
1 NU omits *behold*

10 a Luke 1:13, 30
b Gen. 12:3

11 a Is. 9:6
b Matt. 1:21
c Acts 2:36

12 1 *feed trough*

13 a Dan. 7:10

14 a Luke 19:38
b Is. 57:19
c [Eph. 2:4, 7]
1 NU *toward men of goodwill*

17 1 NU omits *widely*

19 a Gen. 37:11

20 a Luke 19:37

Luke 2:1–4

WHO IS IN CHARGE?

Caesar Augustus had an impressive amount of power. On a whim, he could order a taxation where everyone in the world had to go back to their hometown to register for the taxation. That is pretty powerful. But there is more to the story.

Back in Micah 5:2, it had been prophesied that the Messiah would be born in Bethlehem. This was a problem because Mary and Joseph lived in Nazareth, which was about 80 miles away from Bethlehem. So what did God do? He tapped Caesar on the shoulder and whispered in his ear, "Order a taxation that will require everyone to go to their hometown." He then made Caesar think it was his idea.

This little autocratic ruler, sitting on the throne in Rome, was not who he thought he was. He was just a puppet in the hand of God.

CIRCUMCISION OF JESUS

21 a And when eight days were completed ¹for the circumcision of the Child, His name was called b JESUS, the name given by the angel c before He was conceived in the womb.

JESUS PRESENTED IN THE TEMPLE

22 Now when a the days of her purification according to the law of Moses were completed, they brought Him to Jerusalem to present *Him* to the Lord 23 a (as it is written in the law of the Lord, b *"Every male who opens the womb shall be called holy to the LORD"*), 24 and to offer a sacrifice according to what is said in the law of the Lord, a *"A pair of turtledoves or two young pigeons."*

Luke 2:24

A Pair of Birds. When women went to observe the rites of purification after childbirth, they were supposed to bring a lamb to sacrifice. But Leviticus 12:8 tells us that, if they couldn't afford a lamb, they were allowed to bring two doves or pigeons instead. The fact that Mary and Joseph brought birds instead of a lamb reveals their poverty.

This verse also lets us know that the wise men hadn't arrived yet with their gifts of gold, frankincense, and myrrh. Jesus wasn't born in the lap of luxury.

SIMEON SEES GOD'S SALVATION

25 And behold, there was a man in Jerusalem whose name *was* Simeon, and this man *was* just and devout, a waiting for the Consolation of Israel, and the Holy Spirit was upon him. 26 And it had been revealed to him by the Holy Spirit that he would not a see death before he had seen the Lord's Christ. 27 So he came a by the Spirit into the temple. And when the parents brought in the Child Jesus, to do for Him according to the custom of the law, 28 he took Him up in his arms and blessed God and said:

29 "Lord, a now You are letting Your servant depart in peace, According to Your word;
30 For my eyes a have seen Your salvation

31 Which You have prepared before the face of all peoples,
32 a A light to *bring* revelation to the Gentiles, And the glory of Your people Israel."

33 ¹ And Joseph and His mother marveled at those things which were spoken of Him. 34 Then Simeon blessed them, and said to Mary His mother, "Behold, this *Child* is destined for the a fall and rising of many in Israel, and for b a sign which will be spoken against 35 (yes, a a sword will pierce through your own soul also), that the thoughts of many hearts may be revealed."

ANNA BEARS WITNESS TO THE REDEEMER

36 Now there was one, Anna, a prophetess, the daughter of Phanuel, of the tribe of a Asher. She was of a great age, and had lived with a husband seven years from her virginity; 37 and this woman *was* a widow ¹ of about eighty-four years, who did not depart from the temple, but served God with fastings and prayers a night and day. 38 And coming in that instant she gave thanks to ¹ the Lord, and spoke of Him to all those who a looked for redemption in Jerusalem.

THE FAMILY RETURNS TO NAZARETH

39 So when they had performed all things according to the law of the Lord, they returned to Galilee, to their *own* city, Nazareth. 40 a And the Child grew and became strong ¹ in spirit, filled with wisdom; and the grace of God was upon Him.

THE BOY JESUS AMAZES THE SCHOLARS

41 His parents went to a Jerusalem b every year at the Feast of the Passover. 42 And when He was twelve years old, they went up to Jerusalem according to the a custom of the feast. 43 When they had finished the a days, as they returned, the Boy Jesus lingered behind in Jerusalem. And ¹ Joseph and His mother did not know *it*; 44 but supposing Him to have been in the company, they went a day's journey, and sought Him among *their* relatives and acquaintances. 45 So when they did not find Him, they returned to Jerusalem, seeking Him. 46 Now so it was *that* after three days they found Him in the temple, sitting in the midst of the teachers, both listening

21 a Lev. 12:3
b [Matt. 1:21]
c Luke 1:31
1 NU *for His circumcision*

22 a Lev. 12:2–8

23 a Deut. 18:4
b Ex. 13:2, 12, 15

24 a Lev. 12:2, 8

25 a Mark 15:43

26 a [Heb. 11:5]

27 a Matt. 4:1

29 a Gen. 46:30

30 a [Is. 52:10]

32 a Acts 10:45; 13:47; 28:28

33 1 NU *And His father and mother*

34 a [1 Pet. 2:7, 8]
b Acts 4:2; 17:32; 28:22

35 a Ps. 42:10

36 a Josh. 19:24

37 a 1 Tim. 5:5
1 NU *until she was eighty-four*

38 a Mark 15:43
1 NU *God*

40 a Luke 1:80; 2:52
1 NU omits *in spirit*

41 a John 4:20
b Deut. 16:1, 16

42 a Ex. 23:14, 15

43 a Ex. 12:15
1 NU *His parents*

to them and asking them questions. ⁴⁷And ᵃall who heard Him were astonished at His understanding and answers. ⁴⁸So when they saw Him, they were amazed; and His mother said to Him, "Son, why have You done this to us? Look, Your father and I have sought You anxiously." ⁴⁹And He said to them, "Why did you seek Me? Did you not know that I must be ᵃabout ᵇMy Father's business?" ⁵⁰But ᵃthey did not understand the statement which He spoke to them.

JESUS ADVANCES IN WISDOM AND FAVOR

⁵¹Then He went down with them and came to Nazareth, and was ¹subject to them, but His mother ᵃkept all these things in her heart. ⁵²And Jesus ᵃincreased in wisdom and stature, ᵇand in favor with God and men.

Luke 2:52

The Silent Years. All that we know about Jesus, from the age of twelve to perhaps the age of thirty, is contained in this one verse. "And Jesus increased in wisdom and stature, and in favor with God and men."

Jesus grew intellectually, physically, spiritually, and socially. This is a great outline for our own personal development and as we minister to our own children. It demonstrates the importance of a balanced life and upbringing and a balanced education.

But this is all we know about these years, which represent the majority of Jesus' life. It was mostly a time of preparation.

JOHN THE BAPTIST PREPARES THE WAY

3 Now in the fifteenth year of the reign of Tiberius Caesar, ᵃPontius Pilate being governor of Judea, Herod being tetrarch of Galilee, his brother Philip tetrarch of Iturea and the region of Trachonitis, and Lysanias tetrarch of Abilene, ² ¹while ᵃAnnas and Caiaphas were high priests, the word of God came to ᵇJohn the son of Zacharias in the wilderness. ³ᵃAnd he went into all the region around the Jordan, preaching

---

47 ᵃMatt. 7:28; 13:54; 22:33

49 ᵃJohn 9:4 ᵇ[Luke 4:22, 32]

50 ᵃJohn 7:15, 46

51 ᵃDan. 7:28 ¹obedient

52 ᵃ[Col. 2:2, 3] ᵇ1 Sam. 2:26

CHAPTER 3

1 ᵃMatt. 27:2

2 ᵃActs 4:6 ᵇLuke 1:13 ¹NU, M in the high priesthood of Annas and Caiaphas

3 ᵃMark 1:4 ᵇLuke 1:77

4 ᵃIs. 40:3–5

6 ᵃIs. 52:10

7 ᵃMatt. 3:7; 12:34; 23:33 ¹Offspring

8 ᵃ[2 Cor. 7:9–11]

9 ᵃMatt. 7:19

10 ᵃ[Acts 2:37, 38; 16:30, 31]

11 ᵃ2 Cor. 8:14 ᵇIs. 58:7

12 ᵃLuke 7:29

---

a baptism of repentance ᵇfor the remission of sins, ⁴as it is written in the book of the words of Isaiah the prophet, saying:

ᵃ"*The voice of one crying in the wilderness:*
   '*Prepare the way of the LORD;*
   Make His paths straight.
⁵ *Every valley shall be filled*
   And every mountain and hill
      brought low;
   The crooked places shall be made
      straight
   And the rough ways smooth;
⁶ *And ᵃall flesh shall see the*
      salvation of God.'"

Luke 3:3–6

Get Straightened Up. In New Testament days, when a king was going to be traveling through an area, people would be sent ahead to prepare the way. They would fill in the chuckholes and flatten out the bumps, so the way would be smooth for the king. They wanted the place to look its best.

John the Baptist, in calling people to repentance, used this same imagery, as was prophesied in Isaiah 40. He was essentially saying, "Straighten out your lives! The King is coming. Get ready for the Messiah!"

JOHN PREACHES TO THE PEOPLE

⁷Then he said to the multitudes that came out to be baptized by him, ᵃ"Brood ¹of vipers! Who warned you to flee from the wrath to come? ⁸Therefore bear fruits ᵃworthy of repentance, and do not begin to say to yourselves, 'We have Abraham as our father.' For I say to you that God is able to raise up children to Abraham from these stones. ⁹And even now the ax is laid to the root of the trees. Therefore ᵃevery tree which does not bear good fruit is cut down and thrown into the fire."

¹⁰So the people asked him, saying, ᵃ"What shall we do then?"

¹¹He answered and said to them, ᵃ"He who has two tunics, let him give to him who has none; and he who has food, ᵇlet him do likewise."

¹²Then ᵃtax collectors also came to be baptized, and said to him, "Teacher, what shall we do?"

13And he said to them, a"Collect no more than what is appointed for you."

14Likewise the soldiers asked him, saying, "And what shall we do?"

So he said to them, "Do not 1intimidate anyone aor accuse falsely, and be content with your wages."

15Now as the people were in expectation, and all reasoned in their hearts about John, whether he was the Christ or not, 16John answered, saying to all, a"I indeed baptize you with water; but One mightier than I is coming, whose sandal strap I am not worthy to loose. He will bbaptize you with the Holy Spirit and fire. 17His winnowing fan is in His hand, and He will thoroughly clean out His threshing floor, and agather the wheat into His barn; but the chaff He will burn with unquenchable fire."

18And with many other exhortations he preached to the people. 19aBut Herod the tetrarch, being rebuked by him concerning Herodias, his 1brother Philip's wife, and for all the evils which Herod had done, 20also added this, above all, that he shut John up in prison.

Luke 3:19–20

Making Enemies. John the Baptist didn't pull any punches. And as he was calling everyone who listened to him to repentance, we see here that he spoke out against Herod and his ungodly union with Herodias, his brother's wife. This caused him to be imprisoned and ultimately killed.

If you speak the truth, you certainly risk making some enemies, especially if you speak out against powerful people. But speak the truth anyway.

JOHN BAPTIZES JESUS

21When all the people were baptized, ait came to pass that Jesus also was baptized; and while He prayed, the heaven was opened. 22And the Holy Spirit descended in bodily form like a dove upon Him, and a voice came from heaven which said, "You are My beloved Son; in You I am awell pleased."

THE GENEALOGY OF JESUS CHRIST

23Now Jesus Himself began His ministry at aabout thirty years of age, being

(as was supposed) bthe son of Joseph, the son of Heli, 24the son of Matthat, the son of Levi, the son of Melchi, the son of Janna, the son of Joseph, 25the son of Mattathiah, the son of Amos, the son of Nahum, the son of Esli, the son of Naggai, 26the son of Maath, the son of Mattathiah, the son of Semei, the son of Joseph, the son of Judah, 27the son of Joannas, the son of Rhesa, the son of aZerubbabel, the son of Shealtiel, the son of Neri, 28the son of Melchi, the son of Addi, the son of Cosam, the son of Elmodam, the son of Er, 29the son of Jose, the son of Eliezer, the son of Jorim, the son of Matthat, the son of Levi, 30the son of Simeon, the son of Judah, the son of Joseph, the son of Jonan, the son of Eliakim, 31the son of Melea, the son of Menan,

Luke 3:23–38

THE EARTHLY GENEALOGY OF JESUS

Matthew 1 gave us the genealogy of Jesus legally, through Joseph. This established His right to reign, being legally, through His stepfather Joseph, descended from David.

Here in Luke we have the genealogy of Jesus through His mother Mary. This was His biological line, traced all the way back to Adam. This emphasizes the humanity of Jesus. Notice here that Joseph is said to be the son of Heli. In Matthew, he was the son of Jacob. He was the son of Heli by marriage or, as we would say, "the son-in-law." Heli was the father of Mary.

So Matthew gave us the legal genealogy of Jesus through His stepfather Joseph. Luke gave us the human genealogy of Jesus through His mother Mary. And John gave us the divine genealogy of Jesus in John 1:1 as he wrote, "In the beginning was the Word, and the Word was with God, and the Word was God."

---

13 aLuke 19:8

14 aEx. 20:16; 23:1
1 Lit. *shake down* for money

16 aMatt. 3:11, 12
bJohn 7:39; 20:22

17 aMatt. 13:24–30

19 aMark 6:17
1 NU *brother's wife*

21 aMatt. 3:13–17

22 a2Pet. 1:17

23 a[Num. 4:3, 35, 39, 43, 47]
bJohn 6:42

27 aEzra 2:2; 3:8

the son of Mattathah, the son of ªNathan, ᵇthe son of David, 32ªthe son of Jesse, the son of Obed, the son of Boaz, the son of Salmon, the son of Nahshon, 33the son of Amminadab, the son of Ram, the son of Hezron, the son of Perez, the son of Judah, 34the son of Jacob, the son of Isaac, the son of Abraham, ªthe son of Terah, the son of Nahor, 35the son of Serug, the son of Reu, the son of Peleg, the son of Eber, the son of Shelah, 36ªthe son of Cainan, the son of ᵇArphaxad, ᶜthe son of Shem, the son of Noah, the son of Lamech, 37the son of Methuselah, the son of Enoch, the son of Jared, the son of Mahalalel, the son of Cainan, 38the son of Enosh, the son of Seth, the son of Adam, ªthe son of God.

SATAN TEMPTS JESUS

4 Then ªJesus, being filled with the Holy Spirit, returned from the Jordan and ᵇwas led by the Spirit ¹into the wilderness, ²being ¹tempted for forty days by the devil. And ªin those days He ate nothing, and afterward, when they had ended, He was hungry. ³And the devil said to Him, "If You are ªthe Son of God, command this stone to become bread."

⁴But Jesus answered him, saying, "It is written, ª'Man shall not live by bread alone, ¹but by every word of God.'"

⁵¹Then the devil, taking Him up on a high mountain, showed Him all the kingdoms of the world in a moment of time. ⁶And the devil said to Him, "All this authority I will give You, and their glory; for ªthis has been delivered to me, and I give it to whomever I wish. ⁷Therefore, if You will worship before me, all will be Yours."

⁸And Jesus answered and said to

him, ¹"Get behind Me, Satan! ²For it is written, ª'You shall worship the LORD your God, and Him only you shall serve.'"

⁹ªThen he brought Him to Jerusalem, set Him on the pinnacle of the temple, and said to Him, "If You are the Son of God, throw Yourself down from here. ¹⁰For it is written:

ª'He shall give His angels charge over you,
To keep you,'

¹¹and,

ª'In their hands they shall bear you up,
Lest you dash your foot against a stone.'"

¹²And Jesus answered and said to him, "It has been said, ª'You shall not ¹tempt the LORD your God.'"

¹³Now when the devil had ended every ¹temptation, he departed from Him ªuntil an opportune time.

JESUS BEGINS HIS GALILEAN MINISTRY

¹⁴ªThen Jesus returned ᵇin the power of the Spirit to ᶜGalilee, and ᵈnews of Him went out through all the surrounding region. ¹⁵And He ªtaught in their synagogues, ᵇbeing glorified by all.

JESUS REJECTED AT NAZARETH

¹⁶So He came to ªNazareth, where He had been brought up. And as His custom was, ᵇHe went into the synagogue on the Sabbath day, and stood up to read. ¹⁷And He was handed the

---

Cross references (center column):

31 ªZech. 12:12 ᵇ2Sam. 5:14; 7:12
32 ª Ruth 4:18–22
34 ª Gen. 11:24, 26–30; 12:3
36 ª Gen. 11:12 ᵇGen. 10:22, 24; 11:10–13 ᶜGen. 5:6–32; 9:27; 11:10
38 ª Gen. 5:1, 2

CHAPTER 4

1 ªMatt. 4:1–11 ᵇLuke 2:27 ¹NU in
2 ªEx. 34:28 ¹tested
3 ª John 20:31
4 ªDeut. 8:3 ¹NU omits but by every word of God
5 ¹NU And taking Him up, he showed Him
6 ª [Rev. 13:2, 7]
8 ªDeut. 6:13; 10:20 ¹NU omits Get behind Me, Satan ²NU, M omit For
9 ªMatt. 4:5–7
10 ªPs. 91:11
11 ªPs. 91:12
12 ªDeut. 6:16 ¹test
13 ª[Heb. 4:15] ¹testing
14 ªMatt. 4:12 ᵇJohn 4:43 ᶜActs 10:37 ᵈMatt. 4:24
15 ªMatt. 4:23 ᵇIs. 52:13 16 ªMark 6:1 ᵇActs 13:14–16; 17:2

THE ANSWER IS IN THE WORD   Luke 4:1–15

A s Jesus was being tempted by Satan, He answered him every time by quoting passages from Deuteronomy. Jesus obviously knew the Word of God. David said, in Psalm 1, speaking of the man who is blessed by God, "His delight is in the law of the LORD, and in His law he meditates day and night."

I think one of the weaknesses of the church today is the lack of the Word of God in the hearts of the people. Many people are following sensationalism, seeking exciting experiences. Others are looking for practical advice, with steps to success and things like that. But what we need more than anything is the Word of God. That is what will give us the depth and power to resist temptation. People need the foundation that comes from studying the Word of God.

Notice here how Jesus was filled with the Spirit before the temptation, He was led by the Spirit into the temptation, but He emerged from the temptation "in the power of the Spirit."

Luke 4:16–21

HALF A SERMON

Jesus stood up in the synagogue to read the Scriptures. He opened the book to Isaiah 61 and began reading. He read verse 1 and half of verse 2. He read the part of verse 2 that says "to proclaim the acceptable year of the LORD," and then He shut the book and sat down. The second half of the verse says, to proclaim "the day of vengeance of our God; to comfort all who mourn."

Why did Jesus stop mid-sentence? Because verse 1 and the first part of verse 2 were to be fulfilled by Jesus at His first coming, while the rest is a reference to His second coming.

After Jesus read the passage, closing the book in mid-sentence, everyone was staring at Him, expecting Him to say something more. He just stated, "Today this Scripture is fulfilled in your hearing." In other words, "I am the Messiah."

book of the prophet Isaiah. And when He had opened the book, He found the place where it was written:

18 "The ᵃ *Spirit of the LORD is upon Me,*
    Because He has anointed Me
    To preach the gospel to the poor;
    He has sent Me ¹*to heal the brokenhearted,*
    To proclaim liberty to the captives
    And recovery of sight to the blind,
    To ᵇ*set at liberty those who are* ²*oppressed;*
19 *To proclaim the acceptable year of the LORD."*

20 Then He closed the book, and gave *it* back to the attendant and sat down. And the eyes of all who were in the synagogue were fixed on Him. 21 And He began to say to them, "Today this Scripture is ᵃfulfilled in your hearing." 22 So all bore witness to Him, and ᵃmarveled at the gracious words which pro-

ceeded out of His mouth. And they said, ᵇ"Is this not Joseph's son?"

23 He said to them, "You will surely say this proverb to Me, 'Physician, heal yourself! Whatever we have heard done in ᵃCapernaum,¹ do also here in ᵇYour country.'" 24 Then He said, "Assuredly, I say to you, no ᵃprophet is accepted in his own country. 25 But I tell you truly, ᵃmany widows were in Israel in the days of Elijah, when the heaven was shut up three years and six months, and there was a great famine throughout all the land; 26 but to none of them was Elijah sent except to ¹Zarephath, *in the region* of Sidon, to a woman *who was* a widow. 27 ᵃAnd many lepers were in Israel in the time of Elisha the prophet, and none of them was cleansed except Naaman the Syrian."

28 So all those in the synagogue, when they heard these things, were ᵃfilled with ¹wrath, 29 ᵃand rose up and thrust Him out of the city; and they led Him to the brow of the hill on which their city was built, that they might throw Him down over the cliff. 30 Then ᵃpassing through the midst of them, He went His way.

JESUS CASTS OUT AN UNCLEAN SPIRIT

31 Then ᵃHe went down to Capernaum, a city of Galilee, and was teaching them on the Sabbaths. 32 And they were ᵃastonished at His teaching, ᵇfor His word was with authority. 33 ᵃNow in the synagogue there was a man who had a spirit of an unclean demon. And he cried out with a loud voice, 34 saying, "Let *us* alone! What have we to do with

---

Luke 4:32

Teaching with Authority. The people were used to hearing teaching from rabbis who were unsure of themselves. They would say, "Some rabbis say this" and "Others suppose this." They mostly taught by quoting others.

But Jesus was different. He would say, "I say to you" as if He had some authority that the others didn't have. They hadn't heard anything like it, and they were astonished. The clarity of His teachings is still authoritative and astonishing.

Cross-references:

18 ᵃIs. 49:8, 9; 61:1, 2
   ᵇ[Dan. 9:24]
   1 NU omits *to heal the brokenhearted*
   2 *downtrodden*

21 ᵃActs 13:29

22 ᵃ[Ps. 45:2]
   ᵇJohn 6:42

23 ᵃMatt. 4:13; 11:23
   ᵇMatt. 13:54
   1 NU *Capharnaum,* here and elsewhere

24 ᵃJohn 4:44

25 ᵃ1 Kin. 17:9

26 1 Gr. *Sarepta*

27 ᵃ2 Kin. 5:1–14

28 ᵃLuke 6:11
   1 *rage*

29 ᵃJohn 8:37; 10:31

30 ᵃJohn 8:59; 10:39

31 ᵃMatt. 4:13

32 ᵃMatt. 7:28, 29
   ᵇ[John 6:63; 7:46; 8:26, 28, 38, 47; 12:49, 50]

33 ᵃMark 1:23

You, Jesus of Nazareth? Did You come to destroy us? [a]I know who You are—[b]the Holy One of God!"

[35]But Jesus rebuked him, saying, [1]"Be quiet, and come out of him!" And when the demon had thrown him in *their* midst, it came out of him and did not hurt him. [36]Then they were all amazed and spoke among themselves, saying, "What a word this *is*! For with authority and power He commands the unclean spirits, and they come out." [37]And the report about Him went out into every place in the surrounding region.

PETER'S MOTHER-IN-LAW HEALED

[38][a]Now He arose from the synagogue and entered Simon's house. But Simon's wife's mother was [1]sick with a high fever, and they [b]made request of Him concerning her. [39]So He stood over her and [a]rebuked the fever, and it left her. And immediately she arose and served them.

MANY HEALED AFTER SABBATH SUNSET

[40][a]When the sun was setting, all those who had any that were sick with various diseases brought them to Him; and He laid His hands on every one of them and healed them. [41][a]And demons also came out of many, crying out and saying, [b]"You are [1]the Christ, the Son of God!"

And He, [c]rebuking *them*, did not allow them to [2]speak, for they knew that He was the Christ.

JESUS PREACHES IN GALILEE

[42][a]Now when it was day, He departed and went into a deserted place. And the crowd sought Him and came to Him, and tried to keep Him from leaving them; [43]but He said to them, "I must [a]preach the kingdom of God to the other cities also, because for this purpose I have been sent." [44][a]And He was preaching in the synagogues of [1]Galilee.

FOUR FISHERMEN CALLED AS DISCIPLES

5 So[a] it was, as the multitude pressed about Him to [b]hear the word of God, that He stood by the Lake of Gennesaret, [2]and saw two boats standing by the lake; but the fishermen had gone from them and were washing *their* nets. [3]Then He got into one of the boats, which was Simon's, and asked him to put out a little from the land. And He

[a]sat down and taught the multitudes from the boat.

[4]When He had stopped speaking, He said to Simon, [a]"Launch out into the deep and let down your nets for a catch."

[5]But Simon answered and said to Him, "Master, we have toiled all night and caught [a]nothing; nevertheless [b]at Your word I will let down the net." [6]And when they had done this, they caught a great number of fish, and their net was breaking. [7]So they signaled to *their* partners in the other boat to come and help them. And they came and filled both the boats, so that they began to sink. [8]When Simon Peter saw *it*, he fell down at Jesus' knees, saying, [a]"Depart from me, for I am a sinful man, O Lord!"

Luke 5:4–8

PERSPECTIVE

Peter had spent most of the night fishing and hadn't caught anything. Now Jesus told him to head out into deeper water, and Peter knew it was useless. But he went ahead and did it, just to humor Jesus. Of course, he and those with him caught so many fish that their boats began to sink. As the boats were sinking, it began to sink into Peter who Jesus really was. He knew Jesus wasn't just a man, but that He was the Messiah. But as he recognized Jesus for who He is, Peter also saw himself for who he was. He said, "Depart from me, for I am a sinful man, O Lord!"

Whenever we get a vision of who Jesus really is, it will always give us a realistic perspective of who we really are, as well. We fail to see the truth about ourselves until we see ourselves in His light. Seeing ourselves in His light always brings conviction.

[9]For he and all who were with him were [a]astonished at the catch of fish which they had taken; [10]and so also *were* James and John, the sons of Zebedee, who were partners with Simon.

Marginal references:

34 [a] Luke 4:41
[b] Ps. 16:10

35 [1] Lit. Be muzzled

38 [a] Mark 1:29–31
[b] Mark 5:23
[1] afflicted with

39 [a] Luke 8:24

40 [a] Matt. 8:16, 17

41 [a] Mark 1:34; 3:11
[b] Mark 8:29
[c] Mark 1:25, 34; 3:11
[1] NU omits the Christ
[2] Or say that they knew

42 [a] Mark 1:35–38

43 [a] [John 9:4]

44 [a] Matt. 4:23; 9:35
[1] NU Judea

CHAPTER 5

1 [a] Mark 1:16–20
[b] Acts 13:44

3 [a] John 8:2

4 [a] John 21:6

5 [a] John 21:3
[b] Ps. 33:9

8 [a] 1 Kin. 17:18

9 [a] Mark 5:42; 10:24, 26

And Jesus said to Simon, "Do not be afraid. ^aFrom now on you will catch men." ¹¹So when they had brought their boats to land, ^athey ¹forsook all and followed Him.

JESUS CLEANSES A LEPER

^{12 a}And it happened when He was in a certain city, that behold, a man who was full of ^bleprosy saw Jesus; and he fell on his face and ¹implored Him, saying, "Lord, if You are willing, You can make me clean."

¹³Then He put out His hand and touched him, saying, "I am willing; be cleansed." ^aImmediately the leprosy left him. ^{14 a}And He charged him to tell no one, "But go and show yourself to the priest, and make an offering for your cleansing, as a testimony to them, ^bjust as Moses commanded."

¹⁵However, ^athe report went around concerning Him all the more; and ^bgreat multitudes came together to hear, and to be healed by Him of their infirmities. ^{16 a}So He Himself often withdrew into the wilderness and ^bprayed.

Luke 5:16

Time to Pray. The greater the pressure, the more Jesus saw the necessity of getting alone in prayer. "So He Himself often withdrew into the wilderness and prayed."

If Jesus, being who He was, saw the necessity of prayer, who in the world do we think we are as we try to survive the pressures of the world without prayer? Jesus shows us that prayer needs to be an integral part of our very being. We need to depend upon the strength that comes from prayer.

JESUS FORGIVES AND HEALS A PARALYTIC

¹⁷Now it happened on a certain day, as He was teaching, that there were Pharisees and teachers of the law sitting by, who had come out of every town of Galilee, Judea, and Jerusalem. And the power of the Lord was present ¹to heal them. ^{18 a}Then behold, men brought on a bed a man who was paralyzed, whom they sought to bring in and lay before Him. ¹⁹And when they

could not find how they might bring him in, because of the crowd, they went up on the housetop and let him down with <i>his</i> bed through the tiling into the midst ^abefore Jesus.

²⁰When He saw their faith, He said to him, "Man, your sins are forgiven you."

^{21 a}And the scribes and the Pharisees began to reason, saying, "Who is this who speaks blasphemies? ^bWho can forgive sins but God alone?"

²²But when Jesus ^aperceived their thoughts, He answered and said to them, "Why are you reasoning in your hearts? ²³Which is easier, to say, 'Your sins are forgiven you,' or to say, 'Rise up and walk'? ²⁴But that you may know that the Son of Man has power on earth to forgive sins"—He said to the man who was paralyzed, ^a"I say to you, arise, take up your bed, and go to your house."

²⁵Immediately he rose up before them, took up what he had been lying on, and departed to his own house, ^aglorifying God. ²⁶And they were all amazed, and they ^aglorified God and were filled with fear, saying, "We have seen strange things today!"

MATTHEW THE TAX COLLECTOR

^{27 a}After these things He went out and saw a tax collector named Levi, sitting at the tax office. And He said to him, ^b"Follow Me." ²⁸So he left all, rose up, and ^afollowed Him.

^{29 a}Then Levi gave Him a great feast in his own house. And ^bthere were a great number of tax collectors and others who sat down with them. ^{30 1}And their scribes and the Pharisees ²complained against His disciples, saying, ^a"Why do You eat and drink with tax collectors and sinners?"

³¹Jesus answered and said to them, "Those who are well have no need of a physician, but those who are sick. ^{32 a}I have not come to call the righteous, but sinners, to repentance."

JESUS IS QUESTIONED ABOUT FASTING

³³Then they said to Him, ^a"Why ¹do the disciples of John fast often and make prayers, and likewise those of the Pharisees, but Yours eat and drink?"

³⁴And He said to them, "Can you make the friends of the bridegroom fast while the ^abridegroom is with them? ³⁵But the days will come when the bridegroom will be taken away

10 ^a Matt. 4:19
11 ^a Matt. 4:20; 19:27
1 left behind
12 ^a Mark 1:40–44
^b Lev. 13:14
1 begged
13 ^a John 5:9
14 ^a Matt. 8:4
^b Lev. 13:1–3; 14:2–32
15 ^a Mark 1:45
^b John 6:2
16 ^a Luke 9:10
^b Matt. 14:23
17 1 NU with Him to heal
18 ^a Mark 2:3–12
19 ^a Matt. 15:30
21 ^a Mark 2:6, 7
^b Is. 43:25
22 ^a John 2:25
24 ^a Luke 7:14
25 ^a Acts 3:8
26 ^a Luke 1:65; 7:16
27 ^a Matt. 9:9–17
^b John 12:26; 21:19, 22
28 ^a Mark 10:28
29 ^a Matt. 9:9, 10
^b Luke 15:1
30 ^a Luke 15:2
1 NU But the Pharisees and their scribes
2 grumbled
32 ^a 1 Tim. 1:15
33 ^a Matt. 9:14
1 NU omits Why do, making the verse a statement
34 ^a John 3:29

Luke 5:30-32

Eating with Sinners. Eating together is one of the more intimate things we can do. As we eat from the same food, it becomes a part of me as my body assimilates it, and it also becomes a part of you. In a sense, then, we become a part of each other. For Jews of Jesus' day, eating together implied a deep sharing. This is why the religious leaders were so shocked and scandalized that Jesus would eat with tax collectors and sinners.

But Jesus came to get close to sinners. No person is beyond the grace of God.

---

from them; then they will fast in those days."

36 [a]Then He spoke a parable to them: "No one [1]puts a piece from a new garment on an old one; otherwise the new makes a tear, and also the piece that was *taken* out of the new does not match the old. 37And no one puts new wine into old wineskins; or else the new wine will burst the wineskins and be spilled, and the wineskins will be ruined. 38But new wine must be put into new wineskins, [1]and both are preserved. 39And no one, having drunk old *wine,* [1]immediately desires new; for he says, 'The old is [2]better.' "

JESUS IS LORD OF THE SABBATH

6 Now [a]it happened [1]on the second Sabbath after the first that He went through the grainfields. And His disciples plucked the heads of grain and ate *them,* rubbing *them* in *their* hands. 2And some of the Pharisees said to them, "Why are you doing [a]what is not lawful to do on the Sabbath?"

3But Jesus answering them said, "Have you not even read this, [a]what David did when he was hungry, he and those who were with him: 4how he went into the house of God, took and ate the showbread, and also gave some to those with him, [a]which is not lawful for any but the priests to eat?" 5And He said to them, "The Son of Man is also Lord of the Sabbath."

HEALING ON THE SABBATH

6 [a]Now it happened on another Sabbath, also, that He entered the syna-

---

36 [a]Mark 2:21, 22
[1]NU *tears a piece from a new garment and puts it on an old one*

38 [1]NU omits *and both are preserved*

39 [1]NU omits *immediately*
[2]NU *good*

CHAPTER 6

1 [a]Matt. 12:1-8
[1]NU *on a Sabbath that He went*

2 [a]Ex. 20:10

3 [a]1Sam. 21:6

4 [a]Lev. 24:9

6 [a]Mark 3:1-6

7 [a]Luke 13:14; 14:1-6
[b]Luke 20:20

8 [a]Matt. 9:4

9 [a]John 7:23
[1]M *to kill*

10 [1]NU, M *him*
[2]NU omits *as whole as the other*

12 [a]Mark 1:35

13 [a]John 6:70
[b]Matt. 10:1

14 [a]John 1:42

---

gogue and taught. And a man was there whose right hand was withered. 7So the scribes and Pharisees watched Him closely, whether He would [a]heal on the Sabbath, that they might find an [b]accusation against Him. 8But He [a]knew their thoughts, and said to the man who had the withered hand, "Arise and stand here." And he arose and stood. 9Then Jesus said to them, "I will ask you one thing: [a]Is it lawful on the Sabbath to do good or to do evil, to save life or [1]to destroy?" 10And when He had looked around at them all, He said to [1]the man, "Stretch out your hand." And he did so, and his hand was restored [2]as whole as the other. 11But they were filled with rage, and discussed with one another what they might do to Jesus.

Luke 6:6-7

WHO JESUS NOTICES

I t is interesting that when the scribes and Pharisees saw a man in the synagogue who had a withered hand, they watched carefully to see what Jesus would do. They knew He would be interested in that man and would want to help him. They knew that Jesus would focus His attention on whatever person in the congregation had the greatest need. They understood Jesus more than we do sometimes.

If we are feeling low and pathetic, we don't feel like going to church. We feel like we don't really belong there, where everyone is so holy and spiritual. But Jesus is always interested in the one who has the greatest need. He is looking for you.

THE TWELVE APOSTLES

12Now it came to pass in those days that He went out to the mountain to pray, and continued all night in [a]prayer to God. 13And when it was day, He called His disciples to *Himself;* [a]and from them He chose [b]twelve whom He also named apostles: 14Simon, [a]whom He also named Peter, and Andrew his

brother; James and John; Philip and Bartholomew; [15]Matthew and Thomas; James the *son* of Alphaeus, and Simon called the Zealot; [16]Judas [a]*the son* of James, and [b]Judas Iscariot who also became a traitor.

Luke 6:12

All-Night Prayer. Luke has given us so much insight into the prayer life of Jesus. He mentioned that, as Jesus was baptized, He was praying when the Spirit descended upon Him. He also tells us here that Jesus prayed all night before selecting the twelve apostles. How important it is to be directed by God in choosing leadership and to spend time with Him in prayer.

JESUS HEALS A GREAT MULTITUDE

[17]And He came down with them and stood on a level place with a crowd of His disciples [a]and a great multitude of people from all Judea and Jerusalem, and from the seacoast of Tyre and Sidon, who came to hear Him and be healed of their diseases, [18]as well as those who were tormented with unclean spirits. And they were healed. [19]And the whole multitude [a]sought to [b]touch Him, for [c]power went out from Him and healed *them* all.

THE BEATITUDES

[20]Then He lifted up His eyes toward His disciples, and said:

[a]"Blessed *are you* poor,
For yours is the kingdom of
God.
[21] [a]Blessed *are you* who hunger
now,
For you shall be [b]filled. [1]
[c]Blessed *are you* who weep now,
For you shall [d]laugh.
[22] [a]Blessed are you when men hate
you,
And when they [b]exclude you,
And revile *you*, and cast out
your name as evil,
For the Son of Man's sake.
[23] [a]Rejoice in that day and leap for
joy!
For indeed your reward *is* great
in heaven,
For [b]in like manner their fathers
did to the prophets.

16 [a]Jude 1
[b]Luke 22:3–6

17 [a]Mark 3:7, 8

19 [a]Matt. 9:21; 14:36
[b]Mark 5:27, 28
[c]Luke 8:46

20 [a]Matt. 5:3–12; [11:5]

21 [a]Is. 55:1; 65:13
[b][Rev. 7:16]
[c][Is. 61:3]
[d]Ps. 126:5
[1]*satisfied*

22 [a]1 Pet. 2:19; 3:14; 4:14
[b][John 16:2]

23 [a]James 1:2
[b]Acts 7:51

24 [a]James 5:1–6
[b]Luke 12:21
[c]Luke 16:25

25 [a][Is. 65:13]
[b][Prov. 14:13]
[c]James 4:9

26 [a][John 15:19]
[1]NU, M omit *to you*
[2]M omits *all*

27 [a]Rom. 12:20

28 [a]Rom. 12:14
[b]Acts 7:60

29 [a]Matt. 5:39–42
[b][1 Cor. 6:7]

30 [a]Deut. 15:7, 8

31 [a]Matt. 7:12

32 [a]Matt. 5:46

34 [a]Matt. 5:42

JESUS PRONOUNCES WOES

[24] "But[a]woe to you [b]who are rich,
For [c]you have received your
consolation.
[25] [a]Woe to you who are full,
For you shall hunger.
[b]Woe to you who laugh now,
For you shall mourn and [c]weep.
[26] [a]Woe [1]to you when [2]all men speak
well of you,
For so did their fathers to the
false prophets.

LOVE YOUR ENEMIES

[27][a]"But I say to you who hear: Love your enemies, do good to those who hate you, [28][a]bless those who curse you, and [b]pray for those who spitefully use you. [29][a]To him who strikes you on the *one* cheek, offer the other also. [b]And from him who takes away your cloak, do not withhold *your* tunic either. [30][a]Give to everyone who asks of you. And from him who takes away your goods do not ask *them* back. [31][a]And just as you want men to do to you, you also do to them likewise.

[32][a]"But if you love those who love you, what credit is that to you? For even sinners love those who love them. [33]And if you do good to those who do good to you, what credit is that to you? For even sinners do the same. [34][a]And if you lend *to those* from whom you hope to receive back, what credit is that to

Luke 6:35

KIND TO THE EVIL

Loving your enemies is a difficult thing to do. You can try to appreciate them, forgive them, and be nice to them, but then they'll do something that reminds you why they are your enemy. But Jesus used God as the example: "For He is kind to the unthankful and evil." God blesses people who don't deserve it. His kindness is poured out on all.

You may say, "But I can't do that. That is impossible!" Yes, it is. God wants to do the supernatural within us, that we can show forth His love.

you? For even sinners lend to sinners to receive as much back. 35But a love your enemies, b do good, and c lend, 1hoping for nothing in return; and your reward will be great, and d you will be sons of the Most High. For He is kind to the unthankful and evil. 36 a Therefore be merciful, just as your Father also is merciful.

DO NOT JUDGE

37 a "Judge not, and you shall not be judged. Condemn not, and you shall not be condemned. b Forgive, and you will be forgiven. 38 a Give, and it will be given to you: good measure, pressed down, shaken together, and running over will be put into your b bosom. For c with the same measure that you use, it will be measured back to you."

39And He spoke a parable to them: a "Can the blind lead the blind? Will they not both fall into the ditch? 40 a A disciple is not above his teacher, but everyone who is perfectly trained will be like his teacher. 41 a And why do you look at the speck in your brother's eye, but do not perceive the plank in your own eye? 42 Or how can you say to your brother, 'Brother, let me remove the speck that is in your eye,' when you yourself do not see the plank that is in your own eye? Hypocrite! First remove the plank from your own eye, and then you will see clearly to remove the speck that is in your brother's eye.

A TREE IS KNOWN BY ITS FRUIT

43 a "For a good tree does not bear bad fruit, nor does a bad tree bear good fruit. 44 For a every tree is known by its own fruit. For men do not gather figs from thorns, nor do they gather grapes from a bramble bush. 45 a A good man out of the good treasure of his heart brings forth good; and an evil man out of the evil 1 treasure of his heart brings forth evil. For out b of the abundance of the heart his mouth speaks.

BUILD ON THE ROCK

46 a "But why do you call Me 'Lord, Lord,' and not do the things which I say? 47 a Whoever comes to Me, and hears My sayings and does them, I will show you whom he is like: 48 He is like a man building a house, who dug deep and laid the foundation on the rock. And when the flood arose, the stream beat vehemently against that house, and could not shake it, for it was 1 founded on the rock. 49 But he who heard and did nothing is like a man

---

35 a [Rom. 13:10]
b Heb. 13:16
c Ps. 37:26
d Matt. 5:46
1 expecting

36 a Matt. 5:48

37 a Matt. 7:1–5
b Matt. 18:21–35

38 a [Prov. 19:17; 28:27]
b Ps. 79:12
c James 2:13

39 a Matt. 15:14; 23:16

40 a [John 13:16; 15:20]

41 a Matt. 7:3

43 a Matt. 7:16–18, 20

44 a Matt. 12:33

45 a Matt. 12:35
b Matt. 12:34
1 NU omits treasure of his heart

46 a Mal. 1:6

47 a James 1:22–25

48 1 NU well built

49 1 NU collapsed

CHAPTER 7

1 a Matt. 8:5–13

---

who built a house on the earth without a foundation, against which the stream beat vehemently; and immediately it 1 fell. And the ruin of that house was great."

JESUS HEALS A CENTURION'S SERVANT

7 Now when He concluded all His sayings in the hearing of the people, He a entered Capernaum. 2 And a certain centurion's servant, who was dear to him, was sick and ready to die. 3 So when he heard about Jesus, he sent elders of the Jews to Him, pleading with Him to come and heal his servant. 4 And when they came to Jesus, they begged Him earnestly, saying that the one for whom He should do this was deserving, 5 "for he loves our nation, and has built us a synagogue." 6 Then Jesus went with them. And when He was already not far from the

Luke 7:1–10

UNWORTHY FAITH

This centurion desired for Jesus to heal his servant and sent a message to Jesus through the Jewish elders. They gave the centurion a good recommendation and said that he was deserving. But as Jesus was approaching his house, the centurion sent messengers to Jesus, telling Him that he wasn't worthy to come to Jesus or to have Jesus come to his house. He just wanted Jesus to say the word, and he knew that is all it would take. Jesus commended him for his faith and healed his servant.

We can't come to God based on our worthiness because of what we have done. We must approach Him in our unworthiness and in submission to His authority. When we do that, we are walking by faith. "For by grace you have been saved through faith, and that not of yourselves; it is the gift of God, not of works, lest anyone should boast" (Eph. 2:8–9).

house, the centurion sent friends to Him, saying to Him, "Lord, do not trouble Yourself, for I am not worthy that You should enter under my roof. [7]Therefore I did not even think myself worthy to come to You. But [a]say the word, and my servant will be healed. [8]For I also am a man placed under [a]authority, having soldiers under me. And I say to one, 'Go,' and he goes; and to another, 'Come,' and he comes; and to my servant, 'Do this,' and he does *it*."

[9]When Jesus heard these things, He marveled at him, and turned around and said to the crowd that followed Him, "I say to you, I have not found such great faith, not even in Israel!" [10]And those who were sent, returning to the house, found the servant well [1]who had been sick.

JESUS RAISES THE SON OF THE WIDOW OF NAIN

[11]Now it happened, the day after, *that* He went into a city called Nain; and many of His disciples went with Him, and a large crowd. [12]And when He came near the gate of the city, behold, a dead man was being carried out, the only son of his mother; and she was a widow. And a large crowd from the city was with her. [13]When the Lord saw her, He had [a]compassion on her and said to her, [b]"Do not weep." [14]Then He came and touched the open coffin, and those who carried *him* stood still. And He said, "Young man, I say to you, [a]arise." [15]So he who was dead [a]sat up and began to speak. And He [b]presented him to his mother.

[16][a]Then fear [1]came upon all, and they [b]glorified God, saying, [c]"A great prophet has risen up among us"; and,

---

Luke 7:11–17

Interrupting a Funeral. Jesus just happened to come across a large funeral procession for a young boy who had died. He reached out and touched the coffin and spoke to the boy, "Young man, I say to you, arise." Immediately the boy sat up and started talking.

What a way to break up a funeral procession! The people were transformed from mourning into rejoicing in just a moment's time.

---

[d]"God has visited His people." [17]And this report about Him went throughout all Judea and all the surrounding region.

JOHN THE BAPTIST SENDS MESSENGERS TO JESUS

[18][a]Then the disciples of John reported to him concerning all these things. [19]And John, calling two of his disciples to *him*, sent *them* to [1]Jesus, saying, "Are You [a]the Coming One, or [2]do we look for another?"

[20]When the men had come to Him, they said, "John the Baptist has sent us to You, saying, 'Are You the Coming One, or do we look for another?'" [21]And that very hour He cured many of [1]infirmities, afflictions, and evil spirits; and to many blind He gave sight.

[22][a]Jesus answered and said to them, "Go and tell John the things you have seen and heard: [b]that *the* blind [c]see, *the* lame [d]walk, *the* lepers are [e]cleansed, *the* deaf [f]hear, *the* dead are raised, [g]*the* poor have the gospel preached to them. [23]And blessed is *he* who is not [1]offended because of Me."

[24][a]When the messengers of John had departed, He began to speak to the multitudes concerning John: "What did you go out into the wilderness to see? A reed shaken by the wind? [25]But what did you go out to see? A man clothed in soft garments? Indeed those who are gorgeously appareled and live in luxury are in kings' courts. [26]But what did you go out to see? A prophet? Yes, I say to you, and more than a prophet. [27]This is *he* of whom it is written:

[a]'*Behold, I send My messenger
before Your face,
Who will prepare Your way
before You.*'

[28]For I say to you, among those born of women there is [1]not a [a]greater prophet than John the Baptist; but he who is least in the kingdom of God is greater than he."

[29]And when all the people heard *Him*, even the tax collectors [1]justified God, [a]having been baptized with the baptism of John. [30]But the Pharisees and [1]lawyers rejected [a]the will of God for themselves, not having been baptized by him.

[31][1]And the Lord said, [a]"To what then shall I liken the men of this generation, and what are they like? [32]They are like children sitting in the marketplace and calling to one another, saying:

Center column notes

7 [a]Ps. 33:9; 107:20
8 [a][Mark 13:34]
10 [1]NU omits *who had been sick*
13 [a]John 11:35 [b]Luke 8:52
14 [a]Acts 9:40
15 [a]John 11:44 [b]2 Kin. 4:36
16 [a]Luke 1:65 [b]Luke 5:26 [c]Luke 24:19 [d]Luke 1:68 [1]*seized them all*
18 [a]Matt. 11:2–19
19 [a][Zech. 9:9] [1]NU *the Lord* [2]*should we expect*
21 [1]*illnesses*
22 [a]Matt. 11:4 [b]Is. 35:5 [c]John 9:7 [d]Matt. 15:31 [e]Luke 17:12–14 [f]Mark 7:37 [g][Is. 61:1–3]
23 [1]*caused to stumble*
24 [a]Matt. 11:7
27 [a]Mal. 3:1
28 [a][Luke 1:15] [1]NU *none greater than John;*
29 [a]Luke 3:12 [1]*declared the righteousness of*
30 [a]Acts 20:27 [1]*the experts in the law*
31 [a]Matt. 11:16 [1]NU, M omit *And the Lord said*

'We played the flute for you,
      And you did not dance;
We mourned to you,
      And you did not weep.'

33For aJohn the Baptist came bneither eating bread nor drinking wine, and you say, 'He has a demon.' 34The Son of Man has come aeating and drinking, and you say, 'Look, a glutton and a Iwinebibber, a friend of tax collectors and sinners!' 35aBut wisdom is justified by all her children."

A SINFUL WOMAN FORGIVEN

36aThen one of the Pharisees asked Him to eat with him. And He went to the Pharisee's house, and sat down to eat. 37And behold, a woman in the city who was a sinner, when she knew that *Jesus* sat at the table in the Pharisee's house, brought an alabaster flask of fragrant oil, 38and stood at His feet behind *Him* weeping; and she began to wash His feet with her tears, and wiped *them* with the hair of her head; and she kissed His feet and anointed *them* with the fragrant oil. 39Now when the Pharisee who had invited Him saw *this*, he spoke to himself, saying, a"This Man, if He were a prophet, would know who and what manner of woman *this is* who is touching Him, for she is a sinner."

40And Jesus answered and said to him, "Simon, I have something to say to you."

So he said, "Teacher, say it."

41"There was a certain creditor who had two debtors. One owed five hundred adenarii, and the other fifty. 42And when they had nothing with which to repay, he freely forgave them both. Tell Me, therefore, which of them will love him more?"

43Simon answered and said, "I suppose the *one* whom he forgave more."

And He said to him, "You have rightly judged." 44Then He turned to the woman and said to Simon, "Do you see this woman? I entered your house; you gave Me no awater for My feet, but she has washed My feet with her tears and wiped *them* with the hair of her head. 45You gave Me no akiss, but this woman has not ceased to kiss My feet since the time I came in. 46aYou did not anoint My head with oil, but this woman has anointed My feet with fragrant oil. 47aTherefore I say to you, her sins, which *are* many, are forgiven, for she loved much. But to whom little is forgiven, *the same* loves little."

48Then He said to her, a"Your sins are forgiven."

49And those who sat at the table with Him began to say to themselves, a"Who is this who even forgives sins?"

50Then He said to the woman, a"Your faith has saved you. Go in peace."

Luke 7:37–50

Sinner Woman. A woman who was described as a sinner was anointing Jesus' feet with ointment. The Pharisees were scandalized that He would allow such a woman to even touch Him. But Jesus came to touch people like her; and His message to her was, "Your sins are forgiven...Your faith has saved you. Go in peace." And that is the message He has for any sinner, no matter how vile, who will come to Him.

MANY WOMEN MINISTER TO JESUS

8 Now it came to pass, afterward, that He went through every city and village, preaching and Ibringing the glad tidings of the kingdom of God. And the twelve *were* with Him, 2and acertain women who had been healed of evil spirits and Iinfirmities—Mary called Magdalene, bout of whom had come seven demons, 3and Joanna the wife of Chuza, Herod's steward, and Susanna, and many others who provided for IHim from their 2substance.

THE PARABLE OF THE SOWER

4aAnd when a great multitude had gathered, and they had come to Him from every city, He spoke by a parable: 5"A sower went out to sow his seed. And as he sowed, some fell by the wayside; and it was trampled down, and the birds of the air devoured it. 6Some fell on rock; and as soon as it sprang up, it withered away because it lacked moisture. 7And some fell among thorns, and the thorns sprang up with it and choked it. 8But others fell on good ground, sprang up, and yielded Ia crop a hundredfold." When He had said these things He cried, a"He who has ears to hear, let him hear!"

THE PURPOSE OF PARABLES

9aThen His disciples asked Him, saying, "What does this parable mean?" 10And He said, "To you it has been

Center column references

33 aMatt. 3:1
b Luke 1:15

34 aLuke 15:2
1 An excessive drinker

35 aMatt. 11:19

36 aJohn 11:2

39 aLuke 15:2

41 aMatt. 18:28

44 aGen. 18:4; 19:2; 43:24

45 aRom. 16:16

46 aPs. 23:5

47 a[1 Tim. 1:14]

48 aMatt. 9:2

49 aLuke 5:21

50 aMatt. 9:22

CHAPTER 8

1 1proclaiming the good news

2 aMatt. 27:55
b Mark 16:9
1 sicknesses

3 1NU, M them
2 possessions

4 aMark 4:1–9

8 aLuke 14:35
1 Lit. fruit

9 aMatt. 13:10–23

given to know the [1]mysteries of the kingdom of God, but to the rest *it is given* in parables, that

a'*Seeing they may not see,*
And hearing they may not understand.'

THE PARABLE OF THE SOWER EXPLAINED

11 a"Now the parable is this: The seed is the bword of God. 12Those by the wayside are the ones who hear; then the devil comes and takes away the word out of their hearts, lest they should believe and be saved. 13But the ones on the rock *are those* who, when they hear, receive the word with joy; and these have no root, who believe for

---

Luke 8:13

Saved and Lost? In the case of seed that is sown on the wayside, they hear the word, but it never germinates or comes to life. But in the case of the seeds sown on the rock, they do spring forth into life, and "believe for a while." But they ultimately fall away. Were they saved and then lost? I don't know, but it is something you should think about. I am only asking the questions. I don't have all the answers.

---

a while and in time of [1]temptation fall away. 14Now the ones *that* fell among thorns are those who, when they have heard, go out and are choked with cares, ariches, and pleasures of life, and bring no fruit to maturity. 15But the ones *that* fell on the good ground are those who, having heard the word with a noble and good heart, keep *it* and bear fruit with apatience.[1]

THE PARABLE OF THE REVEALED LIGHT

16a"No one, when he has lit a lamp, covers it with a vessel or puts *it* under a bed, but sets *it* on a lampstand, that those who enter may see the blight. 17aFor nothing is secret that will not be brevealed, nor *anything* hidden that will not be known and come to light. 18Therefore take heed how you hear. aFor whoever has, to him *more* will be given; and whoever does not have, even what he [1]seems to bhave will be taken from him."

JESUS' MOTHER AND BROTHERS COME TO HIM

19aThen His mother and brothers came to Him, and could not approach Him because of the crowd. 20And it was told Him *by some,* who said, "Your mother and Your brothers are standing outside, desiring to see You." 21But He answered and said to them, "My mother and My brothers are these who hear the word of God and do it."

Cross references (center column)

10 aIs. 6:9
[1] *secret or hidden truths*

11 a[1 Pet. 1:23]
bLuke 5:1; 11:28

13 [1] *testing*

14 a1 Tim. 6:9, 10

15 a[Heb. 10:36–39]
[1] *endurance*

16 aLuke 11:33
bMatt. 5:14

17 aLuke 12:2
b[2 Cor. 5:10]

18 aMatt. 25:29
bMatt. 13:12
[1] *thinks that he has*

19 aMark 3:31–35

BRINGING PEOPLE TOGETHER   Luke 8:2–3

There was a group of women who helped Jesus and His disciples, probably financially supporting Him and arranging the logistics of His travel and accommodations. Three of the names are mentioned here, but there were others as well. The first one mentioned is Mary Magdalene, whose life had been touched by Jesus when He delivered her from seven demons. Joanna is named, and she was the wife of a very important man in Herod's government. Susanna is also listed, and we don't know anything about her except that she was most likely a financial supporter of Jesus.

Where else but at the foot of Jesus could you find a gathering that included both former demon-possessed women and some upper-class socialites? Jesus so often brings together opposites, pulling together an interesting blend of people. Paul said that Jesus is One who breaks down walls (Eph. 2:14).

We saw in the early days of Calvary Chapel how the Lord brought together high-powered businessmen with hippies, young people and old, longhaired, shorthaired, all different types of people, in order to form one body. And it was a glorious thing to see people who were so different, and who would normally be suspicious of each other, brought together by the love of Jesus Christ. This is what Jesus does. He brings different people together, as a testimony that He has broken down the walls that separate us.

Luke 8:21

Hearing and Doing. The family of Jesus had come to talk to Him, as they were worried about Him working too hard and not taking care of Himself. But Jesus defined who His family really is by saying, "My mother and My brothers are these who hear the Word of God and do it."

It isn't just hearing the Word of God that matters. Many people listen to the Lord, year after year. But it is all about hearing and doing.

WIND AND WAVE OBEY JESUS

22 aNow it happened, on a certain day, that He got into a boat with His disciples. And He said to them, "Let us cross over to the other side of the lake." And they launched out. 23But as they sailed He fell asleep. And a windstorm came down on the lake, and they were filling *with water,* and were in *1*jeopardy. 24And they came to Him and awoke Him, saying, "Master, Master, we are perishing!"

Then He arose and rebuked the wind and the raging of the water. And they ceased, and there was a calm. 25But He said to them, a"Where is your faith?"

And they were afraid, and marveled, saying to one another, b"Who can this be? For He commands even the winds and water, and they obey Him!"

A DEMON-POSSESSED MAN HEALED

26aThen they sailed to the country of the *1*Gadarenes, which is opposite Galilee. 27And when He stepped out on the land, there met Him a certain man from the city who had demons *1*for a long time. And he wore no clothes, nor did he live in a house but in the tombs. 28When he saw Jesus, he acried out, fell down before Him, and with a loud voice said, b"What have I to do with cYou, Jesus, Son of the Most High God? I beg You, do not torment me!" 29For He had commanded the unclean spirit to come out of the man. For it had often seized him, and he was kept under guard, bound with chains and shackles; and he broke the bonds and was driven by the demon into the wilderness.

30Jesus asked him, saying, "What is your name?"

And he said, "Legion," because many demons had entered him. 31And they begged Him that He would not command them to go out ainto the abyss.

32Now a herd of many aswine was feeding there on the mountain. So they begged Him that He would permit them to enter them. And He permitted them. 33Then the demons went out of the man and entered the swine, and the herd ran violently down the steep place into the lake and drowned.

34When those who fed *them* saw what had happened, they fled and told *it* in the city and in the country. 35Then they went out to see what had happened, and came to Jesus, and found the man from whom the demons had departed, asitting at the bfeet of Jesus, clothed and in his cright mind. And they were afraid. 36They also who had seen *it* told them by what means he who had been demon-possessed was *1*healed. 37aThen the whole multitude of the surrounding region of the *1*Gadarenes basked Him to cdepart from them, for they were seized with great dfear. And He got into the boat and returned.

38Now athe man from whom the demons had departed begged Him that he might be with Him. But Jesus sent him away, saying, 39"Return to your own house, and tell what great things God has done for you." And he went his way and proclaimed throughout the whole city what great things Jesus had done for him.

A GIRL RESTORED TO LIFE AND A WOMAN HEALED

40So it was, when Jesus returned, that the multitude welcomed Him, for they were all waiting for Him. 41aAnd behold, there came a man named Jairus, and he was a ruler of the synagogue. And he fell down at Jesus' feet and begged Him to come to his house, 42for he had an only daughter about twelve years of age, and she awas dying.

But as He went, the multitudes thronged Him. 43aNow a woman, having a bflow of blood for twelve years, who had spent all her livelihood on physicians and could not be healed by any, 44came from behind and atouched the border of His garment. And immediately her flow of blood stopped.

45And Jesus said, "Who touched Me?"

When all denied it, Peter *1*and those with him said, "Master, the multitudes

Cross references

22 aMatt. 8:23–27

23 *1*danger

25 aLuke 9:41
bLuke 4:36; 5:26

26 aMark 5:1–17
*1*NU Gerasenes

27 *1*NU and for a long time wore no clothes

28 aMark 1:26; 9:26
bMark 1:23, 24
cLuke 4:41

31 a[Rev. 20:1, 3]

32 aLev. 11:7

35 a[Matt. 11:28]
bLuke 10:39; 17:16
c[2 Tim. 1:7]

36 *1*delivered

37 aMatt. 8:34
bLuke 4:34
cActs 16:39
dLuke 5:26
*1*NU Gerasenes

38 aMark 5:18–20

41 aMark 5:22–43

42 aLuke 7:2

43 aMatt. 9:20
bLuke 15:19–22

44 aMark 6:56

45 *1*NU omits and those with him

throng and press You, [2]and You say, 'Who touched Me?'"

[46]But Jesus said, "Somebody touched Me, for I perceived [a]power going out from Me." [47]Now when the woman saw that she was not hidden, she came trembling; and falling down before Him, she declared to Him in the presence of all the people the reason she had touched Him and how she was healed immediately.

[48]And He said to her, "Daughter, [1]be of good cheer; [a]your faith has made you well. [b]Go in peace."

[49a]While He was still speaking, someone came from the ruler of the synagogue's *house*, saying to him, "Your daughter is dead. Do not trouble the [1]Teacher."

[50]But when Jesus heard *it*, He answered him, saying, "Do not be afraid; [a]only believe, and she will be made well." [51]When He came into the house, He permitted no one to go [1]in except [2]Peter, James, and John, and the father and mother of the girl. [52]Now all wept and mourned for her; but He said, [a]"Do not weep; she is not dead, [b]but sleeping." [53]And they ridiculed Him, knowing that she was dead.

[54]But He [1]put them all outside, took her by the hand and called, saying, "Little girl, [a]arise." [55]Then her spirit returned, and she arose immediately. And He commanded that she be given *something* to eat. [56]And her parents were astonished, but [a]He charged them to tell no one what had happened.

SENDING OUT THE TWELVE

9 Then [a]He called His twelve disciples together and [b]gave them power and authority over all demons, and to cure diseases. [2a]He sent them to preach the kingdom of God and to heal the sick. [3a]And He said to them, "Take nothing for the journey, neither staffs nor bag nor bread nor money; and do not have two tunics apiece. [4a]"Whatever house you enter, stay there, and from there depart. [5a]And whoever will not receive you, when you go out of that city, [b]shake off the very dust from your feet as a testimony against them."

[6a]So they departed and went through the towns, preaching the gospel and healing everywhere.

HEROD SEEKS TO SEE JESUS

[7a]Now Herod the tetrarch heard of all that was done by Him; and he was

---

45 [2]NU omits the rest of v. 45.

46 [a]Mark 5:30

48 [a]Luke 7:50
[b]John 8:11
[1]NU omits *be of good cheer*

49 [a]Mark 5:35
[1]NU adds *anymore*

50 [a][Mark 11:22–24]

51 [1]NU adds *with Him*
[2]NU, M *Peter, John, and James*

52 [a]Luke 7:13
[b][John 11:11, 13]

54 [a]John 11:43
[1]NU omits *them all outside*

56 [a]Matt. 8:4; 9:30

CHAPTER 9

1 [a]Matt. 10:1,
2 [b][John 14:12]

2 [a]Matt. 10:7, 8

3 [a]Luke 10:4–12; 22:35

4 [a]Mark 6:10

5 [a]Matt. 10:14
[b]Acts 13:51

6 [a]Mark 6:12

7 [a]Matt. 14:1, 2

9 [a]Luke 23:8

10 [a]Mark 6:30
[b]Matt. 14:13

12 [a]John 6:1, 5

16 [a]Luke 22:19; 24:30

Luke 9:2–6

Traveling Light. It is interesting how Jesus sent the disciples out with almost nothing. He sent them forth so that they could learn the lessons of faith and trust in God.

I am so thankful for the years of ministry when the times were difficult financially. Often we didn't know where our next meal would come from, but we saw how God always supplied our needs. I learned lessons that were invaluable, and I wouldn't trade those lessons for anything.

---

perplexed, because it was said by some that John had risen from the dead, [8]and by some that Elijah had appeared, and by others that one of the old prophets had risen again. [9]Herod said, "John I have beheaded, but who is this of whom I hear such things?" [a]So he sought to see Him.

FEEDING THE FIVE THOUSAND

[10a]And the apostles, when they had returned, told Him all that they had done. [b]Then He took them and went aside privately into a deserted place belonging to the city called Bethsaida. [11]But when the multitudes knew *it*, they followed Him; and He received them and spoke to them about the kingdom of God, and healed those who had need of healing. [12a]When the day began to wear away, the twelve came and said to Him, "Send the multitude away, that they may go into the surrounding towns and country, and lodge and get provisions; for we are in a deserted place here."

[13]But He said to them, "You give them something to eat."

And they said, "We have no more than five loaves and two fish, unless we go and buy food for all these people." [14]For there were about five thousand men.

Then He said to His disciples, "Make them sit down in groups of fifty." [15]And they did so, and made them all sit down.

[16]Then He took the five loaves and the two fish, and looking up to heaven, He [a]blessed and broke them, and gave *them* to the disciples to set before the multitude. [17]So they all ate and were

---

Luke 9:13–17

Loaves and Fishes. There was just no way you could feed over five thousand people with five loaves and two fishes. But Jesus did it.

So often we think what we have is so paltry compared to the need. We look at the overwhelming needs and think, *What can I do? I have so little.* But the little that we have, in the hands of Jesus, can provide for a multitude. The whole key is, take what you have, give it to Jesus, and watch Him multiply it.

---

[1]filled, and twelve baskets of the left-over fragments were taken up by them.

PETER CONFESSES JESUS AS THE CHRIST

18 [a]And it happened, as He was alone praying, *that* His disciples joined Him, and He asked them, saying, "Who do the crowds say that I am?"

19 So they answered and said, [a]"John the Baptist, but some *say* Elijah; and others *say* that one of the old prophets has risen again."

20 He said to them, "But who do you say that I am?"

[a]Peter answered and said, "The Christ of God."

JESUS PREDICTS HIS DEATH AND RESURRECTION

21 [a]And He strictly warned and commanded them to tell this to no one, 22 saying, [a]"The Son of Man must suffer many things, and be rejected by the elders and chief priests and scribes, and be killed, and be raised the third day."

TAKE UP THE CROSS AND FOLLOW HIM

23 [a]Then He said to *them* all, "If anyone desires to come after Me, let him deny himself, and take up his cross [1]daily, and follow Me. 24 [a]For whoever desires to save his life will lose it, but whoever loses his life for My sake will save it. 25 [a]For what profit is it to a man if he gains the whole world, and is himself destroyed or lost? 26 [a]For whoever is ashamed of Me and My words, of him the Son of Man will be [b]ashamed when He comes in His *own* glory, and

---

17 [1] satisfied

18 [a] Matt. 16:13–16

19 [a] Matt. 14:2

20 [a] John 6:68, 69

21 [a] Matt. 8:4; 16:20

22 [a] Matt. 16:21; 17:22

23 [a] Matt. 10:38; 16:24 [1] M omits *daily*

24 [a] [John 12:25]

25 [a] Mark 8:36

26 [a] [Rom. 1:16] [b] Matt. 10:33

27 [a] Matt. 16:28

28 [a] Mark 9:2–8

30 [a] Heb. 11:23–29 [b] 2 Kin. 2:1–11

31 [1] Death, lit. *departure*

32 [a] Dan. 8:18; 10:9

33 [1] tents

34 [a] Ex. 13:21

35 [a] [Matt. 3:17; 12:18] [b] Acts 3:22 [1] NU *My Son, the Chosen One*

36 [a] Matt. 17:9

37 [a] Mark 9:14–27

---

in *His* Father's, and of the holy angels. 27 [a]But I tell you truly, there are some standing here who shall not taste death till they see the kingdom of God."

Luke 9:23

Take Up Your Cross Daily. To deny yourself, dying to yourself, dying to your flesh, is not easy or quick. Crucifixion is a long, painful process of torture and death. So is self-denial. So we are to take up our cross on a daily basis. It is a difficult, slow, painful process to die to self, but we are to reckon ourselves to be dead to sin, but alive to God in Christ (Rom. 6:11).

JESUS TRANSFIGURED ON THE MOUNT

28 [a]Now it came to pass, about eight days after these sayings, that He took Peter, John, and James and went up on the mountain to pray. 29 As He prayed, the appearance of His face was altered, and His robe *became* white *and* glistening. 30 And behold, two men talked with Him, who were [a]Moses and [b]Elijah, 31 who appeared in glory and spoke of His [1]decease which He was about to accomplish at Jerusalem. 32 But Peter and those with him [a]were heavy with sleep; and when they were fully awake, they saw His glory and the two men who stood with Him. 33 Then it happened, as they were parting from Him, *that* Peter said to Jesus, "Master, it is good for us to be here; and let us make three [1]tabernacles: one for You, one for Moses, and one for Elijah"—not knowing what he said.

34 While he was saying this, a cloud came and overshadowed them; and they were fearful as they entered the [a]cloud. 35 And a voice came out of the cloud, saying, [a]"This is [1]My beloved Son. [b]Hear Him!" 36 When the voice had ceased, Jesus was found alone. [a]But they kept quiet, and told no one in those days any of the things they had seen.

A BOY IS HEALED

37 [a]Now it happened on the next day, when they had come down from the mountain, that a great multitude met Him. 38 Suddenly a man from the multitude cried out, saying, "Teacher, I implore You, look on my son, for he is

my only child. 39And behold, a spirit seizes him, and he suddenly cries out; it convulses him so that he foams *at the mouth;* and it departs from him with great difficulty, bruising him. 40So I implored Your disciples to cast it out, but they could not."

41Then Jesus answered and said, "O 1faithless and perverse generation, how long shall I be with you and 2bear with you? Bring your son here." 42And as he was still coming, the demon threw him down and convulsed *him.* Then Jesus rebuked the unclean spirit, healed the child, and gave him back to his father.

JESUS AGAIN PREDICTS HIS DEATH

43And they were all amazed at the majesty of God.

But while everyone marveled at all the things which Jesus did, He said to His disciples, 44a"Let these words sink down into your ears, for the Son of Man is about to be betrayed into the hands of men." 45aBut they did not understand this saying, and it was hidden from them so that they did not perceive it; and they were afraid to ask Him about this saying.

WHO IS THE GREATEST?

46aThen a dispute arose among them as to which of them would be greatest. 47And Jesus, aperceiving the thought of their heart, took a blittle child and set him by Him, 48and said to them, a"Whoever receives this little child in My name receives Me; and bwhoever receives Me creceives Him who sent Me. dFor he who is least among you all will be great."

JESUS FORBIDS SECTARIANISM

49aNow John answered and said, "Master, we saw someone casting out demons in Your name, and we forbade him because he does not follow with us." 50But Jesus said to him, "Do not forbid *him,* for ahe who is not against 1us is on 2our side."

A SAMARITAN VILLAGE REJECTS THE SAVIOR

51Now it came to pass, when the time had come for aHim to be received up, that He steadfastly set His face to go to Jerusalem, 52and sent messengers before His face. And as they went, they entered a village of the Samaritans, to prepare for Him. 53But athey did not receive Him, because His face was *set* for the journey to Jerusalem. 54And

when His disciples aJames and John saw *this,* they said, "Lord, do You want us to command fire to come down from heaven and consume them, 1just as bElijah did?"

55But He turned and rebuked them, 1and said, "You do not know what manner of aspirit you are of. 56 1For athe Son of Man did not come to destroy men's lives but to save *them.*" And they went to another village.

Luke 9:51–56

Fire from Heaven? When Jesus was shunned by this Samaritan village, James and John were incensed, and asked Jesus if they should call down fire from heaven to consume the village. This gives us a clue as to why Jesus called them "the sons of thunder."

But Jesus told them that they just didn't get it. He hadn't come to destroy men's lives, but to save them. Jesus received this rejection with such gentleness. How many of us responded to Jesus the first time He called? It is a good thing He is patient.

THE COST OF DISCIPLESHIP

57aNow it happened as they journeyed on the road, *that* someone said to Him, "Lord, I will follow You wherever You go."

58And Jesus said to him, "Foxes have holes and birds of the air *have* nests, but the Son of Man ahas nowhere to lay *His* head."

59aThen He said to another, "Follow Me."

But he said, "Lord, let me first go and bury my father."

60Jesus said to him, "Let the dead bury their own dead, but you go and preach the kingdom of God."

61And another also said, "Lord, aI will follow You, but let me first go *and* bid them farewell who are at my house."

62But Jesus said to him, "No one, having put his hand to the plow, and looking back, is afit for the kingdom of God."

THE SEVENTY SENT OUT

10 After these things the Lord appointed 1seventy others also, and asent them two by two before His

---

Center column notes:

41 1 *unbelieving* 2 *put up with*

44 aMatt. 17:22

45 aMark 9:32

46 aMatt. 18:1–5

47 aMatt. 9:4 bLuke 18:17

48 aMatt. 18:5 bJohn 12:44 cJohn 13:20 dEph. 3:8

49 aMark 9:38–40

50 aLuke 11:23 1NU *you* 2NU *your*

51 aMark 16:19

53 aJohn 4:4, 9

54 aMark 3:17 b2Kin. 1:10, 12 1NU omits *just as Elijah did*

55 a[2Tim. 1:7] 1NU omits the rest of v. 55.

56 aJohn 3:17; 12:47 1NU omits *For the Son of Man did not come to destroy men's lives but to save them.*

57 aMatt. 8:19–22

58 aLuke 2:7; 8:23

59 aMatt. 8:21, 22

61 a1Kin. 19:20

62 a2Tim. 4:10

CHAPTER 10

1 aMark 6:7 1NU *seventy-two others*

PRAY THE LORD OF THE HARVEST

It is time for a great harvest, but we need to pray that God will send for the laborers.

At the end of World War II, when General MacArthur had signed the accord with Japan, he put out a call for missionaries to go to Japan. He felt like the United States should send ten thousand missionaries to Japan. They were ready to hear the gospel. But the church didn't respond, while the commercial interests came into Japan in a big way. As a result, Japan became a huge, materialistic empire, with very little interest in Christianity. Business succeeded, but the church failed.

Today, there are other areas of the world where the harvest is plentiful. There is a window of opportunity in places like Eastern Europe and Africa. We are doing what we can to saturate these places with the gospel, but we need to "pray the Lord of the harvest to send out laborers into His harvest."

Luke 10:2

2 a John 4:35
b 2 Thess. 3:1

3 a Matt. 10:16

4 a Luke 9:3–5
b 2 Kin. 4:29

5 a Matt. 10:12

7 a Matt. 10:11
b 1 Cor. 10:27
c 1 Tim. 5:18

9 a Mark 3:15
b Matt. 3:2; 10:7

11 a Acts 13:51
1 NU our feet

12 a Matt. 10:15; 11:24
1 NU, M omit But

13 a Matt. 11:21–23
b Ezek. 3:6

15 a Matt. 11:23
b Is. 14:13–15
c Ezek. 26:20
1 NU will you be exalted to heaven? You will be thrust down to Hades!

16 a John 13:20
b 1 Thess. 4:8
c John 5:23

17 a Luke 10:1
1 NU seventy-two

18 a John 12:31

19 a Mark 16:18

20 a Is. 4:3
1 NU, M omit rather

21 a Matt. 11:25–27

22 a John 3:35; 5:27; 17:2
b [John 1:18; 6:44, 46]
1 M And turning to the disciples He said, "All

23 a Matt. 13:16, 17

24 a 1 Pet. 1:10, 11

---

face into every city and place where He Himself was about to go. 2 Then He said to them, a "The harvest truly *is* great, but the laborers *are* few; therefore b pray the Lord of the harvest to send out laborers into His harvest. 3 Go your way; a behold, I send you out as lambs among wolves. 4 a Carry neither money bag, knapsack, nor sandals; and b greet no one along the road. 5 a But whatever house you enter, first say, 'Peace to this house.' 6 And if a son of peace is there, your peace will rest on it; if not, it will return to you. 7 a And remain in the same house, b eating and drinking such things as they give, for c the laborer is worthy of his wages. Do not go from house to house. 8 Whatever city you enter, and they receive you, eat such things as are set before you. 9 a And heal the sick there, and say to them,

---

b 'The kingdom of God has come near to you.' 10 But whatever city you enter, and they do not receive you, go out into its streets and say, 11 a 'The very dust of your city which clings to 1 us we wipe off against you. Nevertheless know this, that the kingdom of God has come near you.' 12 1 But I say to you that a it will be more tolerable in that Day for Sodom than for that city.

WOE TO THE IMPENITENT CITIES

13 a "Woe to you, Chorazin! Woe to you, Bethsaida! b For if the mighty works which were done in you had been done in Tyre and Sidon, they would have repented long ago, sitting in sackcloth and ashes. 14 But it will be more tolerable for Tyre and Sidon at the judgment than for you. 15 a And you, Capernaum, 1 who are b exalted to heaven, c will be brought down to Hades. 16 a He who hears you hears Me, b he who rejects you rejects Me, and c he who rejects Me rejects Him who sent Me."

THE SEVENTY RETURN WITH JOY

17 Then a the 1 seventy returned with joy, saying, "Lord, even the demons are subject to us in Your name." 18 And He said to them, a "I saw Satan fall like lightning from heaven. 19 Behold, a I give you the authority to trample on serpents and scorpions, and over all the power of the enemy, and nothing shall by any means hurt you. 20 Nevertheless do not rejoice in this, that the spirits are subject to you, but 1 rather rejoice because a your names are written in heaven."

JESUS REJOICES IN THE SPIRIT

21 a In that hour Jesus rejoiced in the Spirit and said, "I thank You, Father, Lord of heaven and earth, that You have hidden these things from *the* wise and prudent and revealed them to babes. Even so, Father, for so it seemed good in Your sight. 22 a All 1 things have been delivered to Me by My Father, and b no one knows who the Son is except the Father, and who the Father is except the Son, and *the one* to whom the Son wills to reveal *Him*."

23 Then He turned to *His* disciples and said privately, a "Blessed *are* the eyes which see the things you see; 24 for I tell you a that many prophets and kings have desired to see what you see, and have not seen *it*, and to hear what you hear, and have not heard *it*."

Luke 10:21

Revealed to Babes. Upon hearing the exciting reports of all that God had done through the disciples who went out, Jesus rejoiced and praised God and said, "You have hidden these things from the wise and prudent and revealed them to babes." There wasn't a Ph.D. in the bunch. These were just simple guys who went out and shared the gospel.

We sometimes think that to be in the ministry you need to go to seminary for many years to become wise and prudent. All you need is a call from God and the power of the Spirit.

THE PARABLE OF THE GOOD SAMARITAN

25And behold, a certain ¹lawyer stood up and tested Him, saying, a"Teacher, what shall I do to inherit eternal life?"
26He said to him, "What is written in the law? What is your reading *of it?*"
27So he answered and said, a"'*You shall love the* LORD *your God with all your heart, with all your soul, with all your strength, and with all your mind,'* and b'*your neighbor as yourself.'* "
28And He said to him, "You have answered rightly; do this and ªyou will live."
29But he, wanting to ªjustify himself, said to Jesus, "And who is my neighbor?"
30Then Jesus answered and said: "A certain *man* went down from Jerusalem to Jericho, and fell among ¹thieves, who stripped him of his clothing, wounded *him,* and departed, leaving *him* half dead. 31Now by chance a certain priest came down that road. And when he saw him, ªhe passed by on the other side. 32Likewise a Levite, when he arrived at the place, came and looked, and passed by on the other side. 33But a certain ªSamaritan, as he journeyed, came where he was. And when he saw him, he had bcompassion. 34So he went to *him* and bandaged his wounds, pouring on oil and wine; and he set him on his own animal, brought him to an inn, and took care of him. 35On the next day, ¹when he departed,

25 ª Matt.
19:16–19; 22:35
¹ expert in the
law

27 ª Deut. 6:5
b Lev. 19:18

28 ª Ezek.
20:11, 13, 21

29 ª Luke 16:15

30 ¹ robbers

31 ª Ps. 38:11

33 ª John 4:9
b Luke 15:20

35 ª Matt. 20:2
¹ NU omits
when he departed

37 ª Prov. 14:21

38 ª John 11:1;
12:2, 3

39 ª [1 Cor.
7:32–40]
b Acts 22:3
¹ NU *the Lord's*

41 ¹ NU *the
Lord*

42 ª [Ps. 27:4]

he took out two ªdenarii, gave *them* to the innkeeper, and said to him, 'Take care of him; and whatever more you spend, when I come again, I will repay you.' 36So which of these three do you think was neighbor to him who fell among the thieves?"
37And he said, "He who showed mercy on him."
Then Jesus said to him, ª"Go and do likewise."

Luke 10:29–37

Who Is My Neighbor? In response to the question, "Who is my neighbor?" Jesus told the story of a man who was mugged and injured and lying on the side of the road. A priest and a Levite both came by and ignored him, but a Samaritan stopped and helped him. The real neighbor was obviously the one who showed mercy. Jesus then said, "Go and do likewise."

The lesson is simple and clear. You are to love your neighbor as yourself, and your neighbor is any person who is in need or distress. Now do it.

MARY AND MARTHA WORSHIP AND SERVE

38Now it happened as they went that He entered a certain village; and a certain woman named ªMartha welcomed Him into her house. 39And she had a sister called Mary, ªwho also bsat at ¹Jesus' feet and heard His word. 40But Martha was distracted with much serving, and she approached Him and said, "Lord, do You not care that my sister has left me to serve alone? Therefore tell her to help me."
41And ¹Jesus answered and said to her, "Martha, Martha, you are worried and troubled about many things. 42But ªone thing is needed, and Mary has chosen that good part, which will not be taken away from her."

THE MODEL PRAYER

11 Now it came to pass, as He was praying in a certain place, when He ceased, *that* one of His disciples said to Him, "Lord, teach us to pray, as John also taught his disciples."
2So He said to them, "When you pray, say:

Luke 11:2

Our Father. The first thing in prayer is relationship. God is our Father. You see, if you are not a child of God, you have no access to the Father. In Old Testament times, you had to come to God through priests and sacrifices. You could not come directly to God. But now, through Jesus Christ, we have a relationship with God as His children. And thus, we come on the basis of this relationship.

a Our[1] Father [2]in heaven,
Hallowed be Your name.
Your kingdom come.
[3] Your will be done
On earth as *it is* in heaven.
3   Give us day by day our daily
bread.
4   And [a]forgive us our sins,
For we also forgive everyone who
is indebted to us.
And do not lead us into
temptation,
[1] But deliver us from the evil one."

CHAPTER 11

2 [a] Matt. 6:9–13
[1] NU omits *Our*
[2] NU omits *in heaven*
[3] NU omits the rest of v. 2.

4 [a] [Eph. 4:32]
[1] NU omits *But deliver us from the evil one*

8 [a] [Luke 18:1–5]

9 [a] [John 15:7]
[b] Is. 55:6

11 [a] Matt. 7:9
[1] NU omits *bread from any father among you, will he give him a stone? Or if he asks for*

13 [a] James 1:17

A FRIEND COMES AT MIDNIGHT

[5]And He said to them, "Which of you shall have a friend, and go to him at midnight and say to him, 'Friend, lend me three loaves; [6]for a friend of mine has come to me on his journey, and I have nothing to set before him'; [7]and he will answer from within and say, 'Do not trouble me; the door is now shut, and my children are with me in bed; I cannot rise and give to you'? [8]I say to you, [a]though he will not rise and give to him because he is his friend, yet because of his persistence he will rise and give him as many as he needs.

KEEP ASKING, SEEKING, KNOCKING

[9][a]"So I say to you, ask, and it will be given to you; [b]seek, and you will find; knock, and it will be opened to you. [10]For everyone who asks receives, and he who seeks finds, and to him who knocks it will be opened. [11][a]If a son asks for [1]bread from any father among you, will he give him a stone? Or if *he asks* for a fish, will he give him a serpent instead of a fish? [12]Or if he asks for an egg, will he offer him a scorpion? [13]If you then, being evil, know how to give [a]good gifts to your children, how much more will *your* heavenly Father give the Holy Spirit to those who ask Him!"

ASKING FOR THE HOLY SPIRIT   Luke 11:9–13

If an earthly son asks his father for food and nourishment, the father won't respond by giving him something harmful. So also, as we have need for spiritual nourishment, as we recognize the need we have for the Holy Spirit to fill and empower our lives, we can be assured that our loving heavenly Father will respond to that prayer as we ask Him to fill us with the Spirit.

There are some people who will tell you that it is dangerous to ask for the Holy Spirit. They will tell you that you may be opening yourself up to all sorts of dangerous phenomena if you ask God to give you His Spirit. That is blasphemous. An earthly father wouldn't give his son a scorpion when he asks for an egg. How much more likely that your heavenly Father would never give you something harmful when you are asking for something that is as needful as the Holy Spirit!

Now, I do think there is sometimes a danger in seeking a particular experience. Everyone experiences the working of the Spirit in their lives in a different way; and if you are seeking the experience that someone else has, it may lead to something harmful. For instance, Charles Finney described his experience of being filled with the Spirit as if it were waves of liquid love poured over him, from head to toe. Now, if you decide that you want that experience and you seek to have the feeling of liquid love pouring over you, there may be many different ways of finding that particular experience; and it may come in some way other than through the Spirit.

Don't seek a particular experience. God works differently, as He wills. Don't ask for an experience; just ask for the Holy Spirit, and however you experience Him, let that be in His hands.

A HOUSE DIVIDED CANNOT STAND

14a And He was casting out a demon, and it was mute. So it was, when the demon had gone out, that the mute spoke; and the multitudes marveled. 15 But some of them said, a "He casts out demons by 1 Beelzebub, the ruler of the demons."

16 Others, testing *Him*, a sought from Him a sign from heaven. 17 a But b He, knowing their thoughts, said to them: "Every kingdom divided against itself is brought to desolation, and a house *divided* against a house falls. 18 If Satan also is divided against himself, how will his kingdom stand? Because you say I cast out demons by Beelzebub. 19 And if I cast out demons by Beelzebub, by whom do your sons cast *them* out? Therefore they will be your judges. 20 But if I cast out demons a with the finger of God, surely the kingdom of God has come upon you. 21 a When a strong man, fully armed, guards his own palace, his goods are in peace. 22 But a when a stronger than he comes upon him and overcomes him, he takes from him all his armor in which he trusted, and divides his 1 spoils. 23 a He who is not with Me is against Me, and he who does not gather with Me scatters.

AN UNCLEAN SPIRIT RETURNS

24 a "When an unclean spirit goes out of a man, he goes through dry places, seeking rest; and finding none, he says, 'I will return to my house from which I came.' 25 And when he comes, he finds *it* swept and put in order. 26 Then he goes and takes with *him* seven other spirits more wicked than himself, and they enter and dwell there; and a the last *state* of that man is worse than the first."

KEEPING THE WORD

27 And it happened, as He spoke these things, that a certain woman from the crowd raised her voice and said to Him, a "Blessed *is* the womb that bore You, and *the* breasts which nursed You!"

28 But He said, a "More than that, blessed *are* those who hear the word of God and keep it!"

SEEKING A SIGN

29 a And while the crowds were thickly gathered together, He began to say, "This is an evil generation. It seeks a b sign, and no sign will be given to it except the sign of Jonah 1 the prophet. 30 For as a Jonah became a sign to the Ninevites, so also the Son of Man will

Cross references (center column)

14 a Matt. 9:32–34; 12:22, 24

15 a Matt. 9:34; 12:24
1 NU, M *Beelzebul*

16 a Matt. 12:38; 16:1

17 a Matt. 12:25–29
b John 2:25

20 a Ex. 8:19

21 a Mark 3:27

22 a [Is. 53:12]
1 *plunder*

23 a Matt. 12:30

24 a Matt. 12:43–45

26 a [2 Pet. 2:20]

27 a Luke 1:28, 48

28 a [Luke 8:21]

29 a Matt. 12:38–42
b 1 Cor. 1:22
1 NU omits *the prophet*

30 a Jon. 1:17; 2:10; 3:3–10

31 a 1 Kin. 10:1–9
b [Rom. 9:5]

32 a Jon. 3:5

33 a Mark 4:21
b Matt. 5:15

34 a Matt. 6:22, 23
1 Clear, or *healthy*
2 Evil, or *unhealthy*

38 a Mark 7:2, 3

Luke 11:27–28

BLESSED

Mary was certainly blessed as a result of her privilege of giving birth to Jesus, and she is to be appreciated. This woman blessed Mary by saying, "Blessed is the womb that bore You, and the breasts which nursed You!" But Jesus said, "More than that, blessed are those who hear the Word of God and keep it!"

Everything comes down to our obedience and response to God. We will all be judged by the same standard. What did you do with Jesus? What did you do with the Word of God?

be to this generation. 31 a The queen of the South will rise up in the judgment with the men of this generation and condemn them, for she came from the ends of the earth to hear the wisdom of Solomon; and indeed a b greater than Solomon *is* here. 32 The men of Nineveh will rise up in the judgment with this generation and condemn it, for a they repented at the preaching of Jonah; and indeed a greater than Jonah *is* here.

THE LAMP OF THE BODY

33 a "No one, when he has lit a lamp, puts *it* in a secret place or under a b basket, but on a lampstand, that those who come in may see the light. 34 a The lamp of the body is the eye. Therefore, when your eye is 1 good, your whole body also is full of light. But when *your eye* is 2 bad, your body also *is* full of darkness. 35 Therefore take heed that the light which is in you is not darkness. 36 If then your whole body *is* full of light, having no part dark, *the* whole *body* will be full of light, as when the bright shining of a lamp gives you light."

WOE TO THE PHARISEES AND LAWYERS

37 And as He spoke, a certain Pharisee asked Him to dine with him. So He went in and sat down to eat. 38 a When the Pharisee saw *it*, he marveled that He had not first washed before dinner.

39 a Then the Lord said to him, "Now you Pharisees make the outside of the cup and dish clean, but b your inward part is full of *1*greed and wickedness. 40 Foolish ones! Did not a He who made the outside make the inside also? 41 a But rather give alms of *1*such things as you have; then indeed all things are clean to you.

42 a "But woe to you Pharisees! For you tithe mint and rue and all manner of herbs, and b pass by justice and the c love of God. These you ought to have done, without leaving the others undone. 43 a Woe to you Pharisees! For you love the *1*best seats in the synagogues and greetings in the marketplaces. 44 a Woe to you, *1*scribes and Pharisees, hypocrites! b For you are like graves which are not seen, and the men who walk over *them* are not aware of *them*."

45 Then one of the lawyers answered and said to Him, "Teacher, by saying these things You reproach us also."

46 And He said, "Woe to you also, lawyers! a For you load men with burdens hard to bear, and you yourselves do not touch the burdens with one of your fingers. 47 a Woe to you! For you build the tombs of the prophets, and your fathers killed them. 48 In fact, you bear witness that you approve the deeds of your fathers; for they indeed killed them, and you build their tombs. 49 Therefore the wisdom of God also said, a 'I will send them prophets and apostles, and *some* of them they will kill and persecute,' 50 that the blood of all the prophets which was shed from the foundation of the world may be required of this generation, 51 a from the blood of Abel to b the blood of Zechariah who perished between the altar and the temple. Yes, I say to you, it shall be required of this generation.

52 a "Woe to you lawyers! For you have taken away the key of knowledge. You did not enter in yourselves, and those who were entering in you hindered."

53 *1*And as He said these things to them, the scribes and the Pharisees began to assail *Him* vehemently, and to cross-examine Him about many things, 54 lying in wait for Him, *1*and a seeking to catch Him in something He might say, 2 that they might accuse Him.

BEWARE OF HYPOCRISY

12 In a the meantime, when an innumerable multitude of people had gathered together, so that they trampled one another, He began to say to

His disciples first *of all*, b "Beware of the *1*leaven of the Pharisees, which is hypocrisy. 2 a For there is nothing covered that will not be revealed, nor hidden that will not be known. 3 Therefore whatever you have spoken in the dark will be heard in the light, and what you have spoken in the ear in inner rooms will be proclaimed on the housetops.

JESUS TEACHES THE FEAR OF GOD

4 a "And I say to you, b My friends, do not be afraid of those who kill the body, and after that have no more that they can do. 5 But I will show you whom you should fear: Fear Him who, after He has killed, has power to cast into hell; yes, I say to you, a fear Him! 6 "Are not five sparrows sold for two *1*copper coins? And a not one of them is forgotten before God. 7 But the very hairs of your head are all numbered. Do not fear therefore; you are of more value than many sparrows.

CONFESS CHRIST BEFORE MEN

8 a "Also I say to you, whoever confesses Me b before men, him the Son of Man also will confess before the angels of God. 9 But he who a denies Me before men will be denied before the angels of God.

10 "And a anyone who speaks a word against the Son of Man, it will be forgiven him; but to him who blasphemes against the Holy Spirit, it will not be forgiven. 11 a "Now when they bring you to the synagogues and magistrates and authorities, do not worry about how or what you should answer, or what you should say. 12 For the Holy Spirit will a teach you in that very hour what you ought to say."

THE PARABLE OF THE RICH FOOL

13 Then one from the crowd said to Him, "Teacher, tell my brother to divide the inheritance with me."

14 But He said to him, a "Man, who made Me a judge or an arbitrator over you?" 15 And He said to them, a "Take heed and beware of *1*covetousness, for one's life does not consist in the abundance of the things he possesses."

16 Then He spoke a parable to them, saying: "The ground of a certain rich man yielded plentifully. 17 And he thought within himself, saying, 'What shall I do, since I have no room to store my crops?' 18 So he said, 'I will do this: I will pull down my barns and build greater, and there I will store all my

Cross-references

39 a Matt. 23:25
b Titus 1:15
1 Lit. eager grasping or robbery
40 a Gen. 1:26, 27
41 a [Luke 12:33; 16:9]
1 Or what is inside
42 a Matt. 23:23
b [Mic. 6:7, 8]
c John 5:42
43 a Mark 12:38, 39
1 Or places of honor
44 a Matt. 23:27
b Ps. 5:9
1 NU omits scribes and Pharisees, hypocrites
46 a Matt. 23:4
47 a Matt. 23:29
49 a Matt. 23:34
51 a Gen. 4:8
b 2 Chr. 24:20, 21
52 a Matt. 23:13
53 *1* NU And when He left there
54 a Mark 12:13
1 NU omits and seeking
2 NU omits that they might accuse Him

CHAPTER 12
1 a Mark 8:15
b Matt. 16:12
1 yeast
2 a Matt. 10:26; [1 Cor. 4:5]
4 a Is. 51:7, 8, 12, 13
b [John 15:13–15]
5 a Ps. 119:120
6 a Matt. 6:26
1 Gr. assarion, a coin worth about 1/16 of a denarius
8 a Matt. 10:32
b Ps. 119:46
9 a Matt. 10:33
10 a [Matt. 12:31, 32]
11 a Mark 13:11
12 a [John 14:26]
14 a [John 18:36]
15 a [1 Tim. 6:6–10]
1 NU all covetousness

Luke 12:15

Life Isn't About Things. "One's life does not consist in the abundance of the things he possesses." How that goes against the common ideas of man today. Somehow we think that life **does** consist in abundance of possessions.

People constantly try to amass more and more, thinking to themselves that as soon as they can reach certain material goals, then they will find satisfaction and contentment. But they will always be looking for more and more, because things can't satisfy.

Luke 12:31

Priorities. God is first. Seek the kingdom of God first. He will take care of all the other things you need if you put Him first.

But what if you don't put Him first? Your whole life will be spent trying to get enough food, trying to get enough clothes, striving to get more of everything, and never being satisfied. And if you don't put Him first, you won't have time for Him at all. He will be crowded out by all the other concerns.

If you put God first, He promises to take care of all your other needs.

---

crops and my goods. 19And I will say to my soul, a"Soul, you have many goods laid up for many years; take your ease; beat, drink, and be merry." ' 20But God said to him, 'Fool! This night ayour soul will be required of you; bthen whose will those things be which you have provided?'
21"So *is* he who lays up treasure for himself, aand is not rich toward God."

DO NOT WORRY

22Then He said to His disciples, "Therefore I say to you, ado not worry about your life, what you will eat; nor about the body, what you will put on. 23Life is more than food, and the body *is more* than clothing. 24Consider the ravens, for they neither sow nor reap, which have neither storehouse nor barn; and aGod feeds them. Of how much more value are you than the birds? 25And which of you by worrying can add one cubit to his stature? 26If you then are not able to do *the* least, why 1are you anxious for the rest? 27Consider the lilies, how they grow: they neither toil nor spin; and yet I say to you, even aSolomon in all his glory was not 1arrayed like one of these. 28If then God so clothes the grass, which today is in the field and tomorrow is thrown into the oven, how much more will He clothe you, O *you* of alittle faith?
29"And do not seek what you should eat or what you should drink, nor have an anxious mind. 30For all these things the nations of the world seek after, and your Father aknows that you need these things. 31aBut seek 1the kingdom

of God, and all these things shall be added to you.
32"Do not fear, little flock, for ait is your Father's good pleasure to give you the kingdom. 33aSell what you have and give balms; cprovide yourselves money bags which do not grow old, a treasure in the heavens that does not fail, where no thief approaches nor moth destroys. 34For where your treasure is, there your heart will be also.

THE FAITHFUL SERVANT AND THE EVIL SERVANT

35a"Let your waist be girded and byour lamps burning; 36and you yourselves be like men who wait for their master, when he will return from the wedding, that when he comes and knocks they may open to him immediately. 37aBlessed *are* those servants whom the master, when he comes, will find watching. Assuredly, I say to you that he will gird himself and have them sit down *to eat,* and will come and serve them. 38And if he should come in the second watch, or come in the third watch, and find *them* so, blessed are those servants. 39aBut know this, that if the master of the house had known what hour the thief would come, he would 1have watched and not allowed his house to be broken into. 40aTherefore you also be ready, for the Son of Man is coming at an hour you do not expect."
41Then Peter said to Him, "Lord, do You speak this parable *only* to us, or to all *people?*"

Cross references (center column):

19 aEccl. 11:9
b[Eccl. 2:24; 3:13; 5:18; 8:15]

20 aPs. 52:7
bPs. 39:6

21 a[James 2:5; 5:1–5]

22 aMatt. 6:25–33

24 aJob 38:41

26 1do you worry

27 a1Kin. 10:4–7
1clothed

28 aMatt. 6:30; 8:26; 14:31; 16:8

30 aMatt. 6:31, 32

31 aMatt. 6:33
1NU *His kingdom, and these things*

32 a[Matt. 11:25, 26]

33 aMatt. 19:21
bLuke 11:41
cMatt. 6:20

35 a[1 Pet. 1:13]
b[Matt. 25:1–13]

37 aMatt. 24:46

39 aRev. 3:3; 16:15
1NU *not have allowed*

40 aMark 13:33

Luke 12:40
When You Least Expect Him.
I am always disappointed when I hear someone predicting the Lord's return, setting dates based on some calculations based on an interpretation of prophecy. You see, Jesus has told us right here that "the Son of Man is coming at an hour you do not expect." So, once someone sets a date, it is pretty sure it won't happen then.

How about today? Do you think Jesus will come today, really? No? That's great, because He will come when we least expect Him, like maybe today?

42 And the Lord said, a"Who then is that faithful and wise steward, whom *his* master will make ruler over his household, to give *them their* portion of food *1*in due season? 43Blessed *is* that servant whom his master will find so doing when he comes. 44 a Truly, I say to you that he will make him ruler over all that he has. 45 a But if that servant says in his heart, 'My master is delaying his coming,' and begins to beat the male and female servants, and to eat and drink and be drunk, 46the master of that servant will come on a a day when he is not looking for *him*, and at an hour when he is not aware, and will cut him in two and appoint *him* his portion with the unbelievers. 47 And a that servant who b knew his master's will, and did not prepare *himself* or do according to his will, shall be beaten with many *stripes*. 48 a But he who did not know, yet committed things deserving of stripes, shall be beaten with few. For everyone to whom much is given, from him much will be required; and to whom much has been committed, of him they will ask the more.

CHRIST BRINGS DIVISION
49 a "I came to send fire on the earth, and how I wish it were already kindled! 50 But a I have a baptism to be baptized with, and how distressed I am till it is b accomplished! 51 a Do *you* suppose that I came to give peace on earth? I tell you, not at all, b but rather division. 52 a For from now on five in one house will be divided: three against two, and two against three. 53 a Father will be

42 a Matt. 24:45, 46; 25:21
1 at the right time

44 a Matt. 24:47; 25:21

45 a 2 Pet. 3:3, 4

46 a 1 Thess. 5:3

47 a Deut. 25:2
b [James 4:17]

48 a [Lev. 5:17]

49 a Luke 12:51

50 a Mark 10:38
b John 12:27; 19:30

51 a Matt. 10:34–36
b John 7:43; 9:16; 10:19

52 a Mark 13:12

53 a Matt. 10:21, 36

54 a Matt. 16:2, 3

55 a Job 37:17

56 a Luke 19:41–44

58 a Prov. 25:8
b [Is. 55:6]

CHAPTER 13

1 *1 mixed*

6 a Matt. 21:19

7 *1 waste*

divided against son and son against father, mother against daughter and daughter against mother, mother-in-law against her daughter-in-law and daughter-in-law against her mother-in-law."

DISCERN THE TIME
54Then He also said to the multitudes, a"Whenever you see a cloud rising out of the west, immediately you say, 'A shower is coming'; and so it is. 55And when *you see* the a south wind blow, you say, 'There will be hot weather'; and there is. 56Hypocrites! You can discern the face of the sky and of the earth, but how *is it* you do not discern a this time?

MAKE PEACE WITH YOUR ADVERSARY
57"Yes, and why, even of yourselves, do you not judge what is right? 58 a When you go with your adversary to the magistrate, make every effort b along the way to settle with him, lest he drag you to the judge, the judge deliver you to the officer, and the officer throw you into prison. 59I tell you, you shall not depart from there till you have paid the very last mite."

REPENT OR PERISH
13 There were present at that season some who told Him about the Galileans whose blood Pilate had *1*mingled with their sacrifices. 2And Jesus answered and said to them, "Do you suppose that these Galileans were worse sinners than all *other* Galileans, because they suffered such things? 3I tell you, no; but unless you repent you will all likewise perish. 4Or those eighteen on whom the tower in Siloam fell and killed them, do you think that they were worse sinners than all *other* men who dwelt in Jerusalem? 5I tell you, no; but unless you repent you will all likewise perish."

THE PARABLE OF THE BARREN FIG TREE
6He also spoke this parable: a"A certain *man* had a fig tree planted in his vineyard, and he came seeking fruit on it and found none. 7Then he said to the keeper of his vineyard, 'Look, for three years I have come seeking fruit on this fig tree and find none. Cut it down; why does it *1*use up the ground?' 8But he answered and said to him, 'Sir, let it alone this year also, until I dig around

Luke 13:6–9

ONE LAST CHANCE

Jesus told this parable of a fig tree that hadn't borne fruit for several years. It was about to be destroyed, but the caretaker of the tree asked for one more chance to tend it and water it to see if it could bear fruit.

The fig tree is often used in the Bible as a symbol of Israel as a nation. At this point, they were obviously in the process of rejecting their Messiah, but Jesus was letting them know that He was giving them another chance.

How many times do we fail to bear fruit and yet Jesus asks for another chance for us? We need to be aware that the last chance will come. We can't afford to assume that we will keep getting more chances. We won't.

it and fertilize *it*. ⁹¹And if it bears fruit, *well*. But if not, after that you can ᵃcut it down.'"

A SPIRIT OF INFIRMITY

¹⁰Now He was teaching in one of the synagogues on the Sabbath. ¹¹And behold, there was a woman who had a spirit of infirmity eighteen years, and was bent over and could in no way

---

9 ᵃ[John 15:2]
¹NU *And if it bears fruit after that, well. But if not, you can*

11 ¹*straighten up*

12 ᵃLuke 7:21; 8:2

13 ᵃActs 9:17

14 ᵃ[Luke 6:6–11; 14:1–6]
ᵇEx. 20:9; 23:12
ᶜMark 3:2

15 ᵃLuke 14:5
¹NU, M *Hypocrites*

16 ᵃLuke 19:9

17 ᵃMark 5:19, 20

18 ᵃMark 4:30–32

19 ¹NU omits *large*

21 ᵃMatt. 13:33
¹*yeast*
²Gr. *sata*, same as Heb. *seah*; approximately 2 pecks in all

---

¹raise *herself* up. ¹²But when Jesus saw her, He called *her* to *Him* and said to her, "Woman, you are loosed from your ᵃinfirmity." ¹³ᵃAnd He laid *His* hands on her, and immediately she was made straight, and glorified God.

¹⁴But the ruler of the synagogue answered with indignation, because Jesus had ᵃhealed on the Sabbath; and he said to the crowd, ᵇ"There are six days on which men ought to work; therefore come and be healed on them, and ᶜnot on the Sabbath day."

¹⁵The Lord then answered him and said, ¹"Hypocrite! ᵃDoes not each one of you on the Sabbath loose his ox or donkey from the stall, and lead *it* away to water it? ¹⁶So ought not this woman, ᵃbeing a daughter of Abraham, whom Satan has bound—think of it—for eighteen years, be loosed from this bond on the Sabbath?" ¹⁷And when He said these things, all His adversaries were put to shame; and all the multitude rejoiced for all the glorious things that were ᵃdone by Him.

THE PARABLE OF THE MUSTARD SEED

¹⁸ᵃThen He said, "What is the kingdom of God like? And to what shall I compare it? ¹⁹It is like a mustard seed, which a man took and put in his garden; and it grew and became a ¹large tree, and the birds of the air nested in its branches."

THE PARABLE OF THE LEAVEN

²⁰And again He said, "To what shall I liken the kingdom of God? ²¹It is like ¹leaven, which a woman took and hid in three ᵃmeasures² of meal till it was all leavened."

CHURCH GROWTH   Luke 13:18–19

Jesus told this parable about His kingdom, growing from a mustard seed into a great tree, with lots of birds nesting in its branches. First of all, mustard doesn't grow into trees. Mustard grows on a bush. So the growth here was unnatural. And sometimes birds represent evil in the Bible. Therefore, Jesus was predicting the great growth of the church, but acknowledging that it won't all be good. All kinds of birds will build nests in the outward church.

Today there are so many people who put "Reverend" in front of their names and do things in the name of a "church," and yet they do not submit to Jesus Christ and His teachings. They want to be a part of the church, but they aren't interested in the faith and Scripture that is the basis for the church. They use the name of Jesus, but have no relationship with Him. They brand anyone who speaks up for the truth as being "intolerant." But Jesus said, "Not everyone who says to Me, 'Lord, Lord,' shall enter the kingdom of heaven, but he who does the will of My Father in heaven" (Matt. 7:21).

THE NARROW WAY

22a And He went through the cities and villages, teaching, and journeying toward Jerusalem. 23Then one said to Him, "Lord, are there a few who are saved?"

And He said to them, 24a "Strive to enter through the narrow gate, for bmany, I say to you, will seek to enter and will not be able. 25a When once the Master of the house has risen up and bshut the door, and you begin to stand outside and knock at the door, saying, c'Lord, Lord, open for us,' and He will answer and say to you, d'I do not know you, where you are from,' 26then you will begin to say, 'We ate and drank in Your presence, and You taught in our streets.' 27a But He will say, 'I tell you I do not know you, where you are from. bDepart from Me, all you workers of iniquity.' 28a There will be weeping and gnashing of teeth, bwhen you see Abraham and Isaac and Jacob and all the prophets in the kingdom of God, and yourselves thrust out. 29They will come from the east and the west, from the north and the south, and sit down in the kingdom of God. 30a And indeed there are last who will be first, and there are first who will be last."

31 1On that very day some Pharisees came, saying to Him, "Get out and depart from here, for Herod wants to kill You."

32 And He said to them, "Go, tell that fox, 'Behold, I cast out demons and perform cures today and tomorrow, and the third day a I shall be 1 perfected.' 33 Nevertheless I must journey today,

---

Luke 13:34

I Wanted To. The prophets had been sent by God to warn the people, and yet the people mistreated them and killed them. Yet Jesus still loved Jerusalem, despite what they had done. His desire had always been to gather them and love them, but they exercised their will against His.

I wonder how many times Jesus looks at us, lamenting, "How often I wanted to help you, I wanted to protect you, I wanted to draw close to you, but you were not willing." The failure is not on God's part. The failure is on our part.

---

22 a Mark 6:6

23 a [Matt. 7:14; 20:16]

24 a [Matt. 7:13]
b [John 7:34; 8:21; 13:33]

25 a Is. 55:6
b Matt. 25:10
c Luke 6:46
d Matt. 7:23; 25:12

27 a [Matt. 7:23; 25:41]
b Ps. 6:8

28 a Matt. 8:12; 13:42; 24:51
b Matt. 8:11

30 a [Matt. 19:30; 20:16]

31 1 NU In that very hour

32 a [Heb. 2:10; 5:9; 7:28]
1 Resurrected

34 a Matt. 23:37–39

35 a Lev. 26:31, 32
b Ps. 118:26; Matt. 21:9
1 NU, M omit assuredly

CHAPTER 14

3 a Matt. 12:10
1 NU adds or not

5 a [Ex. 23:5]
1 NU, M son

10 a Prov. 25:6, 7

11 a Matt. 23:12
1 put down

---

tomorrow, and the day following; for it cannot be that a prophet should perish outside of Jerusalem.

JESUS LAMENTS OVER JERUSALEM

34a "O Jerusalem, Jerusalem, the one who kills the prophets and stones those who are sent to her! How often I wanted to gather your children together, as a hen gathers her brood under her wings, but you were not willing! 35See! a Your house is left to you desolate; and 1assuredly, I say to you, you shall not see Me until the time comes when you say, b'Blessed is He who comes in the name of the LORD!'"

A MAN WITH DROPSY HEALED ON THE SABBATH

14 Now it happened, as He went into the house of one of the rulers of the Pharisees to eat bread on the Sabbath, that they watched Him closely. 2And behold, there was a certain man before Him who had dropsy. 3And Jesus, answering, spoke to the lawyers and Pharisees, saying, a "Is it lawful to heal on the 1Sabbath?"

4But they kept silent. And He took him and healed him, and let him go. 5Then He answered them, saying, a "Which of you, having a 1 donkey or an ox that has fallen into a pit, will not immediately pull him out on the Sabbath day?" 6And they could not answer Him regarding these things.

TAKE THE LOWLY PLACE

7So He told a parable to those who were invited, when He noted how they chose the best places, saying to them: 8"When you are invited by anyone to a wedding feast, do not sit down in the best place, lest one more honorable than you be invited by him; 9and he who invited you and him come and say to you, 'Give place to this man,' and then you begin with shame to take the lowest place. 10a But when you are invited, go and sit down in the lowest place, so that when he who invited you comes he may say to you, 'Friend, go up higher.' Then you will have glory in the presence of those who sit at the table with you. 11a For whoever exalts himself will be 1humbled, and he who humbles himself will be exalted."

12Then He also said to him who invited Him, "When you give a dinner or a supper, do not ask your friends, your brothers, your relatives, nor rich neighbors, lest they also invite you back, and you be repaid. 13But when you give a

Luke 14:11

Exalting and Humbling. Jesus here gave a basic biblical principle: "For whoever exalts himself will be humbled, and he who humbles himself will be exalted." James wrote: "God resists the proud, but gives grace to the humble" (James 4:6). This is the opposite of what the philosophies of the world teach.

The world honors the aggressive, go-getter, self-made man. Jesus said the opposite. If you want to be exalted, allow yourself to be abased. He then showed us how on the cross (Phil. 2:5–11).

feast, invite ᵃthe poor, the ¹maimed, the lame, the blind. ¹⁴And you will be ᵃblessed, because they cannot repay you; for you shall be repaid at the resurrection of the just."

THE PARABLE OF THE GREAT SUPPER

¹⁵Now when one of those who sat at the table with Him heard these things, he said to Him, ᵃ"Blessed is he who shall eat ¹bread in the kingdom of God!"

¹⁶ᵃThen He said to him, "A certain man gave a great supper and invited

Luke 14:13–14

God Will Repay You. Jesus suggested one way of laying up treasure in heaven. He told a Pharisee and his other guests that if they invited people to their houses who could reciprocate, they would receive a reward on earth. Favors would be done in return. But if they reached out to the poor, the maimed, the lame, and the blind, and invited them over for a feast, these guests couldn't possibly repay them; and God would repay them instead.

One way to guarantee treasures in heaven is to do things for people down here who can't possibly repay you. God will cover their tab.

13 ᵃNeh. 8:10,
12 ¹crippled

14 ᵃ[Matt. 25:34–40]

15 ᵃRev. 19:9
¹M dinner

16 ᵃMatt. 22:2–14

17 ᵃProv. 9:2, 5

21 ¹crippled

24 ᵃ[Acts 13:46]

26 ᵃDeut. 13:6; 33:9
ᵇRom. 9:13
ᶜRev. 12:11

27 ᵃLuke 9:23

28 ᵃProv. 24:27

33 ᵃMatt. 19:27

34 ᵃ[Mark 9:50]

35 ¹rubbish heap

many, ¹⁷and ᵃsent his servant at supper time to say to those who were invited, 'Come, for all things are now ready.' ¹⁸But they all with one accord began to make excuses. The first said to him, 'I have bought a piece of ground, and I must go and see it. I ask you to have me excused.' ¹⁹And another said, 'I have bought five yoke of oxen, and I am going to test them. I ask you to have me excused.' ²⁰Still another said, 'I have married a wife, and therefore I cannot come.' ²¹So that servant came and reported these things to his master. Then the master of the house, being angry, said to his servant, 'Go out quickly into the streets and lanes of the city, and bring in here the poor and the ¹maimed and the lame and the blind.' ²²And the servant said, 'Master, it is done as you commanded, and still there is room.' ²³Then the master said to the servant, 'Go out into the highways and hedges, and compel them to come in, that my house may be filled. ²⁴For I say to you ᵃthat none of those men who were invited shall taste my supper.'"

LEAVING ALL TO FOLLOW CHRIST

²⁵Now great multitudes went with Him. And He turned and said to them, ²⁶ᵃ"If anyone comes to Me ᵇand does not hate his father and mother, wife and children, brothers and sisters, ᶜyes, and his own life also, he cannot be My disciple. ²⁷And ᵃwhoever does not bear his cross and come after Me cannot be My disciple. ²⁸For ᵃwhich of you, intending to build a tower, does not sit down first and count the cost, whether he has enough to finish it— ²⁹lest, after he has laid the foundation, and is not able to finish, all who see it begin to mock him, ³⁰saying, 'This man began to build and was not able to finish'? ³¹Or what king, going to make war against another king, does not sit down first and consider whether he is able with ten thousand to meet him who comes against him with twenty thousand? ³²Or else, while the other is still a great way off, he sends a delegation and asks conditions of peace. ³³So likewise, whoever of you ᵃdoes not forsake all that he has cannot be My disciple.

TASTELESS SALT IS WORTHLESS

³⁴ᵃ"Salt is good; but if the salt has lost its flavor, how shall it be seasoned? ³⁵It is neither fit for the land nor for the ¹dunghill, but men throw it out. He who has ears to hear, let him hear!"

Luke 14:26–27

HATING YOUR FAMILY

This passage is difficult for many people to understand. It sounds like Jesus is saying that if you don't hate your family then you can't be His disciple. And yet we know that we are commanded to love our families. Husbands are supposed to love their wives as Christ loved the church and gave Himself for her (Eph. 5:25).

We don't understand partly because in our Western culture we tend to view love and hate as opposites. In the Eastern mindset, love and hate were more comparative terms, on a continuum. What Jesus was saying was that your love for Me has to be so strong that your love for your family looks like hatred by comparison.

The greatest commandment was that we should love God with all our heart, soul, and mind. There is no other second place that can compare. Not even our families. Our love for Him is supreme.

THE PARABLE OF THE LOST SHEEP

15 Then ᵃall the tax collectors and the sinners drew near to Him to hear Him. ²And the Pharisees and scribes complained, saying, "This Man ¹receives sinners ᵃand eats with them." ³So He spoke this parable to them, saying:

⁴ ᵃ"What man of you, having a hundred sheep, if he loses one of them, does not leave the ninety-nine in the wilderness, and go after the one which is lost until he finds it? ⁵And when he has found *it*, he lays *it* on his shoulders, rejoicing. ⁶And when he comes home, he calls together *his* friends and neighbors, saying to them, ᵃ'Rejoice with me, for I have found my sheep ᵇwhich was lost!' ⁷I say to you that likewise there will be more joy in heaven over one sinner who repents ᵃthan over

---

CHAPTER 15

1 ᵃ[Matt. 9:10–13]

2 ᵃGal. 2:12
1 *welcomes*

4 ᵃMatt. 18:12–14

6 ᵃ[Rom. 12:15]
ᵇ[1 Pet. 2:10, 25]

7 ᵃ[Luke 5:32]
ᵇ[Mark 2:17]
1 *upright*

8 1 Gr. *drachma*, a valuable coin often worn in a ten-piece garland by married women

12 ᵃMark 12:44

---

ninety-nine ¹just persons who ᵇneed no repentance.

THE PARABLE OF THE LOST COIN

⁸"Or what woman, having ten silver ¹coins, if she loses one coin, does not light a lamp, sweep the house, and search carefully until she finds it? ⁹And when she has found *it*, she calls *her* friends and neighbors together, saying, 'Rejoice with me, for I have found the piece which I lost!' ¹⁰Likewise, I say to you, there is joy in the presence of the angels of God over one sinner who repents."

THE PARABLE OF THE LOST SON

¹¹Then He said: "A certain man had two sons. ¹²And the younger of them said to *his* father, 'Father, give me the portion of goods that falls *to me.*' So he divided to them ᵃhis livelihood. ¹³And not many days after, the younger son gathered all together, journeyed to a

Luke 15:1–2

BEING WITH COMMON PEOPLE

The Pharisees and scribes were offended that Jesus was associating and eating with "sinners." He had just eaten with the Pharisees in the previous chapter, but now He left their midst and was with the common people. Jesus seemed to be much more comfortable with the common people, and I can certainly relate to that. Common people are just easier to be around. They are real people.

So often the sophisticated religious people are constantly putting on an act, always scrutinizing, playing games, and it just isn't comfortable to be with them. They are often hypocrites, as Jesus called the Pharisees.

It is just much more relaxing and enjoyable to be with common people. They aren't watching you and judging you. They are just real people.

Luke 15:7

THE HEART OF HEAVEN

Jesus expressed the fact that there is incredible joy in heaven over one sinner who repents. These Pharisees who were criticizing Jesus for associating with sinners thought two of the worst things you could ever do were to touch sinners and to eat with them. Jesus let them know that their hearts were out of harmony with heaven. If they shared the heart of heaven, they, too, would be rejoicing that sinners were being reached.

Is our attitude toward sinners more in line with the heart of heaven, or is it more like that of the Pharisees?

---

far country, and there wasted his possessions with [1]prodigal living. 14But when he had spent all, there arose a severe famine in that land, and he began to be in want. 15Then he went and joined himself to a citizen of that country, and he sent him into his fields to feed swine. 16And he would gladly have filled his stomach with the [1]pods that the swine ate, and no one gave him *anything*.

17"But when he came to himself, he said, 'How many of my father's hired servants have bread enough and to spare, and I perish with hunger! 18I will arise and go to my father, and will say to him, "Father, [a]I have sinned against heaven and before you, 19and I am no longer worthy to be called your son. Make me like one of your hired servants."'

20"And he arose and came to his father. But [a]when he was still a great way off, his father saw him and had compassion, and ran and fell on his neck and kissed him. 21And the son said to him, 'Father, I have sinned against heaven [a]and in your sight, and am no longer worthy to be called your son.'

22"But the father said to his servants, [1]'Bring out the best robe and put *it* on him, and put a ring on his hand and

---

Side notes (center column)

13 [1]wasteful

16 [1]carob pods

18 [a]2 Sam. 12:13; 24:10, 17

20 [a][Eph. 2:13, 17]

21 [a]Ps. 51:4

22 [1]NU *Quickly bring*

24 [a]Luke 9:60; 15:32

---

sandals on *his* feet. 23And bring the fatted calf here and kill *it*, and let us eat and be merry; 24[a]for this my son was dead and is alive again; he was lost and is found.' And they began to be merry.

25"Now his older son was in the field. And as he came and drew near to the house, he heard music and dancing. 26So he called one of the servants and asked what these things meant. 27And he said to him, 'Your brother has come, and because he has received him safe and sound, your father has killed the fatted calf.'

28"But he was angry and would not go in. Therefore his father came out and pleaded with him. 29So he answered and said to *his* father, 'Lo, these many years I have been serving you; I never transgressed your commandment at any time; and yet you never gave me a young goat, that I might make merry with my friends. 30But as soon as this son of yours came, who has devoured your livelihood with harlots, you killed the fatted calf for him.'

31"And he said to him, 'Son, you are

Luke 15:20

THE FATHER'S EMBRACE

The disgraceful son had returned home. He was a real mess, having been working in the pigpen. But the father didn't ask him to clean up first, before touching him. He just ran to him and embraced him and kissed him. He had compassion on him. His older brother, in the meantime, wanted nothing to do with him. He was disgusted by his sinning brother.

The attitude of the older brother was the attitude of the Pharisees. "I'm not going to soil my hands by touching this sinner!" The heart of the father was the heart of God; and Jesus reached out at every opportunity to touch sinners, to touch lepers, to heal those who were hurting.

Are we prepared to embrace the filthy? That is our Father's heart.

always with me, and all that I have is yours. [32]It was right that we should make merry and be glad, [a]for your brother was dead and is alive again, and was lost and is found.'"

THE PARABLE OF THE UNJUST STEWARD

16 He also said to His disciples: "There was a certain rich man who had a steward, and an accusation was brought to him that this man was [1]wasting his goods. [2]So he called him and said to him, 'What is this I hear about you? Give an [a]account of your stewardship, for you can no longer be steward.'

[3]"Then the steward said within himself, 'What shall I do? For my master is taking the stewardship away from me. I cannot dig; I am ashamed to beg. [4]I have resolved what to do, that when

Luke 16:1–13

THE UNJUST STEWARD

This story could be very misleading, if it is misunderstood.

It is a story about a man who was losing his job because of embezzlement. When he knew he was going to be fired, he went to many of his company's accounts and agreed to settle their bills at a discount. This way they would be grateful to him, and perhaps they would return the favor to him in the future. This dishonest worker was then commended and was said to be wiser than God's children.

Jesus certainly wasn't advocating embezzlement or justifying this crooked behavior. What He was teaching was that at least this crook was thinking about the future and making decisions in the present that would affect his future. The example and exhortation to us is, "Think about and plan for eternity. Use your money here and now to prepare for the future. Invest in heaven."

---

32 [a] Luke 15:24

CHAPTER 16

1 [1] squandering

2 [a] [Rom. 14:12]

6 [1] Gr. batos, same as Heb. bath; 8 or 9 gallons each

7 [1] Gr. koros, same as Heb. kor; 10 or 12 bushels each

8 [a] [Eph. 5:8]

9 [a] Dan. 4:27
[1] Lit., in Aram., wealth
[2] NU it fails

10 [a] Matt. 25:21

12 [a] [1 Pet. 1:3, 4]

13 [a] Matt. 6:24

14 [a] Matt. 23:13
[1] Lit. turned up their nose at

I am put out of the stewardship, they may receive me into their houses.'

[5]"So he called every one of his master's debtors to *him*, and said to the first, 'How much do you owe my master?' [6]And he said, 'A hundred [1]measures of oil.' So he said to him, 'Take your bill, and sit down quickly and write fifty.' [7]Then he said to another, 'And how much do you owe?' So he said, 'A hundred [1]measures of wheat.' And he said to him, 'Take your bill, and write eighty.' [8]So the master commended the unjust steward because he had dealt shrewdly. For the sons of this world are more shrewd in their generation than [a]the sons of light.

[9]"And I say to you, [a]make friends for yourselves by unrighteous [1]mammon, that when [2]you fail, they may receive you into an everlasting home. [10][a]He who *is* faithful in *what is* least is faithful also in much; and he who is unjust in *what is* least is unjust also in much. [11]Therefore if you have not been faithful in the unrighteous mammon, who will commit to your trust the true *riches*? [12]And if you have not been faithful in what is another man's, who will give you what is your [a]own?

[13][a]"No servant can serve two masters; for either he will hate the one and love the other, or else he will be loyal to the one and despise the other. You cannot serve God and mammon."

Luke 16:13

Serving God and Money. "You cannot serve God and mammon [money]." Money represents the strongest power available to mankind, in the flesh. Money gives you the ability to control others and to control your own environment. Having a lot of money will make you feel omnipotent. But it will also make you impotent, because money can't meet our deepest needs.

If money is the driving force in your life, it will crowd out God. You'll have to choose between serving God and serving money.

THE LAW, THE PROPHETS, AND THE KINGDOM

[14]Now the Pharisees, [a]who were lovers of money, also heard all these things, and they [1]derided Him. [15]And

He said to them, "You are those who ajustify yourselves bbefore men, but cGod knows your hearts. For dwhat is highly esteemed among men is an abomination in the sight of God.

16a"The law and the prophets *were* until John. Since that time the kingdom of God has been preached, and everyone is pressing into it. 17aAnd it is easier for heaven and earth to pass away than for one *l*tittle of the law to fail.

18a"Whoever divorces his wife and marries another commits adultery; and whoever marries her who is divorced from *her* husband commits adultery.

THE RICH MAN AND LAZARUS

19"There was a certain rich man who was clothed in purple and fine linen and *l*fared sumptuously every day. 20But there was a certain beggar named Lazarus, full of sores, who was laid at his gate, 21desiring to be fed with *l*the crumbs which fell from the rich man's table. Moreover the dogs came and licked his sores. 22So it was that the beggar died, and was carried by the angels to aAbraham's bosom. The rich man also died and was buried. 23And being in torments in Hades, he lifted up his eyes and saw Abraham afar off, and Lazarus in his bosom.

24"Then he cried and said, 'Father Abraham, have mercy on me, and send

15 aLuke 10:29
b[Matt. 6:2, 5, 16]
cPs. 7:9
d1Sam. 16:7

16 aMatt. 3:1–12; 4:17; 11:12, 13

17 aIs. 40:8; 51:6
lThe smallest stroke in a Heb. letter

18 a1Cor. 7:10, 11

19 l lived in luxury

21 lNU what fell

22 aMatt. 8:11

24 aZech. 14:12
b[Mark 9:42–48]

25 aLuke 6:24

29 aActs 15:21; 17:11

31 a[John 5:46]
bJohn 12:10, 11

CHAPTER 17

1 a[1Cor. 11:19]
b[2Thess. 1:6]
1stumbling blocks

Lazarus that he may dip the tip of his finger in water and acool my tongue; for I bam tormented in this flame.' 25But Abraham said, 'Son, aremember that in your lifetime you received your good things, and likewise Lazarus evil things; but now he is comforted and you are tormented. 26And besides all this, between us and you there is a great gulf fixed, so that those who want to pass from here to you cannot, nor can those from there pass to us.'

27"Then he said, 'I beg you therefore, father, that you would send him to my father's house, 28for I have five brothers, that he may testify to them, lest they also come to this place of torment.' 29Abraham said to him, a'They have Moses and the prophets; let them hear them.' 30And he said, 'No, father Abraham; but if one goes to them from the dead, they will repent.' 31But he said to him, a'If they do not hear Moses and the prophets, bneither will they be persuaded though one rise from the dead.'"

JESUS WARNS OF OFFENSES

17 Then He said to the disciples, a"It is impossible that no *l*offenses should come, but bwoe *to him* through whom they do come! 2It would be better for him if a millstone were hung around his neck, and he were thrown

---

LIFE AFTER DEATH   Luke 16:19–31

In this story Jesus told about Lazarus and the rich man, we learn much about life after death and especially about what happened to people who died before Jesus rose from the dead.

We learn that there were two destinies: a place of torment and flames and a place of comfort called "Abraham's bosom." Abraham was in the place of comfort. There was a gulf between the two locations so that once you went to either destination you couldn't move from one place to the other. The people who were suffering had memories of life on earth and were aware of the choices that were made that contributed to their destiny. At this time, the righteous were not able to come into the presence of God, but were in a holding place, receiving comfort and waiting for deliverance.

By looking at several other Scriptures, we learn about the rest of the story of life after death. Paul wrote in Ephesians 4:8–10 concerning Jesus: "When He ascended on high, He led captivity captive, and gave gifts to men." He went on to say that Jesus ascended after He "first descended into the lower parts of the earth" and that He then "ascended far above all the heavens, that He might fill all things." So, after Jesus died, He led the captives from their captivity and took them to heaven. Before Jesus' death, the Old Testament saints who died were unable to go into the presence of God. They were waiting until their sins would be dealt with. Once Jesus died, the door to heaven was opened, and He personally escorted them in.

Christians who die today don't need to go to Abraham's bosom. For us, when we die, since the price of our sin has now been paid, we go immediately into the presence of the Lord in heaven. For us, being absent from the body is to be present with the Lord (2 Cor. 5:8).

Luke 17:2

OFFENDING THE LITTLE ONES

Jesus told His disciples that the person who offends, or causes a child to stumble, is in serious trouble. "It would be better for him if a millstone were hung around his neck, and he were thrown into the sea."

There are people who get hold of baby Christians and try to destroy their faith. There are others who have access to children and who challenge their immature faith, putting doubts in their minds. I think of some of the college professors, who try to destroy the faith of young people. Then there are those who treat children abusively and harmfully, stumbling them. I also think of those who promote the awful practice of abortion, stealing the lives of millions of children before they can even take their first breath.

These people will answer severely for what they have done to God's children. Their fate will be much worse than violent drowning.

---

into the sea, than that he should *1*offend one of these little ones. 3Take heed to yourselves. aIf your brother sins *1*against you, brebuke him; and if he repents, forgive him. 4And if he sins against you seven times in a day, and seven times in a day returns *1*to you, saying, 'I repent,' you shall forgive him."

FAITH AND DUTY

5And the apostles said to the Lord, "Increase our faith."

6aSo the Lord said, "If you have faith as a mustard seed, you can say to this mulberry tree, 'Be pulled up by the roots and be planted in the sea,' and it would obey you. 7And which of you, having a servant plowing or tending sheep, will say to him when he has come in from the field, 'Come at once and sit down to eat'? 8But will he not

---

Marginal notes:

2 *1 cause one of these little ones to stumble*

3 a[Matt. 18:15, 21]
b[Prov. 17:10]
1 NU omits against you

4 *1 M omits to you*

6 a[Mark 9:23; 11:23]

8 a[Luke 12:37]

9 *1 NU omits the rest of v. 9; M omits him*

10 aRom. 3:12; 11:35

11 aLuke 9:51, 52

12 aLev. 13:46

14 aMatt. 8:4

---

rather say to him, 'Prepare something for my supper, and gird yourself aand serve me till I have eaten and drunk, and afterward you will eat and drink'? 9Does he thank that servant because he did the things that were commanded *1*him? I think not. 10So likewise you, when you have done all those things which you are commanded, say, 'We are aunprofitable servants. We have done what was our duty to do.'"

TEN LEPERS CLEANSED

11Now it happened aas He went to Jerusalem that He passed through the midst of Samaria and Galilee. 12Then as He entered a certain village, there met Him ten men who were lepers, awho stood afar off. 13And they lifted up *their* voices and said, "Jesus, Master, have mercy on us!"

14So when He saw *them*, He said to them, a"Go, show yourselves to the priests." And so it was that as they went, they were cleansed.

Luke 17:12–19

CLEANSED OR WELL?

Ten lepers were cleansed of their leprosy, which was a wonderful miracle. This awful disease that robs you of your life after isolating you from others, this incurable condition, taken away by a miracle of God.

But one man came back to express his thanks. Only one man out of ten returned to thank Jesus. And Jesus said to that man, "Your faith has made you well." He received an extra blessing from Jesus that was missed by the others. In his thankful attitude, and because of his faith, he was healed spiritually, as well as physically. His sins were forgiven.

It is nice to receive physical healing, but that is nothing compared to having your sins forgiven eternally. We who have come to Jesus in an attitude of thanksgiving are not just healed; we are well.

15And one of them, when he saw that he was healed, returned, and with a loud voice aglorified God, 16and fell down on *his* face at His feet, giving Him thanks. And he was a aSamaritan. 17So Jesus answered and said, "Were there not ten cleansed? But where *are* the nine? 18Were there not any found who returned to give glory to God except this foreigner?" 19aAnd He said to him, "Arise, go your way. Your faith has made you well."

THE COMING OF THE KINGDOM

20Now when He was asked by the Pharisees when the kingdom of God would come, He answered them and said, "The kingdom of God does not come with observation; 21anor will they say, 1'See here!' or 'See there!' For indeed, bthe kingdom of God is 2within you." 22Then He said to the disciples, a"The days will come when you will desire to see one of the days of the Son of Man, and you will not see *it.* 23aAnd they will say to you, 1'Look here!' or 'Look there!' Do not go after *them* or follow *them.* 24aFor as the lightning that flashes out

IT WON'T BE A SECRET

Luke 17:20–24

The second coming of Jesus won't be a secret. Some have tried to spiritualize the event and say that it has already happened. But everyone will know what it is when it actually takes place. It will be like lightning, lighting up the whole sky. He will come in judgment, gathering everyone in the world to be divided between those who have accepted Him and those who haven't. The righteous will enter His glorious kingdom, while the unrighteous will go to the place of judgment.

Of course, we will be taken away in the rapture before this time of judgment arrives. Like Noah and Lot, we will be removed before judgment is poured out.

of one *part* under heaven shines to the other *part* under heaven, so also the Son of Man will be in His day. 25aBut first He must suffer many things and be brejected by this generation. 26aAnd as it bwas in the cdays of dNoah, so it will be also in the days of the Son of Man: 27They ate, they drank, they married wives, they were given in marriage, until the aday that Noah entered the ark, and the flood came and bdestroyed them all. 28aLikewise as it was also in the days of Lot: They ate, they drank, they bought, they sold, they planted, they built; 29but on athe day that Lot went out of Sodom it rained fire and brimstone from heaven and destroyed *them* all. 30Even so will it be in the day when the Son of Man ais revealed.

31"In that day, he awho is on the housetop, and his 1goods *are* in the house, let him not come down to take them away. And likewise the one who is in the field, let him not turn back. 32aRemember Lot's wife. 33aWhoever seeks to save his life will lose it, and whoever loses his life will preserve it. 34aI tell you, in that night there will be two 1men in one bed: the one will be taken and the other will be left. 35aTwo *women* will be grinding together: the one will be taken and the other left. 361Two *men* will be in the field: the one will be taken and the other left."

37And they answered and said to Him, a"Where, Lord?"

So He said to them, "Wherever the body is, there the eagles will be gathered together."

THE PARABLE OF THE PERSISTENT WIDOW

18 Then He spoke a parable to them, that men aalways ought to pray and not lose heart, 2saying: "There was in a certain city a judge who did not fear God nor 1regard man. 3Now there was a widow in that city; and she came to him, saying, 1'Get justice for me from my adversary.' 4And he would not for a while; but afterward he said within himself, 'Though I do not fear God nor regard man, 5ayet because this widow troubles me I will 1avenge her, lest by her continual coming she weary me.'"

6Then the Lord said, "Hear what the unjust judge said. 7And ashall God not avenge His own elect who cry out day and night to Him, though He bears long with them? 8I tell you athat He will avenge them speedily. Nevertheless,

15 aLuke 5:25; 18:43
16 a2Kin. 17:24
19 aMatt. 9:22
21 aLuke 17:23 b[Rom. 14:17] 1NU reverses here and there 2in your midst
22 aMatt. 9:15
23 aMatt. 24:23 1NU reverses here and there
24 aMatt. 24:27
25 aMark 8:31; 9:31; 10:33 bLuke 9:22
26 aMatt. 24:37–39 b[Gen. 6:5–7] c[Gen. 6:8–13] d1Pet. 3:20
27 aGen. 7:1–16 bGen. 7:19–23
28 aGen. 19
29 aGen. 19:16, 24, 29
30 a[2Thess. 1:7]
31 aMark 13:15 1possessions
32 aGen. 19:26
33 aMatt. 10:39; 16:25
34 a[1Thess. 4:17] 1Or people
35 aMatt. 24:40, 41
36 1NU, M omit v. 36.
37 aMatt. 24:28
CHAPTER 18
1 aLuke 11:5–10
2 1respect
3 1Avenge me on
5 aLuke 11:8 1vindicate
7 aRev. 6:10
8 aHeb. 10:37

CRYING DAY AND NIGHT

Luke 18:1–7

Sometimes God doesn't answer our prayers immediately. But He isn't like this unjust judge, who was finally just badgered into response. God is contrasted with this unjust judge. God always has a purpose to His delays in answering, and He will always respond right on time.

Remember the story of Hannah? She desired to have a son and was praying so intensely about it that, when Eli saw her, he thought she was drunk. But as she prayed, she eventually pledged to God that, if He would give her a son, her son would be dedicated completely to His service (1 Sam. 1:11). That was exactly what God was waiting for. God wanted to raise up a righteous man to lead Israel, and Hannah's son Samuel would be that man. But God waited to answer her prayer until she was desperate enough to dedicate her future son to the Lord.

God wants to work in us through our prayers, and they usually are more about changing us than anything else. This is why it is so important that "men always ought to pray and not lose heart" (v. 1).

Luke 18:9–14

TWO PRAYER ATTITUDES

Jesus told this parable to address "some who trusted in themselves that they were righteous, and despised others." There was a Pharisee and a tax collector who both went to the temple to pray. The Pharisee was bragging to God about what a wonderful person he was and how he was so much better than others. His prayer was all about him, and he kept praying "I, I, I, I, I." The tax collector, on the other hand, knew he was a sinner and humbly cried out for mercy. The tax collector was justified, which means "declared righteous."

We can either come to God in our own righteousness, or we can come in humility and brokenness to receive His righteousness.

when the Son of Man comes, will He really find faith on the earth?"

THE PARABLE OF THE PHARISEE AND THE TAX COLLECTOR

9 Also He spoke this parable to some ᵃwho trusted in themselves that they

9 ᵃLuke 10:29; 16:15

11 ᵃPs. 135:2
ᵇIs. 1:15; 58:2

14 ᵃLuke 14:11
¹put down

15 ᵃMark 10:13–16

16 ᵃ1Pet. 2:2

17 ᵃMark 10:15

18 ᵃMatt. 19:16–29

19 ᵃPs. 86:5; 119:68

20 ᵃEx. 20:12–16; Deut. 5:16–20

were righteous, and despised others: ¹⁰"Two men went up to the temple to pray, one a Pharisee and the other a tax collector. ¹¹The Pharisee ᵃstood and prayed thus with himself, ᵇ'God, I thank You that I am not like other men—extortioners, unjust, adulterers, or even as this tax collector. ¹²I fast twice a week; I give tithes of all that I possess.' ¹³And the tax collector, standing afar off, would not so much as raise *his* eyes to heaven, but beat his breast, saying, 'God, be merciful to me a sinner!' ¹⁴I tell you, this man went down to his house justified *rather* than the other; ᵃfor everyone who exalts himself will be ¹humbled, and he who humbles himself will be exalted."

JESUS BLESSES LITTLE CHILDREN

¹⁵ᵃThen they also brought infants to Him that He might touch them; but when the disciples saw *it*, they rebuked them. ¹⁶But Jesus called them to *Him* and said, "Let the little children come to Me, and do not forbid them; for ᵃof such is the kingdom of God. ¹⁷ᵃAssuredly, I say to you, whoever does not receive the kingdom of God as a little child will by no means enter it."

JESUS COUNSELS THE RICH YOUNG RULER

¹⁸ᵃNow a certain ruler asked Him, saying, "Good Teacher, what shall I do to inherit eternal life?" ¹⁹So Jesus said to him, "Why do you call Me good? No one *is* good but ᵃOne, *that is*, God. ²⁰You know the commandments: ᵃ'Do not commit adultery,' 'Do not murder,' 'Do not steal,' 'Do not bear

false witness,' ᵇ'Honor your father and your mother.' "

²¹And he said, "All ᵃthese things I have kept from my youth."

²²So when Jesus heard these things, He said to him, "You still lack one thing. ᵃSell all that you have and distribute to the poor, and you will have treasure in heaven; and come, follow Me."

²³But when he heard this, he became very sorrowful, for he was very rich.

WITH GOD ALL THINGS ARE POSSIBLE

²⁴And when Jesus saw that he became very sorrowful, He said, ᵃ"How hard it is for those who have riches to enter the kingdom of God! ²⁵For it is easier for a camel to go through the eye of a needle than for a rich man to enter the kingdom of God."

²⁶And those who heard it said, "Who then can be saved?"

²⁷But He said, ᵃ"The things which are impossible with men are possible with God."

²⁸ᵃThen Peter said, "See, we have left ¹all and followed You."

²⁹So He said to them, "Assuredly, I say to you, ᵃthere is no one who has left house or parents or brothers or wife or children, for the sake of the kingdom of God, ³⁰ᵃwho shall not receive many times more in this present time, and in the age to come eternal life."

JESUS A THIRD TIME PREDICTS HIS DEATH AND RESURRECTION

³¹ᵃThen He took the twelve aside and said to them, "Behold, we are going up to Jerusalem, and all things ᵇthat are written by the prophets concerning the Son of Man will be ¹accomplished. ³²For ᵃHe will be delivered to the Gentiles and will be mocked and insulted and spit upon. ³³They will scourge Him and kill Him. And the third day He will rise again."

³⁴ᵃBut they understood none of these things; this saying was hidden from them, and they did not know the things which were spoken.

A BLIND MAN RECEIVES HIS SIGHT

³⁵ᵃThen it happened, as He was coming near Jericho, that a certain blind man sat by the road begging. ³⁶And hearing a multitude passing by, he asked what it meant. ³⁷So they told him that Jesus of Nazareth was passing by. ³⁸And he cried out, saying, "Jesus, ᵃSon of David, have mercy on me!"

20 ᵇ Eph. 6:2; Col. 3:20

21 ᵃ Phil. 3:6

22 ᵃ Matt. 6:19, 20; 19:21

24 ᵃ Mark 10:23

27 ᵃ Jer. 32:17

28 ᵃ Matt. 19:27
¹ NU our own

29 ᵃ Deut. 33:9

30 ᵃ Job 42:10

31 ᵃ Matt. 16:21; 17:22; 20:17
ᵇ Ps. 22
¹ fulfilled

32 ᵃ Acts 3:13

34 ᵃ Luke 2:50; 9:45

35 ᵃ Matt. 20:29–34

38 ᵃ Matt. 9:27

42 ᵃ Luke 17:19

43 ᵃ Luke 5:26

CHAPTER 19

1 ᵃ Josh. 6:26

3 ᵃ John 12:21

5 ¹ NU omits and saw him
² hurry

Luke 18:35

Coming or Going? In this account of the healing of a blind man (Mark names him as Bartimaeus), the passage says that Jesus encountered him as He was approaching Jericho. The account in Mark 10:46, however, says it happened as He was leaving Jericho. Which is it? Was He coming or going?

Bible critics used to point this out as a contradiction in the Bible. But archaeologists have discovered that there were two Jerichos in those days; and they were about three miles apart. The lower section was the poorer section, while the upper was richer. So Jesus was probably leaving one section and going toward the other and was therefore coming and going.

³⁹Then those who went before warned him that he should be quiet; but he cried out all the more, "Son of David, have mercy on me!"

⁴⁰So Jesus stood still and commanded him to be brought to Him. And when he had come near, He asked him, ⁴¹saying, "What do you want Me to do for you?"

He said, "Lord, that I may receive my sight."

⁴²Then Jesus said to him, "Receive your sight; ᵃyour faith has made you well." ⁴³And immediately he received his sight, and followed Him, ᵃglorifying God. And all the people, when they saw it, gave praise to God.

JESUS COMES TO ZACCHAEUS' HOUSE

19 Then *Jesus* entered and passed through ᵃJericho. ²Now behold, there *was* a man named Zacchaeus who was a chief tax collector, and he was rich. ³And he sought to ᵃsee who Jesus was, but could not because of the crowd, for he was of short stature. ⁴So he ran ahead and climbed up into a sycamore tree to see Him, for He was going to pass that *way*. ⁵And when Jesus came to the place, He looked up ¹and saw him, and said to him, "Zacchaeus, ²make haste and come down, for today I must stay at your house."

⁶So he ¹made haste and came down, and received Him joyfully. ⁷But when they saw *it*, they all ¹complained, saying, ᵃ"He has gone to be a guest with a man who is a sinner."

⁸Then Zacchaeus stood and said to the Lord, "Look, Lord, I give half of my goods to the ᵃpoor; and if I have taken anything from anyone by ᵇfalse accusation, ᶜI restore fourfold."

⁹And Jesus said to him, "Today salvation has come to this house, because ᵃhe also is ᵇa son of Abraham; ¹⁰ᵃfor the Son of Man has come to seek and to save that which was lost."

Luke 19:2–10
The Sign of Salvation. Zacchaeus, this little Jewish tax collector, brought Jesus home to entertain Him and listen to His teachings. After listening to Jesus, Zacchaeus announced that he intended to pay back all the people he had ripped off and to give half of his goods to the poor. Jesus said, "Today salvation has come to this house."

If God is working in your life, you will begin to act out of character. There will be a definite change.

THE PARABLE OF THE MINAS
¹¹Now as they heard these things, He spoke another parable, because He was near Jerusalem and because ᵃthey thought the kingdom of God would appear immediately. ¹²ᵃTherefore He said: "A certain nobleman went into a far country to receive for himself a kingdom and to return. ¹³So he called ten of his servants, delivered to them ten ¹minas, and said to them, ˎDo business till I come.' ¹⁴ᵃBut his citizens hated him, and sent a delegation after him, saying, 'We will not have this *man* to reign over us.'

¹⁵"And so it was that when he returned, having received the kingdom, he then commanded these servants, to whom he had given the money, to be called to him, that he might know how much every man had gained by trading. ¹⁶Then came the first, saying, 'Master, your mina has earned ten minas.' ¹⁷And he said to him, ᵃ'Well *done*, good servant; because you were ᵇfaithful in a very little, have authority over ten

Luke 19:12–27
Take Care of Business. In this parable, in which Jesus told of a nobleman who left his estate in the care of his servants for an indefinite period of time, the nobleman left them each with some money and gave them the mandate, "Do business till I come."

Jesus has left each of us with a certain amount of time, talents, and resources; and we don't know exactly when He will return. But He expects us to be investing what we have while we wait. He wants us to work at using what He has given us.

cities.' ¹⁸And the second came, saying, 'Master, your mina has earned five minas.' ¹⁹Likewise he said to him, 'You also be over five cities.'

²⁰"Then another came, saying, 'Master, here is your mina, which I have kept put away in a handkerchief. ²¹ᵃFor I feared you, because you are ¹an austere man. You collect what you did not deposit, and reap what you did not sow.' ²²And he said to him, ᵃ'Out of your own mouth I will judge you, *you* wicked servant. ᵇYou knew that I was an austere man, collecting what I did not deposit and reaping what I did not sow. ²³Why then did you not put my money in the bank, that at my coming I might have collected it with interest?'

²⁴"And he said to those who stood by, 'Take the mina from him, and give *it* to him who has ten minas.' ²⁵(But they said to him, 'Master, he has ten minas.') ²⁶'For I say to you, ᵃthat to everyone who has will be given; and from him who does not have, even what he has will be taken away from him. ²⁷But bring here those enemies of mine, who did not want me to reign over them, and slay *them* before me.'"

THE TRIUMPHAL ENTRY
²⁸When He had said this, ᵃHe went on ahead, going up to Jerusalem. ²⁹ᵃAnd it came to pass, when He drew near to ¹Bethphage and ᵇBethany, at the mountain called ᶜOlivet, *that* He sent two of His disciples, ³⁰saying, "Go into the village opposite *you*, where as you enter you will find a colt tied, on which no one has ever sat. Loose it and bring *it* here. ³¹And if anyone asks you,

Cross-references: 6 ¹hurried | 7 ᵃLuke 5:30; 15:2 ¹grumbled | 8 ᵃ[Ps. 41:1] ᵇLuke 3:14 ᶜEx. 22:1 | 9 ᵃ[Gal. 3:7] ᵇ[Luke 13:16] | 10 ᵃMatt. 18:11 | 11 ᵃActs 1:6 | 12 ᵃMatt. 25:14–30 | 13 ¹Gr. *mna*, same as Heb. *minah*, each worth about three months' salary | 14 ᵃ[John 1:11] | 17 ᵃMatt. 25:21, 23 ᵇLuke 16:10 | 21 ᵃMatt. 25:24 ¹*a severe* | 22 ᵃJob 15:6 ᵇMatt. 25:26 | 26 ᵃLuke 8:18 | 28 ᵃMark 10:32 | 29 ᵃMatt. 21:1 ᵇJohn 12:1 ᶜActs 1:12 ¹M *Bethphage*

'Why are you loosing *it?*' thus you shall say to him, 'Because the Lord has need of it.'"
32So those who were sent went their way and found *it* just ªas He had said to them. 33But as they were loosing the colt, the owners of it said to them, "Why are you loosing the colt?" 34And they said, "The Lord has need of him." 35Then they brought him to Jesus. ªAnd they threw their own clothes on the colt, and they set Jesus on him. 36And as He went, *many* spread their clothes on the road.

37Then, as He was now drawing near the descent of the Mount of Olives, the whole multitude of the disciples began to ªrejoice and praise God with a loud voice for all the mighty works they had seen, 38saying:

a"'*Blessed is the King who comes in the name of the LORD!*'
b Peace in heaven and glory in the highest!"

39And some of the Pharisees called to Him from the crowd, "Teacher, rebuke Your disciples."
40But He answered and said to them, "I tell you that if these should keep silent, ªthe stones would immediately cry out."

Luke 19:39–40

Talking Rocks. As the people were declaring that Jesus was the Messiah, the Pharisees were irate and demanded that He silence them. His response was, "I tell you that if these should keep silent, the stones would immediately cry out."

Somehow I wish they had kept silent. I'd love to hear the stones crying out, declaring Jesus to be the Messiah. Actually, creation does speak of God, if we are tuned in to hear it.

JESUS WEEPS OVER JERUSALEM

41Now as He drew near, He saw the city and ªwept over it, 42saying, "If you had known, even you, especially in this ªyour day, the things *that* bmake for your cpeace! But now they are hidden from your eyes. 43For days will come upon you when your enemies will ªbuild an embankment around you, surround you and close you in on every

side, 44ªand level you, and your children within you, to the ground; and bthey will not leave in you one stone upon another, cbecause you did not know the time of your visitation."

JESUS CLEANSES THE TEMPLE

45ªThen He went into the temple and began to drive out those who 1bought and sold in it, 46saying to them, "It is written, ª'*My house* 1*is a house of prayer,*' but you have made it a b'*den of thieves.*'"

47And He ªwas teaching daily in the temple. But bthe chief priests, the scribes, and the leaders of the people sought to destroy Him, 48and were unable to do anything; for all the people were very attentive to ªhear Him.

JESUS' AUTHORITY QUESTIONED

20 Now ªit happened on one of those days, as He taught the people in the temple and preached the gospel, *that* the chief priests and the scribes, together with the elders, confronted *Him* 2and spoke to Him, saying, "Tell us, ªby what authority are You doing these things? Or who is he who gave You this authority?"
3But He answered and said to them, "I also will ask you one thing, and answer Me: 4The ªbaptism of John— was it from heaven or from men?"

Luke 20:3–4

Taking Control. The Jewish leaders were trying to trap Jesus with their question about whose authority He used in cleansing the temple. He turned the situation around and asked them a question about John the Baptist, which He knew they couldn't answer without a riot breaking out.

It is interesting to me how Jesus was always the Master of every situation. They tried to put Him on the defensive, but He turned it right around on them. He is always in control.

5And they reasoned among themselves, saying, "If we say, 'From heaven,' He will say, 'Why 1then did you not believe him?' 6But if we say, 'From men,' all the people will stone us, ªfor they are persuaded that John was a

Side column references:
32 ªLuke 22:13
35 ª2Kin. 9:13
37 ªLuke 13:17; 18:43
38 ªPs. 118:26 b[Eph. 2:14]
40 ªHab. 2:11
41 ªJohn 11:35
42 ªHeb. 3:13 b[Acts 10:36] c[Rom. 5:1]
43 ªJer. 6:3, 6
44 ª1Kin. 9:7, 8 bMatt. 24:2 c[1Pet. 2:12]
45 ªMark 11:11, 15–17 1NU were selling, saying
46 ªIs. 56:7 bJer. 7:11 1NU shall be
47 ªLuke 21:37; 22:53 bJohn 7:19; 8:37
48 ªLuke 21:38
CHAPTER 20
1 ªMatt. 21:23–27
2 ªActs 4:7; 7:27
4 ªJohn 1:26, 31
5 1NU, M omit then
6 ªLuke 7:24–30

prophet." ⁷So they answered that they did not know where *it was* from.

⁸And Jesus said to them, "Neither will I tell you by what authority I do these things."

THE PARABLE OF THE WICKED VINEDRESSERS

⁹Then He began to tell the people this parable: ᵃ"A certain man planted a vineyard, leased it to ¹vinedressers, and went into a far country for a long time. ¹⁰Now at ¹vintage-time he ᵃsent a servant to the vinedressers, that they might give him some of the fruit of the vineyard. But the vinedressers beat him and sent *him* away empty-handed. ¹¹Again he sent another servant; and they beat him also, treated *him* shamefully, and sent *him* away empty-handed. ¹²And again he sent a third; and they wounded him also and cast *him* out.

¹³"Then the owner of the vineyard said, 'What shall I do? I will send my beloved son. Probably they will respect *him* when they see him.' ¹⁴But when the vinedressers saw him, they reasoned among themselves, saying, 'This is the ᵃheir. Come, ᵇlet us kill him, that the inheritance may be ᶜours.' ¹⁵So they cast him out of the vineyard and ᵃkilled *him*. Therefore what will the owner of the vineyard do to them? ¹⁶He will come and destroy those vinedressers and give the vineyard to ᵃothers."

And when they heard *it* they said, "Certainly not!"

Luke 20:14–15

Prophetic Parable. As Jesus was telling this parable about the evil vinedressers who plotted against and then killed the son of the vineyard owner, it was obvious to the religious leaders that He was talking about them. They had been plotting to kill Jesus for some time, and Jesus exposed their plan. But He also prophesied that it would work, just three days later. "So they cast him out of the vineyard and killed him."

Jesus knew what was happening, and He knew why and how. It was all according to prophetic plan.

---

9 ᵃMark 12:1–12
1 tenant farmers

10 ᵃ[1 Thess. 2:15]
1 Lit. the season

14 ᵃ[Heb. 1:1–3]
ᵇMatt. 27:21–23
ᶜJohn 11:47, 48

15 ᵃLuke 23:33

16 ᵃRom. 11:1, 11

17 ᵃPs. 118:22

18 ᵃIs. 8:14, 15
ᵇ[Dan. 2:34, 35, 44, 45]

19 ¹M were afraid—for

20 ᵃMatt. 22:15

21 ᵃMark 12:14

23 ¹NU omits Why do you test Me?

25 ᵃ[1 Pet. 2:13–17]
1 Pay

---

¹⁷Then He looked at them and said, "What then is this that is written:

ᵃ'*The stone which the builders rejected*
Has become the chief cornerstone'?

¹⁸Whoever falls on that stone will be ᵃbroken; but ᵇon whomever it falls, it will grind him to powder."

¹⁹And the chief priests and the scribes that very hour sought to lay hands on Him, but they ¹feared the people—for they knew He had spoken this parable against them.

THE PHARISEES: IS IT LAWFUL TO PAY TAXES TO CAESAR?

²⁰ᵃSo they watched *Him*, and sent spies who pretended to be righteous, that they might seize on His words, in order to deliver Him to the power and the authority of the governor. ²¹Then they asked Him, saying, ᵃ"Teacher, we know that You say and teach rightly, and You do not show personal favoritism, but teach the way of God in truth: ²²Is it lawful for us to pay taxes to Caesar or not?"

²³But He perceived their craftiness, and said to them, ¹"Why do you test Me? ²⁴Show Me a denarius. Whose image and inscription does it have?"

They answered and said, "Caesar's."

²⁵And He said to them, ᵃ"Render¹ therefore to Caesar the things that are Caesar's, and to God the things that are God's."

²⁶But they could not catch Him in His words in the presence of the people. And they marveled at His answer and kept silent.

Luke 20:25

Paying Our Dues. "Render therefore to Caesar the things that are Caesar's, and to God the things that are God's." As Christians, we are commanded to pay our taxes, whether they are fair or not. We are not to rebel against the government by being tax protesters. But we must also adhere to the more important part of this verse, as we give God what is due Him.

You are paying your taxes? Great. You should do that. But are you giving God His due?

THE SADDUCEES: WHAT ABOUT THE RESURRECTION?

27a Then some of the Sadducees, b who deny that there is a resurrection, came to Him and asked Him, 28 saying: "Teacher, Moses wrote to us *that* if a man's brother dies, having a wife, and he dies without children, his brother should take his wife and raise up offspring for his brother. 29 Now there were seven brothers. And the first took a wife, and died without children. 30 And the second *l* took her as wife, and he died childless. 31 Then the third took her, and in like manner the seven *l* also; and they left no children, and died. 32 Last of all the woman died also. 33 Therefore, in the resurrection, whose wife does she become? For all seven had her as wife."

34 Jesus answered and said to them, "The sons of this age marry and are given in marriage. 35 But those who are a counted worthy to attain that age, and the resurrection from the dead, neither marry nor are given in marriage; 36 nor can they die anymore, for a they are equal to the angels and are sons of God, b being sons of the resurrection. 37 But even Moses showed in the *burning* bush *passage* that the dead are raised, when he called the Lord a *'the God of Abraham, the God of Isaac, and the God of Jacob.'* 38 For He is not the God of the dead but of the living, for a all live to Him."

39 Then some of the scribes answered and said, "Teacher, You have spoken well." 40 But after that they dared not question Him anymore.

JESUS: HOW CAN DAVID CALL HIS DESCENDANT LORD?

41 And He said to them, a "How can they say that the Christ is the Son of David? 42 Now David himself said in the Book of Psalms:

a *'The LORD said to my Lord,*
  "Sit at My right hand,
43   *Till I make Your enemies Your*
    footstool."'

44 Therefore David calls Him *'Lord'*; a how is He then his Son?"

BEWARE OF THE SCRIBES

45a Then, in the hearing of all the people, He said to His disciples, 46a "Beware of the scribes, who desire to go around in long robes, b love greetings in the marketplaces, the best seats in the synagogues, and the best places at feasts,

Cross references (center column)

27 a Mark 12:18–27
b Acts 23:6, 8
30 1 NU omits the rest of v. 30.
31 1 NU, M *also* left no children
35 a Phil. 3:11
36 a [1 John 3:2]
b Rom. 8:23
37 a Ex. 3:1–6, 15
38 a [Rom. 6:10, 11; 14:8, 9]
41 a Matt. 22:41–46
42 a Ps. 110:1
44 a Rom. 1:3; 9:4, 5
45 a Matt. 23:1–7
46 a Matt. 23:5
b Luke 11:43; 14:7
47 a Matt. 23:14
b [Matt. 6:5, 6]

CHAPTER 21

1 a Mark 12:41–44
2 a [2 Cor. 6:10]
b Mark 12:42
1 Gr. *lepta*, very small copper coins
3 a [2 Cor. 8:12]
4 a [2 Cor. 8:12]
1 NU omits for God
5 a Mark 13:1
1 decorated
6 a Luke 19:41–44
8 a Eph. 5:6
1 NU omits Therefore
2 follow
9 a Rev. 6:4
10 a Matt. 24:7
11 a Rev. 6:12
12 a [Rev. 2:10]
b Acts 4:3; 5:18; 12:4; 16:24
c Acts 25:23
d 1 Pet. 2:13
13 a [Phil. 1:12–14, 28]
14 a Luke 12:11
1 say in defense
15 a Acts 6:10
1 withstand
16 a Mic. 7:6
b Acts 7:59; 12:2

47a who devour widows' houses, and for a b pretense make long prayers. These will receive greater condemnation."

THE WIDOW'S TWO MITES

21 And He looked up a and saw the rich putting their gifts into the treasury, 2 and He saw also a certain a poor widow putting in two b mites. *l* 3 So He said, "Truly I say to you a that this poor widow has put in more than all; 4 for all these out of their abundance have put in offerings *l* for God, but she out of her poverty put in a all the livelihood that she had."

JESUS PREDICTS THE DESTRUCTION OF THE TEMPLE

5a Then, as some spoke of the temple, how it was *l* adorned with beautiful stones and donations, He said, 6 "These things which you see—the days will come in which a not *one* stone shall be left upon another that shall not be thrown down."

THE SIGNS OF THE TIMES AND THE END OF THE AGE

7 So they asked Him, saying, "Teacher, but when will these things be? And what sign *will there be* when these things are about to take place?"

8 And He said: a "Take heed that you not be deceived. For many will come in My name, saying, 'I am *He,*' and, 'The time has drawn near.' *l* Therefore do not 2 go after them. 9 But when you hear of a wars and commotions, do not be terrified; for these things must come to pass first, but the end *will* not *come* immediately."

10a Then He said to them, "Nation will rise against nation, and kingdom against kingdom. 11 And there will be great a earthquakes in various places, and famines and pestilences; and there will be fearful sights and great signs from heaven. 12a But before all these things, they will lay their hands on you and persecute *you,* delivering *you* up to the synagogues and b prisons. c You will be brought before kings and rulers d for My name's sake. 13 But a it will turn out for you as an occasion for testimony. 14a Therefore settle *it* in your hearts not to meditate beforehand on what you will *l* answer; 15 for I will give you a mouth and wisdom a which all your adversaries will not be able to contradict or *l* resist. 16a You will be betrayed even by parents and brothers, relatives and friends; and they will put b *some* of

Luke 21:12–13

Witnessing Opportunity. As Jesus predicted the coming persecution and imprisonment of His disciples, He pointed out, "It will turn out for you as an occasion for testimony." That is exactly what took place, as we learn in the book of Acts. Every occasion of persecution turned into an occasion for witnessing.

The same is true for us, if we keep our eyes opened to the opportunities. Often our greatest testimony times will be in the midst of persecution and suffering.

you to death. 17And ayou will be hated by all for My name's sake. 18aBut not a hair of your head shall be lost. 19By your patience possess your souls.

Luke 21:19

Patience in Persecution. "By your patience possess your souls." In the midst of persecution, remain patient. Stay in control by being patient. Don't panic.

We so often want to fly off the handle when times are tough. We want to respond. We want action. We get all tense, and we make everyone around us tense.

"Possess your soul" is the idea that you should keep your soul under control. Self-control takes patience when things don't seem to be going well. Hang in there.

THE DESTRUCTION OF JERUSALEM

20a"But when you see Jerusalem surrounded by armies, then know that its desolation is near. 21Then let those who are in Judea flee to the mountains, let those who are in the midst of her depart, and let not those who are in the country enter her. 22For these are the days of vengeance, that aall things which are written may be fulfilled. 23aBut woe to those who are pregnant and to those who are nursing babies in those days! For there will be great distress in the

17 a Matt. 10:22

18 a Matt. 10:30

20 a Mark 13:14

22 a [Dan. 9:24–27]

23 a Matt. 24:19

24 a [Dan. 9:27; 12:7]

25 a [2 Pet. 3:10–12]

26 a Matt. 24:29

27 a Rev. 1:7; 14:14

28 a [Rom. 8:19, 23]

land and wrath upon this people. 24And they will fall by the edge of the sword, and be led away captive into all nations. And Jerusalem will be trampled by Gentiles auntil the times of the Gentiles are fulfilled.

THE COMING OF THE SON OF MAN

25a"And there will be signs in the sun, in the moon, and in the stars; and on the earth distress of nations, with perplexity, the sea and the waves roaring; 26men's hearts failing them from fear and the expectation of those things which are coming on the earth, afor the powers of the heavens will be shaken. 27Then they will see the Son of Man acoming in a cloud with power and great glory. 28Now when these things begin to happen, look up and lift up your heads, because ayour redemption draws near."

Luke 21:25–28

LOOK UP!

When all these prophecies concerning the coming of cataclysmic events are beginning to be fulfilled, Jesus said, "Look up and lift up your heads, because your redemption draws near."

Notice it is "when these things begin to happen." They have certainly begun to happen today. We aren't seeing them in full fruition, but we are seeing the developments beginning to unfold. There are wars that have been fought between multiple nations. Israel has come back into the land God gave them. The world is turning against Israel. God's people are being attacked all over the world, including in our court system. There are more impending threats against Christianity.

And our response should be to look up. Jesus is coming soon! I am "looking for the blessed hope and glorious appearing of our great God and Savior Jesus Christ" (Titus 2:13).

THE PARABLE OF THE FIG TREE

29a Then He spoke to them a parable: "Look at the fig tree, and all the trees. 30When they are already budding, you see and know for yourselves that summer is now near. 31So you also, when you see these things happening, know that the kingdom of God is near. 32Assuredly, I say to you, this generation will by no means pass away till all things take place. 33a Heaven and earth will pass away, but My bwords will by no means pass away.

THE IMPORTANCE OF WATCHING

34"But atake heed to yourselves, lest your hearts be weighed down with 1carousing, drunkenness, and bcares of this life, and that Day come on you unexpectedly. 35For ait will come as a snare on all those who dwell on the face of the whole earth. 36a Watch therefore, and bpray always that you may 1be counted cworthy to escape all these things that will come to pass, and dto stand before the Son of Man."

37a And in the daytime He was teaching in the temple, but bat night He went out and stayed on the mountain called Olivet. 38Then early in the morning all the people came to Him in the temple to hear Him.

THE PLOT TO KILL JESUS

22 Now athe Feast of Unleavened Bread drew near, which is called Passover. 2And athe chief priests and the scribes sought how they might kill Him, for they feared the people.

3a Then Satan entered Judas, surnamed Iscariot, who was numbered among the btwelve. 4So he went his way and conferred with the chief priests and captains, how he might betray Him to them. 5And they were glad, and aagreed to give him money. 6So he promised and sought opportunity to abetray Him to them in the absence of the multitude.

JESUS AND HIS DISCIPLES PREPARE THE PASSOVER

7a Then came the Day of Unleavened Bread, when the Passover must be 1killed. 8And He sent Peter and John, saying, "Go and prepare the Passover for us, that we may eat."

9So they said to Him, "Where do You want us to prepare?"

10And He said to them, "Behold, when you have entered the city, a man will meet you carrying a pitcher of water; follow him into the house which

he enters. 11Then you shall say to the master of the house, 'The Teacher says to you, "Where is the guest room where I may eat the Passover with My disciples?" ' 12Then he will show you a large, furnished upper room; there make ready."

13So they went and afound it just as He had said to them, and they prepared the Passover.

JESUS INSTITUTES THE LORD'S SUPPER

14a When the hour had come, He sat down, and the 1twelve apostles with Him. 15Then He said to them, "With fervent desire I have desired to eat this Passover with you before I suffer; 16for I say to you, I will no longer eat of it auntil it is fulfilled in the kingdom of God."

17Then He took the cup, and gave thanks, and said, "Take this and divide it among yourselves; 18for aI say to you, 1I will not drink of the fruit of the vine until the kingdom of God comes."

19a And He took bread, gave thanks and broke it, and gave it to them, saying, "This is My bbody which is given for you; cdo this in remembrance of Me."

20Likewise He also took the cup after supper, saying, a"This cup is the new covenant in My blood, which is shed for you. 21a But behold, the hand of My betrayer is with Me on the table. 22a And truly the Son of Man goes bas it has been determined, but woe to that man by whom He is betrayed!"

23a Then they began to question among

Cross References

29 a Mark 13:28

33 a Matt. 24:35
b Is. 40:8

34 a 1 Thess. 5:6
b Luke 8:14
1 dissipation

35 a Rev. 3:3; 16:15

36 a Matt. 24:42; 25:13
b Luke 18:1
c Luke 20:35
d [Eph. 6:13]
1 NU have strength to

37 a John 8:1, 2
b Luke 22:39

CHAPTER 22

1 a Matt. 26:2–5

2 a John 11:47

3 a Mark 14:10, 11
b Matt. 10:2–4

5 a Zech. 11:12

6 a Ps. 41:9

7 a Matt. 26:17–19
1 Sacrificed

13 a Luke 19:32

14 a Mark 14:17
1 NU omits twelve

16 a [Rev. 19:9]

18 a Mark 14:25
1 NU adds from now on

19 a Matt. 26:26
b [1 Pet. 2:24]
c 1 Cor. 11:23–26

20 a 1 Cor. 10:16

21 a John 13:21, 26, 27

22 a Matt. 26:24
b Acts 2:23

23 a John 13:22, 25

Luke 22:14–16

This Is It. As Jesus sat down with His disciples to eat the Passover meal, He told them, "With fervent desire I have desired to eat this Passover with you before I suffer; for I say to you, I will no longer eat of it until it is fulfilled in the kingdom of God."

Jesus had been looking forward to this night ever since the first Passover, there in Egypt. It was all looking forward to this time, and the time had finally arrived. The ultimate Passover Lamb was about to be offered, willingly.

themselves, which of them it was who would do this thing.

THE DISCIPLES ARGUE ABOUT GREATNESS

24 a Now there was also a dispute among them, as to which of them should be considered the greatest. 25 a And He said to them, "The kings of the Gentiles exercise lordship over them, and those who exercise authority over them are called 'benefactors.' 26 a But not so *among* you; on the contrary, b he who is greatest among you, let him be as the younger, and he who governs as he who serves. 27 a For who *is* greater, he who sits at the table, or he who serves? *Is* it not he who sits at the table? Yet b I am among you as the One who serves. 28 "But you are those who have continued with Me in a My trials. 29 And a I bestow upon you a kingdom, just as My Father bestowed *one* upon Me, 30 that a you may eat and drink at My table in My kingdom, b and sit on thrones judging the twelve tribes of Israel."

JESUS PREDICTS PETER'S DENIAL

31 1 And the Lord said, "Simon, Simon! Indeed, a Satan has asked for you, that he may b sift *you* as wheat. 32 But a I have prayed for you, that your faith should not fail; and when you have returned to *Me*, b strengthen your brethren."

33 But he said to Him, "Lord, I am ready to go with You, both to prison and to death."

34 a Then He said, "I tell you, Peter, the rooster shall not crow this day before you will deny three times that you know Me."

SUPPLIES FOR THE ROAD

35 a And He said to them, "When I sent you without money bag, knapsack, and sandals, did you lack anything?"

So they said, "Nothing."

36 Then He said to them, "But now, he who has a money bag, let him take *it*, and likewise a knapsack; and he who has no sword, let him sell his garment and buy one. 37 For I say to you that this which is written must still be 1 accomplished in Me: a '*And He was numbered with the transgressors.*' For the things concerning Me have an end."

38 So they said, "Lord, look, here *are* two swords."

And He said to them, "It is enough."

Cross-references

24 a Mark 9:34

25 a Mark 10:42–45

26 a [1 Pet. 5:3]
b Luke 9:48

27 a [Luke 12:37]
b Phil. 2:7

28 a [Heb. 2:18; 4:15]

29 a Matt. 24:47

30 a [Matt. 8:11]
b [Rev. 3:21]

31 a 1 Pet. 5:8
b Amos 9:9
1 NU omits *And the Lord said*

32 a [John 17:9, 11, 15]
b John 21:15–17

34 a John 13:37, 38

35 a Matt. 10:9

37 a Is. 53:12
1 *fulfilled*

39 a John 18:1
b Luke 21:37

40 a Mark 14:32–42

41 a Matt. 26:39

42 a John 4:34; 5:30; 6:38; 8:29

43 a Matt. 4:11
1 NU brackets vv. 43 and 44 as not in the original text.

44 a [Heb. 5:7]

46 a Luke 9:32
b Luke 22:40

THE PRAYER IN THE GARDEN

39 a Coming out, b He went to the Mount of Olives, as He was accustomed, and His disciples also followed Him. 40 a When He came to the place, He said to them, "Pray that you may not enter into temptation." 41 a And He was withdrawn from them about a stone's throw, and He knelt down and prayed, 42 saying, "Father, if it is Your will, take this cup away from Me; nevertheless a not My will, but Yours, be done." 43 1 Then a an angel appeared to Him from heaven, strengthening Him. 44 a And being in agony, He prayed more earnestly. Then His sweat became like great drops of blood falling down to the ground.

45 When He rose up from prayer, and had come to His disciples, He found them sleeping from sorrow. 46 Then He said to them, "Why a do you sleep? Rise and b pray, lest you enter into temptation."

Luke 22:31–32

SIFTED LIKE WHEAT

N otice how Jesus prayed for Peter, in anticipation of his coming time of testing by Satan. "Simon, Simon! Indeed, Satan has asked for you, that he may sift you as wheat. But I have prayed for you, that your faith should not fail."

We have a tendency to pray that we will be protected from being attacked and hurt. We would like to escape every bit of pain and suffering that could come our way. We don't enjoy trials. None of us likes to be tested. But the testing and trials actually are used by God to make us who He wants us to be. Our faith grows when we are tested.

Sometimes we may want to pray for faith instead of deliverance from trials. If we do that, we may enjoy more opportunities to strengthen our fellow Christians as we share our experiences.

BETRAYAL AND ARREST IN GETHSEMANE

47And while He was still speaking, abehold, a multitude; and he who was called bJudas, one of the twelve, went before them and drew near to Jesus to kiss Him. 48But Jesus said to him, "Judas, are you betraying the Son of Man with a akiss?"

49When those around Him saw what was going to happen, they said to Him, "Lord, shall we strike with the sword?" 50And aone of them struck the servant of the high priest and cut off his right ear. 51But Jesus answered and said, "Permit even this." And He touched his ear and healed him.

52aThen Jesus said to the chief priests, captains of the temple, and the elders who had come to Him, "Have you come out, as against a brobber, with swords and clubs? 53When I was with you daily in the atemple, you did not try to seize Me. But this is your bhour, and the power of darkness."

PETER DENIES JESUS, AND WEEPS BITTERLY

54aHaving arrested Him, they led Him and brought Him into the high priest's house. bBut Peter followed at a distance. 55aNow when they had kindled a fire in the midst of the courtyard and sat down together, Peter sat among them. 56And a certain servant girl, seeing him as he sat by the fire, looked intently at him and said, "This man was also with Him." 57But he denied 1Him, saying, "Woman, I do not know Him." 58aAnd after a little while another

saw him and said, "You also are of them."

But Peter said, "Man, I am not!" 59aThen after about an hour had passed, another confidently affirmed, saying, "Surely this fellow also was with Him, for he is a bGalilean."

60But Peter said, "Man, I do not know what you are saying!"

Immediately, while he was still speaking, 1the rooster crowed. 61And the Lord turned and looked at Peter. Then aPeter remembered the word of the Lord, how He had said to him, b"Before the rooster 1crows, you will deny Me three times." 62So Peter went out and wept bitterly.

JESUS MOCKED AND BEATEN

63aNow the men who held Jesus mocked Him and bbeat Him. 641And having blindfolded Him, they astruck Him on the face and asked Him, saying, "Prophesy! Who is the one who struck You?" 65And many other things they blasphemously spoke against Him.

JESUS FACES THE SANHEDRIN

66aAs soon as it was day, bthe elders of the people, both chief priests and scribes, came together and led Him into their council, saying, 67a"If You are the Christ, tell us."

But He said to them, "If I tell you, you will bby no means believe. 68And if I 1also ask you, you will by no means answer 2Me or let Me go. 69aHereafter the Son of Man will sit on the right hand of the power of God."

70Then they all said, "Are You then the Son of God?"

So He said to them, a"You rightly say that I am."

Cross References

47 a John 18:3–11
b Acts 1:16, 17
48 a [Prov. 27:6]
50 a Matt. 26:51
52 a Matt. 26:55
b Luke 23:32
53 a Luke 19:47, 48
b [John 12:27]
54 a Matt. 26:57
b John 18:15
55 a Mark 14:66–72
57 1 NU it
58 a John 18:25
59 a Mark 14:70
b Acts 1:11; 2:7
60 1 NU, M a rooster
61 a Matt. 26:75
b John 13:38
1 NU adds today
63 a Ps. 69:1, 4, 7–9
b Is. 50:6
64 a Zech. 13:7
1 NU And having blindfolded Him, they asked Him
66 a Matt. 27:1
b Acts 4:26
67 a Matt. 26:63–66
b Luke 20:5–7
68 1 NU omits also
2 NU omits the rest of v. 68.
69 a Heb. 1:3; 8:1
70 a Matt. 26:64; 27:11

THE LOOK
Luke 22:61

After Peter had denied Jesus three times, he was in a location where he could see Jesus; and this verse says, "And the Lord turned and looked at Peter."

How do you think Peter felt at that moment? And what do you think the Lord's expression was as He looked at Peter? Was it a look of absolute disgust and disdain? Like, "How could you do that, Peter?" Was it a look that said, "I told you so"? Or was it a look that said, "I understand, Peter. I know you love Me. I forgive you, Peter"?

How you think Jesus looked at Peter testifies as to how well you know Jesus. If you see in His eyes anger and condemnation, you don't know Him very well. If you see Him taunting and rubbing it in, saying, "I told you so," then you also don't know Him very well. But those who see in His eyes that infinite love, understanding, compassion, and forgiveness—those are the ones who really know Him. Because that's the kind of Lord He is, and that's the attitude He has toward our weaknesses. The Bible says, "For He knows our frame; He remembers that we are dust" (Ps. 103:14).

71 ªAnd they said, "What further testimony do we need? For we have heard it ourselves from His own mouth."

JESUS HANDED OVER TO PONTIUS PILATE

23 Then ªthe whole multitude of them arose and led Him to bPilate. 2And they began to ªaccuse Him, saying, "We found this *fellow* bperverting *1*the nation, and cforbidding to pay taxes to Caesar, saying dthat He Himself is Christ, a King."

3 ªThen Pilate asked Him, saying, "Are You the King of the Jews?"

He answered him and said, "*It is as you say.*"

4So Pilate said to the chief priests and the crowd, ª"I find no fault in this Man."

5But they were the more fierce, saying, "He stirs up the people, teaching throughout all Judea, beginning from ªGalilee to this place."

JESUS FACES HEROD

6When Pilate heard *1*of Galilee, he asked if the Man were a Galilean. 7And as soon as he knew that He belonged to ªHerod's jurisdiction, he sent Him to Herod, who was also in Jerusalem at that time. 8Now when Herod saw Jesus, ªhe was exceedingly glad; for he had desired for a long *time* to see Him, because bhe had heard many things about Him, and he hoped to see some miracle done by Him. 9Then he questioned Him with many words, but He answered him ªnothing. 10And the chief priests and scribes stood and vehemently accused Him. 11 ªThen Herod, with his *1*men of war, treated Him with contempt and mocked *Him,*

Luke 23:9
Nothing to Say. Herod had been looking forward to meeting Jesus. He had heard a lot about Him, but had never met Him. He was probably hoping to be entertained by some clever teaching or fantastic miracle. But Jesus "answered him nothing."

Herod had gone so far into sin and debauchery that he was irredeemable. A man has fallen pretty deep into sin when he gets to the point where Jesus has nothing to say to him.

---

71 ªMark 14:63

CHAPTER 23

1 ªJohn 18:28
bLuke 3:1; 13:1

2 ªActs 24:2
bActs 17:7
cMatt. 17:27
dJohn 19:12
*1*NU *our*

3 ª1Tim. 6:13

4 ª[1Pet. 2:22]

5 ªJohn 7:41

6 *1*NU omits *of Galilee*

7 ªLuke 3:1; 9:7; 13:31

8 ªLuke 9:9
bMatt. 14:1

9 ªJohn 19:9

11 ªIs. 53:3
*1*troops

12 ªActs 4:26, 27

13 ªMark 15:14

14 ªLuke 23:1, 2
bLuke 23:4

15 *1*NU *he sent Him back to us*

16 ªJohn 19:1

17 ªJohn 18:39
*1*NU omits v. 17.

18 ªActs 3:13–15

23 *1*NU omits *and of the chief priests*

24 ªMark 15:15

25 ªIs. 53:8
*1*NU, M omit *to them*

26 ªMatt. 27:32

29 ªMatt. 24:19

---

arrayed Him in a gorgeous robe, and sent Him back to Pilate. 12That very day ªPilate and Herod became friends with each other, for previously they had been at enmity with each other.

TAKING THE PLACE OF BARABBAS

13 ªThen Pilate, when he had called together the chief priests, the rulers, and the people, 14said to them, ª"You have brought this Man to me, as one who misleads the people. And indeed, bhaving examined *Him* in your presence, I have found no fault in this Man concerning those things of which you accuse Him; 15no, neither did Herod, for *1*I sent you back to him; and indeed nothing deserving of death has been done by Him. 16ªI will therefore chastise Him and release *Him*" 17ª(for *1*it was necessary for him to release one to them at the feast).

18And ªthey all cried out at once, saying, "Away with this *Man*, and release to us Barabbas"— 19who had been thrown into prison for a certain rebellion made in the city, and for murder.

20Pilate, therefore, wishing to release Jesus, again called out to them. 21But they shouted, saying, "Crucify *Him*, crucify Him!"

22Then he said to them the third time, "Why, what evil has He done? I have found no reason for death in Him. I will therefore chastise Him and let *Him* go."

23But they were insistent, demanding with loud voices that He be crucified. And the voices of these men *1*and of the chief priests prevailed. 24So ªPilate gave sentence that it should be as they requested. 25 ªAnd he released *1*to them the one they requested, who for rebellion and murder had been thrown into prison; but he delivered Jesus to their will.

THE KING ON A CROSS

26ªNow as they led Him away, they laid hold of a certain man, Simon a Cyrenian, who was coming from the country, and on him they laid the cross that he might bear *it* after Jesus.

27And a great multitude of the people followed Him, and women who also mourned and lamented Him. 28But Jesus, turning to them, said, "Daughters of Jerusalem, do not weep for Me, but weep for yourselves and for your children. 29ªFor indeed the days are coming in which they will say, 'Blessed *are* the barren, wombs that never bore, and breasts which never nursed!' 30Then

they will begin a*'to say to the mountains, "Fall on us!" and to the hills, "Cover us!"'* 31aFor if they do these things in the green wood, what will be done in the dry?"

32aThere were also two others, criminals, led with Him to be put to death. 33And awhen they had come to the place called Calvary, there they crucified Him, and the criminals, one on the right hand and the other on the left. 34 1Then Jesus said, "Father, aforgive them, for bthey do not know what they do."

And cthey divided His garments and cast lots. 35And athe people stood looking on. But even the brulers with them sneered, saying, "He saved others; let Him save Himself if He is the Christ, the chosen of God."

36The soldiers also mocked Him, coming and offering Him asour wine, 37and saying, "If You are the King of the Jews, save Yourself."

38aAnd an inscription also was 1written over Him in letters of Greek, Latin, and Hebrew:

THIS IS THE KING OF THE JEWS.

39aThen one of the criminals who were hanged blasphemed Him, saying, 1"If You are the Christ, save Yourself and us."

40But the other, answering, rebuked him, saying, "Do you not even fear God, seeing you are under the same condemnation? 41And we indeed justly, for we receive the due reward of our deeds; but this Man has done anothing wrong." 42Then he said 1to Jesus, "Lord, remember me when You come into Your kingdom."

43And Jesus said to him, "Assuredly, I say to you, today you will be with Me in aParadise."

JESUS DIES ON THE CROSS

44aNow it 1was about the sixth hour, and there was darkness over all the earth until the ninth hour. 45Then the sun was 1darkened, and athe veil of the temple was torn in 2two. 46And when Jesus had cried out with a loud voice, He said, "Father, a*'into Your hands I commit My spirit.'* " bHaving said this, He breathed His last.

47aSo when the centurion saw what had happened, he glorified God, saying, "Certainly this was a righteous Man!"

48And the whole crowd who came together to that sight, seeing what had been done, beat their breasts and returned. 49aBut all His acquaintances,

---

30 aHos. 10:8; Rev. 6:16, 17; 9:6

31 a[Jer. 25:29]

32 aIs. 53:9, 12

33 a John 19:17–24

34 a1 Cor. 4:12
bActs 3:17
cMatt. 27:35
1NU brackets the first sentence as a later addition.

35 aPs. 22:17
bMatt. 27:39

36 aPs. 69:21

38 aJohn 19:19
1NU omits *written* and *in letters of Greek, Latin, and Hebrew*

39 aMark 15:32
1NU *Are You not the Christ? Save*

41 a[Heb. 7:26]

42 1NU "Jesus, remember me

43 a[Rev. 2:7]

44 aMatt. 27:45–56
1NU adds *already*

45 aMatt. 27:51
1NU *obscured*
2 *the middle*

46 aPs. 31:5
bJohn 19:30

47 aMark 15:39

49 aPs. 38:11

50 aMatt. 27:57–61

Luke 23:42–43

WITH ME IN PARADISE

In the midst of His agony, as He hung there on the cross, Jesus reached out to save one of the criminals hanging next to Him.

In Hebrews, we are told that Jesus "for the joy that was set before Him endured the cross" (Heb. 12:2). What was the joy that was set before Him that caused Him to endure? It was you and me and all of those who would be saved by His sacrifice. Perhaps this is why God arranged to have the thief hanging next to Jesus and crying out to Him for mercy. After hours of pain and torment, Jesus would be able to announce to the thief, "Today you will be with Me in Paradise."

Hearing the faith of the thief and being able to reach out to him with the good news of salvation gave Jesus a little taste of the joy that was set before Him.

---

and the women who followed Him from Galilee, stood at a distance, watching these things.

JESUS BURIED IN JOSEPH'S TOMB

50aNow behold, *there was* a man named Joseph, a council member, a

---

Luke 23:46

Giving His Life. Jesus willingly committed His life into the hands of the Father and gave it up. In John's gospel, Jesus said of His life, "No one takes it from Me, but I lay it down of Myself. I have power to lay it down, and I have power to take it again" (John 10:18). So, as He said, "Father, into Your hands I commit My spirit," and then breathed His last breath, it was His choice to give His life for us.

good and just man. [51]He had not con-
sented to their decision and deed. *He
was* from Arimathea, a city of the
Jews, [a]who[1]himself was also waiting
for the kingdom of God. [52]This man
went to Pilate and asked for the body
of Jesus. [53a]Then he took it down,
wrapped it in linen, and laid it in a
tomb *that was* hewn out of the rock,
where no one had ever lain before.
[54]That day was [a]the Preparation, and
the Sabbath drew near.

[55]And the women [a]who had come
with Him from Galilee followed after,
and [b]they observed the tomb and how
His body was laid. [56]Then they returned
and [a]prepared spices and fragrant oils.
And they rested on the Sabbath
[b]according to the commandment.

HE IS RISEN

24 Now [a]on the first *day* of the
week, very early in the morning,
they, [1]and certain *other women* with
them, came to the tomb [b]bringing the
spices which they had prepared. [2a]But
they found the stone rolled away from
the tomb. [3a]Then they went in and did
not find the body of the Lord Jesus.
[4]And it happened, as they were [a]great-
ly perplexed about this, that [a]behold,
two men stood by them in shining garments. [5]Then, as they were afraid and
bowed *their* faces to the earth, they
said to them, "Why do you seek the living among the dead? [6]He is not here,
but is risen! [a]Remember how He spoke
to you when He was still in Galilee,
[7]saying, 'The Son of Man must be
[a]delivered into the hands of sinful men,
and be crucified, and the third day rise
again.'"

[8]And [a]they remembered His words.
[9a]Then they returned from the tomb
and told all these things to the eleven
and to all the rest. [10]It was Mary
Magdalene, [a]Joanna, Mary *the mother*
of James, and the other *women* with
them, who told these things to the
apostles. [11a]And their words seemed to
them like [1]idle tales, and they did not
believe them. [12a]But Peter arose and
ran to the tomb; and stooping down, he
saw the linen cloths [1]lying by themselves; and he departed, marveling to
himself at what had happened.

THE ROAD TO EMMAUS

[13a]Now behold, two of them were
traveling that same day to a village
called Emmaus, which was [1]seven
miles from Jerusalem. [14]And they talked together of all these things which

had happened. [15]So it was, while they
conversed and reasoned, that [a]Jesus
Himself drew near and went with them.
[16]But [a]their eyes were restrained, so
that they did not know Him.

[17]And He said to them, "What kind
of conversation *is* this that you have
with one another as you [1]walk and are
sad?"

[18]Then the one [a]whose name was
Cleopas answered and said to Him,
"Are You the only stranger in Jerusalem, and have You not known the
things which happened there in these
days?"

[19]And He said to them, "What things?"
So they said to Him, "The things concerning Jesus of Nazareth, [a]who was a
Prophet [b]mighty in deed and word
before God and all the people, [20a]and
how the chief priests and our rulers
delivered Him to be condemned to
death, and crucified Him. [21]But we
were hoping [a]that it was He who was
going to redeem Israel. Indeed, besides
all this, today is the third day since
these things happened. [22]Yes, and [a]cer-
tain women of our company, who
arrived at the tomb early, astonished
us. [23]When they did not find His body,
they came saying that they had also
seen a vision of angels who said He
was alive. [24]And [a]certain of those *who
were* with us went to the tomb and
found *it* just as the women had said;
but Him they did not see."

[25]Then He said to them, "O foolish
ones, and slow of heart to believe in all
that the prophets have spoken!
[26a]Ought not the Christ to have suffered these things and to enter into His
[b]glory?" [27]And beginning at [a]Moses
and [b]all the Prophets, He [1]expounded
to them in all the Scriptures the things
concerning Himself.

Cross-references (center column)

51 [a]Luke 2:25,
38
[1]NU *who was
waiting*

53 [a]Mark 15:46

54 [a]Matt. 27:62

55 [a]Luke 8:2
[b]Mark 15:47

56 [a]Mark 16:1
[b]Ex. 20:10

CHAPTER 24

1 [a]John 20:1–8
[b]Luke 23:56
[1]NU *and
certain other
women with
them*

2 [a]Mark 16:4

3 [a]Mark 16:5

4 [a]John 20:12
[1]NU omits
greatly

6 [a]Luke 9:22

7 [a]Luke 9:44;
11:29, 30;
18:31–33

8 [a]John 2:19–
22

9 [a]Mark 16:10

10 [a]Luke 8:3

11 [a]Luke 24:25
[1]*nonsense*

12 [a]John 20:3–
6
[1]NU omits *lying*

13 [a]Mark 16:12
[1]Lit. *60 stadia*

15 [a][Matt.
18:20]

16 [a]John 20:14;
21:4

17 [1]NU *walk?
And they stood
still, looking sad.*

18 [a]John 19:25

19 [a]Matt. 21:11
[b]Acts 7:22

20 [a]Acts 13:27,
28

21 [a]Luke 1:68;
2:38

22 [a]Mark 16:10

24 [a]Luke 24:12

26 [a]Acts 17:2,
3
[b][1 Pet. 1:10–
12]

27 [a][Deut.
18:15]
[b][Is. 7:14; 9:6]
[1]*explained*

THE DISCIPLES' EYES OPENED

28Then they drew near to the village where they were going, and ªHe ¹indicated that He would have gone farther. 29But ªthey constrained Him, saying, b"Abide with us, for it is toward evening, and the day is far spent." And He went in to stay with them. 30Now it came to pass, as ªHe sat at the table with them, that He took bread, blessed and broke *it*, and gave it to them. 31Then their eyes were opened and they knew Him; and He vanished from their sight. 32And they said to one another, "Did not our heart burn within us while He talked with us on the road, and while He opened the Scriptures to us?" 33So they rose up that very hour and returned to Jerusalem, and found the eleven and those *who were* with them gathered together, 34saying, "The Lord is risen indeed, and ªhas appeared to Simon!" 35And they told about the things *that had happened* on the road, and how He was ¹known to them in the breaking of bread.

28 ª Mark 6:48
¹ acted as if

29 ª Gen. 19:2, 3
b [John 14:23]

30 ª Matt. 14:19

34 ª 1 Cor. 15:5

35 ¹ recognized

36 ª Mark 16:14

37 ª Mark 6:49

39 ª John 20:20, 27
b [1 Cor. 15:50]

40 ¹ Some printed New Testaments omit v. 40. It is found in nearly all Gr. mss.

41 ª Gen. 45:26
b John 21:5

42 ¹ NU omits *and some honeycomb*

43 ª Acts 10:39–41

44 ª Matt. 16:21; 17:22; 20:18

JESUS APPEARS TO HIS DISCIPLES

36ªNow as they said these things, Jesus Himself stood in the midst of them, and said to them, "Peace to you." 37But they were terrified and frightened, and supposed they had seen ªa spirit. 38And He said to them, "Why are you troubled? And why do doubts arise in your hearts? 39Behold My hands and My feet, that it is I Myself. ªHandle Me and see, for a bspirit does not have flesh and bones as you see I have." 40¹When He had said this, He showed them His hands and His feet. 41But while they still did not believe ªfor joy, and marveled, He said to them, b"Have you any food here?" 42So they gave Him a piece of a broiled fish ¹and some honeycomb. 43ªAnd He took *it* and ate in their presence.

THE SCRIPTURES OPENED

44Then He said to them, ª"These *are* the words which I spoke to you while I was still with you, that all things must

Luke 24:32

BURNING HEARTS

As Jesus taught Cleopas and his fellow traveler, their hearts were burning. They could feel something special as He spoke. You see, the problem with these disciples was that their fire had burned out. They had hoped that Jesus was the Messiah and that He would set up His kingdom; but when He died, their hopes were dashed. But as Jesus spoke to them from the Scriptures, the fire in their hearts was fanned into a flame, and they knew it was true. They couldn't wait to go out and tell the others.

If the fire burns low in our lives, how we need to sit at Jesus' feet and hear from His Word! Then, as our hearts begin to burn once again, as we get on fire for Him, we will go out to share the good news.

Luke 24:45

OPEN UNDERSTANDING

Jesus "opened their understanding, that they might comprehend the Scriptures." How important it is that He opens our understanding so that the Bible will make sense!

You can't just come to the Bible from an intellectual approach. That won't cut it. "The natural man does not receive the things of the Spirit of God, for they are foolishness to him; nor can he know them, because they are spiritually discerned" (1 Cor. 2:14). We need to pray that God will open the eyes of our understanding.

And it's wonderful when the Spirit of God begins to move on a person's heart, drawing them to Jesus. The light clicks on, the understanding begins to open up, and suddenly God's Word makes sense to them. Pray that He will do that for you.

be fulfilled which were written in the Law of Moses and *the* Prophets and *the* Psalms concerning Me." [45]And [a]He opened their understanding, that they might comprehend the Scriptures.

[46]Then He said to them, [a]"Thus it is written, [1]and thus it was necessary for the Christ to suffer and to rise from the dead the third day, [47]and that repentance and [a]remission of sins should be preached in His name [b]to all nations, beginning at Jerusalem. [48]And [a]you are witnesses of these things. [49][a]Behold, I send the Promise of My Father upon you; but tarry in the city [1]of Jerusalem until you are endued with power from on high."

THE ASCENSION

[50]And He led them out [a]as far as Bethany, and He lifted up His hands and blessed them. [51][a]Now it came to pass, while He blessed them, that He was parted from them and carried up into heaven. [52][a]And they worshiped Him, and returned to Jerusalem with great joy, [53]and were continually [a]in the temple [1]praising and blessing God. [2]Amen.

45 [a] Acts 16:14
46 [a] Acts 17:3
[1] NU *that the Christ should suffer and rise*
47 [a] Acts 5:31; 10:43; 13:38; 26:18
[b] [Jer. 31:34]
48 [a] [Acts 1:8]
49 [a] Joel 2:28
[1] NU omits *of Jerusalem*
50 [a] Acts 1:12
51 [a] Mark 16:19
52 [a] Matt. 28:9
53 [a] Acts 2:46   [1] NU omits *praising and*   [2] NU omits *Amen.*

THE GOSPEL ACCORDING TO
JOHN

INTRODUCTION **T**he gospel of John is quite different than the other three Gospels, which collectively are called the Synoptic Gospels.

John was written much later than the other three Gospels, probably around AD 90. Because the other three Gospels were in wide distribution by this time, John provides stories and teachings that fill in the gaps left by the other accounts. The book was no doubt written by John, the disciple of Jesus, as can be seen by the last few verses of the book, and as is supported by early church history.

John gives the purpose of the book in John 20:31, where he says, "These are written that you may believe that Jesus is the Christ, the Son of God, and that believing you may have life in His name." In other words, John wrote this gospel so that people could understand and believe who Jesus is—the Messiah and God in the flesh—and that this awareness would lead to an abundant life.

Matthew was written to present Jesus as the fulfillment of the Old Testament prophecies concerning the Messiah. Mark was written to present Jesus as the perfect servant, and Luke showed Him as the perfect human. John shows that Jesus was God.

Matthew chapter 1 gives the genealogy of Jesus through His adopted father Joseph, showing that He had the legal right to rule. Mark doesn't contain a genealogy at all, emphasizing just the life and actions of Jesus. Luke chapter 3 gives the genealogy of Jesus through His mother Mary, showing Him to be biologically a descendant of Adam, through the line of David. But in John's gospel, the genealogy is found in the first verse, as he says, "In the beginning was the Word, and the Word was with God, and the Word was God." Jesus was around before Adam, because He always existed, before time began, as God.

John's gospel gives numerous evidences of the deity of Christ. You will see how many times Jesus described Himself in John beginning with the words "I am." That was the way God introduced Himself to Moses in the book of Exodus, and Jesus used this self-description many times in this book.

We should also mention that, although the gospel of John distinctly emphasizes the deity of Christ, it also presents very clearly that Jesus was the Messiah, as when Jesus told the Samaritan woman that He was the Messiah (John 4:25–26).

John also presents Jesus as a servant, such as when He washed the feet of the disciples (John 13:1–17), and shows Him to be a human, "and the Word became flesh" (John 1:14).

Thus the gospel of John paints a complete picture of who Jesus is, and so is a powerful source for bringing someone into a relationship with Jesus. This is why I usually recommend this book to a new Christian, or to someone who is wanting to learn more about Jesus. It tells the whole story, and was written for the purpose of giving life.

THE ETERNAL WORD

1 In the beginning ^awas the Word, and the ^bWord was ^cwith God, and the Word was ^dGod. ^{2 a}He was in the beginning with God. ^{3 a}All things were made through Him, and without Him nothing was made that was made. ^{4 a}In Him was life, and ^bthe life was the light of men. ⁵And ^athe light shines in the darkness, and the darkness did not ¹comprehend it.

JOHN'S WITNESS: THE TRUE LIGHT

⁶There was a ^aman sent from God, whose name *was* John. ⁷This man came for a ^awitness, to bear witness of the Light, that all through him might

JESUS THE CREATOR GOD

John didn't want his readers to miss who Jesus is and opened up by saying, "The Word was God." And to remove any doubts about which god, he further clarified, "All things were made through Him, and without Him nothing was made that was made." Paul made the same point in Colossians 1:16 when he said, "For by Him all things were created that are in heaven and that are on earth, visible and invisible, whether thrones or dominions or principalities or powers. All things were created through Him and for Him."

There are many gods who are objects of worship in this world, but Jesus is the true God, the Creator God.

CHAPTER 1

1 ^a 1 John 1:1
^b Rev. 19:13
^c [John 17:5]
^d [1 John 5:20]

2 ^a Gen. 1:1

3 ^a [Col. 1:16, 17]

4 ^a [1 John 5:11]
^b John 8:12; 9:5; 12:46

5 ^a [John 3:19]
¹ Or *overcome*

6 ^a Matt. 3:1–17

7 ^a John 3:25–36; 5:33–35
^b [John 3:16]

8 ^a Is. 9:2; 49:6

9 ^a Is. 49:6
¹ Or *That was the true Light which, coming into the world, gives light to every man.*

10 ^a Heb. 1:2

11 ^a [Luke 19:14]
¹ His own things or domain
² His own people

12 ^a Gal. 3:26
¹ authority

13 ^a [1 Pet. 1:23]

14 ^a Rev. 19:13
^b Gal. 4:4
^c Heb. 2:11
^d Is. 40:5
^e [John 8:32; 14:6; 18:37]

15 ^a John 3:32
^b [Matt. 3:11]
^c [Col. 1:17]
¹ ranks higher than I

16 ^a [Col. 1:19; 2:9]
¹ NU *For*

17 ^a [Ex. 20:1]

^bbelieve. ⁸He was not that Light, but *was sent* to bear witness of that ^aLight. ^{9 a}That ¹was the true Light which gives light to every man coming into the world.

¹⁰He was in the world, and the world was made through Him, and ^athe world did not know Him. ^{11 a}He came to His ¹own, and His ²own did not receive Him. ¹²But ^aas many as received Him, to them He gave the ¹right to become children of God, to those who believe in His name: ^{13 a}who were born, not of blood, nor of the will of the flesh, nor of the will of man, but of God.

THE WORD BECOMES FLESH

^{14 a}And the Word ^bbecame ^cflesh and dwelt among us, and ^dwe beheld His glory, the glory as of the only begotten of the Father, ^efull of grace and truth.

John 1:14

The Incarnation. "And the Word became flesh and dwelt among us." This is amazing! The same God who created the universe took on a body of flesh, and He dwelt, or "tabernacled," among us. He pitched His tent with us and made Himself at home with us.

Paul said, "Great is the mystery of godliness: God was manifested in the flesh" (1 Tim. 3:16). How could there be a more profound miracle than that? But God went to that length just because He loved us that much.

^{15 a}John bore witness of Him and cried out, saying, "This was He of whom I said, ^b'He who comes after me ¹is preferred before me, ^cfor He was before me.'"

^{16 1}And of His ^afullness we have all received, and grace for grace. ¹⁷For ^athe law was given through Moses, *but*

bgrace and ctruth came through Jesus Christ. 18aNo one has seen God at any time. bThe only begotten 1Son, who is in the bosom of the Father, He has declared *Him.*

A VOICE IN THE WILDERNESS

19Now this is athe testimony of John, when the Jews sent priests and Levites from Jerusalem to ask him, "Who are you?"

20aHe confessed, and did not deny, but confessed, "I am not the Christ."

21And they asked him, "What then? Are you Elijah?"

He said, "I am not."

"Are you athe Prophet?"

And he answered, "No."

22Then they said to him, "Who are you, that we may give an answer to those who sent us? What do you say about yourself?"

23He said: a"I *am*

b'*The voice of one crying in the wilderness:*
"*Make straight the way of the LORD,*"'

as the prophet Isaiah said."

24Now those who were sent were from the Pharisees. 25And they asked him, saying, "Why then do you baptize if you are not the Christ, nor Elijah, nor the Prophet?"

26John answered them, saying, a"I baptize with water, bbut there stands One among you whom you do not know. 27aIt is He who, coming after me, 1is preferred before me, whose sandal strap I am not worthy to loose."

28These things were done ain 1Bethabara beyond the Jordan, where John was baptizing.

THE LAMB OF GOD

29The next day John saw Jesus coming toward him, and said, "Behold! aThe Lamb of God bwho takes away the sin of the world! 30This is He of whom I said, 'After me comes a Man who 1is preferred before me, for He was before me.' 31I did not know Him; but that He should be revealed to Israel, atherefore I came baptizing with water."

32aAnd John bore witness, saying, "I saw the Spirit descending from heaven like a dove, and He remained upon Him. 33I did not know Him, but He who sent me to baptize with water said to me, 'Upon whom you see the Spirit descending, and remaining on Him, athis is He who baptizes with the Holy

Spirit.' 34And I have seen and testified that this is the aSon of God."

THE FIRST DISCIPLES

35Again, the next day, John stood with two of his disciples. 36And looking at Jesus as He walked, he said, a"Behold the Lamb of God!"

37The two disciples heard him speak, and they afollowed Jesus. 38Then Jesus turned, and seeing them following, said to them, "What do you seek?"

They said to Him, "Rabbi" (which is to say, when translated, Teacher), "where are You staying?"

39He said to them, "Come and see." They came and saw where He was staying, and remained with Him that day (now it was about the tenth hour).

40One of the two who heard John *speak,* and followed Him, was aAndrew, Simon Peter's brother. 41He first found his own brother Simon, and said to him, "We have found the 1Messiah"

Cross references (center column)

17 b [Rom. 5:21; 6:14]
c [John 8:32; 14:6; 18:37]

18 a Ex. 33:20
b 1 John 4:9
1 NU *God*

19 a John 5:33

20 a Luke 3:15

21 a Deut. 18:15, 18

23 a Matt. 3:3
b Is. 40:3

26 a Matt. 3:11
b Mal. 3:1

27 a Acts 19:4
1 *ranks higher than I*

28 a Judg. 7:24
1 NU, M *Bethany*

29 a Rev. 5:6–14
b [1 Pet. 2:24]

30 1 *ranks higher than I*

31 a Matt. 3:6

32 a Mark 1:10

33 a Matt. 3:11

34 a John 11:27

36 a John 1:29

37 a Matt. 4:20, 22

40 a Matt. 4:18

41 1 Lit. *Anointed One*

John 1:29

THE LAMB OF GOD

Jewish people were very familiar with lambs being used as a sacrifice. They remembered the lambs that were killed when the Israelites were about to be freed from Egypt, and they put the blood of the lambs on their doorposts and lintels. Growing up, they saw how many lambs were killed as a covering for their sins. Now Jesus was being called "the Lamb of God who takes away the sin of the world!" Their only frame of reference for a man being sacrificed would have been the story of Abraham, who had prepared to offer his son Isaac on Mount Moriah. (See Gen. 22:2.)

Now in just a few years the people would see the fulfillment of that event, as Jesus would be offered up on Mount Moriah, to take away our sins once and for all. This is the fulfillment of all the sacrifices ever offered.

(which is translated, the Christ). 42And he brought him to Jesus.

Now when Jesus looked at him, He said, "You are Simon the son of 1Jonah. aYou shall be called Cephas" (which is translated, 2A Stone).

PHILIP AND NATHANAEL

43The following day Jesus wanted to go to Galilee, and He found aPhilip and said to him, "Follow Me." 44Now aPhilip was from Bethsaida, the city of Andrew and Peter. 45Philip found aNathanael and said to him, "We have found Him of whom bMoses in the law, and also the cprophets, wrote—Jesus dof Nazareth, the eson of Joseph."

46And Nathanael said to him, a"Can anything good come out of Nazareth?"

Philip said to him, "Come and see."

47Jesus saw Nathanael coming toward Him, and said of him, "Behold, aan Israelite indeed, in whom is no deceit!"

48Nathanael said to Him, "How do You know me?"

Jesus answered and said to him, "Before Philip called you, when you were under the fig tree, I saw you."

49Nathanael answered and said to Him, "Rabbi, aYou are the Son of God! You are bthe King of Israel!"

50Jesus answered and said to him, "Because I said to you, 'I saw you under the fig tree,' do you believe? You will

42 a Matt. 16:18
1 NU John
2 Gr. Petros, usually translated Peter

43 a John 6:5; 12:21, 22; 14:8, 9

44 a John 12:21

45 a John 21:2
b Luke 24:27
c [Zech. 6:12]
d [Matt. 2:23]
e Luke 3:23

46 a John 7:41, 42, 52

47 a Ps. 32:2; 73:1

49 a Matt. 14:33
b Matt. 21:5

51 a Gen. 28:12
1 NU omits hereafter

CHAPTER 2

1 a [Heb. 13:4]
b John 4:46
c John 19:25

4 a John 19:26
b 2 Sam. 16:10
c John 7:6, 8, 30; 8:20

6 a [Mark 7:3]

9 a John 4:46

see greater things than these." 51And He said to him, "Most assuredly, I say to you, ahereafter1 you shall see heaven open, and the angels of God ascending and descending upon the Son of Man."

WATER TURNED TO WINE

2 On the third day there was a awedding in bCana of Galilee, and the cmother of Jesus was there. 2Now both Jesus and His disciples were invited to the wedding. 3And when they ran out of wine, the mother of Jesus said to Him, "They have no wine."

4Jesus said to her, a"Woman, bwhat does your concern have to do with Me? cMy hour has not yet come."

5His mother said to the servants, "Whatever He says to you, do it."

6Now there were set there six waterpots of stone, aaccording to the manner of purification of the Jews, containing twenty or thirty gallons apiece. 7Jesus said to them, "Fill the waterpots with water." And they filled them up to the brim. 8And He said to them, "Draw some out now, and take it to the master of the feast." And they took it. 9When the master of the feast had tasted athe water that was made wine, and did not know where it came from (but the servants who had drawn the water knew), the master of the feast called the bridegroom. 10And he said to him, "Every man at the beginning sets out the good

NOT YET   John 2:3–4

Mary knew from the very beginning that her Son Jesus was very special. An angel had appeared to her, telling her about the Son she would have, and she conceived without having physical relations with a man. For thirty years she had watched Jesus growing up, wondering when He would reveal His nature to the world. For thirty years the people around her had whispered, suggesting that she had given birth to an illegitimate son. But now Jesus had been baptized and had chosen some disciples, and it looked like something was going to start happening. And if Jesus would reveal Himself openly, it would exonerate her from all the whispers.

So, as they were guests at this wedding and the wine had run out, she came to Jesus and said, "They have no wine." No doubt she thought this would be an excellent opportunity for Him to demonstrate His power. He responded by saying, "Woman, what does your concern have to do with Me? My hour has not yet come." In other words, "Mom, what am I going to do with you? This isn't the time."

Everyone was in a hurry for Jesus to be introduced as the Messiah except Jesus. He knew it was a matter of timing in order to fulfill the Scriptures. It would have to be exactly 483 years from the declaration to restore and rebuild Jerusalem (Dan. 9:25). He would need to be riding on a donkey (Zech. 9:9). Jesus wouldn't let anyone but the Father dictate His timing. And His timing is always perfect. Then He proceeded to change the water to wine, quietly and simply.

wine, and when the *guests* have well drunk, then the inferior. You have kept the good wine until now!"

11This abeginning of signs Jesus did in Cana of Galilee, band 1manifested His glory; and His disciples believed in Him.

12After this He went down to aCapernaum, He, His mother, bHis brothers, and His disciples; and they did not stay there many days.

JESUS CLEANSES THE TEMPLE

13aNow the Passover of the Jews was at hand, and Jesus went up to Jerusalem. 14aAnd He found in the temple those who sold oxen and sheep and doves, and the money changers 1doing business. 15When He had made a whip of cords, He drove them all out of the temple, with the sheep and the oxen, and poured out the changers' money and overturned the tables. 16And He said to those who sold doves, "Take these things away! Do not make aMy Father's house a house of merchandise!" 17Then His disciples remembered that it was written, a*"Zeal for Your house 1has eaten Me up."*

John 2:14–17

A HOUSE OF MERCHANDISE

Jesus saw the people selling animals in the temple courtyard, and He drove them out. He really had two problems with them.

First of all, the money changers were ripping off the people who were being forced to buy special certified animals from them at highly inflated prices. God is always angry at people who profiteer off religion. They were making money off the people in the name of the Lord. God still hates that.

But second, by selling animals right there at the temple, they were trying to make it easy and convenient. You could basically just buy your way into good standing before God. But you can't take a shortcut to God. You only come to Him through the costly sacrifice of His Son.

Marginal references:

11 aJohn 4:54
b[John 1:14]
1revealed

12 aMatt. 4:13
bMatt. 12:46;
13:55

13 aDeut. 16:1–6

14 aMark 11:15, 17
1Lit. *sitting*

16 aLuke 2:49

17 aPs. 69:9
1NU, M *will eat*

18 aMatt. 12:38

19 aMatt. 26:61; 27:40

21 a[1 Cor. 3:16; 6:19]

22 aLuke 24:8
1NU, M omit *to them*

23 a[Acts 2:22]

24 aRev. 2:23

25 aMatt. 9:4

CHAPTER 3

2 aJohn 7:50; 19:39

18So the Jews answered and said to Him, a"What sign do You show to us, since You do these things?"

19Jesus answered and said to them, a"Destroy this temple, and in three days I will raise it up."

20Then the Jews said, "It has taken forty-six years to build this temple, and will You raise it up in three days?"

21But He was speaking aof the temple of His body. 22Therefore, when He had risen from the dead, aHis disciples remembered that He had said this 1to them; and they believed the Scripture and the word which Jesus had said.

THE DISCERNER OF HEARTS

23Now when He was in Jerusalem at the Passover, during the feast, many believed in His name when they saw the asigns which He did. 24But Jesus did not commit Himself to them, because He aknew all *men*, 25and had no need that anyone should testify of man, for aHe knew what was in man.

John 2:23–25

DIDN'T COMMIT TO THEM

As Jesus began to work miracles and healings, many people began to follow Him. But it didn't lead to a relationship with Him, as "Jesus did not commit Himself to them."

It is great to experience miracles from God and to have great feelings about God. I have seen plenty of those miracles and felt those wonderful feelings. But lasting faith doesn't come from experiencing the spectacular. That is a shallow faith.

Lasting faith comes from trusting Jesus when we don't see what He is doing. It is the "evidence of things not seen" (Heb. 11:1).

THE NEW BIRTH

3 There was a man of the Pharisees named Nicodemus, a ruler of the Jews. 2aThis man came to Jesus by night and said to Him, "Rabbi, we know that You are a teacher come from God;

for ^bno one can do these signs that You do unless ^cGod is with him."

³Jesus answered and said to him, "Most assuredly, I say to you, ^aunless one is born ¹again, he cannot see the kingdom of God."

⁴Nicodemus said to Him, "How can a man be born when he is old? Can he enter a second time into his mother's womb and be born?"

⁵Jesus answered, "Most assuredly, I say to you, ^aunless one is born of water and the Spirit, he cannot enter the kingdom of God. ⁶That which is born of the flesh is ^aflesh, and that which is born of the Spirit is spirit. ⁷Do not marvel that I said to you, 'You must be born again.' ⁸^aThe wind blows where it wishes, and you hear the sound of it, but cannot tell where it comes from

Cross references:
2 ^b John 9:16, 33
^c [Acts 10:38]
3 ^a [1 Pet. 1:23]
¹ Or *from above*
5 ^a [Acts 2:38]
6 ^a 1 Cor. 15:50
8 ^a Eccl. 11:5

BORN AGAIN   John 3:3

Nicodemus came to Jesus to hear what God wanted to say to man. The Israelites hadn't heard from God in over four hundred years, and now there was One who was clearly from God, so Nicodemus wanted to hear from God.

Jesus threw Nicodemus a curveball by telling him, "Unless one is born again, he cannot see the kingdom of God." Jesus was telling him that without a new birth, a spiritual birth, it would be impossible to comprehend what God was saying. This is what Paul pointed out when he said, "The natural man does not receive the things of the Spirit of God, for they are foolishness to him; nor can he know them, because they are spiritually discerned" (1 Cor. 2:14). In Romans 6:4, Paul referred to this new birth as "newness of life." Peter described it as being "begotten again" (1 Pet. 1:3). There is a work of God's Spirit within a person's life whereby that person comes into a whole new dimension of life, the dimension of the Spirit.

Man was created as a threefold being, with a body, a soul, and a spirit. We were designed to have our spirit rule over our body and soul. But because of our rebellion against God, we become spiritually dead, and our flesh rules. What God wants to do is to revive our spirit bringing it back to life by its being filled with the Spirit of God. Then, walking in the Spirit, we experience a new life; and being born again, of the Spirit, we can now understand what God wants to say to us.

This brings up this issue we all must face. Have I been born again? Have I been born of the Spirit? If you haven't, you can't enter the kingdom of God. If you haven't, you can't understand the things of God. All you need to do is ask: "God, I want to be born again. I want to accept Jesus as my Savior. I give my life to You." If you do that, you will be born again, entering into a whole new life in the spiritual realm.

BORN OF WATER AND SPIRIT   John 3:5–6

There are two basic interpretations regarding what Jesus was referring to when He said, "born of water and the Spirit." We know what being born of the Spirit is. It is the new birth when we accept Jesus Christ. But what is being born of water?

Some say it is water baptism. Water baptism is something we do to symbolize the death of the flesh and the new life in Christ. In that case, being born of water and Spirit would refer to two aspects of being born again, with one being the outward sign and the second being the inward work of the Spirit.

The second interpretation is that being born of water referred to physical birth (as the mother's water breaks and birth follows). In this case, Jesus would have been saying, "You need to be born twice, physically and spiritually." This certainly fits the context of being born "again." Jesus also followed it up by talking about being born of the flesh and the Spirit.

We can't be certain as to which interpretation is correct. Each expresses truth. I lean toward the second interpretation, and I like the saying, "Born once, die twice. Born twice, die once."

and where it goes. So is everyone who is born of the Spirit."

9Nicodemus answered and said to Him, a"How can these things be?" 10Jesus answered and said to him, "Are you the teacher of Israel, and do not know these things? 11aMost assuredly, I say to you, We speak what We know and testify what We have seen, and byou do not receive Our witness. 12If I have told you earthly things and you do not believe, how will you believe if I tell you heavenly things? 13aNo one has ascended to heaven but He who came down from heaven, *that is,* the Son of Man 1who is in heaven. 14aAnd as Moses lifted up the serpent in the wilderness, even so bmust the Son of Man be lifted up, 15that whoever abelieves in Him should 1not perish but bhave eternal life. 16aFor God so loved the world that He gave His only begotten bSon, that whoever believes in Him should not perish but have everlasting life. 17aFor God did not send His Son into the world to condemn the world, but that the world through Him might be saved.

John 3:16

EVERLASTING LIFE

Jesus wasn't just talking about quantity of life here. He was talking about a quality of life. Quantity of life without quality is hell. Jesus has given us a rich life of inestimable quality that also happens to go on forever. What a glorious truth!

God's purpose for your life is not that you would perish, but that you would have a rich, full life that lasts forever. Truth so profound that with all my years of study I can't fully comprehend it. Yet so simple that my great-grandchildren understand it and believe in Jesus.

18a"He who believes in Him is not condemned; but he who does not believe is condemned already, because he has not believed in the name of the only begotten Son of God. 19And this is the condemnation, athat the light has

---

9 a John 6:52, 60

11 a [Matt. 11:27]
b John 3:32; 8:14

13 a Eph. 4:9
1 NU omits *who is in heaven*

14 a Num. 21:9
b John 8:28; 12:34; 19:18

15 a John 6:47
b John 3:36
1 NU omits *not perish but*

16 a Rom. 5:8
b [Is. 9:6]

17 a Luke 9:56

18 a John 5:24; 6:40, 47; 20:31

19 a [John 1:4, 9–11]

20 a Eph. 5:11, 13

21 a 1 Cor. 15:10

22 a John 4:1, 2

23 a 1 Sam. 9:4
b Matt. 3:5, 6

24 a Matt. 4:12; 14:3

26 a John 1:7, 15, 27, 34
b Mark 2:2; 3:10; 5:24

27 a 1 Cor. 3:5, 6; 4:7

28 a John 1:19–27
b Mal. 3:1

29 a [2 Cor. 11:2]
b Song 5:1

30 a [Is. 9:7]

31 a John 3:13; 8:23
b Matt. 28:18
c 1 Cor. 15:47
d John 6:33

32 a John 3:11; 15:15

33 a 1 John 5:10

34 a John 7:16
b John 1:16

35 a [Heb. 2:8]

36 a John 3:16; 17; 6:47
b Rom. 1:18

CHAPTER 4

1 a John 3:22, 26

---

come into the world, and men loved darkness rather than light, because their deeds were evil. 20For aeveryone practicing evil hates the light and does not come to the light, lest his deeds should be exposed. 21But he who does the truth comes to the light, that his deeds may be clearly seen, that they have been adone in God."

JOHN THE BAPTIST EXALTS CHRIST

22After these things Jesus and His disciples came into the land of Judea, and there He remained with them aand baptized. 23Now John also was baptizing in Aenon near aSalim, because there was much water there. bAnd they came and were baptized. 24For aJohn had not yet been thrown into prison.

25Then there arose a dispute between *some* of John's disciples and the Jews about purification. 26And they came to John and said to him, "Rabbi, He who was with you beyond the Jordan, ato whom you have testified—behold, He is baptizing, and all bare coming to Him!"

27John answered and said, a"A man can receive nothing unless it has been given to him from heaven. 28You yourselves bear me witness, that I said, a'I am not the Christ,' but, b'I have been sent before Him.' 29aHe who has the bride is the bridegroom; but bthe friend of the bridegroom, who stands and hears him, rejoices greatly because of the bridegroom's voice. Therefore this joy of mine is fulfilled. 30aHe must increase, but I *must* decrease. 31aHe who comes from above bis above all; che who is of the earth is earthly and speaks of the earth. dHe who comes from heaven is above all. 32And awhat He has seen and heard, that He testifies; and no one receives His testimony. 33He who has received His testimony ahas certified that God is true. 34aFor He whom God has sent speaks the words of God, for God does not give the Spirit bby measure. 35aThe Father loves the Son, and has given all things into His hand. 36aHe who believes in the Son has everlasting life; and he who does not believe the Son shall not see life, but the bwrath of God abides on him."

A SAMARITAN WOMAN MEETS HER MESSIAH

4 Therefore, when the Lord knew that the Pharisees had heard that Jesus made and abaptized more disciples than John 2(though Jesus Himself did

not baptize, but His disciples), ³He left Judea and departed again to Galilee. ⁴But He needed to go through Samaria.

⁵So He came to a city of Samaria which is called Sychar, near the plot of ground that ªJacob ᵇgave to his son Joseph. ⁶Now Jacob's well was there. Jesus therefore, being wearied from *His* journey, sat thus by the well. It was about the sixth hour.

⁷A woman of Samaria came to draw water. Jesus said to her, "Give Me a drink." ⁸For His disciples had gone away into the city to buy food.

⁹Then the woman of Samaria said to Him, "How is it that You, being a Jew, ask a drink from me, a Samaritan woman?" For ªJews have no dealings with ᵇSamaritans.

¹⁰Jesus answered and said to her, "If you knew the ªgift of God, and who it is who says to you, 'Give Me a drink,' you would have asked Him, and He would have given you ᵇliving water."

¹¹The woman said to Him, "Sir, You have nothing to draw with, and the well is deep. Where then do You get that living water? ¹²Are You greater than our father Jacob, who gave us the well, and drank from it himself, as well as his sons and his livestock?"

¹³Jesus answered and said to her, "Whoever drinks of this water will thirst again, ¹⁴but ªwhoever drinks of the water that I shall give him will never thirst. But the water that I shall give him ᵇwill become in him a foun-

tain of water springing up into everlasting life."

¹⁵ªThe woman said to Him, "Sir, give me this water, that I may not thirst, nor come here to draw."

¹⁶Jesus said to her, "Go, call your husband, and come here."

¹⁷The woman answered and said, "I have no husband."

Jesus said to her, "You have well said, 'I have no husband,' ¹⁸for you have had five husbands, and the one whom you now have is not your husband; in that you spoke truly."

¹⁹The woman said to Him, "Sir, ªI perceive that You are a prophet. ²⁰Our fathers worshiped on ªthis mountain, and you *Jews* say that in ᵇJerusalem is the place where one ought to worship."

²¹Jesus said to her, "Woman, believe Me, the hour is coming ªwhen you will neither on this mountain, nor in Jerusalem, worship the Father. ²²You worship ªwhat you do not know; we know what we worship, for ᵇsalvation is of the Jews. ²³But the hour is coming, and now is, when the true worshipers will ªworship the Father in ᵇspirit ᶜand truth; for the Father is seeking such to worship Him. ²⁴ªGod *is* Spirit, and those who worship Him must worship in spirit and truth."

²⁵The woman said to Him, "I know that Messiah ªis coming" (who is called

---

Cross references:

5 ªGen. 33:19
ᵇGen. 48:22

9 ªActs 10:28
ᵇ2Kin. 17:24

10 ª[Rom. 5:15]
ᵇIs. 12:3; 44:3

14 ª[John 6:35, 58]
ᵇJohn 7:37, 38

15 ªJohn 6:34, 35; 17:2, 3

19 ªLuke 7:16, 39; 24:19

20 ªJudg. 9:7
ᵇDeut. 12:5, 11

21 ª1Tim. 2:8

22 ª[2Kin. 17:28–41]
ᵇ[Rom. 3:1; 9:4, 5]

23 ª[Heb. 13:10–14]
ᵇPhil. 3:3
ᶜ[John 1:17]

24 ª2Cor. 3:17

25 ªDeut. 18:15

John 4:13

Thirst Again. An extremely profound statement: "Whoever drinks of this water will thirst again." This statement should be written over every ambition you have.

What is it that you are hoping to attain in life? What is it that you think will bring you satisfaction and fulfillment? What goals are you pressing toward? What possessions are you striving to acquire? Whatever it is, write over the top of it, "Drink of this water, but you will thirst again." There is nothing in the material realm that will satisfy our spiritual thirst.

John 4:24

SPIRIT AND TRUTH

Jesus told the righteous Pharisee, Nicodemus, that he could only come to God by being born of the Spirit. Now His message to this immoral woman was basically the same. You must come to God on the spiritual plane, worshiping Him in spirit and truth.

The woman had a thirst and an emptiness that could only be filled by the Spirit of God. And that is true of every one of us, whether we are the elite of society or the dregs of society. God will meet all our needs, but only on His terms, by His Spirit.

Christ). "When He comes, ᵇHe will tell us all things."

²⁶Jesus said to her, ᵃ"I who speak to you am *He*."

THE WHITENED HARVEST

²⁷And at this *point* His disciples came, and they marveled that He talked with a woman; yet no one said, "What do You seek?" or, "Why are You talking with her?"

²⁸The woman then left her waterpot, went her way into the city, and said to the men, ²⁹"Come, see a Man ᵃwho told me all things that I ever did. Could this be the Christ?" ³⁰Then they went out of the city and came to Him.

³¹In the meantime His disciples urged Him, saying, "Rabbi, eat." ³²But He said to them, "I have food to eat of which you do not know." ³³Therefore the disciples said to one another, "Has anyone brought Him *anything* to eat?"

³⁴Jesus said to them, ᵃ"My food is to do the will of Him who sent Me, and to ᵇfinish His work. ³⁵Do you not say, 'There are still four months and *then* comes ᵃthe harvest'? Behold, I say to you, lift up your eyes and look at the fields, ᵇfor they are already white for harvest! ³⁶ᵃAnd he who reaps receives wages, and gathers fruit for eternal life, that ᵇboth he who sows and he who

---

John 4:34

FINISHING HIS WORK

Jesus came to do the work of the Father. He was doing that work as He shared the truth with the woman at the well. That was food to Him. It was what He lived for. But He said, "My food is to do the will of Him who sent Me, and to finish His work."

When Jesus hung on the cross to die for our sins, He said, "It is finished!" (John 19:30). That was when He finished the work of providing for our salvation.

Jesus lived to declare the truth, but He died to make it a reality.

Margin references:

25 ᵇ John 4:29, 39

26 ᵃ Matt. 26:63, 64

29 ᵃ John 4:25

34 ᵃ Ps. 40:7, 8
ᵇ [John 6:38; 17:4; 19:30]

35 ᵃ Gen. 8:22
ᵇ Matt. 9:37

36 ᵃ Dan. 12:3
ᵇ 1 Thess. 2:19

37 ᵃ 1 Cor. 3:5–9

38 ᵃ [1 Pet. 1:12]

39 ᵃ John 4:29

41 ᵃ Luke 4:32

42 ᵃ 1 John 4:14
1 NU omits *the Christ*

44 ᵃ Matt. 13:57

45 ᵃ John 2:13, 23; 3:2
ᵇ Deut. 16:16

46 ᵃ John 2:1, 11
1 *royal official*

48 ᵃ 1 Cor. 1:22

---

reaps may rejoice together. ³⁷For in this the saying is true: ᵃ'One sows and another reaps.' ³⁸I sent you to reap that for which you have not labored; ᵃothers have labored, and you have entered into their labors."

THE SAVIOR OF THE WORLD

³⁹And many of the Samaritans of that city believed in Him ᵃbecause of the word of the woman who testified, "He told me all that I *ever* did." ⁴⁰So when the Samaritans had come to Him, they urged Him to stay with them; and He stayed there two days. ⁴¹And many more believed because of His own ᵃword.

⁴²Then they said to the woman, "Now we believe, not because of what you said, for ᵃwe ourselves have heard *Him* and we know that this is indeed ¹the Christ, the Savior of the world."

WELCOME AT GALILEE

⁴³Now after the two days He departed from there and went to Galilee. ⁴⁴For ᵃJesus Himself testified that a prophet has no honor in his own country. ⁴⁵So when He came to Galilee, the Galileans received Him, ᵃhaving seen all the things He did in Jerusalem at the feast; ᵇfor they also had gone to the feast.

A NOBLEMAN'S SON HEALED

⁴⁶So Jesus came again to Cana of Galilee ᵃwhere He had made the water wine. And there was a certain ¹nobleman whose son was sick at Capernaum. ⁴⁷When he heard that Jesus had come out of Judea into Galilee, he went to Him and implored Him to come down and heal his son, for he was at the point of death. ⁴⁸Then Jesus said to him, ᵃ"Unless you *people* see signs and wonders, you will by no means believe."

⁴⁹The nobleman said to Him, "Sir, come down before my child dies!"

⁵⁰Jesus said to him, "Go your way; your son lives." So the man believed the word that Jesus spoke to him, and he went his way. ⁵¹And as he was now going down, his servants met him and told *him*, saying, "Your son lives!"

⁵²Then he inquired of them the hour when he got better. And they said to him, "Yesterday at the seventh hour the fever left him." ⁵³So the father knew that *it was* at the same hour in which Jesus said to him, "Your son lives." And he himself believed, and his whole household.

54This again *is* the second sign Jesus did when He had come out of Judea into Galilee.

A MAN HEALED AT THE POOL OF BETHESDA

5 After ªthis there was a feast of the Jews, and Jesus ᵇwent up to Jerusalem. 2Now there is in Jerusalem ªby the Sheep *Gate* a pool, which is called in Hebrew, ¹Bethesda, having five porches. 3In these lay a great multitude of sick people, blind, lame, ¹paralyzed, 2waiting for the moving of the water. 4For an angel went down at a certain time into the pool and stirred up the water; then whoever stepped in first, after the stirring of the water, was made well of whatever disease he had. 5Now a certain man was there who had an infirmity thirty-eight years. 6When Jesus saw him lying there, and knew that he already had been *in that condition* a long time, He said to him, "Do you want to be made well?"

7The sick man answered Him, "Sir, I have no man to put me into the pool when the water is stirred up; but while I am coming, another steps down before me."

8Jesus said to him, ª"Rise, take up your bed and walk." 9And immediately the man was made well, took up his bed, and walked.

And ªthat day was the Sabbath. 10The Jews therefore said to him who was cured, "It is the Sabbath; ªit is not lawful for you to carry your bed."

11He answered them, "He who made

John 5:8–9

Commanding the Impossible. Jesus commanded this lame man to pick up his bed and walk. The man could have argued with Jesus, explaining why it was impossible for him to get up and walk. But instead he somehow found the faith to obey the impossible command from a perfect stranger.

When we will to obey what is for us an impossible command, at the moment we obey it, we will discover that God has given us the ability to obey it. If He commands us to do something, He will enable us to do it.

CHAPTER 5

1 ªDeut. 16:16
ᵇJohn 2:13

2 ªNeh. 3:1, 32; 12:39
¹NU *Bethzatha*

3 ¹ *withered*
2NU omits the rest of v. 3 and all of v. 4.

8 ªLuke 5:24

9 ªJohn 9:14

10 ªJer. 17:21, 22

13 ªLuke 13:14; 22:51

14 ªJohn 8:11

16 ªJohn 8:37; 10:39
¹NU omits *and sought to kill Him*

17 ª[John 9:4; 17:4]

18 ªJohn 7:1, 19
ᵇJohn 10:30

19 ªJohn 5:30; 6:38; 8:28; 12:49; 14:10

20 ªMatt. 3:17
ᵇ[Matt. 11:27]

21 ª[John 11:25]

22 ª[Acts 17:31]

---

me well said to me, 'Take up your bed and walk.'"

12Then they asked him, "Who is the Man who said to you, 'Take up your bed and walk'?" 13But the one who was ªhealed did not know who it was, for Jesus had withdrawn, a multitude being in *that* place. 14Afterward Jesus found him in the temple, and said to him, "See, you have been made well. ªSin no more, lest a worse thing come upon you."

15The man departed and told the Jews that it was Jesus who had made him well.

HONOR THE FATHER AND THE SON

16For this reason the Jews ªpersecuted Jesus, ¹and sought to kill Him, because He had done these things on the Sabbath. 17But Jesus answered them, ª"My Father has been working until now, and I have been working."

18Therefore the Jews ªsought all the more to kill Him, because He not only broke the Sabbath, but also said that God was His Father, ᵇmaking Himself equal with God. 19Then Jesus answered and said to them, "Most assuredly, I say to you, ªthe Son can do nothing of Himself, but what He sees the Father do; for whatever He does, the Son also does in like manner. 20For ªthe Father loves the Son, and ᵇshows Him all things that He Himself does; and He will show Him greater works than these, that you may marvel. 21For as the Father raises the dead and gives life to *them,* ªeven so the Son gives life to whom He will. 22For the Father judges no one, but ªhas committed all judgment to the Son, 23that all should honor the Son just as they honor the Father.

John 5:18

Equality with God. The Jews understood Jesus much better than some of those today who call themselves Christians but then deny the deity of Christ. They understood what Jesus was declaring—that as the Son of God, He was equal with God. They caught on in a hurry, and it upset them greatly that He was claiming equality with God.

Anyone who makes Jesus less than equal with God doesn't understand Jesus at all.

aHe who does not honor the Son does not honor the Father who sent Him.

LIFE AND JUDGMENT ARE THROUGH THE SON

24 "Most assuredly, I say to you, ahe who hears My word and believes in Him who sent Me has everlasting life, and shall not come into judgment, bbut has passed from death into life. 25 Most assuredly, I say to you, the hour is coming, and now is, when athe dead will hear the voice of the Son of God; and those who hear will live. 26 For aas the Father has life in Himself, so He has granted the Son to have blife in Himself, 27 and ahas given Him authority to execute judgment also, bbecause He is the Son of Man. 28 Do not marvel at this; for the hour is coming in which all who are in the graves will ahear His voice 29 aand come forth—bthose who have done good, to the resurrection of life, and those who have done evil, to the resurrection of condemnation. 30 aI can of Myself do nothing. As I hear, I judge; and My judgment is righteous, because bI do not seek My own will but the will of the Father who sent Me.

THE FOURFOLD WITNESS

31 a"If I bear witness of Myself, My witness is not 1true. 32 aThere is another who bears witness of Me, and I know that the witness which He witnesses of Me is true. 33 You have sent to John, aand he has borne witness to the truth. 34 Yet I do not receive testimony from man, but I say these things that you may be saved. 35 He was the burning and ashining lamp, and byou were willing for a time to rejoice in his light. 36 But aI have a greater witness than John's; for bthe works which the Father has given Me to finish—the very cworks that I do—bear witness of Me, that the Father has sent Me. 37 And the Father Himself, who sent Me, ahas testified of Me. You have neither heard His voice at any time, bnor seen His form. 38 But you do not have His word abiding in you, because whom He sent, Him you do not believe. 39 aYou search the Scriptures, for in them you think you have eternal life; and bthese are they which testify of Me. 40 aBut you are not willing to come to Me that you may have life.

41 a"I do not receive honor from men. 42 But I know you, that you do not have the love of God in you. 43 I have come in My Father's name, and you do not

Cross references

23 a 1 John 2:23
24 a John 3:16, 18; 6:47
b [1 John 3:14]
25 a [Col. 2:13]
26 a Ps. 36:9
b 1 Cor. 15:45
27 a [Acts 10:42; 17:31]
b Dan. 7:13
28 a [1 Thess. 4:15–17]
29 a Is. 26:19
b Dan. 12:2
30 a John 5:19
b Matt. 26:39
31 a John 8:14
1 valid as testimony
32 a [Matt. 3:17]
33 a [John 1:15, 19, 27, 32]
35 a 2 Pet. 1:19
b Mark 6:20
36 a 1 John 5:9
b John 3:2; 10:25; 17:4
c John 9:16; 10:38
37 a Matt. 3:17
b 1 John 4:12
39 a Is. 8:20; 34:16
b Luke 24:27
40 a [John 1:11; 3:19]
41 a 1 Thess. 2:6
44 a John 12:43
b [Rom. 2:29]
45 a Rom. 2:12
46 a Deut. 18:15, 18
47 a Luke 16:29, 31

CHAPTER 6

1 a Mark 6:32
b John 6:23; 21:1
2 a Matt. 4:23; 8:16; 9:35; 14:36; 15:30; 19:2
1 sick
4 a Deut. 16:1
5 a Matt. 14:14
b John 1:43
7 a Num. 11:21, 22
8 a John 1:40

John 5:39–40

You Search the Scriptures. What a tragedy when someone searches the Scriptures, studying the Bible and theology, and yet they miss the One it is all about!

The Jews had studied hard to learn the Old Testament. But they couldn't even see that it was talking about Jesus. He fulfilled over three hundred prophecies from the Scriptures and shed light on so much of the Word through His teaching, and yet the Jews chose to reject Him ("you are not willing to come to Me") even though He offered them life.

How sad when one knows the Book without knowing the Author!

---

receive Me; if another comes in his own name, him you will receive. 44 aHow can you believe, who receive honor from one another, and do not seek bthe honor that comes from the only God? 45 Do not think that I shall accuse you to the Father; athere is one who accuses you—Moses, in whom you trust. 46 For if you believed Moses, you would believe Me; afor he wrote about Me. 47 But if you ado not believe his writings, how will you believe My words?"

FEEDING THE FIVE THOUSAND

6 After athese things Jesus went over the Sea of Galilee, which is the Sea of bTiberias. 2 Then a great multitude followed Him, because they saw His signs which He performed on those who were adiseased.1 3 And Jesus went up on the mountain, and there He sat with His disciples.

4 aNow the Passover, a feast of the Jews, was near. 5 aThen Jesus lifted up His eyes, and seeing a great multitude coming toward Him, He said to bPhilip, "Where shall we buy bread, that these may eat?" 6 But this He said to test him, for He Himself knew what He would do.

7 Philip answered Him, a"Two hundred denarii worth of bread is not sufficient for them, that every one of them may have a little."

8 One of His disciples, aAndrew,

Simon Peter's brother, said to Him, [9] "There is a lad here who has five barley loaves and two small fish, [a]but what are they among so many?"

[10]Then Jesus said, "Make the people sit down." Now there was much grass in the place. So the men sat down, in number about five thousand. [11]And Jesus took the loaves, and when He had given thanks He distributed *them* [1]to the disciples, and the disciples to those sitting down; and likewise of the fish, as much as they wanted. [12]So when they were filled, He said to His disciples, "Gather up the fragments that remain, so that nothing is lost." [13]Therefore they gathered *them* up, and filled twelve baskets with the fragments of the five barley loaves which were left over by those who had eaten. [14]Then those men, when they had seen the sign that Jesus did, said, "This is truly [a]the Prophet who is to come into the world."

JESUS WALKS ON THE SEA

[15]Therefore when Jesus perceived that they were about to come and take Him by force to make Him [a]king, He departed again to the mountain by Himself alone.

John 6:15

Forcible Coronation. After Jesus fed five thousand people with five loaves and two fish, the people were ecstatic, and wanted to forcibly make Him king. But He resisted their desires and departed.

These people wanted to proclaim Jesus as the Messiah, which He was, but they were doing it on the basis of His miracle and their filled stomachs. He had met their physical needs, and that was all they understood. But they didn't yet understand their spiritual needs and that their spiritual needs would necessitate His death before the glory could come.

[16][a]Now when evening came, His disciples went down to the sea, [17]got into the boat, and went over the sea toward Capernaum. And it was already dark, and Jesus had not come to them. [18]Then the sea arose because a great wind was blowing. [19]So when they had rowed

about [1]three or four miles, they saw Jesus walking on the sea and drawing near the boat; and they were [a]afraid. [20]But He said to them, [a]"It is I; do not be afraid." [21]Then they willingly received Him into the boat, and immediately the boat was at the land where they were going.

THE BREAD FROM HEAVEN

[22]On the following day, when the people who were standing on the other side of the sea saw that there was no other boat there, except [1]that one [2]which His disciples had entered, and that Jesus had not entered the boat with His disciples, but His disciples had gone away alone— [23]however, other boats came from Tiberias, near the place where they ate bread after the Lord had given thanks— [24]when the people therefore saw that Jesus was not there, nor His disciples, they also got into boats and came to Capernaum, [a]seeking Jesus. [25]And when they found Him on the other side of the sea, they said to Him, "Rabbi, when did You come here?"

[26]Jesus answered them and said, "Most assuredly, I say to you, you seek Me, not because you saw the signs, but because you ate of the loaves and were filled. [27][a]Do not labor for the food which perishes, but [b]for the food which endures to everlasting life, which the Son of Man will give you, [c]because God the Father has set His seal on Him."

[28]Then they said to Him, "What shall we do, that we may work the works of God?"

[29]Jesus answered and said to them, [a]"This is the work of God, that you believe in Him whom He sent."

[30]Therefore they said to Him, [a]"What sign will You perform then, that we may see it and believe You? What work will You do? [31][a]Our fathers ate the manna in the desert; as it is written, [b]'He gave them bread from heaven to eat.' "

[32]Then Jesus said to them, "Most assuredly, I say to you, Moses did not give you the bread from heaven, but [a]My Father gives you the true bread from heaven. [33]For the bread of God is He who comes down from heaven and gives life to the world."

[34][a]Then they said to Him, "Lord, give us this bread always."

[35]And Jesus said to them, [a]"I am the bread of life. [b]He who comes to Me shall never hunger, and he who believes

Cross references (center column)

9 [a] 2 Kin. 4:43

11 [1] NU omits *to the disciples, and the disciples*

14 [a] Gen. 49:10

15 [a] [John 18:36]

16 [a] Matt. 14:23

19 [a] Matt. 17:6
[1] Lit. *25 or 30 stadia*

20 [a] Is. 43:1, 2

22 [1] NU omits *that*
[2] NU omits *which His disciples had entered*

24 [a] Luke 4:42

27 [a] Matt. 6:19
[b] John 4:14
[c] Acts 2:22

29 [a] [1 John 3:23]

30 [a] Matt. 12:38; 16:1

31 [a] Ex. 16:15
[b] Ex. 16:4, 15; Neh. 9:15; Ps. 78:24

32 [a] John 3:13, 16

34 [a] John 4:15

35 [a] John 6:48, 58
[b] John 4:14; 7:37

in Me shall never cthirst. 36aBut I said to you that you have seen Me and yet bdo not believe. 37aAll that the Father gives Me will come to Me, and bthe one who comes to Me I will lby no means cast out. 38For I have come down from heaven, anot to do My own will, bbut the will of Him who sent Me. 39This is the will of the Father who sent Me, athat of all He has given Me I should lose nothing, but should raise it up at the last day. 40And this is the will of Him who sent Me, athat everyone who sees the Son and believes in Him may have everlasting life; and I will raise him up at the last day."

John 6:31–35

I AM THE BREAD OF LIFE

Jesus contrasted Himself with the manna that came down from heaven in the time of Moses.

The manna provided temporary miraculous sustenance for the people, as Jesus had just done by feeding five thousand people. But physical sustenance is not what people ultimately need. If you eat bread today, you will need it again tomorrow. Jesus, as the Bread of Life, would fill their spiritual hunger eternally.

When God revealed Himself to Moses, He identified Himself as the "I AM." Now Jesus said, "I AM the bread of life."

REJECTED BY HIS OWN

41The Jews then lcomplained about Him, because He said, "I am the bread which came down from heaven." 42And they said, a"Is not this Jesus, the son of Joseph, whose father and mother we know? How is it then that He says, 'I have come down from heaven'?"

43Jesus therefore answered and said to them, l"Do not murmur among yourselves. 44aNo one can come to Me unless the Father who sent Me bdraws him; and I will raise him up at the last day. 45It is written in the prophets, a'And they shall all be taught by God.'

Center column references:
35 cIs. 55:1, 2
36 a John 6:26, 64; 15:24
b John 10:26
37 a John 6:45
b 2Tim. 2:19
l certainly not
38 a Matt. 26:39
b John 4:34
39 a John 10:28; 17:12; 18:9
40 a John 3:15, 16; 4:14; 6:27, 47, 54
41 l grumbled
42 a Matt. 13:55
43 l Stop grumbling
44 a Song 1:4
b [Phil. 1:29; 2:12, 13]
45 a Is. 54:13
b John 6:37
l M hears and has learned
46 a John 1:18
b Matt. 11:27
47 a [John 3:16, 18]
l NU omits in Me
48 a John 6:33, 35
49 a John 6:31, 58
50 a John 6:51, 58
51 a John 3:13
b Heb. 10:5
52 a John 7:43; 9:16; 10:19
53 a Matt. 26:26
54 a John 4:14; 6:27, 40
55 l NU true food
2 NU true drink
56 a [1John 3:24; 4:15, 16]
58 a John 6:49–51
b Ex. 16:14–35
60 a John 6:66
l difficult
61 l grumbled
2 make you stumble
62 a Acts 1:9; 2:32, 33
63 a 2Cor. 3:6
b John 3:6
c [John 6:68; 14:24]
64 a John 6:36
b John 2:24, 25; 13:11
65 a John 6:37, 44, 45
66 a Luke 9:62
l Or away; lit. to the back

bTherefore everyone who lhas heard and learned from the Father comes to Me. 46aNot that anyone has seen the Father, bexcept He who is from God; He has seen the Father. 47Most assuredly, I say to you, ahe who believes lin Me has everlasting life. 48aI am the bread of life. 49aYour fathers ate the manna in the wilderness, and are dead. 50aThis is the bread which comes down from heaven, that one may eat of it and not die. 51I am the living bread awhich came down from heaven. If anyone eats of this bread, he will live forever; and bthe bread that I shall give is My flesh, which I shall give for the life of the world."

52The Jews therefore aquarreled among themselves, saying, "How can this Man give us His flesh to eat?"

53Then Jesus said to them, "Most assuredly, I say to you, unless ayou eat the flesh of the Son of Man and drink His blood, you have no life in you. 54aWhoever eats My flesh and drinks My blood has eternal life, and I will raise him up at the last day. 55For My flesh is lfood indeed, and My blood is 2drink indeed. 56He who eats My flesh and drinks My blood aabides in Me, and I in him. 57As the living Father sent Me, and I live because of the Father, so he who feeds on Me will live because of Me. 58aThis is the bread which came down from heaven—not bas your fathers ate the manna, and are dead. He who eats this bread will live forever."

59These things He said in the synagogue as He taught in Capernaum.

MANY DISCIPLES TURN AWAY

60aTherefore many of His disciples, when they heard this, said, "This is a lhard saying; who can understand it?" 61When Jesus knew in Himself that His disciples lcomplained about this, He said to them, "Does this 2offend you? 62aWhat then if you should see the Son of Man ascend where He was before? 63aIt is the Spirit who gives life; the bflesh profits nothing. The cwords that I speak to you are spirit, and they are life. 64But athere are some of you who do not believe." For bJesus knew from the beginning who they were who did not believe, and who would betray Him. 65And He said, "Therefore aI have said to you that no one can come to Me unless it has been granted to him by My Father."

66aFrom that time many of His disciples went lback and walked with Him

John 6:66–69

WHERE ELSE?

Many of Jesus' disciples deserted Him, being confused by His teaching. When He started talking about eating His body and drinking His blood, they decided they had heard enough. It was just too bizarre. But He then turned to those who were left and asked them if they were leaving too. Peter said, "Lord, to whom shall we go? You have the words of eternal life." They didn't really understand everything Jesus was saying; and it sounded weird to them too. But they had committed to Him and knew of no better options.

Sometimes we don't understand everything God is saying and doing. We have problems and difficulties. But where else can we go? We have already learned that the world has nothing for us. It can't solve our problems. There is really nothing to go back to. So we trust the One who has the words of eternal life.

no more. ⁶⁷Then Jesus said to the twelve, "Do you also want to go away?" ⁶⁸But Simon Peter answered Him, "Lord, to whom shall we go? You have ᵃthe words of eternal life. ⁶⁹ᵃAlso we have come to believe and know that You are the ¹Christ, the Son of the living God."

⁷⁰Jesus answered them, ᵃ"Did I not choose you, the twelve, ᵇand one of you is a devil?" ⁷¹He spoke of ᵃJudas Iscariot, *the son* of Simon, for it was he who would ᵇbetray Him, being one of the twelve.

JESUS' BROTHERS DISBELIEVE

7 After these things Jesus walked in Galilee; for He did not want to walk in Judea, ᵃbecause the ¹Jews sought to kill Him. ²ᵃNow the Jews' Feast of Tabernacles was at hand. ³ᵃHis brothers therefore said to Him, "Depart from here and go into Judea, that Your disciples also may see the works that You are doing. ⁴For no one does anything in

secret while he himself seeks to be known openly. If You do these things, show Yourself to the world." ⁵For ᵃeven His ᵇbrothers did not believe in Him.

⁶Then Jesus said to them, ᵃ"My time has not yet come, but your time is always ready. ⁷ᵃThe world cannot hate you, but it hates Me ᵇbecause I testify of it that its works are evil. ⁸You go up to this feast. I am not ¹yet going up to this feast, ᵃfor My time has not yet fully come." ⁹When He had said these things to them, He remained in Galilee.

John 7:7

Why the World Hates Jesus.

Jesus said that the world hated Him "because I testify of it that its works are evil."

Things haven't changed. The world still hates Jesus and for the same reason. People don't like to be told they are wrong. They don't want to be called evil. They want their sin to be accepted. They want you to be tolerant of their evil even though it is their evil that is destroying them.

Jesus is trying to rescue them with the truth because He loves them, but they hate Him for it.

THE HEAVENLY SCHOLAR

¹⁰But when His brothers had gone up, then He also went up to the feast, not openly, but as it were in secret. ¹¹Then ᵃthe Jews sought Him at the feast, and said, "Where is He?" ¹²And ᵃthere was much complaining among the people concerning Him. ᵇSome said, "He is good"; others said, "No, on the contrary, He deceives the people." ¹³However, no one spoke openly of Him ᵃfor fear of the Jews.

¹⁴Now about the middle of the feast Jesus went up into the temple and ᵃtaught. ¹⁵ᵃAnd the Jews marveled, saying, "How does this Man know letters, having never studied?"

¹⁶¹Jesus answered them and said, ᵃ"My doctrine is not Mine, but His who sent Me. ¹⁷ᵃIf anyone wills to do His will, he shall know concerning the doctrine, whether it is from God or *whether* I speak on My own *authority*. ¹⁸ᵃHe who speaks from himself seeks

Cross-references

68 ᵃActs 5:20

69 ᵃLuke 9:20
¹NU *Holy One of God.*

70 ᵃLuke 6:13
ᵇ[John 13:27]

71 ᵃJohn 12:4; 13:2, 26
ᵇMatt. 26:14–16

CHAPTER 7

1 ᵃJohn 5:18; 7:19, 25; 8:37, 40
¹The ruling authorities

2 ᵃLev. 23:34

3 ᵃMatt. 12:46

5 ᵃPs. 69:8
ᵇMark 3:21

6 ᵃJohn 2:4; 8:20

7 ᵃ[John 15:19]
ᵇJohn 3:19

8 ᵃJohn 8:20
¹NU omits *yet*

11 ᵃJohn 11:56

12 ᵃJohn 9:16; 10:19
ᵇLuke 7:16

13 ᵃ[John 9:22; 12:42; 19:38]

14 ᵃMark 6:34

15 ᵃMatt. 13:54

16 ᵃJohn 3:11
¹NU, M *So Jesus*

17 ᵃJohn 3:21; 8:43

18 ᵃJohn 5:41

his own glory; but He who [b]seeks the glory of the One who sent Him is true, and [c]no unrighteousness is in Him. [19a]Did not Moses give you the law, yet none of you keeps the law? [b]Why do you seek to kill Me?"

[20]The people answered and said, [a]"You have a demon. Who is seeking to kill You?"

[21]Jesus answered and said to them, "I did one work, and you all marvel. [22a]Moses therefore gave you circumcision (not that it is from Moses, [b]but from the fathers), and you circumcise a man on the Sabbath. [23]If a man receives circumcision on the Sabbath, so that the law of Moses should not be broken, are you angry with Me because [a]I made a man completely well on the Sabbath? [24a]Do not judge according to appearance, but judge with righteous judgment."

COULD THIS BE THE CHRIST?

[25]Now some of them from Jerusalem said, "Is this not He whom they seek to [a]kill? [26]But look! He speaks boldly, and they say nothing to Him. [a]Do the rulers know indeed that this is [1]truly the Christ? [27a]However, we know where this Man is from; but when the Christ comes, no one knows where He is from."

[28]Then Jesus cried out, as He taught in the temple, saying, [a]"You both know Me, and you know where I am from; and [b]I have not come of Myself, but He who sent Me [c]is true, [d]whom you do not know. [29] [1]But [a]I know Him, for I am from Him, and He sent Me."

[30]Therefore [a]they sought to take Him; but [b]no one laid a hand on Him, because His hour had not yet come. [31]And [a]many of the people believed in

Him, and said, "When the Christ comes, will He do more signs than these which this *Man* has done?"

JESUS AND THE RELIGIOUS LEADERS

[32]The Pharisees heard the crowd murmuring these things concerning Him, and the Pharisees and the chief priests sent officers to take Him. [33]Then Jesus said [1]to them, [a]"I shall be with you a little while longer, and *then* I [b]go to Him who sent Me. [34]You [a]will seek Me and not find *Me*, and where I am you [b]cannot come."

[35]Then the Jews said among themselves, "Where does He intend to go that we shall not find Him? Does He intend to go to [a]the Dispersion among the Greeks and teach the Greeks? [36]What is this thing that He said, 'You will seek Me and not find Me, and where I am you cannot come'?"

THE PROMISE OF THE HOLY SPIRIT

[37a]On the last day, that great *day* of the feast, Jesus stood and cried out, saying, [b]"If anyone thirsts, let him come to Me and drink. [38a]He who believes in Me, as the Scripture has said, [b]out of his heart will flow rivers of living water." [39a]But this He spoke concerning the Spirit, whom those [1]believing in Him would receive; for the [2]Holy Spirit was not yet *given*, because Jesus was not yet [b]glorified.

WHO IS HE?

[40]Therefore [1]many from the crowd, when they heard this saying, said, "Truly this is [a]the Prophet." [41]Others said, "This is [a]the Christ."

---

18 [b] John 8:50 [c] [2 Cor. 5:21]
19 [a] Deut. 33:4 [b] Matt. 12:14
20 [a] John 8:48, 52
22 [a] Lev. 12:3 [b] Gen. 17:9–14
23 [a] John 5:8, 9, 16
24 [a] Prov. 24:23
25 [a] Matt. 21:38; 26:4
26 [a] John 7:48 [1] NU omits *truly*
27 [a] Luke 4:22
28 [a] John 8:14 [b] John 5:43 [c] Rom. 3:4 [d] John 1:18; 8:55
29 [a] Matt. 11:27 [1] NU, M omit *But*
30 [a] Mark 11:18 [b] John 7:32, 44; 8:20; 10:39
31 [a] Matt. 12:23
33 [a] John 13:33 [b] [1 Pet. 3:22] [1] NU, M omit *to them*
34 [a] Hos. 5:6 [b] [Matt. 5:20]
35 [a] James 1:1
37 [a] Lev. 23:36 [b] [Is. 55:1]
38 [a] Deut. 18:15 [b] Is. 12:3; 43:20; 44:3; 55:1
39 [a] Is. 44:3 [b] John 12:16; 13:31; 17:5 [1] NU *who believed* [2] NU omits *Holy*
40 [a] Deut. 18:15, 18 [1] NU *some* **41** [a] John 4:42; 6:69

IF ANYONE THIRSTS
John 7:37–39

Everyone is thirsting for God. We all have a huge spiritual need that can only be filled by God. We know we are thirsty, but we try to satisfy that thirst with physical things or with emotional experiences. But all of these things offer only temporary relief, as the excitement of the new toys or the emotional experiences give way to that nagging thirst that we all have deep down inside. So we pursue an endless quest of unsatisfying acquisitions, supposing that we will experience satisfaction eventually, or we give up on ultimate satisfaction and settle for temporary relief that comes in spurts.

But Jesus announced that He is the One who can satisfy the thirst that is in the heart of every individual. And He will do it by overflowing our hearts with the Spirit. He offers complete satisfaction. For the one who comes to Him, He promises that out of that person's life will gush forth torrents of living water.

If you have not experienced this overflowing, and if you are trying to fill your need with other things, come to Jesus. He is the only One who can satisfy the deepest longings of your heart.

But some said, "Will the Christ come out of Galilee? 42 [a]Has not the Scripture said that the Christ comes from the seed of David and from the town of Bethlehem, [b]where David was?" 43So [a]there was a division among the people because of Him. 44Now [a]some of them wanted to take Him, but no one laid hands on Him.

REJECTED BY THE AUTHORITIES

45Then the officers came to the chief priests and Pharisees, who said to them, "Why have you not brought Him?"

46The officers answered, [a]"No man ever spoke like this Man!"

47Then the Pharisees answered them, "Are you also deceived? 48Have any of the rulers or the Pharisees believed in Him? 49But this crowd that does not know the law is accursed."

John 7:49

Spiritual Elitism. As so many people were coming to Jesus and following Him, the religious leaders were trying to figure it all out. In doing so, they discounted the crowds who followed Jesus because they were seen as being unlearned and unsophisticated. "This crowd that does not know the law is accursed." They had a religious hierarchy, and their spiritual snobbery kept them from seeing the truth.

Knowing God and understanding the things of God doesn't require a seminary education. All you need to know is Jesus. He is the Mediator between God and man (1 Tim. 2:5).

50Nicodemus [a](he who came to [1]Jesus [2]by night, being one of them) said to them, 51 [a]"Does our law judge a man before it hears him and knows what he is doing?"

52They answered and said to him, "Are you also from Galilee? Search and look, for [a]no prophet [1]has arisen out of Galilee."

AN ADULTERESS FACES THE LIGHT OF THE WORLD

53 [1]And everyone went to his *own* house.

---

42 [a]Mic. 5:2
[b]1Sam. 16:1, 4
43 [a]John 7:12
44 [a]John 7:30
46 [a]Luke 4:22
50 [a]John 3:1, 2;
19:39
[1]Lit. *Him*
[2]NU *before*
51 [a]Deut. 1:16,
17; 19:15
52 [a][Is. 9:1, 2]
[1]NU *is to rise*
53 [1]NU brackets 7:53 through 8:11 as not in the original text. They are present in over 900 mss. of John.

CHAPTER 8
2 [a]John 8:20;
18:20
[1]M *very early*
4 [a]Ex. 20:14
[1]M *we found this woman*
5 [a]Lev. 20:10
[1]M *in our law Moses commanded*
[2]NU, M *to stone such*
[3]M adds *about her*
6 [a]Matt. 22:15
[1]NU, M omit *as though He did not hear*
7 [a]Deut. 17:7
[1]M *He looked up*
9 [a]Rom. 2:22
[1]NU, M omit *being convicted by their conscience*
10 [1]NU omits *and saw no one but the woman;* M *He saw her and said,*
[2]NU, M *omit of yours*
11 [a][John 3:17]
[b][John 5:14]
[1]NU, M add *from now on*
12 [a]John 1:4; 9:5; 12:35
[b]1Thess. 5:5
13 [a]John 5:31
[1]*valid* as testimony
14 [a]John 7:28; 9:29
15 [a]John 7:24
[b][John 3:17; 12:47; 18:36]
16 [a]John 16:32
17 [a]Deut. 17:6; 19:15
18 [a]John 5:37

8

But Jesus went to the Mount of Olives.

2Now [1]early in the morning He came again into the temple, and all the people came to Him; and He sat down and [a]taught them. 3Then the scribes and Pharisees brought to Him a woman caught in adultery. And when they had set her in the midst, 4they said to Him, "Teacher, [1]this woman was caught in [a]adultery, in the very act. 5 [a]Now [1]Moses, in the law, commanded us [2]that such should be stoned. But what do You [3]say?" 6This they said, testing Him, that they [a]might have *something* of which to accuse Him. But Jesus stooped down and wrote on the ground with *His* finger, [1]as though He did not hear.

7So when they continued asking Him, He [1]raised Himself up and said to them, [a]"He who is without sin among you, let him throw a stone at her first." 8And again He stooped down and wrote on the ground. 9Then those who heard *it*, [a]being[1] convicted by *their* conscience, went out one by one, beginning with the oldest *even* to the last. And Jesus was left alone, and the woman standing in the midst. 10When Jesus had raised Himself up [1]and saw no one but the woman, He said to her, "Woman, where are those accusers [2]of yours? Has no one condemned you?"

11She said, "No one, Lord."

And Jesus said to her, [a]"Neither do I condemn you; go [1]and [b]sin no more."

12Then Jesus spoke to them again, saying, [a]"I am the light of the world. He who [b]follows Me shall not walk in darkness, but have the light of life."

JESUS DEFENDS HIS SELF-WITNESS

13The Pharisees therefore said to Him, [a]"You bear witness of Yourself; Your witness is not [1]true."

14Jesus answered and said to them, "Even if I bear witness of Myself, My witness is true, for I know where I came from and where I am going; but [a]you do not know where I come from and where I am going. 15 [a]You judge according to the flesh; [b]I judge no one. 16And yet if I do judge, My judgment is true; for [a]I am not alone, but I *am* with the Father who sent Me. 17 [a]It is also written in your law that the testimony of two men is true. 18I am One who bears witness of Myself, and [a]the Father who sent Me bears witness of Me."

19Then they said to Him, "Where is Your Father?"

Jesus answered, a"You know neither Me nor My Father. bIf you had known Me, you would have known My Father also."

20These words Jesus spoke in athe treasury, as He taught in the temple; and bno one laid hands on Him, for cHis hour had not yet come.

JESUS PREDICTS HIS DEPARTURE

21Then Jesus said to them again, "I am going away, and ayou will seek Me, and bwill die in your sin. Where I go you cannot come."

22So the Jews said, "Will He kill Himself, because He says, 'Where I go you cannot come'?"

23And He said to them, a"You are from beneath; I am from above. bYou are of this world; I am not of this world. 24aTherefore I said to you that you will die in your sins; bfor if you do not believe that I am He, you will die in your sins."

25Then they said to Him, "Who are You?"

And Jesus said to them, "Just what I ahave been saying to you from the beginning. 26I have many things to say and to judge concerning you, but aHe who sent Me is true; and bI speak to the world those things which I heard from Him."

27They did not understand that He spoke to them of the Father. 28Then Jesus said to them, "When you alift1 up the Son of Man, bthen you will know that I am He, and cthat I do nothing of Myself; but das My Father taught Me, I speak these things. 29And aHe who sent Me is with Me. bThe Father has not

19 a John 16:3
b John 14:7

20 a Mark 12:41, 43
b John 2:4; 7:30
c John 7:8

21 a John 7:34; 13:33
b John 8:24

23 a John 3:31
b 1 John 4:5

24 a John 8:21
b [Mark 16:16]

25 a John 4:26

26 a John 7:28
b John 3:32; 15:15

28 a John 3:14; 12:32; 19:18
b [Rom. 1:4]
c John 5:19, 30
d John 3:11
1 Crucify

29 a John 14:10
b John 8:16; 16:32
c John 4:34; 5:30; 6:38

30 a John 7:31; 10:42; 11:45

left Me alone, cfor I always do those things that please Him." 30As He spoke these words, amany believed in Him.

John 8:24

THE ONLY WAY

Jesus made one of His most radical statements here. "If you do not believe that I am He, you will die in your sins."

You may notice in your English Bible that the word "He" appears in italics, as it isn't in the original but was added by the translators. The verse literally says, "If you do not believe that I am, you will die in your sins." Of course, "I AM" is the personal name for God in the Hebrew. Here Jesus was saying that every man's eternal destiny is determined by whether or not they believe that Jesus is the great I AM. That He is Yahweh or Jehovah.

Now that sounds pretty narrow-minded, but it is true. Jesus said, "Narrow is the gate and difficult is the way which leads to life, and there are few who find it" (Matt. 7:14). The way to avoiding dying in your sins? Believe that Jesus is God. That is the only way.

I DON'T CONDEMN YOU
John 8:3–11

The scribes and Pharisees brought to Jesus a woman who had been caught in the act of adultery. They were trying to trap Him by asking Him what to do. If He responded with grace and mercy, as they expected, they would show that He was in disagreement with the Old Testament Law. But if He said she should be stoned, as the Law dictated, He would be in violation of Roman law, which had taken away from the Jews the right of capital punishment.

Instead, Jesus turned the whole thing around by shining a light on their own unrighteousness. "He who is without sin among you, let him throw a stone at her first." Then, as He wrote silently in the dirt, perhaps writing each of their personal sins, they each left until no one remained except the woman and Jesus. He was the only One there who was without sin and who had the right to condemn the woman. But He chose to forgive her and set her free. He had already explained to Nicodemus, "For God did not send His Son into the world to condemn the world, but that the world through Him might be saved" (John 3:17).

Jesus looked at this immoral woman with compassion. She was one for whom He would die. And so are you.

THE TRUTH SHALL MAKE YOU FREE

31Then Jesus said to those Jews who believed Him, "If you ᵃabide in My word, you are My disciples indeed. 32And you shall know the ᵃtruth, and ᵇthe truth shall make you free."

33They answered Him, ᵃ"We are Abraham's descendants, and have never been in bondage to anyone. How *can* You say, 'You will be made free'?"

34Jesus answered them, "Most assuredly, I say to you, ᵃwhoever commits sin is a slave of sin. 35And ᵃa slave does not abide in the house forever, *but* a son abides forever. 36ᵃTherefore if the Son makes you free, you shall be free indeed.

ABRAHAM'S SEED AND SATAN'S

37"I know that you are Abraham's descendants, but ᵃyou seek to kill Me, because My word has no place in you. 38ᵃI speak what I have seen with My Father, and you do what you have ¹seen with your father."

39They answered and said to Him, ᵃ"Abraham is our father."

Jesus said to them, ᵇ"If you were Abraham's children, you would do the works of Abraham. 40ᵃBut now you seek to kill Me, a Man who has told you the truth ᵇwhich I heard from God. Abraham did not do this. 41You do the deeds of your father."

Then they said to Him, "We were not born of fornication; ᵃwe have one Father—God."

42Jesus said to them, ᵃ"If God were your Father, you would love Me, for ᵇI proceeded forth and came from God; ᶜnor have I come of Myself, but He sent Me. 43ᵃWhy do you not understand My speech? Because you are not able to listen to My word. 44ᵃYou are of *your* father the devil, and the ᵇdesires of your father you want to ᶜdo. He was a murderer from the beginning, and ᵈdoes not stand in the truth, because there is no truth in him. When he speaks a lie, he speaks from his own *resources*, for he is a liar and the father of it. 45But because I tell the truth, you do not believe Me. 46Which of you convicts Me of sin? And if I tell the truth, why do you not believe Me? 47ᵃHe who is of God hears God's words; therefore you do not hear, because you are not of God."

BEFORE ABRAHAM WAS, I AM

48Then the Jews answered and said to Him, "Do we not say rightly that You are a Samaritan and ᵃhave a demon?"

49Jesus answered, "I do not have a demon; but I honor My Father, and ᵃyou dishonor Me. 50And ᵃI do not seek My *own* glory; there is One who seeks and judges. 51Most assuredly, I say to you, ᵃif anyone keeps My word he shall never see death."

52Then the Jews said to Him, "Now we know that You ᵃhave a demon! ᵇAbraham is dead, and the prophets; and You say, 'If anyone keeps My word he shall never taste death.' 53Are You greater than our father Abraham, who is dead? And the prophets are dead. ᵃWho do You make Yourself out to be?"

54Jesus answered, ᵃ"If I honor Myself, My honor is nothing. ᵇIt is My Father who honors Me, of whom you say that He is ¹your God. 55Yet ᵃyou have not known Him, but I know Him. And if I say, 'I do not know Him,' I shall be a liar like you; but I do know Him and ᵇkeep His word. 56Your father

Cross references

31 ᵃ[John 14:15, 23]
32 ᵃ[John 1:14, 17; 14:6] ᵇ[Rom. 6:14, 18, 22]
33 ᵃ[Matt. 3:9]
34 ᵃ2 Pet. 2:19
35 ᵃGal. 4:30
36 ᵃGal. 5:1
37 ᵃJohn 7:19
38 ᵃ[John 3:32; 5:19, 30; 14:10, 24] ¹NU *heard from*
39 ᵃMatt. 3:9 ᵇ[Rom. 2:28]
40 ᵃJohn 8:37 ᵇJohn 8:26
41 ᵃIs. 63:16
42 ᵃ1 John 5:1 ᵇJohn 16:27; 17:8, 25 ᶜGal. 4:4
43 ᵃ[John 7:17]
44 ᵃMatt. 13:38 ᵇ1 John 2:16, 17 ᶜ[1 John 3:8–10, 15] ᵈ[Jude 6]
47 ᵃ1 John 4:6
48 ᵃJohn 7:20; 10:20
49 ᵃJohn 5:41
50 ᵃJohn 5:41; 7:18
51 ᵃJohn 5:24; 11:26
52 ᵃJohn 7:20; 10:20 ᵇZech. 1:5
53 ᵃJohn 10:33; 19:7
54 ᵃJohn 5:31, 32 ᵇActs 3:13 ¹NU, M *our*
55 ᵃJohn 7:28, 29 ᵇ[John 15:10]

John 8:56–58

WHAT ABRAHAM SAW

These Jewish leaders revered Abraham and were incensed that Jesus claimed that Abraham rejoiced to see His day. But Abraham had met Jesus personally, as he experienced several theophanies, or appearances of Christ in the Old Testament.

The first was when the Angel of the Lord appeared to him in Genesis 17 to announce the coming birth of Isaac. Then again, in Genesis 18, in announcing the coming destruction of Sodom. It is also quite likely that the appearance of Melchizedek in Genesis 14 was actually Jesus Himself.

But Jesus took it even further than just saying that Abraham saw Him. He told the leaders, "Before Abraham was, I AM." That is when they really lost it. He was claiming to be the I AM, Yahweh—the God of Abraham, Isaac, and Jacob. Outrageous! But true.

Abraham arejoiced to see My day, band he saw *it* and was glad."

57Then the Jews said to Him, "You are not yet fifty years old, and have You seen Abraham?"

58Jesus said to them, "Most assuredly, I say to you, abefore Abraham was, bI AM."

59Then athey took up stones to throw at Him; but Jesus hid Himself and went out of the temple, bgoing*1* through the midst of them, and so passed by.

A MAN BORN BLIND RECEIVES SIGHT

9 Now as *Jesus* passed by, He saw a man who was blind from birth. 2And His disciples asked Him, saying, "Rabbi, awho sinned, this man or his parents, that he was born blind?"

3Jesus answered, "Neither this man nor his parents sinned, abut that the works of God should be revealed in him. 4aI*1* must work the works of Him who sent Me while it is bday; *the* night is coming when no one can work. 5As long as I am in the world, aI am the light of the world."

6When He had said these things, aHe spat on the ground and made clay with the saliva; and He anointed the eyes of the blind man with the clay. 7And He

---

John 9:1–3

WHOSE FAULT IS IT?

Jesus encountered this man who was born blind, and His disciples asked Him whose sin had caused the blindness. Jesus responded, "Neither this man nor his parents sinned, but that the works of God should be revealed in him."

God at times allows us to experience difficulty, hardship, and suffering in order that He might accomplish His works in our lives. The apostle Paul spoke of his sufferings and said, "I consider that the sufferings of this present time are not worthy to be compared with the glory which shall be revealed in us" (Rom. 8:18).

---

56 a Luke 10:24
b Heb. 11:13

58 a Mic. 5:2
b Rev. 1:8

59 a John 10:31; 11:8
b Luke 4:30
1 NU omits the rest of v. 59.

CHAPTER 9

2 a John 9:34

3 a John 11:4

4 a [John 4:34; 5:19, 36; 17:4]
b John 11:9, 10; 12:35
1 NU *We*

5 a [John 1:5, 9; 3:19; 8:12; 12:35, 46]

6 a Mark 7:33; 8:23

7 a Neh. 3:15
b 2 Kin. 5:14

8 1 NU *a beggar*

9 1 NU *"No, but he is like him."*

11 a John 9:6, 7

---

said to him, "Go, wash ain the pool of Siloam" (which is translated, Sent). So bhe went and washed, and came back seeing.

John 9:6–7

BREAKING THE RULES

The Jewish leaders had developed a complicated interpretation of the Old Testament Law that was ridiculous. If you had nails in your sandals, you couldn't wear them on the Sabbath. It would be considered carrying a burden, because of the weight of the nails. Of course, they created loopholes, as well. Today some Orthodox Jews will go shopping on the Sabbath day, but they think if they pay with a credit card they aren't violating the Sabbath law to not do business, since they will pay for it later. The elevators stop at every floor in Israel on the Sabbath, so they don't have to push the buttons.

Here on this occasion, Jesus intentionally violated the Sabbath regulations in at least two ways. He healed the blind man, which the Jewish leaders deemed improper on the Sabbath; and He spit and made clay to do it, and they taught that making clay was a violation of the Sabbath laws. He went out of His way to break their rules, to show that He was above their human rules. He was the One who had given the Law. He was the Lord of the Sabbath.

8Therefore the neighbors and those who previously had seen that he was *1*blind said, "Is not this he who sat and begged?"

9Some said, "This is he." Others *said*, *1*"He is like him."

He said, "I am *he*."

10Therefore they said to him, "How were your eyes opened?"

11He answered and said, a"A Man

called Jesus made clay and anointed my eyes and said to me, 'Go to [1]the pool of Siloam and wash.' So I went and washed, and I received sight."

12 Then they said to him, "Where is He?"

He said, "I do not know."

THE PHARISEES EXCOMMUNICATE THE HEALED MAN

13 They brought him who formerly was blind to the Pharisees. 14 Now it was a Sabbath when Jesus made the clay and opened his eyes. 15 Then the Pharisees also asked him again how he had received his sight. He said to them, "He put clay on my eyes, and I washed, and I see."

16 Therefore some of the Pharisees said, "This Man is not from God, because He does not [1]keep the Sabbath."

Others said, [a]"How can a man who is a sinner do such signs?" And [b]there was a division among them.

17 They said to the blind man again, "What do you say about Him because He opened your eyes?"

He said, [a]"He is a prophet."

18 But the Jews did not believe concerning him, that he had been blind and received his sight, until they called the parents of him who had received his sight. 19 And they asked them, saying, "Is this your son, who you say was born blind? How then does he now see?"

20 His parents answered them and said, "We know that this is our son, and that he was born blind; 21 but by what means he now sees we do not know, or who opened his eyes we do not know. He is of age; ask him. He will speak for himself." 22 His parents said these *things* because [a]they feared the Jews, for the Jews had agreed already that if anyone confessed *that* He *was* Christ, he [b]would be put out of the synagogue. 23 Therefore his parents said, "He is of age; ask him."

24 So they again called the man who was blind, and said to him, [a]"Give God the glory! [b]We know that this Man is a sinner."

25 He answered and said, "Whether He is a sinner *or not* I do not know. One thing I know: that though I was blind, now I see."

26 Then they said to him again, "What did He do to you? How did He open your eyes?"

27 He answered them, "I told you already, and you did not listen. Why do you want to hear *it* again? Do you also want to become His disciples?"

> **John 9:25**
>
> **Basic Apologetics.** The Jews were trying to pin the healed man down in his explanation as to what had happened to him and how Jesus healed him on the Sabbath day. He didn't get caught up in their theological debate though. He just offered an argument that was impossible to refute. "Though I was blind, now I see."
>
> It is tough to argue with that kind of evidence. The kind of apologetics that is most effective is the personal attestation that "I used to be blind, and now I see. I used to be dead, and now I'm alive."

28 Then they reviled him and said, "You are His disciple, but we are Moses' disciples. 29 We know that God [a]spoke to [b]Moses; *as for* this *fellow*, [c]we do not know where He is from."

30 The man answered and said to them, [a]"Why, this is a marvelous thing, that you do not know where He is from; yet He has opened my eyes! 31 Now we know that [a]God does not hear sinners; but if anyone is a worshiper of God and does His will, He hears him. 32 Since the world began it has been unheard of that anyone opened the eyes of one who was born blind. 33 [a]If this Man were not from God, He could do nothing."

34 They answered and said to him, [a]"You were completely born in sins, and are you teaching us?" And they [1]cast him out.

TRUE VISION AND TRUE BLINDNESS

35 Jesus heard that they had cast him out; and when He had [a]found him, He said to him, "Do you [b]believe in [c]the Son of [1]God?"

36 He answered and said, "Who is He, Lord, that I may believe in Him?"

37 And Jesus said to him, "You have both seen Him and [a]it is He who is talking with you."

38 Then he said, "Lord, I believe!" And he [a]worshiped Him.

39 And Jesus said, [a]"For judgment I have come into this world, [b]that those who do not see may see, and that those who see may be made blind."

40 Then *some* of the Pharisees who

11 [1] NU omits *the pool of*
16 [a] John 3:2; 9:33 [b] John 7:12, 43; 10:19 [1] *observe*
17 [a] [John 4:19; 6:14]
22 [a] Acts 5:13 [b] John 16:2
24 [a] Josh. 7:19 [b] John 9:16
29 [a] Num. 12:6–8 [b] [John 5:45–47] [c] John 7:27, 28; 8:14
30 [a] John 3:10
31 [a] Zech. 7:13
33 [a] John 3:2; 9:16
34 [a] John 9:2 [1] Excommunicated him
35 [a] John 5:14 [b] John 1:7; 16:31 [c] Matt. 14:33; 16:16 [1] NU *Man*
37 [a] John 4:26
38 [a] Matt. 8:2
39 [a] [John 3:17; 5:22, 27; 12:47] [b] Matt. 13:13; 15:14

John 9:35–38

Progressive Revelation of Jesus.
When Jesus healed the blind man, he received physical sight and knew Jesus was a powerful man. Then under the interrogation of the Jews, he said that Jesus must be a prophet. Here Jesus revealed to him that He was the Son of God, the Messiah. Upon this revelation, the man said, "Lord, I believe!" and he fell down and worshiped Jesus.

As Jesus is revealed to us, step by step, we will ultimately be led to worship Him.

were with Him heard these words, [a]and said to Him, "Are we blind also?" [41]Jesus said to them, [a]"If you were blind, you would have no sin; but now you say, 'We see.' Therefore your sin remains.

JESUS THE TRUE SHEPHERD

10 "Most assuredly, I say to you, he who does not enter the sheepfold by the door, but climbs up some other way, the same is a thief and a robber. [2]But he who enters by the door is the shepherd of the sheep. [3]To him the doorkeeper opens, and the sheep hear his voice; and he calls his own sheep by [a]name and leads them out. [4]And when he brings out his own sheep, he goes before them; and the sheep follow him, for they know his voice. [5]Yet they will by no means follow a [a]stranger, but will flee from him, for they do not know the voice of strangers." [6]Jesus used this illustration, but they did not understand the things which He spoke to them.

JESUS THE GOOD SHEPHERD

[7]Then Jesus said to them again, "Most assuredly, I say to you, I am the door of the sheep. [8]All who *ever* came [1]before Me are thieves and robbers, but the sheep did not hear them. [9][a]I am the door. If anyone enters by Me, he will be saved, and will go in and out and find pasture. [10]The thief does not come except to steal, and to kill, and to destroy. I have come that they may have life, and that they may have *it* more abundantly.

[11][a]"I am the good shepherd. The good shepherd gives His life for the sheep. [12]But a [1]hireling, *he who is* not

---

40 [a][Rom. 2:19]

41 [a]John 15:22, 24

CHAPTER 10

3 [a]John 20:16

5 [a][2 Cor. 11:13–15]

8 [1]M omits *before Me*

9 [a][Eph. 2:18]

11 [a]Is. 40:11

12 [a]Zech. 11:16, 17
[1]*hired man*

14 [a]2 Tim. 2:19
[b]2 Tim. 1:12

15 [a]Matt. 11:27
[b][John 15:13; 19:30]

16 [a]Is. 42:6; 56:8
[b]Eph. 2:13–18

17 [a]John 5:20
[b][Heb. 2:9]

18 [a][John 2:19; 5:26]
[b][John 6:38; 14:31; 17:4];
Acts 2:24, 32]

19 [a]John 7:43; 9:16

20 [a]John 7:20
[1]*insane*

21 [a][Ex. 4:11]
[b]John 9:6, 7, 32, 33

John 10:10–11

LIFE ON THE HIGHEST PLANE

Jesus came to give, not to take. The true servant of Jesus Christ will give rather than take, following His example.

Many people today have the wrong concept of Jesus Christ because of those who beg and rip off the people in His name. That isn't of Jesus. He came to give. "I have come that they may have life, and that they may have it more abundantly."

Jesus came to offer life, when we were facing the death sentence. But it was more than just life. It was abundant life. It is life on a higher plane. He came to give us a life that is better than we could ever imagine. He is our Good Shepherd.

the shepherd, one who does not own the sheep, sees the wolf coming and [a]leaves the sheep and flees; and the wolf catches the sheep and scatters them. [13]The hireling flees because he is a hireling and does not care about the sheep. [14]I am the good shepherd; and [a]I know My *sheep*, and [b]am known by My own. [15][a]As the Father knows Me, even so I know the Father; [b]and I lay down My life for the sheep. [16]And [a]other sheep I have which are not of this fold; them also I must bring, and they will hear My voice; [b]and there will be one flock *and* one shepherd.

[17]"Therefore My Father [a]loves Me, [b]because I lay down My life that I may take it again. [18]No one takes it from Me, but I lay it down of Myself. I [a]have power to lay it down, and I have power to take it again. [b]This command I have received from My Father."

[19]Therefore [a]there was a division again among the Jews because of these sayings. [20]And many of them said, [a]"He has a demon and is [1]mad. Why do you listen to Him?" [21]Others said, "These are not the words of one who has a demon. [a]Can a demon [b]open the eyes of the blind?"

John 10:17–18

Who Killed Jesus? Many people have blamed the Jews for killing Jesus. Generations of Jews have been persecuted and called "Christ Killers." The Jews blamed the Romans because it was the Romans who executed Him. We personalize it and say that since it was our sins that sent Him to the cross, we are responsible.

But Jesus made it clear here: "I lay down My life that I may take it again. No one takes it from Me, but I lay it down of Myself." Jesus offered Himself for our sins. He took ultimate responsibility for His own death.

THE SHEPHERD KNOWS HIS SHEEP

²²Now it was the Feast of Dedication in Jerusalem, and it was winter. ²³And Jesus walked in the temple, ᵃin Solomon's porch. ²⁴Then the Jews surrounded Him and said to Him, "How long do You keep us in ᴵdoubt? If You are the Christ, tell us plainly." ²⁵Jesus answered them, "I told you, and you do not believe. ᵃThe works that I do in My Father's name, they ᵇbear witness of Me. ²⁶But ᵃyou do not believe, because you are not of My sheep, ᴵas I said to you. ²⁷ᵃMy sheep hear My voice, and I know them, and they follow Me. ²⁸And I give them eternal life, and they shall never perish; neither shall anyone snatch them out of My hand. ²⁹ᵃMy Father, ᵇwho has given *them* to Me, is greater than all; and no one is able to snatch *them* out of My Father's hand. ³⁰ᵃI and *My* Father are one."

RENEWED EFFORTS TO STONE JESUS

³¹Then ᵃthe Jews took up stones again to stone Him. ³²Jesus answered them, "Many good works I have shown you from My Father. For which of those works do you stone Me?" ³³The Jews answered Him, saying, "For a good work we do not stone You, but for ᵃblasphemy, and because You, being a Man, ᵇmake Yourself God." ³⁴Jesus answered them, "Is it not written in your law, ᵃ'I said, "You are gods"'? ³⁵If He called them gods, ᵃto whom the word of God came (and the Scripture ᵇcannot be broken), ³⁶do you

---

23 ᵃActs 3:11; 5:12

24 ᴵSuspense

25 ᵃJohn 5:36; 10:38
ᵇMatt. 11:4

26 ᵃ[John 8:47]
ᴵNU omits *as I said to you*

27 ᵃJohn 10:4, 14

29 ᵃJohn 14:28
ᵇ[John 17:2, 6, 12, 24]

30 ᵃJohn 17:11, 21–24

31 ᵃJohn 8:59

33 ᵃMatt. 9:3
ᵇJohn 5:18

34 ᵃPs. 82:6

35 ᵃMatt. 5:17, 18 ᵇ1 Pet. 1:25

36 ᵃJohn 6:27
ᵇJohn 3:17
ᶜJohn 5:17, 18
ᵈLuke 1:35

37 ᵃJohn 10:25; 15:24

38 ᵃJohn 5:36
ᵇJohn 14:10, 11
ᴵNU *understand*

39 ᵃJohn 7:30, 44

40 ᵃJohn 1:28

41 ᵃ[John 1:29, 36; 3:28–36; 5:33]

CHAPTER 11

1 ᵃLuke 10:38, 39

2 ᵃMatt. 26:7

John 10:27–30

HIS SHEEP ARE SAFE

The sheep know the voice of their shepherd. There can be many different flocks all mixed together in the fold or at the watering trough. But when each shepherd gets up and calls to his sheep, the sheep know their shepherd's voice, and they follow. The sheep feel secure when they are with their shepherd. And we, as children of God, are secure in Jesus, our Good Shepherd. We are safe in the hand of the Father, and no one is able to snatch us out of His hand.

But how do I know if I am really one of His sheep? How do I know if I am secure? Are you listening to His voice and following Him? Then you are one of His sheep.

---

say of Him ᵃwhom the Father sanctified and ᵇsent into the world, 'You are blaspheming,' ᶜbecause I said, 'I am ᵈthe Son of God'? ³⁷ᵃIf I do not do the works of My Father, do not believe Me; ³⁸but if I do, though you do not believe Me, ᵃbelieve the works, that you may know and ᴵbelieve ᵇthat the Father *is* in Me, and I in Him." ³⁹ᵃTherefore they sought again to seize Him, but He escaped out of their hand.

THE BELIEVERS BEYOND JORDAN

⁴⁰And He went away again beyond the Jordan to the place ᵃwhere John was baptizing at first, and there He stayed. ⁴¹Then many came to Him and said, "John performed no sign, ᵃbut all the things that John spoke about this Man were true." ⁴²And many believed in Him there.

THE DEATH OF LAZARUS

11 Now a certain *man* was sick, Lazarus of Bethany, the town of ᵃMary and her sister Martha. ²ᵃIt was *that* Mary who anointed the Lord with fragrant oil and wiped His feet with her hair, whose brother Lazarus was sick. ³Therefore the sisters sent to

Him, saying, "Lord, behold, he whom You love is sick." [6 a John 10:40]
4When Jesus heard *that*, He said, "This sickness is not unto death, but for the glory of God, that the Son of God may be glorified through it."
5Now Jesus loved Martha and her sister and Lazarus. 6So, when He heard that he was sick, aHe stayed two more days in the place where He was. 7Then after this He said to *the* disciples, "Let us go to Judea again."
8*The* disciples said to Him, "Rabbi, lately the Jews sought to astone You, and are You going there again?"
9Jesus answered, "Are there not twelve hours in the day? aIf anyone walks in the day, he does not stumble, because he sees the blight of this world. 10But aif one walks in the night, he stumbles, because the light is not in him." 11These things He said, and after that He said to them, "Our friend Lazarus asleeps, but I go that I may wake him up."
12Then His disciples said, "Lord, if he sleeps he will get well." 13However, Jesus spoke of his death, but they thought that He was speaking about taking rest in sleep.
14Then Jesus said to them plainly, "Lazarus is dead. 15And I am glad for your sakes that I was not there, that you may believe. Nevertheless let us go to him."
16Then aThomas, who is called the Twin, said to his fellow disciples, "Let us also go, that we may die with Him."

I AM THE RESURRECTION AND THE LIFE
17So when Jesus came, He found that he had already been in the tomb four days. 18Now Bethany was near Jerusalem, about ltwo miles away. 19And many of the Jews had joined the women around Martha and Mary, to comfort them concerning their brother.
20Now Martha, as soon as she heard that Jesus was coming, went and met Him, but Mary was sitting in the house. 21Now Martha said to Jesus, "Lord, if You had been here, my brother would not have died. 22But even now I know that awhatever You ask of God, God will give You."
23Jesus said to her, "Your brother will rise again."
24Martha said to Him, a"I know that he will rise again in the resurrection at the last day."
25Jesus said to her, "I am athe resurrection and the life. bHe who believes

Marginal references (left column):
8 a John 8:59; 10:31
9 a John 9:4; 12:35
  b ls. 9:2
10 a John 12:35
11 a Matt. 9:24
16 a John 14:5; 20:26–28
18 1 Lit. *15 stadia*
22 a [John 9:31; 11:41]
24 a [John 5:29]
25 a John 5:21; 6:39, 40, 44
  b 1 John 5:10
  c 1 Cor. 15:22
27 a Matt. 16:16

in Me, though he may cdie, he shall live. 26And whoever lives and believes in Me shall never die. Do you believe this?"
27She said to Him, "Yes, Lord, aI believe that You are the Christ, the Son of God, who is to come into the world."

John 11:20–27

THE RESURRECTION AND THE LIFE

Martha was upset because her brother Lazarus had died, and she was blaming Jesus by saying that if Jesus had been there he would not have died. This was probably true. If Jesus had been there, He probably would have just healed Lazarus.

But Jesus had something bigger in mind. He then made this radical statement, "I am the resurrection and the life. He who believes in Me, though he may die, he shall live. And whoever lives and believes in Me shall never die." He was talking about spiritual death, that eternal separation from God.

Believing in Jesus as Lord makes spiritual death something that we will never experience. But He went on to prove what He was saying by showing His authority over physical death, as He broke the laws of nature and brought Lazarus back to life. By believing in Him we know that we will never experience separation from God. He is the resurrection and the life.

JESUS AND DEATH, THE LAST ENEMY
28And when she had said these things, she went her way and secretly called Mary her sister, saying, "The Teacher has come and is calling for you." 29As soon as she heard *that*, she arose quickly and came to Him. 30Now Jesus had not yet come into the town,

but ¹was in the place where Martha met Him. ³¹ᵃThen the Jews who were with her in the house, and comforting her, when they saw that Mary rose up quickly and went out, followed her, ¹saying, "She is going to the tomb to weep there."

³²Then, when Mary came where Jesus was, and saw Him, she ᵃfell down at His feet, saying to Him, ᵇ"Lord, if You had been here, my brother would not have died."

³³Therefore, when Jesus saw her weeping, and the Jews who came with her weeping, He groaned in the spirit and was troubled. ³⁴And He said, "Where have you laid him?"

They said to Him, "Lord, come and see."

³⁵ᵃJesus wept. ³⁶Then the Jews said, "See how He loved him!"

³⁷And some of them said, "Could not this Man, ᵃwho opened the eyes of the blind, also have kept this man from dying?"

John 11:35

Jesus Wept. When Jesus saw all the pain and suffering of the people, He wept. Why did He weep? He knew that He was going to raise Lazarus from the dead in a few minutes. What was He sad about?

He was sad because He saw the consequences of man's sin. He saw all the pain in the world that is caused by man's rebellion against God. Seeing the sorrow and bitterness and pain that sin brings, Jesus was moved with compassion and wept. His heart is still broken when He sees what we've done to ourselves.

LAZARUS RAISED FROM THE DEAD

³⁸Then Jesus, again groaning in Himself, came to the tomb. It was a cave, and a ᵃstone lay against it. ³⁹Jesus said, "Take away the stone."

Martha, the sister of him who was dead, said to Him, "Lord, by this time there is a stench, for he has been *dead* four days."

⁴⁰Jesus said to her, "Did I not say to you that if you would believe you would ᵃsee the glory of God?" ⁴¹Then they took away the stone ¹*from the place where the dead man was lying. And*

Marginal notes:

30 ¹NU *was still*

31 ᵃJohn 11:19, 33
¹NU *supposing that she was going*

32 ᵃRev. 1:17
ᵇJohn 11:21

35 ᵃLuke 19:41

37 ᵃJohn 9:6, 7

38 ᵃMatt. 27:60, 66

40 ᵃ[John 11:4, 23]

41 ¹NU omits *from the place where the dead man was lying*

42 ᵃJohn 12:30; 17:21

44 ᵃJohn 19:40
ᵇJohn 20:7

45 ᵃJohn 2:23; 10:42; 12:11, 18

46 ᵃJohn 5:15

47 ᵃPs. 2:2
ᵇActs 4:16

49 ᵃLuke 3:2

50 ᵃJohn 18:14
¹NU *you*

Jesus lifted up *His* eyes and said, "Father, I thank You that You have heard Me. ⁴²And I know that You always hear Me, but ᵃbecause of the people who are standing by I said *this*, that they may believe that You sent Me." ⁴³Now when He had said these things, He cried with a loud voice, "Lazarus, come forth!" ⁴⁴And he who had died came out bound hand and foot with ᵃgraveclothes, and ᵇhis face was wrapped with a cloth. Jesus said to them, "Loose him, and let him go."

John 11:40–44

LAYING IT ON THE LINE

Jesus had just told Martha that He is the resurrection and the life. But here He boldly stepped up to prove it. They opened the tomb. Jesus prayed to the Father, then called out to His friend who had been dead four days, "Lazarus, come forth!"

Jesus was laying it all on the line in one moment. All the bystanders and mourners were wondering what would happen. If Lazarus didn't come to life, Jesus would be discredited. But Lazarus came shuffling out of the tomb, proving that Jesus could back up His words with action.

THE PLOT TO KILL JESUS

⁴⁵Then many of the Jews who had come to Mary, ᵃand had seen the things Jesus did, believed in Him. ⁴⁶But some of them went away to the Pharisees and ᵃtold them the things Jesus did. ⁴⁷ᵃThen the chief priests and the Pharisees gathered a council and said, ᵇ"What shall we do? For this Man works many signs. ⁴⁸If we let Him alone like this, everyone will believe in Him, and the Romans will come and take away both our place and nation." ⁴⁹And one of them, ᵃCaiaphas, being high priest that year, said to them, "You know nothing at all, ⁵⁰ᵃnor do you consider that it is expedient for ¹us that one man should die for the people, and not that the whole nation

should perish." [51]Now this he did not say on his own *authority;* but being high priest that year he prophesied that Jesus would die for the nation, [52]and [a]not for that nation only, but [b]also that He would gather together in one the children of God who were scattered abroad.

[53]Then, from that day on, they plotted to [a]put Him to death. [54][a]Therefore Jesus no longer walked openly among the Jews, but went from there into the country near the wilderness, to a city called [b]Ephraim, and there remained with His disciples.

[55][a]And the Passover of the Jews was near, and many went from the country up to Jerusalem before the Passover, to [b]purify themselves. [56][a]Then they sought Jesus, and spoke among themselves as they stood in the temple, "What do you think—that He will not come to the feast?" [57]Now both the chief priests and the Pharisees had given a command, that if anyone knew where He was, he should report *it,* that they might [a]seize Him.

THE ANOINTING AT BETHANY

12 Then, six days before the Passover, Jesus came to Bethany, [a]where Lazarus was [1]who had been dead, whom He had raised from the dead. [2][a]There they made Him a supper; and Martha served, but Lazarus was one of those who sat at the table with Him. [3]Then [a]Mary took a pound of very costly oil of [b]spikenard, anointed the feet of Jesus, and wiped His feet with her hair. And the house was filled with the fragrance of the oil.

[4]But one of His disciples, [a]Judas Iscariot, Simon's *son,* who would betray Him, said, [5]"Why was this fragrant oil not sold for [1]three hundred denarii and given to the poor?" [6]This he said, not that he cared for the poor, but because he was a thief, and [a]had the money box; and he used to take what was put in it.

[7]But Jesus said, "Let her alone; [1]she has kept this for the day of My burial. [8]For [a]the poor you have with you always, but Me you do not have always."

THE PLOT TO KILL LAZARUS

[9]Now a great many of the Jews knew that He was there; and they came, not for Jesus' sake only, but that they might also see Lazarus, [a]whom He had raised from the dead. [10][a]But the chief priests

52 [a] Is. 49:6
[b] [Eph. 2:14–17]
53 [a] Matt. 26:4
54 [a] John 4:1, 3; 7:1
[b] 2 Chr. 13:19
55 [a] John 2:13; 5:1; 6:4
[b] Num. 9:10, 13; 31:19, 20
56 [a] John 7:11
57 [a] Matt. 26:14–16

CHAPTER 12

1 [a] John 11:1, 43
[1] NU omits who had been dead
2 [a] Mark 14:3; Luke 10:38–41
3 [a] John 11:2
[b] Song 1:12
4 [a] John 13:26
5 [1] About one year's wages for a worker
6 [a] John 13:29
7 [1] NU that she may keep
8 [a] Mark 14:7
9 [a] John 11:43, 44
10 [a] Luke 16:31
11 [a] John 11:45; 12:18
12 [a] Matt. 21:4–9
13 [a] Ps. 118:25, 26
14 [a] Matt. 21:7
15 [a] Zech. 9:9
16 [a] Luke 18:34
[b] John 7:39; 12:23
[c] [John 14:26]
18 [a] John 12:11
19 [a] John 11:47, 48
20 [a] Acts 17:4
[b] 1 Kin. 8:41, 42
21 [a] John 1:43, 44; 14:8–11
23 [a] John 13:32
24 [1] Cor. 15:36
[1] Lit. *fruit*
25 [a] Mark 8:35
26 [a] [Matt. 16:24]
[b] John 14:3; 17:24

plotted to put Lazarus to death also, [11][a]because on account of him many of the Jews went away and believed in Jesus.

THE TRIUMPHAL ENTRY

[12][a]The next day a great multitude that had come to the feast, when they heard that Jesus was coming to Jerusalem, [13]took branches of palm trees and went out to meet Him, and cried out:

"Hosanna!
[a]'*Blessed is He who comes in the name of the LORD!*'
The King of Israel!"

[14][a]Then Jesus, when He had found a young donkey, sat on it; as it is written:

[15] "*Fear* [a] *not, daughter of Zion;*
Behold, your King is coming,
Sitting on a donkey's colt."

[16][a]His disciples did not understand these things at first; [b]but when Jesus was glorified, [c]then they remembered that these things were written about Him and *that* they had done these things to Him.

[17]Therefore the people, who were with Him when He called Lazarus out of his tomb and raised him from the dead, bore witness. [18][a]For this reason the people also met Him, because they heard that He had done this sign. [19]The Pharisees therefore said among themselves, [a]"You see that you are accomplishing nothing. Look, the world has gone after Him!"

THE FRUITFUL GRAIN OF WHEAT

[20]Now there [a]were certain Greeks among those [b]who came up to worship at the feast. [21]Then they came to Philip, [a]who was from Bethsaida of Galilee, and asked him, saying, "Sir, we wish to see Jesus."

[22]Philip came and told Andrew, and in turn Andrew and Philip told Jesus. [23]But Jesus answered them, saying, [a]"The hour has come that the Son of Man should be glorified. [24]Most assuredly, I say to you, [a]unless a grain of wheat falls into the ground and dies, it remains alone; but if it dies, it produces much [1]grain. [25][a]He who loves his life will lose it, and he who hates his life in this world will keep it for eternal life. [26]If anyone serves Me, let him [a]follow Me; and [b]where I am, there My servant will be also. If anyone serves Me, him *My* Father will honor.

John 12:16

THEY DIDN'T GET IT

In his account of the Triumphal Entry, John gives us this special insight, not recorded in any of the other Gospels. "His disciples did not understand these things at first; but when Jesus was glorified, then they remembered that these things were written about Him and that they had done these things to Him." How interesting!

Even though Zechariah had prophesied that the Messiah would ride into town on a donkey (Zech. 9:9), and even though the words of the praise of the crowd had been predicted in the Psalms (Ps. 118:24–26), and even though Daniel had predicted this exact day (Dan. 9:25), the disciples still didn't understand what it was all about until later, after the resurrection. It is often only as we look back at fulfilled prophecy that it soaks into us that we can trust God's predictions about the future and claim His promises for us.

JESUS PREDICTS HIS DEATH ON THE CROSS

27 a"Now My soul is troubled, and what shall I say? 'Father, save Me from this hour'? b But for this purpose I came to this hour. 28 Father, glorify Your name."

a Then a voice came from heaven, saying, "I have both glorified it and will glorify it again."

29 Therefore the people who stood by and heard it said that it had thundered. Others said, "An angel has spoken to Him."

30 Jesus answered and said, a"This voice did not come because of Me, but for your sake. 31 Now is the judgment of this world; now a the ruler of this world will be cast out. 32 And I, a if I am 1 lifted up from the earth, will draw b all *peoples* to Myself." 33 a This He said, signifying by what death He would die.

---

27 a [Matt. 26:38, 39]
b Luke 22:53

28 a Matt. 3:17; 17:5

30 a John 11:42

31 a [2 Cor. 4:4]

32 a John 3:14; 8:28
b [Rom. 5:18]
1 Crucified

33 a John 18:32; 21:19

34 a Mic. 4:7

35 a [John 1:9; 7:33; 8:12]
b Eph. 5:8
c [1 John 2:9–11]

36 a Luke 16:8
b John 8:59

37 a John 11:47

38 a Is. 53:1

---

34 The people answered Him, a"We have heard from the law that the Christ remains forever; and how *can* You say, 'The Son of Man must be lifted up'? Who is this Son of Man?"

35 Then Jesus said to them, "A little while longer a the light is with you. b Walk while you have the light, lest darkness overtake you; c he who walks in darkness does not know where he is going. 36 While you have the light, believe in the light, that you may become a sons of light." These things Jesus spoke, and departed, and b was hidden from them.

WHO HAS BELIEVED OUR REPORT?

37 But although He had done so many a signs before them, they did not believe in Him, 38 that the word of Isaiah the prophet might be fulfilled, which he spoke:

a*"Lord, who has believed our report?*
And to whom has the arm of the LORD been revealed?"

John 12:37–41

DID NOT, SO COULD NOT

The religious leaders chose not to believe in Jesus. They rejected Him. "Although He had done so many signs before them, they did not believe in Him." John pointed this out as a fulfillment of Isaiah 53:1, which asked, "Who has believed our report?" But as a result of their rejection of Jesus, their eyes were then blinded so they "could not believe."

If you choose to reject Jesus and harden your heart to Him, the day may come when your chances are all used up. God may confirm your choice by hardening your heart further, as He did with Pharaoh in his dealings with Moses (Ex. 8:15, 32; 9:34; 10:1). Beware of the day when "did not" becomes "could not."

³⁹Therefore they could not believe, because Isaiah said again:

⁴⁰ "He ᵃ has blinded their eyes and
hardened their hearts,
ᵇLest they should see with their
eyes,
Lest they should understand with
their hearts and turn,
So that I should heal them."

⁴¹ᵃThese things Isaiah said ¹when he saw His glory and spoke of Him.

WALK IN THE LIGHT

⁴²Nevertheless even among the rulers many believed in Him, but ᵃbecause of the Pharisees they did not confess Him, lest they should be put out of the synagogue; ⁴³ᵃfor they loved the praise of men more than the praise of God. ⁴⁴Then Jesus cried out and said, ᵃ"He who believes in Me, ᵇbelieves not in Me ᶜbut in Him who sent Me. ⁴⁵And ᵃhe who sees Me sees Him who sent Me. ⁴⁶ᵃI have come as a light into the world, that whoever believes in Me should not abide in darkness. ⁴⁷And if anyone hears My words and does not ¹believe, ᵃI do not judge him; for ᵇI did not come to judge the world but to save the world. ⁴⁸ᵃHe who rejects Me, and does not receive My words, has that which judges him—ᵇthe word that I have spoken will judge him in the last day. ⁴⁹For ᵃI have not spoken on My own authority;

but the Father who sent Me gave Me a command, ᵇwhat I should say and what I should speak. ⁵⁰And I know that His command is everlasting life. Therefore, whatever I speak, just as the Father has told Me, so I ᵃspeak."

JESUS WASHES THE DISCIPLES' FEET

13 Now ᵃbefore the Feast of the Passover, when Jesus knew that ᵇHis hour had come that He should depart from this world to the Father, having loved His own who were in the world, He ᶜloved them to the end. ²And ¹supper being ended, ᵃthe devil having already put it into the heart of Judas Iscariot, Simon's son, to betray Him, ³Jesus, knowing ᵃthat the Father had given all things into His hands, and that He ᵇhad come from God and ᶜwas going to God, ⁴ᵃrose from supper and laid aside His garments, took a towel and girded Himself. ⁵After that, He poured water into a basin and began to wash the disciples' feet, and to wipe them with the towel with which He was girded. ⁶Then He came to Simon Peter. And Peter said to Him, ᵃ"Lord, are You washing my feet?"

Reference column

40 ᵃ Is. 6:9, 10
ᵇ Matt. 13:14

41 ᵃ Is. 6:1
¹ NU because

42 ᵃ John 7:13; 9:22

43 ᵃ John 5:41, 44

44 ᵃ Mark 9:37
ᵇ [John 3:16, 18, 36; 11:25, 26]
ᶜ [John 5:24]

45 ᵃ [John 14:9]

46 ᵃ John 1:4, 5; 8:12; 12:35, 36

47 ᵃ John 5:45
ᵇ John 3:17
¹ NU keep them

48 ᵃ [Luke 10:16]
ᵇ Deut. 18:18, 19

49 ᵃ John 8:38
ᵇ Deut. 18:18

50 ᵃ John 5:19; 8:28

CHAPTER 13

1 ᵃ Matt. 26:2
ᵇ John 12:23; 17:1
ᶜ John 15:9

2 ᵃ Luke 22:3
¹ NU during supper

3 ᵃ Acts 2:36
ᵇ John 8:42; 16:28
ᶜ John 17:11; 20:17

4 ᵃ [Luke 22:27]

6 ᵃ Matt. 3:14

John 12:44–50

A FINAL APPEAL

Jesus again explained that He was just bringing a message from God. And it was a message that brought light and life. "I did not come to judge the world but to save the world." The world is already judged. "Whatever I speak, just as the Father has told Me, so I speak."

When we share the truths of God with people, as we tell them what God says, we can have the same confidence in our message. "And I know that His command is everlasting life." We are the messengers of that which can bring life.

John 13:3–4

WHAT TO DO WITH POWER

The power of the universe is vested in Jesus. He said in Matthew 28:18, "All authority has been given to Me in heaven and on earth." Here verse 3 says that Jesus knew "that the Father had given all things into His hands." What do you do with that kind of power? How do you use all that authority? Jesus, on the basis of that power, girded Himself, took a towel, and washed the feet of His disciples. He used His power to serve.

It has been said that "power tends to corrupt, and absolute power corrupts absolutely." It may be true for most people, but not for the One who truly had absolute power.

7 Jesus answered and said to him, "What I am doing you ᵃdo not understand now, ᵇbut you will know after this."

8 Peter said to Him, "You shall never wash my feet!"

Jesus answered him, ᵃ"If I do not wash you, you have no part with Me."

9 Simon Peter said to Him, "Lord, not my feet only, but also *my* hands and *my* head!"

10 Jesus said to him, "He who is bathed needs only to wash *his* feet, but is completely clean; and ᵃyou are clean, but not all of you." 11 For ᵃHe knew who would betray Him; therefore He said, "You are not all clean."

12 So when He had washed their feet, taken His garments, and sat down again, He said to them, "Do you *l*know what I have done to you? 13 ᵃYou call Me Teacher and Lord, and you say well, for *so* I am. 14 If I then, *your* Lord and Teacher, have washed *your* feet, ᵇyou also ought to wash one another's feet. 15 For ᵃI have given you an example, that you should do as I have done to you. 16 ᵃMost assuredly, I say to you, a servant is not greater than his master; nor is he who is sent greater than he who sent him. 17 ᵃIf you know these things, blessed are you if you do them.

JESUS IDENTIFIES HIS BETRAYER

18 "I do not speak concerning all of you. I know whom I have chosen; but that the ᵃScripture may be fulfilled, ᵇ'*He who eats ¹bread with Me has lifted up his heel against Me.*' 19 ᵃNow I tell you before it comes, that when it does come to pass, you may believe that I am He. 20 ᵃMost assuredly, I say to you, he who receives whomever I send receives Me; and he who receives Me receives Him who sent Me."

21 ᵃWhen Jesus had said these things, ᵇHe was troubled in spirit, and testified and said, "Most assuredly, I say to you, ᶜone of you will betray Me." 22 Then the disciples looked at one another, perplexed about whom He spoke.

23 Now ᵃthere was ¹leaning on Jesus' bosom one of His disciples, whom Jesus loved. 24 Simon Peter therefore motioned to him to ask who it was of whom He spoke.

25 Then, leaning ¹back on Jesus' breast, he said to Him, "Lord, who is it?"

26 Jesus answered, "It is he to whom I shall give a piece of bread when I have dipped *it*." And having dipped the

---

7 ᵃ John 12:16; 16:12
ᵇ John 13:19

8 ᵃ [1 Cor. 6:11]

10 ᵃ [John 15:3]

11 ᵃ John 6:64; 18:4

12 ¹ *understand*

13 ᵃ Matt. 23:8, 10

14 ᵃ Luke 22:27
ᵇ [Rom. 12:10]

15 ᵃ [1 Pet. 2:21–24]

16 ᵃ Matt. 10:24

17 ᵃ [James 1:25]

18 ᵃ John 15:25; 17:12
ᵇ Ps. 41:9
¹ NU *My bread has*

19 ᵃ John 14:29; 16:4

20 ᵃ Matt. 10:40

21 ᵃ Luke 22:21
ᵇ John 12:27
ᶜ 1 John 2:19

23 ᵃ John 19:26; 20:2; 21:7, 20
¹ *reclining*

25 ¹ NU, M add *thus*

26 ᵃ John 6:70, 71; 12:4

27 ᵃ Luke 22:3

29 ᵃ John 12:6

John 13:23

The Disciple Jesus Loved. John described himself several times as "the disciple Jesus loved." It is interesting that none of the other Gospels describe John that way, or call him "John the beloved." But John had a strong sense that he was loved by Jesus. And it is great to know that Jesus loves you. That is the feeling we should all have ("He loves me!") as we lean on Him.

---

bread, He gave *it* to ᵃJudas Iscariot, *the son* of Simon. 27 ᵃNow after the piece of bread, Satan entered him. Then Jesus said to him, "What you do, do quickly." 28 But no one at the table knew for what reason He said this to him. 29 For some thought, because ᵃJudas had the money box, that Jesus had said to him, "Buy *those things* we need for the feast," or that he should give something to the poor.

John 13:34

A NEW COMMANDMENT

This is an amazing commandment Jesus gave to His disciples: "Love one another; as I have loved you, that you also love one another." He had already taught them that the most important commandment in the Law was "love the LORD your God" and the second was "love your neighbor as yourself" (Matt. 22:37–39). But now He gave them a new commandment.

The new commandment is to love each other as He loved us. This is a love that was impossible before Jesus came. But He set a whole new standard of love and gave this new commandment. My own self-love is no longer the basis. It had been the highest form of love we could know, but the selfless love of Jesus brought love to a new level.

30Having received the piece of bread, he then went out immediately. And it was night.

THE NEW COMMANDMENT

31So, when he had gone out, Jesus said, a"Now the Son of Man is glorified, and bGod is glorified in Him. 32If God is glorified in Him, God will also glorify Him in Himself, and aglorify Him immediately. 33Little children, I shall be with you a alittle while longer. You will seek Me; band as I said to the Jews, 'Where I am going, you cannot come,' so now I say to you. 34aA new commandment I give to you, that you love one another; as I have loved you, that you also love one another. 35aBy this all will know that you are My disciples, if you have love for one another."

JESUS PREDICTS PETER'S DENIAL

36Simon Peter said to Him, "Lord, where are You going?"

John 14:1

REMEDY FOR A TROUBLED HEART

Jesus knew that His disciples were heading into some difficult times. Peter would deny Jesus and feel terrible about it. They would all see Him hanging on a cross. None of this would make sense to them. It isn't what they had expected from the Messiah. But Jesus said, "Let not your heart be troubled." But how could they help but be troubled with all they were facing?

The remedy is in the same sentence. "You believe in God, believe also in Me." Jesus was basically saying, "If your heart is troubled, just trust Me." That is hard to do when things don't make sense to us. But when we go through difficult trials and nothing makes sense to us and our hearts are troubled, that is when we need to hear the voice of Jesus saying, "Just trust Me."

Cross References

31 a John 12:23　b [1 Pet. 4:11]
32 a John 12:23
33 a John 12:35; 14:19; 16:16–19　b [John 7:34; 8:21]
34 a 1 Thess. 4:9
35 a 1 John 2:5
36 a John 13:33; 14:2; 16:5　b 2 Pet. 1:14
37 a Mark 14:29–31
38 a John 18:25–27

CHAPTER 14

1 a [John 14:27; 16:22, 24]
2 a John 13:33, 36　1 Lit. dwellings　2 NU would I have told you that I go or I would have told you; for I go
3 a [Acts 1:11]　b [John 12:26]
5 a Matt. 10:3
6 a [Heb. 9:8; 10:19, 20]　b [John 1:14, 17; 8:32; 18:37]　c [John 11:25]　d 1 Tim. 2:5　e [John 10:7–9]
7 a John 8:19

Jesus answered him, "Where I aam going you cannot follow Me now, but byou shall follow Me afterward." 37Peter said to Him, "Lord, why can I not follow You now? I will alay down my life for Your sake." 38Jesus answered him, "Will you lay down your life for My sake? Most assuredly, I say to you, the rooster shall not acrow till you have denied Me three times.

THE WAY, THE TRUTH, AND THE LIFE

14 "Let anot your heart be troubled; you believe in God, believe also in Me. 2In My Father's house are many 1mansions; if it were not so, 2I would have told you. aI go to prepare a place for you. 3And if I go and prepare a place for you, aI will come again and receive you to Myself; that bwhere I am, there you may be also. 4And where I go you know, and the way you know."

5aThomas said to Him, "Lord, we do not know where You are going, and how can we know the way?"

6Jesus said to him, "I am athe way, bthe truth, and cthe life. dNo one comes to the Father eexcept through Me.

THE FATHER REVEALED

7a"If you had known Me, you would have known My Father also; and from now on you know Him and have seen Him."

John 14:7–11

SEEING THE FATHER

We often have the concept of God the Father as being kind of cold and distant and vengeful. We see Jesus as the good, kind, benevolent member of the God-head, interceding for us with the Father who wants to judge us. Nothing could be further from the truth.

Jesus came so we could see the Father. Everything Jesus did the Father also did. The heart of the Father is the heart of Jesus. "He who has seen Me has seen the Father." Jesus came to represent the Father, and He did it perfectly.

8Philip said to Him, "Lord, show us the Father, and it is sufficient for us." 9Jesus said to him, "Have I been with you so long, and yet you have not known Me, Philip? aHe who has seen Me has seen the Father; so how can you say, 'Show us the Father'? 10Do you not believe that aI am in the Father, and the Father in Me? The words that I speak to you bI do not speak on My own *authority*; but the Father who dwells in Me does the works. 11Believe Me that I *am* in the Father and the Father in Me, aor else believe Me for the sake of the works themselves.

THE ANSWERED PRAYER

12a"Most assuredly, I say to you, he who believes in Me, the works that I do he will do also; and greater *works* than these he will do, because I go to My Father. 13aAnd whatever you ask in My name, that I will do, that the Father may be bglorified in the Son. 14If you lask anything in My name, I will do *it*.

JESUS PROMISES ANOTHER HELPER

15a"If you love Me, lkeep My commandments. 16And I will pray the Father, and aHe will give you another lHelper, that He may abide with you forever— 17athe Spirit of truth, bwhom the world cannot receive, because it neither sees Him nor knows Him; but you know Him, for He dwells with you cand will be in you. 18aI will not leave you orphans; bI will come to you.

INDWELLING OF THE FATHER AND THE SON

19"A little while longer and the world will see Me no more, but ayou will see Me. bBecause I live, you will live also. 20At that day you will know that aI am in My Father, and you in Me, and I in you. 21aHe who has My commandments and keeps them, it is he who loves Me. And he who loves Me will be loved by My Father, and I will love him and lmanifest Myself to him." 22aJudas (not Iscariot) said to Him, "Lord, how is it that You will manifest Yourself to us, and not to the world?" 23Jesus answered and said to him, "If anyone loves Me, he will keep My word; and My Father will love him, aand We will come to him and make Our home with him. 24He who does not love Me does not keep My words; and athe word which you hear is not Mine but the Father's who sent Me.

9 aCol. 1:15
10 aJohn 10:38; 14:11, 20
bJohn 5:19; 14:24
11 aJohn 5:36; 10:38
12 aLuke 10:17
13 aMatt. 7:7
bJohn 13:31
14 1NU *ask Me*
15 a1John 5:3
1NU *you will keep*
16 aRom. 8:15
1*Comforter*, Gr. *Parakletos*
17 a[1John 4:6; 5:7]
b[1Cor. 2:14]
c[1John 2:27]
18 a[Matt. 28:20]
b[John 14:3, 28]
19 aJohn 16:16, 22
b[1Cor. 15:20]
20 aJohn 10:38; 14:11
21 a1John 2:5
1*reveal*
22 aLuke 6:16
23 aRev. 3:20; 21:3
24 aJohn 5:19
26 aLuke 24:49
bJohn 15:26
c1Cor. 2:13
dJohn 2:22; 12:16
1*Comforter*, Gr. *Parakletos*
27 a[Phil. 4:7]
28 aJohn 14:3, 18
bJohn 16:16
c[Phil. 2:6]
1NU omits *I said*
29 aJohn 13:19
30 a[John 12:31]
b[Heb. 4:15]
31 aJohn 10:18

CHAPTER 15

2 aMatt. 15:13

John 14:26

THE HELPER

The word translated "Helper" is the Greek word *parakletos*. It means "one who is called alongside to help." The Holy Spirit is there alongside us, helping us. "He will teach you all things, and bring to your remembrance all things that I said to you."

Isn't it wonderful to be instructed by the Author of the Book? It is such a blessing to me to have the Holy Spirit open up my understanding to a passage of Scripture. Maybe I've wrestled with it, searched it out in the Greek, and tried to figure out what it means. Then suddenly the Holy Spirit turns the light on, and it just makes sense. It really helps to have the God of heaven as your tutor, right there alongside you.

THE GIFT OF HIS PEACE

25"These things I have spoken to you while being present with you. 26But aHelper, the Holy Spirit, whom the Father will bsend in My name, cHe will teach you all things, and bring to your dremembrance all things that I said to you. 27aPeace I leave with you, My peace I give to you; not as the world gives do I give to you. Let not your heart be troubled, neither let it be afraid. 28You have heard Me asay to you, 'I am going away and coming *back* to you.' If you loved Me, you would rejoice because lI said, b'I am going to the Father,' for cMy Father is greater than I.

29"And anow I have told you before it comes, that when it does come to pass, you may believe. 30I will no longer talk much with you, afor the ruler of this world is coming, and he has bnothing in Me. 31But that the world may know that I love the Father, and aas the Father gave Me commandment, so I do. Arise, let us go from here.

THE TRUE VINE

15 "I am the true vine, and My Father is the vinedresser. 2aEvery branch in Me that does not bear fruit

He ¹takes away; and every *branch* that bears fruit He prunes, that it may bear ᵇmore fruit. ³ᵃYou are already clean because of the word which I have spoken to you. ⁴ᵃAbide in Me, and I in you. As the branch cannot bear fruit of itself, unless it abides in the vine, neither can you, unless you abide in Me. ⁵"I am the vine, you *are* the branches. He who abides in Me, and I in him, bears much ᵃfruit; for without Me you can do ᵇnothing. ⁶If anyone does not abide in Me, ᵃhe is cast out as a branch and is withered; and they gather them and throw *them* into the fire, and they are burned. ⁷If you abide in Me, and My words ᵃabide in you, ᵇyou¹ will ask what you desire, and it shall be done for you. ⁸ᵃBy this My Father is glorified, that you bear much fruit; ᵇso you will be My disciples.

2 ᵇ[Matt. 13:12]
¹ Or *lifts up*

3 ᵃ[John 13:10; 17:17]

4 ᵃ[Col. 1:23]

5 ᵃHos. 14:8
ᵇ2 Cor. 3:5

6 ᵃMatt. 3:10

7 ᵃ1 John 2:14
ᵇJohn 14:13; 16:23
¹ NU omits *you will*

8 ᵃ[Matt. 5:16]
ᵇJohn 8:31

9 ᵃJohn 5:20; 17:26

10 ᵃJohn 14:15

11 ᵃ1 John 1:4

12 ᵃ1 John 3:11
ᵇRom. 12:9

13 ᵃ1 John 3:16

14 ᵃ[Matt. 12:50; 28:20]

15 ᵃGen. 18:17

16 ᵃJohn 6:70; 13:18; 15:19
ᵇ[Col. 1:6]
ᶜJohn 14:13; 16:23, 24

John 15:1–8

ETERNAL SECURITY

Many people endlessly debate about the issue of eternal security. Can you lose your salvation once you are a child of God? This passage is one of the passages that seems to indicate the possibility that you can lose your salvation. "If anyone does not abide in Me, he is cast out as a branch and is withered; and they gather them and throw them into the fire, and they are burned."

But this passage doesn't make me insecure at all. I intend to always abide in Him. Why would I ever want to cease abiding in Him? If I abide in Him, I live a life of fruitfulness. If I abide in Him, He answers my prayers. If I abide in Him, I abide in His love. If I abide in Him, my joy is full. I am eternally secure as long as I abide in Him, and I am going to do just that. I will leave the arguments to the theologians. I am abiding in Him.

LOVE AND JOY PERFECTED

⁹"As the Father ᵃloved Me, I also have loved you; abide in My love. ¹⁰ᵃIf you keep My commandments, you will abide in My love, just as I have kept My Father's commandments and abide in His love.

¹¹"These things I have spoken to you, that My joy may remain in you, and ᵃthat your joy may be full. ¹²This is My ᵇcommandment, that you love one another as I have loved you. ¹³ᵃGreater love has no one than this, than to lay down one's life for his friends. ¹⁴ᵃYou are My friends if you do whatever I command you. ¹⁵No longer do I call you servants, for a servant does not know what his master is doing; but I have called you friends, ᵃfor all things that I heard from My Father I have made known to you. ¹⁶ᵃYou did not choose Me, but I chose you and ᵇappointed you that you should go and bear fruit, and *that* your fruit should remain, that whatever you ask the Father ᶜin My name He may give you. ¹⁷These things I command you, that you love one another.

John 15:11

HIS JOY

Jesus said, "These things I have spoken to you, that My joy may remain in you, and that your joy may be full." But He was about to face the cross, and He knew it. He knew the ugly experience He would go through the next day. He would be mocked, jeered, buffeted, scourged, insulted, and humiliated. With all that He was about to go through, we might rightfully ask, "Your joy? What joy?"

But Hebrews 12:2 tells us that He endured the cross "for the joy that was set before Him." His joy was the redemption of man. His joy is the ability to say to you, "Your sins are forgiven. Enter into the joy of your Lord." And if we abide in Him, we gain the eternal perspective and receive the joy that comes from seeing the future.

I CHOSE YOU

This enters into the difficult area of divine election. "You did not choose Me, but I chose you." This is something that I don't think any person really fully understands. How do the sovereignty of God and divine election line up with human responsibility? How are they reconciled?

There are some people who think they understand this; but when they think they understand, it is usually because they've watered down one concept or the other. Either they emphasize divine election and the sovereignty of God, at the expense of human responsibility and choice, as the Calvinists do, or they recognize human responsibility while denying the reality of divine election, as do the Arminians.

Each extreme is correct in what they assert, but they err in what they deny. We shouldn't deny the sovereignty of God; we should revel in the fact that God chose us before the foundation of the world (Eph. 1:4). But it is also wrong to ignore the responsibility that each person has to answer the call of God.

It is also important that we acknowledge that God makes the invitation to everyone. He did not only send His Son for a chosen few, but He "so loved the world that He gave His only begotten Son, that whoever believes in Him should not perish but have everlasting life" (John 3:16). His invitation is always, "Whoever desires, let him take the water of life freely" (Rev. 22:17). "Whoever" means "whoever," and the invitation is open to all. But you must respond to the invitation. The door to heaven says, "Whoever desires"; but once we get inside, we'll realize that He chose us.

You may say, "I don't think that is fair. What if I'm just not chosen?" Well, why don't you accept Him? Then you will be chosen. "But I don't want to accept Jesus." Then why do you care if you were chosen or not?

THE WORLD'S HATRED

18 a"If the world hates you, you know that it hated Me before *it hated* you. 19 aIf you were of the world, the world would love its own. Yet bbecause you are not of the world, but I chose you out of the world, therefore the world hates you. 20 Remember the word that I said to you, a'A servant is not greater than his master.' If they persecuted Me, they will also persecute you. bIf they kept My word, they will keep yours also. 21 But aall these things they will do to you for My name's sake, because they do not know Him who sent Me. 22 aIf I had not come and spoken to them, they would have no sin, bbut now they have no excuse for their sin. 23 aHe who hates Me hates My Father also. 24 If I had not done among them athe works which no one else did, they would have no sin; but now they have bseen and also hated both Me and My Father. 25 But *this happened* that the word might be fulfilled which is written in their law, a'*They hated Me without a cause.*'

THE COMING REJECTION

26 a"But when the ʲHelper comes, whom I shall send to you from the

Father, the Spirit of truth who proceeds from the Father, bHe will testify of Me. 27 And ayou also will bear witness, because byou have been with Me from the beginning.

16 "These things I have spoken to you, that you ashould not be made to stumble. 2 aThey will put you out of the synagogues; yes, the time is coming bthat whoever kills you will think that he offers God service. 3 And athese things they will do ʲto you because they have not known the Father nor Me. 4 But these things I have told you, that when ʲthe time comes, you may remember that I told you of them.

"And these things I did not say to you at the beginning, because I was with you.

THE WORK OF THE HOLY SPIRIT

5 "But now I ago away to Him who sent Me, and none of you asks Me, 'Where are You going?' 6 But because I have said these things to you, asorrow has filled your heart. 7 Nevertheless I tell you the truth. It is to your advantage that I go away; for if I do not go away, the Helper will not come to you;

18 a 1 John 3:13
19 a 1 John 4:5
b John 17:14
20 a John 13:16
b Ezek. 3:7
21 a Matt. 10:22; 24:9
22 a John 9:41; 15:24
b [James 4:17]
23 a 1 John 2:23
24 a John 3:2
b John 14:9
25 a Ps. 35:19; 69:4; 109:3–5
26 a Luke 24:49
b 1 John 5:6
1 *Comforter,* Gr. *Parakletos*
27 a Luke 24:48
b Luke 1:2

CHAPTER 16
1 a Matt. 11:6
2 a John 9:22
b Acts 8:1
3 a John 8:19; 15:21
1 NU, M omit *to you*
4 1 NU *their*
5 a John 7:33; 13:33; 14:28; 17:11
6 a [John 16:20, 22]

John 16:3

They Don't Know Him. Jesus warned His disciples that there would be those of the Jewish faith who would persecute and reject them because these devout Jews "have not known the Father nor Me." It is possible to be very religious, yet not know God. Paul was that way, as he was so zealous for God he was killing Christians.

How sad, though, when someone gets involved with religion with a heart to find God, but they get caught up in religious activity, going through the motions, yet never really meeting God. They miss Him along the way.

but ªif I depart, I will send Him to you. 8And when He has ªcome, He will convict the world of sin, and of righteousness, and of judgment: 9ªof sin, because they do not believe in Me; 10ªof righteousness, ᵇbecause I go to My Father

John 16:7

TO YOUR ADVANTAGE

The disciples were sad because Jesus was saying that He would go away. But He told them that His going away would be to their advantage, because the Holy Spirit would come. They would be better off as a result. As long as Jesus was with them, He was limited by space and time in His material body.

But when the Holy Spirit came, He could be inside us all the time. And He is with us right now; but He is also at the other churches in the area right now, and He is also halfway around the world. What a tremendous advantage to us, that God can be everywhere at the same time!

7 ª Acts 2:33

8 ª Acts 1:8; 2:1–4, 37

9 ª Acts 2:22

10 ª Acts 2:32
ᵇ John 5:32

11 ª Acts 26:18
ᵇ [Luke 10:18]

12 ª Mark 4:33

13 ª [John 14:17]
ᵇ John 14:26

14 ª John 15:26

15 ª Matt. 11:27
1 NU, M takes of Mine and will declare

16 ª John 7:33; 12:35; 13:33; 14:19; 19:40–42; 20:19
ᵇ John 13:3

18 1 understand

20 ª Mark 16:10
ᵇ Luke 24:32, 41

21 ª Is. 13:8; 26:17; 42:14

22 ª 1 Pet. 1:8

23 ª Matt. 7:7

24 ª John 17:13
ᵇ John 15:11

and you see Me no more; 11ªof judgment, because ᵇthe ruler of this world is judged. 12"I still have many things to say to you, ªbut you cannot bear *them* now. 13However, when He, ªthe Spirit of truth, has come, ᵇHe will guide you into all truth; for He will not speak on His own *authority*, but whatever He hears He will speak; and He will tell you things to come. 14ªHe will glorify Me, for He will take of what is Mine and declare *it* to you. 15ªAll things that the Father has are Mine. Therefore I said that He 1will take of Mine and declare *it* to you.

SORROW WILL TURN TO JOY

16"A ªlittle while, and you will not see Me; and again a little while, and you will see Me, ᵇbecause I go to the Father." 17Then *some* of His disciples said among themselves, "What is this that He says to us, 'A little while, and you will not see Me; and again a little while, and you will see Me'; and, 'because I go to the Father'?" 18They said therefore, "What is this that He says, 'A little while'? We do not 1know what He is saying."

19Now Jesus knew that they desired to ask Him, and He said to them, "Are you inquiring among yourselves about what I said, 'A little while, and you will not see Me; and again a little while, and you will see Me'? 20Most assuredly, I say to you that you will weep and ªlament, but the world will rejoice; and you will be sorrowful, but your sorrow will be turned into ᵇjoy. 21ªA woman, when she is in labor, has sorrow because her hour has come; but as soon as she has given birth to the child, she no longer remembers the anguish, for joy that a human being has been born into the world. 22Therefore you now have sorrow; but I will see you again and ªyour heart will rejoice, and your joy no one will take from you. 23"And in that day you will ask Me nothing. ªMost assuredly, I say to you, whatever you ask the Father in My name He will give you. 24Until now you have asked nothing in My name. Ask, and you will receive, ªthat your joy may be ᵇfull.

JESUS CHRIST HAS OVERCOME THE WORLD

25"These things I have spoken to you in figurative language; but the time is coming when I will no longer speak to

you in figurative language, but I will tell you ᵃplainly about the Father. ²⁶In that day you will ask in My name, and I do not say to you that I shall pray the Father for you; ²⁷ᵃfor the Father Himself loves you, because you have loved Me, and ᵇhave believed that I came forth from God. ²⁸ᵃI came forth from the Father and have come into the world. Again, I leave the world and go to the Father."

²⁹His disciples said to Him, "See, now You are speaking plainly, and using no figure of speech! ³⁰Now we are sure that ᵃYou know all things, and have no need that anyone should question You. By this ᵇwe believe that You came forth from God."

³¹Jesus answered them, "Do you now believe? ³²ᵃIndeed the hour is coming, yes, has now come, that you will be scattered, ᵇeach to his ᶦown, and will leave Me alone. And ᶜyet I am not alone, because the Father is with Me. ³³These things I have spoken to you, that ᵃin Me you may have peace. ᵇIn

---

John 16:33

OVERCOMING THE WORLD

Jesus promised to give His disciples peace in the midst of tribulation. This peace would be based on the fact that "I have overcome the world."

Jesus has defeated Satan through the cross. The only power Satan can exercise over you now is the power you allow him. He has been dethroned, and any power he has is usurped power. When we, as children of God, come against Satan in the name of Jesus, on the basis of the cross, he must yield to the authority of Jesus.

Through Jesus Christ, the weakest child of God has authority and power over Satan. That should give us such peace, knowing that our enemy has already been defeated. We just need to thank God for the victory.

---

25 ᵃ John 7:13

27 ᵃ [John 14:21, 23]
ᵇ John 3:13

28 ᵃ John 13:1, 3; 16:5, 10, 17

30 ᵃ John 21:17
ᵇ John 17:8

32 ᵃ Matt. 26:31, 56
ᵇ John 20:10
ᶜ John 8:29
ᶦ own things or place

33 ᵃ [Eph. 2:14]
ᵇ 2 Tim. 3:12
ᶜ Rom. 8:37
ᶦ NU, M omit will

CHAPTER 17

1 ᵃ John 12:23

2 ᵃ John 3:35
ᵇ John 6:37, 39; 17:6, 9, 24
ᶦ M shall

3 ᵃ Jer. 9:23, 24
ᵇ 1 Cor. 8:4
ᶜ John 3:34

4 ᵃ John 13:31
ᵇ John 4:34; 19:30
ᶜ John 14:31

5 ᵃ Phil. 2:6
ᶦ Lit. alongside

6 ᵃ Ps. 22:22
ᵇ John 6:37
ᶜ Ezek. 18:4
ᶦ revealed

8 ᵃ John 8:28
ᵇ John 8:42; 16:27, 30
ᶜ Deut. 18:15, 18

9 ᵃ [1 John 5:19]

10 ᵃ John 16:15

11 ᵃ John 13:1

---

the world you ᶦwill have tribulation; but be of good cheer, ᶜI have overcome the world."

JESUS PRAYS FOR HIMSELF

17 Jesus spoke these words, lifted up His eyes to heaven, and said: "Father, ᵃthe hour has come. Glorify Your Son, that Your Son also may glorify You, ²ᵃas You have given Him authority over all flesh, that He ᶦshould give eternal life to as many ᵇas You have given Him. ³And ᵃthis is eternal life, that they may know You, ᵇthe only true God, and Jesus Christ ᶜwhom You have sent. ⁴ᵃI have glorified You on the earth. ᵇI have finished the work ᶜwhich You have given Me to do. ⁵And now, O Father, glorify Me together ᶦwith Yourself, with the glory ᵃwhich I had with You before the world was.

JESUS PRAYS FOR HIS DISCIPLES

⁶ᵃ"I have ᶦmanifested Your name to the men ᵇwhom You have given Me out of the world. ᶜThey were Yours, You gave them to Me, and they have kept Your word. ⁷Now they have known that all things which You have given Me are from You. ⁸For I have given to them the words ᵃwhich You have given Me; and they have received *them,* ᵇand have known surely that I came forth from You; and they have believed that ᶜYou sent Me.

⁹"I pray for them. ᵃI do not pray for the world but for those whom You have given Me, for they are Yours. ¹⁰And all Mine are Yours, and ᵃYours are Mine, and I am glorified in them. ¹¹ᵃNow I

John 17:9–10

Glorified in Us. Jesus prayed about all those who had been given to Him, that is, about His disciples and those who would later believe, including us. And He said, "I am glorified in them."

How can He be glorified in us? As we trust in Him and obey Him, He is glorified. Paul said that we are "to the praise of the glory of His grace" (Eph. 1:6). God is glorified when we respond to what He has done for us by praising Him for His love and grace. He is blessed and, seeing us, says, "That's My boy!"

John 17:15–16

IN THE WORLD

We are here in the world to fulfill the purposes of God, and that's why He's left us here. He wouldn't leave us in this dark, sinful world unless He had a good reason; and His reason is that we could be a light in this world, bearing witness of His love. So He has left us in the world, praying that we will be protected from the evil one.

In the next verse, Jesus said that we are "not of the world." We are in the world, to share the love of Jesus, but we are not of the world. We are just aliens, passing through on our way to heaven.

am no longer in the world, but these are in the world, and I come to You. Holy Father, b keep 1 through Your name those whom You have given Me, that they may be one c as We *are*. 12 While I was with them 1 in the world, a I kept them in 2 Your name. Those whom You gave Me I have kept; and b none of them is 3 lost c except the son of 4 perdition, d that the Scripture might be fulfilled. 13 But now I come to You, and these things I speak in the world, that they may have My joy fulfilled in themselves. 14 I have given them Your word; a and the world has hated them because they are not of the world, b just as I am not of the world. 15 I do not pray that You should take them out of the world, but a that You should keep them from the evil one. 16 They are not of the world, just as I am not of the world. 17 a Sanctify 1 them by Your truth. b Your word is truth. 18 a As You sent Me into the world, I also have sent them into the world. 19 And a for their sakes I sanctify Myself, that they also may be sanctified by the truth.

JESUS PRAYS FOR ALL BELIEVERS

20 "I do not pray for these alone, but also for those who 1 will believe in Me through their word; 21 a that they all may be one, as b You, Father, *are* in Me, and I in You; that they also may be one in Us, that the world may believe that

11 b [1 Pet. 1:5]
c John 10:30
1 NU, M *keep them through Your name which You have given Me*

12 a Heb. 2:13
b 1 John 2:19
c John 6:70
d Ps. 41:9; 109:8
1 NU omits *in the world*
2 NU *Your name which You gave Me. And I guarded them;* (or *it;*)
3 *destroyed*
4 *destruction*

14 a John 15:19
b John 8:23

15 a 1 John 5:18

17 a [Eph. 5:26]
b Ps. 119:9, 142, 151
1 *Set them apart*

18 a John 4:38; 20:21

19 a [Heb. 10:10]

20 1 NU, M omit *will*

21 a [Gal. 3:28]
b John 10:38; 17:11, 23

22 a 1 John 1:3
b [2 Cor. 3:18]

23 a [Col. 3:14]

24 a [1 Thess. 4:17]
b John 17:5

25 a John 15:21
b John 7:29; 8:55; 10:15
c John 3:17; 17:3, 8, 18, 21, 23

26 a John 17:6
b John 15:9

CHAPTER 18

1 a Mark 14:26, 32
b 2 Sam. 15:23

You sent Me. 22 And the a glory which You gave Me I have given them, b that they may be one just as We are one: 23 I in them, and You in Me; a that they may be made perfect in one, and that the world may know that You have sent Me, and have loved them as You have loved Me.

John 17:21–23

PRAYER FOR UNITY

How the squabbles, fighting, and division in the church must hurt our heavenly Father and the Son, who prayed, "that they all may be one." And His prayer is that we would be one so "the world may believe that You sent Me."

If we bring division to the body of Christ, we are working directly contrary to the prayer of Jesus and we are blowing our witness to the world. The witness of the unity of the church is a powerful evidence of who God is, as He brings together diverse people from different backgrounds and makes them one. Division in the body drives people away. They can have that anywhere.

24 a "Father, I desire that they also whom You gave Me may be with Me where I am, that they may behold My glory which You have given Me; b for You loved Me before the foundation of the world. 25 O righteous Father! a The world has not known You, but b I have known You; and c these have known that You sent Me. 26 a And I have declared to them Your name, and will declare *it*, that the love b with which You loved Me may be in them, and I in them."

BETRAYAL AND ARREST IN GETHSEMANE

18 When Jesus had spoken these words, a He went out with His disciples over b the Brook Kidron, where there was a garden, which He and His disciples entered. 2 And Judas, who

betrayed Him, also knew the place; ªfor Jesus often met there with His disciples. 3ªThen Judas, having received a detachment *of troops*, and officers from the chief priests and Pharisees, came there with lanterns, torches, and weapons. 4Jesus therefore, ªknowing all things that would come upon Him, went forward and said to them, "Whom are you seeking?"

5They answered Him, ª"Jesus 1of Nazareth."

Jesus said to them, "I am *He*." And Judas, who ᵇbetrayed Him, also stood with them. 6Now when He said to them, "I am *He*," they drew back and fell to the ground.

John 18:5–6

The Powerful Name. When Jesus asked the soldiers who they were looking for, they told Him "Jesus of Nazareth." He responded by saying, "*ego eimi*" in the Greek, or "I am" in English. The word "He" after that is in italics, indicating that it is not in the original manuscripts. Jesus just said, "I AM." That is the same name God had used to reveal Himself in the Old Testament. "I AM WHO I AM."

There is so much power in that name that the soldiers fell over backwards to the ground. Who was in control?

7Then He asked them again, "Whom are you seeking?"

And they said, "Jesus of Nazareth." 8Jesus answered, "I have told you that I am *He*. Therefore, if you seek Me, let these go their way," 9that the saying might be fulfilled which He spoke, ª"Of those whom You gave Me I have lost none."

10ªThen Simon Peter, having a sword, drew it and struck the high priest's servant, and cut off his right ear. The servant's name was Malchus.

11So Jesus said to Peter, "Put your sword into the sheath. Shall I not drink ªthe cup which My Father has given Me?"

BEFORE THE HIGH PRIEST

12Then the detachment *of troops* and the captain and the officers of the Jews arrested Jesus and bound Him. 13And

---

2 ªLuke 21:37; 22:39

3 ªLuke 22:47–53

4 ªJohn 6:64; 13:1, 3; 19:28

5 ªMatt. 21:11 ᵇPs. 41:9 1Lit. *the Nazarene*

9 ª[John 6:39; 17:12]

10 ªMatt. 26:51

11 ªMatt. 20:22; 26:39

13 ªMatt. 26:57 ᵇLuke 3:2 ᶜMatt. 26:3

14 ªJohn 11:50 1*advantageous*

15 ªMark 14:54 ᵇJohn 20:2–5 1M *the other*

16 ªMatt. 26:69

17 ªMatt. 26:34

20 ªLuke 4:15 ᵇJohn 6:59 ᶜMark 14:49 1NU *all the Jews meet*

21 ªMark 12:37

ªthey led Him away to ᵇAnnas first, for he was the father-in-law of ᶜCaiaphas who was high priest that year. 14ªNow it was Caiaphas who advised the Jews that it was 1expedient that one man should die for the people.

John 18:12

What Bound Him? The soldiers who were taking Jesus captive bound Him. How foolish! Did they really think those little ropes or chains could hold Him? He could have said the word, and the Father would have sent twelve legions of angels (Matt. 26:53). In fact, I suspect that God had to restrain the angels at this point, as they saw what was happening to Jesus.

They didn't need to bind Jesus. He was bound by cords much stronger than the ropes they used. He was bound by His love for you.

PETER DENIES JESUS

15ªAnd Simon Peter followed Jesus, and so *did* ᵇanother 1 disciple. Now that disciple was known to the high priest, and went with Jesus into the courtyard of the high priest. 16ªBut Peter stood at the door outside. Then the other disciple, who was known to the high priest, went out and spoke to her who kept the door, and brought Peter in. 17Then the servant girl who kept the door said to Peter, "You are not also *one* of this Man's disciples, are you?"

He said, "I am ªnot."

18Now the servants and officers who had made a fire of coals stood there, for it was cold, and they warmed themselves. And Peter stood with them and warmed himself.

JESUS QUESTIONED BY THE HIGH PRIEST

19The high priest then asked Jesus about His disciples and His doctrine. 20Jesus answered him, ª"I spoke openly to the world. I always taught ᵇin synagogues and ᶜin the temple, where 1the Jews always meet, and in secret I have said nothing. 21Why do you ask Me? Ask ªthose who have heard Me what I said to them. Indeed they know what I said."

22And when He had said these things,

one of the officers who stood by [a]struck[1] Jesus with the palm of his hand, saying, "Do You answer the high priest like that?"

23 Jesus answered him, "If I have spoken evil, bear witness of the evil; but if well, why do you strike Me?"

24 [a]Then Annas sent Him bound to [b]Caiaphas the high priest.

PETER DENIES TWICE MORE

25 Now Simon Peter stood and warmed himself. [a]Therefore they said to him, "You are not also *one* of His disciples, are you?"

He denied *it* and said, "I am not!"

26 One of the servants of the high priest, a relative *of him* whose ear Peter cut off, said, "Did I not see you in the garden with Him?" 27 Peter then denied again; and [a]immediately a rooster crowed.

IN PILATE'S COURT

28 [a]Then they led Jesus from Caiaphas to the Praetorium, and it was early morning. [b]But they themselves did not go into the [1]Praetorium, lest they should be defiled, but that they might eat the Passover. 29 [a]Pilate then went out to them and said, "What accusation do you bring against this Man?"

30 They answered and said to him, "If He were not [1]an evildoer, we would not have delivered Him up to you."

31 [1]Then Pilate said to them, "You take Him and judge Him according to your law."

Therefore the Jews said to him, "It is not lawful for us to put anyone to death," 32 [a]that the saying of Jesus might be fulfilled which He spoke, [b]signifying by what death He would die.

33 [a]Then Pilate entered the [1]Praetorium again, called Jesus, and said to Him, "Are You the King of the Jews?"

34 Jesus answered him, "Are you speaking for yourself about this, or did others tell you this concerning Me?"

35 Pilate answered, "Am I a Jew? Your own nation and the chief priests have delivered You to me. What have You done?"

36 [a]Jesus answered, [b]"My kingdom is not of this world. If My kingdom were of this world, My servants would fight, so that I should not be delivered to the Jews; but now My kingdom is not from here."

37 Pilate therefore said to Him, "Are You a king then?"

Jesus answered, "You say *rightly* that I am a king. For this cause I was born,

---

22 [a] Jer. 20:2
[1] Lit. *gave Jesus a slap,*

24 [a] Matt. 26:57
[b] John 11:49

25 [a] Luke 22:58–62

27 [a] John 13:38

28 [a] Mark 15:1
[b] Acts 10:28; 11:3
[1] The governor's headquarters

29 [a] Matt. 27:11–14

30 [1] *a criminal*

32 [a] Matt. 20:17–19; 26:2
[b] John 3:14; 8:28; 12:32, 33

33 [a] Matt. 27:11
[1] The governor's headquarters

36 [a] 1 Tim. 6:13
[b] [Dan. 2:44; 7:14]

37 [a] [Matt. 5:17; 20:28]
[b] Is. 55:4
[c] [John 14:6]
[d] John 8:47; 10:27

38 [a] John 19:4, 6

39 [a] Luke 23:17–25

40 [a] Acts 3:14
[b] Luke 23:19

CHAPTER 19

1 [a] Matt. 20:19; 27:26

3 [a] Is. 50:6
[1] NU *And they came up to Him and said*

4 [a] John 18:33, 38

John 18:36–37

MY KINGDOM IS NOT FROM HERE

Jesus acknowledged to Pilate that He is a king. But His kingdom is not from this world. He was born and came into the world to establish a spiritual kingdom. His kingdom will be in the transformed hearts of men. It is about changed lives. And if you have received Jesus Christ as your Lord and Savior by asking Him to forgive you and be the Lord of your life, then you have entered the kingdom. You are a part of the kingdom of God.

Jesus rules in the hearts of those who have heard His voice and responded to His call. And it is so wonderful to be a part of the kingdom of Jesus Christ. It is out of this world!

---

and for this cause I have come into the world, [a]that I should bear [b]witness to the truth. Everyone who [c]is of the truth [d]hears My voice."

38 Pilate said to Him, "What is truth?" And when he had said this, he went out again to the Jews, and said to them, [a]"I find no fault in Him at all.

TAKING THE PLACE OF BARABBAS

39 [a]"But you have a custom that I should release someone to you at the Passover. Do you therefore want me to release to you the King of the Jews?"

40 [a]Then they all cried again, saying, "Not this Man, but Barabbas!" [b]Now Barabbas was a robber.

THE SOLDIERS MOCK JESUS

19 So then [a]Pilate took Jesus and scourged *Him.* 2 And the soldiers twisted a crown of thorns and put *it* on His head, and they put on Him a purple robe. 3 [1]Then they said, "Hail, King of the Jews!" And they [a]struck Him with their hands.

4 Pilate then went out again, and said to them, "Behold, I am bringing Him out to you, [a]that you may know that I find no fault in Him."

John 19:5

Crown of Thorns. Why a crown of thorns? Back in Genesis 3:17–19, after Adam and Eve had sinned in the garden of Eden, the curse upon the earth was that thorns and thistles would grow from it.

It is said that thorns are just blossoms that never come to fruition. So here, as Jesus was being tortured in order to redeem the earth from the power of sin and death, it is appropriate that the King would wear a crown of thorns as a symbol of the stunted growth that resulted from sin.

PILATE'S DECISION

5Then Jesus came out, wearing the crown of thorns and the purple robe. And *Pilate* said to them, "Behold the Man!"

6aTherefore, when the chief priests and officers saw Him, they cried out, saying, "Crucify *Him*, crucify *Him!*"

Pilate said to them, "You take Him and crucify *Him*, for I find no fault in Him."

7The Jews answered him, a"We have a law, and according to 1our law He ought to die, because bHe made Himself the Son of God."

8Therefore, when Pilate heard that saying, he was the more afraid, 9and went again into the Praetorium, and said to Jesus, "Where are You from?" aBut Jesus gave him no answer.

10Then Pilate said to Him, "Are You not speaking to me? Do You not know that I have 1power to crucify You, and 2power to release You?"

11Jesus answered, a"You could have no power at all against Me unless it had been given you from above. Therefore bthe one who delivered Me to you has the greater sin."

12From then on Pilate sought to release Him, but the Jews cried out, saying, "If you let this Man go, you are not Caesar's friend. aWhoever makes himself a king speaks against Caesar."

13aWhen Pilate therefore heard that saying, he brought Jesus out and sat down in the judgment seat in a place that is called *The* Pavement, but in Hebrew, Gabbatha. 14Now ait was the

6 a Acts 3:13

7 a Lev. 24:16
b Matt. 26:63–66
1 NU the law

9 a Is. 53:7

10 1 authority

11 a [Luke 22:53]
b Rom. 13:1

12 a Luke 23:2

13 a 1 Sam. 15:24

14 a Matt. 27:62

15 a [Gen. 49:10]

16 a Luke 23:24
1 NU omits and led Him away

17 a Mark 15:21, 22
b Num. 15:36

18 a Is. 53:12

19 a Matt. 27:37

23 a Luke 23:34

24 a Ps. 22:18

25 a Mark 15:40
b Luke 24:18

26 a John 13:23; 20:2; 21:7, 20, 24
b John 2:4

27 a John 1:11; 16:32

Preparation Day of the Passover, and about the sixth hour. And he said to the Jews, "Behold your King!"

15But they cried out, "Away with *Him*, away with *Him!* Crucify Him!"

Pilate said to them, "Shall I crucify your King?"

The chief priests answered, a"We have no king but Caesar!"

16aThen he delivered Him to them to be crucified. Then they took Jesus 1and led *Him* away.

THE KING ON A CROSS

17aAnd He, bearing His cross, bwent out to a place called *the Place* of a Skull, which is called in Hebrew, Golgotha, 18where they crucified Him, and atwo others with Him, one on either side, and Jesus in the center. 19aNow Pilate wrote a title and put *it* on the cross. And the writing was:

JESUS OF NAZARETH,
THE KING OF THE JEWS.

20Then many of the Jews read this title, for the place where Jesus was crucified was near the city; and it was written in Hebrew, Greek, *and* Latin. 21Therefore the chief priests of the Jews said to Pilate, "Do not write, 'The King of the Jews,' but, 'He said, "I am the King of the Jews." '"

22Pilate answered, "What I have written, I have written."

23aThen the soldiers, when they had crucified Jesus, took His garments and made four parts, to each soldier a part, and also the tunic. Now the tunic was without seam, woven from the top in one piece. 24They said therefore among themselves, "Let us not tear it, but cast lots for it, whose it shall be," that the Scripture might be fulfilled which says:

a"*They divided My garments among them,*
And for My clothing they cast lots."

Therefore the soldiers did these things.

BEHOLD YOUR MOTHER

25aNow there stood by the cross of Jesus His mother, and His mother's sister, Mary the *wife* of bClopas, and Mary Magdalene. 26When Jesus therefore saw His mother, and athe disciple whom He loved standing by, He said to His mother, b"Woman, behold your son!" 27Then He said to the disciple, "Behold your mother!" And from that hour that disciple took her ato his own *home.*

John 19:23–24

His Clothes. The four soldiers who would lead a person to their execution would often divide up any valuables belonging to the prisoner. These soldiers divided up Jesus' clothes into four parts, but His tunic was left. It was nice, woven in one piece; they didn't want to cut it up, so they cast lots for it.

Even this small detail was predicted by Scripture. Psalm 22:18 said, "They divided My garments among them, and for My clothing they cast lots." A divine plan was meticulously unfolding.

IT IS FINISHED

28 After this, Jesus, 1knowing that all things were now accomplished, athat the Scripture might be fulfilled, said, "I thirst!" 29 Now a vessel full of sour wine was sitting there; and athey filled a sponge with sour wine, put it on hyssop, and put it to His mouth. 30 So when Jesus had received the sour wine, He said, a"It is finished!" And bowing His head, He gave up His spirit.

JESUS' SIDE IS PIERCED

31 aTherefore, because it was the Preparation Day, bthat the bodies should not remain on the cross on the Sabbath (for that Sabbath was a chigh day), the Jews asked Pilate that their

28 a Ps. 22:15
1 M seeing

29 a Matt. 27:48, 50

30 a John 17:4

31 a Mark 15:42
b Deut. 21:23
c Ex. 12:16

34 a [1 John 5:6, 8]

35 a John 21:24
b [John 20:31]

36 a [Ex. 12:46; Num. 9:12]; Ps. 34:20

37 a Zech. 12:10; 13:6

38 a Luke 23:50–56
b [John 7:13; 9:22; 12:42]

39 a John 3:1, 2; 7:50
b Matt. 2:11

40 a John 20:5, 7

42 a Is. 53:9
b John 19:14, 31

legs might be broken, and *that* they might be taken away. 32 Then the soldiers came and broke the legs of the first and of the other who was crucified with Him. 33 But when they came to Jesus and saw that He was already dead, they did not break His legs. 34 But one of the soldiers pierced His side with a spear, and immediately ablood and water came out. 35 And he who has seen has testified, and his testimony is atrue; and he knows that he is telling the truth, so that you may bbelieve. 36 For these things were done that the Scripture should be fulfilled, a"Not one of His bones shall be broken." 37 And again another Scripture says, a"They shall look on Him whom they pierced."

JESUS BURIED IN JOSEPH'S TOMB

38 aAfter this, Joseph of Arimathea, being a disciple of Jesus, but secretly, bfor fear of the Jews, asked Pilate that he might take away the body of Jesus; and Pilate gave *him* permission. So he came and took the body of Jesus. 39 And aNicodemus, who at first came to Jesus by night, also came, bringing a mixture of bmyrrh and aloes, about a hundred pounds. 40 Then they took the body of Jesus, and abound it in strips of linen with the spices, as the custom of the Jews is to bury. 41 Now in the place where He was crucified there was a garden, and in the garden a new tomb in which no one had yet been laid. 42 So athere they laid Jesus, bbecause of the Jews' Preparation *Day*, for the tomb was nearby.

THE DAY OF HIS DEATH   John 19:31

Many people have been confused concerning the day of the death of Jesus. We know it was the day before the Sabbath, because the Jews wanted to get Him off the cross before the Sabbath. So traditionally people have believed Jesus died on Friday afternoon. But He had said He would be dead for three days and three nights, and we know He rose on Sunday morning, so that would only be two nights. Several explanations have been offered, but this passage here gives us a possible clue.

John tells us "that Sabbath was a high day." The day after Passover was the beginning of the Feast of Unleavened Bread. The first day of the Feast of Unleavened Bread was always considered a high Sabbath, no matter what day of the week it fell on. It was a special Sabbath day.

So I believe that Jesus was actually crucified on a Thursday, on the Day of Passover, with the next day, Friday, being the High Sabbath, the following day being the normal Saturday Sabbath, and the third day being Easter Sunday, the day He rose from the dead. This makes three days and nights. It also explains why His followers couldn't come to the tomb to anoint His body until three days later, as they couldn't do that on either Sabbath. We still celebrate the traditional Good Friday, but technically I believe it should be Good Thursday.

THE EMPTY TOMB

20 Now the ᵃfirst *day* of the week Mary Magdalene went to the tomb early, while it was still dark, and saw *that* the ᵇstone had been taken away from the tomb. ²Then she ran and came to Simon Peter, and to the ᵃother disciple, ᵇwhom Jesus loved, and said to them, "They have taken away the Lord out of the tomb, and we do not know where they have laid Him."

³ᵃPeter therefore went out, and the other disciple, and were going to the tomb. ⁴So they both ran together, and the other disciple outran Peter and came to the tomb first. ⁵And he, stooping down and looking in, saw ᵃthe linen cloths lying *there*; yet he did not go in. ⁶Then Simon Peter came, following him, and went into the tomb; and he saw the linen cloths lying *there*, ⁷and ᵃthe ¹handkerchief that had been around His head, not lying with the linen cloths, but folded together in a place by itself. ⁸Then the ᵃother disciple,

---

John 20:8–9

HEARING PROBLEM

When Peter and John saw the burial garments of Jesus, left as if His body had dematerialized out of them, they believed. "For as yet they did not know the Scripture, that He must rise again from the dead."

This shows the blindness of preconceived ideas. Jesus had told His followers repeatedly that He would die and rise from the dead. Yet, when you don't want to hear something, you can just block it out of your mind. They wanted to see Jesus coming in His glory to establish His kingdom, and they just didn't catch on to what He was saying about death and resurrection.

It is so important for us to hear everything God is saying to us and not just what we want to hear or what we expect to hear.

CHAPTER 20

1 ᵃMatt. 28:1–8
ᵇMatt. 27:60, 66; 28:2

2 ᵃJohn 21:23, 24
ᵇJohn 13:23; 19:26; 21:7, 20, 24

3 ᵃLuke 24:12

5 ᵃJohn 19:40

7 ᵃJohn 11:44
¹ *face cloth*

8 ᵃJohn 21:23, 24

9 ᵃPs. 16:10
¹ *understand*

11 ᵃMark 16:5

14 ᵃMatt. 28:9
ᵇJohn 21:4

16 ᵃJohn 10:3
¹NU adds *in Hebrew*

17 ᵃHeb. 4:14
ᵇHeb. 2:11
ᶜJohn 16:28; 17:11
ᵈEph. 1:17

18 ᵃLuke 24:10, 23
¹NU *disciples, "I have seen the Lord,"*

19 ᵃLuke 24:36
ᵇJohn 9:22; 19:38
ᶜJohn 14:27; 16:33
¹NU omits *assembled*

20 ᵃActs 1:3
ᵇJohn 16:20, 22

21 ᵃJohn 17:18, 19

23 ᵃMatt. 16:19; 18:18

---

who came to the tomb first, went in also; and he saw and believed. ⁹For as yet they did not ¹know the ᵃScripture, that He must rise again from the dead. ¹⁰Then the disciples went away again to their own homes.

MARY MAGDALENE SEES THE RISEN LORD

¹¹ᵃBut Mary stood outside by the tomb weeping, and as she wept she stooped down *and looked* into the tomb. ¹²And she saw two angels in white sitting, one at the head and the other at the feet, where the body of Jesus had lain. ¹³Then they said to her, "Woman, why are you weeping?"

She said to them, "Because they have taken away my Lord, and I do not know where they have laid Him."

¹⁴ᵃNow when she had said this, she turned around and saw Jesus standing *there*, and ᵇdid not know that it was Jesus. ¹⁵Jesus said to her, "Woman, why are you weeping? Whom are you seeking?"

She, supposing Him to be the gardener, said to Him, "Sir, if You have carried Him away, tell me where You have laid Him, and I will take Him away."

¹⁶Jesus said to her, ᵃ"Mary!"

She turned and said to ¹Him, "Rabboni!" (which is to say, Teacher).

¹⁷Jesus said to her, "Do not cling to Me, for I have not yet ᵃascended to My Father; but go to ᵇMy brethren and say to them, ᶜ'I am ascending to My Father and your Father, and *to* ᵈMy God and your God.'"

¹⁸ᵃMary Magdalene came and told the ¹disciples that she had seen the Lord, and *that* He had spoken these things to her.

THE APOSTLES COMMISSIONED

¹⁹ᵃThen, the same day at evening, being the first *day* of the week, when the doors were shut where the disciples were ¹assembled, for ᵇfear of the Jews, Jesus came and stood in the midst, and said to them, ᶜ"Peace *be* with you." ²⁰When He had said this, He ᵃshowed them *His* hands and His side. ᵇThen the disciples were glad when they saw the Lord.

²¹So Jesus said to them again, "Peace to you! ᵃAs the Father has sent Me, I also send you." ²²And when He had said this, He breathed on *them*, and said to them, "Receive the Holy Spirit. ²³ᵃIf you forgive the sins of any, they

John 20:16–17

DON'T CLING
TO ME

Mary Magdalene had a deep love for Jesus. He had delivered her from the horror of demon possession and had changed her life completely. Now Jesus had died, and she was intent on finding His body when she ran into Him in the garden.

She didn't recognize Him at first, in the dawn's early light and as she looked through tear-filled eyes; but when He called her name, there was no mistaking it. Here He was. And Mary grabbed onto Him and just wouldn't let go. She had a death grip around His neck. Her attitude was probably, *You got away from me once, but You'll never get away from me again!*

He told her to stop hanging onto Him and to go tell the disciples the news of the resurrection and that He would soon be ascending back to His Father in heaven.

---

24 ᵃ John 11:16

27 ᵃ 1 John 1:1
ᵇ Mark 16:14

29 ᵃ 1 Pet. 1:8
1 NU, M omit
Thomas

30 ᵃ John 21:25

31 ᵃ Luke 1:4
ᵇ 1 John 5:13
ᶜ Luke 2:11
ᵈ John 3:15, 16;
5:24

---

are forgiven them; if you retain the *sins* of any, they are retained."

SEEING AND BELIEVING

24Now Thomas, ᵃcalled the Twin, one of the twelve, was not with them when Jesus came. 25The other disciples therefore said to him, "We have seen the Lord."

So he said to them, "Unless I see in His hands the print of the nails, and put my finger into the print of the nails, and put my hand into His side, I will not believe."

26And after eight days His disciples were again inside, and Thomas with them. Jesus came, the doors being shut, and stood in the midst, and said, "Peace to you!" 27Then He said to Thomas, "Reach your finger here, and look at My hands; and ᵃreach your hand *here*, and put *it* into My side. Do not be ᵇunbelieving, but believing."

28And Thomas answered and said to Him, "My Lord and my God!"

29Jesus said to him, 1"Thomas, because you have seen Me, you have believed. ᵃBlessed *are* those who have not seen and *yet* have believed."

THAT YOU MAY BELIEVE

30And ᵃtruly Jesus did many other signs in the presence of His disciples, which are not written in this book; 31ᵃbut these are written that ᵇyou may believe that Jesus ᶜis the Christ, the Son of God, ᵈand that believing you may have life in His name.

RECEIVE THE HOLY SPIRIT   John 20:22

As Jesus breathed on His disciples and said, "Receive the Holy Spirit," they were receiving the second part of the threefold relationship of the believer with the Holy Spirit.

In John 14:16–17, Jesus told them that the Holy Spirit would be sent to them as a Helper. He told them, "He dwells with you and will be in you." So the Holy Spirit had already been with them, but Jesus said that in the future He would be in them. Then, in Acts 1:8, Jesus said, "But you shall receive power when the Holy Spirit has come upon you."

So the Holy Spirit was always with them, as He is everywhere. Now the Holy Spirit came into them as Jesus breathed on them. This was their spiritual birth as they experienced the indwelling of the Holy Spirit. And on the Day of Pentecost, as the Holy Spirit would be poured out on them, they would experience the power that comes on a believer for service.

If you have never before accepted Jesus Christ as your Savior, the Holy Spirit is with you. He is the One who draws you to God and convicts you of sin. If you have accepted Jesus, then the Holy Spirit is inside you. But He wants to come upon you, as well, to give you the power to live the Christian life, and to serve Him in a fruitful way. Don't stop short of all that God has for you. Ask for the power of the Spirit to come upon you and to stay upon you.

John 20:31

THE PURPOSE OF THE GOSPEL

Here John gave us his reason for writing this book. He wanted people to know that Jesus is the Christ, or the Messiah, and also that He is the Son of God, or God Himself. But John wasn't just trying to write an apologetic argument for who Jesus is. It was his intent and desire that through this book many would discover the meaning of life, finding that rich, full existence that comes from being in relationship with Jesus.

It isn't enough to just know who Jesus is intellectually. He wants to give you life.

BREAKFAST BY THE SEA

21 After these things Jesus showed Himself again to the disciples at the ᵃSea of Tiberias, and in this way He showed *Himself:* ²Simon Peter, ᵃThomas called the Twin, ᵇNathanael of ᶜCana in Galilee, ᵈthe *sons* of Zebedee, and two others of His disciples were together. ³Simon Peter said to them, "I am going fishing."

They said to him, "We are going with you also." They went out and ¹immediately got into the boat, and that night they caught nothing. ⁴But when the morning had now come, Jesus stood on the shore; yet the disciples ᵃdid not know that it was Jesus. ⁵Then ᵃJesus said to them, "Children, have you any food?"

They answered Him, "No."

⁶And He said to them, ᵃ"Cast the net on the right side of the boat, and you will find *some.*" So they cast, and now they were not able to draw it in because of the multitude of fish.

⁷Therefore ᵃthat disciple whom Jesus loved said to Peter, "It is the Lord!" Now when Simon Peter heard that it was the Lord, he put on *his* outer garment (for he had removed it), and plunged into the sea. ⁸But the other disciples came in the little boat (for they were not far from land, but about two

CHAPTER 21

1 ᵃ John 6:1

2 ᵃ John 20:24
ᵇ John 1:45–51
ᶜ John 2:1
ᵈ Matt. 4:21

3 ¹ NU omits *immediately*

4 ᵃ John 20:14

5 ᵃ Luke 24:41

6 ᵃ Luke 5:4, 6, 7

7 ᵃ John 13:23; 20:2

12 ᵃ Acts 10:41

14 ᵃ John 20:19, 26

John 21:5–6

Have You Caught Anything? The disciples had been fishing all night and hadn't caught anything. The fishing trip was a failure. But now Jesus told them to throw the net on the other side of the boat, and they caught a net full of fish.

What a difference there is between self-directed service and God-directed service! God knows what He is doing. When we let Him direct us, we will be blessed. When we do it our way, it means certain failure. Whose instructions are you following?

hundred cubits), dragging the net with fish. ⁹Then, as soon as they had come to land, they saw a fire of coals there, and fish laid on it, and bread. ¹⁰Jesus said to them, "Bring some of the fish which you have just caught."

¹¹Simon Peter went up and dragged the net to land, full of large fish, one hundred and fifty-three; and although there were so many, the net was not broken. ¹²Jesus said to them, ᵃ"Come *and* eat breakfast." Yet none of the disciples dared ask Him, "Who are You?"—knowing that it was the Lord. ¹³Jesus then came and took the bread and gave it to them, and likewise the fish.

¹⁴This *is* now ᵃthe third time Jesus showed Himself to His disciples after He was raised from the dead.

JESUS RESTORES PETER

¹⁵So when they had eaten breakfast, Jesus said to Simon Peter, "Simon, *son*

John 21:7

It Is the Lord! When Peter saw all the fish they had caught, he knew there was only one explanation: "It is the Lord!" Whenever the net gets so full that you can't drag it in, there is only one possibility. It is the Lord.

As I look at what God has done through Calvary Chapel over all these years, I see nets that are so full, and I realize there is only one reason. It is the Lord!

of [1]Jonah, do you love Me more than these?"

He said to Him, "Yes, Lord; You know that I [2]love You."

He said to him, a"Feed My lambs."

[16]He said to him again a second time, "Simon, son of [1]Jonah, do you love Me?"

He said to Him, "Yes, Lord; You know that I [2]love You."

aHe said to him, "Tend My bsheep."

[17]He said to him the third time, "Simon, son of [1]Jonah, do you [2]love Me?" Peter was grieved because He said to him the third time, "Do you love Me?"

And he said to Him, "Lord, aYou know all things; You know that I love You."

Jesus said to him, "Feed My sheep. [18]aMost assuredly, I say to you, when you were younger, you girded yourself and walked where you wished; but when you are old, you will stretch out your hands, and another will gird you and carry you where you do not wish."

[19]This He spoke, signifying aby what death he would glorify God. And when He had spoken this, He said to him, b"Follow Me."

THE BELOVED DISCIPLE AND HIS BOOK

[20]Then Peter, turning around, saw the disciple awhom Jesus loved following, bwho also had leaned on His breast at the supper, and said, "Lord, who is the one who betrays You?" [21]Peter, seeing him, said to Jesus, "But Lord, what about this man?"

[22]Jesus said to him, "If I [1]will that he remain atill I come, what is that to you? You follow Me."

[23]Then this saying went out among the brethren that this disciple would not die. Yet Jesus did not say to him that he would not die, but, "If I will that he remain till I come, what is that to you?"

[24]This is the disciple who atestifies of these things, and wrote these things; and we know that his testimony is true.

[25]aAnd there are also many other things that Jesus did, which if they were written one by one, bI suppose that even the world itself could not contain the books that would be written. Amen.

Side references:

15 a Acts 20:28 [1]NU John [2]have affection for
16 a Heb. 13:20 b Ps. 79:13 [1]NU John [2]have affection for
17 a John 2:24, 25; 16:30 [1]NU John [2]have affection for
18 a Acts 12:3, 4
19 a 2 Pet. 1:13, 14 b [Matt. 4:19; 16:24]
20 a John 13:23; 20:2 b John 13:25
22 a [Rev. 2:25; 3:11; 22:7, 20] [1]desire
24 a John 19:35
25 a John 20:30 b Amos 7:10

DO YOU LOVE ME MORE THAN THESE?

John 21:15–19

Jesus asked Peter if he loved Him supremely. The disciples had just had the biggest day in their lives as fishermen. The fish were flopping all over the place, and this represented professional success to Peter. But Jesus wanted to know if he loved Him more than professional success.

To serve Jesus, you need to love Him more than anything else. "These" represents something different to each of us, but we need to ask ourselves if there is anything in our lives more important than our relationship with Jesus.

Jesus continued to ask Peter if he loved Him, using the word *agape* for love. This word was the word in Greek that to the New Testament writers represented supreme, sacrificial love. Peter responded by saying that he was fond of Jesus. He used the word for love that is in the Greek *phileo*. It usually denotes a brotherly love. The third time Jesus used the word *phileo* as He asked Peter if he loved Him. This grieved Peter, and he eventually responded that he had *phileo* love for Jesus. He never rose to the level of *agape* love for Jesus until after the Day of Pentecost.

Jesus was basically asking Peter where He fit in Peter's life. "What priority am I in your life? How far down am I on the list of things you care about?" And I believe He would ask each of us, "How much do you love Me? How many things in your life are more important to you than I am?" Tough question, but it is an important question.

THE
ACTS OF THE APOSTLES

The book of Acts was written by Luke and was a continuation of the gospel of Luke. Luke was a physician and historian, who kept detailed records of the events that were relayed to him, as well as the events to which he was an eyewitness. He accompanied Paul on his later missionary journeys, and it is thought that he joined him in Troas as Acts 16:10 has a shifting of pronouns from "they" to "we" which continues to the end of the book. Luke was the only Gentile to write a book of the New Testament, and he wrote two of them, Luke and Acts.

The book was written sometime after AD 60 as we know Paul was imprisoned in Rome around that time and the book ends with Paul in Rome. There is no mention of the destruction of Jerusalem, which happened in AD 70, so it was written sometime between AD 60 and 69.

The title in our Bible is "The Acts of the Apostles" but it would probably be more accurate to entitle it "The Acts of the Holy Spirit Through the Apostles." The theme of the book is found in Acts 1:8, where Jesus told His disciples, "But you shall receive power when the Holy Spirit has come upon you; and you shall be witnesses to Me in Jerusalem, and in all Judea and Samaria, and to the end of the earth." This provides a threefold outline of the book, as chapters 1–7 chronicle the spread of the gospel in Jerusalem, chapters 8–12 show it spreading to Judea and Samaria, with chapters 13–28 taking it to the rest of the known world. So the book tells the story of how the Holy Spirit established the church, and it is both exciting and challenging for us today as we seek to be empowered and used by the Holy Spirit.

Acts begins with the resurrection of Jesus and it figures prominently throughout the book. The apostles were driven to declare the reality of the resurrection.

The book is addressed to someone named Theophilus. Tradition says that Theophilus was a wealthy Roman official who had purchased Luke's freedom for him. Luke was investigating the accounts of Jesus and the establishment of His church and reporting the facts back to him. Some people have suggested that the name Theophilus might be a pseudonym, to protect the identity of the man Luke was writing to. The name Theophilus means "lover of God," and I kind of like the idea that perhaps it was a pseudonym. If that were the case, then we could say that it is addressed to all lovers of God, which would include us.

PROLOGUE

1 The former account I made, O ªThe-ophilus, of all that Jesus began both to do and teach, ²ªuntil the day in which ¹He was taken up, after He through the Holy Spirit ᵇhad given commandments to the apostles whom He had chosen, ³ªto whom He also presented Himself alive after His suffering by many ¹infallible proofs, being seen by them during forty days and speaking of the things pertaining to the kingdom of God.

THE HOLY SPIRIT PROMISED

4ªAnd being assembled together with them, He commanded them not to depart from Jerusalem, but to wait for the Promise of the Father, "which," He said, "you have ᵇheard from Me; ⁵ªfor John truly baptized with water, ᵇbut you shall be baptized with the Holy Spirit not many days from now." ⁶Therefore, when they had come together, they asked Him, saying, "Lord, will You at this time restore the kingdom to Israel?" ⁷And He said to them, ª"It is not for you to ᵇknow times or seasons which the Father has put in His own authority. ⁸ªBut you shall receive power ᵇwhen the Holy Spirit has come upon you; and ᶜyou shall be ¹witnesses to Me in Jerusalem, and in all Judea and ᵈSamaria, and to the ᵉend of the earth."

CHAPTER 1

1 ª Luke 1:3

2 ª Mark 16:19
ᵇ Matt. 28:19
1 He ascended
into heaven.

3 ª Mark 16:12,
14
1 unmistakable

4 ª Luke 24:49
ᵇ [John 14:16,
17, 26; 15:26]

5 ª Matt. 3:11
ᵇ [Joel 2:28]

7 ª 1 Thess. 5:1
ᵇ Matt. 24:36

8 ª [Acts 2:1, 4]
ᵇ Luke 24:49
ᶜ Luke 24:48
ᵈ Acts 8:1, 5, 14
ᵉ Col. 1:23
1 NU My witnesses

9 ª Luke 24:50,
51
ᵇ Acts 1:2

JESUS ASCENDS TO HEAVEN

⁹ªNow when He had spoken these things, while they watched, ᵇHe was taken up, and a cloud received Him out of their sight. ¹⁰And while they looked

Acts 1:1–2

THE FINAL CHAPTER

L uke's gospel presents the beginning of Jesus' ministry. Acts presents the continuation of Jesus' ministry. His ministry did not end with His ascension!

Jesus continued to heal; Jesus continued to work. Jesus continued to pour forth His grace, mercy, and love. Only, in Acts, He did it by the power of the Holy Spirit through His apostles. In that sense, the book of Acts is an open-ended book because the Lord continues to work to the present day through people filled with the Holy Spirit. The final chapter of the book has not been written yet.

MANY INFALLIBLE PROOFS

Acts 1:3

F acts are determined in our jurisprudence system by the testimony of eyewitnesses—that is, by two or three people who bear witness that on a certain date they saw a certain event. If they make this testimony under oath and there are sufficient witnesses to give an account, to corroborate, then it can be determined to be an actual fact.

Jesus appeared after His resurrection, first to Mary Magdalene; then to the other women; then to Peter; then to the two disciples on the road to Emmaus; and, on that first Sunday night, to ten of the apostles, Thomas not being present. The following Sunday night, Jesus appeared to the apostles again with Thomas present. We have the account in the last chapter of the gospel of John of His appearance to seven disciples in Galilee. He appeared another time to James (1 Cor. 15:7). Paul also wrote that Jesus appeared to more than five hundred people at once (1 Cor. 15:6).

Jesus showed by many infallible proofs that He was alive. He ate fish and honey to show His followers that He was not a ghost or a spirit. He said, "Touch Me. Feel Me." So they handled Him. They touched Him, and they realized He wasn't just an apparition. He had risen bodily from the dead and He was alive.

The people who saw Him bore witness to the fact that they had seen the resurrected Lord. Many gave their lives as martyrs because of their witness to His resurrection. If He had not risen from the dead, surely these witnesses would have confessed to fraud to save their lives. Instead, many suffered violent deaths, maintaining to the very end that their story was true. They had seen Him. Jesus was alive!

Acts 1:8

WITNESSES TO HIM

Jesus said that when the Holy Spirit has come upon you, you will receive power to live in such a way that you will become a reflection of Him. That's what being a witness is.

It is interesting that in Antioch the people began to call Jesus' followers "Christians" because they were like Christ. The term "Christians" was not one His followers took upon themselves. It was a term given to them by the media of that day because they were so Christlike. It was sort of a derisive term, like when they used to call us "Jesus freaks" because we were so crazy about Jesus!

God's desire is that our lives reflect Jesus. Peter said we should follow in His steps (1 Pet. 2:21), but we can't do that by our own power. We cannot forgive. We cannot love. We cannot be kind and considerate like Jesus. But by the power of the Holy Spirit, we can be transformed into His image and be witnesses to Him.

steadfastly toward heaven as He went up, behold, two men stood by them ᵃin white apparel, ¹¹who also said, "Men of Galilee, why do you stand gazing up into heaven? This *same* Jesus, who was taken up from you into heaven, ᵃwill so come in like manner as you saw Him go into heaven."

THE UPPER ROOM PRAYER MEETING

¹²ᵃThen they returned to Jerusalem from the mount called Olivet, which is near Jerusalem, a Sabbath day's journey. ¹³And when they had entered, they went up ᵃinto the upper room where they were staying: ᵇPeter, James, John, and Andrew; Philip and Thomas; Bartholomew and Matthew; James *the son* of Alphaeus and ᶜSimon the Zealot; and ᵈJudas *the son* of James. ¹⁴ᵃThese

10 ᵃJohn 20:12

11 ᵃDan. 7:13

12 ᵃLuke 24:52

13 ᵃActs 9:37, 39; 20:8
ᵇMatt. 10:2–4
ᶜLuke 6:15
ᵈJude 1

14 ᵃActs 2:1, 46
ᵇLuke 23:49, 55 ᶜMatt. 13:55
¹ *purpose* or *mind*
²NU omits *and supplication*

15 ᵃRev. 3:4
¹NU *brethren*

16 ᵃPs. 41:9
ᵇLuke 22:47

17 ᵃMatt. 10:4
ᵇActs 1:25

18 ᵃMatt. 27:3–10
ᵇMark 14:21
¹ *reward of unrighteousness*
² *intestines*

20 ᵃPs. 69:25
¹ *deserted*

all continued with one ¹accord in prayer ²and supplication, with ᵇthe women and Mary the mother of Jesus, and with ᶜHis brothers.

MATTHIAS CHOSEN

¹⁵And in those days Peter stood up in the midst of the ¹disciples (altogether the number ᵃof names was about a hundred and twenty), and said, ¹⁶"Men *and* brethren, this Scripture had to be fulfilled, ᵃwhich the Holy Spirit spoke before by the mouth of David concerning Judas, ᵇwho became a guide to those who arrested Jesus; ¹⁷for ᵃhe was numbered with us and obtained a part in ᵇthis ministry."

Acts 1:16

INSPIRED AND INERRANT

There are two things I want you to notice.

Number one, the disciples' confidence in the Scriptures: Because it was written, it had to come to pass. They had great confidence in the Word of God. Because God said it, it had to happen!

Second, notice the recognition that the Scriptures were inspired by the Holy Spirit, "which the Holy Spirit spoke before by the mouth of David."

So the disciples believed in the inspiration and inerrancy of the Scriptures. These are two important fundamental beliefs we must have concerning the Word of God.

¹⁸ᵃ(Now this man purchased a field with ᵇthe ¹wages of iniquity; and falling headlong, he burst open in the middle and all his ²entrails gushed out. ¹⁹And it became known to all those dwelling in Jerusalem; so that field is called in their own language, Akel Dama, that is, Field of Blood.) ²⁰"For it is written in the Book of Psalms:

ᵃ'*Let his dwelling place be ¹desolate, And let no one live in it*';

and,

ᵇ'*Let another take his* ²*office.*'

²¹"Therefore, of these men who have accompanied us all the time that the Lord Jesus went in and out among us, ²²beginning from the baptism of John to that day when ªHe was taken up from us, one of these must ᵇbecome a witness with us of His resurrection."

²³And they proposed two: Joseph called ªBarsabas, who was surnamed Justus, and Matthias. ²⁴And they prayed and said, "You, O Lord, ªwho know the hearts of all, show which of these two You have chosen ²⁵ªto take part in this ministry and apostleship from which Judas by transgression fell, that he might go to his own place." ²⁶And they cast their lots, and the lot fell on Matthias. And he was numbered with the eleven apostles.

COMING OF THE HOLY SPIRIT

2 When ªthe Day of Pentecost had fully come, ᵇthey were all ¹with one accord in one place. ²And suddenly there came a sound from heaven, as of a rushing mighty wind, and ªit filled the whole house where they were sitting. ³Then there appeared to them ¹divided tongues, as of fire, and *one* sat upon each of them. ⁴And ªthey were all filled with the Holy Spirit and began ᵇto speak with other tongues, as the Spirit gave them utterance.

THE CROWD'S RESPONSE

⁵And there were dwelling in Jerusalem Jews, ªdevout men, from every nation under heaven. ⁶And when this sound occurred, the ªmultitude came together, and were confused, because everyone heard them speak in his own language. ⁷Then they were all amazed and marveled, saying to one another, "Look, are not all these who speak ªGalileans? ⁸And how *is it that* we hear, each in our own ¹language in which we were born? ⁹Parthians and Medes and Elamites, those dwelling in Mesopotamia, Judea and ªCappadocia, Pontus and Asia, ¹⁰Phrygia and Pamphylia, Egypt and the parts of Libya adjoining Cyrene, visitors from Rome, both Jews and proselytes, ¹¹Cretans and ¹Arabs—we hear them speaking in our own tongues the wonderful works of God." ¹²So they were all amazed and perplexed, saying to one another, "Whatever could this mean?"

¹³Others mocking said, "They are full of new wine."

---

20 ᵇ Ps. 109:8
² Gr. *episkopen*, position of overseer

22 ª Acts 1:9
ᵇ Acts 1:8; 2:32

23 ª Acts 15:22

24 ª 1 Sam. 16:7

25 ª Acts 1:17

CHAPTER 2

1 ª Lev. 23:15
ᵇ Acts 1:14
¹ NU *together*

2 ª Acts 4:31

3 ¹ Or *tongues as of fire, distributed and resting on each*

4 ª Acts 1:5
ᵇ Mark 16:17

5 ª Acts 8:2

6 ª Acts 4:32

7 ª Acts 1:11

8 ¹ *dialect*

9 ª 1 Pet. 1:1

11 ¹ *Arabians*

15 ª 1 Thess. 5:7
¹ 9 A.M.

17 ª Joel 2:28–32
ᵇ Acts 10:45
ᶜ Acts 21:9

18 ª 1 Cor. 12:10

19 ª Joel 2:30

Acts 2:2–4

THE FIRST, BUT NOT THE LAST

Notice there were different supernatural phenomena accompanying the outpouring of the Holy Spirit upon the church. First, there was a sound like a mighty rushing wind. Second, there were divided tongues of fire that appeared above the followers' heads. Third, they were all speaking in other tongues as the Spirit gave them utterance.

The Greek word for "other tongues" is *glossa*. It means "an unknown tongue," that is, a tongue unknown to the person speaking it. Speaking in tongues is a gift mentioned several times in the Bible. Here is the first mention of its exercise. Interestingly, of the three phenomena that accompanied the outpouring of the Holy Spirit, the speaking of tongues is the only one repeated on other occasions.

PETER'S SERMON

¹⁴But Peter, standing up with the eleven, raised his voice and said to them, "Men of Judea and all who dwell in Jerusalem, let this be known to you, and heed my words. ¹⁵For these are not drunk, as you suppose, ªsince it is *only* ¹the third hour of the day. ¹⁶But this is what was spoken by the prophet Joel:

17 '*And* ª *it shall come to pass in the last days, says God,*
    ᵇ *That I will pour out of My Spirit on all flesh;*
    Your sons and ᶜ *your daughters shall prophesy,*
    Your young men shall see visions,
    Your old men shall dream dreams.
18 *And on My menservants and on My maidservants*
    I will pour out My Spirit in those days;
    ª *And they shall prophesy.*
19 ª *I will show wonders in heaven above*
    And signs in the earth beneath:

Acts 2:16–21

STAND ON SOLID GROUND

Peter said that the events that occurred when the Holy Spirit was poured out on the day of Pentecost were a fulfillment of what had been spoken by the prophet Joel. It is of ultimate importance that if there be any spiritual manifestation or phenomena taking place, we be able to give people a scriptural basis for what is happening. I am not interested in any spiritual phenomena for which I do not have a solid scriptural basis.

One of the problems today is there are lots of spiritual phenomena taking place for which there is no scriptural support. Thus, I question the validity of these phenomena and I attribute them to something other than a genuine work of the Holy Spirit. Whether it is a psychological or metaphysical phenomenon, unless there is a scriptural basis for it, you are on dangerous ground. You cannot use experience as a criterion for truth because people come along with all kinds of weird experiences. The Scriptures are our basis for truth. If we stand on the Scriptures, we stand on solid ground.

Blood and fire and vapor of smoke.
20   a The sun shall be turned into
      darkness,
      And the moon into blood,
      Before the coming of the great
      and awesome day of the LORD.
21   And it shall come to pass
      That awhoever calls on the name
      of the LORD
      Shall be saved.'

22"Men of Israel, hear these words: Jesus of Nazareth, a Man attested by God to you aby miracles, wonders, and signs which God did through Him in your midst, as you yourselves also know— 23Him, abeing delivered by the

---

20 a Matt. 24:29

21 a Rom. 10:13

22 a John 3:2; 5:6

23 a Luke 22:22
b Acts 5:30
1 NU omits have taken

24 a [Rom. 8:11]
1 destroyed or abolished
2 Lit. birth pangs

25 a Ps. 16:8–11

27 a Acts 13:30–37

29 a Acts 13:36

30 a Ps. 132:11
1 NU He would seat one on his throne,

31 a Ps. 16:10

---

determined purpose and foreknowledge of God, byou 1have taken by lawless hands, have crucified, and put to death; 24awhom God raised up, having 1loosed the 2pains of death, because it was not possible that He should be held by it. 25For David says concerning Him:

a'I foresaw the LORD always before
   my face,
   For He is at my right hand, that I
   may not be shaken.
26   Therefore my heart rejoiced, and
   my tongue was glad;
   Moreover my flesh also will rest
   in hope.
27   For You will not leave my soul in
   Hades,
   Nor will You allow Your Holy
   One to see acorruption.
28   You have made known to me the
   ways of life;
   You will make me full of joy in
   Your presence.'

Acts 2:23

GOD'S PLAN

Peter pointed out that the crucifixion of Jesus was not an accident. It wasn't mankind out of control. It was the plan of God. This is proved by the fact that it was prophesied in the Scriptures (for example, in Ps. 22 and Isa. 53) many years before it occurred. This is why it is foolish to blame Jesus' crucifixion on the Jews.

If you want to place blame for Jesus' death, look in the mirror. It was for your sins and mine that Jesus died on the cross, and it was God's plan that Jesus should come to give His life for us.

29"Men and brethren, let me speak freely to you aof the patriarch David, that he is both dead and buried, and his tomb is with us to this day. 30Therefore, being a prophet, aand knowing that God had sworn with an oath to him that of the fruit of his body, 1according to the flesh, He would raise up the Christ to sit on his throne, 31he, foreseeing this, spoke concerning the resurrection of the Christ, athat His

soul was not left in Hades, nor did His flesh see corruption. 32aThis Jesus God has raised up, bof which we are all witnesses. 33Therefore abeing exalted Ito bthe right hand of God, and chaving received from the Father the promise of the Holy Spirit, He dpoured out this which you now see and hear.

34"For David did not ascend into the heavens, but he says himself:

a'The LORD said to my Lord,
  "Sit at My right hand,
35   Till I make Your enemies Your
        footstool."'

36"Therefore let all the house of Israel know assuredly that God has made this Jesus, whom you crucified, both Lord and Christ."

37Now when they heard this, athey were cut to the heart, and said to Peter and the rest of the apostles, "Men and brethren, what shall we do?" 38Then Peter said to them, a"Repent, and let every one of you be baptized in the name of Jesus Christ for the Iremission of sins; and you shall receive the gift of the Holy Spirit. 39For the promise is to you and ato your children, and bto all who are afar off, as many as the Lord our God will call."

A VITAL CHURCH GROWS

40And with many other words he testified and exhorted them, saying, "Be saved from this Iperverse generation." 41Then those who Igladly received his word were baptized; and that day about three thousand souls were added to them. 42aAnd they continued steadfastly in the apostles' Idoctrine and fellowship, in the breaking of bread, and in prayers. 43Then fear came upon every soul, and amany wonders and signs were done through the apostles. 44Now all who believed were together, and ahad all things in common, 45and Isold their possessions and goods, and adivided2 them among all, as anyone had need.

46aSo continuing daily with one accord bin the temple, and cbreaking bread from house to house, they ate their food with gladness and simplicity of heart, 47praising God and having favor with all the people. And athe Lord added Ito the church daily those who were being saved.

A LAME MAN HEALED

3 Now Peter and John went up together ato the temple at the hour of prayer, bthe ninth hour. 2And aa certain

Reference column

32 a Acts 2:24
b Acts 1:8; 3:15

33 a [Acts 5:31]
b [Heb. 10:12]
c [John 14:26]
d Acts 2:1–11, 17; 10:45
I Possibly by

34 a Ps. 68:18; 110:1

37 a Luke 3:10, 12, 14

38 a Luke 24:47
I forgiveness

39 a Joel 2:28, 32
b Eph. 2:13

40 I crooked

41 I NU omits gladly

42 a Acts 1:14
I teaching

43 a Acts 2:22

44 a Acts 4:32, 34, 37; 5:2

45 a Is. 58:7
I would sell
2 distributed

46 a Acts 1:14
b Luke 24:53
c Acts 2:42; 20:7

47 a Acts 5:14
I NU omits to the church

CHAPTER 3

1 a Acts 2:46
b Ps. 55:17

2 a Acts 14:8
b John 9:8
I Beg

6 a Acts 4:10

8 a Is. 35:6

9 a Acts 4:16, 21

10 a John 9:8

11 a John 10:23

man lame from his mother's womb was carried, whom they laid daily at the gate of the temple which is called Beautiful, bto Iask alms from those who entered the temple; 3who, seeing Peter and John about to go into the temple, asked for alms. 4And fixing his eyes on him, with John, Peter said, "Look at us." 5So he gave them his attention, expecting to receive something from them. 6Then Peter said, "Silver and gold I do not have, but what I do have I give you: aIn the name of Jesus Christ of Nazareth, rise up and walk." 7And he took him by the right hand and lifted him up, and immediately his feet and ankle bones received strength. 8So he, aleaping up, stood and walked and entered the temple with them—walking, leaping, and praising God. 9aAnd all the people saw him walking and praising God. 10Then they knew that it was he who asat begging alms at the Beautiful Gate of the temple; and they were filled with wonder and amazement at what had happened to him.

PREACHING IN SOLOMON'S PORTICO

11Now as the lame man who was healed held on to Peter and John, all the people ran together to them in the porch awhich is called Solomon's, greatly amazed. 12So when Peter saw it, he responded to the people: "Men of Israel, why do you marvel at this? Or

Acts 3:1

MEN OF PRAYER

It is interesting to note the characteristics of the people used by God. Here are two men God used. Of course, right off the top we see they were men of prayer. God uses men of prayer. That should not surprise us.

Surely, if I want God to use my life, I need to be in daily contact with Him. I need to seek His guidance. I need to seek His counsel. I should not act apart from God's directions.

Peter and John were men of prayer; they were looking to the Lord for guidance, strength, and wisdom.

why look so intently at us, as though by our own power or godliness we had made this man walk? [13a]The God of Abraham, Isaac, and Jacob, the God of our fathers, [b]glorified His Servant Jesus, whom you [c]delivered up and

---

Acts 3:12–13

Glory to God. There is a danger for the person who is exercising the gifts of the Holy Spirit when they start receiving admiration from the crowd. The moment you begin to accept the adulation, your ministry is placed in a precarious position.

Notice how Peter immediately disassociated himself from the miracle. He corrected the people immediately. Then he explained the miracle.

The people God uses are people who are not seeking glory for themselves. They give the glory to God.

---

13 [a]John 5:30
[b]John 7:39;
12:23; 13:31
[c]Matt. 27:2
[d]Matt. 27:20

14 [a]Mark 1:24
[b]Acts 7:52
[c]John 18:40

15 [a]Acts 2:24
[b]Acts 2:32
[1]Or Originator

16 [a]Matt. 9:22

17 [a]Luke 23:34

18 [a]Acts 26:22
[b]1Pet. 1:10

19 [a][Acts 2:38;
26:20]

20 [1]NU, M
Christ Jesus
[2]NU, M
ordained for you
before

21 [a]Acts 1:11
[b]Matt. 17:11
[c]Luke 1:70
[1]Or time

---

[d]denied in the presence of Pilate, when he was determined to let *Him* go. [14]But you denied [a]the Holy One [b]and the Just, and [c]asked for a murderer to be granted to you, [15]and killed the [1]Prince of life, [a]whom God raised from the dead, [b]of which we are witnesses. [16a]And His name, through faith in His name, has made this man strong, whom you see and know. Yes, the faith which *comes* through Him has given him this perfect soundness in the presence of you all.

[17]"Yet now, brethren, I know that [a]you did *it* in ignorance, as *did* also your rulers. [18]But [a]those things which God foretold [b]by the mouth of all His prophets, that the Christ would suffer, He has thus fulfilled. [19a]Repent therefore and be converted, that your sins may be blotted out, so that times of refreshing may come from the presence of the Lord, [20]and that He may send [1]Jesus Christ, who was [2]preached to you before, [21a]whom heaven must receive until the times of [b]restoration of all things, [c]which God has spoken by the mouth of all His holy prophets since [1]the world began. [22]For Moses

---

THE GIFT OF FAITH   Acts 3:7

I believe it took a great deal of faith for Peter to take the man by the right hand and lift him to his feet. Can you imagine doing such a thing? What do you suppose was going through Peter's mind? I know what would be going through my mind: *I hope this guy stands up. I hope he doesn't collapse.*

The New Testament teaches in 1 Corinthians 12 that there is a special gift of faith God gives to us for certain situations. It isn't something we have all of the time. But there are times when God assures our heart that He is going to do a work, and then He gives us a special faith that enables us to boldly step out upon a strong impression that comes to us by His Spirit.

Many years ago, some young people wheeled their grandfather to the front of the church and asked me to pray for him. As I was praying, I got a strong impression to speak a word of faith and to lift him up. When I was through praying, I said to him, "Stand up and walk," and I lifted the man out of the wheelchair. He began to walk! The grandkids were so excited. They told me, "He hasn't walked in five years! We just wanted you to pray for his cold." Of course, we all rejoiced in the power of the Lord.

The following Wednesday night, I was invited to speak at a church in Arizona. After the service, a man came up with his wife in a wheelchair. She had had a stroke, and he asked me to pray that God would heal her. After I prayed, I said, "We will continue to pray. We know God is able to do exceedingly abundantly above all we could ever ask or think." Then her husband wheeled her out of the church. Afterwards, my son asked me, "Why didn't you lift her out of the wheelchair like you did that guy on Sunday morning?" "Because," I responded, "God didn't give me the faith to do it." I don't make a practice of lifting people up out of wheelchairs. In fact, I have only done it once. But God sometimes will give men the supernatural ability to step out in faith.

truly said to the fathers, a'*The LORD your God will raise up for you a Prophet like me from your brethren. Him you shall hear in all things, whatever He says to you.* 23*And it shall be that every soul who will not hear that Prophet shall be utterly destroyed from among the people.'* 24Yes, and aall the prophets, from Samuel and those who follow, as many as have spoken, have also 1foretold these days. 25a You are sons of the prophets, and of the covenant which God made with our fathers, saying to Abraham, b'*And in your seed all the families of the earth shall be blessed.'* 26To you afirst, God, having raised up His Servant Jesus, sent Him to bless you, bin turning away every one *of you* from your iniquities."

PETER AND JOHN ARRESTED

4 Now as they spoke to the people, the priests, the captain of the temple, and the aSadducees came upon them, 2being greatly disturbed that they taught the people and preached in Jesus the resurrection from the dead. 3And they laid hands on them, and put *them* in custody until the next day, for it was already evening. 4However, many of those who heard the word believed; and the number of the men came to be about five thousand.

ADDRESSING THE SANHEDRIN

5And it came to pass, on the next day, that their rulers, elders, and scribes, 6as well as aAnnas the high priest, Caiaphas, John, and Alexander, and as many as were of the family of the high priest, were gathered together at Jerusalem. 7And when they had set them in the midst, they asked, a"By what power or by what name have you done this?"

8aThen Peter, filled with the Holy Spirit, said to them, "Rulers of the people and elders of Israel: 9If we this day are judged for a good deed *done* to a helpless man, by what means he has been made well, 10let it be known to you all, and to all the people of Israel, athat by the name of Jesus Christ of Nazareth, whom you crucified, bwhom God raised from the dead, by Him this man stands here before you whole. 11This is the a'*stone which was rejected by you builders, which has become the chief cornerstone.'* 12aNor is there salvation in any other, for there is no other name under heaven given among men by which we must be saved."

Cross references

22 a Deut. 18:15, 18, 19

24 a Luke 24:25
1 NU, M *proclaimed*

25 a [Rom. 9:4, 8]
b Gen. 12:3; 18:18; 22:18; 26:4; 28:14

26 a [Rom. 1:16; 2:9]
b Matt. 1:21

CHAPTER 4

1 a Matt. 22:23

6 a Luke 3:2

7 a Matt. 21:23

8 a Luke 12:11, 12

10 a Acts 2:22; 3:6, 16
b Acts 2:24

11 a Ps. 118:22

12 a [1 Tim. 2:5, 6]

13 a [1 Cor. 1:27]

14 a Acts 3:11

16 a John 11:47
b Acts 3:7–10
1 *remarkable sign*
2 *well known*

THE NAME OF JESUS FORBIDDEN

13Now when they saw the boldness of Peter and John, aand perceived that they were uneducated and untrained men, they marveled. And they realized that they had been with Jesus. 14And seeing the man who had been healed astanding with them, they could say nothing against it. 15But when they had commanded them to go aside out of the council, they conferred among themselves, 16saying, a"What shall we do to these men? For, indeed, that a 1notable miracle has been done through them *is* bevident2 to all who dwell in Jerusalem,

Acts 4:14–17

MISTAKEN IDENTITY

The Sadducees had false perceptions of Peter and John.

First, they perceived they were unlearned and ignorant men. In fact, Peter and John had a better working knowledge of the Scriptures than the Sadducees did. After all, they had had three years of private tutoring by Jesus. They were in seminary with the Author Himself teaching them. Every time Peter spoke in Acts, he was quoting the Scriptures. True, these men didn't go to the University of Jerusalem, but they were far from unlearned.

Second, it was a misperception for the Sadducees to think their relationship with Christ was past tense. This passage says the Sadducees realized Peter and John had been with Jesus. How wonderful it is to be with Jesus, and for Peter and John this experience wasn't past tense! Jesus was still with them.

The third mistake the Sadducees made was to think they could quiet Peter and John by a strong warning. You can't quiet men filled with the Holy Spirit and walking with Jesus.

Clearly, the Sadducees did not know the truth about these men.

and we cannot deny *it*. [17]But so that it spreads no further among the people, let us severely threaten them, that from now on they speak to no man in this name."

[18a]So they called them and commanded them not to speak at all nor teach in the name of Jesus. [19]But Peter and John answered and said to them, [a]"Whether it is right in the sight of God to listen to you more than to God, you judge. [20a]For we cannot but speak the things which [b]we have seen and heard." [21]So when they had further threatened them, they let them go, finding no way of punishing them, [a]because of the people, since they all [b]glorified God for [c]what had been done. [22]For the man was over forty years old on whom this miracle of healing had been performed.

PRAYER FOR BOLDNESS

[23]And being let go, [a]they went to their own *companions* and reported all that the chief priests and elders had said to them. [24]So when they heard that, they raised their voice to God with one accord and said: "Lord, [a]You *are* God, who made heaven and earth and the sea, and all that is in them, [25]who [1]by the mouth of Your servant David have said:

[a]' *Why did the nations rage,*
  And the people plot vain
    things?
[26] *The kings of the earth took their*
    stand,

Acts 4:24

Pray About It. Here we have an important key in our struggle with the worldly powers that often are antagonistic to righteous causes. It doesn't say the Christians all got together, painted signs, and protested in front of the temple. Instead, they went to God. They took their concerns to God in prayer.

When we see injustices in our world, we can do much more through prayer than we can through public demonstrations. I am not really one to picket, to carry signs; but if you want to get together and pray about it, I'm ready.

Marginal references:

18 [a] Acts 5:28, 40

19 [a] Acts 5:29

20 [a] Acts 1:8; 2:32
[b] [1 John 1:1, 3]

21 [a] Acts 5:26
[b] Matt. 15:31
[c] Acts 3:7, 8

23 [a] Acts 2:44–46; 12:12

24 [a] Ex. 20:11

25 [a] Ps. 2:1, 2
[1] NU *through the Holy Spirit, by the mouth of our father, Your servant David,*

27 [a] Luke 22:2; 23:1, 8
[b] [Luke 1:35]
[c] John 10:36

28 [a] Acts 2:23; 3:18

29 [a] Acts 4:13, 31; 9:27; 13:46; 14:3; 19:8; 26:26

30 [a] Acts 2:43; 5:12
[b] Acts 3:6, 16
[c] Acts 4:27

31 [a] Acts 2:2, 4; 16:26
[b] Acts 4:29

32 [a] Rom. 15:5, 6
[b] Acts 2:44

33 [a] [Acts 1:8]
[b] Acts 1:22
[c] Rom. 6:15

34 [a] Acts 2:45

35 [a] Acts 4:37; 5:2
[b] Acts 2:45; 6:1

     And the rulers were gathered
       together
     Against the LORD and against His
       Christ.'

[27]"For [a]truly against [b]Your holy Servant Jesus, [c]whom You anointed, both Herod and Pontius Pilate, with the Gentiles and the people of Israel, were gathered together [28a]to do whatever Your hand and Your purpose determined before to be done. [29]Now, Lord, look on their threats, and grant to Your servants [a]that with all boldness they may speak Your word, [30]by stretching out Your hand to heal, [a]and that signs and wonders may be done [b]through the name of [c]Your holy Servant Jesus."

Acts 4:29

Taking Time to Worship. Interesting, the Christian disciples didn't just rush into their petition. They took time, first of all, to worship God.

I think prayer should always begin with worship; a time of quietness before the Lord, recognizing the greatness of God, acknowledging the One to whom we are coming to for help, and realizing that God has it all under control. Worship gives us perspective and strength. Then we are ready to bring our petitions to Him.

---

[31]And when they had prayed, [a]the place where they were assembled together was shaken; and they were all filled with the Holy Spirit, [b]and they spoke the word of God with boldness.

SHARING IN ALL THINGS

[32]Now the multitude of those who believed [a]were of one heart and one soul; [b]neither did anyone say that any of the things he possessed was his own, but they had all things in common. [33]And with [a]great power the apostles gave [b]witness to the resurrection of the Lord Jesus. And [c]great grace was upon them all. [34]Nor was there anyone among them who lacked; [a]for all who were possessors of lands or houses sold them, and brought the proceeds of the things that were sold, [35a]and laid *them* at the apostles' feet; [b]and they distributed to each as anyone had need.

³⁶And ¹Joses, who was also named Barnabas by the apostles (which is translated Son of ²Encouragement), a Levite of the country of Cyprus, ³⁷ᵃhaving land, sold *it*, and brought the money and laid *it* at the apostles' feet.

LYING TO THE HOLY SPIRIT

5 But a certain man named Ananias, with Sapphira his wife, sold a possession. ²And he kept back *part* of the proceeds, his wife also being aware *of it*, and brought a certain part and laid *it* at the apostles' feet. ³ᵃBut Peter said, "Ananias, why has ᵇSatan filled your heart to lie to the Holy Spirit and keep back *part* of the price of the land for yourself? ⁴While it remained, was it not your own? And after it was sold, was it not in your own control? Why have you conceived this thing in your heart? You have not lied to men but to God."

Acts 5:3

HYPOCRISY JUDGED

Hypocrisy—pretending to be something you are not—is a horrible evil that has plagued the church through the years. God dealt very severely with hypocrisy during the birth of the church.

Here Ananias and Sapphira were making a pretense of giving everything and yet they were holding back, obviously by agreement between themselves. So Peter, exercising the gift of the word of knowledge or perhaps discernment, challenged Ananias. "Why would you pretend to give everything to God when you are actually holding something back?" Notice Peter told Ananias that he was lying to the Holy Spirit. Later, Peter said that he'd not lied to man, but to God.

Lying to the Holy Spirit is equivalent to lying to God, which indicates the Holy Spirit is God, one of the three persons of the divine Trinity. Ananias paid a high price for his hypocrisy.

---

36 ¹NU *Joseph*
2 Or *Consolation*

37 ª Acts 4:34, 35; 5:1, 2

CHAPTER 5

3 ª Deut. 23:21
ᵇ Luke 22:3

5 ª Acts 5:10, 11

6 ª John 19:40

9 ª Acts 5:3, 4

10 ª Acts 5:5

11 ª Acts 2:43; 5:5; 19:17

12 ª Acts 2:43; 4:30; 6:8; 14:3; 15:12
ᵇ Acts 3:11; 4:32

13 ª John 9:22
ᵇ Acts 2:47; 4:21

---

⁵Then Ananias, hearing these words, ᵃfell down and breathed his last. So great fear came upon all those who heard these things. ⁶And the young men arose and ᵃwrapped him up, carried *him* out, and buried *him*. ⁷Now it was about three hours later when his wife came in, not knowing what had happened. ⁸And Peter answered her, "Tell me whether you sold the land for so much?"

She said, "Yes, for so much."

⁹Then Peter said to her, "How is it that you have agreed together ᵃto test the Spirit of the Lord? Look, the feet of those who have buried your husband *are* at the door, and they will carry you out." ¹⁰ᵃThen immediately she fell down at his feet and breathed her last. And the young men came in and found her dead, and carrying *her* out, buried *her* by her husband. ¹¹ᵃSo great fear came upon all the church and upon all who heard these things.

Acts 5:10

THEY BREATHED THEIR LAST

If you are living without consciousness of God, then the Bible declares that you are dead! You can have all the bodily functions, breathing, thinking, singing, but if your conscience is separated from God—if you have made no place for God in your life—then you're spiritually dead.

Spiritual death is worse than physical death. It is much more to be feared than physical death. Jesus said, "Do not fear those who kill the body but cannot kill the soul. But rather fear Him who is able to destroy both soul and body in hell" (Matt. 10:28).

CONTINUING POWER IN THE CHURCH

¹²And ᵃthrough the hands of the apostles many signs and wonders were done among the people. ᵇAnd they were all with one accord in Solomon's Porch. ¹³Yet ᵃnone of the rest dared join them, ᵇbut the people esteemed them highly.

14And believers were increasingly added to the Lord, multitudes of both men and women, 15so that they brought the sick out into the streets and laid *them* on beds and couches, ᵃthat at least the shadow of Peter passing by might fall on some of them. 16Also a multitude gathered from the surrounding cities to Jerusalem, bringing ᵃsick people and those who were tormented by unclean spirits, and they were all healed.

IMPRISONED APOSTLES FREED

17ᵃThen the high priest rose up, and all those who *were* with him (which is the sect of the Sadducees), and they were filled with ¹indignation, 18ᵃand laid their hands on the apostles and put them in the common prison. 19But at night ᵃan angel of the Lord opened the prison doors and brought them out, and said, 20"Go, stand in the temple and speak to the people ᵃall the words of this life."

21And when they heard *that*, they entered the temple early in the morning and taught. ᵃBut the high priest and those with him came and called the ¹council together, with all the ²elders of the children of Israel, and sent to the prison to have them brought.

APOSTLES ON TRIAL AGAIN

22But when the officers came and did not find them in the prison, they

15 ᵃActs 19:12
16 ᵃMark 16:17, 18
17 ᵃActs 4:1, 2, 6
¹jealousy
18 ᵃLuke 21:12
19 ᵃActs 12:7; 16:26
20 ᵃ[John 6:63, 68; 17:3]
21 ᵃActs 4:5, 6
¹Sanhedrin
²council of elders or senate
23 ¹NU, M omit outside
24 ᵃActs 4:1; 5:26
¹NU omits the high priest
25 ¹NU, M omit saying
26 ᵃMatt. 21:26
28 ᵃActs 4:17, 18
ᵇActs 2:23, 36
ᶜMatt. 23:35
29 ᵃActs 4:19
30 ᵃActs 3:13, 15
ᵇ[1 Pet. 2:24]
31 ᵃ[Acts 2:33, 36]
ᵇActs 3:15
ᶜMatt. 1:21
ᵈLuke 24:47
32 ᵃJohn 15:26, 27

returned and reported, 23saying, "Indeed we found the prison shut securely, and the guards standing ¹outside before the doors; but when we opened them, we found no one inside!" 24Now when ¹the high priest, ᵃthe captain of the temple, and the chief priests heard these things, they wondered what the outcome would be. 25So one came and told them, ¹saying, "Look, the men whom you put in prison are standing in the temple and teaching the people!"

26Then the captain went with the officers and brought them without violence, ᵃfor they feared the people, lest they should be stoned. 27And when they had brought them, they set *them* before the council. And the high priest asked them, 28saying, ᵃ"Did we not strictly command you not to teach in this name? And look, you have filled Jerusalem with your doctrine, ᵇand intend to bring this Man's ᶜblood on us!"

29But Peter and the *other* apostles answered and said: ᵃ"We ought to obey God rather than men. 30ᵃThe God of our fathers raised up Jesus whom you murdered by ᵇhanging on a tree. 31ᵃHim God has exalted to His right hand *to be* ᵇPrince and ᶜSavior, ᵈto give repentance to Israel and forgiveness of sins. 32And ᵃwe are His

SAVED BY FAITH

Acts 5:14–16

When I was living in Tucson in the very early years of ministry, I lived next door to an Air Force captain and his wife, Jan. Jim had been a professor at Cornell. He was in the reserves and had been called to active duty.

One evening, Chuck Jr. was not well. I went off to church, and Kay stayed home with the children. Jan came over and said, "You need to call the doctor." Kay said, "No, we have prayed for him." "Oh, but that is pushing it," Jan said. "You should take him to a doctor." Kay said, "No, we believe the Lord can heal him, so we are going to trust the Lord." The next morning Chuck Jr. was out playing with the kids.

Jan was so amazed that he was fine, she called me over and said, "Tell me more." So we shared with Jan about the Lord, and she accepted the Lord. Her husband was an agnostic, so she wanted to wait for the right timing to share with him that she had accepted Christ. But when her husband Jim came home from the air base that evening, his daughters were jumping around asking her whether she was going to tell him what had happened when I was over during the afternoon. Jim asked her what had been going on while he was not at home, so she had to share with him.

Then Jim started talking with us. We gave him Henry Morris's *That Ye Might Believe,* which had just been published. Jim started reading the book, and he couldn't put it down. He called me the next morning. He said he had finished the book at two o'clock in the morning, and he said that he thought I would be interested to hear that he had been on his knees when he finished the book. Jim had accepted the Lord.

witnesses to these things, and *so* also *is* the Holy Spirit ᵇwhom God has given to those who obey Him."

GAMALIEL'S ADVICE

³³When they heard *this*, they were ᵃfuriousᴵ and plotted to kill them. ³⁴Then one in the council stood up, a Pharisee named ᵃGamaliel, a teacher of the law held in respect by all the people, and commanded them to put the apostles outside for a little while. ³⁵And he said to them: "Men of Israel, ᴵtake heed to yourselves what you intend to do regarding these men. ³⁶For some time ago Theudas rose up, claiming to be somebody. A number of men, about four hundred, ᴵjoined him. He was slain, and all who obeyed him were scattered and came to nothing. ³⁷After this man, Judas of Galilee rose up in the days of the census, and drew away many people after him. He also perished, and all who obeyed him were dispersed. ³⁸And now I say to you, keep away from these men and let them alone; for if this plan or this work is of men, it will come to nothing; ³⁹ᵃbut if it is of God, you cannot overthrow it—lest you even be found ᵇto fight against God."

⁴⁰And they agreed with him, and when they had ᵃcalled for the apostles ᵇand beaten *them*, they commanded that they should not speak in the name of Jesus, and let them go. ⁴¹So they departed from the presence of the council, ᵃrejoicing that they were counted worthy to suffer shame for ᴵHis name. ⁴²And daily ᵃin the temple, and in every house, ᵇthey did not cease teaching and preaching Jesus *as* the Christ.

SEVEN CHOSEN TO SERVE

6 Now in those days, ᵃwhen *the num-ber of* the disciples was multiplying, there arose a complaint against the Hebrews by the ᵇHellenists,ᴵ because their widows were neglected ᶜin the daily distribution. ²Then the twelve summoned the multitude of the disciples and said, ᵃ"It is not desirable that we should leave the word of God and serve tables. ³Therefore, brethren, ᵃseek out from among you seven men of *good* reputation, full of the Holy Spirit and wisdom, whom we may appoint over this ᵇbusiness; ⁴but we ᵃwill give ourselves continually to prayer and to the ministry of the word." ⁵And the saying pleased the whole multitude. And they chose Stephen, ᵃa

---

32 ᵇActs 2:4; 10:44

33 ᵃActs 2:37; 7:54
ᴵ *cut to the quick*

34 ᵃActs 22:3

35 ᴵ *be careful*

36 ᴵ *followed*

39 ᵃ1Cor. 1:25
ᵇActs 7:51; 9:5

40 ᵃActs 4:18
ᵇMatt. 10:17

41 ᵃ[1Pet. 4:13–16]
ᴵ NU *the name;*
M *the name of Jesus*

42 ᵃActs 2:46
ᵇActs 4:20, 29

CHAPTER 6

1 ᵃActs 2:41; 4:4
ᵇActs 9:29; 11:20
ᶜActs 4:35; 11:29
ᴵ Greek-speaking Jews

2 ᵃEx. 18:17

3 ᵃ1Tim. 3:7
ᵇ1Tim. 3:8–13

4 ᵃActs 2:42

5 ᵃActs 6:3; 11:24
ᵇActs 8:5, 26; 21:8
ᶜRev. 2:6, 15

6 ᵃActs 1:24
ᵇ[2Tim. 1:6]

7 ᵃActs 12:24
ᵇJohn 12:42

8 ᵃActs 2:43; 5:12; 8:15; 14:3
ᴵ NU *grace*

10 ᵃLuke 21:15

---

man full of faith and the Holy Spirit, and ᵇPhilip, Prochorus, Nicanor, Timon, Parmenas, and ᶜNicolas, a proselyte from Antioch, ⁶whom they set before the apostles; and ᵃwhen they had prayed, ᵇthey laid hands on them.

⁷Then ᵃthe word of God spread, and the number of the disciples multiplied greatly in Jerusalem, and a great many ᵇof the priests were obedient to the faith.

STEPHEN ACCUSED OF BLASPHEMY

⁸And Stephen, full of ᴵfaith and power, did great ᵃwonders and signs among the people. ⁹Then there arose some from what is called the Synagogue of the Freedmen (Cyrenians, Alexandrians, and those from Cilicia and Asia), disputing with Stephen. ¹⁰And ᵃthey were not able to resist the wisdom and the Spirit by which he

spoke. ¹¹ᵃThen they secretly induced men to say, "We have heard him speak blasphemous words against Moses and God." ¹²And they stirred up the people,

Acts 6:8

FAITHFUL TO HIS CALL

Stephen, a man full of faith and power, was waiting tables in obedience to God's call. I've heard ministry referred to as "the highest calling." There is no one "highest calling."

Whatever God has called you to do is your highest calling. If it's waiting tables, great! Do it as unto the Lord. "And whatever you do in word or deed, do all in the name of the Lord Jesus" (Col. 3:17). I am what I am for the Lord because of His calling upon me. It is important that I be faithful to His call.

Acts 6:14–15

STEPHEN AND SAUL

As you study Stephen's response in chapter 7, I want you to realize that sitting there listening to him was a young man named Saul. Now Saul's first response was extremely negative as is often the case of a person under conviction.

A lot of times when a person comes under conviction, he becomes intolerable. You can't be around him. He responds in a very negative way because God is speaking to him, and he is fighting against God. As Jesus said to Paul, "It is hard for you to kick against the goads" (Acts 9:5). But it was through Stephen that the Spirit of God began to work in Saul's heart.

the elders, and the scribes; and they came upon *him*, seized him, and brought *him* to the council. ¹³They also set up false witnesses who said, "This man does not cease to speak ¹blasphemous words against this holy place and the law; ¹⁴ᵃfor we have heard him say that this Jesus of Nazareth will destroy this place and change the customs which Moses delivered to us." ¹⁵And all who sat in the council, looking steadfastly at him, saw his face as the face of an angel.

STEPHEN'S ADDRESS: THE CALL OF ABRAHAM

7 Then the high priest said, "Are these things so?" ²And he said, ᵃ"Brethren and fathers, listen: The ᵇGod of glory appeared to our father Abraham when he was in Mesopotamia, before he dwelt in ᶜHaran, ³and said to him, ᵃ'*Get out of your country and from your relatives, and come to a land that I will show you.*' ⁴Then ᵃhe came out of the land of the Chaldeans and dwelt in Haran. And from there, when his father was ᵇdead, He moved him to this land in which you now dwell. ⁵And *God* gave him no inheritance in it, not even *enough* to set his foot on. But even when *Abraham* had no child, ᵃHe promised to give it to him for a possession, and to his descen-

Acts 7:1

OPEN DOOR

The high priest said, "Are these things so?" That was all that Stephen needed, an open door, and he began to give witness.

Jesus told His disciples they would be brought before the kings and magistrates. Jesus told them not to give any forethought to what they would say in that hour because the Holy Spirit would give them the words. (See Luke 12:11.)

So we find this modeled for us throughout the book of Acts. Every time Christians stood before the courts, the kings, the judges; when God gave them an open door, they used it to share the gospel.

Cross-references

11 ᵃ 1 Kin. 21:10, 13

13 ¹ NU omits blasphemous

14 ᵃ Acts 10:38; 25:8

CHAPTER 7

2 ᵃ Acts 22:1
ᵇ Ps. 29:3
ᶜ Gen. 11:31, 32

3 ᵃ Gen. 12:1

4 ᵃ Gen. 11:31; 15:7
ᵇ Gen. 11:32

5 ᵃ Gen. 12:7; 13:15; 15:3, 18; 17:8; 26:3

dants after him. [6]But God spoke in this way: [a]that his descendants would dwell in a foreign land, and that they would bring them into [b]bondage and oppress *them* four hundred years. [7][a]'*And the nation to whom they will be in bondage I will* [b]*judge,'* said God, [c]'*and after that they shall come out and serve Me in this place.'* [8][a]Then He gave him the covenant of circumcision; [b]and so Abraham begot Isaac and circumcised him on the eighth day; [c]and Isaac begot Jacob, and [d]Jacob begot the twelve patriarchs.

THE PATRIARCHS IN EGYPT

[9][a]"And the patriarchs, becoming envious, [b]sold Joseph into Egypt. [c]But God was with him [10]and delivered him out of all his troubles, [a]and gave him favor and wisdom in the presence of Pharaoh, king of Egypt; and he made him governor over Egypt and all his house. [11][a]Now a famine and great [1]trouble came over all the land of Egypt and Canaan, and our fathers found no sustenance. [12][a]But when Jacob heard that there was grain in Egypt, he sent out our fathers first. [13]And the [a]second *time* Joseph was made known to *his* brothers, and Joseph's family became known to the Pharaoh. [14][a]Then Joseph sent and called his father Jacob and [b]all his relatives to *him*, [1]seventy-five people. [15][a]So Jacob went down to Egypt; [b]and he died, he and our fathers. [16]And [a]they were carried back to Shechem and laid in [b]the tomb that Abraham bought for a sum of money from the sons of Hamor, *the father of* Shechem.

GOD DELIVERS ISRAEL BY MOSES

[17]"But when [a]the time of the promise drew near which God had sworn to Abraham, [b]the people grew and multiplied in Egypt [18]till another king [a]arose who did not know Joseph. [19]This man dealt treacherously with our people, and oppressed our forefathers, [a]making them expose their babies, so that they might not live. [20][a]At this time Moses was born, and [b]was well pleasing to God; and he was brought up in his father's house for three months. [21]But [a]when he was set out, [b]Pharaoh's daughter took him away and brought him up as her own son. [22]And Moses was learned in all the wisdom of the Egyptians, and was [a]mighty in words and deeds.

[23][a]"Now when he was forty years old, it came into his heart to visit his brethren, the children of Israel. [24]And seeing one of *them* suffer wrong, he defended and avenged him who was oppressed, and struck down the Egyptian. [25]For he supposed that his brethren would have understood that God would deliver them by his hand, but they did not understand. [26]And the next day he appeared to *two of* them as they were fighting, and *tried* to reconcile them, saying, 'Men, you are brethren; why do you wrong one another?' [27]But he who did his neighbor wrong pushed him away, saying, [a]'*Who made you a ruler and a judge over us? [28]Do you want to kill me as you did the Egyptian yesterday?'* [29][a]Then, at this saying, Moses fled and became a dweller in the land of Midian, where he [b]had two sons.

Cross-references (center column):

6 [a] Gen. 15:13, 14, 16; 47:11, 12 [b] Ex. 1:8–14; 12:40, 41
7 [a] Gen. 15:14 [b] Ex. 14:13–31 [c] Ex. 3:12
8 [a] Gen. 17:9–14 [b] Gen. 21:1–5 [c] Gen. 25:21–26 [d] Gen. 29:31—30:24; 35:18, 22–26
9 [a] Gen. 37:4, 11, 28 [b] Gen. 37:28 [c] Gen. 39:2, 21, 23
10 [a] Gen. 41:38–44
11 [a] Gen. 41:54; 42:5 [1] *affliction*
12 [a] Gen. 42:1, 2
13 [a] Gen. 45:4, 16
14 [a] Gen. 45:9, 27 [b] Deut. 10:22 [1] Or *seventy,* Ex. 1:5
15 [a] Gen. 46:1–7 [b] Gen. 49:33
16 [a] Josh. 24:32 [b] Gen. 23:16
17 [a] Gen. 15:13 [b] Ex. 1:7–9
18 [a] Ex. 1:8
19 [a] Ex. 1:22
20 [a] Ex. 2:1, 2 [b] Heb. 11:23
21 [a] Ex. 2:3, 4 [b] Ex. 2:5–10
22 [a] Luke 24:19   23 [a] Ex. 2:11, 12   27 [a] Ex. 2:14
29 [a] Heb. 11:27 [b] Ex. 2:15, 21, 22; 4:20; 18:3

GOD IS WITH US   Acts 7:9

Even in those difficult circumstances of life that we don't understand, God is with us. The prophet said to King Asa, "The LORD is with you while you are with Him" (2 Chr. 15:2).

Not always do the circumstances indicate that God is with us. There are times when it would seem God has forsaken us. Certainly that must have seemed to be the case with Joseph. Not only did his brothers sell him to traders going to Egypt, he was sold on the slave market to one of the headmen, Potiphar. Then Potiphar's wife got a crush on Joseph, and she tried to force him to go to bed with her. When Joseph steadfastly refused, well, "Hell hath no fury like a woman scorned." She cried rape and falsely accused him. He was put in prison for several years. I mean, it says, "God was with him." Oh, man. It's hard to see God in these circumstances. (See Gen. 39.)

That's true with us so many times when we're going through trying, dark times. It's hard for us to see that God is with us; and yet, when we get the whole story, we see that, yes indeed, God was there directing the situation the entire time.

30 a"And when forty years had passed, an Angel *1*of the Lord appeared to him in a flame of fire in a bush, in the wilderness of Mount Sinai. 31When Moses saw *it*, he marveled at the sight; and as he drew near to observe, the voice of the Lord came to him, 32*saying,* a*'I am the God of your fathers—the God of Abraham, the God of Isaac, and the God of Jacob.'* And Moses trembled and dared not look. 33 a*'Then the LORD said to him, "Take your sandals off your feet, for the place where you stand is holy ground.* 34*I have surely* a*seen the oppression of My people who are in Egypt; I have heard their groaning and have come down to deliver them. And now come, I will* b*send you to Egypt."'*

35"This Moses whom they rejected, saying, a*'Who made you a ruler and a judge?'* is the one God sent *to be* a ruler and a deliverer b by the hand of the Angel who appeared to him in the bush. 36 a He brought them out, after he had b shown wonders and signs in the land of Egypt, c and in the Red Sea, d and in the wilderness forty years.

ISRAEL REBELS AGAINST GOD

37"This is that Moses who said to the children of Israel, a*'The LORD your God will raise up for you a Prophet like me from your brethren.* b*Him1 you shall hear.'* 38 a"This is he who was in the *1*congregation in the wilderness with b the Angel who spoke to him on Mount Sinai, and *with* our fathers, c the one who received the living d oracles2 to give to us, 39whom our fathers a would not obey, but rejected. And in their hearts they turned back to Egypt, 40 a saying to Aaron, *'Make us gods to go before us; as for this Moses who brought us out of the land of Egypt, we do not know what has become of him.'* 41 a And they made a calf in those days, offered sacrifices to the idol, and b rejoiced in the works of their own hands. 42Then a God turned and gave them up to worship b the host of heaven, as it is written in the book of the Prophets:

> c*'Did you offer Me slaughtered animals and sacrifices during forty years in the wilderness, O house of Israel?*
> 43　*You also took up the tabernacle of Moloch, And the star of your god Remphan,*

Images which you made to worship; And a*I will carry you away beyond Babylon.'*

GOD'S TRUE TABERNACLE

44"Our fathers had the tabernacle of witness in the wilderness, as He appointed, instructing Moses a to make it according to the pattern that he had seen, 45 a which our fathers, having received it in turn, also brought with Joshua into the land possessed by the Gentiles, b whom God drove out before the face of our fathers until the c days of David, 46 a who found favor before God and b asked to find a dwelling for the God of Jacob. 47 a But Solomon built Him a house. 48"However, a the Most High does not dwell in temples made with hands, as the prophet says:

> 49　*'Heaven*a *is My throne, And earth is My footstool. What house will you build for Me? says the LORD, Or what is the place of My rest?*
> 50　*Has My hand not* a*made all these things?'*

ISRAEL RESISTS THE HOLY SPIRIT

51"*You* a stiff-necked *1*and b uncircumcised in heart and ears! You always resist the Holy Spirit; as your fathers did, so do you. 52 a Which of the prophets did your fathers not persecute? And they killed those who foretold the coming of b the Just One, of whom you now have become the betrayers and murderers, 53 a who have received the law by the direction of angels and have not kept *it*."

STEPHEN THE MARTYR

54 a When they heard these things they were *1*cut to the heart, and they gnashed at him with *their* teeth. 55But he, a being full of the Holy Spirit, gazed into heaven and saw the b glory of God, and Jesus standing at the right hand of God, 56and said, "Look! a I see the heavens opened and the b Son of Man standing at the right hand of God!" 57Then they cried out with a loud voice, stopped their ears, and ran at him with one accord; 58and they cast *him* out of the city and stoned *him*. And a the witnesses laid down their clothes at the feet of a young man named Saul. 59And they stoned Stephen as he was calling on God and saying, "Lord Jesus, a receive my spirit." 60Then he knelt

---

30 a Ex. 3:1–10
1 NU omits of the Lord
32 a Ex. 3:6, 15
33 a Ex. 3:5, 7, 8, 10
34 a Ex. 2:24, 25 b Ps. 105:26
35 a Ex. 2:14 b Ex. 14:21
36 a Ex. 12:41; 33:1 b Ps. 105:27 c Ex. 14:21 d Ex. 16:1, 35
37 a Deut. 18:15, 18, 19 b Matt. 17:5 1 NU, M omit Him you shall hear
38 a Ex. 19:3 b Gal. 3:19 c Deut. 5:27 d Heb. 5:12 1 Gr. ekklesia, assembly or church 2 sayings
39 a Ps. 95:8–11
40 a Ex. 32:1, 23
41 a Deut. 9:16 b Ex. 32:6, 18, 19
42 a [2 Thess. 2:11] b 2 Kin. 21:3 c Amos 5:25–27
43 a Jer. 25:9–12
44 a [Heb. 8:5]
45 a Josh. 3:14; 18:1; 23:9 b Ps. 44:2 c 2 Sam. 6:2–15
46 a 2 Sam. 7:1–13 b 1 Chr. 22:7
47 a 1 Kin. 6:1–38; 8:20, 21
48 a 1 Kin. 8:27
49 a Is. 66:1, 2
50 a Ps. 102:25
51 a Ex. 32:9 b Lev. 26:41 1 stubborn
52 a 2 Chr. 36:16 b Acts 3:14; 22:14
53 a Ex. 20:1
54 a Acts 5:33 1 furious
55 a Acts 6:5 b [Ex. 24:17]
56 a Matt. 3:16 b Dan. 7:13
58 a Acts 22:20
59 a Ps. 31:5

down and cried out with a loud voice, a"Lord, do not charge them with this sin." And when he had said this, he fell asleep.

Acts 7:60

ETERNAL LIFE

Now, when referring to the end of life on earth for a Christian, the Bible usually uses the phrase "fell asleep." That's because what happens to the Christian is different from what happens to the sinner. Christians do not really die. There is a transition that takes place, but they are still alive. Jesus said, "And whoever lives and believes in Me shall never die" (John 11:26). So it would be wrong to say that Stephen died. Because he believed in Jesus, the promise is that he will never die.

Someday, if the Lord should tarry, you'll perhaps pick up the morning newspaper and it will say that Chuck Smith, pastor of Calvary Chapel, died last night. Don't believe it. Typical reporting—wrong! To report it accurately, they would have to say, "Chuck Smith moved last night out of his worn-out tent into a beautiful new mansion, into a building of God not made with hands, eternal in the heavens."

SAUL PERSECUTES THE CHURCH

8 Now Saul was consenting to his death.

At that time a great persecution arose against the church which was at Jerusalem; and athey were all scattered throughout the regions of Judea and Samaria, except the apostles. 2And devout men carried Stephen to his burial, and amade great lamentation over him.

3As for Saul, ahe made havoc of the church, entering every house, and dragging off men and women, committing them to prison.

CHRIST IS PREACHED IN SAMARIA

4Therefore athose who were scattered went everywhere preaching the

word. 5Then aPhilip went down to 1the city of Samaria and preached Christ to them. 6And the multitudes with one accord heeded the things spoken by Philip, hearing and seeing the miracles which he did. 7For aunclean spirits, crying with a loud voice, came out of many who were possessed; and many who were paralyzed and lame were healed. 8And there was great joy in that city.

Acts 8:8

THE JOY OF THE LORD

You know that wherever God is working, one of the by-products of the work of God is joy. What a joy it is to see God at work! It's just a thrill!

So often throughout the New Testament, the result of the work of God's Spirit in a person's life is joy. It is interesting that as Paul spoke of the fruit of the Spirit, which is love, the first characteristic of this love is joy (Gal. 5:22).

There is just such joy in the Lord! And so there was great joy in Samaria.

THE SORCERER'S PROFESSION OF FAITH

9But there was a certain man called Simon, who previously apracticed 1sorcery in the city and bastonished the 2people of Samaria, claiming that he was someone great, 10to whom they all gave heed, from the least to the greatest, saying, "This man is the great power of God." 11And they heeded him because he had astonished them with his 1sorceries for a long time. 12But when they believed Philip as he preached the things aconcerning the kingdom of God and the name of Jesus Christ, both men and women were baptized. 13Then Simon himself also believed; and when he was baptized he continued with Philip, and was amazed, seeing the miracles and signs which were done.

CHAPTER 8

60 a Matt. 5:44
1 a Acts 8:4; 11:19
2 a Gen. 23:2
3 a Phil. 3:6
4 a Matt. 10:23
5 a Acts 6:5; 8:26, 30
1 Or a
7 a Mark 16:17
9 a Acts 8:11; 13:6
b Acts 5:36
1 magic
2 Or nation
11 1 magic arts
12 a Acts 1:3; 8:4

THE SORCERER'S SIN

[14]Now when the [a]apostles who were at Jerusalem heard that Samaria had received the word of God, they sent Peter and John to them, [15]who, when they had come down, prayed for them [a]that they might receive the Holy Spirit. [16]For [a]as yet He had fallen upon none of them. [b]They had only been baptized in [c]the name of the Lord Jesus. [17]Then [a]they laid hands on them, and they received the Holy Spirit.

Acts 8:16

LIVING WATER

Notice these people in Samaria were believers, and they had been baptized. This means the Holy Spirit was in them, but He had not fallen (epi) upon them. This Greek preposition "epi" is used to describe a relationship to the Holy Spirit where He overflows from you. You see, it is one thing to have the Holy Spirit within you doing the work of conforming you into the image of Jesus Christ. It is quite another thing to have the Holy Spirit flowing forth from you.

This is what they were receiving, a releasing of the Holy Spirit. He was not just within them, but He was flowing forth from them. This is what Jesus was describing when He said, "If anyone thirsts, let him come to Me and drink. He who believes in Me, as the Scripture has said, out of his heart will flow rivers of living water" (John 7:37–38).

[18]And when Simon saw that through the laying on of the apostles' hands the Holy Spirit was given, he offered them money, [19]saying, "Give me this power also, that anyone on whom I lay hands may receive the Holy Spirit."
[20]But Peter said to him, "Your money perish with you, because [a]you thought that [b]the gift of God could be purchased with money! [21]You have neither part nor portion in this matter, for your [a]heart is not right in the sight of God.

[22]Repent therefore of this your wickedness, and pray God [a]if perhaps the thought of your heart may be forgiven you. [23]For I see that you are [a]poisoned by bitterness and bound by iniquity."
[24]Then Simon answered and said, [a]"Pray to the Lord for me, that none of the things which you have spoken may come upon me."
[25]So when they had testified and preached the word of the Lord, they returned to Jerusalem, preaching the gospel in many villages of the Samaritans.

CHRIST IS PREACHED TO AN ETHIOPIAN

[26]Now an angel of the Lord spoke to [a]Philip, saying, "Arise and go toward the south along the road which goes down from Jerusalem to Gaza." This is [1]desert. [27]So he arose and went. And behold, [a]a man of Ethiopia, a eunuch of great authority under Candace the queen of the Ethiopians, who had charge of all her treasury, and [b]had come to Jerusalem to worship, [28]was returning. And sitting in his chariot, he was reading Isaiah the prophet. [29]Then the Spirit said to Philip, "Go near and overtake this chariot."
[30]So Philip ran to him, and heard him reading the prophet Isaiah, and said, "Do you understand what you are reading?"

Acts 8:29

HUNGRY HEART

The man of Ethiopia had a yearning for God. In his search for God, he had gone to Jerusalem. There he got the Scriptures, and he was heading back toward Ethiopia, still searching.

I believe God honors the heart that is searching after Him. I believe God will reveal Himself to an honest heart that is truly seeking Him. There are stories of people in remote areas who, when missionaries came to share the truth of Jesus Christ, these people said, "We've always believed in Him. We just didn't know His name!" God is faithful to reveal Himself to every hungry heart.

Cross references

14 [a] Acts 5:12, 29, 40
15 [a] Acts 2:38; 19:2
16 [a] Acts 19:2 [b] Matt. 28:19 [c] Acts 10:48; 19:5
17 [a] Acts 6:6; 19:6
20 [a] [Matt. 10:8] [b] [Acts 2:38; 10:45; 11:17]
21 [a] Jer. 17:9
22 [a] 2 Tim. 2:25
23 [a] Heb. 12:15
24 [a] James 5:16
26 [a] Acts 6:5 [1] Or a deserted place
27 [a] Ps. 68:31; 87:4 [b] John 12:20

31And he said, "How can I, unless someone guides me?" And he asked Philip to come up and sit with him. 32The place in the Scripture which he read was this:

a"He was led as a sheep to the slaughter;
And as a lamb before its shearer is silent,
b So He opened not His mouth.
33   In His humiliation His ajustice was taken away,
And who will declare His generation?
For His life is btaken from the earth."

34So the eunuch answered Philip and said, "I ask you, of whom does the prophet say this, of himself or of some other man?" 35Then Philip opened his mouth, aand beginning at this Scripture, preached Jesus to him. 36Now as they went down the road, they came to some water. And the eunuch said, "See, here is water. aWhat hinders me from being baptized?"

37 1Then Philip said, a"If you believe with all your heart, you may."
And he answered and said, b"I believe that Jesus Christ is the Son of God."
38So he commanded the chariot to stand still. And both Philip and the eunuch went down into the water, and he baptized him. 39Now when they came up out of the water, athe Spirit of the Lord caught Philip away, so that the eunuch saw him no more; and he went on his way rejoicing. 40But Philip was found at 1Azotus. And passing through, he preached in all the cities till he came to aCaesarea.

THE DAMASCUS ROAD: SAUL CONVERTED

9 Then aSaul, still breathing threats and murder against the disciples of the Lord, went to the high priest 2and asked aletters from him to the synagogues of Damascus, so that if he found any who were of the Way, whether men or women, he might bring them bound to Jerusalem.

3aAs he journeyed he came near Damascus, and suddenly a light shone around him from heaven. 4Then he fell to the ground, and heard a voice saying to him, "Saul, Saul, awhy are you persecuting Me?"

5And he said, "Who are You, Lord?"
Then the Lord said, "I am Jesus,

Side notes:
32 aIs. 53:7, 8 bJohn 19:9
33 aLuke 23:1–25 bLuke 23:33–46
35 aLuke 24:27
36 aActs 10:47; 16:33
37 a[Mark 16:16] bMatt. 16:16 1NU, M omit v. 37. It is found in Western texts, including the Latin tradition.
39 aEzek. 3:12, 14
40 aActs 21:8 1Same as Heb. Ashdod
CHAPTER 9
1 aActs 7:57; 8:1, 3; 26:10, 11
2 aActs 22:5
3 a1 Cor. 15:8
4 a[Matt. 25:40]
5 1NU, M omit the rest of v. 5 and begin v. 6 with But arise and go
7 a[Acts 22:9; 26:13]
10 aActs 22:12
11 aActs 21:39; 22:3

whom you are persecuting. 1It is hard for you to kick against the goads."
6So he, trembling and astonished, said, "Lord, what do You want me to do?"
Then the Lord said to him, "Arise and go into the city, and you will be told what you must do."
7And athe men who journeyed with him stood speechless, hearing a voice but seeing no one. 8Then Saul arose from the ground, and when his eyes were opened he saw no one. But they led him by the hand and brought him into Damascus. 9And he was three days without sight, and neither ate nor drank.

ANANIAS BAPTIZES SAUL

10Now there was a certain disciple at Damascus anamed Ananias; and to him the Lord said in a vision, "Ananias."
And he said, "Here I am, Lord."
11So the Lord said to him, "Arise and go to the street called Straight, and inquire at the house of Judas for one called Saul aof Tarsus, for behold, he is praying. 12And in a vision he has seen a man named Ananias coming in and putting his hand on him, so that he might receive his sight."
13Then Ananias answered, "Lord, I have heard from many about this man,

Acts 9:13

CALLED TO BE SAINTS

This is the first time believers are called "saints." In the gospel of Matthew, Matthew spoke about the saints of the Old Testament rising from their graves after Jesus' resurrection (Matt. 27:52). But here this term is being applied to the church in Jerusalem.

As far as God is concerned, you who are followers of Jesus Christ are saints. You don't have to be canonized to be a saint. As a believer in Jesus Christ, you are one. Paul told the Ephesians (Eph. 1:18) that we are called to be saints. St. Charles, what a great ring that has to it!

ªhow much ¹harm he has done to Your saints in Jerusalem. ¹⁴And here he has authority from the chief priests to bind all ªwho call on Your name."

¹⁵But the Lord said to him, "Go, for ªhe is a chosen vessel of Mine to bear My name before ᵇGentiles, ᶜkings, and the ᵈchildren¹ of Israel. ¹⁶For ªI will show him how many things he must suffer for My ᵇname's sake."

¹⁷ªAnd Ananias went his way and entered the house; and ᵇlaying his hands on him he said, "Brother Saul, the Lord ¹Jesus, who appeared to you on the road as you came, has sent me that you may receive your sight and ᶜbe filled with the Holy Spirit." ¹⁸Immediately there fell from his eyes *something* like scales, and he received his sight at once; and he arose and was baptized.

¹⁹So when he had received food, he was strengthened. ªThen Saul spent some days with the disciples at Damascus.

SAUL PREACHES CHRIST

²⁰Immediately he preached ¹the Christ in the synagogues, that He is the Son of God.

²¹Then all who heard were amazed, and said, ª"Is this not he who destroyed those who called on this name in Jerusalem, and has come here for that purpose, so that he might bring them bound to the chief priests?"

²²But Saul increased all the more in strength, ªand confounded the Jews who dwelt in Damascus, proving that this *Jesus* is the Christ.

SAUL ESCAPES DEATH

²³Now after many days were past, ªthe Jews plotted to kill him. ²⁴ªBut their plot became known to Saul. And they watched the gates day and night, to kill him. ²⁵Then the disciples took him by night and ªlet *him* down through the wall in a large basket.

SAUL AT JERUSALEM

²⁶And ªwhen Saul had come to Jerusalem, he tried to join the disciples; but they were all afraid of him, and did not

---

Side references

13 ª Acts 9:1
¹ *bad things*

14 ª Acts 7:59; 9:2, 21

15 ª Eph. 3:7, 8
ᵇ Rom. 1:5; 11:13
ᶜ Acts 25:22, 23; 26:1
ᵈ Rom. 1:16; 9:1–5
¹ Lit. *sons*

16 ª Acts 20:23
ᵇ 2 Cor. 4:11

17 ª Acts 22:12, 13
ᵇ Acts 8:17
ᶜ Acts 2:4; 4:31; 8:17; 13:52
¹ M omits *Jesus*

19 ª Acts 26:20

20 ¹ NU *Jesus*

21 ª Gal. 1:13, 23

22 ª Acts 18:28

23 ª 2 Cor. 11:26

24 ª 2 Cor. 11:32

25 ª Josh. 2:15

26 ª Acts 22:17–20; 26:20

Acts 9:26

PRIVATE LESSONS

Between verses 25 and 26, there is a gap of about three years. Paul did not go immediately to Jerusalem upon leaving Damascus, but he went down to the area of Mt. Sinai in Arabia. He was there for three years as the Lord readjusted his understanding of the Scriptures.

It was a time of solitude. It was a time of seeking God. It was a time of tremendous spiritual revelation. God used that time to reveal to him His marvelous grace, apart from the Law. For three years, Paul was instructed personally by the Lord.

ANY ALTERNATIVE PLANS?   **Acts 9:16**

Here the Lord said an interesting thing about Paul to Ananias, "For I will show him how many things he must suffer for My name's sake."

In 2 Corinthians, Paul listed the many things he suffered for the cause of Jesus Christ: "Are they ministers of Christ?—I speak as a fool—I am more: in labors more abundant, in stripes above measure, in prisons more frequently, in deaths often. From the Jews five times I received forty stripes minus one. Three times I was beaten with rods; once I was stoned; three times I was shipwrecked; a night and a day I have been in the deep; in journeys often, in perils of waters, in perils of robbers, in perils of my own countrymen, in perils of the Gentiles, in perils in the city, in perils in the wilderness, in perils in the sea, in perils among false brethren; in weariness and toil, in sleeplessness often, in hunger and thirst, in fastings often, in cold and nakedness—besides the other things, what comes upon me daily: my deep concern for all the churches" (2 Cor. 11:23–28).

Do you suppose the Lord showed Paul all of these things? The amazing thing to me is that Paul would still follow Him. I mean, if the Lord had shown me that kind of a future, I think I would have asked Him, "Lord, are there any alternative plans?"

believe that he was a disciple. ²⁷^aBut Barnabas took him and brought *him* to the apostles. And he declared to them how he had seen the Lord on the road, and that He had spoken to him, ^band how he had preached boldly at Damascus in the name of Jesus. ²⁸So ^ahe was with them at Jerusalem, coming in and going out. ²⁹And he spoke boldly in the name of the Lord Jesus and disputed against the ^aHellenists,¹ ^bbut they attempted to kill him. ³⁰When the brethren found out, they brought him down to Caesarea and sent him out to Tarsus.

THE CHURCH PROSPERS

³¹^aThen the ¹churches throughout all Judea, Galilee, and Samaria had peace and were ^bedified.² And walking in the ^cfear of the Lord and in the ^dcomfort of the Holy Spirit, they were ^emultiplied.

AENEAS HEALED

³²Now it came to pass, as Peter went ^athrough all *parts of the country*, that he also came down to the saints who dwelt in Lydda. ³³There he found a certain man named Aeneas, who had been bedridden eight years and was paralyzed. ³⁴And Peter said to him, "Aeneas, ^aJesus the Christ heals you. Arise and make your bed." Then he arose immediately. ³⁵So all who dwelt at Lydda and ^aSharon saw him and ^bturned to the Lord.

DORCAS RESTORED TO LIFE

³⁶At Joppa there was a certain disciple named ¹Tabitha, which is translated ²Dorcas. This woman was full ^aof good works and charitable deeds which she did. ³⁷But it happened in those days that she became sick and died. When they had washed her, they laid *her* in ^aan upper room. ³⁸And since Lydda was near Joppa, and the disciples had heard that Peter was there, they sent two men to him, imploring *him* not to delay in coming to them. ³⁹Then Peter arose and went with them. When he had come, they brought *him* to the upper room. And all the widows stood by him weeping, showing the tunics and garments which Dorcas had made while she was with them. ⁴⁰But Peter ^aput them all out, and ^bknelt down and prayed. And turning to the body he ^csaid, "Tabitha, arise." And she opened her eyes, and when she saw Peter she sat up. ⁴¹Then he gave her *his* hand and lifted her up; and when he had called

the saints and widows, he presented her alive. ⁴²And it became known throughout all Joppa, ^aand many believed on the Lord. ⁴³So it was that he stayed many days in Joppa with ^aSimon, a tanner.

CORNELIUS SENDS A DELEGATION

10 There was a certain man in ^aCaesarea called Cornelius, a centurion of what was called the Italian ¹Regiment, ²^aa devout *man* and one who ^bfeared God with all his household, who gave ¹alms generously to the people, and prayed to God always. ³About ¹the ninth hour of the day ^ahe saw clearly in a vision an angel of God coming in and saying to him, "Cornelius!"

⁴And when he observed him, he was afraid, and said, "What is it, lord?"

So he said to him, "Your prayers and your alms have come up for a memorial before God. ⁵Now ^asend men to Joppa, and send for Simon whose surname is Peter. ⁶He is lodging with ^aSimon, a tanner, whose house is by the sea. ^bHe¹ will tell you what you must do." ⁷And when the angel who spoke to him had departed, Cornelius called two of his household servants and a devout soldier from among those who waited on him continually. ⁸So

---

Marginal references (center column)

27 ^aActs 4:36; 13:2
^bActs 9:20, 22
28 ^aGal. 1:18
29 ^aActs 6:1; 11:20
^b2Cor. 11:26
¹Greek-speaking Jews
31 ^aActs 5:11; 8:1; 16:5
^b[Eph. 4:16, 29]
^cPs. 34:9
^dJohn 14:16
^eActs 16:5
¹NU church . . . was
²built up
32 ^aActs 8:14
34 ^a[Acts 3:6, 16; 4:10]
35 ^a1Chr. 5:16; 27:29
^bActs 11:21; 15:19
36 ^a1Tim. 2:10
¹Lit., in Aram., Gazelle
²Lit., in Gr., Gazelle
37 ^aActs 1:13; 9:39
40 ^aMatt. 9:25
^bActs 7:60
^cMark 5:41, 42
42 ^aJohn 11:45
43 ^aActs 10:6

CHAPTER 10
1 ^aActs 8:40; 23:23
¹Cohort
2 ^aActs 8:2; 9:22; 22:12
^b[Acts 10:22, 35; 13:16, 26]
¹charitable gifts
3 ^aActs 10:30; 11:13
¹3 P.M.
5 ^aActs 11:13, 14
6 ^aActs 9:43
^bActs 11:14
¹NU, M omit the rest of v. 6.

Acts 10:1–9

GOD WORKS ON BOTH ENDS

It's interesting to me how God works on both ends to bring His purposes to pass. He was working in the heart of Cornelius. And, on the other end, he was working in the heart of Peter.

There are times when people come to me and declare that God has spoken to them concerning me. Quite often, God has already been working in my own heart on that same issue.

God works on both ends. He'll work in your heart, and then that work will be confirmed by someone coming and sharing with you.

when he had explained all *these* things to them, he sent them to Joppa.

PETER'S VISION

9The next day, as they went on their journey and drew near the city, ªPeter went up on the housetop to pray, about ¹the sixth hour. ¹⁰Then he became very hungry and wanted to eat; but while they made ready, he fell into a trance ¹¹and ªsaw heaven opened and an object like a great sheet bound at the four corners, descending to him and let down to the earth. ¹²In it were all kinds of four-footed animals of the earth, wild beasts, creeping things, and birds of the air. ¹³And a voice came to him, "Rise, Peter; kill and eat."

¹⁴But Peter said, "Not so, Lord! ªFor I have never eaten anything common or unclean."

¹⁵And a voice *spoke* to him again the second time, ª"What God has ¹cleansed you must not call common." ¹⁶This was done three times. And the object was taken up into heaven again.

Acts 10:15

TRADITION!

As far as the Jews were concerned, the Gentiles were unclean. For a person with a strong Jewish background, it would have been extremely difficult to rise above the hold tradition had on him. Traditions, many times, are stronger than doctrine; and we hold to our traditions even when they are not doctrinally sound.

Peter, growing up in the Jewish tradition, looked upon the Gentiles as unclean. Now the Lord was going to bring about in Peter a very radical and dramatic change—the realization that God would save Gentiles! The Jews did not believe a Gentile could be saved. They believed the Gentiles had to proselytize into the Jewish faith in order to be saved. This was the belief of the early church. Now the Lord was trying to break Peter and the early church from this tradition.

---

9 ª Acts 10:9–32; 11:5–14
1 Noon

11 ª Acts 7:56

14 ª Deut. 14:3, 7

15 ª [Rom. 14:14]
1 Declared clean

17 1 was perplexed

19 ª Acts 11:12

20 ª Acts 15:7–9

21 1 NU, M omit who had been sent to him from Cornelius

22 ª Acts 22:12

23 ª Acts 10:45; 11:12

26 ª Acts 14:14, 15

28 ª John 4:9; 18:28
b [Acts 10:14, 35; 15:8, 9]

30 ª Acts 1:10
b Matt. 28:3
1 NU Four days ago to this hour, at the ninth hour

31 ª Dan. 10:12
b Heb. 6:10
1 charitable gifts

32 1 NU omits the rest of v. 32.

SUMMONED TO CAESAREA

¹⁷Now while Peter ¹wondered within himself what this vision which he had seen meant, behold, the men who had been sent from Cornelius had made inquiry for Simon's house, and stood before the gate. ¹⁸And they called and asked whether Simon, whose surname was Peter, was lodging there.

¹⁹While Peter thought about the vision, ªthe Spirit said to him, "Behold, three men are seeking you. ²⁰ªArise therefore, go down and go with them, doubting nothing; for I have sent them."

²¹Then Peter went down to the men ¹who had been sent to him from Cornelius, and said, "Yes, I am he whom you seek. For what reason have you come?"

²²And they said, "Cornelius *the* centurion, a just man, one who fears God and ªhas a good reputation among all the nation of the Jews, was divinely instructed by a holy angel to summon you to his house, and to hear words from you." ²³Then he invited them in and lodged *them.*

On the next day Peter went away with them, ªand some brethren from Joppa accompanied him.

PETER MEETS CORNELIUS

²⁴And the following day they entered Caesarea. Now Cornelius was waiting for them, and had called together his relatives and close friends. ²⁵As Peter was coming in, Cornelius met him and fell down at his feet and worshiped *him.* ²⁶But Peter lifted him up, saying, ª"Stand up; I myself am also a man." ²⁷And as he talked with him, he went in and found many who had come together. ²⁸Then he said to them, "You know how ªunlawful it is for a Jewish man to keep company with or go to one of another nation. But ᵇGod has shown me that I should not call any man common or unclean. ²⁹Therefore I came without objection as soon as I was sent for. I ask, then, for what reason have you sent for me?"

³⁰So Cornelius said, ¹"Four days ago I was fasting until this hour; and at the ninth hour I prayed in my house, and behold, ªa man stood before me ᵇin bright clothing, ³¹and said, 'Cornelius, ªyour prayer has been heard, and ᵇyour ¹alms are remembered in the sight of God. ³²Send therefore to Joppa and call Simon here, whose surname is Peter. He is lodging in the house of Simon, a tanner, by the sea. ¹When he comes, he will speak to you.' ³³So I sent to you

immediately, and you have done well to come. Now therefore, we are all present before God, to hear all the things commanded you by God."

PREACHING TO CORNELIUS' HOUSEHOLD

34Then Peter opened *his* mouth and said: a"In truth I perceive that God shows no partiality. 35But ain every nation whoever fears Him and works righteousness is baccepted by Him. 36The word which *God* sent to the *I*children of Israel, apreaching peace through Jesus Christ—bHe is Lord of all— 37that word you know, which was proclaimed throughout all Judea, and abegan from Galilee after the baptism which John preached: 38how aGod anointed Jesus of Nazareth with the Holy Spirit and with power, who bwent about doing good and healing all who were oppressed by the devil, cfor God was with Him. 39And we are awitnesses of all things which He did both in the land of the Jews and in Jerusalem, whom *I*they bkilled by hanging on a tree. 40Him aGod raised up on the third day, and showed Him openly, 41anot to all the people, but to witnesses chosen before by God, *even* to us bwho ate and drank with Him after He arose from the dead. 42And aHe commanded us to preach to the people, and to testify

Acts 10:45

NO PARTIALITY

Here is the beginning of the Gentile church. God poured out His Spirit and called out from among the Gentiles a bride for Jesus Christ. This is a beautiful picture for which we can give thanks to God because the door has been opened to the Gentiles.

God receives each one of us on an equal footing. He doesn't close the door to any man. We are wrong if we believe one race is superior to another. No matter who the man is, no matter where he is from, if he will call upon God, he will be saved!

bthat it is He who was ordained by God *to be* Judge cof the living and the dead. 43aTo Him all the prophets witness that, through His name, bwhoever believes in Him will receive cremission*I* of sins."

THE HOLY SPIRIT FALLS ON THE GENTILES

44While Peter was still speaking these words, athe Holy Spirit fell upon all those who heard the word. 45aAnd *I*those of the circumcision who believed were astonished, as many as came with Peter, bbecause the gift of the Holy Spirit had been poured out on the Gentiles also. 46For they heard them speak with tongues and magnify God.

Then Peter answered, 47"Can anyone forbid water, that these should not be baptized who have received the Holy Spirit ajust as we *have*?" 48aAnd he commanded them to be baptized bin the name of the Lord. Then they asked him to stay a few days.

PETER DEFENDS GOD'S GRACE

11 Now the apostles and brethren who were in Judea heard that the Gentiles had also received the word of God. 2And when Peter came up to Jerusalem, athose of the circumcision contended with him, 3saying, a"You went in to uncircumcised men band ate with them!"

4But Peter explained *it* to them ain order from the beginning, saying: 5a"I was in the city of Joppa praying; and in a trance I saw a vision, an object descending like a great sheet, let down from heaven by four corners; and it came to me. 6When I observed it intently and considered, I saw four-footed animals of the earth, wild beasts, creeping things, and birds of the air. 7And I heard a voice saying to me, 'Rise, Peter; kill and eat.' 8But I said, 'Not so, Lord! For nothing common or unclean has at any time entered my mouth.' 9But the voice answered me again from heaven, 'What God has cleansed you must not call common.' 10Now this was done three times, and all were drawn up again into heaven. 11At that very moment, three men stood before the house where I was, having been sent to me from Caesarea. 12Then athe Spirit told me to go with them, doubting nothing. Moreover bthese six brethren accompanied me, and we entered the man's house. 13aAnd he told me how he had seen an angel standing in his

Cross references

34 aDeut. 10:17

35 a[Eph. 2:13]
bPs. 15:1, 2

36 aIs. 57:19
bRom. 10:12
1Lit. sons

37 aLuke 4:14

38 aLuke 4:18
bMatt. 4:23
cJohn 3:2; 8:29

39 aActs 1:8
bActs 2:23
1NU, M they also

40 aActs 2:24

41 a[John 14:17, 19, 22; 15:27]
bLuke 24:30, 41–43

42 aMatt. 28:19
bJohn 5:22, 27
c1Pet. 4:5

43 aZech. 13:1
bGal. 3:22
cActs 13:38, 39
1forgiveness

44 aActs 4:31

45 aActs 10:23
bActs 11:18
1The Jews

47 aActs 2:4; 10:44; 11:17; 15:8

48 a1Cor. 1:14–17
bActs 2:38; 8:16; 19:5

CHAPTER 11

2 aActs 10:45

3 aActs 10:28
bGal. 2:12

4 aLuke 1:3

5 aActs 10:9

12 a[John 16:13]
bActs 10:23

13 aActs 10:30

Acts 11:5

DREAMS AND VISIONS

God often spoke to men through dreams (Abimelech, Jacob, Joseph, Daniel, Pharaoh, Gideon) and visions (Abram, Jacob, Samuel, Elijah, Nathan, Job, Isaiah, Ezekiel, Daniel, Obadiah, Zechariah, Ananias, Paul). Visions are like dreams, only you are awake but in sort of a trance. A vision is a gift whereby a person can see into the spiritual realm.

In the Old Testament, we find this gift of seeing into the spirit world exercised many times by the prophets, especially by Elijah and Ezekiel. God has often communicated to people by dreams and visions. In Joel, God said that in the last day, "I will pour out My Spirit on all flesh; your sons and your daughters shall prophesy, your old men shall dream dreams, your young men shall see visions" (Joel 2:28).

house, who said to him, 'Send men to Joppa, and call for Simon whose surname is Peter, 14who will tell you words by which you and all your household will be saved.' 15And as I began to speak, the Holy Spirit fell upon them, ªas upon us at the beginning. 16Then I remembered the word of the Lord, how He said, ª'John indeed baptized with water, but byou shall be baptized with the Holy Spirit.' 17aIf therefore God gave them the same gift as *He gave* us when we believed on the Lord Jesus Christ, bwho was I that I could withstand God?"

18When they heard these things they became silent; and they glorified God, saying, ª"Then God has also granted to the Gentiles repentance to life."

BARNABAS AND SAUL AT ANTIOCH

19aNow those who were scattered after the persecution that arose over Stephen traveled as far as Phoenicia, Cyprus, and Antioch, preaching the word to no one but the Jews only. 20But

15 ª Acts 2:1–4; 15:7–9

16 ª John 1:26, 33
b Is. 44:3

17 ª [Acts 15:8, 9]
b Acts 10:47

18 ª Rom. 10:12, 13; 15:9, 16

19 ª Acts 8:1, 4

20 ª Acts 6:1; 9:29

21 ª Luke 1:66
b Acts 9:35; 14:1

22 ª Acts 4:36; 9:27

23 ª Acts 13:43; 14:22

24 ª Acts 6:5
b Acts 5:14; 11:21

25 ª Acts 9:11, 30

27 ª 1 Cor. 12:28

Acts 11:4–17

A STORY WORTH REPEATING

Now in Bible days, writing was not the easiest thing in the world. You wrote on parchment. Thus, you wanted to conserve your words because parchment was rather scarce. When Luke first wrote the book of Acts, he wrote it on parchment. The book of Acts would have taken a parchment about thirty feet long. If it got longer than that, it would have gotten quite bulky. So writers tried to limit their words.

But this story is told twice. We read the story in chapter 10 as it was happening; and here, Luke repeated it as Peter told the entire story to the church in Jerusalem. For Luke to tell the entire story twice indicates this story of the Gentiles receiving the grace of God was a very important juncture for the church.

some of them were men from Cyprus and Cyrene, who, when they had come to Antioch, spoke to ªthe Hellenists, preaching the Lord Jesus. 21And ªthe hand of the Lord was with them, and a great number believed and bturned to the Lord.

22Then news of these things came to the ears of the church in Jerusalem, and they sent out ªBarnabas to go as far as Antioch. 23When he came and had seen the grace of God, he was glad, and ªencouraged them all that with purpose of heart they should continue with the Lord. 24For he was a good man, ªfull of the Holy Spirit and of faith. bAnd a great many people were added to the Lord.

25Then Barnabas departed for ªTarsus to seek Saul. 26And when he had found him, he brought him to Antioch. So it was that for a whole year they assembled with the church and taught a great many people. And the disciples were first called Christians in Antioch.

RELIEF TO JUDEA

27And in these days ªprophets came from Jerusalem to Antioch. 28Then one

ALL THE WAY, MY SAVIOR LEADS ME

Acts 11:25

Now it is interesting as you see the progression of things, how that each subsequent event was tied to an earlier thing. God is weaving the whole thing together. The Holy Spirit is fully directing the activity of His church.

It's awfully interesting when you get to be my age, if you make it that far, to look back and see how God was intertwining the events and circumstances all along the way. Things I didn't understand at the time. Things I was even at certain times rebelling against because I didn't understand them. But now, as I look back, I can see, yes, God brought to pass this relationship. He had me there in order that He might put me here, and so you see how the whole thing is linked together and you see that God's hand was there all along the way.

And thus you see here in the book of Acts how each event relates to the others. It is wonderful to see how God works through a wide variety of ministries and in different ways, building up His body, the church. So we have a part, and we are thrilled to have this part in the work of God's Holy Spirit—seeing the hand of God at work with each new event being related to some event in the past, seeing His hand at work all the way.

---

of them, named ªAgabus, stood up and showed by the Spirit that there was going to be a great famine throughout all the world, which also happened in the days of ᵇClaudius Caesar. ²⁹Then the disciples, each according to his ability, determined to send ªrelief to the brethren dwelling in Judea. ³⁰ªThis they also did, and sent it to the elders by the hands of Barnabas and Saul.

28 ª Acts 21:10
ᵇ Acts 18:2

29 ª 1 Cor. 16:1

30 ª Acts 12:25

HEROD'S VIOLENCE TO THE CHURCH

CHAPTER 12

12 Now about that time Herod the king stretched out *his* hand to harass some from the church. ²Then he killed James ªthe brother of John with the sword. ³And because he saw that it pleased the Jews, he proceeded further to seize Peter also. Now it was *during* ªthe Days of Unleavened Bread. ⁴So ªwhen he had arrested him, he put *him* in prison, and delivered *him* to four ¹squads of soldiers to keep him, intending to bring him before the people after Passover.

2 ª Matt. 4:21;
20:23

3 ª Ex. 12:15,
23:15

4 ª John 21:18
¹ Gr. *tetrads,*
squads of four

PETER FREED FROM PRISON

⁵Peter was therefore kept in prison, but ¹constant prayer was offered to God for him by the church. ⁶And when Herod was about to bring him out, that night Peter was sleeping, bound with two chains between two soldiers; and the guards before the door were ¹keeping the prison. ⁷Now behold, ªan angel of the Lord stood by *him,* and a light shone in the prison; and he struck Peter on the side and raised him up, saying, "Arise quickly!" And his chains fell off *his* hands. ⁸Then the angel said

5 ¹ NU *constantly* or *earnestly*

6 ¹ *guarding*

7 ª Acts 5:19

9 ª Ps. 126:1
ᵇ Acts 10:3, 17;
11:5

10 ª Acts 5:19;
16:26

to him, "Gird yourself and tie on your sandals"; and so he did. And he said to him, "Put on your garment and follow me." ⁹So he went out and followed him, and ªdid not know that what was done by the angel was real, but thought ᵇhe was seeing a vision. ¹⁰When they were past the first and the second guard posts, they came to the iron gate that leads to the city, ªwhich opened to

Acts 12:7

SHOW ME YOUR WAYS, O LORD

It's interesting to me that God is not limited to one method. He can work, and often does work, by a variety of methods. Later on, God would release Paul and Silas from the Philippian jail. But rather than sending an angel to open the doors, He would send an earthquake to shake the walls down.

Our God is a God of variety. Don't try to put Him in a box. Be open to what God wants to do. If He wants to have a new movement, or if He wants to work in a new way, praise the Lord! Let's be open to the moving of the Holy Spirit.

them of its own accord; and they went out and went down one street, and immediately the angel departed from him.

11 And when Peter had come to himself, he said, "Now I know for certain that ᵃthe Lord has sent His angel, and ᵇhas delivered me from the hand of Herod and *from* all the expectation of the Jewish people."

12 So, when he had considered *this*, ᵃhe came to the house of Mary, the mother of ᵇJohn whose surname was Mark, where many were gathered together ᶜpraying. 13 And as Peter knocked at the door of the gate, a girl named Rhoda came to answer. 14 When she recognized Peter's voice, because of *her* gladness she did not open the gate, but ran in and announced that Peter stood before the gate. 15 But they said to her, "You are beside yourself!" Yet she kept insisting that it was so. So they said, ᵃ"It is his angel."

Acts 12:15

O You of Little Faith. I wonder if sometimes we put an overemphasis on our faith as a necessity for answered prayer. Obviously, in this story, the Christians gathered at Mary's house didn't have faith. God works in sovereign ways His wonders to perform. And though there was a lack of faith in their prayers, God still answered them.

Have you ever been surprised when God answered your prayer? I have! I have prayed earnestly for things; and, when God answered, wow! I couldn't believe it. So they were astonished when Peter was released from jail.

---

16 Now Peter continued knocking; and when they opened *the door* and saw him, they were astonished. 17 But ᵃmotioning to them with his hand to keep silent, he declared to them how the Lord had brought him out of the prison. And he said, "Go, tell these things to James and to the brethren." And he departed and went to another place.

18 Then, as soon as it was day, there was no small ¹stir among the soldiers

---

Cross references (center column):

11 ᵃ [Ps. 34:7]
ᵇ Job 5:19

12 ᵃ Acts 4:23
ᵇ Acts 13:5, 13; 15:37
ᶜ Acts 12:5

15 ᵃ [Matt. 18:10]

17 ᵃ Acts 13:16; 19:33; 21:40

18 ¹ *disturbance*

20 ᵃ Matt. 11:21
ᵇ Ezek. 27:17
¹ *who was in charge of the king's bedchamber*
² Lit. *nourished*

23 ᵃ 2 Sam. 24:16, 17
ᵇ Ps. 115:1
¹ *breathed his last*

24 ᵃ Acts 6:7; 19:20

25 ᵃ Acts 11:30
ᵇ Acts 11:30
ᶜ Acts 13:5, 13
¹ NU, M *to*

---

about what had become of Peter. 19 But when Herod had searched for him and not found him, he examined the guards and commanded that *they* should be put to death.

And he went down from Judea to Caesarea, and stayed *there.*

HEROD'S VIOLENT DEATH

20 Now Herod had been very angry with the people of ᵃTyre and Sidon; but they came to him with one accord, and having made Blastus ¹the king's personal aide their friend, they asked for peace, because ᵇtheir country was ²supplied with food by the king's *country.*

21 So on a set day Herod, arrayed in royal apparel, sat on his throne and gave an oration to them. 22 And the people kept shouting, "The voice of a god and not of a man!" 23 Then immediately an angel of the Lord ᵃstruck him, because ᵇhe did not give glory to God. And he was eaten by worms and ¹died.

24 But ᵃthe word of God grew and multiplied.

Acts 12:24

THE WORD MULTIPLIED

Herod set himself against the work of God. He was going to curry favor with the Jews by putting to death the leadership of the early church. So he took one of the major leaders, James, and had him beheaded. When he saw this was pleasing to the Jews, he put Peter in jail and planned to kill him too. Herod was going to kill off the leadership and destroy the church.

But rather than the church being destroyed, the Word of God grew and multiplied. Jesus told His disciples that He would build His church and the gates of Hades (KJV: "hell") would not prevail against it (Matt. 16:18).

BARNABAS AND SAUL APPOINTED

25 And ᵃBarnabas and Saul returned ¹from Jerusalem when they had ᵇfulfilled *their* ministry, and they also ᶜtook

with them dJohn whose surname was Mark.

13 Now ain the church that was at Antioch there were certain prophets and teachers: bBarnabas, Simeon who was called Niger, cLucius of Cyrene, Manaen who had been brought up with Herod the tetrarch, and Saul. 2As they ministered to the Lord and fasted, the Holy Spirit said, a"Now separate to Me Barnabas and Saul for the work bto which I have called them." 3Then, ahaving fasted and prayed, and laid hands on them, they sent *them* away.

Acts 13:2

Minister to the Lord. At Antioch, certain prophets and teachers were ministering to the Lord. We usually think of ministering to the congregation. These men were ministering to the Lord.

I believe the primary purpose of the church is to minister to the Lord. I think the Lord created us for His glory in order that, through the church, He might receive praise and glory. As Paul stated to the Ephesians, we were created "to the praise of the glory of His grace" (Eph. 1:6). And the outflow, of course, of ministry to the Lord is ministry to others.

PREACHING IN CYPRUS

4So, being sent out by the Holy Spirit, they went down to Seleucia, and from there they sailed to aCyprus. 5And when they arrived in Salamis, athey preached the word of God in the synagogues of the Jews. They also had bJohn as *their* assistant.

6Now when they had gone through lthe island to Paphos, they found aa certain sorcerer, a false prophet, a Jew whose name *was* Bar-Jesus, 7who was with the proconsul, Sergius Paulus, an intelligent man. This man called for Barnabas and Saul and sought to hear the word of God. 8But aElymas the sorcerer (for so his name is translated) lwithstood them, seeking to turn the proconsul away from the faith. 9Then Saul, who also *is called* Paul, afilled with the Holy Spirit, looked intently at him 10and said, "O full of all deceit and

25 dActs 12:12; 15:37

CHAPTER 13

1 aActs 14:26
bActs 11:22
cRom. 16:21

2 aGal. 1:15; 2:9
bHeb. 5:4

3 aActs 6:6

4 aActs 4:36

5 a[Acts 13:46]
bActs 12:25; 15:37

6 aActs 8:9
lNU the whole island

8 aEx. 7:11
lopposed

9 aActs 2:4; 4:8

10 aMatt. 13:38

11 a1Sam. 5:6

13 aActs 15:38

14 aActs 16:13

15 aLuke 4:16
bHeb. 13:22
lencouragement

16 aActs 10:35

17 aDeut. 7:6–8
bActs 7:17
cEx. 14:8
1M omits Israel
2Mighty power

18 aNum. 14:34

19 aDeut. 7:1
bJosh. 14:1, 2; 19:51

20 aJudg. 2:16
b1Sam. 3:20

21 a1Sam. 8:5
b1Sam. 10:20–24

22 a1Sam. 15:23, 26, 28
b1Sam. 16:1, 12, 13
cPs. 89:20
d1Sam. 13:14

23 aIs. 11:1
bPs. 132:11
c[Matt. 1:21]
1M salvation, after

24 a[Luke 3:3]

25 aMark 1:7
bJohn 1:20, 27

all fraud, ayou son of the devil, *you* enemy of all righteousness, will you not cease perverting the straight ways of the Lord? 11And now, indeed, athe hand of the Lord *is* upon you, and you shall be blind, not seeing the sun for a time."

And immediately a dark mist fell on him, and he went around seeking someone to lead him by the hand. 12Then the proconsul believed, when he saw what had been done, being astonished at the teaching of the Lord.

AT ANTIOCH IN PISIDIA

13Now when Paul and his party set sail from Paphos, they came to Perga in Pamphylia; and aJohn, departing from them, returned to Jerusalem. 14But when they departed from Perga, they came to Antioch in Pisidia, and awent into the synagogue on the Sabbath day and sat down. 15And aafter the reading of the Law and the Prophets, the rulers of the synagogue sent to them, saying, "Men *and* brethren, if you have bany word of lexhortation for the people, say on."

16Then Paul stood up, and motioning with *his* hand said, "Men of Israel, and ayou who fear God, listen: 17The God of this people lIsrael achose our fathers, and exalted the people bwhen they dwelt as strangers in the land of Egypt, and with 2an uplifted arm He cbrought them out of it. 18Now afor a time of about forty years He put up with their ways in the wilderness. 19And when He had destroyed aseven nations in the land of Canaan, bHe distributed their land to them by allotment.

20"After that aHe gave *them* judges for about four hundred and fifty years, buntil Samuel the prophet. 21aAnd afterward they asked for a king; so God gave them bSaul the son of Kish, a man of the tribe of Benjamin, for forty years. 22And awhen He had removed him, bHe raised up for them David as king, to whom also He gave testimony and said, c'I have found David the *son* of Jesse, da man after My own heart, who will do all My will.' 23aFrom this man's seed, according bto *the* promise, God raised up for Israel cal Savior—Jesus— 24aafter John had first preached, before His coming, the baptism of repentance to all the people of Israel. 25And as John was finishing his course, he said, a'Who do you think I am? I am not *He.* But behold, bthere comes One after me, the sandals of whose feet I am not worthy to loose.'

26"Men *and* brethren, sons of the [1]family of Abraham, and [a]those among you who fear God, [b]to you the [2]word of this salvation has been sent. 27For those who dwell in Jerusalem, and their rulers, [a]because they did not know Him, nor even the voices of the Prophets which are read every Sabbath, have fulfilled *them* in condemning *Him.* 28[a]And though they found no cause for death *in Him,* they asked Pilate that He should be put to death. 29[a]Now when they had fulfilled all that was written concerning Him, [b]they took *Him* down from the tree and laid *Him* in a tomb. 30[a]But God raised Him from the dead. 31[a]He was seen for many days by those who came up with Him from Galilee to Jerusalem, who are His witnesses to the people. 32And we declare to you glad tidings—[a]that promise which was made to the fathers. 33God has fulfilled this for us their children, in that He has raised up Jesus. As it is also written in the second Psalm:

a'*You are My Son,*
Today I have begotten You.'

34And that He raised Him from the dead, no more to return to [1]corruption, He has spoken thus:

a'*I will give you the sure* [2]*mercies*
of David.'

35Therefore He also says in another *Psalm:*

a'*You will not allow Your Holy One*
to see corruption.'

36"For David, after he had served [1]his own generation by the will of God, [a]fell asleep, was buried with his fathers, and [2]saw corruption; 37but He whom God raised up [1]saw no corruption. 38Therefore let it be known to you, brethren, that [a]through this Man is preached to you the forgiveness of sins; 39and [a]by Him everyone who believes is justified from all things from which you could not be justified by the law of Moses. 40Beware therefore, lest what has been spoken in the prophets come upon you:

41 '*Behold,*[a] *you despisers,*
Marvel and perish!
For I work a work in your days,
A work which you will by no
means believe,
Though one were to declare it to
you.' "

26 [a] Ps. 66:16
[b] Matt. 10:6
[1] stock
[2] message

27 [a] Luke 23:34

28 [a] Matt. 27:22, 23

29 [a] Luke 18:31
[b] Matt. 27:57–61

30 [a] Matt. 12:39, 40; 28:6

31 [a] Acts 1:3, 11

32 [a] [Gen. 3:15]

33 [a] Ps. 2:7

34 [a] Is. 55:3
[1] the state of decay
[2] blessings

35 [a] Ps. 16:10

36 [a] Acts 2:29
[1] in his
[2] underwent decay

37 [1] underwent no decay

38 [a] Jer. 31:34

39 [a] [Is. 53:11]

41 [a] Hab. 1:5

42 [1] Or And when they went out of the synagogue of the Jews; NU And when they went out, they begged

43 [a] Acts 11:23
[b] Titus 2:11

45 [a] 1 Pet. 4:4

46 [a] Rom. 1:16
[b] Ex. 32:10
[c] Acts 18:6

Acts 13:32

THE MESSAGE

Notice that Paul shared with those in Antioch how Christ died for our sins, that He was buried, and that He rose again the third day, according to the Scriptures. Paul preached the gospel to these people. The promise that God made to David had been fulfilled. He had sent the Savior, that is, Jesus! The Word of God spoke of the Messiah being put to death, suffering, being despised and rejected, and all that had happened. Those prophecies were fulfilled. All the way through, Paul showed his listeners that God's purposes were fulfilled in Jesus.

If you will compare Paul's sermon here with Peter's sermon back in the second chapter of Acts, you will find there are many parallels in their messages. Basically, their messages are the death of Jesus Christ for our sins, His burial, and His resurrection, and that these events are the fulfillment of the Old Testament prophecies.

BLESSING AND CONFLICT AT ANTIOCH

42 [1]So when the Jews went out of the synagogue, the Gentiles begged that these words might be preached to them the next Sabbath. 43Now when the congregation had broken up, many of the Jews and devout proselytes followed Paul and Barnabas, who, speaking to them, [a]persuaded them to continue in [b]the grace of God.

44On the next Sabbath almost the whole city came together to hear the word of God. 45But when the Jews saw the multitudes, they were filled with envy; and contradicting and blaspheming, they [a]opposed the things spoken by Paul. 46Then Paul and Barnabas grew bold and said, [a]"It was necessary that the word of God should be spoken to you first; but [b]since you reject it, and judge yourselves unworthy of everlasting life, behold, [c]we turn to the Gentiles. 47For so the Lord has commanded us:

a'*I have set you as a light to the Gentiles, That you should be for salvation to the ends of the earth.'* "

48Now when the Gentiles heard this, they were glad and glorified the word of the Lord. ªAnd as many as had been appointed to eternal life believed. 49And the word of the Lord was being spread throughout all the region. 50But the Jews stirred up the devout and prominent women and the chief men of the city, ªraised up persecution against Paul and Barnabas, and expelled them from their region. 51aBut they shook off the dust from their feet against them, and came to Iconium. 52And the disciples ªwere filled with joy and bwith the Holy Spirit.

AT ICONIUM

14 Now it happened in Iconium that they went together to the synagogue of the Jews, and so spoke that a great multitude both of the Jews and of the ªGreeks believed. 2But the unbelieving Jews stirred up the Gentiles and 1poisoned their 2minds against the brethren. 3Therefore they stayed there a long time, speaking boldly in the Lord, ªwho was bearing witness to the word of His grace, granting signs and bwonders to be done by their hands. 4But the multitude of the city was ªdivided: part sided with the Jews, and part with the bapostles. 5And when a violent attempt was made by both the Gentiles and Jews, with their rulers, ªto abuse and stone them, 6they became aware of it and ªfled to Lystra and Derbe, cities of Lycaonia, and to the

47 ª Is. 42:6; 49:6
48 ª [Acts 2:47]
50 ª 2 Tim. 3:11
51 ª Matt. 10:14
52 ª John 16:22 b Acts 2:4; 4:8, 31; 13:9

CHAPTER 14

1 ª Acts 18:4
2 1 embittered 2 Lit. souls
3 ª Heb. 2:4 b Acts 5:12
4 ª Luke 12:51 b Acts 13:2, 3
5 ª 2 Tim. 3:11
6 ª Matt. 10:23

Acts 14:3

SIGNS AND WONDERS

The interesting thing to me is that, as Paul and Barnabas were in Iconium, the Lord granted signs and wonders to be done by their hands, which gave testimony to the word of grace they were sharing. In the gospel of Mark, as Jesus commanded the disciples to go into all the world and preach the gospel, He said that certain signs would follow those who believed (Mark 16:17). In other words, miraculous signs would be done in order to prove the Word of God to the people.

In the present time, there is a serious mistake that has been made in the endeavor to promote signs and wonders within the church. There is quite an emphasis on signs and wonders, hoping they will attract the unconverted. But that is not how it happened in the early church. The chief emphasis of their ministry was the teaching of the Word of God. The signs and wonders followed the teaching to confirm the Word of God in the hearts of the people.

APPOINTED TO ETERNAL LIFE   Acts 13:48

This is an interesting verse. These are divine mysteries, truths we cannot reconcile with our finite minds, the election of God and the free will of man. "As many as had been appointed to eternal life believed." Who appointed these Gentiles to eternal life? God. Yet, though God is sovereign and He has elected that we should be in Christ before the foundation of the earth, God has also ordained that we must exercise the free choice He has given to us. So the gospel is "to whosoever will, let him come," but the coming is still up to you. You must come! You must exercise your free will to choose to come to Jesus Christ. So we have the mystery of the sovereignty of God and the responsibility of man.

This remains a mystery, unsolved by the theologians through all their arguments, throughout all the centuries. There are men lining up on one side and men lining up on the other side, but both sides are correct. That's why the argument has never been resolved. God is sovereign; and as many as were appointed, or ordained, to eternal life believed. But their belief was always a matter of choice, a matter of free will.

surrounding region. [7] And they were preaching the gospel there.

IDOLATRY AT LYSTRA

[8a] And in Lystra a certain man without strength in his feet was sitting, a cripple from his mother's womb, who had never walked. [9] This man heard Paul speaking. [1] Paul, observing him intently and seeing that he had faith to be healed, [10] said with a loud voice, [a] "Stand up straight on your feet!" And he leaped and walked. [11] Now when the people saw what Paul had done, they raised their voices, saying in the Lycaonian language, [a] "The gods have come down to us in the likeness of men!" [12] And Barnabas they called [1] Zeus, and Paul, [2] Hermes, because he was the chief speaker. [13] Then the priest of Zeus, whose temple was in front of their city, brought oxen and garlands to the gates, [a] intending to sacrifice with the multitudes.

[14] But when the apostles Barnabas and Paul heard this, [a] they tore their clothes and ran in among the multitude, crying out [15] and saying, "Men, [a] why are you doing these things? [b] We also are men with the same nature as you, and preach to you that you should turn from [c] these useless things [d] to the living God, [e] who made the heaven, the earth, the sea, and all things that are in them, [16a] who in bygone generations allowed all nations to walk in their own ways. [17a] Nevertheless He did not leave Himself without witness, in that He did good, [b] gave us rain from heaven and fruitful seasons, filling our hearts with [c] food and gladness." [18] And with these sayings they could scarcely restrain the multitudes from sacrificing to them.

STONING, ESCAPE TO DERBE

[19a] Then Jews from Antioch and Iconium came there; and having persuaded the multitudes, [b] they stoned Paul *and* dragged *him* out of the city, supposing him to be [c] dead. [20] However, when the disciples gathered around him, he rose up and went into the city. And the next day he departed with Barnabas to Derbe.

STRENGTHENING THE CONVERTS

[21] And when they had preached the gospel to that city [a] and made many disciples, they returned to Lystra, Iconium, and Antioch, [22] strengthening the souls of the disciples, [a] exhorting *them* to continue in the faith, and *saying,* [b] "We

---

Cross references:

8 [a] Acts 3:2
9 [1] Lit. Who
10 [a] [Is. 35:6]
11 [a] Acts 8:10; 28:6
12 [1] Jupiter [2] Mercury
13 [a] Dan. 2:46
14 [a] Matt. 26:65
15 [a] Acts 10:26 [b] James 5:17 [c] 1 Cor. 8:4 [d] 1 Thess. 1:9 [e] Rev. 14:7
16 [a] Ps. 81:12
17 [a] Rom. 1:19, 20 [b] Deut. 11:14 [c] Ps. 145:16
19 [a] Acts 13:45, 50; 14:2–5 [b] 2 Cor. 11:25 [c] [2 Cor. 12:1–4]
21 [a] Matt. 28:19
22 [a] Acts 11:23 [b] [2 Tim. 2:12; 3:12]
23 [a] Titus 1:5
27 [a] Acts 15:4, 12 [b] 2 Cor. 2:12

Acts 14:15

ORDINARY MEN

"**W**e are men of like passions" or "we also are men with the same nature as you." That is hard for us to believe, isn't it?

When you read in the Old Testament of Elijah calling fire down from heaven, don't you believe Elijah was some kind of super saint? I mean look at the power Elijah had! But the Bible says Elijah was a man with a nature like ours (James 5:17).

Then, you read of Paul telling a lame man who had never walked before to "stand up on your feet," and the lame man stood up and walked. You say, "Oh my, Paul is something special." But Paul said here, "No, we are men with the same nature as you."

God uses common people. God uses ordinary men to accomplish His work. God wants to use you! You say, "Oh no, not me!" Yes, you! The men God uses are always surprised that God would use them. Who knows what God could do through your life if you were fully yielded to Him?

---

must through many tribulations enter the kingdom of God." [23] So when they had [a] appointed elders in every church, and prayed with fasting, they commended them to the Lord in whom they had believed. [24] And after they had passed through Pisidia, they came to Pamphylia. [25] Now when they had preached the word in Perga, they went down to Attalia. [26] From there they sailed to Antioch, where they had been commended to the grace of God for the work which they had completed.

[27] Now when they had come and gathered the church together, [a] they reported all that God had done with them, and that He had [b] opened the door of faith to the Gentiles. [28] So they stayed there a long time with the disciples.

CONFLICT OVER CIRCUMCISION

15 And ªcertain *men* came down from Judea and taught the brethren, b"Unless you are circumcised according to the custom of Moses, you cannot be saved." ²Therefore, when Paul and Barnabas had no small dissension and dispute with them, they determined that ªPaul and Barnabas and certain others of them should go up to Jerusalem, to the apostles and elders, about this question.

³So, ªbeing sent on their way by the church, they passed through Phoenicia and Samaria, bdescribing the conversion of the Gentiles; and they caused great joy to all the brethren. ⁴And when they had come to Jerusalem, they were received by the church and the apostles and the elders; and they reported all things that God had done with them. ⁵But some of the sect of the Pharisees who believed rose up, saying, "It is necessary to circumcise them, and to command *them* to keep the law of Moses."

THE JERUSALEM COUNCIL

⁶Now the apostles and elders came together to consider this matter. ⁷And when there had been much dispute, Peter rose up *and* said to them: ª"Men *and* brethren, you know that a good while ago God chose among us, that by my mouth the Gentiles should hear the word of the gospel and believe. ⁸So God, ªwho knows the heart, ¹acknowledged them by bgiving them the Holy Spirit, just as *He did* to us, ⁹ªand made no distinction between us and them, bpurifying their hearts by faith. ¹⁰Now therefore, why do you test God ªby putting a yoke on the neck of the disciples which neither our fathers nor we were able to bear? ¹¹But ªwe believe that through the grace of the Lord Jesus ¹Christ we shall be saved in the same manner as they."

¹²Then all the multitude kept silent and listened to Barnabas and Paul declaring how many miracles and wonders God had ªworked through them among the Gentiles. ¹³And after they had ¹become silent, ªJames answered, saying, "Men *and* brethren, listen to me: ¹⁴ªSimon has declared how God at the first visited the Gentiles to take out of them a people for His name. ¹⁵And with this the words of the prophets agree, just as it is written:

16   'Afterª this I will return
     And will rebuild the tabernacle of
     David, which has fallen down;

CHAPTER 15

1 ªGal. 2:12
b Phil. 3:2

2 ªGal. 2:1

3 ªRom. 15:24
b Acts 14:27;
15:4, 12

7 ªActs 10:20

8 ªActs 1:24
b Acts 2:4;
10:44, 47
¹ *bore witness to*

9 ªRom. 10:12
b Acts 10:15, 28

10 ªMatt. 23:4

11 ªRom. 3:4;
5:15
¹ NU, M omit
Christ

12 ªActs 14:27;
15:3, 4

13 ªActs 12:17
¹ *stopped speaking*

14 ªActs 15:7

16 ªAmos 9:11,
12

17 ¹ NU *LORD*,
who makes
these things

18 ¹ NU (continuing v. 17)
known from eternity (of old).'

19 ªActs 15:28;
21:25
b 1 Thess. 1:9

20 ªActs 21:25
b [1 Cor. 8:1;
10:20, 28]
c [1 Cor. 6:9]
d Lev. 3:17
¹ Or *fornication*

21 ªActs 13:15,
27

Acts 15:8

GOD KNOWS THE HEART

Here, Peter declared the omniscience of God. "God knows the heart" of men. As David said in Psalm 139, "LORD, You have searched me and known me. You know my sitting down and my rising up; You understand my thought afar off." This doesn't mean God is way up in heaven and I'm way down here; and from that distance, He knows my thoughts. In the Hebrew it is, "You know my thoughts in their origin." It's interesting to me how God knows my thoughts from their origin. He knows my thoughts before I think them.

A little later in this same discussion, James would say, "Known to God from eternity are all His works" (Acts 15:18). It is interesting how God's omniscience is woven right in here with their common discussion. God knows the heart.

     I will rebuild its ruins,
     And I will set it up;
17   *So that the rest of mankind may*
     seek the LORD,
     Even all the Gentiles who are
     called by My name,
     Says the ¹LORD who does all
     these things.'

18 ¹"Known to God from eternity are all His works. ¹⁹Therefore ªI judge that we should not trouble those from among the Gentiles who bare turning to God, ²⁰but that we ªwrite to them to abstain bfrom things polluted by idols, cfrom ¹sexual immorality, dfrom things strangled, and *from* blood. ²¹For Moses has had throughout many generations those who preach him in every city, ªbeing read in the synagogues every Sabbath."

THE JERUSALEM DECREE

²²Then it pleased the apostles and elders, with the whole church, to send

chosen men of their own company to Antioch with Paul and Barnabas, *namely*, Judas who was also named ªBarsabas,¹ and Silas, leading men among the brethren.

23They wrote this, *letter* by them:

The apostles, the elders, and the brethren,

To the brethren who are of the Gentiles in Antioch, Syria, and Cilicia:

Greetings.

24 Since we have heard that ªsome who went out from us have troubled you with words, bunsettling your souls, ¹saying, "*You must* be circumcised and keep the law"— to whom we gave no *such* commandment—25it seemed good to us, being assembled with one ¹accord, to send chosen men to you with our beloved Barnabas and Paul, 26ªmen who have risked their lives for the name of our Lord Jesus Christ. 27We have therefore sent Judas and Silas, who will also report the same things by word of mouth. 28For it seemed good to the Holy Spirit, and to us, to lay upon you no

greater burden than these necessary things: 29ªthat you abstain from things offered to idols, bfrom blood, from things strangled, and from csexual¹ immorality. If you keep yourselves from these, you will do well.

Farewell.

CONTINUING MINISTRY IN SYRIA

30So when they were sent off, they came to Antioch; and when they had gathered the multitude together, they delivered the letter. 31When they had read it, they rejoiced over its encouragement. 32Now Judas and Silas, themselves being ªprophets also, bexhorted and strengthened the brethren with many words. 33And after they had stayed *there* for a time, they were ªsent back with greetings from the brethren to ¹the apostles.

34 ¹However, it seemed good to Silas to remain there. 35ªPaul and Barnabas also remained in Antioch, teaching and preaching the word of the Lord, with many others also.

DIVISION OVER JOHN MARK

36Then after some days Paul said to Barnabas, "Let us now go back and

Cross-references (center column)

22 ªActs 1:23
¹NU, M *Barsabbas*

24 ªTitus 1:10, 11
bGal. 1:7; 5:10
¹NU omits *saying, "You must be circumcised and keep the law"*

25 ¹ *purpose or mind*

26 ªActs 13:50; 14:19

29 ªActs 15:20; 21:25
bLev. 17:14
cCol. 3:5
¹ Or *fornication*

32 ªEph. 4:11
bActs 14:22; 18:23

33 ªHeb. 11:31
¹NU *those who had sent them*

34 ¹NU, M omit v. 34.

35 ªActs 13:1

RIGHTEOUSNESS COMES BY FAITH ALONE

Acts 15:10

Peter was very honest here. He acknowledged that the Law as it was being taught by the Pharisees was unbearable.

It should be noted that Jesus was in continual dispute with the Pharisees over the Law. They were constantly accusing Jesus of violating the Law. Now Jesus did not violate the Law, but He did violate the traditions that grew out of the Law. So Peter said, "Look, why do we tempt God by putting on their neck a yoke of bondage? Why put this yoke on them? It's been too heavy for us."

Now Paul later wrote of the interesting paradox concerning the Gentiles and Jews. "That Gentiles, who did not pursue righteousness, have attained to righteousness, even the righteousness of faith; but Israel, pursuing the law of righteousness, has not attained to the law of righteousness. Why? Because they did not seek it by faith, but as it were, by the works of the law" (Rom. 9:30–32). By the Law is knowledge of sin. The Law can only point a finger at you and declare you guilty. The Law cannot absolve you from your guilt. It can only condemn you. But by faith in Jesus Christ, we have attained the righteousness of God. There is "no condemnation to those who are in Christ Jesus" (Rom. 8:1).

This is the very issue that was splitting the early church. This is an issue that is still being faced today by the church as there are many who will add to the faith the necessity of doing certain works that put on people a yoke of bondage. They declare it is necessary to submit to certain rituals in order to be saved. Rituals do not save. Ordinances do not save. You are saved by your faith in Jesus Christ.

visit our brethren in every city where we have preached the word of the Lord, *and see* how they are doing." 37Now Barnabas *l*was determined to take with them ªJohn called Mark. 38But Paul insisted that they should not take with them ªthe one who had departed from them in Pamphylia, and had not gone with them to the work. 39Then the contention became so sharp that they parted from one another. And so Barnabas took Mark and sailed to ªCyprus; 40but Paul chose Silas and departed, ªbeing *l*commended by the brethren to the grace of God. 41And he went through Syria and Cilicia, ªstrengthening the churches.

Acts 15:39–41

TWO TEAMS

Here two powerful church leaders got into an argument so severe they split company. How is it that men of God cannot agree?

Is it possible God wanted two missionary teams instead of one to cover twice the territory and so God allowed the contention to arise? That was the net result of the contention. Barnabas took Mark and headed off to Cyprus. Paul took Silas and headed off to Syria, Cilicia, and beyond. They went all the way into Europe on this journey.

Thus, the overall effect of the contention was good because it broadened the whole missionary endeavor.

TIMOTHY JOINS PAUL AND SILAS

16 Then he came to ªDerbe and Lystra. And behold, a certain disciple was there, ªnamed Timothy, ª*the* son of a certain Jewish woman who believed, but his father *was* Greek. 2He was well spoken of by the brethren who were at Lystra and Iconium. 3Paul wanted to have him go on with him. And he ªtook *him* and circumcised him because of the Jews who were in that region, for they all knew that his father was Greek. 4And as they went through the cities, they delivered to them the ªdecrees to keep, ªwhich were determined by the apostles and elders at Jerusalem. 5ªSo the churches were strengthened in the faith, and increased in number daily.

Notes:
37 ªActs 12:12, 25 *l* resolved
38 ªActs 13:13
39 ªActs 4:36; 13:4
40 ªActs 11:23; 14:26 *l* committed
41 ªActs 16:5

CHAPTER 16

1 ªActs 14:6 ᵇRom. 16:21 ᶜ2 Tim. 1:5; 3:15
3 ª[Gal. 2:3; 5:2]
4 ªActs 15:19–21 ᵇActs 15:28, 29
5 ªActs 2:47; 15:41
6 ªGal. 1:1, 2 *l* The Roman province of Asia
7 *l* NU adds *of Jesus*
8 ª2 Cor. 2:12
9 ªActs 10:30
10 ª2 Cor. 2:13
12 ªPhil. 1:1 *l* Lit. *first*
14 ªRev. 1:11; 2:18, 24 ᵇLuke 24:45
15 ªJudg. 19:21
16 ª1 Sam. 28:3, 7 ᵇActs 19:24
18 ªMark 1:25, 34 ᵇMark 16:17 *l* distressed
19 ªActs 16:16; 19:25, 26 ᵇMatt. 10:18

THE MACEDONIAN CALL

6Now when they had gone through Phrygia and the region of ªGalatia, they were forbidden by the Holy Spirit to preach the word in *l*Asia. 7After they had come to Mysia, they tried to go into Bithynia, but the *l*Spirit did not permit them. 8So passing by Mysia, they ªcame down to Troas. 9And a vision appeared to Paul in the night. A ªman of Macedonia stood and pleaded with him, saying, "Come over to Macedonia and help us." 10Now after he had seen the vision, immediately we sought to go ªto Macedonia, concluding that the Lord had called us to preach the gospel to them.

LYDIA BAPTIZED AT PHILIPPI

11Therefore, sailing from Troas, we ran a straight course to Samothrace, and the next *day* came to Neapolis, 12and from there to ªPhilippi, which is the *l*foremost city of that part of Macedonia, a colony. And we were staying in that city for some days. 13And on the Sabbath day we went out of the city to the riverside, where prayer was customarily made; and we sat down and spoke to the women who met *there.* 14Now a certain woman named Lydia heard *us.* She was a seller of purple from the city of ªThyatira, who worshiped God. ᵇThe Lord opened her heart to heed the things spoken by Paul. 15And when she and her household were baptized, she begged *us,* saying, "If you have judged me to be faithful to the Lord, come to my house and stay." So ªshe persuaded us.

PAUL AND SILAS IMPRISONED

16Now it happened, as we went to prayer, that a certain slave girl ªpossessed with a spirit of divination met us, who brought her masters ᵇmuch profit by fortune-telling. 17This girl followed Paul and us, and cried out, saying, "These men are the servants of the Most High God, who proclaim to us the way of salvation." 18And this she did for many days.

But Paul, ªgreatly *l*annoyed, turned and said to the spirit, "I command you in the name of Jesus Christ to come out of her." ᵇAnd he came out that very hour. 19But ªwhen her masters saw that their hope of profit was gone, they seized Paul and Silas and ᵇdragged *them* into the marketplace to the authorities.

20And they brought them to the magistrates, and said, "These men, being

Jews, ªexceedingly trouble our city; ²¹and they teach customs which are not lawful for us, being Romans, to receive or observe." ²²Then the multitude rose up together against them; and the magistrates tore off their clothes ªand commanded *them* to be beaten with rods. ²³And when they had laid many stripes on them, they threw *them* into prison, commanding the jailer to keep them securely. ²⁴Having received such a charge, he put them into the inner prison and fastened their feet in the stocks.

THE PHILIPPIAN JAILER SAVED

²⁵But at midnight Paul and Silas were praying and singing hymns to God, and the prisoners were listening to them.

20 ª Acts 17:8

22 ª 1 Thess. 2:2

26 ª Acts 4:31
b Acts 5:19;
12:7, 10

30 ª Acts 2:37;
9:6; 22:10

31 ª [John 3:16,
36; 6:47]

²⁶ªSuddenly there was a great earthquake, so that the foundations of the prison were shaken; and immediately ball the doors were opened and everyone's chains were loosed. ²⁷And the keeper of the prison, awaking from sleep and seeing the prison doors open, supposing the prisoners had fled, drew his sword and was about to kill himself. ²⁸But Paul called with a loud voice, saying, "Do yourself no harm, for we are all here."

²⁹Then he called for a light, ran in, and fell down trembling before Paul and Silas. ³⁰And he brought them out and said, ª"Sirs, what must I do to be saved?" ³¹So they said, ª"Believe on the Lord Jesus Christ, and you will be saved, you

INFILTRATION BY THE ENEMY   Acts 16:18

One of Satan's tactics to hinder the work of God is to become involved in the work of God. One of the great curses of the church has been its compromise with the world.

In the book of Revelation, you find Jesus rebuking the churches because they had left their first love. They had allowed the doctrines of the Nicolaitans to infiltrate the church. They had embraced the doctrines of Balaam. They had allowed that woman Jezebel, who called herself a prophetess, to influence the church. It was by this infiltration that the church's influence was greatly weakened. So, although this woman was speaking the truth, Paul would not accept her advertisement of them. "These men are the servants of the Most High God!" Yes, they were. "They proclaim the way of salvation." Yes, they did! Even Jesus did not allow demons to speak. They would cry out, "We know You are the Holy One of God," and Jesus would command them to be silent. (See Mark 1:24–25, Luke 4:34–35.)

The Bible asks the question, "What communion has light with darkness?" (2 Cor. 6:14). Yet there has been an attempt to combine them. Today there is a strong movement toward ecumenism. Its proponents say we need to put aside the differences in our doctrinal beliefs so that we might all be unified. We can't do it. The church must maintain its doctrinal purity and refuse the infiltration of the enemy.

MAGNIFY THE LORD   Acts 16:25

Singing is a tremendous way to alter our attitude and bring glory to God. After the victories and after the work of God, so often God's people would write songs to remind them of what God had done.

Moses sang after God delivered Israel from the Egyptians, "I will sing to the LORD, for He has triumphed gloriously!" (Ex. 15:1). In Deuteronomy 32:1–43, you have another song of Moses. This is a glorious song of God's power, God's deliverance. "Their rock is not like our Rock!" After the victory God brought over Sisera, Deborah wrote a song of God's deliverance (Judg. 5:1–31). David, of course, was constantly writing songs to and about God. "Oh, magnify the LORD with me, and let us exalt His name together" (Ps. 34:3).

Singing to the Lord and about the Lord is a great way to buoy your spirit and to keep your focus on the Lord. As we focus on the Lord in song, it's amazing how our problems diminish into nothingness. Paul and Silas sang in prison, and the prisoners listened attentively. They were probably wondering, *Who in the world are these guys—singing in these conditions?*

Acts 16:30

ONLY BELIEVE

To the Philippian jailer who wanted to know what he had to do to be saved, Paul answered, "Believe on the Lord Jesus Christ, and you will be saved." Notice he didn't say, "Join our church." He didn't give him a list of rules and regulations. He didn't lay any trip on him. Just believe on the Lord Jesus Christ, and you will be saved.

Is it possible that it is that simple? Is it possible we have complicated the matter by adding so many other requirements? Is it possible God will save a person by their simple belief in Jesus Christ? That was Paul's answer.

and your household." 32Then they spoke the word of the Lord to him and to all who were in his house. 33And he took them the same hour of the night and washed *their* stripes. And immediately he and all his *family* were baptized. 34Now when he had brought them into his house, ªhe set food before them; and he rejoiced, having believed in God with all his household.

PAUL REFUSES TO DEPART SECRETLY

35And when it was day, the magistrates sent the ¹officers, saying, "Let those men go."

36So the keeper of the prison reported these words to Paul, saying, "The magistrates have sent to let you go. Now therefore depart, and go in peace."

37But Paul said to them, "They have beaten us openly, uncondemned ªRomans, *and* have thrown *us* into prison. And now do they put us out secretly? No indeed! Let them come themselves and get us out."

38And the officers told these words to the magistrates, and they were afraid when they heard that they were Romans. 39Then they came and pleaded with them and brought *them* out, and ªasked *them* to depart from the city. 40So they went out of the prison ªand entered *the house of* Lydia; and

34 ª Luke 5:29; 19:6

35 ¹ *lictors,* lit. *rod bearers*

37 ª Acts 22:25–29

39 ª Matt. 8:34

40 ª Acts 16:14

CHAPTER 17

1 ª 1 Thess. 1:1

2 ª Luke 4:16
b 1 Thess. 2:1–16

3 ª Acts 18:5, 28

4 ª Acts 28:24

when they had seen the brethren, they encouraged them and departed.

PREACHING CHRIST AT THESSALONICA

17 Now when they had passed through Amphipolis and Apollonia, they came to ªThessalonica, where there was a synagogue of the Jews. 2Then Paul, as his custom was, ªwent in to them, and for three Sabbaths ᵇreasoned with them from the Scriptures, 3explaining and demonstrating ªthat the Christ had to suffer and rise again from the dead, and *saying,* "This Jesus whom I preach to you is the Christ." 4ªAnd some of them were persuaded; and a great multitude of the devout Greeks, and not a few of

Acts 17:2

LET US REASON TOGETHER

The gospel of Jesus Christ is reasonable. Salvation is a reasonable offer. It makes sense to commit your life to God.

Paul said, "I beseech you therefore, brethren, by the mercies of God, that you present your bodies a living sacrifice, holy, acceptable to God, which is your reasonable service" (Rom. 12:1). It makes sense! God has a much better plan for your life than anything you could devise for yourself.

"Come now," God said, "and let us reason together, though your sins are like scarlet, they shall be as white as snow" (Isa. 1:18). The gospel is reasonable. In fact, I believe the rejection of the gospel is unreasonable. I think the only reason some people reject the gospel is that Satan has deceived them and is holding them captive so that they cannot reason.

So Paul reasoned with the Jews at Thessalonica, showing them from the Scriptures that Jesus was the Messiah.

the leading women, joined Paul and [b]Silas.

ASSAULT ON JASON'S HOUSE

[5]But the Jews [1]who were not persuaded, [2]becoming [a]envious, took some of the evil men from the marketplace, and gathering a mob, set all the city in an uproar and attacked the house of [b]Jason, and sought to bring them out to the people. [6]But when they did not find them, they dragged Jason and some brethren to the rulers of the city, crying out, [a]"These who have turned the world upside down have come here too. [7]Jason has [1]harbored them, and these are all acting contrary to the decrees of Caesar, [a]saying there is another king—Jesus." [8]And they troubled the crowd and the rulers of the city when they heard these things. [9]So when they had taken security from Jason and the rest, they let them go.

MINISTERING AT BEREA

[10]Then [a]the brethren immediately sent Paul and Silas away by night to Berea. When they arrived, they went into the synagogue of the Jews. [11]These were more [1]fair-minded than those in Thessalonica, in that they received the word with all readiness, and [a]searched the Scriptures daily to find out whether these things were so. [12]Therefore many of them believed, and also not a few of the Greeks, prominent women as well as men. [13]But when the Jews from Thessalonica learned that the word of God was preached by Paul at Berea, they came there also and stirred up the crowds. [14a]Then immediately the brethren sent Paul away, to go to the sea; but both Silas and Timothy remained there. [15]So those who conducted Paul brought him to Athens; and [a]receiving a command for Silas and Timothy to come to him with all speed, they departed.

THE PHILOSOPHERS AT ATHENS

[16]Now while Paul waited for them at Athens, [a]his spirit was provoked within him when he saw that the city was [1]given over to idols. [17]Therefore he reasoned in the synagogue with the Jews and with the *Gentile* worshipers, and in the marketplace daily with those who happened to be there. [18 1]Then certain Epicurean and Stoic philosophers encountered him. And some said, "What does this [2]babbler want to say?"

Others said, "He seems to be a proclaimer of foreign gods," because he preached to them [a]Jesus and the resurrection. [19]And they took him and brought him to the [1]Areopagus, saying, "May we know what this new doctrine *is* of which you speak? [20]For you are bringing some strange things to our ears. Therefore we want to know what these things mean." [21]For all the Athenians and the foreigners who were there spent their time in nothing else but either to tell or to hear some new thing.

ADDRESSING THE AREOPAGUS

[22]Then Paul stood in the midst of the [1]Areopagus and said, "Men of Athens, I perceive that in all things you are very religious; [23]for as I was passing through and considering the objects of your worship, I even found an altar with this inscription:

TO THE UNKNOWN GOD.

Therefore, the One whom you worship without knowing, Him I proclaim to you: [24a]God, who made the world and everything in it, since He is [b]Lord of heaven and earth, [c]does not dwell in temples made with hands. [25]Nor is He

Acts 17:22–28

THE UNKNOWN GOD

Some of the most marvelous temples built by man were in Athens. Paul was surrounded by them, and he was saying, "The true and living God, the Lord of heaven and earth, does not dwell in temples made with hands. This God you worship ignorantly, the unknown God, He doesn't dwell in temples. Neither is He worshiped with men's hands as though He needs anything from you."

You can't give anything to God. He doesn't need anything from you, but you need an awful lot from Him! You need God for life. "In Him we live and move and have our being."

Marginal notes:

4 [b]Acts 15:22, 27, 32, 40

5 [a]Acts 13:45
[b]Rom. 16:21
[1]NU omits who were not persuaded
[2]M omits becoming envious

6 [a][Acts 16:20]

7 [a]1 Pet. 2:13
[1]welcomed

10 [a]Acts 9:25; 17:14

11 [a]John 5:39
[1]Lit. *noble*

14 [a]Matt. 10:23

15 [a]Acts 18:5

16 [a]2 Pet. 2:8
[1]*full of idols*

18 [a]1 Cor. 15:12
[1]NU, M add *also*
[2]Lit. *seed picker,* an idler who makes a living picking up scraps

19 [1]Lit. *Hill of Ares,* or *Mars' Hill*

22 [1]Lit. *Hill of Ares,* or *Mars' Hill*

24 [a]Acts 14:15
[b]Matt. 11:25
[c]Acts 7:48–50

worshiped with men's hands, as though He needed anything, since He [a]gives to all life, breath, and all things. [26]And He has made from one [1]blood every nation of men to dwell on all the face of the earth, and has determined their preappointed times and [a]the boundaries of their dwellings, [27]so that they should seek the Lord, in the hope that they might grope for Him and find Him, [b]though He is not far from each one of us; [28]for [a]in Him we live and move and have our being, [b]as also some of your own poets have said, 'For we are also His offspring.' [29]Therefore, since we are the offspring of God, [a]we ought not to think that the Divine Nature is like gold or silver or stone, something shaped by art and man's devising. [30]Truly, [a]these times of ignorance God overlooked, but [b]now commands all men everywhere to repent, [31]because He has appointed a day on which [a]He will judge the world in righteousness by the Man whom He has ordained. He has given assurance of this to all by [b]raising Him from the dead."

[32]And when they heard of the resurrection of the dead, some mocked, while others said, "We will hear you again on this *matter*." [33]So Paul departed from among them. [34]However, some men joined him and believed, among them Dionysius the Areopagite, a woman named Damaris, and others with them.

MINISTERING AT CORINTH

18 After these things Paul departed from Athens and went to Corinth. [2]And he found a certain Jew named [a]Aquila, born in Pontus, who had recently come from Italy with his wife Priscilla (because Claudius had commanded all the Jews to depart from Rome); and he came to them. [3]So, because he was of the same trade, he stayed with them [a]and worked; for by occupation they were tentmakers. [4a]And he reasoned in the synagogue every Sabbath, and persuaded both Jews and Greeks.

[5a]When Silas and Timothy had come from Macedonia, Paul was [b]compelled [1]by the Spirit, and testified to the Jews *that* Jesus *is* the Christ. [6]But [a]when they opposed him and blasphemed, [b]he shook *his* garments and said to them, [c]"Your blood *be* upon your *own* heads; [d]I *am* clean. [e]From now on I will go to the Gentiles." [7]And he departed from there and entered the house of a certain

---

Acts 17:32–34

How Say You? Note the varied reactions to the gospel. Some mocked. Some procrastinated. Others believed. It's like Jesus said about the sown seed. Some fell on the wayside, some among thorns, some on stony ground, and some on good soil.

What is your reaction? Are you among those that mock the message? Are you among those who are delaying the decision? Or, are you among those who have believed and committed yourself to Jesus Christ? It's important for you to know because one day God is going to judge the world in righteousness through Jesus Christ.

Cross references:

25 [a] Is. 42:5

26 [a] Deut. 32:8
[1] NU omits blood

27 [a] [Rom. 1:20]
[b] Jer. 23:23, 24

28 [a] [Heb. 1:3]
[b] Titus 1:12

29 [a] Is. 40:18, 19

30 [a] [Rom. 3:25]
[b] [Titus 2:11, 12]

31 [a] Acts 10:42
[b] Acts 2:24

CHAPTER 18

2 [a] 1 Cor. 16:19

3 [a] Acts 20:34

4 [a] Acts 17:2

5 [a] Acts 17:14, 15
[b] Acts 18:28
[1] Or *in his spirit* or *in the Spirit*

6 [a] Acts 13:45
[b] Neh. 5:13
[c] 2 Sam. 1:16
[d] [Ezek. 3:18, 19]
[e] Acts 13:46–48; 28:28

DELIVER YOUR SOUL   Acts 18:6

Paul said, "I am not ashamed of the gospel of Christ, for it is the power of God to salvation for everyone who believes, for the Jew first and also for the Greek" (Rom. 1:16). Paul always went to the Jews first. When they rejected, he went to the Greeks.

In chapter 20, we find Paul speaking with elders of Ephesus about being innocent of the blood of all men because he had not failed to declare to them the whole counsel of God. Paul looked upon himself as a debtor to Jesus Christ because he had received the gospel and it had transformed his life. He was probably so tireless in his efforts to spread the gospel because he felt he would otherwise be responsible for their eternal damnation and their blood would be on his hands. So he really pushed to share the gospel because then those who had heard would be responsible to accept or reject it. He would have fulfilled his responsibility by witnessing to them. We don't seem to have that same sense of urgency in sharing the gospel today.

man named [1]Justus, one who worshiped God, whose house was next door to the synagogue. [8a]Then Crispus, the ruler of the synagogue, believed on the Lord with all his household. And many of the Corinthians, hearing, believed and were baptized.

[9]Now [a]the Lord spoke to Paul in the night by a vision, "Do not be afraid, but speak, and do not keep silent; [10a]for I am with you, and no one will attack you to hurt you; for I have many people in this city." [11]And he continued there a year and six months, teaching the word of God among them.

Acts 18:9–10

AN UNLIKELY PLACE

In a vision, the Lord promised to be with Paul in Corinth and said that no one would be able to hurt him. The Lord told Paul to speak, for "I have many people in this city."

Corinth was probably the most unlikely place you would ever expect to have successful evangelism. But God so often works in the unlikely places. Some of the places, you think, *Oh, that would be a great place to go with the gospel and establish a church,* and it isn't. Some of the places, you think, *Stay away from there! That's the last place in the world you want to go,* and that's the place where God says, "Speak, for I have many people in this city."

[12]When Gallio was proconsul of Achaia, the Jews with one accord rose up against Paul and brought him to the [1]judgment seat, [13]saying, "This *fellow* persuades men to worship God contrary to the law."

[14]And when Paul was about to open *his* mouth, Gallio said to the Jews, "If it were a matter of wrongdoing or wicked crimes, O Jews, there would be reason why I should bear with you. [15]But if it is a [a]question of words and names and your own law, look *to it* yourselves; for I do not want to be a judge of such *matters.*" [16]And he drove them from the

judgment seat. [17]Then [1]all the Greeks took [a]Sosthenes, the ruler of the synagogue, and beat *him* before the judgment seat. But Gallio took no notice of these things.

PAUL RETURNS TO ANTIOCH

[18]So Paul still remained [1]a good while. Then he took leave of the brethren and sailed for Syria, and Priscilla and Aquila *were* with him. [a]He had *his* hair cut off at [b]Cenchrea, for he had taken a vow. [19]And he came to Ephesus, and left them there; but he himself entered the synagogue and reasoned with the Jews. [20]When they asked *him* to stay a longer time with them, he did not consent, [21]but took leave of them, saying, [a]"I [1]must by all means keep this coming feast in Jerusalem; but I will return again to you, [b]God willing." And he sailed from Ephesus.

Acts 18:18

A VOW OF COMMITMENT

When you wanted to show a special appreciation to God, or thanksgiving for the blessings of God, you would shave your head and for a period of thirty days or whatever you had proscribed, you would not eat meat or drink wine. The vow of the Nazirite was the vow of full commitment to God. When people are totally committed to God, they are people of great strength. There is power in commitment. Tremendous!

The reason communism was able to make such great strides was the commitment the people had to communism. The reason tree huggers are able to do so much is that they are committed to their cause. There is a lot to be said for commitment.

[22]And when he had landed at [a]Caesarea, and [1]gone up and greeted the church, he went down to Antioch. [23]After he had spent some time *there,* he departed and went over the region

7 [1]NU *Titius Justus*

8 [a]1 Cor. 1:14

9 [a]Acts 23:11

10 [a]Jer. 1:18, 19

12 [1]Gr. *bema*

15 [a]Acts 23:29; 25:19

17 [a]1 Cor. 1:1 [1]NU *they all*

18 [a]Acts 21:24 [b]Rom. 16:1 [1]Lit. *many days*

21 [a]Acts 19:21; 20:16 [b]1 Cor. 4:19 [1]NU omits *I must by all means keep this coming feast in Jerusalem*

22 [a]Acts 8:40 [1]To Jerusalem

of ᵃGalatia and Phrygia ˡin order, ᵇstrengthening all the disciples.

MINISTRY OF APOLLOS

24ᵃNow a certain Jew named Apollos, born at Alexandria, an eloquent man *and* mighty in the Scriptures, came to Ephesus. 25This man had been instructed in the way of the Lord; and being ᵃfervent in spirit, he spoke and taught accurately the things of the Lord, ᵇthough he knew only the baptism of John. 26So he began to speak boldly in the synagogue. When Aquila and Priscilla heard him, they took him aside and explained to him the way of God more accurately. 27And when he desired to cross to Achaia, the brethren wrote, exhorting the disciples to receive him; and when he arrived, ᵃhe greatly helped those who had believed through grace; 28for he vigorously refuted the Jews publicly, ᵃshowing from the Scriptures that Jesus is the Christ.

PAUL AT EPHESUS

19 And it happened, while ᵃApollos was at Corinth, that Paul, having passed through ᵇthe upper regions, came to Ephesus. And finding some disciples 2he said to them, "Did you receive the Holy Spirit when you believed?"

So they said to him, ᵃ"We have not so much as heard whether there is a Holy Spirit."

3And he said to them, "Into what then were you baptized?"

So they said, ᵃ"Into John's baptism."

4Then Paul said, ᵃ"John indeed baptized with a baptism of repentance, saying to the people that they should believe on Him who would come after him, that is, on Christ Jesus."

5When they heard *this*, they were baptized ᵃin the name of the Lord Jesus. 6And when Paul had ᵃlaid hands on them, the Holy Spirit came upon them, and ᵇthey spoke with tongues and prophesied. 7Now the men were about twelve in all.

8ᵃAnd he went into the synagogue and spoke boldly for three months, reasoning and persuading ᵇconcerning the things of the kingdom of God. 9But ᵃwhen some were hardened and did not believe, but spoke evil ᵇof the Way before the multitude, he departed from them and withdrew the disciples, reasoning daily in the school of Tyrannus. 10And ᵃthis continued for two years, so that all who dwelt in Asia heard the

Cross References

23 ᵃGal. 1:2
ᵇActs 14:22; 15:32, 41
ˡ *successively*

24 ᵃTitus 3:13

25 ᵃRom. 12:11
ᵇActs 19:3

27 ᵃ1 Cor. 3:6

28 ᵃActs 9:22; 17:3; 18:5

CHAPTER 19

1 ᵃ1 Cor. 1:12; 3:5, 6
ᵇActs 18:23

2 ᵃ1 Sam. 3:7

3 ᵃActs 18:25

4 ᵃMatt. 3:11

5 ᵃActs 8:12, 16; 10:48

6 ᵃActs 6:6; 8:17
ᵇActs 2:4; 10:46

8 ᵃActs 17:2; 18:4
ᵇActs 1:3; 28:23

9 ᵃ2 Tim. 1:15
ᵇActs 9:2; 19:23; 22:4; 24:14

10 ᵃActs 19:8; 20:31

11 ᵃMark 16:20

12 ᵃActs 5:15

13 ᵃMatt. 12:27
ᵇMark 9:38
ᶜ1 Cor. 1:23; 2:2
ˡNU *I*
²*adjure*, solemnly command

Acts 19:2

COME, HOLY SPIRIT

Now here in Acts, when Paul said to the Ephesians, "Did you receive the Holy Spirit since you believed?" (or "when you believed?"), Paul was acknowledging that you can believe and yet be filled with the Holy Spirit at a later time. Paul probably asked the question because he observed a lack of fervency, a lack of love, a lack of passion or fire.

There were and are many Christians lacking the real dynamic of the Spirit in their lives. They are sort of ho-hum Christians. There is no real fire. "Yes, I'm a Christian. I believe in Jesus," but it doesn't go beyond that. There is no real enthusiasm for the things of the Lord. And perhaps Paul observed a spiritual deadness. So he asked, "Did you receive the Holy Spirit?" because the Holy Spirit is dynamic! He is power! He makes us alive to the things of God! He brings in us a fire and enthusiasm! He brings joy! So "did you receive the Holy Spirit when you believed?"

---

word of the Lord Jesus, both Jews and Greeks.

MIRACLES GLORIFY CHRIST

11Now ᵃGod worked unusual miracles by the hands of Paul, 12ᵃso that even handkerchiefs or aprons were brought from his body to the sick, and the diseases left them and the evil spirits went out of them. 13ᵃThen some of the itinerant Jewish exorcists ᵇtook it upon themselves to call the name of the Lord Jesus over those who had evil spirits, saying, ˡ"We ²exorcise you by the Jesus whom Paul ᶜpreaches." 14Also there were seven sons of Sceva, a Jewish chief priest, who did so.

15And the evil spirit answered and said, "Jesus I know, and Paul I know; but who are you?"

16Then the man in whom the evil

Acts 19:11
Lord, Make Me Your Instrument.
Notice that it was God who worked the miracles, not Paul. It was the hands of Paul. God uses human instruments to accomplish His work.

What a thrill and what a blessing it is to be an instrument in God's hands! What a blessing that God would do His work through me. I may become the instrument that God uses, but it is God's work. God wants to work through you.

16 [1] M and they overpowered them
2 NU both of them

17 [a] Luke 1:65; 7:16

18 [a] Matt. 3:6

20 [a] Acts 6:7; 12:24

21 [a] Rom. 15:25
[b] Acts 20:22
[c] Acts 20:1
[d] Rom. 1:13; 15:22–29

22 [a] 1 Tim. 1:2
[b] Rom. 16:23

23 [a] 2 Cor. 1:8
[b] Acts 9:2

24 [a] Acts 16:16, 19
[1] Gr. Artemis

spirit was leaped on them, [1]overpowered them, and prevailed against [2]them, so that they fled out of that house naked and wounded. [17]This became known both to all Jews and Greeks dwelling in Ephesus; and [a]fear fell on them all, and the name of the Lord Jesus was magnified. [18]And many who had believed came [a]confessing and telling their deeds. [19]Also, many of those who had practiced magic brought their books together and burned them in the sight of all. And they counted up the value of them, and it totaled fifty thousand pieces of silver. [20][a]So the word of the Lord grew mightily and prevailed.

THE RIOT AT EPHESUS
[21][a]When these things were accomplished, Paul [b]purposed in the Spirit, when he had passed through [c]Macedonia and Achaia, to go to Jerusalem, saying, "After I have been there, [d]I must also see Rome." [22]So he sent into Macedonia two of those who ministered to him, [a]Timothy and [b]Erastus, but he himself stayed in Asia for a time. [23]And [a]about that time there arose a great commotion about [b]the Way. [24]For a certain man named Demetrius, a silversmith, who made silver shrines of [1]Diana, brought [a]no small profit to the

DON'T LET YOUR LOVE GROW COLD

Acts 19:40

Where do you suppose the greatest danger lies in this story—from Demetrius or from the government officials?

It's interesting that the church has always prospered under persecution. Whenever the church is protected by the government, it becomes weak. The early church suffering persecution from the Roman government grew and thrived. But once it was embraced by the government, it became weak.

It's interesting that when Jesus addressed the church of Ephesus in the book of Revelation, He said, "I have this against you, that you have left your first love. . . . repent and do the first works, or else I will come to you quickly and remove your lampstand" (Rev. 2:4–5). Now, in the vision John had, Jesus was walking in the midst of the seven golden lampstands, which were representative of the church. The seven churches of Asia were represented by the lampstands, and Jesus is walking in their midst. The warning of Jesus to the church of Ephesus was: "If you don't repent and go back to your first works, your first love, I will remove My presence from the church." In Ephesus today, you see the ruins of a once great city. Nearby there's a little Muslim village, but there is not one single Christian in or around Ephesus today. The presence of Christ has been removed from the city.

The Lord wants our love to remain fervent. He wants us to be continuously filled with the Spirit. Their "first love" refers to when Paul came and they received the Holy Spirit. But gradually, by the end of the first century, other forces had crept in and the church had lost its vitality, its love, and its power until finally there was no church at all.

This is a warning to us concerning the importance of maintaining fervor, love, and excitement for the things of Jesus. May we not let our love grow cold, but let the fire of God's Spirit ever burn in our hearts and lives as we seek to reach our Jerusalems, our Judeas, our Samarias, and the uttermost parts of our world.

craftsmen. [25]He called them together with the workers of similar occupation, and said: "Men, you know that we have our prosperity by this trade. [26]Moreover you see and hear that not only at Ephesus, but throughout almost all Asia, this Paul has persuaded and turned away many people, saying that [a]they are not gods which are made with hands. [27]So not only is this trade of ours in danger of falling into disrepute, but also the temple of the great goddess Diana may be despised and [1]her magnificence destroyed, whom all Asia and the world worship."

[28]Now when they heard *this,* they were full of wrath and cried out, saying, "Great is Diana of the Ephesians!" [29]So the whole city was filled with confusion, and rushed into the theater with one accord, having seized [a]Gaius and [b]Aristarchus, Macedonians, Paul's travel companions. [30]And when Paul wanted to go in to the people, the disciples would not allow him. [31]Then some of the [1]officials of Asia, who were his friends, sent to him pleading that he would not venture into the theater. [32]Some therefore cried one thing and some another, for the assembly was confused, and most of them did not know why they had come together. [33]And they drew Alexander out of the multitude, the Jews putting him forward. And [a]Alexander [b]motioned with his hand, and wanted to make his defense to the people. [34]But when they found out that he was a Jew, all with one voice cried out for about two hours, "Great is Diana of the Ephesians!"

[35]And when the city clerk had quieted the crowd, he said: "Men of Ephesus, what man is there who does not know that the city of the Ephesians is temple guardian of the great goddess [1]Diana, and of the *image* which fell down from [2]Zeus? [36]Therefore, since these things cannot be denied, you ought to be quiet and do nothing rashly. [37]For you have brought these men here who are neither robbers of temples nor blasphemers of [1]your goddess. [38]Therefore, if Demetrius and his fellow craftsmen have a [1]case against anyone, the courts are open and there are proconsuls. Let them bring charges against one another. [39]But if you have any other inquiry to make, it shall be determined in the lawful assembly. [40]For we are in danger of being [1]called in question for today's uproar, there being no reason which we may give to

account for this disorderly gathering." [41]And when he had said these things, he dismissed the assembly.

JOURNEYS IN GREECE

20 After the uproar had ceased, Paul called the disciples to *himself,* embraced *them,* and [a]departed to go to Macedonia. [2]Now when he had gone over that region and encouraged them with many words, he came to [a]Greece [3]and stayed three months. And [a]when the Jews plotted against him as he was about to sail to Syria, he decided to return through Macedonia. [4]And Sopater of Berea accompanied him to Asia—also [a]Aristarchus and Secundus of the Thessalonians, and [b]Gaius of Derbe, and [c]Timothy, and [d]Tychicus and [e]Trophimus of Asia. [5]These men, going ahead, waited for us at [a]Troas. [6]But we sailed away from Philippi after [a]the Days of Unleavened Bread, and in five days joined them [b]at Troas, where we stayed seven days.

MINISTERING AT TROAS

[7]Now on [a]the first *day* of the week, when the disciples came together [b]to break bread, Paul, ready to depart the next day, spoke to them and continued his message until midnight. [8]There were many lamps [a]in the upper room

26 [a] Is. 44:10–20

27 [1] NU *she be deposed from her magnificence*

29 [a] Rom. 16:23
[b] Col. 4:10

31 [1] *Asiarchs, rulers of Asia, the province*

33 [a] 2 Tim. 4:14
[b] Acts 12:17

35 [1] Gr. *Artemis*
[2] *heaven*

37 [1] NU *our*

38 [1] Lit. *matter*

40 [1] Or *charged with rebellion concerning today*

CHAPTER 20

1 [a] 1 Tim. 1:3

2 [a] Acts 17:15; 18:1

3 [a] 2 Cor. 11:26

4 [a] Col. 4:10
[b] Acts 19:29
[c] Acts 16:1
[d] Eph. 6:21
[e] 2 Tim. 4:20

5 [a] 2 Tim. 4:13

6 [a] Ex. 12:14, 15
[b] 2 Tim. 4:13

7 [a] 1 Cor. 16:2
[b] Acts 2:42, 46; 20:11

8 [a] Acts 1:13

Acts 20:7

THE LORD'S DAY

This is an indication the Gentile church began early to meet on Sundays. They gathered together on the first day of the week to break bread. When Paul was writing to the Corinthians, he also referred to when they gathered together on the first day of the week (1 Cor. 16:2).

Often I'm asked, "What day of the week should we worship the Lord?" Well, I go back to Romans where Paul said, "One person esteems one day above another; another esteems every day alike" (Rom. 14:5). I'm the guy that considers every day alike. As far as I am concerned, every day is the Lord's Day. I worship Him every day of the week.

where ¹they were gathered together. ⁹And in a window sat a certain young man named Eutychus, who was sinking into a deep sleep. He was overcome by sleep; and as Paul continued speaking, he fell down from the third story and was taken up dead. ¹⁰But Paul went down, ªfell on him, and embracing *him* said, ᵇ"Do not trouble yourselves, for his life is in him." ¹¹Now when he had come up, had broken bread and eaten, and talked a long while, even till daybreak, he departed. ¹²And they brought the young man in alive, and they were not a little comforted.

FROM TROAS TO MILETUS

¹³Then we went ahead to the ship and sailed to Assos, there intending to take Paul on board; for so he had ¹given orders, intending himself to go on foot. ¹⁴And when he met us at Assos, we took him on board and came to Mitylene. ¹⁵We sailed from there, and the next *day* came opposite Chios. The following *day* we arrived at Samos and stayed at Trogyllium. The next *day* we came to Miletus. ¹⁶For Paul had decided to sail past Ephesus, so that he would not have to spend time in Asia; for ªhe was hurrying ᵇto be at Jerusalem, if possible, on ᶜthe Day of Pentecost.

THE EPHESIAN ELDERS EXHORTED

¹⁷From Miletus he sent to Ephesus and called for the elders of the church. ¹⁸And when they had come to him, he said to them: "You know, ªfrom the first day that I came to Asia, in what manner I always lived among you, ¹⁹serving the Lord with all humility, with many tears and trials which happened to me ªby the plotting of the Jews; ²⁰how ªI kept back nothing that was helpful, but proclaimed it to you, and taught you publicly and from house to house, ²¹ªtestifying to Jews, and also to Greeks, ᵇrepentance toward God and faith toward our Lord Jesus Christ. ²²And see, now ªI go bound in the spirit to Jerusalem, not knowing the things that will happen to me there, ²³except that ªthe Holy Spirit testifies in every city, saying that chains and tribulations await me. ²⁴ ¹But ªnone of these things move me; nor do I count my life dear to myself, ᵇso that I may finish my ²race with joy, ᶜand the ministry ᵈwhich I received from the Lord Jesus, to testify to the gospel of the grace of God.

8 ¹NU, M *we*

10 ª 1 Kin. 17:21
ᵇ Matt. 9:23, 24

13 ¹ *arranged it*

16 ª Acts 18:21; 19:21; 21:4
ᵇ Acts 24:17
ᶜ Acts 2:1

18 ª Acts 18:19; 19:1, 10; 20:4, 16

19 ª Acts 20:3

20 ª Acts 20:27

21 ª Acts 18:5; 19:10
ᵇ Mark 1:15

22 ª Acts 19:21

23 ª Acts 21:4, 11

24 ª Acts 21:13
ᵇ 2 Tim. 4:7
ᶜ Acts 1:17
ᵈ Gal. 1:1
¹ NU *But I do not count my life of any value or dear to myself*
² *course*

26 ª Acts 18:6
¹ Lit. *clean*

27 ª Luke 7:30
¹ *avoided declaring*

28 ª 1 Pet. 5:2
ᵇ 1 Cor. 12:28
ᶜ Eph. 1:7, 14
ᵈ Heb. 9:14
¹ M *of the Lord and God*

29 ª Matt. 7:15

30 ª 1 Tim. 1:20
¹ *misleading*

31 ª Acts 19:8, 10; 24:17

Acts 20:19

HUMILITY

Humility—what a tremendous characteristic! So often a person who has been used of God gets an exalted attitude where they begin to have a sense of self-importance. Not Paul.

When God uses a person in a mighty way, there is a tendency for people to exalt that person, thinking that he or she is really above the rest when indeed they are not. But because people treat them that way, they become used to being treated that way, and then they begin to expect to be treated that way. It's really sad when a person is demanding special treatment or begins to have a feeling of self-importance and greatness because people have been treating them in a special way. Billy Graham is a prime example of what Paul is saying here. He is a man who has been mightily used by God, and yet I've never met a more humble man in all my life. He is absolutely beautiful in that humility, and I see him as a tremendous example, just like Paul, of serving the Lord with all humility.

²⁵"And indeed, now I know that you all, among whom I have gone preaching the kingdom of God, will see my face no more. ²⁶Therefore I testify to you this day that I *am* ªinnocent¹ of the blood of all *men.* ²⁷For I have not ¹shunned to declare to you ªthe whole counsel of God. ²⁸ªTherefore take heed to yourselves and to all the flock, among which the Holy Spirit ᵇhas made you overseers, to shepherd the church ¹of God ᶜwhich He purchased ᵈwith His own blood. ²⁹For I know this, that after my departure ªsavage wolves will come in among you, not sparing the flock. ³⁰Also ªfrom among yourselves men will rise up, speaking ¹perverse things, to draw away the disciples after themselves. ³¹Therefore watch, and remember that ªfor three years I

did not cease to warn everyone night and day with tears.

32 "So now, brethren, I commend you to God and [a]to the word of His grace, which is able [b]to build you up and give you [c]an inheritance among all those who are sanctified. 33 I have coveted no one's silver or gold or apparel. 34 [1]Yes, you yourselves know [a]that these hands have provided for my necessities, and for those who were with me. 35 I have shown you in every way, [a]by laboring like this, that you must support the weak. And remember the words of the Lord Jesus, that He said, 'It is more blessed to give than to receive.'"

Acts 20:35

IT IS MORE BLESSED TO GIVE

You won't find this quotation in the Gospels. Paul was no doubt quoting Jesus, but the Gospel writers did not record this statement. However, as John said at the end of his gospel, if all of the things Jesus did were written, "the world itself could not contain the books that would be written" (John 21:25).

So there were many things Jesus said that were not recorded in the Gospels, but Paul was aware that one of Jesus' teachings was, "It is more blessed to give than to receive." Oh, the blessedness of giving!

36 And when he had said these things, he knelt down and prayed with them all. 37 Then they all [a]wept [1]freely, and [b]fell on Paul's neck and kissed him, 38 sorrowing most of all for the words which he spoke, that they would see his face no more. And they accompanied him to the ship.

WARNINGS ON THE JOURNEY TO JERUSALEM

21 Now it came to pass, that when we had departed from them and set sail, running a straight course we came to Cos, the following *day* to Rhodes, and from there to Patara. 2 And finding a ship sailing over to Phoenicia,

---

Marginal notes (center column):

32 [a] Heb. 13:9
[b] Acts 9:31
[c] [Heb. 9:15]

34 [a] Acts 18:3
[1] NU, M omit Yes

35 [a] Rom. 15:1

37 [a] Acts 21:13
[b] Gen. 45:14
[1] Lit. *much*

CHAPTER 21

4 [a] [Acts 20:23; 21:12]
[1] NU *the disciples*

5 [a] Acts 9:40; 20:36

6 [a] John 1:11

8 [a] Acts 8:40; 21:16
[b] Eph. 4:11
[c] Acts 6:5
[1] NU omits *who were Paul's companions*

9 [a] Joel 2:28

10 [a] Acts 11:28

11 [a] Acts 20:23; 21:33; 22:25

13 [a] Acts 20:24, 37

---

we went aboard and set sail. 3 When we had sighted Cyprus, we passed it on the left, sailed to Syria, and landed at Tyre; for there the ship was to unload her cargo. 4 And finding [1]disciples, we stayed there seven days. [a]They told Paul through the Spirit not to go up to Jerusalem. 5 When we had come to the end of those days, we departed and went on our way; and they all accompanied us, with wives and children, till *we were* out of the city. And [a]we knelt down on the shore and prayed. 6 When we had taken our leave of one another, we boarded the ship, and they returned [a]home.

Acts 21:4

Through the Spirit. Now there is a question whether the Holy Spirit was directly forbidding Paul to go to Jerusalem or whether the Holy Spirit was warning that Paul would be imprisoned and afflicted in Jerusalem. It is quite possible the Spirit told the disciples at Tyre concerning Paul's impending imprisonment, and they misinterpreted that warning as a message from the Holy Spirit that Paul should not go to Jerusalem. I guess we won't know until we talk to Paul.

7 And when we had finished *our* voyage from Tyre, we came to Ptolemais, greeted the brethren, and stayed with them one day. 8 On the next *day* we [1]who were Paul's companions departed and came to [a]Caesarea, and entered the house of Philip [b]the evangelist, [c]who was *one* of the seven, and stayed with him. 9 Now this man had four virgin daughters [a]who prophesied. 10 And as we stayed many days, a certain prophet named [a]Agabus came down from Judea. 11 When he had come to us, he took Paul's belt, bound his *own* hands and feet, and said, "Thus says the Holy Spirit, [a]'So shall the Jews at Jerusalem bind the man who owns this belt, and deliver *him* into the hands of the Gentiles.'"

12 Now when we heard these things, both we and those from that place pleaded with him not to go up to Jerusalem. 13 Then Paul answered, [a]"What do you mean by weeping and breaking

Acts 21:8

PHILIP
AND PAUL

After Stephen was stoned, Paul led the persecution of the church. He wreaked havoc on the church in Jerusalem. As a result of the persecution that Paul spearheaded, the disciples were spread throughout Judea.

One of those who had to flee Jerusalem because of Paul was Philip. He went to Samaria. He preached to the Ethiopian eunuch. Here Philip, twenty years later, hosted Paul in his home in Caesarea. Philip had opened the gates, but Paul knocked the walls down as far as taking the gospel to the Gentiles. Now they were together.

my heart? For I am ready not only to be bound, but also to die at Jerusalem for the name of the Lord Jesus." 14So when he would not be persuaded, we ceased, saying, a"The will of the Lord be done."

PAUL URGED TO MAKE PEACE
15And after those days we 1packed and went up to Jerusalem. 16Also some of the disciples from Caesarea went with us and brought with them a certain Mnason of Cyprus, an early disciple, with whom we were to lodge.
17aAnd when we had come to Jerusalem, the brethren received us gladly. 18On the following day Paul went in with us to aJames, and all the elders were present. 19When he had greeted them, ahe told in detail those things which God had done among the Gentiles bthrough his ministry. 20And when they heard it, they glorified the Lord. And they said to him, "You see, brother, how many myriads of Jews there are who have believed, and they are all azealous for the law; 21but they have been informed about you that you teach all the Jews who are among the Gentiles to forsake Moses, saying that they ought not to circumcise their children nor to walk according to the customs. 22 1What then? The assembly must certainly meet, for they will hear

that you have come. 23Therefore do what we tell you: We have four men who have taken a vow. 24Take them and be purified with them, and pay their expenses so that they may ashave their heads, and that all may know that those things of which they were informed concerning you are nothing, but that you yourself also walk orderly and keep the law. 25But concerning the Gentiles who believe, awe have written and decided 1that they should observe no such thing, except that they should keep themselves from things offered to idols, from blood, from things strangled, and from 2sexual immorality."

ARRESTED IN THE TEMPLE
26Then Paul took the men, and the next day, having been purified with them, aentered the temple bto announce the 1expiration of the days of purification, at which time an offering should be made for each one of them.
27Now when the seven days were almost ended, athe Jews from Asia, seeing him in the temple, stirred up the whole crowd and blaid hands on him, 28crying out, "Men of Israel, help! This is the man awho teaches all men everywhere against the people, the law, and this place; and furthermore he also brought Greeks into the temple and has defiled this holy place." 29(For they had 1previously seen aTrophimus the Ephesian with him in the city, whom they supposed that Paul had brought into the temple.)
30And aall the city was disturbed; and the people ran together, seized Paul, and dragged him out of the temple; and immediately the doors were shut. 31Now as they were aseeking to kill him, news came to the commander of the 1garrison that all Jerusalem was in an uproar. 32aHe immediately took soldiers and centurions, and ran down to them. And when they saw the commander and the soldiers, they stopped beating Paul. 33Then the acommander came near and took him, and bcommanded him to be bound with two chains; and he asked who he was and what he had done. 34And some among the multitude cried one thing and some another.

So when he could not ascertain the truth because of the tumult, he commanded him to be taken into the barracks. 35When he reached the stairs, he had to be carried by the soldiers because of the violence of the mob.

14 a Luke 11:2; 22:42

15 1 made preparations

17 a Acts 15:4

18 a Gal. 1:19; 2:9

19 a Rom. 15:18, 19
b Acts 1:17; 20:24

20 a Acts 15:1; 22:3

22 1 NU What then is to be done? They will certainly hear

24 a Acts 18:18

25 a Acts 15:19, 20, 29
1 NU omits that they should observe no such thing, except
2 fornication

26 a Acts 21:24; 24:18
b Num. 6:13
1 completion

27 a Acts 20:19; 24:18
b Acts 26:21

28 a Acts 6:13; 24:6

29 a Acts 20:4
1 M omits previously

30 a Acts 16:19; 26:21

31 a 2 Cor. 11:23
1 cohort

32 a Acts 23:27; 24:7

33 a Acts 24:7
b Acts 20:23; 21:11

³⁶For the multitude of the people followed after, crying out, ᵃ"Away with him!"

ADDRESSING THE JERUSALEM MOB

³⁷Then as Paul was about to be led into the barracks, he said to the commander, "May I speak to you?"

He replied, "Can you speak Greek? ³⁸ᵃAre you not the Egyptian who some time ago stirred up a rebellion and led the four thousand assassins out into the wilderness?"

³⁹But Paul said, ᵃ"I am a Jew from Tarsus, in Cilicia, a citizen of no ¹mean city; and I implore you, permit me to speak to the people."

⁴⁰So when he had given him permission, Paul stood on the stairs and ᵃmotioned with his hand to the people. And when there was a great silence, he spoke to *them* in the ᵇHebrew language, saying,

22 "Brethrenᵃ and fathers, hear my defense before you now." ²And when they heard that he spoke to them in the ᵃHebrew language, they kept all the more silent.

Then he said: ³ᵃ"I am indeed a Jew, born in Tarsus of Cilicia, but brought up in this city ᵇat the feet of ᶜGamaliel, taught ᵈaccording to the strictness of our fathers' law, and ᵉwas zealous toward God ᶠas you all are today. ⁴ᵃI persecuted this Way to the death, binding and delivering into prisons both men and women, ⁵as also the high priest bears me witness, and ᵃall the council of the elders, ᵇfrom whom I also received letters to the brethren, and went to Damascus ᶜto bring in chains even those who were there to Jerusalem to be punished.

36 ᵃJohn 19:15

38 ᵃActs 5:36

39 ᵃActs 9:11; 22:3
¹ *insignificant*

40 ᵃActs 12:17
ᵇActs 22:2

CHAPTER 22

1 ᵃActs 7:2

2 ᵃActs 21:40

3 ᵃ2 Cor. 11:22
ᵇDeut. 33:3
ᶜActs 5:34
ᵈActs 23:6; 26:5
ᵉGal. 1:14
ᶠ[Rom. 10:2]

4 ᵃ1 Tim. 1:13

5 ᵃActs 23:14; 24:1; 25:15
ᵇLuke 22:66
ᶜActs 9:2

6 ᵃActs 9:3; 26:12, 13

Acts 22:6

THERE'S NO DENYING IT

It's interesting that Paul did not give these Jews in Jerusalem some theological treatise. It may be that was his intention, or this could just be Paul's introduction. But Paul witnessed to them with his personal testimony.

One of the most powerful witnesses you can give a person is the testimony of your personal experience with Jesus Christ. Telling people what Jesus Christ has done in your life, of the changes He has wrought in you, is often one of the most powerful testimonies because it can't be denied. When you hear some Calvary Chapel pastors such as Raul Ries or Mike MacIntosh give their testimonies, what can you say? You know that God has done wonders in their lives. There is no denying it. They are miraculous examples of God's grace and love and of the Holy Spirit's power to transform lives. The personal witness always makes a great testimony. Here, Paul is giving them his personal testimony.

HEART FOR ISRAEL

Acts 21:40

Here Paul experienced the moment he had been waiting for, an opportunity to share with the zealots the gospel of Jesus Christ. Paul had always desired to bring the gospel to the Jews. He felt he understood them sufficiently so that he could convince them Jesus was the Messiah. Paul's heart and prayer for Israel was that they might be saved. He had such an intense desire to reach the Jews, he was willing to die for the privilege.

Paul must have been a really charismatic person, and surely he was filled with the Spirit; but here were all of the people, as the soldiers were carrying him off, crying, "Kill him, kill him, away with him," and Paul pleaded for permission to address the angry multitude! So when he had been given permission, he stood up and he waved his hand to the people. Suddenly, they were all silent, and Paul began to speak to them in Hebrew. This was it, Paul's opportunity to share the gospel of Jesus Christ with the Jews in Jerusalem, the moment he had been waiting for since his conversion.

6"Now ᵃit happened, as I journeyed and came near Damascus at about noon, suddenly a great light from heaven shone around me. 7And I fell to the ground and heard a voice saying to me, 'Saul, Saul, why are you persecuting Me?' 8So I answered, 'Who are You, Lord?' And He said to me, 'I am Jesus of Nazareth, whom you are persecuting.'

9"And ᵃthose who were with me indeed saw the light ᴵand were afraid, but they did not hear the voice of Him who spoke to me. 10So I said, 'What shall I do, Lord?' And the Lord said to me, 'Arise and go into Damascus, and there you will be told all things which are appointed for you to do.' 11And since I could not see for the glory of that light, being led by the hand of those who were with me, I came into Damascus.

12"Then ᵃa certain Ananias, a devout man according to the law, ᵇhaving a good testimony with all the ᶜJews who dwelt there, 13came to me; and he stood and said to me, 'Brother Saul, receive your sight.' And at that same hour I looked up at him. 14Then he said, ᵃ'The God of our fathers ᵇhas chosen you that you should ᶜknow His will, and ᵈsee the Just One, ᵉand hear the voice of His mouth. 15ᵃFor you will be His witness to all men of ᵇwhat you have seen and heard. 16And now why are you waiting? Arise and be baptized, ᵃand wash away your sins, ᵇcalling on the name of the Lord.'

17"Now ᵃit happened, when I returned to Jerusalem and was praying in the temple, that I was in a trance 18and ᵃsaw Him saying to me, ᵇ'Make haste and get out of Jerusalem quickly, for they will not receive your testimony concerning Me.' 19So I said, 'Lord, ᵃthey know that in every synagogue I imprisoned and ᵇbeat those who believe on You. 20ᵃAnd when the blood of Your martyr Stephen was shed, I also was standing by ᵇconsenting ᴵto his death, and guarding the clothes of those who were killing him.' 21Then He said to me, 'Depart, ᵃfor I will send you far from here to the Gentiles.'"

PAUL'S ROMAN CITIZENSHIP

22And they listened to him until this word, and then they raised their voices and said, ᵃ"Away with such a fellow from the earth, for ᵇhe is not fit to live!" 23Then, as they cried out and ᴵtore off their clothes and threw dust into the air, 24the commander ordered him to be brought into the barracks, and said that he should be examined under scourging, so that he might know why they shouted so against him. 25And as they bound him with thongs, Paul said to the centurion who stood by, ᵃ"Is it lawful for you to scourge a man who is a Roman, and uncondemned?"

26When the centurion heard that, he went and told the commander, saying, "Take care what you do, for this man is a Roman."

27Then the commander came and said to him, "Tell me, are you a Roman?" He said, "Yes."

28The commander answered, "With a large sum I obtained this citizenship."

Cross-references

9 ᵃ Acts 9:7
1 NU omits and were afraid

12 ᵃ Acts 9:17
ᵇ Acts 10:22
ᶜ 1 Tim. 3:7

14 ᵃ Acts 3:13; 5:30
ᵇ Acts 9:15; 26:16
ᶜ Acts 3:14; 7:52
ᵈ 1 Cor. 9:1; 15:8
ᵉ Gal. 1:12

15 ᵃ Acts 23:11
ᵇ Acts 4:20; 26:16

16 ᵃ Heb. 10:22
ᵇ Rom. 10:13

17 ᵃ Acts 9:26; 26:20

18 ᵃ Acts 22:14
ᵇ Matt. 10:14

19 ᵃ Acts 8:3; 22:4
ᵇ Matt. 10:17

20 ᵃ Acts 7:54—8:1
ᵇ Luke 11:48
1 NU omits to his death

21 ᵃ Acts 9:15

22 ᵃ Acts 21:36
ᵇ Acts 25:24

23 1 Lit. threw

25 ᵃ Acts 16:37

THE LORD KNOWS BEST   Acts 22:18–21

Notice that in these verses, Paul was arguing with the Lord. Whenever you find yourself arguing with the Lord, just know that you are wrong. So many times we find ourselves arguing, "But, Lord, I know what they are feeling. I'm sure, Lord, I can convince them."

The Lord said, "Paul, they're not going to receive you; get out of Jerusalem." Now I believe that for seventeen years Paul felt the Lord was wrong. I believe deep down in his heart that Paul felt that if he could just talk to the Jews, he could convince them. It isn't our words of wisdom that convince a man to follow Jesus Christ. It is the Holy Spirit speaking to a person's heart that opens their heart to the truth.

Seventeen years before, the Lord had told Paul to flee Jerusalem; and I think that for this entire seventeen years, Paul felt the Lord had been wrong. Paul believed he could convince them. So here he was. He was shining. They were quiet. They were listening.

And then, Paul mentioned the word "Gentiles"; and a huge uproar ensued. The Jews tore their clothes. They threw dirt in the air. They were an emotional group, and Paul had pushed the wrong button. Finally, Paul had had his chance to speak to the Jews in Jerusalem, and they wanted to kill him.

And Paul said, "But I was born *a citizen.*" [CHAPTER 23]
29Then immediately those who were about to examine him withdrew from him; and the commander was also afraid after he found out that he was a Roman, and because he had bound him.

THE SANHEDRIN DIVIDED

30The next day, because he wanted to know for certain why he was accused by the Jews, he released him from *his* bonds, and commanded the chief priests and all their council to appear, and brought Paul down and set him before them.

Acts 22:30

NOT MY WILL, BUT YOURS BE DONE

The most difficult thing in the world is to try to be something God didn't make you. The most wonderful thing in the world is to do what God wants you to do. That's glorious. So many times I've found myself trying to be something God didn't make me and God had to teach me.

So God works in each of us. He is working in you. He's preparing you. He's giving you the background and experiences that will be a part of His plan as He is working out His eternal purposes for your life. As you yield yourself to Him, the picture will begin to unfold and you will begin to see exactly the purpose and the plan that God has for you—that wonderful life when it's committed fully to Jesus Christ.

23 Then Paul, looking earnestly at the council, said, "Men *and* brethren, aI have lived in all good conscience before God until this day." 2And the high priest Ananias commanded those who stood by him ato strike him on the mouth. 3Then Paul said to him, "God will strike you, *you*

1 a2Tim. 1:3

2 aJohn 18:22

3 aDeut. 25:1, 2

5 aLev. 5:17, 18
bEx. 22:28

6 aPhil. 3:5
bActs 24:15, 21; 26:6; 28:20

8 aMatt. 22:23

Acts 23:3

WHITEWASHED SEPULCHER

In those days, under the Law, a Jew could not touch a dead body. So there were these rock-hewn sepulchers all over the countryside. Over the years, some of them became half hidden or buried. So it was possible to inadvertently stumble across a sepulcher. If you touched it, you would have to go through purification rites before you could enter the temple because you would be considered unclean. You'd have touched something that was touching a dead body. To protect people from touching the sepulchers, the Jews would paint these tombs with whitewash so they would stand out.

Concerning the Pharisees, Jesus said they were whitewashed tombs, meaning they appeared nice on the outside, all white and painted; but on the inside, Jesus said, they were "full of dead men's bones" (Matt. 23:27). So Paul picked up this use of the term from the Lord, and he said to the high priest, "God will strike you, you whitewashed wall!"

whitewashed wall! For you sit to judge me according to the law, and ado you command me to be struck contrary to the law?"
4And those who stood by said, "Do you revile God's high priest?"
5Then Paul said, a"I did not know, brethren, that he was the high priest; for it is written, b*You shall not speak evil of a ruler of your people.*'"
6But when Paul perceived that one part were Sadducees and the other Pharisees, he cried out in the council, "Men *and* brethren, aI am a Pharisee, the son of a Pharisee; bconcerning the hope and resurrection of the dead I am being judged!"
7And when he had said this, a dissension arose between the Pharisees and the Sadducees; and the assembly was divided. 8aFor Sadducees say that

there is no resurrection—and no angel or spirit; but the Pharisees confess both. [9]Then there arose a loud outcry. And the scribes of the Pharisees' party arose and protested, saying, a"We find no evil in this man; [1]but [b]if a spirit or an angel has spoken to him, [c]let us not fight against God."

[10]Now when there arose a great dissension, the commander, fearing lest Paul might be pulled to pieces by them, commanded the soldiers to go down and take him by force from among them, and bring *him* into the barracks.

THE PLOT AGAINST PAUL

[11]But [a]the following night the Lord stood by him and said, [1]"Be of good cheer, Paul; for as you have testified for Me in [b]Jerusalem, so you must also bear witness at [c]Rome."

[12]And when it was day, [a]some of the Jews banded together and bound themselves under an oath, saying that they would neither eat nor drink till they had [b]killed Paul. [13]Now there were more than forty who had formed this conspiracy. [14]They came to the chief priests and [a]elders, and said, "We have bound ourselves under a great oath that we will eat nothing until we have killed Paul. [15]Now you, therefore, together with the council, suggest to the commander that he be brought down to you [1]tomorrow, as though you were going to make further inquiries concerning him; but we are ready to kill him before he comes near."

[16]So when Paul's sister's son heard of their ambush, he went and entered the barracks and told Paul. [17]Then Paul called one of the centurions to *him* and said, "Take this young man to the commander, for he has something to tell

him." [18]So he took him and brought *him* to the commander and said, "Paul the prisoner called me to *him* and asked *me* to bring this young man to you. He has something to say to you."

[19]Then the commander took him by the hand, went aside, and asked privately, "What is it that you have to tell me?"

[20]And he said, a"The Jews have agreed to ask that you bring Paul down to the council tomorrow, as though they were going to inquire more fully about him. [21]But do not yield to them, for more than forty of them lie in wait for him, men who have bound themselves by an oath that they will neither eat nor drink till they have killed him; and now they are ready, waiting for the promise from you."

[22]So the commander let the young man depart, and commanded *him*, "Tell no one that you have revealed these things to me."

SENT TO FELIX

[23]And he called for two centurions, saying, "Prepare two hundred soldiers, seventy horsemen, and two hundred spearmen to go to [a]Caesarea at the third hour of the night; [24]and provide mounts to set Paul on, and bring *him* safely to Felix the governor." [25]He wrote a letter in the following manner:

[26]   Claudius Lysias,

To the most excellent governor Felix:

Greetings.

[27]   [a]This man was seized by the Jews and was about to be killed by them. Coming with the troops I rescued him, having learned

Center column notes

9 [a] Acts 25:25; 26:31
[b] Acts 22:6, 7, 17, 18
[c] Acts 5:39
[1] NU *what if a spirit or an angel has spoken to him?* omitting the last clause

11 [a] Acts 18:9; 27:23, 24
[b] Acts 21:18, 19; 22:1–21
[c] Acts 28:16, 17, 23
[1] *Take courage*

12 [a] Acts 23:21, 30; 25:3
[b] Acts 9:23, 24; 25:3; 26:21; 27:42

14 [a] Acts 4:5, 23; 6:12; 22:5; 24:1; 25:15

15 [1] NU omits *tomorrow*

20 [a] Acts 23:12

23 [a] Acts 8:40; 23:33

27 [a] Acts 21:30, 33; 24:7

BE OF GOOD COURAGE
Acts 23:11

Paul was back in prison at a very low point in his life. That which he had dreamed of for many years, to bear witness of Christ before the Jews, had been a disaster. He was rejected by his brethren for whom he had such a deep love and desire to win to Christ. He was discouraged.

So the Lord encouraged Paul. He said, "Paul, you've testified of Me in Jerusalem. It was a total fiasco, but that's all right; you testified. Now you must testify of Me in Rome." So the Lord took him out of the doldrums of his past and gave him a call for his future. He set the past aside, reaching for what God had in the future, and it's important that we do the same.

There may be times in your life when you have been forsaken by your friends, maybe even by the body of Christ. But the Lord will never forsake you. You can be certain of that. Though Paul was forsaken by his brethren, he was not forsaken by his Lord. The Lord stood with him in those dark experiences of his life even as the Lord will always stand by you.

that he was a Roman. 28ªAnd when I wanted to know the reason they accused him, I brought him before their council. 29I found out that he was accused aconcerning questions of their law, bbut had nothing charged against him deserving of death or chains. 30And awhen it was told me that *l*the Jews lay in wait for the man, I sent him immediately to you, and balso commanded his accusers to state before you the charges against him.

Farewell.

31Then the soldiers, as they were commanded, took Paul and brought *him* by night to Antipatris. 32The next day they left the horsemen to go on with him, and returned to the barracks. 33When they came to aCaesarea and had delivered the bletter to the governor, they also presented Paul to him. 34And when the governor had read *it*, he asked what province he was from. And when he understood that *he was* from aCilicia, 35he said, a"I will hear you when your accusers also have come." And he commanded him to be kept in bHerod's *l*Praetorium.

ACCUSED OF SEDITION

24 Now after afive days bAnanias the high priest came down with the elders and a certain orator *named* Tertullus. These gave evidence to the governor against Paul.

2And when he was called upon, Tertullus began his accusation, saying: "Seeing that through you we enjoy great peace, and *l*prosperity is being brought to this nation by your foresight, 3we accept *it* always and in all places, most noble Felix, with all thankfulness. 4Nevertheless, not to be tedious to you any further, I beg you to hear, by your *l*courtesy, a few words from us. 5aFor we have found this man a plague, a creator of dissension among all the Jews throughout the world, and a ringleader of the sect of the Nazarenes. 6aHe even tried to profane the temple, and we seized him, *l*and wanted bto judge him according to our law. 7aBut the commander Lysias came by and with great violence took *him* out of our hands, 8acommanding his accusers to come to you. By examining him yourself you may ascertain all these things of which we accuse him." 9And the Jews also *l*assented, maintaining that these things were so.

Cross-references (center column)

28 ª Acts 22:30
29 ª Acts 18:15; 25:19
b Acts 25:25; 26:31
30 ª Acts 23:20
b Acts 24:8; 25:6
1 NU *there would be a plot against the man*
33 ª Acts 8:40
b Acts 23:26–30
34 ª Acts 6:9; 21:39
35 ª Acts 24:1, 10; 25:16
b Matt. 27:27
1 *Headquarters*

CHAPTER 24

1 ª Acts 21:27
b Acts 23:2, 30, 35; 25:2
2 1 Or *reforms are*
4 1 *graciousness*
5 ª 1 Pet. 2:12, 15
6 ª Acts 21:28
b John 18:31
1 NU ends the sentence here and omits the rest of v. 6, all of v. 7, and the first clause of v. 8.
7 ª Acts 21:33; 23:10
8 ª Acts 23:30
9 1 NU, M *joined the attack*
11 ª Acts 21:15, 18, 26, 27; 24:17
12 ª Acts 25:8; 28:17
14 ª Acts 9:2; 24:22
b 2 Tim. 1:3
c Acts 26:22; 28:23
15 ª Acts 23:6; 26:6, 7; 28:20
b [Dan. 12:2]
1 NU omits *of the dead*
16 ª Acts 23:1
17 ª Rom. 15:25–28
18 ª Acts 21:27; 26:21 b Acts 21:26
19 ª [Acts 23:30; 25:16]
20 1 NU, M *what wrongdoing they found*

THE DEFENSE BEFORE FELIX

10Then Paul, after the governor had nodded to him to speak, answered: "Inasmuch as I know that you have been for many years a judge of this nation, I do the more cheerfully answer for myself, 11because you may ascertain that it is no more than twelve days since I went up to Jerusalem ato worship. 12aAnd they neither found me in the temple disputing with anyone nor inciting the crowd, either in the synagogues or in the city. 13Nor can they prove the things of which they now accuse me. 14But this I confess to you, that according to athe Way which they call a sect, so I worship the bGod of my fathers, believing all things which are written in cthe Law and in the Prophets. 15ªI have hope in God, which they themselves also accept, bthat there will be a resurrection *l*of *the* dead, both of *the* just and *the* unjust. 16aThis *being* so, I myself always strive to have a conscience without offense toward God and men.

17"Now after many years aI came to bring alms and offerings to my nation, 18ain the midst of which some Jews from Asia found me bpurified in the temple, neither with a mob nor with tumult. 19aThey ought to have been here before you to object if they had anything against me. 20Or else let those who are *here* themselves say *l*if they found any wrongdoing in me while I stood before the council, 21unless *it is* for this one statement which I cried out, standing among them, a'Concerning the resurrection of the dead I am being judged by you this day.'"

FELIX PROCRASTINATES

22But when Felix heard these things, having more accurate knowledge of *the* aWay, he adjourned the proceedings and said, "When bLysias the commander comes down, I will make a decision on your case." 23So he commanded the centurion to keep Paul and to let *him* have liberty, and atold him not to forbid any of his friends to provide for or visit him.

24And after some days, when Felix came with his wife Drusilla, who was Jewish, he sent for Paul and heard him concerning the afaith in Christ. 25Now as he reasoned about righteousness, self-control, and the judgment to come, Felix was afraid and answered, "Go away for now; when I have a convenient

21 ª [Acts 23:6; 24:15; 28:20] 22 ª Acts 9:2; 18:26; 19:9, 23; 22:4 b Acts 23:26; 24:7 23 ª Acts 23:16; 27:3; 28:16
24 ª [Rom. 10:9]

Acts 24:23

HOUSE ARREST

Scholars dispute the authorship of Hebrews, but I believe it was during this time that Paul wrote his letter. Paul was there near the church in Jerusalem where many of those who had embraced Christianity were leaning back toward Judaism.

Paul had visited the church in Jerusalem and seen the influence of tradition on the believers. He had seen how some were being drawn back into Judaism. Thus, he wrote this great letter to the Hebrews, warning them against going back and trying to find a righteous standing before God by the Law and showing them the superiority of Christianity over Judaism. A better way. Better promises. A better hope. A better High Priest.

This outstanding letter to the Hebrew believers was written probably during the two years Paul was under house arrest in Caesarea.

26 ª Ex. 23:8
1 NU omits *that he might release him*

27 ª Acts 12:3; 23:35; 25:9, 14

CHAPTER 25

1 ª Acts 8:40; 25:4, 6, 13

2 ª Acts 24:1; 25:15
1 NU *chief priests*

Acts 24:26

A Clear Conscience. Felix was a corrupt man. He was looking for a bribe. Paul had brought an offering to the nation of Israel. He testified of that fact. So Felix knew that Paul had funds available.

It's interesting to me that Paul would not, even for the sake of his own freedom, bribe an official. He had a conscience that was clear before God and man. He would rather be in prison than to get out by bribing the governor. And yet, this corrupt Felix was waiting for a bribe.

time I will call for you." 26Meanwhile he also hoped that ªmoney would be given him by Paul, 1that he might release him. Therefore he sent for him more often and conversed with him. 27But after two years Porcius Festus succeeded Felix; and Felix, ªwanting to do the Jews a favor, left Paul bound.

PAUL APPEALS TO CAESAR

25 Now when Festus had come to the province, after three days he went up from ªCaesarea to Jerusalem. 2ªThen the 1high priest and the chief men of the Jews informed him against Paul; and they petitioned him, 3asking a favor against him, that he would

A MORE CONVENIENT TIME   Acts 24:25

Paul testified to Felix about these things. "Felix, there is a day of judgment that is going to come. You have not been living a righteous life. You've indulged yourself in all kinds of evil, and it's going to catch up with you." Felix was afraid, but he put off making a decision.

This is the pattern of man. Indecision. Deferring the decision. Putting it off for a more convenient time. Being convicted by the Spirit, even a powerful experience of conviction, does not guarantee conversion. It takes acting on that conviction to bring conversion, and that step Felix wouldn't take. Convicted? Yes. Afraid? Yes. Conversion? No. He put it off. "Go your way now, Paul. When it's more convenient, I'll call you." He was deferring the most important decision of his life.

How many people have made this same mistake, putting off the decision to commit their lives to Jesus Christ? When the moment came, when that hour of God's Spirit was there, they put it off! With Felix, the convenient time never came. Tragic! It never came. This is true of so many people who put off their decision for Jesus Christ, waiting for a more convenient time, only to discover that they sinned away the day of grace and that more convenient time never came! Hell is filled with people who decided to wait for a more convenient time.

summon him to Jerusalem—a while they lay in ambush along the road to kill him. 4But Festus answered that Paul should be kept at Caesarea, and that he himself was going there shortly. 5"Therefore," he said, "let those who have authority among you go down with me and accuse this man, to see a if there is any fault in him."

6And when he had remained among them more than ten days, he went down to Caesarea. And the next day, sitting on the judgment seat, he commanded Paul to be brought. 7When he had come, the Jews who had come down from Jerusalem stood about a and laid many serious complaints against Paul, which they could not prove, 8while he answered for himself, a "Neither against the law of the Jews, nor against the temple, nor

Acts 25:10–11

APPEAL TO CAESAR

Paul exercised his prerogative as a Roman citizen and appealed to Caesar for the final decision. A Roman citizen, unless he was guilty of murder, could always make his appeal to Caesar if he was getting an unjust decision from the court. Caesar reserved the right for the final disposition. Paul was getting the runaround. Paul was innocent. He had declared to Felix, "You know these charges are not true."

Now it's interesting to me that Paul said, "Look, if I have done something that deserves the death penalty, I'll die, but I'm not going to let you deliver me to them." We are not to put ourselves deliberately into a position of jeopardy. There are some people who intentionally court disaster. It's not wise.

Paul said, "As much as depends on you, live peaceably with all men" (Rom. 12:18). Don't try to create disturbances. Don't try to be a martyr. Paul was not willing to be martyred by the Jews on unconfirmed charges. So Paul appealed to Caesar.

---

3 a Acts 23:12, 15

5 a Acts 18:14; 25:18

7 a Acts 24:5, 13

8 a Acts 6:13; 24:12; 28:17

9 a Acts 12:2; 24:27
b Acts 25:20

11 a Acts 18:14; 23:29; 25:25; 26:31
b Acts 26:32; 28:19

Acts 25:12

BOUND FOR ROME

It's interesting how so often the Lord reveals an overall plan, but yet many times there is an interval of time before God works out that plan. Sometimes in that interval of time, we get a little impatient and take things into our own hands. *Doesn't God want me to go to Rome? Well, let me figure out a way there because the Lord told me I had to bear witness in Rome.* But the Lord has His ways of fulfilling His purposes in our lives. And we've got to watch our impatience because so often we get ahead of God.

When Jesus said, "You are going to bear witness of Me in Rome," you can be sure Paul was going to get to Rome. Now Paul probably wasn't planning to get there the way he did. He was probably planning on paying his own transportation. Instead, he got to Rome courtesy of the Roman government.

against Caesar have I offended in anything at all."

9But Festus, a wanting to do the Jews a favor, answered Paul and said, b "Are you willing to go up to Jerusalem and there be judged before me concerning these things?"

10So Paul said, "I stand at Caesar's judgment seat, where I ought to be judged. To the Jews I have done no wrong, as you very well know. 11a For if I am an offender, or have committed anything deserving of death, I do not object to dying; but if there is nothing in these things of which these men accuse me, no one can deliver me to them. b I appeal to Caesar."

12Then Festus, when he had conferred with the council, answered, "You have appealed to Caesar? To Caesar you shall go!"

PAUL BEFORE AGRIPPA

13And after some days King Agrippa and Bernice came to Caesarea to greet

Festus. 14When they had been there many days, Festus laid Paul's case before the king, saying: a"There is a certain man left a prisoner by Felix, 15aabout whom the chief priests and the elders of the Jews informed me, when I was in Jerusalem, asking for a judgment against him. 16aTo them I answered, 'It is not the custom of the Romans to deliver any man 1to destruction before the accused meets the accusers face to face, and has opportunity to answer for himself concerning the charge against him.' 17Therefore when they had come together, awithout any delay, the next day I sat on the judgment seat and commanded the man to be brought in. 18When the accusers stood up, they brought no accusation against him of such things as I 1supposed, 19abut had some questions against him about their own religion and about a certain Jesus, who had died, whom Paul affirmed to be alive. 20And because I was uncertain of such questions, I asked whether he was willing to go to Jerusalem and there be judged concerning these matters. 21But

Acts 25:19

HE LIVES

Paul affirmed that Jesus was alive. The resurrection is the heart of the gospel. Without the resurrection, there is no gospel. The cross has no power and no meaning if Jesus did not rise from the dead. The whole Christian belief system is founded on the resurrection of Jesus from the dead.

Peter said, "Blessed be the God and Father of our Lord Jesus Christ, who according to His abundant mercy has begotten us again to a living hope through the resurrection of Jesus Christ from the dead, to an inheritance incorruptible and undefiled and that does not fade away, reserved in heaven for you" (1 Pet. 1:3). The resurrection gives us a hope for the future. I have no fear of death because Jesus rose from the dead.

14 a Acts 24:27

15 a Acts 24:1; 25:2, 3

16 a Acts 25:4, 5
1 NU omits to destruction, although it is implied

17 a Acts 25:6, 10

18 1 suspected

19 a Acts 18:14, 15; 23:29

21 a Acts 25:11, 12

22 a Acts 9:15

23 a Acts 9:15
1 pageantry

24 a Acts 25:2, 3, 7
b Acts 21:36; 22:22

25 a Acts 23:9, 29; 26:31
b Acts 25:11, 12

CHAPTER 26

2 a [1 Pet. 3:14; 4:14]
b [1 Pet. 3:15, 16]
c Acts 21:28; 24:5, 6

5 a Phil. 3:5

6 a Acts 23:6
b Acts 13:32

7 a James 1:1
b 1 Thess. 3:10
c Phil. 3:11

when Paul aappealed to be reserved for the decision of Augustus, I commanded him to be kept till I could send him to Caesar."

22Then aAgrippa said to Festus, "I also would like to hear the man myself."

"Tomorrow," he said, "you shall hear him."

23So the next day, when Agrippa and Bernice had come with great 1pomp, and had entered the auditorium with the commanders and the prominent men of the city, at Festus' command aPaul was brought in. 24And Festus said: "King Agrippa and all the men who are here present with us, you see this man about whom athe whole assembly of the Jews petitioned me, both at Jerusalem and here, crying out that he was bnot fit to live any longer. 25But when I found that ahe had committed nothing deserving of death, band that he himself had appealed to Augustus, I decided to send him. 26I have nothing certain to write to my lord concerning him. Therefore I have brought him out before you, and especially before you, King Agrippa, so that after the examination has taken place I may have something to write. 27For it seems to me unreasonable to send a prisoner and not to specify the charges against him."

PAUL'S EARLY LIFE

26 Then Agrippa said to Paul, "You are permitted to speak for yourself."

So Paul stretched out his hand and answered for himself: 2"I think myself ahappy, King Agrippa, because today I shall answer bfor myself before you concerning all the things of which I am caccused by the Jews, 3especially because you are expert in all customs and questions which have to do with the Jews. Therefore I beg you to hear me patiently.

4"My manner of life from my youth, which was spent from the beginning among my own nation at Jerusalem, all the Jews know. 5They knew me from the first, if they were willing to testify, that according to athe strictest sect of our religion I lived a Pharisee. 6aAnd now I stand and am judged for the hope of bthe promise made by God to our fathers. 7To this promise aour twelve tribes, earnestly serving God bnight and day, chope to attain. For this hope's sake, King Agrippa, I am accused by the Jews. 8Why should it be

---

Acts 26:2

Happy to Answer. Like Paul, King Agrippa was a student of Jewish Scriptures. Paul was happy to present his case to Agrippa. Festus didn't know the Scriptures. He didn't know the promises of Messiah. He was not familiar with the Jews' customs. But Agrippa was a Jew, not by nationality, but by religious practice. He had proselytized and religiously became a Jew, but he was also an avid student of the Scriptures.

The writers of Agrippa's day acknowledged his understanding of the Scriptures. So Paul was pleased to answer and share his personal faith in Jesus Christ with King Agrippa.

---

thought incredible by you that God raises the dead?

9 a"Indeed, I myself thought I must do many things 1contrary to the name of bJesus of Nazareth. 10aThis I also did in Jerusalem, and many of the saints I shut up in prison, having received authority bfrom the chief priests; and when they were put to death, I cast my vote against *them*.

Acts 26:8

Is Anything Too Difficult for God? Difficulty must be measured by the capacity of the agent doing the work.

Was it difficult to remodel Murrieta Hot Springs? Well, if we had had a bunch of trained French Poodles doing the work, it would have been impossible. Even though they can jump through hoops and turn somersaults in the air, they don't have the capacity. But when you get knowledgeable, skilled men, it's not difficult.

When God is the agent doing the work, talk of difficulty is absurd. Why should it be thought an incredible thing that God raises the dead?

---

9 a 1Tim. 1:12, 13
b Acts 2:22; 10:38
1 against

10 a Acts 8:1–3; 9:13
b Acts 9:14

11 a Acts 22:19

12 a Acts 9:3–8; 22:6–11; 26:12–18

16 a Acts 22:15

17 a Acts 22:21
1 rescue
2 NU, M omit now

18 a Is. 35:5; 42:7, 16
b 1 Pet. 2:9
c Luke 1:77
d Col. 1:12
e Acts 20:32
1 set apart

---

11 aAnd I punished them often in every synagogue and compelled *them* to blaspheme; and being exceedingly enraged against them, I persecuted *them* even to foreign cities.

PAUL RECOUNTS HIS CONVERSION

12 a"While thus occupied, as I journeyed to Damascus with authority and commission from the chief priests, 13at midday, O king, along the road I saw a light from heaven, brighter than the sun, shining around me and those who journeyed with me. 14And when we all had fallen to the ground, I heard a voice speaking to me and saying in the Hebrew language, 'Saul, Saul, why are you persecuting Me? *It is* hard for you to kick against the goads.' 15So I said, 'Who are You, Lord?' And He said, 'I am Jesus, whom you are persecuting. 16But rise and stand on your feet; for I have appeared to you for this purpose, ato make you a minister and a witness both of the things which you have seen and of the things which I will yet reveal to you. 17I will 1deliver you from the *Jewish* people, as well as *from* the Gentiles, ato whom I 2now send you, 18ato open their eyes, *in order* bto turn them from darkness to light, and *from* the power of Satan to God, cthat they may receive forgiveness of sins and dan inheritance among those who are esanctified1 by faith in Me.'

PAUL'S POST-CONVERSION LIFE

19"Therefore, King Agrippa, I was not disobedient to the heavenly vision,

---

Acts 26:18

Open Their Eyes, Lord. So our prayer for our unsaved loved ones is that the Lord delivers them from the power of Satan, who has blinded their eyes to the truth. We pray that their eyes be opened so they can actually consider the claims of the gospel without this heavy prejudicial pressure Satan has put upon their mind. He has blinded them!

Paul wrote to Timothy that through our gentleness, patience, and humility "they may come to their senses and escape the snare of the devil, having been taken captive by him to do his will" (2 Tim. 2:26).

20but ªdeclared first to those in Damascus and in Jerusalem, and throughout all the region of Judea, and *then* to the Gentiles, that they should repent, turn to God, and do bworks befitting repentance. 21For these reasons the Jews seized me in the temple and tried to kill *me.* 22Therefore, having obtained help from God, to this day I stand, witnessing both to small and great, saying no other things than those ªwhich the prophets and bMoses said would come— 23 ªthat the Christ would suffer, bthat He would be the first to rise from the dead, and cwould proclaim light to the *Jewish* people and to the Gentiles."

AGRIPPA PARRIES PAUL'S CHALLENGE

24Now as he thus made his defense, Festus said with a loud voice, "Paul, ªyou are beside yourself! Much learning is driving you mad!"

25But he said, "I am not *1*mad, most noble Festus, but speak the words of truth and reason. 26For the king, before whom I also speak freely, ªknows these things; for I am convinced that none of these things escapes his attention, since this thing was not done in a corner. 27King Agrippa, do you believe the prophets? I know that you do believe."

28Then Agrippa said to Paul, "You almost persuade me to become a Christian."

29And Paul said, ª"I would to God that not only you, but also all who hear me today, might become both almost and altogether such as I am, except for these chains."

30When he had said these things, the king stood up, as well as the governor and Bernice and those who sat with them; 31and when they had gone aside, they talked among themselves, saying, ª"This man is doing nothing deserving of death or chains."

32Then Agrippa said to Festus, "This man might have been set ªfree bif he had not appealed to Caesar."

THE VOYAGE TO ROME BEGINS

27 And when ªit was decided that we should sail to Italy, they delivered Paul and some other prisoners to *one* named Julius, a centurion of the Augustan Regiment. 2So, entering a ship of Adramyttium, we put to sea, meaning to sail along the coasts of Asia. ªAristarchus, a Macedonian of Thessalonica, was with us. 3And the next *day* we landed at Sidon. And

Reference column

20 ª Acts 9:19, 20, 22; 11:26
b Matt. 3:8

22 ª Rom. 3:21
b John 5:46

23 ª Luke 24:26
b 1 Cor. 15:20, 23
c Luke 2:32

24 ª [1 Cor. 1:23; 2:13, 14; 4:10]

25 1 *out of my mind*

26 ª Acts 26:3

29 ª 1 Cor. 7:7

31 ª Acts 23:9, 29; 25:25

32 ª Acts 28:18
b Acts 25:11

CHAPTER 27

1 ª Acts 25:12, 25

2 ª Acts 19:29

3 ª Acts 24:23; 28:16

6 ª Acts 28:11

7 ª Titus 1:5, 12

9 ª Lev. 16:29–31; 23:27–29
1 The Day of Atonement, late September or early October

Acts 27:1

Soldier to Soldier. Julius, a centurion of the Augustan Regiment, was one of the personal guards of Caesar. He was one of the elite of the elite. Being a centurion, he was over a hundred or so men. Centurions were very fine men.

No doubt, Julius was a seasoned and brave soldier. So there was a bond between Julius and Paul because it was one brave soldier meeting another. Paul had a respect for Julius, as one of Caesar's soldiers; and Julius, no doubt, developed a tremendous respect for Paul, a soldier of the cross of Jesus Christ.

Julius ªtreated Paul kindly and gave *him* liberty to go to his friends and receive care. 4When we had put to sea from there, we sailed under *the shelter of* Cyprus, because the winds were contrary. 5And when we had sailed over the sea which is off Cilicia and Pamphylia, we came to Myra, *a city* of Lycia. 6There the centurion found ªan Alexandrian ship sailing to Italy, and he put us on board.

7When we had sailed slowly many days, and arrived with difficulty off Cnidus, the wind not permitting us to proceed, we sailed under *the shelter of* ªCrete off Salmone. 8Passing it with difficulty, we came to a place called Fair Havens, near the city *of* Lasea.

PAUL'S WARNING IGNORED

9Now when much time had been spent, and sailing was now dangerous ªbecause 1the Fast was already over, Paul advised them, 10saying, "Men, I perceive that this voyage will end with disaster and much loss, not only of the cargo and ship, but also our lives." 11Nevertheless the centurion was more persuaded by the helmsman and the owner of the ship than by the things spoken by Paul. 12And because the harbor was not suitable to winter in, the majority advised to set sail from there also, if by any means they could reach Phoenix, a harbor of Crete opening toward the southwest and northwest, *and* winter *there.*

IN THE TEMPEST

13When the south wind blew softly, supposing that they had obtained *their* desire, putting out to sea, they sailed close by Crete. 14But not long after, a tempestuous head wind arose, called 1Euroclydon. 15So when the ship was caught, and could not head into the wind, we let *her* 1drive. 16And running under *the shelter of* an island called 1Clauda, we secured the skiff with difficulty. 17When they had taken it on board, they used cables to undergird the ship; and fearing lest they should run aground on the 1Syrtis *Sands,* they struck sail and so were driven. 18And because we were exceedingly tempest-tossed, the next *day* they lightened the ship. 19On the third *day* awe threw the ship's tackle overboard with our own hands. 20Now when neither sun nor stars appeared for many days, and no small tempest beat on *us,* all hope that we would be saved was finally given up.

21But after long abstinence from food, then Paul stood in the midst of them and said, "Men, you should have listened to me, and not have sailed from Crete and incurred this disaster and loss. 22And now I urge you to take 1heart, for there will be no loss of life among you, but only of the ship. 23aFor there stood by me this night an angel of the God to whom I belong and bwhom I serve, 24saying, 'Do not be afraid, Paul; you must be brought before Caesar; and indeed God has granted you all those who sail with you.' 25Therefore take heart, men, afor I believe God that it will be just as it was told me. 26However, awe must run aground on a certain island."

27Now when the fourteenth night had come, as we were driven up and down in the Adriatic *Sea,* about midnight the sailors sensed that they were drawing near some land. 28And they took soundings and found *it* to be twenty fathoms; and when they had gone a little farther, they took soundings again and found *it* to be fifteen fathoms. 29Then, fearing lest we should run aground on the rocks, they dropped four anchors from the stern, and 1prayed for day to come. 30And as the sailors were seeking to escape from the ship, when they had let down the skiff into the sea, under pretense of putting out anchors from the prow, 31Paul said to the centurion and the soldiers, "Unless these men stay in the ship, you cannot be saved." 32Then the soldiers

Marginal notes

14 1A southeast wind that stirs up broad waves; NU *Euraquilon,* a northeaster

15 1be driven

16 1NU *Cauda*

17 1M *Syrtis*

19 aJon. 1:5

22 1courage

23 aActs 18:9; 23:11
bDan. 6:16

25 aRom. 4:20, 21

26 aActs 28:1

29 1Or *wished*

34 1[Matt. 10:30]

35 a[1 Tim. 4:3, 4]

37 aActs 2:41; 7:14

Acts 27:23–25

THE PRECIOUS PROMISES OF JESUS

There in the midst of the storm, the Lord ministered to Paul. The Lord encouraged Paul. The Lord assured Paul of his mission: "You've got to bear witness before Caesar." So he had the promise, the Lord's word, that he was going to get to Caesar.

It's wonderful to have that assurance of the Lord of His purpose for your life. When the storms come and we are prone to despair; when we are filled with anxiety and doubt, we can rest upon the precious promises of God.

"You shall bear witness of Me in Rome." Paul said, "I believe God that it will be just as it was told me." That's confidence in the Word of God! I love that.

cut away the ropes of the skiff and let it fall off.

33And as day was about to dawn, Paul implored *them* all to take food, saying, "Today is the fourteenth day you have waited and continued without food, and eaten nothing. 34Therefore I urge you to take nourishment, for this is for your survival, asince not a hair will fall from the head of any of you." 35And when he had said these things, he took bread and agave thanks to God in the presence of them all; and when he had broken *it* he began to eat. 36Then they were all encouraged, and also took food themselves. 37And in all we were two hundred and seventy-six apersons on the ship. 38So when they had eaten enough, they lightened ship and threw out the wheat into the sea.

SHIPWRECKED ON MALTA

39When it was day, they did not recognize the land; but they observed a bay with a beach, onto which they

THE REST OF THE STORY   Acts 27:44

It had been a very dark journey filled with difficulties. Months had passed since Paul and the soldiers first set out for Italy. They had been in this vicious storm. They hadn't seen the sun or stars for over fourteen days. The winds had been howling with huge waves crashing over the ship. They despaired of life itself. They weren't able to govern their own destiny. They had to leave themselves to the mercy of the winds and the heavy seas.

Now they had come to a strange island. The ship, which was stuck, was being broken apart by the fierceness of the waves. They made it safely to shore. There was still a driving rain; it was still cold. But God had a purpose in it all. He had a purpose in landing right where they did. God's hand was guiding this whole affair. God was bringing Paul deliberately to the island of Malta because God had a work for Paul to accomplish there.

When you read the final chapter in Acts, suddenly you will see the whole story. What a difference it makes when you can see the whole story, when you can understand the purposes of God in the trials. Then you can look back and follow the hand of God in all of the circumstances. You see the plan of God, and this suddenly gives new life and new understanding to all of your difficult experiences.

As we go through difficult experiences in our lives; when all seems to be dark and we despair of ever getting out of it, God's hand is at work. One day, looking back on all of the difficult experiences, you will see how God was guiding and preparing you the entire time.

planned to run the ship if possible. ⁴⁰And they ¹let go the anchors and left *them* in the sea, meanwhile loosing the rudder ropes; and they hoisted the mainsail to the wind and made for shore. ⁴¹But striking ¹a place where two seas met, ᵃthey ran the ship aground; and the prow stuck fast and remained immovable, but the stern was being broken up by the violence of the waves.

⁴²And the soldiers' plan was to kill the prisoners, lest any of them should swim away and escape. ⁴³But the centurion, wanting to save Paul, kept them from *their* purpose, and commanded that those who could swim should jump *overboard* first and get to land, ⁴⁴and the rest, some on boards and some on *parts* of the ship. And so it was ᵃthat they all escaped safely to land.

PAUL'S MINISTRY ON MALTA

28 Now when they had escaped, they then found out that ᵃthe island was called Malta. ²And the ᵃnatives¹ showed us unusual kindness; for they kindled a fire and made us all welcome, because of the rain that was falling and because of the cold. ³But when Paul had gathered a bundle of sticks and laid *them* on the fire, a viper came out because of the heat, and fastened on his hand. ⁴So when the natives saw the creature hanging from his

hand, they said to one another, "No doubt this man is a murderer, whom, though he has escaped the sea, yet justice does not allow to live." ⁵But he shook off the creature into the fire and ᵃsuffered no harm. ⁶However, they were expecting that he would swell up or suddenly fall down dead. But after they had looked for a long time and saw no harm come to him, they changed their minds and ᵃsaid that he was a god.

⁷In that region there was an estate of the ¹leading citizen of the island, whose name was Publius, who received us and entertained us courteously for three days. ⁸And it happened that the father of Publius lay sick of a fever and dysentery. Paul went in to him and ᵃprayed, and ᵇhe laid his hands on him and healed him. ⁹So when this was done, the rest of those on the island who had diseases also came and were healed. ¹⁰They also honored us in many ᵃways; and when we departed, they provided such things as were ᵇnecessary.

ARRIVAL AT ROME

¹¹After three months we sailed in ᵃan Alexandrian ship whose figurehead was the ¹Twin Brothers, which had wintered at the island. ¹²And landing at Syracuse, we stayed three days. ¹³From there we circled round and reached Rhegium. And after one day the south

40 ¹ *cast off*

41 ᵃ 2 Cor. 11:25
¹ A reef

44 ᵃ Acts 27:22, 31

CHAPTER 28

1 ᵃ Acts 27:26

2 ᵃ Col. 3:11
¹ Lit. *barbarians*

5 ᵃ Mark 16:18

6 ᵃ Acts 12:22; 14:11

7 ¹ Magistrate

8 ᵃ [James 5:14, 15]
ᵇ Mark 5:23; 6:5; 7:32; 16:18

10 ᵃ Matt. 15:6
ᵇ [Phil. 4:19]

11 ᵃ Acts 27:6
¹ Gr. *Dioskouroi,* Zeus's sons Castor and Pollux

wind blew; and the next day we came to Puteoli, [14]where we found [a]brethren, and were invited to stay with them seven days. And so we went toward Rome. [15]And from there, when the brethren heard about us, they came to meet us as far as Appii Forum and Three Inns. When Paul saw them, he thanked God and took courage.

[16]Now when we came to Rome, the centurion delivered the prisoners to the captain of the guard; but [a]Paul was permitted to dwell by himself with the soldier who guarded him.

PAUL'S MINISTRY AT ROME

[17]And it came to pass after three days that Paul called the leaders of the Jews together. So when they had come together, he said to them: "Men *and* brethren, [a]although I have done nothing against our people or the customs of our fathers, yet [b]I was delivered as a prisoner from Jerusalem into the hands of the Romans, [18]who, [a]when they had examined me, wanted to let *me* go, because there was no cause for putting me to death. [19]But when the [1]Jews spoke against *it*, [a]I was compelled to appeal to Caesar, not that I had anything of which to accuse my nation. [20]For this reason therefore I have called for you, to see *you* and speak with *you*, because [a]for the hope of Israel I am bound with [b]this chain."

[21]Then they said to him, "We neither received letters from Judea concerning you, nor have any of the brethren who came reported or spoken any evil of you. [22]But we desire to hear from you what you think; for concerning this sect, we know that [a]it is spoken against everywhere."

[23]So when they had appointed him a

Reference column

14 [a] Rom. 1:8

16 [a] Acts 23:11; 24:25; 27:3

17 [a] Acts 23:29; 24:12, 13; 26:31
[b] Acts 21:33

18 [a] Acts 22:24; 24:10; 25:8; 26:32

19 [a] Acts 25:11, 21, 25
[1] The ruling authorities

20 [a] Acts 26:6, 7
[b] Eph. 3:1; 4:1; 6:20

22 [a] [1 Pet. 2:12; 3:16; 4:14, 16]

23 [a] Luke 24:27
[b] Acts 26:6, 22

24 [a] Acts 14:4; 19:9

25 [1] NU *your*

26 [a] Is. 6:9, 10

Acts 28:20

The Hope of Israel. What is "the hope of Israel"? "The hope of Israel" was the hope that God would send the anointed King, the promised Messiah.

Paul said, "I don't really have anything against the Jews, though they forced me to appeal to Caesar." He was assuring the Jewish leadership that he was not going there to condemn the Jewish nation or the Jewish people. He was there because of his hope and in chains because of the hope of Israel.

day, many came to him at *his* lodging, [a]to whom he explained and solemnly testified of the kingdom of God, persuading them concerning Jesus [b]from both the Law of Moses and the Prophets, from morning till evening. [24]And [a]some were persuaded by the things which were spoken, and some disbelieved. [25]So when they did not agree among themselves, they departed after Paul had said one word: "The Holy Spirit spoke rightly through Isaiah the prophet to [1]our fathers, [26]saying,

[a]'*Go to this people and say:*
"*Hearing you will hear, and shall not understand;*
And seeing you will see, and not perceive;
27　*For the hearts of this people have grown dull.*
Their ears are hard of hearing,

DIVINE APPOINTMENT

Acts 28:9

Now God had a purpose even in a venomous viper fastening onto Paul (28:3). The purpose of God was to cause the people of Malta to realize that divine power was at work in this man's life. It opened the door for Paul to be able to minister to the people because they looked up to him, realizing the power of God was upon his life. Had the venomous viper not fastened onto Paul and been shaken off without any harm, he probably wouldn't have been noticed at all. But because of what could be looked at as a very unfortunate, horrible experience, God used it to open doors for ministry.

We've got to be careful of snap judgments concerning our situations. We need to realize God is at work and God has a purpose in all that He allows. Through the storms, God will guide us to those places where He knows there are people who need ministry.

So a great ministry opened to Paul. Many sick people were healed; and, of course, this gave him the opportunity to share the gospel of Jesus Christ.

And their eyes they have closed,
Lest they should see with their
eyes and hear with their ears,
Lest they should understand with
their hearts and turn,
So that I should heal them."'

28"Therefore let it be known to you that the salvation of God has been sent ato the Gentiles, and they will hear it!"

28 a Rom. 11:11

29 1 NU omits v. 29.

31 a Eph. 6:19

29 1And when he had said these words, the Jews departed and had a great dispute among themselves. 30Then Paul dwelt two whole years in his own rented house, and received all who came to him, 31apreaching the kingdom of God and teaching the things which concern the Lord Jesus Christ with all confidence, no one forbidding him.

FRUIT FROM PAUL'S CHAINS   Acts 28:30

Paul was chained in Rome. As a prisoner, he could not move about Rome freely. This gave Paul time to write letters to the Ephesian church, to the Colossians, to the Philippians, and to Philemon.

Imagine what we would have lost if we didn't have the glorious message to the Ephesian church that tells of the glory of Jesus Christ. Think of what we would have lost if we didn't have Paul's letter to the Philippians that speaks of the joy we can have in the midst of hardships. Think of what we would have lost if we didn't have Paul's letter to the Colossians that speaks of the excellency and preeminence of Jesus Christ. Think of what we would have lost if we didn't have Paul's letter to Philemon, which speaks so beautifully of the glorious intercessory work of Jesus Christ.

God brought Paul to this wicked city in chains to bring the glorious light of the gospel of Jesus Christ. Then He left Paul in his chains so he would have the time to write these epistles that were not only a blessing to the churches to whom they were sent, but they have been a blessing to us throughout all of church history. We are blessed today because God allowed Paul to be chained in Rome.

THE EPISTLE OF PAUL THE APOSTLE TO THE
ROMANS

INTRODUCTION This book was a letter written by the apostle Paul to the church in Rome. He was writing from Corinth, probably around AD 57. At this point Paul had never been to Rome, but he had desired to go to Rome for a long time. He wouldn't actually get to Rome until around AD 60, as we see in the end of the book of Acts.

Paul obviously knew many of the Christians in Rome, and many of them were probably converted as a result of his ministry in other places. The church in Rome was primarily made up of Gentiles, with some Jews mixed in. As Peter was called to minister to the Jews, Paul was the apostle to the Gentiles, even though he was a Jew himself. Paul was making plans to come to Rome, to minister to the Christians there, and this book was somewhat a preparation for his visit, as he encouraged the Christians, and gave them advance training preceding his personal ministry to them.

The book of Romans stands out among all the books of the New Testament as being the most theological and systematic. It is a detailed teaching, outlining the essentials of the faith, and serves as a profound explanation of the gospel. The entire book explains the need for salvation, and how God is able to give us righteousness. Paul makes clear the purpose and need for the death of Jesus and the practical implications of the great doctrinal truths, including the unity of Jews and Gentiles that comes by faith in Jesus Christ.

For me personally, the book of Romans will always stand out as the vehicle God used to teach me about the glorious grace of God. The hopeless lament, "O wretched man that I am! Who will deliver me from this body of death?" (Rom. 7:24) that gives way to the glorious truths of Romans 8:1, "There is therefore now no condemnation to those who are in Christ Jesus" is positively life-changing.

Understanding the truth of the grace of God through the book of Romans revolutionized my life and my ministry, as I discovered who I am in Christ. The victory that comes from understanding that "if God is for us, who can be against us?" is just glorious! (Rom. 8:31). We are "more than conquerors through Him who loved us" (Rom. 8:37).

GREETING

1 Paul, a bondservant of Jesus Christ, ᵃcalled *to be* an apostle, ᵇseparated to the gospel of God ²ᵃwhich He promised before ᵇthrough His prophets in

CHAPTER 1
1 ᵃ1Tim. 1:11
ᵇActs 9:15; 13:2
2 ᵃActs 26:6
ᵇGal. 3:8

the Holy Scriptures, ³concerning His Son Jesus Christ our Lord, who ¹was ᵃborn of the seed of David according to the flesh, ⁴*and* ᵃdeclared *to be* the

3 ᵃGal. 4:4 ¹came 4 ᵃActs 9:20; 13:33

Rom. 1:5
Grace Through Him. Paul had experienced the grace of God. Though he considered himself to be the chief of sinners (1 Tim. 1:15), yet he had been touched by God's grace.

You, too, can experience the wonderful grace of Jesus. God's grace, His unmerited favor, is a constant theme throughout the book of Romans. My prayer is that as you read Romans you will come to a fuller, richer understanding of God's grace toward you.

Son of God with power according bto the Spirit of holiness, by the resurrection from the dead. 5Through Him awe have received grace and apostleship for bobedience to the faith among all nations cfor His name, 6among whom you also are the called of Jesus Christ;

7To all who are in Rome, beloved of God, acalled to be saints:

bGrace to you and peace from God our Father and the Lord Jesus Christ.

DESIRE TO VISIT ROME
8First, aI thank my God through Jesus Christ for you all, that byour faith is spoken of throughout the whole world. 9For aGod is my witness, bwhom

Rom. 1:11–12
Encouraged Together. Paul was longing to see the Roman Christians "that I may be encouraged together with you by the mutual faith both of you and me." That should be our experience when we get together. When the body of Christ gets together, we should be mutually edified.

As I come and share what God is doing in my life and you share what God is doing in your life, our visit becomes beneficial and encouraging to both of us. That is true fellowship.

4 b [Heb. 9:14]

5 a Eph. 3:8
b Acts 6:7
c Acts 9:15

7 a 1 Cor. 1:2, 24
b 1 Cor. 1:3

8 a 1 Cor. 1:4
b Rom. 16:19

9 a Rom. 9:1
b Acts 27:23
c 1 Thess. 3:10
1 Or in

11 a Rom. 15:29

12 a Titus 1:4

13 a [1 Thess. 2:18]
b Phil. 4:17

16 a Ps. 40:9, 10
b 1 Cor. 1:18, 24
c Acts 3:26
1 NU omits of Christ

17 a Rom. 3:21; 9:30

I serve 1with my spirit in the gospel of His Son, that cwithout ceasing I make mention of you always in my prayers, 10making request if, by some means, now at last I may find a way in the will of God to come to you. 11For I long to see you, that aI may impart to you some spiritual gift, so that you may be established— 12that is, that I may be encouraged together with you by athe mutual faith both of you and me.

13Now I do not want you to be unaware, brethren, that I often planned to come to you (but awas hindered until now), that I might have some bfruit among you also, just as among the other Gentiles. 14I am a debtor both to Greeks and to barbarians, both to wise and to unwise. 15So, as much as is in me, I am ready to preach the gospel to you who are in Rome also.

THE JUST LIVE BY FAITH
16For aI am not ashamed of the gospel 1of Christ, for bit is the power of God to salvation for everyone who believes, cfor the Jew first and also for the Greek. 17For ain it the righteousness of God is revealed from faith to

Rom. 1:16–17

NOT ASHAMED

The gospel, the good news of what Jesus has done for us, is powerful truth. In it we see the righteousness of God that comes by faith. This righteousness of God is in direct contrast with human righteousness, which is by works. The Pharisees tried hard to be righteous by their own efforts. But Jesus said it would take more righteousness than that to get to heaven (Matt. 5:20).

As we accept Jesus Christ, by faith, He gives us His righteousness, and therefore we are not ashamed to declare that it is not about us, but it is all about Him. If I stand in my own righteousness, I stand ashamed. But to stand in His righteousness, I don't need to be ashamed.

faith; as it is written, [b]*"The just shall live by faith."*

GOD'S WRATH ON UNRIGHTEOUSNESS

18[a]For the wrath of God is revealed from heaven against all ungodliness and [b]unrighteousness of men, who [1]suppress the truth in unrighteousness, 19because [a]what may be known of God is [1]manifest [2]in them, for [b]God has shown *it* to them. 20For since the creation of the world [a]His invisible *attributes* are clearly seen, being understood by the things that are made, *even* His eternal power and [1]Godhead, so that they are without excuse, 21because, although they knew God, they did not glorify *Him* as God, nor were thankful, but [a]became futile in their thoughts, and their foolish hearts were darkened. 22[a]Professing to be wise, they became fools, 23and changed the glory of the [a]incorruptible [b]God into an image made like [1]corruptible man—and birds and four-footed animals and creeping things.

24[a]Therefore God also gave them up to uncleanness, in the lusts of their hearts, [b]to dishonor their bodies [c]among themselves, 25who exchanged [a]the truth of God [b]for the lie, and worshiped and served the creature rather than the Creator, who is blessed forever. Amen.

26For this reason God gave them up to [a]vile passions. For even their [1]women exchanged the natural use for what is against nature. 27Likewise also the [1]men, leaving the natural use of the [2]woman, burned in their lust for one another, [1]men with [1]men committing what is shameful, and receiving in themselves the penalty of their error which was due.

28And even as they did not like to retain God in *their* knowledge, God gave them over to a debased mind, to do those things [a]which are not fitting; 29being filled with all unrighteousness, [1]sexual immorality, wickedness, [2]covetousness, [3]maliciousness; full of envy, murder, strife, deceit, evil-mindedness; *they are* whisperers, 30[a]backbiters, haters of God, violent, proud, boasters, inventors of evil things, disobedient to parents, 31[1]undiscerning, untrustworthy, unloving, [2]unforgiving, unmerciful; 32who, [a]knowing the righteous judgment of God, that those who practice such things [b]are deserving of death, not only do the same but also [c]approve of those who practice them.

GOD'S RIGHTEOUS JUDGMENT

2 Therefore you are [a]inexcusable, O man, whoever you are who judge, [b]for in whatever you judge another you condemn yourself; for you who judge practice the same things. 2But we know that the judgment of God is according to truth against those who practice such things. 3And do you think this, O man, you who judge those practicing such things, and doing the same, that you will escape the judgment of God? 4Or do you despise [a]the riches of His goodness, [b]forbearance, and [c]longsuffering, [d]not knowing that the goodness of God leads you to repentance? 5But in accordance with your hardness and your [1]impenitent heart [a]you are [2]treasuring up for yourself wrath in the day of wrath and revelation of the righteous judgment of

Rom. 2:4

THE GOODNESS OF GOD

Everything that God does in our lives is designed to bring us to repentance. Our only hope is that we turn around and change directions from the natural bent of our flesh.

But people often mistake God's forbearance and longsuffering for tolerance or indifference. Because of God's patience and love, they get the idea that He doesn't care about their sin. But the purpose of His goodness is to turn us around. God loves you more than you can ever realize; and in spite of what you are doing, He patiently allows you the time and space to repent.

But there comes a day, make no mistake about it, when God will judge. If we respond to His goodness by repenting of our sins, the day of judgment will be a time of rewards and celebration. But if we ignore His goodness and refuse to repent, we will face the wrath of God.

---

17 [b] Hab. 2:4

18 [a] [Acts 17:30]
[b] 2 Thess. 2:10
[1] *hold down*

19 [a] [Acts 14:17; 17:24]
[b] [John 1:9]
[1] *evident*
[2] *among*

20 [a] Ps. 19:1–6
[1] *divine nature, deity*

21 [a] Jer. 2:5

22 [a] Jer. 10:14

23 [a] 1 Tim. 1:17; 6:15, 16
[b] Deut. 4:16–18
[1] *perishable*

24 [a] Eph. 4:18, 19
[b] 1 Cor. 6:18
[c] Lev. 18:22

25 [a] 1 Thess. 1:9
[b] Is. 44:20

26 [a] Lev. 18:22
[1] Lit. *females*

27 [1] Lit. *males*
[2] Lit. *female*

28 [a] Eph. 5:4

29 [1] NU omits *sexual immorality*
[2] *greed*
[3] *malice*

31 [1] *without understanding*
[2] NU omits *unforgiving*

32 [a] [Rom. 2:2]
[b] [Rom. 6:21]
[c] Hos. 7:3

CHAPTER 2

1 [a] [Rom. 1:20]
[b] [Matt. 7:1–5]

4 [a] [Eph. 1:7, 18; 2:7]
[b] [Rom. 3:25]
[c] Ex. 34:6
[d] Is. 30:18

5 [a] [Deut. 32:34]
[1] *unrepentant*
[2] *storing*

God, ⁶who ^a*"will render to each one according to his deeds"* : ⁷eternal life to those who by patient continuance in doing good seek for glory, honor, and immortality; ⁸but to those who are self-seeking and ^ado not obey the truth, but obey unrighteousness—indignation and wrath, ⁹tribulation and anguish, on every soul of man who does evil, of the Jew ^afirst and also of the ¹Greek; ¹⁰abut glory, honor, and peace to everyone who works what is good, to the Jew first and also to the Greek. ¹¹For ^athere is no partiality with God.

¹²For as many as have sinned without law will also perish without law, and as many as have sinned in the law will be judged by the law ¹³(for ^anot the hearers of the law *are* just in the sight of God, but the doers of the law will be justified; ¹⁴for when Gentiles, who do not have the law, by nature do the things in the law, these, although not having the law, are a law to themselves, ¹⁵who show the ^awork of the law written in their hearts, their ^bconscience also bearing witness, and between themselves *their* thoughts accusing or else excusing *them*) ¹⁶ain the day when God will judge the secrets of men ^bby Jesus Christ, ^caccording to my gospel.

THE JEWS GUILTY AS THE GENTILES

¹⁷ ¹Indeed ^ayou are called a Jew, and ^brest² on the law, ^cand make your boast

---

Rom. 2:11

NO PARTIALITY

You are as important to God as anyone else in the world. God loves you supremely, and He is not a respecter of persons.

I am sometimes embarrassed when people come up to me and say, "Will you pray for me? I know you are much closer to God than I am." Not so! I am not closer to God than you are. We are all equally close to God. God will receive you as readily as He receives me.

Man elevates other men, but God doesn't. We are all on the same level to Him. You are infinitely important to God!

---

6 ^aPs. 62:12; Prov. 24:12

8 ^a[2 Thess. 1:8]

9 ^a1 Pet. 4:17
¹Gentile

10 ^a[1 Pet. 1:7]

11 ^aDeut. 10:17

13 ^a[James 1:22, 25]

15 ^a1 Cor. 5:1
^bActs 24:25

16 ^a[Matt. 25:31]
^bActs 10:42; 17:31
^c1 Tim. 1:11

17 ^aJohn 8:33
^bMic. 3:11
^cIs. 48:1, 2
¹NU *But if*
²*rely*

18 ^aDeut. 4:8
^bPhil. 1:10

19 ^aMatt. 15:14

20 ^a[2 Tim. 3:5]

21 ^aMatt. 23:3

22 ^aMal. 3:8

23 ^aRom. 2:17; 9:4

24 ^aEzek. 16:27
^bIs. 52:5; Ezek. 36:22

25 ^a[Gal. 5:3]

26 ^a[Acts 10:34]

27 ^aMatt. 12:41
¹Lit. *letter*

28 ^a[Gal. 6:15]

29 ^a[1 Pet. 3:4]
^bPhil. 3:3
^cDeut. 30:6
^d[1 Cor. 4:5]
¹A play on words—*Jew* is literally *praise.*

---

in God, ¹⁸and ^aknow *His* will, and ^bapprove the things that are excellent, being instructed out of the law, ¹⁹and ^aare confident that you yourself are a guide to the blind, a light to those who are in darkness, ²⁰an instructor of the foolish, a teacher of babes, ^ahaving the form of knowledge and truth in the law. ²¹aYou, therefore, who teach another, do you not teach yourself? You who preach that a man should not steal, do you steal? ²²You who say, "Do not commit adultery," do you commit adultery? You who abhor idols, ^ado you rob temples? ²³You who ^amake your boast in the law, do you dishonor God through breaking the law? ²⁴For ^a*"the name of God is* ^b*blasphemed among the Gentiles because of you,"* as it is written.

CIRCUMCISION OF NO AVAIL

²⁵aFor circumcision is indeed profitable if you keep the law; but if you are a breaker of the law, your circumcision has become uncircumcision. ²⁶Therefore, ^aif an uncircumcised man keeps the righteous requirements of the law, will not his uncircumcision be counted as circumcision? ²⁷And will not the physically uncircumcised, if he fulfills the law, ^ajudge you who, *even* with your ¹written *code* and circumcision, *are* a transgressor of the law? ²⁸For ^ahe is not a Jew who *is one* outwardly, nor *is* circumcision that which *is* outward in the flesh; ²⁹but *he is* a Jew ^awho *is one* inwardly; and ^bcircumcision *is that* of the heart, ^cin the Spirit, not in the letter; ^dwhose ¹praise *is* not from men but from God.

GOD'S JUDGMENT DEFENDED

3 What advantage then has the Jew, or what *is* the profit of circumcision? ²Much in every way! Chiefly

---

Rom. 2:25–29

A Matter of the Heart. God has never cared about the outward observance of religion. The only value of outward observance is when it reflects an inward reality. True commitment, true circumcision, is a matter of the heart, in the Spirit. Faith isn't something that is inherited or that you attain by going through the motions. It is a personal commitment that happens in your heart.

because [a]to them were committed the [1]oracles of God. [3]For what if [a]some did not believe? [b]Will their unbelief make the faithfulness of God without effect? [4a]Certainly not! Indeed, let [b]God be [1]true but [c]every man a liar. As it is written:

[d]"*That You may be justified in Your words,*
And may overcome when You are judged."

[5]But if our unrighteousness demonstrates the righteousness of God, what shall we say? *Is* God unjust who inflicts wrath? [a](I speak as a man.) [6]Certainly not! For then [a]how will God judge the world? [7]For if the truth of God has increased through my lie to His glory, why am I also still judged as a sinner? [8]And *why* not *say,* [a]"Let us do evil that good may come"?—as we are slanderously reported and as some affirm that we say. Their [1]condemnation is just.

ALL HAVE SINNED

[9]What then? Are we better *than* they? Not at all. For we have previously charged both Jews and Greeks that [a]they are all under sin. [10]As it is written:

[a]"*There is none righteous, no, not one;*
[11]   *There is none who understands;*
    There is none who seeks after God.
[12]   *They have all turned aside;*
    They have together become unprofitable;
    There is none who does good, no, not one."
[13] "*Their* [a] *throat is an open* [1]*tomb;*
    With their tongues they have practiced deceit";
    [b]"*The poison of asps is under their lips";*
[14] "*Whose* [a] *mouth is full of cursing and bitterness.*"
[15] "*Their* [a] *feet are swift to shed blood;*
[16]   *Destruction and misery are in their ways;*
[17]   *And the way of peace they have not known.*"
[18] "*There* [a] *is no fear of God before their eyes.*"

[19]Now we know that whatever [a]the law says, it says to those who are under the law, that [b]every mouth may be stopped, and all the world may become [1]guilty before God. [20]Therefore [a]by the

---

CHAPTER 3

2 [a] Deut. 4:5–8
[1] sayings, Scriptures

3 [a] Heb. 4:2
[b] [2 Tim. 2:13]

4 [a] Job 40:8
[b] [John 3:33]
[c] Ps. 62:9
[d] Ps. 51:4
[1] Found true

5 [a] Gal. 3:15

6 [a] [Gen. 18:25]

8 [a] Rom. 5:20
[1] Lit. *judgment*

9 [a] Gal. 3:22

10 [a] Ps. 14:1–3; 53:1–3; Eccl. 7:20

13 [a] Ps. 5:9
[b] Ps. 140:3
[1] *grave*

14 [a] Ps. 10:7

15 [a] Prov. 1:16; Is. 59:7, 8

18 [a] Ps. 36:1

19 [a] John 10:34
[b] Job 5:16
[1] *accountable*

20 [a] [Gal. 2:16]

21 [a] Acts 15:11
[b] John 5:46
[c] 1 Pet. 1:10

22 [a] [Col. 3:11]
[1] NU omits *and on all*

23 [a] Gal. 3:22

24 [a] [Eph. 2:8]
[1] *without any cost*

Rom. 3:10–18

NO ONE IS GOOD

The Jews looked down on the Gentiles with an attitude of superiority, which carried over into the early church. But Paul made it clear that we are all in the same boat. No one is righteous, no one understands, no one seeks God, no one does good on his own.

Apart from the work of God's grace, we are all worthless. We all stand guilty before God. Our natural state is one of depravation. Our lips are poison, and our ways are destruction and misery. We were all a complete mess when Jesus found us.

deeds of the law no flesh will be justified in His sight, for by the law *is* the knowledge of sin.

GOD'S RIGHTEOUSNESS THROUGH FAITH

[21]But now [a]the righteousness of God apart from the law is revealed, [b]being witnessed by the Law [c]and the Prophets, [22]even the righteousness of God, through faith in Jesus Christ, to all [1]and on all who believe. For [a]there is no difference; [23]for [a]all have sinned and fall short of the glory of God, [24]being justified [1]freely [a]by His grace

---

Rom. 3:20

Law Can't Justify. All that the Law can do is show us what sin is, and that awareness of sin should drive us to God for help and forgiveness. The Law only reveals that we are sinners. Once it does that, it has fulfilled its purpose.

It is a mistake to try to live under a set of rules, as many churches attempt to do. We can't keep the rules, no matter what the rules are. The rules can only teach us to cry out for help.

Rom. 3:23–27

NO BOASTING

We have all sinned. We have all missed the mark. If we were both in a boat heading over to Catalina Island and the boat sank, we could try to swim to Catalina. But I'm so out of shape, I might make it 100 yards before I drown. But if you are a good swimmer and you get within a mile of Catalina, you can see Avalon Harbor. You may see the boats and the people, and yet if you get exhausted and go under and drown, you may have come closer than me, but we both drowned. We both came up short.

Some people may be better than others, but we all come short of the glory of God. And we all will only be justified by His grace, through faith in Jesus. That excludes any boasting. We all make it only because of Him.

ᵇthrough the redemption that is in Christ Jesus, 25whom God set forth ᵃ*as* a *1*propitiation ᵇby His blood, through faith, to demonstrate His righteousness, because in His forbearance God had passed over ᶜthe sins that were previously committed, 26to demonstrate at the present time His righteousness, that He might be just and the justifier of the one who has faith in Jesus.

BOASTING EXCLUDED

27ᵃWhere *is* boasting then? It is excluded. By what law? Of works? No, but by the law of faith. 28Therefore we conclude ᵃthat a man is *1*justified by faith apart from the deeds of the law. 29Or *is* He the God of the Jews only? *Is* He not also the God of the Gentiles? Yes, of the Gentiles also, 30since ᵃ*there is* one God who will justify the circumcised by faith and the uncircumcised through faith. 31Do we then make void the law through faith? Certainly not! On the contrary, we establish the law.

---

24 ᵇ[Heb. 9:12, 15]

25 ᵃLev. 16:15
ᵇCol. 1:20
ᶜActs 14:16; 17:30
1 mercy seat

27 ᵃ[1 Cor. 1:29]

28 ᵃGal. 2:16
1 declared righteous

30 ᵃ[Gal. 3:8, 20]

CHAPTER 4

1 ᵃIs. 51:2
ᵇJames 2:21
1 Or (fore)father according to the flesh has found?

2 ᵃRom. 3:20, 27

3 ᵃGen. 15:6
1 imputed, credited, reckoned, counted

4 ᵃRom. 11:6
1 according to

5 ᵃ[Eph. 2:8, 9]
ᵇJosh. 24:2

6 ᵃPs. 32:1, 2

7 ᵃPs. 32:1, 2

ABRAHAM JUSTIFIED BY FAITH

4What then shall we say that ᵃAbraham our ᵇfather*1*has found according to the flesh? 2For if Abraham was ᵃjustified by works, he has *something* to boast about, but not before God. 3For what does the Scripture say? ᵃ*"Abraham believed God, and it was 1accounted to him for righteousness."* 4Now ᵃto him who works, the wages are not counted *1*as grace but *1*as debt.

Rom. 4:1–3

Abraham Believed God. The Jews look back to Abraham as their father and hero. So Paul used Abraham as an example of righteousness. He went back to Genesis 15:6, as God instituted His covenant with Abraham. The testimony of the Scriptures was that "[Abraham] believed in the LORD, and He accounted it to him for righteousness."

Some things never change. Abraham couldn't be justified by his works and had nothing to boast about. And today, as in the days of Abraham, we will only be justified by grace, through believing God.

DAVID CELEBRATES THE SAME TRUTH

5But to him who ᵃdoes not work but believes on Him who justifies ᵇthe ungodly, his faith is accounted for righteousness, 6just as David also ᵃdescribes the blessedness of the man to whom God imputes righteousness apart from works:

7 *"Blessed*ᵃ *are those whose lawless deeds are forgiven,*
    And whose sins are covered;
8   *Blessed is the man to whom the LORD shall not impute sin."*

ABRAHAM JUSTIFIED BEFORE CIRCUMCISION

9*Does* this blessedness then *come* upon the circumcision *only,* or upon the uncircumcised also? For we say that faith was accounted to Abraham for righteousness. 10How then was it accounted? While he was circumcised, or uncircumcised? Not while circumcised, but while

Rom. 4:6–8

DAVID WAS FORGIVEN

Davis was another of the great heroes of Israel. David was a man after God's own heart (1 Sam. 13:14), and yet he failed in a big way. He committed adultery, then let his act lead to murder. Yet, when confronted with his sin, he repented and received forgiveness.

In Psalm 51, we see David's gratefulness to God for His forgiveness that was "imputed" to him by grace. Paul quoted David's prayer of receiving forgiveness here to show that even David could only stand before God because of what God had done, not because of what David had done. And like David, how blessed and happy we are to be forgiven, to be the objects of the grace of God.

uncircumcised. [11] And [a]he received the sign of circumcision, a seal of the righteousness of the faith which *he had while still* uncircumcised, that [b]he might be the father of all those who believe, though they are uncircumcised, that righteousness might be imputed to them also, [12]and the father of circumcision to those who not only *are* of the circumcision, but who also walk in the steps of the faith which our father [a]Abraham *had while still* uncircumcised.

THE PROMISE GRANTED THROUGH FAITH

[13]For the promise that he would be the [a]heir of the world *was* not to Abraham or to his seed through the law, but through the righteousness of faith. [14]For [a]if those who are of the law *are* heirs, faith is made void and the promise made of no effect, [15]because [a]the law brings about wrath; for where there is no law *there is* no transgression.

[16]Therefore *it is* of faith that *it might be* [a]according to grace, [b]so that the promise might be [1]sure to all the seed, not only to those who are of the law,

11 [a] Gen. 17:10
[b] Luke 19:9

12 [a] Rom. 4:18–22

13 [a] Gen. 17:4–6; 22:17

14 [a] Gal. 3:18

15 [a] Rom. 3:20

16 [a] [Rom. 3:24]
[b] [Gal. 3:22]
[c] Is. 51:2
[1] certain

17 [a] Gen. 17:5
[b] [Rom. 8:11]
[c] Rom. 9:26

18 [a] Gen. 15:5

19 [a] Gen. 17:17
[b] Heb. 11:11

21 [a] [Heb. 11:19]

22 [a] Gen. 15:6

23 [a] Rom. 15:4

24 [a] Acts 2:24

25 [a] Is. 53:4, 5
[b] [1 Cor. 15:17]

but also to those who are of the faith of Abraham, [c]who is the father of us all [17](as it is written, [a]"*I have made you a father of many nations*") in the presence of Him whom he believed—God, [b]who gives life to the dead and calls those [c]things which do not exist as though they did; [18]who, contrary to hope, in hope believed, so that he became the father of many nations, according to what was spoken, [a]"*So shall your descendants be.*" [19]And not being weak in faith, [a]he did not consider his own body, already dead (since he was about a hundred years old), [b]and the deadness of Sarah's womb. [20]He did not waver at the promise of God through unbelief, but was strengthened in faith, giving glory to God, [21]and being fully convinced that what He had promised [a]He was also able to perform. [22]And therefore [a]"*it was accounted to him for righteousness.*"

[23]Now [a]it was not written for his sake alone that it was imputed to him, [24]but also for us. It shall be imputed to us who believe [a]in Him who raised up Jesus our Lord from the dead, [25][a]who was delivered up because of our offenses, and [b]was raised because of our justification.

Rom. 4:16

ASSURANCE AND SECURITY

If salvation ever depended on us and on our goodness, we would be in big trouble. Even if God graded on the curve and you just had to be more righteous than most, how would you ever know if you were doing enough? But because salvation is simply by grace through faith, the promise is "sure to all the seed."

We have the wonderful assurance that comes from knowing that it depends on Him and on His faithfulness and not on us. And as verse 21 points out, He is able to keep His promises.

Rom. 5:1

PEACE WITH GOD

Before we came to Christ we were at war with God. We were rebels against the laws of God, feeling that they were too restrictive. We believed the lies of Satan as he made sin seem attractive. He blinded us to the fact that sin was destroying us. So we fought against God, not realizing that He was trying to save us. We knew we were at war, but we didn't know that we were fighting against God.

Then Jesus told us, "Come to Me . . . and I will give you rest" (Matt. 11:28). And when we surrender to Him and accept Jesus Christ as our Lord and Savior, we suddenly realize that the war is over. I'm no longer fighting against God. There is such peace! There is such rest! To know that God is now on my side!

FAITH TRIUMPHS IN TROUBLE

5 Therefore, ªhaving been justified by faith, ¹we have ᵇpeace with God through our Lord Jesus Christ, ²ªthrough whom also we have access by faith into this grace ᵇin which we stand, and ᶜrejoice in hope of the glory

Rom. 5:8

Demonstration of God's Love. There are so many imitations of love that it is difficult to really know what true love is. Deep inside each of us, there is a yearning and a need for true love, and the world is more than happy to provide us with phony substitutes.

But God has shown us what real love is. While we were still sinners, in rebellion against God, Christ died for us. We didn't deserve it, and there was nothing attractive about us. But He died for us. That is love!

CHAPTER 5

1 ªIs. 32:17
ᵇ[Eph. 2:14]
1 Some ancient mss. *let us have*

2 ª[Eph. 2:18; 3:12]
ᵇ1 Cor. 15:1
ᶜHeb. 3:6

3 ªMatt. 5:11, 12
ᵇJames 1:3
1 *endurance*

4 ª[James 1:12]
1 *approved character*

5 ªPhil. 1:20
ᵇ2 Cor. 1:22

6 ª[Rom. 4:25; 5:8; 8:32]
1 *at the right time*

8 ª[John 3:16; 15:13]

9 ªEph. 2:13
ᵇ1 Thess. 1:10

10 ª[Rom. 8:32]
ᵇ2 Cor. 5:18
ᶜJohn 14:19

11 ª[Gal. 4:9]

12 ª1 Cor. 15:21]
ᵇGen. 2:17

13 ª1 John 3:4

14 ª[1 Cor. 15:21, 22]

15 ª[Is. 53:11]
1 *trespass or false step*

16 1 *trespasses*

17 1 *trespass*

18 ª[1 Cor. 15:21, 45]
1 Or *one trespass*
2 Or *one righteous act*

of God. ³And not only *that,* but ªwe also glory in tribulations, ᵇknowing that tribulation produces ¹perseverance; ⁴ªand perseverance, ¹character; and character, hope. ⁵ªNow hope does not disappoint, ᵇbecause the love of God has been poured out in our hearts by the Holy Spirit who was given to us.

CHRIST IN OUR PLACE

⁶For when we were still without strength, ¹in due time ªChrist died for the ungodly. ⁷For scarcely for a righteous man will one die; yet perhaps for a good man someone would even dare to die. ⁸But ªGod demonstrates His own love toward us, in that while we were still sinners, Christ died for us. ⁹Much more then, having now been justified ªby His blood, we shall be saved ᵇfrom wrath through Him. ¹⁰For ªif when we were enemies ᵇwe were reconciled to God through the death of His Son, much more, having been reconciled, we shall be saved ᶜby His life. ¹¹And not only *that,* but we also ªrejoice in God through our Lord Jesus Christ, through whom we have now received the reconciliation.

DEATH IN ADAM, LIFE IN CHRIST

¹²Therefore, just as ªthrough one man sin entered the world, and ᵇdeath through sin, and thus death spread to all men, because all sinned— ¹³(For until the law sin was in the world, but ªsin is not imputed when there is no law. ¹⁴Nevertheless death reigned from Adam to Moses, even over those who had not sinned according to the likeness of the transgression of Adam, ªwho is a type of Him who was to come. ¹⁵But the free gift *is* not like the ¹offense. For if by the one man's offense many died, much more the grace of God and the gift by the grace of the one Man, Jesus Christ, abounded ªto many. ¹⁶And the gift *is* not like *that which* came through the one who sinned. For the judgment *which came* from one *offense resulted* in condemnation, but the free gift *which came* from many ¹offenses *resulted* in justification. ¹⁷For if by the one man's ¹offense death reigned through the one, much more those who receive abundance of grace and of the gift of righteousness will reign in life through the One, Jesus Christ.)

¹⁸Therefore, as through ¹one man's offense *judgment came* to all men, resulting in condemnation, even so through ªone² Man's righteous act *the*

Rom. 5:12–19

ONE MAN

We, as descendants of Adam, inherited a sin nature. He sinned first, and we followed suit. We inherited guilt. And even as it took only one man to pollute the gene pool, so it would only take one Man to make it right.

If we become related to Jesus, by faith, we inherit His righteousness. Death spread through the first Adam, but life spreads through Jesus Christ, the Second Adam. His righteous act of sacrifice brought the free gift of forgiveness to all who will trust in Him.

We are related to Adam, but we have the opportunity to also be related to Christ. One Man makes all the difference in the world.

free gift came [b]to all men, resulting in justification of life. [19]For as by one man's disobedience many were made sinners, so also by [a]one Man's obedience many will be made righteous. [20]Moreover [a]the law entered that the offense might abound. But where sin abounded, grace [b]abounded much more, [21]so that as sin reigned in death, even so grace might reign through righteousness to eternal life through Jesus Christ our Lord.

DEAD TO SIN, ALIVE TO GOD

6 What shall we say then? [a]Shall we continue in sin that grace may abound? [2]Certainly not! How shall we who [a]died to sin live any longer in it? [3]Or do you not know that [a]as many of us as were baptized into Christ Jesus [b]were baptized into His death? [4]Therefore we were [a]buried with Him through baptism into death, that [b]just as Christ was raised from the dead by [c]the glory of the Father, [d]even so we also should walk in newness of life. [5a]For if we have been united together in the likeness of His death, certainly we also shall be *in the likeness* of *His* resurrection, [6]knowing this, that [a]our old man was crucified with *Him,* that

---

18 [b] [John 12:32]

19 [a] [Phil. 2:8]

20 [a] John 15:22
[b] 1 Tim. 1:14

CHAPTER 6

1 [a] Rom. 3:8; 6:15

2 [a] [Gal. 2:19]

3 [a] [Gal. 3:27]
[b] [1 Cor. 15:29]

4 [a] Col. 2:12
[b] 1 Cor. 6:14
[c] John 2:11
[d] [Gal. 6:15]

5 [a] Phil. 3:10

6 [a] Gal. 2:20; 5:24; 6:14
[b] Col. 2:11
[1] rendered inoperative

7 [a] 1 Pet. 4.1
[1] cleared

8 [a] 2 Tim. 2:11

9 [a] Rev. 1:18

10 [a] Heb. 9:27
[b] Luke 20:38

11 [a] [Rom. 6:2; 7:4, 6]
[b] [Gal. 2:19]
[1] consider

12 [a] Ps. 19:13

13 [a] Col. 3:5
[b] 1 Pet. 2:24; 4:2
[1] Or weapons

14 [a] [Gal. 5:18]

15 [a] 1 Cor. 9:21

16 [a] 2 Pet. 2:19

---

[b]the body of sin might be [1]done away with, that we should no longer be slaves of sin. [7]For [a]he who has died has been [1]freed from sin. [8]Now [a]if we died with Christ, we believe that we shall also live with Him, [9]knowing that [a]Christ, having been raised from the dead, dies no more. Death no longer has dominion over Him. [10]For *the death* that He died, [a]He died to sin once for all; but *the life* that He lives, [b]He lives to God. [11]Likewise you also, [1]reckon yourselves to be [a]dead indeed to sin, but [b]alive to God in Christ Jesus our Lord.

[12a]Therefore do not let sin reign in your mortal body, that you should obey it in its lusts. [13]And do not present your [a]members *as* [1]instruments of unrighteousness to sin, but [b]present yourselves to God as being alive from the dead, and your members *as* [1]instruments of righteousness to God. [14]For [a]sin shall not have dominion over you, for you are not under law but under grace.

FROM SLAVES OF SIN TO SLAVES OF GOD

[15]What then? Shall we sin [a]because we are not under law but under grace? Certainly not! [16]Do you not know that [a]to whom you present yourselves

Rom. 6:1–2

SHALL WE SIN FOR GRACE?

As Paul was teaching the principle of grace and the reality that our salvation has nothing to do with our works, the inevitable question was raised, "Then why should we stop sinning?" The way he put it was, "Shall we continue in sin that grace may abound?" His answer was, "Certainly not!"

It is interesting how people can take one truth and then carry it through to a logical conclusion that is totally wrong. Paul would develop, in this chapter, the proper relationship of a believer to sin. We are to be dead to sin.

WHOSE SLAVE ARE YOU?

When you were walking in the flesh, without a relationship with the Lord, you were a slave of sin. Sin, by its very nature, enslaves us. All sin is addictive. If it were not addictive, no one would even want to do it. The results are so unsatisfying and ultimately devastating that no one would continue in sin if it were not so addicting. So Paul pointed out that we were all slaves of sin, as we presented our bodies to be abused by the forces of evil. Sin had us trapped, and it was killing us.

But Jesus Christ came to set us free from sin. He gives us the choice of either being slaves to sin or becoming His servants. We can now reckon ourselves dead to sin and alive to God in Christ Jesus our Lord. The result of slavery to sin is death. The result of slavery to God is eternal life. "But now having been set free from sin, and having become slaves of God, you have your fruit to holiness, and the end, everlasting life." We can either serve the one who brings death or the One who gives eternal life. And if you've really been set free from the awful clutches of sin, you won't want to go back to it. It is death.

---

slaves to obey, you are that one's slaves whom you obey, whether of sin *leading* to death, or of obedience *leading* to righteousness? [17]But God be thanked that *though* you were slaves of sin, yet you obeyed from the heart [a]that form of doctrine to which you were [1]delivered. [18]And [a]having been set free from sin, you became slaves of righteousness. [19]I speak in human *terms* because of the weakness of your flesh. For just as you presented your members *as* slaves of uncleanness, and of lawlessness *leading* to *more* lawlessness, so now present your members *as* slaves of righteousness [1]for holiness.

[20]For when you were [a]slaves of sin, you were free in regard to righteousness. [21][a]What fruit did you have then in the things of which you are now ashamed? For [b]the end of those things *is* death. [22]But now [a]having been set free from sin, and having become slaves of God, you have your fruit [1]to holiness, and the end, everlasting life.

Rom. 6:23

Payday Is Coming. We will one day answer for how we've lived our lives. If we have lived after the flesh, we will ultimately face death, that spiritual death that is eternal separation from God. That is the natural end of a life of sin.

But God has given us a gift, and that gift is eternal life. We only need to trust in Him in order to receive the gift.

---

17 [a] 2 Tim. 1:13
[1] *entrusted*

18 [a] John 8:32

19 [1] *unto sancti-fication*

20 [a] John 8:34

21 [a] Rom. 7:5
[b] Rom. 1:32

22 [a] Rom. 6:18;
8:2
[1] *unto sanctifi-cation*

23 [a] Gen. 2:17
[b] 1 Pet. 1:4
[1] *free gift*

CHAPTER 7

1 [1] *rules*

2 [a] 1 Cor. 7:39

3 [a] [Matt. 5:32]

4 [a] Gal. 2:19;
5:18
[b] Gal. 5:22

5 [a] Rom. 6:13
[b] James 1:15

6 [a] Rom. 2:29

7 [a] Rom. 3:20
[b] Ex. 20:17;
Deut. 5:21; Acts
20:33

8 [a] Rom. 4:15

---

[23]For [a]the wages of sin *is* death, but [b]the [1]gift of God *is* eternal life in Christ Jesus our Lord.

FREED FROM THE LAW

7 Or do you not know, brethren (for I speak to those who know the law), that the law [1]has dominion over a man as long as he lives? [2]For [a]the woman who has a husband is bound by the law to *her* husband as long as he lives. But if the husband dies, she is released from the law of *her* husband. [3]So then [a]if, while *her* husband lives, she marries another man, she will be called an adulteress; but if her husband dies, she is free from that law, so that she is no adulteress, though she has married another man. [4]Therefore, my brethren, you also have become [a]dead to the law through the body of Christ, that you may be married to another—to Him who was raised from the dead, that we should [b]bear fruit to God. [5]For when we were in the flesh, the sinful passions which were aroused by the law [a]were at work in our members [b]to bear fruit to death. [6]But now we have been delivered from the law, having died to what we were held by, so that we should serve [a]in the newness of the Spirit and not *in* the oldness of the letter.

SIN'S ADVANTAGE IN THE LAW

[7]What shall we say then? *Is* the law sin? Certainly not! On the contrary, [a]I would not have known sin except through the law. For I would not have known covetousness unless the law had said, [b]*"You shall not covet."* [8]But [a]sin, taking opportunity by the commandment, produced in me all *manner*

Rom. 7:6

8 b 1 Cor. 15:56

Rom. 7:7–13

THE LETTER OR THE SPIRIT

O beying the rules can only allow you to follow the letter of the law, as best you can. But even if you are really good at obeying the rules, there will still be something missing.

God wants to have a relationship with you, and relationships aren't based on rules but they are a thing of the Spirit. This is why Jesus was so attractive to people, while the Pharisees were so unattractive. The Pharisees were following the letter of the Law, while missing the Spirit. Jesus embodied the Spirit of the Law. He made it look so natural, as opposed to the artificial religion of the Pharisees.

Living by the letter of the Law will always end in frustration. Living in the Spirit will always lead to an abundant, genuine life that is lived in relationship with God.

WHAT'S THE POINT OF THE LAW?

T he Law was given as a revealer of sin. We wouldn't understand God's righteous standards apart from the Law. Thus, the Law is a good thing. But the Law can never be a set of rules we live by in order to make us righteous before God. It won't do that.

The Law lets me know how far I really am from true righteousness and causes me to cry out for help. The Law, properly understood, reveals our sinful nature. Then God steps in with the remedy, which is the gospel of Jesus Christ.

longer I who do it, but sin that dwells in me. 18For I know that ain me (that is, in my flesh) nothing good dwells; for to will is present with me, but *how* to perform what is good I do not find. 19For the good that I will *to do*, I do not do; but the evil I will not *to do*, that I practice. 20Now if I do what I will not *to do*, it is no longer I who do it, but sin that

10 a Lev. 18:5

12 a Ps. 19:8

14 a 2 Kin. 17:17

dwells in me.

21I find then a law, that evil is present

of evil desire. For bapart from the law sin *was* dead. 9I was alive once without the law, but when the commandment came, sin revived and I died. 10And the commandment, awhich *was* to *bring* life, I found to *bring* death. 11For sin, taking occasion by the commandment, deceived me, and by it killed *me*. 12Therefore athe law *is* holy, and the commandment holy and just and good.

LAW CANNOT SAVE FROM SIN

13Has then what is good become death to me? Certainly not! But sin, that it might appear sin, was producing death in me through what is good, so that sin through the commandment might become exceedingly sinful. 14For we know that the law is spiritual, but I am carnal, asold under sin. 15For what I will to do, I do not understand. aFor what I will to do, that I do not practice; but what I hate, that I do. 16If, then, I do what I will not to do, I agree with the law that *it is* good. 17But now, *it is* no

Rom. 7:14–25

The Inward Struggle. Paul described the struggle that is within every person who is trying to lead a good life. We want to do the right things, and we are determined to do them. We want to stop doing things that are wrong. But there is a battle going on inside, and we often end up doing things we hate and neglecting the things we really want to do. It makes us feel wretched!

We can't fix it on our own. We are unable to reform ourselves. We need outside help. And God comes along to do just that.

15 a [Gal. 5:17]

18 a [Gen. 6:5; 8:21]

with me, the one who wills to do good. [22]For I ᵃdelight in the law of God according to ᵇthe inward man. [23]But ᵃI see another law in ᵇmy members, warring against the law of my mind, and bringing me into captivity to the law of sin which is in my members. [24]O wretched man that I am! Who will deliver me ᵃfrom this body of death? [25]ᵃI thank God—through Jesus Christ our Lord!

So then, with the mind I myself serve the law of God, but with the flesh the law of sin.

FREE FROM INDWELLING SIN

8 There is therefore now no condemnation to those who are in Christ Jesus, ᵃwho[1] do not walk according to the flesh, but according to the Spirit. [2]For ᵃthe law of ᵇthe Spirit of life in Christ Jesus has made me free from ᶜthe law of sin and death. [3]For ᵃwhat

Rom. 8:1

NO CONDEMNATION

Because Jesus died for our sins, freeing us from the bondage of sin and death, we can now live our lives in the realm of the Spirit. Our spirits were dead, but He made us alive in the Spirit, allowing us to be filled with the Holy Spirit, who enables us to walk in the Spirit. As a result we are in Christ Jesus, and "there is therefore now no condemnation to those who are in Christ Jesus, who do not walk according to the flesh, but according to the Spirit."

Jesus told Nicodemus that He didn't come into the world to condemn the world, but to save the world. "He who believes in Him is not condemned; but he who does not believe is condemned already" (John 3:18). Belief in Jesus removes all condemnation, because He gives His righteousness to us. And how wonderful it is to know that I've been set free from any condemnation!

22 ᵃPs. 1:2
ᵇ[2 Cor. 4:16]

23 ᵃ[Gal. 5:17]
ᵇRom. 6:13, 19

24 ᵃ[1 Cor. 15:51, 52]

25 ᵃ1 Cor. 15:57

CHAPTER 8

1 ᵃGal. 5:16
1 NU omits the rest of v. 1.

2 ᵃRom. 6:18, 22
ᵇ[1 Cor. 15:45]
ᶜRom. 7:24, 25

3 ᵃActs 13:39
ᵇ[2 Cor. 5:21]

4 ᵃGal. 5:16, 25

5 ᵃJohn 3:6
ᵇ[Gal. 5:22–25]

6 ᵃGal. 6:8
1 fleshly

7 ᵃJames 4:4
ᵇ1 Cor. 2:14
1 fleshly

11 ᵃActs 2:24
ᵇ1 Cor. 6:14
1 Or because of

12 ᵃ[Rom. 6:7, 14]

13 ᵃGal. 6:8
ᵇEph. 4:22

14 ᵃ[Gal. 5:18]

15 ᵃHeb. 2:15
ᵇ2 Tim. 1:7
ᶜ[Is. 56:5]
ᵈMark 14:36
1 Lit., in Aram., Father

16 ᵃEph. 1:13

17 ᵃActs 26:18
ᵇPhil. 1:29

18 ᵃ2 Cor. 4:17

19 ᵃ[2 Pet. 3:13]

20 ᵃGen. 3:17–19

the law could not do in that it was weak through the flesh, ᵇGod did by sending His own Son in the likeness of sinful flesh, on account of sin: He condemned sin in the flesh, [4]that the righteous requirement of the law might be fulfilled in us who ᵃdo not walk according to the flesh but according to the Spirit. [5]For ᵃthose who live according to the flesh set their minds on the things of the flesh, but those who live according to the Spirit, ᵇthe things of the Spirit. [6]For ᵃto be [1]carnally minded is death, but to be spiritually minded is life and peace. [7]Because ᵃthe [1]carnal mind is enmity against God; for it is not subject to the law of God, ᵇnor indeed can be. [8]So then, those who are in the flesh cannot please God.

[9]But you are not in the flesh but in the Spirit, if indeed the Spirit of God dwells in you. Now if anyone does not have the Spirit of Christ, he is not His. [10]And if Christ is in you, the body is dead because of sin, but the Spirit is life because of righteousness. [11]But if the Spirit of ᵃHim who raised Jesus from the dead dwells in you, ᵇHe who raised Christ from the dead will also give life to your mortal bodies [1]through His Spirit who dwells in you.

SONSHIP THROUGH THE SPIRIT

[12]ᵃTherefore, brethren, we are debtors—not to the flesh, to live according to the flesh. [13]For ᵃif you live according to the flesh you will die; but if by the Spirit you ᵇput to death the deeds of the body, you will live. [14]For ᵃas many as are led by the Spirit of God, these are sons of God. [15]For ᵃyou did not receive the spirit of bondage again ᵇto fear, but you received the ᶜSpirit of adoption by whom we cry out, ᵈ"Abba,[1] Father." [16]ᵃThe Spirit Himself bears witness with our spirit that we are children of God, [17]and if children, then ᵃheirs—heirs of God and joint heirs with Christ, ᵇif indeed we suffer with Him, that we may also be glorified together.

FROM SUFFERING TO GLORY

[18]For I consider that ᵃthe sufferings of this present time are not worthy to be compared with the glory which shall be revealed in us. [19]For ᵃthe earnest expectation of the creation eagerly waits for the revealing of the sons of God. [20]For ᵃthe creation was subjected to futility, not willingly, but because of Him who subjected it in hope; [21]because the creation itself also will

Rom. 8:14–17

ADOPTED BY GOD

God wants to have a relationship with us as our Father. He adopts us and then wants us to call Him "Abba, Father." The word *Abba* is the Hebrew word for "father." It was used as a term of endearment, rather like our word "Daddy."

My children never called me "Father" or "Chuck"; they called me "Daddy" and, as they got older, "Dad." I would never want a formal relationship with my kids. I want them to feel close to me and comfortable with me.

Our heavenly Father is the same way. We are now His kids, and He wants a close relationship with us. That relationship is discovered on a spiritual level. His Spirit communes with our spirit and lets us know that we are His. This is almost too wonderful to comprehend! God has adopted me as His child, and I am now an heir of God! And He likes me to call Him Daddy.

be delivered from the bondage of [1]corruption into the glorious [a]liberty of the children of God. 22For we know that the whole creation [a]groans and labors with birth pangs together until now. 23Not only *that*, but we also who have [a]the firstfruits of the Spirit, [b]even we ourselves groan [c]within ourselves, eagerly waiting for the adoption, the [d]redemption of our body. 24For we were saved in this hope, but [a]hope that is seen is not hope; for why does one still hope for what he sees? 25But if we hope for what we do not see, we eagerly wait for *it* with perseverance.

26Likewise the Spirit also helps in our weaknesses. For [a]we do not know what we should pray for as we ought, but [b]the Spirit Himself makes intercession [1]for us with groanings which cannot be uttered. 27Now [a]He who searches the hearts knows what the

---

21 [a][2 Cor. 3:17]
[1]decay

22 [a]Jer. 12:4, 11

23 [a]2 Cor. 5:5
[b]2 Cor. 5:2, 4
[c][Luke 20:36]
[d]Eph. 1:14; 4:30

24 [a]Heb. 11:1

26 [a]Matt. 20:22
[b]Eph. 6:18
[1]NU omits *for us*

27 [a]1 Chr. 28:9
[b]1 John 5:14

28 [a]2 Tim. 1:9

29 [a]2 Tim. 2:19
[b]Eph. 1:5, 11
[c][2 Cor. 3:18]
[d]Heb. 1:6

30 [a][1 Pet. 2:9; 3:9]
[b][Gal. 2:16]
[c]John 17:22

31 [a]Num. 14:9

32 [a]Rom. 5:6, 10 [b][Rom. 4:25]

33 [a]Is. 50:8, 9

34 [a]John 3:18
[b]Mark 16:19
[c]Heb. 7:25; 9:24

---

mind of the Spirit *is*, because He makes intercession for the saints [b]according to *the will of* God.

28And we know that all things work together for good to those who love God, to those [a]who are the called according to *His* purpose. 29For whom [a]He foreknew, [b]He also predestined [c]*to be* conformed to the image of His Son, [d]that He might be the firstborn among many brethren. 30Moreover whom He predestined, these He also [a]called; whom He called, these He also [b]justified; and whom He justified, these He also [c]glorified.

GOD'S EVERLASTING LOVE

31What then shall we say to these things? [a]If God *is* for us, who *can be* against us? 32[a]He who did not spare His own Son, but [b]delivered Him up for us all, how shall He not with Him also freely give us all things? 33Who shall bring a charge against God's elect? [a]*It is* God who justifies. 34[a]Who *is* he who condemns? *It is* Christ who died, and furthermore is also risen, [b]who is even at the right hand of God, [c]who also makes intercession for us. 35Who shall separate us from the love of Christ? *Shall* tribulation, or distress,

Rom. 8:37

MORE THAN CONQUERORS

What does it mean to be more than a conqueror? A conqueror is one who goes to war, fights a battle, and wins. To be more than a conqueror is to go into the battle having already won, going in as a victor. And that is what we are. Satan has already been defeated. There is no condemnation for us and no way for us to be separated from the love of God.

Death can't beat us, demons can't beat us, tribulation doesn't threaten us, and we can't lose because of the love of God that is in Christ Jesus our Lord. We enjoy the battle because we already know the outcome!

or persecution, or famine, or nakedness, or peril, or sword? 36As it is written:

a"*For Your sake we are killed all day long;*
We are accounted as sheep for the slaughter."

37aYet in all these things we are more than conquerors through Him who loved us. 38For I am persuaded that neither death nor life, nor angels nor aprincipalities nor powers, nor things present nor things to come, 39nor height nor depth, nor any other created thing, shall be able to separate us from the love of God which is in Christ Jesus our Lord.

ISRAEL'S REJECTION OF CHRIST

9 I atell the truth in Christ, I am not lying, my conscience also bearing me witness in the Holy Spirit, 2athat I have great sorrow and continual grief in my heart. 3For aI could wish that I myself were accursed from Christ for my brethren, my lcountrymen according to the flesh, 4who are Israelites, ato whom *pertain* the adoption, bthe glory, cthe covenants, dthe giving of the law, ethe service of God, and fthe promises; 5aof whom *are* the fathers and from bwhom, according to the flesh, Christ came, cwho is over all, *the* eternally blessed God. Amen.

ISRAEL'S REJECTION AND GOD'S PURPOSE

6aBut it is not that the word of God has taken no effect. For bthey *are* not all Israel who *are* of Israel, 7anor *are* they all children because they are the seed of Abraham; but, b"*In Isaac your seed shall be called.*" 8That is, those who *are* the children of the flesh, these

are not the children of God; but athe children of the promise are counted as the seed. 9For this *is* the word of promise: a"*At this time I will come and Sarah shall have a son.*"

10And not only *this*, but when aRebecca also had conceived by one man, *even* by our father Isaac 11(for *the children* not yet being born, nor having done any good or evil, that the purpose of God according to election might stand, not of works but of aHim who calls), 12it was said to her, a"*The older shall serve the younger.*" 13As it is written, a"*Jacob I have loved, but Esau I have hated.*"

ISRAEL'S REJECTION AND GOD'S JUSTICE

14What shall we say then? aIs there unrighteousness with God? Certainly not! 15For He says to Moses, a"*I will have mercy on whomever I will have mercy, and I will have compassion on whomever I will have compassion.*" 16So then it *is* not of him who wills, nor of him who runs, but of God who shows mercy. 17For athe Scripture says to the Pharaoh, b"*For this very purpose I have raised you up, that I may show My power in you, and that My name may be declared in all the earth.*" 18Therefore He has mercy on whom He wills, and whom He wills He ahardens.

19You will say to me then, "Why does He still find fault? For awho has resisted His will?" 20But indeed, O man, who are you to reply against God? aWill the thing formed say to him who formed *it*, "Why have you made me like this?" 21Does not the apotter have power over the clay, from the same lump to make bone vessel for honor and another for dishonor?

Cross-references

36 a Ps. 44:22
37 a 1 Cor. 15:57
38 a [Eph. 1:21]

CHAPTER 9

1 a 2 Cor. 1:23
2 a Rom. 10:1
3 a Ex. 32:32
1 Or *relatives*
4 a Ex. 4:22
b 1 Sam. 4:21
c Acts 3:25
d Ps. 147:19
e Heb. 9:1, 6
f [Acts 2:39; 13:32]
5 a Deut. 10:15
b [Luke 1:34, 35; 3:23]
c Jer. 23:6
6 a Num. 23:19
b [Gal. 6:16]
7 a [Gal. 4:23]
b Gen. 21:12
8 a Gal. 4:28
9 a Gen. 18:10, 14
10 a Gen. 25:21
11 a [Rom. 4:17; 8:28]
12 a Gen. 25:23
13 a Mal. 1:2, 3
14 a Deut. 32:4
15 a Ex. 33:19
17 a Gal. 3:8
b Ex. 9:16
18 a Ex. 4:21
19 a 2 Chr. 20:6
20 a Is. 29:16
21 a Prov. 16:4
b 2 Tim. 2:20

SUCH LOVE!   Rom. 9:1–3

Paul was estranged from some of his Jewish friends because they didn't understand how a Jew like Paul could focus his attention on ministering to the Gentiles. But he made it clear here how much he loved his Jewish neighbors. He had a constant sorrow and grief for Israel, nagging away at him. He loved them so much that he wished that he himself could be sent to hell if it would help the Jews to be saved.

I frankly don't understand that depth of love. When I see the direction our country is going, I sometimes think it is headed that way, too. But, I don't wish myself to be accursed so that our nation could be saved.

Jesus said, "Greater love has no one than this, than to lay down one's life for his friends" (John 15:13). Then Jesus demonstrated that love by laying down His life for us. Such love! And Paul showed that same heart for his people. That is amazing to me.

Rom. 9:14–16

God Does Whatever He Wants.

"Is there unrighteousness with God?" Of course not! He is God, and everything that He does is right. We would be foolish to judge Him. The nature of mercy is that no one deserves it. It is a gift. And God says, "I will have mercy on whomever I will have mercy."

God doesn't owe mercy to anyone, and He doesn't have to give it to everyone just because He gives it to someone. Whatever He does is fair because it all comes from His mercy, and He is God.

22 What if God, wanting to show *His* wrath and to make His power known, endured with much longsuffering ᵃthe vessels of wrath ᵇprepared for destruction, 23 and that He might make known ᵃthe riches of His glory on the vessels of mercy, which He had ᵇprepared beforehand for glory, 24 even us whom He ᵃcalled, ᵇnot of the Jews only, but also of the Gentiles?

25 As He says also in Hosea:

ᵃ"*I will call them My people, who were not My people,*
And her beloved, who was not beloved."
26 "*And* ᵃ *it shall come to pass in the place where it was said to them,*
'*You are not My people,*'

Rom. 9:22–23

Vessels of Mercy.
God shows His mercy to people so that others can see the riches of His glory. As He turned His back on Israel for a period of time and showed grace on the Gentiles, it demonstrated His wrath against continual patterns of sin, while at the same time demonstrating His love and mercy on people who really didn't deserve it.

When Gentiles started getting saved, it got everyone's attention. We are trophies of His mercy.

---

22 ᵃ[1 Thess. 5:9]
ᵇ[1 Pet. 2:8]

23 ᵃ[Col. 1:27]
ᵇ[Rom. 8:28–30]

24 ᵃ[Rom. 8:28]
ᵇ Rom. 3:29

25 ᵃ Hos. 2:23

26 ᵃ Hos. 1:10

27 ᵃ Is. 10:22, 23
ᵇ Rom. 11:5

28 ᵃ Is. 10:23; 28:22
1 NU the LORD will finish the work and cut it short upon the earth

29 ᵃ Is. 1:9
ᵇ Is. 13:19
1 Lit., in Heb., Hosts

30 ᵃ Rom. 4:11
ᵇ Rom. 1:17; 3:21; 10:6

31 ᵃ[Rom. 10:2–4]
ᵇ[Gal. 5:4]
1 NU omits of righteousness

32 ᵃ[1 Cor. 1:23]
1 NU by works, omitting of the law

33 ᵃ Is. 8:14; 28:16
ᵇ Rom. 5:5; 10:11

CHAPTER 10

1 1 NU them

2 ᵃ Acts 21:20

3 ᵃ[Rom. 1:17]
ᵇ[Phil. 3:9]

4 ᵃ[Gal. 3:24; 4:5]

5 ᵃ Lev. 18:5

6 ᵃ Deut. 30:12–14

7 ᵃ Deut. 30:13

8 ᵃ Deut. 30:14

There they shall be called sons of the living God."

27 Isaiah also cries out concerning Israel:

ᵃ"*Though the number of the children of Israel be as the sand of the sea,*
ᵇ *The remnant will be saved.*
28 *For* ¹*He will finish the work and cut it short in righteousness,*
ᵃ *Because the LORD will make a short work upon the earth.*"

29 And as Isaiah said before:

ᵃ"*Unless the LORD of* ¹*Sabaoth had left us a seed,*
ᵇ *We would have become like Sodom,*
And we would have been made like Gomorrah."

PRESENT CONDITION OF ISRAEL

30 What shall we say then? ᵃThat Gentiles, who did not pursue righteousness, have attained to righteousness, ᵇeven the righteousness of faith; 31 but Israel, ᵃpursuing the law of righteousness, ᵇhas not attained to the law ¹of righteousness. 32 Why? Because *they* did not seek it by faith, but as it were, ¹by the works of the law. For ᵃthey stumbled at that stumbling stone. 33 As it is written:

ᵃ"*Behold, I lay in Zion a stumbling stone and rock of offense,*
And ᵇ*whoever believes on Him will not be put to shame.*"

ISRAEL NEEDS THE GOSPEL

10 Brethren, my heart's desire and prayer to God for ¹Israel is that they may be saved. 2 For I bear them witness ᵃthat they have a zeal for God, but not according to knowledge. 3 For they being ignorant of ᵃGod's righteousness, and seeking to establish their own ᵇrighteousness, have not submitted to the righteousness of God. 4 For ᵃChrist is the end of the law for righteousness to everyone who believes.

5 For Moses writes about the righteousness which is of the law, ᵃ"*The man who does those things shall live by them.*" 6 But the righteousness of faith speaks in this way, ᵃ"*Do not say in your heart, 'Who will ascend into heaven?*'" (that is, to bring Christ down from above) 7 or, ᵃ"'*Who will descend into the abyss?*'" (that is, to bring Christ up from the dead). 8 But what does it say? ᵃ"*The word is near you, in*

9 [a] Luke 12:8

Rom. 10:1–3

Zeal Without Knowledge. Paul saw the unbelieving Jews as having "a zeal for God, but not according to knowledge." Paul had personal experience in this. Before his conversion, he had been persecuting the church, thinking it was for God (Phil. 3:6). I think of the many, many people today who are following misguided causes with all their hearts, working themselves to death for nothing. They often put us to shame when it comes to zeal.

But it isn't enough to be sincere. You have to know the truth about God's righteousness. Zeal without knowledge is a tragic waste and nothing more.

11 [a] Is. 28:16

12 [a] Rom. 3:22, 29
[b] Acts 10:36
[c] Eph. 1:7

13 [a] Joel 2:32
[b] Acts 9:14

14 [a] Titus 1:3

your mouth and in your heart" (that is, the word of faith which we preach): 9that [a]if you confess with your mouth the Lord Jesus and believe in your heart that God has raised Him from the dead, you will be saved. 10For with the heart one believes unto righteousness, and with the mouth confession is made unto salvation. 11For the Scripture says, [a]*"Whoever believes on Him will₁ not be put to shame."* 12For [a]there is no distinction between Jew and Greek, for [b]the same Lord over all [c]is rich to all who call upon Him. 13For [a]*"whoever calls* [b]*on the name of the LORD shall be saved."*

15 [a] Is. 52:7;
Nah. 1:15
[1] NU omits *preach the gospel of peace,*
Who

16 [a] Is. 53:1

Rom. 10:6–13

You Are So Close. It doesn't take some great majestic act to be saved. You don't have to ascend into heaven or descend into the abyss. It is as close as a simple confession. It takes acknowledging that Jesus is the Lord, and believing in your heart that He was raised from the dead; your heart must line up with what you say, as you make Jesus the Lord of your life. "For 'whoever calls on the name of the LORD shall be saved.'" It is so simple many people miss it.

ISRAEL REJECTS THE GOSPEL

14How then shall they call on Him in whom they have not believed? And how shall they believe in Him of whom they have not heard? And how shall they hear [a]without a preacher? 15And how shall they preach unless they are sent? As it is written:

> [a]*"How beautiful are the feet of those who [1]preach the gospel of peace,*
> *Who bring glad tidings of good things!"*

16But they have not all obeyed the gospel. For Isaiah says, [a]*"LORD, who has believed our report?"* 17So then faith *comes* by hearing, and hearing by the word of God.

18But I say, have they not heard? Yes indeed:

HEARING THE WORD OF GOD   Rom. 10:17–21

The Jews were totally confused by Jesus being the Messiah and were now baffled that Gentiles could be saved. But God had spoken to them in many ways and they refused to hear. "Faith comes by hearing, and hearing by the word of God."

Paul cited Psalm 19:4 to show that David saw the program of God reaching the world. Then he quoted Moses, as God said, "I will provoke them to jealousy by those who are not a nation; I will move them to anger by a foolish nation" (Deut. 32:21). He then quoted Isaiah, "I was found by those who did not seek Me . . . I have stretched out My hands all day long to a rebellious people" (Is. 65:1–2). If they had been paying attention, they would have realized that all God ever wanted to do was to save the world. If they had been listening to His word, it would have been clear that God wanted to use them to accomplish that, but they didn't hear Him.

God told Abraham, "In you all the families of the earth shall be blessed" (Gen. 12:3). That was God's eternal plan.

a*"Their sound has gone out to all
the earth,
And their words to the ends of the
world."*

¹⁹But I say, did Israel not know? First Moses says:

a*"I will provoke you to jealousy by
those who are not a nation,
I will move you to anger by a
^bfoolish nation."*

²⁰But Isaiah is very bold and says:

a*"I was found by those who did not
seek Me;
I was made manifest to those who
did not ask for Me."*

²¹But to Israel he says:

a*"All day long I have stretched out
My hands
To a disobedient and contrary
people."*

ISRAEL'S REJECTION NOT TOTAL

11 I say then, ^ahas God cast away His people? ^bCertainly not! For ^cI also am an Israelite, of the seed of Abraham, *of* the tribe of Benjamin. ²God has not cast away His people whom ^aHe foreknew. Or do you not know what the Scripture says of Elijah, how he pleads with God against Israel, saying, ³a*"LORD, they have killed Your*

Rom. 11:2–5

A REMNANT

Paul reminded Israel of the time of Elijah when the people had turned from God to worship idols, and yet there was a remnant of seven thousand people who hadn't bowed their knees to Baal. Now seven thousand people isn't very many out of a nation of over a million, but it is something.

Paul said that he was a part of the remnant in his day, a Jew who had accepted Jesus as his Messiah. God always has a remnant in every period of history. May we be a part of His faithful remnant, walking in His grace.

---

18 ^aPs. 19:4

19 ^aDeut. 32:21
   ^bTitus 3:3

20 ^aIs. 65:1

21 ^aIs. 65:2

CHAPTER 11

1 ^aJer. 46:28
   ^b1 Sam. 12:22
   ^c2 Cor. 11:22

2 ^a[Rom. 8:29]

3 ^a1 Kin. 19:10, 14

4 ^a1 Kin. 19:18

5 ^aRom. 9:27

6 ^aRom. 4:4
   ¹NU omits the rest of v. 6.

7 ^aRom. 9:31
   ^b2 Cor. 3:14

8 ^aIs. 29:10, 13
   ^bDeut. 29:3, 4

9 ^aPs. 69:22, 23

11 ^aIs. 42:6, 7
   ^bRom. 10:19
   ¹trespass

12 ¹trespass

13 ^aActs 9:15; 22:21

14 ^a1 Cor. 9:22

15 ^a[Is. 26:16–19]

16 ^aLev. 23:10

17 ^aJer. 11:16
   ^b[Eph. 2:12]
   ¹richness

18 ^a[1 Cor. 10:12]

---

*prophets and torn down Your altars,
and I alone am left, and they seek my
life"*? ⁴But what does the divine response say to him? ^a*"I have reserved for Myself seven thousand men who have not bowed the knee to Baal."* ⁵Even so then, at this present time there is a remnant according to the election of grace. ⁶And ^aif by grace, then *it is* no longer of works; otherwise grace is no longer grace. ¹But if *it is* of works, it is no longer grace; otherwise work is no longer work.

⁷What then? ^aIsrael has not obtained what it seeks; but the elect have obtained it, and the rest were ^bblinded. ⁸Just as it is written:

a*"God has given them a spirit of
stupor,
^bEyes that they should not see
And ears that they should not
hear,
To this very day."*

⁹And David says:

a*"Let their table become a snare
and a trap,
A stumbling block and a
recompense to them.
¹⁰ Let their eyes be darkened, so
that they do not see,
And bow down their back
always."*

ISRAEL'S REJECTION NOT FINAL

¹¹I say then, have they stumbled that they should fall? Certainly not! But ^athrough their ¹fall, to provoke them to ^bjealousy, salvation *has come* to the Gentiles. ¹²Now if their ¹fall *is* riches for the world, and their failure riches for the Gentiles, how much more their fullness!

¹³For I speak to you Gentiles; inasmuch as ^aI am an apostle to the Gentiles, I magnify my ministry, ¹⁴if by any means I may provoke to jealousy *those who are* my flesh and ^asave some of them. ¹⁵For if their being cast away is the reconciling of the world, what *will* their acceptance *be* ^abut life from the dead?

¹⁶For if ^athe firstfruit *is* holy, the lump *is* also *holy;* and if the root *is* holy, so *are* the branches. ¹⁷And if ^asome of the branches were broken off, ^band you, being a wild olive tree, were grafted in among them, and with them became a partaker of the root and ¹fatness of the olive tree, ¹⁸a do not boast against the branches. But if you do boast, *remember that* you do not

support the root, but the root *supports* you.

19You will say then, "Branches were broken off that I might be grafted in." 20Well *said.* Because of aunbelief they were broken off, and you stand by faith. Do not be haughty, but fear. 21For if God did not spare the natural branches, He may not spare you either. 22Therefore consider the goodness and severity of God: on those who fell, severity; but toward you, 1goodness, aif you continue in *His* goodness. Otherwise byou also will be cut off. 23And they also, aif they do not continue in unbelief, will be grafted in, for God is able to graft them in again. 24For if you were cut out of the olive tree which is wild by nature, and were grafted contrary to nature into a cultivated olive tree, how much more will these, who *are* natural *branches,* be grafted into their own olive tree?

25For I do not desire, brethren, that you should be ignorant of this mystery, lest you should be awise in your own 1opinion, that bblindness in part has happened to Israel cuntil the fullness of the Gentiles has come in. 26And so all Israel will be 1saved, as it is written:

> a"*The Deliverer will come out of Zion,*
> *And He will turn away ungodliness from Jacob;*

Rom. 11:26–29

ISRAEL WILL BE SAVED

The church is being used by God to make Israel jealous, but the church has not taken the place of Israel. "All Israel will be saved." The day will come when God will deal with Israel as a nation once again, and the Jews will turn back to God and acknowledge Jesus as their Messiah.

At the end of the church age, after the Lord raptures His church, He will once again focus on Israel. "For the gifts and the calling of God are irrevocable." God will still keep His unconditional promises to Israel.

Marginal references (center column):

20 a Heb. 3:19

22 a 1 Cor. 15:2
b [John 15:2]
1 NU adds of God

23 a [2 Cor. 3:16]

25 a Rom. 12:16
b 2 Cor. 3:14
c Luke 21:24
1 estimation

26 a Is. 59:20, 21
1 Or delivered

27 a Is. 27:9

28 a Deut. 7:8; 10:15

29 a Num. 23:19

30 a [Eph. 2:2]

32 a [Gal. 3:22]
1 shut them all up in

34 a Is. 40:13; Jer. 23:18
b Job 36:22

35 a Job 41:11

36 a Heb. 2:10
b Heb. 13:21

Rom. 11:33–36

GOD IS AMAZING!

As Paul reflected on God's incredible plan of redemption, how He saved the Gentiles, and yet will still keep His promises to Israel, he was just overwhelmed. "Oh, the depth of the riches both of the wisdom and knowledge of God! How unsearchable are His judgments and His ways past finding out!"

We don't always understand what God is doing, as His ways are so much higher than ours (Is. 55:9); but as His plan unfolds, we are just amazed at the brilliance of His strategy. He is God. Don't question Him; just watch Him!

27 For a*this is My covenant with them,*
When I take away their sins."

28Concerning the gospel *they are* enemies for your sake, but concerning the election *they are* abeloved for the sake of the fathers. 29For the gifts and the calling of God *are* airrevocable. 30For as you awere once disobedient to God, yet have now obtained mercy through their disobedience, 31even so these also have now been disobedient, that through the mercy shown you they also may obtain mercy. 32For God has 1committed them aall to disobedience, that He might have mercy on all.

33Oh, the depth of the riches both of the wisdom and knowledge of God! How unsearchable *are* His judgments and His ways past finding out!

34 "*For who has known the* amind of *the* LORD?
Or b *who has become His counselor?*"
35 "*Or* a *who has first given to Him*
And it shall be repaid to him?"

36For aof Him and through Him and to Him *are* all things, bto whom *be* glory forever. Amen.

Rom. 12:1–2

LIVING SACRIFICES

Paul, on the basis of the mercies of God and all that He has done for us, begged his readers to present their bodies to the Lord as a living sacrifice, instead of being conformed to this world. This world is becoming more pagan all the time, and it is programming us to think in a certain way. But God wants to renew our minds so we can walk in His will, which will take sacrifice.

We will need to deny our flesh of some of the things it wants to do, knowing that it is unfruitful. We will have to give up some of our time-wasting activities in order to spend time in the Word and in fellowship and prayer.

The payoff? Being holy and "acceptable to God." There should be no higher goal for a child of God than to please our Lord. It is just reasonable.

LIVING SACRIFICES TO GOD

12 I [a]beseech[1] you therefore, brethren, by the mercies of God, that you present your bodies [b]a living sacrifice, holy, acceptable to God, *which is* your [2]reasonable service. 2And [a]do not be conformed to this world, but [b]be transformed by the renewing of your mind, that you may [c]prove what *is* that good and acceptable and perfect will of God.

SERVE GOD WITH SPIRITUAL GIFTS

3For I say, [a]through the grace given to me, to everyone who is among you, [b]not to think *of himself* more highly than he ought to think, but to think soberly, as God has dealt [c]to each one a measure of faith. 4For [a]as we have many members in one body, but all the members do not have the same function, 5so [a]we, *being* many, are one body in Christ, and individually members of

CHAPTER 12

1 [a]2 Cor. 10:1–4
[b] Heb. 10:18, 20
[1] *urge*
[2] *rational*

2 [a] 1 John 2:15
[b] Eph. 4:23
[c] [1 Thess. 4:3]

3 [a] Gal. 2:9
[b] Prov. 25:27
[c] [Eph. 4:7]

4 [a] 1 Cor. 12:12–14

5 [a] [1 Cor. 10:17]

6 [a] [John 3:27]
[b] Acts 11:27

7 [a] Eph. 4:11

8 [a] Acts 15:32
[b] [Matt. 6:1–3]
[c] [Acts 20:28]
[d] 2 Cor. 9:7

9 [a] 1 Tim. 1:5
[b] Ps. 34:14

10 [a] Heb. 13:1
[b] Phil. 2:3

12 [a] Luke 10:20
[b] Luke 21:19
[c] Luke 18:1
[1] *persevering*

13 [a] 1 Cor. 16:1
[b] 1 Tim. 3:2
[1] Lit. *pursuing*

14 [a] [Matt. 5:44]

15 [a] [1 Cor. 12:26]

16 [a] [Phil. 2:2; 4:2]
[b] Jer. 45:5

17 [a] [Matt. 5:39]
[b] 2 Cor. 8:21
[1] Or *Provide good*

18 [a] Heb. 12:14

19 [a] Lev. 19:18

one another. 6Having then gifts differing according to the grace that is [a]given to us, *let us use them:* if prophecy, *let us* [b]*prophesy* in proportion to our faith; 7or ministry, *let us use it* in *our* ministering; [a]he who teaches, in teaching; 8[a]he who exhorts, in exhortation; [b]he who gives, with liberality; [c]he who leads, with diligence; he who shows mercy, [d]with cheerfulness.

BEHAVE LIKE A CHRISTIAN

9[a]*Let* love *be* without hypocrisy. [b]Abhor what is evil. Cling to what is good. 10[a]*Be* kindly affectionate to one another with brotherly love, [b]in honor giving preference to one another; 11not lagging in diligence, fervent in spirit, serving the Lord; 12[a]rejoicing in hope, [b]patient[1] in tribulation, [c]continuing steadfastly in prayer; 13[a]distributing to the needs of the saints, [b]given[1] to hospitality.

14[a]Bless those who persecute you; bless and do not curse. 15[a]Rejoice with those who rejoice, and weep with those who weep. 16[a]Be of the same mind toward one another. [b]Do not set your mind on high things, but associate with the humble. Do not be wise in your own opinion.

17[a]Repay no one evil for evil. [b]Have[1] regard for good things in the sight of all men. 18If it is possible, as much as depends on you, [a]live peaceably with all men. 19Beloved, [a]do not avenge

Rom. 12:4–8

DO YOUR JOB

God has given each of us certain gifts and ministries to be used in the body; and though we are all different, He calls us to work together to accomplish His purposes. We are connected and need to depend on each other.

If we all just do our own jobs, the body will function beautifully. But if we are not humbly working together; or if we neglect our job to worry about what someone else is doing, the body will be flopping around, out of control. Find your job in the body, and just do it.

Rom. 12:18

Live Peaceably with All. "If it is possible, as much as depends on you, live peaceably with all men." It isn't possible to be at peace with everyone. But do as much as you can do. You can't always prevent friction between people, but don't let the friction be from your side. Live peaceably, as much as you possibly can.

Too much energy and time are wasted fighting with people over things that don't matter. Be a peacemaker. You will be blessed.

yourselves, but *rather* give place to wrath; for it is written, b*"Vengeance is Mine, I will repay,"* says the Lord. 20Therefore

a*"If your enemy is hungry, feed him;
If he is thirsty, give him a drink;
For in so doing you will heap
coals of fire on his head."*

21Do not be overcome by evil, but aovercome evil with good.

SUBMIT TO GOVERNMENT

13 Let every soul be asubject to the governing authorities. For there is no authority except from God, and the authorities that exist are appointed by God. 2Therefore whoever resists athe authority resists the ordinance of God, and those who resist will 1bring judgment on themselves. 3For rulers are not a terror to good works, but to evil. Do you want to be unafraid of the authority? aDo what is good, and you will have praise from the same. 4For he is God's minister to you for good. But if you do evil, be afraid; for he does not bear the sword in vain; for he is God's minister, an avenger to *execute* wrath on him who practices evil. 5Therefore ayou must be subject, not only because of wrath bbut also for conscience' sake. 6For because of this you also pay taxes, for they are God's ministers attending continually to this very thing. 7aRender therefore to all their due: taxes to whom taxes *are* due, customs to whom customs, fear to whom fear, honor to whom honor.

LOVE YOUR NEIGHBOR

8Owe no one anything except to love one another, for ahe who loves another

19 bDeut. 32:35

20 aProv. 25:21, 22

21 a[Rom. 12:1, 2]

CHAPTER 13

1 a1Pet. 2:13

2 a[Titus 3:1]
1Lit. *receive*

3 a1Pet. 2:14

5 aEccl. 8:2
b[1Pet. 2:13, 19]

7 aMatt. 22:21

8 a[Gal. 5:13, 14]

9 aEx. 20:13–17; Deut. 5:17–21
1NU omits *"You shall not bear false witness,"*

Rom. 13:1

GOVERNMENT ORDAINED BY GOD

I confess that I have a problem with the notion that every government authority is ordained by God. When I see some of the corrupt people who come into power, I wonder how these crooked politicians could possibly be chosen by God. But when Paul was writing to the Christians in Rome and saying these things, the Roman Empire was at its apex of evil, and it was being ruled by the horrible tyrant Nero.

We can't always understand the plans of God. Sometimes when people reject God's leadership, He then gives them the leadership they deserve. If people want to rebel against God, He lets them. Our role is to accept whatever leadership God puts over us, realizing that He has a purpose in mind. He is still in ultimate control.

has fulfilled the law. 9For the commandments, a*"You shall not commit adultery," "You shall not murder," "You shall not steal,"* 1*"You shall not*

Rom. 13:8–10

Love Fulfills the Law. Jesus said that the Law can be summed up by two rules. Love God, and love your neighbor (Matt. 22:37–40). Paul here, in commenting on the second tablet of the Law—the commandments regarding our behavior toward people—reiterated this.

We fulfill the Law in relationship to others if we love our neighbor as ourselves. And if you need a practical definition of loving your neighbor, "Love does no harm to a neighbor."

Rom. 13:11–14

KNOW THE TIME

I believe that Jesus intended for the church to be constantly expecting His return at any time. He didn't give any prophecies that had to come before His return, because He wanted them to live with the expectancy that it could happen at any moment.

There were rumors in the early church that Jesus would come back before John would die (John 21:23). In Thessalonica, the people were concerned that those who died would miss the kingdom, because they had missed out on the rapture (1 Thess. 4). Throughout church history, there has remained in the hearts of the children of God that anticipation of His imminent return, and I believe God intended it that way.

Living in the anticipation of Jesus' return keeps us focused on what matters and keeps us living with our eyes open, awake to the possibility that today might be the day. We need to wake up. The day is at hand.

---

bear false witness," "You shall not covet" and if there is any other commandment, are all summed up in this saying, namely, b"You shall love your neighbor as yourself." 10Love does no harm to a neighbor; therefore alove is the fulfillment of the law.

PUT ON CHRIST

11And do this, knowing the time, that now it is high time ato awake out of sleep; for now our salvation is nearer than when we first believed. 12The night is far spent, the day is at hand. aTherefore let us cast off the works of darkness, and blet us put on the armor of light. 13aLet us walk 1properly, as in the day, bnot in revelry and drunkenness, cnot in lewdness and lust, dnot in strife and envy. 14But aput on the Lord Jesus Christ, and bmake no provision for the flesh, to fulfill its lusts.

---

9 b Lev. 19:18

10 a [Matt. 7:12; 22:39, 40]

11 a [1 Cor. 15:34]

12 a Eph. 5:11
b [Eph. 6:11, 13]

13 a Phil. 4:8
b Prov. 23:20
c [1 Cor. 6:9]
d James 3:14
1 decently

14 a Gal. 3:27
b [Gal. 5:16]

CHAPTER 14

1 a [1 Cor. 8:9; 9:22]

2 a [Titus 1:15]

3 a [Col. 2:16]

4 a James 4:11, 12

5 a Gal. 4:10

6 a Gal. 4:10
b [1 Tim. 4:3]
1 NU omits the rest of this sentence.

7 a [Gal. 2:20]

8 a 2 Cor. 5:14, 15

9 a 2 Cor. 5:15

THE LAW OF LIBERTY

14 Receivea one who is weak in the faith, but not to disputes over doubtful things. 2For one believes he amay eat all things, but he who is weak eats only vegetables. 3Let not him who eats despise him who does not eat, and alet not him who does not eat judge him who eats; for God has received him. 4aWho are you to judge another's servant? To his own master he stands or falls. Indeed, he will be made to stand, for God is able to make him stand.

5aOne person esteems one day above another; another esteems every day alike. Let each be fully convinced in his own mind. 6He who aobserves the day, observes it to the Lord; 1and he who does not observe the day, to the Lord he does not observe it. He who eats, eats to the Lord, for bhe gives God thanks; and he who does not eat, to the Lord he does not eat, and gives God thanks. 7For anone of us lives to himself, and no one dies to himself. 8For if we alive, we live to the Lord; and if we die, we die to the Lord. Therefore, whether we live or die, we are the Lord's. 9For ato this end Christ died

---

Rom. 14:1–4

JUDGING OTHERS

We all have different convictions about what we should and shouldn't do. Some people are vegetarians; others eat meat at every meal. It is important that we not look down on those whose convictions differ from ours. There is way too much of this in the body of Christ.

If someone else has the liberty to do something that I am convicted about, I wonder if he is really a Christian. If someone else has a hang-up about something that I have the liberty to do, I judge him as a prude and a legalist. But we all answer only to God, our Master. Let's not allow ourselves to get dragged into these silly "disputes over doubtful things."

SPECIAL DAYS

People have always argued over which day should be observed as a day of worship. In the early church, Christians began to worship on Sunday, as that was the day on which Jesus had risen from the dead (Acts 20:7). This pattern was continued throughout history and was discussed by Justin Martyr, Tertullian, and other church fathers. But some of the Jews in the early church were pushing for Saturday worship, according to the Jewish tradition. There are still those today, including the Seventh-day Adventists, who advocate Saturday worship. Paul pointed out here that some people esteem "one day above another; another esteems every day alike." It is acceptable to have these differences of opinion and these differences of practice. What isn't acceptable is to judge each other based on these convictions. Paul said in Colossians 2:16 to not let anyone judge you according to Sabbath days.

I am personally the kind of person who "esteems every day alike." To me, every day is the Lord's day. I wake up every morning and dedicate the day to the Lord. It is irrelevant to me what day it is, as they are all the Lord's days. But I won't judge you if you see it differently, and I hope you won't judge me. These are not the kinds of issues that the body of Christ should be dividing over and arguing about.

[1]and rose and lived again, that He might be [b]Lord of both the dead and the living. [10]But why do you judge your brother? Or why do you show contempt for your brother? For [a]we shall all stand before the judgment seat of [1]Christ. [11]For it is written:

[a]"As I live, says the LORD,
Every knee shall bow to Me,
And every tongue shall confess to God."

[12]So then [a]each of us shall give account of himself to God. [13]Therefore let us not judge one another [1]anymore, but rather resolve this, [a]not to put a stumbling block or a cause to fall in our brother's way.

THE LAW OF LOVE

[14]I know and am convinced by the Lord Jesus [a]that there is nothing unclean of itself; but to him who considers anything to be unclean, to him it is unclean. [15]Yet if your brother is grieved because of your food, you are no longer walking in love. [a]Do not destroy with your food the one for whom Christ died. [16][a]Therefore do not let your good be spoken of as evil; [17][a]for the kingdom of God is not eating and drinking, but righteousness and [b]peace and joy in the Holy Spirit. [18]For he who serves Christ in [1]these things [a]is acceptable to God and approved by men.
[19][a]Therefore let us pursue the things which make for peace and the things

9 [b]Acts 10:36
1 NU omits and rose

10 [a]2 Cor. 5:10
1 NU God

11 [a]Is. 45:23

12 [a]1 Pet. 4:5

13 [a]1 Cor. 8:9
1 any longer

14 [a]1 Cor. 10:25

15 [a]1 Cor. 8:11

16 [a][Rom. 12:17]

17 [a]1 Cor. 8:8
[b][Rom. 8:6]

18 [a]2 Cor. 8:21
1 NU this thing

19 [a]Rom. 12:18
[b]1 Cor. 14:12
1 build up

20 [a]Rom. 14:15
[b]Acts 10:15
[c]1 Cor. 8:9–12

by which [b]one may [1]edify another. [20][a]Do not destroy the work of God for the sake of food. [b]All things indeed are pure, [c]but it is evil for the man who

Rom. 14:17–20

RIGHTEOUSNESS, PEACE AND JOY

How we need to emphasize the positive qualities of what God wants to do in our lives, rather than the negative disagreements we have. The body of Christ is constantly being splintered because there are those who insist on emphasizing the differences that divide us rather than the qualities that unite us.

I feel sorry for the people who think they have the corner on all truth and that, if you disagree with them, you probably aren't really a Christian. We shouldn't be tearing each other down. We need to find ways to build each other up. The kingdom of God isn't about fighting and arguing. It is about righteousness, peace, joy, and our mutual love for each other.

eats with [1]offense. [21]*It is* good neither to eat [a]meat nor drink wine nor *do anything* by which your brother stumbles [1]or is offended or is made weak. [22]*I*Do you have faith? Have *it* to yourself before God. [a]Happy *is* he who does not condemn himself in what he approves. [23]But he who doubts is condemned if he eats, because *he does* not eat from faith; for [a]whatever *is* not from faith is [1]sin.

BEARING OTHERS' BURDENS

15 We [a]then who are strong ought to bear with the [1]scruples of the weak, and not to please ourselves. [2]a Let each of us please *his* neighbor for *his* good, leading to [1]edification. [3]a For even Christ did not please Himself; but as it is written, [b]*"The reproaches of those who reproached You fell on Me."* [4]For [a]whatever things were written before were written for our learning, that we through the [1]patience and comfort of the Scriptures might have hope. [5]a Now may the God of patience and comfort grant you to be like-minded toward one another, according to Christ Jesus, [6]that you may [a]with one mind *and* one mouth glorify the God and Father of our Lord Jesus Christ.

Rom. 15:4–5

Patience and Comfort. Paul explained that one purpose for the Old Testament is that we would have the hope that comes from "the patience and comfort of the Scriptures." We learn patience when we see how patient God is.

It is interesting to me that God is never in a hurry. Throughout the Scriptures, everyone else was in a hurry, but God never was. He is patient in the working out of His purposes. We will do well to be the same. His patience is comforting, and it brings hope.

GLORIFY GOD TOGETHER

[7]Therefore [a]receive one another, just [b]as Christ also received [1]us, to the glory of God. [8]Now I say that [a]Jesus Christ has become a [1]servant to the circumcision for the truth of God, [b]to confirm the promises *made* to the fathers, [9]and [a]that the Gentiles might glorify God for *His* mercy, as it is written:

---

20 [1] A feeling of giving offense

21 [a] 1 Cor. 8:13
[1] NU omits the rest of v. 21.

22 [a] [1 John 3:21]
[1] NU *The faith which you have*—*have*

23 [a] Titus 1:15
[1] M puts Rom. 16:25–27 here.

CHAPTER 15

1 [a] [Gal. 6:1, 2]
[1] *weaknesses*

2 [a] 1 Cor. 9:22; 10:24, 33
[1] *building up*

3 [a] Matt. 26:39
[b] Ps. 69:9

4 [a] 1 Cor. 10:11
[1] *perseverance*

5 [a] 1 Cor. 1:10

6 [a] Acts 4:24

7 [a] Rom. 14:1, 3
[b] Rom. 5:2
[1] NU, M *you*

8 [a] Matt. 15:24
[b] 2 Cor. 1:20
[1] *minister*

9 [a] John 10:16
[b] 2 Sam. 22.50;
Ps. 18:49

10 [a] Deut. 32:43

11 [a] Ps. 117:1

12 [a] Is. 11:1, 10

13 [a] Rom. 12:12; 14:17

14 [a] 2 Pet. 1:12
[b] 1 Cor. 1:5; 8:1, 7, 10
[1] M *others*

15 [a] Rom. 1:5; 12:3

16 [a] Rom. 11:13
[b] [Is. 66:20]
[1] *Consisting of*

17 [a] Heb. 2:17; 5:1

Rom. 15:7

Receive One Another. We are told to "receive one another, just as Christ also received us, to the glory of God." Ephesians 1:6 says that we are "accepted in the Beloved." He has accepted us. Then let us accept each other.

Let's not put up artificial barriers that divide us from the rest of the body of Christ. We need to break down these walls that men build to define their own territory. Let's leave it open for the whole body of Christ.

---

[b]*"For this reason I will confess to You among the Gentiles,*
And sing to Your name."

[10]And again he says:

[a]*"Rejoice, O Gentiles, with His people!"*

[11]And again:

[a]*"Praise the Lord, all you Gentiles! Laud Him, all you peoples!"*

[12]And again, Isaiah says:

[a]*"There shall be a root of Jesse;*
And He who shall rise to reign over the Gentiles,
In Him the Gentiles shall hope."

[13]Now may the God of hope fill you with all [a]joy and peace in believing, that you may abound in hope by the power of the Holy Spirit.

FROM JERUSALEM TO ILLYRICUM

[14]Now [a]I myself am confident concerning you, my brethren, that you also are full of goodness, [b]filled with all knowledge, able also to admonish [1]one another. [15]Nevertheless, brethren, I have written more boldly to you on *some* points, as reminding you, [a]because of the grace given to me by God, [16]that [a]I might be a minister of Jesus Christ to the Gentiles, ministering the gospel of God, that the [b]offering [1]of the Gentiles might be acceptable, sanctified by the Holy Spirit. [17]Therefore I have reason to glory in Christ Jesus [a]in the things *which pertain* to God. [18]For I will not dare to speak of any of those things

a which Christ has not accomplished through me, in word and deed, b to make the Gentiles obedient— 19 a in mighty signs and wonders, by the power of the Spirit of God, so that from Jerusalem and round about to Illyricum I have fully preached the gospel of Christ. 20 And so I have made it my aim to preach the gospel, not where Christ was named, a lest I should build on another man's foundation, 21 but as it is written:

a "*To whom He was not announced,
they shall see;
And those who have not heard
shall understand.*"

PLAN TO VISIT ROME

22 For this reason a I also have been much hindered from coming to you. 23 But now no longer having a place in these parts, and a having a great desire these many years to come to you, 24 whenever I journey to Spain, 1 I shall come to you. For I hope to see you on my journey, a and to be helped on my way there by you, if first I may b enjoy your *company* for a while. 25 But now a I am going to Jerusalem to 1 minister to the saints. 26 For a it pleased those from Macedonia and Achaia to make a certain contribution for the poor among the saints who are in Jerusalem. 27 It pleased them indeed, and they are their debtors. For a if the Gentiles have been partakers of their spiritual things, b their duty is also to minister to them in material things. 28 Therefore, when I have performed this and have sealed to them a this fruit, I shall go by way of you to Spain. 29 a But I know that when I come to you, I shall come in the fullness of the blessing 1 of the gospel of Christ. 30 Now I beg you, brethren, through the Lord Jesus Christ, and a through the love of the Spirit, b that you strive together with me in prayers to God for me, 31 a that I may be delivered from those in Judea who 1 do not believe, and that b my service for Jerusalem may be acceptable to the saints, 32 a that I may come to you with joy b by the will of God, and may c be refreshed together with you. 33 Now a the God of peace *be* with you all. Amen.

SISTER PHOEBE COMMENDED

16 I commend to you Phoebe our sister, who is a servant of the church in a Cenchrea, 2 a that you may receive her in the Lord b in a manner worthy of the saints, and assist her in

---

18 a Acts 15:12; 21:19
b Rom. 1:5

19 a Acts 19:11

20 a [2 Cor. 10:13, 15, 16]

21 a Is. 52:15

22 a Rom. 1:13

23 a Acts 19:21; 23:11

24 a Acts 15:3
b Rom. 1:12
1 NU omits *I shall come to you* and joins *Spain* with the next sentence.

25 a Acts 19:21
1 *serve*

26 a 1 Cor. 16:1

27 a Rom. 11:17
b 1 Cor. 9:11

28 a Phil. 4:17

29 a [Rom. 1:11]
1 NU omits *of the gospel*

30 a Phil. 2:1
b 2 Cor. 1:11

31 a 2 Tim. 3:11; 4:17
b 2 Cor. 8:4
1 *are disobedient*

32 a Rom. 1:10
b Acts 18:21
c 1 Cor. 16:18

33 a 1 Cor. 14:33

CHAPTER 16

1 a Acts 18:18

2 a Phil. 2:29
b Phil. 1:27

3 a Acts 18:2, 18, 26

5 a 1 Cor. 16:19

Rom. 15:30

Striving in Prayer. Paul didn't know what awaited him in Jerusalem, where he had a lot of enemies. So he requested that his fellow Christians "strive together with [him] in prayers to God for [him]." The word "strive" here is the Greek word *agonidzo* from which we get our English word "agonize." He begged them to agonize in prayer for him.

I don't know if you have ever really agonized in prayer, but there is a depth of prayer and intercession that is agonizing. And it is the fervent prayer of a righteous man that "avails much" (James 5:16).

---

whatever business she has need of you; for indeed she has been a helper of many and of myself also.

GREETING ROMAN SAINTS

3 Greet a Priscilla and Aquila, my fellow workers in Christ Jesus, 4 who risked their own necks for my life, to whom not only I give thanks, but also all the churches of the Gentiles. 5 Likewise *greet* a the church that is in their house.

Rom. 16:3–5

Priscilla and Aquila. Priscilla and Aquila were an interesting couple. They are mentioned six times in the New Testament. They had a home in Rome and one in Ephesus. They had a tent-making business, and Paul sometimes worked with them in their business. They helped teach Apollos when he was new in the ministry (Acts 18:26). They had a church that met in both of their homes. They were a wonderful couple who helped support Paul and ministered wherever they were.

How thankful I am for those faithful, anointed laymen who are raised up by God to assist in ministry.

Greet my beloved Epaenetus, who is [b]the firstfruits of [1]Achaia to Christ. [6]Greet Mary, who labored much for us. [7]Greet Andronicus and Junia, my countrymen and my fellow prisoners, who are of note among the [a]apostles, who also [b]were in Christ before me.

[8]Greet Amplias, my beloved in the Lord. [9]Greet Urbanus, our fellow worker in Christ, and Stachys, my beloved. [10]Greet Apelles, approved in Christ. Greet those who are of the *household* of Aristobulus. [11]Greet Herodion, my [1]countryman. Greet those who are of the *household* of Narcissus who are in the Lord.

[12]Greet Tryphena and Tryphosa, who have labored in the Lord. Greet the beloved Persis, who labored much in the Lord. [13]Greet Rufus, [a]chosen in the Lord, and his mother and mine. [14]Greet Asyncritus, Phlegon, Hermas, Patrobas, Hermes, and the brethren who are with them. [15]Greet Philologus and Julia, Nereus and his sister, and Olympas, and all the saints who are with them.

[16a]Greet one another with a holy kiss. [1]The churches of Christ greet you.

AVOID DIVISIVE PERSONS

[17]Now I urge you, brethren, note those [a]who cause divisions and offenses, contrary to the doctrine which you learned, and [b]avoid them. [18]For those who are such do not serve our Lord [1]Jesus Christ, but [a]their own belly, and [b]by smooth words and flattering speech deceive the hearts of the simple. [19]For [a]your obedience has become known to all. Therefore I am glad on your behalf; but I want you to be [b]wise in what is good, and [1]simple concerning evil. [20]And [a]the God of peace [b]will crush Satan under your feet shortly.

[c]The grace of our Lord Jesus Christ *be* with you. Amen.

GREETINGS FROM PAUL'S FRIENDS

[21a]Timothy, my fellow worker, and [b]Lucius, [c]Jason, and [d]Sosipater, my countrymen, greet you.

[22]I, Tertius, who wrote *this* epistle, greet you in the Lord.

[23a]Gaius, my host and *the host* of the whole church, greets you. [b]Erastus, the treasurer of the city, greets you, and Quartus, a brother. [24a]The[1] grace of our Lord Jesus Christ *be* with you all. Amen.

5 [b]1 Cor. 16:15
[1]NU *Asia*

7 [a]Acts 1:13, 26
[b]Gal. 1:22

11 [1]Or *relative*

13 [a]2 John 1

16 [a]1 Cor. 16:20
[1]NU *All the churches*

17 [a][Acts 15:1]
[b][1 Cor. 5:9]

18 [a]Phil. 3:19
[b]Col. 2:4
[1]NU, M omit *Jesus*

19 [a]Rom. 1:8
[b]Matt. 10:16
[1]*innocent*

20 [a]Rom. 15:33
[b]Gen. 3:15
[c]1 Cor. 16:23

21 [a]Acts 16:1
[b]Acts 13:1
[c]Acts 17:5
[d]Acts 20:4

23 [a]1 Cor. 1:14
[b]Acts 19:22

24 [a]1 Thess. 5:28
[1]NU omits v. 24.

25 [a][Eph. 3:20]
[b]Rom. 2:16
[c]Eph. 1:9
[d]Col. 1:26; 2:2; 4:3
[1]M puts Rom. 16:25–27 after Rom. 14:23.

26 [a]Eph. 1:9 [b]Rom. 1:5

27 [a]Jude 25

BENEDICTION

[25] [1]Now [a]to Him who is able to establish you [b]according to my gospel and the preaching of Jesus Christ, [c]according to the revelation of the mystery [d]kept secret since the world began [26]but [a]now made manifest, and by the prophetic Scriptures made known to all nations, according to the commandment of the everlasting God, for [b]obedience to the faith— [27]to [a]God, alone wise, *be* glory through Jesus Christ forever. Amen.

Rom. 16:19

WISE BUT SIMPLE

This is a good idea! "Be wise in what is good, and simple concerning evil."

Some people seem to have a morbid curiosity about evil things. They want to know all about the various practices of the world of evil. They are curious about séances, spiritism, and the occult. They want to learn more and more about these evil practices. There are some who feel that if you are going to minister to youth you need to watch MTV in order to understand what makes youth tick.

I would rather be wise in what is good, and innocent about evil. Why pollute your mind with garbage? There are many things that we'd be much better off not knowing about.

THE FIRST EPISTLE OF PAUL THE APOSTLE TO THE

CORINTHIANS

INTRODUCTION The book of 1 Corinthians was written by Paul around AD 56. Paul had founded the church in Corinth as it was described in the eighteenth chapter of the book of Acts. After starting the church in Corinth, Paul went on to Ephesus, from where he wrote this letter.

Corinth was a large city that had two major ports, and was an important center of trade in Greece. It was also known as an extremely immoral city. It was the location of a major temple for the goddess Aphrodite, which was mainly just a religious house of prostitution.

The church of Corinth was a church that was functioning in the middle of a horrible environment of debauchery, and the challenges to the church were enormous. The temptation to compromise and conform to the immoral world around them was huge, as it is in our society today.

Paul had received several reports of things that were happening within the Corinthian church that were particularly disturbing to him, and he wrote the letter to correct some of their misconduct. The church was characterized by a strong partisan spirit, with various people polarizing themselves around certain individuals. Unity was sorely lacking. There were serious moral problems, whereby the people of the church were priding themselves for being so tolerant of evil, neglecting the church discipline that is necessary for protecting the purity of the church. The people were abusing the Lord's Supper, sometimes using it as an occasion for getting drunk. And they were also confused about the resurrection of Jesus and about the future resurrection of Christians. They were very gifted people, but they were abusing spiritual gifts, exercising the gifts without control or restraint, and without love.

Some of the most helpful Scriptures are those that were written in response to errors or questions, and the book of 1 Corinthians gives us much useful information and instruction as Paul corrects their errors by laying the truth out in a straightforward and practical way. And when we read the book today we can't help but see the similarities between the church in Corinth and the modern-day church. As they were ridden with moral problems, false doctrine, and division, so today these same issues are those that threaten the effectiveness of the church. This is a practical book, relevant for us today, calling us to a pure faith and a walk of love.

GREETING

1 Paul, ᵃcalled *to be* an apostle of Jesus Christ ᵇthrough the will of God, and ᶜSosthenes *our* brother,

2 To the church of God which is at Corinth, to those who ᵃare *1*sanctified in Christ Jesus, ᵇcalled *to be* saints, with all who in every place call on the name of Jesus Christ ᶜour Lord, ᵈboth theirs and ours:

3 ᵃGrace to you and peace from God our Father and the Lord Jesus Christ.

SPIRITUAL GIFTS AT CORINTH

4 ᵃI thank my God always concerning you for the grace of God which was given to you by Christ Jesus, 5 that you were enriched in everything by Him ᵃin all *1*utterance and all knowledge, 6 even as ᵃthe testimony of Christ was confirmed *1*in you, 7 so that you come short in no gift, eagerly ᵃwaiting for the revelation of our Lord Jesus Christ, 8 ᵃwho will also confirm you to the end, ᵇ*that you may be* blameless in the day of our Lord Jesus Christ. 9 ᵃGod *is* faithful, by whom you were called into ᵇthe fellowship of His Son, Jesus Christ our Lord.

SECTARIANISM IS SIN

10 Now I plead with you, brethren, by the name of our Lord Jesus Christ, ᵃthat you all *1*speak the same thing, and *that* there be no *2*divisions among you, but *that* you be perfectly joined together in the same mind and in the same judgment. 11 For it has been declared to me concerning you, my

CHAPTER 1

1 ᵃRom. 1:1
ᵇ2 Cor. 1:1
ᶜActs 18:17

2 ᵃ[Acts 15:9]
ᵇRom. 1:7
ᶜ[1 Cor. 8:6]
ᵈ[Rom. 3:22]
1 set apart

3 ᵃRom. 1:7

4 ᵃRom. 1:8

5 ᵃ[1 Cor. 12:8]
1 speech

6 ᵃ2 Tim. 1:8
1 Or *among*

7 ᵃPhil. 3:20

8 ᵃ1 Thess. 3:13; 5:23
ᵇCol. 1:22; 2:7

9 ᵃIs. 49:7
ᵇ[John 15:4]

10 ᵃ2 Cor. 13:11
1 Have a uniform testimony
2 schisms or dissensions

11 *1* quarrels

12 ᵃ1 Cor. 3:4
ᵇActs 18:24
ᶜJohn 1:42

13 ᵃ2 Cor. 11:4

14 ᵃJohn 4:2
ᵇActs 18:8
ᶜRom. 16:23

16 ᵃ1 Cor. 16:15, 17

17 ᵃ[1 Cor. 2:1, 4, 13]

---

1 Cor. 1:14–17

Paul and Baptism. In the context of division in the body, Paul talked about baptism, one of the things that was a source of division among the church, even as it is today. He took an almost flippant attitude about it, saying that he had only baptized a few of them, and he couldn't even remember how many. "Christ did not send me to baptize, but to preach the gospel." This presents a real problem for those who teach that baptism is needed for salvation. Paul was making it clear that baptism is not a part of the gospel.

brethren, by those of Chloe's *household*, that there are *1*contentions among you. 12 Now I say this, that ᵃeach of you says, "I am of Paul," or "I am of ᵇApollos," or "I am of ᶜCephas," or "I am of Christ." 13 ᵃIs Christ divided? Was Paul crucified for you? Or were you baptized in the name of Paul?

14 I thank God that I baptized ᵃnone of you except ᵇCrispus and ᶜGaius, 15 lest anyone should say that I had baptized in my own name. 16 Yes, I also baptized the household of ᵃStephanas. Besides, I do not know whether I baptized any other. 17 For Christ did not send me to baptize, but to preach the gospel, ᵃnot with wisdom of words, lest

---

DIVISIONS AND CONTENTIONS   1 Cor. 1:10–13

Paul had heard that there were divisions in the body in Corinth, and he was pleading with them for unity.

There is a great variety among Christians, and this is a beautiful thing. There are some people who relate to God in a formal, liturgical way. Others enjoy a more casual worship atmosphere. Some people enjoy a more academic approach to Bible teaching, while others lean more toward a devotional perspective.

It is great that we have different types of churches to meet the needs of different people. But the problem comes in when the different groups begin to argue and fight, looking down on those who are different. This leads to the state Paul said Corinth was in: "There are contentions among you." There is nothing wrong with denominations. The problem comes in when the various denominations and churches become argumentative and divisive over their differences.

We can be different and express those differences; but we also need to be one in Christ, loving each other, accepting each other, praying for each other, and supporting each other.

the cross of Christ should be made of no effect.

CHRIST THE POWER AND WISDOM OF GOD

18For the 1message of the cross is afoolishness to bthose who are perishing, but to us cwho are being saved it is the dpower of God. 19For it is written:

a"*I will destroy the wisdom of the wise,*
And bring to nothing the understanding of the prudent."

20aWhere is the wise? Where is the scribe? Where is the 1disputer of this age? bHas not God made foolish the wisdom of this world? 21For since, in the awisdom of God, the world through wisdom did not know God, it pleased God through the foolishness of the message preached to save those who believe. 22For aJews request a sign, and Greeks seek after wisdom; 23but we preach Christ crucified, ato the Jews a 1stumbling block and to the 2Greeks bfoolishness, 24but to those who are

---

1 Cor. 1:26–29

CHOOSING THE FOOLISH

God didn't choose many of the "wise according to the flesh." There are some exceptions, but most of us are not college professors with doctorates. God usually chooses plain, simple people. And why does He choose that way? "That no flesh should glory in His presence."

If I were some great scholar, with several advanced degrees from Harvard and Oxford, people would see what God has done and say, "My, Harvard is some institution to turn out someone like this." But when they see what God has done and realize that I am just a regular guy without an Ivy League education, then they say, "That is amazing! God can use a simple guy like this?" And the glory is God's for the great things He has done!

---

18 a 1 Cor. 2:14
b 2 Cor. 2:15
c [1 Cor. 15:2]
d Rom. 1:16
1 Lit. *word*

19 a Is. 29:14

20 a Is. 19:12; 33:18
b Job 12:17
1 *debater*

21 a Dan. 2:20

22 a Matt. 12:38

23 a Luke 2:34
b [1 Cor. 2:14]
1 Gr. *skandalon, offense*
2 NU *Gentiles*

24 a [Rom. 1:4]
b Col. 2:3

26 a John 7:48
1 *consider*
2 *well-born*

27 a Matt. 11:25

28 1 *insignificant or lowly*

30 a [2 Cor. 5:21]

31 a Jer. 9:23, 24

CHAPTER 2

1 1 NU *mystery*

2 a Gal. 6:14

3 a Acts 18:1
b [2 Cor. 4:7]

4 a 2 Pet. 1:16
b Rom. 15:19
1 NU omits *human*

5 a 1 Thess. 1:5

---

called, both Jews and Greeks, Christ athe power of God and bthe wisdom of God. 25Because the foolishness of God is wiser than men, and the weakness of God is stronger than men.

GLORY ONLY IN THE LORD

26For 1you see your calling, brethren, athat not many wise according to the flesh, not many mighty, not many 2noble, are called. 27But aGod has chosen the foolish things of the world to put to shame the wise, and God has chosen the weak things of the world to put to shame the things which are mighty; 28and the 1base things of the world and the things which are despised God has chosen, and the things which are not, to bring to nothing the things that are, 29that no flesh should glory in His presence. 30But of Him you are in Christ Jesus, who became for us wisdom from God—and arighteousness and sanctification and redemption— 31that, as it is written, a"*He who glories, let him glory in the LORD.*"

CHRIST CRUCIFIED

2 And I, brethren, when I came to you, did not come with excellence of speech or of wisdom declaring to you the 1testimony of God. 2For I determined not to know anything among you aexcept Jesus Christ and Him crucified. 3aI was with you bin weakness, in fear, and in much trembling. 4And my speech and my preaching awere not with persuasive words of 1human wisdom, bbut in demonstration of the Spirit and of power, 5that your faith should not be in the wisdom of men but in the apower of God.

---

1 Cor. 2:1–2

Jesus Christ, and Him Crucified. When Paul came to Corinth, which was the academic and philosophical center of the world at that time, he didn't come with fancy speeches or deep philosophical discourses. He was highly educated, and certainly capable of impressing people with his intellectual prowess. But he chose rather to preach a simple message about Jesus Christ, who gave His life for them. That is all that really matters, in the final analysis. Jesus died for you.

SPIRITUAL WISDOM

6However, we speak wisdom among those who are mature, yet not the wisdom of this age, nor of the rulers of this age, who are coming to nothing. 7But we speak the wisdom of God in a mystery, the hidden *wisdom* which God 1ordained before the ages for our glory, 8which none of the rulers of this age knew; for ahad they known, they would not have bcrucified the Lord of glory.

9But as it is written:

a"*Eye has not seen, nor ear heard,*
Nor have entered into the heart of
man
The things which God has
prepared for those who love
Him."

---

1 Cor. 2:9

Eye Has Not Seen. How often we have heard this verse quoted concerning heaven! "Eye has not seen, nor ear heard, nor have entered into the heart of man the things which God has prepared for those who love Him." It certainly applies to heaven; but, in context, it is talking about what we have right now because of the cross.

People are blind to the glorious grace and forgiveness of God that could be theirs if they would only accept Jesus. How many of us really appreciate what we have right here and now?

10But aGod has revealed *them* to us through His Spirit. For the Spirit searches all things, yes, the deep things of God. 11For what man knows the things of a man except the aspirit of the man which is in him? bEven so no one knows the things of God except the Spirit of God. 12Now we have received, not the spirit of the world, but athe Spirit who is from God, that we might know the things that have been freely given to us by God. 13These things we also speak, not in words which man's wisdom teaches but which the 1Holy Spirit teaches, comparing spiritual things with spiritual. 14aBut the natural man does not receive the things of the Spirit of God,

---

Marginal references:

7 1 predetermined

8 a Luke 23:34
b Matt. 27:33–50

9 a [Is. 64:4; 65:17]

10 a Matt. 11:25; 13:11; 16:17

11 a [James 2:26]
b Rom. 11:33

12 a [Rom. 8:15]

13 1 NU omits Holy

14 a Matt. 16:23

16 a Is. 40:13
b [John 15:15]

CHAPTER 3

1 a Heb. 5:13

2 a 1 Pet. 2:2
b John 16:12

---

1 Cor. 2:13–14

Spiritual Discernment. The things of the Lord cannot be understood apart from the supernatural work of the Holy Spirit. It isn't just that the natural man chooses not to understand or doesn't take the time to understand, but he can't know them because they are spiritually discerned.

This is why it is fruitless to try to argue with non-Christians about Christian theology. They don't have the spiritual capacity to understand. What they need to hear is the simple gospel of Jesus Christ. Anything else is putting the cart before the horse.

---

for they are foolishness to him; nor can he know *them*, because they are spiritually discerned. 15But he who is spiritual judges all things, yet he himself is *rightly* judged by no one. 16For a"*who has known the mind of the LORD that he may instruct Him?*" bBut we have the mind of Christ.

SECTARIANISM IS CARNAL

3 And I, brethren, could not speak to you as to spiritual *people* but as to carnal, as to ababes in Christ. 2I fed you with amilk and not with solid food; bfor

---

1 Cor. 3:1–4

The Marks of Carnality. The Corinthian Christians were carnal and fleshly. Paul called them babies and said he couldn't teach them the things they really needed to learn because they hadn't even mastered the basics of Christianity. What was the evidence of their carnality and immaturity? They had envy, strife, and divisions among them.

Not much has changed in almost two thousand years. Churches are still marked by the evidence of carnality, as we see envy, strife, and divisions. Isn't it time we grew up?

until now you were not able *to receive it*, and even now you are still not able; [3]for you are still carnal. For where *there are* envy, strife, and divisions among you, are you not carnal and [1]behaving like *mere* men? [4]For when one says, "I am of Paul," and another, "I *am* of Apollos," are you not carnal?

WATERING, WORKING, WARNING

[5]Who then is Paul, and who *is* Apollos, but [a]ministers through whom you believed, as the Lord gave to each one? [6a]I planted, [b]Apollos watered, [c]but God gave the increase. [7]So then [a]neither he who plants is anything, nor he who waters, but God who gives the increase. [8]Now he who plants and he who waters are one, [a]and each one will receive his own reward according to his own labor.

[9]For [a]we are God's fellow workers; you are God's field, *you are* [b]God's building. [10a]According to the grace of God which was given to me, as a wise master builder I have laid [b]the foundation, and another builds on it. But let each one take heed how he builds on it. [11]For no other foundation can anyone lay than [a]that which is laid, [b]which is

---

1 Cor. 3:11–15

BUILDING ON THE FOUNDATION

Jesus Christ is our foundation and everything we do in this life builds on that foundation.

We can build with gold, silver, and precious stones, or with wood, hay, and straw. In other words, we can use permanent materials or disposable materials, as we build our lives. But when this life is over and we face the Lord, what we have done for eternity will last and give us rewards. What we have done that was temporal and earthly will be gone, and we will lose the rewards we could have received, had we lived our lives with eternity in mind.

Are you doing things today that will matter for eternity? If not, then you are wasting valuable time.

Marginal references:

3 [1] Lit. *walking according to man*

5 [a] 2 Cor. 3:3, 6; 4:1; 5:18; 6:4

6 [a] Acts 18:4 [b] Acts 18:24–27 [c] [2 Cor. 3:5]

7 [a] [Gal. 6:3]

8 [a] Ps. 62:12

9 [a] 2 Cor. 6:1 [b] [Eph. 2:20–22]

10 [a] Rom. 1:5 [b] 1 Cor. 4:15

11 [a] Is. 28:16 [b] Eph. 2:20

13 [a] 1 Pet. 1:7 [b] Luke 2:35

16 [a] 2 Cor. 6:16

17 [1] *destroys*

18 [a] Prov. 3:7

19 [a] Job 5:13

20 [a] Ps. 94:11

21 [a] [2 Cor. 4:5]

Jesus Christ. [12]Now if anyone builds on this foundation *with* gold, silver, precious stones, wood, hay, straw, [13]each one's work will become clear; for the Day [a]will declare it, because [b]it will be revealed by fire; and the fire will test each one's work, of what sort it is. [14]If anyone's work which he has built on *it* endures, he will receive a reward. [15]If anyone's work is burned, he will suffer loss; but he himself will be saved, yet so as through fire. [16a]Do you not know that you are the temple of God and *that* the Spirit of God dwells in you? [17]If anyone [1]defiles the temple of God, God will destroy him. For the temple of God is holy, which *temple* you are.

---

1 Cor. 3:16–17

TEMPLE OF GOD

If you are a child of God, the Holy Spirit lives inside you. You are a temple of God. And Paul here reminded his readers that the temple of God is holy and shouldn't be mistreated or defiled.

Some people use this passage to teach against smoking cigarettes. That could certainly be a good application; but to be consistent, we should include candy bars and everything else that is bad for us.

What Paul was really talking about here was the abuse of our bodies that takes place as we use our bodies for immoral behavior. Our bodies are His holy temples, and we need to keep them pure.

AVOID WORLDLY WISDOM

[18a]Let no one deceive himself. If anyone among you seems to be wise in this age, let him become a fool that he may become wise. [19]For the wisdom of this world is foolishness with God. For it is written, [a]*"He catches the wise in their own craftiness"*; [20]and again, [a]*"The LORD knows the thoughts of the wise, that they are futile."* [21]Therefore let no one boast in men. For [a]all things are yours: [22]whether Paul or Apollos or Cephas, or the world or life or death, or things present or things to come—all

are yours. 23And ayou *are* Christ's, and Christ *is* God's.

STEWARDS OF THE MYSTERIES OF GOD

4 Let a man so consider us, as aservants of Christ band stewards of the mysteries of God. 2Moreover it is required in stewards that one be found faithful. 3But with me it is a very small thing that I should be judged by you or by a human 1court. In fact, I do not even judge myself. 4For I know of nothing against myself, yet I am not justified by this; but He who judges me is the Lord. 5aTherefore judge nothing before the time, until the Lord comes, who will both bring to blight the hidden things of darkness and creveal the 1counsels of the hearts. dThen each one's praise will come from God.

---

1 Cor. 4:2

Requirement of a Steward. The primary requirement of a steward was that he be faithful to his master. When someone entrusts responsibility to you, you are expected to do what you are told to do.

Jesus told many parables about stewards, some who were faithful and some who weren't. We are stewards of God, and He has entrusted us with carrying on His work. We aren't required to be brilliant, or even successful. That is His department. We are just required to be faithful, carrying out our duties as stewards.

FOOLS FOR CHRIST'S SAKE

6Now these things, brethren, I have figuratively transferred to myself and Apollos for your sakes, that you may learn in us not to think beyond what is written, that none of you may be 1puffed up on behalf of one against the other. 7For who 1makes you differ *from another*? And awhat do you have that you did not receive? Now if you did indeed receive *it*, why do you boast as if you had not received *it*?

8You are already full! aYou are already rich! You have reigned as kings without us—and indeed I could wish you did reign, that we also might reign with you! 9For I think that God

---

23 a2Cor. 10:7

CHAPTER 4

1 aCol. 1:25
b Titus 1:7

3 1Lit. *day*

5 aMatt. 7:1
b Matt. 10:26
c 1Cor. 3:13
d Rom. 2:29
1 *motives*

6 1*arrogant*

7 aJohn 3:27
1 *distinguishes you*

8 aRev. 3:17

9 aHeb. 10:33
1Lit. *theater*

10 aActs 17:18;
26:24
b2Cor. 13:9

12 aActs 18:3;
20:34
b Matt. 5:44

13 aLam. 3:45
1*exhort,
encourage*

14 a1Thess.
2:11

15 aGal. 4:19

16 a[1Cor.
11:1]

---

1 Cor. 4:6–7

WHO MAKES YOU DIFFERENT?

Members of the church at Corinth were bragging and boasting about how they were better than others. But Paul asked them, "Who makes you differ from another? And what do you have that you did not receive? Now if you did indeed receive it, why do you boast as if you had not received it?"

Everything we have was given to us by God. Our talents, our abilities, our knowledge, our gifts, our possessions, are all from God. It is so foolish when we think we are better than someone else because our talents, abilities, knowledge, gifts, and possessions are superior to theirs. Ours were given to us by the One who tells us not to think more highly of ourselves than we think of others (Phil. 2:3–4).

has displayed us, the apostles, last, as men condemned to death; for we have been made a aspectacle1 to the world, both to angels and to men. 10We *are* afools for Christ's sake, but you *are* wise in Christ! bWe *are* weak, but you *are* strong! You *are* distinguished, but we *are* dishonored! 11To the present hour we both hunger and thirst, and we are poorly clothed, and beaten, and homeless. 12aAnd we labor, working with our own hands. bBeing reviled, we bless; being persecuted, we endure; 13being defamed, we 1entreat. aWe have been made as the filth of the world, the offscouring of all things until now.

PAUL'S PATERNAL CARE

14I do not write these things to shame you, but aas my beloved children I warn *you*. 15For though you might have ten thousand instructors in Christ, yet *you do* not *have* many fathers; for ain Christ Jesus I have begotten you through the gospel. 16Therefore I urge you, aimitate me.

YOUR SPIRITUAL FATHER

Paul appealed to Corinthian Christians as his children in the faith, since he was the one who had led them to the Lord. They had many instructors (he suggested that they might have ten thousand instructors in Christ), but they had only one father, since Paul was the one who had led them to Christ. Many of these other instructors were leading the people astray, teaching them things that were contrary to sound doctrine. And in the process they were defaming Paul, teaching that he was not worth listening to.

Over the years I have seen many thousands of people come to a knowledge of Jesus Christ here at Calvary Chapel. Many of them move on to other places and are taught by other people. And that is great. I don't want to be their only teacher for life. But it is sad when some of them get under the teaching of a person who leads them astray, and then they come to me and try to teach me all that they have learned. They try to show me how I have been wrong all these years and that I need to follow them.

I really don't doubt their sincerity at all. But I find it tragic when I see those who I once fathered in the faith but are now led astray by those who desire to attract a following by pulling people from the simple Word of God into some complex intellectual nonsense. It is enough to break a father's heart.

17For this reason I have sent aTimothy to you, bwho is my beloved and faithful son in the Lord, who will cremind you of my ways in Christ, as I dteach everywhere ein every church. 18aNow some are 1puffed up, as though I were not coming to you. 19aBut I will come to you shortly, bif the Lord wills, and I will know, not the word of those who are puffed up, but the power. 20For athe kingdom of God is not in word but in bpower. 21What do you want? aShall I come to you with a rod, or in love and a spirit of gentleness?

IMMORALITY DEFILES THE CHURCH

5 It is actually reported that there is sexual immorality among you, and such sexual immorality as is not even 1named among the Gentiles—that a man has his father's awife! 2aAnd you are 1puffed up, and have not rather bmourned, that he who has done this deed might be taken away from among you. 3aFor I indeed, as absent in body but present in spirit, have already judged (as though I were present) him who has so done this deed. 4In the aname of our Lord Jesus Christ, when you are gathered together, along with my spirit, bwith the power of our Lord Jesus Christ, 5adeliver such a one to bSatan for the destruction of the flesh, that his spirit may be saved in the day of the Lord 1Jesus.
6aYour glorying is not good. Do you not know that ba little leaven leavens the whole lump? 7Therefore 1purge out

the old leaven, that you may be a new lump, since you truly are unleavened. For indeed aChrist, our bPassover, was sacrificed 2for us. 8Therefore alet us keep the feast, bnot with old leaven, nor cwith the leaven of malice and wickedness, but with the unleavened bread of sincerity and truth.

IMMORALITY MUST BE JUDGED

9I wrote to you in my epistle anot to 1keep company with sexually immoral people. 10Yet I certainly did not mean

---

17 a Acts 19:22
b 1 Tim. 1:2, 18
c 1 Cor. 11:2
d 1 Cor. 7:17
e 1 Cor. 14:33

18 a 1 Cor. 5:2
1 arrogant

19 a Acts 19:21; 20:2
b Acts 18:21

20 a 1 Thess. 1:5
b 1 Cor. 2:4

21 a 2 Cor. 10:2

CHAPTER 5

1 a Lev. 18:6–8
1 NU omits named

2 a 1 Cor. 4:18
b 2 Cor. 7:7–10
1 arrogant

3 a Col. 2:5

4 a [Matt. 18:20]
b [John 20:23]

5 a 1 Tim. 1:20
b [Acts 26:18]
1 NU omits Jesus

6 a 1 Cor. 3:21
b Gal. 5:9

7 a Is. 53:7
b John 19:14
1 clean out
2 NU omits for us

8 a Ex. 12:15
b Deut. 16:3
c Matt. 16:6

9 a 2 Cor. 6:14
1 associate

---

1 Cor. 5:1–2

Proud of Tolerance. There was an evil, incestuous relationship going on within the Corinthian church. The people should have been mournful. It should have bro -ken their hearts that such a thing was occurring. Instead, they were not only tolerant of the sin, but they were proud to be so tolerant.

In our society today, even within churches, there is often a pride in our tolerance of sin. We should be embarrassed to stand by and let people destroy themselves without speaking up and taking action. Ignoring destructive sin in the body is nothing to be proud of.

1 Cor. 5:5

EXCOMMUNICATION

Paul told the Corinthians to remove the immoral person from their midst. "Deliver such a one to Satan for the destruction of the flesh, that his spirit may be saved in the day of the Lord Jesus." The idea is to cut the immoral person off from Christian fellowship, so that they can realize what the fleshly life does to a person. As they experience the isolation and realize what it feels like to be alienated from the body of Christ and from fellowship, they will then hopefully repent of their sins and turn back to the Lord.

The goal of all church discipline should be restoration. It worked in this case, as Paul later encouraged them to love this man and to reinstate him to fellowship (2 Cor. 2:6–9). Church discipline fails if we neglect to use it, instead ignoring sin within the body, or if we hammer people with their failure and never give them an opportunity to be restored. It works if we apply it in a biblical way, with a heart of love and restoration.

with the sexually immoral people of this world, or with the covetous, or extortioners, or idolaters, since then you would need to go ªout of the world. ¹¹But now I have written to you not to keep company ªwith anyone named a brother, who is sexually immoral, or covetous, or an idolater, or a reviler, or a drunkard, or an extortioner—ᵇnot even to eat with such a person.

¹²For what *have* I *to do* with judging those also who are outside? Do you not judge those who are inside? ¹³But those who are outside God judges. Therefore ª*"put away from yourselves the evil person."*

DO NOT SUE THE BRETHREN

6 Dare any of you, having a matter against another, go to law before the unrighteous, and not before the ªsaints? ²Do you not know that ªthe

---

10 ª John 17:15

11 ª Matt. 18:17
ᵇ Gal. 2:12

13 ª Deut. 13:5;
17:7, 12; 19:19;
21:21; 22:21,
24; 24:7

CHAPTER 6

1 ª Dan. 7:22

2 ª Ps. 49:14

3 ª 2 Pet. 2:4

4 ¹ *courts*

7 ª [Prov. 20:22]

9 ª Gal. 5:21
¹ *catamites,*
those submitting
to homosexuals
² *male homo-sexuals*

11 ª [1 Cor.
12:2]
ᵇ Heb. 10:22
¹ *set apart*

12 ª 1 Cor.
10:23
¹ *profitable*
² Or *anything*

---

1 Cor. 5:12–13

Judging Outsiders. It isn't our job to fix the world. It is our job to share the gospel with the world. I don't make rules for how the world should live. I think it is a mistake to endeavor to write Christian legislation. You can't make men holy with laws. They need a change of heart.

We can't fix the world by judging it, but rather by introducing them to the One who can change them from the inside. The changed believer will change the world.

saints will judge the world? And if the world will be judged by you, are you unworthy to judge the smallest matters? ³Do you not know that we shall ªjudge angels? How much more, things that pertain to this life? ⁴If then you have ¹judgments concerning things pertaining to this life, do you appoint those who are least esteemed by the church to judge? ⁵I say this to your shame. Is it so, that there is not a wise man among you, not even one, who will be able to judge between his brethren? ⁶But brother goes to law against brother, and that before unbelievers!

⁷Now therefore, it is already an utter failure for you that you go to law against one another. ªWhy do you not rather accept wrong? Why do you not rather *let yourselves* be cheated? ⁸No, you yourselves do wrong and cheat, and *you do* these things *to your* brethren! ⁹Do you not know that the unrighteous will not inherit the kingdom of God? Do not be deceived. ªNeither fornicators, nor idolaters, nor adulterers, nor ¹homosexuals, nor ²sodomites, ¹⁰nor thieves, nor covetous, nor drunkards, nor revilers, nor extortioners will inherit the kingdom of God. ¹¹And such were ªsome of you. ᵇBut you were washed, but you were ¹sanctified, but you were justified in the name of the Lord Jesus and by the Spirit of our God.

GLORIFY GOD IN BODY AND SPIRIT

¹²ªAll things are lawful for me, but all things are not ¹helpful. All things are lawful for me, but I will not be brought under the power of ²any.

TAKING YOUR BROTHER TO COURT

1 Cor. 6:1–7

It is a shame when Christians are not able to settle their disagreements within the church and instead go to the secular courts to solve their problems. What a horrible witness it is if we can't solve our problems without worldly help! The judicial system is so inept anyway, why would we ever turn to them for help?

Paul said in verse 7, "It is already an utter failure for you that you go to law against one another. Why do you not rather accept wrong?" In other words, if you go to court, you have lost already. So take the loss and move on. At least, you haven't been a bad witness to the nonbelievers who see what is happening and to those in the legal system.

So if you have a dispute with a brother, try to resolve it within the church. Today we have Christian arbitration as a viable option, to avoid the courts. That is the way it should be. It is shameful when we can't work things out among Christians.

13 aFoods for the stomach and the stomach for foods, but God will destroy both it and them. Now the body *is* not for bsexual immorality but cfor the Lord, dand the Lord for the body. 14And aGod both raised up the Lord and will also raise us up bby His power.

15Do you not know that ayour bodies are members of Christ? Shall I then take the members of Christ and make *them* members of a harlot? Certainly not! 16Or do you not know that he who is joined to a harlot is one body *with her*? For a*"the two,"* He says, *"shall become one flesh."* 17aBut he who is joined to the Lord is one spirit *with Him.*

18aFlee sexual immorality. Every sin that a man does is outside the body, but he who commits sexual immorality sins bagainst his own body. 19Or ado you not know that your body is the temple of the Holy Spirit *who is* in you, whom you have from God, band you are not your own? 20For ayou were bought at a price; therefore glorify God in your body 1and in your spirit, which are God's.

PRINCIPLES OF MARRIAGE

7 Now concerning the things of which you wrote to me:
aIt is good for a man not to touch a

Notes (center column):

13 a Matt. 15:17
b Gal. 5:19
c 1 Thess. 4:3
d [Eph. 5:23]

14 a 2 Cor. 4:14
b Eph. 1:19

15 a Rom. 12:5

16 a Gen. 2:24

17 a [John 17:21–23]

18 a Heb. 13:4
b Rom. 1:24

19 a 2 Cor. 6:16
b Rom. 14:7

20 a 2 Pet. 2:1
1 NU omits the rest of v. 20.

CHAPTER 7

1 a 1 Cor. 7:8, 26

---

1 Cor. 6:9–11

Don't Be Deceived. There were people who were fooling themselves into thinking that they could live in immorality and still be Christians. Paul made it clear that fornicators, idolaters, adulterers, homosexuals, sodomites, thieves, covetous, drunkards, revilers, and extortioners will not "inherit the kingdom of God." That was a part of your past life. "But you were washed, but you were sanctified, but you were justified."

If you are God's child, He will clean up your life. Don't fool yourself.

---

1 Cor. 6:12

BROUGHT UNDER THE POWER

As a Christian, I have been set free from the bondage of the flesh and the slavery to sin. I have the most incredible liberty. How much more free can you get than to say, "All things are lawful for me"? But Paul said that he wouldn't exercise his freedom in a way that would bring him back into bondage.

I am so free in Jesus Christ! I can do whatever I want. But I don't want to do things that enslave me. It would be foolish if, after being set free, you were to sell yourself into slavery again. "I will not be brought under the power of any."

woman. 2Nevertheless, because of sexual immorality, let each man have his own wife, and let each woman have her own husband. 3aLet the husband render to his wife the affection due her, and likewise also the wife to her husband. 4The wife does not have authority over her own body, but the husband *does*. And likewise the husband does not have authority over his own body, but the wife *does*. 5aDo not deprive one another except with consent for a time, that you may give yourselves to fasting and prayer; and come together again so that bSatan does not tempt you because of your lack of self-control. 6But I say this as a concession, anot as a commandment. 7For aI wish that all men were even as I myself. But each one has his own gift from God, one in this manner and another in that.

8But I say to the unmarried and to the widows: aIt is good for them if they remain even as I am; 9but aif they cannot exercise self-control, let them marry. For it is better to marry than to burn *with passion.*

---

1 Cor. 7:7–9

The Gift of Celibacy. God had given Paul the gift of celibacy, where he was able to handle being single for the rest of his life. And he saw that, in his situation, with everything he had to deal with, it was very convenient for him to have that gift. But he said that not everyone has this gift; and if you are burning with passion, and you just can't handle the temptation of being single, "it is better to marry than to burn with passion." Celibacy is a useful gift, but it's not for everyone.

KEEP YOUR MARRIAGE VOWS

10Now to the married I command, *yet* not I but the aLord: bA wife is not to depart from *her* husband. 11But even if she does depart, let her remain unmarried or be reconciled to *her* husband. And a husband is not to divorce *his* wife.

12But to the rest I, not the Lord, say: If any brother has a wife who does not believe, and she is willing to live with him, let him not divorce her. 13And a woman who has a husband who does

---

Cross-references (center column):

3 a Ex. 21:10

5 a Joel 2:16
b 1 Thess. 3:5

6 a 2 Cor. 8:8

7 a Acts 26:29

8 a 1 Cor. 7:1, 26

9 a 1 Tim. 5:14

10 a Mark 10:6–10
b [Matt. 5:32]

14 a Mal. 2:15

15 a Rom. 12:18

16 a 1 Pet. 3:1

17 a 1 Cor. 4:17
1 *direct*

18 a Acts 15:1

19 a [Gal. 3:28; 5:6; 6:15]
b [John 15:14]

---

not believe, if he is willing to live with her, let her not divorce him. 14For the unbelieving husband is sanctified by the wife, and the unbelieving wife is sanctified by the husband; otherwise ayour children would be unclean, but now they are holy. 15But if the unbeliever departs, let him depart; a brother or a sister is not under bondage in such *cases.* But God has called us ato peace. 16For how do you know, O wife, whether you will asave *your* husband? Or how do you know, O husband, whether you will save *your* wife?

---

1 Cor. 7:14

SANCTIFIED BY ASSOCIATION

In discussing Christians who are married to unbelievers, Paul told them to not just automatically leave their spouse because they aren't saved. "For the unbelieving husband is sanctified by the wife, and the unbelieving wife is sanctified by the husband." This doesn't mean that they are saved just because they are married to a Christian. The word "sanctified" means "to be set apart."

If you are married to a Christian who lives a godly and exemplary life, you are in a unique situation, as you get to see the reality of Jesus up close and personal. It is an advantage to have that kind of example, and it can lead to salvation (v. 16).

LIVE AS YOU ARE CALLED

17But as God has distributed to each one, as the Lord has called each one, so let him walk. And aso I 1ordain in all the churches. 18Was anyone called while circumcised? Let him not become uncircumcised. Was anyone called while uncircumcised? aLet him not be circumcised. 19aCircumcision is nothing and uncircumcision is nothing, but bkeeping the commandments of God *is what matters.* 20Let each one remain in the same calling in which he was called. 21Were you called *while* a slave? Do not be concerned about it; but if you

can be made free, rather use it. ²²For he who is called in the Lord while a slave is ^athe Lord's freedman. Likewise he who is called while free is ^bChrist's slave. ^{23 a}You were bought at a price; do not become slaves of men. ²⁴Brethren, let each one remain with ^aGod in that state in which he was called.

TO THE UNMARRIED AND WIDOWS

²⁵Now concerning virgins: ^aI have no commandment from the Lord; yet I give judgment as one ^bwhom the Lord in His mercy has made ^ctrustworthy. ²⁶I suppose therefore that this is good because of the present distress—^athat it is good for a man to remain as he is: ²⁷Are you bound to a wife? Do not seek to be loosed. Are you loosed from a wife? Do not seek a wife. ²⁸But even if you do marry, you have not sinned; and if a virgin marries, she has not sinned. Nevertheless such will have trouble in the flesh, but I would spare you.

²⁹But ^athis I say, brethren, the time is short, so that from now on even those who have wives should be as though they had none, ³⁰those who weep as though they did not weep, those who rejoice as though they did not rejoice, those who buy as though they did not possess, ³¹and those who use this world as not ^amisusing it. For ^bthe form of this world is passing away.

³²But I want you to be without ¹care. ^aHe who is unmarried ²cares for the things of the Lord—how he may please the Lord. ³³But he who is married cares about the things of the world— how he may please his wife. ³⁴There is a difference between a wife and a virgin. The unmarried woman ^acares about the things of the Lord, that she may be holy both in body and in spirit. But she who is married cares about the things of the world—how she may please her husband. ³⁵And this I say for your own profit, not that I may put a leash on you, but for what is proper, and that you may serve the Lord without distraction.

³⁶But if any man thinks he is behaving improperly toward his ¹virgin, if she is past the flower of youth, and thus it must be, let him do what he wishes. He does not sin; let them marry. ³⁷Nevertheless he who stands steadfast in his heart, having no necessity, but has power over his own will, and has so determined in his heart that he will keep his ¹virgin, does well.

22 ^a[John 8:36]
^b1 Pet. 2:16

23 ^a1 Pet. 1:18, 19

24 ^a[Col. 3:22–24]

25 ^a2 Cor. 8:8
^b1 Tim. 1:13, 16
^c1 Tim. 1:12

26 ^a1 Cor. 7:1, 8

29 ^a1 Pet. 4:7

31 ^a1 Cor. 9:18
^b[1 John 2:17]

32 ^a1 Tim. 5:5
¹concern
²is concerned about

34 ^aLuke 10:40

36 ¹Or virgin daughter

37 ¹Or virgin daughter

38 ^aHeb. 13:4
¹NU his own virgin

39 ^aRom. 7:2
^b2 Cor. 6:14

40 ^a1 Cor. 7:6, 25
^b1 Thess. 4:8

CHAPTER 8

1 ^aActs 15:20
^bRom. 14:14
^cRom. 14:3
¹makes arrogant
²builds up

2 ^a[1 Cor. 13:8–12]

4 ^aIs. 41:24
^bDeut. 4:35, 39; 6:4

1 Cor. 7:32

WITHOUT CARE

According to Jesus, the cares of this world can choke out the Word of God, making it unfruitful (Matt. 13:22). The Bible often reminds us to not be worried and anxious. It is easy for us to get so caught up in things that we become distracted from the important things of the Lord.

How many times I have seen happy, carefree people lose all their joy when they become more financially successful. It is easy for our possessions to begin to possess us. Hebrews 12:1–2 reminds us to "lay aside every weight, and the sin which so easily ensnares us, and let us run with endurance the race that is set before us, looking unto Jesus."

This world holds a lot of distractions. Some of them are sins, but some of them are just weights. Either way, we can't afford to get sidetracked. Paul's advice is excellent. Live "without care."

^{38 a}So then he who gives ¹her in marriage does well, but he who does not give her in marriage does better.

^{39 a}A wife is bound by law as long as her husband lives; but if her husband dies, she is at liberty to be married to whom she wishes, ^bonly in the Lord. ⁴⁰But she is happier if she remains as she is, ^aaccording to my judgment— and ^bI think I also have the Spirit of God.

BE SENSITIVE TO CONSCIENCE

⁸Now ^aconcerning things offered to idols: We know that we all have ^bknowledge. ^cKnowledge ¹puffs up, but love ²edifies. ²And ^aif anyone thinks that he knows anything, he knows nothing yet as he ought to know. ³But if anyone loves God, this one is known by Him.

⁴Therefore concerning the eating of things offered to idols, we know that ^aan idol is nothing in the world, ^band

1 Cor. 8:1

Knowledge and Love. "Knowledge puffs up, but love edifies." One of the tragic things about the great institutions of education is the intellectual snobbery that is so often developed around these institutions. It is sad that once a person learns some things they tend to look down on others who haven't had the same opportunity for learning.

But knowledge and love are not set off as opposites here. If you had to choose between knowledge and love, you would certainly pick love, but the ideal is to have knowledge with love.

that *there is* no other God but one. ⁵For even if there are ᵃso-called gods, whether in heaven or on earth (as there are many gods and many lords), ⁶yet ᵃfor us *there is* one God, the Father, ᵇof whom *are* all things, and we for Him; and ᶜone Lord Jesus Christ, ᵈthrough whom *are* all things, and ᵉthrough whom we *live.*

⁷However, *there is* not in everyone that knowledge; for some, ᵃwith consciousness of the idol, until now eat *it* as a thing offered to an idol; and their conscience, being weak, is ᵇdefiled. ⁸But ᵃfood does not commend us to God; for neither if we eat are we the better, nor if we do not eat are we the worse.

Cross references (center column):

5 ᵃ [John 10:34]

6 ᵃ Mal. 2:10
ᵇ Acts 17:28
ᶜ John 13:13
ᵈ John 1:3
ᵉ Rom. 5:11

7 ᵃ [1 Cor. 10:28]
ᵇ Rom. 14:14, 22

8 ᵃ [Rom. 14:17]

9 ᵃ Gal. 5:13
ᵇ Rom. 14:13, 21
ᶦ *cause of offense*

1 Cor. 8:8

FOOD DOESN'T MATTER

The Corinthian Christians were arguing about whether or not they should eat meat that had been offered to idols. Paul told them, "Food does not commend us to God; for neither if we eat are we the better, nor if we do not eat are we the worse."

We don't become spiritual by what we eat or drink. It is our faith in Jesus Christ that makes us righteous. There are some people who believe that you can't drink beer and be a Christian or that you can't go to movies and be a Christian. But that isn't what Christianity is about. The only thing that commends us to God is our relationship with Jesus Christ.

I personally have never had a drink of an alcoholic beverage and don't intend to. But that isn't what makes me acceptable to God. I am acceptable to God because of the cross.

⁹But ᵃbeware lest somehow this liberty of yours become ᵇa ᶦstumbling block to those who are weak. ¹⁰For if anyone sees you who have knowledge

A STUMBLING BLOCK
1 Cor. 8:9–13

Some people, especially new Christians, have hang-ups about all sorts of things that relate to their past lives. But as we mature in the Lord and experience the liberty that is in Christ, we get a different perspective, and we may have less hang-ups. But Paul warned Christians to be careful not to cause those who are weak to stumble.

If my behavior hurts someone who is weaker, then it is better for me to not do something, even if I realize there would really be nothing wrong with it. For example, I personally don't see anything wrong with Christmas trees. But I realize there are some people who feel strongly that, because of the pagan roots of many of the Christmas traditions, including the tree, that for them Christmas trees are offensive. Even though I may love the sight of a decorated tree and the smell of the fresh pine scent, for the sake of the people who may be offended, I don't put one up in my house. If there is even one person who would stumble by finding out that their pastor had a Christmas tree, it would not be worth it to me. I don't want my liberty to become a stumbling block.

eating in an idol's temple, will not ᵃthe conscience of him who is weak be emboldened to eat those things offered to idols? ¹¹And ᵃbecause of your knowledge shall the weak brother perish, for whom Christ died? ¹²But ᵃwhen you thus sin against the brethren, and wound their weak conscience, you sin against Christ. ¹³Therefore, ᵃif food makes my brother stumble, I will never again eat meat, lest I make my brother stumble.

A PATTERN OF SELF-DENIAL

9 Am ᵃI not an apostle? Am I not free? ᵇHave I not seen Jesus Christ our Lord? ᶜAre you not my work in the Lord? ²If I am not an apostle to others, yet doubtless I am to you. For you are ᵃthe ˡseal of my apostleship in the Lord.

---

1 Cor. 9:1–15

The Minister's Pay. Paul was getting a lot of criticism from others, questioning his authority and apostleship. So now he argued that he had every right to be financially supported by them, but that he had never exercised that right. He reasoned from logic and from the Scriptures that, as one who ministered to them, he should have been paid by them. "Those who preach the gospel should live from the gospel."

But Paul went on to say that he didn't want their money. A minister is entitled to be paid, but that shouldn't be his motive.

---

³My defense to those who examine me is this: ⁴ᵃDo we have no ˡright to eat and drink? ⁵Do we have no right to take along ˡa believing wife, as *do* also the other apostles, ᵃthe brothers of the Lord, and ᵇCephas? ⁶Or *is it* only Barnabas and I ᵃwho have no right to refrain from working? ⁷Who ever ᵃgoes to war at his own expense? Who ᵇplants a vineyard and does not eat of its fruit? Or who ᶜtends a flock and does not drink of the milk of the flock? ⁸Do I say these things as a *mere* man? Or does not the law say the same also? ⁹For it is written in the law of Moses, ᵃ*"You shall not muzzle an ox while it treads out the grain."* Is it oxen

---

10 ᵃ1 Cor. 10:28

11 ᵃRom. 14:15, 20

12 ᵃMatt. 25:40

13 ᵃRom. 14:21

CHAPTER 9

1 ᵃActs 9:15
ᵇ1 Cor. 15:8
ᶜ1 Cor. 3:6; 4:15

2 ᵃ2 Cor. 12:12
ˡ certification

4 ᵃ[1 Thess. 2:6, 9]
ˡ authority

5 ᵃMatt. 13:55
ᵇMatt. 8:14
ˡLit. a sister, a wife

6 ᵃActs 4:36

7 ᵃ2 Cor. 10:4
ᵇDeut. 20:6
ᶜJohn 21:15

9 ᵃDeut. 25:4

10 ᵃ2 Tim. 2:6

11 ᵃRom. 15:27

12 ᵃ[Acts 18:3; 20:33]
ᵇ2 Cor. 11:12

13 ᵃLev. 6:16, 26; 7:6, 31
ᵇNum. 18:8–31

14 ᵃMatt. 10:10
ᵇRom. 10:15

15 ᵃActs 18:3; 20:33
ᵇ2 Cor. 11:10

16 ᵃ[Rom. 1:14]

17 ᵃ1 Cor. 3:8, 14; 9:18
ᵇGal. 2:7

18 ᵃ1 Cor. 10:33
ᵇ1 Cor. 7:31; 9:12
ˡNU omits of Christ

19 ᵃ1 Cor. 9:1
ᵇGal. 5:13
ᶜMatt. 18:15

20 ᵃActs 16:3; 21:23–26
ˡNU adds though not being myself under the law

God is concerned about? ¹⁰Or does He say *it* altogether for our sakes? For our sakes, no doubt, *this* is written, that ᵃhe who plows should plow in hope, and he who threshes in hope should be partaker of his hope. ¹¹ᵃIf we have sown spiritual things for you, *is it* a great thing if we reap your material things? ¹²If others are partakers of *this* right over you, *are* we not even more?

ᵃNevertheless we have not used this right, but endure all things ᵇlest we hinder the gospel of Christ. ¹³ᵃDo you not know that those who minister the holy things eat *of the things* of the ᵇtemple, and those who serve at the altar partake of *the offerings of* the altar? ¹⁴Even so ᵃthe Lord has commanded ᵇthat those who preach the gospel should live from the gospel.

¹⁵But ᵃI have used none of these things, nor have I written these things that it should be done so to me; for ᵇit *would be* better for me to die than that anyone should make my boasting void. ¹⁶For if I preach the gospel, I have nothing to boast of, for ᵃnecessity is laid upon me; yes, woe is me if I do not preach the gospel! ¹⁷For if I do this willingly, ᵃI have a reward; but if against my will, ᵇI have been entrusted with a stewardship. ¹⁸What is my reward then? That ᵃwhen I preach the gospel, I may present the gospel ˡof Christ without charge, that I ᵇmay not abuse my authority in the gospel.

---

1 Cor. 9:16–17

Woe Is Me. Paul had God's call upon his heart to preach the gospel. He said that his preaching was not to his glory. He couldn't help but do it. "Woe is me if I do not preach the gospel!"

When God calls you to preach the gospel, you really can't do anything else. Nothing will stand in the way. It isn't something to brag about. You just have to do it.

SERVING ALL MEN

¹⁹For though I am ᵃfree from all men, ᵇI have made myself a servant to all, ᶜthat I might win the more; ²⁰and ᵃto the Jews I became as a Jew, that I might win Jews; to those *who are* under the law, as under the ˡlaw, that I might win those *who are* under the

law; [21]ato bthose *who are* without law, as without law c(not being without ¹law toward God, but under ²law toward Christ), that I might win those *who are* without law; [22]ato the weak I became ¹as weak, that I might win the weak. bI have become all things to all *men*, cthat I might by all means save some. [23]Now this I do for the gospel's sake, that I may be partaker of it with *you.*

1 Cor. 9:19–23

All Things to All Men. Paul's great desire was to win people for Jesus Christ. This desire drove him to adapt to whatever culture he was ministering to. He understood the Jews because that was his native culture. He could relate to them. He also related to the Gentiles.

Paul found ways to connect with everyone, because he knew that was the basis on which he could reach them. Adaptability for the sake of the gospel, to reach the lost.

STRIVING FOR A CROWN

[24]Do you not know that those who run in a race all run, but one receives the prize? aRun in such a way that you may ¹obtain it. [25]And everyone who competes *for the prize* ¹is temperate in all things. Now they *do it* to obtain a perishable crown, but we *for* aan imperishable

crown. [26]Therefore I run thus: anot with uncertainty. Thus I fight: not as *one who* beats the air. [27]aBut I discipline my body and bbring *it* into subjection, lest, when I have preached to others, I myself should become cdisqualified.

OLD TESTAMENT EXAMPLES

10 Moreover, brethren, I do not want you to be unaware that all our fathers were under athe cloud, all passed through bthe sea, [2]all were baptized into Moses in the cloud and in the sea, [3]all ate the same aspiritual food, [4]and all drank the same aspiritual drink. For they drank of that spiritual Rock that followed them, and that Rock was Christ. [5]But with most of them God was not well pleased, for *their bodies* awere scattered in the wilderness.
[6]Now these things became our examples, to the intent that we should not lust after evil things as athey also lusted. [7]aAnd do not become idolaters as *were* some of them. As it is written, b*"The people sat down to eat and drink, and rose up to play."* [8]aNor let us commit sexual immorality, as bsome of them did, and cin one day twenty-three thousand fell; [9]nor let us ¹tempt Christ, as asome of them also tempted, and bwere destroyed by serpents; [10]nor complain, as asome of them also complained, and bwere destroyed by cthe destroyer. [11]Now ¹all these things happened to them as examples, and athey were written for our ²admonition, bupon whom the ends of the ages have come.

21 a [Gal. 2:3; 3:2]
b [Rom. 2:12, 14]
c [1 Cor. 7:22]
1 NU *God's law*
2 NU *Christ's law*

22 a Rom. 14:1; 15:1
b 1 Cor. 10:33
c Rom. 11:14
1 NU omits *as*

24 a Gal. 2:2
1 *win*

25 a James 1:12
1 *exercises self-control*

26 a 2 Tim. 2:5

27 a [Rom. 8:13]
b [Rom. 6:18]
c Jer. 6:30

CHAPTER 10

1 a Ex. 13:21, 22
b Ex. 14:21, 22, 29

3 a Ex. 16:4, 15, 35

4 a Ex. 17:5–7

5 a Num. 14:29, 37; 26:65

6 a Num. 11:4, 34

7 a 1 Cor. 5:11; 10:14
b Ex. 32:6

8 a Rev. 2:14
b Num. 25:1–9
c Ps. 106:29

9 a Ex. 17:2, 7
b Num. 21:6–9
1 *test*

10 a Ex. 16:2 b Num. 14:37 c Ex. 12:23 **11** a Rom. 15:4
b Phil. 4:5 1 NU omits *all* 2 *instruction*

WILDERNESS EXPERIENCES
1 Cor. 10:5

There is a legitimate wilderness experience for God's people and an illegitimate wilderness experience. The children of Israel were led out into the wilderness by God, on their way to the Promised Land. The journey from Egypt to their new home should have taken about a month. Instead it took forty years because of their lack of faith.

Sometimes God leads us into the wilderness because that is the way to get where we are going with Him. But He wants us to pass through, not to be left scattered in the wilderness. But if we don't trust Him and we rebel against Him, we may end up spending a much longer time in the wilderness than He intended. The purpose of our legitimate wilderness experiences is that God uses them to prepare us to enter into the blessings that He has for us. But if we resist His work in our lives and we allow the wilderness experiences to make us bitter, we will find ourselves spending much more time in the wilderness than was necessary, which will be an illegitimate wilderness experience.

Legitimate wilderness experiences are important parts of our growth as children of God. Illegitimate wilderness experiences are a complete waste of time.

1 Cor. 10:12–13

A Way of Escape. Beware of becoming overly confident in your own abilities. "Let him who thinks he stands take heed lest he fall." All temptations are "common to man." We are all alike. You are not an exception. You are not better or worse than anyone else. We all face failure at every turn.

But God is faithful. He will always give us a way out if we listen to Him. That doesn't mean necessarily that we always take the way of escape, but He always offers it. If I fail, it is because of my unfaithfulness, not His.

[12]Therefore [a]let him who thinks he stands take heed lest he fall. [13]No temptation has overtaken you except such as is common to man; but [a]God is faithful, [b]who will not allow you to be tempted beyond what you are able, but with the temptation will also make the way of escape, that you may be able to [1]bear it.

FLEE FROM IDOLATRY

[14]Therefore, my beloved, [a]flee from idolatry. [15]I speak as to [a]wise men; judge for yourselves what I say. [16a]The cup of blessing which we bless, is it not the [1]communion of the blood of Christ? [b]The bread which we break, is it not the communion of the body of Christ? [17]For [a]we, though many, are one bread and one body; for we all partake of that one bread.

[18]Observe [a]Israel [b]after the flesh: [c]Are not those who eat of the sacrifices [1]partakers of the altar? [19]What am I saying then? [a]That an idol is anything, or what is offered to idols is anything? [20]Rather, that the things which the Gentiles [a]sacrifice [b]they sacrifice to demons and not to God, and I do not want you to have fellowship with demons. [21a]You cannot drink the cup of the Lord and [b]the cup of demons; you cannot partake of the [c]Lord's table and of the table of demons. [22]Or do we [a]provoke the Lord to jealousy? [b]Are we stronger than He?

ALL TO THE GLORY OF GOD

[23]All things are lawful [1]for me, but not all things are [a]helpful; all things

are lawful [2]for me, but not all things [3]edify. [24]Let no one seek his own, but each one [a]the other's *well-being*.

[25a]Eat whatever is sold in the meat market, asking no questions for conscience' sake; [26]for [a]*"the earth is the LORD's, and all its fullness."* [27]If any of those who do not believe invites you *to dinner*, and you desire to go, [a]eat whatever is set before you, asking no question for conscience' sake. [28]But if anyone says to you, "This was offered to idols," do not eat it [a]for the sake of the one who told you, and for conscience' sake; [1]for [b]*"the earth is the LORD's, and all its fullness."* [29]"Conscience," I say, not your own, but that of the other. For [a]why is my liberty judged by another *man's* conscience? [30]But if I partake with thanks, why am I evil spoken of for *the food* [a]over which I give thanks?

[31a]Therefore, whether you eat or drink, or whatever you do, do all to the glory of God. [32a]Give no offense, either to the Jews or to the Greeks or to the church of God, [33]just [a]as I also please all *men* in all *things*, not seeking my own profit, but the *profit* of many, that they may be saved.

1 Cor. 10:31

All to the Glory of God. What a great bottom line principle! Oh God, if we don't grasp anything else, help us to grasp this! I am to live for the glory of God. That is the purpose of my existence. Just bringing God glory. If you can do something to the glory of God, you are on solid ground.

This should be the standard by which I should judge what I do and don't do: Can I do it for the glory of God?

11 Imitate[a] me, just as I also *imitate* Christ.

HEAD COVERINGS

[2]Now I praise you, brethren, that you remember me in all things and keep the traditions just as I delivered *them* to you. [3]But I want you to know that [a]the head of every man is Christ, [b]the head of woman *is* man, and [c]the head of Christ *is* God. [4]Every man praying or [a]prophesying, having *his* head

Center column references

12 [a] Rom. 11:20

13 [a] 1 Cor. 1:9
[b] Ps. 125:3
[1] endure

14 [a] 2 Cor. 6:17

15 [a] 1 Cor. 8:1

16 [a] Matt. 26:26–28
[b] Acts 2:42
[1] fellowship or sharing

17 [a] 1 Cor. 12:12, 27

18 [a] Rom. 4:12
[b] Rom. 4:1
[c] Lev. 3:3; 7:6, 14
[1] fellowshippers or sharers

19 [a] 1 Cor. 8:4

20 [a] Lev. 17:7
[b] Deut. 32:17

21 [a] 2 Cor. 6:15, 16
[b] Deut. 32:38
[c] [1 Cor. 11:23–29]

22 [a] Deut. 32:21
[b] Ezek. 22:14

23 [a] 1 Cor. 6:12
[1] NU omits for me
[2] build up

24 [a] Phil. 2:4

25 [a] [1 Tim. 4:4]

26 [a] Ps. 24:1

27 [a] Luke 10:7, 8

28 [a] [1 Cor. 8:7, 10, 12]
[b] Ps. 24:1
[1] NU omits the rest of v. 28.

29 [a] Rom. 14:16

30 [a] Rom. 14:6

31 [a] Col. 3:17

32 [a] Rom. 14:13

33 [a] Rom. 15:2

CHAPTER 11

1 [a] Eph. 5:1

3 [a] Eph. 1:22; 4:15; 5:23
[b] Gen. 3:16
[c] John 14:28

4 [a] 1 Cor. 12:10

DIVINE ORDER

God created men and women with differences, some of them obvious and some not so obvious. In this passage, Paul exhorted them to respect the differences that God ordered.

It is a shame if women would dress in such a way that they would look like prostitutes. It is a shame if men look like women. In the same way that God is the head of Christ, so also Christ is the head of man, and man is the head of woman. Christ is God and is equal with God, but His role in the Godhead is to do the will of the Father. So, also, although women are equal in value, and often equal or superior in ability to men, God has ordained an order that puts the man as the leader over his wife.

Today there are many who would overthrow these role differences. But this divine order is declared by God, and men and women can only be happy and fulfilled if this divine order is respected and adhered to. Paul went on to say in verse 16 that he wasn't going to fight about it. This is just the way it is, whether you want to accept it or not.

---

covered, dishonors his head. 5But every woman who prays or prophesies with *her* head uncovered dishonors her head, for that is one and the same as if her head were ªshaved. 6For if a woman is not covered, let her also be shorn. But if it is ªshameful for a woman to be shorn or shaved, let her be covered. 7For a man indeed ought not to cover *his* head, since ªhe is the image and glory of God; but woman is the glory of man. 8For man is not from woman, but woman ªfrom man. 9Nor was man created for the woman, but woman ªfor the man. 10For this reason the woman ought to have *a symbol of* authority on *her* head, because of the angels. 11Nevertheless, ªneither *is* man independent of woman, nor woman independent of man, in the Lord. 12For as woman *came* from man, even so man also *comes* through woman; but all things are from God.

13Judge among yourselves. Is it proper for a woman to pray to God with her head uncovered? 14Does not even nature itself teach you that if a man has long hair, it is a dishonor to him? 15But if a woman has long hair, it is a glory to her; for *her* hair is given *1*to her for a covering. 16But ªif anyone seems to be contentious, we have no such custom, ʰnor *do* the churches of God.

CONDUCT AT THE LORD'S SUPPER

17Now in giving these instructions I do not praise *you*, since you come together not for the better but for the worse. 18For first of all, when you come together as a church, ªI hear that there are divisions among you, and in part I

believe it. 19For ªthere must also be factions among you, ʰthat those who are approved may be *1*recognized among you. 20Therefore when you come together in one place, it is not to eat the Lord's Supper. 21For in eating, each one takes his own supper ahead of *others*; and one is hungry and ªanother is drunk. 22What! Do you not have houses to eat and drink in? Or do you despise ªthe church of God and ʰshame *1*those who have nothing? What shall I say to you? Shall I praise you in this? I do not praise *you*.

INSTITUTION OF THE LORD'S SUPPER

23For ªI received from the Lord that which I also delivered to you: ʰthat the

---

5 ª Deut. 21:12

6 ª Num. 5:18

7 ª Gen. 1:26, 27; 5:1; 9:6

8 ª Gen. 2:21–23

9 ª Gen. 2:18

11 ª [Gal. 3:28]

15 *1* M omits *to her*

16 ª 1 Tim. 6:4
ʰ 1 Cor. 7:17

18 ª 1 Cor. 1:10–12; 3:3

19 ª 1 Tim. 4:1
ʰ [Deut. 13:3]
1 Lit. *manifest, evident*

21 ª Jude 12

22 ª 1 Cor. 10:32
ʰ James 2:6
1 The poor

23 ª 1 Cor. 15:3
ʰ Matt. 26:26–28

---

1 Cor. 11:23

Receiving from the Lord. As Paul was instructing the Corinthian Christians on the Lord's Supper, he told them, "I received from the Lord that which I also delivered to you."

My desire is that every message I preach and every book I write could be prefaced by this. My study time is precious and exciting to me, as the Lord ministers to me so I can deliver it to others. As God speaks to my heart and I have the privilege of sharing it with others, I always want to be able to say, "Here is what I received from the Lord."

Lord Jesus on the *same* night in which He was betrayed took bread; 24and when He had given thanks, He broke *it* and said, *1*"Take, eat; this is My body which is *2*broken for you; do this in remembrance of Me." 25In the same manner *He* also *took* the cup after supper, saying, "This cup is the new covenant in My blood. This do, as often as you drink *it*, in remembrance of Me." 26For as often as you eat this bread and drink this cup, you proclaim the Lord's death atill He comes.

EXAMINE YOURSELF

27Therefore whoever eats athis bread or drinks *this* cup of the Lord in an unworthy manner will be guilty of the body and *1*blood of the Lord. 28But alet a man examine himself, and so let him eat of the bread and drink of the cup. 29For he who eats and drinks *1*in an unworthy manner eats and drinks judgment to himself, not discerning the *2*Lord's body. 30For this reason many *are* weak and sick among you, and many *1*sleep. 31For aif we would judge ourselves, we would not be judged. 32But when we are judged, awe are chastened by the Lord, that we may not be condemned with the world.

---

1 Cor. 11:28

Self-Examination. Communion is a good time for self-examination. God, search me, and know my heart. Lord, is there anything within me that is displeasing to You?

It is interesting how proficient we are at examining others, but how blind we can be to our own faults. It isn't easy to examine yourself, because our hearts are deceitful and wicked (Jer. 17:9–10). So, before we partake of the bread and the cup, it is a great time to examine ourselves, as we hold in our hands the emblems of the price He paid to forgive our sins.

33Therefore, my brethren, when you acome together to eat, wait for one another. 34But if anyone is hungry, let him eat at home, lest you come together for judgment. And the rest I will set in order when I come.

Cross References (center column)

24 *1*NU omits *Take, eat;* *2*NU omits *bro-ken*

26 a John 14:3

27 a[John 6:51] *1*NU, M *the blood*

28 a 2 Cor. 13:5

29 *1*NU omits *in an unworthy manner* *2*NU omits *Lord's*

30 *1*Are dead

31 a[1 John 1:9]

32 a Ps. 94:12

33 a 1 Cor. 14:26

CHAPTER 12

1 a 1 Cor. 12:4; 14:1, 37

2 a Eph. 2:11 b Ps. 115:5 *1*NU, M *that when* *2*mute, silent

3 a Matt. 16:17 *1*Gr. anathema

4 a Rom. 12:3–8 b Eph. 4:4 *1*allotments or various kinds

5 a Rom. 12:6

6 a 1 Cor. 15:28 *1*all things in

8 a 1 Cor. 2:6, 7 b Rom. 15:14

9 a 2 Cor. 4:13 b Mark 3:15; 16:18 *1*NU one

10 a Mark 16:17 b Rom. 12:6 c 1 John 4:1 d Acts 2:4–11

11 a Rom. 12:6 b[John 3:8]

12 a Rom. 12:4, 5 b[Gal. 3:16]

13 a[Rom. 6:5]

SPIRITUAL GIFTS: UNITY IN DIVERSITY

12 Now aconcerning spiritual *gifts*, brethren, I do not want you to be ignorant: 2You know athat*1* you were Gentiles, carried away to these bdumb*2* idols, however you were led. 3Therefore I make known to you that no one speaking by the Spirit of God calls Jesus *1*accursed, and ano one can say that Jesus is Lord except by the Holy Spirit.

4aThere are *1*diversities of gifts, but bthe same Spirit. 5aThere are differences of ministries, but the same Lord. 6And there are diversities of activities, but it is the same God awho works *1*all in all. 7But the manifestation of the Spirit is given to each one for the profit *of all:* 8for to one is given athe word of wisdom through the Spirit, to another bthe word of knowledge through the same Spirit, 9ato another faith by the same Spirit, to another bgifts of healings by *1*the same Spirit, 10ato another the working of miracles, to another bprophecy, to another cdiscerning of spirits, to another ddifferent kinds of tongues, to another the interpretation of tongues. 11But one and the same Spirit works all these things, adistrib-uting to each one individually bas He wills.

UNITY AND DIVERSITY IN ONE BODY

12For aas the body is one and has many members, but all the members of that one body, being many, are one body, bso also *is* Christ. 13For aby one

---

1 Cor. 12:4–6

Diversities of Gifts. God works uniquely in each of us, as He has given us each different gifts, and He works in us and through us in different ways. We make a great mistake in trying to reduce God to a pattern or system. He doesn't operate in our lives by a formula. I may experience the gifts of the Spirit and the filling of the Spirit in a different way than you do.

Don't look to duplicate someone else's experience in your life. There is one Spirit, but different gifts, ministries, activities, and manifestations.

DISTRIBUTING AS HE WILLS   1 Cor. 12:11

God uses the gifts of the Spirit, "distributing to each one individually as He wills." We can't work up the faith to perform a miracle; it comes from Him as a gift.

Several years back, after the morning service at Calvary Chapel, some kids wheeled their grandfather up to the front of the church. He was in a wheelchair, and they asked me to pray for him. I said "sure" and laid my hands on him and began to pray. I had just been reading in Acts 3 where Peter pulled the lame man to his feet, and it came into my mind to do the same. I lifted him up out of his wheelchair and said, "In the name of Jesus, walk!" And the man started walking! His grandkids were so excited they were almost doing cartwheels through the church. Then they told me that their grandpa had a cold, and they wanted me to pray for him to be healed of his cold!

Where did that faith come from? I don't make a practice of pulling people out of wheelchairs; but at that instant, God gave me the faith to do that, and God gave me that gift of faith and healing at that moment. He does what He wants when He wants, and it is a blessing when He uses us and gives us the gifts that are needed.

Spirit we were all baptized into one body—b whether Jews or Greeks, whether slaves or free—and c have all been made to drink 1 into one Spirit. 14 For in fact the body is not one member but many.

15 If the foot should say, "Because I am not a hand, I am not of the body," is it therefore not of the body? 16 And if the ear should say, "Because I am not an eye, I am not of the body," is it therefore not of the body? 17 If the whole body were an eye, where would be the hearing? If the whole were hearing, where would be the smelling? 18 But now a God has set the members, each one of them, in the body b just as He pleased. 19 And if they were all one member, where would the body be?

20 But now indeed there are many members, yet one body. 21 And the eye cannot say to the hand, "I have no need of you"; nor again the head to the feet, "I have no need of you." 22 No, much rather, those members of the body which seem to be weaker are necessary. 23 And those members of the body which we think to be less honorable, on these we bestow greater honor; and our unpresentable parts have greater modesty, 24 but our presentable parts have no need. But God composed the body, having given greater honor to that part which lacks it, 25 that there should be no 1 schism in the body, but that the members should have the same care for one another. 26 And if one member suffers, all the members suffer with it; or if one member is honored, all the members rejoice with it.

27 Now a you are the body of Christ,

13 b Col. 3:11
c [John 7:37–39]
1 NU omits into

18 a 1 Cor. 12:28
b Rom. 12:3

25 1 division

27 a Rom. 12:5
b Eph. 5:30

28 a Eph. 4:11
b [Eph. 2:20; 3:5]
c Acts 13:1
d 1 Cor. 12:10, 29
e 1 Cor. 12:9, 30
f Num. 11:17
g Rom. 12:8

and b members individually. 28 And a God has appointed these in the church: first b apostles, second c prophets, third teachers, after that d miracles, then e gifts of healings, f helps, g administrations, varieties of tongues. 29 Are all

1 Cor. 12:14–24

EACH MEMBER IS NECESSARY

It is so important for me to realize that I am a part of the body. I may not be a very visible or noticeable part, but I am an important part of the body. I am needed for the whole body to function properly.

There are parts of your body that you can't see, but they are still vitally important. What would you do without your digestive system? How about your heart or your lungs?

We need to know that God made us and has a unique place for each of us in His body. And we need to be satisfied where God has placed us, knowing that He put us there for His purposes. Though we may not draw a lot of attention, our contributions are vitally important to the whole functioning of the body.

apostles? *Are* all prophets? *Are* all teachers? *Are* all workers of miracles? ³⁰Do all have gifts of healings? Do all speak with tongues? Do all interpret? ³¹But ᵃearnestly desire the ¹best gifts. And yet I show you a more excellent way.

THE GREATEST GIFT

13 Though I speak with the tongues of men and of angels, but have not love, I have become sounding brass or a clanging cymbal. ²And though I have *the gift of* ᵃprophecy, and understand all mysteries and all knowledge, and though I have all faith, ᵇso that I could remove mountains, but have not love, I am nothing. ³And ᵃthough I bestow all my goods to feed *the poor,* and though I give my body ¹to be burned, but have not love, it profits me nothing.

⁴ᵃLove suffers long *and* is ᵇkind; love ᶜdoes not envy; love does not parade itself, is not ¹puffed up; ⁵does not

GIFTS WITHOUT LOVE

1 Cor. 13:1–3

The Corinthian church was a gifted church. They were experiencing the exercise of all the spiritual gifts, and yet they were a divided and carnal church. As wonderful as the gifts of the Spirit are, they are nothing without love. Paul closed chapter 12 by saying, "But earnestly desire the best gifts. And yet I show you a more excellent way." Love is the more excellent way.

The ability to speak in tongues without love is a clanging cymbal. Prophecy, knowledge, and faith in infinite supply are still nothing without love. Giving sacrificially without love is totally unprofitable. Love is the key. If we miss that, everything else we do is a waste of time and effort.

John said, "He who does not love does not know God, for God is love" (1 John 4:8). That is what it all comes down to, and that is the fruit of the Spirit (Gal. 5:22).

31 ᵃ1 Cor. 14:1, 39
¹ NU *greater*

CHAPTER 13

2 ᵃ1 Cor. 12:8–10, 28; 14:1
ᵇ Matt. 17:20; 21:21

3 ᵃ Matt. 6:1, 2
¹ NU *so I may boast*

4 ᵃ Prov. 10:12; 17:9
ᵇ Eph. 4:32
ᶜ Gal. 5:26
¹ *arrogant*

5 ᵃ1 Cor. 10:24
¹ *keeps no accounts of evil*

6 ᵃ Rom. 1:32
ᵇ 2 John 4

7 ᵃ Gal. 6:2

9 ᵃ1 Cor. 8:2; 13:12

10 ¹ *complete*

12 ᵃ Phil. 3:12
ᵇ [1 John 3:2]

CHAPTER 14

1 ᵃ1 Cor. 12:31; 14:39
ᵇ Num. 11:25, 29

2 ᵃ Acts 2:4; 10:46

1 Cor. 13:4–8

THIS IS A TEST

Back in chapter 11, Paul told us to examine ourselves. This chapter gives us a great opportunity to do that. Take this passage, and whenever it says "love" insert your name instead. "Chuck suffers long and is kind. Chuck doesn't envy. Chuck does not think evil. Chuck never fails." Go ahead and laugh, but insert your name, and see how you do. Then insert the name of Jesus. "Jesus suffers long and is kind. Jesus doesn't envy. Jesus isn't provoked. Jesus never fails."

This is a great test, to see how far I am down the road toward what the Lord would have me to be. This is describing what God wants us to be. He wants His love to be operating in our lives. Go ahead. Examine yourself.

behave rudely, ᵃdoes not seek its own, is not provoked, ¹thinks no evil; ⁶ᵃdoes not rejoice in iniquity, but ᵇrejoices in the truth; ⁷ᵃbears all things, believes all things, hopes all things, endures all things.

⁸Love never fails. But whether *there are* prophecies, they will fail; whether *there are* tongues, they will cease; whether *there is* knowledge, it will vanish away. ⁹ᵃFor we know in part and we prophesy in part. ¹⁰But when that which is ¹perfect has come, then that which is in part will be done away. ¹¹When I was a child, I spoke as a child, I understood as a child, I thought as a child; but when I became a man, I put away childish things. ¹²For ᵃnow we see in a mirror, dimly, but then ᵇface to face. Now I know in part, but then I shall know just as I also am known.

¹³And now abide faith, hope, love, these three; but the greatest of these *is* love.

PROPHECY AND TONGUES

14 Pursue love, and ᵃdesire spiritual *gifts*, ᵇbut especially that you may prophesy. ²For he who ᵃspeaks in

1 Cor. 13:8–10

WHEN THE PERFECT HAS COME

The gifts will continue in use until "that which is perfect has come." There are some people who deny the use of some of the spiritual gifts for today who suggest that "the perfect" refers to the completion of the canon of Scripture, and thus some of these gifts ceased with the first-century church. However, it is clear from the context that the perfect is referring to the coming of Jesus Christ. It says then we will see "face to face" in verse 12.

But also in Joel 2:28–32, as Joel predicted the coming pouring out of the gifts of the Spirit, he made it clear that they are for the last days, right before the day of the Lord. We need all the gifts until our perfect Lord returns for us. Then they won't be necessary anymore.

a tongue does not speak to men but to God, for no one understands *him;* however, in the spirit he speaks mysteries. [3]But he who prophesies speaks [a]edification and [b]exhortation and comfort to men. [4]He who speaks in a tongue edifies himself, but he who prophesies

1 Cor. 14:2

Speaking in Tongues to God. The gift of tongues is the gift whereby God enables us to communicate with Him in the Spirit, bypassing the narrow channel of our intellect. So often we find that words are inadequate to express our feelings of gratefulness to God for all His blessings. So the Spirit helps us by allowing us to commune with God in the Spirit, as we worship Him in Spirit and truth, with "groanings which cannot be uttered" (Rom. 8:26).

3 [a] Rom. 14:19; 15:2 [b] 1 Tim. 4:13

5 [1] NU *and*

6 [a] 1 Cor. 14:26

10 [1] *meaning*

11 [1] Lit. *barbarian*

12 [1] *eager* [2] *building up*

13 [a] 1 Cor. 12:10

1 Cor. 14:3–5

Superiority of Prophecy. The gift of tongues is wonderful for someone to exercise in their private times of worship with the Lord; but in the church service, when other people are around, Paul stressed that the gift of prophecy is much more beneficial, because everyone can understand it.

Prophecy is defined here as speaking "edification and exhortation and comfort" to the people. That is what we do as we teach the Word. Speaking in tongues is self-edifying, and that is good; but speaking prophetically edifies the whole body, and that is better in the assembly.

edifies the church. [5]I wish you all spoke with tongues, but even more that you prophesied; [1]for he who prophesies *is* greater than he who speaks with tongues, unless indeed he interprets, that the church may receive edification.

TONGUES MUST BE INTERPRETED

[6]But now, brethren, if I come to you speaking with tongues, what shall I profit you unless I speak to you either by [a]revelation, by knowledge, by prophesying, or by teaching? [7]Even things without life, whether flute or harp, when they make a sound, unless they make a distinction in the sounds, how will it be known what is piped or played? [8]For if the trumpet makes an uncertain sound, who will prepare for battle? [9]So likewise you, unless you utter by the tongue words easy to understand, how will it be known what is spoken? For you will be speaking into the air. [10]There are, it may be, so many kinds of languages in the world, and none of them *is* without [1]significance. [11]Therefore, if I do not know the meaning of the language, I shall be a [1]foreigner to him who speaks, and he who speaks *will be* a foreigner to me. [12]Even so you, since you are [1]zealous for spiritual *gifts, let it be* for the [2]edification of the church *that* you seek to excel.

[13]Therefore let him who speaks in a tongue pray that he may [a]interpret.

14For if I pray in a tongue, my spirit prays, but my understanding is unfruitful. 15What is *the conclusion* then? I will pray with the spirit, and I will also pray with the understanding. aI will sing with the spirit, and I will also sing bwith the understanding. 16Otherwise, if you bless with the spirit, how will he who occupies the place of the uninformed say "Amen" aat your giving of thanks, since he does not understand what you say? 17For you indeed give thanks well, but the other is not edified. 18I thank my God I speak with tongues more than you all; 19yet in the church I would rather speak five words with my understanding, that I may teach others also, than ten thousand words in a tongue.

TONGUES A SIGN TO UNBELIEVERS

20Brethren, ado not be children in understanding; however, in malice bbe babes, but in understanding be mature. 21aIn the law it is written:

b"*With men of other tongues and other lips
I will speak to this people;
And yet, for all that, they will not hear Me,*"

says the Lord. 22Therefore tongues are for a asign, not to those who believe but to unbelievers; but prophesying is not for unbelievers but for those who believe. 23Therefore if the whole church comes together in one place, and all speak with tongues, and there come in *those who are* uninformed or unbelievers, awill they not say that you are *l*out of your mind? 24But if all prophesy, and an unbeliever or an uninformed person comes in, he is convinced by all, he is convicted by all. 25*l*And thus the secrets of his heart are revealed; and so, falling down on *his* face, he will worship God and report athat God is truly among you.

ORDER IN CHURCH MEETINGS

26How is it then, brethren? Whenever you come together, each of you has a psalm, ahas a teaching, has a tongue, has a revelation, has an interpretation. bLet all things be done *l*edification. 27If anyone speaks in a tongue, *let there be* two or at the most three, *each* in turn, and let one interpret. 28But if there is no interpreter, let him keep silent in church, and let him speak to himself and to God. 29Let two

or three prophets speak, and alet the others judge. 30But if *anything* is revealed to another who sits by, alet the first keep silent. 31For you can all prophesy one by one, that all may learn and all may be encouraged. 32And athe spirits of the prophets are subject to the prophets. 33For God is not *the author* of *l*confusion but of peace, aas in all the churches of the saints. 34aLet *l*your women keep silent in the churches, for they are not permitted to speak; but *they are* to be submissive, as the blaw also says. 35And if they want to learn something, let them ask their own husbands at home; for it is shameful for women to speak in church. 36Or did the word of God come *originally* from you? Or *was it* you only that it reached? 37aIf anyone thinks himself to be a prophet or spiritual, let him acknowledge that the things which I write to you are the commandments of the Lord. 38But *l*if anyone is ignorant, let him be ignorant. 39Therefore, brethren, adesire earnestly to prophesy, and do not forbid to speak with tongues. 40aLet all things be done decently and in order.

---

1 Cor. 14:40

Decently and in Order. The bottom line of all Paul had to say in this chapter is found in this last verse: "Let all things be done decently and in order." Apparently the church services in Corinth were out of control. People were speaking out in tongues without any interpretation. Several people would be speaking out at the same time. Women were yelling out questions in the middle of church. Visitors who came to the church didn't understand what was going on and thought the people were crazy.

Church services should be orderly, and they should make sense.

THE RISEN CHRIST, FAITH'S REALITY

15 Moreover, brethren, I declare to you the gospel awhich I preached to you, which also you received and bin which you stand, 2aby which also you

---

Cross references (center column):

15 aCol. 3:16
bPs. 47:7

16 a1 Cor. 11:24

20 aPs. 131:2
b[1 Pet. 2:2]

21 aJohn 10:34
bIs. 28:11, 12

22 aMark 16:17

23 aActs 2:13
*l*insane

25 aIs. 45:14
*l*NU omits *And thus*

26 a1 Cor. 12:8–10; 14:6
b[2 Cor. 12:19]
*l*building up

29 a1 Cor. 12:10

30 a[1 Thess. 5:19, 20]

32 a1 John 4:1

33 a1 Cor. 11:16
*l*disorder

34 a1 Tim. 2:11
bGen. 3:16
*l*NU omits *your*

37 a2 Cor. 10:7

38 *l*NU *if anyone does not recognize this, he is not recognized.*

39 a1 Cor. 12:31

40 a1 Cor. 14:33

CHAPTER 15

1 a[Gal. 1:11]
b[Rom. 5:2; 11:20]

2 aRom. 1:16

are saved, if you hold fast that word which I preached to you—unless [b]you believed in vain.

[3]For [a]I delivered to you first of all that [b]which I also received: that Christ died for our sins [c]according to the Scriptures, [4]and that He was buried, and that He rose again the third day [a]according to the Scriptures, [5a]and that He was seen by [1]Cephas, then [b]by the twelve. [6]After that He was seen by over five hundred brethren at once, of whom the greater part remain to the present, but some have [1]fallen asleep. [7]After that He was seen by James, then [a]by all the apostles. [8a]Then last of all He was seen by me also, as by one born out of due time.

[9]For I am [a]the least of the apostles, who am not worthy to be called an apostle, because [b]I persecuted the

1 Cor. 15:1–8

THE GOSPEL

Paul summed up in these verses what the gospel is. The word "gospel" means "good news," and this is the good news that Paul was preaching.

First of all, "Christ died for our sins according to the Scriptures." This is what we call the "substitutionary atonement." He took our sins on Himself and died in our place. This had been prophesied in Isaiah 53:6, which says, "The LORD has laid on Him the iniquity of us all."

Second, "He was buried." This was also prophesied in Isaiah 53, in verse 9, which says, "They made His grave with the wicked—but with the rich at His death."

Third, He rose again on the third day and was seen by many witnesses, including Paul himself.

This is great news for us; and as Paul made the declaration of this message the sole purpose of his life, we, too, should take every opportunity to declare the good news to those around us.

church of God. [10]But [a]by the grace of God I am what I am, and His grace toward me was not in vain; but I labored more abundantly than they all, [b]yet not I, but the grace of God *which was* with me. [11]Therefore, whether *it was* I or they, so we preach and so you believed.

THE RISEN CHRIST, OUR HOPE

[12]Now if Christ is preached that He has been raised from the dead, how do some among you say that there is no resurrection of the dead? [13]But if there is no resurrection of the dead, [a]then Christ is not risen. [14]And if Christ is not risen, then our preaching *is* empty and your faith *is* also empty. [15]Yes, and we are found false witnesses of God, because [a]we have testified of God that He raised up Christ, whom He did not raise up—if in fact the dead do not rise. [16]For if *the* dead do not rise, then Christ is not risen. [17]And if Christ is not risen, your faith *is* futile; [a]you are still in your sins! [18]Then also those who have [1]fallen [a]asleep in Christ have perished. [19a]If in this life only we have hope in Christ, we are of all men the most pitiable.

THE LAST ENEMY DESTROYED

[20]But now [a]Christ is risen from the dead, *and* has become [b]the firstfruits of those who have [1]fallen asleep. [21]For [a]since by man *came* death, [b]by Man also *came* the resurrection of the dead. [22]For as in Adam all die, even so in

---

1 Cor. 15:12–20

If Christ Is Not Risen. There are many so-called "ministers" today who do not believe that Jesus really rose from the dead. This is nothing new or enlightened. There were those in Paul's day who said the same thing. But Paul made it clear in these verses that, if Jesus didn't rise from the dead, then we are hopelessly lost in our sins.

Any preaching that denies the resurrection is empty. And a church without a risen Lord is pathetic and pitiable. But Paul went on to say, "But now Christ is risen from the dead." Hallelujah!

---

2 [b] Gal. 3:4

3 [a] 1 Cor. 11:2, 23
[b] [Gal. 1:12]
[c] Ps. 22:15

4 [a] Ps. 16:9–11; 68:18; 110:1

5 [a] Luke 24:34
[b] Matt. 28:17
[1] Peter

6 [1] Died

7 [a] Acts 1:3, 4

8 [a] [Acts 9:3–8; 22:6–11; 26:12–18]

9 [a] Eph. 3:8
[b] Acts 8:3

10 [a] Eph. 3:7, 8
[b] Phil. 2:13

13 [a] [1 Thess. 4:14]

15 [a] Acts 2:24

17 [a] [Rom. 4:25]

18 [a] Job 14:12
[1] Died

19 [a] 2 Tim. 3:12

20 [a] 1 Pet. 1:3
[b] Acts 26:23
[1] Died

21 [a] Rom. 5:12; 6:23
[b] John 11:25

Christ all shall [a]be made alive. 23But [a]each one in his own order: Christ the firstfruits, afterward those *who are* Christ's at His coming. 24Then *comes* the end, when He delivers [a]the kingdom to God the Father, when He puts an end to all rule and all authority and power. 25For He must reign [a]till He has put all enemies under His feet. 26[a]The last enemy *that* will be destroyed *is* death. 27For [a]"*He has put all things under His feet.*" But when He says "all things are put under Him," *it is* evident that He who put all things under Him is excepted. 28[a]Now when all things are made subject to Him, then [b]the Son Himself will also be subject to Him who put all things under Him, that God may be all in all.

EFFECTS OF DENYING THE RESURRECTION

29Otherwise, what will they do who are baptized for the dead, if the dead do not rise at all? Why then are they baptized for the dead? 30And [a]why do we stand in [1]jeopardy every hour? 31I affirm, by [a]the boasting in you which I have in Christ Jesus our Lord, [b]I die daily. 32If, in the manner of men, [a]I have fought with beasts at Ephesus, what advantage *is it* to me? If *the* dead do not rise, [b]"*Let us eat and drink, for tomorrow we die!*"

33Do not be deceived: [a]"Evil company corrupts good habits." 34[a]Awake to

righteousness, and do not sin; [b]for some do not have the knowledge of God. [c]I speak *this* to your shame.

A GLORIOUS BODY

35But someone will say, [a]"How are the dead raised up? And with what body do they come?" 36Foolish one, [a]what you sow is not made alive unless it dies. 37And what you sow, you do not sow that body that shall be, but mere grain—perhaps wheat or some other *grain.* 38But God gives it a body as He pleases, and to each seed its own body.

39All flesh is not the same flesh, but *there is* one *kind* [1]of flesh of men, another flesh of animals, another of fish, *and* another of birds.

40*There are* also [1]celestial bodies and [2]terrestrial bodies; but the glory of the celestial *is* one, and the *glory* of the terrestrial *is* another. 41*There is* one glory of the sun, another glory of the moon, and another glory of the stars; for *one* star differs from *another* star in glory.

42[a]So also *is* the resurrection of the dead. *The body* is sown in corruption, it is raised in incorruption. 43[a]It is sown in dishonor, it is raised in glory. It is sown in weakness, it is raised in power. 44It is sown a natural body, it is raised a spiritual body. There is a natural body, and there is a spiritual body. 45And so it is written, [a]"*The first man Adam became a living being.*" [b]The last Adam became [c]a life-giving spirit.

Cross references

22 [a][John 5:28, 29]
23 [a][1 Thess. 4:15–17]
24 [a][Dan. 2:44; 7:14, 27]
25 [a]Ps. 110:1
26 [a][2 Tim. 1:10]
27 [a]Ps. 8:6
28 [a][Phil. 3:21]
   [b][1 Cor. 3:23; 11:3; 12:6]
30 [a]2 Cor. 11:26
   [1]*danger*
31 [a]1 Thess. 2:19
   [b]Rom. 8:36
32 [a]2 Cor. 1:8
   [b]Is. 22:13; 56:12
33 [a][1 Cor. 5:6]
34 [a]Rom. 13:11
   [b][1 Thess. 4:5]
   [c]1 Cor. 6:5
35 [a]Ezek. 37:3
36 [a]John 12:24
39 [1]NU, M omit *of flesh*
40 [1]*heavenly*
   [2]*earthly*
42 [a][Dan. 12:3]
43 [a][Phil. 3:21]
45 [a]Gen. 2:7
   [b][Rom. 5:14]
   [c]John 5:21; 6:57

THE RESURRECTION BODY　　1 Cor. 15:35–50

Paul responded here to the question as to what kind of body we will have after the resurrection. These bodies are temporary and disposable. "Flesh and blood cannot inherit the kingdom of God."

Paul likened it to a seed. Unless the seed is planted in the ground and dies, it will never become what it is designed to be. You plant a seed, it dies, but from it grows a beautiful carnation. The seed is related to the carnation, and all the carnation is was contained in the DNA of the seed, but what a difference!

Paul explained that there are "celestial bodies and terrestrial bodies." That is, there are bodies designed to function on earth and those designed for heaven. Our present bodies are not designed for heaven. They are terrestrial bodies. When we die, our natural bodies are sown, planted in the ground, but they are "raised a spiritual body."

The real me is spirit. My physical body is the expression of who I am, but it isn't the real me. In fact, my physical body is constantly being destroyed and replaced, with every cell of my body being replaced every seven years. What remains constant is my spirit, and that's what makes me who I am. So when God gives me my new body, after this one wears out, my spirit will be at home in a body that perfectly represents who I am. So, when we get to heaven and you look for me, look for the guy with a head full of beautiful, bushy, curly hair. I'll be wearing a new body, and I can hardly wait!

⁴⁶However, the spiritual is not first, but the natural, and afterward the spiritual. ⁴⁷ᵃThe first man *was* of the earth, ᵇ*made¹* of dust; the second Man *is* ²the Lord ᶜfrom heaven. ⁴⁸As *was* the *¹man* of dust, so also *are* those *who are* ²*made* of dust; ᵃand as *is* the heavenly *Man*, so also *are* those *who are* heavenly. ⁴⁹And ᵃas we have borne the image of the *man* of dust, ᵇwe¹ shall also bear the image of the heavenly *Man*.

OUR FINAL VICTORY

⁵⁰Now this I say, brethren, that ᵃflesh and blood cannot inherit the kingdom of God; nor does corruption inherit incorruption. ⁵¹Behold, I tell you a ¹mystery: ᵃWe shall not all sleep, ᵇbut we shall all be changed— ⁵²in a moment, in the twinkling of an eye, at the last trumpet. ᵃFor the trumpet will sound, and the dead will be raised incorruptible, and we shall be changed. ⁵³For this corruptible must put on incorruption, and ᵃthis mortal *must* put on immortality. ⁵⁴So when this corruptible has put on incorruption, and this mortal has put on immortality, then shall be brought to pass the saying that is written: ᵃ*"Death is swallowed up in victory."*

⁵⁵ *"O ᵃ¹ Death, where is your sting?*
   O Hades, where is your victory?"

1 Cor. 15:51–57

IN THE TWINKLING
OF AN EYE

Most people will get their new bodies after they die. Their old bodies are planted in the ground, and new bodies spring forth. But there are also many Christians who won't have to die. "We shall not all sleep, but we shall all be changed—in a moment, in the twinkling of an eye."

When Jesus returns for His church, just prior to the tribulation, He will catch us up to be with Him. If we are alive at that time, and I hope we are, our bodies will be transformed in the twinkling of an eye. Instant heavenly body! Glorious!

47 ᵃ John 3:31
ᵇ Gen. 2:7; 3:19
ᶜ John 3:13
¹ *earthy*
² NU omits *the Lord*

48 ᵃ Phil. 3:20
¹ *earthy*

49 ᵃ Gen. 5:3
ᵇ Rom. 8:29
¹ M *let us also bear*

50 ᵃ [John 3:3, 5]

51 ᵃ [1 Thess. 4:15]
ᵇ [Phil. 3:21]
¹ *hidden truth*

52 ᵃ Matt. 24:31

53 ᵃ 2 Cor. 5:4

54 ᵃ Is. 25:8

55 ᵃ Hos. 13:14
¹ NU *O Death, where is your victory? O Death, where is your sting?*

56 ᵃ [Rom. 3:20; 4:15; 7:8]

57 ᵃ [Rom. 7:25]
ᵇ [1 John 5:4]

58 ᵃ 2 Pet. 3:14
ᵇ [1 Cor. 3:8]

CHAPTER 16

1 ᵃ Gal. 2:10

2 ᵃ Acts 20:7

3 ᵃ 2 Cor. 3:1; 8:18

4 ᵃ 2 Cor. 8:4, 19

5 ᵃ 2 Cor. 1:15, 16

6 ᵃ Acts 15:3

7 ᵃ James 4:15

⁵⁶The sting of death *is* sin, and ᵃthe strength of sin *is* the law. ⁵⁷ᵃBut thanks *be* to God, who gives us ᵇthe victory through our Lord Jesus Christ.

⁵⁸ᵃTherefore, my beloved brethren, be steadfast, immovable, always abounding in the work of the Lord, knowing ᵇthat your labor is not in vain in the Lord.

COLLECTION FOR THE SAINTS

16 Now concerning ᵃthe collection for the saints, as I have given orders to the churches of Galatia, so you must do also: ²ᵃOn the first *day* of the week let each one of you lay something aside, storing up as he may prosper, that there be no collections when I come. ³And when I come, ᵃwhomever you approve by *your* letters I will send to bear your gift to Jerusalem. ⁴ᵃBut if it is fitting that I go also, they will go with me.

---

1 Cor. 16:2

First Day of the Week. The Jerusalem church was going through some difficult times, so Paul wanted the churches in Galatia and Corinth to take up a collection for them. He didn't want them to collect it when he arrived, but to do it beforehand.

It is interesting that he told them to take up the collection "on the first day of the week." This is an indication that the church at this time was meeting on Sunday. This is also mentioned in Acts 20:7. Extrabiblical church history indicates that early Christians met on Sunday because Jesus rose from the dead on Sunday.

In reality, I think every day is the Lord's day, and I worship Him every day.

PERSONAL PLANS

⁵Now I will come to you ᵃwhen I pass through Macedonia (for I am passing through Macedonia). ⁶And it may be that I will remain, or even spend the winter with you, that you may ᵃsend me on my journey, wherever I go. ⁷For I do not wish to see you now on the way; but I hope to stay a while with you, ᵃif the Lord permits. ⁸But I will tarry in Ephesus until

1 Cor. 16:7

BLESSED ARE THE FLEXIBLE

Paul shared his travel plans with the Corinthians, but then threw in "if the Lord permits." James said that, rather than say what we are going to do tomorrow, we should instead say, "If the Lord wills" (James 4:15). This is a good approach to take to our plans and schedules.

As the people of God, we need to stay flexible, making our plans subject to change or alteration. We don't want to make our plans so rigid that God has to break us in order to change our direction. He will do that if necessary, but it is better to stay flexible. I always say, "Blessed are the flexible, for they shall not be broken."

ᵃPentecost. ⁹For ᵃa great and effective door has opened to me, and ᵇthere are many adversaries.

¹⁰And ᵃif Timothy comes, see that he may be with you without fear; for ᵇhe does the work of the Lord, as I also do. ¹¹ᵃTherefore let no one despise him. But send him on his journey ᵇin peace, that he may come to me; for I am waiting for him with the brethren.

¹²Now concerning our brother ᵃApollos, I strongly urged him to come to you with the brethren, but he was quite unwilling to come at this time; however, he will come when he has a convenient time.

FINAL EXHORTATIONS

¹³ᵃWatch, ᵇstand fast in the faith, be brave, ᶜbe strong. ¹⁴ᵃLet all that you do be done with love.

---

8 ᵃLev. 23:15–22

9 ᵃActs 14:27
ᵇActs 19:9

10 ᵃActs 19:22
ᵇPhil. 2:20

11 ᵃ1Tim. 4:12
ᵇActs 15:33

12 ᵃ1Cor. 1:12; 3:5

13 ᵃMatt. 24:42
ᵇPhil. 1:27; 4:1
ᶜ[Eph. 3:16; 6:10]

14 ᵃ[1 Pet. 4:8]

15 ᵃ1Cor. 1:16
ᵇRom. 16:5
ᶜ2Cor. 8:4

16 ᵃHeb. 13:17
ᵇ[Heb. 6:10]

17 ᵃ2Cor. 11:9

18 ᵃCol. 4:8
ᵇPhil. 2:29

19 ᵃRom. 16:5

20 ᵃRom. 16:16

21 ᵃCol. 4:18

22 ᵃEph. 6:24
ᵇGal. 1:8, 9
ᶜJude 14, 15
ˡGr. anathema
²Aram. Marana tha; possibly Maran atha, Our Lord has come

23 ᵃRom. 16:20

---

¹⁵I urge you, brethren—you know ᵃthe household of Stephanas, that it is ᵇthe firstfruits of Achaia, and that they have devoted themselves to ᶜthe ministry of the saints— ¹⁶ᵃthat you also submit to such, and to everyone who works and ᵇlabors with us.

¹⁷I am glad about the coming of Stephanas, Fortunatus, and Achaicus, ᵃfor what was lacking on your part they supplied. ¹⁸ᵃFor they refreshed my spirit and yours. Therefore ᵇacknowledge such men.

GREETINGS AND A SOLEMN FAREWELL

¹⁹The churches of Asia greet you. Aquila and Priscilla greet you heartily in the Lord, ᵃwith the church that is in their house. ²⁰All the brethren greet you.

ᵃGreet one another with a holy kiss. ²¹ᵃThe salutation with my own hand—Paul's.

²²If anyone ᵃdoes not love the Lord Jesus Christ, ᵇlet him be ˡaccursed. ᶜO² Lord, come!

²³ᵃThe grace of our Lord Jesus Christ be with you. ²⁴My love be with you all in Christ Jesus. Amen.

---

1 Cor. 16:8–9

Many Adversaries. I love this about Paul! He said that he is going to stay in Ephesus for a while because "a great and effective door has opened to me, and there are many adversaries." Paul would never run from a fight. When he saw the enemies, he took it as evidence that God was about to do something exciting.

I wonder how many great opportunities we miss and how many open doors we walk away from, because we get scared away by adversity. Our attitude should be, "Resist the devil and he will flee from you" (James 4:7).

CORINTHIANS

INTRODUCTION
Paul had written the book of 1 Corinthians from Ephesus. He wrote it to address many of the problems that existed in the church at Corinth. In the end of the book he expressed his desire to come to Corinth in the near future, "if the Lord permits" (1 Cor. 16:5–7).

But Paul had learned to be flexible, and trouble in Ephesus caused him to have to leave suddenly and he went to Troas, where he was hoping to meet up with Titus, to hear how things were going in Corinth. He had probably sent the first letter to Corinth with Titus; and as the letter was a difficult one for them to receive, since it pointed out so many errors in their church, Paul was anxious to hear how they had received it. But Titus wasn't in Troas, so Paul went on to Philippi where he met up with Titus, got the latest news from Corinth, and wrote this second letter in AD 56–57.

This letter is more encouraging than the first letter, as he commended them for their positive response to his first letter, and for the fact that they had taken corrective measures. However, there was a growing faction of false teachers arising in Corinth who were attacking Paul. They accused him of being a liar, of being cruel in his writings, of being a con man, and they questioned his qualifications as an apostle. So, in 2 Corinthians Paul was forced to defend his character and his ministry.

It is never pleasant to be under attack. No matter how strong you are, it hurts for someone to attack your ministry. Years ago there was a man who was traveling all over the country, claiming that I was a part of the Illuminati and that the church of Satan had once given me seven million dollars to start a Christian music company to corrupt Christian young people with evil rock-and-roll music. Of course this was ridiculous, and my wife, Kay, eventually confronted the man publicly, and he backed off his claims; but as ridiculous as these accusations were, they still hurt. They didn't hurt because I cared what this man thought of me, but they hurt because I knew innocent people were being deceived. People all over the country who were new Christians, and had been studying the Bible with the help of our tapes, were now confused and hurt. So sometimes, to protect innocent sheep, you have to defend yourself against false charges. And that is what Paul did in 2 Corinthians.

The result is that we learned a lot about Paul in this book. He shares personal details about his life and ministry that we would have never known of otherwise, and

God gives us much information about the nature of the ministry and the call to the ministry through these writings. We receive a personal view of "Paul, an apostle of Jesus Christ by the will of God" (2 Cor. 1:1).

GREETING

1 Paul, [a]an apostle of Jesus Christ by the will of God, and [b]Timothy *our* brother,

To the church of God which is at Corinth, [c]with all the saints who are in all Achaia:

2[a]Grace to you and peace from God our Father and the Lord Jesus Christ.

COMFORT IN SUFFERING

3[a]Blessed *be* the God and Father of our Lord Jesus Christ, the Father of mercies and God of all comfort, 4who [a]comforts us in all our tribulation, that we may be able to comfort those who are in any [1]trouble, with the comfort with which we ourselves are comforted by God. 5For as [a]the sufferings of Christ abound in us, so our [1]consolation also abounds through Christ. 6Now if we are afflicted, [a]*it is* for your consolation and salvation, which is effective for enduring the same sufferings which we also suffer. Or if we are comforted, *it is* for your consolation and salvation. 7And our hope for you *is* steadfast, because we know that [a]as you are partakers of the sufferings, so also *you will partake* of the consolation.

DELIVERED FROM SUFFERING

8For we do not want you to be ignorant, brethren, of [a]our [1]trouble which

CHAPTER 1

1 [a]2 Tim. 1:1
 [b]1 Cor. 16:10
 [c]Col. 1:2

2 [a]Rom. 1:7

3 [a]1 Pet. 1:3

4 [a]Is. 51:12; 66:13
 [1]*tribulation*

5 [a]2 Cor. 4:10
 [1]*comfort*

6 [a]2 Cor. 4:15; 12:15

7 [a][Rom. 8:17]

8 [a]Acts 19:23
 [1]*tribulation*

9 [a]Jer. 17:5, 7

10 [a][2 Pet. 2:9]
 [1]NU *shall*

11 [a]Rom. 15:30
 [1]M *your behalf*

came to us in Asia: that we were burdened beyond measure, above strength, so that we despaired even of life. 9Yes, we had the sentence of death in ourselves, that we should [a]not trust in ourselves but in God who raises the dead, 10awho delivered us from so great a death, and [1]does deliver us; in whom we trust that He will still deliver *us*, 11you also [a]helping together in prayer for us, that thanks may be given by many persons on [1]our behalf

---

2 Cor. 1:8–9

Trusting in Yourself. Paul told the Corinthians about a difficult situation he had just gone through in Asia. He was "burdened beyond measure, above strength, so that we despaired even of life." It was beyond what he could handle, and he thought it would kill him. But he recognized God's purpose in the whole ordeal was that Paul would learn to trust in God instead of himself.

Sometimes God will put us in situations that we can't handle, just to remind us to trust in Him rather than in ourselves.

THE GOD OF ALL COMFORT   2 Cor. 1:3–7

I t is interesting when we think of the apostle Paul, we think of him as some kind of super saint, like he could leap tall buildings in a single bound. But Paul was like everyone else and seemed to be prone to discouragement and fear. He went through many afflictions and trials, and sometimes wondered whether he would be better off just dying and going to heaven. But God always comforted Paul, and kept him going. Here he talked about how when you have been comforted it gives you the ability to comfort others.

I went through the experience of losing my father and brother in a plane crash. So whenever I hear of someone who loses a family member, especially in a plane crash, I feel a tremendous empathy with them. I have been there and know what they are feeling, and I can offer comfort to them because I experienced the Lord comforting me.

So Paul told the people, "I've been there. And in those dark hours the Lord was with me and strengthened me." He is the God of all comfort.

bfor the gift *granted* to us through many.

PAUL'S SINCERITY

12For our boasting is this: the testimony of our conscience that we conducted ourselves in the world in 1simplicity and agodly sincerity, bnot with fleshly wisdom but by the grace of God, and more abundantly toward you. 13For we are not writing any other things to you than what you read or understand. Now I trust you will understand, even to the end 14(as also you have understood us in part), athat we are your boast as byou also *are* ours, in the day of the Lord Jesus.

---

2 Cor. 1:13

No Double Talk. There were people who were attacking Paul's ministry by suggesting that he had a hidden agenda and that what he said wasn't what he meant. So Paul told them, "We are not writing any other things to you than what you read or understand."

That is the way we should all communicate. Just say what you mean, straight out, without any hidden meaning. And when we listen to each other, we should take what people say at face value, giving them the benefit of the doubt. Don't wonder what they really mean.

SPARING THE CHURCH

15And in this confidence aI intended to come to you before, that you might have ba second benefit— 16to pass by way of you to Macedonia, ato come again from Macedonia to you, and be helped by you on my way to Judea. 17Therefore, when I was planning this, did I do it lightly? Or the things I plan, do I plan aaccording to the flesh, that with me there should be Yes, Yes, and No, No? 18But *as* God *is* afaithful, our 1word to you was notYes and No. 19For athe Son of God, Jesus Christ, who was preached among you by us—by me, bSilvanus, and cTimothy—was not Yes and No, dbut in Him wasYes. 20 aFor all the promises of God in Him *are* Yes, and in Him Amen, to the glory of God through us. 21Now He who establishes

us with you in Christ and ahas anointed us *is* God, 22who aalso has sealed us and bgiven us the Spirit in our hearts as a guarantee. 23Moreover aI call God as witness against my soul, bthat to spare you I came no more to Corinth. 24Not athat we 1have dominion over your faith, but are fellow workers for your joy; for bby faith you stand.

2 But I determined this within myself, athat I would not come again to you in sorrow. 2For if I make you asorrowful, then who is he who makes me glad but the one who is made sorrowful by me?

FORGIVE THE OFFENDER

3And I wrote this very thing to you, lest, when I came, aI should have sorrow over those from whom I ought to have joy, bhaving confidence in you all that my joy is *the joy* of you all. 4For out of much 1affliction and anguish of heart I wrote to you, with many tears, anot that you should be grieved, but that you might know the love which I have so abundantly for you.

---

2 Cor. 2:1–4

The Heart Behind Discipline. Paul had written the first letter to Corinth to rebuke them for some of the glaring problems and sins that existed in the church there. But now he also wanted them to know the spirit in which he was correcting them.

"For out of much affliction and anguish of heart I wrote to you, with many tears, not that you should be grieved, but that you might know the love which I have so abundantly for you." What if we had that kind of heart of love every time we corrected or disciplined one another?

5But aif anyone has caused grief, he has not bgrieved me, but all of you to some extent—not to be too severe. 6This punishment which *was inflicted* aby the majority *is* sufficient for such a man, 7aso that, on the contrary, you *ought* rather to forgive and comfort *him*, lest perhaps such a one be swallowed up with too much sorrow. 8Therefore I urge you to reaffirm *your*

Center column references:

11 b2Cor. 4:15; 9:11

12 a2Cor. 2:17
b[1 Cor. 2:4]
1 The opposite of duplicity

14 a2Cor. 5:12
bPhil. 2:16

15 a1Cor. 4:19
bRom. 1:11; 15:29

16 a1Cor. 16:3–6

17 a2Cor. 10:2; 11:18

18 a1John 5:20
1 *message*

19 aMark 1:1
b1Pet. 5:12
c2Cor. 1:1
d[Heb. 13:8]

20 a[Rom. 15:8, 9]

21 a[1John 2:20, 27]

22 a[Eph. 4:30]
b[Eph. 1:14]

23 aGal. 1:20
b1Cor. 4:21

24 a[1Pet. 5:3]
bRom. 11:20
1 *rule*

CHAPTER 2

1 a2Cor. 1:23

2 a2Cor. 7:8

3 a2Cor. 12:21
bGal. 5:10

4 a[2Cor. 2:9; 7:8, 12]
1 *tribulation*

5 a[1Cor. 5:1]
bGal. 4:12

6 a1Cor. 5:4, 5

7 aGal. 6:1

RESTORING YOUR BROTHER   2 Cor. 2:6–8

In his first letter, Paul had addressed an issue of immorality that was going on in Corinth (1 Cor. 5), and he had told the Corinthian Christians to remove the offending party from fellowship in order to try to save his soul. Now after some time had gone by, the man had repented, and Paul told the church, "This punishment which was inflicted by the majority is sufficient for such a man, so that, on the contrary, you ought rather to forgive and comfort him, lest perhaps such a one be swallowed up with too much sorrow."

In the body of Christ, there has to be a place of forgiveness. There has to be a place of restoring someone back into fellowship. When a person has sinned, it is tragic. If they continue in sin, it is necessary to separate them. But when there is confession of sin and repentance, there has to be restoration into full fellowship with the body of Christ. Unfortunately, there are always people who take a harsh attitude and want to cut off a person forever. But we have to allow, in the body of Christ, a place of restoration into the fellowship for those who have stumbled and fallen.

love to him. 9For to this end I also wrote, that I might put you to the test, whether you are aobedient in all things. 10Now whom you forgive anything, I also forgive. For 1if indeed I have forgiven anything, I have forgiven that one for your sakes in the presence of Christ, 11lest Satan should take advantage of us; for we are not ignorant of his devices.

TRIUMPH IN CHRIST

12Furthermore, awhen I came to Troas to preach Christ's gospel, and ba 1door was opened to me by the Lord, 13aI had no rest in my spirit, because I did not find Titus my brother; but taking my leave of them, I departed for Macedonia.

---

2 Cor. 2:17

Peddling the Word of God. In those days, as in our day, there were those who saw the ministry as a business. They used the Word to cash in on the ministry for their own enrichment. The gospel is not something to be marketed. God is insulted and offended when we use telemarketing and other gimmicks to support what is purportedly His work.

What a horrible indictment, that it could be said that we are "peddling the word of God." Paul said, "But as of sincerity, but as from God, we speak in the sight of God." Beware. God sees.

---

9 a 2 Cor. 7:15; 10:6
10 1 NU indeed, what I have forgiven, if I have forgiven anything, I did it for your sakes
12 a Acts 16:8
b 1 Cor. 16:9
1 Opportunity
13 a 2 Cor. 7:6, 13; 8:6
14 1 manifests
15 a [1 Cor. 1:18]
b [2 Cor. 4:3]
16 a Luke 2:34
b [1 Cor. 15:10]
17 a 2 Pet. 2:3
b 2 Cor. 1:12
1 M the rest
2 adulterating for gain

CHAPTER 3

1 a 2 Cor. 5:12; 10:12, 18; 12:11
b Acts 18:27
2 a 1 Cor. 9:2
3 a 1 Cor. 3:5
b Ex. 24:12; 31:18; 32:15
c Ps. 40:8
5 a [John 15:5]
b 1 Cor. 15:10
6 a 1 Cor. 3:5
b Jer. 31:31
c Rom. 2:27
d Gal. 3:10
e John 6:63
1 Or spirit
7 a Rom. 7:10
b Ex. 34:1

14Now thanks be to God who always leads us in triumph in Christ, and through us 1diffuses the fragrance of His knowledge in every place. 15For we are to God the fragrance of Christ aamong those who are being saved and bamong those who are perishing. 16aTo the one we are the aroma of death leading to death, and to the other the aroma of life leading to life. And bwho is sufficient for these things? 17For we are not, as 1so many, apeddling2 the word of God; but as bof sincerity, but as from God, we speak in the sight of God in Christ.

CHRIST'S EPISTLE

3 Do awe begin again to commend ourselves? Or do we need, as some others, bepistles of commendation to you or letters of commendation from you? 2aYou are our epistle written in our hearts, known and read by all men; 3clearly you are an epistle of Christ, aministered by us, written not with ink but by the Spirit of the living God, bon tablets of stone but con tablets of flesh, that is, of the heart.

THE SPIRIT, NOT THE LETTER

4And we have such trust through Christ toward God. 5aNot that we are sufficient of ourselves to think of anything as being from ourselves, but bour sufficiency is from God, 6who also made us sufficient as aministers of bthe new covenant, not cof the letter but of the 1Spirit; for dthe letter kills, ebut the Spirit gives life.

GLORY OF THE NEW COVENANT

7But if athe ministry of death, bwritten and engraved on stones, was glorious,

2 Cor. 3:1–3

FRUIT OF MINISTRY

Paul was being attacked by some people who were questioning his qualifications as a minister. But he told the Corinthians that he didn't need any letters of commendation, because their lives were commendation enough. He had led them to the Lord and grounded them in the faith.

Looking at the fruit of a ministry is an excellent way to assess the ministry. Jesus said, concerning false prophets, "You will know them by their fruits" (Matt. 7:16). We should always ask of those who would criticize another ministry, "What is the fruit of your ministry?" Paul's credentials were the faith in Christ and the walk with the Lord of those to whom he had ministered.

7 c Ex. 34:29

8 a [Gal. 3:5]

9 a [Rom. 1:17; 3:21]

12 a Eph. 6:19

13 a Ex. 34:33–35
b [Gal. 3:23]

14 a Acts 28:26

16 a Rom. 11:23
b Is. 25:7

17 a [1 Cor. 15:45]
b Gal. 5:1, 13

18 a 1 Cor. 13:12
b [2 Cor. 4:4, 6]
c [Rom. 8:29, 30]

2 Cor. 3:5–6

WE ARE NOT SUFFICIENT

Paul said, "Not that we are sufficient of ourselves to think of anything as being from ourselves." How important it is for us to remember that we are not sufficient in ourselves to do the work of God! He is the only One who is sufficient, and we need Him if we are to do anything productive for the kingdom.

I am amazed at all the seminars and books that are available from people who want to show you how to make your church grow. The only explanation as to how Calvary Chapel has grown so much is just the sovereign work of the grace of God. We had no gimmicks, no secrets, no plans, no procedures, no special skills, no geniuses. It was just the Spirit of God working in the hearts and lives of the people. Nothing more. And that was sufficient, because He is sufficient.

cso that the children of Israel could not look steadily at the face of Moses because of the glory of his countenance, which *glory* was passing away, 8how will athe ministry of the Spirit not be more glorious? 9For if the ministry of condemnation *had* glory, the ministry aof righteousness exceeds much more in glory. 10For even what was made glorious had no glory in this respect, because of the glory that excels. 11For if what is passing away *was* glorious, what remains *is* much more glorious.

12Therefore, since we have such hope, awe use great boldness of speech— 13unlike Moses, awho put a veil over his face so that the children of Israel could not look steadily at bthe end of what was passing away. 14But atheir minds were blinded. For until this day the same veil remains unlifted in the reading of the Old Testament, because the *veil* is taken away in Christ. 15But even to this day, when Moses is read, a veil lies on their heart. 16Nevertheless awhen one turns to the Lord, bthe veil is taken away. 17Now athe Lord is the Spirit; and where the Spirit of the Lord *is*, there *is* bliberty.

18But we all, with unveiled face, beholding aas in a mirror bthe glory of the Lord, care being transformed into the

2 Cor. 3:18

From Glory to Glory. The Jews had a veil over their eyes from the time of Moses and couldn't see the Lord clearly. But the veil has been lifted for us; and as we see Him, we "are being transformed into the same image from glory to glory, just as by the Spirit of the Lord."

Man was originally created in the image of God, but the image was distorted by the fall. Now it is God's desire and purpose to restore you back into the image of God as you look at the glory of Jesus.

same image from glory to glory, just as ¹by the Spirit of the Lord.

THE LIGHT OF CHRIST'S GOSPEL

4 Therefore, since we have this ministry, ᵃas we have received mercy, we ᵇdo not lose heart. ²But we have renounced the hidden things of shame, not walking in craftiness nor ¹handling the word of God deceitfully, but by manifestation of the truth ᵃcommending ourselves to every man's conscience in the sight of God. ³But even if our gospel is veiled, ᵃit is veiled to those who are perishing, ⁴whose minds ᵃthe god of this age ᵇhas blinded, who do not believe, lest ᶜthe light of the gospel of the glory of Christ, ᵈwho is the image of God, should shine on them. ⁵ᵃFor we do not preach ourselves, but Christ Jesus the Lord, and ᵇourselves your bondservants for Jesus' sake. ⁶For it is the God ᵃwho commanded light to shine out of darkness, who has ᵇshone in our hearts to *give* the light of the knowledge of the glory of God in the face of Jesus Christ.

---

2 Cor. 4:2

Handling the Word Deceitfully. Paul just taught the simple truth. He didn't use craftiness nor did he handle the Word of God deceitfully." There are those who twist the Scriptures to make them say whatever they want them to say. For instance, the Bible tells us that Jesus wore a robe that was woven from top to bottom, without a seam. Some advocates of the prosperity doctrine use this to say Jesus wore designer clothes.

Twisting the Scriptures to make them say what we want them to say should terrify us. It is God's Word. Use it honestly.

CAST DOWN BUT UNCONQUERED

⁷But we have this treasure in earthen vessels, ᵃthat the excellence of the power may be of God and not of us. ⁸*We are* ᵃhard-pressed on every side, yet not crushed; *we are* perplexed, but not in despair; ⁹persecuted, but not ᵃforsaken; ᵇstruck down, but not destroyed— ¹⁰ᵃalways carrying about in the body the dying of the Lord Jesus,

---

Cross references:

18 ¹Or *from the Lord, the Spirit*

CHAPTER 4

1 ᵃ1Cor. 7:25
ᵇ2Cor. 4:16

2 ᵃ2Cor. 5:11
¹*adulterating the word of God*

3 ᵃ[1Cor. 1:18]

4 ᵃJohn 12:31
ᵇJohn 12:40
ᶜ[2Cor. 3:8, 9]
ᵈ[John 1:18]

5 ᵃ1Cor. 1:13
ᵇ1Cor. 9:19

6 ᵃGen. 1:3
ᵇ2Pet. 1:19

7 ᵃ1Cor. 2:5

8 ᵃ2Cor. 1:8;
7:5

9 ᵃ[Heb. 13:5]
ᵇPs. 37:24

10 ᵃPhil. 3:10
ᵇRom. 8:17

11 ᵃRom. 8:36

13 ᵃ2Pet. 1:1
ᵇPs. 116:10

14 ᵃ[Rom. 8:11]

15 ᵃCol. 1:24
ᵇ2Cor. 1:11

16 ᵃ2Cor. 4:1
ᵇ[Is. 40:29, 31]

---

2 Cor. 4:7

EARTHEN VESSELS

What an absolute treasure is this glorious truth of the gospel! Eternal life is a priceless treasure! And yet God chooses to place this treasure into earthen vessels, or pots made from clay. He doesn't put it into a gold treasure chest, but into us, and we are made from earth. That way we won't draw people to ourselves, but to God.

You wouldn't give someone a present where the package is more valuable than the present. And you would feel pretty strange if you gave a gift to someone and they just kept going on about how beautiful the wrapping was without ever opening the present.

God uses clay pots like us so that no one will glory in who we are, but they will glory in who He is. It is foolish for us to exalt ourselves. He chose us because we aren't exalted; and if we seek to exalt ourselves, it will render us useless to Him.

ᵇthat the life of Jesus also may be manifested in our body. ¹¹For we who live ᵃare always delivered to death for Jesus' sake, that the life of Jesus also may be manifested in our mortal flesh. ¹²So then death is working in us, but life in you.

¹³And since we have ᵃthe same spirit of faith, according to what is written, ᵇ*"I believed and therefore I spoke,"* we also believe and therefore speak, ¹⁴knowing that ᵃHe who raised up the Lord Jesus will also raise us up with Jesus, and will present *us* with you. ¹⁵For ᵃall things *are* for your sakes, that ᵇgrace, having spread through the many, may cause thanksgiving to abound to the glory of God.

SEEING THE INVISIBLE

¹⁶Therefore we ᵃdo not lose heart. Even though our outward man is perishing, yet the inward *man* is ᵇbeing

renewed day by day. [17]For [a]our light affliction, which is but for a moment, is working for us a far more exceeding *and* eternal weight of glory, [18a]while we do not look at the things which are seen, but at the things which are not seen. For the things which are seen *are* temporary, but the things which are not seen *are* eternal.

---

2 Cor. 4:18

Looking at the Unseen. If Paul had been focusing on the things going on around him, he would have been greatly discouraged. He was enduring tremendous persecution, and it was taking its toll on his body. But his focus was on the spiritual realm.

The man who can see into the spiritual world is the man who will ultimately prevail. The material world is a phony world, full of phony people. The spiritual world is the real world, and that is where we live. Our citizenship is in heaven (Phil. 3:20).

ASSURANCE OF THE RESURRECTION

5 For we know that if [a]our earthly [1]house, *this* tent, is destroyed, we have a building from God, a house [b]not made with hands, eternal in the heavens. [2]For in this [a]we groan, earnestly desiring to be clothed with our [1]habitation which is from heaven, [3]if indeed, [a]having been clothed, we shall not be found naked. [4]For we who are in *this* tent groan, being burdened, not because we want to be unclothed, [a]but further clothed, that mortality may be swallowed up by life. [5]Now He who has prepared us for this very thing *is* God, who also [a]has given us the Spirit as [1]a guarantee.

[6]So *we are* always confident, knowing that while we are at home in the body we are absent from the Lord. [7]For [a]we walk by faith, not by sight. [8]We are confident, yes, [a]well pleased rather to be absent from the body and to be present with the Lord.

THE JUDGMENT SEAT OF CHRIST

[9]Therefore we make it our aim, whether present or absent, to be well pleasing to Him. [10a]For we must all appear before the judgment seat of Christ, [b]that each one may receive the

---

17 [a]Rom. 8:18

18 [a][Heb. 11:1, 13]

CHAPTER 5

1 [a]Job 4:19
[b]Mark 14:58
[1]Physical body

2 [a]Rom. 8:23
[1]dwelling

3 [a]Rev. 3:18

4 [a]1 Cor. 15:53

5 [a]Rom. 8:23
[1]down payment, earnest

7 [a]Heb. 11:1

8 [a]Phil. 1:23

10 [a]Rom. 2:16; 14:10, 12
[b]Eph. 6:8

11 [a][Heb. 10:31; 12:29]

---

2 Cor. 5:1–4

THESE TENTS

Paul described our physical bodies as temporary dwelling places, tents that will one day be discarded. But God is preparing new bodies for us, "a house not made with hands, eternal in the heavens." The real me isn't my body; it is my spirit. And when this body wears out, I will move into a new body that He has prepared for me. The new body will be related to this body, perhaps genetically, but will be designed for heaven and eternity.

Someday you may read in the newspaper that Chuck Smith died. Don't you believe it! Accurate reporting would say, "Chuck Smith moved!" Out of an old, worn-out tent, and into a glorious new body like Jesus has. No more groaning, no more pain, no more suffering. Just perfect fellowship with the Lord forever!

---

things *done* in the body, according to what he has done, whether good or bad. [11]Knowing, therefore, [a]the terror of the Lord, we persuade men; but we are well known to God, and I also trust are well known in your consciences.

---

2 Cor. 5:6–8

Present with the Lord. Paul wasn't afraid to die. In fact, he really looked forward to it because he realized that as long as he was here on the earth, he would be absent from the Lord. He said that he would be "well pleased rather to be absent from the body and to be present with the Lord."

When my spirit leaves my body, I am dead, by definition. But for a Christian, when my spirit leaves my body, I go immediately into the presence of the Lord, in my new body. I can hardly wait!

THE JUDGMENT SEAT OF CHRIST   2 Cor. 5:10

Every person who does not accept Jesus Christ will one day stand before the great white throne of judgment, to be judged for their sins (Rev. 20:11). But every Christian will appear before the judgment seat of Christ. These are two different kinds of judgments.

At the judgment seat of Christ, it will be about rewards that are given. The word for "judgment" here in the Greek is *bema* which was the word used for the judging stands in the Olympics. The Olympic judges would place the laurel wreath on the head of the winner, in front of the bema seat. When we Christians stand before Jesus and the judgment seat of Christ, we will be rewarded based on what we have done for the Lord and especially for the motives we had for what we did.

If I do good things to impress people, my reward is here on earth. I receive the adulation of men. But the things I do that are motivated by a love for God and a love for people, those will be rewarded by Jesus on this day of judgment. This was a significant motivation for Paul to want to please the Lord. Just to stand in front of the judge's stand and hear Jesus say, "Well done!" (Matt. 25:21).

BE RECONCILED TO GOD

12For awe do not commend ourselves again to you, but give you opportunity bto boast on our behalf, that you may have *an answer* for those who boast in appearance and not in heart. 13For aif we are beside ourselves, *it is* for God;

2 Cor. 6:2

NOW IS THE TIME

God has done so much for us by sending Jesus to die for us and offering salvation as a free gift. And yet, there are those who put off getting right with God.

They intend to get right with God one of these days. But why put it off? It doesn't make sense. It would be like if you had a horrible migraine headache and someone gave you some new medicine that would knock it out immediately. Would you just put the medicine on the shelf and maybe take it tomorrow? "I think I'll just suffer one more night, and maybe I'll take it in the morning." Why?

Procrastination in getting right with God makes no sense. Don't wait! Don't put it off! Now is the day of salvation.

12 a 2 Cor. 3:1
b 2 Cor. 1:14

13 a 2 Cor. 11:1, 16; 12:11

14 a [Rom. 5:15; 6:6]

15 a [Rom. 6:11]

16 a 2 Cor. 10:3
b [Matt. 12:50]

17 a [John 6:63]
b [Rom. 8:9]
c Is. 43:18; 65:17
d [Rom. 6:3–10]

18 a Rom. 5:10

19 a [Rom. 3:24]
1 *reckoning*

20 a Eph. 6:20

21 a Is. 53:6, 9
b [Rom. 1:17; 3:21]

CHAPTER 6

1 a 1 Cor. 3:9
b 2 Cor. 5:20

2 a Is. 49:8

or if we are of sound mind, *it is* for you. 14For the love of Christ compels us, because we judge thus: that aif One died for all, then all died; 15and He died for all, athat those who live should live no longer for themselves, but for Him who died for them and rose again.

16aTherefore, from now on, we regard no one according to the flesh. Even though we have known Christ according to the flesh, byet now we know Him *thus* no longer. 17Therefore, if anyone ais in Christ, he is ba new creation; cold things have passed away; behold, all things have become dnew. 18Now all things *are* of God, awho has reconciled us to Himself through Jesus Christ, and has given us the ministry of reconciliation, 19that is, that aGod was in Christ reconciling the world to Himself, not 1imputing their trespasses to them, and has committed to us the word of reconciliation.

20Now then, we are aambassadors for Christ, as though God were pleading through us: we implore *you* on Christ's behalf, be reconciled to God. 21For aHe made Him who knew no sin *to be* sin for us, that we might become bthe righteousness of God in Him.

MARKS OF THE MINISTRY

6We then, *as* aworkers together *with Him* also bplead with *you* not to receive the grace of God in vain. 2For He says:

> a"*In an acceptable time I have heard you,*
> *And in the day of salvation I have helped you.*"

Behold, now *is* the accepted time; behold, now *is* the day of salvation. [3 ᵃRom. 14:13]

3ᵃWe give no offense in anything, that our ministry may not be blamed. [4 ᵃ1Cor. 4:1; 1 endurance] 4But in all *things* we commend ourselves ᵃas ministers of God: in much 1patience, in tribulations, in needs, in distresses, [5 ᵃ2Cor. 11:23] 5ᵃin stripes, in imprisonments, in tumults, in labors, in sleeplessness, in fastings; 6by purity, by [6 1Lit. *unhypo-critical*] knowledge, by longsuffering, by kindness, by the Holy Spirit, by 1sincere love, [7 ᵃ2Cor. 7:14; b1Cor. 2:4; c2Cor. 10:4] 7ᵃby the word of truth, by bthe power of God, by cthe armor of righteousness on the right hand and on the left, 8by honor and dishonor, by evil report and good report; as deceivers, and *yet* true; [9 ᵃ2Cor. 4:2; 5:11; b1Cor. 4:9, 11; cPs. 118:18] 9as unknown, and ᵃ*yet* well known; bas dying, and behold we live; cas chastened, and *yet* not killed; 10as sorrowful, yet always rejoicing; as poor, yet making many ᵃrich; as having nothing, and *yet* possessing all things. [10 ᵃ[2Cor. 8:9]]

BE HOLY

11O Corinthians! 1We have spoken openly to you, ᵃour heart is wide open. [11 ᵃ2Cor. 7:3; 1Lit. *Our mouth is open*] 12You are not restricted by us, but ᵃyou are restricted by your *own* affections. 13Now in return for the same ᵃ(I speak [12 ᵃ2Cor. 12:15] as to children), you also be open. 14ᵃDo not be unequally yoked together with unbelievers. For bwhat [13 ᵃ1Cor. 4:14]

2 Cor. 6:4–10

IN, BY, AND AS

Paul described the ministry in these verses as he experienced it. He started with a list of the problems of the ministry, preceded by the word "in." These are all the kinds of trials he faced. Then he gave a list of provisions and resources for the ministry, each preceded by the word "by." Then he described some of the contrasts between perception and reality in the ministry. These are each preceded by "as."

By going through this list, we discover so much about the ministry, its problems, provisions, and perceptions, as well as its power.

[14 ᵃ1Cor. 5:9; bEph. 5:6, 7, 11; 1 *in common*; 2 *fellowship*]

[16 ᵃ[1Cor. 3:16, 17; 6:19]; bEzek. 37:26, 27; 1NU *we*]

[17 ᵃIs. 52:11]

[18 ᵃ2Sam. 7:14; b[Rom. 8:14]]

CHAPTER 7

[1 ᵃ[1John 3:3]]

[2 ᵃActs 20:33]

1fellowship has righteousness with lawlessness? And what 2communion has light with darkness? 15And what accord has Christ with Belial? Or what part has a believer with an unbeliever? 16And what agreement has the temple of God with idols? For ᵃyou1 are the temple of the living God. As God has said:

b"*I will dwell in them
And walk among them.
I will be their God,
And they shall be My people.*"

17Therefore

ᵃ"*Come out from among them
And be separate, says the Lord.
Do not touch what is unclean,
And I will receive you.*"

18 "*I ᵃwill be a Father to you,
And you shall be My bsons and daughters,
Says the LORD Almighty.*"

7Therefore,ᵃ having these promises, beloved, let us cleanse ourselves from all filthiness of the flesh and spirit, perfecting holiness in the fear of God.

THE CORINTHIANS' REPENTANCE

2Open *your hearts* to us. We have wronged no one, we have corrupted no one, ᵃwe have cheated no one. 3I do not

2 Cor. 7:1

CLEANSED FROM FILTH

On the basis of all that God has done for us, Paul has exhorted us to "cleanse ourselves from all filthiness of the flesh and spirit, perfecting holiness in the fear of God."

Trying to fulfill the lust of the flesh is a one-way road to hell. You can never satisfy your flesh. It will always demand more and more. There are so many lives and so many families today that are being destroyed by pornography. People are living in this fantasy world that promises fulfillment, but always leaves them wanting more.

We need to cleanse ourselves of all filth and not allow the flesh to take over our lives. The key is the fear of God. If we have a healthy respect for God and know that He is always with us, it has a purifying effect on our lives. I would be afraid to do things that offend Him.

say *this* to condemn; for [a]I have said before that you are in our hearts, to die together and to live together. [4][a]Great *is* my boldness of speech toward you, [b]great *is* my boasting on your behalf. [c]I am filled with comfort. I am exceedingly joyful in all our tribulation. [5]For indeed, [a]when we came to Macedonia, our bodies had no rest, but [b]we were troubled on every side. [c]Outside *were* conflicts, inside *were* fears. [6]Nevertheless [a]God, who comforts the downcast, comforted us by [b]the coming of Titus, [7]and not only by his coming, but also by the [1]consolation with which he was comforted in you, when he told us of your earnest desire, your mourning, your zeal for me, so that I rejoiced even more. [8]For even if I made you [a]sorry with my letter, I do not regret it; [b]though I did regret it. For I perceive that the same epistle made you sorry, though only for a while. [9]Now I rejoice, not that you were made sorry, but that

Cross references
3 [a]2 Cor. 6:11, 12
4 [a]2 Cor. 3:12 [b]1 Cor. 1:4 [c]Phil. 2:17
5 [a]2 Cor. 2:13 [b]2 Cor. 4:8 [c]Deut. 32:25
6 [a]2 Cor. 1:3, 4 [b]2 Cor. 2:13; 7:13
7 [1]comfort
8 [a]2 Cor. 2:2 [b]2 Cor. 2:4
10 [a]Matt. 26:75 [b]Prov. 17:22
11 [a]Eph. 5:11 [b]2 Cor. 2:5–11

2 Cor. 7:5–7

The Depressed Apostle. We often get the idea that God only uses those people who have been elevated to super-saint status. Yet all of those men who have been used mightily by God were no different from us. They experienced the same struggles we do.

Paul struggled with depression. He had fears and discouragement. But he was comforted by the God "who comforts the downcast." The same God, the God of all comfort, is there for you, as well.

your sorrow led to repentance. For you were made sorry in a godly manner, that you might suffer loss from us in nothing. [10]For [a]godly sorrow produces repentance *leading* to salvation, not to be regretted; [b]but the sorrow of the world produces death. [11]For observe this very thing, that you sorrowed in a godly manner: What diligence it produced in you, what [a]clearing *of yourselves*, what indignation, what fear, what vehement desire, what zeal, what vindication! In all *things* you proved yourselves to be [b]clear in this matter. [12]Therefore, although I wrote

2 Cor. 7:9–10

Sorrow and Repentance. Paul had written a letter to the Corinthians that was rather harsh, pointing out many of the serious problems that existed in their church. He was hesitant to write it, knowing that it would hurt them. But he pointed out that, although it had produced sorrow, that sorrow had led to repentance.

It is good to be sorry for your sins, but the real question is, are you going to change? To repent means to change directions. Is that what you do after feeling sorry for your sins? If not, your sorrow means nothing. "Godly sorrow produces repentance."

to you, *I did* not *do it* for the sake of him who had done the wrong, nor for the sake of him who suffered wrong, ᵃbut that our care for you in the sight of God might appear to you.

THE JOY OF TITUS

¹³Therefore we have been comforted in your comfort. And we rejoiced exceedingly more for the joy of Titus, because his spirit ᵃhas been refreshed by you all. ¹⁴For if in anything I have boasted to him about you, I am not ashamed. But as we spoke all things to you in truth, even so our boasting to Titus was found true. ¹⁵And his affections are greater for you as he remembers ᵃthe obedience of you all, how with fear and trembling you received him. ¹⁶Therefore I rejoice that ᵃI have confidence in you in everything.

EXCEL IN GIVING

8 Moreover, brethren, we make known to you the grace of God bestowed on the churches of Macedonia: ²that in a great trial of affliction the abundance of their joy and ᵃtheir deep poverty abounded in the riches of their liberality. ³For I bear witness that according to *their* ability, yes, and beyond *their* ability, *they were* freely willing, ⁴imploring us with much urgency *ⁱthat* we would receive the gift and ᵃthe fellowship of the ministering to the saints. ⁵And not *only* as we had hoped, but they first ᵃgave themselves to the Lord, and *then* to us by the ᵇwill

of God. ⁶So ᵃwe urged Titus, that as he had begun, so he would also complete this grace in you as well. ⁷But as ᵃyou abound in everything—in faith, in speech, in knowledge, in all diligence, and in your love for us—*see* ᵇthat you abound in this grace also.

CHRIST OUR PATTERN

⁸ᵃI speak not by commandment, but I am testing the sincerity of your love by the diligence of others. ⁹For you know the grace of our Lord Jesus Christ, ᵃthat though He was rich, yet for your sakes He became poor, that you through His poverty might become ᵇrich.

¹⁰And in this ᵃI give advice: ᵇIt is to your advantage not only to be doing what you began and ᶜwere desiring to do a year ago; ¹¹but now you also must complete the doing *of it*; that as *there was* a readiness to desire *it*, so *there* also *may be* a completion out of what *you* have. ¹²For ᵃif there is first a willing mind, *it is* accepted according to what one has, *and* not according to what he does not have.

¹³For *I do* not *mean* that others should be eased and you burdened; ¹⁴but by an equality, *that* now at this time your abundance *may supply* their lack, that their abundance also may *supply* your lack—that there may be equality. ¹⁵As it is written, ᵃ*"He who gathered much had nothing left over, and he who gathered little had no lack."*

Cross-references

12 ᵃ 2 Cor. 2:4

13 ᵃ Rom. 15:32

15 ᵃ 2 Cor. 2:9

16 ᵃ 2 Thess. 3:4

CHAPTER 8

2 ᵃ Mark 12:44

4 ᵃ Rom. 15:25, 26
1 NU, M omit *that we would receive,* thus changing text to *urgency for the favor and fellowship*

5 ᵃ [Rom. 12:1, 2]
ᵇ [Eph. 6:6]

6 ᵃ 2 Cor. 8:17; 12:18

7 ᵃ [1 Cor. 1:5; 12:13]
ᵇ 2 Cor. 9:8

8 ᵃ 1 Cor. 7:6

9 ᵃ Phil. 2:6, 7
ᵇ Rom. 9:23

10 ᵃ 1 Cor. 7:25, 40
ᵇ [Heb. 13:16]
ᶜ 2 Cor. 9:2

12 ᵃ Mark 12:43, 44

15 ᵃ Ex. 16:18

---

2 Cor. 8:5

Where Giving Starts. Paul was commending the Macedonian Christians, who had given so generously to the Jerusalem church, despite the fact that they themselves were not very well off. This generosity was a great thing, but their generosity started when "they first gave themselves to the Lord."

Once we commit ourselves completely to the Lord, recognizing that everything we have came from Him and belongs to Him, then giving becomes a natural outgrowth of that realization. If you can give yourself, the rest is easy and natural.

---

2 Cor. 8:13–15

Taking Care of Each Other. Paul intended that there would be mutual caring among the churches.

At this time, Corinth was in a time of abundance while other parts of the body in other cities were struggling. Thus, it was only appropriate that out of their abundance they would contribute to the needs of their brothers and sisters, knowing that the day might come when the shoe would be on the other foot, and they might need assistance.

That is the church of Jesus Christ, functioning like a body and acting like a family.

COLLECTION FOR THE JUDEAN SAINTS

16But thanks *be* to God who [1]puts the same earnest care for you into the heart of Titus. 17For he not only accepted the exhortation, but being more diligent, he went to you of his own accord. 18And we have sent with him [a]the brother whose praise *is* in the gospel throughout all the churches, 19and not only *that*, but who was also [a]chosen by the churches to travel with us with this gift, which is administered by us [b]to the glory of the Lord Himself and *to show* your ready mind, 20avoiding this: that anyone should blame us in this lavish gift which is administered by us— 21[a]providing honorable things, not only in the sight of the Lord, but also in the sight of men.

22And we have sent with them our brother whom we have often proved diligent in many things, but now much more diligent, because of the great

2 Cor. 8:18–21

HONORABLE HANDLING OF MONEY

In handling this large financial offering, Paul gave Titus the responsibility to transport it. But Titus was accompanied by an unnamed brother who was praised throughout the churches as having a good reputation. This high level of accountability was for the purpose of being above reproach, "not only in the sight of the Lord, but also in the sight of men."

It is very important that we maintain a high level of accountability with the Lord's money. We have double signatures on all the checks our church issues. I don't write the checks myself. There is always a full accounting of everything we do, and any member of the church may come in and see how the money is spent. I believe this is pleasing to God; and I think the people appreciate it, as well.

confidence which *we have* in you. 23If anyone inquires about [a]Titus, *he is* my partner and fellow worker concerning you. Or if our brethren *are inquired about, they are* [b]messengers[1] of the churches, the glory of Christ. 24Therefore show to them, [1]and before the churches, the proof of your love and of our [a]boasting on your behalf.

ADMINISTERING THE GIFT

9 Now concerning [a]the ministering to the saints, it is superfluous for me to write to you; 2for I know your willingness, about which I boast of you to the Macedonians, that Achaia was ready a [a]year ago; and your zeal has stirred up the majority. 3[a]Yet I have sent the brethren, lest our boasting of you should be in vain in this respect, that, as I said, you may be ready; 4lest if *some* Macedonians come with me and find you unprepared, we (not to mention you!) should be ashamed of this [1]confident boasting. 5Therefore I thought it necessary to [1]exhort the brethren to go to you ahead of time, and prepare your generous gift beforehand, which *you had* previously promised, that it may be ready as *a matter of* generosity and not as a [2]grudging obligation.

THE CHEERFUL GIVER

6[a]But this *I say:* He who sows sparingly will also reap sparingly, and he who sows [1]bountifully will also reap [2]bountifully. 7*So let* each one *give* as he purposes in his heart, [a]not grudgingly or of [1]necessity; for [b]God loves a cheerful giver. 8[a]And God *is* able to make all grace abound toward you, that you, always having all sufficiency in all *things*, may have an abundance for every good work. 9As it is written:

[a]"*He has dispersed abroad,*
He has given to the poor;
His righteousness endures
forever."

10Now [1]may He who [a]supplies seed to the sower, and bread for food, [2]supply and multiply the seed you have *sown* and increase the fruits of your [b]righteousness, 11while *you are* enriched in everything for all liberality, [a]which causes thanksgiving through us to God. 12For the administration of this service not only [a]supplies the needs of the saints, but also is abounding through many thanksgivings to God, 13while, through the proof of this ministry, they [a]glorify God for the obedience

16 [1]NU has *put*

18 [a]2 Cor. 12:18

19 [a]1 Cor. 16:3, 4
[b]2 Cor. 4:15

21 [a]Rom. 12:17

23 [a]2 Cor. 7:13, 14
[b]Phil. 2:25
[1]Lit. *apostles, "sent ones"*

24 [a]2 Cor. 7:4, 14; 9:2
[1]NU, M omit *and*

CHAPTER 9

1 [a]Gal. 2:10

2 [a]2 Cor. 8:10

3 [a]2 Cor. 8:6, 17

4 [1]NU *confidence.*

5 [1]*encourage*
[2]Lit. *covetousness*

6 [a]Prov. 11:24; 22:9
[1]*with blessings*

7 [a]Deut. 15:7
[b]Rom. 12:8
[1]*compulsion*

8 [a][Prov. 11:24]

9 [a]Ps. 112:9

10 [a]Is. 55:10
[b]Hos. 10:12
[1]NU omits *may*
[2]NU *will supply*

11 [a]2 Cor. 1:11

12 [a]2 Cor. 8:14

13 [a][Matt. 5:16]

SOWING AND REAPING

2 Cor. 9:6

Paul knew that the Christians in Corinth were planning on giving to the Lord's work, and he had been bragging about their generosity. But in the middle of this discussion he reminded them of a great spiritual principle: "He who sows sparingly will also reap sparingly, and he who sows bountifully will also reap bountifully."

It is impossible to outgive God. When we give to Him, He always gives back more to us. It doesn't make sense mathematically, but it works practically. There are many people who think they can't afford to give to the Lord. But perhaps the reason they don't have money to give to the Lord is because of their lack of obedience in this area.

I learned this years ago, right after I graduated from college. I was planning an evangelistic trip back to Missouri, and I didn't know how I was going to pay for the trip. Right before I was scheduled to leave, I went to a missions rally and heard a man speak about the needs in Puerto Rico where he was a missionary. I only had five dollars to my name, but I felt like God was telling me to put it in the missions offering. Inside I felt like it was foolish because I didn't have money to get to Missouri; and here I was, giving my last five dollars to a missionary. But I gave the money because that is what I thought God wanted me to do.

The very next day an attorney called who was representing a woman who was in an accident I had witnessed months before. They needed me to come and testify in the trial. I told them I was supposed to leave for Missouri, and they told me they would pay my way to Missouri if I could stay around an extra day to testify.

When you give to God, He will always go to great lengths to pay you back.

---

13 b [Heb. 13:16]

NOT GRUDGINGLY OR OF NECESSITY

2 Cor. 9:7

The only way to give to God is from a willing and grateful heart. God never wants you to feel pressured to give, and I never want to say anything to anyone that pressures him to give. It is between you and the Lord.

And don't complain about how much you have given. God doesn't want your gift if that is your attitude. Keep your gift.

The Greek word for "cheerful" means "hilarious." If you aren't hilarious about your opportunity to participate in what God is doing by giving, keep your money. God doesn't want it.

14 a 2 Cor. 8:1

15 a [James 1:17]

Abounding Grace.

2 Cor. 9:8

If you are giving to the Lord with the right heart, willingly and cheerfully, the result will be that you will always have everything you need. You will have "all sufficiency in all things." He will be good to you, and provide for you, if you have trusted your finances to Him.

You can keep all your possessions and money to yourself if you want; but if you give it to Him, He will "make all grace abound toward you." It is a great deal. It helps make me cheerful to give.

CHAPTER 10

prayer for you, who long for you because of the exceeding a grace of God in you. 15Thanks be to God a for His indescribable gift!

THE SPIRITUAL WAR

10 Now a I, Paul, myself am pleading with you by the meekness and gentleness of Christ—b who in presence am lowly among you, but being absent

---

of your confession to the gospel of Christ, and for your liberal b sharing with them and all men, 14and by their

1 a Rom. 12:1
b 1 Thess. 2:7

2 Cor. 10:3–4

Our Weapons. We are living in the flesh in this material world, but our warfare isn't of this world. Our war is in the spirit realm, and our weapons are mighty spiritual weapons. Our problem is that we keep getting tangled up in battles of the flesh; and when we get in the flesh, we are defeated. If we get in the flesh, Satan has an advantage over us.

If we remain in the Spirit, the advantage is ours, and we can't lose. We are indestructible if we wear the whole armor of God (Eph. 6:10–18).

am bold toward you. [2]But I beg you [a]that when I am present I may not be bold with that confidence by which I intend to be bold against some, who think of us as if we walked according to the flesh. [3]For though we walk in the flesh, we do not war according to the flesh. [4][a]For the weapons [b]of our warfare are not [1]carnal but [c]mighty in God [d]for pulling down strongholds, [5][a]casting down arguments and every high thing that exalts itself against the knowledge of God, bringing every thought into captivity to the obedience of Christ, [6][a]and being ready to punish all disobedience when [b]your obedience is fulfilled.

REALITY OF PAUL'S AUTHORITY

[7][a]Do you look at things according to the outward appearance? [b]If anyone is convinced in himself that he is Christ's, let him again consider this in himself, that just as he is Christ's, even [1]so [c]we are Christ's. [8]For even if I should boast somewhat more [a]about our authority, which the Lord gave [1]us for [2]edification and not for your destruction, [b]I shall not be ashamed— [9]lest I seem to terrify you by letters. [10]"For his letters," they say, "are weighty and powerful, but [a]his bodily presence is weak, and his [b]speech contemptible." [11]Let such a person consider this, that what we are in word by letters when we are absent, such we will also be in deed when we are present.

LIMITS OF PAUL'S AUTHORITY

[12][a]For we dare not class ourselves or compare ourselves with those who

Reference column

2 [a]1 Cor. 4:21

4 [a]Eph. 6:13
[b]1 Tim. 1:18
[c]Acts 7:22
[d]Jer. 1:10
[1]of the flesh

5 [a]1 Cor. 1:19

6 [a]2 Cor. 13:2, 10
[b]2 Cor. 7:15

7 [a][John 7:24]
[b]1 Cor. 1:12; 14:37
[c]1 Cor. 3:23
[1]NU as we are.

8 [a]2 Cor. 13:10
[b]2 Cor. 7:14
[1]NU omits us
[2]building up

10 [a]Gal. 4:13
[b]2 Cor. 11:6

12 [a]2 Cor. 5:12

13 [a]2 Cor. 10:15

14 [a]1 Cor. 3:5, 6

15 [a]Rom. 15:20

17 [a]Jer. 9:24

18 [a]Prov. 27:2
[b]Rom. 2:29

CHAPTER 11

1 [a]2 Cor. 11:4, 16, 19

2 [a]Gal. 4:17
[b]Hos. 2:19
[c]Col. 1:28
[d]Lev. 21:13

2 Cor. 10:12

GRADING ON THE CURVE

Paul says that it is unwise to compare ourselves among ourselves. It is so easy for me to get complacent and overlook my failures and sins if I am looking at others. I may think, *I am wrong, but at least I'm not as wrong as he is.* On the other hand, if I compare myself with others, I may also judge myself too harshly, thinking I don't measure up to what someone else has accomplished. It is all foolishness.

If we judge ourselves by comparing ourselves to Jesus, we all fall so short that we need Him constantly. And that is the point. Any other comparison is meaningless.

commend themselves. But they, measuring themselves by themselves, and comparing themselves among themselves, are not wise. [13][a]We, however, will not boast beyond measure, but within the limits of the sphere which God appointed us—a sphere which especially includes you. [14]For we are not overextending ourselves (as though *our authority* did not extend to you), [a]for it was to you that we came with the gospel of Christ; [15]not boasting of things beyond measure, *that is,* [a]in other men's labors, but having hope, *that* as your faith is increased, we shall be greatly enlarged by you in our sphere, [16]to preach the gospel in the *regions* beyond you, *and* not to boast in another man's sphere of accomplishment.

[17]But [a]*"he who glories, let him glory in the LORD."* [18]For [a]not he who commends himself is approved, but [b]whom the Lord commends.

CONCERN FOR THEIR FAITHFULNESS

11 Oh, that you would bear with me in a little [a]folly—and indeed you do bear with me. [2]For I am [a]jealous for you with godly jealousy. For [b]I have betrothed you to one husband, [c]that I may present you [d]as a chaste virgin to

2 Cor. 10:17–18

Glory in the Lord. We make fools of ourselves when we glory in ourselves. The only accomplishments that matter are those done through us by the Lord, and how can we boast about those? Our self-commendation means nothing. It is only the commendation that comes from God that matters.

God said to the prophet Jeremiah, "Let not the wise man glory in his wisdom, let not the mighty man glory in his might, nor let the rich man glory in his riches; but let him who glories glory in this, that he understands and knows Me" (Jer. 9:23–24).

Christ. ³But I fear, lest somehow, as ᵃthe serpent deceived Eve by his craftiness, so your minds ᵇmay be corrupted from the ¹simplicity that is in Christ. ⁴For if he who comes preaches another Jesus whom we have not preached, or *if* you receive a different spirit which you have not received, or a ᵃdifferent gospel which you have not accepted— you may well put up with it!

PAUL AND FALSE APOSTLES

⁵For I consider that ᵃI am not at all inferior to the most eminent apostles.

2 Cor. 11:3

Simplicity in Christ. The gospel is so simple. Just "believe on the Lord Jesus Christ, and you will be saved" (Acts 16:31). Just believe that Jesus came from God, took my sin, died in my place, and rose again. Simple!

But it is amazing how men can complicate something so simple. It is amazing all the requirements they can add. You have to keep the law. You have to be circumcised. You need to be baptized. You need to pray three hours a day. You need to tithe. They make it so complicated. Don't lose the simplicity of the gospel.

3 ᵃGen. 3:4, 13
ᵇEph. 6:24
1 NU adds *and purity*

4 ᵃGal. 1:6–8

5 ᵃ2 Cor. 12:11

6 ᵃ[1 Cor. 1:17]
ᵇ[Eph. 3:4]
ᶜ[2 Cor. 12:12]
1 NU omits *been*

7 ᵃ1 Cor. 9:18
1 *putting myself down*

9 ᵃActs 20:33
ᵇPhil. 4:10

10 ᵃRom. 1:9; 9:1
ᵇ1 Cor. 9:15

11 ᵃ2 Cor. 6:11; 12:15

12 ᵃ1 Cor. 9:12

13 ᵃPhil. 1:15
ᵇPhil. 3:2

14 ᵃGal. 1:8

15 ᵃ[Phil. 3:19]

17 ᵃ1 Cor. 7:6

⁶Even though ᵃI *am* untrained in speech, yet *I am* not ᵇin knowledge. But ᶜwe have ¹been thoroughly manifested among you in all things.

⁷Did I commit sin in ¹humbling myself that you might be exalted, because I preached the gospel of God to you ᵃfree of charge? ⁸I robbed other churches, taking wages *from them* to minister to you. ⁹And when I was present with you, and in need, ᵃI was a burden to no one, for what I lacked ᵇthe brethren who came from Macedonia supplied. And in everything I kept myself from being burdensome to you, and so I will keep *myself.* ¹⁰ᵃAs the truth of Christ is in me, ᵇno one shall stop me from this boasting in the regions of Achaia. ¹¹Why? ᵃBecause I do not love you? God knows!

¹²But what I do, I will also continue to do, ᵃthat I may cut off the opportunity from those who desire an opportunity to be regarded just as we are in the things of which they boast. ¹³For such ᵃ*are* false apostles, ᵇdeceitful workers, transforming themselves into apostles of Christ. ¹⁴And no wonder! For Satan himself transforms himself into ᵃan angel of light. ¹⁵Therefore *it is* no great thing if his ministers also transform themselves into ministers of righteousness, ᵃwhose end will be according to their works.

2 Cor. 11:13–15

Angel of Light. Things aren't always as they appear to be. Satan can transform himself into an angel of light. He can make himself look very attractive. And if he can do it, Paul wasn't surprised that some of these false prophets could also be very convincing.

You can't accurately judge people by outward appearances. Satan is sneaky and deliberately deceptive, and so are many of his followers. They look really slick until you inspect their fruit.

RELUCTANT BOASTING

¹⁶I say again, let no one think me a fool. If otherwise, at least receive me as a fool, that I also may boast a little. ¹⁷What I speak, ᵃI speak not according to the Lord, but as it were, foolishly, in this confidence of boasting. ¹⁸Seeing

that many boast according to the flesh, I also will boast. [19]For you put up with fools gladly, [a]since you *yourselves* are wise! [20]For you put up with it [a]if one brings you into bondage, if one devours *you*, if one takes *from you*, if one exalts himself, if one strikes you on the face. [21]To our shame [a]I say that we were too weak for that! But [b]in whatever anyone is bold—I speak foolishly—I am bold also.

SUFFERING FOR CHRIST

[22]Are they [a]Hebrews? So *am* I. Are they Israelites? So *am* I. Are they the seed of Abraham? So *am* I. [23]Are they ministers of Christ?—I speak as a fool—I *am* more: [a]in labors more abundant, [b]in stripes above measure, in prisons more frequently, [c]in deaths often. [24]From the Jews five times I received [a]forty [b]*stripes* minus one. [25]Three times I was [a]beaten with rods; [b]once I was stoned; three times I [c]was shipwrecked; a night and a day I have been in the deep; [26]*in* journeys often, *in* perils of waters, *in* perils of robbers, [a]*in* perils of *my own* countrymen, [b]*in* perils of the Gentiles, *in* perils in the city, *in* perils in the wilderness, *in* perils in the sea, *in* perils among false brethren; [27]*in* weariness and toil, [a]*in* sleeplessness often, [b]*in* hunger and thirst, *in* [c]fastings often, in cold and nakedness— [28]besides the other things, what comes upon me daily: [a]my deep concern for all the churches. [29][a]Who is weak, and I am not weak? Who is made to stumble, and I do not burn *with indignation*?

[30]If I must boast, [a]I will boast in the things which concern my [1]infirmity.

Reference column

19 [a]1 Cor. 4:10
20 [a][Gal. 2:4; 4:3, 9; 5:1]
21 [a]2 Cor. 10:10
[b]Phil. 3:4
22 [a]Phil. 3:4–6
23 [a]1 Cor. 15:10
[b]Acts 9:16
[c]1 Cor. 15:30
24 [a]Deut. 25:3
[b]2 Cor. 6:5
25 [a]Acts 16:22, 23; 21:32
[b]Acts 14:5, 19
[c]Acts 27:1–44
26 [a]Acts 9:23, 24; 13:45, 50; 17:5, 13
[b]Acts 14:5, 19; 19:23; 27:42
27 [a]Acts 20:31
[b]1 Cor. 4:11
[c]Acts 9:9; 13:2, 3; 14:23
28 [a]Acts 20:18
29 [a][1 Cor. 8:9, 13; 9:22]
30 [a][2 Cor. 12:5, 9, 10]
[1]weakness
31 [a]1 Thess. 2:5
[b]Rom. 9:5
32 [a]Acts 9:19–25

CHAPTER 12

1 [a]Acts 16:9; 18:9; 22:17, 18; 23:11; 26:13–15; 27:23 [b][Gal. 1:12; 2:2] [1]NU *necessary, though not profitable, to boast*
2 [a]Rom. 16:7
[b]Acts 22:17

Sidebar

2 Cor. 11:23–30

Glory in Infirmities. Paul had been the victim of a lot of negative talk about him. People had been putting him down by questioning his credentials, his background, his motives, and even his teaching style.

In response, though Paul said he was being forced to boast, he didn't brag about all his converts or all the churches he had started or the books he had written. Instead, he chose to boast about all the problems and sufferings he had endured. What could they say to that? He had certainly paid his dues.

Main text continued

[31][a]The God and Father of our Lord Jesus Christ, [b]who is blessed forever, knows that I am not lying. [32][a]In Damascus the governor, under Aretas the king, was guarding the city of the Damascenes with a garrison, desiring to arrest me; [33]but I was let down in a basket through a window in the wall, and escaped from his hands.

THE VISION OF PARADISE

12 It is [1]doubtless not profitable for me to boast. I will come to [a]visions and [b]revelations of the Lord: [2]I know a man [a]in Christ who fourteen years ago—whether in the body I do not know, or whether out of the body I do not know, God knows—such a one [b]was caught up to the third heaven.

THE THIRD HEAVEN
2 Cor. 12:1–6

Paul had experienced a revelation of the third heaven. The first heaven would be our atmosphere here on the earth. The second heaven would be outer space. The third heaven would be the dwelling place of God.

As Paul saw heaven, he wasn't sure if he had actually died and gone to heaven or whether he was just given a vision. At any rate, he experienced paradise, and he "heard inexpressible words, which it is not lawful for a man to utter." In other words, it was indescribable. Words couldn't express the beauty that was there. And Paul also realized that, if he were able to describe it, people would then put him on a pedestal and think more highly of him than they should.

Our tendency, if we had such an experience, would be to write a book about it, go on a nationwide speaking tour, and plan a movie of the week. Paul just quietly went about his business and kept the experience to himself for many years. All of our experiences with God aren't meant to be shared. Some of them are just personal, between us and God.

3And I know such a man—whether in the body or out of the body I do not know, God knows— 4how he was caught up into aParadise and heard inexpressible words, which it is not lawful for a man to utter. 5Of such a one I will boast; yet of myself I will not aboast, except in my infirmities. 6For though I might desire to boast, I will not be a fool; for I will speak the truth. But I refrain, lest anyone should think of me above what he sees me *to be* or hears from me.

THE THORN IN THE FLESH

7And lest I should be exalted above measure by the abundance of the revelations, a athorn in the flesh was given to me, ba messenger of Satan to *l*buffet me, lest I be exalted above measure. 8aConcerning this thing I pleaded with the Lord three times that it might depart from me. 9And He said to me, "My grace is sufficient for you, for My strength is made perfect in weakness." Therefore most gladly aI will rather boast in my infirmities, bthat the power of Christ may rest upon me. 10There-

fore aI take pleasure in infirmities, in reproaches, in needs, in persecutions, in distresses, for Christ's sake. bFor when I am weak, then I am strong.

SIGNS OF AN APOSTLE

11I have become aa fool *l*in boasting; you have compelled me. For I ought to have been commended by you; for bin nothing was I behind the most eminent apostles, though cI am nothing. 12aTruly the signs of an apostle were accomplished among you with all perseverance, in signs and bwonders and mighty cdeeds. 13For what is it in which you were inferior to other churches, except that I myself was not burdensome to you? Forgive me this wrong!

LOVE FOR THE CHURCH

14aNow *for* the third time I am ready to come to you. And I will not be burdensome to you; for bI do not seek yours, but you. cFor the children ought not to lay up for the parents, but parents for the children. 15And I will very gladly spend and be spent afor your souls; though bthe more abundantly I love you, the less I am loved.

Cross references

4 a Luke 23:43

5 a 2 Cor. 11:30

7 a Ezek. 28:24
b Job 2:7
1 *beat*

8 a Matt. 26:44

9 a 2 Cor. 11:30
b [1 Pet. 4:14]

10 a [Rom. 5:3; 8:35]
b 2 Cor. 13:4

11 a 2 Cor. 5:13; 11:1, 16; 12:6
b 2 Cor. 11:5
c 1 Cor. 3:7; 13:2; 15:9
1 NU omits *in boasting*

12 a Rom. 15:18
b Acts 15:12
c Acts 14:8–10; 16:16–18; 19:11, 12, 20:6–12; 28:1–10

14 a 2 Cor. 1:15; 13:1, 2
b [1 Cor. 10:24–33]
c 1 Cor. 4:14

15 a [2 Tim. 2:10]
b 2 Cor. 6:12, 13

16 a 2 Cor. 11:9

18 a 2 Cor. 8:18

2 Cor. 12:7–10

PERFECT STRENGTH IN WEAKNESS

Paul had been given a "thorn in the flesh." This was probably a physical malady, perhaps an eye ailment, but we don't know exactly what it was. It was bothering him so much that he continued to ask God to heal him, and God didn't. Instead, God said, "My grace is sufficient for you, for My strength is made perfect in weakness." Paul went on to say that he had learned "when I am weak, then I am strong."

Sometimes we find that we will never truly experience the strength of God until we first experience our own weakness in some glaring way. Do you want power? It might come through infirmities.

2 Cor. 12:15

I Will Be Spent for You. Paul was not ministering to the Corinthians so that he could get something out of it. He said that he'd do it at his own expense, even if it cost him his life. His reason was his love for them, even though it seemed like the more he loved them, the less they loved him.

How different this attitude is from what is typical in so many ministries today, where gimmicks and fundraising are all designed to separate the people from their money. Paul said, "I'm not seeking your money; I'm seeking you!"

16But be that *as it may*, aI did not burden you. Nevertheless, being crafty, I caught you by cunning! 17Did I take advantage of you by any of those whom I sent to you? 18I urged Titus, and sent our abrother with *him*. Did Titus take advantage of you? Did we not walk in the same spirit? Did *we* not *walk* in the same steps?

[19a]Again,[1] do you think that we excuse ourselves to you? [b]We speak before God in Christ. [c]But *we do* all things, beloved, for your edification. [20]For I fear lest, when I come, I shall not find you such as I wish, and *that* [a]I shall be found by you such as you do not wish; lest *there be* contentions, jealousies, outbursts of wrath, selfish ambitions, backbitings, whisperings, conceits, tumults; [21]lest, when I come again, my God [a]will humble me among you, and I shall mourn for many [b]who have sinned before and have not repented of the uncleanness, [c]fornica-tion, and lewdness which they have practiced.

COMING WITH AUTHORITY

13 This *will be* [a]the third *time* I am coming to you. [b]*"By the mouth of two or three witnesses every word shall be established."* [2a]I have told you before, and foretell as if I were present the second time, and now being absent [1]I write to those [b]who have sinned before, and to all the rest, that if I come again [c]I will not spare— [3]since you seek a proof of Christ [a]speaking in me, who is not weak toward you, but mighty [b]in you. [4a]For though He was crucified in weakness, yet [b]He lives by the power of God. For [c]we also are weak in Him, but we shall live with Him by the power of God toward you.

[5]Examine yourselves *as to* whether you are in the faith. Test yourselves. Do you not know yourselves, [a]that Jesus Christ is in you?—unless indeed you [1]are [b]disqualified. [6]But I trust that you will know that we are not disqualified.

PAUL PREFERS GENTLENESS

[7]Now [1]I pray to God that you do no evil, not that we should appear approved, but that you should do what

---

2 Cor. 13:5

Test Yourselves. The Corinthians were attacking Paul. So he gave them a good piece of advice. "Examine yourselves as to whether you are in the faith. Test yourselves."

Many practice sin, while believing themselves to be Christians. How important it is that we each examine ourselves! Are we really in the faith? Is the evidence of regeneration flowing forth from our lives?

---

19 [a]2 Cor. 5:12
[b][Rom. 9:1, 2]
[c]1 Cor. 10:33
1 NU You have been thinking for a long time that we

20 [a]1 Cor. 4:21

21 [a]2 Cor. 2:1, 4
[b]2 Cor. 13:2
[c]1 Cor. 5:1

CHAPTER 13

1 [a]2 Cor. 12:14
[b]Deut. 17:6; 19:15

2 [a]2 Cor. 10:2
[b]2 Cor. 12:21
[c]2 Cor. 1:23; 10:11
1 NU omits I write

3 [a]Matt. 10:20
[b][1 Cor. 9:2]

4 [a][1 Pet. 3:18]
[b][Rom. 1:4; 6:4]
[c][2 Cor. 10:3, 4]

5 [a][Gal. 4:19]
[b]1 Cor. 9:27
1 do not stand the test

7 [a]2 Cor. 6:9
1 NU we

9 [a]1 Cor. 4:10
[b][1 Thess. 3:10]

10 [a]1 Cor. 4:21
[b]2 Cor. 10:8 **11**
[a]Rom. 12:16, 18
[b]Rom. 15:33

12 [a]Rom. 16:16

14 [a]Rom. 16:24 [b]Phil. 2:1 1 fellowship

---

2 Cor. 13:10

Edification, Not Destruction. Paul told the Corinthian Christians some difficult things by letter so that they could absorb it, pray about it, and deal with it, before he got there in person. He wanted to build them up, not to destroy them.

Sometimes God has a tough message to deliver to us, and it hurts. But He is only hurting us to keep us from hurting ourselves even more. He is trying to build us up, but some demolition may be necessary first.

---

is honorable, though [a]we may seem disqualified. [8]For we can do nothing against the truth, but for the truth. [9]For we are glad [a]when we are weak and you are strong. And this also we pray, [b]that you may be made complete. [10a]Therefore I write these things being absent, lest being present I should use sharpness, according to the [b]authority which the Lord has given me for edification and not for destruction.

GREETINGS AND BENEDICTION

[11]Finally, brethren, farewell. Become complete. [a]Be of good comfort, be of one mind, live in peace; and the God of love [b]and peace will be with you. [12a]Greet one another with a holy kiss. [13]All the saints greet you. [14a]The grace of the Lord Jesus Christ, and the love of God, and [b]the [1]communion of the Holy Spirit *be* with you all. Amen.

---

2 Cor. 13:14

A Trinitarian Benediction. Paul ended this book by referring to the three members of the Godhead. "The grace of the Lord Jesus Christ, and the love of God, and the communion of the Holy Spirit be with you all. Amen." Three persons, but one God. They all work together, but they are distinct from each other. Do I understand it? Not even close. Do I believe it? Absolutely!

GALATIANS

INTRODUCTION This is the only letter Paul wrote that was addressed to a group of churches rather than to just one specific church. Galatia wasn't a city but rather a whole region in Asia Minor. The Galatian people were originally Celtic people who had migrated from Gaul to the area south of the Black Sea, near present-day Armenia. Paul had evidently been instrumental in starting several churches in the area of Galatia and was now hearing about some false teaching that was circulating there. He wrote to correct these dangerous heresies.

We don't know when this letter was written, but probably during Paul's third missionary journey in the mid 50s. The Galatian churches had apparently become infected by Judaizers, who were teaching that salvation would only come to those who kept the law of Moses. Paul was deeply concerned for the Galatians, because he saw them leaving the truth of the gospel and adding legalism to the gospel, watering down the grace of God.

Whereas the book of Romans presents the truth of the gospel in a doctrinal outline, the book of Galatians defends it in a personal and practical appeal. It is one of the most passionate books Paul wrote; in it he stressed to them what was at stake if they left the grace of God and traded it for a legalism that would destroy them.

In this book, there are no preliminary thanksgivings or prayer requests as there are in most of Paul's epistles. There are no personal greetings to individuals, or from individuals, as is also often the case. Paul expressed his amazement, right off the bat, that they had begun to follow after "a different gospel," which wasn't really "good news" at all (Gal. 1:6-7). He confronted, head-on, the false teachers who were trying to "pervert the gospel of Christ." So what we have in Galatians is a beautiful and powerful presentation of "the gospel of grace."

Paul not only reiterates that salvation is by grace alone, but he goes on to describe the life of grace as life in the Spirit. Legalists would argue that the teaching of grace results in a fleshly, self-indulgent life. Paul demonstrates that just the opposite is true. When we understand the grace of God, we receive the power of the Holy Spirit to walk in the Spirit in a wonderful relationship with the Lord. Only grace can make a person righteous.

This book served as an inspiration to Martin Luther and John Wesley and so many others, and my prayer is that it will inspire you, as well, to accept the grace of God and enter into the life in the Spirit.

GREETING

1 Paul, an apostle (not from men nor through man, but ᵃthrough Jesus Christ and God the Father ᵇwho raised Him from the dead), ²and all the brethren who are with me,

To the churches of Galatia:

³Grace to you and peace from God the Father and our Lord Jesus Christ, ⁴ᵃwho gave Himself for our sins, that He might deliver us ᵇfrom this present evil age, according to the will of our God and Father, ⁵to whom *be* glory forever and ever. Amen.

ONLY ONE GOSPEL

⁶I marvel that you are turning away so soon ᵃfrom Him who called you in the grace of Christ, to a different gospel, ⁷ᵃwhich is not another; but there are some ᵇwho trouble you and want to ᶜpervert¹ the gospel of Christ. ⁸But even if ᵃwe, or an angel from heaven, preach any other gospel to you than what we have preached to you, let him be ¹accursed. ⁹As we have said before, so now I say again, if anyone preaches any other gospel to you ᵃthan what you have received, let him be accursed.

Gal. 1:4

DELIVER US FROM EVIL

We are living in an evil world. The world has a very strong hold on people because all of us are searching for meaning and fulfillment. But meaning and fulfillment can never come from worldly things. That is the big lie.

Yet, because of its promises, we gravitate toward the world in hopes of finding fulfillment. We go from one pursuit to another. Then the emptiest moment of your life comes when you have achieved and attained all that you had hoped would bring you fulfillment, and you find you are still empty.

Fulfillment is in the Son, Jesus Christ! He gave Himself to deliver you from this present evil age.

CHAPTER 1

1 ᵃActs 9:6
  ᵇActs 2:24

4 ᵃ[Matt. 20:28]
  ᵇHeb. 2:5

6 ᵃGal. 1:15;
  5:8

7 ᵃ2Cor. 11:4
  ᵇGal. 5:10, 12
  ᶜ2Cor. 2:17
  ¹distort

8 ᵃ1Cor. 16:22
  ¹Gr. anathema

9 ᵃDeut. 4:2

10 ᵃ1Thess. 2:4
   ᵇ1Sam. 24:7
   ᶜ1Thess. 2:4

11 ᵃ1Cor. 15:1

12 ᵃ1Cor. 15:1
   ᵇ[Eph. 3:3–5]

13 ᵃActs 9:1
   ᵇActs 8:3; 22:
   4, 5

14 ᵃActs 26:9
   ᵇJer. 9:14

15 ᵃIs. 49:1, 5

16 ᵃ[2Cor. 4:5–
   7]
   ᵇActs 9:15
   ᶜMatt. 16:17

18 ᵃActs 9:26
   ¹NU Cephas

19 ᵃ1Cor. 9:5
   ᵇMatt. 13:55

Gal. 1:6

Good News. "Gospel" means "good news." Trying to be approved of God by our works and our efforts is not good news. The good news is that God has accepted the finished work of Jesus Christ and imputed the righteousness of Jesus to you through your faith in Jesus. That's the good news!

It's not by works but by His grace that I stand. You stand not in your righteousness, but in the righteousness that is of Christ through faith. The good news is the grace of God through Jesus Christ by which we are accepted by God.

¹⁰For ᵃdo I now ᵇpersuade men, or God? Or ᶜdo I seek to please men? For if I still pleased men, I would not be a bondservant of Christ.

CALL TO APOSTLESHIP

¹¹ᵃBut I make known to you, brethren, that the gospel which was preached by me is not according to man. ¹²For ᵃI neither received it from man, nor was I taught *it*, but *it* came ᵇthrough the revelation of Jesus Christ. ¹³For you have heard of my former conduct in Judaism, how ᵃI persecuted the church of God beyond measure and ᵇ*tried to* destroy it. ¹⁴And I advanced in Judaism beyond many of my contemporaries in my own nation, ᵃbeing more exceedingly zealous ᵇfor the traditions of my fathers. ¹⁵But when it pleased God, ᵃwho separated me from my mother's womb and called *me* through His grace, ¹⁶ᵃto reveal His Son in me, that ᵇI might preach Him among the Gentiles, I did not immediately confer with ᶜflesh and blood, ¹⁷nor did I go up to Jerusalem to those *who were* apostles before me; but I went to Arabia, and returned again to Damascus.

CONTACTS AT JERUSALEM

¹⁸Then after three years ᵃI went up to Jerusalem to see ¹Peter, and remained with him fifteen days. ¹⁹But ᵃI saw none of the other apostles except ᵇJames, the Lord's brother. ²⁰(Now *concerning* the things which I

Gal. 1:8

ONLY ONE GOSPEL

"**I**f we, or an angel from heaven" were to awaken you in the night with a bright, shining light and say, "I've come to bring to you new revelation to give to the world, a new way to be saved. Here are the rules people must follow. If they fulfill these requirements, they can have salvation. Now I commission you to share this gospel with the world." Paul said let them be accursed! There is only one gospel, the gospel of the grace of God through Jesus Christ!

Did you receive the Spirit through the works of the law or the hearing of faith? Not by the law but by what Jesus has done for us. The Bible always emphasizes the work of God in your redemption, not your works. And whenever you get that twisted, you have a twisted gospel. You have another gospel. And if any man preaches any other gospel than that which you have already received, Paul said, "Let him be accursed!"

write to you, indeed, before God, I do not lie.)

²¹ᵃAfterward I went into the regions of Syria and Cilicia. ²²And I was unknown by face to the churches of Judea which ᵃ*were* in Christ. ²³But they were ᵃhearing only, "He who formerly ᵇpersecuted us now preaches the faith which he once *tried to* destroy." ²⁴And they ᵃglorified God in me.

DEFENDING THE GOSPEL

2 Then after fourteen years ᵃI went up again to Jerusalem with Barnabas, and also took Titus with *me.* ²And I went up ¹by revelation, and communicated to them that gospel which I preach among the Gentiles, but ᵃprivately to those who were of reputation, lest by any means ᵇI might run, or had run, in vain. ³Yet not even Titus who

---

21 ᵃActs 9:30

22 ᵃRom. 16:7

23 ᵃActs 9:20, 21   ᵇActs 8:3

24 ᵃActs 11:18

CHAPTER 2

1 ᵃActs 15:2

2 ᵃActs 15:1–4   ᵇPhil. 2:16   ¹*because of*

4 ᵃActs 15:1, 24   ᵇGal. 3:25; 5:1, 13   ᶜGal. 4:3, 9

5 ᵃ[Gal. 1:6; 2:14; 3:1]

6 ᵃGal. 2:9; 6:3   ᵇActs 10:34   ᶜ2 Cor. 11:5; 12:11   ¹Lit. *does not receive the face of a man*

7 ᵃActs 9:15; 13:46; 22:21   ᵇ1 Thess. 2:4

8 ᵃ1 Pet. 1:1   ᵇActs 9:15   ᶜ[Gal. 3:5]

9 ᵃMatt. 16:18   ᵇRom. 1:5   ᶜGal. 13:3   ¹Peter

10 ᵃActs 11:30

---

was with me, being a Greek, was compelled to be circumcised. ⁴And *this occurred* because of ᵃfalse brethren secretly brought in (who came in by stealth to spy out our ᵇliberty which we have in Christ Jesus, ᶜthat they might bring us into bondage), ⁵to whom we did not yield submission even for an hour, that ᵃthe truth of the gospel might continue with you.

⁶But from those ᵃwho seemed to be something—whatever they were, it makes no difference to me; ᵇGod ¹shows personal favoritism to no man—for those who seemed to *be something* ᶜadded nothing to me. ⁷But on the contrary, ᵃwhen they saw that the gospel for the uncircumcised ᵇhad been committed to me, as *the gospel* for the circumcised *was* to Peter ⁸(for He who worked effectively in Peter for the apostleship to the ᵃcircumcised ᵇalso ᶜworked effectively in me toward the Gentiles), ⁹and when James, ¹Cephas, and John, who seemed to be ᵃpillars, perceived ᵇthe grace that had been given to me, they gave me and Barnabas the right hand of fellowship, ᶜthat we *should go* to the Gentiles and they to the circumcised. ¹⁰*They desired* only that we should remember the poor, ᵃthe very thing which I also was eager to do.

Gal. 2:6

HE LOVES YOU

God is no respecter of persons. God shows favoritism to no man. That I love. You see, you are as important to God as anybody else. The world may hold up this or that man or woman as great people of God, sort of in a category above the rest of us. Not so. You are so important to God! I think we lose sight of that.

We think of ourselves as so insignificant as we stand around others who have such great ministries. "Oooh. The way they stand, the way they talk. These guys are big shots." But God doesn't look at it that way. God sees us all on the same plane, and He loves us all equally.

NO RETURN TO THE LAW

11aNow when 1Peter had come to Antioch, I 2withstood him to his face, because he was to be blamed; 12for before certain men came from James, ahe would eat with the Gentiles; but when they came, he withdrew and separated himself, fearing 1those who were of the circumcision. 13And the rest of the Jews also played the hypocrite with him, so that even Barnabas was carried away with their hypocrisy. 14But when I saw that they were not straightforward about athe truth of the gospel, I said to Peter bbefore *them* all, c"If you, being a Jew, live in the manner of Gentiles and not as the Jews, 1why do you compel Gentiles to live as 2Jews? 15aWe *who are* Jews by nature, and not bsinners of the Gentiles, 16aknowing that a man is not 1justified by the works of the law but bby faith in Jesus Christ, even we have believed in Christ Jesus, that we might be justified by faith in Christ and not cby the works of the law; for by the works of the law no flesh shall be justified. 17"But if, while we seek to be justified by Christ, we ourselves also are found asinners, *is* Christ therefore a minister of sin? Certainly not! 18For if I build again those things which I destroyed, I make myself a transgressor. 19For I

11 a Acts 15:35
1 NU *Cephas*
2 *opposed*

12 a [Acts 10:28; 11:2, 3]
1 Jewish Christians

14 a Gal. 1:6; 2:5
b 1 Tim. 5:20
c [Acts 10:28]
1 NU *how can you*
2 Some interpreters stop the quotation here.

15 a [Acts 15:10]
b Matt. 9:11

16 a Acts 13:38, 39
b Rom. 1:17
c Ps. 143:2
1 *declared righteous*

17 a [1 John 3:8]

19 a Rom. 8:2
b [Rom. 6:2, 14; 7:4]
c [Rom. 6:11]

20 a [Rom. 6:6]
b 2 Cor. 5:15
c Eph. 5:2

21 a Heb. 7:11
1 *for nothing*

Gal. 2:21

Did Christ Die in Vain? This is a tremendously powerful statement, one that you need to really meditate on. If I could be made righteous by keeping the law, then Christ did not need to die for me.

In the garden of Gethsemane, Jesus prayed, "Father, if it is possible, let this cup pass from Me" (Matt. 26:39). He was talking about His death. God would not have sent His Son to the cross if we could be saved by the law. If justification was possible by the keeping of the law, then Christ died in vain

athrough the law bdied to the law that I might clive to God. 20I have been acrucified with Christ; it is no longer I who live, but Christ lives in me; and the *life* which I now live in the flesh bI live by faith in the Son of God, cwho loved me and gave Himself for me. 21I do not set aside the grace of God; for aif righteousness *comes* through the law, then Christ died 1in vain."

JUSTIFIED BY FAITH   Gal. 2:16

There is something almost inherent in man that seeks to be worthy of salvation. We seek by good works to counterbalance the sin or the bad works we have done. Now, it is interesting that this has become the whole basis for the Jewish justification today.

The Day of Atonement, Yom Kippur, used to be the day for the national atonement for sin. It was the day the high priest would go into the Most Holy Place to intercede for the nation. It was the day the goat was killed as a sin offering.

Today, when the Jews celebrate the Day of Atonement, there is no sacrifice for sin. Instead, the Day of Atonement has become a day of reflection. They sit in meditation, reflecting on the past year and weighing on a scale all the bad things and the good things they have done. These were bad things. These were good things. They're hoping the good will outweigh the bad. Thus, they feel they will have atoned for their sins by their good works. They feel that so long as they counterbalance the evil with good works, they will be accepted by God.

But there is no biblical basis for that whatsoever. The Bible says that "without shedding of blood there is no remission" for sin (Heb. 9:22). Their Bible says their righteousness is as filthy rags in the eyes of God (Is. 64:6). Yet, this is exactly what they are offering to God. So their Day of Atonement is meaningless because they are seeking to be justified by works. But "by the works of the law no flesh shall be justified."

So Paul declared now the gospel. Man is not justified by the works of the law but by faith in Jesus Christ.

JUSTIFICATION BY FAITH

3 O foolish Galatians! Who has bewitched you [1]that you should not obey the truth, before whose eyes Jesus Christ was clearly portrayed [2]among you as crucified? [2]This only I want to learn from you: Did you receive the Spirit by the works of the law, [a]or by the hearing of faith? [3]Are you so foolish? [a]Having begun in the Spirit, are you now being made perfect by [b]the flesh? [4][a]Have you suffered so [1]many things in vain—if indeed it was in vain? [5]Therefore He who supplies the Spirit to you and works miracles among you, does He do it by the works of the law, or by the hearing of faith?— [6]just as Abraham [a]"believed God, and it was accounted to him for righteousness." [7]Therefore know that only [a]those who are of faith are sons of Abraham. [8]And [a]the Scripture, foreseeing that God would justify the Gentiles by faith, preached the gospel to Abraham beforehand, saying, [b]"In you all the nations shall be blessed." [9]So then those who are of faith are blessed with believing Abraham.

THE LAW BRINGS A CURSE

[10]For as many as are of the works of the law are under the curse; for it is written, [a]"Cursed is everyone who does not continue in all things which are written in the book of the law, to do them." [11]But that no one is [1]justified by

CHAPTER 3

1 [1]NU omits *that you should not obey the truth*
2 NU omits *among you*

2 [a]Rom. 10:16, 17

3 [a][Gal. 4:9]
[b]Heb. 7:16

4 [a]Heb. 10:35
[1]Or *great*

6 [a]Gen. 15:6

7 [a]John 8:39

8 [a]Rom. 9:17
[b]Gen. 12:3; 18:18; 22:18; 26:4; 28:14

10 [a]Deut. 27:26

11 [1]*declared righteous*

Gal. 3:3

O FOOLISH GALATIANS!

Let me say that I think this is probably one of the greatest dangers we as Christians face. And surely it is one of the greatest dangers the church has faced through the years. Every genuine revival and move of God, it seems, ends up with man trying to perfect it by the flesh. God began a work in the Spirit. Now we need to get it organized. We need to form committees. We need to hire consultants. So you see, we are now going to perfect that which God began in the Spirit.

This was the problem with the Galatians. Having begun in the Spirit, trusting in Jesus for their salvation, putting their faith in Christ to be accounted by God for righteousness, they were endeavoring to improve their righteousness. Paul said, "Are you so foolish?" The righteousness of Christ is complete!

THE JUST SHALL LIVE BY FAITH   Gal. 3:11

When Habakkuk, the prophet, saw the deteriorating conditions of Judah, the prophet cried to God. He told Him that things were getting horrible, and "the law is powerless" (Hab. 1:4). God said, "I will work a work in your days which you would not believe, though it were told you" (Hab. 1:5).

So the Lord began to share with Habakkuk His intention of using the Babylonians to judge Judah. The prophet couldn't understand why God would use a people like the Babylonians, who were even more evil than Israel, to judge Israel. Habakkuk said, "I don't understand it. I'm going to go into my tower and wait to see what You will say to me." And, as he was sitting in his tower waiting to see what God would say, the Word of the Lord came to Habakkuk, saying, "The just shall live by his faith" (Hab. 2:4). In other words, "Habakkuk, you're going to see things that are going to shake you, but 'the just shall live by his faith.'"

So we have that great declaration of God, "The just shall live by his faith." This, of course, was the passage that set Martin Luther free when he was reading Galatians. He had been trying as a monk to mortify the flesh, to get rid of his sinful nature. He was troubled and guilt-ridden. He was trying to observe all the works the church had put upon him as they were trying to be perfected in the flesh. Then he came across this passage, "the just shall live by faith," and this verse set him free!

the law in the sight of God *is* evident, for a*"the just shall live by faith."* 12Yet athe law is not of faith, but b*"the man who does them shall live by them."*

13aChrist has redeemed us from the curse of the law, having become a curse for us (for it is written, b*"Cursed is everyone who hangs on a tree"*), 14athat the blessing of Abraham might come upon the bGentiles in Christ Jesus, that we might receive cthe promise of the Spirit through faith.

THE CHANGELESS PROMISE

15Brethren, I speak in the manner of men: aThough *it is* only a man's covenant, yet *if it is* confirmed, no one annuls or adds to it. 16Now to Abraham and his Seed were the promises made. He does not say, "And to seeds," as of many, but as of aone, b*"And to your Seed,"* who is cChrist. 17And this I say, *that* the law, awhich was four hundred and thirty years later, cannot annul the covenant that was confirmed before by God *l*in Christ, bthat it should make the promise of no effect. 18For if athe inheritance *is* of the law, b*it is* no longer of promise; but God gave *it* to Abraham by promise.

Gal. 3:24

THE LAW IS A TUTOR

The law was our tutor, or in the King James Version our schoolmaster, to bring us to Christ. Now, this is probably not the best translation for us because we think of the tutor as the teacher. But in reality, it was the servant who led the child to school where he would learn. So the law is that which God uses to bring us to Jesus Christ so that we might learn how desperately sinful we are and how helpless we are to overcome sin. This drives us to Jesus Christ.

But the law can't make us righteous. Its purpose is to show us our sin in order to make us guilty before God so we are driven to faith in Jesus Christ.

11 aHab. 2:4
12 aRom. 4:4, 5
bLev. 18:5
13 a[Rom. 8:3]
bDeut. 21:23
14 a[Rom. 4:1–5, 9, 16]
bRom. 3:29, 30
cIs. 32:15
15 aHeb. 9:17
16 aGen. 22:18
bGen. 12:3, 7; 13:15; 24:7
c[1 Cor. 12:12]
17 aEx. 12:40
b[Rom. 4:13]
1NU omits *in Christ*
18 a[Rom. 8:17]
bRom. 4:14
19 aJohn 15:22
bGal. 4:4
cActs 7:53
dEx. 20:19
20 a[Rom. 3:29]
22 aRom. 11:32
bRom. 4:11
23 1Lit. confined
24 aRom. 10:4
bActs 13:39
1In a household, the guardian responsible for the care and discipline of the children
26 aJohn 1:12
27 a[Rom. 6:3]
bRom. 10:12; 13:14
28 aCol. 3:11
b[1 Cor. 12:13]
c[Eph. 2:15, 16]
29 aGen. 21:10
bRom. 4:11
cRom. 8:17

CHAPTER 4
3 aCol. 2:8, 20
4 a[Gen. 49:10]
b[John 1:14]
cGen. 3:15
dLuke 2:21, 27
1Or *made*
5 a[Matt. 20:28]
b[John 1:12]
6 a[Rom. 5:5; 8:9, 15, 16]
1Lit., in Aram., *Father*
7 a[Rom. 8:16, 17]
1NU *through God*
2NU omits *through Christ*
8 aEph. 2:12 bRom. 1:25
9 a[1 Cor. 8:3]

PURPOSE OF THE LAW

19What purpose then *does* the law serve? aIt was added because of transgressions, till the bSeed should come to whom the promise was made; *and it was* cappointed through angels by the hand dof a mediator. 20Now a mediator does not *mediate* for one *only,* abut God is one.

21*Is* the law then against the promises of God? Certainly not! For if there had been a law given which could have given life, truly righteousness would have been by the law. 22But the Scripture has confined aall under sin, bthat the promise by faith in Jesus Christ might be given to those who believe. 23But before faith came, we were kept under guard by the law, *l*kept for the faith which would afterward be revealed. 24Therefore athe law was our *l*tutor *to bring us* to Christ, bthat we might be justified by faith. 25But after faith has come, we are no longer under a tutor.

SONS AND HEIRS

26For you aare all sons of God through faith in Christ Jesus. 27For aas many of you as were baptized into Christ bhave put on Christ. 28aThere is neither Jew nor Greek, bthere is neither slave nor free, there is neither male nor female; for you are all cone in Christ Jesus. 29And aif you *are* Christ's, then you are Abraham's bseed, and cheirs according to the promise.

4 Now I say *that* the heir, as long as he is a child, does not differ at all from a slave, though he is master of all, 2but is under guardians and stewards until the time appointed by the father. 3Even so we, when we were children, awere in bondage under the elements of the world. 4But awhen the fullness of the time had come, God sent forth His Son, bborn*l*cof a woman, dborn under the law, 5ato redeem those who were under the law, bthat we might receive the adoption as sons.

6And because you are sons, God has sent forth athe Spirit of His Son into your hearts, crying out, *l*"Abba, Father!" 7Therefore you are no longer a slave but a son, aand if a son, then an heir *l*of God 2through Christ.

FEARS FOR THE CHURCH

8But then, indeed, awhen you did not know God, byou served those which by nature are not gods. 9But now aafter

Gal. 4:6

ABBA, FATHER

The word *Abba* is the Hebrew word for "father." But it's more like our English word, "daddy," because it's a term of endearment. It's a term of closeness. It's a term of coziness.

"Father" can be a formal kind of a relationship. When I think of "father," I think of sitting straight at the table, you know, and not saying a word with "father" at the other end. You think of a formal, don't-speak-until-you're-spoken-to kind of a thing. With "daddy," you think of climbing up on his lap, listening to stories, and getting hugs. Both are proper. There is a balance in "Abba, Father."

God desires to have a close relationship with us, where He touches us and can be touched by us. But, also, realizing who God is—the awesome power, authority, the eternal, omnipotent, omniscient God—there is always that reverence and respect that comes with Father. It's a fine balance.

---

9 b Col. 2:20
c Heb. 7:18

10 a Rom. 14:5

11 a 1 Thess. 3:5

12 a 2 Cor. 2:5

13 a 1 Cor. 2:3

14 a Mal. 2:7
b [Luke 10:16]
1 Or *messenger*

15 1 NU *Where*

17 a Rom. 10:2

19 a 1 Cor. 4:15

22 a Gen. 16:15
b Gen. 21:2

23 a Rom. 9:7, 8
b Heb. 11:11

24 a Deut. 33:2
1 NU, M omit *the*

26 a [Is. 2:2]

---

you have known God, or rather are known by God, b how *is it that* you turn again to c the weak and beggarly elements, to which you desire again to be in bondage? 10 a You observe days and months and seasons and years. 11 I am afraid for you, a lest I have labored for you in vain.

12 Brethren, I urge you to become like me, for I *became* like you. a You have not injured me at all. 13 You know that a because of physical infirmity I preached the gospel to you at the first. 14 And my trial which was in my flesh you did not despise or reject, but you received me a as an 1 angel of God, b *even* as Christ Jesus. 15 1 What then was the blessing you *enjoyed?* For I bear you witness that, if possible, you would have plucked out your own eyes and given them to me. 16 Have I there-

---

fore become your enemy because I tell you the truth?

17 They a zealously court you, *but* for no good; yes, they want to exclude you, that you may be zealous for them. 18 But it is good to be zealous in a good thing always, and not only when I am present with you. 19 a My little children, for whom I labor in birth again until Christ is formed in you, 20 I would like to be present with you now and to change my tone; for I have doubts about you.

Gal. 4:19

FATHER'S HEART

Here the Galatians were—little children. They were not well grounded in the faith. Paul wasn't with them that long. Paul saw false teachers had come in bringing heresies and upsetting these babes. And Paul's heart went out to them. Paul said, "I'm laboring in birth until Christ is formed in you."

Paul's desire was to bring them into a full relationship with God through Jesus Christ. He desired to see their lives transformed by the indwelling presence and power of Christ in them. Thus, in prayer, Paul was laboring to this end.

TWO COVENANTS

21 Tell me, you who desire to be under the law, do you not hear the law? 22 For it is written that Abraham had two sons: a the one by a bondwoman, b the other by a freewoman. 23 But he *who was* of the bondwoman a was born according to the flesh, b and he of the freewoman through promise, 24 which things are symbolic. For these are 1 the two covenants: the one from Mount a Sinai which gives birth to bondage, which is Hagar— 25 for this Hagar is Mount Sinai in Arabia, and corresponds to Jerusalem which now is, and is in bondage with her children— 26 but the a Jerusalem above is free, which is the mother of us all. 27 For it is written:

Gal. 4:25

TWO COVENANTS

Paul picked up an allegory from Abraham, who had two sons.

The first son, Ishmael, was the son of expediency. He was a demonstration of the lack of faith in the promises of God. He was a product of a fleshly endeavor to accomplish the purposes of God. Now, that is quite common and, of course, it's part of the Law. It is a fleshly endeavor to attempt to attain the promises of God through the Law.

The other son, Isaac, was the son of promise. God promised to give Abraham a son; and, thus, Isaac was the spiritual son.

Now, when Isaac grew older, God said to Abraham, "Take now your son, your only son Isaac" (Gen. 22:2). Wait a minute, aren't You forgetting Ishmael? What do You mean, your only son? Ishmael was a son of the flesh. God doesn't acknowledge the works of the flesh. So those who are endeavoring in their flesh to please God need to take note that God doesn't recognize the works of the flesh.

a"*Rejoice, O barren,*
    You who do not bear!
Break forth and shout,
    You who are not in labor!
For the desolate has many more
    children
Than she who has a husband."

28Now awe, brethren, as Isaac *was*, are bchildren of promise. 29But, as ahe who was born according to the flesh then persecuted him *who was born* according to the Spirit, beven so *it is* now. 30Nevertheless what does athe Scripture say? b"*Cast out the bond-woman and her son, for* c*the son of the bondwoman shall not be heir with the son of the freewoman.*" 31So then, brethren, we are not children of the bondwoman but of the free.

27 a Is. 54:1

28 a Gal. 3:29
b Acts 3:25

29 a Gen. 21:9
b Gal. 5:11

30 a [Gal. 3:8, 22]
b Gen. 21:10, 12
c [John 8:35]

CHAPTER 5

1 a Phil. 4:1
b Acts 15:10
1 NU *For freedom Christ has made us free; stand fast therefore, and*

2 a Acts 15:1

3 a [Rom. 2:25]
1 *obligated*

4 a [Rom. 9:31]
b Heb. 12:15

5 a Rom. 8:24

6 a [Gal. 6:15]
b 1 Thess. 1:3

7 a 1 Cor. 9:24

CHRISTIAN LIBERTY

5 Stand a 1fast therefore in the liberty by which Christ has made us free, and do not be entangled again with a byoke of bondage. 2Indeed I, Paul, say to you that aif you become circumcised, Christ will profit you nothing. 3And I testify again to every man who becomes circumcised athat he is 1a debtor to keep the whole law. 4 aYou have become estranged from Christ, you who *attempt to* be justified by law; byou have fallen from grace. 5For we through the Spirit eagerly await for the hope of righteousness by faith. 6For ain Christ Jesus neither circumcision nor uncircumcision avails anything, but bfaith working through love.

LOVE FULFILLS THE LAW

7You aran well. Who hindered you from obeying the truth? 8This persua-

---

Gal. 5:8

Just Read the Bible. This is a very important Scripture! There are a lot of people who have weird interpretations of the Scripture. When I talk to those caught up in various cults and false religions, I often ask them, "Where did you get this idea? Where did you get this concept? I can guarantee you did not get it by just reading the Scriptures because you could read the Scriptures forever and you would never come up with that crazy interpretation. It isn't scriptural. Unless you had been taught it, you would have never come to it." The positions they hold are ones taught to them. They are not positions they have come to by reading the Scriptures. That is why cults are constantly promoting their own books because they know that if you would just read the Bible, you would not come to their persuasion.

Paul said, "This persuasion did not come to you from the Lord." I encourage you to read the Bible. I'm not afraid of what you will come to believe by just reading the Bible.

sion does not *come* from Him who calls you. [9][a] A little leaven leavens the whole lump. [10] I have confidence in you, in the Lord, that you will have no other mind; but he who troubles you shall bear his judgment, whoever he is.

[11] And I, brethren, if I still preach circumcision, [a] why do I still suffer persecution? Then [b] the offense of the cross has ceased. [12][a] I could wish that those [b] who trouble you would even [1] cut themselves off!

[13] For you, brethren, have been called to liberty; only [a] do not *use* liberty as an [b] opportunity for the flesh, but [c] through love serve one another. [14] For [a] all the law is fulfilled in one word, *even* in this: [b] *"You shall love your neighbor as yourself."* [15] But if you bite and devour one another, beware lest you be consumed by one another!

WALKING IN THE SPIRIT

[16] I say then: [a] Walk in the Spirit, and you shall not fulfill the lust of the flesh.

---

[9] [a] 1 Cor. 5:6

[11] [a] 1 Cor. 15:30
[b] [1 Cor. 1:23]

[12] [a] Josh. 7:25
[b] Acts 15:1, 2
[1] *mutilate themselves*

[13] [a] 1 Cor. 8:9
[b] 1 Pet. 2:16
[c] 1 Cor. 9:19

[14] [a] Matt. 7:12; 22:40
[b] Lev. 19:18

[16] [a] Rom. 6:12

[17] [a] Rom. 7:18, 22, 23; 8:5
[b] Rom. 7:15

[18] [a] [Rom. 6:14; 7:4; 8:14]

[19] [a] Eph. 5:3, 11
[1] NU omits *adultery*
[2] *sexual immorality*

[21] [a] 1 Cor. 6:9, 10
[1] NU omits *murders*

[22] [a] [John 15:2]
[b] [Col. 3:12–15]
[c] Rom. 15:14
[d] 1 Cor. 13:7

[23] [a] 1 Tim. 1:9
[1] *meekness*

[24] [a] Rom. 6:6

[25] [a] [Rom. 8:4, 5]

[26] [a] Phil. 2:3

---

[17] For [a] the flesh lusts against the Spirit, and the Spirit against the flesh; and these are contrary to one another, [b] so that you do not do the things that you wish. [18] But [a] if you are led by the Spirit, you are not under the law.

[19] Now [a] the works of the flesh are evident, which are: [1] adultery, [2] fornication, uncleanness, lewdness, [20] idolatry, sorcery, hatred, contentions, jealousies, outbursts of wrath, selfish ambitions, dissensions, heresies, [21] envy, [1] murders, drunkenness, revelries, and the like; of which I tell you beforehand, just as I also told *you* in time past, that [a] those who practice such things will not inherit the kingdom of God.

[22] But [a] the fruit of the Spirit is [b] love, joy, peace, longsuffering, kindness, [c] goodness, [d] faithfulness, [23] [1] gentleness, self-control. [a] Against such there is no law. [24] And those *who are* Christ's [a] have crucified the flesh with its passions and desires. [25] [a] If we live in the Spirit, let us also walk in the Spirit. [26] [a] Let us not become conceited, provoking one another, envying one another.

Gal. 5:16

WALK IN THE SPIRIT

Man is a trinity made up of body, mind, and spirit. Man, basically, is a spirit, living in a body, possessing a consciousness or mind.

Now my mind is either going to be controlled by fleshly desires, or it is going to be controlled by spiritual desires. If I am living after the flesh, giving in to the passions and desires of my flesh, then the result will be that I will have a carnal mind. Paul said we are to bring "every thought into captivity to the obedience of Christ" (2 Cor. 10:5).

When we find our minds absorbed in the things of the flesh, it's important to take control and say, "I don't want to think on those things." Start to sing a worship chorus or just turn your mind toward the Lord. Get into the Scriptures. We want to live in the Spirit. We want to walk in the Spirit. If we do, we will not fulfill the lusts of our flesh.

Gal. 5:22–23

THE FRUIT OF THE SPIRIT

In contrast to the works of the law, we have the fruit of the Spirit. Works suggest a factory. Fruit gives you the idea of a garden. Works are production, sweat, and toil. Fruit is the natural outgrowth of a relationship.

If you have a relationship with Jesus Christ, these are the characteristics that will begin to mark your life. There are not really nine fruits of the Spirit. There is only one fruit of the Spirit, and that is love! But this kind of love is not the Greek *eros*, or the Greek *phileo*. It is the word *agape* which was used in the New Testament to describe a depth of love beyond man's capacity—a love marked by joy, peace, longsuffering, kindness, goodness, faithfulness, gentleness, and self-control.

Gal. 6:1

GENTLENESS

We want to seek to restore in the spirit of gentleness, not in a condemning way, because, but for the grace of God, there go I! None of us is so holy or righteous that we are immune from temptation. We are told to consider ourselves under similar circumstances, knowing that we might be tempted, too.

The word here for "trespass" means "taken suddenly in this trespass." This isn't a person who has deliberately turned his back on Jesus. It's one who has been caught up in the moment and taken captive by the enemy. We are to seek to restore such a person in a spirit of gentleness.

BEAR AND SHARE THE BURDENS

6 Brethren, if a man is ¹overtaken in any trespass, you who *are* spiritual restore such a one in a spirit of ᵃgentleness, considering yourself lest you also be tempted. ²ᵃBear one another's burdens, and so fulfill ᵇthe law of Christ. ³For ᵃif anyone thinks himself to be something, when ᵇhe is nothing, he deceives himself. ⁴But ᵃlet each one examine his own work, and then he will have rejoicing in himself alone, and ᵇnot in another. ⁵For ᵃeach one shall bear his own load.

BE GENEROUS AND DO GOOD

⁶ᵃLet him who is taught the word share in all good things with him who teaches.

⁷Do not be deceived, God is not mocked; for ᵃwhatever a man sows, that he will also reap. ⁸For he who sows to his flesh will of the flesh reap corruption, but he who sows to the Spirit will of the Spirit reap ᵃeverlasting life. ⁹And ᵃlet us not grow weary while doing good, for in due season we shall reap ᵇif we do not lose heart. ¹⁰ᵃTherefore, as we have opportunity, ᵇlet us do good to all, ᶜespecially to those who are of the household of faith.

CHAPTER 6

1 ᵃEph. 4:2
1 *caught*

2 ᵃRom. 15:1
ᵇ[James 2:8]

3 ᵃRom. 12:3
ᵇ[2Cor. 3:5]

4 ᵃ1Cor. 11:28
ᵇLuke 18:11

5 ᵃ[Rom. 2:6]

6 ᵃ1Cor. 9:11, 14

7 ᵃ[Rom. 2:6]

8 ᵃ[Rom. 6:8]

9 ᵃ1Cor. 15:58
ᵇ[James 5:7, 8]

10 ᵃProv. 3:27
ᵇTitus 3:8
ᶜRom. 12:13

12 ᵃGal. 5:11

14 ᵃ[1Cor. 1:18]

GLORY ONLY IN THE CROSS

¹¹See with what large letters I have written to you with my own hand! ¹²As many as desire to make a good showing in the flesh, these *would* compel you to be circumcised, ᵃonly that they may not suffer persecution for the cross of Christ. ¹³For not even those who are circumcised keep the law, but they desire to have you circumcised that they may boast in your flesh. ¹⁴But God forbid that I should boast except in the ᵃcross of our Lord Jesus Christ, by ¹whom the world has been crucified to me, and ᵇI to the world. ¹⁵For ᵃin Christ Jesus neither circumcision nor

Gal. 6:14

GLORY IN THE CROSS

When I was a child, I considered myself righteous because I didn't go to the movies, go to dances, smoke, or drink. My whole righteousness was predicated on these kinds of negatives and a few positives. I went to church every Sunday and Wednesday night. Yet, my righteousness was in keeping the rules that had been set by the church.

I didn't know what it was to glory in the cross, in the finished work of Jesus Christ. I was always endeavoring to do better. Failing, but promising God, "I'm going to do better." Struggling, trying in my flesh to please God.

Then I discovered the grace of God and learned that righteousness was through Jesus Christ. Oh, what a relief that was! What freedom!

So God forbid! Others may boast in their fleshly accomplishments, but God forbid that I should glory except in the finished work of my redemption on the cross of Jesus Christ!

Gal. 6:8

Sow to the Spirit. How do you sow to the Spirit? The Bible tells us "the Word of God is living and powerful, and sharper than any two-edged sword" (Heb. 4:12). It is the Word of God that feeds the Spirit.

If you feed your mind the Word of God, reading the Bible and listening to the Word of God being taught, you are sowing to the Spirit. As you feed your Spirit, you will reap of the Spirit. Spiritual reaping is glorious, but you reap what you sow. If you sow to the Spirit, you will reap everlasting life.

14 b Col. 2:20
1 Or *which,* the cross

15 a 1 Cor. 7:19

uncircumcision avails anything, but a new creation.

BLESSING AND A PLEA

16And as many as walk according to this rule, peace and mercy *be* upon them, and upon the Israel of God.

17From now on let no one trouble me, for I bear in my body the marks of the Lord Jesus.

18Brethren, the grace of our Lord Jesus Christ *be* with your spirit. Amen.

EPHESIANS

INTRODUCTION

Ephesians was the first of what are called Paul's Prison Epistles, along with Colossians, Philippians, and Philemon. He wrote them while he was a prisoner, awaiting trial in Rome.

Ephesus was a prominent capital of the Roman Empire in Asia, located in present-day Turkey. Paul visited there toward the end of his second missionary journey, and the leaders of the church at that time were Priscilla and Aquila, along with Apollos.

Later, during Paul's third missionary journey, he stayed and ministered in Ephesus for three years with great success. The ministry had such an impact that it was a threat to the business at the Temple of Diana, which was one of the seven wonders of the ancient world. Since Paul had stayed longer in Ephesus than anywhere else he went, the Ephesians were well-taught people, and when he wrote this letter he was able to teach about some of the deepest and greatest truths of the Bible because of the strong foundation he had laid with them.

In the first three chapters, Paul outlines for Christians all the riches that are ours in Christ. He gives the deepest teaching in the Bible on what it means to be the church, the body of Christ, and he lists all our possessions and our standing because of what Christ has done for us. He takes the Ephesian Christians, and us, into the heavenlies, presenting the lofty truths of the mystery of the gospel and our salvation. He makes it clear that everything we have in Him is because of grace and doesn't come from our human effort.

In the last three chapters, Paul applies these truths in a practical way, outlining the walk of the believer in light of the truth of who we are in Christ. While the first three chapters present some of the heaviest doctrinal truths of the Bible, the last three chapters share the practical implications of this doctrine in a way that is clear and understandable.

Paul offers practical teaching on the church, the family, and the work place, and gives also a powerful description of how to experience victory in spiritual warfare, by putting on the armor of God. He also outlines the purpose of the church, stating that God gave apostles, prophets, evangelists, and pastor-teachers "for the equipping of the saints for the work of the ministry, for the edifying of the body of Christ" (Eph. 4:11–12).

It is interesting that the church in Ephesus was the first church Jesus wrote to in Revelation 4, and they were seen as still being doctrinally solid. The problem He

addressed with them is the same problem that is always a danger, especially to churches that pride themselves on their doctrinal purity. They had left their first love. In a sense they had soaked up the first half of the book of Ephesians, but had neglected the second half, especially Ephesians 5:1–2 where Paul says, "Be imitators of God as dear children. And walk in love, as Christ also has loved us and given Himself for us."

GREETING

1 Paul, an apostle of Jesus Christ by the will of God,

To the saints who are in Ephesus, and faithful in Christ Jesus:

2 Grace to you and peace from God our Father and the Lord Jesus Christ.

REDEMPTION IN CHRIST

3 a Blessed *be* the God and Father of our Lord Jesus Christ, who has blessed us with every spiritual blessing in the heavenly *places* in Christ, 4 just as a He chose us in Him b before the foundation

CHAPTER 1

3 a 2 Cor. 1:3

4 a Rom. 8:28
b 1 Pet. 1:2
c Luke 1:75

5 a [Rom. 8:29]
b John 1:12
c [1 Cor. 1:21]

6 a [Rom. 3:24]
b Matt. 3:17
1 Lit. *bestowed grace (favor) upon us*

7 a [Heb. 9:12]
b [Rom. 3:24, 25]

8 1 *understanding*

9 a [Rom. 16:25]

of the world, that we should c be holy and without blame before Him in love, 5 a having predestined us to b adoption as sons by Jesus Christ to Himself, c according to the good pleasure of His will, 6 to the praise of the glory of His grace, a by which He 1 made us accepted in b the Beloved.

7 a In Him we have redemption through His blood, the forgiveness of sins, according to b the riches of His grace 8 which He made to abound toward us in all wisdom and 1 prudence, 9 a having made known to us the mystery of His

---

Eph. 1:1

BY THE WILL OF GOD

"**P**aul, an apostle of Jesus Christ by the will of God." Take out the name Paul and put in your name. Take out the word "apostle" and fill in the blank. What are you, by the will of God?

God has given each of us gifts and callings according to His will. What is it that He has called you to do? I would have to write, "Chuck Smith, a pastor-teacher of Jesus Christ by the will of God." That is what God has called me to do, in serving Him.

It is important that you know what you are by the will of God. It's extremely difficult to try to be something you aren't. Ask God to show you who you are, by His will, and then go for it with all your heart.

Eph. 1:4–6

CHOSEN IN HIM

If you are a Christian, it is because God chose you. Jesus told His disciples, "You did not choose Me, but I chose you" (John 15:16). And for each of us who have received Jesus Christ as our Savior, we discover that He chose us. This confuses many people because they realize that we have the ability to choose, and that is true. But God, who knows all things, knows what we will choose; and He doesn't pick losers. He picks winners.

You may say, "But that isn't fair? What if God didn't choose me?" Have you accepted Jesus Christ? If so, then He chose you. If you haven't accepted Him, do it and you'll find out you were chosen. If you don't want to accept Him, why do you care if you were chosen or not?

will, according to His good pleasure bwhich He purposed in Himself, 10that in the dispensation of athe fullness of the times bHe might gather together in one call things in Christ, 1both which are in heaven and which are on earth—in Him. 11aIn Him also we have obtained an inheritance, being predestined according to bthe purpose of Him who works all things according to the counsel of His will, 12athat we bwho first trusted in Christ should be to the praise of His glory.

13In Him you also *trusted*, after you heard athe word of truth, the gospel of your salvation; in whom also, having believed, byou were sealed with the Holy Spirit of promise, 14who1 is the 2guarantee of our inheritance buntil the redemption of cthe purchased possession, dto the praise of His glory.

PRAYER FOR SPIRITUAL WISDOM

15Therefore I also, aafter I heard of your faith in the Lord Jesus and your love for all the saints, 16ado not cease to give thanks for you, making mention of you in my prayers: 17that athe God of our Lord Jesus Christ, the Father of glory, bmay give to you the spirit of wisdom and revelation in the knowledge of Him, 18athe eyes of your 1understanding being enlightened; that you may know what is bthe hope of His calling, what are the riches of the glory of His inheritance in the saints, 19and what is the exceeding greatness of His power toward us who believe, aaccording to the working of His mighty power 20which He worked in Christ when aHe raised Him from the dead and bseated *Him* at His right hand in the heavenly *places*, 21afar above all bprincipality1

Eph. 1:18

The Riches of His Inheritance.
Paul prayed that the Ephesian Christians would understand "what are the riches of the glory of His inheritance in the saints."

You are God's inheritance, and He treasures you. Do you want to know how much He values you? He values you so highly that He sent His only begotten Son to die for you and make you His child. Paul prayed, "Oh, if you only knew how much God treasures you!"

---

9 b [2 Tim. 1:9]
10 a Gal. 4:4
b 1 Cor. 3:22
c [Col. 1:16, 20]
1 NU, M omit both

11 a Rom. 8:17
b Is. 46:10

12 a 2 Thess. 2:13
b James 1:18

13 a John 1:17
b [2 Cor. 1:22]

14 a 2 Cor. 5:5
b Rom. 8:23
c [Acts 20:28]
d 1 Pet. 2:9
1 NU which
2 down payment, earnest

15 a Col. 1:4

16 a Rom. 1:9

17 a John 20:17
b Col. 1:9

18 a Acts 26:18
b Eph. 2:12
1 NU, M hearts

19 a Col. 2:12

20 a Acts 2:24
b Ps. 110:1

21 a Phil. 2:9, 10
b [Rom. 8:38, 39]
1 rule
2 authority
3 power

22 a Ps. 8:6; 110:1
b Heb. 2:7

23 a Rom. 12:5
b Col. 2:9
c [1 Cor. 12:6]

CHAPTER 2

1 a Col. 2:13
b Eph. 4:18

2 a Col. 1:21
b Eph. 6:12
c Col. 3:6
1 Gr. aion, aeon

3 a 1 Pet. 4:3
b Gal. 5:16
c [Ps. 51:5]

4 a Rom. 10:12
b John 3:16

5 a Rom. 5:6, 8
b [Rom. 6:4, 5]

6 a Eph. 1:20

7 a Titus 3:4

8 a [2 Tim. 1:9]
b Rom. 4:16
c [John 1:12, 13]

9 a Rom. 4:4, 5; 11:6
b Rom. 3:27

10 a Is. 19:25

---

and 2power and 3might and dominion, and every name that is named, not only in this age but also in that which is to come.

22And aHe put all *things* under His feet, and gave Him b*to be* head over all *things* to the church, 23awhich is His body, bthe fullness of Him cwho fills all in all.

BY GRACE THROUGH FAITH

2 And ayou *He made alive*, bwho were dead in trespasses and sins, 2ain which you once walked according to the 1course of this world, according to bthe prince of the power of the air, the spirit who now works in cthe sons of disobedience, 3aamong whom also we all once conducted ourselves in bthe lusts of our flesh, fulfilling the desires of the flesh and of the mind, and cwere by nature children of wrath, just as the others.

Eph. 2:2

Prince of the Power of the Air.

The current, or flow of the world is being orchestrated and directed by Satan. He is guiding the direction of this world system.

When you were walking in the world, meandering through life, believing you were in control, in reality you were under the power of Satan. You were in his grip, flowing along, being governed by Satan, without even knowing it. But God came along and made you alive, for the first time.

4But God, awho is rich in mercy, because of His bgreat love with which He loved us, 5aeven when we were dead in trespasses, bmade us alive together with Christ (by grace you have been saved), 6and raised *us* up together, and made *us* sit together ain the heavenly *places* in Christ Jesus, 7that in the ages to come He might show the exceeding riches of His grace in a*His* kindness toward us in Christ Jesus. 8aFor by grace you have been saved bthrough faith, and that not of yourselves; cit is the gift of God, 9not of aworks, lest anyone should bboast. 10For we are aHis workmanship, created in Christ Jesus for good works, which God prepared beforehand that we should walk in them.

Eph. 2:8–9

By Grace Through Faith. There is no way you can earn your salvation. It is only by grace, that unearned, undeserved blessing from God. It is a gift from Him.

There are no rules you can follow that will qualify you for it. If you will have faith in the promises of God and in Jesus Christ, He gives you eternal salvation. If it could come by doing good works, we would brag about it. But it is free. The wonderful, amazing grace of Jesus!

BROUGHT NEAR BY HIS BLOOD

11Therefore remember that you, once Gentiles in the flesh—who are called Uncircumcision by what is called ᵃthe Circumcision made in the flesh by hands— 12that at that time you were without Christ, being aliens from the commonwealth of Israel and strangers from the covenants of promise, having no hope and without God in the world. 13But now in Christ Jesus you who once were far off have been brought near by the blood of Christ.

CHRIST OUR PEACE

14For He Himself is our peace, who has made both one, and has broken down the middle wall of separation,

Eph. 2:14

Broken Walls. I think it is tragic that, while Jesus came to break down the walls, to make us all one, people are so often trying to build up walls of separation. Unless you see things just the way they do, they'll get on the radio and castigate you because you don't see eye-to-eye with them.

If God can break down the walls between Jews and Gentiles, certainly He can break down the walls between Christians who are building up walls that He tore down and are fencing themselves into little, exclusive boxes. God help us!

---

11 ᵃ[Col. 2:11]

15 ᵃGal. 6:15

16 ᵃ[Col. 1:20–22]
b[Rom. 6:6]

18 ᵃJohn 10:9
b1Cor. 12:13

20 ᵃ1Pet. 2:4
bMatt. 16:18
c1Cor. 12:28
dPs. 118:22

21 ᵃ1Cor. 3:16, 17

22 ᵃ1Pet. 2:5
bJohn 17:23

CHAPTER 3

2 ᵃActs 9:15
1stewardship

3 ᵃActs 22:17, 21; 26:16
b[Rom. 11:25; 16:25]

6 ᵃGal. 3:28, 29

7 ᵃRom. 15:16
bRom. 1:5
cRom. 15:18

8 ᵃ[1Cor. 15:9]
b[Col. 1:27; 2:2, 3]

9 ᵃHeb. 1:2
1NU, M stewardship (dispensation)
2NU omits through Jesus Christ

10 ᵃ1Pet. 1:12
b[1Tim. 3:16]
cCol. 1:16; 2:10, 15
1variegated or many-sided
2rulers

11 ᵃ[Eph. 1:4, 11]

15having abolished in His flesh the enmity, *that is,* the law of commandments *contained* in ordinances, so as to create in Himself one ᵃnew man *from* the two, *thus* making peace, 16and that He might ᵃreconcile them both to God in one body through the cross, thereby bputting to death the enmity. 17And He came and preached peace to you who were afar off and to those who were near. 18For ᵃthrough Him we both have access bby one Spirit to the Father.

CHRIST OUR CORNERSTONE

19Now, therefore, you are no longer strangers and foreigners, but fellow citizens with the saints and members of the household of God, 20having been ᵃbuilt bon the foundation of the ᶜapostles and bon prophets, Jesus Christ Himself being dthe chief corner*stone,* 21in whom the whole building, being fitted together, grows into ᵃa holy temple in the Lord, 22ᵃin whom you also are being built together for a bdwelling place of God in the Spirit.

THE MYSTERY REVEALED

3 For this reason I, Paul, the prisoner of Christ Jesus for you Gentiles— 2if indeed you have heard of the *1*dispensation of the grace of God ᵃwhich was given to me for you, 3ᵃhow that by revelation bHe made known to me the mystery (as I have briefly written already, 4by which, when you read, you may understand my knowledge in the mystery of Christ), 5which in other ages was not made known to the sons of men, as it has now been revealed by the Spirit to His holy apostles and prophets: 6that the Gentiles ᵃshould be fellow heirs, of the same body, and partakers of His promise in Christ through the gospel, 7ᵃof which I became a minister baccording to the gift of the grace of God given to me by cthe effective working of His power.

PURPOSE OF THE MYSTERY

8To me, ᵃwho am less than the least of all the saints, this grace was given, that I should preach among the Gentiles bthe unsearchable riches of Christ, 9and to make all see what *is* the *1*fellow-ship of the mystery, which from the beginning of the ages has been hidden in God who ᵃcreated all things 2through Jesus Christ; 10ᵃto the intent that now bthe *1*manifold wisdom of God might be made known by the church cto the 2principalities and powers in the heavenly *places,* 11ᵃaccording

LESS THAN THE LEAST

Paul's estimate of himself was that he was "less than the least of all the saints." In another place Paul called himself the chief of sinners (1 Tim. 1:15).

Paul was certainly the most accomplished of all the apostles. He wrote thirteen or fourteen books of the New Testament. He started some of the greatest churches of the day. And yet he considered himself to be less than the least of the saints. Paul remained amazed at the fact that God would save him.

It is sad when people think that God was lucky to get them. "God got someone really special when He got me." I have to confess, when I see some of these fellows on Christian television, strutting across the stage, acting like professional wrestlers, I wonder, where is the humility that Paul had?

---

12 a Heb. 4:16; 10:19, 35

13 a Phil. 1:14
b 2 Cor. 1:6

14 a Eph. 1:3
1 NU omits *of our Lord Jesus Christ*

16 a [Phil. 4:19]
b Col. 1:11
c Rom. 7:22

17 a John 14:23
b Col. 1:23

18 a Eph. 1:18
b Rom. 8:39

19 a Eph. 1:23

20 a Rom. 16:25
b 1 Cor. 2:9
c Col. 1:29

21 a Rom. 11:36

CHAPTER 4

1 a 1 Thess. 2:12
1 Lit. *in*
2 *exhort, encourage*

3 a Col. 3:14

4 a Rom. 12:5

5 a 1 Cor. 1:13
b Jude 3
c [Heb. 6:6]

6 a Mal. 2:10
b Rom. 11:36
1 NU omits *you;*
M *us*

7 a [1 Cor. 12:7, 11]

BOLDNESS AND ACCESS

In Christ we have "boldness and access with confidence through faith in Him." When Jesus died, the veil in the temple was torn in two. By His death we received access to the presence of God. "Let us therefore come boldly to the throne of grace, that we may obtain mercy and find grace to help in time of need" (Heb. 4:16). Our access only comes through Jesus Christ.

There is only one Mediator between God and man, and that is Jesus Christ (1 Tim. 2:5). Although the Catholic Church has debated for years concerning Mary's role as co-redemptrix with Christ, we believe that Christ is the only Redeemer, the only Mediator, and the only Savior. He gives us bold access to the presence of God, and no other help is necessary.

---

to the eternal purpose which He accomplished in Christ Jesus our Lord, 12in whom we have boldness and access awith confidence through faith in Him. 13aTherefore I ask that you do not lose heart at my tribulations for you, bwhich is your glory.

APPRECIATION OF THE MYSTERY

14For this reason I bow my knees to the aFather 1of our Lord Jesus Christ, 15from whom the whole family in heaven and earth is named, 16that He would grant you, aaccording to the riches of His glory, bto be strengthened with might through His Spirit in cthe inner man, 17athat Christ may dwell in your hearts through faith; that you, bbeing rooted and grounded in love, 18amay be able to comprehend with all the saints bwhat *is* the width and length and depth and height— 19to know the love of Christ which passes knowledge; that you may be filled awith all the fullness of God.

20Now ato Him who is able to do exceedingly abundantly babove all that we ask or think, caccording to the power that works in us, 21ato Him *be* glory in the church by Christ Jesus to all generations, forever and ever. Amen.

WALK IN UNITY

4 I, therefore, the prisoner 1of the Lord, 2beseech you to awalk worthy of the calling with which you were called, 2with all lowliness and gentleness, with longsuffering, bearing with one another in love, 3endeavoring to keep the unity of the Spirit ain the bond of peace. 4aThere is one body and one Spirit, just as you were called in one hope of your calling; 5aone Lord, bone faith, cone baptism; 6aone God and Father of all, who *is* above all, and bthrough all, and 1you all.

SPIRITUAL GIFTS

7But ato each one of us grace was given according to the measure of Christ's gift. 8Therefore He says:

Eph. 3:17

DWELLING IN OUR HEARTS

Paul prayed for the Ephesians that "Christ may dwell in your hearts through faith." The word for "dwell" in the Greek means to "settle down and be at home with." So he was praying that God would be at home in their hearts.

Robert Munger wrote a great little booklet entitled *My Heart, Christ's Home*. I highly recommend it to you. It concerns all the aspects of inviting Christ to be at home in your life. Do you think He feels at home with you? Or is there a little tension and discomfort? Think about it.

a"*When He ascended on high,
He led captivity captive,
And gave gifts to men.*"

9 a(Now this, "*He ascended*"—what does it mean but that He also 1first descended into the lower parts of the earth? 10He who descended is also the One awho ascended far above all the heavens, bthat He might fill all things.) 11And He Himself gave some *to be* apostles, some prophets, some evangelists, and some pastors and teachers, 12for the equipping of the saints for the work of ministry, afor the 1edifying of

---

8 a Ps. 68:18

9 a John 3:13;
20:17
1 NU omits *first*

10 a Acts 1:9
b [Eph. 1:23]

12 a 1 Cor.
14:26
b Col. 1:24
1 *building up*

13 a Col. 2:2
b 1 Cor. 14:20

14 a 1 Cor.
14:20
b Rom. 16:18

15 a Eph. 1:22

16 a Col. 2:19

Eph. 4:1

Walk Worthy. Paul spent the last three chapters outlining the glorious calling of the believer. Here he turned to practical matters of application, saying, "Walk worthy of the calling with which you were called." What calling?

We have been called to be saints. We have been called to be children of God by faith. We have been called to be heirs of salvation. So walk worthy of your calling, as a saint, as a child of God, and as an heir of God.

bthe body of Christ, 13till we all come to the unity of the faith aand of the knowledge of the Son of God, to ba perfect man, to the measure of the stature of the fullness of Christ; 14that we should no longer be achildren, tossed to and fro and carried about with every wind of doctrine, by the trickery of men, in the cunning craftiness of bdeceitful plotting, 15but, speaking the truth in love, may grow up in all things into Him who is the ahead—Christ— 16afrom whom the whole body, joined and knit together by what every joint supplies, according to the effective working by which every part does its share, causes growth of the body for the edifying of itself in love.

THE PURPOSE OF THE CHURCH   Eph. 4:11–12

For years, in the early part of my ministry, most of my sermons were evangelistic sermons, because I believed that the primary purpose of the church was to evangelize the world. It was only when I began a careful study of Ephesians and read these verses that I came to the conclusion that the purpose of the church is not to evangelize the world, but to equip the saints for the work of ministry, to build up the body of Christ.

The problem with evangelistic messages is that they don't help the people to grow and mature. I kept church members in a state of perpetual infancy by preaching the same basic sermons to them over and over again and not taking them on into maturity in Christ.

I have discovered that the real need in the church is solid, systematic, expository teaching of the Scriptures. That is what leads to spiritual growth in the people and equips them to go out and do the work of the ministry. If I do my job, all those who listen and learn will then go out and evangelize and minister in many other ways, which will lead to the body of Christ being built up. It just works.

THE NEW MAN

17This I say, therefore, and testify in the Lord, that you should ano longer walk as 1the rest of the Gentiles walk, in the futility of their mind, 18having their understanding darkened, being alienated from the life of God, because of the ignorance that is in them, because of the ablindness of their heart; 19awho, being past feeling, bhave given themselves over to lewdness, to work all uncleanness with greediness.

20But you have not so learned Christ, 21if indeed you have heard Him and have been taught by Him, as the truth is in Jesus: 22that you aput off, concerning your former conduct, the old man which grows corrupt according to the deceitful lusts, 23and abe renewed in the spirit of your mind, 24and that you aput on the new man which was created according to God, in true righteousness and holiness.

DO NOT GRIEVE THE SPIRIT

25Therefore, putting away lying, a"Let each one of you speak truth with

Eph. 4:29

OUT OF YOUR MOUTH

We sometimes think that the Christian life is just a bunch of negatives and things we aren't supposed to do. Here, Paul wrote, "Let no corrupt word proceed out of your mouth," and that is certainly good advice for what not to do. It isn't appropriate for a child of God to have garbage coming from his mouth.

But Paul also gave the positive: "But what is good for necessary edification, that it may impart grace to the hearers." The message is a positive message. God wants us to build each other up and be full of grace. The negative is only mentioned because of how it can overpower the positive. It is really a positive message of all the positive changes God wants to bring into our lives.

17 a Eph. 2:2; 4:22
1 NU omits the rest of

18 a Rom. 1:21

19 a 1 Tim. 4:2
b 1 Pet. 4:3

22 a Col. 3:8

23 a [Rom. 12:2]

24 a [Rom. 6:4; 7:6; 12:2]

25 a Zech. 8:16
b Rom. 12:5

26 a Ps. 4:4; 37:8

27 a [Rom. 12:19]
1 an opportunity

28 a Acts 20:35
b Luke 3:11

29 a Col. 3:8
b 1 Thess. 5:11
c Col. 3:16
1 building up

30 a Is. 7:13

31 a Col. 3:8, 19
b James 4:11
c Titus 3:3
1 loud quarreling

32 a 2 Cor. 6:10
b [Mark 11:25]

CHAPTER 5

1 a Luke 6:36
b 1 Pet. 1:14–16

2 a 1 Thess. 4:9
b Gal. 1:4
c 2 Cor. 2:14, 15

3 a Col. 3:5–7
b [Luke 12:15]

Eph. 5:5–6

NOT DECEIVED BY EMPTY WORDS

This is a very serious statement here. If you are involved in sexual impurity, according to the Scriptures, you have no place or inheritance in the kingdom of Christ and God. After making this strong statement, he says further, "Let no one deceive you with empty words." Don't let anyone tell you that it isn't a big deal.

The Bible makes it clear that if you really have a walk with God, you will stop living after the flesh. If you are still living after the flesh, don't be surprised if heaven's gates are closed to you or you are left behind when the rapture comes. Don't blame me. I warned you.

his neighbor," for bwe are members of one another. 26a"Be angry, and do not sin": do not let the sun go down on your wrath, 27anor give 1place to the devil. 28Let him who stole steal no longer, but rather alet him labor, working with his hands what is good, that he may have something bto give him who has need. 29aLet no corrupt word proceed out of your mouth, but bwhat is good for necessary 1edification, cthat it may impart grace to the hearers. 30And ado not grieve the Holy Spirit of God, by whom you were sealed for the day of redemption. 31aLet all bitterness, wrath, anger, 1clamor, and bevil speaking be put away from you, cwith all malice. 32And abe kind to one another, tenderhearted, bforgiving one another, even as God in Christ forgave you.

WALK IN LOVE

5 Thereforea be imitators of God as dear bchildren. 2And awalk in love, bas Christ also has loved us and given Himself for us, an offering and a sacrifice to God cfor a sweet-smelling aroma.

3But fornication and all auncleanness or bcovetousness, let it not even be named among you, as is fitting for

NOT DRUNK, BUT FILLED

It's sort of interesting that Paul would put two seemingly different things together—being drunk with wine and being filled with the Spirit. The two seem incongruous.

But when you think about it, what is a person trying to do when they get drunk? They are usually looking for some relief from the pressures and pains of life. The alcohol provides for an altered state of consciousness, to temporarily escape from problems.

And what happens when we are filled with the Spirit? Our problems are taken care of. We commit them to the Lord. We don't worry about them anymore. We know He will take care of things. And there is no hangover later.

Eph. 5:18

4 ᵃMatt. 12:34, 35
ᵇTitus 3:9
ᶜRom. 1:28
ᵈPhil. 4:6

5 ᵃ1 Cor. 6:9, 10
¹NU *know this*

7 ᵃ1 Tim. 5:22

8 ᵃ1 Thess. 5:5

9 ᵃGal. 5:22
¹NU *light*

10 ᵃ[Rom. 12:1, 2]

11 ᵃ2 Cor. 6:14
¹*reprove*

12 ᵃRom. 1:24

13 ᵃ[John 3:20, 21]
¹*reproved*

14 ᵃ[Is. 26:19; 60:1]

15 ᵃCol. 4:5
¹*carefully*

16 ᵃCol. 4:5
ᵇEccl. 11:2

17 ᵃCol. 4:5
ᵇ[Rom. 12:2]
ᶜ1 Thess. 4:3

18 ᵃProv. 20:1; 23:31

19 ᵃActs 16:25
ᵇJames 5:13

20 ᵃPs. 34:1
ᵇ[1 Pet. 2:5]

21 ᵃ[Phil. 2:3]
¹NU *Christ*

22 ᵃCol. 3:18—4:1

23 ᵃ[1 Cor. 11:3]
ᵇCol. 1:18

24 ᵃTitus 2:4, 5

25 ᵃCol. 3:19

saints; 4 ᵃneither filthiness, nor ᵇfoolish talking, nor coarse jesting, ᶜwhich are not fitting, but rather ᵈgiving of thanks. 5For ¹this you know, that no fornicator, unclean person, nor covetous man, who is an idolater, has any ᵃinheritance in the kingdom of Christ and God. 6Let no one deceive you with empty words, for because of these things the wrath of God comes upon the sons of disobedience. 7Therefore do not be ᵃpartakers with them.

WALK IN LIGHT
8For you were once darkness, but now you are ᵃlight in the Lord. Walk as children of light 9(for ᵃthe fruit of the ¹Spirit *is* in all goodness, righteousness, and truth), 10ᵃfinding out what is acceptable to the Lord. 11And have ᵃno fellowship with the unfruitful works of darkness, but rather ¹expose *them.* 12ᵃFor it is shameful even to speak of those things which are done by them in secret. 13But ᵃall things that are ¹exposed are made manifest by the light, for whatever makes manifest is light. 14Therefore He says:

ᵃ"Awake, you who sleep,
Arise from the dead,
And Christ will give you light."

WALK IN WISDOM
15ᵃSee then that you walk ¹circumspectly, not as fools but as wise, 16ᵃredeeming the time, ᵇbecause the days are evil. 17ᵃTherefore do not be unwise, but ᵇunderstand ᶜwhat the will of the Lord *is.* 18And ᵃdo not be drunk with wine, in which is dissipation; but be filled with the Spirit, 19speaking to one another ᵃin psalms and hymns and spiritual songs, singing and making ᵇmelody in your heart to the Lord, 20ᵃgiving thanks always for all things to God the Father ᵇin the name of our Lord Jesus Christ, 21ᵃsubmitting to one another in the fear of ¹God.

MARRIAGE—CHRIST AND THE CHURCH
22Wives, ᵃsubmit to your own husbands, as to the Lord. 23For ᵃthe husband is head of the wife, as also ᵇChrist is head of the church; and He is the Savior of the body. 24Therefore, just as the church is subject to Christ, so *let* the wives *be* to their own husbands ᵃin everything.
25ᵃHusbands, love your wives, just as

Eph. 5:22–25

WIVES, SUBMIT; HUSBANDS, LOVE

"Wives, submit to your own husbands, as to the Lord." Why did you submit your life to the Lord? It was because you came to understand how much He loved you. Thus, the command to the husbands: "Husbands, love your wives, just as Christ also loved the church and gave Himself for her."

If husbands are sacrificially loving their wives as they should, wives will naturally want to submit to them. If wives are submitting, husbands will be more inclined to continue to love them and sacrifice for them. If you have both, this works great!

Christ also loved the church and ᵇgave Himself for her, ²⁶that He might ¹sanctify and cleanse her ᵃwith the washing of water ᵇby the word, ²⁷ᵃthat He might present her to Himself a glorious church, ᵇnot having spot or wrinkle or any such thing, but that she should be holy and without blemish. ²⁸So husbands ought to love their own wives as their own bodies; he who loves his wife loves himself. ²⁹For no one ever hated his own flesh, but nourishes and cherishes it, just as the Lord *does* the church. ³⁰For ᵃwe are members of His body, ¹of His flesh and of His bones. ³¹ᵃ*"For this reason a man shall leave his father and mother and be joined to his wife, and the* ᵇ*two shall become one flesh."* ³²This is a great mystery, but I speak concerning Christ and the church. ³³Nevertheless ᵃlet each one of you in particular so love his own wife as himself, and let the wife *see* that she ᵇrespects *her* husband.

CHILDREN AND PARENTS

6 Children, ᵃobey your parents in the Lord, for this is right. ²ᵃ*"Honor your father and mother,"* which is the first commandment with promise: ³*"that it may be well with you and you may live long on the earth."*

⁴And ᵃyou, fathers, do not provoke your children to wrath, but ᵇbring them

Eph. 6:1–3

IN THE LORD

If you had a godly home and came from a godly heritage, count your blessings. It is such a wonderful thing for children to learn to obey and honor their parents "in the Lord."

I thank God for the godly home that I was privileged to grow up in and for my parents who taught me the things of the Lord. I thank God over and over for that!

Parents, give your children a home that is in the Lord—a loving environment where they can grow up, knowing that they are loved by God and where they can be taught to honor God. It will be well with them, and they may live long.

---

25 ᵇActs 20:28

26 ᵃJohn 3:5
ᵇ[John 15:3; 17:17]
¹ *set it apart*

27 ᵃCol. 1:22
ᵇSong 4:7

30 ᵃGen. 2:23
1 NU omits the rest of v. 30.

31 ᵃGen. 2:24
ᵇ[1 Cor. 6:16]

33 ᵃCol. 3:19
ᵇ1 Pet. 3:1, 6

CHAPTER 6

1 ᵃCol. 3:20

2 ᵃDeut. 5:16

4 ᵃCol. 3:21
ᵇGen. 18:19

5 ᵃ[1 Tim. 6:1]
ᵇ2 Cor. 7:15
ᶜ1 Chr. 29:17

6 ᵃCol. 3:22

8 ᵃRom. 2:6

9 ᵃCol. 4:1
ᵇRom. 2:11
1 NU *He who is both their Master and yours is*

11 ᵃ[2 Cor. 6:7]
1 *schemings*

12 ᵃRom. 8:38
ᵇLuke 22:53
1 NU *this darkness,*

13 ᵃ[2 Cor. 10:4]
ᵇEph. 5:16

14 ᵃIs. 11:5
ᵇIs. 59:17

---

up in the training and admonition of the Lord.

BONDSERVANTS AND MASTERS

⁵ᵃBondservants, be obedient to those who are your masters according to the flesh, ᵇwith fear and trembling, ᶜin sincerity of heart, as to Christ; ⁶ᵃnot with eyeservice, as men-pleasers, but as bondservants of Christ, doing the will of God from the heart, ⁷with goodwill doing service, as to the Lord, and not to men, ⁸ᵃknowing that whatever good anyone does, he will receive the same from the Lord, whether *he is* a slave or free.

Eph. 6:5–7

As to the Lord. In every workplace, there are those who work hard all the time. But there are others who are always sloughing off until the boss comes in; then they jump up and put on a big show for the boss.

Paul said that, as employees, we shouldn't be men-pleasers, but we should do all that we do at work as if God were our boss. In all that we do, we should be doing it for Him; thus, we should do it all diligently, honestly, and fervently, whether anyone is watching or not. Someone **is** watching.

---

⁹And you, masters, do the same things to them, giving up threatening, knowing that ¹your own ᵃMaster also is in heaven, and ᵇthere is no partiality with Him.

THE WHOLE ARMOR OF GOD

¹⁰Finally, my brethren, be strong in the Lord and in the power of His might. ¹¹ᵃPut on the whole armor of God, that you may be able to stand against the ¹wiles of the devil. ¹²For we do not wrestle against flesh and blood, but against ᵃprincipalities, against powers, against ᵇthe rulers of ¹the darkness of this age, against spiritual *hosts* of wickedness in the heavenly *places*. ¹³ᵃTherefore take up the whole armor of God, that you may be able to withstand ᵇin the evil day, and having done all, to stand. ¹⁴Stand therefore, ᵃhaving girded your waist with truth, ᵇhaving put on

Eph. 6:12

NOT FLESH AND BLOOD

I t is important for us to realize that we are in a battle and that it is a spiritual battle.

Satan often uses his wily tactics to hide behind people or other physical things to make us believe that we are battling against flesh and blood. He wants to draw us into a physical battle with him. If Satan can draw you into the flesh, he has the decided advantage over you.

But if we fight against him in the Spirit, with the spiritual resources and armor that God provides, we can't lose. So it is vital that we un-derstand the spiritual nature of all our conflicts.

---

15 ᵃ Is. 52:7

16 ᵃ 1 John 5:4

17 ᵃ 1 Thess. 5:8
b [Heb. 4:12]

18 ᵃ Luke 18:1
b [Matt. 26:41]
c Phil. 1:4

19 ᵃ Col. 4:3

20 ᵃ 2 Cor. 5:20

21 ᵃ Acts 20:4
b 1 Cor. 4:1, 2

22 ᵃ Col. 4:8
b 2 Cor. 1:6

---

the breastplate of righteousness, 15ᵃand having shod your feet with the preparation of the gospel of peace; 16above all, taking ᵃthe shield of faith with which you will be able to quench all the fiery darts of the wicked one. 17And ᵃtake the helmet of salvation, and bthe sword of the Spirit, which is the word of God; 18apraying always with all prayer and supplication in the Spirit, bbeing watchful to this end with all perseverance and csupplication for all the saints— 19and for me, that utterance may be given to me, ᵃthat I may open my mouth boldly to make known the mystery of the gospel, 20for which ᵃI am an ambassador in chains; that in it I may speak boldly, as I ought to speak.

A GRACIOUS GREETING

21But that you also may know my affairs and how I am doing, ᵃTychicus, a beloved brother and bfaithful minister in the Lord, will make all things known to you; 22ᵃwhom I have sent to you for this very purpose, that you may know our affairs, and that he may bcomfort your hearts.

23Peace to the brethren, and love with faith, from God the Father and the Lord Jesus Christ. 24Grace be with all those who love our Lord Jesus Christ in sincerity. Amen.

THE EPISTLE OF PAUL THE APOSTLE TO THE

PHILIPPIANS

As Paul was writing this letter around AD 62 to the church in Philippi (which was located in present-day Greece and was a capital city), he was in prison in Rome, waiting for his final appeal. He had already had his preliminary hearing, and he was waiting for his appeal before Caesar. He was in the Mamartine Prison, down in the lower dungeon, and was chained to a prison guard. Epaphroditus and Timothy were both with him, helping with his writings, and waiting to carry his letters to the various churches. Epaphroditus would deliver the letter to the church in Philippi, and Tychicus would take another letter to Ephesus.

This letter to Philippi is a very special letter. Paul had obvious love for this church and he wrote to them to thank them for a gift they had recently sent to him. He used this occasion to thank them and also to give them some instructions on unity within the church. The theme of the book is joy, which is especially notable since he was writing from an uncomfortable and ominous position in prison, awaiting his fate at the hands of Caesar. Despite the terrible circumstances, Paul had learned the secret to contentment and joy and wanted to share this with a church for which he had so much affection.

Paul had founded the church in Philippi on his second missionary journey. He and Silas had been thrown into jail there and were miraculously delivered by the Lord, which led to the conversion of the jailer. Acts 16 tells this story, as well as of Paul's encounter with Lydia and of the girl who was delivered from demons. These people comprised the early church in Philippi, and the church grew into a healthy body that supported Paul more than any other church.

It was appropriate that Paul would write to them from prison, exhorting them to have the joy of the Lord, since he had been in prison in Philippi and was singing while in chains there years earlier. These Christians had seen firsthand how joy can come while in the most difficult of circumstances, and Paul was encouraging them so they would know that nothing had changed and that God was still in charge.

Philippians is a special book that shows us how to live above the present circumstances, rising above adversity not just by surviving, but by thriving in the joy of the Lord.

GREETING

1 Paul and Timothy, bondservants of Jesus Christ,

To all the saints in Christ Jesus who are in Philippi, with the [1]bishops and [a]deacons:

2Grace to you and peace from God our Father and the Lord Jesus Christ.

THANKFULNESS AND PRAYER

3[a]I thank my God upon every remembrance of you, 4always in [a]every prayer of mine making request for you all with joy, 5[a]for your fellowship in the gospel from the first day until now, 6being confident of this very thing, that He who has begun [a]a good work in you will complete *it* until the day of Jesus Christ; 7just as it is right for me to think this of you all, because I have you in my heart, inasmuch as both in my chains and in the defense and confirmation of the gospel, you all are partakers with me of grace. 8For God is my witness, how greatly I long for you all with the affection of Jesus Christ. 9And this I pray, that your love may abound still more and more in knowledge and all discernment, 10that you may approve the things that are excellent, that you may be sincere and without offense till the day of Christ, 11being filled with the fruits of righteousness [a]which *are* by Jesus Christ, [b]to the glory and praise of God.

CHAPTER 1

1 [a][1 Tim. 3:8–13]
1 Lit. *overseers*

3 [a]1 Cor. 1:4

4 [a]Eph. 1:16

5 [a][Rom. 12:13]

6 [a][John 6:29]

11 [a]Col. 1:6
[b]John 15:8

13 [a]Phil. 4:22
1 Or *Praetorium*

Phil. 1:6
He Will Complete His Work.

I love this! God has started a good work in you, and He will not give up. He is not going to stop!

The Lord will perform His perfect work in our lives. He will keep working in you until the day you see Jesus Christ, either when you go to heaven to be with Him or when He catches up Christians in the rapture.

The work of the Spirit of God will continue in you. It is based on the faithfulness of God. He hasn't taken you this far to dump you now!

CHRIST IS PREACHED

12But I want you to know, brethren, that the things *which happened* to me have actually turned out for the furtherance of the gospel, 13so that it has become evident [a]to the whole [1]palace guard, and to all the rest, that my chains are in Christ; 14and most of the brethren in the Lord, having become confident by my chains, are much more bold to speak the word without fear. 15Some indeed preach Christ even

---

SINCERE AND WITHOUT OFFENSE

Phil. 1:10

The English word "sincere" comes from the Latin word *sincerus,* which means "without wax."

The Romans loved statues and put them everywhere. Sometimes when a statue was being made, a little piece of the stone would break off. Rather than throwing away a statue just because the tip of the nose broke off, they became very adept at mixing marble powder with wax and then patching the statue. This worked fine until the statue was exposed to heat. On a hot day, the wax would just melt right down the side of statue. So the more expensive statues were those that were made without wax, and those would have a sign on them that said *sincerus.*

The Greek word used here for "sincere" means "judged in the brightness of the sun." The idea was that you would hold something up to the light of the sun to inspect it. This is what Paul was praying for the Philippians. That they would have a faith that would hold together in the heat and that would hold up under close scrutiny. A relationship with God that would be the real thing.

What a great prayer to pray for someone. I would love for people to pray that I would be sincere and without offense until the day of Christ.

from envy and strife, and some also from goodwill: 16 *1*The former preach Christ from selfish ambition, not sincerely, supposing to add affliction to my chains; 17but the latter out of love, knowing that I am appointed for the defense of the gospel. 18What then? Only *that* in every way, whether in pretense or in truth, Christ is preached; and in this I rejoice, yes, and will rejoice.

TO LIVE IS CHRIST

19For I know that athis will turn out for my deliverance through your prayer and the supply of the Spirit of Jesus Christ, 20according to my earnest expectation and hope that in nothing I shall be ashamed, but awith all boldness, as always, so now also Christ will be magnified in my body, whether by life bor by death. 21For to me, to live *is* Christ, and to die *is* gain. 22But if *I* live on in the flesh, this *will mean* fruit from *my* labor; yet what I shall choose I *1*cannot tell. 23 *1*For I am hard-pressed between the two, having a adesire to depart and be with Christ, *which is* bfar better. 24Nevertheless to remain in the flesh *is* more needful for you. 25And being confident of this, I know that I shall remain and continue with you all for your progress and joy of faith, 26that ayour rejoicing for me may be more abundant in Jesus Christ by my coming to you again.

STRIVING AND SUFFERING FOR CHRIST

27Only alet your conduct be worthy of the gospel of Christ, so that whether

---

Phil. 1:20–21

By Life or By Death. Paul was going to face Caesar Nero, and he didn't know if he would be set free or if he would be executed. It could go either way.

But Paul didn't seem to care whether he lived or died. All he wanted was for Christ to be magnified. And if his death accomplished more for Christ than his life, he was ready to go. He saw death as better for him ("to die is gain"), but he was willing to stick around if God had more for him to do. That is commitment!

---

16 *1* NU reverses vv. 16 and 17.

19 a Job 13:16, LXX

20 a Eph. 6:19, 20
b [Rom. 14:8]

22 *1* do not know

23 a [2 Cor. 5:2, 8]
b [Ps. 16:11]
1 NU, M *But*

26 a 2 Cor. 1:14

27 a Eph. 4:1
b Eph. 4:3
c Jude 3

28 *1* NU *of your salvation*

29 a [Matt. 5:11, 12]
b Eph. 2:8
c [2 Tim. 3:12]

30 a Col. 1:29; 2:1
b Acts 16:19–40

CHAPTER 2

1 a Col. 3:12
1 Or encouragement

2 a John 3:29
b Rom. 12:16
c Phil. 4:2

3 a Gal. 5:26
b Rom. 12:10

4 a 1 Cor. 13:5
b Rom. 15:1, 2

5 a [Matt. 11:29]

6 a 2 Cor. 4:4
1 Or something to be held onto to be equal

7 a Ps. 22:6
b Is. 42:1
c [John 1:14]
1 emptied Himself of His privileges

8 a Matt. 26:39
b Heb. 5:8

I come and see you or am absent, I may hear of your affairs, that you stand fast in one spirit, bwith one mind cstriving together for the faith of the gospel, 28and not in any way terrified by your adversaries, which is to them a proof of perdition, but *1*to you of salvation, and that from God. 29For to you ait has been granted on behalf of Christ, bnot only to believe in Him, but also to csuffer for His sake, 30ahaving the same conflict bwhich you saw in me and now hear *is* in me.

UNITY THROUGH HUMILITY

2 Therefore if *there is* any *1*consolation in Christ, if any comfort of love, if any fellowship of the Spirit, if any aaffection and mercy, 2afulfill my joy bby being like-minded, having the same love, *being* of cone accord, of one mind. 3aLet nothing *be done* through selfish ambition or conceit, but bin lowliness of mind let each esteem others better than himself. 4aLet each of you look out not only for his own interests, but also for the interests of bothers.

THE HUMBLED AND EXALTED CHRIST

5aLet this mind be in you which was also in Christ Jesus, 6who, abeing in the form of God, did not consider it *1*robbery to be equal with God, 7abut *1*made Himself of no reputation, taking the form bof a bondservant, *and* ccoming in the likeness of men. 8And being found in appearance as a man, He humbled Himself and abecame bobedient to *the point of* death, even the

---

Phil. 2:5–8

From the Highest to the Lowest. You can't get any higher than equality with God, being God Himself. And you can't get any lower than a death on the cross. But Jesus submitted Himself to the will of the Father and took these steps down, making Himself of "no reputation." Why did He do it? Because that was the only way we could be saved.

Jesus' love for us drove Him to this voluntary and obedient descent from the highest high to the lowest low. He loves you that much.

Phil. 2:9–11

EVERY KNEE, EVERY TONGUE

Sooner or later, every knee will bow to Jesus, and every tongue will confess that He is the Christ, the Messiah, and that He is the Lord God. Isaiah prophesied that someday every knee will bow and every tongue will confess (Is. 45:23). Romans 10:9 says "that if you confess with your mouth the Lord Jesus and believe in your heart that God has raised Him from the dead, you will be saved."

We choose to confess now and to bow our knee willingly now. That is what saves us. But for those who reject His salvation now, their day of reckoning will come. They will all bow.

---

death of the cross. 9 aTherefore God also bhas highly exalted Him and cgiven Him the name which is above every name, 10 athat at the name of Jesus every knee should bow, of those in heaven, and of those on earth, and of those under the earth, 11 and athat every tongue should confess that Jesus Christ is Lord, to the glory of God the Father.

LIGHT BEARERS

12 Therefore, my beloved, aas you have always obeyed, not as in my presence only, but now much more in my absence, bwork out your own salvation with cfear and trembling; 13 for ait is God who works in you both to will and to do bfor His good pleasure.

14 Do all things awithout 1 complaining and bdisputing,2 15 that you may become blameless and 1 harmless, children of God without fault in the midst of a crooked and perverse generation, among whom you shine as alights in the world, 16 holding fast the word of life, so that aI may rejoice in the day of Christ that bI have not run in vain or labored in cvain.

17 Yes, and if aI am being poured out as a drink offering on the sacrifice band

Cross references
9 a Heb. 2:9
b Acts 2:33
c Eph. 1:21
10 a Is. 45:23
11 a John 13:13
12 a Phil. 1:5, 6; 4:15
b John 6:27, 29
c Eph. 6:5
13 a Heb. 13:20, 21
b Eph. 1:5
14 a 1 Pet. 4:9
b Rom. 14:1
1 grumbling
2 arguing
15 a Matt. 5:15, 16
1 innocent
16 a 2 Cor. 1:14
b Gal. 2:2
c 1 Thess. 3:5
17 a 2 Tim. 4:6
b Rom. 15:16
c 2 Cor. 7:4
19 a Rom. 16:21
1 condition
20 a 2 Tim. 3:10
22 a 1 Cor. 4:17
25 a Phil. 4:18
b Philem. 2
c 2 Cor. 8:23
d 2 Cor. 11:9
26 a Phil. 1:8

---

service of your faith, cI am glad and rejoice with you all. 18 For the same reason you also be glad and rejoice with me.

TIMOTHY COMMENDED

19 But I trust in the Lord Jesus to send aTimothy to you shortly, that I also may be encouraged when I know your 1 state. 20 For I have no one alike-minded, who will sincerely care for your state. 21 For all seek their own, not the things which are of Christ Jesus. 22 But you know his proven character, athat as a son with his father he served with me in the gospel. 23 Therefore I hope to send him at once, as soon as I see how it goes with me. 24 But I trust in the Lord that I myself shall also come shortly.

EPAPHRODITUS PRAISED

25 Yet I considered it necessary to send to you aEpaphroditus, my brother, fellow worker, and bfellow soldier, cbut your messenger and dthe one who ministered to my need; 26 asince he was longing for you all, and was distressed because you had heard that he was sick. 27 For indeed he was sick almost unto death; but God had mercy on him, and not only on him but on me also, lest I should have sorrow upon sorrow. 28 Therefore I sent him the more eagerly,

Phil. 2:14–15

COMPLAINING AND DISPUTING

"Do all things without complaining and disputing." Wouldn't you like to put that up in your kid's bedroom? But it isn't just kids who have a problem with this. They learn it from their parents.

Many non-Christians see Christians as people who are always complaining and fighting, even among themselves. But we are in the middle of a crooked and perverse generation, and we should be showing them what great attitudes we have so they can see that we are children of God, shining as lights in a dark world.

that when you see him again you may rejoice, and I may be less sorrowful. [29]Receive him therefore in the Lord with all gladness, and hold such men in esteem; [30]because for the work of Christ he came close to death, [1]not regarding his life, [a]to supply what was lacking in your service toward me.

ALL FOR CHRIST

3 Finally, my brethren, [a]rejoice in the Lord. For me to write the same things to you is not tedious, but for you it is safe.

[2][a]Beware of dogs, beware of [b]evil workers, [c]beware of the mutilation! [3]For we are [a]the circumcision, [b]who worship [1]God in the Spirit, rejoice in Christ Jesus, and have no confidence in the flesh, [4]though [a]I also might have confidence in the flesh. If anyone else thinks he may have confidence in the flesh, I [b]more so: [5]circumcised the eighth day, of the stock of Israel, [a]of the tribe of Benjamin, [b]a Hebrew of the Hebrews; concerning the law, [c]a Pharisee; [6]concerning zeal, [a]persecuting the church; concerning the righteousness which is in the law, blameless. [7]But [a]what things were gain to me, these I have counted loss for Christ. [8]Yet indeed I also count all things loss

Phil. 3:7–8

COUNT ALL THINGS LOSS

P aul had just told the Philippians how righteous he was as a Pharisee. As far as their interpretation of the Law, he was blameless.

But despite all his religious accomplishments, Paul had turned his back on all that and had given it up. He had given up his confidence in his flesh; he had given up his reputation with the Jewish leaders. He counted his righteousness as rubbish compared to knowing Christ and receiving righteousness from Him.

When we come to Christ, we need to count all our assets as rubbish. He is everything we need.

Reference column

30 [a] 1 Cor. 16:17
1 risking

CHAPTER 3

1 [a] 1 Thess. 5:16

2 [a] Gal. 5:15
[b] Ps. 119:115
[c] Rom. 2:28

3 [a] Deut. 30:6
[b] Rom. 7:6
1 NU, M in the Spirit of God

4 [a] 2 Cor. 5:16; 11:18
[b] 2 Cor. 11:22, 23

5 [a] Rom. 11:1
[b] 2 Cor. 11:22
[c] Acts 23:6

6 [a] Acts 8:3; 22:4, 5; 26:9–11

7 [a] Matt. 13:44

8 [a] Jer. 9:23

9 [a] Rom. 10:3
[b] Rom. 1:17

10 [a] Eph. 1:19, 20
[b] [Rom. 6:3–5]

11 [a] Acts 26:6–8
1 Lit. arrive at

12 [a] [1 Tim. 6:12, 19]
[b] Heb. 12:23
1 obtained it

[a]for the excellence of the knowledge of Christ Jesus my Lord, for whom I have suffered the loss of all things, and count them as rubbish, that I may gain Christ [9]and be found in Him, not having [a]my own righteousness, which is from the law, but [b]that which is through faith in Christ, the righteousness which is from God by faith; [10]that I may know Him and the [a]power of His resurrection, and [b]the fellowship of His sufferings, being conformed to His death, [11]if, by any means, I may [a]attain[1] to the resurrection from the dead.

PRESSING TOWARD THE GOAL

[12]Not that I have already [a]attained,[1] or am already [b]perfected; but I press on, that I may lay hold of that for which Christ Jesus has also laid hold of me. [13]Brethren, I do not count myself

Phil. 3:13–14

PRESSING TOWARD THE GOAL

P aul said that he was forgetting the past and reaching forward to the future. It is awfully difficult to move forward when you are looking backward. Many people are hindered in their progress because they are always looking at the past, either hung up by their failures, or bitter against those who have hurt them, or resting on the laurels of their past successes. I want to look forward to what God is going to do in the future, and I believe our best days are ahead of us.

As Paul talked about pressing "toward the goal for the prize," I think of how runners in distance races hold a certain amount of energy back for that final lap and their finishing kick. That is how I want to live my life. I am getting older and I have the finish line in sight. Now is the time for me to turn on my final kick and give it everything I've got. I'm pressing forward, leaning into the tape! No time to look back!

to have [1]apprehended; but one thing I do, [a]forgetting those things which are behind and [b]reaching forward to those things which are ahead, [14][a]I press toward the goal for the prize of [b]the upward call of God in Christ Jesus.

[15]Therefore let us, as many as are [a]mature, [b]have this mind; and if in anything you think otherwise, [c]God will reveal even this to you. [16]Nevertheless, to *the degree* that we have already [1]attained, [a]let us walk [b]by the same [2]rule, let us be of the same mind.

OUR CITIZENSHIP IN HEAVEN

[17]Brethren, [a]join in following my example, and note those who so walk, as [b]you have us for a pattern. [18]For many walk, of whom I have told you often, and now tell you even weeping, *that they are* [a]the enemies of the cross of Christ: [19][a]whose end *is* destruction, [b]whose god *is their* belly, and [c]*whose* glory *is* in their shame—[d]who set their mind on earthly things. [20]For [a]our citizenship is in heaven, [b]from which we also [c]eagerly wait for the Savior, the Lord Jesus Christ, [21][a]who will transform our lowly body that it may be [b]conformed to His glorious body, [c]according to the working by which He is able even to [d]subdue all things to Himself.

Phil. 3:20–21

Heavenly Citizenship. Our minds aren't set on earthly things. Our goal is not to achieve worldly success or to see how many toys we can accumulate. Our earthly estate isn't what we live for. We are interested in building up an estate in heaven. Our real citizenship is in heaven. We are just camping out here. Heaven is our home. And we are keeping our eyes on heaven as we wait for our Lord's return. We "eagerly wait for the Savior."

4 Therefore, my beloved and [a]longed-for brethren, [b]my joy and crown, so [c]stand fast in the Lord, beloved.

BE UNITED, JOYFUL, AND IN PRAYER

[2]I implore Euodia and I implore Syntyche [a]to be of the same mind in the Lord. [3][1]And I urge you also, true companion, help these women who [a]labored with me in the gospel, with Clement also, and the rest of my fellow

---

13 [a] Luke 9:62
[b] Heb. 6:1
[1] *laid hold of it*
14 [a] 2 Tim. 4:7
[b] Heb. 3:1
15 [a] 1 Cor. 2:6
[b] Gal. 5:10
[c] Hos. 6:3
16 [a] Gal. 6:16
[b] Rom. 12:16;
15:5
[1] *arrived*
[2] NU omits *rule*
and the rest of
v. 16.
17 [a] [1 Cor.
4:16; 11:1]
[b] Titus 2:7, 8
18 [a] Gal. 1:7
19 [a] 2 Cor.
11:15
[b] 1 Tim. 6:5
[c] Hos. 4:7
[d] Rom. 8:5
20 [a] Eph. 2:6,
19
[b] Acts 1:11
[c] 1 Cor. 1:7
21 [a] [1 Cor.
15:43–53]
[b] 1 John 3:2
[c] Eph. 1:19
[d] [1 Cor. 15:28]

CHAPTER 4
1 [a] Phil. 1:8
[b] 2 Cor. 1:14
[c] Phil. 1:27
2 [a] Phil. 2:2;
3:16
3 [a] Rom. 16:3
[b] Luke 10:20
[1] NU, M *Yes*
4 [a] Rom. 12:12
5 [a] [James 5:7–
9]
[1] *graciousness*
or *forbearance*
6 [a] Matt. 6:25
[b] [1 Thess. 5:17,
18]
7 [a] [John 14:27]
8 [a] Eph. 4:25
[b] 2 Cor. 8:21
[c] Deut. 16:20
[d] 1 Thess. 5:22
[e] 1 Cor. 13:4–7
9 [a] Rom. 15:33
10 [a] 2 Cor. 11:9
[1] *you have
revived your
care*
11 [a] 1 Tim. 6:6,
8
12 [a] 1 Cor. 4:11
[1] *live humbly*
[2] *live in prosperity*
13 [a] John 15:5
[1] NU *Him who*

Phil. 4:4

Rejoice in the Lord. Paul was writing from a prison cell in Rome, and yet he was telling the Philippians to rejoice. He kept reiterating this. Although he was a prisoner, God was using him to reach many within the palace with the gospel; and he was rejoicing over that.

The major theme of this book is rejoicing in the Lord. Christians, above all people, should be the most joyful people in the world! We have so much to rejoice in. I can't always rejoice in my circumstances, but I can always rejoice in the Lord!

---

workers, whose names *are* in [b]the Book of Life.

[4][a]Rejoice in the Lord always. Again I will say, rejoice!

[5]Let your [1]gentleness be known to all men. [a]The Lord *is* at hand.

[6][a]Be anxious for nothing, but in everything by prayer and supplication, with [b]thanksgiving, let your requests be made known to God; [7]and [a]the peace of God, which surpasses all understanding, will guard your hearts and minds through Christ Jesus.

MEDITATE ON THESE THINGS

[8]Finally, brethren, whatever things are [a]true, whatever things *are* [b]noble, whatever things *are* [c]just, [d]whatever things *are* pure, whatever things *are* [e]lovely, whatever things *are* of good report, if *there is* any virtue and if *there is* anything praiseworthy—meditate on these things. [9]The things which you learned and received and heard and saw in me, these do, and [a]the God of peace will be with you.

PHILIPPIAN GENEROSITY

[10]But I rejoiced in the Lord greatly that now at last [a]your[1] care for me has flourished again; though you surely did care, but you lacked opportunity. [11]Not that I speak in regard to need, for I have learned in whatever state I am, [a]to be content: [12][a]I know how to [1]be abased, and I know how to [2]abound. Everywhere and in all things I have learned both to be full and to be hungry, both to abound and to suffer need. [13]I can do all things [a]through [1]Christ who strengthens me.

THE LORD IS AT HAND
Phil. 4:5

The early church had a strong sense that Jesus was coming soon. In fact, there was a rumor in the early church that Jesus would return before John would die (John 21:23). The people in Thessalonica expected Jesus to return at any time and were concerned for those who had died and missed the rapture (1 Thess. 4:13–18).

I believe that God has wanted every generation of the church to live in the expectation of the return of Jesus Christ. We live differently if we believe in the imminent return of Jesus.

Belief in the imminent return of our Lord has several beneficial effects on our lives. First of all, it gives us an urgency to share the gospel. If we don't have much time, we need to get the word out. Second, it gives us a healthier sense of priorities. We have a tendency to put value on material things and to put spiritual things on the back burner. But a conscious awareness of the soon return of Jesus helps us see what really matters most, and we will value eternal things over temporal things. Third, the belief that the Lord is coming soon gives a purity to our walk and our lives. If Jesus could come back at any time, I don't want to be doing things I would be ashamed of when He returns.

I believe the Lord is coming soon. I think we are blessed to be in the generation that will witness His coming. Now, I could be wrong. He may not come for another thousand years. But my hope is that He will come back soon, and I believe God intended that to be the hope of each generation—that we would live in this anticipation. The Lord is at hand!

14Nevertheless you have done well that ayou shared in my distress. 15Now you Philippians know also that in the beginning of the gospel, when I departed from Macedonia, ano church shared with me concerning giving and receiving but you only. 16For even in Thessalonica you sent *aid* once and again for my necessities. 17Not that I seek the gift, but I seek athe fruit that abounds to your account. 18Indeed I *l*have all and abound. I am full, having received from aEpaphroditus the things *sent* from you, ba sweet-smelling aroma, cacceptable sacrifice, well pleasing to God. 19And my God ashall supply all your need according to His riches in glory by Christ Jesus. 20aNow to our God and Father *be* glory forever and ever. Amen.

GREETING AND BLESSING

21Greet every saint in Christ Jesus. The brethren awho are with me greet you. 22All the saints greet you, but especially those who are of Caesar's household.

23The grace of our Lord Jesus Christ be with *l*you all. Amen.

14 a Phil. 1:7

15 a 2 Cor. 11:8, 9

17 a Titus 3:14

18 a Phil. 2:25
b Heb. 13:16
c 2 Cor. 9:12
1 Or *have received all*

19 a Ps. 23:1

20 a Rom. 16:27

21 a Gal. 1:2

23 1 NU *your spirit*

Phil. 4:13

I Can Do All Things. There are two verses that I think should be underlined in every Bible. One of them is this verse: "I can do all things through Christ who strengthens me." The other is John 15:5, where Jesus said, "Without Me you can do nothing."

How we need to keep these two truths at the forefront of our minds. Apart from Christ, we are nothing and can do nothing. But thank God, through Christ I can do all things!

COLOSSIANS

INTRODUCTION Colossians is another of what are called the Prison Epistles. These are the letters that Paul wrote as he was imprisoned in Rome around AD 62. (The other Prison Epistles are Ephesians, Philippians, and Philemon.)

Colosse was a church that was not formally founded by Paul, as he had never been there personally. It was most likely founded by someone who had been converted in Ephesus while Paul was ministering there.

Colosse was around a hundred miles from Ephesus. It was at one time a great city, but it was on the decline at the time of Paul's writing and was destroyed shortly thereafter by an earthquake.

The book was closely related to the book of Philemon, and was probably delivered at the same time as Philemon by Onesimus. It was also related to the book of Ephesians, which was written about the same time. But whereas Ephesians was written to teach about the church, Colossians was written to teach about Jesus. At this time in Colosse, there were several heresies that were sprouting up concerning the nature of Jesus. It would seem that there was a growing Gnosticism, combined with Jewish legalism.

The Gnostics believed that they had a special, mystical understanding of who Jesus was, believing Him to be less than God. They saw Him as a step in the progression from God to man, but they denied His deity and also His humanity. This mystical philosophy was combined with a legalism that held to the teaching that you could somehow earn status with God by keeping the outward rules of the Law. Paul responded to this heresy by presenting Jesus as the Creator God, "By Him all things were created" (Col. 1:16). He declared Him to be completely God and completely man, as he said, "For in Him dwells all the fullness of the Godhead bodily" (Col. 2:9).

Jesus was God in a body. He wasn't a spirit being, nor was He any less than completely God. And because He died to fulfill the requirements of the Law, and He is the reality of which the Law was only a mere shadow (Col. 2:17), we should not allow others to judge us according to the outward rituals of the Law (Col. 2:16).

The book then goes on to give practical application of the truth of who Jesus is and forms a beautiful outline of the Christian life, centered around the Person of Jesus Christ, God in the flesh.

GREETING

1 Paul, [a]an apostle of Jesus Christ by the will of God, and Timothy our brother,

2 To the saints [a]and faithful brethren in Christ *who are* in Colosse:

[b]Grace to you and peace from God our Father [1]and the Lord Jesus Christ.

THEIR FAITH IN CHRIST

3 [a]We give thanks to the God and Father of our Lord Jesus Christ, praying always for you, 4 [a]since we heard of your faith in Christ Jesus and of [b]your love for all the saints; 5 because of the hope [a]which is laid up for you in heaven, of which you heard before in the word of the truth of the gospel, 6 which has come to you, [a]as *it has* also in all the world, and [b]is bringing forth [1]fruit, as *it is* also among you since the day you heard and knew [c]the grace of God in truth; 7 as you also learned from [a]Epaphras, our dear fellow servant, who is [b]a faithful minister of Christ on your behalf, 8 who also declared to us your [a]love in the Spirit.

PREEMINENCE OF CHRIST

9 [a]For this reason we also, since the day we heard it, do not cease to pray for you, and to ask [b]that you may be filled with [c]the knowledge of His will [d]in all wisdom and spiritual understanding; 10 [a]that you may walk worthy of the Lord, [b]fully pleasing *Him*, [c]being fruitful in every good work and increasing in the [d]knowledge of God; 11 [a]strengthened with all might, according to His

glorious power, [b]for all patience and longsuffering [c]with joy; 12 [a]giving thanks to the Father who has qualified us to be partakers of [b]the inheritance of the saints in the light. 13 He has delivered us from [a]the power of darkness [b]and [1]conveyed *us* into the kingdom of the Son of His love, 14 [a]in whom we have redemption [1]through His blood, the forgiveness of sins.

15 He is [a]the image of the invisible God, [b]the firstborn over all creation. 16 For [a]by Him all things were created that are in heaven and that are on earth, visible and invisible, whether thrones or [b]dominions or [1]principalities or [2]powers. All things were created [c]through Him and for Him. 17 [a]And He is before all things, and in Him [b]all things consist. 18 And [a]He is the head of the body, the church, who is the beginning, [b]the firstborn from the dead, that in all things He may have the preeminence.

RECONCILED IN CHRIST

19 For it pleased *the Father that* [a]in Him all the fullness should dwell, 20 and [a]by Him to reconcile [b]all things to Himself, by Him, whether things on earth or things in heaven, [c]having made peace through the blood of His cross.

21 And you, [a]who once were alienated and enemies in your mind [b]by wicked works, yet now He has [c]reconciled

---

CHAPTER 1

1 [a]Eph. 1:1

2 [a]1Cor. 4:17
[b]Gal. 1:3
[1]NU omits *and the Lord Jesus Christ*

3 [a]Phil. 1:3

4 [a]Eph. 1:15
[b][Heb. 6:10]

5 [a][1Pet. 1:4]

6 [a]Matt. 24:14
[b]John 15:16
[c]Eph. 3:2
[1]NU, M add *and growing*

7 [a]Philem. 23
[b]2Cor. 11:23

8 [a]Rom. 15:30

9 [a]Eph. 1:15–17
[b]1Cor. 1:5
[c][Rom. 12:2]
[d]Eph. 1:8

10 [a]Eph. 4:1
[b]1Thess. 4:1
[c]Heb. 13:21
[d]2Pet. 3:18

11 [a][Eph. 3:16; 6:10]
[b]Eph. 4:2
[c][Acts 5:41]

12 [a][Eph. 5:20]
[b]Eph. 1:11

13 [a]Eph. 6:12
[b]2Pet. 1:11
[1]*transferred*

14 [a]Eph. 1:7
[1]NU, M omit *through His blood*

15 [a]2Cor. 4:4
[b]Rev. 3:14

16 [a]Heb. 1:2, 3 [b][Eph. 1:20, 21] [c]Heb. 2:10 [1]*rulers* [2]*authorities* 17 [a][John 17:5] [b]Heb. 1:3 18 [a]Eph. 1:22 [b]Rev. 1:5 19 [a]John 1:16 20 [a]Eph. 2:14 [b]2Cor. 5:18 [c]Eph. 1:10 21 [a][Eph. 2:1] [b]Titus 1:15 [c]2Cor. 5:18, 19

THE FIRSTBORN OVER ALL CREATION

Col. 1:15

There are many people who struggle with the idea of Jesus as the "firstborn," using this term to say Jesus is something less than God. But "firstborn" here doesn't mean that Jesus was born. It is a term of position and preeminence.

In the Old Testament, we read about Joseph having two sons, Ephraim and Manasseh. Manasseh was born first. But when Jacob blessed them, he placed his right hand on Ephraim, giving him the greater blessing. Joseph tried to get him to give Manasseh the greater blessing, but Jacob intentionally gave it to Ephraim (Gen. 48:13–20). Later on, in Jeremiah 31:9, God said, "I am a Father to Israel, and Ephraim is My firstborn." So we can clearly see that "firstborn" refers to the most prominent one, not to one who was literally born first.

Jesus is the most important One in the universe; and thus, He is the firstborn over all creation. Again, verse 18 refers to Him as "the firstborn from the dead." He wasn't the first one to rise from the dead, but He was the greatest to rise from the dead. The whole point of the book of Colossians is that Jesus Christ is preeminent over all and that He is God in the flesh.

Col. 1:17

HE HOLDS IT ALL TOGETHER

"**I**n Him all things consist" means that Christ is the One who holds everything together

We know that all matter is made up of atoms, which are made up of protons and electrons. The nucleus is the proton, which is positively charged; and the electrons, which are negatively charged, revolve around the nucleus. But how do we get the atoms to hold together to form matter? We know that like charges repel, while opposite charges attract. So what holds the atoms together, when the laws of electricity say they should repel and explode?

The force that holds them together is so strong that, when it is interrupted, a nuclear explosion is the result. So what is the force that is equal to an atomic blast in every atom? It is Jesus, the One who holds it all together.

22 ain the body of His flesh through death, bto present you holy, and blameless, and above reproach in His sight— 23if indeed you continue ain the faith, grounded and steadfast, and are bnot moved away from the hope of the gospel which you heard, cwhich was preached to every creature under heaven, dof which I, Paul, became a minister.

SACRIFICIAL SERVICE FOR CHRIST

24aI now rejoice in my sufferings bfor you, and fill up in my flesh cwhat is lacking in the afflictions of Christ, for dthe sake of His body, which is the church, 25of which I became a minister according to athe 1stewardship from God which was given to me for you, to fulfill the word of God, 26athe 1mystery which has been hidden from ages and from generations, bbut now has been revealed to His saints. 27aTo them God willed to make known what are bthe

22 a 2 Cor. 5:18
b [Eph. 5:27]

23 a Eph. 3:17
b [John 15:6]
c Col. 1:6
d Col. 1:25

24 a 2 Cor. 7:4
b Eph. 3:1, 13
c [2 Cor. 1:5; 12:15]
d Eph. 1:23

25 a Gal. 2:7
1 dispensation or administration

26 a [1 Cor. 2:7]
b [2 Tim. 1:10]
1 secret or hidden truth

27 a 2 Cor. 2:14
b Rom. 9:23
c [Rom. 8:10, 11]
d 1 Tim. 1:1
1 M who

28 a Acts 20:20
b Eph. 5:27

29 a Eph. 3:7

CHAPTER 2

1 a Phil. 1:30
1 struggle

2 1 NU omits both of the Father and

3 a 1 Cor. 1:24, 30

4 a Rom. 16:18

5 a 1 Thess. 2:17
b 1 Cor. 14:40
c 1 Pet. 5:9
1 Lit. and seeing

6 a 1 Thess. 4:1

7 a Eph. 2:21

Col. 1:22–23

If You Continue in the Faith.

Paul said that we will be presented holy and blameless to God, "if indeed you continue in the faith, grounded and steadfast, and are not moved away from the hope of the gospel." This verse presents a real problem to advocates of a "once saved, always saved" position. It begs the question, "What if you don't continue?" If it is impossible to not continue, then what is Paul warning against?

I believe that we are eternally secure if we continue in the faith and if we abide in Jesus. And that is exactly what I am going to do, and thus I feel very secure. But I wouldn't want to say anything that would make someone feel secure if they don't continue and abide.

riches of the glory of this mystery among the Gentiles: 1which is cChrist in you, dthe hope of glory. 28Him we preach, awarning every man and teaching every man in all wisdom, bthat we may present every man perfect in Christ Jesus. 29To this *end* I also labor, striving according to His working which works in me amightily.

NOT PHILOSOPHY BUT CHRIST

2 For I want you to know what a great aconflict1 I have for you and those in Laodicea, and *for* as many as have not seen my face in the flesh, 2that their hearts may be encouraged, being knit together in love, and *attaining* to all riches of the full assurance of understanding, to the knowledge of the mystery of God, 1both of the Father and of Christ, 3ain whom are hidden all the treasures of wisdom and knowledge. 4Now this I say alest anyone should deceive you with persuasive words. 5For athough I am absent in the flesh, yet I am with you in spirit, rejoicing 1to see byour *good* order and the csteadfastness of your faith in Christ.

6aAs you therefore have received Christ Jesus the Lord, so walk in Him, 7arooted and built up in Him and established in the faith, as you have been

Col. 2:3

All the Treasures of Wisdom and Knowledge. All the treasures of wisdom and knowledge are hidden in Jesus. In other words, because He is God, He is omniscient and knows everything there is to know.

When I get into those situations where I just can't predict what the future will hold, and I don't know what to do, it is so wonderful to know that, as I commit my ways to Him, He uses all the wisdom and knowledge there is to help me and guide me!

taught, abounding [1]in it with thanksgiving.

[8]Beware lest anyone [1]cheat you through philosophy and empty deceit, according to [a]the tradition of men, according to the [b]basic principles of the world, and not according to Christ. [9]For [a]in Him dwells all the fullness of the Godhead [1]bodily; [10]and you are complete in Him, who is the [a]head of all [1]principality and power.

NOT LEGALISM BUT CHRIST

[11]In Him you were also [a]circumcised with the circumcision made without hands, by [b]putting off the body [1]of the sins of the flesh, by the circumcision of Christ, [12a]buried with Him in baptism, in which you also were raised with *Him*

Col. 2:9–10

All the Fullness. This is the strongest affirmation possible of the deity of Christ. "In Him dwells all the fullness of the Godhead bodily." The word for "fullness" here is the strong Greek word *pleroma*, meaning "the whole package." Everything that there is to God was in Jesus Christ in a bodily form.

The glorious part for us is in verse 10 where Paul said, "and you are complete in Him." The word translated "complete" is from the same Greek word *pleroma*. You are complete in Him! He is all you need!

7 [1]NU omits *in it*

8 [a]Gal. 1:14
[b]Gal. 4:3, 9, 10
[1]Lit. *plunder you* or *take you captive*

9 [a][John 1:14]
[1]*in bodily form*

10 [a][Eph. 1:20, 21]
[1]*rule and authority*

11 [a]Deut. 10:16
[b]Rom. 6:6; 7:24
[1]NU omits *of the sins*

12 [a]Rom. 6:4
[b]Eph. 1:19, 20
[c]Acts 2:24

14 [a][Eph. 2:15, 16]
[1]*certificate of debt with its*

15 [a][Is. 53:12]
[b]Eph. 6:12

16 [a]Rom. 14:3
[1]*feast day*

17 [a]Heb. 8:5; 10:1
[1]Lit. *body*

18 [1]NU omits *not*

19 [a]Eph. 4:15
[b]Eph. 1:23; 4:16

20 [a]Rom. 6:2–5
[1]NU, M omit *Therefore*

through [b]faith in the working of God, [c]who raised Him from the dead. [13]And you, being dead in your trespasses and the uncircumcision of your flesh, He has made alive together with Him, having forgiven you all trespasses, [14a]having wiped out the [1]handwriting of requirements that was against us, which was contrary to us. And He has taken it out of the way, having nailed it to the cross. [15a]Having disarmed [b]principalities and powers, He made a public spectacle of them, triumphing over them in it.

[16]So let no one [a]judge you in food or in drink, or regarding a [1]festival or a new moon or sabbaths, [17a]which are a shadow of things to come, but the [1]substance is of Christ. [18]Let no one cheat you of your reward, taking delight in *false* humility and worship of angels, intruding into those things which he has [1]not seen, vainly puffed up by his fleshly mind, [19]and not holding fast to [a]the Head, from whom all the body, nourished and knit together by joints and ligaments, [b]grows with the increase *that is* from God.

[20][1]Therefore, if you [a]died with Christ from the basic principles of the world,

Col. 2:16–17

LET NO MAN JUDGE YOU

In view of the finished work of Jesus Christ on the cross, Paul wanted to stress the danger of going back to a legalistic relationship with God, so he warned the Colossians, "Let no one judge you in food or in drink, or regarding a festival or a new moon or sabbaths, which are a shadow of things to come, but the substance is of Christ."

There are those today who still desire to judge us. They stress their belief that we are still bound to keep the Sabbath, for instance. But the Sabbath, as a day of rest, was just a shadow of Christ, who would give us true rest. He is our Sabbath. Don't let anyone judge you.

bwhy, as *though* living in the world, do you subject yourselves to regulations— 21a"Do not touch, do not taste, do not handle," 22which all concern things which perish with the using—aaccording to the commandments and doctrines of men? 23aThese things indeed have an appearance of wisdom in self-imposed religion, *false* humility, and 1neglect of the body, *but are* of no value against the indulgence of the flesh.

NOT CARNALITY BUT CHRIST

3 If then you were araised with Christ, seek those things which are above, bwhere Christ is, sitting at the right hand of God. 2Set your mind on things above, not on things on the aearth. 3aFor you died, band your life is hidden with Christ in God. 4aWhen Christ *who is* bour life appears, then you also will appear with Him in cglory.

5aTherefore put to death byour members which are on the earth: cfornication, uncleanness, passion, evil desire, and covetousness, dwhich is idolatry. 6aBecause of these things the wrath of God is coming upon bthe sons of disobedience, 7ain which you yourselves once walked when you lived in them.

8aBut now you yourselves are to put off all these: anger, wrath, malice, blasphemy, filthy language out of your mouth. 9Do not lie to one another, since you have put off the old man with his deeds, 10and have put on the new *man* who ais renewed in knowledge baccording to the image of Him who

---

Col. 3:10

According to His Image. We are being renewed into the glorious image of our Creator. The Holy Spirit is changing us into the image and likeness of Jesus Christ.

Sometimes we look at what is happening in our lives and we think, Lord, what are You doing? But He is just chipping off the rough edges to make us into what He wants us to be. It is painful, and we often don't understand; but if you want to see what you will eventually look like, look at the model, Jesus Christ.

---

20 bGal. 4:3, 9

21 a1Tim. 4:3

22 aTitus 1:14

23 a1Tim. 4:8
1 *severe treatment, asceticism*

CHAPTER 3

1 aCol. 2:12
bEph. 1:20

2 a[Matt. 6:19–21]

3 a[Rom. 6:2]
b[2Cor. 5:7]

4 a[1John 3:2]
bJohn 14:6
c1Cor. 15:43

5 a[Rom. 8:13]
b[Rom. 6:13]
cEph. 5:3
dEph. 4:19; 5:3, 5

6 aRom. 1:18
b[Eph. 2:2]

7 a1Cor. 6:11

8 aEph. 4:22

10 aRom. 12:2
b[Rom. 8:29]
c[Eph. 2:10]

11 aGal. 3:27, 28
bEph. 1:23

12 a[1Pet. 1:2]
b1John 3:17

13 a[Mark 11:25]

14 a1Pet. 4:8
b[1Cor. 13]
cEph. 4:3

15 a[John 14:27]
b1Cor. 7:15
cEph. 4:4
d[1Thess. 5:18]

16 aEph. 5:19

17 a1Cor. 10:31

18 a1Pet. 3:1
b[Eph. 5:22—6:9]

---

ccreated him, 11where there is neither aGreek nor Jew, circumcised nor uncircumcised, barbarian, Scythian, slave *nor* free, bbut Christ *is* all and in all.

CHARACTER OF THE NEW MAN

12Therefore, aas *the* elect of God, holy and beloved, bput on tender mercies, kindness, humility, meekness, longsuffering; 13abearing with one another, and forgiving one another, if anyone has a complaint against another; even as Christ forgave you, so you also *must do.* 14aBut above all these things bput on love, which is the cbond of perfection. 15And let athe peace of God rule in your hearts, bto which also you were called cin one body; and dbe thankful. 16Let the word of Christ dwell in you richly in all wisdom, teaching and admonishing one another ain psalms and hymns and spiritual songs, singing with grace in your hearts to the Lord. 17And awhatever you do in word or deed, *do* all in the name of the Lord Jesus, giving thanks to God the Father through Him.

THE CHRISTIAN HOME

18aWives, submit to your own husbands, bas is fitting in the Lord.

Col. 3:16

LET HIS WORD DWELL IN YOU

We study the Word of God so that as we become rich in our understanding and knowledge of God, His word becomes at home in our lives. How can you tell if His word is dwelling richly within you? You will be "teaching and admonishing one another in psalms and hymns and spiritual songs, singing with grace in your hearts to the Lord."

Rich and varied worship is a sign that the word of Christ is dwelling richly in your heart. But it is also a great way to plant His Word in your heart as we sing songs that teach us the Word of God and help us meditate on His truth. Let it happen!

Col. 3:21

Fathers, Don't Provoke and Discourage. As fathers, we need to make sure that we are being reasonable with our children, taking the time to explain things to them. Don't put demands on them and hide behind "because I'm the dad, that's why!"

We often put unreasonable demands on our children, and expect them to live up to impossible expectations. Our unreasonable expectations will only lead them to frustration. Don't discourage them; love and accept them.

19 a Husbands, love your wives and do not be b bitter toward them.
20 a Children, obey your parents b in all things, for this is well pleasing to the Lord.
21 a Fathers, do not provoke your children, lest they become discouraged.
22 a Bondservants, obey in all things your masters according to the flesh, not with eyeservice, as men-pleasers, but in sincerity of heart, fearing God. 23 a And whatever you do, do it heartily, as to the Lord and not to men, 24 a knowing that from the Lord you will receive the reward of the inheritance; b for 1 you serve the Lord Christ. 25 But he who does wrong will be repaid for what he has done, and a there is no partiality.

4 Masters, a give your bondservants what is just and fair, knowing that you also have a Master in heaven.

---

19 a [Eph. 5:25]
b Eph. 4:31

20 a Eph. 6:1
b Eph. 5:24

21 a Eph. 6:4

22 a Eph. 6:5

23 a [Eccl. 9:10]

24 a Eph. 6:8
b 1 Cor. 7:22
1 NU omits *for*

25 a Rom. 2:11

CHAPTER 4

1 a Eph. 6:9

2 a Luke 18:1
b Col. 2:7

3 a Eph. 6:19
b 1 Cor. 16:9
c Eph. 3:3, 4;
6:19
d Eph. 6:20
1 *hidden truth*

5 a Eph. 5:15
b [Matt. 10:16]
c Eph. 5:16

6 a Eccl. 10:12
b Mark 9:50
c 1 Pet. 3:15

Col. 4:1

MASTERS, BE MASTERED

It is so important for Christian employers to remember that they have a Master in heaven. No one can really rule properly unless he is ruled. We need to remember that we will all answer to the Lord someday. Whenever you put a man into leadership who doesn't understand that he is under authority, a tyranny will always develop, whether in government or in business.

If you are a leader, treat those who are following you well. Pay your employees a good wage. God surely pays you well and treats you graciously!

CHRISTIAN GRACES

2 a Continue earnestly in prayer, being vigilant in it b with thanksgiving; 3 a meanwhile praying also for us, that God would b open to us a door for the word, to speak c the 1 mystery of Christ, d for which I am also in chains, 4 that I may make it manifest, as I ought to speak.
5 a Walk in b wisdom toward those *who are* outside, c redeeming the time. 6 *Let* your speech always *be* a with grace, b seasoned with salt, c that you may know how you ought to answer each one.

WISDOM TOWARD OUTSIDERS   Col. 4:5

Once in a while I flip the TV channel over to one of the Christian television shows, and my heart is always grieved by what I see. What bothers me is that I know there are so many non-Christians who are desperately looking for answers; and they turn on their television, and what they find is this phony nonsense. I am so sad that this will be the only picture of Christianity that millions will ever see.

How we need to walk in wisdom toward those who are outside the faith. Our time is limited; and if they are going to get the message of the good news, we need to share it with them. It isn't a message of screaming and yelling, or of phony, worked-up emotionalism. It is the positive truth of who Jesus is and of what He has done for us.

Let your life be a positive witness for Jesus Christ. There is a lot of foolishness out there, and there isn't much time.

FINAL GREETINGS

7[a]Tychicus, a beloved brother, faithful minister, and fellow servant in the Lord, will tell you all the news about me. 8[a]I am sending him to you for this very purpose, that [1]he may know your circumstances and comfort your hearts, 9with [a]Onesimus, a faithful and beloved brother, who is *one* of you. They will make known to you all things which *are happening* here.

10[a]Aristarchus my fellow prisoner

Col. 4:17

Fulfill Your Ministry. Paul's exhortation to Archippus is a good one for all of us. "Take heed to the ministry which you have received in the Lord, that you may fulfill it."

God has given you a ministry. He has a place of service for each of us in the body, and it is important that we discover our ministries. But it is also important that we fulfill those ministries. We fulfill our ministries when we accept what it is God has called us to and then go for it with everything we've got, just full-on serving Him!

---

7 [a] 2 Tim. 4:12

8 [a] Eph. 6:22
[1] NU *you may know our circumstances and he may comfort*

9 [a] Philem. 10

10 [a] Acts 19:29; 20:4; 27:2
[b] 2 Tim. 4:11

12 [a] Philem. 23
[b] Rom. 15:30
[c] Matt. 5:48
[1] NU *fully assured*

13 [1] NU *concern*

14 [a] 2 Tim. 4:11
[b] 2 Tim. 4:10

15 [a] Rom. 16:5
[1] NU *Nympha*
[2] NU *her*

16 [a] 1 Thess. 5:27

17 [a] Philem. 2
[b] 2 Tim. 4:5

18 [a] 1 Cor. 16:21
[b] Heb. 13:3

---

greets you, with [b]Mark the cousin of Barnabas (about whom you received instructions: if he comes to you, welcome him), 11and Jesus who is called Justus. These *are my* only fellow workers for the kingdom of God who are of the circumcision; they have proved to be a comfort to me.

12[a]Epaphras, who is *one* of you, a bondservant of Christ, greets you, always [b]laboring fervently for you in prayers, that you may stand [c]perfect and [1]complete in all the will of God. 13For I bear him witness that he has a great [1]zeal for you, and those who are in Laodicea, and those in Hierapolis. 14[a]Luke the beloved physician and [b]Demas greet you. 15Greet the brethren who are in Laodicea, and [1]Nymphas and [a]the church that *is* in [2]his house.

CLOSING EXHORTATIONS AND BLESSING

16Now when [a]this epistle is read among you, see that it is read also in the church of the Laodiceans, and that you likewise read the *epistle* from Laodicea. 17And say to [a]Archippus, "Take heed to [b]the ministry which you have received in the Lord, that you may fulfill it."

18[a]This salutation by my own hand—Paul. [b]Remember my chains. Grace *be* with you. Amen.

THESSALONIANS

INTRODUCTION The church in Thessalonica was a healthy, vibrant church that had been founded by Paul when he was on his second missionary journey with Silas, Timothy, and Luke. Paul was only there in Thessalonica for less than a month and taught them for three consecutive Saturdays, according to Acts 17. He moved on after a few weeks because of all the trouble that was going on there, but left behind a young but healthy church.

Paul continued on his journey to Berea, then to Athens and Corinth. Apparently, while in Corinth, Paul received a report about how things were going in Thessalonica, including some questions the church had concerning some of his teachings. This letter was written to answer their questions and to correct some of their misunderstandings. It was probably one of the first letters Paul wrote, in around AD 52.

First Thessalonians contains profound teachings on the nature of the gospel, the methodology of ministry, and the life of the believer, but its most distinguishing trait is the extensive teachings concerning the end times and the rapture of the church.

Paul had obviously taught the Thessalonians concerning the return of Christ that could come at any moment. Since a little time had gone by and some of their members had already died, no doubt from persecution, they were now afraid that those who had died were missing out on something and that they would especially miss the rapture of the church. Paul wrote with the intent of comforting them (1 Thess. 4:18; 5:11), letting them know that those who have already died won't be missing anything. He had already comforted them with the teaching of the rapture, which would deliver us "from the wrath to come," but he also wanted to make it clear that those who die before the rapture will be equally blessed as they go immediately to be with the Lord, later meeting up with us in the air.

One of the striking features of this book is the depth of the teaching that Paul had communicated during only three weeks of a church's existence. There are people today who feel that teaching eschatology (the study of last days prophecy) is too advanced and complicated for newer Christians, and there are some who feel that it is too complicated even for mature Christians. Paul didn't feel that way. He included it in his new believers class. Why? Because it provides tremendous comfort for those who are suffering and powerful motivation for us to live our lives with the right priorities.

GREETING

1 Paul, a Silvanus, and Timothy,
To the church of the b Thessalonians in God the Father and the Lord Jesus Christ:

Grace to you and peace 1 from God our Father and the Lord Jesus Christ.

THEIR GOOD EXAMPLE

2 a We give thanks to God always for you all, making mention of you in our prayers, 3 remembering without ceasing a your work of faith, b labor of love, and patience of hope in our Lord Jesus Christ in the sight of our God and Father, 4 knowing, beloved brethren, a your election by God. 5 For a our gospel did not come to you in word only, but also in power, b and in the Holy Spirit c and in much assurance, as you know what kind of men we were among you for your sake.

6 And a you became followers of us and of the Lord, having received the word in much affliction, b with joy of the Holy Spirit, 7 so that you became examples to all in Macedonia and Achaia who believe. 8 For from you the word of the Lord a has sounded forth,

CHAPTER 1

1 a 1 Pet. 5:12
b Acts 17:1–9
1 NU omits from God our Father and the Lord Jesus Christ

2 a Rom. 1:8

3 a John 6:29
b Rom. 16:6

4 a Col. 3:12

5 a Mark 16:20
b 2 Cor. 6:6
c Heb. 2:3

6 a 1 Cor. 4:16;
11:1
b Acts 5:41;
13:52

8 a Rom. 10:18
b Rom. 1:8;
16:19

9 a 1 Thess. 2:1
b 1 Cor. 12:2

10 a [Rom. 2:7]
b Rom. 5:9

1 Thess. 1:6

Joy of the Lord. May God help our church to be an example of what it is to have the joy of the Holy Spirit. And may people see the power of God working in our midst so that we become examples. Surely, we may have persecution or tribulation or affliction, but, oh, may that never rob us of that joy of the Holy Spirit, and may our joy be a real witness and example to all!

not only in Macedonia and Achaia, but also b in every place. Your faith toward God has gone out, so that we do not need to say anything. 9 For they themselves declare concerning us a what manner of entry we had to you, b and how you turned to God from idols to serve the living and true God, 10 and a to wait for His Son from heaven, whom He raised from the dead, *even* Jesus who delivers us b from the wrath to come.

JESUS, NAME ABOVE ALL NAMES   1 Thess. 1:1

"Lord Jesus Christ" is not first, middle, and last name.

It is unfortunate we so often think of Lord as the name for Jesus. His name is Jesus. His title is Lord. When you say Lord, you are talking about a relationship. He is the Master. You are the servant. It implies obedience.

The name Jesus is the Greek adaptation of the Hebrew name Joshua or Yeshua, which means "Yahweh is salvation." It is a beautiful name. When the angel instructed Joseph, he said, "You shall call his name JESUS, for He will save His people from their sins" (Matt. 1:21). So His name implies His mission. He came to save His people from their sins.

But Jesus was also the promised Messiah. The word "Messiah" means "Anointed One." Priests and kings were anointed for their office. You remember how the oil was poured on Aaron's head (Lev. 8:12). It's a symbol of the Holy Spirit coming upon you. The idea of "Anointed One," *Mashiach,* or "Messiah," is that Jesus was anointed by God to be King. And, of course, when He comes again, He will have written on His garment and His side, "KING OF KINGS AND LORD OF LORDS" (Rev. 19:16). The word "Messiah" in Greek is *Christos,* from which we get our word "Christ."

If I had the time, I would write a New Testament and give the definition for the word "Lord." Also, I would put a comma after the word "Lord" because Lord is His title and Jesus is His name. Then, instead of the Greek *Christos* or "Christ," I would put "Messiah" because then people would not think of "Christ" as His name.

He is the Lord. His name is Jesus. He is Messiah. So whenever you find "Lord Jesus Christ," that's the whole implication.

ELECTION BY GOD

One day, Jesus said to His disciples, "You did not choose Me, but I chose you" (John 15:16). Now I don't have any problem with that because He chose me.

You say, "It's not fair for God to choose because I don't know if He chose me," and I'll say, "Well, you can find out. All you have to do is ask Jesus Christ to be the Lord of your life. Turn your life over to Him, and you'll discover that He chose you."

You say, "Maybe I don't want to." Well, maybe He didn't choose you then, but you can't blame Him.

You say, "He didn't choose me." Well, you don't know that until you accept Him. And when you do, you'll find out He did. So the ball is in your court.

PAUL'S CONDUCT

2 For you yourselves know, brethren, that our coming to you was not in vain. ²But ¹even after we had suffered before and were spitefully treated at ªPhilippi, as you know, we were ᵇbold in our God to speak to you the gospel of God in much conflict. ³ªFor our exhortation *did* not *come* from error or uncleanness, nor *was it* in deceit.

⁴But as ªwe have been approved by God ᵇto be entrusted with the gospel, even so we speak, ᶜnot as pleasing men, but God ᵈwho tests our hearts. ⁵For ªneither at any time did we use flattering words, as you know, nor a ¹cloak for covetousness—ᵇGod *is* witness. ⁶ªNor did we seek glory from men, either from you or from others, when we might have ᶜmade demands ᵈas apostles of Christ. ⁷But ªwe were gentle among you, just as a nursing *mother* cherishes her own children. ⁸So, affectionately longing for you, we were well pleased ªto impart to you not only the gospel of God, but also ᵇour

---

CHAPTER 2

2 ª Acts 14:5; 16:19–24
ᵇ Acts 17:1–9
¹ NU, M omit even

3 ª 2 Cor. 7:2

4 ª 1 Cor. 7:25
ᵇ Titus 1:3
ᶜ Gal. 1:10
ᵈ Prov. 17:3

5 ª 2 Cor. 2:17
ᵇ Rom. 1:9
¹ pretext for greed

6 ª 1 Tim. 5:17
ᵇ 1 Cor. 9:4
ᶜ 2 Cor. 11:9
ᵈ 1 Cor. 9:1

7 ª 1 Cor. 2:3

8 ª Rom. 1:11
ᵇ 2 Cor. 12:15

9 ª Acts 18:3; 20:34, 35
ᵇ 2 Cor. 12:13

10 ª 1 Thess. 1:5
ᵇ 2 Cor. 7:2

11 ¹ NU, M implored

12 ª Eph. 4:1
ᵇ 1 Cor. 1:9

13 ª 1 Thess. 1:2, 3
ᵇ Mark 4:20
ᶜ [Gal. 4:14]
ᵈ [1 Pet. 1:23]

14 ª Gal. 1:22
ᵇ Acts 17:5

NO CHARGE

I love the services we have at Calvary Chapel where we are seeking to reach out to the community, such as Good Friday midday and evening services and Easter sunrise service. We don't take offerings. I like that! We are not a burden on anyone. We just present the Word.

So many people say, "All they want is the money." Well, you can destroy that argument if you don't ask for money, you don't pass the plate, and there is no box to drop money in when you leave. You're just offering the gospel to people without charge. That's great!

Here Paul was rejoicing because when he was in Thessalonica, he was able to work with his own hands, laboring among them day and night, so that he would not be a burden to them as he shared the gospel.

---

own lives, because you had become dear to us. ⁹For you remember, brethren, our ªlabor and toil; for laboring night and day, ᵇthat we might not be a burden to any of you, we preached to you the gospel of God.

¹⁰ªYou *are* witnesses, and God *also*, ᵇhow devoutly and justly and blamelessly we behaved ourselves among you who believe; ¹¹as you know how we exhorted, and comforted, and ¹charged every one of you, as a father *does* his own children, ¹²ªthat you would walk worthy of God ᵇwho calls you into His own kingdom and glory.

THEIR CONVERSION

¹³For this reason we also thank God ªwithout ceasing, because when you ᵇreceived the word of God which you heard from us, you welcomed *it* ᶜnot as the word of men, but as it is in truth, the word of God, which also effectively ᵈworks in you who believe. ¹⁴For you, brethren, became imitators ªof the churches of God which are in Judea in Christ Jesus. For ᵇyou also suffered the

1 Thess. 2:13

The Effective Word. The glorious thing about the gospel of Jesus Christ is that it works. More than two thousand years ago, it was effective in Thessalonica.

Today, at the beginning of the twenty-first century, the power of the gospel has not changed. It is still effectual! It still transforms lives! It still brings people from darkness to light! It still delivers people from the power of Satan into the kingdom of God! The glorious gospel of Jesus Christ transforms hearts and lives. It brings man from sorrow to joy, from unrest to peace. The glorious Word of God. It works.

same things from your own countrymen, just as they *did* from the Judeans, 15 a who killed both the Lord Jesus and b their own prophets, and have persecuted us; and they do not please God c and are 1 contrary to all men, 16 a forbidding us to speak to the Gentiles that they may be saved, so as always b to fill up *the measure of* their sins; c but wrath has come upon them to the uttermost.

LONGING TO SEE THEM

17 But we, brethren, having been taken away from you for a short time

1 Thess. 2:19

Together Again. The coming of Jesus is a prominent theme throughout this book. Paul was only among the Thessalonians for a short time, but he shared with them the glorious kingdom of God that was going to come. He shared with them how Jesus died, rose again, and ascended into heaven; but he also shared that Jesus was coming back again. Over and over in this epistle, Paul referred to the return of the Lord.

What is our hope or joy or crown? Paul said it's being with you when our Lord returns and we will be together again!

---

15 a Acts 2:23
b Matt. 5:12;
23:34, 35
c Esth. 3:8
1 hostile

16 a Luke 11:52
b Gen. 15:16
c Matt. 24:6

17 a 1 Cor. 5:3

18 a Rom. 1:13;
15:22

19 a 2 Cor. 1:14
b Prov. 16:31
c Jude 24
d 1 Cor. 15:23

CHAPTER 3

2 a Rom. 16:21

3 a Eph. 3:13
b Acts 9:16;
14:22

4 a Acts 20:24

5 a 1 Cor. 7:5
b Gal. 2:2

6 a Acts 18:5
b Phil. 1:8

7 a 2 Cor. 1:4

8 a Phil. 4:1

10 a 2 Cor. 13:9

11 a Mark 1:3

12 a Phil. 1:9

13 a 2 Thess.
2:17

---

a in presence, not in heart, endeavored more eagerly to see your face with great desire. 18 Therefore we wanted to come to you—even I, Paul, time and again—but a Satan hindered us. 19 For a what *is* our hope, or joy, or b crown of rejoicing? *Is it* not even you in the c presence of our Lord Jesus Christ d at His coming? 20 For you are our glory and joy.

CONCERN FOR THEIR FAITH

3 Therefore, when we could no longer endure it, we thought it good to be left in Athens alone, 2 and sent a Timothy, our brother and minister of God, and our fellow laborer in the gospel of Christ, to establish you and encourage you concerning your faith, 3 a that no one should be shaken by these afflictions; for you yourselves know that b we are appointed to this. 4 a For, in fact, we told you before when we were with you that we would suffer tribulation, just as it happened, and you know. 5 For this reason, when I could no longer endure it, I sent to know your faith, a lest by some means the tempter had tempted you, and b our labor might be in vain.

ENCOURAGED BY TIMOTHY

6 a But now that Timothy has come to us from you, and brought us good news of your faith and love, and that you always have good remembrance of us, greatly desiring to see us, b as we also *to see* you— 7 therefore, brethren, in all our affliction and distress a we were comforted concerning you by your faith. 8 For now we live, if you a stand fast in the Lord.

9 For what thanks can we render to God for you, for all the joy with which we rejoice for your sake before our God, 10 night and day praying exceedingly that we may see your face a and perfect what is lacking in your faith?

PRAYER FOR THE CHURCH

11 Now may our God and Father Himself, and our Lord Jesus Christ, a direct our way to you. 12 And may the Lord make you increase and a abound in love to one another and to all, just as we *do* to you, 13 so that He may establish a your hearts blameless in holiness before our God and Father at the coming of our Lord Jesus Christ with all His saints.

A MAN OF PRAYER

To almost every church Paul wrote, he told them how he had been praying for them without ceasing. Paul was a man of prayer. Prayer was his life. When he could not be there in person, he was there in the Spirit praying for them.

One of the beautiful things about prayer is that it is not restricted by time, space, or material obstacles. You can go into your closet, shut the door, and spend fifteen or twenty minutes in China. You can journey with our missionaries to China and help them get past the border guards. Then, you can head over to Moscow and join the several Calvary Chapels that have been opened there. Next, you can head over to Poland to spend time with our missionaries there; and then travel on down to Bulgaria and Romania. You can travel the world in your closet doing a work for God through prayer.

That was Paul's life. Though he was in Corinth, he was praying night and day for those in Thessalonica. Paul was a man of prayer. No wonder he accomplished so much for the kingdom of God!

---

1 Thess. 3:13

Be Holy. One of the greatest weaknesses in the church today is the lack of holiness. You rarely hear sermons preached on holiness anymore.

We go back to the writings of the Puritans, and the theme of the Puritans was holy living. But somehow, sadly, that theme has been lost. Yet that is a requirement of God. God said, "Be holy, for I am holy" (1 Pet. 1:16).

Paul prayed that the Thessalonians might be blameless in holiness before God. May God make you pure. May God make you holy.

PLEA FOR PURITY

4 Finally then, brethren, we urge and exhort in the Lord Jesus ᵃthat you should abound more and more, ᵇjust as you received from us how you ought to walk and to please God; ²for you know what commandments we gave you through the Lord Jesus. ³For this is ᵃthe will of God, ᵇyour sanctification: ᶜthat you should abstain from sexual immorality; ⁴ᵃthat each of you should know how to possess his own vessel in sanctification and honor, ⁵ᵃnot in passion of lust, ᵇlike the Gentiles ᶜwho do not know God; ⁶that no one should take advantage of and defraud his brother in this matter, because the Lord ᵃis the avenger of all

CHAPTER 4

1 ᵃ1 Cor. 15:58
ᵇPhil. 1:27

3 ᵃ[Rom. 12:2]
ᵇEph. 5:27
ᶜ[1 Cor. 6:15–20]

4 ᵃRom. 6:19

5 ᵃCol. 3:5
ᵇEph. 4:17, 18
ᶜ1 Cor. 15:34

6 ᵃ2 Thess. 1:8

7 ᵃLev. 11:44

8 ᵃLuke 10:16

---

1 Thess. 3:13

HIS IMMINENT RETURN

Paul prayed that the Thessalonians would be ready when the Lord came with all of His saints. This is something Paul was constantly concerned about and expecting. I believe it was by design that God wanted every period of church history to live in a constant expectation of His coming for us.

I believe the purpose of His wanting that was, first of all, to give to us a sense of urgency in getting the gospel out to as many as possible. In addition, he wanted to give us a good sense of priority because, when Jesus comes, we're going to leave behind all our wealth and whatever else we've acquired. Our priority should be the things of the Spirit. Also, because the Lord may return at any time, we have a real impetus to walk in holiness. The hope of the imminent return of Jesus is a purifying hope.

such, as we also forewarned you and testified. ⁷For God did not call us to uncleanness, ᵃbut in holiness. ⁸ᵃTherefore he who rejects *this* does not reject

PLEASE GOD

We make a great mistake when we try to determine how close we can live to the world and still be a Christian. People want us to set guidelines for what is right and wrong, or what is sinful and what is not, so that they can live on the edge.

I don't believe the real issue is trying to walk a fine line between right and wrong. The real issue is, "Does my life please the Lord?" This should be the basis upon which we judge how we live. "Would God be pleased with my doing this?" "Would I want to be doing this when Jesus comes again for the church?"

Jesus said, "I always do those things that please" the Father (John 8:29). I think that's a great standard! Our chief desire should be to please God.

YOU SHALL NEVER DIE

The term "sleep" is used in the New Testament to refer to a Christian's death. It probably began with Jesus.

Word came from Mary and Martha that Lazarus was sick (John 11:3, 6). Talking to the disciples, Jesus said, "Our friend Lazarus sleeps" (John 11:11). His disciples said, "If he sleeps, he will get well" (John 11:12). But then Jesus told them plainly that Lazarus was dead (John 11:14).

Jesus had used the term "sleep" because what happens to a child of God is not the same thing that happens to a sinner who dies. Jesus told Martha, "I am the resurrection and the life. He who believes in Me, though he may die, he shall live. And whoever lives and believes in Me shall never die" (John 11:25). Jesus was referring to spiritual death, which is the separation of consciousness from God. Jesus was saying that anyone who believes in Him will never be consciously separated from God!

---

man, but God, [b]who[1] has also given us His Holy Spirit.

A BROTHERLY AND ORDERLY LIFE

[9]But concerning brotherly love you have no need that I should write to you, for [a]you yourselves are taught by God [b]to love one another; [10]and indeed you do so toward all the brethren who are in all Macedonia. But we urge you, brethren, [a]that you increase more and more; [11]that you also aspire to lead a quiet life, [a]to mind your own business, and [b]to work with your own hands, as we commanded you, [12][a]that you may walk properly toward those who are outside, and *that* you may lack nothing.

THE COMFORT OF CHRIST'S COMING

[13]But I do not want you to be ignorant, brethren, concerning those who have fallen [1]asleep, lest you sorrow [a]as others [b]who have no hope. [14]For [a]if we believe that Jesus died and rose again, even so God will bring with Him [b]those who [1]sleep in Jesus.

[15]For this we say to you [a]by the word of the Lord, that [b]we who are alive *and* remain until the coming of the Lord will by no means precede those who are [1]asleep. [16]For [a]the Lord Himself will descend from heaven with a shout, with the voice of an archangel, and with [b]the trumpet of God. [c]And the dead in Christ will rise first. [17][a]Then we who are alive *and* remain shall be caught up together with them [b]in the clouds to meet the Lord in the air. And thus [c]we shall always be with the Lord. [18][a]Therefore comfort one another with these words.

THE DAY OF THE LORD

5 But concerning [a]the times and the seasons, brethren, you have no need that I should write to you. [2]For

---

Cross references (center column):

8 [b] 1 Cor. 2:10
[1] NU *who also gives*

9 [a] [Jer. 31:33, 34]
[b] Matt. 22:39

10 [a] 1 Thess. 3:12

11 [a] 2 Thess. 3:11
[b] Acts 20:35

12 [a] Rom. 13:13

13 [a] Lev. 19:28
[b] [Eph. 2:12]
[1] Died

14 [a] 1 Cor. 15:13
[b] 1 Cor. 15:20, 23
[1] Or *through Jesus sleep*

15 [a] 1 Kin. 13:17; 20:35
[b] 1 Cor. 15:51, 52
[1] Dead

16 [a] [Matt. 24:30, 31]
[b] [1 Cor. 15:52]
[c] [1 Cor. 15:23]

17 [a] [1 Cor. 15:51–53]
[b] Acts 1:9
[c] John 14:3; 17:24

18 [a] 1 Thess. 5:11

CHAPTER 5

1 [a] Matt. 24:3

1 Thess. 4:17

CAUGHT UP
TO THE LORD

The words "caught up" are a translation of the Greek word *harpazo*. *Harpazo* means to be snatched away or taken away by force. We will be taken away by the force of God's Spirit at the call of Jesus. We'll be caught up, together with our loved ones who died in Christ, to meet the Lord in the air.

This is not the second coming of Jesus. He is coming *for* His church prior to His second coming *with* His church. There will be a period of time when we will be with the Lord in heaven. Then, when He returns to earth, we'll come back and reign with Him for a thousand years, and we will ever be with the Lord.

Paul said comfort one another with these words. Get your mind on the eternal glories that God has for those who walk in fellowship with Him.

you yourselves know perfectly that ªthe day of the Lord so comes as a thief in the night. ³For when they say, "Peace and safety!" then ªsudden destruction comes upon them, ᵇas labor pains upon a pregnant woman. And they shall not escape. ⁴ªBut you, brethren, are not in darkness, so that this Day should overtake you as a thief. ⁵You are all ªsons of light and sons of the day. We are not of the night nor of darkness. ⁶ªTherefore let us not sleep, as others *do*, but ᵇlet us watch and be ¹sober. ⁷For ªthose who sleep, sleep at night, and those who get drunk ᵇare drunk at night. ⁸But let us who are of the day be sober, ªputting on the breastplate of faith and love, and *as* a helmet the hope of salvation. ⁹For ªGod did not appoint us to wrath, ᵇbut to obtain salvation through our Lord Jesus Christ, ¹⁰ªwho died for us, that whether we wake or sleep, we should live together with Him.

2 ª[2 Pet. 3:10]
3 ªIs. 13:6–9 ᵇHos. 13:13
4 ª1 John 2:8
5 ªEph. 5:8
6 ªMatt. 25:5 ᵇ[1 Pet. 5:8] ¹*self-controlled*
7 ª[Luke 21:34] ᵇActs 2:15
8 ªEph. 6:14
9 ªRom. 9:22 ᵇ[2 Thess. 2:13]
10 ª2 Cor. 5:15
11 ¹*Or encourage* ²*build one another up*
12 ª1 Cor. 16:18 ¹*instruct or warn*
13 ªMark 9:50
14 ª2 Thess. 3:6, 7, 11 ᵇHeb. 12:12 ᶜRom. 14:1; 15:1 ᵈGal. 5:22 ¹*encourage* ²*insubordinate or idle*
15 ªLev. 19:18 ᵇGal. 6:10
16 ª[2 Cor. 6:10]
17 ªEph. 6:18
19 ªEph. 4:30
20 ª1 Cor. 14:1, 31
21 ª1 John 4:1 ᵇPhil. 4:8
23 ªPhil. 4:9 ᵇ1 Thess. 3:13 ᶜ1 Cor. 1:8, 9 ¹*set you apart*
24 ª[1 Cor. 10:13] ᵇPhil. 1:6

1 Thess. 5:6

WATCH, AND
BE READY!

This is an important warning. You should not be in darkness so that the coming of the Lord takes you by surprise.

There are a lot of things in this world that cloud our spiritual awareness and conscience. People get caught up in the things of the world. And today the rottenness of the world is so easily accessible that we can become spiritually dull rather than spiritually alert.

Thus, the warning of Jesus is to watch and be ready for you don't know the day or the hour your Lord is coming (Matt. 24:42).

¹¹Therefore ¹comfort each other and ²edify one another, just as you also are doing.

VARIOUS EXHORTATIONS

¹²And we urge you, brethren, ªto recognize those who labor among you, and are over you in the Lord and ¹admonish you, ¹³and to esteem them very highly in love for their work's sake. ªBe at peace among yourselves.

¹⁴Now we ¹exhort you, brethren, ªwarn those who are ²unruly, ᵇcomfort the fainthearted, ᶜuphold the weak, ᵈbe patient with all. ¹⁵ªSee that no one renders evil for evil to anyone, but always ᵇpursue what is good both for yourselves and for all.

¹⁶ªRejoice always, ¹⁷ªpray without ceasing, ¹⁸in everything give thanks; for this is the will of God in Christ Jesus for you.

¹⁹ªDo not quench the Spirit. ²⁰ªDo not despise prophecies. ²¹ªTest all things; ᵇhold fast what is good. ²²Abstain from every form of evil.

BLESSING AND ADMONITION

²³Now may ªthe God of peace Himself ᵇsanctify¹ you completely; and may your whole spirit, soul, and body ᶜbe preserved blameless at the coming of our Lord Jesus Christ. ²⁴He who calls

you *is* ᵃfaithful, who also will ᵇdo *it.* | **27** ¹*letter* | ²⁷I charge you by the Lord that this
25Brethren, pray for us. | ²NU omits *holy* | ¹epistle be read to all the ²holy brethren.
26Greet all the brethren with a holy | | ²⁸The grace of our Lord Jesus Christ
kiss. | | *be* with you. Amen.

NOT APPOINTED TO WRATH

1 Thess. 5:9

This is a glorious verse. When the great tribulation, the day of the Lord's wrath and judgment comes upon the earth, we will not be here! Thank God, He has not appointed us to wrath.

There are many today who teach that the church will go through the great tribulation. I believe that teaching is unscriptural and contrary to the whole thrust of the Scriptures in regard to God's children. You can go back to the Old Testament and see that when God sent the angels to destroy Sodom, Abraham questioned the Lord, "Would you also destroy the righteous with the wicked? . . . Shall not the Judge of all the earth do right?" (Gen. 18:22–25). The Lord affirmed to Abraham that the righteous would be spared (Gen. 18:26–32).

Now the thing to recognize is that the judgment coming upon Sodom was from God. When the angels arrived at Sodom, it was extremely wicked; but Lot, Abraham's righteous nephew, was living there. In the morning, the angels said, "Lot, get out of here! We're going to destroy this place, but we can't destroy it until you are out of here" (Gen. 19:15–22). As Peter made reference to this event, he said, "The Lord knows how to deliver the godly out of temptations and to reserve the unjust under punishment for the day of judgment" (2 Pet. 2:9).

When judgment proceeds from God, the righteous are spared because God's judgment is against sin. But thank God, through Jesus Christ our sins have been forgiven! Thus, when the judgment of God comes on this earth, His people will not be here. This is the blessed hope of every believer. Well, not every believer, because some believe they are going to go through the great tribulation. But it is the blessed hope for those who believe in a pretribulation rapture.

I am very strong in that particular persuasion because of the Lord's answer to Abraham's question, "Shall not the Judge of all the earth do right?" It wouldn't be fair for God to destroy the righteous with the wicked, and the Lord affirmed that He would not do that. The judgment of God will not come upon the earth until the Lord has taken His church out of here.

THE WILL OF GOD

1 Thess. 5:16–18

Paul declared three short little exhortations. First, "Rejoice always." What does that mean? It means the church should be a joyful people. We should be the most joyful people on the face of the earth because God has forgiven our sins, and we have the hope of eternal life with Jesus Christ.

Also, the church should be a praying church, "Pray without ceasing." Now, this doesn't mean you have to be on your knees twenty-four hours a day. Prayer is the constant awareness of and communion with God and the awe that I have as I worship Him.

Finally, the church should be thankful: "In everything give thanks." This is impossible to do unless I know my life is in God's hands. Nothing can happen to me except God allows it. And if God allows it to happen to me, He has a purpose for it.

So we are to be a joyful church, a praying church, and a thankful church. "This is the will of God in Christ Jesus for you."

THE SECOND EPISTLE OF PAUL THE APOSTLE TO THE
THESSALONIANS

INTRODUCTION **T**he church in Thessalonica was a healthy, vibrant church, which had been founded by Paul when he was on his second missionary journey with Silas, Timothy, and Luke. Paul was only there in Thessalonica for less than a month and taught them for three consecutive Saturdays, according to Acts 17. He moved on after a few weeks because of all the trouble that was going on there, but left behind a young but healthy church.

Paul continued on his journey to Berea, then to Athens and Corinth. Apparently, while in Corinth, Paul received a report about how things were going in Thessalonica, including some questions the church had concerning some of his teachings. The book of 1 Thessalonians was written to answer their questions and to correct some of their misunderstandings. Shortly after sending them the first letter, he received reports of other questions and misunderstandings they had, and wrote this second letter to further clarify what he had taught them previously.

First Thessalonians was primarily focused on the rapture of the church. Members had been worried that those who had recently died would miss the rapture, and Paul comforted them by letting them know that those who died would precede us and meet us in the air.

Second Thessalonians is more directed at the great tribulation and the second coming of Christ. There were people who were teaching that the great tribulation was already upon them and that believers were going to go through the great tribulation. Paul corrected this error by letting them know that, although they were going through tribulation, it was not the great tribulation. That period of time will be clearly distinguishable by the rising of the Antichrist as a world leader, and it will end when Jesus returns to the earth to destroy His enemies. Paul distinguishes between the rapture, where Jesus takes us up into the air to meet Him and the second coming, following the great tribulation, where He will return to subdue the earth and set up His earthly thousand-year reign.

So again, the first letter comforts Christians by telling us that the rapture is coming, while the second letter comforts us by letting us know that we are not presently in the great tribulation, and we will not go through the great tribulation. Glorious assurance, especially to those who are presently suffering.

GREETING

1 Paul, Silvanus, and Timothy,
To the church of the Thessalonians in God our Father and the Lord Jesus Christ:

2 aGrace to you and peace from God our Father and the Lord Jesus Christ.

GOD'S FINAL JUDGMENT AND GLORY

3We are bound to thank God always for you, brethren, as it is fitting, because your faith grows exceedingly, and the love of every one of you all abounds toward each other, 4so that awe ourselves boast of you among the churches of God bfor your patience

CHAPTER 1

2 a 1 Cor. 1:3

4 a 2 Cor. 7:4
b 1 Thess. 1:3
c 1 Thess. 2:14
1 afflictions

---

2 Thess. 1:3–4

FERVENT IN SPIRIT

What a great church! Paul thanked God continually for the Thessalonians. Persecution arose very early, yet these people were sincere in seeking God, their faith was growing exceedingly, and their love toward each was abounding! That is the kind of fellowship you want to be in. Where you have faith and love that are abounding toward each other.

This church was enduring heavy persecution and tribulations. Perhaps that was the reason for their growing faith and abounding love. It's interesting how persecution seems to bind the church together.

You know, you really can't serve the Lord unless you have genuine commitment. It isn't, "Well, if it isn't raining and there's not a basketball game on, I'll go to church." It takes a real commitment to Jesus Christ in times of persecution. Thus, there is usually a tremendous depth of relationship with the Lord. And with that relationship, there comes tremendous faith and a great love for fellow believers.

5 a Phil. 1:28
b 1 Thess. 2:14
1 plain

6 a Rev. 6:10
1 affliction

7 a Rev. 14:13
b Jude 14

9 a Phil. 3:19
b Deut. 33:2

10 a Matt. 25:31
b John 17:10
1 NU, M have believed

---

and faith cin all your persecutions and 1tribulations that you endure, 5which is amanifest1 evidence of the righteous judgment of God, that you may be counted worthy of the kingdom of God, bfor which you also suffer; 6asince it is a righteous thing with God to repay with 1tribulation those who trouble you, 7and to give you who are troubled arest with us when bthe Lord Jesus is revealed from heaven with His mighty angels, 8in flaming fire taking vengeance on those who do not know God, and on those who do not obey the gospel of our Lord Jesus Christ. 9aThese shall be punished with everlasting destruction from the presence of the Lord and bfrom the glory of His power, 10when He comes, in that Day, ato be bglorified in His saints and to be admired among all those who 1believe, because our testimony among you was believed.

---

2 Thess. 1:10

THE GLORY OF GOD

One day when Jesus comes and He begins to reign over the earth, you will see the world as God intended it to be!

You will not see any disabled people. The blind will behold the glory of the Lord! The mute will sing praises to God, and the lame will leap for joy (Is. 35:5, 6). There will be no sickness. There will be no sorrow. The former things will pass away (Rev. 21:4).

You will see a world in which people live together in harmony and love. It will be a world filled with love, a world of peace, a world of total sharing of all resources. It will be a glorious world, the kingdom age (Rev. 21:24–27).

So in that day, Jesus will be glorified in His saints and admired among all who believe. Our Lord will reign in glory!

2 Thess. 1:11

Pray Always! Jesus, talking about the great tribulation and the cataclysmic judgments of God that will take place during that time, said to His disciples, "Pray always that you may be counted worthy to escape all these things that will come to pass, and to stand before the Son of Man" (Luke 21:36).

If Jesus told us to pray always to be counted worthy, I think it would be a wise thing for us to pray, "Lord, I want to be worthy to escape the great judgment coming upon the earth. I want to stand, Lord, before You in glory."

[11] Therefore we also pray always for you that our God would a count you worthy of *this* calling, and fulfill all the good pleasure of *His* goodness and b the work of faith with power, [12] a that the name of our Lord Jesus Christ may

2 Thess. 2:3

APOSTASY OF THE CHURCH

Before the day of the Lord comes, there's going to be a falling away. The word translated "falling away" is the Greek word *apostasia*. The root word means "to depart." Through usage, it has come to mean "a falling away from the faith," or "apostasy." But the word itself simply means "departing."

Now I do believe many will depart from the faith. In fact, as you look at the so-called church today, you realize the church is in a state of apostasy. But also the word can refer to the departure of the saints, the rapture of the church. The day of the Lord will not take place until there is first a departure, such as when the church departs to be with the Lord.

11 a Col. 1:12
b 1 Thess. 1:3

12 a [Col. 3:17]

CHAPTER 2

1 a [1 Thess. 4:15–17]
b Matt. 24:31

2 a Matt. 24:4
1 NU *the Lord*

3 a 1 Tim. 4:1
b Dan. 7:25; 8:25; 11:36
c John 17:12
1 NU *lawlessness*

4 a Is. 14:13, 14
b 1 Cor. 8:5
1 NU omits *as God*

7 a 1 John 2:18
1 *hidden truth*

2 Thess. 2:4

A SIGN FOR THE JEWS

Paul said here that the Antichrist will sit in the temple of God declaring that he is God and demanding to be worshiped as God. This is the final event that will trigger the wrath and judgment of God. In Matthew 24, Jesus said, "When you see this abomination of desolation that Daniel spoke about, standing in the holy place, it's time for you Jews to flee out of Jerusalem." He said, "Let him who reads, understand" (Matt. 24:15).

We are told in Revelation that God will give the Jews the wings of a great eagle to fly them to a wilderness place, where God will watch over them and keep the remnant safe for three-and-one-half years (Rev. 12:14).

It is this event that will trigger the beginning of the end.

be glorified in you, and you in Him, according to the grace of our God and the Lord Jesus Christ.

THE GREAT APOSTASY

2 Now, brethren, a concerning the coming of our Lord Jesus Christ b and our gathering together to Him, we ask you, [2] a not to be soon shaken in mind or troubled, either by spirit or by word or by letter, as if from us, as though the day of [1] Christ had come. [3] Let no one deceive you by any means; for *that Day will not come* a unless the falling away comes first, and b the man of [1] sin is revealed, c the son of perdition, [4] who opposes and a exalts himself b above all that is called God or that is worshiped, so that he sits [1] as God in the temple of God, showing himself that he is God.

[5] Do you not remember that when I was still with you I told you these things? [6] And now you know what is restraining, that he may be revealed in his own time. [7] For a the [1] mystery of

THOSE WHO WILL PERISH   2 Thess. 2:10–11

I t's tragic! People who reject the truth of God, people who do not receive the love of the truth that they might be saved. They will be deceived. They will perish.

There are some who interpret these passages to mean that if you have ever heard the truth of Jesus Christ and rejected it, there will be no opportunity for you to be saved after the church has been taken away. I don't know if they are correct.

We know the Antichrist will cause everyone to receive a mark on their right hand or forehead, and no one will be able to buy or sell without it (Rev. 13:16–17). We also know he will put to death those who refuse to take the mark (Rev. 20:4). We know that for anyone who takes the mark, there will be no hope for their salvation, ever! (Rev. 14:9–11).

In Revelation, chapter 20, John sees those who are martyred for Christ during the great tribulation, so we also know many will be saved during this time. Yet, there are commentators who interpret this passage as saying, if you reject Jesus now, knowingly, there will be no opportunity for you to be saved during the great tribulation. So just beware in case you have been holding that out as your safety net. You know, "I'll live like the devil now; and as soon as the church is gone, I'll repent and get right." One tough old guy told me, "They will never put a mark on me!" But I said, "If you can't live for Christ now, how are you going to die for Him then?" They have not the love of the truth that they might be saved.

I don't know if these commentators are correct or not, but I'll tell you what, when you are talking about eternal life, I don't want any question marks! I want to be sure of my salvation. I want to love the truth and follow the truth so there is no question about my destiny. Eternity is too long to live with a question mark.

---

lawlessness is already at work; only [7] He who now restrains *will do so* until [2] He is taken out of the way. [8] And then the lawless one will be revealed, [a]whom the Lord will consume [b]with the breath of His mouth and destroy [c]with the brightness of His coming. [9] The coming of the *lawless one* is [a]according to the working of Satan, with all power, [b]signs, and lying wonders, [10] and with all unrighteous deception among [a]those who perish, because they did not receive [b]the love of the truth, that they might be saved. [11] And [a]for this reason God will send them strong delusion, [b]that they should believe the lie, [12] that they all may be condemned who did not believe the truth but [a]had pleasure in unrighteousness.

STAND FAST

[13] But we are [1]bound to give thanks to God always for you, brethren beloved by the Lord, because God [a]from the beginning [b]chose you for salvation [c]through [2]sanctification by the Spirit and belief in the truth, [14] to which He called you by our gospel, for [a]the obtaining of the glory of our Lord Jesus Christ. [15] Therefore, brethren, [a]stand fast and hold [b]the traditions which you were taught, whether by word or our [1]epistle.

[16] Now may our Lord Jesus Christ Himself, and our God and Father, [a]who has loved us and given *us* everlasting consolation and [b]good hope by grace, [17] comfort your hearts [a]and [1]establish you in every good word and work.

PRAY FOR US

3 Finally, brethren, [a]pray for us, that the word of the Lord may run *swiftly* and be glorified, just as *it is* with you, [2] and [a]that we may be delivered from unreasonable and wicked men; [b]for not all have faith. [3] But [a]the Lord is faithful, who will establish you and [b]guard *you* from the evil one. [4] And [a]we have confidence in the Lord concerning you, both that you do and will do the things we command you. [5] Now may [a]the Lord direct your hearts into the love of God and into the patience of Christ.

WARNING AGAINST IDLENESS

[6] But we command you, brethren, in the name of our Lord Jesus Christ, [a]that you withdraw [b]from every brother who walks [c]disorderly and not according to the tradition which [1]he

7 [2]Or *he*
8 [a]Dan. 7:10
[b]Is. 11:4
[c]Heb. 10:27
9 [a]John 8:41
[b]Deut. 13:1
10 [a]2 Cor. 2:15
[b]1 Cor. 16:22
11 [a]Rom. 1:28
[b]1 Tim. 4:1
12 [a]Rom. 1:32
13 [a]Eph. 1:4
[b]1 Thess. 1:4
[c][1 Pet. 1:2]
1 *under obligation*
2 *being set apart by*
14 [a]1 Pet. 5:10
15 [a]1 Cor. 16:13
[b]1 Cor. 11:2
1 *letter*
16 [a][Rev. 1:5]
[b]1 Pet. 1:3
17 [a]1 Cor. 1:8
1 *strengthen*

CHAPTER 3
1 [a]Eph. 6:19
2 [a]Rom. 15:31
[b]Acts 28:24
3 [a]1 Cor. 1:9
[b]John 17:15
4 [a]2 Cor. 7:16   5 [a]1 Chr. 29:18   6 [a]Rom. 16:17 [b]1 Cor. 5:1 [c]1 Thess. 4:11   1 NU, M *they*

2 Thess. 2:17

COMFORT OUR HEARTS, LORD

Father, thank You for the way You have laid out the map so that we know where we are going. We can look on the map and see where we are; and we are thankful, Lord, that we are almost home and the journey is about over.

Lord, with anxious hearts, we wait in excitement for that day when You shall come and receive Your church, and gather us to Yourself that we might see You in the glory that You had before the world was (John 17:5). Lord, we look forward to the day we will be united together forever in Your Kingdom.

Lord, comfort our hearts with Your Word and hope in a world that is so distraught, a world being torn apart at the seams, a world drowning in iniquity. Lord, comfort our hearts with the hope of our future with You.

---

received from us. 7For you yourselves know how you ought to follow us, for we were not disorderly among you; 8nor did we eat anyone's bread 1free of charge, but worked with alabor and toil night and day, that we might not be a burden to any of you, 9not because we do not have aauthority, but to make ourselves an example of how you should follow us.

10For even when we were with you, we commanded you this: If anyone will not work, neither shall he eat. 11For we hear that there are some who walk among you in a disorderly manner, not working at all, but are abusybodies. 12Now those who are such we command and 1exhort through our Lord Jesus Christ athat they work in quietness and eat their own bread.

13But *as for* you, brethren, ado not grow weary *in* doing good. 14And if anyone does not obey our word in this 1epistle, note that person and ado not

---

Side notes (center column):

8 a 1 Thess. 2:9
1 Lit. *for nothing*

9 a 1 Cor. 9:4, 6–14

11 a 1 Pet. 4:15

12 a Eph. 4:28
1 *encourage*

13 a Gal. 6:9

14 a Matt. 18:17
1 *letter*

15 a Lev. 19:17
b Titus 3:10
1 *warn*

16 a Rom. 15:33
17 a 1 Cor. 16:21
1 *letter*

18 a Rom. 16:20, 24

---

2 Thess. 3:1

Pray for Us. It's interesting how Paul was always soliciting the prayers of the various churches. The Bible says, "Bear one another's burdens" (Gal. 6:2). "Pray one for another" (James 5:16). It is important that we pray, especially for those in leadership.

---

keep company with him, that he may be ashamed. 15aYet do not count *him* as an enemy, bbut 1admonish *him* as a brother.

BENEDICTION

16Now may athe Lord of peace Himself give you peace always in every way. The Lord *be* with you all. 17aThe salutation of Paul with my own hand, which is a sign in every 1epistle; so I write.

18aThe grace of our Lord Jesus Christ *be* with you all. Amen.

---

2 Thess. 3:5

THE LOVE OF GOD

Oh, I love that! "May the Lord direct your hearts into the love of God."

It's interesting how Satan often comes with doubt and questions concerning God's love, especially when things have gone wrong. Satan comes along and says, "If God really loves you, why did He allow this to happen?" He is seeking to cause you to question God's love for you.

God does love us, and He is working in all of the circumstances in our lives a good purpose. That I know! May God direct your hearts into the love of God.

THE FIRST EPISTLE OF PAUL THE APOSTLE TO
TIMOTHY

INTRODUCTION The book of 1 Timothy is the first of the three books we call the Pastoral Epistles. First and 2 Timothy and Titus were written by the apostle Paul to young pastors to tell them how to lead the church.

First Timothy was written by Paul, from Macedonia, probably around AD 62. Timothy had been an assistant to Paul, traveling with him on his second and third missionary journeys. Paul called him "my son" so we assume he came to the Lord under Paul's teaching at Troas, where Timothy grew up. Timothy's father was Greek, but his mother and grandmother were godly Jewish women who trained him in the things of the Lord.

At the time of this writing, Paul had established the church in Ephesus and had left Timothy there to oversee the church when Paul left. So Timothy, who had traveled and worked with Paul so much and who had been personally trained by him, was now in a position of leadership. He was, no doubt, nervous about this new role; and Paul wrote this letter to give him encouragement and advice.

There were certain heresies that were cropping up in Ephesus that needed to be addressed, and there were also issues concerning leadership within the church. The church was growing and it was important that it be established in sound doctrine, and that the leaders in the church know how they should conduct themselves.

One of Timothy's jobs in the church would be to identify and train other men for the ministry, so much of the book focuses on the qualifications and character of the men who would lead the church. This was for Timothy's personal benefit, in his own spiritual development, but was also to help him in developing other leaders within the church.

This book has much to say to any young person who aspires to be used by God in Christian service and ministry. It is also of inestimable value to those currently leading within a local church. The practical advice of Paul that is contained in this book can help a church or minister to stay on course, fulfilling the calling of God on their lives, or it can help a church or minister who has veered off track to return to the roots of what a New Testament church ought to be.

GREETING

1 Paul, an apostle of Jesus Christ, by the commandment of God our Savior and the Lord Jesus Christ, our hope,

2 To Timothy, a ᵃtrue son in the faith:

ᵇGrace, mercy, *and* peace from God our Father and Jesus Christ our Lord.

NO OTHER DOCTRINE

3 As I urged you ᵃwhen I went into Macedonia—remain in Ephesus that you may ¹charge some ᵇthat they teach no other doctrine, 4 ᵃnor give heed to fables and endless genealogies, which cause disputes rather than godly edification which is in faith. 5 Now ᵃthe purpose of the commandment is love ᵇfrom a pure heart, *from* a good conscience, and *from* ¹sincere faith, 6 from which some, having strayed, have turned aside to ᵃidle talk, 7 desiring to be teachers of the law, understanding neither what they say nor the things which they affirm.

---

1 Tim. 1:6

Idle Talk. Paul warned Timothy about those timewasters, who turn away from what matters to "idle talk."

There are some people who spend all their time and energy trying to debate and discuss nitpicky issues that don't matter. I get letters from people who I can tell only want to debate with me. Sometimes they start with an honest-sounding question, but when you give them an honest answer they respond by writing a lengthy diatribe, advocating some strange theory.

I try to avoid these disputes. I know I won't get anywhere with them, so why waste time in idle talk?

---

8 But we know that the law *is* ᵃgood if one uses it lawfully, 9 knowing this: that the law is not made for a righteous person, but for *the* lawless and insubordinate, for *the* ungodly and for sinners, for *the* unholy and profane, for murderers of fathers and murderers of mothers, for manslayers, 10 for fornicators, for sodomites, for kidnappers, for

---

CHAPTER 1

2 ᵃTitus 1:4
ᵇGal. 1:3

3 ᵃActs 20:1, 3
ᵇGal. 1:6, 7
1 command

4 ᵃTitus 1:14

5 ᵃRom. 13:8–10
ᵇEph. 6:24
1 Lit. unhypocritical

6 ᵃ1 Tim. 6:4, 20

8 ᵃRom. 7:12, 16

10 ¹opposed

11 ᵃ1 Tim. 6:15
ᵇ1 Cor. 9:17

12 ᵃ1 Cor. 15:10
ᵇ1 Cor. 7:25
ᶜCol. 1:25

13 ᵃActs 8:3
ᵇJohn 4:21
1 violently arrogant

14 ᵃRom. 5:20
ᵇ2 Tim. 1:13; 2:22

15 ᵃ2 Tim. 2:11
ᵇMatt. 1:21; 9:13

17 ᵃPs. 10:16
ᵇRom. 1:23
ᶜHeb. 11:27
ᵈRom. 16:27
1 NU *the only God,*

---

liars, for perjurers, and if there is any other thing that is ¹contrary to sound doctrine, 11 according to the glorious gospel of the ᵃblessed God which was ᵇcommitted to my trust.

GLORY TO GOD FOR HIS GRACE

12 And I thank Christ Jesus our Lord who has ᵃenabled me, ᵇbecause He counted me faithful, ᶜputting *me* into the ministry, 13 although ᵃI was formerly a blasphemer, a persecutor, and an ¹insolent man; but I obtained mercy because ᵇI did *it* ignorantly in unbelief. 14 ᵃAnd the grace of our Lord was exceedingly abundant, ᵇwith faith and love which are in Christ Jesus. 15 ᵃThis *is* a faithful saying and worthy of all acceptance, that ᵇChrist Jesus came into the world to save sinners, of whom I am chief. 16 However, for this reason I obtained mercy, that in me first Jesus Christ might show all longsuffering, as a pattern to those who are going to believe on Him for everlasting life. 17 Now to ᵃthe King eternal, ᵇimmortal, ᶜinvisible, to ¹God ᵈwho alone is wise,

---

1 Tim. 1:12

HIS ENABLEMENT

I am so thankful that God has counted me faithful, putting me into the ministry. But I am even more thankful that He has enabled me.

We often hear the call of God in our lives, to serve Him in some capacity. But it doesn't take long before we come across a situation where our natural abilities just aren't enough, and we feel like we are over our heads. At that point, we have to decide whether we will try to obey, or whether we will just quit, giving in to our natural limitations.

God's callings are always accompanied by His enabling. He will never call us to do something without also enabling us to do it. Many times the Lord asks us to do something that is impossible. And then, working in us, by His Spirit, He proceeds to do the impossible.

1 Tim. 1:15–16

The Chief Sinner. Paul considered himself to be chief among sinners, because of the things he did as he was persecuting the church, trying to destroy the church. But, he said, "for this reason I obtained mercy, that in me first Jesus Christ might show all long-suffering, as a pattern to those who are going to believe on Him for everlasting life."

God showed mercy to the chief of sinners so that no one would feel that they are out of reach of God's love and grace. God saved Paul so that others would have hope.

_e*be* honor and glory forever and ever. Amen.

FIGHT THE GOOD FIGHT

18This ¹charge I commit to you, son Timothy, according to the prophecies previously made concerning you, that by them you may wage the good warfare, 19having faith and a good conscience, which some having rejected, concerning the faith have suffered shipwreck, 20of whom are ^aHymenaeus and ^bAlexander, whom I delivered to Satan that they may learn not to ^cblaspheme.

17 ^e 1 Chr. 29:11

18 ¹ *command*

20 ^a 2 Tim. 2:17, 18
^b 2 Tim. 4:14
^c Acts 13:45

CHAPTER 2

1 ¹ *encourage*

2 ^a Ezra 6:10
^b [Rom. 13:1]
¹ *a prominent place*
² *dignity*

3 ^a Rom. 12:2
^b 2 Tim. 1:9

PRAY FOR ALL MEN

2 Therefore I ¹exhort first of all that supplications, prayers, intercessions, *and* giving of thanks be made for all men, 2^afor kings and ^ball who are in ¹authority, that we may lead a quiet and peaceable life in all godliness and 2reverence. 3For this *is* ^agood and acceptable in the sight ^bof God our

1 Tim. 2:1–3

PRAYING FOR LEADERS

Praying for our leaders is "good and acceptable in the sight of God our Savior."

It is much easier to criticize the failures and weaknesses of our national leaders than to pray for them. When we see some of the things that our government does, and so often what they are doing goes directly against the Word of God, and the will of God, we become frustrated and angry.

But we are commanded to pray for these leaders, whether we agree with them or not. Let's hold them up in prayer. God likes that.

SAVED THROUGH CHILDBEARING

1 Tim. 2:15

The ideal place for a woman is in the home, raising godly children, rather than as a prominent teacher within the church. Raising children is an incredibly important ministry and a place where women can experience God's blessing on their lives.

When I wanted to marry Kay, I told her I wasn't looking for an assistant pastor. I love children, and I was looking for a mother for my children. And the fact that all our children are walking with the Lord, and serving the Lord, is the result of her being a godly mother in the home.

After our children were grown, Kay was then able to draw from the vast experience she gained as a mother, in order to share this with the other women in our church. She teaches the women of our church from her heart, out of all that God taught her while she was raising our children. But it was in raising children that she found a richness and fulfillment in life, which was her salvation.

Of course, it was also through childbirth, the birth of Jesus to Mary, that salvation came to all of us.

Savior, [4][a]who desires all men to be saved [b]and to come to the knowledge of the truth. [5][a]For *there is* one God and [b]one Mediator between God and men, *the* Man Christ Jesus, [6][a]who gave Himself a ransom for all, to be testified in due time, [7][a]for which I was appointed a preacher and an apostle—I am speaking the truth [1]in Christ *and* not lying—[b]a teacher of the Gentiles in faith and truth.

---

1 Tim. 2:5

A Narrow-Minded Message.
"There is one God and one Mediator between God and men, the Man Christ Jesus." All roads do not lead to God! All religions are not good! There is only one road that leads to God and that is Jesus Christ. He said, "I am the way, the truth, and the life. No one comes to the Father except through Me" (John 14:6).

I sometimes hear from people who are very upset because I speak a narrow, bigoted message that there is only one way. I didn't say it. Jesus said it!

MEN AND WOMEN IN THE CHURCH

[8]I desire therefore that the men pray [a]everywhere, [b]lifting up holy hands, without wrath and doubting; [9]in like manner also, that the [a]women adorn themselves in modest apparel, with propriety and [1]moderation, not with braided hair or gold or pearls or costly clothing, [10][a]but, which is proper for women professing godliness, with good works. [11]Let a woman learn in silence with all submission. [12]And [a]I do not permit a woman to teach or to have authority over a man, but to be in silence. [13]For Adam was formed first, then Eve. [14]And Adam was not deceived, but the woman being deceived, fell into transgression. [15]Nevertheless she will be saved in childbearing if they continue in faith, love, and holiness, with self-control.

QUALIFICATIONS OF OVERSEERS

3 This *is* a faithful saying: If a man desires the position of a [1]bishop, he desires a good work. [2]A bishop then must be blameless, the husband of one wife, temperate, sober-minded, of good behavior, hospitable, able to teach;

---

4 [a] Ezek. 18:23, 32
[b] [John 17:3]

5 [a] Gal. 3:20
[b] [Heb. 9:15]

6 [a] Mark 10:45

7 [a] Eph. 3:7, 8
[b] [Gal. 1:15, 16]
[1] NU omits *in Christ*

8 [a] Luke 23:34
[b] Ps. 134:2

9 [a] 1 Pet. 3:3
[1] *discretion*

10 [a] 1 Pet. 3:4

12 [a] 1 Cor. 14:34

CHAPTER 3

1 [1] Lit. *overseer*

3 [1] *addicted*
[2] NU omits *not greedy for money*
[3] *loving money*

6 [1] *new convert*

7 [a] 2 Tim. 2:26

8 [a] Ezek. 44:21

9 [1] *hidden truth*

11 [1] *malicious gossips*

---

1 Tim. 3:1

DESIRING A GOOD WORK

Paul says that if you desire to be a bishop (or an elder or leader within the church) that you desire a good work. The word for "desire" in the Greek means much more than just that you'd like to do it or that you are open to doing it. The word describes an intense, burning desire from the heart.

It is a great privilege to serve in leadership in the church, and I am so thankful for those men God has raised up over the years to serve at Calvary Chapel with me. It is a good work. And if someone really wants to share in these leadership roles, he would do well to study this passage concerning the qualifications of leadership in the church.

As our lives line up with these requirements, others will recognize the hand of God on our lives and will look to us as leaders.

---

[3]not [1]given to wine, not violent, [2]not greedy for money, but gentle, not quarrelsome, not [3]covetous; [4]one who rules his own house well, having *his* children in submission with all reverence [5](for if a man does not know how to rule his own house, how will he take care of the church of God?); [6]not a [1]novice, lest being puffed up with pride he fall into the *same* condemnation as the devil. [7]Moreover he must have a good testimony among those who are outside, lest he fall into reproach and the [a]snare of the devil.

QUALIFICATIONS OF DEACONS

[8]Likewise deacons *must be* reverent, not double-tongued, [a]not given to much wine, not greedy for money, [9]holding the [1]mystery of the faith with a pure conscience. [10]But let these also first be tested; then let them serve as deacons, being *found* blameless. [11]Likewise, *their* wives *must be* reverent, not [1]slanderers, temperate, faithful in all things.

1 Tim. 3:6

Not a Novice. It is sad when people are elevated in ministry within the church too rapidly. They may be clever business people, or prominent citizens in the community, or perhaps talented entertainers or athletes; and when they come to the Lord, we see how gifted they are and immediately put them into a visible and public position.

They are not given the time to develop, and quite often the result is that they are lifted up in pride. We need to give people a chance to be grounded in the faith before they are put into positions of leadership.

1 Tim. 3:16

THE MYSTERY OF GODLINESS

"Great is the mystery of godliness." That a man could become like God in his character, and in his life. That he can take on godlike characteristics, is such an amazing feat and an incomprehensible mystery. And yet it is something that happens in the life of everyone who yields his life to the Lord.

Lives are changed mysteriously! A heroin addict, who has tried every kind of program imaginable, suddenly is delivered from years of slavery to the needle. An alcoholic leaves the bottle and never touches it again. A person who is filled with bitterness and anger comes to Jesus and is softened immediately by the touch of the gospel. Great is the mystery of godlikeness!

12Let deacons be the husbands of one wife, ruling *their* children and their own houses well. 13For those who have served well as deacons aobtain for

---

13 ᵃMatt. 25:21

15 1 foundation, mainstay

16 ᵃ[John 1:14]
ᵇ[Matt. 3:16]
ᶜMatt. 28:2
ᵈRom. 10:18
ᵉCol. 1:6, 23
ᶠLuke 24:51
1 hidden truth
2 NU Who

CHAPTER 4

1 ᵃRev. 16:14
1 explicitly

2 ᵃMatt. 7:15
ᵇEph. 4:19

5 1 set apart

6 ᵃ2Tim. 3:14

7 ᵃ2Tim. 2:16
ᵇHeb. 5:14

8 ᵃ1Cor. 8:8
ᵇPs. 37:9

10 ᵃPs. 36:6
1 NU we labor and strive,

12 ᵃ1Pet. 5:3
1 look down on your youthfulness
2 NU omits in spirit

---

themselves a good standing and great boldness in the faith which is in Christ Jesus.

THE GREAT MYSTERY

14These things I write to you, though I hope to come to you shortly; 15but if I am delayed, *I write* so that you may know how you ought to conduct yourself in the house of God, which is the church of the living God, the pillar and 1ground of the truth. 16And without controversy great is the 1mystery of godliness:

    ᵃ God2 was manifested in the flesh,
    ᵇ Justified in the Spirit,
    ᶜ Seen by angels,
    ᵈ Preached among the Gentiles,
    ᵉ Believed on in the world,
    ᶠ Received up in glory.

THE GREAT APOSTASY

4 Now the Spirit 1expressly says that in latter times some will depart from the faith, giving heed ᵃto deceiving spirits and doctrines of demons, 2ᵃspeaking lies in hypocrisy, having their own conscience ᵇseared with a hot iron, 3forbidding to marry, *and commanding* to abstain from foods which God created to be received with thanksgiving by those who believe and know the truth. 4For every creature of God *is* good, and nothing is to be refused if it is received with thanksgiving; 5for it is 1sanctified by the word of God and prayer.

A GOOD SERVANT OF JESUS CHRIST

6If you instruct the brethren in these things, you will be a good minister of Jesus Christ, ᵃnourished in the words of faith and of the good doctrine which you have carefully followed. 7But ᵃreject profane and old wives' fables, and ᵇexercise yourself toward godliness. 8For ᵃbodily exercise profits a little, but godliness is profitable for all things, ᵇhaving promise of the life that now is and of that which is to come. 9This *is* a faithful saying and worthy of all acceptance. 10For to this *end* 1we both labor and suffer reproach, because we trust in the living God, ᵃwho is *the* Savior of all men, especially of those who believe. 11These things command and teach.

TAKE HEED TO YOUR MINISTRY

12Let no one 1despise your youth, but be an ᵃexample to the believers in word, in conduct, in love, 2in spirit, in faith, in purity. 13Till I come, give

1 Tim. 4:8

Exercise. Bodily exercise does profit a little; but spiritual exercise, where we work on our spiritual health, is of much more benefit.

Many people get so involved in physical exercise that they become obsessed with their bodies. It is certainly a good thing to take care of your body, as it is the temple of the Holy Spirit. But real and lasting benefit comes from spiritual exercise as we do those things that make us more like God.

Godliness reaps eternal rewards. Therefore let's not neglect our spiritual workout.

attention to reading, to exhortation, to ¹doctrine. ¹⁴ᵃDo not neglect the gift that is in you, which was given to you by prophecy ᵇwith the laying on of the hands of the eldership. ¹⁵Meditate on

1 Tim. 4:10

THE SAVIOR OF ALL MEN

God has provided salvation for all men. When Christ died, He died for the sins of the world. His offer is open to all. "Whoever desires, let him take the water of life freely" (Rev. 22:17). Whoever wants to can drink freely.

But many people reject Him and refuse His gift of salvation. So, although He died for all and makes the offer to all, only those who accept Jesus Christ receive the benefit, so He "is the Savior of all men, especially of those who believe." In other words, He died for everyone, but it takes acceptance by faith to really know Him as your personal Savior. His death doesn't do you any good unless you receive His forgiveness.

13 ¹teaching

14 ᵃ2Tim. 1:6
ᵇActs 6:6

CHAPTER 5

4 ᵃGen. 45:10
¹NU, M omit
good and

5 ᵃActs 26:7

6 ¹*indulgence*

8 ᵃIs. 58:7
ᵇ2Tim. 3:5
ᶜMatt. 18:17

1 Tim. 4:12

AN EXAMPLE TO THE BELIEVERS

Timothy was probably in his thirties by now, but in his culture there were certain spiritual functions that couldn't be performed unless you were at least forty.

When young people have wisdom, it is sometimes not perceived as such just because of their youth. But Paul told Timothy that the best way to deal with that was to be an example by the way he lived his life. If his life was exemplary and if he practiced what he preached, he could win over those who were skeptical of him because of his age.

No matter what age we are, our lives should always confirm the truths we are teaching.

these things; give yourself entirely to them, that your progress may be evident to all. ¹⁶Take heed to yourself and to the doctrine. Continue in them, for in doing this you will save both yourself and those who hear you.

TREATMENT OF CHURCH MEMBERS

5 Do not rebuke an older man, but exhort *him* as a father, younger men as brothers, ²older women as mothers, younger women as sisters, with all purity.

HONOR TRUE WIDOWS

³Honor widows who are really widows. ⁴But if any widow has children or grandchildren, let them first learn to show piety at home and ᵃto repay their parents; for this is ¹good and acceptable before God. ⁵Now she who is really a widow, and left alone, trusts in God and continues in supplications and prayers ᵃnight and day. ⁶But she who lives in ¹pleasure is dead while she lives. ⁷And these things command, that they may be blameless. ⁸But if anyone does not provide for his own, ᵃand especially for those of his household, ᵇhe has denied the faith ᶜand is worse than an unbeliever.

1 Tim. 5:8

PROVIDE FOR YOUR OWN

Nowadays we tend to delegate taking care of the elderly to the government. When that isn't an option, we look to churches and other charities to take responsibility.

In this chapter Paul had much to say about taking care of those who are in need, especially widows, but his central point is that it is the role of a family to take care of their own.

Thus, the one who neglects to do this is worse than an unbeliever. If we believe in Jesus Christ, it should be shown tangibly, as we help our own.

9 Do not let a widow under sixty years old be taken into the number, *and not unless* she has been the wife of one man, 10 well reported for good works: if she has brought up children, if she has lodged strangers, if she has washed the saints' feet, if she has relieved the afflicted, if she has diligently followed every good work.

1 Tim. 5:17–18

Double Honor. Those who are leading God's people should be honored and respected, especially those whose main ministry is teaching the Word. This should include paying them and supporting them financially, as we are exhorted to "not muzzle an ox" but to give wages to a laborer as he is worthy.

Financial gain should never be the motivation for someone to minister to people. However, when they have proven themselves, they should be provided for, which should free them up to give more of their time and efforts to preparation for ministry.

---

11 1 Refuse to enroll

12 1 Or *solemn promise*

16 1 NU omits *man or* 2 *give aid to*

18 a Deut. 25:4 b Luke 10:7

19 a Deut. 17:6; 19:15

21 a Deut. 1:17 1 *chosen*

22 a Eph. 5:6, 7

23 1 *illnesses*

24 a Gal. 5:19–21

CHAPTER 6

1 a Eph. 6:5

---

11 But 1 refuse *the* younger widows; for when they have begun to grow wanton against Christ, they desire to marry, 12 having condemnation because they have cast off their first 1 faith. 13 And besides they learn *to be* idle, wandering about from house to house, and not only idle but also gossips and busybodies, saying things which they ought not. 14 Therefore I desire that *the* younger *widows* marry, bear children, manage the house, give no opportunity to the adversary to speak reproachfully. 15 For some have already turned aside after Satan. 16 If any believing 1 man or woman has widows, let them 2 relieve them, and do not let the church be burdened, that it may relieve those who are really widows.

HONOR THE ELDERS

17 Let the elders who rule well be counted worthy of double honor, especially those who labor in the word and doctrine. 18 For the Scripture says, a "You shall not muzzle an ox while it treads out the grain," and, b "The laborer *is* worthy of his wages." 19 Do not receive an accusation against an elder except a from two or three witnesses. 20 Those who are sinning rebuke in the presence of all, that the rest also may fear.

21 I charge *you* before God and the Lord Jesus Christ and the 1 elect angels that you observe these things without a prejudice, doing nothing with partiality. 22 Do not lay hands on anyone hastily, nor a share in other people's sins; keep yourself pure.

23 No longer drink only water, but use a little wine for your stomach's sake and your frequent 1 infirmities.

24 Some men's sins are a clearly evident, preceding *them* to judgment, but those of some *men* follow later. 25 Likewise, the good works *of some* are clearly evident, and those that are otherwise cannot be hidden.

HONOR MASTERS

6 Let as many a bondservants as are under the yoke count their own masters worthy of all honor, so that the name of God and *His* doctrine may not be blasphemed. 2 And those who have believing masters, let them not despise *them* because they are brethren, but rather serve *them* because those who are benefited are believers and beloved. Teach and exhort these things.

1 Tim. 5:21

A HEAVY EXHORTATION

Paul was making a very serious charge to Timothy. He said, "I charge you before God," and if that isn't enough, "and the Lord Jesus Christ," and finally, "and the elect angels." What was this serious charge? "That you observe these things without prejudice, doing nothing with partiality." The exhortation was against being a respecter of persons, giving preferential treatment to some.

Every person is equal in God's eyes. So if I, as a minister of God, become a respecter of persons, then I am misrepresenting God. How important it is that we understand that everyone is of equal importance in the eyes of God.

God loves us all the same. He doesn't have favorites. He loves us all supremely, and we should follow His example. We need to treat all people, regardless of their status in life, with dignity and respect. To do less is to offend Him.

ERROR AND GREED

3If anyone teaches otherwise and does not consent to ᵃwholesome words, *even* the words of our Lord Jesus Christ, ᵇand to the ¹doctrine which accords with godliness, 4he is proud, knowing nothing, but is obsessed with disputes and arguments over words, from which come envy, strife, reviling, evil suspicions, 5¹useless wranglings of men of corrupt minds and destitute of the truth, who suppose that godliness is a *means of* gain. 2From ᵃsuch withdraw yourself.

6Now godliness with ᵃcontentment is great gain. 7For we brought nothing into *this* world, *¹and it is* ᵃcertain we can carry nothing out. 8And having food and clothing, with these we shall be ᵃcontent. 9But those who desire to be rich fall into temptation and a snare,

---

3 ᵃ2Tim. 1:13
ᵇTitus 1:1
¹ *teaching*

5 ᵃ2Tim. 3:5
¹ NU, M *constant friction*
² NU omits the rest of v. 5.

6 ᵃHeb. 13:5

7 ᵃJob 1:21
¹ NU omits *and it is certain*

8 ᵃProv. 30:8, 9

---

1 Tim. 6:5–6

Godliness and Gain. There are some who use the guise of godliness as a means of profit. They take advantage of people who want to know God better and convince them that if they send money they will achieve status with God. They are motivated by greed and often use greed to motivate their followers.

Paul said to turn away from those kinds of people. Turn the channel. The alternative is to realize that real gain comes when we learn to be content with what we have and pursue godliness with all our hearts.

and *into* many foolish and harmful lusts which drown men in destruction and perdition. 10For the love of money is a root of all *kinds of* evil, for which some have strayed from the faith in their greediness, and pierced themselves through with many sorrows.

THE GOOD CONFESSION

11But you, O man of God, flee these things and pursue righteousness,

1 Tim. 6:11–12

FIGHT THE GOOD FIGHT OF FAITH

Money can lead you into all sorts of dangerous diversions and all kinds of evil. So it is the job of the man of God to flee materialism and to follow after the fruit of the Spirit, including righteousness, godliness, faith, love, patience, and gentleness.

It isn't easy but we must fight the good fight of faith, getting a hold on eternal life and the eternal perspective. When we follow after money, we are fighting the wrong battle. We need to fight the good fight, which is the battle to focus on the eternal.

godliness, faith, love, patience, gentleness. [12]Fight the good fight of faith, lay hold on eternal life, to which you were also called and have confessed the good confession in the presence of many witnesses. [13]I urge you in the sight of God who gives life to all things, and *before* Christ Jesus [a]who witnessed the good confession before Pontius Pilate, [14]that you keep *this* commandment without spot, blameless until our Lord Jesus Christ's appearing, [15]which He will manifest in His own time, *He who is* the blessed and only [1]Potentate, the King of kings and Lord of lords, [16]who alone has immortality, dwelling in [a]unapproachable light, [b]whom no man has seen or can see, to whom *be* honor and everlasting power. Amen.

INSTRUCTIONS TO THE RICH

[17]Command those who are rich in this present age not to be haughty, nor to trust in uncertain [a]riches but in the living God, who gives us richly all things [b]to enjoy. [18]*Let them* do good, that they be rich in good works, ready to give, willing to share, [19][a]storing up for themselves a good foundation for the time to come, that they may lay hold on eternal life.

GUARD THE FAITH

[20]O Timothy! [a]Guard what was committed to your trust, [b]avoiding the

13 [a] John 18:36, 37

15 [1] *Sovereign*

16 [a] Dan. 2:22
[b] John 6:46

17 [a] Jer. 9:23; 48:7
[b] Eccl. 5:18, 19

19 [a] [Matt. 6:20, 21; 19:21]

20 [a] [2 Tim. 1:12, 14]
[b] Titus 1:14
[1] *empty chatter*

1 Tim. 6:17–19

TRUSTING RICHES

Wealthy people learn that they can count on their riches to help them out of a lot of problem situations. Money can buy you a lot, and it is easy for those who have a lot of money to trust in their riches. But Paul told Timothy to warn wealthy people to not trust in those riches but to trust in the living God, who is richer than they can imagine. They should use their earthly resources to help others, thus storing up treasure in heaven.

All of the toys one might accumulate here on earth mean nothing for eternity. Don't trust these earthly possessions. Invest in the kingdom of God, and you'll have riches where it counts most.

profane *and* [1]idle babblings and contradictions of what is falsely called knowledge— [21]by professing it some have strayed concerning the faith.
Grace *be* with you. Amen.

THE SECOND EPISTLE OF PAUL THE APOSTLE TO

TIMOTHY

INTRODUCTION

This book was written by Paul from his Roman prison cell. He knew his death was imminent, and he wanted to give some last-minute instructions to his young protégé Timothy. This was the last book Paul wrote, probably in AD 67. As his last recorded words, we see a more personal communication from Paul than any of his other books. When you know your time is short you have a tendency to boil everything down to what matters most, and that is what Paul did here.

Timothy was serving as the pastor in Ephesus, and Paul really wanted to see him one more time before his death. He had been deserted by others; and he knew Timothy was a true friend, who was like a son to Paul. Paul was unabashed in this letter as he declared his affection for Timothy and his need of him. There was a certain sadness, as Paul talked about his race being almost over, but there was also the strong declaration that he knew he had finished his race and kept the faith. Paul really wanted to see Timothy, as soon as possible, but if Timothy wasn't able to make it to Rome before Paul was martyred, he wanted to give him some final instructions and to share his heart once more.

Paul warned Timothy against the many false teachings that were going around. He challenged Timothy to remain faithful and loyal to the gospel. But if there is one thing that stands out in this book more than anything else, it is Paul's exhortation to Timothy to preach the Word. Paul knew that if Timothy would stick with the Word, everything else would be taken care of. And staying in the Word is still the key to being consistent, faithful, loyal, and solidly dependable.

There are many other ideas out there that tempt young ministers to turn aside, and to grab onto the latest gimmick. There are thousands of books being written that profess to give instructions for living your life or for leading a church. But there is still just one book that is the key, and that is the Bible. And I can't think of a better piece of advice to leave to the next generation than "Preach the Word!"

GREETING

1 Paul, an apostle of [1]Jesus Christ by the will of God, according to the [a]promise of life which is in Christ Jesus,

[2]To Timothy, a [a]beloved son:

Grace, mercy, *and* peace from God the Father and Christ Jesus our Lord.

TIMOTHY'S FAITH AND HERITAGE

[3]I thank God, whom I serve with a pure conscience, as *my* [a]forefathers *did*, as without ceasing I remember you in my prayers night and day, [4]greatly desiring to see you, being mindful of your tears, that I may be filled with joy, [5]when I call to remembrance [a]the [1]genuine faith that is in you, which dwelt

2 Tim. 1:3

PRAYERS NIGHT AND DAY

Paul, no doubt, had a tremendous prayer life. He often mentioned to the churches he was writing to that he was praying for them constantly, and here he tells Timothy that he prayed for him "night and day." Of course, when you are in jail, chained to a Roman soldier, there isn't much else to do other than to pray. But Paul realized that, although he was stuck in a jail cell, yet through prayer he could still be touching the world for Christ.

That is one of the glorious things about prayer. It is not limited to space or geography. Prayers can travel and do a work for God around the world. I wonder if God doesn't sometimes take us out of circulation for a time in order that we might be used in a greater way through prayer.

---

first in your grandmother Lois and ᵇyour mother Eunice, and I am persuaded is in you also. ⁶Therefore I remind you ᵃto stir up the gift of God which is in you through the laying on of my hands. ⁷For ᵃGod has not given us a spirit of fear, ᵇbut of power and of love and of a sound mind.

NOT ASHAMED OF THE GOSPEL

⁸ᵃTherefore do not be ashamed of ᵇthe testimony of our Lord, nor of me ᶜHis prisoner, but share with me in the sufferings for the gospel according to the power of God, ⁹who has saved us and called *us* with a holy calling, ᵃnot according to our works, but ᵇaccording to His own purpose and grace which was given to us in Christ Jesus ᶜbefore time began, ¹⁰but ᵃhas now been revealed by the appearing of our Savior Jesus Christ, *who* has abolished death and brought life and immortality to light through the gospel, ¹¹ᵃto which I was appointed a

---

5 ᵇActs 16:1

6 ᵃ1Tim. 4:14

7 ᵃRom. 8:15
ᵇ[Acts 1:8]

8 ᵃ[Rom. 1:16]
ᵇ1Tim. 2:6
ᶜEph. 3:1

9 ᵃ[Rom. 3:20]
ᵇRom. 8:28
ᶜRom. 16:25

10 ᵃEph. 1:9

11 ᵃActs 9:15
¹NU omits *of the Gentiles*

12 ᵃ1Pet. 4:19

13 ᵃTitus 1:9
ᵇRom. 2:20;
6:17
ᶜ1Tim. 6:3

---

preacher, an apostle, and a teacher ¹of the Gentiles. ¹²For this reason I also suffer these things; nevertheless I am not ashamed, ᵃfor I know whom I have believed and am persuaded that He is able to keep what I have committed to Him until that Day.

2 Tim. 1:12

Committed to Him. The word for "committed" is the same word you would use to refer to a deposit that was given to the bank. You trust the bank to keep your money safe, and to pay interest on that money.

Paul said that on the basis of his personal knowledge of God, he has committed his whole life to Him and knows that his commitment is a wise decision and will be worth it, whether he lives or dies. Total commitment to the God who is able!

BE LOYAL TO THE FAITH

¹³ᵃHold fast ᵇthe pattern of ᶜsound words which you have heard from me, in faith and love which are in Christ Jesus. ¹⁴That good thing which was committed to you, keep by the Holy Spirit who dwells in us. ¹⁵This you know, that all those in Asia have turned away from me, among whom are Phygellus and Hermogenes. ¹⁶The Lord grant mercy to

2 Tim. 1:6–7

Stirring Up Your Gifts. The Greek word that is here translated "stir up" is a word that was used to describe stirring up the dying embers of a fire, to stoke them back into flames. You would stir up the coals, and add fresh wood to the fire.

It would appear that Paul was concerned that Timothy might perhaps be in danger of letting his gifts die off into embers, perhaps as a result of fear. Timothy needed to keep the fire in his heart burning strong, not allowing his gifts to go dormant. We all need this reminder.

the [a]household of Onesiphorus, for he often refreshed me, and was not ashamed of my chain; [17]but when he arrived in Rome, he sought me out very zealously and found *me*. [18]The Lord [a]grant to him that he may find mercy from the Lord [b]in that Day—and you know very well how many ways he [c]ministered [1]*to me* at Ephesus.

BE STRONG IN GRACE

2 You therefore, [a]my son, [b]be strong in the grace that is in Christ Jesus. [2]And the things that you have heard from me among many witnesses, commit these to faithful men who will be able to teach others also. [3]You therefore must [a]endure[1] hardship [b]as a good soldier of Jesus Christ. [4] [a]No one engaged in warfare entangles himself with the affairs of *this* life, that he may please him who enlisted him as a soldier. [5]And also [a]if anyone competes in athletics, he is not crowned unless he competes according to the rules. [6]The hardworking farmer must be first to partake of the crops. [7]Consider what I say, and [1]may the Lord [a]give you understanding in all things.

[8]Remember that Jesus Christ, [a]of the seed of David, [b]was raised from the dead [c]according to my gospel, [9] [a]for which I suffer trouble as an evildoer, [b]*even* to the point of chains; [c]but the word [a]of God is not chained. [10]Therefore [a]I endure all things for the sake of the [1]elect, [b]that they also may obtain the salvation which is in Christ Jesus with eternal glory.

16 [a] 2 Tim. 4:19
18 [a] Mark 9:41
[b] 2 Thess. 1:10
[c] Heb. 6:10
[1] *to me* from Vg., a few Gr. mss.

CHAPTER 2

1 [a] 1 Tim. 1:2
[b] Eph. 6:10
3 [a] 2 Tim. 4:5
[b] 1 Tim. 1:18
[1] NU *You must share*
4 [a] [2 Pet. 2:20]
5 [a] [1 Cor. 9:25]
7 [a] Prov. 2:6
[1] NU *the Lord will give you*
8 [a] Rom. 1:3, 4
[b] 1 Cor. 15:4
[c] Rom. 2:16
9 [a] Acts 9:16
[b] Eph. 3:1
[c] Acts 28:31
10 [a] Eph. 3:13
[b] 2 Cor. 1:6
[1] *chosen ones*
11 [a] Rom. 6:5, 8
12 [a] [Rom. 5:17; 8:17]
[b] Matt. 10:33
13 [a] Num. 23:19
14 [a] Titus 3:9
[1] *battle*
15 [a] 2 Pet. 1:10

[11]*This is* a faithful saying:

> For [a]if we died with *Him*,
> We shall also live with *Him*.
> [12] [a]If we endure,
> We shall also reign with *Him*.
> [b]If we deny *Him*,
> He also will deny us.
> [13] If we are faithless,
> He remains faithful;
> He [a]cannot deny Himself.

APPROVED AND DISAPPROVED WORKERS

[14]Remind *them* of these things, [a]charging *them* before the Lord not to [1]strive about words to no profit, to the ruin of the hearers. [15] [a]Be diligent to present yourself approved to God, a worker who does not need to be ashamed, rightly dividing the word of truth. [16]But shun profane *and* [1]idle babblings, for they will [2]increase to more ungodliness. [17]And their message will spread like cancer. [a]Hymenaeus and Philetus are of this sort, [18]who have strayed concerning the truth, [a]saying that the resurrection is already past; and they overthrow the faith of some. [19]Nevertheless [a]the solid foundation of God stands, having this seal: "The Lord [b]knows those who are His," and, "Let everyone who names the name of [1]Christ depart from iniquity."

[20]But in a great house there are not only [a]vessels of gold and silver, but also

16 [1] *empty chatter* [2] *lead*　**17** [a] 1 Tim. 1:20　**18** [a] 1 Cor. 15:12　**19** [a] [1 Cor. 3:11] [b] [Nah. 1:7] [1] NU, M *the Lord*　**20** [a] Rom. 9:21

HOW THE WORD SPREADS　　2 Tim. 2:2

Paul shows the pattern of ministry here. Paul taught Timothy and others, who in turn passed the Word on to other faithful men who will teach others.

People who are taught will teach others. I have had such a great personal thrill in my life to see people who were sitting in the pews at Calvary Chapel Costa Mesa, soaking up the teaching of the Word, then going out to start churches all over the world.

But it hasn't stopped there. Each of the churches that was started from our church then becomes its own sending base; and men like Mike MacIntosh, Greg Laurie, Skip Heitzig, and so many others, who initially were taught the Word here at Calvary, have themselves raised up those who were taught by them and sent them out to start other churches. Every year at our pastors conferences I am amazed to see how many more new churches there are, many of them third or fourth generation from us, and yet they are thriving ministries that are carrying on what the Lord has done here in Costa Mesa.

I have sometimes been asked how I feel about the fact that there are so many Calvary Chapel pastors who I don't know and have never even met. The truth is, I love it! It just shows that things are working the way they are supposed to, and that this is a move of the Spirit and not a personality cult.

2 Tim. 2:15

Approved to God. In the old King James Version, this verse said, "Study to show thyself approved unto God." Here we have "be diligent," and both phrases convey the message that we are to work at pleasing God. Learning the Word takes time and effort, if we are to "rightly divide the word of truth," which could also be translated "accurately handle the Word of truth."

As we read the Word of God, and study it, God is pleased. He approves when we work on our knowledge and understanding of the Bible.

of wood and clay, some for honor and some for dishonor. 21Therefore if anyone cleanses himself from the latter, he will be a vessel for honor, 1sanctified and useful for the Master, aprepared for every good work. 22aFlee also youthful lusts; but pursue righteousness, faith, love, peace with those who call on the Lord out of a pure heart. 23But avoid foolish and ignorant disputes, knowing that they generate strife. 24And aa servant of the Lord must not quarrel but be gentle to all, bable to teach, cpatient, 25ain humility correcting those who are in opposition, bif God perhaps will

2 Tim. 2:20–21

Vessels of Honor. In biblical days, people didn't have plumbing, so pots were used for many different purposes. Certain pots were set aside for drinking water or for food. Other pots were used to collect the dirty water and the garbage and refuse. You wouldn't want to confuse these different vessels, and you certainly wouldn't mix their uses.

Paul here exhorted Timothy to keep himself pure. Once a pot was used for refuse, it would be a vessel of dishonor, not fit for higher uses. We need to keep ourselves pure and fit for the Master's use.

---

21 a 2 Tim. 3:17
1 set apart

22 a 1 Tim. 6:11

24 a Titus 3:2
b Titus 1:9
c 1 Tim. 3:3

25 a Gal. 6:1
b Acts 8:22
c 1 Tim. 2:4

26 a 1 Tim. 3:7

CHAPTER 3

1 a 1 Tim. 4:1
1 times of stress

3 1 irreconcilable

4 a 2 Pet. 2:10

5 a Titus 1:16
b 1 Tim. 5:8

---

grant them repentance, cso that they may know the truth, 26and *that* they may come to their senses *and* aescape the snare of the devil, having been taken captive by him to do his will.

PERILOUS TIMES AND PERILOUS MEN

3 But know this, that ain the last days 1perilous times will come: 2For men will be lovers of themselves, lovers of money, boasters, proud, blasphemers, disobedient to parents, unthankful, unholy, 3unloving, 1unforgiving, slanderers, without self-control, brutal, despisers of good, 4atraitors, headstrong, haughty, lovers of pleasure rather than lovers of God, 5ahaving a form of godliness but bdenying its

---

2 Tim. 3:5

A FORM OF GODLINESS

"Having a form of godliness but denying its power." That is an accurate description of much of the church today. They observe rituals, and have a form of godliness, but there is no power there. Churches have often just become social centers, where you can get some entertaining messages dealing with psychological issues, and hear some inspiring music, but the power of God is lacking.

You can learn all the practical steps toward having a better life, how to communicate, how to quit smoking, how to raise your children, how to invest your money, and it is often good advice; but the power of God is left out. Jesus said, "Without Me you can do nothing" (John 15:5).

Our first and foremost need is to realize that we need the power of the Holy Spirit working in our lives. To ignore that is at best teaching people how to get along in life without God, and without Him we can't do anything meaningful.

power. And cfrom such people turn away! 6For aof this sort are those who creep into households and make captives of gullible women loaded down with sins, led away by various lusts, 7always learning and never able ato come to the knowledge of the truth. 8aNow as Jannes and Jambres resisted Moses, so do these also resist the truth: bmen of corrupt minds, cdisapproved concerning the faith; 9but they will progress no further, for their folly will be manifest to all, aas theirs also was.

THE MAN OF GOD AND THE WORD OF GOD

10aBut you have carefully followed my doctrine, manner of life, purpose, faith, longsuffering, love, perseverance, 11persecutions, afflictions, which happened to me aat Antioch, bat Iconium, cat Lystra—what persecutions I endured. And dout of them all the Lord delivered me. 12Yes, and aall who desire to live godly in Christ Jesus will suffer persecution. 13aBut evil men and impostors will grow worse and worse, deceiving and being deceived.

2 Tim. 3:12

A PROMISE OF PERSECUTION

This is one of my least favorite promises in the Bible. I don't think anyone prints this promise on a promise card or in a book of promises, but it is a promise just the same. "All who desire to live godly in Christ Jesus will suffer persecution." You can't escape it, so don't even try.

Jesus said, "If the world hates you, you know that it hated Me before it hated you. If you were of the world, the world would love its own. Yet because you are not of the world, but I chose you out of the world, therefore the world hates you" (John 15:18–19). It is a dangerous thing to try to curry favor from the world. If you seek godliness, you will be persecuted.

---

5 c 2 Thess. 3:6

6 a Matt. 23:14

7 a 1 Tim. 2:4

8 a Ex. 7:11, 12, 22; 8:7; 9:11
b 1 Tim. 6:5
c Rom. 1:28

9 a Ex. 7:11, 12; 8:18; 9:11

10 a 1 Tim. 4:6

11 a Acts 13:44–52
b Acts 14:1–6, 19
c Acts 14:8–20
d Ps. 34:19

12 a [Ps. 34:19]

13 a 2 Thess. 2:11

14 a 2 Tim. 1:13

15 a John 5:39

16 a [2 Pet. 1:20]
b Rom. 4:23; 15:4
1 training, discipline

17 a 1 Tim. 6:11
b 2 Tim. 2:21

CHAPTER 4

1 a 1 Tim. 5:21
b Acts 10:42
1 NU omits therefore
2 NU and by

2 a Titus 2:15
b 1 Tim. 5:20
c 1 Tim. 4:13

3 a 2 Tim. 3:1
b 1 Tim. 1:10
c 2 Tim. 3:6

4 a 1 Tim. 1:4

5 a 2 Tim. 1:8
b Acts 21:8

14But you must acontinue in the things which you have learned and been assured of, knowing from whom you have learned them, 15and that from childhood you have known athe Holy Scriptures, which are able to make you wise for salvation through faith which is in Christ Jesus.

16aAll Scripture is given by inspiration of God, band is profitable for doctrine, for reproof, for correction, 1instruction in righteousness, 17athat the man of God may be complete, bthoroughly equipped for every good work.

2 Tim. 3:16–17

ALL SCRIPTURE

How much of the Scriptures are inspired by God and profitable for us? All!

There are those today who would take away parts of the Bible as they decide which parts are inspired and which aren't. "Let's take a vote of the scholars, to decide what Jesus really said."

How presumptuous and foolish to throw out parts of the Bible. It is all inspired and without error, and we need every word of it. This is why we study all the way through the Bible. We want to be completely equipped for every good work.

PREACH THE WORD

4 I acharge you 1therefore before God and the Lord Jesus Christ, bwho will judge the living and the dead 2at His appearing and His kingdom: 2Preach the word! Be ready in season and out of season. aConvince, brebuke, cexhort, with all longsuffering and teaching. 3aFor the time will come when they will not endure bsound doctrine, cbut according to their own desires, because they have itching ears, they will heap up for themselves teachers; 4and they will turn their ears away from the truth, and abe turned aside to fables. 5But you be watchful in all things, aendure afflictions, do the work of ban evangelist, fulfill your ministry.

2 Tim. 4:2

PREACH THE WORD!

Paul reiterated over and over to Timothy the importance of sticking to the Word of God in his preaching.

God's Word is so versatile. It can help convince us that God's way is better than our way. It can rebuke us, correcting our many errors when we get off track. It also exhorts us, as it encourages us to keep going and to not quit. And it communicates with the patience of a good teacher, "with all longsuffering and teaching."

In season and out of season, the Bible is always timely.

PAUL'S VALEDICTORY

6For aI am already being poured out as a drink offering, and the time of bmy departure is at hand. 7aI have fought the good fight, I have finished the race, I have kept the faith. 8Finally, there is laid up for me athe crown of righteousness, which the Lord, the righteous bJudge, will give to me con that Day, and not to me only but also to all who have loved His appearing.

THE ABANDONED APOSTLE

9Be diligent to come to me quickly; 10for aDemas has forsaken me, bhaving loved this present world, and has departed for Thessalonica—Crescens for Galatia, Titus for Dalmatia. 11Only Luke is with me. Get aMark and bring him with you, for he is useful to me for ministry. 12And aTychicus I have sent to Ephesus. 13Bring the cloak that I left with Carpus at Troas when you come—and the books, especially the parchments.

14aAlexander the coppersmith did me much harm. May the Lord repay him according to his works. 15You also must beware of him, for he has greatly resisted our words.

Cross references (center column)

6 a Phil. 2:17
b [Phil. 1:23]

7 a 1 Cor. 9:24–27

8 a James 1:12
b John 5:22
c 2 Tim. 1:12

10 a Col. 4:14
b 1 John 2:15

11 a Acts 12:12, 25; 15:37–39

12 a Acts 20:4

14 a 1 Tim. 1:20

16 a Acts 7:60

17 a Acts 23:11
b Acts 9:15
c 1 Sam. 17:37

18 a Ps. 121:7
b Rom. 11:36

19 a Acts 18:2
b 2 Tim. 1:16

20 a Rom. 16:23
b Acts 20:4; 21:29 22 1 NU omits *Jesus Christ*

2 Tim. 4:3–4

ITCHING EARS

Paul prophesied of a coming day when audiences would insist on only hearing teaching that is easy to listen to—teaching that only tells them what they want to hear. He described this as "having itching ears."

This is a graphic description of the "seeker friendly" movement within the church today. Entertain the people, and tell them what they want to hear. It is like cotton candy, sweet to the taste but without substance. Paul warned against the day when "church lite" takes the place of sound doctrine. If that happens no one will ever be truly changed, and change is what we really need.

16At my first defense no one stood with me, but all forsook me. aMay it not be charged against them.

THE LORD IS FAITHFUL

17aBut the Lord stood with me and strengthened me, bso that the message might be preached fully through me, and *that* all the Gentiles might hear. Also I was delivered cout of the mouth of the lion. 18aAnd the Lord will deliver me from every evil work and preserve *me* for His heavenly kingdom. bTo Him *be* glory forever and ever. Amen!

COME BEFORE WINTER

19Greet aPrisca and Aquila, and the household of bOnesiphorus. 20aErastus stayed in Corinth, but bTrophimus I have left in Miletus sick.

21Do your utmost to come before winter.

Eubulus greets you, as well as Pudens, Linus, Claudia, and all the brethren.

FAREWELL

22The Lord 1Jesus Christ be with your spirit. Grace be with you. Amen.

INTRODUCTION

This is the third of Paul's Pastoral Epistles. The two letters to Timothy and this letter to Titus were personal letters written to pastors, to instruct them concerning the conduct of the church and the ministers.

We don't know much about Titus. He isn't mentioned in the book of Acts. We know that he traveled with Paul and that Paul used him to deliver the second letter to the Corinthians and that he was also the one who collected money for the needy church in Jerusalem. One of the first outreaches of Paul was to the island of Crete, and Paul eventually sent Titus there to help get the church established.

As Paul was writing this letter to Titus, Paul was probably in Macedonia, while Titus was in Crete. It is thought that this letter was written around AD 62, probably at about the same time Paul wrote his first letter to Timothy.

In Titus 1:5, Paul says that he left Titus in Crete so that he could "set in order the things that are lacking, and appoint elders in every city." So the emphasis of this book is the orderliness and organization of the church and the qualifications of the leaders of the church. He also exhorted the church to live a life of grace and to demonstrate it by their good works.

As he described the qualifications for church leaders, Paul reminded Titus that the proper perspective of any church leader is "looking for the blessed hope and glorious appearing of our great God and Savior Jesus Christ" (Titus 2:13). Besides being one of the strongest declarations of the deity of Jesus Christ in the New Testament, this verse also reminds us to keep our eye on the sky, waiting for the rapture of the church and living our lives knowing that Jesus could come back at any time.

Paul really packed some precious jewels into this short book, and it should be read often by every Christian and especially by every church leader or pastor.

GREETING

CHAPTER 1

1 Paul, a bondservant of God and an apostle of Jesus Christ, according to the faith of God's elect and ^athe acknowledgment of the truth ^bwhich accords with godliness, ²in hope of eternal life which God, who ^acannot lie, promised before time began, ³but has in due time manifested His word through preaching, which was committed to me according to the commandment of God our Savior;

⁴To ^aTitus, a true son in *our* common faith:

Grace, mercy, *and* peace from God the Father and ¹the Lord Jesus Christ our Savior.

QUALIFIED ELDERS

⁵For this reason I left you in Crete, that you should ^aset in order the things that are lacking, and appoint elders in every city as I commanded you— ⁶if a man is blameless, the husband of one

1 ^a2Tim. 2:25
^b[1Tim. 3:16]

2 ^aNum. 23:19

4 ^a2Cor. 2:13;
8:23
1NU *Christ Jesus*

5 ^a1Cor. 11:34

Titus 1:2

Hope of Eternal Life. When the Bible uses the word "hope," it isn't referring to hope the way we tend to use the word. It refers to something that is certain.

Today I have the hope of eternal life, through Jesus Christ. He died in order that I might experience the life of God. God imparts His eternal life to me; and as He imparts that life to me, I have the hope and the certainty for the future. I'm going to spend eternity in the kingdom of God!

wife, [a]having faithful children not accused of [1]dissipation or insubordination. [7]For a [1]bishop must be blameless, as a steward of God, not self-willed, not quick-tempered, [a]not given to wine, not violent, not greedy for money, [8]but hospitable, a lover of what is good, sober-minded, just, holy, self-controlled, [9]holding fast the faithful word as he has been taught, that he may be able, by sound doctrine, both to exhort and convict those who contradict.

THE ELDERS' TASK

[10]For there are many insubordinate, both idle [a]talkers and deceivers, especially those of the circumcision, [11]whose mouths must be stopped, who subvert whole households, teaching things which they ought not, [a]for the sake of dishonest gain. [12][a]One of them, a prophet of their own, said, "Cretans *are* always liars, evil beasts, lazy gluttons." [13]This testimony is true. [a]There-

6 [a] 1 Tim. 3:2–4
[1] *debauchery,* lit. *incorrigibility*

7 [a] Lev. 10:9
[1] Lit. *overseer*

10 [a] James 1:26

11 [a] 1 Tim. 6:5

12 [a] Acts 17:28

13 [a] 2 Cor. 13:10

14 [a] Is. 29:13

15 [a] 1 Cor. 6:12

16 [a] Matt. 7:20–23; 25:12
[b] [2 Tim. 3:5, 7]
[c] Rom. 1:28
[1] *detestable*

fore rebuke them sharply, that they may be sound in the faith, [14]not giving heed to Jewish fables and [a]commandments of men who turn from the truth. [15][a]To the pure all things are pure, but to those who are defiled and unbelieving nothing is pure; but even their mind and conscience are defiled. [16]They profess to [a]know God, but [b]in works they deny *Him,* being [1]abominable, disobedient, [c]and disqualified for every good work.

Titus 1:16

Professing to Know God. Many people today profess to know God. It is always interesting to me whenever I read about the nation-wide polls that show how many people in this country consider themselves to be Christians.

The vast majority of Americans profess to know God and to believe in Him. But if they really knew God they wouldn't be living the way they are. Our country would be radically different. Like the people in Paul's day, there are many who "profess to know God, but in works they deny Him." Talk is cheap.

QUALITIES OF A SOUND CHURCH

2 But as for you, speak the things which are proper for sound doctrine: [2]that the older men be sober, reverent, temperate, sound in faith, in love, in patience; [3]the older women likewise, that they be reverent in behavior, not slanderers, not given to

TO THE PURE
Titus 1:15

If your heart is pure before God, all things are pure. But for a person whose mind is corrupt and polluted, everything is filthy. How important it is that we keep our minds pure and undefiled. Paul said in Philippians 4:8 to meditate on the things that are true, noble, just, pure, lovely, of good report, virtuous, and praiseworthy. When we do that, he says, "the God of peace will be with you" (v. 9).

But for those who allow their minds to dwell on impure thoughts, they will always live with the worldly pollution of a corrupt mind. To those who watch worldly entertainment, and who hang around with people who talk dirty, and who listen to filthy jokes and stories, their minds become corrupted, and everything they hear sounds dirty. It is so hard to get something filthy out of your mind, once you put it in.

But if you remain pure, your mind will be uncorrupted, and you will see things and hear things in the best and most positive light possible. A pure mind is a glorious thing!

Titus 2:3

TEACHING GOOD THINGS

Paul exhorts the older women to be "teachers of good things." By the time we get older, we have gained a lot of experiences. We've been through the University of Hard Knocks. As we've learned a lot of hard lessons, it is so important that we pass those lessons on to the next generation in such a way that they can benefit, and be encouraged.

It is sometimes easy for older people to become bitter and angry, about the difficult times they've had. But it is important that we pass on good things to the next generation, giving them an enthusiasm and optimism about the future, and about what God will do. Remember, the gospel is "good news."

much wine, teachers of good things— 4that they admonish the young women to love their husbands, to love their children, 5to be discreet, chaste, ahomemakers, good, bobedient to their own husbands, cthat the word of God may not be blasphemed.

6Likewise, exhort the young men to be sober-minded, 7in all things showing yourself to be aa pattern of good works; in doctrine showing integrity, reverence, bincorruptibility,1 8sound speech that cannot be condemned, that one who is an opponent may be ashamed, having nothing evil to say of 1you.

9Exhort abondservants to be obedient to their own masters, to be well pleasing in all things, not answering back, 10not 1pilfering, but showing all good 2fidelity, that they may adorn the doctrine of God our Savior in all things.

TRAINED BY SAVING GRACE

11For athe grace of God that brings salvation has appeared to all men, 12teaching us that, denying ungodliness and worldly lusts, we should live soberly, righteously, and godly in the

CHAPTER 2

5 a 1 Tim. 5:14
b 1 Cor. 14:34
c Rom. 2:24

7 a 1 Tim. 4:12
b Eph. 6:24
1 NU omits
incorruptibility

8 1 NU, M us

9 a 1 Tim. 6:1

10 1 thieving
2 honesty

11 a [Rom. 5:15]

13 a 1 Cor. 1:7
b [Col. 3:4]

present age, 13alooking for the blessed bhope and glorious appearing of our great God and Savior Jesus Christ, 14awho gave Himself for us, that He might redeem us from every lawless deed band purify for Himself cHis own special people, zealous for good works. 15Speak these things, aexhort, and rebuke with all authority. Let no one despise you.

GRACES OF THE HEIRS OF GRACE

3Remind them ato be subject to rulers and authorities, to obey, bto be ready for every good work, 2to speak evil of no one, to be peaceable, gentle, showing all humility to all men. 3For awe ourselves were also once foolish, disobedient, deceived, serving various lusts and pleasures, living in malice and envy, hateful and hating one another. 4But when athe kindness and the love of bGod our Savior toward man appeared, 5anot by works of righteousness which we have done, but according to His mercy He saved us, through bthe washing of regeneration and renewing of the Holy Spirit,

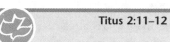

Titus 2:11–12

WHAT GRACE TEACHES US

How thankful we are for the grace of God! But what does it teach us?

First of all, it teaches us to "deny ungodliness and worldly lusts." Some people think that the grace of God teaches us that we can do whatever we want because grace covers it. But the lesson of grace is that we can be free from our sinful nature and deny the pull of the flesh. That is what true gratitude for grace will do.

This then teaches us to live "soberly, righteously, and godly in this present age." Grace teaches me to live in a way that pleases the One who showed grace to me by dying for me. He died for me, so I want to live for Him..

6 ªwhom He poured out on us abundantly through Jesus Christ our Savior, 7that having been justified by His grace ªwe should become heirs according to the hope of eternal life.

8 ªThis is a faithful saying, and these things I want you to affirm constantly, that those who have believed in God should be careful to maintain good works. These things are good and profitable to men.

AVOID DISSENSION

9But ªavoid foolish disputes, genealogies, contentions, and strivings about the law; for they are unprofitable and useless. 10ªReject a divisive man after the first and second ¹admonition, 11knowing that such a person is warped and sinning, being self-condemned.

FINAL MESSAGES

12When I send Artemas to you, or ªTychicus, be diligent to come to me at Nicopolis, for I have decided to spend the winter there. 13Send Zenas the lawyer and ªApollos on their journey

Titus 3:1

SUBJECT TO RULERS

The Bible does not teach civil disobedience. It teaches us to be in subjection to those in authority over us. Paul said in Romans 13:1, "Let every soul be subject to the governing authorities. For there is no authority except from God, and the authorities that exist are appointed by God."

This doesn't mean that God always allows good men to reign. When Paul wrote this, Nero was in charge in Rome. God sometimes allows evil men to reign, as a way of judging sin and causing His people to turn back to Him. Our role is to submit to our leaders, and to be good citizens, unless they order us to do something that directly contradicts the commandments of God, in which case "we ought to obey God rather than men" (Acts 5:29).

---

14 ª Gal. 1:4
b [Heb. 1:3; 9:14]
c Ex. 15:16

15 ª 2 Tim. 4:2

CHAPTER 3

1 ª 1 Pet. 2:13
b Col. 1:10

3 ª 1 Cor. 6:11

4 ª Titus 2:11
b 1 Tim. 2:3

5 ª [Rom. 3:20]
b John 3:3

6 ª Ezek. 36:26

7 ª [Rom. 8:17, 23, 24]

8 ª 1 Tim. 1:15

9 ª 2 Tim. 2:23

10 ª Matt. 18:17 ¹ warning

12 ª Acts 20:4

13 ª Acts 18:24

Titus 3:5

Renewing of the Spirit. The Holy Spirit is in the process of transforming us from what we used to be into what God wants us to be. I'm not yet complete, as far as my progress is concerned, but the process of renewal is underway, to conform me into the image of Jesus Christ. I'm not what I should be but, thank God, I'm not what I used to be, and I know that since God has begun a good work in me, He will finish it (Phil. 1:6). He is in the process of making me new!

with haste, that they may lack nothing. 14And let our *people* also learn to maintain good works, to *meet* urgent needs, that they may not be unfruitful.

FAREWELL

15All who *are* with me greet you. Greet those who love us in the faith. Grace *be* with you all. Amen.

Titus 3:14

MAINTAIN FRUITFULNESS

God's purpose for your life is that you would be fruitful. Jesus said that the Father is glorified when you "bear much fruit" (John 15:8).

It is a good idea for us to look at our lives once in a while to see if we are really bearing fruit for the kingdom of God. Jesus said that if a branch doesn't bear fruit it is taken away (John 15:2).

God left us here to bear fruit. It is important that we fulfill our purpose by "maintain[ing] good works" so that we "may not be unfruitful."

THE EPISTLE OF PAUL THE APOSTLE TO

PHILEMON

INTRODUCTION The epistle to Philemon is the last of the Prison Epistles, written while Paul was imprisoned in Rome. It was a personal letter addressed to a wealthy Christian named Philemon who had been converted probably while Paul was ministering in Ephesus. Philemon had a church meeting at his home in Colosse, which was in present-day Turkey. There is no biblical record of Paul ever visiting Colosse, but it is apparent that the church was started by some of his converts and that they looked to him as their spiritual leader.

Philemon was a slave owner; and one of his slaves, Onesimus, had run away. Onesimus had probably headed to Rome, as it would be easy to get lost in the big city; but while in Rome, he must have encountered Paul and gotten saved. Paul had encouraged Onesimus to go back to his owner, Philemon, to make restitution for leaving while owing Philemon. But in sending him back, Paul gave him this letter to take to Philemon, in which he encouraged Philemon to accept Onesimus as a brother rather than a slave. Paul told Philemon that if Onesimus owed him anything to charge it to Paul's account. Philemon owed Paul his eternal life, and Paul figured that should cover it.

Besides being an interesting historical anecdote, this book illustrates several important points. First of all, it demonstrates the radical truth that God makes all people, whether slaves or free, one in Christ. The book also shows the importance of restitution after a person comes to Christ. And finally it illustrates the freedom that is in Christ, as He loosens the chains that bind all those who don't know Him.

GREETING

Paul, a ᵃprisoner of Christ Jesus, and Timothy *our* brother,

To Philemon our beloved *friend* and fellow laborer, [2]to [1]the beloved Apphia, ᵃArchippus our fellow soldier, and to the church in your house:

[3]Grace to you and peace from God our Father and the Lord Jesus Christ.

PHILEMON'S LOVE AND FAITH

[4]ᵃI thank my God, making mention of you always in my prayers, [5]ᵃhearing of your love and faith which you have toward the Lord Jesus and toward all the saints, [6]that the sharing of your faith may become effective ᵃby the acknowledgment of ᵇevery good thing which is

in [1]you in Christ Jesus. [7]For we [1]have great [2]joy and [3]consolation in your love, because the [4]hearts of the saints have been refreshed by you, brother.

THE PLEA FOR ONESIMUS

[8]Therefore, though I might be very bold in Christ to command you what is fitting, [9]yet for love's sake I rather appeal *to you*—being such a one as Paul, the aged, and now also a prisoner of Jesus Christ— [10]I appeal to you for my son ᵃOnesimus, whom I have begotten *while* in my chains, [11]who once was unprofitable to you, but now is profitable to you and to me. [12]I am sending him [1]back. You therefore receive him, that is, my own [2]heart, [13]whom I wished to keep with

1 ᵃEph. 3:1
2 ᵃCol. 4:17
[1] NU *our sister* Apphia
4 ᵃ2 Thess. 1:3
5 ᵃCol. 1:4
6 ᵃPhil. 1:9
  ᵇ[1 Thess. 5:18]
7 [1] NU had
  [2] M thanksgiving
  [3] comfort
  [4] Lit. *inward parts, heart, liver, and lungs*
10 ᵃCol. 4:9
12 [1] NU *back to you in person, that is, my own heart,*

Philem. 1

A Prisoner of Christ Jesus.

Notice, Paul didn't say, "Paul, a prisoner of the Roman government." He was a prisoner of Jesus Christ. It was his love for Jesus that had placed him in bondage.

It makes such a difference in how you regard your chains and limitations. If you are a prisoner of Rome then you can sit there in your cell and sulk. But if a prisoner of Jesus, you rejoice! I'm a prisoner of Jesus! I'm bound by Him!

me, that on your behalf he might minister to me in my chains for the gospel. [14]But without your consent I wanted to do nothing, [a]that your good deed might not be by compulsion, as it were, but voluntary. [15]For perhaps he departed for a while for this *purpose*, that you might receive him forever, [16]no longer as a slave but

Philem. 8–10

APOSTOLIC AUTHORITY

Paul could have given a bold command to Philemon, appealing to his apostolic authority. But he didn't do that. Instead, he appealed "for love's sake" begging him to do the right thing for love.

It is tragic when church leaders appeal to their positions to exercise authority and wield power over people. The old maxim that "power corrupts" can sadly be demonstrated in the church, as well as in human secular government and in the business world.

Paul demonstrated, on the other hand, the servant leadership taught by Jesus. He didn't throw his weight around, but appealed to love. Godly leaders will always do that. Leaders who flex their muscles and intimidate people only show their lack of Christlikeness.

12 [2]See v. 7.

14 [a]2 Cor. 9:7

16 [a]Col. 3:22

19 [a]1 Cor. 16:21

21 [a]2 Cor. 7:16

22 [a]Phil. 1:25; 2:24
[b]2 Cor. 1:11

23 [a]Col. 1:7; 4:12

24 [a]Acts 12:12, 25; 15:37–39
[b]Acts 19:29; 27:2
[c]Col. 4:14
[d]2 Tim. 4:11

25 [a]2 Tim. 4:22

more than a slave—a beloved brother, especially to me but how much more to you, both in the [a]flesh and in the Lord.

PHILEMON'S OBEDIENCE ENCOURAGED

[17]If then you count me as a partner, receive him as *you would* me. [18]But if he has wronged you or owes anything, put that on my account. [19]I, Paul, am writing with my own [a]hand. I will repay—not to mention to you that you owe me even your own self besides. [20]Yes, brother, let me have joy from you in the Lord; refresh my heart in the Lord. [21][a]Having confidence in your obedience, I write to you, knowing that you will do even more than I say. [22]But, meanwhile, also prepare a guest room for me, for [a]I trust that [b]through your prayers I shall be granted to you.

Philem. 17–18

AN EXAMPLE OF INTERCESSION

Paul's intercession to Philemon, for the benefit of Onesimus, is a beautiful example of intercession, and a glorious picture of the intercession of Jesus before the Father on our behalf. Paul said, "Receive him as you would me"; in other words, "I will stand in his place."

Satan is the accuser of the brethren, accusing us before God day and night (Rev. 12:10). But Jesus Christ took our sins upon Himself, paying the penalty on our behalf. And He is at the right hand of the Father, making intercession for us (Heb. 7:25). "If he has wronged you or owes you anything, put that on My account."

FAREWELL

[23][a]Epaphras, my fellow prisoner in Christ Jesus, greets you, [24]*as do* [a]Mark, [b]Aristarchus, [c]Demas, [d]Luke, my fellow laborers.

[25][a]The grace of our Lord Jesus Christ *be* with your spirit. Amen.

THE EPISTLE TO THE
HEBREWS

INTRODUCTION The book of Hebrews was written to Jewish Christians. They had related to God under the old covenant, but now Jesus had come and introduced a new covenant, which was confusing for them. The Old Testament hadn't really prepared them for this transition, and it was difficult to find a balance.

This book outlines and establishes that Christianity is the natural successor to Judaism, and that Jesus is superior to angels, prophets, and past revelations of God. He is the fulfillment of the Law. Hebrews is one of the most systematic and doctrinal books in the New Testament, along with Romans. It paints a beautiful picture of Jesus Christ as our High Priest and God. For a Jewish audience, this book builds the bridge between the Old and New Testaments.

Hebrews addresses a very real danger to these new believers too. As Christianity was regarded more and more as a cult by the Jewish establishment and as they were beginning to undergo severe persecution, there was a great temptation for Jewish Christians to return to Judaism and turn away from Christianity. There were also attempts to make Christianity more Jewish, in order to make it more palatable to the establishment. This book addresses and corrects these errors. Christianity did flow forth as the natural progression from Judaism, but it is much more than Judaism. It is a new covenant.

The book doesn't tell us who wrote it or when it was written. It would seem almost certain that it would have had to have been written before AD 70, when the temple was destroyed, as a book that had so much to say about the temple would likely have mentioned such an event. There is much controversy as to who wrote the book. Tradition attributed it to the apostle Paul, and that is who I believe wrote it. Its style varies somewhat from Paul's, but that is to be expected because he was writing to an audience different from those addressed in his other epistles. Hebrews certainly contains a lot of teaching that agrees with Paul's other teachings, and the author was working with Timothy, according to Hebrews 13:23.

But whether or not Paul was the human author, the important thing is that the Holy Spirit wrote and inspired this book, and it is a treasure trove of blessing for us, as it paints a graphic picture of Jesus.

GOD'S SUPREME REVELATION

1 God, who [1]at various times and [a]in various ways spoke in time past to the fathers by the prophets, [2]has in these last days spoken to us by *His* Son,

CHAPTER 1

1 [a]Num. 12:6,
8
[1]Or *in many portions*

whom He has appointed heir of all things, through whom also He made the [1]worlds; [3][a]who being the brightness of *His* glory and the express

2 [1]Or *ages*, Gr. *aiones*, aeons   3 [a]John 1:14

bimage of His person, and cupholding all things by the word of His power, dwhen He had 1by Himself 2purged 3our sins, esat down at the right hand of the Majesty on high, 4having become so much better than the angels, as aHe has by inheritance obtained a more excellent name than they.

Heb. 1:3

Express Image. Jesus was the "express image" of the Person of God. He could say, "He who has seen Me has seen the Father" (John 14:9).

The Greek word used for "express image" is a word that referred to an image made when a signet ring is placed in wax, then applied to a document. It is an exact duplicate of the ring. So Jesus is exactly God. You couldn't express it any more strongly.

Heb. 1:4

Better Than the Angels. Jesus is "so much better than the angels." He is infinitely superior to the angels, as this chapter makes abundantly clear. Yet there are still those who teach that Jesus is an angel. The Jehovah's Witnesses teach that He is Michael the archangel. The Mormons teach that He is the brother of Lucifer; and since Lucifer is a fallen angel, this would make Jesus an angel, also. Any suggestion that Jesus is an angel is heresy. He created the angels and is much superior to them.

THE SON EXALTED ABOVE ANGELS

5For to which of the angels did He ever say:

a"You are My Son,
  Today I have begotten You"?

And again:

b"I will be to Him a Father,
  And He shall be to Me a Son"?

6But when He again brings athe firstborn into the world, He says:

---

3 b 2 Cor. 4:4
c Col. 1:17
d [Heb. 7:27]
e Ps. 110:1
1 NU omits by Himself
2 cleansed
3 NU omits our

4 a [Phil. 2:9, 10]

5 a Ps. 2:7
b 2 Sam. 7:14

6 a [Rom. 8:29]
b Deut. 32:43, LXX, DSS; Ps. 97:7

7 a Ps. 104:4

8 a Ps. 45:6, 7
1 A ruler's staff

9 a Is. 61:1, 3

10 a Ps. 102:25–27

11 a [Is. 34:4]
b Is. 50:9; 51:6

12 a Heb. 13:8

13 a Ps. 110:1

14 a Ps. 103:20
b Rom. 8:17

---

b"Let all the angels of God worship Him."

7And of the angels He says:

a"Who makes His angels spirits
  And His ministers a flame of fire."

8But to the Son He says:

a"Your throne, O God, is forever
    and ever;
  A 1scepter of righteousness is the
    scepter of Your kingdom.
9 You have loved righteousness and
    hated lawlessness;
  Therefore God, Your God, ahas
    anointed You
  With the oil of gladness more
    than Your companions."

Heb. 1:8–9

God Called Jesus God. Here the author of Hebrews quoted Psalm 45:6–7 and made it clear that this passage referred to God the Father speaking to Jesus and saying, "Your throne, O God, is forever and ever." So God called Jesus God! How much clearer could He make it?

If God the Father called Jesus God, then how dare I call Him anything less? If God calls Him God, the case is closed. He is God!

10And:

a"You, LORD, in the beginning laid
    the foundation of the earth,
  And the heavens are the work of
    Your hands.
11 aThey will perish, but You remain;
    And bthey will all grow old like a
    garment;
12 Like a cloak You will fold them
    up,
  And they will be changed.
  But You are the asame,
  And Your years will not fail."

13But to which of the angels has He ever said:

a"Sit at My right hand,
  Till I make Your enemies Your
    footstool"?

14aAre they not all ministering spirits sent forth to minister for those who will binherit salvation?

DO NOT NEGLECT SALVATION

2 Therefore we must give [1]the more earnest heed to the things we have heard, lest we drift away. [2]For if the word [a]spoken through angels proved steadfast, and [b]every transgression and disobedience received a just [1]reward, [3a]how shall we escape if we neglect so great a salvation, [b]which at the first began to be spoken by the Lord, and was [c]confirmed to us by those who heard *Him*, [4a]God also bearing witness [b]both with signs and wonders, with various miracles, and [c]gifts[1] of the Holy Spirit, [d]according to His own will?

Heb. 2:3

NO ESCAPE

If the words of the Law came to pass and people suffered the consequences of their sins that were predicted by prophets and angels, then you can believe God will keep His word. You can't just think you'll slide by and escape His notice. "How shall we escape if we neglect so great a salvation?" You are only fooling yourself if you think you can escape the judgment of God—if you think you can hide from God.

The only way of escape from coming judgment is to accept the forgiveness that has been provided by Jesus Christ, on the basis of His death on the cross for you. Jesus told us that He is the only way (John 14:6). To try to find another path is foolish. Either your sins will be judged on the cross, if you accept His sacrifice for you, or you will be personally judged for them for all eternity. There is no escape.

THE SON MADE LOWER THAN ANGELS

[5]For He has not put [a]the world to come, of which we speak, in subjection to angels. [6]But one testified in a certain place, saying:

   [a]"*What is man that You are mindful of him,*

CHAPTER 2

1 [1]all the more careful attention

2 [a]Acts 7:53
[b]Num. 15:30
[1]retribution or penalty

3 [a]Heb. 10:28
[b]Matt. 4:17
[c]Luke 1:2

4 [a]Mark 16:20
[b]Acts 2:22, 43
[c]1 Cor. 12:4, 7, 11
[d]Eph. 1:5, 9
[1]distributions

5 [a][2 Pet. 3:13]

6 [a]Ps. 8:4–6

7 [1]Or *for a little while*
[2]NU, M omit the rest of v. 7.

8 [a]Matt. 28:18
[b]1 Cor. 15:25, 27

9 [a]Phil. 2:7–9
[b]Acts 2:33; 3:13
[c][John 3:16]
[1]Or *for a little while*

10 [a]Col. 1:16
[b]Heb. 5:8, 9; 7:28

11 [a]Heb. 10:10
[b]Acts 17:26
[c]Matt. 28:10
[1]sets apart

12 [a]Ps. 22:22

   Or the son of man that You take care of him?
[7]   *You have made him* [1a]*little lower than the angels;*
   You have crowned him with glory and honor,
   [2]*And set him over the works of Your hands.*
[8]   [a]*You have put all things in subjection under his feet.*"

For in that He put all in subjection under him, He left nothing *that is* not put under him. But now [b]we do not yet see all things put under him. [9]But we see Jesus, [a]who was made [1]a little lower than the angels, for the suffering of death [b]crowned with glory and honor, that He, by the grace of God, might taste death [c]for everyone.

BRINGING MANY SONS TO GLORY

[10]For it was fitting for Him, [a]for whom *are* all things and by whom *are* all things, in bringing many sons to glory, to make the captain of their salvation [b]perfect through sufferings. [11]For [a]both He who [1]sanctifies and those who are being sanctified [b]are all of one, for which reason [c]He is not ashamed to call them brethren, [12]saying:

   [a]"*I will declare Your name to My brethren;*
   In the midst of the assembly I will sing praise to You."

Heb. 2:11

ONE WITH HIM

As a result of what Jesus has done for us, we are at one with Him, and He calls us brothers. How glorious that is!

Jesus, in talking with His disciples, after telling them, "I am in the Father and the Father in Me" (John 14:11), went on to tell them of the day when "you will know that I am in My Father, and you in Me, and I in you" (John 14:20). The fellowship that has always been enjoyed within the Trinity is now ours, as we are in Him, at one with Him. And He isn't ashamed to call us brothers. Wow!

¹³And again:

ª"*I will put My trust in Him.*"

And again:

ᵇ"*Here am I and the children whom God has given Me.*"

¹⁴Inasmuch then as the children have partaken of flesh and blood, He ªHimself likewise shared in the same, ᵇthat through death He might destroy him who had the power of ᶜdeath, that is, the devil, ¹⁵and release those who ªthrough fear of death were all their lifetime subject to bondage. ¹⁶For indeed He does not ¹give aid to angels, but He does ²give aid to the seed of Abraham. ¹⁷Therefore, in all things He had ªto be made like *His* brethren, that He might be ᵇa merciful and faithful High Priest in things *pertaining* to God, to make propitiation for the sins of the people. ¹⁸ªFor in that He Himself has suffered, being ¹tempted, He is able to aid those who are tempted.

Heb. 2:17–18

A Merciful and Faithful High Priest. Jesus became a man. He experienced temptation. He knows what it is like to be tempted, so He is able to help us when we are tempted. He understands. He knows what it's like to bear the frailties of the flesh. He knows what it is to be hungry and thirsty, and He knows how strong the desires of the flesh can get. Thus, He is equipped to sympathize with us and qualified to represent us before the Father.

THE SON WAS FAITHFUL

3 Therefore, holy brethren, partakers of the heavenly calling, consider the Apostle and High Priest of our confession, Christ Jesus, ²who was faithful to Him who appointed Him, as ªMoses also *was faithful* in all His house. ³For this One has been counted worthy of more glory than Moses, inasmuch as ªHe who built the house has more honor than the house. ⁴For every house is built by someone, but ªHe who built all things *is* God. ⁵ªAnd Moses indeed *was* faithful in all His house as ᵇa servant, ᶜfor a testimony of those things

---

Marginal references:

13 ª 2 Sam. 22:3; Is. 8:17
ᵇ Is. 8:18

14 ª John 1:14
ᵇ Col. 2:15
ᶜ 2 Tim. 1:10

15 ª [Luke 1:74]

16 ¹ Or *take on the nature of*
² Or *take on*

17 ª Phil. 2:7
ᵇ [Heb. 4:15; 5:1–10]

18 ª [Heb. 4:15, 16]
¹ *tested*

CHAPTER 3

2 ª Num. 12:7

3 ª Zech. 6:12, 13

4 ª [Eph. 2:10]

5 ª Heb. 3:2
ᵇ Ex. 14:31
ᶜ Deut. 18:15, 18, 19

6 ª Heb. 1:2
ᵇ [1 Cor. 3:16]
ᶜ [Matt. 10:22]
¹ NU omits *firm to the end*

7 ª Acts 1:16
ᵇ Ps. 95:7–11

---

which would be spoken *afterward,* ⁶but Christ as ªa Son over His own house, ᵇwhose house we are ᶜif we hold fast the confidence and the rejoicing of the hope ¹firm to the end.

Heb. 3:5–6

SERVANT OR SON

Moses brought the Law, which allowed people to relate to God in a legal relationship. Jesus, as the Son of God, brings us into a loving, family relationship with God. God doesn't want a formal, legal relationship with us. He wants a relationship of love.

In a legal relationship, there is a tendency to see how far we can go without breaking the law. We usually look for loopholes in the law, to see what we can get away with. But in a love relationship, we want to know how close we can get to the object of our love.

I believe that is the relationship to which God calls us. Not a legal relationship whereby we calculate what is the bare minimum we can do to get to heaven, but a love relationship where we want to please Him, and we hang onto Him, staying as close as we possibly can. I'd rather be His son rather than His employee.

BE FAITHFUL

⁷Therefore, as ªthe Holy Spirit says:

  ᵇ"*Today, if you will hear His voice,*
8   *Do not harden your hearts as in the rebellion,*
    In the day of trial in the wilderness,
9   *Where your fathers tested Me, tried Me,*
    And saw My works forty years.
10   *Therefore I was angry with that generation,*
    And said, 'They always go astray in their heart,
    And they have not known My ways.'

Heb. 3:10

God's Anger. The generation that perished in the wilderness provoked God to anger. "Therefore I was angry with that generation, and said, 'They always go astray in their heart, and they have not known My ways.'" I would never want to make God mad, but the way to do it is to have a heart of unbelief and a lack of knowledge of God.

It is so important for us to study the Scriptures because that is how we get to know God. And the more I know God, the easier it is for me to trust and serve Him.

11   *So I swore in My wrath,*
      'They shall not enter My rest.'"

12Beware, brethren, lest there be in any of you an evil heart of unbelief in departing from the living God; 13but ¹exhort one another daily, while it is called *"Today,"* lest any of you be hardened through the deceitfulness of sin. 14For we have become partakers of Christ if we hold the beginning of our confidence steadfast to the end, 15while it is said:

ᵃ*"Today, if you will hear His voice,*
   Do not harden your hearts as in
   the rebellion."

Heb. 3:14

Partakers of Christ. Oh, my! What a verse of Scripture! "We have become partakers of Christ." We are partakers of His divine nature. To think that Jesus would dwell in us is a concept that we really can't fully comprehend or grasp. But this is exactly what the Bible teaches. I may not understand it, but I believe it and I love it!

FAILURE OF THE WILDERNESS WANDERERS

16ᵃFor who, having heard, rebelled? Indeed, *was it* not all who came out of Egypt, *led* by Moses? 17Now with whom was He angry forty years? *Was*

13 ¹encourage

15 ᵃPs. 95:7, 8

16 ᵃNum. 14:2, 11, 30

17 ᵃNum. 14:22, 23

18 ᵃNum. 14:30

19 ᵃ1 Cor. 10:11, 12

CHAPTER 4

1 ᵃHeb. 12:15

2 ¹NU, M since they were not united by faith with those who heeded it

3 ᵃPs. 95:11

4 ᵃGen. 2:2

5 ᵃPs. 95:11

7 ᵃPs. 95:7, 8

8 ᵃJosh. 22:4
¹Gr. *Jesus,* same as Heb. *Joshua*

11 ᵃ2 Pet. 1:10

12 ᵃPs. 147:15
ᵇIs. 49:2
ᶜEph. 6:17
ᵈ1 Cor. 14:24, 25

13 ᵃPs. 33:13–15; 90:8
ᵇJob 26:6

it not with those who sinned, ᵃwhose corpses fell in the wilderness? 18And ᵃto whom did He swear that they would not enter His rest, but to those who did not obey? 19So we see that they could not enter in because of ᵃunbelief.

THE PROMISE OF REST

4 Therefore, since a promise remains of entering His rest, ᵃlet us fear lest any of you seem to have come short of it. 2For indeed the gospel was preached to us as well as to them; but the word which they heard did not profit them, ¹not being mixed with faith in those who heard *it.* 3For we who have believed do enter that rest, as He has said:

ᵃ*"So I swore in My wrath,*
   'They shall not enter My rest,'"

although the works were finished from the foundation of the world. 4For He has spoken in a certain place of the seventh *day* in this way: ᵃ*"And God rested on the seventh day from all His works"*; 5and again in this *place:* ᵃ*"They shall not enter My rest."*

6Since therefore it remains that some *must* enter it, and those to whom it was first preached did not enter because of disobedience, 7again He designates a certain day, saying in David, *"Today,"* after such a long time, as it has been said:

ᵃ*"Today, if you will hear His voice,*
   Do not harden your hearts."

8For if ¹Joshua had ᵃgiven them rest, then He would not afterward have spoken of another day. 9There remains therefore a rest for the people of God. 10For he who has entered His rest has himself also ceased from his works as God *did* from His.

THE WORD DISCOVERS OUR CONDITION

11ᵃLet us therefore be diligent to enter that rest, lest anyone fall according to the same example of disobedience. 12For the word of God *is* ᵃliving and powerful, and ᵇsharper than any ᶜtwo-edged sword, piercing even to the division of soul and spirit, and of joints and marrow, and is ᵈa discerner of the thoughts and intents of the heart. 13ᵃAnd there is no creature hidden from His sight, but all things *are* ᵇnaked and open to the eyes of Him to whom we *must* give account.

Heb. 4:10

Resting. When God created the world, He rested on the seventh day. He didn't rest because He was tired. He rested because He was through. His work was finished, so He stopped.

In the same way that God stopped after finishing the work of creation, we can also enter into the rest of the finished work of Jesus Christ on the cross. It is finished! It's a done deal! I don't have to work to achieve my own salvation. I am saved by grace. As far as my salvation is concerned, He is resting and so am I.

Heb. 4:12

DIVISION OF SOUL AND SPIRIT

The soul and spirit are so intricately integrated within us that it is almost impossible for us to recognize whether or not an experience we have is a soulish experience or a spiritual experience. There are many people who are having soulish, emotional experiences, but who are interpreting them as spiritual experiences. So how can you tell the difference? How can you know if your experiences are legitimately from the Holy Spirit or if they are just from your emotions and psyche? That is where the Word of God comes in.

As we compare our experiences to the teachings of the Bible, and as we spend time studying and meditating on the Word, the living Word of God helps us divide between the soul and spirit. By comparing our experiences to the teachings of the Bible we have an objective standard by which we can evaluate our experiences. It is a living and powerful soul and spirit detector.

---

14 ᵃ Heb. 2:17; 7:26
ᵇ Heb. 10:23

15 ᵃ Is. 53:3–5
ᵇ Luke 22:28
ᶜ 2 Cor. 5:21

16 ᵃ [Eph. 2:18]

CHAPTER 5

1 ᵃ Heb. 2:17; 8:3

2 ᵃ Heb. 7:28
¹ deal gently with

3 ᵃ Lev. 9:7; 16:6

4 ᵃ Ex. 28:1

5 ᵃ John 8:54

OUR COMPASSIONATE HIGH PRIEST

14Seeing then that we have a great ᵃHigh Priest who has passed through the heavens, Jesus the Son of God, ᵇlet us hold fast *our* confession. 15For ᵃwe do not have a High Priest who cannot sympathize with our weaknesses, but ᵇwas in all *points* tempted as *we are*, ᶜ*yet* without sin. 16ᵃLet us therefore come boldly to the throne of grace, that we may obtain mercy and find grace to help in time of need.

Heb. 4:16

COME BOLDLY

We can enter into God's presence through our great High Priest, Jesus Christ. He has made access to the Father possible, and we can now come boldly into the presence of God.

Jesus opened up the door of heaven to us when He died on the cross for us. There is a path we follow, lined with His precious blood, that leads us home to God. Access is ours, as we come in His name to find mercy and grace.

Under the old covenant, only the high priest could gain access to the mercy seat and only once a year on the Day of Atonement. But we enter boldly any time we want.

QUALIFICATIONS FOR HIGH PRIESTHOOD

5For every high priest taken from among men ᵃis appointed for men in things *pertaining* to God, that he may offer both gifts and sacrifices for sins. 2He can ¹have compassion on those who are ignorant and going astray, since he himself is also subject to ᵃweakness. 3Because of this he is required as for the people, so also for ᵃhimself, to offer *sacrifices* for sins. 4And no man takes this honor to himself, but he who is called by God, just as ᵃAaron *was*.

A PRIEST FOREVER

5ᵃSo also Christ did not glorify Himself to become High Priest, but *it was* He who said to Him:

Heb. 5:2

Compassion on the Ignorant Strays. Earthly high priests were supposed to have compassion on those who were ignorant and went astray. They were weak themselves and, thus, should understand the weaknesses of others. So, also, none of us is perfect, and we should have compassion for the weaknesses of others.

We sometimes become very judgmental of others, and God then forces us to see our own failures so that we will be more understanding of those who don't get it. Our sins look terrible when we see them in others.

b*"You are My Son,
Today I have begotten You."*

6As He also says in another *place*:

a*"You are a priest forever
According to the order of
Melchizedek"*;

Heb. 5:8–9

LEARNING OBEDIENCE

It is hard to grasp the concept that Jesus "learned obedience" and was "perfected." But there are certain things you can only learn by experience.

When Jesus prayed in the garden of Gethsemane, "Take this cup away from Me," He was expressing His own desire. But it didn't stop there, because He went on to say, "Not My will, but Yours, be done" (Luke 22:42). He learned obedience as He submitted His will to the will of the Father, and we, too, learn obedience when we submit our will to His. Thus, He was "perfected" or "made completely ready" to save us.

---

5 b Ps. 2:7

6 a Ps. 110:4

7 a Matt. 26:39, 42, 44
b Ps. 22:1
c Matt. 26:53
d Matt. 26:39

8 a Phil. 2:8

9 a Heb. 2:10

10 a Ps. 110:4

11 a [John 16:12]
b [Matt. 13:15]

12 a 1 Cor. 3:1–3
1 *sayings,* Scriptures

13 a Eph. 4:14

14 a Is. 7:15
1 *mature*
2 *practice*

CHAPTER 6

1 a Heb. 5:12
b [Heb. 9:14]
1 *maturity*

2 a Acts 19:3–5

7who, in the days of His flesh, when He had aoffered up prayers and supplications, bwith vehement cries and tears to Him cwho was able to save Him from death, and was heard dbecause of His godly fear, 8though He was a Son, *yet* He learned aobedience by the things which He suffered. 9And ahaving been perfected, He became the author of eternal salvation to all who obey Him, 10called by God as High Priest a*"according to the order of Melchizedek,"* 11of whom awe have much to say, and hard to explain, since you have become bdull of hearing.

SPIRITUAL IMMATURITY

12For though by this time you ought to be teachers, you need *someone* to teach you again the first principles of the 1oracles of God; and you have come to need amilk and not solid food. 13For everyone who partakes *only* of milk *is* unskilled in the word of righteousness, for he is aa babe. 14But solid food belongs to those who are 1of full age, *that is,* those who by reason of 2use have their senses exercised ato discern both good and evil.

Heb. 5:12–14

Spiritual Infancy. By this time, many of these Christians should have been teaching others; but, instead, they were like irresponsible babies. They hadn't really developed from their state of spiritual infancy.

The writer of Hebrews couldn't tell them much of what he wanted to say because they had not matured enough. Their immaturity was due to their admixture of Law and faith. They were still partly looking to their own works for a righteous standing with God. They needed to grow up into an understanding of grace. Legalism will always stunt your growth.

THE PERIL OF NOT PROGRESSING

6Therefore, aleaving the discussion of the elementary *principles* of Christ, let us go on to 1perfection, not laying again the foundation of repentance from bdead works and of faith toward God, 2aof the doctrine of

baptisms, bof laying on of hands, cof resurrection of the dead, dand of eternal judgment. 3And this 1we will do if God permits.

4For *it is* impossible for those who were once enlightened, and have tasted athe heavenly gift, and bhave become partakers of the Holy Spirit, 5and have tasted the good word of God

2 b [Acts 8:17]	
c Acts 17:31	
d Acts 24:25	
3 1 M let us do	
4 a [John 4:10]	
b [Gal. 3:2, 5]	
6 a Heb. 10:29	
1 Or and have fallen away	
7 a Ps. 65:10	

and the powers of the age to come, 6 1if they fall away, to renew them again to repentance, asince they crucify again for themselves the Son of God, and put *Him* to an open shame.

7For the earth which drinks in the rain that often comes upon it, and bears herbs useful for those by whom it is cultivated, areceives blessing from

MOVING PAST ELEMENTARY
Heb. 6:1–3

For many years I was seeking to be an evangelist, although I was a pastor of a church. Every Sunday, I preached evangelistic topics of repentance, faith in God, baptism, and the life and death nature of the gospel, even as Paul talks about here. Just the basics. I never really led my congregation into a maturity in their Christian walk. They continued as babes in Christ because I was only feeding them milk.

Then I discovered, when reading Ephesians 4, that the work of a pastor is to equip the saints for the work of the ministry (Eph. 4:12). This revolutionized my understanding of the ministry, and I set out to make my people the best-equipped and best-taught people around. We began to teach systematically through the Bible, from Genesis to Revelation.

In Acts 20:27, as Paul was talking with the elders from Ephesus, he told them, "I have not shunned to declare to you the whole counsel of God." By taking my congregation through the Bible, I can say the same thing: "I have declared the whole counsel of God to you." That is how you bring people into maturity.

There is a place for evangelism, and we still explain the gospel for those who haven't yet heard, and I thank God for the many people we see saved every week, but the primary focus of our ministry is to bring the people into maturity. The time comes when you need to graduate from elementary school.

IMPOSSIBLE TO REPENT?
Heb. 6:4–6

This is a difficult passage of Scripture to interpret. For those Calvinists and others who believe in eternal security, it introduces the problem of a person who is apparently saved but who then falls away. They try to bend these verses to imply that the person referred to is not a Christian, but it is really a stretch to say that someone who has been enlightened, who has been a partaker of the Holy Spirit, and who has tasted the good Word of God and the powers of the age to come could not be a Christian. This passage is also problematic for those Arminians who believe that people can get saved and lost as many times as they want; because, in this case, if one is lost, it is impossible for them to get saved again. It is important to remember that the people who were being addressed were those who were leaving the faith to go back into Judaism and the Law. If they fell back into Judaism, there was no other hope for salvation for them. They wouldn't be saved by following the Law.

There may also be an application to certain people today who leave the faith and who turn radically against God, doing everything they can to lead others astray. It may be possible to sink so far in not only rejecting Christ but in destroying the faith of others that you get to a point of no return.

But this passage is certainly not teaching that if you fall into sin you can never repent. That is contrary to all of the Bible and would leave us all lost.

God; [8a]but if it bears thorns and briers, it is rejected and near to being cursed, whose end is to be burned.

A BETTER ESTIMATE

[9]But, beloved, we are confident of better things concerning you, yes, things that accompany salvation, though we speak in this manner. [10]For [a]God is not unjust to forget [b]your work and [1]labor of love which you have shown toward His name, in that you have [c]ministered to the saints, and do minister. [11]And we desire that each one of you show the same diligence [a]to the full assurance of hope until the end, [12]that you do not become [1]sluggish, but imitate those who through faith and patience [a]inherit the promises.

GOD'S INFALLIBLE PURPOSE IN CHRIST

[13]For when God made a promise to Abraham, because He could swear by no one greater, [a]He swore by Himself, [14]saying, [a]*"Surely blessing I will bless you, and multiplying I will multiply you."* [15]And so, after he had patiently endured, he obtained the [a]promise. [16]For men indeed swear by the greater, and [a]an oath for confirmation is for them an end of all dispute. [17]Thus God, determining to show more abundantly to [a]the heirs of promise [b]the [1]immutability of His counsel, [2]confirmed it by an oath, [18]that by two [1]immutable

---

Heb. 6:19

AN ANCHOR FOR THE SOUL

The hope we have in Jesus and the confidence that we have in His Word is an anchor for our souls. We are living in a rapidly changing world, and we see the tide of the world as it drifts away from the things of God. It is so easy to get pulled with the tide.

We need an anchor, and God's Word does that for us. His Word is sure and steadfast. It won't fail. And we have access to God through Jesus Christ. Our souls are solidly anchored and will not go adrift.

---

8 [a] Is. 5:6

10 [a] Rom. 3:4
[b] 1 Thess. 1:3
[c] Rom. 15:25
[1] NU omits *labor of*

11 [a] Col. 2:2

12 [a] Heb. 10:36
[1] *lazy*

13 [a] Gen. 22:16, 17

14 [a] Gen. 22:16, 17

15 [a] Gen. 12:4; 21:5

16 [a] Ex. 22:11

17 [a] Heb. 11:9
[b] Rom. 11:29
[1] *unchangeableness of His purpose*
[2] *guaranteed*

18 [a] Num. 23:19
[b] [Col. 1:5]
[1] *unchangeable*
[2] M omits *might*

19 [a] Lev. 16:2, 15

20 [a] [Heb. 4:14]
[b] Heb. 3:1; 5:10, 11

CHAPTER 7

1 [a] Gen. 14:18–20

4 [1] *plunder*

5 [a] Num. 18:21–26

6 [a] Gen. 14:19, 20
[b] [Rom. 4:13]

8 [a] Heb. 5:6; 6:20

11 [a] Heb. 7:18; 8:7

13 [1] *served*

14 [a] Is. 1:1

---

things, in which it is impossible for God to [a]lie, we [2]might have strong consolation, who have fled for refuge to lay hold of the hope [b]set before us.

[19]This *hope* we have as an anchor of the soul, both sure and steadfast, [a]and which enters the *Presence* behind the veil, [20a]where the forerunner has entered for us, *even* Jesus, [b]having become High Priest forever according to the order of Melchizedek.

THE KING OF RIGHTEOUSNESS

7 For this [a]Melchizedek, king of Salem, priest of the Most High God, who met Abraham returning from the slaughter of the kings and blessed him, [2]to whom also Abraham gave a tenth part of all, first being translated "king of righteousness," and then also king of Salem, meaning "king of peace," [3]without father, without mother, without genealogy, having neither beginning of days nor end of life, but made like the Son of God, remains a priest continually.

[4]Now consider how great this man *was*, to whom even the patriarch Abraham gave a tenth of the [1]spoils. [5]And indeed [a]those who are of the sons of Levi, who receive the priesthood, have a commandment to receive tithes from the people according to the law, that is, from their brethren, though they have come from the loins of Abraham; [6]but he whose genealogy is not derived from them received tithes from Abraham [a]and blessed [b]him who had the promises. [7]Now beyond all contradiction the lesser is blessed by the better. [8]Here mortal men receive tithes, but there he *receives them*, [a]of whom it is witnessed that he lives. [9]Even Levi, who receives tithes, paid tithes through Abraham, so to speak, [10]for he was still in the loins of his father when Melchizedek met him.

NEED FOR A NEW PRIESTHOOD

[11a]Therefore, if perfection were through the Levitical priesthood (for under it the people received the law), what further need *was there* that another priest should rise according to the order of Melchizedek, and not be called according to the order of Aaron? [12]For the priesthood being changed, of necessity there is also a change of the law. [13]For He of whom these things are spoken belongs to another tribe, from which no man has [1]officiated at the altar. [14]For *it is* evident that [a]our Lord arose from [b]Judah, of which tribe Moses spoke nothing concerning [1]priesthood.

15And it is yet far more evident if, in the likeness of Melchizedek, there arises another priest 16who has come, not according to the law of a fleshly commandment, but according to the power of an endless life. 17For ¹He testifies:

a" *You are a priest forever*
    According to the order of
    Melchizedek."

18For on the one hand there is an annulling of the former commandment because of ªits weakness and unprofitableness, 19for ªthe law made nothing ¹perfect; on the other hand, *there is the* bringing in of ba better hope, through which cwe draw near to God.

GREATNESS OF THE NEW PRIEST

20And inasmuch as *He was* not *made* priest without an oath 21(for they have become priests without an oath, but He with an oath by Him who said to Him:

14 b Matt. 1:2
1 NU *priests*

17 ª Ps. 110:4
1 NU *it is testified*

18 ª [Rom. 8:3]

19 ª [Acts 13:39]
b Heb. 6:18, 19
c Rom. 5:2
1 *complete*

21 ª Ps. 110:4
1 NU *ends the quotation after forever.*

22 ª Heb. 8:6
1 *guarantee*

25 ª Jude 24
b Rom. 8:34
1 *completely or forever*

26 ª Heb. 4:15
b Eph. 1:20
1 *innocent*

a" *The LORD has sworn*
    And will not relent,
' *You are a priest ¹forever*
    According to the order of
    Melchizedek' "),

22by so much more Jesus has become a ¹surety of a ªbetter covenant. 23Also there were many priests, because they were prevented by death from continuing. 24But He, because He continues forever, has an unchangeable priesthood. 25Therefore He is also ªable to save ¹to the uttermost those who come to God through Him, since He always lives bto make intercession for them.

26For such a High Priest was fitting for us, ªwho is holy, ¹harmless, undefiled, separate from sinners, band has become higher than the heavens; 27who does not need daily, as those high priests, to offer up sacrifices, first for His ªown sins and then for the people's,

MELCHIZEDEK—
A SUPERIOR PRIESTHOOD

Heb. 7:1–10

How could Jesus be our great High Priest, if He was not of the tribe of Levi? The author of Hebrews developed the argument that Jesus is a priest of a higher order than the Levites, that is, the order of Melchizedek. Melchizedek was this interesting character who showed up mysteriously in Genesis 14, when Abraham paid tithes to him. He was mentioned in a messianic prophecy in Psalm 110:4, which said that the Messiah would be "*a priest forever according to the order of Melchizedek.*" We see here that Melchizedek was "without father, without mother, without genealogy, having neither beginning of days nor end of life, but made like the Son of God, remains a priest continually."

There are some who see Melchizedek as a type of Christ, who interpret this passage to say that we have no recording of Melchizedek's genealogy and that his family remains anonymous in order to enhance the symbolic connection to Jesus. Others take the most literal meaning, that Melchizedek had no genealogy because he was, in fact, Jesus Christ Himself, in a Christophany, or appearance of Jesus in His pre-incarnate state and that He had always existed. This would seem to be the most obvious and clear interpretation.

He is called the "king of Salem," which could be a reference to Jerusalem, where Jesus will rule and reign, but it also means "king of peace," which He certainly is. He is called the "Prince of Peace" in Isaiah 9:6. The name Melchizedek means "King of Righteousness," and this certainly also describes Jesus.

In two different passages in the book of Jeremiah, the Messiah is referred to by the name *Yahweh-Tsidkenu*, which means "Yahweh our righteousness" (Jer. 23:6; 33:16). Also, in John 8:56, when Jesus said that Abraham rejoiced to see His day, and saw it, this could easily be a reference to when Abraham saw Jesus in the form of Melchizedek.

We can't be dogmatic concerning the identity of Melchizedek; but whether he was Jesus Himself, or just a type of Jesus, the point here in this passage is that there is a higher priestly order than the Levitical order and that Jesus is of the superior order of Melchizedek, which predates the Levites. Thus, Jesus is eminently qualified to serve as our High Priest.

THE LAW COULDN'T CUT IT

Heb. 7:18–19

The old covenant was insufficient and was annulled, "because of its weakness and unprofitableness." There was nothing wrong with the Law, but there was something wrong with the people. The Law was inadequate to fix what was wrong with the people. "The Law made nothing perfect."

The Law could reveal your sin, but it couldn't take away your sin. It was good at condemning you and showing that you were guilty, but could do nothing else. It still left you distant from God. But Jesus would change all that with a new covenant.

SAVING TO THE UTTERMOST

Heb. 7:25

For those who come to God through Him, Jesus is "able to save to the uttermost."

Saving to the uttermost means that He throws open wide the doors of heaven to all nations and people and says, "Whoever wills." Saving to the uttermost means He will save you from the direst of circumstances. Saving to the uttermost means He can save you from the deepest depths of sin and defilement. Saving to the uttermost means you will be saved ultimately, for all eternity.

And why can He save to the uttermost? Because "He always lives to make intercession for them." What a glorious truth! I am saved to the uttermost!

27 a Lev. 9:7; 16:6

CHAPTER 8

1 a Col. 3:1

2 a Heb. 9:8, 12
b Heb. 9:11, 24
1 Lit. *holies*

3 a Heb. 5:1; 8:4
b [Eph. 5:2]

5 a Heb. 9:23, 24
b Col. 2:17
c Ex. 25:40

6 a [2 Cor. 3:6–8]
b Heb. 7:22

7 a Ex. 3:8; 19:5

for this He did once for all when He offered up Himself. 28For the law appoints as high priests men who have weakness, but the word of the oath, which came after the law, *appoints* the Son who has been perfected forever.

THE NEW PRIESTLY SERVICE

8 Now *this is* the main point of the things we are saying: We have such a High Priest, awho is seated at the right hand of the throne of the Majesty in the heavens, 2a Minister of athe 1sanctuary and of bthe true tabernacle which the Lord erected, and not man.

3For aevery high priest is appointed to offer both gifts and sacrifices. Therefore bit is necessary that this One also have something to offer. 4For if He were on earth, He would not be a priest, since there are priests who offer the gifts according to the law; 5who serve athe copy and bshadow of the heavenly things, as Moses was divinely instructed when he was about to make the tabernacle. For He said, c"See that you make all things according to the pattern shown you on the mountain." 6But now aHe has obtained a more excellent ministry, inasmuch as He is also Mediator of a bbetter covenant, which was established on better promises.

A NEW COVENANT

7For if that afirst covenant had been faultless, then no place would have been sought for a second. 8Because finding fault with them, He says: a"Behold, the days are coming, says the

Heb. 8:8

The Fault Was Theirs. The problem with the old covenant was not with the Law itself. The Law was good. All the people needed to do was to walk in love and obedience to God. He made all sorts of incredible promises to them if they would just keep His commandments.

But they didn't keep His commandments. They broke the Law again and again. They turned to idols and served other gods. So God promised a new covenant because He was "finding fault with them." They were the problem.

Heb. 8:10

WRITTEN ON OUR HEARTS

Now, quoting from Jeremiah 31:31–34, the writer of Hebrews described the new covenant that God has made with His people. This time, the Law will be written on minds and hearts. It is no longer predicated on our ability to keep the Law. Now it is predicated on what Jesus Christ accomplished on the cross and on the faithfulness of God.

And the wonderful thing is, now God is working on our hearts. He is changing our desires from within. And now, rather than longing for the things of the world we are longing for the things of the Spirit!

The glorious result is a genuine, intimate, personal relationship with God. "I will be their God, and they shall be My people."

LORD, when I will make a new covenant with the house of Israel and with the house of Judah— 9not according to the covenant that I made with their fathers in the day when I took them by the hand to lead them out of the land of Egypt; because they did not continue in My covenant, and I disregarded them, says the LORD. 10For this is the covenant that I will make with the house of Israel after those days, says the aLORD: I will put My laws in their mind and write them on their hearts; and bI will be their God, and they shall be My people. 11aNone of them shall teach his neighbor, and none his brother, saying, 'Know the bLORD,' for all shall know Me, from the least of them to the greatest of them. 12For I will be merciful to their unrighteousness, aand their sins 1and their lawless deeds I will remember no more."
13aIn that He says, "A new covenant," He has made the first obsolete. Now what is becoming obsolete and growing old is ready to vanish away.

---

8 aJer. 31:31–34

10 aJer. 31:33
bZech. 8:8

11 aIs. 54:13
bJer. 31:34

12 aRom. 11:27
1 NU omits and their lawless deeds

13 a[2 Cor. 5:17]

CHAPTER 9

1 aEx. 25:8

2 1 holy place, lit. holies

3 aEx. 26:31–35; 40:3

4 aLev. 16:12
bEx. 25:10
cEx. 16:33
dNum. 17:1–10
eEx. 25:16; 34:29

5 aLev. 16:2

6 aNum. 18:2–6; 28:3

7 aEx. 30:10
bHeb. 5:3

8 a[John 14:6]

9 aHeb. 7:19

Heb. 8:12

Remembered No More. Jesus is at the right hand of the Father, making intercession for us. God responds to our unrighteousness with His mercy. And He can't remember our lawless deeds anymore.

We may remember our actions and beat ourselves up over them or remain in the habitual patterns of our past. Satan may remember them and condemn us for our failures of the past. But God can't remember them. We come to God and say, "God, I'm really struggling with guilt over that horrible thing I did years ago." His response is, "What horrible thing?"

THE EARTHLY SANCTUARY

9 Then indeed, even the first covenant had ordinances of divine service and athe earthly sanctuary. 2For a tabernacle was prepared: the first part, in which was the lampstand, the table, and the showbread, which is called the 1sanctuary; 3aand behind the second veil, the part of the tabernacle which is called the Holiest of All, 4which had the agolden censer and bthe ark of the covenant overlaid on all sides with gold, in which were cthe golden pot that had the manna, dAaron's rod that budded, and ethe tablets of the covenant; 5and aabove it were the cherubim of glory overshadowing the mercy seat. Of these things we cannot now speak in detail.

LIMITATIONS OF THE EARTHLY SERVICE

6Now when these things had been thus prepared, athe priests always went into the first part of the tabernacle, performing the services. 7But into the second part the high priest went alone aonce a year, not without blood, which he offered for bhimself and for the people's sins committed in ignorance; 8the Holy Spirit indicating this, that athe way into the Holiest of All was not yet made manifest while the first tabernacle was still standing. 9It was symbolic for the present time in which both gifts and sacrifices are offered awhich cannot make him who

performed the service perfect in regard to the conscience— [10]concerned only with [a]foods and drinks, [b]various [1]washings, [c]and fleshly ordinances imposed until the time of reformation.

THE HEAVENLY SANCTUARY

[11]But Christ came *as* High Priest of [a]the good things [1]to come, with the greater and more perfect tabernacle not made with hands, that is, not of this creation. [12]Not [a]with the blood of goats and calves, but [b]with His own blood He entered the Most Holy Place [c]once for all, [d]having obtained eternal redemption. [13]For if [a]the blood of bulls and goats and [b]the ashes of a heifer, sprinkling the unclean, [1]sanctifies for the [2]purifying of the flesh, [14]how much more shall the blood of Christ, who through the eternal Spirit offered Himself without [1]spot to God, [a]cleanse your conscience from [b]dead works [c]to serve the living God? [15]And for this reason [a]He is the Mediator of the new covenant, by means of death, for the redemption of the transgressions under the first covenant, that [b]those who are called may receive the promise of the eternal inheritance.

THE MEDIATOR'S DEATH NECESSARY

[16]For where there *is* a testament, there must also of necessity be the

---

Heb. 9:11–12

The Real Deal. The earthly priests entered into the tabernacle to offer the blood of the sacrifice. That tabernacle was just a simulation or model of what was in heaven, and it didn't really work in taking away sins. It was just a picture of the real thing, as Jesus entered into heaven itself, offering His own blood once and for all!

There is no need for any further sacrifice. The blood of goats and calves could only foreshadow the reality of Jesus' sacrifice. He was the real deal!

---

death of the testator. [17]For [a]a testament *is* in force after men are dead, since it has no power at all while the testator lives. [18a]Therefore not even the first *covenant* was dedicated without blood. [19]For when Moses had spoken every [1]precept to all the people

Cross references:
- 10 [a]Col. 2:16 [b]Num. 19:7 [c]Eph. 2:15 [1]Lit. *baptisms*
- 11 [a]Heb. 10:1 [1]NU *that have come*
- 12 [a]Heb. 10:4 [b]Eph. 1:7 [c]Zech. 3:9 [d][Dan. 9:24]
- 13 [a]Lev. 16:14, 15 [1]*sets apart* [2]*cleansing*
- 14 [a]1 John 1:7 [b]Heb. 6:1 [c]Luke 1:74 [1]*blemish*
- 15 [a]Rom. 3:25 [b]Heb. 3:1
- 17 [a]Gal. 3:15
- 18 [a]Ex. 24:6
- 19 [a]Ex. 24:5, 6 [b]Lev. 14:4, 7 [1]*command*
- 20 [a][Matt. 26:28] [b]Ex. 24:3–8
- 21 [a]Ex. 29:12, 36
- 22 [a]Lev. 17:11 [1]*cleansed* [2]*forgiveness*
- 23 [a]Heb. 8:5 [1]*cleansed*
- 24 [a]Heb. 6:20 [b]Heb. 8:2 [c]Rom. 8:34 [1]*representations*
- 25 [a]Heb. 9:7
- 27 [a]Gen. 3:19 [b][2 Cor. 5:10]
- 28 [a]Rom. 6:10 [b]1 Pet. 2:24 [c]Matt. 26:28 [d]Titus 2:13

according to the law, [a]he took the blood of calves and goats, [b]with water, scarlet wool, and hyssop, and sprinkled both the book itself and all the people, [20]saying, [a]*"This is the [b]blood of the covenant which God has commanded you."* [21]Then likewise [a]he sprinkled with blood both the tabernacle and all the vessels of the ministry. [22]And according to the law almost all things are [1]purified with blood, and [a]without shedding of blood there is no [2]remission.

GREATNESS OF CHRIST'S SACRIFICE

[23]Therefore *it was* necessary that [a]the copies of the things in the heavens should be [1]purified with these, but the

---

Heb. 9:22

No Remission Without Blood. "Without shedding of blood there is no remission." This verse presents a real problem for the Jews today.

Ever since the temple was destroyed in AD 70, Jews have not been able to offer sacrifices. And if they reject the sacrifice of Jesus on the cross, they are without an avenue for the remission of their sins. They are condemned by their own Scriptures. They may try to keep the Law; but their Law demands a sacrifice, and they can't offer a sacrifice. They are without hope.

---

heavenly things themselves with better sacrifices than these. [24]For [a]Christ has not entered the holy places made with hands, *which are* [1]copies of [b]the true, but into heaven itself, now [c]to appear in the presence of God for us; [25]not that He should offer Himself often, as [a]the high priest enters the Most Holy Place every year with blood of another— [26]He then would have had to suffer often since the foundation of the world; but now, once at the end of the ages, He has appeared to put away sin by the sacrifice of Himself. [27]And as it is appointed for men to die once, [b]but after this the judgment, [28]so [a]Christ was [b]offered once to bear the sins [c]of many. To those who [d]eagerly wait for Him He will appear a second time, apart from sin, for salvation.

DIE ONCE, THEN JUDGMENT
Heb. 9:27

" **I**t is appointed for men to die once, but after this the judgment." Death is not the end. Judgment comes after death. Some people believe in reincarnation, but this verse clearly eliminates that as a possibility. It doesn't say, "It is appointed for men to die six, seven, or eight times"; it says once.

Of course, if your faith has been put in Jesus Christ, your sins were taken upon Him and were judged on the cross. So you will die, but you won't have to face judgment because you have already been judged and declared righteous. But for those who reject the offer of salvation, they will die and then face eternal judgment and separation from God. In a sense, they will die twice; once physically and again spiritually.

If you are born once, you will really die twice. But if you are born twice, once physically and again of the Spirit, then you will only die once. Your judgment has already been dealt with. Your account has been settled. You will die once and then spend an eternity in the presence of God.

ANIMAL SACRIFICES INSUFFICIENT

CHAPTER 10

10 For the law, having a ᵃshadow of the good things to come, *and* not the very image of the things, ᵇcan never with these same sacrifices, which they offer continually year by year, make those who approach perfect. 2For then would they not have ceased to be offered? For the worshipers, once ¹purified, would have had no more consciousness of sins. 3But in those *sacrifices there is* a reminder of sins every year. 4For ᵃ*it is* not possible that the blood of bulls and goats could take away sins.

CHRIST'S DEATH FULFILLS GOD'S WILL

5Therefore, when He came into the world, He said:

ᵃ*"Sacrifice and offering You did not desire,*
But a body You have prepared for Me.
6 *In burnt offerings and sacrifices for sin*
You had no pleasure.
7 *Then I said, 'Behold, I have come—*
In the volume of the book it is written of Me—
To do Your will, O God.'"

8Previously saying, "*Sacrifice and offering, burnt offerings, and offerings for sin You did not desire, nor had pleasure in them*" (which are offered according to the law), 9then He said, "*Behold, I have come to do Your will, 1O God.*" He takes away the first that He may establish the second. 10ᵃBy that will we have been ¹sanctified ᵇthrough the offering of the body of Jesus Christ once *for all.*

Notes
1 ᵃHeb. 8:5
  ᵇHeb. 7:19; 9:9
2 ¹*cleansed*
4 ᵃMic. 6:6, 7
5 ᵃPs. 40:6–8
9 ¹NU, M omit O God
10 ᵃJohn 17:19
  ᵇ[Heb. 9:12]
  ¹*set apart*
11 ᵃNum. 28:3
12 ᵃCol. 3:1
  ᵇPs. 110:1
13 ᵃPs. 110:1
14 ¹*set apart*
16 ᵃJer. 31:33, 34
17 ᵃJer. 31:34

CHRIST'S DEATH PERFECTS THE SANCTIFIED

11And every priest stands ᵃministering daily and offering repeatedly the same sacrifices, which can never take away sins. 12ᵃBut this Man, after He had offered one sacrifice for sins forever, sat down ᵇat the right hand of God, 13from that time waiting ᵃtill His enemies are made His footstool. 14For by one offering He has perfected forever those who are being ¹sanctified.

15But the Holy Spirit also witnesses to us; for after He had said before,
16ᵃ*"This is the covenant that I will make with them after those days, says the LORD: I will put My laws into their hearts, and in their minds I will write them,"* 17then He adds, ᵃ*"Their sins*

Heb. 10:7

In the Volume of the Book. This is quite a statement! That the volume of the book, or the totality of Scripture, is written about Jesus!

The whole Old Testament was really about Him. It was full of prophecies concerning Him. It contained numerous types that foreshadowed Him. All the sacrifices were about Him. All the feasts and festivals depicted Him. The design of the tabernacle and temple was all about Him. Who other than Jesus Christ could say, "In the volume of the book it is written of Me"?

Heb. 10:12

He Sat Down. "But this Man, after He had offered one sacrifice for sins forever, sat down at the right hand of God." He sat down because the work was done. Redemption was a finished work! On the cross Jesus cried, "It is finished!" He finished it. There is nothing that you can do to add to His redemptive work. It is a finished work. He is sitting down. You are complete in Him!

---

and their lawless deeds I will remember no more." [18]Now where there is [1]remission of these, *there is* no longer an offering for sin.

HOLD FAST YOUR CONFESSION

[19]Therefore, brethren, having [a]boldness[1] to enter [b]the Holiest by the blood of Jesus, [20]by a new and [a]living way which He consecrated for us, through the veil, that is, His flesh, [21]and *having* a High Priest over the house of God, [22]let us [a]draw near with a true heart [b]in full assurance of faith, having our hearts sprinkled from an evil conscience and our bodies washed with pure water. [23]Let us hold fast the confession of *our* hope without wavering, for [a]He who promised *is* faithful. [24]And let us consider one another in order to stir up love and good works, [25]not [a]forsaking the assembling of ourselves together, as *is* the manner of some, but exhorting one another, and [b]so much the more as you see [c]the Day approaching.

THE JUST LIVE BY FAITH

[26]For [a]if we sin willfully [b]after we have received the knowledge of the truth, there [c]no longer remains a sacrifice for sins, [27]but a certain fearful expectation of judgment, and [a]fiery indignation which will devour the adversaries. [28]Anyone who has rejected Moses' law dies without mercy on *the testimony of* two or three [a]witnesses. [29][a]Of how much worse punishment, do you suppose, will he be thought worthy who has trampled the Son of God underfoot, [b]counted the blood of the covenant by which he was sanctified a common thing, [c]and insulted the Spirit of grace? [30]For we know Him who said, [a]"*Vengeance is Mine, I will repay*," [1]says the Lord. And again,

---

18 [1] forgiveness

19 [a][Eph. 2:18]
[b]Heb. 9:8, 12
[1] confidence

20 [a]John 14:6

22 [a]Heb. 7:19; 10:1
[b]Eph. 3:12

23 [a]1 Cor. 1:9; 10:13

25 [a]Acts 2:42
[b]Rom. 13:11
[c]Phil. 4:5

26 [a]Num. 15:30
[b]2 Pet. 2:20
[c]Heb. 6:6

27 [a]Zeph. 1:18

28 [a]Deut. 17:2–6; 19:15

29 [a][Heb. 2:3]
[b]1 Cor. 11:29
[c][Matt. 12:31]

30 [a]Deut. 32:35
[b]Deut. 32:36
[1]NU omits says the Lord

31 [a][Luke 12:5]

32 [a]Gal. 3:4
[1] enlightened

33 [a]1 Cor. 4:9
[b]Phil. 1:7

34 [a]2 Tim. 1:16
[b]Matt. 5:12
[c]Matt. 6:20
[1]NU the prisoners instead of me in my chains
[2] possessions
[3]NU omits in heaven

35 [a]Matt. 5:12

36 [a]Luke 21:19
[b][Col. 3:24]

37 [a]Luke 18:8
[b]Hab. 2:3, 4
[1]Or that which
[2] delay

38 [a]Rom. 1:17
[1]NU My just one

39 [a]2 Pet. 2:20
[b]Acts 16:31
[1] destruction

---

[b]"*The LORD will judge His people.*" [31][a]It is a fearful thing to fall into the hands of the living God.

[32]But [a]recall the former days in which, after you were [1]illuminated, you endured a great struggle with sufferings: [33]partly while you were made [a]a spectacle both by reproaches and tribulations, and partly while [b]you became companions of those who were so treated; [34]for you had compassion on [1]me [a]in my chains, and [b]joyfully accepted the plundering of your [2]goods, knowing that [c]you have a better and an enduring possession for yourselves [3]in heaven. [35]Therefore do not cast away your confidence, [a]which has great reward. [36][a]For you have need of endurance, so that after you have done the will of God, [b]you may receive the promise:

[37] "For [a]yet a little while,
    And [b]He[1] *who is coming will
        come and will not* [2]*tarry.*
[38]   Now [a]the[1] *just shall live by faith;
    But if anyone draws back,
    My soul has no pleasure in him.*"

[39]But we are not of those [a]who draw back to [1]perdition, but of those who [b]believe to the saving of the soul.

Heb. 10:24

LOVE AND GOOD WORKS

Part of the purpose of the church, as we gather together, is that we might be encouraged to good works, encouraged to seek the Lord, encouraged to forsake the things of the world, and encouraged to walk close to Christ. This exhortation is part of the reason we gather, along with being built up and edified in our faith, and being comforted together in the Scriptures.

We want to grow in our understanding and knowledge of the purpose and will of God in our lives, so let's "consider one another in order to stir up love and good works." Let's encourage each other to love and to do the right things.

BY FAITH WE UNDERSTAND

11 Now faith is the ¹substance of things hoped for, the ²evidence ᵃof things not seen. ²For by it the elders obtained a *good* testimony. ³By faith we understand that ᵃthe ¹worlds were framed by the word of God, so that the things which are seen were not made of things which are visible.

FAITH AT THE DAWN OF HISTORY

⁴By faith ᵃAbel offered to God a more excellent sacrifice than Cain, through which he obtained witness that he was righteous, God testifying of his gifts; and through it he being dead still ᵇspeaks.

Heb. 11:1

Substance and Evidence. There is a substance to faith. As we look forward to God doing what He says He will do, it is not just fantasizing; it is substantial reality. It is the "evidence of things not seen." That is, although there may not be visible evidence of it at the moment, I believe God will do what He promises, and that is all the evidence I need.

All God has done so far stands as evidence that He will continue to remain faithful. I have the promise of God, and that is sufficient. I rest on that!

---

⁵By faith Enoch was taken away so that he did not see death, ᵃ*"and was not found, because God had taken him"*; for before he was taken he had this testimony, that he pleased God. ⁶But without faith *it is* impossible to please *Him,* for he who comes to God must believe that He is, and *that* He is a rewarder of those who diligently seek Him. ⁷By faith ᵃNoah, being divinely warned of things not yet seen, moved with godly fear, ᵇprepared an ark for the saving of his household, by which he condemned the world and became heir of ᶜthe righteousness which is according to faith.

FAITHFUL ABRAHAM

⁸By faith ᵃAbraham obeyed when he was called to go out to the place which

---

CHAPTER 11

1 ᵃRom. 8:24
1 *realization*
2 Or *confidence*

3 ᵃPs. 33:6
1 Or *ages,* Gr. *aiones, aeons*

4 ᵃGen. 4:3–5
ᵇHeb. 12:24

5 ᵃGen. 5:21–24

7 ᵃGen. 6:13–22
ᵇ1 Pet. 3:20
ᶜRom. 3:22

8 ᵃGen. 12:1–4

9 ᵃGen. 12:8; 13:3, 18; 18:1, 9
ᵇHeb. 6:17

10 ᵃ[Heb. 12:22; 13:14]
ᵇ[Rev. 21:10]

11 ᵃGen. 17:19; 18:11–14; 21:1, 2
ᵇLuke 1:36
ᶜHeb. 10:23
1 NU omits *she bore a child*

12 ᵃRom. 4:19
ᵇGen. 15:5; 22:17; 32:12

13 ᵃHeb. 11:39
ᵇGen. 12:7
ᶜJohn 8:56
ᵈPs. 39:12
1 NU, M omit *were assured of them*

14 ᵃHeb. 13:14

15 ᵃGen. 11:31

16 ᵃEx. 3:6, 15; 4:5
ᵇ[Rev. 21:2]

Heb. 11:6

PLEASING GOD

How God is pleased when we put our faith and trust in Him! It pleases God! It would seem to me that the converse then would also be true. God is displeased when we don't trust Him, when we doubt His promises, and when we live in fear and anxiety.

We are exhorted in the Scriptures, over and over, to trust in the Lord. It pleases God when we take Him at His word. It pleases Him when we believe that He exists and that He rewards those who diligently seek Him—when we know that He will do what He says He will do.

---

he would receive as an inheritance. And he went out, not knowing where he was going. ⁹By faith he dwelt in the land of promise as *in* a foreign country, ᵃdwelling in tents with Isaac and Jacob, ᵇthe heirs with him of the same promise; ¹⁰for he waited for ᵃthe city which has foundations, ᵇwhose builder and maker *is* God.

¹¹By faith ᵃSarah herself also received strength to conceive seed, and ᵇshe¹ bore a child when she was past the age, because she judged Him ᶜfaithful who had promised. ¹²Therefore from one man, and him as good as ᵃdead, were born *as many* as the ᵇstars of the sky in multitude—innumerable as the sand which is by the seashore.

THE HEAVENLY HOPE

¹³These all died in faith, ᵃnot having received the ᵇpromises, but ᶜhaving seen them afar off ¹were assured of them, embraced *them* and ᵈconfessed that they were strangers and pilgrims on the earth. ¹⁴For those who say such things ᵃdeclare plainly that they seek a homeland. ¹⁵And truly if they had called to mind ᵃthat *country* from which they had come out, they would have had opportunity to return. ¹⁶But now they desire a better, that is, a heavenly *country.* Therefore God is not ashamed ᵃto be called their God, for He has ᵇprepared a city for them.

THE FAITH OF THE PATRIARCHS

17By faith Abraham, awhen he was tested, offered up Isaac, and he who had received the promises offered up his only begotten *son*, 18 1of whom it was said, a*"In Isaac your seed shall be called,"* 19concluding that God awas able to raise *him* up, even from the dead, from which he also received him in a figurative sense.

20By faith aIsaac blessed Jacob and Esau concerning things to come.

21By faith Jacob, when he was dying, ablessed each of the sons of Joseph, and worshiped, *leaning* on the top of his staff.

22By faith aJoseph, when he was dying, made mention of the departure of the children of Israel, and gave instructions concerning his bones.

THE FAITH OF MOSES

23By faith aMoses, when he was born, was hidden three months by his parents, because they saw *he was* a beautiful child; and they were not afraid of the king's bcommand.

24By faith aMoses, when he became of age, refused to be called the son of Pharaoh's daughter, 25choosing rather to suffer affliction with the people of God than to enjoy the *1*passing pleasures of sin, 26esteeming athe *1*reproach of Christ greater riches than the treasures 2in Egypt; for he looked to the breward.

27By faith ahe forsook Egypt, not fearing the wrath of the king; for he endured as seeing Him who is invisible.

28By faith ahe kept the Passover and the sprinkling of blood, lest he who destroyed the firstborn should touch them.

29By faith athey passed through the Red Sea as by dry *land, whereas* the Egyptians, attempting to do so, were drowned.

BY FAITH THEY OVERCAME

30By faith athe walls of Jericho fell down after they were encircled for seven days. 31By faith athe harlot Rahab did not perish with those who *1*did not believe, when bshe had received the spies with peace.

32And what more shall I say? For the time would fail me to tell of aGideon and bBarak and cSamson and dJephthah, also *of* eDavid and fSamuel and the prophets: 33who through faith subdued kingdoms, worked righteousness, obtained promises, astopped the mouths of lions, 34aquenched the violence of

---

17 a James 2:21
18 a Gen. 21:12
1 *to*
19 a Rom. 4:17
20 a Gen. 27:26–40
21 a Gen. 48:1, 5, 16, 20
22 a Gen. 50:24, 25
23 a Ex. 2:1–3
b Ex. 1:16, 22
24 a Ex. 2:11–15
25 1 *temporary*
26 a Heb. 13:13
b Rom. 8:18
1 *reviling*
because of
2 NU, M *of*
27 a Ex. 10:28
28 a Ex. 12:21
29 a Ex. 14:22–29
30 a Josh. 6:20
31 a Josh. 2:9; 6:23
b Josh. 2:1
1 *were disobedient*
32 a Judg. 6:11; 7:1–25
b Judg. 4:6–24
c Judg. 13:24—16:31
d Judg. 11:1–29; 12:1–7
e 1 Sam. 16; 17
f 1 Sam. 7:9–14
33 a Dan. 6:22
34 a Dan. 3:23–28
35 a 1 Kin. 17:22
b Acts 22:25
36 a Gen. 39:20
37 a 1 Kin. 21:13
b 2 Kin. 1:8
c Zech. 13:4
1 NU omits *were tempted*
38 a 1 Kin. 18:4, 13; 19:9
39 a Heb. 11:2, 13
40 a Heb. 5:9

CHAPTER 12
1 a Col. 3:8
b 1 Cor. 9:24
c Rom. 12:12
2 a Luke 24:26
b Phil. 2:8
c Ps. 110:1
1 *originator*

Heb. 11:24–27

THE CHOICE OF FAITH

Moses stands as an example of what the life of faith is all about. He could have continued living as a prince in Egypt, having all the luxuries the world can offer. But he chose rather to suffer with the people of God, realizing that even "the reproach of Christ [is] greater riches than the treasures in Egypt."

The worst that God has to offer is better than the best that the world can give. This kind of faith can see the invisible One. When you look at the eternal perspective, the best the world has to offer can't hold a candle to what God offers.

---

fire, escaped the edge of the sword, out of weakness were made strong, became valiant in battle, turned to flight the armies of the aliens. 35aWomen received their dead raised to life again.

Others were btortured, not accepting deliverance, that they might obtain a better resurrection. 36Still others had trial of mockings and scourgings, yes, and aof chains and imprisonment. 37aThey were stoned, they were sawn in two, *1*were tempted, were slain with the sword. bThey wandered about cin sheepskins and goatskins, being destitute, afflicted, tormented— 38of whom the world was not worthy. They wandered in deserts and mountains, a*in* dens and caves of the earth.

39And all these, ahaving obtained a good testimony through faith, did not receive the promise, 40God having provided something better for us, that they should not be amade perfect apart from us.

THE RACE OF FAITH

12 Therefore we also, since we are surrounded by so great a cloud of witnesses, alet us lay aside every weight, and the sin which so easily ensnares *us*, and blet us run cwith endurance the race that is set before us, 2looking unto Jesus, the *1*author and

2finisher of *our* faith, ªwho for the joy that was set before Him ᵇendured the cross, despising the shame, and ᶜhas sat down at the right hand of the throne of God.

THE DISCIPLINE OF GOD

3ªFor consider Him who endured such hostility from sinners against Himself, ᵇlest you become weary and discouraged in your souls. 4ªYou have not yet resisted to bloodshed, striving against sin. 5And you have forgotten

---

Heb. 12:2

Looking Unto Jesus. Keep focused on the goal! Jesus is the author and finisher of our faith. Our faith comes as a gift from Him, and He is the One who will stick with us and finish the work of faith.

We have a confidence in the Lord, knowing that "He who has begun a good work in you will complete it until the day of Jesus Christ" (Phil. 1:6). The Lord hasn't brought you this far to dump you now! He will complete His work. Just stay focused on Him!

---

the exhortation which speaks to you as to sons:

ª"My son, do not despise the
  ¹chastening of the LORD,
Nor be discouraged when you are
  rebuked by Him;
6 For ªwhom the LORD loves He
  chastens,
And scourges every son whom He
  receives."

7ªIf¹ you endure chastening, God deals with you as with sons; for what ᵇson is there whom a father does not chasten? 8But if you are without chastening, ªof which all have become partakers, then you are illegitimate and not sons. 9Furthermore, we have had human fathers who corrected *us*, and we paid *them* respect. Shall we not much more readily be in subjection to ªthe Father of spirits and live? 10For they indeed for a few days chastened *us* as seemed *best* to them, but He for *our* profit, ªthat *we* may be partakers of His holiness. 11Now no ¹chastening seems to be joyful for the present, but painful; nevertheless, afterward it yields ªthe

Side notes (center column)

2 *perfecter*

3 ªMatt. 10:24
ᵇGal. 6:9

4 ª[1 Cor. 10:13]

5 ªProv. 3:11, 12
¹ *discipline*

6 ªRev. 3:19

7 ªDeut. 8:5
ᵇProv. 13:24; 19:18; 23:13
¹ NU, M *It is for discipline that you endure; God*

8 ª1 Pet. 5:9

9 ª[Job 12:10]

10 ªLev. 11:44

11 ªJames 3:17, 18
¹ *discipline*

12 ªIs. 35:3

14 ªPs. 34:14
ᵇMatt. 5:8

15 ªHeb. 4:1
ᵇDeut. 29:18

16 ª[1 Cor. 6:13–18]
ᵇGen. 25:33
¹ *godless*

17 ªGen. 27:30–40

---

peaceable fruit of righteousness to those who have been trained by it.

RENEW YOUR SPIRITUAL VITALITY

12Therefore ªstrengthen the hands which hang down, and the feeble knees, 13and make straight paths for your feet, so that what is lame may not be dislocated, but rather be healed.

14ªPursue peace with all *people*, and

              Heb. 12:6–8

LOVE AND CHASTENING

It is important for us to realize that, although God chastens us, it is because He loves us. The chastening of the Lord is never punitive, but is always corrective. God doesn't punish us; He corrects us. And there is quite a difference between punishment and correction.

We parents know how important it is that we correct our children. When we see our children running out into the street without looking, we realize the danger to our children, and we correct them. Our loving heavenly Father sees us doing things that can destroy us, and He corrects us for our own good. It may be painful at times, but not as painful as if He just allowed us to continue along our deadly path.

When you feel yourself being spanked by the Lord, don't resist it or resent Him for it. Take it as evidence that you are His child and that He loves you very much.

---

holiness, ᵇwithout which no one will see the Lord: 15looking carefully lest anyone ªfall short of the grace of God; lest any ᵇroot of bitterness springing up cause trouble, and by this many become defiled; 16lest there *be* any ªfornicator or ¹profane person like Esau, ᵇwho for one morsel of food sold his birthright. 17For you know that afterward, when he wanted to inherit the blessing, he was ªrejected, for he found no place for repentance, though he sought it diligently with tears.

Heb. 12:14

PURSUE PEACE AND HOLINESS

Our goal should be peace with all people. We certainly won't be able to reach that goal but we should pursue it just the same.

Paul said in Romans 12:18, "If it is possible, as much as depends on you, live peaceably with all men." The idea is that there are some people who will refuse to live in peace with you. But make sure that you have done everything you can do to reconcile.

Let any division be because of someone else's stubbornness, not yours. This is a part of the holiness that God desires.

THE GLORIOUS COMPANY

18For you have not come 1to athe mountain that may be touched and that burned with fire, and to blackness and 2darkness and tempest, 19and the sound of a trumpet and the voice of words, so that those who heard it abegged that the word should not be spoken to them anymore. 20(For they could not endure what was commanded: a"And if so much as a beast touches the mountain, it shall be stoned 1or shot with an arrow." 21And so terrifying was the sight that Moses said, a"I am exceedingly afraid and trembling.")

22But you have come to Mount Zion and to the city of the living God, the heavenly Jerusalem, to an innumerable company of angels, 23to the 1general assembly and church of athe firstborn bwho are registered in heaven, to God cthe Judge of all, to the spirits of just men dmade perfect, 24to Jesus athe Mediator of the new covenant, and to bthe blood of sprinkling that speaks better things cthan that of Abel.

HEAR THE HEAVENLY VOICE

25See that you do not refuse Him who speaks. For aif they did not escape who refused Him who spoke on earth, much more shall we not escape if we

18 aDeut. 4:11; 5:22
1NU to that which
2NU gloom

19 aEx. 20:18–26

20 aEx. 19:12, 13
1NU, M omit the rest of v. 20.

21 aDeut. 9:19

23 a[James 1:18]
bLuke 10:20
cPs. 50:6; 94:2
d[Phil. 3:12]
1 festal gathering

24 aHeb. 8:6; 9:15
bEx. 24:8
cGen. 4:10

25 aHeb. 2:2, 3

26 aHag. 2:6
1NU will shake

27 a[Is. 34:4; 54:10; 65:17]

28 aHeb. 13:15, 21
1M omits may

29 aEx. 24:17

CHAPTER 13

1 aRom. 12:10

2 aMatt. 25:35
bGen. 18:1–22; 19:1

3 aMatt. 25:36

4 aProv. 5:18, 19
b1Cor. 6:9

5 aDeut. 31:6, 8; Josh. 1:5

6 aPs. 27:1; 118:6

7 1lead

turn away from Him who speaks from heaven, 26whose voice then shook the earth; but now He has promised, saying, a"Yet once more I 1shake not only the earth, but also heaven." 27Now this, "Yet once more," indicates the aremoval of those things that are being shaken, as of things that are made, that the things which cannot be shaken may remain.

28Therefore, since we are receiving a kingdom which cannot be shaken, let us have grace, by which we 1may aserve God acceptably with reverence and godly fear. 29For aour God is a consuming fire.

CONCLUDING MORAL DIRECTIONS

13Let abrotherly love continue. 2aDo not forget to entertain strangers, for by so doing bsome have unwittingly entertained angels. 3aRemember the prisoners as if chained with them—those who are mistreated—since you yourselves are in the body also.

4aMarriage is honorable among all, and the bed undefiled; bbut fornicators and adulterers God will judge.

5Let your conduct be without covetousness; be content with such things as you have. For He Himself has said, a"I will never leave you nor forsake you." 6So we may boldly say:

a"The LORD is my helper;
I will not fear.
What can man do to me?"

CONCLUDING RELIGIOUS DIRECTIONS

7Remember those who 1rule over you, who have spoken the word of God

---

Heb. 13:5

Content with What You Have. The Lord has said, "I will never leave you nor forsake you." What more do you really want? What does it take to satisfy a person?

There are those who live their lives pursuing the lust of the flesh. But how much lust is enough? There are those who strive for material wealth. But will they ever be satisfied?

We have God, who promises to take care of us. How rich could we be? Be content because you have Him! He is enough!

THE SACRIFICE OF PRAISE

God instituted a series of sacrifices to be kept by the people of Israel. But after a period of time they were just going through the motions, not really honoring God with their hearts, though they were still offering physical sacrifices. God rejected their sacrifices, because they weren't from the heart.

After David sinned with Bathsheba and was confronted with his sin and repented, he prayed, "You do not desire sacrifice, or else I would give it; You do not delight in burnt offering. The sacrifices of God are a broken spirit, a broken and a contrite heart" (Ps. 51:16–17).

God is interested in our praise, but He wants it to be from the heart. This is why our praise for God is a sacrifice. Often I don't feel like praising God. Oh, there are certainly times when praise for God just overflows from my life, and I can hardly contain it. But there are other times when praise is difficult. It is especially important that I praise God in those times, from the heart. You see, He doesn't need anything from us. But praise is something that He wants from us.

What an incredible privilege to be able to give something to God that He really wants! The sacrifices of praise.

---

to you, whose faith follow, considering the outcome of *their* conduct. [8]Jesus Christ *is* [a]the same yesterday, today, and forever. [9]Do not be carried [1]about with various and strange doctrines. For *it is* good that the heart be established by grace, not with foods which have not profited those who have been occupied with them.

[10]We have an altar from which those who serve the tabernacle have no right to eat. [11]For the bodies of those animals, whose blood is brought into the sanctuary by the high priest for sin, are burned outside the camp. [12]Therefore Jesus also, that He might [1]sanctify the people with His own blood, suffered outside the gate. [13]Therefore let us go forth to Him, outside the camp, bearing [a]His reproach. [14]For here we have no continuing city, but we seek the one to come. [15a]Therefore by Him let us continually offer [b]the sacrifice of praise to God, that is, [c]the fruit of *our* lips, [1]giving thanks to His name. [16a]But do not forget to do good and to share, for [b]with such sacrifices God is well pleased.

[17a]Obey those who [1]rule over you, and be submissive, for [b]they watch out for your souls, as those who must give account. Let them do so with joy and not with grief, for that would be unprofitable for you.

PRAYER REQUESTED

[18a]Pray for us; for we are confident that we have [b]a good conscience, in all things desiring to live honorably. [19]But I especially urge *you* to do this, that I may be restored to you the sooner.

BENEDICTION, FINAL EXHORTATION, FAREWELL

[20]Now may [a]the God of peace [b]who brought up our Lord Jesus from the dead, [c]that great Shepherd of the sheep, [d]through the blood of the everlasting covenant, [21]make you [1]complete in every good work to do His will, [a]working in [2]you what is well pleasing in His sight, through Jesus Christ, to whom *be* glory forever and ever. Amen.

[22]And I appeal to you, brethren, bear with the word of exhortation, for I have written to you in few words. [23]Know that *our* brother Timothy has been set free, with whom I shall see you if he comes shortly.

[24]Greet all those who [1]rule over you, and all the saints. Those from Italy greet you.

[25]Grace *be* with you all. Amen.

---

8 [a] Heb. 1:12

9 [1] NU, M *away*

12 [1] *set apart*

13 [a] 1 Pet. 4:14

15 [a] Eph. 5:20
[b] Lev. 7:12
[c] Hos. 14:2
[1] Lit. *confessing*

16 [a] Rom. 12:13
[b] Phil. 4:18

17 [a] Phil. 2:29
[b] Ezek. 3:17
[1] *lead*

18 [a] Eph. 6:19
[b] Acts 23:1

20 [a] Rom. 5:1,
2, 10; 15:33
[b] Rom. 4:24
[c] 1 Pet. 2:25; 5:4
[d] Zech. 9:11

21 [a] Phil. 2:13
[1] *perfect*
[2] NU, M *us*

24 [1] *lead*

THE EPISTLE OF

JAMES

The book of James is the first of what are called the General Epistles, which include James, 1–2 Peter, 1–3 John, and Jude. These are called the General Epistles because they are addressed to a particular church or individual, but were intended for circulation among the believers.

This book was written by James, the half brother of Jesus. Initially, the brothers of Jesus didn't believe in Him. But after the resurrection, and probably after meeting Him personally in His post-resurrection appearances, they realized that He was really God in the flesh, the Savior of the world, and it changed their lives forever.

It is interesting, however, that in writing this book James didn't cite his relationship to Jesus for his credentials. If it were me, I would have said, "I'm Chuck, the half brother of Jesus." I'd want people to know how important I am. But James didn't do that. Instead, he identified himself just as "James, a bondservant of God and of the Lord Jesus Christ" (James 1:1). It just doesn't get any better than that.

James became the leader of the church in Jerusalem, as we see from Acts 15. Most scholars believe that the book of James is one of the oldest of all the New Testament books. It was probably written around AD 45. The book was addressed to the Jewish Christians who were scattered all over the known world, and it dealt with their condition at the time, as they were beginning to suffer persecution.

James is perhaps the most practical book in the New Testament. Although it contains some important doctrinal teachings, it is mainly practical advice as to how to live the Christian life. The book addresses the prejudices that we are so prone to hold. It talks about money, the tongue, pride, strife, and so many other practical issues we still face every day.

The message that James communicates is that the Christian life should not just be a belief system and philosophy to which we give mental assent. Rather, it is a way of life. It is something to be believed, but also acted upon. If our faith doesn't result in works, and a changed life, then that faith is dead. Fruit follows faith; obedience follows belief. And how important it is for us today to be reminded that Christianity is not a belief system to hold, but a life to be lived.

Whenever I think of the book of James, I can't help but think of Romaine, a man who served me for so many years here at Calvary Chapel as my assistant, until he went home to be with the Lord. Romaine was a retired Marine Sergeant, and he acted like one. He had a tough exterior, but deep inside he had a heart for the Lord and a love for His

people. But Romaine loved the book of James and taught on it often. He had a practical way of applying the Word that was much like the style of James. He would just cut to the chase and call you to an honest application of the Word. Sometimes it hurt, but you knew you needed it.

GREETING TO THE TWELVE TRIBES

1 James, ᵃa bondservant of God and of the Lord Jesus Christ,

To the twelve tribes which are scattered abroad:

Greetings.

PROFITING FROM TRIALS

²My brethren, ᵃcount it all joy ᵇwhen you fall into various trials, ³ᵃknowing that the testing of your faith produces ¹patience. ⁴But let patience have *its* perfect work, that you may be ¹perfect and complete, lacking nothing. ⁵ᵃIf any of you lacks wisdom, ᵇlet him ask of God, who gives to all liberally and without reproach, and ᶜit will be given to him. ⁶ᵃBut let him ask in faith, with no doubting, for he who doubts is like a wave of the sea driven and tossed by the wind. ⁷For let not that man suppose that he will receive anything from the Lord; ⁸*he is* ᵃa double-minded man, unstable in all his ways.

THE PERSPECTIVE OF RICH AND POOR

⁹Let the lowly brother glory in his exaltation, ¹⁰but the rich in his humiliation, because ᵃas a flower of the field he will pass away. ¹¹For no sooner has the sun risen with a burning heat than it withers the grass; its flower falls, and its beautiful appearance perishes. So the rich man also will fade away in his pursuits.

CHAPTER 1

1 ᵃActs 12:17

2 ᵃActs 5:41
ᵇ1 Pet. 1:6

3 ᵃRom. 5:3–5
¹*endurance* or *perseverance*

4 ¹*mature*

5 ᵃ1 Kin. 3:9
ᵇMatt. 7:7
ᶜJer. 29:12

6 ᵃ[Mark 11:23, 24]

8 ᵃJames 4:8

10 ᵃJob 14:2

COUNT IT ALL JOY

God puts our faith to the test. God puts our devotion to the test. God tests us to the breaking point of our abilities and resources so we will learn to trust in the Lord instead of ourselves.

My resources are limited; but when I look to God, I have unlimited resources. My strength is limited; but when I rely on God, I have unlimited strength.

Paul said he took pleasure in his weakness, "for when I am weak, then I am strong" (2 Cor. 12:10). So count it all joy when God puts you to the test.

James 1:3

James 1:5

IT WILL BE GIVEN

Often people ask, "How can I pray for you?" I always say, "Pray that I might have wisdom in making the many decisions that need to be made daily." Our wisdom is fallible. We can all look back and say, "Well, if I'd only . . ." The wonderful thing is God will give us wisdom if we ask Him. That's a glorious promise!

That wonderful proverb tells us, "Trust in the LORD with all your heart, and lean not on your own understanding; in all your ways acknowledge Him, and He shall direct your paths" (Prov. 3:5–6). Notice there are several qualifications to the "He shall direct your paths" part. To receive God's direction, what must I do? First, I must trust in the Lord with all my heart. Then I must acknowledge, or ask, Him. If any of you lacks wisdom, ask God. It will be given to you.

LOVING GOD UNDER TRIALS

12aBlessed *is* the man who endures temptation; for when he has been approved, he will receive bthe crown of life cwhich the Lord has promised to those who love Him. 13Let no one say when he is tempted, "I am tempted by God"; for God cannot be tempted by evil, nor does He Himself tempt anyone. 14But each one is tempted when he is drawn away by his own desires and enticed. 15Then, awhen desire has conceived, it gives birth to sin; and sin, when it is full-grown, bbrings forth death.

16Do not be deceived, my beloved brethren. 17aEvery good gift and every perfect gift is from above, and comes down from the Father of lights, bwith whom there is no variation or shadow

James 1:26

RELIGION

Christianity is not a religion. In fact, it's the opposite of religion.

Religion tells of man's endeavor to reach God. With religion, you have finite man on earth trying to touch an infinite God in heaven. That's impossible! You can never start with a finite being and reach an infinite one. Christianity is an infinite God reaching down to earth to touch man. "For God so loved the world He gave His only begotten Son" (John 3:16).

Religion tells us man can reach God through works. Christianity tells us man can never reach God through his works.

One day the people asked Jesus, "What shall we do, that we may work the works of God?" Jesus said, "This is the work of God, that you believe in Him whom He sent" (John 6:28–29). Your works can't bring you into relationship with God. Relationship with God comes solely from receiving God's love and trusting in God's provision for your sin.

of turning. 18aOf His own will He brought us forth by the bword of truth, cthat we might be a kind of firstfruits of His creatures.

QUALITIES NEEDED IN TRIALS

19 1So then, my beloved brethren, let every man be swift to hear, aslow to speak, bslow to wrath; 20for the wrath of man does not produce the righteousness of God.

DOERS—NOT HEARERS ONLY

21Therefore alay aside all filthiness and 1overflow of wickedness, and receive with meekness the implanted word, bwhich is able to save your souls. 22But abe doers of the word, and not hearers only, deceiving yourselves. 23For aif anyone is a hearer of the word and not a doer, he is like a man observing his natural face in a mirror; 24for he observes himself, goes away, and immediately forgets what kind of man he was. 25But ahe who looks into the perfect law of liberty and continues *in it*, and is not a forgetful hearer but a doer of the work, bthis one will be blessed in what he does.

26If anyone 1among you thinks he is religious, and adoes not bridle his tongue but deceives his own heart, this one's religion *is* useless. 27aPure and undefiled religion before God and the Father is this: bto visit orphans and widows in their trouble, cand to keep oneself unspotted from the world.

BEWARE OF PERSONAL FAVORITISM

2 My brethren, do not hold the faith of our Lord Jesus Christ, a*the Lord* of glory, with bpartiality. 2For if there should come into your assembly a man with gold rings, in 1fine apparel, and there should also come in a poor man in 2filthy clothes, 3and you 1pay attention to the one wearing the fine clothes and say to him, "You sit here in a good place," and say to the poor man, "You stand there," or, "Sit here at my footstool," 4have you not 1shown partiality among yourselves, and become judges with evil thoughts? 5Listen, my beloved brethren: aHas God not chosen the poor of this world *to be* brich in faith and heirs of the kingdom cwhich He promised to those who love Him? 6But ayou have dishonored the poor man. Do not the rich oppress you band drag you into the courts? 7Do they not blaspheme that noble name by which you are acalled?

12 a James 5:11
b [1 Cor. 9:25]
c Matt. 10:22

15 a Job 15:35
b [Rom. 5:12; 6:23]

17 a John 3:27
b Num. 23:19

18 a John 1:13
b [1 Pet. 1:3, 23]
c [Eph. 1:12, 13]

19 a Prov. 10:19; 17:27
b Prov. 14:17; 16:32
1 NU *Know this* or *This you know*

21 a Col. 3:8
b Acts 13:26
1 *abundance*

22 a Matt. 7:21-28

23 a Luke 6:47

25 a James 2:12
b John 13:17

26 a Ps. 34:13
1 NU omits *among you*

27 a Matt. 25:34–36
b Is. 1:17
c [Rom. 12:2]

CHAPTER 2

1 a 1 Cor. 2:8
b Lev. 19:15

2 1 *bright*
2 *vile*

3 1 Lit. *look upon*

4 1 *differentiated*

5 a 1 Cor. 1:27
b Luke 12:21
c Ex. 20:6

6 a 1 Cor. 11:22
b Acts 13:50

7 a 1 Pet. 4:16

James 2:3–4

SHOW NO PARTIALITY

My father was an usher at the church we attended in Ventura, and he also had a prison ministry. He would go every Sunday afternoon to Ventura County Jail to minister to the inmates. Often, when the inmates were released, they would look up my dad at church.

I remember one fellow we dubbed "George the tramp" because he wore filthy clothes and smelled of the Rescue Mission disinfectant. The first time he came to church, he came late. With this verse in mind, my dad ushered George right down to the front row to the chagrin of the congregation. As they walked down the aisle to the front, everyone could smell the disinfectant they put on George at the Rescue Mission.

Yet my dad was right in following James's exhortation not to show favoritism because a person is rich and not to look with disdain because a person is poor. Before God, we all stand on one level. That's what James was telling us here.

⁸If you really fulfill *the* royal law according to the Scripture, ᵃ*"You shall love your neighbor as yourself,"* you do well; ⁹but if you ¹show partiality, you commit sin, and are convicted by the law as ᵃtransgressors. ¹⁰For whoever shall keep the whole law, and yet ᵃstumble in one *point,* ᵇhe is guilty of all. ¹¹For He who said, ᵃ*"Do not commit adultery,"* also said, ᵇ*"Do not murder."* Now if you do not commit adultery, but you do murder, you have become a transgressor of the law. ¹²So speak and so do as those who will be judged by ᵃthe law of liberty. ¹³For ᵃjudgment is without mercy to the one who has shown ᵇno ᶜmercy. ᵈMercy triumphs over judgment.

---

⁸ ᵃLev. 19:18

⁹ ᵃDeut. 1:17
¹Lit. *receive the face*

¹⁰ ᵃGal. 3:10
ᵇDeut. 27:26

¹¹ ᵃEx. 20:14; Deut. 5:18
ᵇEx. 20:13; Deut. 5:17

¹² ᵃJames 1:25

¹³ ᵃJob 22:6
ᵇProv. 21:13
ᶜMic. 7:18
ᵈRom. 12:8

¹⁴ ᵃMatt. 7:21–23, 26; 21:28–32

¹⁵ ᵃLuke 3:11

¹⁶ ᵃ[1 John 3:17, 18]

¹⁸ ᵃHeb. 6:10
ᵇJames 3:13
¹NU omits *your*
²NU omits *my*

²⁰ ¹NU *useless*

²¹ ᵃGen. 22:9, 10, 12, 16–18

²² ᵃHeb. 11:17

FAITH WITHOUT WORKS IS DEAD

¹⁴ᵃWhat *does it* profit, my brethren, if someone says he has faith but does not have works? Can faith save him? ¹⁵ᵃIf a brother or sister is naked and destitute of daily food, ¹⁶and ᵃone of you says to them, "Depart in peace, be warmed and filled," but you do not give them the things which are needed for the body, what *does it* profit? ¹⁷Thus also faith by itself, if it does not have works, is dead.

¹⁸But someone will say, "You have faith, and I have works." ᵃShow me your faith without ¹your works, ᵇand I will show you my faith by ²my works. ¹⁹You believe that there is one God. You do well. Even the demons believe—and tremble! ²⁰But do you want to know, O foolish man, that faith without works is ¹dead? ²¹Was not Abraham our father justified by works ᵃwhen he offered Isaac his son on the altar? ²²Do you see ᵃthat faith was working together with his works, and

James 2:12

THE LAW OF LIBERTY

In Christ Jesus, I have been set free. I'm at liberty from the law of Moses. The law of Moses could not and did not save me. I was saved by faith in Jesus Christ, and Jesus is the end of the law of works to all who believe. My faith in Jesus Christ brought me under a new law, the law of liberty.

Under the law of liberty, I do things not to be saved, but because I am saved. This new law results from God putting His desires upon my heart, and I delight in the things I do for the Lord. This is the law of liberty. Yes, I do good works, but I don't expect my works to save me. I look to Jesus alone for my salvation. But because I have received Jesus as Lord, my belief is manifested in a changed life. And with this, both Paul and James would be in total agreement.

by ᵇworks faith was made ¹perfect? ²³And the Scripture was fulfilled which says, ᵃ"*Abraham believed God, and it was ¹accounted to him for righteousness.*" And he was called ᵇthe friend of God. ²⁴You see then that a man is justified by works, and not by faith only.

²⁵Likewise, ᵃwas not Rahab the harlot also justified by works when she received the messengers and sent *them* out another way?

²⁶For as the body without the spirit is dead, so faith without works is dead also.

James 2:26

FAITH WORKS

It's interesting that Paul used Abraham as the example of a man whose faith in God's Word was accounted to him by God for righteousness (Rom. 4:1–3). Hebrews said that, by faith, Abraham offered up Isaac, believing that God would, if necessary, raise him from the dead to fulfill His word (Heb. 11:17–19).

James looked at Abraham's offering of Isaac from a different standpoint. James said that the offering of Isaac was a practical demonstration of Abraham's faith in God's promises. By his willingness to sacrifice Isaac, Abraham proved the faith that he had in God's promises. Now it wasn't the act of offering Isaac that caused God to account Abraham righteous. He was accounted righteous by his faith alone, but his faith was then acted out in his offering of Isaac.

No man will ever be moved to action without faith. But no man's faith is genuine unless it moves him to action.

THE UNTAMABLE TONGUE

3 My brethren, ᵃlet not many of you become teachers, ᵇknowing that we shall receive a stricter judgment. ²For ᵃwe all stumble in many things. ᵇIf anyone does not stumble in word, ᶜhe *is* a ¹perfect man, able also to bridle the

---

22 ᵇ John 8:39
¹ complete

23 ᵃ Gen. 15:6
ᵇ 2 Chr. 20:7
¹ credited

25 ᵃ Heb. 11:31

CHAPTER 3

1 ᵃ [Matt. 23:8]
ᵇ Luke 6:37

2 ᵃ 1 Kin. 8:46
ᵇ Ps. 34:13
ᶜ [Matt. 12:34–37]
¹ mature

3 ᵃ Ps. 32:9
¹ NU *Now if*

5 ᵃ Prov. 12:18; 15:2
ᵇ Ps. 12:3; 73:8

6 ᵃ Prov. 16:27
ᵇ [Matt. 12:36; 15:11, 18]
¹ unrighteousness
² existence
³ Gr. *Gehenna*

---

whole body. ³¹Indeed, ᵃwe put bits in horses' mouths that they may obey us, and we turn their whole body. ⁴Look also at ships: although they are so large and are driven by fierce winds, they are turned by a very small rudder wherever the pilot desires. ⁵Even so ᵃthe tongue is a little member and ᵇboasts great things.

See how great a forest a little fire kindles! ⁶And ᵃthe tongue *is* a fire, a world of ¹iniquity. The tongue is so set among our members that it ᵇdefiles the whole body, and sets on fire the course of ²nature; and it is set on fire by ³hell. ⁷For every kind of beast and bird, of reptile and creature of the sea, is tamed and has been tamed by mankind. ⁸But no man can tame the tongue. *It is* an

James 3:1

STRICTER JUDGMENT

God has a special ministry of what is referred to in the Bible as the pastor-teacher. As a teacher of the Word of God, I have a tremendous responsibility before God to teach as accurately as I can what the Scriptures say. I'm not called to offer my own opinions. I'm called to teach what God's Word says. Where the Bible is silent, it's important that I am silent. Where the Bible speaks, it's important that I speak.

One day, I'll stand before our Lord Jesus Christ, and I will be judged under a stricter standard because of being a teacher. That's the reason it is vitally important to me to teach through the Word of God from Genesis to Revelation and to accurately represent God and the Word of God to you.

James warns against just anybody getting up and teaching without recognizing the responsibility they have when they stand before God to give an account; and if you're guilty of teaching people falsely, you will have the stricter judgment.

James 3:6

TAME THE
TONGUE

Oh, the destructive power of the tongue once it is set on fire by hell! The tongue has the power to destroy people. How many people have had their reputations destroyed or their lives made miserable because of someone's tongue? And many times, what is being said isn't true.

We need to realize the power of life and death is in the tongue. We can use our tongues to build up or to destroy. May God help us use our tongues in constructive ways: to encourage, to teach, to strengthen, to comfort, and to give hope!

unruly evil, ᵃfull of deadly poison. ⁹With it we bless our God and Father, and with it we curse men, who have been made ᵃin the ¹similitude of God. ¹⁰Out of the same mouth proceed blessing and cursing. My brethren, these things ought not to be so. ¹¹Does a spring send forth fresh *water* and bitter from the same opening? ¹²Can a ᵃfig tree, my brethren, bear olives, or a grapevine bear figs? ¹Thus no spring yields both salt water and fresh.

HEAVENLY VERSUS DEMONIC WISDOM

¹³ᵃWho *is* wise and understanding among you? Let him show by good conduct *that* his works *are done* in the meekness of wisdom. ¹⁴But if you have ᵃbitter envy and ¹self-seeking in your hearts, ᵇdo not boast and lie against the truth. ¹⁵ᵃThis wisdom does not descend from above, but *is* earthly, sensual, demonic. ¹⁶For ᵃwhere envy and self-seeking *exist*, confusion and every evil thing *are* there. ¹⁷But ᵃthe wisdom that is from above is first pure, then peaceable, gentle, willing to yield, full of mercy and good fruits, ᵇwithout partiality ᶜand without hypocrisy. ¹⁸ᵃNow the fruit of righteousness is sown in peace by those who make peace.

---

8 ᵃ Ps. 140:3

9 ᵃ Gen. 1:26; 5:1; 9:6
¹ *likeness*

12 ᵃ Matt. 7:16–20
1 NU *Neither can a salty spring produce fresh water.*

13 ᵃ Gal. 6:4

14 ᵃ Rom. 13:13
ᵇ Rom. 2:17
¹ *selfish ambition*

15 ᵃ Phil. 3:19

16 ᵃ 1 Cor. 3:3

17 ᵃ 1 Cor. 2:6, 7
ᵇ James 2:1
ᶜ Rom. 12:9

18 ᵃ Prov. 11:18

CHAPTER 4

1 ᵃ Rom. 7:23
¹ *battles*

2 ¹ *battle*
2 NU, M omit *Yet*

3 ᵃ Job 27:8, 9

James 3:16–17

MY PEACE
I GIVE TO YOU

God wants us to have peaceable lives. He has offered a peace treaty to you who are at war with Him.

Because of your war with God, there is turmoil in your heart; and that inner turmoil manifests itself in turmoil with the people around you. Because you are a boiling cauldron inside, you are at war with everyone around you.

The wisdom that comes from God brings peace with God. "'Come now, and let us reason together,' says the LORD, 'though your sins are like scarlet, they shall be as white as snow; though they are red like crimson, they shall be as wool'" (Is. 1:18). God is inviting you to enter into His peaceful life.

PRIDE PROMOTES STRIFE

4 Where do ¹wars and fights *come* from among you? Do *they* not *come* from your *desires for* pleasure ᵃthat war in your members? ²You lust and do not have. You murder and covet and cannot obtain. You fight and ¹war. ²Yet you do not have because you do not ask. ³ᵃYou ask and do not receive,

---

James 4:4

Choose. There are two kingdoms, and your allegiance is to one or the other. You are either living in the kingdom of God and God rules your life, or you are living in the kingdom of darkness and Satan rules your life.

As God looks at us, He sees that each one of us is living in one kingdom or the other. It's just that straight. No man can serve both God and mammon (Luke 16:13).

bbecause you ask amiss, that you may spend *it* on your pleasures. ⁴¹Adulterers and adulteresses! Do you not know that ᵃfriendship with the world is enmity with God? ᵇWhoever therefore wants to be a friend of the world makes himself an enemy of God. ⁵Or do you think that the Scripture says in vain, ᵃ"The Spirit who dwells in us yearns jealously"?

⁶But He gives more grace. Therefore He says:

ᵃ"*God resists the proud,*
But gives grace to the humble."

HUMILITY CURES WORLDLINESS

⁷Therefore submit to God. ᵃResist the devil and he will flee from you. ⁸ᵃDraw near to God and He will draw near to you. ᵇCleanse *your* hands, *you*

James 4:3

ASKING AMISS?

When Paul prayed that God would remove the thorn in his flesh, God said, "My grace is sufficient for you, for My strength is made perfect in weakness" (2 Cor. 12:7–9). The Lord didn't remove the thorn, but He gave Paul the strength to endure it. God doesn't always answer our prayers as we ask Him. I take issue with people who believe they can force God to perform through prayer. That's never the purpose of prayer. I do not control God. He is not my servant. I am His servant. He isn't obliged to do anything for me. That He does things for me is a sign of His tremendous love and grace because I deserve nothing.

If you've been praying for something a long time and it hasn't been forthcoming, this doesn't mean God isn't going to answer you. But it might be wise to examine your heart and motive to see if the desire is from your flesh because many times we ask and don't receive because we ask amiss.

---

3 ᵇ [Ps. 66:18]

4 ᵃ 1 John 2:15
ᵇ Gal. 1:4
1 NU omits
Adulterers and

5 ᵃ Gen. 6:5

6 ᵃ Prov. 3:34

7 ᵃ [Eph. 4:27;
6:11]

8 ᵃ 2 Chr. 15:2
ᵇ Is. 1:16
ᶜ 1 Pet. 1:22

9 ᵃ Matt. 5:4

10 ᵃ Job 22:29

11 ᵃ 1 Pet. 2:1–3
ᵇ [Matt. 7:1–5]

12 ᵃ [Matt.
10:28]
ᵇ Rom. 14:4
1 NU adds *and
Judge*
2 NU, M *But
who*
3 NU *a neighbor*

13 1 M *let us*

14 ᵃ Job 7:7

15 ᵃ Acts 18:21

16 ᵃ 1 Cor. 5:6

17 ᵃ [Luke
12:47]

CHAPTER 5

1 ᵃ [Luke 6:24]

2 ᵃ Matt. 6:19
ᵇ Job 13:28
1 *have rotted*

James 4:7

Victory! It's important to know that on the cross, Jesus Christ defeated the powers of darkness. In this spiritual battle, Jesus is the victor. Satan is only exercising usurped authority. He doesn't have any real rights. His power was taken from him when Jesus triumphed at the cross.

Although Satan continues to hold on tenaciously, we can come against him through Jesus Christ. We can resist Satan, and he has to flee from us. He has to submit to the authority of Jesus Christ!

---

sinners; and ᶜpurify *your* hearts, *you* double-minded. ⁹ᵃLament and mourn and weep! Let your laughter be turned to mourning and *your* joy to gloom. ¹⁰ᵃHumble yourselves in the sight of the Lord, and He will lift you up.

DO NOT JUDGE A BROTHER

¹¹ᵃDo not speak evil of one another, brethren. He who speaks evil of a brother ᵇand judges his brother, speaks evil of the law and judges the law. But if you judge the law, you are not a doer of the law but a judge. ¹²There is one ¹Lawgiver, ᵃwho is able to save and to destroy. ᵇWho² are you to judge ³another?

DO NOT BOAST ABOUT TOMORROW

¹³Come now, you who say, "Today or tomorrow ¹we will go to such and such a city, spend a year there, buy and sell, and make a profit"; ¹⁴whereas you do not know what *will happen* tomorrow. For what is your life? ᵃIt is even a vapor that appears for a little time and then vanishes away. ¹⁵Instead you *ought* to say, ᵃ"If the Lord wills, we shall live and do this or that." ¹⁶But now you boast in your arrogance. ᵃAll such boasting is evil.

¹⁷Therefore, ᵃto him who knows to do good and does not do *it*, to him it is sin.

RICH OPPRESSORS WILL BE JUDGED

5 Come now, *you* ᵃrich, weep and howl for your miseries that are coming upon *you!* ²Your ᵃriches ¹are corrupted, and ᵇyour garments are moth-eaten. ³Your gold and silver are corroded, and

their corrosion will be a witness against you and will eat your flesh like fire. [a]You have heaped up treasure in the last days. [4]Indeed [a]the wages of the laborers who mowed your fields, which you kept back by fraud, cry out; and [b]the cries of the reapers have reached the ears of the Lord of [1]Sabaoth. [5]You have lived on the earth in pleasure and [1]luxury; you have [2]fattened your hearts [3]as in a day of slaughter. [6]You have condemned, you have murdered the just; he does not resist you.

BE PATIENT AND PERSEVERING

[7]Therefore be patient, brethren, until the coming of the Lord. See *how* the farmer waits for the precious fruit of the earth, waiting patiently for it until it receives the early and latter rain. [8]You also be patient. Establish your hearts, for the coming of the Lord [1]is at hand.

[9]Do not [1]grumble against one another, brethren, lest you be [2]condemned. Behold, the Judge is standing at the door! [10a]My brethren, take the prophets, who spoke in the name of the Lord, as an example of suffering and [b]patience. [11]Indeed [a]we count them blessed who [b]endure. You have heard of [c]the perseverance of Job and seen [d]the end *intended by* the Lord— that [e]the Lord is very compassionate and merciful.

[12]But above all, my brethren, [a]do not swear, either by heaven or by earth or with any other oath. But let your "Yes" be "Yes," and *your* "No," "No," lest you fall into [1]judgment.

Cross references:

3 [a] Rom. 2:5

4 [a] Lev. 19:13
[b] Deut. 24:15
[1] Lit., in Heb., Hosts

5 [1] indulgence
[2] Lit. nourished
[3] NU omits as

8 [1] has drawn near

9 [1] Lit. groan
[2] NU, M judged

10 [a] Matt. 5:12
[b] Heb. 10:36

11 [a] [Ps. 94:12]
[b] [James 1:12]
[c] Job 1:21, 22; 2:10
[d] Job 42:10
[e] Num. 14:18

12 [a] Matt. 5:34–37
[1] M hypocrisy

13 [a] Ps. 50:14, 15
[b] Eph. 5:19

14 [a] Mark 6:13; 16:18

MEETING SPECIFIC NEEDS

[13]Is anyone among you suffering? Let him [a]pray. Is anyone cheerful? [b]Let him sing psalms. [14]Is anyone among you sick? Let him call for the elders of the church, and let them pray over him, [a]anointing him with oil in the name of

---

James 5:10

HAZARD PAY

Probably one of the most hazardous professions in the world is being a prophet. I imagine the worker's compensation for prophets is probably higher than for any other profession because prophets have always been persecuted.

People don't want to hear what God's prophets have to say because God is usually not too happy with them and the prophets are called to tell them. So the people get angry at the prophets for speaking the truth of God, and they persecute the prophets.

Look to the prophets who have spoken in the name of the Lord for examples of the suffering and patience of men who have dared to speak for the Lord. Blessed are those who have endured that persecution.

BE PATIENT, BRETHREN

James 5:7

The Lord is like a good farmer. He waits for the precious fruit of the earth until it receives the early and the latter rains.

Here James is giving us the reason the Lord hasn't come again yet. The Lord is waiting to reap the precious fruit of the earth. The precious fruit are those souls who will receive Jesus as Lord and Savior and come into the family of God.

The early rain refers to the power of the Holy Spirit manifested through the church in the book of Acts as the Spirit was poured out upon the church. Its ministry was so dynamic in reaching the world with the gospel.

The latter rain refers to the promise that, in the last days, God will pour out His Spirit upon all flesh (Joel 2:28) and there will be one final reaping of the harvest of the earth. Then the Lord will bring to an end the blasphemies and the rebellion of man and set up His kingdom on earth.

The Lord has patience as far as the coming again of Jesus Christ and the establishing of His kingdom. Thus, James has told us to be patient, also.

the Lord. [15]And the prayer of faith will save the sick, and the Lord will raise him up. [a]And if he has committed sins, he will be forgiven. [16][1]Confess your trespasses to one another, and pray for one another, that you may be healed. [a]The effective, [2]fervent prayer of a righteous man avails much. [17]Elijah was a man [a]with a nature like ours, and [b]he prayed earnestly that it would not rain; and it did not rain on the land for three years and six months. [18]And he

prayed [a]again, and the heaven gave rain, and the earth produced its fruit.

BRING BACK THE ERRING ONE

[19]Brethren, if anyone among you wanders from the truth, and someone [a]turns him back, [20]let him know that he who turns a sinner from the error of his way [a]will save [1]a soul from death and [b]cover a multitude of sins.

15 [a] Is. 33:24
16 [a] Num. 11:2 [1] NU *Therefore confess your sins* [2] *supplication*
17 [a] Acts 14:15 [b] 1 Kin. 17:1; 18:1
18 [a] 1 Kin. 18:1, 42
19 [a] Gal. 6:1
20 [a] Rom. 11:14 [b] [1 Pet. 4:8] [1] NU *his soul*

PRAY FOR THE SICK   James 5:14

There is a Law of Scriptural Interpretation that says: If it was taught by Jesus, practiced in the book of Acts, and there is a teaching on it in the epistles, then we accept it for general church practice through the church's history. Of course, we find the healing of the sick in Jesus' ministry. It was very common. Also, prayer for the sick was something practiced in the early church by the apostles. And here, James taught on it in this epistle.

Now much of the church no longer practices prayer for the sick. And many times those who do not practice it say that this ceased with the apostles. But Irenaeus, one of the early church fathers, writing late in the second century, related that the sick were still being healed by hands being laid on them. Tertullian, writing midway through the third century, said the Roman Emperor Alexander Severus was healed by the anointing at the hands of a Christian named Tropasian; and, in his gratitude, Alexander kept Tropasian as a guest in his palace until the day of his death.

Now there is much concerning healing that we don't understand. We don't understand why God doesn't heal everyone. But that's God's business. Our business is to pray for the sick and to anoint them with oil in the name of the Lord.

THE FIRST EPISTLE OF
PETER

INTRODUCTION This book was written by the apostle Peter, and was addressed to the Jewish believers who were in the region of Asia Minor, or present-day Turkey. It was written after the writings of Paul, probably around AD 65 to 67.

There is some question as to where Peter was when he wrote this letter. He offers greetings from the church in Babylon (1 Pet. 5:13), but we aren't sure what he meant by Babylon. There are those who suggest that this is literal Babylon, which was in present-day Iraq. There are others who say that Peter was actually in Rome at this time and was using Babylon as a code word for Rome. This is probably the majority opinion among scholars. (Revelation 17 is another passage of Scripture that seems to refer to Rome as Babylon.) Tradition says that Peter was martyred in Rome, so if it was written from Rome it was probably near the end of Peter's life.

The theme of this book is suffering. The Christians were now undergoing increasingly intense suffering and needed to be instructed and encouraged in light of this suffering. They needed to understand that suffering is a normal part of the Christian life and that it was a way to relate to the suffering of Jesus, which Peter had witnessed personally. They also needed to know how important it is to remain loyal and submissive to the Lord, as Peter learned the hard way as he had denied the Lord. Then they needed to focus on the hope that is in Jesus, and the glory of an eternity in heaven. It is our eternal hope that ultimately puts present suffering into perspective.

There are some who have questioned whether or not Peter could have written this book. They say that an uneducated fisherman could never have written something this profound. But that ignores the change that Peter underwent, following the resurrection of Jesus and the day of Pentecost. The time he spent with Jesus, the experience of being forgiven and restored by Him, and the filling of the Spirit, made Peter a different person. This tough fisherman was now using words like "precious." He was a man who had been forever transformed by his relationship with the Lord Jesus Christ.

GREETING TO THE ELECT PILGRIMS

1 Peter, an apostle of Jesus Christ,

To the ¹pilgrims ᵃof the Dispersion in Pontus, Galatia, Cappadocia, Asia, and Bithynia, ²ᵃelect ᵇaccording to the foreknowledge of God the Father, ᶜin sanctification of the Spirit, for ᵈobedience and ᵉsprinkling of the blood of Jesus Christ:

ᶠGrace to you and peace be multiplied.

CHAPTER 1

1 ᵃJames 1:1
¹ *sojourners, temporary residents*
2 ᵃEph. 1:4
ᵇ[Rom. 8:29]
ᶜ2Thess. 2:13

ᵈRom. 1:5 ᵉHeb. 10:22; 12:24 ᶠRom. 1:7

A HEAVENLY INHERITANCE

3 aBlessed *be* the God and Father of our Lord Jesus Christ, who baccording to His abundant mercy chas begotten us again to a living hope dthrough the resurrection of Jesus Christ from the dead, 4to an inheritance Jincorruptible and undefiled and that does not fade away, areserved in heaven for you, 5awho are kept by the power of God through faith for salvation ready to be revealed in the last time.

3 a Eph. 1:3
b Gal. 6:16
c [John 3:3, 5]
d 1 Cor. 15:20

4 a Col. 1:5
1 *imperishable*

5 a John 10:28

1 Pet. 1:3

LIVING HOPE

The heart of the gospel is that Jesus rose from the dead. Paul said the gospel we preach to you is that Christ died for our sins, was buried, and rose again the third day, according to the Scriptures (1 Cor. 15:3–4). When you look at the preaching of the early church in the book of Acts, you see that it centered on the resurrection of Jesus from the dead. The first message preached by Peter after Pentecost was a sermon concerning the resurrection of Jesus from the dead (Acts 2:30–32).

That is always the heart of the message of the church. Our hope is more than just hope. It's a living hope because of the resurrection of Jesus Christ!

6 a Matt. 5:12
b 2 Cor. 4:17
c James 1:2
1 *distressed*

7 a James 1:3
b Job 23:10
c [Rom. 2:7]

8 a 1 John 4:20
b John 20:29
1 M *known*

6aIn this you greatly rejoice, though now bfor a little while, if need be, cyou have been Jgrieved by various trials, 7that athe genuineness of your faith, *being* much more precious than gold that perishes, though bit is tested by fire, cmay be found to praise, honor, and glory at the revelation of Jesus Christ, 8awhom having not Jseen you love. bThough now you do not see *Him*, yet believing, you rejoice with joy inexpressible and full of glory, 9receiving the end of your faith—the salvation of *your* souls.

10Of this salvation the prophets have inquired and searched carefully, who prophesied of the grace *that would*

11 a 2 Pet. 1:21

12 a Eph. 3:10
1 NU, M *you*

14 a [Rom. 12:2]

15 a [2 Cor. 7:1]

16 a Lev. 11:44, 45; 19:2; 20:7

17 a Acts 10:34
1 *sojourning, dwelling* as residents *aliens*

18 1 *perishable*

1 Pet. 1:4–5

GOD'S PART

Now the Scriptures always have God's part and man's part. God's part is first and predominant. Man's part is secondary. It is interesting, though, that most preaching emphasizes man's part rather than God's part. So often you hear preaching concerning what man should do for God, but the scriptural emphasis is on God's part, what God has done for us.

Here, Peter gave us God's part. He sent His Son to die for our sins. He sent His Spirit by which we might be born again. He has given us an inheritance. He is reserving it for us, and He is keeping us for it by the power of God. So far, nothing for us to do! This is all God's part.

come to you, 11searching what, or what manner of time, athe Spirit of Christ who was in them was indicating when He testified beforehand the sufferings of Christ and the glories that would follow. 12To them it was revealed that, not to themselves, but to Jus they were ministering the things which now have been reported to you through those who have preached the gospel to you by the Holy Spirit sent from heaven—things which aangels desire to look into.

LIVING BEFORE GOD OUR FATHER

13Therefore gird up the loins of your mind, be sober, and rest *your* hope fully upon the grace that is to be brought to you at the revelation of Jesus Christ; 14as obedient children, not aconforming yourselves to the former lusts, *as* in your ignorance; 15abut as He who called you *is* holy, you also be holy in all *your* conduct, 16because it is written, a*"Be holy, for I am holy."*

17And if you call on the Father, who awithout partiality judges according to each one's work, conduct yourselves throughout the time of your Jstay *here* in fear; 18knowing that you were not redeemed with Jcorruptible things, *like* silver or gold, from your aimless conduct

received by tradition from your fathers, [19]but [a]with the precious blood of Christ, [b]as of a lamb without blemish and without spot. [20a]He indeed was foreordained before the foundation of the world, but was [1]manifest [b]in these last times for you [21]who through Him believe in God, [a]who raised Him from the dead and [b]gave Him glory, so that your faith and hope are in God.

1 Pet. 1:20

MEANINGFUL LOVE

Before God created the world, He planned to create man and to place him in this world so He might have meaningful love with him.

In His foreknowledge, God knew man would make wrong choices. God knew man would fail. Yet, God still gave man the capacity to choose because without choice, man becomes a robot, and you can't have a meaningful relationship with a robot. It may obey you, but it can't give you meaningful love.

You can choose to love God or to hate God, but choice must be involved if there's going to be a meaningful relationship.

THE ENDURING WORD

[22]Since you [a]have purified your souls in obeying the truth [1]through the Spirit in [2]sincere [b]love of the brethren, love one another fervently with a pure heart, [23a]having been born again, not of [1]corruptible seed but [2]incorruptible, [b]through the word of God which lives and abides [3]forever, [24]because

[a]*"All flesh is as grass,*
    And all [1]the glory of man as the
        flower of the grass.
    The grass withers,
    And its flower falls away,
[25] [a]*But the [1]word of the LORD*
        endures forever."

[b]Now this is the word which by the gospel was preached to you.

---

19 [a] Acts 20:28
[b] Ex. 12:5

20 [a] Rom. 3:25
[b] Gal. 4:4
[1] *revealed*

21 [a] Acts 2:24
[b] Acts 2:33

22 [a] Acts 15:9
[b] Heb. 13:1
[1] NU omits *through the Spirit*
[2] Lit. *unhypocritical*

23 [a] John 1:13
[b] James 1:18
[1] *perishable*
[2] *imperishable*
[3] NU omits *forever*

24 [a] Is. 40:6–8
[1] NU *its glory as*

25 [a] Is. 40:8
[b] [John 1:1]
[1] *spoken word*

CHAPTER 2

1 [a] Heb. 12:1

2 [a] [Matt. 18:3; 19:14]
[b] 1 Cor. 3:2
[1] NU adds *up to salvation*

3 [a] Heb. 6:5

4 [a] Ps. 118:22

6 [a] Is. 28:16

---

2 Therefore, [a]laying aside all malice, all deceit, hypocrisy, envy, and all evil speaking, [2a]as newborn babes, desire the pure [b]milk of the word, that you may grow [1]thereby, [3]if indeed you have [a]tasted that the Lord *is* gracious.

1 Pet. 2:2

PURE MILK OF THE WORD

The Word of God doesn't return void. It accomplishes the purpose for which it is sent (Is. 55:11). And the beautiful thing is that as you plant the Word of God in your heart, in time of need, the Word will come back to you. Suddenly you'll find yourself quoting a passage of Scripture or speaking some truth, and you didn't even know you knew that verse. But it's been planted in your heart, and the Holy Spirit brings it to your remembrance (John 14:26).

God's Word is spiritual food. We grow by it. If I want to be used of God, it is important that I fill my mind, my heart, and my life with the Word of God. To have a working knowledge of God's Word is vital. That's why we teach the Word of God from Genesis to Revelation at Calvary Chapel. We desire the pure milk of the Word that we might grow thereby.

THE CHOSEN STONE AND HIS CHOSEN PEOPLE

[4]Coming to Him *as to* a living stone, [a]rejected indeed by men, but chosen by God *and* precious, [5]you also, as living stones, are being built up a spiritual house, a holy priesthood, to offer up spiritual sacrifices acceptable to God through Jesus Christ. [6]Therefore it is also contained in the Scripture,

[a]*"Behold, I lay in Zion*
    A chief cornerstone, elect,
        precious,
    And he who believes on Him will
        by no means be put to shame."

7Therefore, to you who believe, *He is* precious; but to those who [1]are disobedient,

a"*The stone which the builders rejected
Has become the chief cornerstone,*"

8and

a"*A stone of stumbling
And a rock of offense.*"

bThey stumble, being disobedient to the word, cto which they also were appointed. 9But you *are* a chosen generation, a royal priesthood, a holy nation, His own special people, that you may proclaim the praises of Him who called you out of adarkness into His marvelous light; 10awho once *were* not a people but *are* now the people of God, who had not obtained mercy but now have obtained mercy.

7 aPs. 118:22
1 NU *disbelieve*

8 aIs. 8:14
b1Cor. 1:23
cRom. 9:22

9 a[Acts 26:18]

10 aHos. 1:9, 10; 2:23

LIVING BEFORE THE WORLD

11Beloved, I beg *you* as sojourners and pilgrims, abstain from fleshly lusts awhich war against the soul, 12ahaving your conduct honorable among the Gentiles, that when they speak against you as evildoers, bthey may, by *your* good works which they observe, glorify God in the day of visitation.

SUBMISSION TO GOVERNMENT

13aTherefore submit yourselves to every [1]ordinance of man for the Lord's sake, whether to the king as supreme, 14or to governors, as to those who are sent by him for the punishment of evildoers and *for the* praise of those who do good. 15For this is the will of God, that by doing good you may put to silence the ignorance of foolish men— 16aas free, yet not busing liberty as a cloak for [1]vice, but as bondservants of God. 17Honor all *people.* Love the brotherhood. Fear aGod. Honor the king.

---

1 Pet. 2:9

WE ARE A CHOSEN GENERATION

A ll these special benefits that the Jewish nation once knew as the chosen instrument of God (Ex. 19:5) have now come to the church. Now you are God's chosen people. You are a royal priesthood. You are a holy nation. You are to be God's special people to proclaim the praises of God. The American Standard translation says, to "show forth the excellencies of [God]." So yours is the privilege, but with that privilege comes the responsibility.

The Jews once had the privilege, but they didn't live up to the responsibility. They didn't bring forth the fruit the Father desired. We, the church, have a tremendous responsibility to bring forth the fruit that God longs for in the world today, that we might show forth the praises of our God who called us out of darkness and into His marvelous light.

11 aJames 4:1

12 aPhil. 2:15
bMatt. 5:16; 9:8

13 aMatt. 22:21
1 *institution*

16 aRom. 6:14, 20, 22
bGal. 5:13
1 *wickedness*

17 aProv. 24:21

---

1 Pet. 2:22–25

PETER TAUGHT ISAIAH 53

I n these verses, Peter alluded to Isaiah 53. He didn't give a word-for-word quotation, and he twisted the order of the things, but he drew out the truths from Isaiah 53 and applied them.

I think it's important that we have the truth of God's Word hidden in our heart. I don't think it is so important that we have the exact word-by-word quotation. God is not the Spirit of chapter and verse. He's the Spirit of truth.

I often tell young pastors that if they are listening to my tapes and the Spirit of God takes a truth and confirms it to their heart, then they should use it. They don't have to say, "Chuck Smith said...." The truth has come to their heart. Grasping the basic truths and then being able to relate them accurately is vitally important. Peter did that here with Isaiah 53.

SUBMISSION TO MASTERS

18 aServants, *be* submissive to *your* masters with all fear, not only to the good and gentle, but also to the harsh. 19For this *is* acommendable, if because of conscience toward God one endures grief, suffering wrongfully. 20For awhat credit *is it* if, when you are beaten for your faults, you take it patiently? But when you do good and suffer, if you take it patiently, this *is* commendable before God. 21For ato this you were called, because Christ also suffered for 1us, bleaving 2us an example, that you should follow His steps:

22 　"Whoa committed no sin,
　　Nor was deceit found in His
　　　mouth";

23awho, when He was reviled, did not revile in return; when He suffered, He did not threaten, but bcommitted *Himself* to Him who judges righteously; 24awho Himself bore our sins in His own body on the tree, bthat we, having died to sins, might live for righteousness—cby whose 1stripes you were healed. 25For ayou were like sheep going astray, but have now returned bto the Shepherd and 1Overseer of your souls.

SUBMISSION TO HUSBANDS

3 Wives, likewise, *be* asubmissive to your own husbands, that even if some do not obey the word, bthey, without a word, may cbe won by the conduct of their wives, 2awhen they observe your chaste conduct *accompanied* by fear. 3aDo not let your adornment be *merely* outward—arranging the hair, wearing gold, or putting on *fine* apparel— 4rather *let it be* athe hidden person of the heart, with the 1incorruptible *beauty* of a gentle and quiet spirit, which is very precious in the sight of God. 5For in this manner, in former times, the holy women who trusted in God also adorned themselves, being submissive to their own husbands, 6as Sarah obeyed Abraham, acalling him lord, whose daughters you are if you do good and are not afraid with any terror.

A WORD TO HUSBANDS

7aHusbands, likewise, dwell with *them* with understanding, giving honor to the wife, bas to the weaker vessel, and as *being* heirs together of the grace of life, cthat your prayers may not be hindered.

18 a Eph. 6:5–8

19 a Matt. 5:10

20 a Luke 6:32–34

21 a Matt. 16:24
b [1 John 2:6]
1 NU you
2 NU, M you

22 a Is. 53:9

23 a Is. 53:7
b Luke 23:46

24 a [Heb. 9:28]
b Rom. 7:6
c Is. 53:5
1 wounds

25 a Is. 53:5, 6
b [Ezek. 34:23]
1 Gr. Episkopos

CHAPTER 3

1 a Eph. 5:22
b 1 Cor. 7:16
c Matt. 18:15

2 a 1 Pet. 2:12;
3:6

3 a 1 Tim. 2:9

4 a Rom. 2:29
1 imperishable

6 a Gen. 18:12

7 a [Eph. 5:25]
b 1 Cor. 12:23
c Job 42:8

8 1 NU humble

9 a [Prov. 17:13]
b Matt. 5:44
c Matt. 25:34

10 a Ps. 34:12–16
b James 1:26
1 restrain

11 a Ps. 37:27
b Rom. 12:18

12 a John 9:31

13 a Prov. 16:7

14 a James 1:12
b Is. 8:12

15 a Ps. 119:46
b [Titus 3:7]
1 set apart
2 NU Christ as
Lord

1 Pet. 3:4

True Beauty. True beauty is the beauty of the heart. Seek to develop that inward beauty. If you would spend as much time seeking to develop your inward beauty as you spend trying to develop your outward beauty, you would have much greater benefits.

It's amazing how your relationship with the Lord can affect your whole being, even your countenance. A relationship with Jesus becomes apparent. Inward beauty results in outward beauty. A life lived in purity and holiness leaves the marks of beauty on a person's countenance. True beauty is in the heart and the character of an individual.

CALLED TO BLESSING

8Finally, all *of you be* of one mind, having compassion for one another; love as brothers, *be* tenderhearted, *be* 1courteous; 9anot returning evil for evil or reviling for reviling, but on the contrary bblessing, knowing that you were called to this, cthat you may inherit a blessing. 10For

　a"He who would love life
　　And see good days,
　　bLet him 1refrain his tongue from
　　　evil,
　　And his lips from speaking deceit.
11　Let him aturn away from evil and
　　　do good;
　　bLet him seek peace and pursue it.
12　For the eyes of the LORD *are on*
　　　the righteous,
　　aAnd His ears are open to their
　　　prayers;
　　But the face of the LORD *is*
　　　against those who do evil."

SUFFERING FOR RIGHT AND WRONG

13aAnd who *is* he who will harm you if you become followers of what is good? 14aBut even if you should suffer for righteousness' sake, *you are* blessed. b"And do not be afraid of their threats, nor be troubled." 15But 1sanctify 2the Lord God in your hearts, and always abe ready to *give* a defense to everyone who asks you a reason for the bhope that is in you, with meekness and fear;

1 Pet. 3:15

THE REASON FOR THE HOPE

So here you are studying the Bible. Great! You are studying to know and to understand the Word of God. And as you study the Word of God, the Holy Spirit is preparing your heart so that you might be able to explain to anyone who asks you the reason for the hope that is in you. How can you have such joy? How can you be so optimistic about the future when the world is in such a mess?

You should be able to give inquirers the reason for the hope that you have in Jesus Christ, to tell them of the kingdom of God to come and the better world that He is going to establish on this earth. The importance of studying and knowing the Word of God is to be able to explain not just what you believe, but why you believe it.

16ahaving a good conscience, that when they defame you as evildoers, those who revile your good conduct in Christ may be ashamed. 17For *it is* better, if it is the will of God, to suffer for doing good than for doing evil.

CHRIST'S SUFFERING AND OURS

18For Christ also suffered once for sins, the just for the unjust, that He might bring 1us to God, being put to death in the flesh but made alive by the Spirit, 19by whom also He went and preached to the spirits in prison, 20who formerly were disobedient, 1when once the Divine longsuffering waited in the days of Noah, while the ark was being prepared, in which a few, that is, eight souls, were saved through water. 21aThere is also an antitype which now saves us—baptism b(not the removal of the filth of the flesh, cbut the answer of a good conscience toward God), through the resurrection of Jesus Christ, 22who has gone into heaven and ais at the right hand of God,

---

16 a Heb. 13:18

18 1 NU, M *you*

20 1 NU, M *when the long-suffering of God waited patiently*

21 a Eph. 5:26
b [Titus 3:5]
c [Rom. 10:10]

22 a Ps. 110:1
b Rom. 8:38

CHAPTER 4

1 1 NU omits *for us*

2 a John 1:13

3 1 NU *time*

5 a Acts 10:42

6 a 1 Pet. 1:12;
3:19
b [Rom. 8:9, 13]

7 a Rom. 13:11

---

1 Pet. 3:16–17

IF THEY ONLY KNEW

When people see the way we are living, they try to find fault with it. "What do you do for fun?" That's what they ask us. "You don't go to bars; you don't get drunk; you don't smoke or do drugs; so what do you do for fun?" They revile our good conduct in Christ.

If people only knew the joy that is ours in this relationship with Jesus! What greater joy is there than walking in fellowship with our Lord? What greater joy than to see Him paint a beautiful sunset or to look at His creation through what you might call sanctified eyes? The joy that we have in the things of the Lord and in the fellowship of the believers is rich and beautiful.

bangels and authorities and powers having been made subject to Him.

4 Therefore, since Christ suffered 1for us in the flesh, arm yourselves also with the same mind, for he who has suffered in the flesh has ceased from sin, 2that he no longer should live the rest of *his* time in the flesh for the lusts of men, abut for the will of God. 3For we *have spent* enough of our past 1lifetime in doing the will of the Gentiles—when we walked in lewdness, lusts, drunkenness, revelries, drinking parties, and abominable idolatries. 4In regard to these, they think it strange that you do not run with *them* in the same flood of dissipation, speaking evil of *you.* 5They will give an account to Him who is ready ato judge the living and the dead. 6For this reason athe gospel was preached also to those who are dead, that they might be judged according to men in the flesh, but blive according to God in the spirit.

SERVING FOR GOD'S GLORY

7But athe end of all things is at hand; therefore be serious and watchful in your prayers. 8And above all things

have fervent love for one another, for a*"love will cover a multitude of sins."* 9aBe hospitable to one another bwithout grumbling. 10aAs each one has received a gift, minister it to one another, bas good stewards of cthe manifold grace of God. 11aIf anyone speaks, *let him speak* as the 1oracles of God. If anyone ministers, *let him do it* as with the ability which God supplies, that bin all things God may be glorified through Jesus Christ, to whom belong the glory and the 2dominion forever and ever. Amen.

STEWARDS OF GOD'S GRACE

1 Pet. 4:10

God has entrusted us with His wonderful grace, and we are to be stewards of that grace. A steward is one who oversees the resources of another. So I am to oversee the resources of God's grace and to show God's grace to others using the gifts God has given to me to minister to others.

The word "minister" means "servant." We've all been called to serve our Lord Jesus Christ, although we are not all called to serve Him in the same capacity. There are many different gifts that God gives to us to enable us to fulfill our service to Him. "There are diversities of gifts, but the same Spirit. There are differences of ministries, but the same Lord. And there are diversities of activities, but it is the same God who works all in all. But the manifestation of the Spirit is given to each one for the profit of all" (1 Cor. 12:4–7). We are stewards of the manifold grace of God for the profit of all.

SUFFERING FOR GOD'S GLORY

12Beloved, do not think it strange concerning the fiery trial which is to try you, as though some strange thing happened to you; 13but rejoice ato the extent that you partake of Christ's sufferings, that bwhen His glory is revealed, you

---

8 a[Prov. 10:12]

9 a Heb. 13:2
b 2 Cor. 9:7

10 a Rom. 12:6–8
b 1 Cor. 4:1, 2
c [1 Cor. 12:4]

11 a Eph. 4:29
b [1 Cor. 10:31]
1 utterances
2 sovereignty

13 a James 1:2
b 2 Tim. 2:12

14 a Matt. 5:11
b Matt. 5:16
1 insulted or reviled
2 NU omits the rest of v. 14.

15 1 meddler

16 1 NU name

17 a Is. 10:12
b Luke 10:12

18 a Prov. 11:31

19 a 2 Tim. 1:12

CHAPTER 5

1 a Matt. 26:37

---

1 Pet. 4:11

TO GOD BE THE GLORY

Paul said, "What do you have that you did not receive? Now if you did indeed receive it, why do you boast as if you had not received it?" (1 Cor. 4:7). Now there is always a danger in the exercise of the gifts that God gives to you of taking the glory that belongs to God unto yourself.

When you begin to use your gifts, there will always be those who want to exalt you rather than to exalt God. You must not allow that to happen. You must not take bows for God. You must always immediately point people away from yourself and to the Lord. We minister "with the ability which God supplies, that in all things God may be glorified."

may also be glad with exceeding joy. 14If you are 1reproached for the name of Christ, ablessed *are you*, for the Spirit of glory and of God rests upon you. 2On their part He is blasphemed, bbut on your part He is glorified. 15But let none of you suffer as a murderer, a thief, an evildoer, or as a 1busybody in other people's matters. 16Yet if *anyone suffers* as a Christian, let him not be ashamed, but let him glorify God in this 1matter. 17For the time *has come* afor judgment to begin at the house of God; and if *it begins* with us first, bwhat will *be* the end of those who do not obey the gospel of God? 18Now

a*"If the righteous one is scarcely saved,*
Where will the ungodly and the
sinner appear?"

19Therefore let those who suffer according to the will of God acommit their souls *to Him* in doing good, as to a faithful Creator.

SHEPHERD THE FLOCK

5 The elders who are among you I exhort, I who am a fellow elder and a awitness of the sufferings of Christ,

1 Pet. 4:12

1 b Rom. 8:17, 18

FIERY TRIALS

It's interesting that our first reaction to a heavy trial is to think something strange is happening to us. We don't understand why God's people have to suffer. That's a real enigma to us because we know God loves us supremely. So we wonder, *If God loves me so much, why does He allow me to suffer?*

When I love someone, I want to save them from suffering. That's how we spoil our kids rotten. In protecting them from the consequences of their actions, we cause them to go deeper into their rebellion.

God does love us, but "whom the LORD loves He chastens" (Heb. 12:6). While others might be able to get away with things, God won't let us get away with them because we're His children, and trials are one way that God purifies His children.

2 a Acts 20:28
b 1 Cor. 9:17
c 1 Tim. 3:3
1 NU adds *according to God*

3 a Ezek. 34:4
b Ps. 33:12
c Phil. 3:17
1 *masters*

1 Pet. 5:3

THE SERVANT LEADER

On the night He was betrayed, Jesus took a towel and washed the feet of His disciples, taking the position of a servant. After He had washed their feet, He said, "You call Me Teacher and Lord, and you say well, for so I am. If I then, your Lord and Teacher, have washed your feet, you also ought to wash one another's feet" (John 13:13–14).

Earlier in His ministry, Jesus told His disciples, "The rulers of the Gentiles lord it over them." But, Jesus said, "It shall be so not be so among you" (Matt. 20:25–26). And in our world this is true, also, but this should not be so in the church. So, no doubt, Peter was thinking of Jesus' words and of the example that Jesus gave us.

and also a partaker of the ᵇglory that will be revealed: ²ᵃShepherd the flock of God which is among you, serving as overseers, ᵇnot by compulsion but ¹willingly, ᶜnot for dishonest gain but eagerly; ³nor as ᵃbeing ¹lords over ᵇthose entrusted to you, but ᶜbeing examples to the flock; ⁴and when ᵃthe Chief Shepherd appears, you will receive ᵇthe crown of glory that does not fade away.

4 a Heb. 13:20
b 2 Tim. 4:8

SUBMIT TO GOD, RESIST THE DEVIL

⁵Likewise you younger people, submit yourselves to *your* elders. Yes, ᵃall of *you* be submissive to one another, and be clothed with humility, for

5 a Eph. 5:21
b Prov. 3:34
c Is. 57:15

ᵇ"*God resists the proud,*
But ᶜgives grace to the humble."

⁶Therefore humble yourselves under the mighty hand of God, that He may exalt you in due time, ⁷casting all your care upon Him, for He cares for you.

⁸Be ¹sober, be ²vigilant; ³because your adversary the devil walks about like a roaring lion, seeking whom he

8 1 *self-controlled*
2 *watchful*
3 NU, M omit *because*

1 Pet. 5:5–6

EXALT THE LORD OUR GOD

There is no place in the body of Christ for the exaltation of any man. There is only One who is to be exalted in the church, and that is Jesus Christ. This business of exalting people is anti-scriptural. So Peter was saying, "All of you be submissive to one another, and be clothed with humility, for 'God resists the proud.'"

Pride is one of seven things that God hates (Prov. 6:16–19). Peter said, "Therefore humble yourselves under the mighty hand of God, that He may exalt you in due time."

1 Pet. 5:7

HE CARES FOR YOU

One of the greatest truths the Bible teaches is that God cares for you. He knows all about you. He knows the number of hairs on your head (Luke 12:7). God knows you better than you know yourself.

And God knows the needs that you have today. He knew them before you were born. And God knows the needs you're going to have five years from now. He knows exactly what you'll be going through. And the beautiful thing is that He is preparing you now for what's going to happen then.

He cares for you. He loves you. He's concerned with your welfare. And thus, you can trust Him. And you can cast your cares on Him with confidence because He cares for you. He's going to do what He knows is best for you.

10 ᵃ 1 Cor. 1:9
¹ NU *the God of all grace,*
² NU, M *you*
³ NU *will perfect*

11 ᵃ Rev. 1:6

12 ᵃ 2 Cor. 1:19
ᵇ Acts 20:24

13 ᵃ Acts 12:12, 25; 15:37, 39

may devour. ⁹Resist him, steadfast in the faith, knowing that the same sufferings are experienced by your brotherhood in the world. ¹⁰But ¹may the God of all grace, ᵃwho called ²us to His eternal glory by Christ Jesus, after you have suffered a while, ³perfect, establish, strengthen, and settle *you*. ¹¹ᵃTo Him *be* the glory and the dominion forever and ever. Amen.

FAREWELL AND PEACE

¹²By ᵃSilvanus, our faithful brother as I consider him, I have written to you briefly, exhorting and testifying ᵇthat this is the true grace of God in which you stand.

¹³She who is in Babylon, elect together with *you*, greets you; and *so does* ᵃMark my son. ¹⁴Greet one another with a kiss of love.

Peace to you all who are in Christ Jesus. Amen.

THE SECOND EPISTLE OF

PETER

INTRODUCTION This book was written by the apostle Peter, probably from Rome, shortly before his death in AD 67.

While the book of 1 Peter was addressed to the Jewish Christians who were spread throughout Asia Minor, this second epistle was written to Christians everywhere. Peter had a sense that his death was rapidly approaching, and this letter was written more or less as a swan song, as he reminded the believers of the things that were ultimately important. In this respect, it is similar to 2 Timothy, which was Paul's final letter.

In 1 Peter, he emphasized suffering and the hope of heaven. In this letter, he addressed the apostasy and heresy that was growing in the church and that would be increasing in the future. The defense against this false teaching was to be a strong adherent to the inspired Word of God. He referred often to knowledge and learning. This emphasis on the Word of God bears a striking similarity to Paul's emphasis in his last book, 2 Timothy. Both men, in their final books, drove home the point that studying the Word of God, and teaching the Word of God, is the only way to continue to grow to be who God wants us to be.

Sanctification is always through the Word. And with all the clever false teachings out there, the answer isn't to become expert in false teachings. The answer is to know the truth and compare every teaching to revealed truth.

Peter also reminded his readers that the Lord could return at any time. He isn't slack concerning His promises, but is patient toward us (2 Pet. 3:9). And since this world will all burn one day, this knowledge should cause us to live with eternity in view (2 Pet. 3:11–12).

The book is basically summarized in the final two verses, which say, "You therefore, beloved, since you know this beforehand, beware lest you also fall from your own steadfastness, being led away with the error of the wicked; but grow in the grace and knowledge of our Lord and Savior Jesus Christ. To Him be the glory both now and forever. Amen" (2 Pet. 3:17–18).

GREETING THE FAITHFUL

CHAPTER 1

1 Simon Peter, a bondservant and ªapostle of Jesus Christ,

To those who have ¹obtained ᵇlike² precious faith with us by the righteousness of our God and Savior Jesus Christ:

2 ªGrace and peace be multiplied to you in the knowledge of God and of Jesus our Lord, 3 as His ªdivine power has given to us all things that *pertain* to life and godliness, through the knowledge of Him ᵇwho called us by

---

1 ª Gal. 2:8
ᵇ Eph. 4:5
¹ received
² faith of the same value

2 ª Dan. 4:1

3 ª 1 Pet. 1:5   ᵇ 1 Thess. 2:12

glory and virtue, [4]aby which have been given to us exceedingly great and precious promises, that through these you may be bpartakers of the divine nature, having escaped the [1]corruption *that is* in the world through lust.

---

2 Pet. 1:4

Precious Promises. An interesting study is to mark all of the promises of the Bible—great and precious promises! Or you can go through the Gospels and underline the promises of Jesus. That would be a good place to start. What tremendous promises Jesus gave us: the promise of eternal life, the promise of the Holy Spirit, promises concerning our prayer life. Wonderful promises.

We used to sing years ago, "Every promise in the Book is mine, every chapter, every verse, every line. And I'm living in His love divine, for every promise in the Book is mine."

FRUITFUL GROWTH IN THE FAITH

[5]But also for this very reason, agiving all diligence, add to your faith virtue, to virtue bknowledge, [6]to knowledge self-control, to self-control [1]perseverance, to perseverance godliness, [7]to godliness brotherly kindness, and ato brotherly kindness love. [8]For if these things are yours and abound, *you* will be neither [1]barren anor unfruitful in the knowledge of our Lord Jesus Christ. [9]For he who lacks these things is ashort-sighted, even to blindness, and has forgotten that he was cleansed from his old sins.

[10]Therefore, brethren, be even more diligent ato make your call and election sure, for if you do these things you will never stumble; [11]for so an entrance will be supplied to you abundantly into the everlasting kingdom of our Lord and Savior Jesus Christ.

PETER'S APPROACHING DEATH

[12]For this reason aI will not be negligent to remind you always of these things, bthough you know and are established in the present truth. [13]Yes, I think it is right, aas long as I am in this [1]tent, bto stir you up by reminding

---

you, [14]aknowing that shortly I must [1]put off my tent, just as bour Lord Jesus Christ showed me. [15]Moreover I will be careful to ensure that you always have a reminder of these things after my [1]decease.

THE TRUSTWORTHY PROPHETIC WORD

[16]For we did not follow acunningly devised fables when we made known to you the bpower and ccoming of our Lord Jesus Christ, but were deyewitnesses of His majesty. [17]For He received from God the Father honor and glory when such a voice came to Him from the Excellent Glory: a"This is My beloved Son, in whom I am well pleased." [18]And we heard this voice which came from heaven when we were with Him on athe holy mountain.

[19][1]And so we have the prophetic word confirmed, which you do well to heed as a alight that shines in a dark place, buntil cthe day dawns and the morning star rises in your dhearts; [20]knowing this first, that ano prophecy of Scripture is of any private [1]interpretation, [21]for aprophecy never came by the will of man, bbut [1]holy men of God spoke *as they were* moved by the Holy Spirit.

---

2 Pet. 1:20

No Private Interpretation. It is interesting that the word "apocalypse," which we translate "revelation," literally means "an unveiling." It isn't a covering or a hiding. It's an unveiling.

God seeks to reveal the truth. It isn't hidden in little secret messages or in codes you have to figure out to find out what God meant. I can assure you that God meant what He said, and He said what He meant, and He said it plainly so that all of us can understand it! There is no secret or private interpretation.

DESTRUCTIVE DOCTRINES

2 But there were also false prophets among the people, even as there will be afalse teachers among you, who will secretly bring in destructive heresies, even denying the Lord who bought them, *and* bring on themselves swift destruction. [2]And many will follow their

---

Center column cross-references:

4 a 2 Cor. 1:20; 7:1
b [2 Pet. 3:18]
1 *depravity*

5 a 2 Pet. 3:18
b 2 Pet. 1:2

6 1 *patience*

7 a Gal. 6:10

8 a [John 15:2]
1 *useless*

9 a 1 John 2:9–11

10 a 1 John 3:19

12 a Phil. 3:1
b 1 Pet. 5:12

13 a [2 Cor. 5:1, 4]
b 2 Pet. 3:1
1 *Body*

14 a [2 Tim. 4:6]
b John 13:36; 21:18, 19
1 *Die and leave this body*

15 1 Lit. *exodus, departure*

16 a 1 Cor. 1:17
b [Eph. 1:19–22]
c [1 Pet. 5:4]
d Matt. 17:1–5

17 a Matt. 17:5

18 a Matt. 17:1

19 a [John 1:4, 5, 9]
b Prov. 4:18
c Rev. 2:28; 22:16
d [2 Cor. 4:5–7]
1 Or *We also have the more sure prophetic word*

20 a [Rom. 12:6]
1 Or *origin*

21 a [2 Tim. 3:16]
b 2 Sam. 23:2
1 NU *men spoke from God*

CHAPTER 2

1 a 1 Tim. 4:1, 2

2 Pet. 1:21

HOLY MEN SPOKE

"**A**ll Scripture is given by inspiration of God" (2 Tim. 3:16). Holy men spoke as they were moved by the Holy Spirit. God has given to us in the Scriptures all that is necessary for a life of godliness (2 Pet. 1:3).

God's Word has a transforming effect upon all who read it, study it, and take it to heart. It will change your life and transform you into the image of our Lord. The Word of God is living and powerful (Heb. 4:12), and it will work in us in a powerful way if we will allow it.

destructive ways, because of whom the way of truth will be blasphemed. ³By covetousness they will exploit you with deceptive words; for a long time their judgment has not been idle, and their destruction ¹does not slumber.

2 Pet. 2:1–2

BEWARE OF FALSE PROPHETS

The Bible declares that Jesus is God. Over and over that assertion is made in the Bible. John said, "In the beginning was the Word, and the Word was with God, and the Word was God" (John 1:1).

False prophets deny the deity of Jesus Christ. They say Jesus was a brother of Lucifer or Jesus was Michael the archangel. They would reduce Jesus to the angelic class, to a created being, making Him something less than God. Peter tells us that false prophets deny the Lord and "bring in destructive heresies" and that "many will follow their destructive ways."

3 ¹ M *will not*

4 ¹ Lit. *Tartarus*

6 ª Gen. 19:1–26

7 ª Gen. 19:16, 29

8 ª Ps. 119:139

9 ª Ps. 34:15–19

10 ª Jude 4, 7, 8

DOOM OF FALSE TEACHERS

⁴For if God did not spare the angels who sinned, but cast *them* down to ¹hell and delivered *them* into chains of darkness, to be reserved for judgment; ⁵and did not spare the ancient world, but saved Noah, *one of* eight *people*, a preacher of righteousness, bringing in the flood on the world of the ungodly; ⁶and turning the cities of ªSodom and Gomorrah into ashes, condemned *them* to destruction, making *them* an example to those who afterward would live ungodly; ⁷and ªdelivered righteous Lot, *who was* oppressed by the filthy conduct of the wicked ⁸(for that righteous man, dwelling among them, ªtormented *his* righteous soul from day to day by seeing and hearing *their* lawless deeds)— ⁹*then* ªthe Lord knows how to deliver the godly out of temptations and to reserve the unjust under punishment for the day of judgment, ¹⁰and especially ªthose who walk according to the flesh in the lust of

2 Pet. 2:10–11

LET THE LORD REBUKE SATAN

In these verses, Peter warned of presumptuous, self-willed people who are not even afraid to make rash accusations against evil powers.

Jude wrote concerning Michael the archangel's dispute with Satan over the body of Moses (Jude 9). Michael and Satan are both extremely powerful, influential angels; and they were contending with each other over the body of Moses. But in the dispute, Michael did not "bring against him a reviling accusation, but said, 'The Lord rebuke you!'" (Jude 9).

I'm bothered when people make light of Satan and talk about how they're going to go against him. I really don't want any direct dealings with him. Like Michael the archangel, I want to keep the Lord between us. Let the Lord rebuke Satan.

uncleanness and despise authority. [b]*They* are presumptuous, self-willed. They are not afraid to speak evil of [1]dignitaries, [11]whereas [a]angels, who are greater in power and might, do not bring a reviling accusation against them before the Lord.

DEPRAVITY OF FALSE TEACHERS

[12]But these, [a]like natural brute beasts made to be caught and destroyed, speak evil of the things they do not understand, and will utterly perish in their own corruption, [13a]*and* will receive the wages of unrighteousness, *as* those who count it pleasure [b]to [1]carouse in the daytime. [c]*They are* spots and blemishes, [2]carousing in their own deceptions while [d]they feast with you, [14]having eyes full of [1]adultery and that cannot cease from sin, enticing unstable souls. [a]They have a heart trained in covetous practices, *and are* accursed children. [15]They have forsaken the right way and gone astray, following the way of [a]Balaam the *son* of Beor, who loved the wages of unrighteousness; [16]but he was rebuked for his iniquity: a dumb donkey speaking with a man's voice restrained the madness of the prophet.

[17a]These are wells without water, [1]clouds carried by a tempest, for whom is reserved the blackness of darkness [2]forever.

DECEPTIONS OF FALSE TEACHERS

[18]For when they speak great swelling *words* of emptiness, they allure through the lusts of the flesh, through lewdness,

---

2 Pet. 2:19

Bondage. Whatever it is that takes control over your life, you are in bondage to it.

As Christians, we are slaves to Jesus Christ. We've accepted Him as our Lord and Master. We have willingly submitted ourselves to Him. And we've discovered that to be a slave of Jesus Christ is much better than to be a slave of Satan or to be a slave to our own flesh.

In becoming a slave to Jesus, I am free. I have a glorious freedom in Jesus because I am no longer forced by my lusts to do those things that were destroying me!

---

10 [b]Jude 8
[1]*glorious ones,*
lit. *glories*

11 [a]Jude 9

12 [a]Jude 10

13 [a]Phil. 3:19
[b]Rom. 13:13
[c]Jude 12
[d]1Cor. 11:20, 21
[1]*revel*
[2]*reveling*

14 [a]Jude 11
[1]Lit. *an adulteress*

15 [a]Num. 22:5, 7

17 [a]Jude 12, 13
[1]NU *and mists*
[2]NU omits *forever*

18 [1]NU *are barely escaping*

19 [a]John 8:34
[1]*depravity*
[2]*slavery*

20 [a]Matt. 12:45
[b][Heb. 6:4–6]

21 [a]Luke 12:47

22 [a]Prov. 26:11

CHAPTER 3

1 [a]2Pet. 1:13

2 [a]2Pet. 1:21
[b]Jude 17
[1]NU, M *the apostles of your Lord and Savior* or *your apostles of the Lord and Savior*

3 [a]2Pet. 2:10

4 [a]Gen. 6:1–7

5 [a]Gen. 1:6, 9
[b]Ps. 24:2; 136:6

6 [a]Gen. 7:11, 12, 21–23

7 [a]2Pet. 3:10, 12
[b][2Thess. 1:8]
[1]*destruction*

8 [a]Ps. 90:4

9 [a]Hab. 2:3
[b]Is. 30:18
[c]Ezek. 33:11
[d][Rom. 2:4]
[1]NU *you*

10 [a]Rev. 3:3; 16:15
[b]Ps. 102:25, 26

---

the ones who [1]have actually escaped from those who live in error. [19]While they promise them liberty, they themselves are slaves of [1]corruption; [a]for by whom a person is overcome, by him also he is brought into [2]bondage. [20]For if, after they [a]have escaped the pollutions of the world through the knowledge of the Lord and Savior Jesus Christ, they are [b]again entangled in them and overcome, the latter end is worse for them than the beginning. [21]For [a]it would have been better for them not to have known the way of righteousness, than having known *it*, to turn from the holy commandment delivered to them. [22]But it has happened to them according to the true proverb: [a]*"A dog returns to his own vomit,"* and, "a sow, having washed, to her wallowing in the mire."

GOD'S PROMISE IS NOT SLACK

3 Beloved, I now write to you this second epistle (in *both of* which [a]I stir up your pure minds by way of reminder), [2]that you may be mindful of the words [a]which were spoken before by the holy prophets, [b]and of the commandment of [1]us, the apostles of the Lord and Savior, [3]knowing this first: that scoffers will come in the last days, [a]walking according to their own lusts, [4]and saying, "Where is the promise of His coming? For since the fathers fell asleep, all things continue as *they were* from the beginning of [a]creation." [5]For this they willfully forget: that [a]by the word of God the heavens were of old, and the earth [b]standing out of water and in the water, [6a]by which the world *that* then existed perished, being flooded with water. [7]But [a]the heavens and the earth *which* are now preserved by the same word, are reserved for [b]fire until the day of judgment and [1]perdition of ungodly men.

[8]But, beloved, do not forget this one thing, that with the Lord one day *is* as a thousand years, and [a]a thousand years as one day. [9a]The Lord is not slack concerning *His* promise, as some count slackness, but [b]is longsuffering toward [1]us, [c]not willing that any should perish but [d]that all should come to repentance.

THE DAY OF THE LORD

[10]But [a]the day of the Lord will come as a thief in the night, in which [b]the heavens will pass away with a great noise, and the elements will melt with

ONE DAY IS AS A THOUSAND YEARS

Scoffers say, "It's been almost 2,000 years since Jesus was here on the earth and promised to come again. Where is the promise of His coming? In the last chapter of Revelation, Jesus said, 'Behold, I am coming quickly' (Rev. 22:12), and look, it's been 2,000 years. That's not very quick!" But Peter has given us an explanation. He said, "Do not forget this one thing, that with the Lord one day is as a thousand years, and a thousand years as one day." God exists outside of time. In the eternal realm, you have a whole different measurement. In the eternal realm, there is no time.

2 Pet. 3:3–8

fervent heat; both the earth and the works that are in it will be ¹burned up. ¹¹Therefore, since all these things will be dissolved, what manner *of persons* ought you to be ᵃin holy conduct and godliness, ¹²ᵃlooking for and hastening the coming of the day of God, because of which the heavens will ᵇbe

Notes column:

10 ¹NU laid bare, lit. *found*

11 ᵃ1 Pet. 1:15

12 ᵃ1 Cor. 1:7, 8
ᵇPs. 50:3
ᶜMic. 1:4

13 ᵃIs. 65:17; 66:22
ᵇRev. 21:1

14 ᵃ1 Cor. 1:8; 15:58

15 ᵃRom. 2:4

16 ᵃ1 Cor. 15:24
ᵇ2 Tim. 3:16

17 ᵃMark 13:23
ᵇEph. 4:14

18 ᵃEph. 4:15
ᵇ2 Tim. 4:18

dissolved, being on fire, and the elements will ᶜmelt with fervent heat? ¹³Nevertheless we, according to His promise, look for ᵃnew heavens and a ᵇnew earth in which righteousness dwells.

BE STEADFAST

¹⁴Therefore, beloved, looking forward to these things, be diligent ᵃto be found by Him in peace, without spot and blameless; ¹⁵and consider *that* ᵃthe longsuffering of our Lord *is* salvation—as also our beloved brother Paul, according to the wisdom given to him, has written to you, ¹⁶as also in all his ᵃepistles, speaking in them of these things, in which are some things hard to understand, which untaught and unstable *people* twist to their own destruction, as *they do* also the ᵇrest of the Scriptures.

¹⁷You therefore, beloved, ᵃsince you know *this* beforehand, ᵇbeware lest you also fall from your own steadfastness, being led away with the error of the wicked; ¹⁸ᵃbut grow in the grace and knowledge of our Lord and Savior Jesus Christ.

ᵇTo Him *be* the glory both now and forever. Amen.

THINGS TO COME

2 Pet. 3:10

The next major event from a biblical standpoint will be the Lord's coming for His church. This is often called the rapture. He will catch believers up to be with Him in heaven for a period of seven years. During these seven years, He will deal with the nation of Israel. This is the beginning of what the Scriptures call the day of the Lord, when the Lord will once again take control and rule of the earth.

Also during this seven-year period, man will come to the culmination of his rebellion against God. The Man of Sin, Satan's advocate, will receive power and authority from Satan; and he will rule over the world. Literally, all hell will break loose. The earth will be subjected to great cataclysmic judgments. This is known as the great tribulation, as described by Jesus in Matthew 24 and as also described in Revelation, chapters 6 through 18.

Then Jesus will come back to earth with His church and establish the kingdom of God on earth. Jesus will rule and reign over the earth for a thousand years, and we will live and reign with Him. Satan will be bound during those thousand years. At the end of the thousand years, Satan will be released again for a short period of time, and people will align themselves with Satan. This will be his final attempt to overthrow Jesus. Michael the archangel and his armies will stand up against Satan and his armies. Michael will prevail, and Satan will be cast into Gehenna. Then, there will be the great white throne judgment of God. Finally, the event Peter described here, the dissolving and disintegrating of the material universe, will occur.

THE FIRST EPISTLE OF

JOHN

INTRODUCTION The apostle John wrote five books of the New Testament. He wrote the gospel of John, the three epistles of John, and the book of Revelation. John died around AD 100, and it is believed that the book of Revelation was written shortly before he died, while the books of 1, 2, and 3 John were written a few years before, around AD 96.

John was ministering as the pastor of the church in Ephesus, a church that had been founded by Paul. By this time the church had matured, getting past the initial excitement of the early church. As Revelation 2:4 points out, they had left their first love. They were doing a lot of good things, but their relationships with the Lord were growing cold.

By this time the heresy called Gnosticism was also sweeping through the church. This was a teaching that denied the fact that Jesus was actually a man with a body, as they believed that everything material is evil and everything spiritual is good. John wanted to set the record straight on that question, and in the first verse he asserted that he had seen Jesus with his own eyes, and handled Him personally. Jesus was not a spirit or philosophy to John, but He is a living person who wants to fellowship with us.

John stated several purposes he had for writing the book of 1 John.

The first purpose is given in 1:3, where he said that his declaration was for the purpose of bringing fellowship with God and man. It was the desire of John that his readers not just know about Jesus, but that they know Him personally, even as John had.

The second purpose is found in 1:4, as he wrote, "These things we write to you that your joy may be full." Joy is a natural outflowing of a personal relationship with Jesus Christ.

His third purpose is found in 2:1: "My little children, these things I write to you, so that you may not sin." A life in relationship with Jesus results in a life of righteousness and obedience. John stressed this throughout the book. Jesus changes people.

John's fourth stated purpose is in 5:13, where he said, "These things I have written to you who believe in the name of the Son of God, that you may know that you have eternal life, and that you may continue to believe in the name of the Son of God." He wanted believers to have assurance of their salvation, and to continue in it.

Look for these purposes being addressed as you read through this book. I know you will enjoy reading it as I have always enjoyed teaching it.

WHAT WAS HEARD, SEEN, AND TOUCHED

1 That ªwhich was from the beginning, which we have heard, which we have ᵇseen with our eyes, ᶜwhich we have looked upon, and ᵈour hands have handled, concerning the ᵉWord of life— ²ªthe life ᵇwas manifested, and we have seen, ᶜand bear witness, and declare to you that eternal life which was ᵈwith the Father and was manifested to us— ³that which we have seen and heard we declare to you, that you also may have fellowship with us; and truly our fellowship *is* ªwith the Father and with His Son Jesus Christ. ⁴And these things we write to you ªthat ¹your joy may be full.

FELLOWSHIP WITH HIM AND ONE ANOTHER

⁵ªThis is the message which we have heard from Him and declare to you,

1 John 1:3

FELLOWSHIP WITH GOD

What an awesome quantum leap! That finite man could live in communion with an infinite God! The One who existed long before the universe was created, the One who transcends space and time, has chosen to become one with man in communion, sharing, and fellowship.

This becomes all the more awesome when you realize how vast and great God is. He fills the universe, and yet He desires to fellowship with me. I have difficulty when I try to comprehend this. But as we study the Bible carefully, we come to understand that this is the very purpose of our existence. You exist for the purpose of having fellowship and intimacy with God. "Truly our fellowship is with the Father and with His Son Jesus Christ." Tremendous, tremendous words. I can have fellowship with God! Awesome!

CHAPTER 1

1 ª [John 1:1]
ᵇ John 1:14
ᶜ 2 Pet. 1:16
ᵈ Luke 24:39
ᵉ [John 1:1, 4, 14]

2 ª John 1:4
ᵇ Rom. 16:26
ᶜ John 21:24
ᵈ [John 1:1, 18; 16:28]

3 ª 1 Cor. 1:9

4 ª John 15:11; 16:24
¹ NU, M *our*

5 ª 1 John 3:11
ᵇ [1 Tim. 6:16]

6 ª [1 John 2:9–11]

7 ª Is. 2:5
ᵇ [1 Cor. 6:11]

9 ª Prov. 28:13
ᵇ [Rom. 3:24–26]
ᶜ Ps. 51:2

10 ª 1 John 5:10

CHAPTER 2

1 ª Heb. 7:25; 9:24

2 ª [Rom. 3:25]

---

1 John 1:4

A Joy That Is Full. What joy it is to realize that I can fellowship with the God who created the universe. He desires to fellowship with me! That's too much!

Sometimes we become sad that there are some people who don't want to be around us. But God desires fellowship with us. He longs for this fellowship. That should give us great joy!

that ᵇGod is light and in Him is no darkness at all. ⁶ªIf we say that we have fellowship with Him, and walk in darkness, we lie and do not practice the truth. ⁷But if we ªwalk in the light as He is in the light, we have fellowship with one another, and ᵇthe blood of Jesus Christ His Son cleanses us from all sin.

1 John 1:6

Walking in Darkness. There are many people who profess to know God and to have fellowship with Him, and yet they are walking in darkness, contrary to the commands of God. They are only fooling themselves.

The idea that you can have fellowship with God without turning away from a life of sin is a lie. Real fellowship with God changes us from within. I can have a wonderful prayer life and feel very close to God, but I am living a lie if I am not also turning away from sin. It is not true fellowship.

⁸If we say that we have no sin, we deceive ourselves, and the truth is not in us. ⁹If we ªconfess our sins, He is ᵇfaithful and just to forgive us *our* sins and to ᶜcleanse us from all unrighteousness. ¹⁰If we say that we have not sinned, we ªmake Him a liar, and His word is not in us.

2 My little children, these things I write to you, so that you may not sin. And if anyone sins, ªwe have an Advocate with the Father, Jesus Christ the righteous. ²And ªHe Himself is the propitiation for our sins, and not for

1 John 2:2
Whom Did Jesus Die For? In Calvinistic theology, there is a doctrine called "limited atonement." According to this theological position, Jesus only died for the elect, or those who were chosen by God. But this verse makes it clear that His atonement was unlimited. He didn't just die for our sins; He died "for the whole world."

How glorious it is that we can declare to any person in this world, "Jesus died for you"!

ours only but ᵇalso for the whole world.

THE TEST OF KNOWING HIM

³Now by this we know that we know Him, if we keep His commandments. ⁴He who says, "I know Him," and does not keep His commandments, is a ᵃliar, and the truth is not in him. ⁵But ᵃwhoever keeps His word, truly the love of God ¹is perfected ᵇin him. By this we know that we are in Him. ⁶ᵃHe who says he abides in Him ᵇought himself also to walk just as He walked.

⁷¹Brethren, I write no new commandment to you, but an old commandment which you have had ᵃfrom the beginning. The old commandment is the word which you heard ²from the beginning. ⁸Again, ᵃa new commandment I write to you, which thing is true in Him and in you, ᵇbecause the darkness is passing away, and ᶜthe true light is already shining.

⁹ᵃHe who says he is in the light, and hates his brother, is in darkness until now. ¹⁰ᵃHe who loves his brother abides in the light, and ᵇthere is no cause for stumbling in him. ¹¹But he who ᵃhates his brother is in darkness and ᵇwalks in darkness, and does not know where he is going, because the darkness has blinded his eyes.

THEIR SPIRITUAL STATE

12 I write to you, little children,
    Because ᵃyour sins are forgiven
        you for His name's sake.
13 I write to you, fathers,
    Because you have known Him
        who is ᵃfrom the beginning.
    I write to you, young men,
    Because you have overcome the
        wicked one.

I write to you, little children,
    Because you have ᵇknown the
        Father.
14 I have written to you, fathers,
    Because you have known Him
        who is from the beginning.
    I have written to you, young men,
    Because ᵃyou are strong, and
        the word of God abides in you,
    And you have overcome the
        wicked one.

1 John 2:14

WINNING THE BATTLE

We are all in a battle. It is a spiritual battle. The object of the battle is the control of our minds, and thus our lives. God wants to control your life, and Satan wants to control your life.

Satan uses force, deceit, and guile, to try to bring you into bondage to him. You will either be a servant of God or a servant of Satan. God wants to bring us out of our bondage to Satan and into His glorious kingdom.

The best defense we can have in this spiritual battle is the Word of God. As we hide His Word in our hearts, we have victory over sin (Ps. 119:11). Paying attention to His Word cleanses our way (Ps. 119:9). When Jesus was tempted by Satan, He relied on the Scriptures as His defense. We become strong when the Word of God abides in us, and this will allow us to overcome the Wicked One.

DO NOT LOVE THE WORLD

¹⁵ᵃDo not love the world or the things in the world. ᵇIf anyone loves the world, the love of the Father is not in him. ¹⁶For all that is in the world—the lust of the flesh, ᵃthe lust of the eyes, and the pride of life—is not of the Father but is of the world. ¹⁷And ᵃthe world is passing away, and the lust of it; but he who does the will of God abides forever.

Notes (center column):
2 ᵇJohn 1:29
4 ᵃRom. 3:4
5 ᵃJohn 14:21, 23 ᵇ[1 John 4:12] ¹has been completed
6 ᵃJohn 15:4 ᵇ1 Pet. 2:21
7 ᵃ1 John 3:11, 23; 4:21 ¹NU Beloved ²NU omits from the beginning
8 ᵃJohn 13:34; 15:12 ᵇRom. 13:12 ᶜ[John 1:9; 8:12; 12:35]
9 ᵃ[1 Cor. 13:2]
10 ᵃ[1 John 3:14] ᵇ2 Pet. 1:10
11 ᵃ[1 John 2:9; 3:15; 4:20] ᵇJohn 12:35
12 ᵃ[1 Cor. 6:11]
13 ᵃJohn 1:1 ᵇ[Rom. 8:15–17]
14 ᵃEph. 6:10
15 ᵃ[Rom. 12:2] ᵇJames 4:4
16 ᵃ[Eccl. 5:10, 11]
17 ᵃ1 Cor. 7:31

1 John 2:15–16

LOVING THE WORLD

This world's system is under the control of Satan. He is the god of this world. You can't love this world system and be attached to its values and still love God. If we are guided by the lust of the flesh, the lust of the eyes, and the pride of life, we are choosing to serve Satan, the god of this world, and we are turning our backs on the one true God.

If we love God, we will turn away from the allure of this present world system and will live our lives serving Him.

DECEPTIONS OF THE LAST HOUR

18 aLittle children, bit is the last hour; and as you have heard that cthe[1] Antichrist is coming, deven now many antichrists have come, by which we know ethat it is the last hour. 19 aThey went out from us, but they were not of us; for bif they had been of us, they would have continued with us; but *they went out* cthat they might be made manifest, that none of them were of us.
20 But ayou have an anointing bfrom the Holy One, and cyou[1] know all things. 21 I have not written to you because you do not know the truth, but because you know it, and that no lie is of the truth.
22 aWho is a liar but he who denies that bJesus is the Christ? He is antichrist who denies the Father and the Son. 23 aWhoever denies the Son does not have the bFather either; che who acknowledges the Son has the Father also.

LET TRUTH ABIDE IN YOU

24 Therefore let that abide in you awhich you heard from the beginning. If what you heard from the beginning abides in you, byou also will abide in the Son and in the Father. 25 aAnd this is the promise that He has promised us—eternal life.
26 These things I have written to you

18 a John 21:5
b 1 Pet. 4:7
c 2 Thess. 2:3
d 2 John 7
e 1 Tim. 4:1
1 NU omits the

19 a Deut. 13:13
b Matt. 24:24
c 1 Cor. 11:19

20 a 2 Cor. 1:21
b Acts 3:14
c [John 16:13]
1 NU you all know.

22 a 2 John 7
b 1 John 4:3

23 a John 15:23
b John 5:23
c 1 John 4:15; 5:1

24 a 2 John 5, 6
b John 14:23

25 a John 3:14–16; 6:40; 17:2, 3

26 1 lead you astray

27 a [John 14:16; 16:13]
b [Jer. 31:33]
c [John 14:16]
1 NU omits will

28 a 1 John 3:21; 4:17; 5:14 1 NU if

29 a Acts 22:14
b 1 John 3:7, 10

CHAPTER 3

1 a [1 John 4:10]
b [John 1:12]
c John 15:18, 21; 16:3
1 NU adds And we are.
2 M you

concerning those who *try to* [1]deceive you. 27 But the aanointing which you have received from Him abides in you, and byou do not need that anyone teach you; but as the same anointing cteaches you concerning all things, and is true, and is not a lie, and just as it has taught you, you [1]will abide in Him.

THE CHILDREN OF GOD

28 And now, little children, abide in Him, that [1]when He appears, we may have aconfidence and not be ashamed before Him at His coming. 29 aIf you know that He is righteous, you know that beveryone who practices righteousness is born of Him.

3 Behold awhat manner of love the Father has bestowed on us, that bwe should be called children of [1]God! Therefore the world does not know [2]us, cbecause it did not know Him.

1 John 3:6

ABIDING, NOT SINNING

At first glance, this verse is disturbing to any of us. "Whoever abides in Him does not sin. Whoever sins has neither seen Him nor known Him." Does this mean that you have to live a perfect life in order to know God? If so, none of us is abiding in Him, or knowing Him. John told us in chapter 1 that we all sin; and if we say we don't sin, we are making God a liar and deceiving ourselves (1 John 1:8, 10).

But the word here for "sin" is in what is called in the Greek the "linear present." What John was saying is, you can't just continue to sin, as a pattern of life, and think you are a Christian. It is not that we don't sin at all. It is just that the pattern of our lives is to grow away from the old sinful habits; and though we will still make mistakes and may fall on occasion, our lives have changed. There is an observable pattern of repentance.

2Beloved, anow we are children of God; and bit has not yet been revealed what we shall be, but we know that when He is revealed, cwe shall be like Him, for dwe shall see Him as He is. 3aAnd everyone who has this hope in Him purifies himself, just as He is pure.

SIN AND THE CHILD OF GOD

4Whoever commits sin also commits lawlessness, and asin is lawlessness. 5And you know athat He was manifested bto take away our sins, and cin Him there is no sin. 6Whoever abides in Him does not sin. Whoever sins has neither seen Him nor known Him. 7Little children, let no one deceive you. He who practices righteousness is righteous, just as He is righteous. 8aHe who sins is of the devil, for the devil has sinned from the beginning. For this purpose the Son of God was manifested, bthat He might destroy the works of the devil. 9Whoever has been aborn of God does not sin, for bHis seed remains in him; and he cannot sin, because he has been born of God.

THE IMPERATIVE OF LOVE

10In this the children of God and the children of the devil are manifest: Whoever does not practice righteousness is not of God, nor is he who does not love his brother. 11For this is the message that you heard from the beginning, athat we should love one another, 12not as aCain who was of the wicked one and murdered his brother. And why did he murder him? Because his works were evil and his brother's righteous.

---

1 John 3:11

This Is the Message. This is the heart of Jesus' message in His teaching. It is the essence of what He wants us to do. "That we should love one another."

The word here for "love" is the Greek word *agapao*. This is the word that the writers of Scripture use to refer to a selfless, Godlike love. It is defined for us in 1 Corinthians 13. Read that chapter, and you'll see the heart of the message of Jesus and the picture of what He wants us to look like.

13Do not marvel, my brethren, if athe world hates you. 14We know that we have passed from death to life, because we love the brethren. He who does not love 1his brother abides in death. 15aWhoever hates his brother is a murderer, and you know that bno murderer has eternal life abiding in him.

THE OUTWORKING OF LOVE

16aBy this we know love, bbecause He laid down His life for us. And we also ought to lay down *our* lives for the brethren. 17But awhoever has this world's goods, and sees his brother in need, and shuts up his heart from him, how does the love of God abide in him? 18My little children, alet us not love in word or in tongue, but in deed and in truth. 19And by this we 1know athat we are of the truth, and shall 2assure our hearts before Him. 20aFor if our heart condemns us, God is greater than our heart, and knows all things. 21Beloved, if our heart does not condemn us, awe have confidence toward God. 22And awhatever we ask we receive from Him, because we keep His commandments band do those things that are pleasing in His sight. 23And this is His commandment: that we should believe on the name of His Son Jesus Christ aand love one another, as He gave 1us commandment.

---

1 John 3:18

LOVING IN DEED AND TRUTH

Our love isn't to be just a verbal love. "I love you, brother. I love you so much." In fact, I often get a little suspicious of a person who is constantly asserting how much they love me.

Love isn't shown by words. Talk is cheap. Love is manifested by deeds. "God demonstrates His own love toward us, in that while we were still sinners, Christ died for us" (Rom. 5:8). Jesus didn't come to earth and say, "I love you," and then let us go to hell. He loved in deed and in truth, and we are to do the same.

Cross references:

2 a [Rom. 8:15, 16]
b [Rom. 8:18, 19, 23]
c Rom. 8:29
d [Ps. 16:11]

3 a 1 John 4:17

4 a Rom. 4:15

5 a 1 John 1:2; 3:8
b John 1:29
c [2 Cor. 5:21]

8 a Matt. 13:38
b Luke 10:18

9 a John 1:3; 3:3
b 1 Pet. 1:23

11 a [John 13:34; 15:12]

12 a Gen. 4:4, 8

13 a [John 15:18; 17:14]

14 1 NU omits his brother

15 a Matt. 5:21
b [Gal. 5:20, 21]

16 a [John 3:16]
b John 10:11; 15:13

17 a Deut. 15:7

18 a Ezek. 33:31

19 a John 18:37
1 NU shall know
2 persuade, set at rest

20 a [1 Cor. 4:4, 5]

21 a [1 John 2:28; 5:14]

22 a Ps. 34:15
b John 8:29

23 a Matt. 22:39
1 M omits us

THE SPIRIT OF TRUTH AND THE SPIRIT OF ERROR

24 Now [a]he who keeps His commandments [b]abides in Him, and He in him. And [c]by this we know that He abides in us, by the Spirit whom He has given us.

4 Beloved, do not believe every spirit, but [a]test the spirits, whether they are of God; because [b]many false prophets have gone out into the world. 2 By this you know the Spirit of God: [a]Every spirit that confesses that Jesus Christ has come in the flesh is of God, 3 and every spirit that does not confess [1]that Jesus [2]Christ has come in the flesh is not of God. And this is the *spirit* of the Antichrist, which you have heard was coming, and is now already in the world.

4 You are of God, little children, and have overcome them, because He who is in you is greater than [a]he who is in the world. 5 [a]They are of the world. Therefore they speak *as* of the world, and [b]the world hears them. 6 We are of God. He who knows God hears us; he

---

1 John 4:4

HE WHO IS IN YOU

W e overcome the enemy because the One who is in us is greater than "he who is in the world." God is infinitely greater than Satan. It isn't even close. God created Satan, and will destroy him by a word from His mouth.

How important it is for us to remember that the victory is already ours because of the One who lives in us. Satan is the god of this world, temporarily, because man handed it over to him. But God lives in us, if we have accepted Him, so we don't have to worry about Satan. God will take care of him.

Christians don't have to worry about getting possessed by demons. We have the Holy Spirit of God living in us. He won't share His temple with those losers. He is greater!

---

24 [a] John 14:23
[b] John 14:21; 17:21
[c] Rom. 8:9, 14, 16

CHAPTER 4

1 [a] 1 Cor. 14:29
[b] Matt. 24:5

2 [a] 1 Cor. 12:3

3 [1] NU omits *that*
[2] NU omits *Christ has come in the flesh*

4 [a] John 14:30; 16:11

5 [a] John 3:31
[b] John 15:19; 17:14

6 [a] [1 Cor. 2:12–16]

7 [a] 1 John 3:10, 11, 23
[b] 1 Thess. 4:9

9 [a] Rom. 5:8
[b] John 3:16

10 [a] Titus 3:5
[b] 1 John 2:2

11 [a] Matt. 18:33

12 [a] John 1:18

13 [a] John 14:20

14 [a] John 1:14
[b] John 3:17; 4:42

15 [a] [Rom. 10:9]

16 [a] [1 John 3:24]
[b] [John 14:23]

17 [a] 1 John 2:28

---

who is not of God does not hear us. [a]By this we know the spirit of truth and the spirit of error.

KNOWING GOD THROUGH LOVE

7 [a]Beloved, let us love one another, for love is of God; and everyone who [b]loves is born of God and knows God. 8 He who does not love does not know God, for God is love. 9 [a]In this the love of God was manifested toward us, that God has sent His only begotten [b]Son into the world, that we might live through Him. 10 In this is love, [a]not that we loved God, but that He loved us and sent His Son [b]*to be* the propitiation for our sins. 11 Beloved, [a]if God so loved us, we also ought to love one another.

SEEING GOD THROUGH LOVE

12 [a]No one has seen God at any time. If we love one another, God abides in us, and His love has been perfected in us. 13 [a]By this we know that we abide in Him, and He in us, because He has given us of His Spirit. 14 And [a]we have seen and testify that [b]the Father has sent the Son *as* Savior of the world. 15 [a]Whoever confesses that Jesus is the Son of God, God abides in him, and he in God. 16 And we have known and believed the love that God has for us. God is love, and [a]he who abides in love abides in God, and God [b]in him.

---

1 John 4:12

Love Perfected. No one has seen God the Father because God is spirit. But He was manifested by Jesus Christ, so that Jesus could say, "He who has seen Me has seen the Father" (John 14:9).

And when we love with the love of Jesus, we can see God in each other, and His love is perfected in us. He gives us a love for people whom we previously couldn't stand. He changes our hearts in a miraculous way. How wonderful it is to see the love of God perfected in our lives!

THE CONSUMMATION OF LOVE

17 Love has been perfected among us in this: that [a]we may have boldness in the day of judgment; because as He is, so are we in this world. 18 There is no fear in love; but perfect love casts out

---

1 John 4:18–19
Love Casts Out Fear. Today there may be things you are worrying about. You can't sleep because of fear. This is an indication that you haven't fully given it to the Lord.

If I commit my life to the Lord, I realize He loves me, and I'm His child. He is going to take care of me. Whatever He allows me to go through, it is within the sphere of His love. And as my heart responds to His love, I love Him in return; and the fear dissolves, cast out by love.

---

fear, because fear involves torment. But he who fears has not been made perfect in love. [19] aWe love [1]Him because He first loved us.

OBEDIENCE BY FAITH

[20] aIf someone says, "I love God," and hates his brother, he is a liar; for he who does not love his brother whom he has seen, [1]how can he love God bwhom he has not seen? [21]And athis commandment we have from Him: that he who loves God *must* love his brother also.

5 Whoever believes that aJesus is the Christ is bborn of God, and everyone who loves Him who begot also loves him who is begotten of Him. [2]By this we know that we love the children of God, when we love God and akeep His commandments. [3]aFor this is the love of God, that we keep His commandments. And bHis commandments are not burdensome. [4]For awhatever is born of God overcomes the world. And this is the victory that bhas overcome the world—[1]our faith. [5]Who is he who overcomes the world, but ahe who believes that Jesus is the Son of God?

THE CERTAINTY OF GOD'S WITNESS

[6]This is He who came aby water and blood—Jesus Christ; not only by water, but by water and blood. bAnd it is the Spirit who bears witness, because the Spirit is truth. [7]For there are three that bear witness [1]in heaven: the Father, athe Word, and the Holy Spirit; band these three are one. [8]And there are three that bear witness on earth: athe Spirit, the water, and the blood; and these three agree as one.

---

19 a 1 John 4:10
[1]NU omits *Him*

20 a [1 John 2:4]
b 1 John 4:12
[1]NU *he cannot*

21 a [Matt. 5:43, 44; 22:39]

CHAPTER 5

1 a 1 John 2:22; 4:2, 15
b John 1:13

2 a John 15:10

3 a John 14:15
b Matt. 11:30; 23:4

4 a John 16:33
b 1 John 2:13; 4:4
[1]M *your*

5 a 1 Cor. 15:57

6 a John 1:31–34
b [John 14:17]

7 a [John 1:1]
b John 10:30
[1]NU, M omit the words from *in heaven* (v. 7) through *on earth* (v. 8). Only 4 or 5 very late mss. contain these words in Greek.

8 a John 15:26

9 a John 5:34, 37; 8:17, 18
b [Matt. 3:16, 17]
[1]NU *God, that*

10 a [Rom. 8:16]
b John 3:18, 33

12 a [John 3:15, 36; 6:47; 17:2, 3]
[1]Or *the life*

13 [1]NU omits the rest of v. 13.

14 a [1 John 2:28; 3:21, 22]

16 a Job 42:8
b [Matt. 12:31]
c Jer. 7:16; 14:11

---

[9]If we receive athe witness of men, the witness of God is greater; bfor this is the witness of [1]God which He has testified of His Son. [10]He who believes in the Son of God ahas the witness in himself; he who does not believe God bhas made Him a liar, because he has not believed the testimony that God has given of His Son. [11]And this is the testimony: that God has given us eternal life, and this life is in His Son. [12]aHe who has the Son has [1]life; he who does not have the Son of God does not have [2]life. [13]These things I have written to you who believe in the name of the Son of God, that you may know that you have eternal life, [1]and that you may *continue to* believe in the name of the Son of God.

---

1 John 5:11–12

GOD'S BOTTOM LINE

Here is God's witness, as clear and concise as it could possibly be. "He who has the Son has life; he who does not have the Son of God does not have life." What could be plainer?

The witness of man says that all roads lead to God. We are told that sincerity is the important thing. As long as you are good intentioned, God will surely receive you.

But I will believe the witness of God over the witness of man. He says that you either have Jesus or you are lost. As simple as that.

CONFIDENCE AND COMPASSION IN PRAYER

[14]Now this is the confidence that we have in Him, that aif we ask anything according to His will, He hears us. [15]And if we know that He hears us, whatever we ask, we know that we have the petitions that we have asked of Him.

[16]If anyone sees his brother sinning a sin *which does* not *lead* to death, he will ask, and aHe will give him life for those who commit sin not *leading* to death. bThere is sin *leading* to death. cI

1 John 5:13

Assurance. John wrote this epistle so that those who believe in Jesus Christ could know that they have eternal life.

There are many people who believe that you can't know for sure that you are saved until you die. What a horrible time to find out! I don't want to wait until I die. I need the assurance now. And we can know now.

Eternal life doesn't start somewhere in the future. Eternal life starts now. We have His assurance.

17 a 1 John 3:4

18 a [1 Pet. 1:23]
b James 1:27
1 *guards*
2 NU *him*

19 a Gal. 1:4

do not say that he should pray about that. 17aAll unrighteousness is sin, and there is sin not *leading* to death.

KNOWING THE TRUE—REJECTING THE FALSE

18We know that awhoever is born of God does not sin; but he who has been born of God bkeeps1 2himself, and the wicked one does not touch him.

19We know that we are of God, and athe whole world lies *under the sway of* the wicked one.

20And we know that the aSon of God has come and bhas given us an understanding, cthat we may know Him who

20 a 1 John 4:2
b Luke 24:45
c John 17:3
d Is. 9:6
e 1 John 5:11, 12

1 John 5:14

ACCORDING TO HIS WILL

Prayer was never intended as a vehicle by which I can get my will done on the earth. Prayer is the vehicle by which I cooperate with God in order to get His will done on the earth. Even Jesus prayed, "not as I will, but as You will" (Matt. 26:39).

I have an agreement with God. If I ask God for anything that is not according to His will, I want Him to just ignore it. Even if I get upset and pout and complain, ignore it!

Sometimes I may think I know best, but I've discovered that God really knows best. So there is a tremendous confidence that comes when I pray in God's will, submitting my concerns to Him.

is true; and we are in Him who is true, in His Son Jesus Christ. dThis is the true God eand eternal life.

21Little children, keep yourselves from idols. Amen.

THE SECOND EPISTLE OF
JOHN

INTRODUCTION This second epistle of John was probably written at about the same time as 1 John, or shortly thereafter. John died around AD 100, so these letters are thought to have been written in the late AD 90s.

We don't know exactly who this letter was written to. It appears to be addressed to a particular Christian lady and her family. She is addressed as "the elect lady and her children." There are some who suggest that "Elect" might have been her name, with "lady" being a title of respect. Others have suggested that this letter was actually written to a particular church, personified as a lady. Still others have believed that a church was meeting in a lady's house, so the lady and the church are being addressed. It really doesn't matter. The book is inspired by God and has application to every Christian in every age.

In 1 John there was a big emphasis on the necessity of love. Second John puts the emphasis on truth.

In the early church it was not unusual for the people to open their homes to traveling ministers. This kind of hospitality was necessary as there were various missionaries who had itinerant ministries, including Paul, Barnabas, Timothy, Silas, and many others.

The problem was, there was also an increasing number of teachers roaming around, spreading false teaching. The false teachers often took advantage of the hospitality of these new Christians and did a lot of damage in the early church. The book of 2 John was written to warn against false teachers, and to tell the well-meaning Christians to be discerning.

In this short book John mentioned truth several times. Love was not to be offered at the expense of truth. Truth comes first, then love. He instructed his readers that if a teacher is denying who Jesus is—that He is God come in the flesh—then that teacher shouldn't even be allowed in the house. Teachers who are wrong about Christ are antichrist. This sounds harsh, but if we allow the truth to be compromised in the church then we lose our foundation.

GREETING THE ELECT LADY

The Elder,

To the [1]elect lady and her children, whom I love in truth, and not only I, but also all those who have known [a]the truth, [2]because of the truth which abides in us and will be with us forever:

[3][a]Grace, mercy, *and* peace will be with [1]you from God the Father and from the Lord Jesus Christ, the Son of the Father, in truth and love.

1 [a]Col. 1:5
[1]*chosen*

3 [a]1 Tim. 1:2
[1]NU, M *us*

WALK IN CHRIST'S COMMANDMENTS

4I ^arejoiced greatly that I have found *some* of your children walking in truth, as we received commandment from the Father. 5And now I plead with you, lady, not as though I wrote a new commandment to you, but that which we have had from the beginning: ^athat we love one another. 6^aThis is love, that we walk according to His commandments. This is the commandment, that ^bas you have heard from the beginning, you should walk in it.

---

2 John 4

Walking in Truth. One of the saddest things throughout church history is that there are so many who do not continue in the truth. There have always been false prophets who attempt to lead others astray, hassling people and turning them from the truth. Instead of going out and reaching non-Christians, the cults and other fringe groups have always found it much easier to prey on those who are nominal Christians, leading them astray.

So it is always encouraging to see those who haven't been swayed from the truth and are still just walking in the simplicity of the truth.

BEWARE OF ANTICHRIST DECEIVERS

7For ^amany deceivers have gone out into the world ^bwho do not confess Jesus Christ *as* coming in the flesh. ^cThis is a deceiver and an antichrist. 8^aLook to yourselves, ^bthat [1]we do not lose those things we worked for, but *that* [2]we may receive a full reward.

9^aWhoever [1]transgresses and does not abide in the doctrine of Christ does not have God. He who abides in the doctrine of Christ has both the Father and the Son. 10If anyone comes to you and ^adoes not bring this doctrine, do not receive him into your house nor greet him; 11for he who greets him shares in his evil deeds.

JOHN'S FAREWELL GREETING

12^aHaving many things to write to you, I did not wish *to do so* with paper

---

Marginal references:

4 ^a 3 John 3, 4

5 ^a [John 13:34, 35; 15:12, 17]

6 ^a 1 John 2:5; 5:3
^b 1 John 2:24

7 ^a 1 John 2:19; 4:1
^b 1 John 4:2
^c 1 John 2:22

8 ^a Mark 13:9
^b Gal. 3:4
[1] NU *you*

9 ^a John 7:16; 8:31
[1] NU *goes ahead*

10 ^a Rom. 16:17

12 ^a 3 John 13, 14
^b John 17:13

13 ^a 1 Pet. 5:13

---

2 John 10-11

Shut the Door. If there are those who deny the doctrine of Christ— that He is God and that He was manifested in the flesh—don't invite them into your house. If they make Jesus out to be less than God, whether they contend He is "the Son of God" and not God Himself (as the Jehovah's Witnesses say) or whether they say He is the spirit brother to Lucifer (as the Mormons teach), don't let them in. Don't let them park in your front yard. And don't let heretics into your house through the television set. Shut the door on false teaching.

---

and ink; but I hope to come to you and speak face to face, ^bthat our joy may be full.

13^aThe children of your elect sister greet you. Amen.

---

2 John 12

FACE-TO-FACE JOY

John had much to say about the fullness of joy. He told us of when Jesus said to abide in His love in order to have fullness of joy (John 15:10–11). In the next chapter, Jesus said that our prayer life will make our joy full (John 16:24). And in 1 John 1:1–5, John related that fellowship with God will fulfill our joy.

Now, here as John talked with his fellow Christians, the disciple Jesus loved told them that he wanted to see them face-to-face so that their joy might be full. This is the joy that comes from fellowshiping with each other.

As we abide in Jesus, pray to the Father, fellowship with God, and fellowship together as the body of Christ, we have fullness of joy.

THE THIRD EPISTLE OF
JOHN

INTRODUCTION The book of 3 John was probably written a little later than John's other two epistles, in the late AD 90s. Some scholars believe this third epistle was written after John wrote Revelation. The book of 1 John emphasized fellowship and love. Second John warned against those who were teaching false doctrine and encouraged discernment. Now his third epistle addressed more personal concerns within the church.

John directed the letter to Gaius. There are several Gaiuses mentioned in the New Testament, but we don't believe this one is mentioned anywhere else, and we know nothing about him other than what we read here. He was apparently a pastor of one of the churches that John was familiar with.

John was writing to encourage Gaius for his faithfulness, especially as he was hospitable to the various itinerant ministers who came through. John also spoke well of a man named Demetrius. But his main purpose in writing the letter was to point out the errors of a man named Diotrephes. His apparently wasn't an error of doctrine, but rather of practice. Diotrephes was a man who was motivated by his ego, and he was speaking against John and others. He was using the church as a way to exert his power, instead of being a servant, and he was abusing people in the process.

Correct doctrine is important but correct behavior is important, also. We need to believe the truth, but also to walk in the truth.

GREETING TO GAIUS

The Elder,

To the beloved Gaius, [a]whom I love in truth:

2Beloved, I pray that you may prosper in all things and be in health, just as your soul prospers. 3For I [a]rejoiced greatly when brethren came and testified of the truth *that is* in you, just as you walk in the truth. 4I have no greater [a]joy than to hear that [b]my children walk in [1]truth.

GAIUS COMMENDED FOR GENEROSITY

5Beloved, you do faithfully whatever you do for the brethren [1]and for strangers, 6who have borne witness of your love before the church. *If* you send them forward on their journey in a manner worthy of God, you will do

well, 7because they went forth for His name's sake, [a]taking nothing from the Gentiles. 8We therefore ought to [a]receive[1] such, that we may become fellow workers for the truth.

DIOTREPHES AND DEMETRIUS

9I wrote to the church, but Diotrephes, who loves to have the preeminence among them, does not receive us. 10Therefore, if I come, I will call to mind his deeds which he does, [a]prating[1] against us with malicious words. And not content with that, he himself does not receive the brethren, and forbids those who wish to, putting *them* out of the church.

11Beloved, [a]do not imitate what is evil, but what is good. [b]He who does good is of God, [1]but he who does evil has not seen [c]God.

---

1 [a] 2 John 1
3 [a] 2 John 4
4 [a] 1 Thess. 2:19, 20
[b] [1 Cor. 4:15]
1 NU *the truth*
5 1 NU *and especially for*
7 [a] 1 Cor. 9:12, 15
8 [a] Matt. 10:40
1 NU *support*
10 [a] Prov. 10:8, 10
1 *talking nonsense*
11 [a] Ps. 34:14; 37:27
[b] [1 John 2:29; 3:10]
[c] [1 John 3:10]
1 NU, M omit *but*

NO GREATER JOY

John the apostle was in his nineties when he wrote this letter. He didn't write long letters anymore. But he was so concerned that the young men he had raised up in the ministry uphold the standards that he had taught them.

As you read the letters to the churches in Revelation 2 and 3, you can see how messed up the churches were, after less than a hundred years. This seems to happen in great movements of God. God will do a powerful work of His Spirit in a group of people, but it usually isn't carried on to the next generation. Liberalism creeps in, and the truth is compromised. This is what generally happens in denominations; and it also happens in institutions of higher learning—even in those founded to train men for the ministry.

So John was thrilled to hear that Gaius was still walking in the truth. And like John, I too have no greater joy than to hear that my children (including all my spiritual children and grandchildren) are walking in the truth.

3 John 5–8

SUPPORTING MINISTERS

Gaius was commended for helping out those who were traveling through, as they ministered. Because he opened his home to them, helping them along, he had become a "fellow worker for the truth."

Jesus said, "He who receives a prophet in the name of a prophet shall receive a prophet's reward" (Matt. 10:41). If we help those who are ministering for the Lord, we will be rewarded as co-laborers with them.

This is why it is such a blessing to support those who go to the mission field. Maybe I can't go to Africa or some other remote place where the gospel needs to be preached; but if I can help support someone who does go there, with my prayers and financial support, it is as if I went myself. I am then a "fellow worker for the truth."

12 a 1 Tim. 3:7
b John 19:35; 21:24
1 *testify*

13 a 2 John 12

12Demetrius ahas a *good* testimony from all, and from the truth itself. And we also 1bear witness, band you know that our testimony is true.

FAREWELL GREETING

13aI had many things to write, but I do not wish to write to you with pen and ink; 14but I hope to see you shortly, and we shall speak face to face.

Peace to you. Our friends greet you. Greet the friends by name.

THE EPISTLE OF

JUDE

INTRODUCTION This rich epistle was written by Jude, the half brother of Jesus Christ. He and James were sons of Mary and Joseph, and thus they were blood relatives of Jesus Christ, through His mother, Mary.

It is interesting, though, that James and Jude did not use their relationship to Jesus to attain a special status. James described himself as "James, a bondservant of God and of the Lord Jesus Christ" (James 1:1), while Jude introduced himself as "Jude, a bondservant of Jesus Christ, and brother of James." Both James and Jude had difficulty accepting who Jesus really was until after the resurrection. Seeing their brother rise from the dead changed everything for them, and they both served as leaders in the early church, as servants of Jesus Christ.

We aren't sure when this book was written, but it is believed to have been written around AD 64. The purpose of this book was to address the apostasy that was creeping into the early church. There were ungodly men who were leading people astray by denying the deity of Christ and by promoting an immoral lifestyle that presumed on the grace of God. Jude's exhortation was to "contend earnestly for the faith" (Jude 3). He went on to cite many of the times in the past when God dealt harshly with apostates. He also alluded to many Old Testament accounts and to other events that we only learn about here, such as the contention between Michael the archangel and the Devil, and the prophecy of Enoch.

Jude didn't give instructions on how to contend for the faith. Rather, he encouraged his readers to maintain a solid walk with the Lord, being built up in the faith and keeping themselves in the love of God. He closed by reminding them that God was able to keep them from stumbling.

Today there are more heretics and apostates than ever before, which makes this little book a relevant and necessary reminder for us to contend for the faith.

GREETING TO THE CALLED

Jude, a bondservant of Jesus Christ, and [a]brother of James,

To those who are [b]called, [1]sanctified by God the Father, and [c]preserved in Jesus Christ:

2 Mercy, [a]peace, and love be multiplied to you.

CONTEND FOR THE FAITH

3 Beloved, while I was very diligent to write to you [a]concerning our common salvation, I found it necessary to write to you exhorting [b]you to contend earnestly for the faith which was once for all delivered to the saints. 4 For certain men have crept in unnoticed, who long ago were marked out for this condemnation, ungodly men, who turn the grace of our God into lewdness and deny the only Lord [1]God and our Lord Jesus Christ.

OLD AND NEW APOSTATES

5 But I want to remind you, though you once knew this, that [a]the Lord,

1 [a] Acts 1:13
[b] Rom. 1:7
[c] John 17:11, 12
1 NU *beloved*

2 [a] 1 Pet. 1:2

3 [a] Titus 1:4
[b] Phil. 1:27

4 1 NU omits *God*

5 [a] 1 Cor. 10:5–10

CONTENDING FOR THE FAITH

There were men with hidden agendas who were creeping into the church, slyly pushing for their own unique, weird twists on the Scriptures. This is still happening today. There are those who want to lead people off on their own tangents, stealing sheep from the church and establishing their own following.

We need to stand up to these people and contend for the basic truths of the Bible. "Contend earnestly for the faith which was once for all delivered to the saints." Stick to the basics. I am not interested in new truth. I am interested in new experiences in the old truth. I don't need to go beyond the Word of God.

---

having saved the people out of the land of Egypt, afterward destroyed those who did not believe. 6And the angels who did not keep their [1]proper domain, but left their own abode, He has reserved in everlasting chains under darkness for the judgment of the great day; 7as aSodom and Gomorrah, and the cities around them in a similar manner to these, having given themselves over to sexual immorality and gone after strange flesh, are set forth as an example, suffering the [1]vengeance of eternal fire.

8aLikewise also these dreamers defile the flesh, reject authority, and bspeak evil of [1]dignitaries. 9Yet Michael the archangel, in [1]contending with the devil, when he disputed about the body of Moses, dared not bring against him a reviling accusation, but said, a"The Lord rebuke you!" 10aBut these speak evil of whatever they do not know; and whatever they know naturally, like brute beasts, in these things they corrupt themselves. 11Woe to them! For they have gone in the way aof Cain, bhave run greedily in the error of Balaam for profit, and perished cin the rebellion of Korah.

---

6 [1]own

7 a Gen. 19:24
[1]punishment

8 a 2Pet. 2:10
b Ex. 22:28
[1]glorious ones,
lit. glories

9 a Zech. 3:2
[1]arguing

10 a 2Pet. 2:12

11 a Gen. 4:3–8
b 2Pet. 2:15
c Num. 16:1–3, 31–35

12 [1]stains, or hidden reefs
[2]NU, M along

13 a Is. 57:20
b [Phil. 3:19]
c 2Pet. 2:17

15 a 1Sam. 2:3

16 a 2Pet. 2:18
b Prov. 28:21

17 a 2Pet. 3:2

FALLEN ANGELS

Jude here refers to "the angels who did not keep their proper domain, but left their own abode."

We are told in Ezekiel that Satan was created by God and that he was an anointed cherub who was perfect until iniquity was found in him (Ezek. 28:12–15). In Isaiah 14, we see the fall of Satan, as he was caught up in pride and cast down from heaven (Is. 14:12–15).

In Revelation 12:4, John refers to the angels who fell with Satan— apparently a third of all the angels, who sided with him. They didn't stay where they belonged, which was in heaven serving the Lord and glorifying Him. And now they await eternal judgment.

APOSTATES DEPRAVED AND DOOMED

12These are [1]spots in your love feasts, while they feast with you without fear, serving only themselves. They are clouds without water, carried [2]about by the winds; late autumn trees without fruit, twice dead, pulled up by the roots; 13araging waves of the sea, bfoaming up their own shame; wandering stars cfor whom is reserved the blackness of darkness forever.

14Now Enoch, the seventh from Adam, prophesied about these men also, saying, "Behold, the Lord comes with ten thousands of His saints, 15to execute judgment on all, to convict all who are ungodly among them of all their ungodly deeds which they have committed in an ungodly way, and of all the aharsh things which ungodly sinners have spoken against Him."

APOSTATES PREDICTED

16These are grumblers, complainers, walking according to their own lusts; and they amouth great swelling words, bflattering people to gain advantage. 17aBut you, beloved, remember the words which were spoken before by the apostles of our Lord Jesus Christ:

[18]how they told you that [a]there would be mockers in the last time who would walk according to their own ungodly lusts. [19]These are [1]sensual persons, who cause divisions, not having the Spirit.

MAINTAIN YOUR LIFE WITH GOD

[20]But you, beloved, [a]building yourselves up on your most holy faith, [b]praying in the Holy Spirit, [21]keep yourselves in the love of God, [a]looking for the mercy of our Lord Jesus Christ unto eternal life.

[22]And on some have compassion, [1]making a distinction; [23]but [a]others save [1]with fear, [b]pulling *them* out of the [2]fire, hating even [c]the garment defiled by the flesh.

GLORY TO GOD

24 [a] Now to Him who is able to keep
[1]you from stumbling,
And [b]to present *you* faultless
Before the presence of His glory
with exceeding joy,
25   To [1]God our Savior,

[2]Who alone is wise,
Be glory and majesty,
Dominion and [3]power,
Both now and forever.
Amen.

18 [a] [1 Tim. 4:1]

19 [1] *soulish* or *worldly*

20 [a] Col. 2:7
[b] [Rom. 8:26]

21 [a] Titus 2:13

22 [1] NU *who are doubting* (or *making distinctions*)

23 [a] Rom. 11:14
[b] Amos 4:11
[c] [Zech. 3:4, 5]
[1] NU omits *with fear*
[2] NU adds *and on some have mercy with fear*

24 [a] [Eph. 3:20]
[b] Col. 1:22
[1] M *them*

25 [1] NU *the only God our*
[2] NU *Through Jesus Christ our Lord, Be glory*
[3] NU adds *Before all time,*

Jude 21

Keeping in God's Love. God loves us. He proved it when He sent His Son to die for us. And He went to that extreme measure because He wants to have fellowship with us. And because God loves you so much, He has many blessings He wants to give you. But you need to be walking with Him, obeying Him, trusting Him, in order for Him to be able to bless you.

So keep yourself in the love of God. Keep yourself in the place where God can do the things for you that He wants to do.

THE
REVELATION
OF JESUS CHRIST

INTRODUCTION The book of Revelation is an exciting book to study. Just as the book of Genesis tells us about when everything started, Revelation is the end of the story, telling us of the culmination of the ages and the end of the world as we know it.

But Revelation is not just an exciting book because it is the last chapter in history and foretells the future. Even more exciting is the fact that the book is the revelation of Jesus Christ, as it says in the first verse.

The word "revelation" means "unveiling" or "disclosure." The Gospels tell the partial story of Jesus, including His birth, life, death, and resurrection. John's gospel even tells about the preexistence and deity of Jesus, in the first chapter. But it is left to the book of Revelation to unveil the rest of the story, as the future and eternal picture of Jesus Christ is developed, and what a glorious picture it is!

The book of Revelation was written by the apostle John, as he was in exile on the isle of Patmos, probably around AD 96. Jesus Himself appeared to John and told him to write this book (Rev. 1:11). It was addressed to seven churches, there in Asia Minor, but is of relevance to anyone who is a part of the church of Jesus Christ.

The outline of the book is found in Revelation 1:19, where Jesus tells John, "Write the things which you have seen, and the things which are, and the things which will take place after this."

The first division, "the things which you have seen," refers to the vision of Jesus as recorded in the first chapter. In this section John saw Jesus in all of His glory.

The second section of the book is chapters 2 and 3, which are the letters to the seven churches. These were specific letters to these churches, but they are also an interesting survey of church history, as each successive church represents a specific phase in the history of the church. The church age is what Jesus is talking about when He says "the things which are."

Then the final section, "the things which will take place after this," refers to the future events that will take place after the rapture of the church; these events are described in chapters 4 to 22.

The Greek words for "after this" are meta tauta. These same words are used in chapter 4, verse 1, and are translated "after these things." The scene there shifts to heaven, as the church has been taken up into heaven, ending the church age. Now all that is

described in the rest of the book involves the events on heaven and earth following the rapture of the church. I expect to be with Jesus during all the rest of the events of the book.

As the book of Revelation has been seen by some as a difficult book to understand, and as there have been many different approaches and interpretations of the book, there are many who have shied away from reading it and studying it. But this is sad.

For one thing, the book contains a promise of blessing to those who study it. In verse 3 of chapter 1, John proclaims, "Blessed is he who reads and those who hear the words of this prophecy." So, there is a built-in blessing for you if you read the book of Revelation.

But remember, also, this book provides a fuller revelation of Jesus Christ Himself. If you want to know Jesus more fully, you need to study this book.

And we have seen over the years what a powerful impact the study of Revelation can have on the lives of believers. Dig in and enjoy!

INTRODUCTION AND BENEDICTION

1 The Revelation of Jesus Christ, ªwhich God gave Him to show His servants—things which must ¹shortly take place. And ᵇHe sent and signified it by His angel to His servant John, ²ªwho bore witness to the word of God, and to the testimony of Jesus Christ, to all things ᵇthat he saw. ³ªBlessed *is* he who reads and those who hear the words of this prophecy, and keep those things which are written in it; for ᵇthe time *is* near.

GREETING THE SEVEN CHURCHES

4John, to the seven churches which are in Asia:

Grace to you and peace from Him ªwho is and ᵇwho was and who is to come, ᶜand from the seven Spirits who are before His throne, 5and from Jesus Christ, ªthe faithful ᵇwitness, the ᶜfirstborn from the dead, and ᵈthe ruler over the kings of the earth.
To Him ᵉwho ¹loved us ᶠand washed us from our sins in His own blood, 6and has ªmade us ¹kings and priests to His God and Father, ᵇto Him *be* glory and dominion forever and ever. Amen.
7Behold, He is coming with ªclouds, and every eye will see Him, even ᵇthey who pierced Him. And all the tribes of the earth will mourn because of Him. Even so, Amen.

CHAPTER 1

1 ª John 3:32
ᵇ Rev. 22:6
¹ *quickly or swiftly*

2 ª 1 Cor. 1:6
ᵇ 1 John 1:1

3 ª Luke 11:28
ᵇ James 5:8

4 ª Ex. 3:14
ᵇ John 1:1
ᶜ [Is. 11:2]

5 ª John 8:14
ᵇ Is. 55:4
ᶜ [Col. 1:18]
ᵈ Rev. 17:14
ᵉ John 13:34
ᶠ Heb. 9:14
¹ NU *loves us and freed;* M *loves us and washed*

6 ª 1 Pet. 2:5, 9
ᵇ 1 Tim. 6:16
¹ NU, M *a kingdom*

7 ª Matt. 24:30
ᵇ Zech. 12:10–14

8 ª Is. 41:4
ᵇ Rev. 4:8; 11:17
ᶜ Is. 9:6
¹ NU, M *omit the Beginning and the End*
²NU, M *Lord God*

---

8 ª"I am the Alpha and the Omega, ¹*the* Beginning and *the* End," says the 2Lord, ᵇ"who is and who was and who is to come, the ᶜAlmighty."

Rev. 1:3

A BUILT-IN BLESSING

There are many people, even pastors, who avoid the book of Revelation. They say that it is a sealed book or that it is just too complicated to understand.

But Revelation is a very important book for us to understand, and God promises a blessing to those who study it. He says you will be blessed if you read it, you'll be blessed if you hear it, and most importantly, you'll be blessed if you keep the words of this book, obeying what God tells us to do.

And "the time is near." This is a good time to read, hear, and keep this book. You will be blessed. God promises.

TO THE SEVEN CHURCHES

Rev. 1:11

This book was addressed and sent to seven literal churches that were in Asia.

Seven is the number of completeness in the Bible, so these churches represented all the churches that were around at that time. But they also can be seen to represent seven stages of church history, as each church seems to coincide with a different consecutive period of time, from the first century to the present. Yet there is also a sense in which each church is applicable to every church, in every age, including today.

So there is a fascinating threefold application.

9 a Phil. 1:7
b [2 Tim. 2:12]
1 NU, M omit both

10 a Acts 10:10
b Acts 20:7
c Rev. 4:1

11 1 NU, M omit "I am the Alpha and the Omega, the First and the Last," and,
2 NU, M omit which are in Asia

12 a Ex. 25:37

13 a Rev. 2:1
b Ezek. 1:26
c Dan. 10:5
d Rev. 15:6

14 a Dan. 7:9
b Dan. 10:6

15 a Ezek. 1:7
b Ezek. 1:24; 43:2

16 a Rev. 1:20; 2:1; 3:1
b Is. 49:2
c Matt. 17:2

VISION OF THE SON OF MAN

⁹I, John, ¹both your brother and ᵃcompanion in the tribulation and ᵇkingdom and patience of Jesus Christ, was on the island that is called Patmos for the word of God and for the testimony of Jesus Christ. ¹⁰ᵃI was in the Spirit on ᵇthe Lord's Day, and I heard behind me ᶜa loud voice, as of a trumpet, ¹¹saying, ¹"I am the Alpha and the Omega, the First and the Last," and, "What you see, write in a book and send it to the seven churches ²which are in Asia: to Ephesus, to Smyrna, to Pergamos, to Thyatira, to Sardis, to Philadelphia, and to Laodicea."

¹²Then I turned to see the voice that spoke with me. And having turned ᵃI saw seven golden lampstands, ¹³ᵃand in the midst of the seven lampstands ᵇOne like the Son of Man, ᶜclothed with a garment down to the feet and ᵈgirded about the chest with a golden band. ¹⁴His head and ᵃhair were white like wool, as white as snow, and ᵇHis eyes like a flame of fire; ¹⁵ᵃHis feet were like fine brass, as if refined in a furnace, and ᵇHis voice as the sound of many waters; ¹⁶ᵃHe had in His right hand seven stars, ᵇout of His mouth went a sharp two-edged sword, ᶜand

---

THE DIVINE KEY TO REVELATION

Rev. 1:19

The key to understanding and interpreting the book of Revelation lies in this verse. "Write the things which you have seen, and the things which are, and the things which will take place after this." This gives us a built-in outline of the book.

First of all, "the things which you have seen" refers to the vision that John had in this chapter of Jesus in His glorified body. Then "the things which are" refers to the letters to the churches in chapters 2 and 3. It is a reference to the church age, which started on the day of Pentecost and continues to the present time, as we are still in the age of the church. Third, "the things which will take place after this" designates the period of time that will follow the church age. After the church is raptured, the earth will enter a new era, beginning with the tribulation, moving into the millennium, and continuing on to the eternal state.

The Greek words found here and translated "after this" are the words *meta tauta,* which mean "after these things." After what things? After the age of the church. So when we come to chapter 4, the chapter begins with the words *meta tauta* as we transition into the discussion of future events after the church is taken.

So it is very logical. The book begins with a revelation of Jesus in chapter 1 ("the things which you have seen"), then moves into the church age in chapters 2 and 3 ("the things which are"), and then moves into the future after the church age in chapters 4 to 22 ("after this").

The book isn't really that hard to understand when you realize that God has given us a built-in key.

His countenance *was* like the sun shining in its strength. [17] And [a]when I saw Him, I fell at His feet as dead. But [b]He laid His right hand on me, saying [1]to me, "Do not be afraid; [c]I am the First and the Last. [18a]I *am* He who lives, and was dead, and behold, [b]I am alive forevermore. Amen. And [c]I have the keys of [1]Hades and of Death. [19] [1]Write the things which you have [a]seen, [b]and the things which are, [c]and the things which will take place after this. [20]The [1]mystery of the seven stars which you saw in My right hand, and the seven golden lampstands: The seven stars are [a]the [2]angels of the seven churches, and [b]the seven lampstands [3]which you saw are the seven churches.

THE LOVELESS CHURCH

2 "To the [1]angel of the church of Ephesus write,

'These things says [a]He who holds the seven stars in His right hand, [b]who walks in the midst of the seven golden lampstands: [2a]"I know your works, your labor, your [1]patience, and that you cannot [2]bear those who are evil. And [b]you have tested those [c]who say they are apostles and are not, and have found them liars; [3]and you have persevered and have patience, and have labored for My name's sake and have [a]not become weary. [4]Nevertheless I have *this* against you, that you have

Rev. 2:4

FIRST LOVE

The church at Ephesus was off to a good start. And they were doing a lot of good things. But Jesus had one complaint against them. They had left their first love.

God wants everything we do to be motivated by our love for Him. The problem in Ephesus was that, although they still had the works, labor, and patience of the past, their motivation had changed. They were no longer motivated by love. Other motivations had crept in.

Jesus called them to remember and repent. Leave the legal relationship and return to the love relationship.

17 [a] Ezek. 1:28
[b] Dan. 8:18; 10:10, 12
[c] Is. 41:4; 44:6; 48:12
[1] NU, M omit *to me*

18 [a] Rom. 6:9
[b] Rev. 4:9
[c] Ps. 68:20
[1] Lit. *Unseen;* the unseen realm

19 [a] Rev. 1:9–18
[b] Rev. 2:1
[c] Rev. 4:1
[1] NU, M *Therefore, write*

20 [a] Rev. 2:1
[b] Zech. 4:2
[1] *hidden truth*
[2] Or *messengers*
[3] NU, M omit *which you saw*

CHAPTER 2

1 [a] Rev. 1:16
[b] Rev. 1:13
[1] Or *messenger*

2 [a] Ps. 1:6
[b] 1 John 4:1
[c] 2 Cor. 11:13
[1] *perseverance*
[2] *endure*

3 [a] Gal. 6:9

5 [a] Matt. 21:41

7 [a] Matt. 11:15
[b] [Rev. 22:2, 14]
[c] [Gen. 2:9; 3:22]

8 [a] Rev. 1:8, 17, 18
[1] Or *messenger*

9 [a] Luke 12:21
[b] Rom. 2:17
[c] Rev. 3:9
[1] *congregation*

10 [a] Matt. 10:22
[b] Matt. 24:13
[c] James 1:12

11 [a] Rev. 13:9
[b] [Rev. 20:6, 14; 21:8]

12 [1] Or *messenger*

left your first love. [5]Remember therefore from where you have fallen; repent and do the first works, [a]or else I will come to you quickly and remove your lampstand from its place—unless you repent. [6]But this you have, that you hate the deeds of the Nicolaitans, which I also hate.

[7a]"He who has an ear, let him hear what the Spirit says to the churches. To him who overcomes I will give [b]to eat from [c]the tree of life, which is in the midst of the Paradise of God."'

THE PERSECUTED CHURCH

[8]"And to the [1]angel of the church in Smyrna write,

'These things says [a]the First and the Last, who was dead, and came to life: [9]"I know your works, tribulation, and poverty (but you are [a]rich); and *I know* the blasphemy of [b]those who say they are Jews and are not, [c]but *are a* [1]synagogue of Satan. [10a]Do not fear any of those things which you are about to suffer. Indeed, the devil is about to throw *some* of you into prison, that you may be tested, and you will have tribulation ten days. [b]Be faithful until death, and I will give you [c]the crown of life.

Rev. 2:9

Poverty and Wealth. The Christians were undergoing intense persecution, and with that came material poverty. Jesus said He knew their poverty, yet they were rich. They were rich in the things that mattered.

You can't really measure your riches by your bank account. The true measure of riches is kept in heaven. The treasures you've laid up in heaven are your eternal wealth.

Many paupers on earth will be wealthy in heaven, and many wealthy people on earth will be impoverished in eternity. Lay up treasures in heaven.

[11a]"He who has an ear, let him hear what the Spirit says to the churches. He who overcomes shall not be hurt by [b]the second death."'

THE COMPROMISING CHURCH

[12]"And to the [1]angel of the church in Pergamos write,

'These things says [a]He who has the sharp two-edged sword: 13"I know your works, and where you dwell, where Satan's throne is. And you hold fast to My name, and did not deny My faith even in the days in which Antipas was My faithful martyr, who was killed among you, where Satan dwells. 14But I have a few things against you, because you have there those who hold the doctrine of [a]Balaam, who taught Balak to put a stumbling block before the children of Israel, [b]to eat things sacrificed to idols, [c]and to commit sexual immorality. 15Thus you also have those who hold the doctrine of the Nicolaitans, [1]which thing I hate. 16Repent, or else I will come to you quickly and [a]will fight against them with the sword of My mouth.

17"He who has an ear, let him hear what the Spirit says to the churches. To him who overcomes I will give some of the hidden [a]manna to eat. And I will give him a white stone, and on the stone [b]a new name written which no one knows except him who receives it."'

Rev. 2:17

A New Name. It was common in the Bible for God to change the name of a person to describe a new character that He was establishing in them. Abram's name was changed to Abraham, Sarai's to Sarah, Saul's to Paul. Jacob's previous name, which meant "Heel Catcher" or "Sneaky," was changed to Israel, which meant "Governed by God." And God has a special name reserved for you that will probably indicate what He plans to do for you in the future. A special name that only you will know. I like that.

THE CORRUPT CHURCH

18"And to the [1]angel of the church in Thyatira write,

'These things says the Son of God, [a]who has eyes like a flame of fire, and His feet like fine brass: 19[a]"I know your works, love, [1]service, faith, and your [2]patience; and as for your works, the last are more than the first. 20Nevertheless I have [1]a few things against you, because you allow [2]that woman [a]Jezebel, who calls herself a prophetess, [3]to teach and seduce My servants

---

12 [a]Rev. 1:16; 2:16
14 [a]Num. 31:16
[b]Acts 15:29
[c]1 Cor. 6:13
15 1 NU, M likewise.
16 [a]2 Thess. 2:8
17 [a]Ex. 16:33, 34
[b]Rev. 3:12
18 [a]Rev. 1:14, 15
1 Or messenger
19 [a]Rev. 2:2
1 NU, M faith, service
2 perseverance
20 [a]1 Kin. 16:31; 21:25
[b]Ex. 34:15
1 NU, M against you that you tolerate
2 M your wife Jezebel
3 NU, M and teaches and seduces
21 [a]Rev. 9:20; 16:9, 11
1 NU, M repent, and she does not want to repent of her sexual immorality.
22 1 NU, M her
23 [a]Jer. 11:20; 17:10
1 examines
24 [a]2 Tim. 3:1–9
[b]Acts 15:28
1 NU, M omit and
2 NU, M omit will
25 [a]Rev. 3:11
26 [a][John 6:29]
[b][Matt. 19:28]
27 [a]Ps. 2:8, 9
28 [a]2 Pet. 1:19

CHAPTER 3
1 [a]Rev. 1:4, 16
1 Or messenger
2 1 NU, M My God
3 [a]1 Tim. 6:20
[b]Rev. 3:19
[c]Matt. 24:42, 43
[d][Rev. 16:15]
4 [a]Acts 1:15
[b][Jude 23]
[c]Rev. 4:4; 6:11
1 NU, M Nevertheless you
2 NU, M omit even
5 [a][Rev. 19:8]
[b]Ex. 32:32
[c]Phil. 4:3
[d]Luke 12:8
6 [a]Rev. 2:7
7 1 Or messenger

---

[b]to commit sexual immorality and eat things sacrificed to idols. 21And I gave her time [a]to [1]repent of her sexual immorality, and she did not repent. 22Indeed I will cast her into a sickbed, and those who commit adultery with her into great tribulation, unless they repent of [1]their deeds. 23I will kill her children with death, and all the churches shall know that I am He who [a]searches[1] the minds and hearts. And I will give to each one of you according to your works.

24"Now to you I say, [1]and to the rest in Thyatira, as many as do not have this doctrine, who have not known the [a]depths of Satan, as they say, [b]I [2]will put on you no other burden. 25But hold fast [a]what you have till I come. 26And he who overcomes, and keeps [a]My works until the end, [b]to him I will give power over the nations—

27 'He[a] shall rule them with a rod of iron;
    They shall be dashed to pieces like the potter's vessels'—

as I also have received from My Father; 28and I will give him [a]the morning star. 29"He who has an ear, let him hear what the Spirit says to the churches."'

THE DEAD CHURCH

3 "And to the [1]angel of the church in Sardis write,

'These things says He who [a]has the seven Spirits of God and the seven stars: "I know your works, that you have a name that you are alive, but you are dead. 2Be watchful, and strengthen the things which remain, that are ready to die, for I have not found your works perfect before [1]God. 3[a]Remember therefore how you have received and heard; hold fast and [b]repent. [c]Therefore if you will not watch, I will come upon you [d]as a thief, and you will not know what hour I will come upon you. 4[1]You have [a]a few names [2]even in Sardis who have not [b]defiled their garments; and they shall walk with Me [c]in white, for they are worthy. 5He who overcomes [a]shall be clothed in white garments, and I will not [b]blot out his name from the [c]Book of Life; but [d]I will confess his name before My Father and before His angels.

6[a]"He who has an ear, let him hear what the Spirit says to the churches."'

THE FAITHFUL CHURCH

7"And to the [1]angel of the church in Philadelphia write,

'These things says [a]He who is holy, [b]He who is true, [c]"He who has the key of David, [d]He who opens and no one shuts, and [e]shuts and no one opens": [8a]"I know your works. See, I have set before you [b]an open door, [1]and no one can shut it; for you have a little strength, have kept My word, and have not denied My name. [9]Indeed I will make [a]those of the synagogue of Satan, who say they are Jews and are not, but lie—indeed [b]I will make them come and worship before your feet, and to know that I have loved you. [10]Because you have kept [1]My command to persevere, [a]I also will keep you from the hour of trial which shall come upon [b]the whole world, to test those who dwell [c]on the earth. [11][1]Behold, [a]I am coming quickly!

Rev. 3:8

Open Doors. I believe that the Lord often leads us by opening and closing doors. When we are seeking God's guidance in our lives, we should look for doors that He may open for us, but we also need to pay attention to doors that He may close.

When God opens a door of opportunity to me, I always want to go through it. But I also want to be sensitive to the fact that He closes doors, as well, and I don't want to force any doors open or break them down if He has closed them.

---

[b]Hold fast what you have, that no one may take [c]your crown. [12]He who overcomes, I will make him [a]a pillar in the temple of My God, and he shall [b]go out no more. [c]I will write on him the name of My God and the name of the city of My God, the [d]New Jerusalem, which [e]comes down out of heaven from My God. [f]And I will write on him My new name.

[13a]"He who has an ear, let him hear what the Spirit says to the churches." '

THE LUKEWARM CHURCH

[14]"And to the [1]angel of the church [2]of the Laodiceans write,

[a]'These things says the Amen, [b]the Faithful and True Witness, [c]the Beginning of the creation of God: [15a]"I know your works, that you are neither cold nor hot. I could wish you were cold or hot. [16]So then, because you are lukewarm, and neither [1]cold nor hot, I will vomit you out of My mouth. [17]Because you say, [a]'I am rich, have become wealthy, and have need of nothing'— and do not know that you are wretched, miserable, poor, blind, and naked— [18]I counsel you [a]to buy from Me gold refined in the fire, that you may be rich; and [b]white garments, that you may be clothed, that the shame of your nakedness may not be revealed; and anoint your eyes with eye salve, that you may see. [19a]As many as I love, I rebuke and [b]chasten[1]. Therefore be [2]zealous and repent. [20]Behold, [a]I stand at the door and knock. [b]If anyone hears My voice and opens the door, [c]I will come in to him and dine with him,

---

Marginal references:

7 [a] Acts 3:14
[b] 1 John 5:20
[c] Is. 9:7; 22:22
[d] [Matt. 16:19]
[e] Job 12:14

8 [a] Rev. 3:1
[b] 1 Cor. 16:9
[1] NU, M *which no one can shut*

9 [a] Rev. 2:9
[b] Is. 45:14;
49:23; 60:14

10 [a] 2 Pet. 2:9
[b] Luke 2:1
[c] Is. 24:17
[1] Lit. *the word of My patience*

11 [a] Phil. 4:5
[b] Rev. 2:25
[c] [Rev. 2:10]
[1] NU, M omit *Behold*

12 [a] 1 Kin. 7:21
[b] Ps. 23:6
[c] [Rev. 14:1; 22:4]
[d] [Heb. 12:22]
[e] Rev. 2:17;
[f] [Rev. 2:17; 22:4]

13 [a] Rev. 2:7

14 [a] 2 Cor. 1:20
[b] Rev. 1:5; 3:7;
19:11
[c] [Col. 1:15]
[1] *Or messenger*
[2] NU, M *in Laodicea*

15 [a] Rev. 3:1

16 [1] NU, M *hot nor cold*

17 [a] Hos. 12:8

18 [a] Is. 55:1
[b] 2 Cor. 5:3

19 [a] Job 5:17
[b] Heb. 12:6
[1] *discipline*
[2] *eager*

20 [a] Song 5:2 [b] Luke 12:36, 37 [c] [John 14:23]

THE PROTESTANT REFORMATION   Rev. 3:1–6

The church of Sardis represents the period of church history called the Protestant Reformation. It began in the 1500s and exists through the present day. This movement started with some great men, such as Martin Luther, John Calvin, John Knox, and others. It was born out of a marvelous renewal and love of the Scriptures and a desire to conform to what the Bible says the church ought to be. It rebelled against many of the abuses of the Catholic Church and its corruption.

But Jesus found the works of the church in Sardis to be imperfect because it retained many of the pagan Babylonian traditions of the Roman church. It developed into an organizational structure that was soon dead. This represents dead Protestantism. How sad it is to see some Protestant churches become as dead as the church they set out to reform.

Jesus told them, "Remember therefore how you have received and heard; hold fast and repent." If those churches would go back to the early teachings of their founders—teachings rooted in the Word—how much more alive they could be. As it is, the return of the Lord will hit them like a thief. They won't be ready. Sad.

Rev. 3:17

GOD'S PERSPECTIVE OF US

The Laodicean church thought they were doing pretty well. They said, "I am rich, have become wealthy, and have need of nothing." But the Lord was saying something quite different about them. From His perspective they were "wretched, miserable, poor, blind, and naked."

It is not important what I think of myself. But it is critically important what God thinks of me. We need to see ourselves through the eyes of God. This is why David prayed, "Search me, O God, and know my heart; try me, and know my anxieties; and see if there is any wicked way in me, and lead me in the way everlasting" (Ps. 139:23-24).

and he with Me. 21To him who overcomes aI will grant to sit with Me on My throne, as I also overcame and sat down with My Father on His throne. 22a"He who has an ear, let him hear what the Spirit says to the churches." '"

THE THRONE ROOM OF HEAVEN

4 After these things I looked, and behold, a door *standing* aopen in heaven. And the first voice which I heard *was* like a btrumpet speaking with me, saying, "Come up here, and I will show you things which must take place after this."

2Immediately aI was in the Spirit; and behold, ba throne set in heaven, and *One* sat on the throne. 31And He who sat there was alike a jasper and a sardius stone in appearance; band *there was* a rainbow around the throne, in appearance like an emerald. 4aAround the throne *were* twenty-four thrones, and on the thrones I saw twenty-four elders sitting, bclothed in white 1robes; and they had crowns of gold on their heads. 5And from the throne proceeded alightnings, 1thunderings, and voices. bSeven lamps of fire *were* burning before the throne, which are cthe 2seven Spirits of God.

Side references

21 a Matt. 19:28

22 a Rev. 2:7

CHAPTER 4

1 a Ezek. 1:1
b Rev. 1:10

2 a Rev. 1:10
b Is. 6:1

3 a Rev. 21:11
b Ezek. 1:28
1 M omits And
He who sat
there was, making the following a description
of the throne.

4 a Rev. 11:16
b Rev. 3:4, 5
1 NU, M robes,
with crowns

5 a Rev. 8:5;
11:19; 16:18
b Ex. 37:23
c [Rev. 1:4]
1 NU, M voices,
and thunderings.
2 M omits the

6 a Rev. 15:2
b Ezek. 1:5
1 NU, M add
something like

7 a Ezek. 1:10;
10:14

8 a Is. 6:2
b Is. 6:3
c Rev. 1:8
d Rev. 1:4
1 M has holy
nine times.

6Before the throne *there* 1was aa sea of glass, like crystal. bAnd in the midst of the throne, and around the throne, *were* four living creatures full of eyes in front and in back. 7aThe first living creature *was* like a lion, the second living creature like a calf, the third living creature had a face like a man, and the fourth living creature *was* like a flying eagle. 8*The* four living creatures, each having asix wings, were full of eyes around and within. And they do not rest day or night, saying:

> b"Holy, 1holy, holy,
> c Lord God Almighty,
> d Who was and is and is to come!"

Rev. 4:1

Come Up Here! This verse introduces the third major section of the book of Revelation, as the verse begins and ends with "after these things." After what things? After the church age.

The previous two chapters are addressed to the church; and when the church's ministry and witness is complete, the church will be taken up into heaven in the rapture. Jesus will say, "Come up here," and we will ascend into heaven to be with the Lord (1 Cor. 15:51-52; 1 Thess. 4:17). This will immediately precede the events of the great tribulation.

Rev. 4:2–5

The Throne of God. Many people wonder what they will see first when they get to heaven. We often think of how anxious we are to see our loved ones or to see some of the heroes of the Bible.

But John, who represented the church, had his attention immediately captured by the throne of God. This awesome throne, with God sitting on it, was just an overpowering sight for John and will probably also be the first thing we notice when we get to heaven.

Rev. 4:8–11

TWENTY-FOUR-HOUR PRAISE

In heaven John saw four angelic beings, who were praising God day and night, without stopping. They were joined in praise by the twenty-four elders. What a worship service!

They praised God for His holiness ("Holy, holy, holy"), His power ("Lord God Almighty"), and His eternality ("Who was and is and is to come"). They offered their glory, honor, and thanks. They proclaimed His worthiness and attested that He is the creator of all things and further asserted that everything exists by His will.

Such will be the activity of heaven. You should get used to praising God now and learn to enjoy worship. We will be doing a lot of that in heaven.

9 Whenever the living creatures give glory and honor and thanks to Him who sits on the throne, ᵃwho lives forever and ever, 10 ᵃthe twenty-four elders fall down before Him who sits on the throne and worship Him who lives forever and ever, and cast their crowns before the throne, saying:

11 "Youᵃ are worthy, ¹O Lord,
      To receive glory and honor and
         power;
   ᵇFor You created all things,
      And by ᶜYour will they ²exist and
         were created."

THE LAMB TAKES THE SCROLL

5 And I saw in the right *hand* of Him who sat on the throne ᵃa scroll written inside and on the back, ᵇsealed with seven seals. ²Then I saw a strong angel proclaiming with a loud voice, ᵃ"Who is worthy to open the scroll and to loose its seals?" ³And no one in heaven or on the earth or under the earth was able to open the scroll, or to look at it. ⁴So I wept much, because no one was found worthy to open ¹and read

9 ᵃRev. 1:18

10 ᵃRev. 5:8, 14; 7:11; 11:16; 19:4

11 ᵃRev. 1:6; 5:12
   ᵇGen. 1:1
   ᶜCol. 1:16
   ¹NU, M our Lord and God
   ²NU, M existed

CHAPTER 5

1 ᵃEzek. 2:9, 10
  ᵇIs. 29:11

2 ᵃRev. 4:11; 5:9

4 ¹NU, M omit and read

5 ᵃGen. 49:9
  ᵇHeb. 7:14
  ᶜIs. 11:1, 10
  ᵈRev. 3:21
  ᵉRev. 6:1
  ¹NU, M omit to loose

6 ᵃ[John 1:29]
  ᵇZech. 3:9; 4:10
  ᶜRev. 1:4; 3:1; 4:5
  ¹NU, M I saw in the midst . . . a Lamb standing

7 ᵃRev. 4:2

8 ᵃRev. 4:8–10; 19:4
  ᵇRev. 8:3

9 ᵃRev. 14:3
  ᵇRev. 4:11
  ᶜJohn 1:29
  ᵈ[Heb. 9:12]

10 ᵃEx. 19:6
   ᵇIs. 61:6
   ¹NU, M them
   ²NU a kingdom
   ³NU, M they

the scroll, or to look at it. ⁵But one of the elders said to me, "Do not weep. Behold, ᵃthe Lion of the tribe of ᵇJudah, ᶜthe Root of David, has ᵈprevailed to open the scroll ᵉand ¹to loose its seven seals."

⁶And I looked, ¹and behold, in the midst of the throne and of the four living creatures, and in the midst of the elders, stood ᵃa Lamb as though it had been slain, having seven horns and ᵇseven eyes, which are ᶜthe seven Spirits of God sent out into all the earth. ⁷Then He came and took the scroll out of the right hand ᵃof Him who sat on the throne.

WORTHY IS THE LAMB

⁸Now when He had taken the scroll, ᵃthe four living creatures and the twenty-four elders fell down before the Lamb, each having a harp, and golden bowls full of incense, which are the ᵇprayers of the saints. ⁹And ᵃthey sang a new song, saying:

   ᵇ"You are worthy to take the scroll,
      And to open its seals;
   For You were slain,
      And ᶜhave redeemed us to God
      ᵈby Your blood
      Out of every tribe and tongue and
         people and nation,
10   And have made ¹us ᵃkings² and
      ᵇpriests to our God;
      And ³we shall reign on the earth."

¹¹Then I looked, and I heard the voice of many angels around the throne, the living creatures, and the elders; and the number of them was ten thousand times ten thousand, and thousands of thousands, ¹²saying with a loud voice:

Rev. 5:8

Prayers as Incense. Prayers are often likened to incense, as "a sweet-smelling aroma" to the Lord.

How God loves for you to commune with Him! How He loves for you to just sit down and open your heart to Him, expressing to Him your love and worship! He hears your prayers, and they are a sweet smell to Him. They are precious to Him.

So John saw the prayers of the saints in heaven as a golden bowl full of incense.

THE TITLE DEED

John saw a scroll, and an angel was asking who was worthy to open the scroll. John wept convulsively because there was no one worthy to open it, until Jesus, the Lion of the tribe of Judah, came along.

Most commentators see this scroll as the title deed to the earth, and I agree with them. God had created the earth and given it over to Adam. But when Adam and Eve sinned, they gave the earth over to the power of Satan. The cost of redeeming back the earth was the blood of Jesus Christ. Jesus has already paid the price of redemption, but He hasn't yet taken possession of the earth. He will finally take possession after the tribulation, and His judgments during the tribulation are the process by which He will take possession.

When I was a child, I was told the story about a little girl who made a gingerbread man. After she had made him and put on the icing and the raisins for buttons and all, the little gingerbread man jumped out of the pan and ran away. As she began to chase him, he called out, "Run, run, as fast as you can, you can't catch me, I'm the gingerbread man!" And she couldn't catch him and went home in tears.

The next day, though, as she passed the bakery, there in the window was her little gingerbread man. She went into the store and told the baker that it was her gingerbread man in the window. He said, "I'm sorry, but if you want the gingerbread man, you'll have to pay ten cents."

She ran back home and broke open her piggy bank and got ten pennies. She hurried back to the store and put the coins on the counter, took her gingerbread man, and held him close to her chest. As she clasped him tightly, she said, "Now you are really mine. First, I made you; then I bought you. You will be mine forever!"

And as Jesus clutches you close to His chest, He says, "Now you are really mine. First, I made you; then I bought you. You will be mine forever!" He redeemed us with His blood.

Rev. 5:9–10

The Song of the Redeemed. This new song being sung in heaven will be the song of the church. It will not be a song from Israel. It will be sung by those from "every tribe and tongue and people and nation."

Israel will still be on the earth, being dealt with during the great tribulation. The church will be in heaven, singing praises to God. And God will have made us kings and priests to our God, and we will reign on the earth with Him during the millennium.

"Worthy is the Lamb who was slain
To receive power and riches and wisdom,
And strength and honor and glory and blessing!"

13And aevery creature which is in heaven and on the earth and under the

---

13 a Phil. 2:10
b 1 Chr. 29:11
c Rev. 4:2, 3; 6:16; 20:11
1 M adds *Amen*

14 1 NU, M omit *twenty-four*
2 NU, M omit *Him who lives forever and ever*

CHAPTER 6

1 a [Rev. 5:5–7, 12; 13:8]
b Rev. 4:7
1 NU, M *seven seals*

2 a Zech. 1:8; 6:3
b Ps. 45:4, 5, LXX
c Zech. 6:11
d Matt. 24:5

3 a Rev. 4:7
1 NU, M omit *and see*

4 a Zech. 1:8; 6:2

---

earth and such as are in the sea, and all that are in them, I heard saying:

b"Blessing and honor and glory and power
Be to Him cwho sits on the throne,
And to the Lamb, forever and 1ever!"

14Then the four living creatures said, "Amen!" And the 1twenty-four elders fell down and worshiped 2Him who lives forever and ever.

FIRST SEAL: THE CONQUEROR

6 Now aI saw when the Lamb opened one of the 1seals; and I heard bone of the four living creatures saying with a voice like thunder, "Come and see." 2And I looked, and behold, aa white horse. bHe who sat on it had a bow; cand a crown was given to him, and he went out dconquering and to conquer.

SECOND SEAL: CONFLICT ON EARTH

3When He opened the second seal, aI heard the second living creature saying, "Come 1and see." 4aAnother horse,

fiery red, went out. And it was granted to the one who sat on it to [b]take peace from the earth, and that *people* should kill one another; and there was given to him a great sword.

THIRD SEAL: SCARCITY ON EARTH

[5]When He opened the third seal, [a]I heard the third living creature say, "Come and see." So I looked, and behold, [b]a black horse, and he who sat on it had a pair of [c]scales[1] in his hand. [6]And I heard a voice in the midst of the four living creatures saying, "A [1]quart of wheat for a [2]denarius, and three quarts of barley for a denarius; and [a]do not harm the oil and the wine."

FOURTH SEAL: WIDESPREAD DEATH ON EARTH

[7]When He opened the fourth seal, [a]I heard the voice of the fourth living creature saying, "Come and see." [8a]So I looked, and behold, a pale horse. And the name of him who sat on it was Death, and Hades followed with him. And [1]power was given to them over a fourth of the earth, [b]to kill with sword, with hunger, with death, [c]and by the beasts of the earth.

FIFTH SEAL: THE CRY OF THE MARTYRS

[9]When He opened the fifth seal, I saw under [a]the altar [b]the souls of those who had been slain [c]for the word of God and for [d]the testimony which they held. [10]And they cried with a loud voice, saying, [a]"How long, O Lord, [b]holy and true, [c]until You judge and avenge our blood on those who dwell on the earth?" [11]Then a [a]white robe was given to each of them; and it was said to them [b]that they should rest a little while longer, until both *the number of* their fellow servants and their brethren, who would be killed as they *were*, was completed.

SIXTH SEAL: COSMIC DISTURBANCES

[12]I looked when He opened the sixth seal, [a]and [1]behold, there was a great earthquake; and [b]the sun became black as sackcloth of hair, and [2]moon became like blood. [13a]And the stars of heaven fell to the earth, as a fig tree drops its late figs when it is shaken by a mighty wind. [14a]Then the sky [1]receded as a scroll when it is rolled up; and [b]every mountain and island was moved out of its place. [15]And the [a]kings of the earth, the great men, [1]the rich men, the commanders, the mighty men, every

Cross References

- **4** [b] Matt. 24:6, 7
- **5** [a] Rev. 4:7 [b] Zech. 6:2, 6 [c] Matt. 24:7 [1] balances
- **6** [a] Rev. 7:3; 9:4 [1] Gr. *choinix*, about 1 quart [2] About 1 day's wage for a worker
- **7** [a] Rev. 4:7
- **8** [a] Zech. 6:3 [b] Ezek. 5:12, 17; 14:21; 29:5 [c] Lev. 26:22 [1] authority
- **9** [a] Rev. 8:3 [b] [Rev. 20:4] [c] Rev. 1:2, 9 [d] 2 Tim. 1:8
- **10** [a] Zech. 1:12 [b] Rev. 3:7 [c] Rev. 11:18
- **11** [a] Rev. 3:4, 5; 7:9 [b] Heb. 11:40
- **12** [a] Matt. 24:7 [b] Joel 2:10, 31; 3:15 [1] NU, M omit behold [2] NU, M whole moon
- **13** [a] Rev. 8:10; 9:1
- **14** [a] Is. 34:4 [b] Rev. 16:20 [1] Or split apart
- **15** [a] Ps. 2:2–4 [1] NU, M the commanders, the rich men,

---

Rev. 6:7–8

Population Devastation. During these first four seals, one-fourth of the earth's population will be destroyed. Just imagine! If there are four billion people on the earth at the beginning of the tribulation period, a billion people will not survive the opening of the first four seals.

You cannot believe the horror that is going to take place upon the earth once the church is taken out of the way and God begins to judge the earth for its sinfulness!

Rev. 6:2

THE MAN ON THE WHITE HORSE

A man will ride in on a white horse, "conquering and to conquer." Later, in the book of Revelation, we read that Jesus will return, riding on a white horse (ch. 19). But the man described here in chapter 6 will be an imposter. He will be a man called "the Antichrist." He is a false Messiah.

But He will come in at first looking like a hero, riding on a white horse, and will arise out of Europe to govern the world and solve all the problems. He will be seen as an economic genius, and he will have the power of Satan at his disposal. But midway through the tribulation, he will turn on the nation of Israel and will stand in the Most Holy Place and declare himself to be God, demanding to be worshiped.

This will be the last straw for God; and He will pour out on the earth His judgments, which are described in the subsequent verses here, beginning with the second seal.

Rev. 6:15–16

THE WRATH OF THE LAMB

"The wrath of the Lamb" sounds like an oxymoron, doesn't it? We don't associate wrath with lambs. Lambs are very mild animals. You don't ever see a sign that says, "Beware of ferocious lambs."

But Jesus is the Lamb of God who gave Himself as a sacrifice for our sin because of the evil of the world. And what makes the Lord angry is the effects of evil on man. And seeing the suffering of innocent people as a result of what evil has done to this earth brings on "the wrath of the Lamb." Look out!

slave and every free man, ᵇhid themselves in the caves and in the rocks of the mountains, 16ᵃand said to the mountains and rocks, "Fall on us and hide us from the face of Him who ᵇsits on the throne and from the wrath of the Lamb! 17For the great day of His wrath has come, ᵃand who is able to stand?"

THE SEALED OF ISRAEL

7 After these things I saw four angels standing at the four corners of the earth, ᵃholding the four winds of the earth, ᵇthat the wind should not blow on the earth, on the sea, or on any tree. 2Then I saw another angel ascending from the east, having the seal of the living God. And he cried with a loud voice to the four angels to whom it was granted to harm the earth and the sea, 3saying, ᵃ"Do not harm the earth, the sea, or the trees till we have sealed the servants of our God ᵇon their foreheads." 4ᵃAnd I heard the number of those who were sealed. ᵇOne hundred *and* forty-four thousand ᶜof all the tribes of the children of Israel *were* sealed:

5   of the tribe of Judah twelve
     thousand *were* sealed;
     of the tribe of Reuben twelve
     thousand *were* 1sealed;
     of the tribe of Gad twelve
     thousand *were* sealed;
6   of the tribe of Asher twelve

---

15 ᵇIs. 2:10, 19, 21; 24:21

16 ᵃLuke 23:29, 30
ᵇRev. 20:11

17 ᵃZeph. 1:14

CHAPTER 7

1 ᵃDan. 7:2
ᵇRev. 7:3; 8:7; 9:4

3 ᵃRev. 6:6
ᵇRev. 22:4

4 ᵃRev. 9:16
ᵇRev. 14:1, 3
ᶜGen. 49:1–27

5 1NU, M omit *sealed* in vv. 5b–8b.

9 ᵃRom. 11:25
ᵇRev. 5:9
ᶜRev. 3:5, 18; 4:4; 6:11

10 ᵃPs. 3:8
ᵇRev. 5:13

11 ᵃRev. 4:6
ᵇRev. 4:11; 5:9, 12, 14; 11:16

12 ᵃRev. 5:13, 14

---

thousand *were* sealed;
of the tribe of Naphtali twelve
thousand *were* sealed;
of the tribe of Manasseh twelve
thousand *were* sealed;
7   of the tribe of Simeon twelve
thousand *were* sealed;
of the tribe of Levi twelve
thousand *were* sealed;
of the tribe of Issachar twelve
thousand *were* sealed;
8   of the tribe of Zebulun twelve
thousand *were* sealed;
of the tribe of Joseph twelve
thousand *were* sealed;
of the tribe of Benjamin twelve
thousand *were* sealed.

Rev. 7:4–8

144,000. There should be no mystery as to the identity of the 144,000. They are "all the tribes of the children of Israel." And to be even more specific, the angel broke them down by tribe.

It couldn't be stated any clearer. And yet, so many groups have attempted to identify themselves as the 144,000 who are sealed by God. It isn't the church; it is Israel. And notice, there are no "lost tribes of Israel." God knows where they are.

A MULTITUDE FROM THE GREAT TRIBULATION

9After these things I looked, and behold, ᵃa great multitude which no one could number, ᵇof all nations, tribes, peoples, and tongues, standing before the throne and before the Lamb, ᶜclothed with white robes, with palm branches in their hands, 10and crying out with a loud voice, saying, ᵃ"Salvation *belongs* to our God ᵇwho sits on the throne, and to the Lamb!" 11ᵃAll the angels stood around the throne and the elders and the four living creatures, and fell on their faces before the throne and ᵇworshiped God, 12ᵃsaying:

"Amen! Blessing and glory and
     wisdom,
Thanksgiving and honor and
     power and might,
Be to our God forever and ever.
Amen."

Rev. 7:9

NO NUMBER

It is a wonderful thing to me that God doesn't keep statistics and flaunt large numbers. This verse speaks of a "great multitude which no one could number." Often in the Bible God just talks about a multitude, or He speaks in round figures. He isn't hung up on or impressed with how many people got saved. He doesn't give specific numbers, as if to glory in numbers. I like that.

People ask me, "How many people have been saved at Calvary Chapel?" or "How many Calvary Chapels are there?" I don't know. God knows. I leave the numbers to Him. He knows those who are His, and that is the important thing.

Rev. 7:14

OUT OF THE GREAT TRIBULATION

The elder identifies the great multitude as "the ones who come out of the great tribulation." I believe the greatest period of revival that the world has ever known will take place immediately after the rapture.

There will be so many people who will have heard the gospel but have not responded to it by committing their lives to Jesus. Their loved ones who have been witnessing to them for a long time will suddenly disappear. I believe this will bring many to their knees, crying out to God for salvation.

¹³Then one of the elders answered, saying to me, "Who are these arrayed in ªwhite robes, and where did they come from?"

Marginal references:

13 ª Rev. 7:9

14 ª Rev. 6:9
b [Heb. 9:14]
1 NU, M *My lord*

15 ª Is. 4:5, 6

16 ª Is. 49:10
b Ps. 121:6

17 ª Ps. 23:1
b Rev. 21:4
1 NU, M *fountains of the waters of life*

CHAPTER 8

1 ª Rev. 6:1

2 ª [Matt. 18:10]
b 2 Chr. 29:25–28

3 ª Rev. 5:8
b Ex. 30:1

4 ª Ps. 141:2

5 ª Rev. 11:19; 16:18
b Rev. 4:5
c 2 Sam. 22:8

---

¹⁴And I said to him, *1*"Sir, you know." So he said to me, ª"These are the ones who come out of the great tribulation, and bwashed their robes and made them white in the blood of the Lamb. ¹⁵Therefore they are before the throne of God, and serve Him day and night in His temple. And He who sits on the throne will ªdwell among them. ¹⁶ªThey shall neither hunger anymore nor thirst anymore; bthe sun shall not strike them, nor any heat; ¹⁷for the Lamb who is in the midst of the throne ªwill shepherd them and lead them to *1*living fountains of waters. bAnd God will wipe away every tear from their eyes."

SEVENTH SEAL: PRELUDE TO THE SEVEN TRUMPETS

8 When ªHe opened the seventh seal, there was silence in heaven for about half an hour. ²ªAnd I saw the seven angels who stand before God, band to them were given seven trumpets. ³Then another angel, having a golden censer, came and stood at the altar. He was given much incense, that he should offer *it* with ªthe prayers of all the saints upon bthe golden altar which was before the throne. ⁴And ªthe smoke of the incense, with the prayers of the saints, ascended before God from the angel's hand. ⁵Then the angel took the censer, filled it with fire from the altar, and threw *it* to the earth. And ªthere were noises, thunderings, blightnings, cand an earthquake.

⁶So the seven angels who had the seven trumpets prepared themselves to sound.

Rev. 8:1

An Eerie Silence. Silence can sometimes be an awesome thing, especially in a large group of people. There will possibly be as many as hundreds of millions of people in heaven. Imagine that many people, with total silence. It is like the calm before a storm.

Weather experts say that there is an awesome silence right before a tornado hits, as there is in the eye of a hurricane. So there will be this silence in heaven, right before the judgment hits.

FIRST TRUMPET: VEGETATION STRUCK

7The first angel sounded: aAnd hail and fire followed, mingled with blood, and they were thrown bto the learth. And a third cof the trees were burned up, and all green grass was burned up.

Rev. 8:7

GRASS AND TREES BURNED

The first of the judgments will strike the first of God's creation upon the earth. After God separated the land from the waters, He created plants and trees. They were the first of God's creation, and they will be the first to experience His judgment. He will destroy a third of them in a tremendous fire.

It is interesting that in the pagan religions that are spreading so much today the trees are worshiped, as Mother Earth, or Gaea, is seen as the primary deity. There is today a legitimate concern for our environment and its destruction. But people are defending the environment, not on a rational basis but on a religious basis, and that is wrong.

Nature is a beautiful and valuable resource; but if man insists on worshiping trees, then trees will be destroyed. God won't allow other gods before Him.

SECOND TRUMPET: THE SEAS STRUCK

8Then the second angel sounded: aAnd *something* like a great mountain burning with fire was thrown into the sea, band a third of the sea cbecame blood. 9aAnd a third of the living creatures in the sea died, and a third of the ships were destroyed.

THIRD TRUMPET: THE WATERS STRUCK

10Then the third angel sounded: aAnd a great star fell from heaven, burning like a torch, band it fell on a third of the

Notes (center column)

7 aEzek. 38:22
bRev. 16:2
cRev. 9:4, 15–18
1NU, M add *and a third of the earth was burned up*

8 aJer. 51:25
bEx. 7:17
cEzek. 14:19

9 aRev. 16:3

10 aIs. 14:12
bRev. 14:7; 16:4

11 aRuth 1:20
bEx. 15:23

12 aIs. 13:10
1*had no light*

13 aRev. 14:6; 19:17
bRev. 9:12; 11:14; 12:12
1NU, M *eagle*

CHAPTER 9

1 aRev. 8:10
bLuke 8:31
1Lit. *shaft of the abyss*

2 aJoel 2:2, 10

3 aJudg. 7:12

4 aRev. 6:6
bRev. 8:7
cRev. 7:2, 3

5 1The locusts

---

rivers and on the springs of water. 11aThe name of the star is Wormwood. bA third of the waters became wormwood, and many men died from the water, because it was made bitter.

Rev. 8:10–11

Water Pollution. The third thing that God will attack in this judgment is the fresh water supply on the earth. Man has done a pretty good job of polluting the lakes, rivers, and streams, and even the ground water. But the pollution of today is nothing compared to this judgment, where a third of all the fresh water on the earth will be polluted and poisoned.

You don't want to be there, and, thank God, you don't have to be there. God has provided a way of escape for His church.

FOURTH TRUMPET: THE HEAVENS STRUCK

12aThen the fourth angel sounded: And a third of the sun was struck, a third of the moon, and a third of the stars, so that a third of them were darkened. A third of the day ldid not shine, and likewise the night.

13And I looked, aand I heard an langel flying through the midst of heaven, saying with a loud voice, b"Woe, woe, woe to the inhabitants of the earth, because of the remaining blasts of the trumpet of the three angels who are about to sound!"

FIFTH TRUMPET: THE LOCUSTS FROM THE BOTTOMLESS PIT

9Then the fifth angel sounded: aAnd I saw a star fallen from heaven to the earth. To him was given the key to bthe lbottomless pit. 2And he opened the bottomless pit, and smoke arose out of the pit like the smoke of a great furnace. So the asun and the air were darkened because of the smoke of the pit. 3Then out of the smoke locusts came upon the earth. And to them was given power, aas the scorpions of the earth have power. 4They were commanded anot to harm bthe grass of the earth, or any green thing, or any tree, but only those men who do not have cthe seal of God on their foreheads. 5And lthey were not given *authority* to

Rev. 9:6

FATE WORSE THAN DEATH

Death will take a holiday for five months. People will not be able to die, even if they want to.

Death isn't the worst thing. Sometimes living is worse than death. When the body can no longer fulfill the purposes for which God designed and created it, it can become a prison of pain. I have seen people who are in agony, kept alive by artificial means, just wanting to die. That's not living.

Can you imagine what it will be like for these people who are being tormented by demons, wanting to die, trying to commit suicide, but they just can't be put out of their misery? It will be a horrible time.

kill them, ªbut to torment them *for* five months. Their torment *was* like the torment of a scorpion when it strikes a man. 6In those days ªmen will seek death and will not find it; they will desire to die, and death will flee from them.
7ªThe shape of the locusts was like horses prepared for battle. bOn their heads were crowns of something like gold, cand their faces *were* like the faces of men. 8They had hair like women's hair, and ªtheir teeth were like lions' *teeth.* 9And they had

Rev. 9:11

The Destroyer. Satan's name given here is *Abaddon* in Hebrew, which means "Destruction"; and in Greek, it is *Apollyon*, which means "Destroyer." What an appropriate name for Satan! The Destroyer. Look at all the lives he has destroyed. People who have given control of their lives and hearts to the powers of darkness. How he has ruined and destroyed their lives!

5 ª[Rev. 9:10; 11:7]

6 ª Jer. 8:3

7 ª Joel 2:4
b Nah. 3:17
c Dan. 7:8

8 ª Joel 1:6

9 ª Joel 2:5–7

11 ª Eph. 2:2
1 Lit. *Destruction*
2 Lit. *Destroyer*

12 ª Rev. 8:13; 11:14

13 ª Rev. 8:3

14 ª Rev. 16:12

15 ª Rev. 8:7–9; 9:18

16 ª Dan. 7:10
b Ezek. 38:4
c Rev. 7:4

breastplates like breastplates of iron, and the sound of their wings *was* ªlike the sound of chariots with many horses running into battle. 10They had tails like scorpions, and there were stings in their tails. Their power *was* to hurt men five months. 11And they had as king over them ªthe angel of the bottomless pit, whose name in Hebrew *is* 1Abaddon, but in Greek he has the name 2Apollyon.
12ªOne woe is past. Behold, still two more woes are coming after these things.

SIXTH TRUMPET: THE ANGELS FROM THE EUPHRATES

13Then the sixth angel sounded: And I heard a voice from the four horns of the ªgolden altar which is before God, 14saying to the sixth angel who had the trumpet, "Release the four angels who are bound ªat the great river Euphrates." 15So the four angels, who had been prepared for the hour and day and month and year, were released to kill a ªthird of mankind. 16Now ªthe number of the army bof the horsemen *was* two hundred million; cI heard the number of them. 17And thus I saw the horses in the vision: those who sat on

Rev. 9:18

MASSIVE SLAUGHTER

In this one trumpet judgment, one-third of the earth's population will be killed!

Now, assuming a world population at the time of the rapture at four billion people left on the planet, we know that one-fourth of that population, or a billion people, will be killed during the first four seal judgments. Now, at the sixth trumpet, another third of the world's population will die, or another billion people. Thus, during just this part of the great tribulation, half the world's population will be wiped out.

As Jesus said, it will be a time of trouble such as the world has never seen or will ever see again!

them had breastplates of fiery red, hyacinth blue, and sulfur yellow; [a]and the heads of the horses *were* like the heads of lions; and out of their mouths came fire, smoke, and brimstone. [18]By these three *plagues* a third of mankind was killed—by the fire and the smoke and the brimstone which came out of their mouths. [19]For [1]their power is in their mouth and in their tails; [a]for their tails *are* like serpents, having heads; and with them they do harm.

[20]But the rest of mankind, who were not killed by these plagues, [a]did not repent of the works of their hands, that they should not worship [b]demons, [c]and idols of gold, silver, brass, stone, and wood, which can neither see nor hear nor walk. [21]And they did not repent of their murders [a]or their [1]sorceries or their sexual immorality or their thefts.

THE MIGHTY ANGEL WITH THE LITTLE BOOK

10 I saw still another mighty angel coming down from heaven, clothed with a cloud. [a]And a rainbow *was* on [b]his head, his face *was* like the sun, and [c]his feet like pillars of fire. [2]He had a little book open in his hand. [a]And he set his right foot on the sea and *his* left *foot* on the land, [3]and cried with a loud voice, as *when* a lion roars. When he cried out, [a]seven thunders uttered their voices. [4]Now when the seven thunders [1]uttered their voices, I was about to write; but I heard a voice from heaven saying [2]to me, [a]"Seal up the things which the seven thunders uttered, and do not write them."

[5]The angel whom I saw standing on the sea and on the land [a]raised up his [1]hand to heaven [6]and swore by Him who lives forever and ever, [a]who created heaven and the things that are in it, the earth and the things that are in it, and the sea and the things that are in it, [b]that there should be delay no longer, [7]but [a]in the days of the sounding of the seventh angel, when he is about to sound, the mystery of God would be finished, as He declared to His servants the prophets.

JOHN EATS THE LITTLE BOOK

[8]Then the voice which I heard from heaven spoke to me again and said, "Go, take the little book which is open in the hand of the angel who stands on the sea and on the earth."

[9]So I went to the angel and said to him, "Give me the little book."

Cross References

17 [a] Is. 5:28, 29

19 [a] Is. 9:15
[1] NU, M *the power of the horses*

20 [a] Deut. 31:29
[b] 1 Cor. 10:20
[c] Dan. 5:23

21 [a] Rev. 21:8; 22:15
[1] NU, M *drugs*

CHAPTER 10

1 [a] Rev. 4:3
[b] Rev. 1:16
[c] Rev. 1:15

2 [a] Matt. 28:18

3 [a] Ps. 29:3–9

4 [a] Dan. 8:26; 12:4, 9
[1] NU, M *sounded,*
[2] NU, M omit *to me*

5 [a] Dan. 12:7
[1] NU, M *right hand*

6 [a] Rev. 4:11
[b] Rev. 16:17

7 [a] Rev. 11:15

9 [a] Jer. 15:16

Rev. 10:1–3

THE MIGHTY ANGEL

The word "angel" means "messenger." We usually think of angels as the spirit beings who were created by God as ministering spirits; but in the Bible, sometimes people are described as angels, and Jesus Christ appears often in the Old Testament as "the Angel of the LORD."

I personally believe that the messenger described here is none other than Jesus Christ, the Angel of the Lord. He is clothed with a cloud. Jesus Himself said that He would return in clouds (Mark 13:26). The rest of this description also sounds so much like the description of Jesus in Revelation 1. Also, He is holding a book, which is probably the scroll He took in chapter 5. Therefore, it is reasonable to believe that this "mighty angel" is Jesus Himself.

Rev. 10:7

The End of the Mystery. The prophets had foretold the day when God would make everything right. Righteousness would cover the earth like a sea. Everything damaged by the fall would be restored. The Messiah would come and make everything as new in the glorious kingdom of God. And now it is about to happen.

That which had been declared to the prophets will now be fulfilled, and "the mystery of God would be finished." The final chapter is about to unfold.

And he said to me, [a]"Take and eat it; and it will make your stomach bitter, but it will be as sweet as honey in your mouth."

[10]Then I took the little book out of

the angel's hand and ate it, [a]and it was as sweet as honey in my mouth. But when I had eaten it, [b]my stomach became bitter. [11]And [1]he said to me,

10 [a]Ezek. 3:3
[b]Ezek. 2:10

11 [1]NU, M *they*

"You must prophesy again about many peoples, nations, tongues, and kings."

THE TWO WITNESSES

11 Then I was given [a]a reed like a measuring rod. [1]And the angel stood, saying, [b]"Rise and measure the temple of God, the altar, and those who worship there. [2]But leave out [a]the court which is outside the temple, and do not measure it, [b]for it has been given to the Gentiles. And they will [c]tread the holy city underfoot *for* [d]forty-two months. [3]And I will give *power* to my two [a]witnesses, [b]and they will prophesy [c]one thousand two hundred and sixty days, clothed in sackcloth."

[4]These are the [a]two olive trees and the two lampstands standing before the [1]God of the earth. [5]And if anyone wants to harm them, [a]fire proceeds from their mouth and devours their enemies. [b]And if anyone wants to harm them, he must be killed in this manner. [6]These [a]have power to shut heaven, so that no rain falls in the days of their prophecy; and they have power over waters to turn them to blood, and to strike the earth with all plagues, as often as they desire.

THE WITNESSES KILLED

[7]When they [a]finish their testimony, [b]the beast that ascends [c]out of the bottomless pit [d]will make war against them, overcome them, and kill them. [8]And their dead bodies *will lie* in the

CHAPTER 11

1 [a]Ezek. 40:3–42:20
[b]Num. 23:18
[1]NU, M omit *And the angel stood*

2 [a]Ezek. 40:17, 20
[b]Ps. 79:1
[c]Dan. 8:10
[d]Rev. 12:6; 13:5

3 [a]Rev. 20:4
[b]Rev. 19:10
[c]Rev. 12:6

4 [a]Zech. 4:2, 3, 11, 14
[1]NU, M *Lord*

5 [a]2 Kin. 1:10–12
[b]Num. 16:29

6 [a]1 Kin. 17:1

7 [a]Luke 13:32
[b]Rev. 13:1, 11; 17:8
[c]Rev. 9:1, 2
[d]Dan. 7:21

Rev. 10:9–10

SWEET AND BITTER

As John devoured the book and as he realized that the kingdom of God was about to be established, it was sweet. Just the thought of the glories of the kingdom, the coming reign of Jesus Christ, the deserts blossoming forth as a rose, the lion and the lamb eating together, no more war! Thinking about it is just as sweet as honey!

But then contemplating the horrible things that must take place beforehand and the judgment that must be poured out on the earth, it just gave him a sick feeling. And it is a bittersweet feeling, as we look forward to the return of Christ, and the glories of His kingdom, while also realizing that it will mean horrible pain and suffering that will come in the process, as sin is judged.

ANTICHRIST'S MIDDLE EAST SOLUTION

Rev. 11:1–2

One of the major factors in the negotiations between the Jews and Moslems in Jerusalem is the problem of the Temple Mount. It is a holy site to the Jewish people; but it is also a holy site for the Moslems as it houses the Al-Aqsa Mosque and the Dome of the Rock. This is a huge problem when you consider that the Jews are going to rebuild their temple during the tribulation period and will be sacrificing there.

I believe this passage gives us a strong hint as to how this will take place. In measuring the temple of God, John was told to not measure the outer court, which had been given to the Gentiles. In Ezekiel 42:20, in measuring the temple area, there was a wall that was said to separate the holy areas from the common or profane. I believe that a likely scenario is that the Antichrist, when negotiating a peace treaty with Israel, will come up with the idea of building a large wall on the Temple Mount and allowing the Jews to rebuild their temple to the north of the Dome of the Rock, on the other side of a large wall.

This could work for the Jews and Arabs alike. And it is likely that this is the reason why the outer court was not measured here. It is in the Moslem area of the Temple Mount. And this would be perceived as a brilliant solution provided by this great world leader.

street of ^athe great city which spiritually is called Sodom and Egypt, ^bwhere also ¹our Lord was crucified. ⁹^aThen *those* from the peoples, tribes, tongues, and nations ¹will see their dead bodies three-and-a-half days, ^band not allow their dead bodies to be put into graves. ¹⁰^aAnd those who dwell on the earth will rejoice over them, make merry, ^band send gifts to one another, ^cbecause these two prophets tormented those who dwell on the earth.

THE WITNESSES RESURRECTED

¹¹^aNow after the three-and-a-half days ^bthe breath of life from God entered them, and they stood on their feet, and great fear fell on those who saw them. ¹²And ¹they heard a loud voice from heaven saying to them, "Come up here." ^aAnd they ascended to heaven ^bin a cloud, ^cand their enemies saw them. ¹³In the same hour ^athere was a great earthquake, ^band a tenth of the city fell. In the earthquake seven thousand people were killed, and the rest were afraid ^cand gave glory to the God of heaven.

¹⁴^aThe second woe is past. Behold, the third woe is coming quickly.

SEVENTH TRUMPET: THE KINGDOM PROCLAIMED

¹⁵Then ^athe seventh angel sounded: ^bAnd there were loud voices in heaven, saying, ^c"The ¹kingdoms of this world

have become *the kingdoms* of our Lord and of His Christ, ^dand He shall reign forever and ever!" ¹⁶And ^athe twenty-four elders who sat before God on their thrones fell on their faces and ^bworshiped God, ¹⁷saying:

"We give You thanks, O Lord God Almighty,
The One ^awho is and who was ¹and who is to come,
Because You have taken Your great power ^band reigned.
18   The nations were ^aangry, and

8 ^aRev. 14:8
^bHeb. 13:12
1 NU, M *their*
9 ^aRev. 17:15
^bPs. 79:2, 3
1 NU, M *see . . . and will not allow*
10 ^aRev. 12:12
^bEsth. 9:19, 22
^cRev. 16:10
11 ^aRev. 11:9
^bEzek. 37:5, 9, 10
12 ^aIs. 14:13
^bActs 1:9
^c2 Kin. 2:11, 12
1 M *I*
13 ^aRev. 6:12; 8:5; 11:19; 16:18
^bRev. 16:19
^cRev. 14:7; 16:9; 19:7
14 ^aRev. 8:13; 9:12
15 ^aRev. 8:2; 10:7
^bIs. 27:13
^cRev. 12:10
^dEx. 15:18
1 NU, M *kingdom . . . has become the kingdom*
16 ^aRev. 4:4
^bRev. 4:11; 5:9, 12, 14; 7:11
17 ^aRev. 16:5
^bRev. 19:6
1 NU, M omit *and who is to come*
18 ^aPs. 2:1

Rev. 11:19

The True Temple. The temples that were built here on earth were only models of the true temple, which is in heaven. That is why the instructions for construction were so precise. They were patterned after the temple in heaven.

We don't know where the ark of the covenant that was in the earthly temple is now, but it was only a model of the real one that is in heaven. I wouldn't spend a whole lot of effort trying to find the ark down here. Someday I will see the real thing.

THE TWO WITNESSES

Rev. 11:4–12

Here we see the account of these two witnesses who will testify during the tribulation, as they are martyred, resurrected, and raptured. There has been much discussion as to the identity of these two witnesses.

Most people agree that one of them is Elijah. In the book of Malachi, in the last words of the Old Testament, it was prophesied that Elijah would be coming before the day of the Lord (Mal. 4:5–6).

But what about the identity of the second prophet? If God wanted us to know for sure, He would have told us, but there is much speculation. Some have thought it will be Enoch, because of the fact that Enoch, like Elijah, never died. There are many other theories, though, such as Zechariah, John the Baptist, and others. The leading candidate would have to be Moses, and that is probably who it is.

The miracles the witnesses will perform are like the miracles of Moses and Elijah. And Moses would be seen as the representative of the Law, while Elijah represents the Prophets. And, of course, when Jesus was transfigured, Moses and Elijah showed up together, so it would seem reasonable that these two would be the two prophets depicted here.

They will be indestructible until "they finish their testimony," and I believe we are, too. Nothing can harm us until God finishes what He wants to do in our lives. At that point, He will say to us, "Come up here," and we will.

Your *wrath has come,
And the time of the ^bdead, that
they should be judged,
And that You should reward Your
servants the prophets and the
saints,
And those who fear Your name,
small and great,
And should destroy those who
destroy the earth."

¹⁹Then ^athe temple of God was opened in heaven, and the ark of *His covenant was seen in His temple. And ^bthere were lightnings, noises, thunderings, an earthquake, ^cand great hail.

THE WOMAN, THE CHILD, AND THE DRAGON

12 Now a great sign appeared in heaven: a woman clothed with the sun, with the moon under her feet, and on her head a garland of twelve stars. ²Then being with child, she cried out ^ain labor and in pain to give birth.

³And another sign appeared in heaven: behold, ^aa great, fiery red dragon having seven heads and ten horns, and seven diadems on his heads. ⁴ ^aHis tail drew a third ^bof the stars of heaven ^cand threw them to the earth. And the dragon stood ^dbefore the woman who was ready to give birth, ^eto devour her

SATAN'S MISSION

Satan, who is here depicted as having been cast out of heaven, along with a third of the angels who chose to rebel with him, had as his primary mission the destruction of Jesus, the Child who was born out of Israel. He knew if he could destroy Jesus he would also destroy mankind.

The plot of Herod to kill the babies was a part of Satan's attempt. The temptation of Jesus to convince Him to take a shortcut by skipping the cross was a part of Satan's evil plan. But he was defeated, and Jesus died and was "caught up to God and His throne," and our salvation was secured, praise God!

Child as soon as it was born. ⁵She bore a male Child ^awho was to rule all nations with a rod of iron. And her Child was ^bcaught up to God and His throne. ⁶Then ^athe woman fled into the wilderness, where she has a place prepared by God, that they should feed her there ^bone thousand two hundred and sixty days.

SATAN THROWN OUT OF HEAVEN

⁷And war broke out in heaven: ^aMichael and his angels fought ^bwith the dragon; and the dragon and his angels fought, ⁸but they *did not prevail, nor was a place found for ²them in heaven any longer. ⁹So ^athe great dragon was cast out, ^bthat serpent of old, called the Devil and Satan, ^cwho deceives the whole world; ^dhe was cast to the earth, and his angels were cast out with him.

¹⁰Then I heard a loud voice saying in heaven, ^a"Now salvation, and strength, and the kingdom of our God, and the power of His Christ have come, for the accuser of our brethren, ^bwho accused them before our God day and night, has been cast down. ¹¹And ^athey

Marginal references

18 ^bDan. 7:10
anger

19 ^aRev. 4:1; 15:5, 8
^bRev. 8:5
^cRev. 16:21
M the covenant of the Lord

CHAPTER 12

2 ^aIs. 26:17; 66:6–9

3 ^aRev. 13:1; 17:3, 7, 9

4 ^aRev. 9:10, 19
^bRev. 8:7, 12
^cDan. 8:10
^dRev. 12:2
^eMatt. 2:16

5 ^aPs. 2:9
^bActs 1:9–11

6 ^aRev. 12:4, 14
^bRev. 11:3; 13:5

7 ^aDan. 10:13, 21; 12:1
^bRev. 20:2

8 *were not strong enough*
²M *him*

9 ^aJohn 12:31
^bGen. 3:1, 4
^cRev. 20:3
^dRev. 9:1

10 ^aRev. 11:15
^bZech. 3:1

11 ^aRom. 16:20

Rev. 12:10

THE ACCUSER

Satan is no friend of ours. He may come on as an angel of light, offering enticing things, but he hates people. And he is always "before our God day and night," accusing us.

If we didn't have an Advocate, Jesus Christ, interceding for us, we would be doomed. But Jesus stands up for us against the accusations of Satan, forever interceding for us (Heb. 7:25). It will still be a happy day when Satan is cast down forever and our enemy is vanquished.

Every once in a while, someone will come up to me and start accusing me of something that they think I've done wrong or said wrong. I have occasionally responded to them, "Who is the accuser of the brethren?" This usually shuts them up.

Rev. 12:11

HOW TO OVERCOME THE ENEMY

We see here three ways in which the dragon was overcome and three ways we can overcome Satan.

First of all, the blood of the Lamb. It was at the cross that Satan was defeated. I claim the victory that was won at the cross.

Second, it was through the word of their testimony. And my testimony is that I have made Jesus my Lord. I am submitting to Him and obeying Him, and that keeps Satan from controlling my life.

Third, they did not love their lives to the death. I am not living for myself. I would rather die for Jesus than live without Him.

These are three things that overcome the enemy.

overcame him by the blood of the Lamb and by the word of their testimony, band they did not love their lives to the death. 12Therefore arejoice, O heavens, and you who dwell in them! bWoe to the inhabitants of the earth and the sea! For the devil has come down to you, having great wrath, cbecause he knows that he has a short time."

THE WOMAN PERSECUTED

13Now when the dragon saw that he had been cast to the earth, he persecuted athe woman who gave birth to the male *Child*. 14aBut the woman was given two wings of a great eagle, bthat she might fly cinto the wilderness to her place, where she is nourished dfor a time and times and half a time, from the presence of the serpent. 15So the serpent aspewed water out of his mouth like a flood after the woman, that he might cause her to be carried away by the flood. 16But the earth helped the woman, and the earth opened its mouth and swallowed up the flood which the dragon had spewed out of his mouth.

---

11 b Luke 14:26

12 a Ps. 96:11
b Rev. 8:13
c Rev. 10:6

13 a Rev. 12:5

14 a Ex. 19:4
b Rev. 12:6
c Rev. 17:3
d Dan. 7:25;
12:7

15 a Is. 59:19

17 1 NU, M omit
Christ

CHAPTER 13

1 a Dan. 7:2, 7
b Rev. 12:3
c Rev. 17:3
1 NU he
2 NU, M ten
horns and seven
heads

2 a Rev. 12:3, 9;
13:4, 12

3 a Rev. 13:12,
14
b Rev. 17:8

4 a Rev. 18:18

5 a Dan. 7:8, 11,
20, 25; 11:36
b Rev. 11:2
1 M make war

17And the dragon was enraged with the woman, and he went to make war with the rest of her offspring, who keep the commandments of God and have the testimony of Jesus 1Christ.

THE BEAST FROM THE SEA

13 Then 1I stood on the sand of the sea. And I saw aa beast rising up out of the sea, bhaving 2seven heads and ten horns, and on his horns ten crowns, and on his heads a cblasphemous name. 2Now the beast which I saw was like a leopard, his feet were like *the feet of* a bear, and his mouth like the mouth of a lion. The adragon gave him his power, his throne, and great authority. 3And I saw one of his heads aas if it had been mortally wounded, and his deadly wound was healed. And ball the world marveled and followed the beast. 4So they worshiped the dragon who gave authority to the beast; and they worshiped the beast, saying, a"Who *is* like the beast? Who is able to make war with him?"

5And he was given aa mouth speaking great things and blasphemies, and he was given authority to 1continue for bforty-two months. 6Then he opened

Rev. 13:7

OVERCOMING THE SAINTS

There are those who see this reference here to "the saints," and they jump to the conclusion that the church must still be here during the tribulation. But this isn't referring to the church. It is referring to Israel.

The Antichrist was allowed here "to make war with the saints and to overcome them." That couldn't be a reference to the church because Jesus said that the gates of hell (Hades) would not prevail against the church (Matt. 16:18). During the tribulation, Israel will be called "the elect" or "the saints" because this will be the time when God will deal with them as a nation again.

his mouth in blasphemy against God, to blaspheme His name, ªHis tabernacle, and those who dwell in heaven. [7]It was granted to him ªto make war with the saints and to overcome them. And [b]authority was given him over every [1]tribe, tongue, and nation. [8]All who dwell on the earth will worship him, ªwhose names have not been written in the Book of Life of the Lamb slain [b]from the foundation of the world.

[9]If anyone has an ear, let him hear. [10]ªHe who leads into captivity shall go into captivity; [b]he who kills with the sword must be killed with the sword. [c]Here is the [1]patience and the faith of the saints.

THE BEAST FROM THE EARTH

[11]Then I saw another beast ªcoming up out of the earth, and he had two horns like a lamb and spoke like a dragon. [12]And he exercises all the authority of the first beast in his presence, and causes the earth and those who dwell in it to worship the first beast, ªwhose deadly wound was healed. [13]ªHe performs great signs, [b]so that he even makes fire come down from heaven on the earth in the sight of men. [14]ªAnd he deceives [1]those who dwell on the earth [b]by those signs which he was granted to do in the sight of the beast, telling those who dwell on the earth to make an image to the beast who was wounded by the sword [c]and lived. [15]He was granted *power* to give breath to the image of the beast, that the image of the beast should both

---

Rev. 13:13–14

Signs and Wonders. The False Prophet, in support of the Beast (or Antichrist), has the power to do great miracles. Jesus said that "false christs and false prophets will rise and show great signs and wonders to deceive, if possible, even the elect" (Matt. 24:24). This is why it is dangerous to follow signs and wonders.

Satan is able to perform supernatural signs and wonders in order to deceive people, and that is what will happen with the Beast and False Prophet during the tribulation. Don't assume that all signs and wonders must come from God. They don't.

Cross references (center column):

6 ª[Col. 2:9]

7 ª Dan. 7:21
b Rev. 11:18
1 NU, M add *and people*

8 ª Ex. 32:32
b Rev. 17:8

9 ª Rev. 2:7

10 ª Is. 33:1
b Gen. 9:6
c Rev. 14:12
1 *perseverance*

11 ª Rev. 11:7

12 ª Rev. 13:3, 4

13 ª Matt. 24:24
b 1 Kin. 18:38

14 ª Rev. 12:9
b 2 Thess. 2:9
c 2 Kin. 20:7
1 M *my own people*

15 ª Rev. 16:2

16 ª Rev. 7:3; 14:9; 20:4

17 ª Rev. 14:9–11
b Rev. 15:2
1 NU, M *the mark, the name*

18 ª Rev. 17:9
b [1 Cor. 2:14]
c Rev. 15:2
d Rev. 21:17

CHAPTER 14

1 ª Rev. 5:6
b Rev. 7:4; 14:3
c Rev. 7:3; 22:4
1 NU, M *the*
2 NU, M add *His name and*

2 ª Rev. 1:15; 19:6
b Rev. 5:8

3 ª Rev. 5:9

4 ª [2 Cor. 11:2]

Rev. 13:16–17

THE MARK

The Antichrist will institute an economic system that is cashless. In the name of efficiency and security, he will place a mark on the right hand or forehead of all who participate, and it will be impossible to buy or sell without it. It will perhaps be a computer identification chip that will link your personal information with a central computer system.

Just a few years ago, people scoffed at this notion. Today, however, with all the problems we are having with identity theft, this will be an idea that is easy to push off on people. And this will give the Antichrist complete economic control of the world.

---

speak ªand cause as many as would not worship the image of the beast to be killed. [16]He causes all, both small and great, rich and poor, free and slave, ªto receive a mark on their right hand or on their foreheads, [17]and that no one may buy or sell except one who has [1]the mark or ªthe name of the beast, [b]or the number of his name. [18]ªHere is wisdom. Let him who has [b]understanding calculate [c]the number of the beast, [d]for it is the number of a man: His number *is* 666.

THE LAMB AND THE 144,000

14 Then I looked, and behold, [1]ª ªLamb standing on Mount Zion, and with Him [b]one hundred *and* forty-four thousand, [2]having His Father's name [c]written on their foreheads. [2]And I heard a voice from heaven, ªlike the voice of many waters, and like the voice of loud thunder. And I heard the sound of [b]harpists playing their harps. [3]They sang as it were a new song before the throne, before the four living creatures, and the elders; and no one could learn that song ªexcept the hundred *and* forty-four thousand who were redeemed from the earth. [4]These are the ones who were not defiled with women, ªfor they are virgins. These are

Rev. 14:3

Special Songs. It seems that each group in heaven will have certain songs that are especially appropriate to that particular group. Earlier, in chapter 5, we saw the song of the redeemed church. Here we see the 144,000 will have a special song that no one can sing except them.

Each of us has a special, unique relationship with God. Our song is a song of being delivered from the great tribulation. The song of the 144,000 will be a song of being delivered through the time of the great tribulation.

Rev. 14:5

Without Fault. That is quite a statement—"without fault before the throne of God." But that is exactly how we will stand before God, if we are in Christ.

Jude, at the close of his little epistle, said, "Now to Him who is able to keep you from stumbling, and to present you faultless before the presence of His glory with exceeding joy" (Jude 24). And that is the way God sees you who are in Jesus Christ! Faultless! Isn't that glorious? What can you say?

the ones ᵇwho follow the Lamb wherever He goes. These ᶜwere ¹redeemed from *among* men, ᵈ*being* firstfruits to God and to the Lamb. ⁵And ᵃin their mouth was found no ¹deceit, for ᵇthey are without fault ²before the throne of God.

THE PROCLAMATIONS OF THREE ANGELS

⁶Then I saw another angel ᵃflying in the midst of heaven, ᵇhaving the everlasting gospel to preach to those who dwell on the earth—ᶜ to every nation, tribe, tongue, and people— ⁷saying with a loud voice, ᵃ"Fear God and give glory to Him, for the hour of His judgment has come; ᵇand worship Him who made heaven and earth, the sea and springs of water."

Marginal references

4 ᵇRev. 3:4; 7:17
ᶜRev. 5:9
ᵈJames 1:18
1 M adds *by Jesus*

5 ᵃPs. 32:2
ᵇEph. 5:27
1 NU, M *falsehood*
2 NU, M omit the rest of v. 5.

6 ᵃRev. 8:13
ᵇEph. 3:9
ᶜRev. 13:7

7 ᵃRev. 11:18
ᵇNeh. 9:6

8 ᵃIs. 21:9
ᵇJer. 51:7
1 NU *Babylon the great is fallen, is fallen, which has made;* M *Babylon the great is fallen. She has made*

9 ᵃRev. 13:14, 15; 14:11
ᵇRev. 13:16

10 ᵃPs. 75:8
ᵇRev. 18:6
ᶜRev. 16:19
ᵈRev. 20:10
ᵉ2 Thess. 1:7

11 ᵃIs. 34:8–10

12 ᵃRev. 13:10
ᵇRev. 12:17
1 *steadfastness, perseverance*
2 NU, M omit *here are those*

⁸And another angel followed, saying, ᵃ"Babylon¹ is fallen, is fallen, that great city, because ᵇshe has made all nations drink of the wine of the wrath of her fornication."

⁹Then a third angel followed them, saying with a loud voice, ᵃ"If anyone worships the beast and his image, and receives *his* ᵇmark on his forehead or on his hand, ¹⁰he himself ᵃshall also drink of the wine of the wrath of God, which is ᵇpoured out full strength into ᶜthe cup of His indignation. ᵈHe shall be tormented with ᵉfire and brimstone in the presence of the holy angels and in the presence of the Lamb. ¹¹And ᵃthe smoke of their torment ascends forever and ever; and they have no rest day or night, who worship the beast and his image, and whoever receives the mark of his name."

¹²ᵃHere is the ¹patience of the saints; ᵇhere² *are* those who keep the commandments of God and the faith of Jesus.

Rev. 14:11

FOREVER AND EVER

The torment of those who reject Jesus Christ as their Savior will last forever and ever.

You may say, "Chuck, do you really believe that God is going to torment forever those who have rebelled against Him? Do you really believe in eternal punishment?" Don't ask me to take away from what God has said. I won't do it. The end of Revelation says that if you take away from the words of this book, your name will be taken out of the Book of Life. You don't want that to happen to me, do you? I am going to leave it as it stands. I won't mess with the Word of God.

Some may ask, "But how long is forever and ever?" In the next chapter, in Revelation 15:7, God is called the One who "lives forever and ever." So the punishment will last as long as God lives.

¹³Then I heard a voice from heaven saying ¹to me, "Write: ^a'Blessed *are* the dead ^bwho die in the Lord from now on.'"

"Yes," says the Spirit, ^c"that they may rest from their labors, and their works follow ^dthem."

REAPING THE EARTH'S HARVEST

¹⁴Then I looked, and behold, a white cloud, and on the cloud sat *One* like the Son of Man, having on His head a golden crown, and in His hand a sharp sickle. ¹⁵And another angel ^acame out of the temple, crying with a loud voice to Him who sat on the cloud, ^b"Thrust in Your sickle and reap, for the time has come ¹for You to reap, for the harvest ^cof the earth is ripe." ¹⁶So He who sat on the cloud thrust in His sickle on the earth, and the earth was reaped.

REAPING THE GRAPES OF WRATH

¹⁷Then another angel came out of the temple which is in heaven, he also having a sharp sickle.

¹⁸And another angel came out from the altar, ^awho had power over fire, and he cried with a loud cry to him who had the sharp sickle, saying, ^b"Thrust in your sharp sickle and gather the clusters of the vine of the earth, for her grapes are fully ripe." ¹⁹So the angel thrust his sickle into the earth and gathered the vine of the earth, and threw *it* into ^athe great winepress of the wrath of God. ²⁰And ^athe winepress was trampled ^boutside the city, and blood came out of the winepress, ^cup to the horses' bridles, for one thousand six hundred ¹furlongs.

PRELUDE TO THE BOWL JUDGMENTS

15 Then ^aI saw another sign in heaven, great and marvelous: ^bseven angels having the seven last plagues, ^cfor in them the wrath of God is complete.

²And I saw *something* like ^aa sea of glass ^bmingled with fire, and those who have the victory over the beast, ^cover his image and ¹over his mark *and* over the ^dnumber of his name, standing on the sea of glass, ^ehaving harps of God. ³They sing ^athe song of Moses, the servant of God, and the song of the ^bLamb, saying:

^c"Great and marvelous *are* Your works,
Lord God Almighty!
^dJust and true *are* Your ways,
O King of the ¹saints!

13 ^aEccl. 4:1, 2 ^b1Cor. 15:18 ^cHeb. 4:9, 10 ^d[1Cor. 3:11–15; 15:58] ¹NU, M omit *to me*

15 ^aRev. 16:17 ^bJoel 3:13 ^cJer. 51:33 ¹NU, M omit *for You*

18 ^aRev. 16:8 ^bJoel 3:13

19 ^aRev. 19:15

20 ^aIs. 63:3 ^bHeb. 13:12 ^cIs. 34:3 ¹Lit. *stadia*, about 184 miles in all

CHAPTER 15

1 ^aRev. 12:1, 3 ^bRev. 21:9 ^cRev. 14:10

2 ^aRev. 4:6 ^b[Matt. 3:11] ^cRev. 13:14, 15 ^dRev. 13:17 ^eRev. 5:8 ¹NU, M omit *over his mark*

3 ^aEx. 15:1–21 ^bRev. 15:3 ^cDeut. 32:3, 4 ^dPs. 145:17 ¹NU, M *nations*

4 ^aEx. 15:14 ^bLev. 11:44 ^cIs. 66:23

5 ^aNum. 1:50 ¹NU, M omit *behold* ²*sanctuary,* the inner shrine

6 ^aEx. 28:6 ¹*sanctuary,* the inner shrine

7 ^aRev. 4:6 ^b1Thess. 1:9

8 ^aEx. 19:18; 40:34 ^b2Thess. 1:9

Rev. 15:1

The Completion of Wrath. We see here in heaven the seven angels, ready to pour out the seven bowl judgments. It is said that "in them the wrath of God is complete." We are coming to the end of the tribulation period.

At the conclusion of these last bowl judgments, God will be through judging the earth and Jesus will return to establish His kingdom. It is almost over.

Rev. 15:3

Great and Marvelous. All the works of our God are truly great and marvelous!

How marvelous is His work of redemption? That He would send His only Son to die for us. How great and marvelous is the work of God in judgment as He pours out all these cataclysmic events on those who have rejected His redemption? How great and marvelous is His work in creation? We can't begin to grasp the magnitude of the universe He created or the precision of its tiniest elements.

Everything God does is truly great and marvelous!

⁴   ^aWho shall not fear You, O Lord,
and glorify Your name?
For *You* alone *are* ^bholy.
For ^call nations shall come and
worship before You,
For Your judgments have been
manifested."

⁵After these things I looked, and ¹behold, ^athe ²temple of the tabernacle of the testimony in heaven was opened. ⁶And out of the ¹temple came the seven angels having the seven plagues, ^aclothed in pure bright linen, and having their chests girded with golden bands. ^{7a}Then one of the four living creatures gave to the seven angels seven golden bowls full of the wrath of God ^bwho lives forever and ever. ^{8a}The temple was filled with smoke ^bfrom the glory of God and from His power, and

Rev. 15:3

JUST AND TRUE

It is interesting that throughout the account of God's judgment on the world, as we see the horrible devastation that will occur, we are again and again reminded that what God does is fair. "Just and true are Your ways, O King of the saints!"

No one can really accuse God of not being fair. There may be things that don't look fair to us, but we don't know the whole story. But when the whole story has been told, we will all declare that God was fair and just.

In the meantime, whenever you come up against something you don't understand, fall back on what you do understand. I know that God is loving. I know that God is just and true and that His judgments are righteous. In the end, we will see just how right He is.

---

no one was able to enter the temple till the seven plagues of the seven angels were completed.

16 Then I heard a loud voice from the temple saying ᵃto the seven angels, "Go and pour out the ¹bowls ᵇof the wrath of God on the earth."

FIRST BOWL: LOATHSOME SORES

2So the first went and poured out his bowl ᵃupon the earth, and a ¹foul and ᵇloathsome sore came upon the men ᶜwho had the mark of the beast and those ᵈwho worshiped his image.

SECOND BOWL: THE SEA TURNS TO BLOOD

3Then the second angel poured out his bowl ᵃon the sea, and ᵇit became blood as of a dead *man;* ᶜand every living creature in the sea died.

THIRD BOWL: THE WATERS TURN TO BLOOD

4Then the third angel poured out his bowl ᵃon the rivers and springs of water, ᵇand they became blood. 5And I heard the angel of the waters saying:

---

1 ᵃRev. 15:1
ᵇRev. 14:10
¹NU, M *seven bowls*

2 ᵃRev. 8:7
ᵇEx. 9:9–11
ᶜRev. 13:15–17; 14:9
ᵈRev. 13:14
¹*severe and malignant,* lit. *bad and evil*

3 ᵃRev. 8:8; 11:6
ᵇEx. 7:17–21
ᶜRev. 8:9

4 ᵃRev. 8:10
ᵇEx. 7:17–20

5 ᵃRev. 15:3, 4
ᵇRev. 1:4, 8
¹NU, M omit *O Lord*
²NU, M *was, the Holy One*

6 ᵃMatt. 23:34
ᵇRev. 11:18
ᶜIs. 49:26
¹NU, M omit *For*

7 ᵃRev. 15:3
ᵇRev. 13:10; 19:2
¹NU, M omit *another from*

8 ᵃRev. 8:12
ᵇRev. 9:17, 18

9 ᵃRev. 16:11
ᵇDan. 5:22
ᶜRev. 11:13

10 ᵃRev. 13:2
ᵇRev. 8:12; 9:2
ᶜRev. 11:10

12 ᵃRev. 9:14

CHAPTER 16

ᵃ"You are righteous, ¹O Lord,
The One ᵇwho is and who ²was
    and who is to be,
Because You have judged these
    things.
6 For ᵃthey have shed the blood ᵇof
    saints and prophets,
    ᶜAnd You have given them blood to
    drink.
¹For it is their just due."

7And I heard ¹another from the altar saying, "Even so, ᵃLord God Almighty, ᵇtrue and righteous *are* Your judgments."

FOURTH BOWL: MEN ARE SCORCHED

8Then the fourth angel poured out his bowl ᵃon the sun, ᵇand power was given to him to scorch men with fire. 9And men were scorched with great heat, and they ᵃblasphemed the name of God who has power over these plagues; ᵇand they did not repent ᶜand give Him glory.

FIFTH BOWL: DARKNESS AND PAIN

10Then the fifth angel poured out his bowl ᵃon the throne of the beast, ᵇand his kingdom became full of darkness; ᶜand they gnawed their tongues because of the pain. 11They blasphemed the God of heaven because of their pains and their sores, and did not repent of their deeds.

SIXTH BOWL: EUPHRATES DRIED UP

12Then the sixth angel poured out his bowl ᵃon the great river Euphrates,

---

Rev. 16:3

Oceanfront Property. During the second trumpet judgment, one-third of all sea life was destroyed. But here all the rest of what lives in the sea will die.

Living close to the Pacific Ocean, we are aware of the effects of even minor water pollution. Occasionally, there is a sewage leak, which causes officials to close the beach for a few days.

But imagine what it will be like when everything in the sea dies suddenly! What smells worse than rotting sea life? You won't want to live on the water in Newport Beach when this happens!

Rev. 16:9, 11, 21

Still No Repentance. Throughout these judgments it is asserted that God's judgments are righteous. Similarly, we also see throughout the passage, the consistency of man's rebellion, as "they blasphemed" and "did not repent."

God's judgment is righteous because man's stubbornness is so unyielding. God has done everything He can to save mankind. Jesus died for people. And yet, even when they experience the results of their sin, some of them just won't repent. Nothing God does can bring them to repentance, so they must be destroyed. There is no other righteous thing God can do.

---

[b]and its water was dried up, [c]so that the way of the kings from the east might be prepared. 13 And I saw three unclean [a]spirits like frogs *coming* out of the mouth of [b]the dragon, out of the mouth of the beast, and out of the mouth of [c]the false prophet. 14 For they are spirits of demons, [a]performing signs, *which* go out to the kings [1]of the earth and of [b]the whole world, to gather them to [c]the battle of that great day of God Almighty.

15 [a]"Behold, I am coming as a thief. Blessed *is* he who watches, and keeps

Rev. 16:13–14

The Unholy Trinity. Even as God is a Trinity, as Father, Son, and Holy Spirit, so we see an unholy trinity bringing the world to Armageddon. We see the Dragon (which is Satan), the Beast (which is the Antichrist), and the False Prophet (who gives his support to the Antichrist).

They each will send out demons to draw the leaders of the earth to the Battle of Armageddon. As God tries to lead all men to heaven, the unholy trinity will lead men to hell.

---

12 [b]Jer. 50:38
[c]Is. 41:2, 25; 46:11

13 [a]1 John 4:1
[b]Rev. 12:3, 9
[c]Rev. 13:11, 14; 19:20; 20:10

14 [a]2 Thess. 2:9
[b]Luke 2:1
[c]Rev. 17:14; 19:19; 20:8
[1]NU, M omit of the earth and

15 [a]Matt. 24:43
[b]2 Cor. 5:3

16 [a]Rev. 19:19
[1]Lit. Mount Megiddo; M Megiddo

17 [a]Rev. 10:6; 21:6

18 [a]Rev. 4:5
[b]Rev. 11:13
[c]Dan. 12:1

19 [a]Rev. 14:8
[b]Rev. 17:5, 18
[c]Rev. 14:8; 18:5
[d]Is. 51:17

20 [a]Rev. 6:14; 20:11

CHAPTER 17

1 [a]Rev. 1:1; 21:9
[b]Rev. 16:19
[c]Nah. 3:4
[d]Jer. 51:13
[1]NU, M omit to me

2 [a]Rev. 2:22; 18:3, 9
[b]Jer. 51:7

3 [a]Rev. 12:6, 14; 21:10
[b]Rev. 12:3
[c]Rev. 13:1

4 [a]Rev. 18:12, 16
[b]Dan. 11:38
[c]Jer. 51:7
[d]Rev. 14:8
[1]M the fornication of the earth

5 [a]2 Thess. 2:7

6 [a]Rev. 18:24
[b]Rev. 13:15
[c]Rev. 6:9, 10

---

his garments, [b]lest he walk naked and they see his shame."

16 [a]And they gathered them together to the place called in Hebrew, [1]Armageddon.

SEVENTH BOWL: THE EARTH UTTERLY SHAKEN

17 Then the seventh angel poured out his bowl into the air, and a loud voice came out of the temple of heaven, from the throne, saying, [a]"It is done!" 18 And [a]there were noises and thunderings and lightnings; [b]and there was a great earthquake, such a mighty and great earthquake [c]as had not occurred since men were on the earth. 19 Now [a]the great city was divided into three parts, and the cities of the nations fell. And [b]great Babylon [c]was remembered before God, [d]to give her the cup of the wine of the fierceness of His wrath. 20 Then [a]every island fled away, and the mountains were not found. 21 And great hail from heaven fell upon men, *each hailstone* about the weight of a talent. Men blasphemed God because of the plague of the hail, since that plague was exceedingly great.

THE SCARLET WOMAN AND THE SCARLET BEAST

17 Then [a]one of the seven angels who had the seven bowls came and talked with me, saying [1]to me, "Come, [b]I will show you the judgment of [c]the great harlot [d]who sits on many waters, 2 [a]with whom the kings of the earth committed fornication, and [b]the inhabitants of the earth were made drunk with the wine of her fornication."

3 So he carried me away in the Spirit [a]into the wilderness. And I saw a woman sitting [b]on a scarlet beast *which was* full of [c]names of blasphemy, having seven heads and ten horns. 4 The woman [a]was arrayed in purple and scarlet, [b]and adorned with gold and precious stones and pearls, [c]having in her hand a golden cup [d]full of abominations and the filthiness of [1]her fornication. 5 And on her forehead a name *was* written:

[a]MYSTERY, BABYLON
THE GREAT, THE MOTHER OF
HARLOTS AND OF THE
ABOMINATIONS OF THE EARTH.

6 I saw [a]the woman, drunk [b]with the blood of the saints and with the blood of [c]the martyrs of Jesus. And when I saw her, I marveled with great amazement.

Rev. 17

THE GREAT HARLOT

Here we see an evil woman who has corrupted the leaders of the earth. In the Bible, the image of prostitution is often used to signify those who venture off into false religion, betraying the God who loves them. False religion is repeatedly called harlotry. So here we see a false religious system that has compromised itself to be in consort with the Beast.

This religious system is connected with the ten kings of the revived Roman Empire, and it is centered around Rome. Rome was built on seven mountains and is clearly delineated in verse 9.

It is important to remember that the corrupt religious system coming out of Rome will be the church that exists after the rapture. When you take all the Christians out of any church, what is left will be awful. And that is what we have here.

THE MEANING OF THE WOMAN AND THE BEAST

7But the angel said to me, "Why did you marvel? I will tell you the ¹mystery of the woman and of the beast that carries her, which has the seven heads and the ten horns. 8The beast that you saw was, and is not, and ªwill ascend out of the bottomless pit and ᵇgo to ¹perdition. And those who ᶜdwell on the earth ᵈwill marvel, ᵉwhose names are not written in the Book of Life from the foundation of the world, when they see the beast that was, and is not, and ²yet is.

9ª"Here *is* the mind which has wisdom: ᵇThe seven heads are seven mountains on which the woman sits. 10There are also seven kings. Five have fallen, one is, *and* the other has not yet come. And when he comes, he must ªcontinue a short time. 11The ªbeast that was, and is not, is himself also the

eighth, and is of the seven, and is going to ¹perdition.
12ª"The ten horns which you saw are ten kings who have received no kingdom as yet, but they receive authority for one hour as kings with the beast. 13These are of one mind, and they will give their power and authority to the beast. 14ªThese will make war with the Lamb, and the Lamb will ᵇovercome them, ᶜfor He is Lord of lords and King of kings; ᵈand those *who are* with Him *are* called, chosen, and faithful."

15Then he said to me, ª"The waters which you saw, where the harlot sits, ᵇare peoples, multitudes, nations, and tongues. 16And the ten horns which you ¹saw on the beast, ªthese will hate the harlot, make her ᵇdesolate ᶜand naked, eat her flesh and ᵈburn her with fire. 17ªFor God has put it into their hearts to fulfill His purpose, to be of one mind, and to give their kingdom to the beast, ᵇuntil the words of God are

Rev. 17:8

THE BEAST WHO WAS

It is said of the Beast that he "was, and is not, and yet is." We are told that after he was and then wasn't, he will ascend out of the bottomless pit. During his evil reign, Caesar Nero was called "the beast" by the early church, because of his beastly activities. And some people suggest that Caesar Nero might even be the Antichrist, that he died and will be brought back. I think this is an interesting possibility.

Nero seemed to start out as a fairly good ruler. We know that Paul had a chance to witness to him. But later in his life he seemed to really flip out and go crazy, and was most likely demon-possessed.

I don't believe in reincarnation, but perhaps the same demon that possessed Caesar Nero will come out of the Abyss to possess the Antichrist. We can't be sure, but it is an interesting possibility.

Margin references

7 ¹ *hidden truth*

8 ª Rev. 11:7
ᵇ Rev. 13:10; 17:11
ᶜ Rev. 3:10
ᵈ Rev. 13:3
ᵉ Rev. 13:8
¹ *destruction*
² NU, M *shall be present*

9 ª Rev. 13:18
ᵇ Rev. 13:1

10 ª Rev. 13:5

11 ª Rev. 13:3, 12, 14; 17:8
¹ *destruction*

12 ª Dan. 7:20

14 ª Rev. 16:14; 19:19
ᵇ Rev. 19:20
ᶜ 1 Tim. 6:15
ᵈ Jer. 50:44

15 ª Is. 8:7
ᵇ Rev. 13:7

16 ª Jer. 50:41
ᵇ Rev. 18:17, 19
ᶜ Ezek. 16:37, 39
ᵈ Rev. 18:8
¹ NU, M *saw, and the beast*

17 ª 2 Thess. 2:11
ᵇ Rev. 10:7

Rev. 17:14

With the Lamb. As the Lamb makes war against these evil forces, we will be the ones who will be with Him. Later we will be seen accompanying Him on white horses (Rev. 19:14).

Paul said in Colossians 3:4, "When Christ who is our life appears, then you also will appear with Him in glory." And Enoch prophesied, "Behold, the Lord comes with ten thousands of His saints" (Jude 14). And the description of us John has given here is beautiful. We are "called, chosen, and faithful."

What a privilege it is to be with the Lamb!

---

fulfilled. [18]And the woman whom you saw [a]is that great city [b]which reigns over the kings of the earth."

THE FALL OF BABYLON THE GREAT

18 After[a] these things I saw another angel coming down from heaven, having great authority, [b]and the earth was illuminated with his glory. [2]And he cried [1]mightily with a loud voice, saying, [a]"Babylon the great is fallen, is fallen, and [b]has become a dwelling place of demons, a prison for every foul spirit, and [c]a cage for every unclean and hated bird! [3]For all the nations [a]have drunk of the wine of the wrath of her fornication, the kings of the earth have committed fornication with her, [b]and the merchants of the earth have become rich through the [1]abundance of her luxury."

[4]And I heard another voice from heaven saying, [a]"Come out of her, my people, lest you share in her sins, and lest you receive of her plagues. [5][a]For her sins [1]have reached to heaven, and [b]God has remembered her iniquities. [6][a]Render to her just as she rendered [1]to you, and repay her double according to her works; [b]in the cup which she has mixed, [c]mix double for her. [7][a]In the measure that she glorified herself and lived [1]luxuriously, in the same measure give her torment and sorrow; for she says in her heart, 'I sit [as] [b]queen, and am no widow, and will not see sorrow.' [8]Therefore her plagues will come [a]in one day—death and

---

Cross-references

18 [a] Rev. 11:8; 16:19
[b] Rev. 12:4

CHAPTER 18

1 [a] Rev. 17:1, 7
[b] Ezek. 43:2

2 [a] Is. 13:19; 21:9
[b] Is. 13:21; 34:11, 13–15
[c] Is. 14:23
[1] NU, M omit _mightily_

3 [a] Rev. 14:8
[b] Is. 47:15
[1] Lit. _strengths_

4 [a] Is. 48:20

5 [a] Gen. 18:20
[b] Rev. 16:19
[1] NU, M _have been heaped up_

6 [a] Ps. 137:8
[b] Rev. 14:10
[c] Rev. 16:19
[1] NU, M omit _to you_

7 [a] Ezek. 28:2–8
[b] Is. 47:7, 8
[1] _sensually_

8 [a] Rev. 18:10
[b] Rev. 17:16
[c] Jer. 50:34
[1] NU, M _has judged_

9 [a] Ezek. 26:16; 27:35
[b] Jer. 50:46
[c] Rev. 19:3

10 [a] Is. 21:9
[b] Rev. 18:17, 19

11 [a] Ezek. 27:27–34

12 [a] Rev. 17:4

13 [a] Ezek. 27:13

---

mourning and famine. And [b]she will be utterly burned with fire, [c]for strong _is_ the Lord God who [1]judges her.

THE WORLD MOURNS BABYLON'S FALL

[9][a]"The kings of the earth who committed fornication and lived luxuriously with her [b]will weep and lament for her, [c]when they see the smoke of her burning, [10]standing at a distance for fear of her torment, saying, [a]'Alas, alas, that great city Babylon, that mighty city! [b]For in one hour your judgment has come.'

[11]"And [a]the merchants of the earth will weep and mourn over her, for no one buys their merchandise anymore: [12][a]merchandise of gold and silver, precious stones and pearls, fine linen and purple, silk and scarlet, every kind of citron wood, every kind of object of ivory, every kind of object of most precious wood, bronze, iron, and marble; [13]and cinnamon and incense, fragrant oil and frankincense, wine and oil, fine flour and wheat, cattle and sheep, horses and chariots, and bodies and [a]souls of men. [14]The fruit that your

---

Rev. 18:3–8

IT'S THE ECONOMY

In the previous chapter, we watched as God destroyed the religious establishment. In this chapter, we read of His destruction of the economic establishment.

Today commercial interests control the world. They are the power brokers. They put politicians into office. And they sit on top of the world, in the lap of luxury, thinking they will never pay for all the years of using people to pad their own nests, using the poor people of the world as pawns in their chess game.

But God will destroy them in a day. We often say about material things, "It's all going to burn someday." Well, this will be the day when it all burns.

Rev. 18:14

WHERE DID
IT ALL GO?

What happened to all the gold and silver and all the other luxurious items? "The fruit that your soul longed for has gone from you, and all the things which are rich and splendid have gone from you, and you shall find them no more at all." The world economic machine is in the business of causing us to long for things. But someday all those things will fail us.

Jesus told the woman at the well, "Whoever drinks of this water will thirst again, but whoever drinks of the water that I shall give him will never thirst" (John 4:13–14). Over every advertisement and over every material thing we desire, we should write, "Whoever drinks of this will thirst again."

Material things cannot satisfy. The salesmen can convince us that if we buy enough we will be happy, but it doesn't work. Jesus is the only One who can satisfy the inner longing of our souls.

soul longed for has gone from you, and all the things which are rich and splendid have [1]gone from you, and you shall find them no more at all. [15]The merchants of these things, who became rich by her, will stand at a distance for fear of her torment, weeping and wailing, [16]and saying, 'Alas, alas, [a]that great city [b]that was clothed in fine linen, purple, and scarlet, and adorned with gold and precious stones and pearls! [17a]For in one hour such great riches [1]came to nothing.' [b]Every shipmaster, all who travel by ship, sailors, and as many as trade on the sea, stood at a distance [18a]and cried out when they saw the smoke of her burning, saying, [b]'What is like this great city?' [19a]"They threw dust on their heads and cried out, weeping and wailing, and saying, 'Alas, alas, that great city, in which all who had ships on the sea

Cross-references

14 [1]NU, M *been lost to you*

16 [a]Rev. 17:18
[b]Rev. 17:4

17 [a]Rev. 18:10
[b]Is. 23:14
[1]*have been laid waste*

18 [a]Ezek. 27:30
[b]Rev. 13:4

19 [a]Josh. 7:6
[b]Rev. 18:8
[1]*have been laid waste*

20 [a]Jer. 51:48
[b]Luke 11:49
[1]NU, M *saints and apostles*

21 [a]Jer. 51:63, 64
[b]Rev. 12:8; 16:20

22 [a]Jer. 7:34; 16:9; 25:10

23 [a]Jer. 25:10
[b]Jer. 7:34; 16:9
[c]Is. 23:8
[d]2 Kin. 9:22

24 [a]Rev. 16:6; 17:6
[b]Jer. 51:49

CHAPTER 19

1 [a]Rev. 11:15; 19:6
[b]Rev. 4:11
[1]NU, M add *something like*
[2]NU, M omit *the Lord*

2 [a]Rev. 15:3; 16:7
[b]Deut. 32:43

became rich by her wealth! [b]For in one hour she [1]is made desolate.'
[20a]"Rejoice over her, O heaven, and *you* [1]holy apostles and prophets, for [b]God has avenged you on her!"

FINALITY OF BABYLON'S FALL

[21]Then a mighty angel took up a stone like a great millstone and threw *it* into the sea, saying, [a]"Thus with violence the great city Babylon shall be thrown down, and [b]shall not be found anymore. [22a]The sound of harpists, musicians, flutists, and trumpeters shall not be heard in you anymore. No craftsman of any craft shall be found in you anymore, and the sound of a millstone shall not be heard in you anymore. [23a]The light of a lamp shall not shine in you anymore, [b]and the voice of bridegroom and bride shall not be heard in you anymore. For [c]your merchants were the great men of the earth, [d]for by your sorcery all the nations were deceived. [24]And [a]in her was found the blood of prophets and saints, and of all who [b]were slain on the earth."

Rev. 18:21–23

Out of Business. God will wipe out the whole economic system as we know it. Those who deceived the nations with their sorcery will be put out of business for good.

Isaiah said, concerning the kingdom, "Ho! Everyone who thirsts, come to the waters; and you who have no money, come, buy and eat. Yes, come, buy wine and milk without money and without price" (Is. 55:1). Commercialism will be gone. In the glorious kingdom of God, there will be an abundance for everyone; and no one will be enslaved to debt.

HEAVEN EXULTS OVER BABYLON

19 After these things [a]I [1]heard a loud voice of a great multitude in heaven, saying, "Alleluia! [b]Salvation and glory and honor and power *belong* to [2]the Lord our God! [2]For [a]true and righteous *are* His judgments, because He has judged the great harlot who corrupted the earth with her fornication; and He [b]has avenged on her the

Rev. 19:1

ALLELUIA!

The word *Alleluia* or *Hallelujah* is transliterated from the Hebrew for "Praise the Lord." The word *Hallel* means "praise," and *Jah* is short for *Yahweh*, which is the personal name of God.

Interestingly enough, this is the first time the word is used in the New Testament. Of course, it is used many times in the Old Testament, especially in the Psalms; but Revelation 19 is the first place it is used in the New Testament, and it is used several times in this chapter. Of course, since the New Testament was written in Greek rather than in Hebrew, you wouldn't expect a Hebrew word to be used a lot.

We use the word quite a bit today, as we have transliterated it, and so do most Christians who speak in other languages.

---

blood of His servants *shed* by her." ³Again they said, "Alleluia! ªHer smoke rises up forever and ever!" ⁴And ªthe twenty-four elders and the four living creatures fell down and worshiped God who sat on the throne, saying, ᵇ"Amen! Alleluia!" ⁵Then a voice came from the throne, saying, ª"Praise our God, all you His servants and those who fear Him, ᵇboth *1* small and great!"

⁶ªAnd I heard, as it were, the voice of a great multitude, as the sound of many waters and as the sound of mighty thunderings, saying, "Alleluia! For ᵇthe *1* Lord God Omnipotent reigns! ⁷Let us be glad and rejoice and give Him glory, for ªthe marriage of the Lamb has come, and His wife has made herself ready." ⁸And ªto her it was granted to be arrayed in fine linen, clean and bright, ᵇfor the fine linen is the righteous acts of the saints.

⁹Then he said to me, "Write: ª'Blessed *are* those who are called to the marriage supper of the Lamb!'" And he said to me, ᵇ"These are the true sayings of God." ¹⁰And ªI fell at his feet to worship him. But he said to me,

---

3 ª Is. 34:10

4 ª Rev. 4:4, 6, 10
ᵇ 1 Chr. 16:36

5 ª Ps. 134:1
ᵇ Rev. 11:18
1 NU, M omit *both*

6 ª Ezek. 1:24
ᵇ Rev. 11:15
1 NU, M *our*

7 ª [Matt. 22:2; 25:10]

8 ª Ezek. 16:10
ᵇ Ps. 132:9

9 ª Luke 14:15
ᵇ Rev. 22:6

10 ª Rev. 22:8
ᵇ Acts 10:26
ᶜ [Heb. 1:14]
ᵈ 1 John 5:10
ᵉ Luke 24:27

11 ª Rev. 15:5
ᵇ Rev. 6:2; 19:19, 21
ᶜ Rev. 3:7, 14
ᵈ Is. 11:4

12 ª Rev. 1:14
ᵇ Rev. 2:17; 19:16
1 M adds *names written, and*

13 ª Is. 63:2, 3
ᵇ [John 1:1, 14]

14 ª Rev. 14:20
ᵇ Matt. 28:3
1 NU, M *pure white linen*

15 ª Is. 11:4
ᵇ Ps. 2:8, 9
ᶜ Is. 63:3–6
1 M *sharp two-edged*

ᵇ"See *that you do* not *do that!* I am your ᶜfellow servant, and of your brethren ᵈwho have the testimony of Jesus. Worship God! For the ᵉtestimony of Jesus is the spirit of prophecy."

CHRIST ON A WHITE HORSE

11ªNow I saw heaven opened, and behold, ᵇa white horse. And He who sat on him *was* called ᶜFaithful and True, and ᵈin righteousness He judges and makes war. 12ªHis eyes *were* like a flame of fire, and on His head *were* many crowns. ᵇHe *1*had a name written that no one knew except Himself. 13ªHe *was* clothed with a robe dipped in blood, and His name is called ᵇThe Word of God. 14ªAnd the armies in heaven, ᵇclothed in *1*fine linen, white and clean, followed Him on white horses. 15Now ªout of His mouth goes a *1*sharp sword, that with it He should strike the nations. And ᵇHe Himself will rule them with a rod of iron. ᶜHe Himself treads the winepress of the fierceness and wrath of Almighty God.

Rev. 19:10

WORSHIP

Under the Law, only God is to be worshiped. Here in this verse John fell down to worship an angel and was rebuked for it. "See that you do not do that! I am your fellow servant, and of your brethren who have the testimony of Jesus. Worship God!" Angels know better than to receive worship.

But Jesus received worship many times. In Matthew 2:11, the wise men worshiped Him. In Matthew 8:2, the leper worshiped Him. After Jesus walked on the water, His disciples worshiped Him (Matt. 14:33). The women who saw Him after His resurrection worshiped Him (Matt. 28:9). Thomas worshiped Him, saying, "My Lord and my God!" (John 20:28).

Jesus received worship because He is God, pure and simple. To suggest otherwise is blasphemy.

16And aHe has on *His* robe and on His thigh a name written:

bKING OF KINGS AND LORD OF LORDS.

Rev. 19:16

KING OF KINGS

Jesus has several names. He has the name "the Word of God." He also has a name that no one knows except Him. And He wears the name "KING OF KINGS AND LORD OF LORDS." He is sovereign and is Lord over all.

The most efficient form of government is a monarchy, but it is only as good as the monarch. It is hell if the monarch is a tyrant.

Jesus is the perfect King. He will rule absolutely, but in righteousness and love, and we will have the privilege of helping Him in His administration.

THE BEAST AND HIS ARMIES DEFEATED

17Then I saw an angel standing in the sun; and he cried with a loud voice, saying to all the birds that fly in the midst of heaven, a"Come and gather together for the *1*supper of the great God, 18athat you may eat the flesh of

16 a Rev. 2:17; 19:12
b Dan. 2:47

17 a Ezek. 39:17
1 NU, M *great supper of God*

18 a Ezek. 39:18–20
1 NU, M *both free*

19 a Rev. 16:13–16

20 a Rev. 16:13
b Rev. 13:8, 12, 13
c Dan. 7:11
d Rev. 14:10

21 a Rev. 19:15
b Rev. 19:17, 18
c Rev. 17:16

CHAPTER 20

1 a Rev. 1:18; 9:1

2 a 2 Pet. 2:4

3 a Dan. 6:17
b Rev. 12:9; 20:8, 10

4 a Dan. 7:9
b [1 Cor. 6:2, 3]
c Rev. 6:9

kings, the flesh of captains, the flesh of mighty men, the flesh of horses and of those who sit on them, and the flesh of all *people,* *1*free and slave, both small and great."

19aAnd I saw the beast, the kings of the earth, and their armies, gathered together to make war against Him who sat on the horse and against His army. 20aThen the beast was captured, and with him the false prophet who worked signs in his presence, by which he deceived those who received the mark of the beast and bthose who worshiped his image. cThese two were cast alive into the lake of fire dburning with brimstone. 21And the rest awere killed with the sword which proceeded from the mouth of Him who sat on the horse. bAnd all the birds cwere filled with their flesh.

SATAN BOUND 1000 YEARS

20 Then I saw an angel coming down from heaven, ahaving the key to the bottomless pit and a great chain in his hand. 2He laid hold of athe dragon, that serpent of old, who is *the* Devil and Satan, and bound him for a thousand years; 3and he cast him into the bottomless pit, and shut him up, and aset a seal on him, bso that he should deceive the nations no more till the thousand years were finished. But after these things he must be released for a little while.

THE SAINTS REIGN WITH CHRIST 1000 YEARS

4And I saw athrones, and they sat on them, and bjudgment was committed to them. Then *I saw* cthe souls of those

---

WHAT TOOK YOU SO LONG?   Rev. 20:1–3

When people see Satan locked up and cast into the bottomless pit, they will ask why God didn't throw him in there long ago. And why will God release him again after a thousand years?

It is important to realize that God has a purpose for Satan, and God will allow him the freedom to fulfill His divine purpose. God wants to test our love for Him; and in order to do so, He sometimes allows Satan to test us. The story of Job is the classic example of this.

God doesn't want us to be just robots. He wants our choosing Him to be a real choice; and in order for it to be a real choice, there has to be an attractive alternative. That is where Satan comes in. As the father of lies, he specializes in making rebellion against God look good. This gives us the opportunity to really choose God's ways and to really love Him, not out of constraint but from the heart.

We couldn't have an honest relationship with God unless we had a choice not to, and Satan provides an option.

who had been beheaded for their witness to Jesus and for the word of God, ^dwho had not worshiped the beast ^eor his image, and had not received *his* mark on their foreheads or on their hands. And they ^flived and ^greigned with Christ for ¹a thousand years. ⁵But the rest of the dead did not live again until the thousand years were finished. This *is* the first resurrection. ⁶Blessed and holy *is* he who has part in the first resurrection. Over such ^athe second death has no power, but they shall be ^bpriests of God and of Christ, ^cand shall reign with Him a thousand years.

SATANIC REBELLION CRUSHED

⁷Now when the thousand years have expired, Satan will be released from his prison ⁸and will go out ^ato deceive the nations which are in the four corners of the earth, ^bGog and Magog, ^cto gather them together to battle, whose number *is* as the sand of the sea. ^{9 a}They went up on the breadth of the earth and surrounded the camp of the saints and the beloved city. And fire came down from God out of heaven and devoured them. ¹⁰The devil, who deceived them, was cast into the lake of fire and brimstone ^awhere ¹ the beast and the false prophet *are*. And they ^bwill be tormented day and night forever and ever.

Rev. 20:7–9

ONE MORE TIME

Here is something that is amazing to me. After the people have had a chance to live in the kingdom of God for a thousand years, living in a perfect environment of total peace and safety, when Satan is loosed there will be countless people who choose to join with him in rebelling against the Lord.

This just goes to show you what is really in the heart of man. It is deceitful and desperately wicked (Jer. 17:9). And this will be demonstrated one last time, as people once again, in a perfect environment like the garden of Eden, still choose to rebel against God.

---

4 ^dRev. 13:12
^eRev. 13:15
^fJohn 14:19
^gRom. 8:17
¹M *the*

6 ^a[Rev. 2:11; 20:14]
^bIs. 61:6
^cRev. 20:4

8 ^aRev. 12:9; 20:3, 10
^bEzek. 38:2; 39:1, 6
^cRev. 16:14

9 ^aEzek. 38:9, 16

10 ^aRev. 19:20; 20:14, 15
^bRev. 14:10
¹NU, M *where also*

11 ^a2 Pet. 3:1
^bDan. 2:35

12 ^aRev. 19:5
^bDan. 7:10
^cPs. 69:28
^dMatt. 16:27
¹NU, M *the throne*

13 ^aRev. 1:18; 6:8; 21:4
^bRev. 2:23; 20:12

14 ^a1 Cor. 15:26
^bRev. 21:8
¹NU, M *death, the lake of fire.*

15 ^aRev. 19:20

THE GREAT WHITE THRONE JUDGMENT

¹¹Then I saw a great white throne and Him who sat on it, from whose face ^athe earth and the heaven fled away. ^bAnd there was found no place for them. ¹²And I saw the dead, ^asmall and great, standing before ¹God, ^band books were opened. And another ^cbook was opened, which is *the Book* of Life. And the dead were judged ^daccording to their works, by the things which were written in the books. ¹³The sea gave up the dead who were in it, ^aand Death and Hades delivered up the dead who were in them. ^bAnd they were judged, each one according to his works. ¹⁴Then ^aDeath and Hades were cast into the lake of fire. ^bThis is the second ¹death. ¹⁵And anyone not found written in the Book of Life ^awas cast into the lake of fire.

Rev. 20:15

THE BOOK OF LIFE

"**A**nd anyone not found written in the Book of Life was cast into the lake of fire." That to me puts at the top of my list of priorities in life to make sure my name is in the Book of Life. How does that happen? By confessing Jesus Christ as my Lord and Savior, and living my life for Him.

It isn't just calling Jesus Lord. Many people will call Him Lord and He will say, "I never knew you" (Matt. 7:23). It is about surrendering your life to Him, making Him Lord.

If you haven't done that, this would be a great time to do it. Just ask Him to save you and to be the Lord of your life. Believe that Jesus died for your sins and rose from the dead. Give Him your life. Then you will know that your name is written in the Book of Life, and this verse won't apply to you.

ALL THINGS MADE NEW

21 Now [a]I saw a new heaven and a new earth, [b]for the first heaven and the first earth had passed away. Also there was no more sea. [2]Then I, [1]John, saw [a]the holy city, New Jerusalem, coming down out of heaven from God, prepared [b]as a bride adorned for her husband. [3]And I heard a loud voice from heaven saying, "Behold, [a]the tabernacle of God is with men, and He will dwell with them, and they shall be His people. God Himself will be with them *and be* their God. [4][a]And God will wipe away every tear from their eyes; [b]there shall be no more death, [c]nor sorrow, nor crying. There shall be no more pain, for the former things have passed away."

[5]Then [a]He who sat on the throne said, [b]"Behold, I make all things new." And He said [1]to me, "Write, for [c]these words are true and faithful."

Rev. 21:4–5

No More Tears. "And God will wipe away every tear from their eyes; there shall be no more death, nor sorrow, nor crying. There shall be no more pain, for the former things have passed away." It sounds like the most beautiful dream you could ever imagine! It sounds too good to be true, doesn't it? But it is true, and God says that "these words are true and faithful." You can take this to the bank. It is really going to happen!

---

[6]And He said to me, [a]"It [1]is done! [b]I am the Alpha and the Omega, the Beginning and the End. [c]I will give of the fountain of the water of life freely to him who thirsts. [7]He who overcomes [1]shall inherit all things, and [a]I will be his God and he shall be My son. [8][a]But the cowardly, [1]unbelieving, abominable, murderers, sexually immoral, sorcerers, idolaters, and all liars shall have their part in [b]the lake which burns with fire and brimstone, which is the second death."

THE NEW JERUSALEM

[9]Then one of [a]the seven angels who had the seven bowls filled with the seven last plagues came [1]to me and talked with me, saying, "Come, I will show you [b]the [2]bride, the Lamb's wife." [10]And he carried me away [a]in the Spirit to a great and high mountain, and showed me [b]the [1]great city, the [2]holy Jerusalem, descending out of heaven from God, [11][a]having the glory of God. Her light *was* like a most precious stone, like a jasper stone, clear as crystal. [12]Also she had a great and high wall with [a]twelve gates, and twelve angels at the gates, and names written on them, which are *the names* of the twelve tribes of the children of Israel: [13][a]three gates on the east, three gates on the north, three gates on the south, and three gates on the west.

[14]Now the wall of the city had twelve foundations, and [a]on them were the [1]names of the twelve apostles of the Lamb. [15]And he who talked with me [a]had a gold reed to measure the city, its gates, and its wall. [16]The city is laid out as a square; its length is as great as its breadth. And he measured the city with the reed: twelve thousand [1]furlongs. Its length, breadth, and height are equal. [17]Then he measured its wall: one hundred *and* forty-four cubits,

Cross references

1 [a] [2 Pet. 3:13]
[b] Rev. 20:11

2 [a] Is. 52:1
[b] 2 Cor. 11:2
[1] NU, M omit John

3 [a] Lev. 26:11

4 [a] Is. 25:8
[b] 1 Cor. 15:26
[c] Is. 35:10;
51:11; 65:19

5 [a] Rev. 4:2, 9;
20:11
[b] Is. 43:19
[c] Rev. 19:9; 22:6
[1] NU, M omit to me

6 [a] Rev. 10:6;
16:17
[b] Rev. 1:8; 22:13
[c] John 4:10
[1] M omits It is done

7 [a] Zech. 8:8
[1] M I shall give him these things

8 [a] 1 Cor. 6:9
[b] Rev. 20:14
[1] M adds and sinners,

9 [a] Rev. 15:1
[b] Rev. 19:7; 21:2
[1] NU, M omit to me
[2] M woman, the Lamb's bride

10 [a] Rev. 1:10
[b] Ezek. 48
[1] NU, M omit great
[2] NU, M holy city, Jerusalem

11 [a] Rev. 15:8;
21:23; 22:5

12 [a] Ezek.
48:31–34

13 [a] Ezek.
48:31–34

14 [a] Eph. 2:20
[1] NU, M twelve names

15 [a] Ezek. 40:3

16 [1] Lit. stadia, about 1,380 miles in all

Rev. 21:16

DIMENSIONS OF THE NEW JERUSALEM

The New Jerusalem is twelve thousand furlongs square, or about fifteen hundred miles square, or 2.25 million square miles. That is pretty big, but the interesting thing is that it is apparently a fifteen-hundred-mile cube, as its "length, breadth, and height are equal."

Now, if you think of it as a skyscraper that is fifteen hundred miles high and fifteen hundred miles square, you get the feel for how big it really will be. Even if each floor is a half-mile high, the total surface area would be bigger than the landmass of the entire world. And who needs half-mile-high ceilings?

The point is, it will be big enough, and there is plenty of room for you.

according to the measure of a man, that is, of an angel. [18]The construction of its wall was *of* jasper; and the city *was* pure gold, like clear glass. [19a]The foundations of the wall of the city *were* adorned with all kinds of precious stones: the first foundation *was* jasper, the second sapphire, the third chalcedony, the fourth emerald, [20]the fifth sardonyx, the sixth sardius, the seventh chrysolite, the eighth beryl, the ninth topaz, the tenth chrysoprase, the eleventh jacinth, and the twelfth amethyst. [21]The twelve gates *were* twelve [a]pearls: each individual gate was of one pearl. [b]And the street of the city *was* pure gold, like transparent glass.

PRECIOUS STONES

I'm sure our jaws will drop when we see the magnificence of heaven, with all these precious metals and stones being used as building materials. We regard these materials as being precious and valuable, but the amazing thing about God is that He just sees them as building materials and decoration. He doesn't treasure them. He treasures you.

We are His treasure; we are what He values most. Peter said that we are "rejected indeed by men, but chosen by God and precious" (1 Pet. 2:4). Value is usually determined by rarity, and God only made one of you. He loves you and values you and has invited you to be a part of His eternal family. What a wonderful thing!

THE GLORY OF THE NEW JERUSALEM

[22a]But I saw no temple in it, for the Lord God Almighty and the Lamb are its temple. [23a]The city had no need of the sun or of the moon to shine [1]in it, for the [2]glory of God illuminated it. The Lamb *is* its light. [24a]And the nations [1]of those who are saved shall walk in its light, and the kings of the earth bring their glory and honor [2]into it. [25a]Its gates shall not be shut at all by

day [b](there shall be no night there). [26a]And they shall bring the glory and the honor of the nations into [1]it. [27]But [a]there shall by no means enter it anything [1]that defiles, or causes an abomination or a lie, but only those who are written in the Lamb's [b]Book of Life.

THE RIVER OF LIFE

22 And he showed me [a]a [1]pure river of water of life, clear as crystal, proceeding from the throne of God and of the Lamb. [2a]In the middle of its street, and on either side of the river, *was* [b]the tree of life, which bore twelve fruits, each *tree* yielding its fruit every month. The leaves of the tree *were* [c]for the healing of the nations. [3]And [a]there shall be no more curse, [b]but the throne of God and of the Lamb shall be in it, and His [c]servants shall serve Him. [4a]They shall see His face, and [b]His name *shall be* on their foreheads. [5a]There shall be no night there: They need no lamp nor [b]light of the sun, for [c]the Lord God gives them light. [d]And they shall reign forever and ever.

Rev. 22:4–5

God's Light. There will be no need for the sun in heaven or for other sources of light because God is the light of heaven. The whole place will be illuminated by Him. And we will see His face.

What an experience it will be to see the face of God! Moses wanted to see God's face, but God told him it would kill him. God passed by and let Moses just get a glimpse of His afterglow.

But in heaven we will look God in the face and live and rule and reign in the light of His presence.

THE TIME IS NEAR

[6]Then he said to me, [a]"These words *are* faithful and true." And the Lord God of the [1]holy prophets [b]sent His angel to show His servants the things which must [c]shortly take place. [7a]"Behold, I am coming quickly! [b]Blessed *is* he who keeps the words of the prophecy of this book." [8]Now I, John, [1]saw and heard these things. And when I heard and saw, [a]I fell down to worship before the feet of the angel who showed me these things. [9]Then he said to me, [a]"See *that you*

Side references: [19]ᵃIs. 54:11 | [21]ᵃMatt. 13:45, 46 ᵇRev. 22:2 | [22]ᵃJohn 4:21, 23 | [23]ᵃIs. 24:23; 60:19, 20 [1]NU, M omit *in it* [2]M *very glory* | [24]ᵃIs. 60:3, 5; 66:12 [1]NU, M omit *of those who are saved* [2]M *of the nations to Him* | [25]ᵃIs. 60:11 ᵇIs. 60:20 | [26]ᵃRev. 21:24 [1]M adds *that they may enter in.* | [27]ᵃJoel 3:17 ᵇPhil. 4:3 [1]NU, M *profane, nor one who causes* | CHAPTER 22 | [1]ᵃEzek. 47:1 [1]NU, M omit *pure* | [2]ᵃEzek. 47:12 ᵇGen. 2:9 ᶜRev. 21:24 | [3]ᵃZech. 14:11 ᵇEzek. 48:35 ᶜRev. 7:15 | [4]ᵃ[Matt. 5:8] ᵇRev. 14:1 | [5]ᵃRev. 21:23 ᵇRev. 7:15 ᶜPs. 36:9 ᵈDan. 7:18, 27 | [6]ᵃRev. 19:9 ᵇRev. 1:1 ᶜHeb. 10:37 [1]NU, M *spirits of the prophets* | [7]ᵃ[Rev. 3:11] ᵇRev. 1:3 | [8]ᵃRev. 19:10 [1]NU, M *am the one who heard and saw* | [9]ᵃRev. 19:10

Rev. 22:7

I Am Coming Quickly. The word "quickly" here doesn't mean "shortly" or "immediately." There are those who would scoff at this and say, "Jesus said He would come quickly, but it has been two thousand years and He still hasn't come."

The idea here is that when He comes, everything will happen quickly. Paul said that it will happen "in a moment, in the twinkling of an eye" (1 Cor. 15:52). When the time is right, things will happen quickly. It will be an almost instantaneous transformation.

do not *do that.* [1]For I am your fellow servant, and of your brethren the prophets, and of those who keep the words of this book. Worship God." [10a]And he said to me, "Do not seal the words of the prophecy of this book, [b]for the time is at hand. [11]He who is unjust, let him be unjust still; he who is filthy, let him be filthy still; he who is righteous, let him [1]be righteous still; he who is holy, let him be holy still."

JESUS TESTIFIES TO THE CHURCHES
[12]"And behold, I am coming quickly, and [a]My reward *is* with Me, [b]to give to every one according to his work. [13a]I am the Alpha and the Omega, *the* [1]Beginning and *the* End, the First and the Last."

[14a]Blessed *are* those who [1]do His commandments, that they may have the right [b]to the tree of life, [c]and may enter through the gates into the city. [15][1]But [a]outside *are* [b]dogs and sorcerers and sexually immoral and murderers and idolaters, and whoever loves and practices a lie.

[16a]"I, Jesus, have sent My angel to testify to you these things in the churches. [b]I am the Root and the Offspring of David, [c]the Bright and Morning Star." [17]And the Spirit and [a]the bride say, "Come!" And let him who hears say, "Come!" [b]And let him who thirsts come. Whoever desires, let him take the water of life freely.

9 [1]NU, M omit *For*

10 [a]Dan. 8:26
[b]Rev. 1:3

11 [1]NU, M *do right*

12 [a]Is. 40:10; 62:11
[b]Rev. 20:12

13 [a]Is. 41:4
[1]NU, M *First and the Last, the Beginning and the End.*

14 [a]Dan. 12:12
[b][Prov. 11:30]
[c]Rev. 21:27
[1]NU *wash their robes,*

15 [a]1 Cor. 6:9
[b]Phil. 3:2
[1]NU, M omit *But*

16 [a]Rev. 1:1
[b]Rev. 5:5
[c]Num. 24:17

17 [a][Rev. 21:2, 9]
[b]Is. 55:1

18 [a]Deut. 4:2; 12:32
[1]NU, M omit *For*
[2]M *may God add*

19 [a]Ex. 32:33
[1]M *may God take away*
[2]NU, M *tree of life*

21 [1]NU *with all;* M *with all the saints*

A WARNING
[18][1]For I testify to everyone who hears the words of the prophecy of this book: [a]If anyone adds to these things, [2]God will add to him the plagues that are written in this book; [19]and if anyone takes away from the words of the book of this prophecy, [a]God [1]shall take away his part from the [2]Book of Life, from the holy city, and *from* the things which are written in this book.

I AM COMING QUICKLY
[20]He who testifies to these things says, "Surely I am coming quickly." Amen. Even so, come, Lord Jesus! [21]The grace of our Lord Jesus Christ *be* [1]with you all. Amen.

Rev. 22:17

THE GRAND INVITATION

"And the Spirit and the bride say, 'Come!' And let him who hears say, 'Come!' And let him who thirsts come. Whoever desires, let him take the water of life freely."

God's Spirit is giving the invitation. We are invited to come to Jesus, to receive forgiveness and cleansing. Come! Come to Jesus! Come and receive God's love. Come and be made a child of God. Come and be blessed by becoming an heir of God, a joint heir through Jesus Christ.

The offer is open to everyone! God hasn't closed the door on anyone. It is "whoever desires." God created you with that ability to choose. You can determine your future by exercising your free will to come to Him. It can't be easier than that! God has left it up to you. You will have no excuse for rejecting His offer of salvation. Whoever desires. Take the water of life freely! Come to Jesus!

AS YOU BEGIN TO READ YOUR BIBLE, you will discover the revelation of Jesus Christ. Book by book, the Word of God declares that Jesus is the only way to God the Father and His everlasting kingdom. It is only through Jesus Christ that you can gain eternal life.

The Bible declares that Jesus came to reveal to you that God loves you. This study is designed to unveil the love of God, the mystery of the Trinity, and Jesus, God's Son, so that you may enjoy an abundant life through knowing and loving Him.

To assist you in learning how the Scriptures apply to you, included are examples in the form of questions and answers covering these five essential topics:

Lesson 1: The Love of God
Lesson 2: The Trinity of God
Lesson 3: Who Is the Son of God?
Lesson 4: The Word of God
Lesson 5: The Eternity of God

Lesson 1

THE LOVE OF GOD

The Word of God clearly defines God's *agape* love for you. The New Testament was originally written in the Greek language. The word *agape* is a Greek word that means "a love that is unconditional, sacrificial, and everlasting."

Using the Old Testament Scriptures, Jeremiah 31:3 as an example, answers the question, *How does God love me?* It reads, "The LORD has appeared of old to me, saying: 'Yes, I have loved you with an everlasting love; therefore with lovingkindness I have drawn you.' "

Answer: God loves me with an everlasting love and has drawn me with His lovingkindness.

Meditate on the following Scriptures. To *meditate* means "to think carefully about, ponder, and study." Write down the description of the depth and intensity of God's love and how He demonstrated His love for you.

1. John 3:16

2. John 15:9

_____

_____

3. Romans 5:5

_____

_____

4. 1 John 3:1

_____

_____

5. 1 John 3:16

_____

_____

_____

_____

6. 1 John 4:9-10

_____

_____

7. 1 John 4:19

_____

ABIDING IN GOD'S LOVE

When you receive Jesus Christ as your Lord and Savior, His love floods into your heart. You want to abide with Him. The word *abide* means "to continue to dwell, be present, remain, and to stay with someone."

Read and meditate on John 15:9-14. Through intimate communion with God by being in His Word, the believer can abide in the love of God.

1. How can you abide in God's love (John 15:9-10)?

_____

2. What will God fill you with (John 15:11)?

_____

3. What does God command you to do in John 15:12-13?

_____

_____

4. What do you become if you obey Christ's commands? (John 15:14)

_____

GOD'S INSEPARABLE LOVE

Nothing can separate you from the love of God! His protective love will enable you to endure and overcome every kind of difficult circumstance. Meditate on Romans 8:35-39.

1. What will never separate you from the love of God? (Romans 8:35)

_____

2. How can you be encouraged as you face trials? (Romans 8:37)

_____

_____

3. The word *principalities* means "organized demonic rulers in the spiritual realm." Why are principalities unable to separate you from God's love? (Romans 8:38-39)

_____

_____

Lesson 2

THE TRINITY OF GOD

The Word of God reveals that God is a Trinity, or three persons in one: God the Father, God the Son, and God the Holy Spirit. The three persons of the Trinity can be clearly seen throughout the Scriptures working in harmony with each other and in the life of the believer as one.

Observe from the following Old Testament Scriptures to answer the question of how the Trinity is revealed.

Genesis 1:1 reads, "In the beginning God created the heavens and the earth."

Answer: The Old Testament was originally written in the Hebrew language. The Hebrew word for *God* used in this Scripture is *Elohim*, the plural form of the word "God."

Genesis 1:26-27 reads "Then God said, 'Let Us make man in Our image, according to Our likeness...so God created man in His own image; in the image of God He created him; male and female."

Answer: God speaks of Himself as (first person plural), "Let Us...Our image...Our likeness." God, who is more than one being, created man and woman in His image.

Observe and describe any of the three persons of the Trinity as they are revealed in the following Scriptures:

1. The birth of Christ in Matthew 1:18-23

_____

_____

2. The baptism of Christ in Matthew 3:16-17

_____

_____

3. The temptation of Christ in Matthew 4:1-11

_____

_____

4. The Great Commission in Matthew 28:18-20

_____

_____

5. In John 1:1-3, 14, the Greek for "the Word" is *Logos*, which means "communication of God" or "the Son of God." Write what you learn about the Trinity.

_____

_____

6. What is revealed about Christ in the following Scriptures?

John 14:16-20

_____

_____

John 14:26

_____

_____

John 16:12-15

_____

_____

7. What is revealed by the Trinity in 1 John 5:7?

_____

_____

Lesson 3

WHO IS THE SON OF GOD?

There have been diverse opinions throughout the ages about who Jesus, the Son of God, is. God in His Word clearly reveals the infinite and magnificent person of His Son.

Observe the Son of God from the following Old Testament Scripture to answer the question, *Who does the Bible say Jesus is?*

Isaiah 9:6 reads, "For unto us a Child is born, unto us a Son is given; and the government will be upon His shoulder. And His name will be called Wonderful, Counselor, Mighty God, Everlasting Father, Prince of Peace."

Answer: The Son of God is a Child, a Son, the government ruler; He is called Wonderful, Counselor, Mighty God, Everlasting Father, and Prince of Peace.

The Gospels, also known as the good news, are the first four books of the New Testament: Matthew, Mark, Luke and John. They tell the story of Jesus' birth, life, death, and resurrection.

Observe who Jesus, the Son of God, is through the following selected passages from the Gospels. Identify the names, titles, and descriptions of Jesus.

1. The genealogy of Jesus is His earthly origin. Read Matthew 1:1-16 and list who Jesus is. (verses 1, 16)

_____

2. Read Matthew 1:18-25. What did the angel of the Lord command His name to be and why? (verse 21)

_____

_____

3. What did the prophet declare that the Son of God would be called? (verses 22-23)

_____

4. What does His name mean? (verse 23)

_____

5. In the Bible, wise men were secular men who were well-versed in the Scriptures. According to Matthew 2:1-6, what title did the wise men give Jesus? (verse 2)

_____

6. What had they seen? (verse 2)

_____

7. In biblical times, scribes were men who copied the Scriptures. What did the chief priests and scribes know about the Christ from Old Testament Scriptures? (verses 3-5)

_____

_____

8. A prophet was a seer who declared the counsel of God. How did the Old Testament prophets reveal the Christ? (verse 6)

_____

_____

9. Read Matthew 2:19-23. What did the angel of the Lord call Jesus? (verses 19-22)

_____

_____

10. What did the prophet predict He would be called? (verse 23)

_____

11. How do these revelations of Jesus the Son of God impact your life?

_____

_____

THE AUTHORITY OF THE SON OF GOD

1. Read Mark 1:21-28. How did Jesus teach in comparison with the scribes? (verse 22)

_____

_____

2. Nazareth is an obscure and insignificant little village in Israel. What did the unclean spirit know about Jesus of Nazareth? (verses 23-24)

_____

3. What does the Son of God have authority to do? (verses 25-27)

_____

_____

4. Read Mark 5:1-20. What did the man with the unclean spirit do at the sight of Christ? (verses 1-6)

_____

5. What did the unclean spirit call the Son of God? (verse 7)

_____

6. A legion was a Roman regiment of about 3,000 to 6,000 men. What was the name of the unclean spirit? (verse 9)

_____

7. What did Jesus do to the demons? (verses 8-13)

_____

_____

8. What did Jesus call Himself? (verse 19)

_____

THE TEMPTATION OF THE SON OF GOD

1. Read Luke 4:1-13. Satan knew that Jesus was the Son of God. How did Satan use the title, "Son of God," to tempt Jesus in the wilderness? (verses 3, 5-7, 9-11)

_____

_____

_____

2. Satan quoted Psalm 91:11-12 to tempt Jesus into taking His life. According to Luke 4:10-11, what do these Scriptures say?

_____

_____

3. Jesus overcame Satan with the Word of God. What Old Testament Scriptures did Jesus quote to resist Satan? (verses 4, 8, 12)

_____

_____

_____

THE REVELATION OF THE SON OF GOD

1. Looking at Luke 7:11-17, what did Jesus do revealing that He is God? (verses 11-15)

2. The Greek word for "Lord" is *Kurios,* which means "one with all authority; sacred name of Jehovah or Yahweh." What title does the author Luke give Jesus in verse 13, and describe His characteristic.

3. The people of Nain glorified God. What did they say? (verse 16)

4. In John 1:35-42, how did John the Baptist introduce Jesus to the world in verse 36?

5. How did the two disciples address Jesus? (verse 38)

6. What revelation did Andrew make about the Son of God? (verse 41)

7. Looking at John 3:14-16, what was God's gift to the world? Why? (verse 16)

THE DIVINITY OF THE SON OF GOD

1. The word *divinity* means "the state of being divine; the Godhead, the eternal, omniscient and omnipotent." As stated in John 8:48-59, certain men challenged Jesus' divinity. Who did they say He was? (verse 48)

2. What did they ask Jesus? (verse 53)

3. In the Hebrew, God is written as *YHWH* (Yahweh, Jehovah), which means "I AM; I exist; I was; I will always be; the eternally existing one." In verse 58, what did Jesus say?

Lesson 4

THE WORD OF GOD

The Word of God is Jesus, the Son of God. As we read and meditate on Psalm 119:89, what does it reveal about the Word of God?

Psalm 119:89 reads, "Forever, O Lord, Your word is settled in heaven."

Answer: God's Word cannot be changed; it is settled.

What does Psalm 119:105 declare about God's Word?

Psalm 119:105 reads, "Your word is a lamp to my feet and a light to my path."

Answer: The Word of God enlightens and guides me in the path of life.

Read the following New Testament Scriptures. What do they declare about the Word of God?

1. Luke 21:33

2. John 1:1-3, 14

3. John 17:17

4. Acts 6:7; 19:20

5. Romans 10:17

6. Ephesians 6:17

7. Colossians 1:25-26

_____

_____

8. 2 Timothy 2:8-9

_____

9. Hebrews 4:12

_____

_____

10. Hebrews 11:3

_____

11. 1 Peter 1:22-25

_____

_____

12. 1 John 1:1

_____

_____

13. 1 John 2:14

_____

_____

14. Revelation 19:11-13

_____

Lesson 5

THE ETERNITY OF GOD

God is eternal. He was, He is, and will always be. God created you in His image and for His infinite purposes. The Scriptures declare that His plan from the beginning of time is that you bring glory to Him and that you spend eternity with Him.

Let the following Scriptures cause you to live your life for the only begotten Son of God, the Lord Jesus Christ, who has given you eternal life.

1. Why did God give His only begotten Son to die for your sins? (John 3:16)

_____

_____

2. Who can have eternal life? (John 3:36)

_____

_____

3. What will be the future of those who do not believe in the Son of God? (John 3:36)

_____

4. How does Jesus encourage you in John 14:1-4?

_____

_____

5. What is His eternal plan for you? (John 14:3)

_____

_____

6. What is eternal life? (John 17:3)

_____

_____

7. What are the wages of sin? (Romans 6:23)

_____

8. What is the gift of God? (Romans 6:23)

_____

9. In Whom is eternal life found? (1 John 5:11)

_____

10. What will you have when you have the Son of God in your heart? (1 John 5:12)

_____

_____

A DISCIPLE OF CHRIST

Once you have confessed Jesus Christ as Savior and Lord of your life, Jesus calls you to follow in His footsteps and become a disciple (Luke 9:18-26). In order to grow in your spiritual walk, you need to:

- Take time to pray and read the Bible every day.
- Find a fellowship of believers whose focus is the study of the Word of God.
- Seek to live your life close to the heart of God.

These things I have written to you who
believe in the name of the Son of God,
that you may know that you have eternal life,
and that you may continue to believe
in the name of the Son of God.

1 JOHN 5:13

BIBLICAL

DEFINITIONS

AS A NEW BELIEVER, you may find that words like "flesh" or "fast" or "the world" have different meanings than what you may be used to. This section gives definitions of these commonly used biblical terms so that when you study the Bible, read Christian books, attend Bible studies or talk with other believers, you'll know what they mean. For further study, we encourage you to go deeper and see the Scriptures listed under the Topical Index.

ANGEL

The word "angel" literally means a "ministering spirit sent forth to minister for those who will inherit salvation" (Hebrews 1:14). Angels can be divided into two categories: those who are obedient unto God and those who rebel. Satan was created as an angel, in one of the highest orders. But he rebelled against God, and when he fell from heaven (Isaiah 14:12-15) one-third of the angels followed his example (Revelation 12:4). There are passages in the Bible where God's angels appeared and talked unto men. We are told in Hebrews 13:2, "Do not forget to entertain strangers, for by so doing some have unwittingly entertained angels." Today, some people worship angels, but the Bible says only God is to be worshiped (see Revelation 22:8).

BACKSLIDING

Backsliding is the opposite of walking faithfully with God (Jeremiah 3:14). Your walk with the Lord should always be progressing—becoming deeper and richer as you experience the fresh work of God's grace within your heart. If there was a time when you experienced His presence and power in your life in a greater measure, then you may be in a backslidden state. God needs to be supreme above everything else in your life.

BORN AGAIN

Jesus said, "Unless one is born again, he cannot see the kingdom of God" (John 3:3). Paul wrote, "The natural man does not receive the things of the Spirit of God, for they are foolishness to him; nor can he know them, because they are spiritually discerned" (1 Corinthians 2:14). We need a spiritual birth. There's a whole other dimension known by a person who is born again of the Spirit that the natural man knows nothing about—its glories and beauties defy description. You'll never know God until you enter into that spiritual dimension by being born again through believing in Jesus Christ (Titus 3:4-7).

CARNALITY

The carnal Christian is one who has claimed Jesus as his Savior but has not denied himself nor taken up his cross to follow Jesus. His life is not ruled by the Holy Spirit but by his own sinful desires. Romans 8:7 tells us that the carnal mind is an enemy against God because it is not subject to His laws. What then is the cure for carnal Christianity? Walk in love—with God and others—and get into God's Word. Better yet, get God's Word into you!

CHURCH

The church is made up of people who have trusted in Jesus Christ. A local church

usually gathers in a building to worship God, but the building is not the church. Some people think they can worship and praise God all on their own, but we need each other more and more as we are living in these last days and evil is abounding (Hebrews 10:24-25). In addition to worshiping and praising God, the primary purposes of the church are to strengthen your faith, to minister to you, to bring you into spiritual maturity, and to help you find your place of service to the Lord.

COMMANDMENTS

We often look at the commandments of God as restrictions—and we rebel against restrictions. But God's commandments are for our good. Let's say you have a great passion to drive your car at 125 mph, so you resent the 65 mph speed limit. And one day, lying in the hospital mangled after you crashed, as the doctor is saying you'll never be able to walk again, you suddenly understand that the law was created for your benefit. Likewise, God's commandments are designed for our own good (Deuteronomy 10:12-13).

COMMUNION

The Jewish people celebrated a special meal called the Feast of the Passover in remembrance of God's deliverance from their torturous slavery in Egypt by slaying a lamb and placing its blood upon the doorposts. But Jesus gave the Passover a new meaning when He (the Lamb of God) took the bread and broke it, saying, "This is My body which is given for you; do this in remembrance of Me."

Likewise He also took the cup after supper, saying, "This cup is the new covenant in My blood, which is shed for you" (Luke 22:19-20). As Christians, communion is a special meal that reminds us of God's deliverance from our sins when Jesus' body was broken and His blood was shed for us when He died on the cross.

CULTS

Many religious groups have wonderful practices and great values, but they deny that Jesus is God who has come in the flesh, putting Jesus in the category of an angel, such as the Jehovah's Witnesses. The Mormons say that He is a brother to Lucifer. These religions say Jesus is something other than God in the flesh.

First John 4:1-3 reads, "Beloved, do not believe every spirit, but test the spirits, whether they are of God; because many false prophets have gone out into the world. By this you know the Spirit of God: every spirit that confesses that Jesus Christ has come in the flesh is of God, and every spirit that does not confess that Jesus Christ has come in the flesh is not of God."

DEATH

The Bible teaches that one day my spirit will leave my body, and the body will return to dust. When through age, accident, illness, or some other cause the body is no longer able to fulfill the purposes for which God created and designed it, then God in His love will release my spirit from my body to live in His glorious kingdom. For the child of God, death is a blessing, not a curse. But the unbeliever must face God and stand before Him in judgment (see Revelation 20:12-15).

DEMONS

Demons are angels who joined Satan in his rebellion against God (see Revelation 12:7-9). The gospel of Mark especially emphasizes the power of Jesus when He healed those who were possessed with demons (see Mark 1:34, 39). When a per-

son is demonized, evil spirits insert themselves somewhere between that person's conscious mind and motor functions, and they have supernatural capacities. However, Jesus has the authority to command demon spirits to leave (see Luke 4:33-36).

DISCERNMENT

Correct doctrine is important, but correct behavior is imperative. This takes discernment. It is possible to hear something without really understanding it. "The natural man does not receive the things of the Spirit of God, for they are foolishness to him; nor can he know them, because they are spiritually discerned" (1 Cor. 2:14). In order to have spiritual discernment, we must have the mind of Christ. In Phil. 2:5-8, Paul describes the mind of Christ as being completely emptied of self and submitted to the purpose and will of the Father. How opposite that is of the world's mind, which seeks to glorify self.

EVOLUTION

God has a plan and a purpose for the creation of man. To believe in evolution—that we evolved through millions of years of accidental mutations from a single-cell protein molecule into this marvelously designed body that we have—is an unreasonable, mathematically unprovable, statistical impossibility. We are the objects of God's love, and God wants fellowship with us. He desires that we spend all of eternity with Him. We are important in the eyes of God. There is a divine eternal purpose in our existence. Knowing this, why would anyone choose to believe in the theory of evolution?

FAITH

Hebrews 11:1 defines faith as "the substance of things hoped for, the evidence of things not seen." There is a substance to faith. It is the "evidence of things not seen." Although there may not be visible evidence of it at the moment, we believe God will do what He promises and He will continue to remain faithful. The writer of Hebrews continues, "But without faith it is impossible to please Him, for he who comes to God must believe that He is, and that He is a rewarder of those who diligently seek Him" (Hebrews 11:6). God is pleased when we put our faith and trust in Him. God is displeased when we don't trust Him, when we doubt His promises, and when we live in fear and anxiety. We are continually exhorted in the Scriptures to trust in the Lord. It pleases God when we take Him at His word.

FASTING

The purpose of fasting is to starve the flesh and feed the spirit. Fasting, reading the Bible, and spending time in prayer will feed the spirit so that we may be more spiritually mature. Some people fast to get things from God, as if God is then obligated to fulfill their desires, but that's contrary to its purpose. Nowadays I think we need to start fasting our minds as well from the corruption of television and movies. Jesus teaches on the subject of fasting in Matthew 6:16-18. You will discover that you are spiritually stronger as a result of fasting and prayer.

FEAR OF THE LORD

"The fear of the Lord is the beginning of wisdom" (Proverbs 9:10). A man who does evil cannot have the fear of the Lord in his heart. If he really had a respect for the sovereignty of God and realized how his life is dependent upon Him, he would flee from evil things (see Proverbs 8:13). We should have the fear of doing something that would displease God. If we love Him, we wouldn't want to do anything that would offend or displease Him.

FORGIVENESS

Even as God has forgiven you, though you were not deserving or worthy, now you are to forgive others (see Matthew 6:14-15). Anger, resentment, and unforgiveness create certain harmful chemicals in your body that can be physically destructive to you. It's of utmost importance emotionally and physically, but more importantly, spiritually, to forgive.

GRACE

Grace is unearned, undeserved favor. It's getting what we *don't* deserve. God has provided salvation and eternal life for us. We can't earn or work for grace; it's God's gift to us through faith in Jesus Christ even though none of us deserve it. There are no rules that we can keep that will qualify us. By grace we are saved through our faith in Jesus Christ and the promises of God.

HEAVEN

The original word for "heaven" means "high" or "lofty" or "that which is above." In heaven there is no sickness, pain, or suffering. There will be no more tears, temptation, sorrow, or death because God will make all things new. Ultimately, in heaven we will live in the immediate presence of God and have a personal intimate fellowship with Him throughout eternity (see Revelation 21:1-4).

HELL

Hell is a place prepared for the Devil and his angels (Matthew 25:41). These angels became evil when they turned away from God (see Jude 6). A common fallacy is often expressed in the question, "How can a God of love consign a man to hell or eternal punishment?" First of all, God has never sent any man to hell, nor will He ever. In fact, the God of love has done everything short of violating man's free will

to keep him out of hell. He sent His Son to die on the cross so men wouldn't have to go to hell. Jesus came "to seek and to save that which was lost" (Luke 19:10). So man, by his own choice, chooses his eternal destiny: heaven or hell.

HOLY SPIRIT

The name of the Holy Spirit in the New Testament is *Parakletos*, which means "Comforter."

Before a person's conversion, the Holy Spirit is **with you** (using the Greek preposition *para*). He convicts the world of sin, of righteousness, and of judgment. When you open your life and heart to Jesus Christ, then the Holy Spirit begins to **indwell you** (using the Greek preposition *en*). This is being *filled* with the Holy Spirit (see John 14:16-17). And finally, when the Holy Spirit is **upon you** (using the Greek preposition *epi*), this is called the baptism of the Holy Spirit (Acts 1:8), giving you a dynamic overflowing power of the Holy Spirit to touch the world around you, and to be a witness for Jesus Christ.

HOPE

There is only One who can give us hope, and that is Jesus Christ. The government can't save us. The United Nations can't save the world. Environmentalism can't save our planet. Science can't save the universe. Unfortunately, when a person has lost all hope, only then will they cry out to God, proclaiming a shallow commitment to Jesus Christ. It's important to realize that your only hope is to surrender your whole heart to God and to be under the control of the Spirit of God.

JESUS (DEATH)

Jesus died to free us from our sin and its damning consequences in our lives. By His

death, He took all of our iniquities and He bore the punishment for our sins. "For He made Him who knew no sin *to be* sin for us, that we might become the righteousness of God in Him" (2 Corinthians 5:21). The crucifixion was planned by God for the purpose of the redemption of man and the revelation of God's love to man (Acts 2:23; Acts 4:28; Romans 5:8).

JESUS (DEITY)

Jesus is God incarnate. He is nothing less than God in the flesh. John 1:14 tells us, "And the Word became flesh and dwelt among us, and we beheld His glory, the glory as of the only begotten of the Father, full of grace and truth." The Bible teaches that God was manifested in His Son. So Jesus, being a manifestation of God, was able to say, "He who has seen Me has seen the Father" (John 14:9).

JESUS (HUMANITY)

"And the Word became flesh and dwelt among us" (John 1:14). Jesus made His tent among us, or more literally, "tabernacled" among us. This is the mystery of the incarnation. Paul speaks about it to Timothy. "Great is the mystery of godliness: God was manifested in the flesh" (1 Timothy 3:16). Jesus is God manifested in the flesh. The Bible is very clear and very distinct in this declaration, affirming over and over that God was manifested in the flesh, in the person of Jesus (Philippians 2:6-7). Many times as we emphasize the divinity of Jesus, we are prone to forget His humanity. The purpose of Jesus taking on a body of flesh was to give us His sympathetic understanding of the weaknesses we experience in our bodies. By taking on a body of flesh, Jesus showed us that despite our weaknesses, we could be victorious. First John 5:4-5 reads, "For whatever is born of God overcomes the world.

And this is the victory that has overcome the world—our faith. Who is he who overcomes the world, but he who believes that Jesus is the Son of God."

JESUS (RESURRECTION)

If Jesus did not rise after He was crucified and laid in the tomb, then there would be no gospel. There would be no church. There would be no Christian faith. Our hope for eternal life rests upon the resurrection of Jesus Christ from the dead. Through faith we can bear witness of many people healed, hopeless drug addicts delivered, alcoholics set free and returned to productive lives, and marriages restored. These changed lives are a testimony to the fact that Jesus is risen from the dead. It's proof of the resurrection. If He is not risen, all of our faith would be in vain. And that makes it more than a hope; it gives to us a living hope. Because Jesus lives, we too shall live.

JESUS (SECOND COMING)

There are two comings of Jesus: the first coming was to offer Himself as the Lamb of God to be slain for the sins of the whole world. His second coming will be to judge the world, establish the kingdom of God, and reign in righteousness. The second coming of Jesus is not the rapture of the church. The church will be caught up in the rapture before His second coming.

LEADING SOMEONE TO CHRIST

We all have friends and loved ones who want to argue with us about God. Paul said to Timothy, "Avoid foolish and ignorant disputes, knowing that they generate strife" (2 Timothy 2:23). The god of this world, Satan, has blinded their eyes; they cannot see the truth (see 1 Corinthians 2:14). So we must first deal with that power holding them captive, and through prayer free them from that strong

prejudice. Then in love, patiently share the truth, praying that they will be open to the Holy Spirit as He reveals the truth, and that they might come to the knowledge of God and be saved.

MERCY

Mercy is the forgiveness of a wrong. But if you don't confess and repent of your sin, you'll get justice. Mercy is **not** getting what you deserve. That is justice. The only way God could be merciful to you, a sinner, and still be a just God, is to place the guilt of your sin on His Son Jesus Christ. Jesus, in turn, died for your sin and paid the penalty for your guilt so that through Him, God could have mercy upon you. Justice has been served because the penalty was paid through Jesus Christ. God is still a just and righteous Judge in His mercy.

OBEDIENCE

We often make it hard on ourselves when we don't obey God. Jesus said, "If you love Me, keep My commandments" (John 14:15). Then as an example to us, He said, "But that the world may know that I love the Father, and as the Father gave Me commandment, so I do" (John 14:31). He demonstrated His love to the Father by keeping His commandments—by submitting to His will and not His own. Love is always proved by obedience to the One that you love.

PEACE

Real peace begins with a right relationship with God. The apostle Paul said, "Therefore, having been justified by faith, we have peace with God through our Lord Jesus Christ" (Romans 5:1).

You are not promised an easy path or a bed of roses; however, you are promised that the Lord will never leave you nor forsake you. The Lord will be with you in every circumstance of life and He will take care of you and provide for you. So when a problem arises, you can believe the words of Jesus when He said, "Come to Me, all you who labor and are heavy laden, and I will give you rest" (Matthew 11:28).

PRAYER

Some people foolishly declare that their belief in God's love was shattered when God didn't answer a prayer. But God never intended prayer as a means by which we can get our will accomplished here on earth. The real purpose of prayer is to align our will with God's will, and surely that is the most important thing—that God's will be done. Prayer opens the door for God to do a glorious work in your life and in the lives of those around you. A dynamic prayer life softens hearts, moves mountains, and brings you into an entirely new and deepened relationship with God.

PROPHECY

One of the most fascinating facets of the Bible is prophecy, especially its predictive element where God speaks of events before they ever take place. Thus, part of the purpose of prophecy is to prove that God is indeed the Author, and that God exists outside of the time continuum. Because God is eternal, He can speak of things that are yet future, and that have not yet come to pass. So God proves His deity by telling us things that are going to happen before they ever take place. It is one of the strongest proofs that the Bible is inspired of God.

PURITY

Purity is oneness of heart toward God and the things of God. Jesus said, "Blessed are the pure in heart, for they shall see God" (Matthew 5:8). This points out the fact that we are all in need of God's grace because

none of us are pure in heart. But God is willing to change our hearts to give us a heart of love, a heart that is after God and after the things of God. Jesus will cleanse us from all sin and create in us a pure heart, and He will then present us faultless before the Father (see Jude 24).

RAPTURE

First Thessalonians 4:17 reads, "Then we who are alive and remain shall be caught up together with them in the clouds to meet the Lord in the air. And thus we shall always be with the Lord." "Caught up" is a translation of the Greek word *harpazo*, which means "snatched away" or "taken away by force." In Latin, it is the word *raptus*, from which we get our word, "rapture." In the rapture, Christians will be taken away by the force of God's Spirit at the call of Jesus to meet Him in the air. This is not the second coming of Jesus, but precedes His second coming to earth. See also 1 Corinthians 15:51-52.

RECONCILIATION

The Bible says, "Be reconciled with God through Jesus Christ." Paul wrote to the Colossians, "And by Him to reconcile all things to Himself, by Him, whether things on earth or things in heaven, having made peace through the blood of His cross. And you, who once were alienated and enemies in your mind by wicked works, yet now He has reconciled in the body of His flesh through death, to present you holy, and blameless, and above reproach in His sight" (Colossians 1:20-22). So Christ was wounded for our transgressions, He was bruised for our iniquities. The chastisement that He took was for our peace, that we might have peace with God. And if we have peace with God, then we can have peace with our fellow man.

REPENTANCE

True repentance is being so sorry that you don't do it again, resulting in a changed life. If a person declares that they have repented of a certain action or sin, but they still continue in it, there is good reason to doubt the genuineness of their repentance. Everything God allows in our lives is designed to bring us to repentance. If we respond to His goodness by repenting of our sins, the day of judgment will be a time of rewards and celebration. But if we ignore His goodness and refuse to repent, we will face His wrath.

SALVATION

Salvation is our deliverance from the power and penalty of sin because sin separates a person from God. When the sins of the world were placed upon Jesus as He died on the cross, He paid the penalty for our sins so that we will never have to be separated from God. But in order to receive God's gift of salvation, we need to repent of our sins and believe in Jesus Christ as our Savior. Only then can we have the gift of salvation and spend eternity with God.

SATAN (ORIGIN, WORK)

The name Satan literally means "adversary." He is an adversary of God. So many people think of Satan as an opposite of God, but rather he is in opposition to God and His kingdom. He is in no way equal to God. Satan was created as an angel, in one of the highest orders. Ezekiel tells us that he was "the anointed cherub" (Ezekiel 28:14). Satan was perfect in beauty and wisdom, until the day he rebelled and iniquity was found in him. At that point, he was cast out from his position. God rules over the whole universe and that includes Satan.

SATAN (RESISTING HIM)

Satan is able to transform himself into an angel of light to deceive (2 Corinthians 11:14). When Satan brings temptation, it always appears to be so beautiful, so desirable. And because he comes in a more charming fashion, many times we are taken unaware. Always keep in mind that Satan seeks to resist whatever work you may desire to do for the Lord. It is important to realize that we are in a spiritual battle. But you can refuse His attacks by utilizing the spiritual armor found in Ephesians 6:10-20. Through the power of Jesus Christ you can have victory over Satan. James 4:7 says, "Submit to God. Resist the devil and he will flee from you."

SINNER'S PRAYER

The sinner's prayer is often used to help someone pray to receive Christ after sharing the gospel with him or her. God requires for a person to be convinced of their sinfulness, their need for repentance, and their need to confess Jesus as their Savior. Romans 10:9-10 states, "If you confess with your mouth the Lord Jesus and believe in your heart that God has raised Him from the dead, you will be saved. For with the heart one believes unto righteousness, and with the mouth confession is made unto salvation." By praying the sinner's prayer, a person is making a commitment to follow God.

TEMPTATION

Satan is out to tempt you so he can ensnare you. His goal is to trap you and bring you into captivity. Some of you may have fallen into temptation already and you don't know how to get out. You're at a tug-of-war with God's Spirit and your flesh, and you feel like you are in a dilemma, and it's ripping you to pieces. If you're in this state of mind, there's only one answer: come to Jesus and confess. "He who covers his sins will not prosper, but whoever confesses and forsakes them will have mercy" (Proverbs 28:13).

TITHING

The word "tithe" means "tenth" and it is first mentioned in the book of Genesis when Abraham gave a tenth of all he had to God (see Genesis 14:18-20). What can we say about giving to God? Well, first of all, we don't give to God because God is in need or because He is on the verge of bankruptcy. But rather we give to God—and should give to God—motivated by love. It is responsive. God has given me so many blessings, so many benefits that my heart desires to just express to God my appreciation and thanksgiving. It is impossible to outgive God. When we give to Him, He always gives back more. I should never give in a grudging way or out of a sense of pressure, but I should always give motivated by love. God loves the cheerful giver (2 Corinthians 9:6-7).

TONGUES

"Tongues" in the Greek is *glossolalia,* and it means "speaking in an unknown tongue." It's the gift whereby God enables us to communicate to Him in the Spirit, bypassing the narrow channel of our intellect. So the Spirit helps the frailty of human language and the weakness of our intellect so we can commune with God. It's a great gift for a person's own devotional life in worshiping God (see 1 Corinthians 14:2-27).

TRIALS

The purpose of a trial is to know what is in your heart. Jeremiah 17:9-10 reaffirms, "The heart is deceitful above all things, and desperately wicked; who can know it? I, the Lord, search the heart, I test the mind." God's testing helps us to under-

stand ourselves and to know our limitations and our weaknesses so we will learn to trust in God and not in ourselves. Another purpose of trials is to refine us (see 1 Peter 1:6-7). Many times God uses fiery trials to get rid of the sin in our lives because He is seeking to make us usable for His glory in ministering to others.

TRINITY

The Bible teaches us there is one God, manifested in three Persons: the Father, the Son, and the Holy Spirit. Because of the difficulty of comprehending the Trinity, there will always be those who deny the three Persons of the one Godhead. But beware! Denial of the Trinity always brings the denial of the deity of Jesus Christ. When Jesus was baptized, we read in Matthew 3:16-17 that the Spirit descended and the Father spoke from heaven. All three members of the Godhead—the Trinity—are clearly at work here.

TRUST

The wisdom of the world would encourage you to trust in yourself whereas the Bible encourages you to trust in the Lord. I have found that trusting in the Lord takes the worry out of the situation. We cannot always understand why God brings certain trials upon us, but in those times, we should learn to just trust God. Have faith in God that He is in control and that He loves you (see 2 Corinthians 1:9).

WITNESSING

When you are witnessing to someone, you are making known who God is and what God has done in your life. In witnessing, we need the power of the Holy Spirit. Jesus said to His disciples, "You shall receive power when the Holy Spirit has come upon you; and you shall be witnesses to Me in Jerusalem, and in all Judea and Samaria, and to the end of the earth" (Acts 1:8). Now, more than something that you do, witnessing is something that you are. Sometimes our witness is totally disallowed because our life doesn't line up with what we say. But this is where the power of the Holy Spirit helps us—and as you live the Christian life, it is then that your life becomes a witness.

WORD OF GOD

The Word of God, the Bible, is God's revelation of Himself to man. The only way man can know the truth about God is through the Bible. We're to reject any other communication if it is not in perfect harmony with what God has already declared in His Word. God does not contradict Himself nor will He lead us into some action which His Word forbids. Through the centuries, the Bible has remained God's eternal truth, and has stood the test of time.

WORLDLINESS

When I was a child, we were taught that we should not go to the movies or dances because doing such things was considered worldliness. And so I didn't—but in reality that isn't what truly defines worldliness. When the Bible talks about being worldly, it's talking about envying, striving, and catering to the desires of the flesh. God's Word exhorts us, "Do not love the world or the things in the world. If anyone loves the world, the love of the Father is not in him" (1 John 2:15). There are two kingdoms, and your allegiance is to one or the other. You are either living in the kingdom of God and God rules your life, or you are living in the kingdom of darkness and Satan rules your life. It's just that straight. So how does one overcome or avoid the sin of worldliness? Jesus said, "But seek first the kingdom of God and His righteous, and all these things shall be added unto you" (Matthew 6:33).

TOPICAL
INDEX

*See the Old Testament for further study

A

ABORTION

Contemplating an abortion
GOD'S PERSPECTIVE
*Psalm 139:13-16
*Jeremiah 1:5
1 Corinthians 6:19-20

GOD'S PROMISES
*Psalm 127:3
Romans 8:28

MAKE A CHANGE
Ephesians 1:4

God's forgiveness after an abortion
GOD'S PERSPECTIVE
*Psalm 103:8-12
*Isaiah 1:18

GOD'S PROMISES
*Psalm 32:1-2; 103:2-5
2 Corinthians 5:17

MAKE A CHANGE
*Psalm 32:5
1 John 1:9

PRAYER
*Psalm 51:9-10

ABUSE

For those abused
GOD'S PERSPECTIVE
*Isaiah 43:18-19
Matthew 11:28-30

GOD'S PROMISES
*2 Samuel 22:2-4
2 Corinthians 4:7-11

MAKE A CHANGE
*Psalm 34:4-5
*Proverbs 3:5-6
*Isaiah 26:3-4
Matthew 6:14-15

BIBLICAL EXAMPLES
*Genesis 37:4-5, 11, 23-24;
50:18-21

To those who have abused
GOD'S PERSPECTIVE
Matthew 18:6-7
1 Corinthians 13:4-7
Galatians 5:22-23
James 1:20

GOD'S PROMISES
1 Corinthians 6:9-11
James 4:6-7
1 Peter 5:6-7

MAKE A CHANGE
*Psalm 34:14
Romans 12:10
1 Corinthians 10:31
Philippians 2:3-4
1 Thessalonians 5:15, 22

For husbands and fathers
GOD'S PERSPECTIVE
*Deuteronomy 6:5-7
Matthew 18:6-7
1 Timothy 3:4

GOD'S PROMISES
*Psalm 27:10
Romans 8:16
Ephesians 3:14-19
1 John 3:1a

MAKE A CHANGE
Ephesians 5:25-30, 33; 6:4
Colossians 3:19, 21
1 Peter 3:7

ADDICTION

GOD'S PERSPECTIVE
*Proverbs 5:22-23
1 Corinthians 6:12-13; 9:24-27
1 Timothy 6:6-10
James 1:14-15
1 Peter 4:1-3
2 Peter 2:19

GOD'S PROMISES
John 8:34-36
Romans 8:12-15

MAKE A CHANGE
*Proverbs 23:20-21
Romans 6:1-2, 11-13, 16; 12:1
1 Corinthians 6:19-20
2 Corinthians 7:1
1 John 1:8-9

BIBLICAL EXAMPLES
*Proverbs 23:29-35

ADULTERY

GOD'S PERSPECTIVE
*Exodus 20:14
*Leviticus 20:10
*Deuteronomy 5:18; 22:22
*Proverbs 5:3-6, 20-23;
6:27-29, 32; 22:14; 23:26-28
Matthew 5:27-28; 15:19; 19:9
Romans 7:2-3
1 Corinthians 6:9-11
Hebrews 13:4
James 1:14-15

GOD'S PROMISES
*Proverbs 28:13
*Isaiah 1:16-18
Revelation 22:14-15

MAKE A CHANGE
*Proverbs 5:15-18; 7:1-5, 21-27
1 Corinthians 6:15-20; 7:3-4
Ephesians 5:3-4
1 John 1:8-9

BIBLICAL EXAMPLES
John 8:2-11

Adultery victims
GOD'S PERSPECTIVE
1 Corinthians 13:4-7
Philippians 4:8

GOD'S PROMISES
*Psalm 34:18; 37:3-8; 46:1-3
*Isaiah 26:3

MAKE A CHANGE
Ephesians 4:26-27
Hebrews 12:14-15
James 5:16
1 Peter 4:8

BIBLICAL EXAMPLES
*Jeremiah 3:6-14
*Hosea 3:1-5

AFFLICTIONS, ADVERSITY, DISABILITIES, TRIALS

GOD'S PERSPECTIVE
*Psalm 62:1-2
Matthew 11:28-30
John 16:33
2 Corinthians 1:8-10;
4:16-18; 5:7
1 Peter 1:6-7

GOD'S PROMISES
*Psalm 55:22; 119:75-76
*Isaiah 26:3; 38:15, 17
Romans 5:3-4; 8:28, 31-32
James 1:2-4

MAKE A CHANGE
*Psalm 119:67-68, 71-72

BIBLICAL EXAMPLES
*Job 1:20-22
*Psalm 31:22
John 9:1-3
Acts 16:22-25
2 Corinthians 12:7-10

AGING

GOD'S PERSPECTIVE
*Genesis 24:1
*Deuteronomy 32:7
*Job 5:26; 12:12; 32:7
*Psalm 90:10; 143:5
*Proverbs 16:31
Matthew 6:10
1 Timothy 5:1-2

GOD'S PROMISES
*1 Kings 3:14
*Psalm 91:16; 92:14
*Proverbs 17:6
*Isaiah 46:4

MAKE A CHANGE
*Proverbs 23:22
*Ecclesiastes 9:10
Titus 2:2-5

BIBLICAL EXAMPLES
*Deuteronomy 34:7
*Joshua 14:7-12
*1 Chronicles 29:28

PRAYER
*Psalm 71:9, 18; 90:12

ALCOHOL ABUSE

GOD'S PERSPECTIVE
*Proverbs 20:1; 21:17; 23:29-32
*Isaiah 5:11, 22
*Habakkuk 2:15
Galatians 5:19-21

GOD'S PROMISES
John 7:37-38; 8:36
1 Corinthians 10:13
2 Corinthians 5:17

MAKE A CHANGE
*Proverbs 23:20-21
Luke 21:34
Romans 13:12-14
1 Corinthians 5:11; 6:19-20
2 Corinthians 7:1
Ephesians 5:18-21

Scriptures concerning alcohol for those who serve in ministry

GOD'S PERSPECTIVE
1 Timothy 3:8-9
Titus 1:7-9

MAKE A CHANGE
2 Timothy 2:4

ALIENATION FROM GOD

GOD'S PERSPECTIVE
John 3:16-17
Ephesians 2:12-13
Colossians 1:21-23

GOD'S PROMISES
Hebrews 4:14-16
James 4:8

MAKE A CHANGE
*Isaiah 1:18

BIBLICAL EXAMPLES
Luke 15:11-24

ANGELS

GOD'S PERSPECTIVE
*Psalm 8:4-6; 103:20-21
Matthew 16:27; 26:52-53
Mark 13:27, 32
Luke 15:10
John 1:51
1 Corinthians 4:9
Galatians 1:8
1 Timothy 3:16
1 Peter 1:12

GOD'S PROMISES
*Psalm 34:7, 91:11-12
Romans 8:38-39
2 Thessalonians 1:6-7
Hebrews 1:14
Revelation 3:5

MAKE A CHANGE
Matthew 18:10
Hebrews 13:2
1 Peter 5:8-9

BIBLICAL EXAMPLES
*Genesis 19:1,15; 28:12
Matthew 4:5-11
Mark 1:13
Luke 1:19; 2:8-14
John 20:11-12
Acts 5:19; 12:7-9

Do not worship angels

GOD'S PERSPECTIVE
*Exodus 20:3-5
*Deuteronomy 5:7-9

GOD'S PROMISES
1 Corinthians 6:3

MAKE A CHANGE
Colossians 2:18

BIBLICAL EXAMPLES
Revelation 19:10

Jesus is not an angel

GOD'S PERSPECTIVE
Colossians 1:16-18
Hebrews 1:4-8; 2:5-9
1 Peter 3:21-22

Fallen angels

GOD'S PERSPECTIVE
*Ezekiel 28:11-19
Matthew 25:41
Luke 10:18
2 Peter 2:4
Jude 1:6
Revelation 12:7-9

BIBLICAL EXAMPLES
*Isaiah 14:12-19

ANGER

GOD'S PERSPECTIVE
*Proverbs 10:12; 12:16; 14:17, 29; 15:1; 19:11; 25:28; 29:22
*Ecclesiastes 7:8-9
Galatians 5:19-21

GOD'S PROMISES
Romans 12:19

MAKE A CHANGE
*Psalm 37:8
*Proverbs 22:24-25
Luke 6:28-29
Ephesians 4:26-27, 30-32
Colossians 3:8
James 1:19-20

God's righteous anger

GOD'S PERSPECTIVE
*Psalm 7:11
Mark 9:42

BIBLICAL EXAMPLES
*Exodus 32:19
*1 Kings 11:9-10
*2 Kings 17:18-19
Mark 3:5; 11:15-17

ANXIETY, WORRY

GOD'S PERSPECTIVE
*Proverbs 12:25
Matthew 6:25-34
Luke 12:27-31
Romans 8:28

GOD'S PROMISES
*Psalm 27:1; 34:4; 42:5; 46:1; 55:22; 62:1-2, 8
*Jeremiah 17:7-8

MAKE A CHANGE
*Psalm 37:7
*Proverbs 3:5-6
Philippians 4:6-7
1 Peter 5:6-7

ARROGANCE

GOD'S PERSPECTIVE
*Psalm 119:21
*Proverbs 8:13; 21:24
*Isaiah 10:12; 13:11; 47:10-11
James 4:16
Revelation 18:5, 7-8

GOD'S PROMISES
*Proverbs 28:14

MAKE A CHANGE
*1 Samuel 2:3
*Proverbs 30:32
Romans 11:20
1 Corinthians 5:6-7
James 3:14

ASSURANCE

GOD'S PERSPECTIVE
John 3:16; 5:24; 10:27-28
Romans 8:16-17, 28-30
1 Corinthians 2:5
Titus 3:4-7
1 John 3:1-3; 4:13-16; 5:11-13

GOD'S PROMISES
*Proverbs 28:13
Romans 5:9-10; 8:37-39
Ephesians 1:13-14; 2:8-9
Philippians 1:6
2 Timothy 1:12
Hebrews 7:25
1 Peter 1:3-5

MAKE A CHANGE
Acts 16:31
Romans 10:9-10
1 John 1:9

BIBLICAL EXAMPLES
*Job 19:25-27

ASTROLOGY
(SEE ALSO HOROSCOPE)

GOD'S PERSPECTIVE
*Deuteronomy 4:19
*Isaiah 47:10, 13-15
*Jeremiah 8:2; 19:13; 31:35
*Zephaniah 1:2, 5

GOD'S PROMISES
*Psalm 19:1-6; 147:4

BIBLICAL EXAMPLES
*Genesis 10:8-9, 11:4-9
*2 Kings 17:15-16

PRAYER
*Psalm 8:3-4

ATHEIST
(SEE ALSO UNBELIEVER)

B

BACKSLIDING

GOD'S PERSPECTIVE
*Deuteronomy 4:9
*Proverbs 14:14
*Jeremiah 2:19; 17:5-6
Luke 9:62
1 Corinthians 3:1-3
Hebrews 10:37-38
2 Peter 2:20-21
1 John 1:6-7, 3:8-10
Revelation 2:4-5

GOD'S PROMISES
*2 Chronicles 7:14
*Isaiah 55:7
*Jeremiah 3:22
*Hosea 14:4
Galatians 6:9
James 5:19-20

MAKE A CHANGE
*Deuteronomy 5:32
*Psalm 105:4-5
Hebrews 3:12-13

BAD HABITS

GOD'S PERSPECTIVE
*Proverbs 28:13
Luke 9:23
Galatians 5:16-18

GOD'S PROMISES
1 John 4:4

MAKE A CHANGE
*Psalm 119:9, 11
Romans 6:11-14; 12:1-2
Colossians 3:5-7
2 Timothy 2:15
James 4:7-8

BAPTISM

GOD'S PERSPECTIVE
Romans 6:4
Ephesians 4:5
Colossians 2:12
1 Peter 3:21

BIBLICAL EXAMPLES
Matthew 3:5-6; 28:19
Mark 1:4
Luke 3:3-6, 21
John 1:33
Acts 2:38; 8:36-37; 19:4

BESTIALITY

GOD'S PERSPECTIVE
*Exodus 22:19
*Leviticus 18:22-25, 29;
20:15-16
*Deuteronomy 27:21
Romans 1:28-32
1 Corinthians 6:13b

GOD'S PROMISES
2 Timothy 2:20-21
Revelation 22:14-15

MAKE A CHANGE
1 Corinthians 6:18-20

BIBLE

GOD'S PERSPECTIVE
*Joshua 1:8
*Psalm 119:105; 138:2
*Jeremiah 23:28
Matthew 24:35
Luke 16:17
Hebrews 4:12

GOD'S PROMISES
*Isaiah 55:10-11
2 Timothy 3:16-17
2 Peter 1:19-21

MAKE A CHANGE
*Psalm 119:9
Ephesians 6:17
Colossians 3:16
2 Timothy 2:15
Titus 1:9
James 1:21-22

BIBLICAL EXAMPLES
Matthew 4:3-4
1 Thessalonians 2:13

PRAYER
*Psalm 119:11

BIRTHDAY

GOD'S PERSPECTIVE
*Isaiah 43:7
John 3:3, 5-8
Acts 17:26-28
1 Peter 1:23

GOD'S PROMISES
*Psalm 100:3; 118:24
Ephesians 2:10

MAKE A CHANGE
John 3:7
2 Corinthians 6:2

PRAYER
*Psalm 119:73; 139:13-16
Revelation 4:11

BITTERNESS, HATE, RESENTMENT, UNFORGIVENESS

GOD'S PERSPECTIVE
*Leviticus 19:17
*Proverbs 26:24-26
Luke 17:3-4
James 3:14-18
1 John 2:9-11; 3:10, 15; 4:20

MAKE A CHANGE
Acts 8:22-23
Galatians 5:15
Ephesians 4:30-32
Colossians 3:8
Hebrews 12:14-15
James 1:19-20
1 Peter 2:19-20

Scriptures related to resentment
GOD'S PERSPECTIVE
Romans 12:17-19

MAKE A CHANGE
Matthew 5:23-24

BIBLICAL EXAMPLES
1 Peter 2:21-23

Scriptures concerning unforgiveness
GOD'S PERSPECTIVE
Matthew 6:14-15
James 2:13

MAKE A CHANGE
Matthew 18:15
Mark 11:25-26
Colossians 3:12-14

BLAME SHIFTING

Blaming others
GOD'S PERSPECTIVE
Matthew 7:1-5

MAKE A CHANGE
Galatians 6:4-5

BIBLICAL EXAMPLES
*Genesis 3:12-13
John 21:20-22

Blaming God
GOD'S PERSPECTIVE
*Proverbs 19:3
James 1:13-14

PRAYER
*Daniel 9:7

BORN AGAIN

GOD'S PERSPECTIVE
*Ezekiel 11:19-20; 36:26-27
John 6:28-29
Acts 4:10, 12
1 John 5:4

GOD'S PROMISES
Romans 8:2-4

MAKE A CHANGE
*Ezekiel 18:31-32
Matthew 18:3

John 3:3-7
1 Peter 1:22-23

BIBLICAL EXAMPLES
John 1:12-13

BROODING, SELF-PITY

GOD'S PROMISES
*Proverbs 15:13

BIBLICAL EXAMPLES
*Jonah 4:3-4
1 Corinthians 4:11-13
2 Corinthians 6:3-10
Philippians 2:4-8; 4:11-12

PRAYER
*Psalm 42:5; 73:21-24

BUSINESS RELATIONSHIPS

GOD'S PERSPECTIVE
*Deuteronomy 22:9-10
*Proverbs 22:24-25
1 Corinthians 5:11; 15:33-34
2 Corinthians 6:14-18
Ephesians 5:11
James 4:4

BIBLICAL EXAMPLES
*Psalm 106:35-36

C

CARNALITY

GOD'S PERSPECTIVE
Mark 7:20-23
Romans 8:6-7
1 Corinthians 3:3
Galatians 5:19-23
James 3:16-18; 4:1-3
2 Peter 2:20-21

GOD'S PROMISES
Galatians 6:7-8

MAKE A CHANGE
Galatians 5:16-17
Ephesians 5:2
Colossians 3:5-8
1 Thessalonians 4:3-7

CATHOLICISM

GOD'S PERSPECTIVE
Matthew 16:6, 12
Romans 3:23-24; 6:23
Ephesians 2:8-9
Titus 3:5

MAKE A CHANGE
John 6:28-29
Romans 10:8-9

Worshiping God only
GOD'S PERSPECTIVE
*Exodus 20:3-6
*Deuteronomy 5:7-10
*Psalm 73:25
*Isaiah 43:10-11; 44:6, 8;
45:21-22
*Jeremiah 25:6
Matthew 4:10
Luke 8:20-21
1 Corinthians 8:5-6
Colossians 2:18
1 Timothy 2:5

MAKE A CHANGE
*Psalm 29:2
Ephesians 5:5-7
1 John 5:20-21

BIBLICAL EXAMPLES
Revelation 19:10; 22:8-9

Being born again
GOD'S PERSPECTIVE
John 1:12-13; 3:3, 5-7
Galatians 6:15
Titus 3:5-7
1 Peter 1:23
1 John 5:4

GOD'S PROMISES
2 Corinthians 5:17

Concerning saints
GOD'S PERSPECTIVE
*Psalm 30:4
Romans 1:7; 12:13
1 Corinthians 6:2
2 Corinthians 13:13
Ephesians 4:11-12
Revelation 14:12

GOD'S PROMISES
*Psalm 31:23

BIBLICAL EXAMPLES
Acts 9:32, 41
2 Timothy 4:7-8

CHANGE (REPENT)
GOD'S PERSPECTIVE
*Ezekiel 18:30-32; 36:25-27
Matthew 4:17
Acts 17:30
Ephesians 4:20-24
Revelation 2:5

GOD'S PROMISES
Luke 24:47
Romans 8:13-14
2 Corinthians 5:17
Philippians 2:12-13

MAKE A CHANGE
Luke 13:3
Romans 6:11-14; 12:1-2
Philippians 3:12-14
Colossians 3:5

CHILD ABUSE
(OVERCOMING THE PAST)
GOD'S PERSPECTIVE
*Psalm 34:17-19; 37:39
Matthew 18:6
Romans 8:28; 15:13

GOD'S PROMISES
*Psalm 18:2; 28:7
*Isaiah 43:18-19; 58:8; 61:7
*Joel 2:25

MAKE A CHANGE
*Psalm 55:4-8
*Isaiah 61:10

PRAYER
*Psalm 6:2
*Jeremiah 17:14
*Lamentations 3:58-59

CHILD DISCIPLINE
GOD'S PERSPECTIVE
*1 Samuel 3:13
*Proverbs 13:24; 17:6; 19:18;
22:15

GOD'S PROMISES
*Proverbs 22:6; 29:17

MAKE A CHANGE
Ephesians 6:4
Colossians 3:21
1 John 4:16-21

The blessing of children
GOD'S PERSPECTIVE
*Genesis 17:7
*Deuteronomy 6:6-7
*Psalm 127:3

GOD'S PROMISES
*Psalm 127:3-5; 128:1-3
Acts 2:38-39

BIBLICAL EXAMPLES
Matthew 19:13-15
Luke 2:51-52

CHURCH
The church as the body of Christ
GOD'S PERSPECTIVE
John 17:25-26
Acts 9:31; 20:28
Romans 12:4-8
1 Corinthians 12:4-7, 12-13,
25-26
Ephesians 1:18-23; 2:19-22
4:11-13; 5:23-25
1 Timothy 5:17
1 Peter 2:5

GOD'S PROMISES
Revelation 21:3

MAKE A CHANGE
1 Corinthians 1:10
Ephesians 4:1-6
Hebrews 10:24-25; 13:17

A physical place to worship God
GOD'S PERSPECTIVE
*Psalm 5:7; 26:8; 84:1-2, 10;
132:7
*Ecclesiastes 5:1

BIBLICAL EXAMPLES
Acts 7:44-49

CHURCH DISCIPLINE
GOD'S PERSPECTIVE
*Psalm 119:21-22, 118
*Proverbs 19:27-29
Romans 15:14
1 Corinthians 5:11-12
1 Timothy 6:10
2 Peter 3:17

GOD'S PROMISES
James 5:19-20

MAKE A CHANGE
Matthew 18:15-18
Romans 16:17
2 Corinthians 2:6-8
Galatians 6:1
Ephesians 5:11
1 Thessalonians 5:12-15
2 Thessalonians 3:6, 14
1 Timothy 6:5
2 Timothy 3:5
Titus 3:10

BIBLICAL EXAMPLES
1 Corinthians 5:1-5
2 Timothy 2:16-23

CLEANLINESS
GOD'S PERSPECTIVE
*Deuteronomy 23:14
*Jeremiah 4:14
Matthew 5:8; 12:33-35

GOD'S PROMISES
*Exodus 15:26
*Deuteronomy 7:12-15
*Ezekiel 36:25-27

MAKE A CHANGE
1 Corinthians 14:40
2 Corinthians 7:1
1 Timothy 3:2-4
Hebrews 10:22
James 4:8
1 Peter 1:22

PRAYER
*Psalm 51:10

COMFORT
GOD'S PERSPECTIVE
*Psalm 119:49-50
Matthew 11:28-29
John 10:14-15, 14:16-17
Romans 8:18, 28
2 Corinthians 4:17-18; 12:9-10

GOD'S PROMISES
*Deuteronomy 31:8
*Psalm 34:18; 55:22, 103:1-14
Matthew 28:20b
2 Corinthians 1:3-5

MAKE A CHANGE
2 Corinthians 13:11
1 Thessalonians 5:11, 14

BIBLICAL EXAMPLES
Colossians 4:7-9

PRAYER
*Psalm 23:1-6; 42:11; 73:23-26;
119:76; 139:1-3

COMMANDMENTS
GOD'S PERSPECTIVE
*Deuteronomy 10:12-13
*1 Samuel 15:22-23
*Isaiah 48:17-19
Matthew 7:21
Romans 13:4
1 John 2:3-6; 3:23-24; 5:2-3
2 John 1:6

GOD'S PROMISES
*Psalm 1:1-2; 19:7-11; 3:1-2
*Proverbs 4:4; 6:23; 7:2, 13:13
Luke 11:28
John 15:10-11

MAKE A CHANGE
John 14:15
James 1:21-25

COMMUNICATION
Cursing or a perverse mouth
GOD'S PERSPECTIVE
*Proverbs 6:12-15; 8:6-8, 13;
17:20; 18:7

MAKE A CHANGE
*Proverbs 4:24
Ephesians 4:31
Colossians 3:8; 4:6
James 1:21
1 Peter 2:1-3

Good communication
GOD'S PERSPECTIVE
*Proverbs 15:1, 7, 23; 18:13
James 3:8-10

MAKE A CHANGE
*Psalm 34:12-13
Ephesians 4:25, 29
James 1:19-20

PRAYER
*Psalm 19:14; 141:3

COMMUNION (THE LORD'S SUPPER)

GOD'S PERSPECTIVE
Matthew 26:26-28
Mark 14:22-24
Luke 22:14-20
1 Corinthians 11:23-26, 27-29

GOD'S PROMISES
1 Corinthians 10:16-17

CONDUCT (BEHAVIOR)

GOD'S PERSPECTIVE
Romans 2:16; 3:10; 14:12
Titus 2:11-13
Hebrews 4:13
2 Peter 3:11-13

GOD'S PROMISES
*Psalm 1:1-6

MAKE A CHANGE
Ephesians 5:8-11
Philippians 1:27
1 Timothy 4:12
James 3:13
1 Peter 1:13-17
1 John 1:9

CONFIDENCE IN GOD

GOD'S PERSPECTIVE
Ephesians 3:8-12
Philippians 4:13
Hebrews 10:35-37, 13:6

GOD'S PROMISES
*Genesis 8:22
*Joshua 1:9
*Proverbs 3:25-26
*Isaiah 32:17
*Jeremiah 17:7
Philippians 1:6
1 John 3:21-22; 5:14-15

MAKE A CHANGE
Ephesians 6:10-11
Hebrews 4:16
1 John 2:28

BIBLICAL EXAMPLES
Acts 28:30-31

CONFUSION (DISORDER)

GOD'S PERSPECTIVE
*1 Chronicles 15:13
*Ezra 9:7
*Jeremiah 3:25
2 Corinthians 12:20
Galatians 5:22-26
James 3:16-18
Titus 1:5

GOD'S PROMISES
Colossians 2:5
2 Thessalonians 3:16

MAKE A CHANGE
Romans 13:13
1 Corinthians 14:33, 40

PRAYER
*Daniel 9:7-8

CONSCIENCE

GOD'S PERSPECTIVE
John 16:8
1 Corinthians 8:12
1 Timothy 1:5, 18-19
Titus 1:15

GOD'S PROMISES
*Isaiah 30:21
Hebrews 9:13-14

MAKE A CHANGE
*Exodus 19:5; 23:22
Acts 24:16
Hebrews 10:22
1 Peter 3:15-16

BIBLICAL EXAMPLES
John 8:9
Acts 23:1

PRAYER
Hebrews 13:18

CONSCIOUSNESS OF SIN

GOD'S PERSPECTIVE
*Leviticus 26:40-42
*Psalm 66:18

GOD'S PROMISES
*Proverbs 28:13

MAKE A CHANGE
*Psalm 38:18
1 John 1:9

BIBLICAL EXAMPLES
*Genesis 3:7-13
*Joshua 7:19
*2 Samuel 12:13; 24:10

PRAYER
*1 Kings 8:46-50
*Psalm 19:12; 32:1-5; 51:1-3, 7;
139:23-24

CONSECRATION (SEE SANCTIFICATION)

CONTENTMENT

GOD'S PERSPECTIVE
*Proverbs 15:16-17; 16:16-17;
17:1; 22:1; 23:4-5
Matthew 6:19-21
1 Timothy 6:6-10

GOD'S PROMISES
*Habakkuk 3:17-19

MAKE A CHANGE
Luke 12:15
1 Corinthians 7:24
Colossians 3:5
Hebrews 13:5

BIBLICAL EXAMPLES
Luke 3:14
Philippians 4:11-13

COVETOUSNESS

GOD'S PERSPECTIVE
*Exodus 20:17
*Psalm 62:10
*Proverbs 12:12; 15:27
Luke 12:15
Romans 13:9
Ephesians 5:3, 5
1 Timothy 3:2-3; 6:17
James 4:2
2 Peter 2:1-3, 14

GOD'S PROMISES
1 Timothy 6:6

MAKE A CHANGE
Colossians 3:5
Hebrews 13:5

BIBLICAL EXAMPLES
*1 Kings 21:4
Luke 12:16-21

PRAYER
*Psalm 119:36
*Proverbs 30:8-9

CULTS, FALSE RELIGIONS

GOD'S PERSPECTIVE
*Deuteronomy 13:1-3; 18:10-12
Matthew 7:15-16; 24:5
John 14:6
Acts 4:12
2 Corinthians 4:3-4; 11:13-15
Galatians 1:8-9
1 Timothy 3:16; 4:1-3
2 Timothy 3:13; 4:3-4
1 Peter 3:18-22
2 Peter 1:16; 2:1-2
1 John 2:22-23; 4:1-3
Jude 1:3-4

GOD'S PROMISES
*Micah 5:12
John 8:32
2 Timothy 3:16-17
Revelation 2:2

MAKE A CHANGE
Ephesians 5:11
Hebrews 13:9

BIBLICAL EXAMPLES
Mark 12:32

PRAYER
*Psalm 25:5

D

DATING

GOD'S PERSPECTIVE
*Exodus 34:16
*Deuteronomy 7:3-4
*Proverbs 22:24-25
1 Corinthians 5:11; 7:39,
15:33-34
2 Corinthians 6:15
James 4:4

GOD'S PROMISES
2 Corinthians 6:16-18

MAKE A CHANGE
*Ezra 9:12
2 Corinthians 6:14

BIBLICAL EXAMPLES
*Nehemiah 13:1-3; 23-26
*Psalm 106:35-36
*Malachi 2:11

PRAYER
*Psalm 101:3-7

The decision to marry or stay single
GOD'S PERSPECTIVE
1 Corinthians 7:2, 8-9, 26-27,
32, 34-35
Philippians 4:11-12
1 Timothy 5:14

Finding a godly wife
GOD'S PERSPECTIVE
*Proverbs 12:4; 31:10-11, 30

GOD'S PROMISES
*Proverbs 18:22; 19:14

Staying pure
GOD'S PERSPECTIVE
1 Corinthians 6:11
1 Thessalonians 4:3-6

GOD'S PROMISES
*Ezekiel 36:25-29
Matthew 5:8
John 1:7

MAKE A CHANGE
*Isaiah 1:16
*Ezekiel 18:31

1 Corinthians 6:18
Hebrews 10:22
James 4:8
1 Peter 1:14-16, 22

PRAYER
*Psalm 51:2, 7

DEATH

GOD'S PERSPECTIVE
*Job 19:25-27
John 10:27-28; 11:25; 14:1-4
Romans 8:38-39
1 Corinthians 15:54-56

GOD'S PROMISES
*Psalm 23:4; 116:15
Luke 23:43
2 Corinthians 5:1-2, 4, 6-8
Philippians 1:21; 3:20-21
1 Thessalonians 4:14
Hebrews 2:14-15; 9:27-28
Revelation 2:7

MAKE A CHANGE
Matthew 10:28

BIBLICAL EXAMPLES
Acts 7:55-60
2 Timothy 4:6-8
2 Peter 1:14

PRAYER
*Job 13:15
*Psalm 23:4

DEBT

GOD'S PERSPECTIVE
*Psalm 37:21
*Proverbs 3:9-10
Matthew 6:31-33
John 6:27
Romans 6:12; 8:5
Galatians 5:17
1 Timothy 6:6-10

GOD'S PROMISES
Matthew 5:6
Ephesians 2:3-5
Philippians 4:19

MAKE A CHANGE
Luke 12:15
Romans 13:13-14
Hebrews 13:5-6

PRAYER
*Proverbs 30:7-9

Paying back debt
GOD'S PERSPECTIVE
*Proverbs 3:27-28; 22:7, 26-27
Luke 16:11-12

MAKE A CHANGE
*Deuteronomy 15:6; 28:12;
10:4; 3:4; 21:5
Romans 13:8

DECISION MAKING

GOD'S PERSPECTIVE
*Deuteronomy 30:19-20
1 Corinthians 2:16; 3:19
Hebrews 3:7-11

GOD'S PROMISES
*Psalm 32:8; 146:5-6
*Proverbs 3:5-6
James 1:5-6

MAKE A CHANGE
*Deuteronomy 12:8
*Psalm 37:3, 5, 7
*Proverbs 14:12; 16:25

Romans 12:1-2
1 Corinthians 10:31
Ephesians 6:18
Philippians 4:6-7
Colossians 3:17, 23

BIBLICAL EXAMPLES
*2 Chronicles 20:12
Hebrews 11:24-26

PRAYER
*Exodus 33:13
*Psalm 25:4-5; 86:11

DEFEATED

GOD'S PERSPECTIVE
*Psalm 34:18
*Isaiah 57:15, 61:1
*Jeremiah 31:25

GOD'S PROMISES
*Psalm 27:1-2; 34:4;
40:1-3; 46:2-4
*Proverbs 24:16
Romans 8:35-39
1 Corinthians 15:57
2 Corinthians 4:8-10
Philippians 4:13
1 Peter 1:6-9

MAKE A CHANGE
*Isaiah 35:3-4
John 16:33
Ephesians 6:10
2 Timothy 2:1
Hebrews 12:11-12

BIBLICAL EXAMPLES
*1 Samuel 30:6
2 Corinthians 1:8-9; 7:5-6

PRAYER
*Psalm 38:15; 42:5; 119:32;
121:1-8, 138:3
2 Corinthians 2:14

DEMONS

GOD'S PERSPECTIVE
Matthew 12:43-45
Romans 8:38-39
1 John 4:1-3

GOD'S PROMISES
1 John 4:4

MAKE A CHANGE
Ephesians 6:10-12
James 4:7
1 Peter 5:8-9

BIBLICAL EXAMPLES
Matthew 12:22; 17:15-20
Mark 1:23-25, 34; 5:2-9;
9:25-29
Luke 4:33-37, 41; 9:38-42
Acts 16:16-18; 19:13-20
Colossians 2:15
1 Peter 3:22
Revelation 12:7-9

PRAYER
Luke 11:4

DEPRESSION

GOD'S PERSPECTIVE
*Proverbs 18:14
*Isaiah 40:28-31
2 Corinthians 10:4-5
1 Peter 1:6-7

GOD'S PROMISES
*Psalm 147:3
Romans 5:3-5
2 Corinthians 1:3-4;
4:16-18; 12:10

Ephesians 3:16-19
Titus 3:5-6
James 1:2-8

MAKE A CHANGE
*Psalm 27:13-14; 37:3-7; 42:5
*Proverbs 3:5-6
Romans 12:2
1 Corinthians 15:58
Philippians 3:1; 4:4

BIBLICAL EXAMPLES
*Job 1:20-22; 2:6-10
2 Corinthians 12:9-10

PRAYER
*Psalm 16:7-8; 55:16-18; 73:26
*Lamentations 3:17-18, 21-26

DIET

GOD'S PERSPECTIVE
*Leviticus 11:45
*Psalm 136:25
Matthew 4:4
Luke 12:29-31
John 6:35
Romans 14:12
1 Corinthians 6:12, 19-20

GOD'S PROMISES
*Deuteronomy 28:1-6

MAKE A CHANGE
1 Corinthians 9:24-25; 10:23, 31
Colossians 3:1-2, 17

BIBLICAL EXAMPLES
*Daniel 1:8

PRAYER
*Psalm 103:2-5

DISABILITY

GOD'S PERSPECTIVE
Luke 13:2-5
John 11:4, 40

GOD'S PROMISES
*Isaiah 35:6
Romans 8:18, 28
2 Corinthians 4:17
1 Peter 1:6-8

MAKE A CHANGE
2 Corinthians 12:9-10

BIBLICAL EXAMPLES
*Exodus 4:10-12
Matthew 11:5
John 9:1-3
Acts 20:24
Hebrews 11:25-26

DISASTER THREATS

GOD'S PERSPECTIVE
*Psalm 46:1-2
*Isaiah 41:10
John 14:1
Romans 8:35-37

GOD'S PROMISES
*Joshua 1:9
*Psalm 46:1-3; 91:9-11;
145:18; 3:25-26; 14:26
Luke 21:18

MAKE A CHANGE
*Psalm 50:15
1 Peter 5:6-7

BIBLICAL EXAMPLES
*Genesis 35:3
Luke 8:22-25

PRAYER
*Psalm 25:16-17; 27:1-2, 118:5-8

DISCERNMENT

GOD'S PERSPECTIVE
*Proverbs 9:7-10; 19:25; 23:9
*Ezekiel 44:23
Matthew 7:6,10:14; 13:45-46
1 Corinthians 2:14
Philippians 3:2-3
Hebrews 5:14
Jude 1:22-23

GOD'S PROMISES
*Malachi 3:18

MAKE A CHANGE
*Proverbs 23:9
John 7:24
Philippians 1:9-10
Hebrews 4:12; 5:14

BIBLICAL EXAMPLES
*1 Kings 3:9, 11-12
Acts 13:45-46

PRAYER
*1 Kings 3:5-14

DISCIPLINE

GOD'S PERSPECTIVE
*Deuteronomy 8:5
*1 Samuel 3:13
*Proverbs 3:11-12
Hebrews 12:5-11
Revelation 3:19

GOD'S PROMISES
*Job 5:17-18
*Psalm 94:12
1 Corinthians 11:32

MAKE A CHANGE
*Psalm 119:67, 71
*Lamentations 3:28-33
2 Timothy 2:24-26

PRAYER
*Psalm 6:1; 118:18
*Jeremiah 10:24

DISCOURAGEMENT

GOD'S PERSPECTIVE
*Genesis 28:15
*Isaiah 43:1-3
*Jeremiah 1:7-8

GOD'S PROMISES
*Deuteronomy 31:8
*Joshua 1:9
*1 Chronicles 22:13
*Psalm 55:22

MAKE A CHANGE
*Psalm 27:14; 31:24
1 Timothy 6:12
Hebrews 10:23; 12:1-3; 12:12
1 Peter 5:6-7

BIBLICAL EXAMPLES
*Deuteronomy 20:1
*2 Kings 6:15-18
Mark 15:43

PRAYER
*Psalm 119:28

DIVORCE

GOD'S PERSPECTIVE
*Genesis 2:24
*Deuteronomy 24:1-4
*Malachi 2:13-16
Matthew 5:31-32,18:15-18;
19:3-9
Mark 10:2-9, 10-12

Romans 7:1-3
1 Corinthians 7:10-15
1 John 4:20-21

MAKE A CHANGE
*Proverbs 5:15-18
Romans 12:18
Ephesians 4:26-27; 5:22-33
Colossians 3:19
Hebrews 12:14-15
1 Peter 3:7

BIBLICAL EXAMPLES
*Isaiah 50:1
*Jeremiah 3:8

DOUBT

GOD'S PERSPECTIVE
*Numbers 14:11; 20:12
*Isaiah 7:9b
Matthew 7:7-8, 11
John 3:18; 8:24; 14:1; 20:29
Revelation 21:8

GOD'S PROMISES
Matthew 17:20; 21:21-22
1 Peter 1:8

MAKE A CHANGE
Hebrews 3:12-13
James 1:5-8

BIBLICAL EXAMPLES
*Psalm 78:21b-24
*Isaiah 49:14-15
Matthew 8:26; 14:29-31
Mark 16:14, 16-18

PRAYER
Mark 9:24
Luke 17:5

DOUBTING GOD'S WORD

GOD'S PERSPECTIVE
Matthew 24:35
Mark 12:24
John 10:35
2 Timothy 3:16-17
Hebrews 3:7-9; 4:12
2 Peter 1:19-21

GOD'S PROMISES
*Psalm 119:89
*Isaiah 40:8
Revelation 3:8

MAKE A CHANGE
Acts 17:11
James 1:21

BIBLICAL EXAMPLES
*2 Kings 7:18-20
1 Thessalonians 2:13

PRAYER
*Psalm 119:89

The effect of God's Word

GOD'S PERSPECTIVE
*Isaiah 55:11
James 1:18
1 Peter 1:23

GOD'S PROMISES
*Psalm 1:1-3
Romans 15:4

MAKE A CHANGE
*Psalm 119:9, 11

BIBLICAL EXAMPLES
Galatians 3:8
1 Thessalonians 2:13
1 Peter 1:22-25

PRAYER
*Psalm 119:114

DOUBTING ONE'S SALVATION

GOD'S PERSPECTIVE
Mark 16:16
John 3:16; 5:24; 6:37
10:27-28
Acts 13:39
Galatians 3:26
Ephesians 2:8-9
Hebrews 7:25
1 John 5:10-12

GOD'S PROMISES
Acts 16:31
Romans 3:24-26; 5:9-10;
8:16; 8:29-30, 38-39; 10:9-10
Ephesians 1:13-14
Philippians 1:6
1 John 5:13

MAKE A CHANGE
Hebrews 10:22
1 Peter 1:22-25
1 John 1:9

DRUG ADDICTION

GOD'S PERSPECTIVE
*1 Samuel 15:23
*Psalm 52:7
*Isaiah 47:9
*Ezekiel 18:30-32
*Malachi 3:5
Galatians 5:19-21
Revelation 21:6-8

GOD'S PROMISES
Revelation 22:14-15

MAKE A CHANGE
1 Corinthians 6:12
Ephesians 5:18

BIBLICAL EXAMPLES
Revelation 9:20-21

E

EMPLOYER/EMPLOYEE RELATIONSHIPS

GOD'S PERSPECTIVE
Luke 12:45-46
Romans 13:1-5
Titus 2:9-10

GOD'S PROMISES
Colossians 3:23-24

MAKE A CHANGE
*Ecclesiastes 9:10a
Ephesians 6:5-9
Colossians 3:17
1 Timothy 6:1-3
1 Peter 2:18-21

BIBLICAL EXAMPLES
*Genesis 31:5-6; 39:2-4
*Daniel 6:4

For employers

GOD'S PERSPECTIVE
*Leviticus 19:13; 25:43
*Deuteronomy 24:14-15
*Jeremiah 22:13
Matthew 20:25-28

GOD'S PROMISES
Ephesians 6:8-9

MAKE A CHANGE
Luke 6:31
Colossians 4:1

BIBLICAL EXAMPLES
*2 Chronicles 10:7

ENCOURAGEMENT

GOD'S PERSPECTIVE
*Psalm 33:20-21
Ephesians 5:19-20
Colossians 3:16

GOD'S PROMISES
*Psalm 32:7
Matthew 28:20b
John 16:33b
Galatians 6:9
Revelation 21:4-7

MAKE A CHANGE
*Psalm 3:5-6; 31:24; 32:11
Philippians 4:6-7
1 Thessalonians 5:11
Hebrews 3:13

BIBLICAL EXAMPLES
*1 Samuel 30:6

PRAYER
*Psalm 43:5; 71:5

ENDURANCE

GOD'S PERSPECTIVE
Luke 8:15
Romans 2:6-7
1 Corinthians 13:4-7

GOD'S PROMISES
Matthew 10:22
Romans 5:3-4
1 Thessalonians 1:3
Hebrews 10:36-37
James 1:12; 5:11
Revelation 3:21

MAKE A CHANGE
Galatians 6:9
Hebrews 6:11-12, 15; 12:1-3
Revelation 2:7, 10, 17, 26; 13:10

BIBLICAL EXAMPLES
Hebrews 11:24-27

ENVY, JEALOUSY, COVETOUSNESS

GOD'S PERSPECTIVE
*Exodus 20:17
*Job 5:2
*Proverbs 3:31-32; 14:30; 23:17-18; 27:4
*Ecclesiastes 4:4
Galatians 5:19-21
Philippians 4:11
1 Timothy 6:6-8
2 Timothy 3:1-2
Titus 3:3-5
James 4:1-4

GOD'S PROMISES
Colossians 3:1-4
Hebrews 13:5
2 Peter 1:2-4

MAKE A CHANGE
Luke 12:15
Romans 13:13
Ephesians 5:3-5
James 3:13-16
1 Peter 2:1-3

BIBLICAL EXAMPLES
*Joshua 7:19-21
*2 Kings 5:20-27
Acts 20:32-34

PRAYER
*Proverbs 30:8-9

ERRATIC, INCONSISTENT BIBLE STUDY

GOD'S PERSPECTIVE
*Proverbs 1:5
Romans 15:4
2 Timothy 3:16-17

GOD'S PROMISES
*Joshua 1:8
*Psalm 1:1-3
1 Thessalonians 2:13

MAKE A CHANGE
1 Timothy 4:15-16
2 Timothy 2:15-16

BIBLICAL EXAMPLES
*Joshua 8:34-35
*2 Kings 23:1-2
*Ezra 7:10
*Nehemiah 8:2-3

PRAYER
*Psalm 119:15-16; 147-148

EVOLUTION

GOD'S PERSPECTIVE
*Genesis 1:1, 26-27; 5:1
*Isaiah 44:24
John 1:3; 3:19-20
Acts 17:24-28
Romans 1:18-19
2 Corinthians 4:3-4
Ephesians 2:10
James 3:8-9

GOD'S PROMISES
*Isaiah 43:1, 7; 44:22
Ephesians 1:11

MAKE A CHANGE
*Psalm 95:5-6; 100:3
*Ecclesiastes 12:1
*Isaiah 55:6-9
1 Timothy 6:20

BIBLICAL EXAMPLES
*Isaiah 45:18

PRAYER
*Psalm 119:73
Revelation 4:11

EXAMPLE (GOOD OR BAD)

Our example to others

GOD'S PERSPECTIVE
Matthew 5:19
Luke 17:1-3
1 Corinthians 8:9-13
1 Thessalonians 1:5-7
2 Thessalonians 3:7-9
1 Peter 2:9

GOD'S PROMISES
1 Peter 5:2-4

MAKE A CHANGE
Philippians 3:17; 4:9
1 Timothy 4:12
Titus 2:7
1 Peter 4:11

BIBLICAL EXAMPLES
1 Corinthians 11:1
1 Thessalonians 2:9-12

God's examples to us

GOD'S PERSPECTIVE
*Leviticus 19:2
John 13:15
1 Corinthians 10:1-11
1 Peter 2:21
Jude 1:7

MAKE A CHANGE
*Micah 6:8
1 Peter 2:17-25
1 John 2:6

BIBLICAL EXAMPLES
John 13:1-7, 15

PRAYER
*Psalm 17:5
Ephesians 3:14-19

EXPOSING SIN

God exposes sin

GOD'S PERSPECTIVE
*Daniel 2:20, 22
Luke 12:2-3
John 3:18-21
Hebrews 4:13

GOD'S PROMISES
*Numbers 32:23

MAKE A CHANGE
*Leviticus 19:17
*Psalm 32:3-5
*Proverbs 28:13
Luke 17:3

BIBLICAL EXAMPLES
2 Timothy 3:8-9

Exposing sin of another

GOD'S PERSPECTIVE
*Proverbs 25:12; 27:5-6

MAKE A CHANGE
Matthew 18:15-17
Ephesians 5:11-14

BIBLICAL EXAMPLES
*2 Samuel 12:1-7; 9

PRAYER
*2 Samuel 12:13
*Psalm 51:4

F

FAITH FOR SALVATION

GOD'S PERSPECTIVE
*Isaiah 43:1-3
Romans 1:17; 10:17
2 Corinthians 1:9
Ephesians 2:8-9
2 Thessalonians 2:13
1 Peter 1:18-2

GOD'S PROMISES
*Psalm 138:8
Romans 10:9
Ephesians 2:4-7
Philippians 2:13
1 Thessalonians 5:23-24
1 Timothy 4:10
Titus 3:4-6
Hebrews 11:6
1 John 5:4

MAKE A CHANGE
John 6:29; 14:1
1 Timothy 6:12
Jude 20-21

BIBLICAL EXAMPLES
John 11:27
Acts 15:11; 16:31

PRAYER
*Psalm 6:4; 25:20; 31:16

FAITH IN THE MIDST OF TRIALS

GOD'S PERSPECTIVE
*Isaiah 41:10
*Jeremiah 32:26-27
Mark 11:24
John 17:15
2 Corinthians 5:7
1 Peter 1:6-9

GOD'S PROMISES
*Psalm 91:3-5
*Lamentations 3:22-24
Luke 21:15-19
2 Timothy 4:18
James 1:2-3

MAKE A CHANGE
*Psalm 27:13-14; 37:7
*Proverbs 3:5-6

BIBLICAL EXAMPLES
Hebrews 11:1-6

PRAYER
*Psalm 16:1; 32:7; 91:15

FAITH (LACK OF)

GOD'S PERSPECTIVE
*Isaiah 41:10
Matthew 6:27, 14:31; 17:20
Mark 4:40; 11:22
Luke 12:28-31

GOD'S PROMISES
Mark 9:23

MAKE A CHANGE
1 Corinthians 16:13
Hebrews 3:12-13; 11:6

BIBLICAL EXAMPLES
Matthew 8:26-27
John 20:29
Romans 4:20

PRAYER
*Psalm 42:11

FALSE PROPHETS

GOD'S PERSPECTIVE
*Deuteronomy 18:21-22
*Jeremiah 23:16
Matthew 7:15; 24:24-25
Mark 13:22-23
2 Corinthians 11:13-15
Colossians 2:8-10
1 Timothy 4:1-3
1 John 4:1-3
2 John 1:9
Revelation 2:2-3

GOD'S PROMISES
*Psalm 91:3

MAKE A CHANGE
Ephesians 5:11
2 John 1:10

BIBLICAL EXAMPLES
*Jeremiah 14:13-14
Acts 17:11
2 Peter 2:1-3

PRAYER
*Psalm 141:9-10

FAMILY

GOD'S PERSPECTIVE
*Deuteronomy 4:9
*Psalm 68:6; 127:3-5; 128
*Proverbs 13:24; 15:5; 17:21
20:11; 22:6, 15
1 Timothy 5:8

GOD'S PROMISES
*Genesis 18:19
*1 Chronicles 17:27

MAKE A CHANGE
*Psalm 78:5-7
Ephesians 6:1, 4
Colossians 3:20, 21

BIBLICAL EXAMPLES
*Joshua 24:15

PRAYER
*2 Samuel 7:29

FASTING

GOD'S PERSPECTIVE
*Isaiah 58:6-9a
*Joel 2:12
*Zechariah 7:5-6
Matthew 6:16-18

MAKE A CHANGE
Romans 7:18; 8:5-8, 13
Galatians 5:17

BIBLICAL EXAMPLES
*1 Samuel 7:6
*2 Samuel 12:16-20
*Ezra 8:22-23
*Esther 4:16
*Psalm 35:13; 69:10; 109:24
*Daniel 1:8; 10:2-3
Matthew 4:2-4
Acts 13:2-4; 14:23

FATIGUE

GOD'S PERSPECTIVE
*Psalm 18:2; 46:1; 121:5
*Proverbs 24:10
*Jeremiah 12:5

GOD'S PROMISES
*Exodus 33:14
*Psalm 68:35
*Isaiah 40:28-31; 41:10
*Jeremiah 31:25
Matthew 11:28-30
Romans 8:31
1 Corinthians 15:58

MAKE A CHANGE
Galatians 6:9-10
Ephesians 6:10
Philippians 4:13
2 Thessalonians 3:13
Hebrews 4:16

PRAYER
*Psalm 28:7; 62:1; 73:26; 138:3
Ephesians 4:14-16

FEAR

GOD'S PERSPECTIVE
*Genesis 15:1
*Isaiah 41:10; 43:1-2
Matthew 10:28-31
Romans 8:15-16
2 Timothy 1:7
Hebrews 2:14-15

GOD'S PROMISES
*Psalm 91:5
*Proverbs 1:32-33
*Jeremiah 17:7-8
John 14:27
Romans 8:28
1 John 4:18

MAKE A CHANGE
*Psalm 27:1; 56:3, 11
*Proverbs 3:25
Philippians 4:6-7

PRAYER
*Psalm 23:4; 27:1; 34:4; 56:3-4
Hebrews 13:6

FEAR OF THE LORD

GOD'S PERSPECTIVE
*Genesis 22:12
*Deuteronomy 6:13; 10:12
*Job 28:28
*Psalm 115:11
*Proverbs 1:7; 8:13; 9:10;
14:26-27; 15:33; 16:6;
19:23; 22:4

GOD'S PROMISES
*Psalm 25:14; 34:9; 111:10;
115:12-13; 66:2
*Jeremiah 32:39
Acts 10:35

MAKE A CHANGE
*Proverbs 3:7

BIBLICAL EXAMPLES
*Exodus 14:31
*Deuteronomy 6:24
*1 Samuel 12:18
*Malachi 3:16
Acts 9:31

PRAYER
*Psalm 61:5; 86:11

FELLOWSHIP

GOD'S PERSPECTIVE
*Psalm 89:7; 107:32; 133:1
*Proverbs 18:1
*Ecclesiastes 4:12
John 17:21-23

MAKE A CHANGE
1 Corinthians 1:9-10
2 Corinthians 6:14
Galatians 6:2, 10
Philippians 2:1-2
Colossians 3:16
Hebrews 10:24-25
1 John 1:3, 6-7

BIBLICAL EXAMPLES
*Psalm 55:14
*Malachi 3:16
Acts 2:42, 46-47
1 John 1:3, 7

PRAYER
*Psalm 22:22; 35:18
2 Corinthians 12:14

FINANCES

GOD'S PERSPECTIVE
*Deuteronomy 8:17-18
*Psalm 34:10; 37:16; 62:10
*Proverbs 11:15; 13:7; 15:16
*Ecclesiastes 5:10
*Isaiah 55:2
Matthew 6:21, 31-33
Luke 12:15
1 Timothy 6:6-10

GOD'S PROMISES
*Proverbs 10:22
*Malachi 3:10
Philippians 4:19

MAKE A CHANGE
*Proverbs 6:1-5; 10:4; 23:4;
28:20, 22
1 Timothy 6:17

BIBLICAL EXAMPLES
*Genesis 13:2; 24:35; 26:12-14;
36:6-7
*Job 31:24-28

FOOD

Food addiction

GOD'S PERSPECTIVE
*Psalm 81:10
*Proverbs 23:19-21; 25:16
Matthew 6:25; 26:41
Luke 12:40-46
John 4:34; 8:36
1 Corinthians 3:16-17; 6:12-13

GOD'S PROMISES
1 Corinthians 10:13

MAKE A CHANGE
*Proverbs 23:2
Romans 12:1
1 Corinthians 6:19-20; 9:27;
10:31
Galatians 5:16
1 Peter 4:1-2

BIBLICAL EXAMPLES
*Daniel 1:8-14

PRAYER
Philippians 4:13

Vegetarian/kosher eating

GOD'S PERSPECTIVE
*Psalm 24:1
1 Timothy 4:1-5

MAKE A CHANGE
Romans 14:1-4, 13-17, 20-21
1 Corinthians 10:25-26, 31-33

BIBLICAL EXAMPLES
Acts 11:5-9

FORGIVENESS (OF OTHERS)

GOD'S PERSPECTIVE
*Leviticus 19:17-18
Matthew 6:12, 14-15; 18:32-35
Mark 11:25-26
Luke 6:37; 11:4; 17:3-4
John 20:23
James 2:8, 10, 12-13
1 John 3:10

MAKE A CHANGE
Ephesians 4:31-32
Colossians 3:12-13
James 5:16
1 Peter 4:8

BIBLICAL EXAMPLES
*Genesis 33:4; 45:5-15; 50:19-21
Matthew 18:21-22
Luke 23:34
2 Corinthians 2:7, 10-11

FORGIVENESS (OF SIN)

GOD'S PERSPECTIVE
*Proverbs 28:13
*Isaiah 1:18; 44:22-23
Matthew 9:6; 11:28-30
Mark 2:10-11
Luke 23:34, 43
John 8:36
Acts 10:43
Romans 3:21-26
Ephesians 1:7-8
Colossians 1:13-14; 2:13-15
Hebrews 8:12

GOD'S PROMISES
*2 Chronicles 7:14
*Proverbs 28:13
*Isaiah 1:18; 55:6-7

MAKE A CHANGE
Acts 3:19
1 John 1:6-9

BIBLICAL EXAMPLES
Luke 5:24-26; 7:47-50
Acts 5:30-31; 13:36-39

PRAYER
*Psalm 32:5; 51:9; 86:5;
103:1-5; 130:3-4
*Micah 7:18-19

FORNICATION

GOD'S PERSPECTIVE
*Proverbs 5:20-23;
6:23-25; 7:4-5
Matthew 15:19-20
Mark 7:21-23
1 Corinthians 6:9-11
Galatians 5:19-21
Hebrews 13:4

GOD'S PROMISES
*Isaiah 55:7
1 John 1:9
Revelation 22:14-15

MAKE A CHANGE
Acts 15:20, 29
1 Corinthians 6:18
Ephesians 5:3-5
Colossians 3:5
1 Timothy 4:12
2 Timothy 2:22

BIBLICAL EXAMPLES
Revelation 2:14

PRAYER
*Psalm 51:7, 10

FOUL LANGUAGE/PROFANITY

GOD'S PERSPECTIVE
*Exodus 20:7
*Proverbs 6:12; 10:32; 12:18;
13:3; 15:28; 21:23
Matthew 12:34, 36-37; 15:11, 18
Luke 6:45
James 1:26; 3:5-8, 10

MAKE A CHANGE
Ephesians 4:29; 5:4
Colossians 3:8, 4:6
1 Peter 3:10

BIBLICAL EXAMPLES
*1 Samuel 17:43

PRAYER
*Psalm 19:14; 141:3

FRIENDSHIPS

GOD'S PERSPECTIVE
*Psalm 1:1
*Proverbs 13:20; 17:17; 18:24;
27:9, 17; 28:7, 23
*Ecclesiastes 4:9-10
John 15:13-15
1 Corinthians 15:33
James 4:4

MAKE A CHANGE
*Proverbs 9:6; 22:24-25
2 Corinthians 6:14

BIBLICAL EXAMPLES
*1 Samuel 18:1-3; 20:17, 42
James 2:23-24

PRAYER
*Psalm 119:63

FRIENDSHIPS AND FAILURE

GOD'S PERSPECTIVE
*Proverbs 17:17; 27:6
*Jeremiah 17:5, 7
*Micah 7:5-7

GOD'S PROMISES
*Deuteronomy 4:31; 31:6, 8
*1 Samuel 12:22
*1 Kings 6:13
*Nehemiah 9:31
*Psalm 94:14
Hebrews 13:15

MAKE A CHANGE
*Psalm 40:4; 62:8;
118:8-9; 146:3
Hebrews 12:2-3

BIBLICAL EXAMPLES
*Psalm 27:10; 41:9; 55:12-14, 16
Mark 14:50
Luke 22:48
John 16:32
2 Timothy 1:15; 4:10, 16-17

PRAYER
*Psalm 22:11; 35:22; 38:21

G

GAMBLING

GOD'S PERSPECTIVE
*Exodus 20:17
*Proverbs 23:4-5; 28:22
*Ecclesiastes 5:10
*Ezekiel 33:31
Matthew 6:24
1 Corinthians 6:12
1 Timothy 6:6-10

GOD'S PROMISES
Matthew 6:33
1 Corinthians 10:13
Hebrews 13:5
1 Peter 5:2-4

MAKE A CHANGE
Luke 12:15
1 Corinthians 10:31
Galatians 5:1
Colossians 3:2, 5-7
1 Timothy 6:17

PRAYER
*Psalm 19:13
*Proverbs 30:8-9

GENERATIONAL SIN

GOD'S PERSPECTIVE
*Exodus 20:5-6; 34:7
*Numbers 14:18
*Deuteronomy 5:9-10
*Psalm 78:1-8
*Jeremiah 31:29-30
Romans 3:24-26

GOD'S PROMISES
*Exodus 20:5-6
*Ezekiel 18:2-3, 14, 17-20
John 8:36
Luke 1:50

MAKE A CHANGE
*Joel 1:3
Galatians 5:1

BIBLICAL EXAMPLES
John 9:1-3

PRAYER
*Psalm 71:18; 78:4, 8;
102:18; 145:4

GIVING

Giving to God

GOD'S PERSPECTIVE
*Exodus 25:2
*Deuteronomy 12:6, 11

*Malachi 3:8
Luke 21:1-4

GOD'S PROMISES
*Proverbs 19:17
*Malachi 3:10
Luke 6:38

MAKE A CHANGE
*Psalm 96:8
*Proverbs 3:9-10
Matthew 6:1-4
2 Corinthians 9:7
Philemon 14

BIBLICAL EXAMPLES
*1 Chronicles 29:16-17
1 Corinthians 16:1-2

Giving to others
GOD'S PERSPECTIVE
*Deuteronomy 15:7-8
*Proverbs 14:21; 19:17; 22:9
*Isaiah 58:7-11
Matthew 25:35, 40

GOD'S PROMISES
*Deuteronomy 15:7, 10-11
*Proverbs 11:24-25; 22:9
1 Timothy 6:17-19

MAKE A CHANGE
*Proverbs 3:28
Acts 20:35
2 Corinthians 9:6-9
Galatians 6:9-10
Hebrews 13:16
1 John 3:16-18

BIBLICAL EXAMPLES
Luke 19:8
Acts 4:32

GOSSIP
GOD'S PERSPECTIVE
*Leviticus 19:16
*Psalm 50:16-21
*Proverbs 11:11-13; 12:18;
16:28; 17:9; 26:20
James 1:26; 3:5-6

GOD'S PROMISES
*Proverbs 21:23
1 Peter 3:10

MAKE A CHANGE
*Psalm 17:3; 34:13
*Proverbs 20:19
Ephesians 4:29
James 1:26; 3:9-10; 4:11
1 Peter 2:1-3

BIBLICAL EXAMPLES
1 Timothy 5:13

PRAYER
*Psalm 15:1-3; 141:3

GRACE
GOD'S PERSPECTIVE
*Exodus 34:6
*Psalm 103:8
John 1:17
Acts 15:11
Romans 3:23-24; 5:8, 20-21
Galatians 2:21
Ephesians 2:8-9
Titus 2:11

GOD'S PROMISES
Romans 5:1-2
Ephesians 1:7-8
2 Timothy 1:9
James 4:6

MAKE A CHANGE
*Joel 2:13
Romans 6:1-2
Hebrews 4:16
1 Peter 1:13
2 Peter 3:18

BIBLICAL EXAMPLES
*Genesis 6:8
Luke 15:11-24
Philemon 1:15-19

PRAYER
*Psalm 86:15

GRADUATION
GOD'S PERSPECTIVE
*Psalm 75:6-7
*Proverbs 1:7; 2:6; 15:33
*Zechariah 4:6
John 6:27
1 Corinthians 3:5; 4:7
2 Corinthians 3:5-6

GOD'S PROMISES
*Proverbs 3:19-24; 9:10
Matthew 6:33
Philippians 2:13
Colossians 2:2-3
2 Thessalonians 3:3

MAKE A CHANGE
1 Corinthians 9:24; 10:31;
15:58
2 Timothy 2:15
2 Peter 1:10

BIBLICAL EXAMPLES
2 Corinthians 1:9
2 Timothy 4:7

PRAYER
Colossians 1:9-10

GRIEF
GOD'S PERSPECTIVE
*Psalms 116:15
John 11:25-26

GOD'S PROMISES
*Psalm 30:5; 34:18
Matthew 5:4
2 Corinthians 1:3-4
Philippians 4:19
Revelation 21:4

MAKE A CHANGE
John 14:1-3
1 Thessalonians 4:13
James 1:2-4

BIBLICAL EXAMPLES
*Genesis 37:30, 35
*2 Samuel 1:11-12, 17-18

PRAYER
*Psalm 23:4-6; 31:9-10, 19

GUIDANCE
GOD'S PERSPECTIVE
*Psalm 37:23; 48:14; 73:23-24
*Proverbs 16:9
*Isaiah 30:21
Romans 12:2

GOD'S PROMISES
*Deuteronomy 31:8
*Psalm 25:9; 32:8-9
*Isaiah 30:21; 42:16; 58:11
John 16:13

MAKE A CHANGE
*Proverbs 3:5-6
Matthew 10:16-20
James 1:5-6

BIBLICAL EXAMPLES
*1 Samuel 23:1-5; 30:7-8
*2 Samuel 2:1; 5:18-19, 22-25
Acts 16:6-10
Hebrews 11:8

PRAYER
*Psalm 31:3; 121:1-2
*Jeremiah 10:23
2 Thessalonians 3:5

GUILT
GOD'S PERSPECTIVE
*Proverbs 20:9
*Ecclesiastes 7:20
*Isaiah 44:22; 64:6
John 16:7-8
Romans 3:22-24
James 2:10, 13

GOD'S PROMISES
*Isaiah 1:18; 43:25
*Micah 7:18-19
John 8:36
Romans 8:1-2

MAKE A CHANGE
*Leviticus 5:5
Romans 7:18-25
Philippians 3:13-14
1 John 1:9

BIBLICAL EXAMPLES
*Psalm 51:1
Luke 18:13-14

PRAYER
*Psalm 32:5; 51:5-7; 143:2

H

HATE
GOD'S PERSPECTIVE
*Leviticus 19:17
*Proverbs 10:12; 15:17;
26:24-26
1 John 2:8-11; 3:15; 4:19-20

MAKE A CHANGE
Luke 6:27-28
Romans 12:9
Galatians 5:15, 19-21
Ephesians 4:31
Hebrews 12:14-15

BIBLICAL EXAMPLES
*Genesis 27:41; 37:4-5, 8
*2 Samuel 6:16
*1 Kings 22:8

Righteous hatred
GOD'S PERSPECTIVE
*Psalm 31:6; 101:3; 119:104, 163
*Proverbs 8:13
*Isaiah 1:14; 61:8

MAKE A CHANGE
*Psalm 97:10
*Amos 5:15
Romans 12:9

BIBLICAL EXAMPLES
Matthew 21:12-13

HEALING
GOD'S PERSPECTIVE
*Exodus 15:26
*Job 5:18
Matthew 10:8

GOD'S PROMISES
*Exodus 15:26; 23:25-26
*Psalm 34:19; 103:2-5
Revelation 22:2

MAKE A CHANGE
James 5:14-16
1 Peter 4:19

BIBLICAL EXAMPLES
*Genesis 20:17
*Numbers 12:13
*2 Kings 5:10-14
Matthew 8:2-3; 9:22; 14:26;
15:28; 3:5; 5:34; 6:56; 10:52;
Luke 6:10
2 Corinthians 12:7-9

PRAYER
*Psalm 30:2
*Jeremiah 17:14

HEAVEN

GOD'S PERSPECTIVE
*Exodus 25:8-9
*Psalm 11:4; 14:2; 33:13-15;
103:19
*Jeremiah 23:23-24
*Ezekiel 1:22-28; 10:1, 3-5, 8-14
Hebrews 8:1-2; 9:23-24
Revelation 4:1-11

GOD'S PROMISES
John 14:2
1 Corinthians 2:9
Revelation 21:4

MAKE A CHANGE
Ephesians 2:6
Colossians 3:1-2

BIBLICAL EXAMPLES
2 Corinthians 12:2-4
Hebrews 11:14-16

PRAYER
*Psalm 16:11; 17:15; 73:25

How to get to heaven
GOD'S PERSPECTIVE
Matthew 7:21; 10:32-33
Luke 12:8-9; 13:23-28
John 6:27-29; 14:6
Acts 4:12
Revelation 21:27

GOD'S PROMISES
Philippians 3:20
1 Peter 1:3-4

MAKE A CHANGE
John 3:3
Romans 10:6-9

BIBLICAL EXAMPLES
John 3:1-3, 5

PRAYER
Luke 23:42-43

HELL

GOD'S PERSPECTIVE
*Psalm 1:6; 9:16-17
*Isaiah 14:11-15
Matthew 23:29-33
2 Thessalonians 1:9
Hebrews 10:29
2 Peter 2:4, 12-17
Jude 1:11-13
Revelation 1:18; 14:10;
20:13-15; 21:8

GOD'S PROMISES
John 3:15, 36; 10:28
2 Peter 2:4-5, 9

MAKE A CHANGE
*Ezekiel 33:11
Matthew 5:30; 18:8-9
Mark 9:43-48
Luke 12:4-5

BIBLICAL EXAMPLES
Luke 16:22-26

PRAYER
*Psalm 86:13

HOLIDAYS

Christmas
GOD'S PERSPECTIVE
Matthew 1:21
Luke 1:25; 2:10-14
John 1:14; 3:16
Galatians 4:4-7
1 Timothy 3:16
2 John 1:7

GOD'S PROMISES
*Isaiah 7:14; 9:6

MAKE A CHANGE
Philippians 2:5-11

BIBLICAL EXAMPLES
Matthew 1:20-25

PRAYER
*Psalm 35:9

Easter
GOD'S PERSPECTIVE
Matthew 12:39-40; 28:5-6
Mark 10:32-34
Luke 24:46
John 2:22; 14:19
Acts 2:30-32
1 Corinthians 15:12-14, 16-17,
42-45

GOD'S PROMISES
*Job 19:26
*Psalm 16:10
*Daniel 12:2
1 Peter 1:3-4

MAKE A CHANGE
Romans 6:6-11
Ephesians 4:21-24
Philippians 3:21
Colossians 3:1-5

BIBLICAL EXAMPLES
Mark 16:1-6
Luke 24:4-8, 23-27

PRAYER
*Psalm 17:15

Halloween
GOD'S PERSPECTIVE
*Deuteronomy 18:10-14
1 Corinthians 10:19-20
Galatians 1:4; 5:19-21
1 Timothy 4:1
Revelation 21:8

GOD'S PROMISES
2 Corinthians 6:17

MAKE A CHANGE
*Leviticus 19:31
Ephesians 6:10-12

BIBLICAL EXAMPLES
Acts 8:9-12; 13:7-11

PRAYER
Matthew 6:13

Thanksgiving
GOD'S PERSPECTIVE
*Deuteronomy 6:11; 8:11-14,
16-20

Matthew 14:19
John 6:23

MAKE A CHANGE
*Leviticus 22:29
*Deuteronomy 8:11-14, 16-20
*1 Chronicles 16:8, 34
*Psalm 30:4; 95:2; 100:1-5;
103:2; 107:21-22; 136:1
Philippians 4:6
Colossians 3:17; 4:2
1 Thessalonians 5:18
Hebrews 13:15

BIBLICAL EXAMPLES
*Daniel 6:10

PRAYER
*Psalm 69:30; 79:13; 116:17
*Jonah 2:9
2 Corinthians 9:15

HOLINESS

GOD'S PERSPECTIVE
*Leviticus 18:24, 30; 20:7
1 Thessalonians 4:7
2 Peter 3:11
1 John 2:5-6

GOD'S PROMISES
Romans 12:1-2
Hebrews 12:10

MAKE A CHANGE
*Leviticus 11:44-45
*Ezra 10:11
*Psalm 34:12; 119:9
*Ezekiel 20:7; 37:23
Romans 6:12-13, 19
2 Corinthians 6:17; 7:1
Ephesians 4:21-24
Colossians 3:1-2, 17
2 Timothy 2:22
Hebrews 12:14
1 Peter 1:15-16

BIBLICAL EXAMPLES
*Genesis 39:7-13
*Ezra 6:21
*Daniel 1:8

PRAYER
*Psalm 19:13; 119:133; 141:4

HOLY SPIRIT, THE

GOD'S PERSPECTIVE
John 16:7-11
Romans 8:14-16, 26-27
1 Corinthians 2:14-16
Ephesians 1:13-14
2 Peter 1:21

GOD'S PROMISES
*Ezekiel 11:19; 36:26
*Joel 2:28-29
John 4:14; 7:38-39; 14:16-17;
16:13-14
Acts 1:5, 8; 11:16
Romans 8:1

MAKE A CHANGE
Matthew 28:19-20
Galatians 5:16, 25
Ephesians 5:18

BIBLICAL EXAMPLES
*Genesis 41:38
*Exodus 31:1-3
*Numbers 11:16-17, 26; 27:18
*Judges 6:34
*1 Samuel 16:13
Acts 6:3, 5

PRAYER
*Psalm 51:11

HOMELESS

506

Holy Spirit (the Baptism)
GOD'S PERSPECTIVE
Matthew 3:11
Mark 1:8
Luke 3:16
John 1:33-34

GOD'S PROMISES
Acts 1:5, 8

MAKE A CHANGE
Acts 2:38

BIBLICAL EXAMPLES
John 1:25-27
Acts 8:14-17

Holy Spirit (Fruit of)
GOD'S PERSPECTIVE
Matthew 7:16-18
Luke 13:6-9
John 15:1-2, 8
Galatians 5:22-23
Ephesians 5:8-10

GOD'S PROMISES
John 15:16
Romans 6:22

MAKE A CHANGE
John 15:4-5
1 Timothy 4:14
2 Timothy 1:6
1 Peter 4:10-11

PRAYER
Colossians 1:9-10

Holy Spirit (Gifts of)
GOD'S PERSPECTIVE
1 Corinthians 12:7-11; 13:1-3
Ephesians 4:11-12

MAKE A CHANGE
Romans 12:6-8

HOMELESS, MINISTERING TO THE POOR

GOD'S PERSPECTIVE
*Proverbs 14:20-21, 31; 17:5
*Isaiah 58:6-11
2 Corinthians 9:13

GOD'S PROMISES
*Proverbs 19:17

MAKE A CHANGE
*Leviticus 25:35
*Deuteronomy 15:7-8, 11
*Job 31:16-23
Luke 6:35, 38; 14:13
Romans 12:10, 13
Galatians 6:10
Titus 3:14
1 John 3:17-18

BIBLICAL EXAMPLES
*Ruth 2:2, 7-8, 15-16
Acts 11:29; 2:44-45
Romans 15:26

HOMOSEXUALITY

GOD'S PERSPECTIVE
*Genesis 1:27; 2:24; 5:2
*Leviticus 18:1, 22; 20:13
*Proverbs 16:5; 18:12; 21:4
*Isaiah 3:9
*Ezekiel 16:49-50
*Obadiah 1:3
Matthew 19:4-5
Romans 1:24-32; 2:8
1 Corinthians 6:9-11
Ephesians 5:31
Jude 1:4, 6-7

GOD'S PROMISES
*Psalm 138:6
*Proverbs 11:21
1 Corinthians 10:13
2 Corinthians 5:17
2 Timothy 1:7
2 Peter 2:4-10

MAKE A CHANGE
1 Corinthians 6:9-11
Ephesians 4:20-24
1 Peter 5:5

BIBLICAL EXAMPLES
*Genesis 19:4-5; 24-25

PRAYER
*Psalm 19:13; 119:133

HONORING PARENTS

GOD'S PERSPECTIVE
*Exodus 20:12; 21:15, 17
*Leviticus 19:3
*Deuteronomy 27:16
*Proverbs 15:20; 19:26; 20:20; 28:24; 30:17
Matthew 15:4-6
Romans 1:28-32
2 Timothy 3:2-5

GOD'S PROMISES
*Deuteronomy 5:16
*Proverbs 1:8-9

MAKE A CHANGE
*Proverbs 6:20-22; 23:22, 25
1 Corinthians 6:9-11
Ephesians 6:1-2

BIBLICAL EXAMPLES
John 19:26-27

HOPE

Hope for our nation
GOD'S PERSPECTIVE
*Job 8:13-15
*Proverbs 13:12
Romans 5:5; 8:24-25; 15:4
Titus 2:13

GOD'S PROMISES
*Psalm 146:5-10; 147:11
*Isaiah 40:28-31
*Jeremiah 29:11
*Lamentations 3:22-26
1 Peter 1:3-5

MAKE A CHANGE
*Psalm 16:8-9; 31:24
Romans 12:10-12
Hebrews 10:23
1 Peter 1:13

PRAYER
*Psalm 39:7; 42:5; 71:5-6
Romans 15:13

HOROSCOPE (SEE ASTROLOGY)

HOT TEMPER

GOD'S PERSPECTIVE
*Proverbs 14:29; 15:1, 18; 25:28; 29:22
*Ecclesiastes 7:9
Galatians 5:19-21
Titus 1:7

MAKE A CHANGE
*Psalm 37:8
*Proverbs 22:24-25
Ephesians 4:31
Colossians 3:8
James 1:19-20

BIBLICAL EXAMPLES
*1 Samuel 20:27-33
*Psalm 106:32-33

HUMILITY

GOD'S PERSPECTIVE
*Psalm 51:17; 101:5; 138:6
*Proverbs 15:33; 16:19; 18:12
*Isaiah 66:2

GOD'S PROMISES
*Proverbs 22:4
Luke 14:11
James 4:6

MAKE A CHANGE
*Proverbs 27:2
Romans 12:3, 16
Philippians 2:3
Colossians 3:12
1 Peter 5:5-6

BIBLICAL EXAMPLES
*2 Chronicles 34:26-28
Luke 18:13
Acts 20:19

HURT

Forgiving those who hurt you
GOD'S PERSPECTIVE
*Psalm 147:3
Luke 4:18
2 Corinthians 1:9

GOD'S PROMISES
*Deuteronomy 33:27
*Psalm 55:22; 121:1-2
*Isaiah 11:9
*Jeremiah 17:7-10
Revelation 21:4

MAKE A CHANGE
Philippians 4:6-7
1 Peter 5:6-7

BIBLICAL EXAMPLES
*Daniel 3:16-18

PRAYER
*Psalm 38:12-15
*Habakkuk 3:17-19

I

ILLNESS

GOD'S PERSPECTIVE
*Jeremiah 30:17
James 1:6
1 Peter 2:24; 4:19

GOD'S PROMISES
*Exodus 23:25
*Deuteronomy 7:15
*Isaiah 35:6; 57:18-19
*Malachi 4:2
2 Corinthians 4:17
James 5:14-16

MAKE A CHANGE
*Proverbs 4:20-22
1 Peter 4:19

BIBLICAL EXAMPLES
*Psalm 107:20
Matthew 8:8
Mark 6:13
2 Corinthians 12:7-10

PRAYER
*Psalm 73:26; 103:2-3
*Jeremiah 17:14

IMITATING JESUS

GOD'S PERSPECTIVE
Matthew 16:24
John 8:29; 13:12-15, 34-35;
15:9-11
Romans 6:10-12
1 Peter 2:20-21
1 John 2:6

GOD'S PROMISES
Romans 8:29-30
2 Corinthians 3:18
1 John 3:2-3

MAKE A CHANGE
Romans 12:10-13; 15:1-3
1 Corinthians 11:1
Ephesians 4:22-24; 5:1-2
Colossians 3:9-10

BIBLICAL EXAMPLES
Galatians 4:19
1 Thessalonians 1:6-7

INCEST

GOD'S PERSPECTIVE
*Leviticus 18:6-18; 20:12, 14,
17, 19-22
*Deuteronomy 22:30; 27:22

BIBLICAL EXAMPLES
*2 Samuel 13:11-12
1 Corinthians 5:1-5

INFERIORITY

GOD'S PERSPECTIVE
*Psalm 62:9-11
Romans 5:8
1 Corinthians 1:26-29
2 Corinthians 1:9; 3:5; 4:7

GOD'S PROMISES
*Psalm 37:5; 55:22
*Proverbs 16:3
2 Corinthians 12:9-10
Ephesians 2:10
Philippians 2:13
1 Thessalonians 2:4; 5:24

MAKE A CHANGE
*Isaiah 26:4
Philippians 4:6-7, 13

BIBLICAL EXAMPLES
*Jeremiah 31:3
Galatians 1:10
1 Corinthians 2:3-5

PRAYER
*Job 5:8
*Psalm 8:3-5; 139:13-16
Galatians 2:20

INFERTILITY

GOD'S PERSPECTIVE
*Isaiah 41:10; 55:8-9
*Jeremiah 33:3

GOD'S PROMISES
*Psalm 18:30; 55:22
*Proverbs 3:5-10
*Hosea 6:3
Romans 8:35-37
Hebrews 10:23

BIBLICAL EXAMPLES
*Genesis 21:2; 25:21; 30:22
*Judges 13:2-3, 24
*1 Samuel 1:18-20
Luke 1:7, 24-25

PRAYER
Psalm 138:8

INSECURITY

GOD'S PERSPECTIVE
*Psalm 62:2; 146:5
*Isaiah 50:10
John 14:12-14
2 Corinthians 3:4-6
Hebrews 10:35-37
1 John 2:28

GOD'S PROMISES
*1 Samuel 2:9
*Psalm 37:23-24; 94:18; 121:3-8
*Proverbs 3:26; 14:26
*Isaiah 26:4
Romans 8:37
Ephesians 1:3-6
Philippians 1:6
2 Timothy 1:7
1 Peter 1:3-5
1 John 5:14-15

BIBLICAL EXAMPLES
*Psalm 22:4-5
*Zechariah 4:6

PRAYER
*Job 13:15
*Psalm 9:10; 16:1, 8-9;
25:20; 34:1
Philippians 4:13

ISLAM
(RELIGION OF THE MUSLIMS)

GOD'S PERSPECTIVE
*Isaiah 64:6
*Jeremiah 17:9
Matthew 10:32-33
John 1:1, 14; 10:7-9, 37-38
Ephesians 2:8-9
Titus 3:5-7

Scriptures showing why the Qur'an is
not of God

GOD'S PERSPECTIVE
*Proverbs 30:6
Galatians 1:8
Revelation 22:18-19

J

JEHOVAH'S WITNESSES

GOD'S PERSPECTIVE
*Isaiah 7:14; 9:6
*Jeremiah 23:5-6
*Micah 5:2
Matthew 13:22; 24:11, 24
John 1:1-3; 5:39-40; 8:58; 10:30
2 Corinthians 11:2-4
Galatians 1:6-9
Colossians 1:15-20
1 Timothy 3:16
Hebrews 1:1-6
1 John 2:22-23; 4:6
2 John 1:7-11
Jude 1:9
Revelation 17:14

GOD'S PROMISES
Titus 2:13

MAKE A CHANGE
Philippians 2:5-8
Colossians 2:8
1 Timothy 1:3
2 Peter 2:1
1 John 4:1

JESTING

GOD'S PERSPECTIVE
*Proverbs 15:4, 21; 26:18-19

GOD'S PROMISES
*Proverbs 16:24

MAKE A CHANGE
*Psalm 34:12-15
Matthew 5:37
Ephesians 4:29; 5:3-4
Colossians 3:8; 4:5-6
James 1:21
1 Peter 3:10

PRAYER
*Psalm 19:14

JESUS (HIS DEATH)

GOD'S PERSPECTIVE
*Psalm 22:1-19
*Isaiah 53:3-7, 10-12
John 10:17-18; 9:28-30
Romans 5:6-8, 10
2 Corinthians 5:19
Galatians 3:13
Philippians 2:7-8
1 Peter 2:22-24; 3:18
1 John 4:10

GOD'S PROMISES
John 3:16
1 John 2:1-2

MAKE A CHANGE
2 Corinthians 5:20b-21
Hebrews 12:2

BIBLICAL EXAMPLES
Luke 23:44-47

PRAYER
*Psalm 79:9; 85:2
Luke 23:34

JESUS (HIS DEITY)

GOD'S PERSPECTIVE
*Psalm 45:6-7
*Isaiah 9:6-7
*Jeremiah 23:5-6
John 1:1-3, 14; 8:56-59
Acts 20:28
Romans 1:3-4
Philippians 2:6-11
Colossians 1:15-20
1 Timothy 3:16
Titus 2:11-14
Hebrews 1:1-4, 6-8
1 John 5:20
Revelation 1:8

GOD'S PROMISES
John 20:31
Hebrews 13:8-9

BIBLICAL EXAMPLES
John 4:25-26; 10:30-33; 20:28
Revelation 5:5-14

JESUS (HIS HUMANITY)

GOD'S PERSPECTIVE
*Isaiah 7:14; 9:6
Luke 2:11
John 1:14
1 Timothy 3:16
Hebrews 4:15
1 John 1:1

MAKE A CHANGE
Philippians 2:5-8

BIBLICAL EXAMPLES
Matthew 1:20-23; 8:20
Luke 1:30-35; 24:39

JESUS (HIS RESURRECTION)

GOD'S PERSPECTIVE
*Job 19:25-26
*Isaiah 26:19
John 11:25-27; 14:19

1 Corinthians 15:1-8, 14, 20-22
Revelation 1:18

GOD'S PROMISES
1 Peter 1:3-5

MAKE A CHANGE
Romans 6:4
Galatians 2:20
Colossians 3:1

BIBLICAL EXAMPLES
Matthew 28:5-6
Luke 24:1-8
John 20:27

PRAYER
*Psalm 16:8-11

JESUS (HIS SECOND COMING)

GOD'S PERSPECTIVE
*Isaiah 61:1-2
*Daniel 7:13-14
*Zechariah 14:4-9
Matthew 26:64
Mark 8:38; 14:62
Luke 4:17-21; 21:25-27
2 Peter 3:1-10

GOD'S PROMISES
Matthew 16:27; 24:30-31
2 Thessalonians 1:6-10

MAKE A CHANGE
Matthew 24:44; 25:13
Luke 12:37-40
Philippians 4:5
1 Thessalonians 1:10
2 Timothy 4:8
Titus 2:13
Hebrews 9:28
James 5:9
Revelation 19:7

BIBLICAL EXAMPLES
Matthew 25:31-32
Revelation 1:7; 19:11-16

PRAYER
Revelation 22:20

JOY

GOD'S PERSPECTIVE
*Nehemiah 8:10
*Psalm 28:7; 35:9; 63:5
*Proverbs 21:15
*Isaiah 49:13; 61:10
Luke 2:10
Romans 14:17
Galatians 5:22-23
1 Peter 4:12-13
1 John 1:3-4

GOD'S PROMISES
*Psalm 5:11; 16:11; 30:5
John 15:10-11; 16:22
Ephesians 3:19
1 Peter 1:6-7

MAKE A CHANGE
*Psalm 98:4; 149:2
*Habakkuk 3:17-18
Luke 10:20
John 16:24
1 Thessalonians 5:16
James 1:2-4

BIBLICAL EXAMPLES
*Nehemiah 12:43
Luke 24:52
Hebrews 12:2

PRAYER
Psalm 51:12

JUDGING

GOD'S PERSPECTIVE
*Isaiah 59:8
Matthew 7:15-18
Luke 16:15
John 7:24
Romans 2:1-2; 14:3-4, 10-13
1 Corinthians 2:15; 13:4-7
2 Corinthians 10:12
James 3:1; 4:11-12
Revelation 2:2

GOD'S PROMISES
1 Corinthians 4:3-5

MAKE A CHANGE
Matthew 7:1-5
Luke 6:36-37
Romans 16:17-18
1 Corinthians 11:30-31
Philippians 2:3
2 Timothy 3:5

BIBLICAL EXAMPLES
2 Timothy 2:16-17; 4:14

K

KINDNESS

GOD'S PERSPECTIVE
*Exodus 23:4-5
*Proverbs 19:22; 25:21-22;
31:26
*Isaiah 54:10
Matthew 5:44-47
Luke 6:27-28, 34-35
1 Corinthians 13:4-8
Galatians 5:22-23
1 Peter 2:23

GOD'S PROMISES
Ephesians 2:4-7

MAKE A CHANGE
*Joel 2:13
Romans 12:10-18, 21
Galatians 6:10
Colossians 3:12
2 Peter 1:5-7

BIBLICAL EXAMPLES
*2 Samuel 9:3, 6-7
*2 Kings 6:22-23
*2 Chronicles 28:15
1 Corinthians 4:12

PRAYER
*Psalm 117:2

L

LAWSUITS

GOD'S PERSPECTIVE
*Exodus 23:1-3, 6-9
*Leviticus 19:15
*Deuteronomy 1:7, 17; 17:8-11
*Proverbs 14:12; 17:14;
25:8-10; 30:33
Matthew 5:25
Luke 12:58
1 Corinthians 6:1-6

MAKE A CHANGE
*Deuteronomy 1:16; 16:18;
17:9; 25:2
Matthew 18:15-17

BIBLICAL EXAMPLES
*Exodus 18:13, 17, 19-24
*1 Kings 3:9, 23-28

PRAYER
*Psalm 35:1
*Lamentations 3:58-59

LAZINESS, WORK

GOD'S PERSPECTIVE
*Proverbs 6:6-11; 10:4-5;
12:11; 12:24; 13:4; 14:23; 15:19;
17:2; 18:9; 19:15; 20:4; 21:25;
26:13-16; 30:24-25
1 Timothy 5:8

MAKE A CHANGE
*Proverbs 20:13; 22:29
Ephesians 4:28
Colossians 3:23
1 Thessalonians 4:11-12
2 Timothy 2:15
Titus 3:14

BIBLICAL EXAMPLES
*2 Chronicles 24:13
*Proverbs 24:30-34
2 Thessalonians 3:7-11
1 Timothy 4:15

LEADING SOMEONE TO CHRIST

GOD'S PERSPECTIVE
Matthew 12:28-30
John 3:16-20; 14:6
Romans 3:23-24; 6:23
1 Corinthians 2:14

GOD'S PROMISES
Ephesians 2:8-9
Titus 3:4-7

MAKE A CHANGE
Romans 10:9
1 Peter 3:15

BIBLICAL EXAMPLES
Acts 2:37-41; 8:29-39; 11:19-21;
16:13-14, 29-34

PRAYER
*Psalm 35:28; 89:1; 119:46, 172
How to lead someone to Christ when
they are ready
THE ROMANS ROAD
Romans 3:10; 3:23; 6:23;
10:9-10; 10:13; 5:1; 8:1; 8:38-39

LONELINESS

GOD'S PERSPECTIVE
*Genesis 28:15
*Deuteronomy 31:6
*Joshua 1:9
Matthew 28:18-20
John 14:23; 16:32c

GOD'S PROMISES
*Psalm 37:25, 28
*Isaiah 41:9-10
*Haggai 1:13
Matthew 11:28-30

MAKE A CHANGE
Hebrews 13:5

BIBLICAL EXAMPLES
*Ezra 9:9
Acts 18:9-11; 23:11; 27:23

PRAYER
*Psalm 9:10; 40:1-5; 139:7-12

LOSS OF JOB

GOD'S PERSPECTIVE
*Psalm 145:18-19
*Jeremiah 29:11-12
Matthew 7:7
Luke 11:9-10

Mark 10:6, 9
1 Corinthians 7:3-4
Hebrews 13:4

GOD'S PROMISES
*Proverbs 31:10-11, 30

MAKE A CHANGE
Ephesians 5:21-28, 33
Colossians 3:18-19
1 Peter 3:1-4, 7

Marriage to an unbeliever
GOD'S PERSPECTIVE
*Exodus 34:12, 16
*Deuteronomy 7:3-4
*Joshua 23:12-13
*Ezra 9:1-2
*Nehemiah 13:23-27
*Proverbs 15:1
*Amos 3:3
2 Corinthians 3:2-3; 6:14-16

GOD'S PROMISES
2 Corinthians 6:16

MAKE A CHANGE
1 Corinthians 7:12-16
1 Peter 3:1-4, 7

MASTURBATION
GOD'S PERSPECTIVE
Romans 6:6
Galatians 5:19, 21-25
2 Timothy 2:25-26
James 1:13-15
1 Peter 2:11
2 Peter 2:19

GOD'S PROMISES
Romans 8:12-13

MAKE A CHANGE
Romans 6:12; 12:2; 13:13-14
1 Corinthians 6:19-20
2 Corinthians 7:1; 10:5
Galatians 5:16-17
Ephesians 4:22-24
Colossians 3:2
1 Peter 4:1-2

PRAYER
*Psalm 19:13; 119:9-12
Philippians 4:13

MATERIALISM
GOD'S PERSPECTIVE
*Psalm 49:6-20; 22:4; 23:4-5
*Ecclesiastes 5:10
Matthew 6:24
Luke 16:13
1 Timothy 6:6-10
Hebrews 11:24-26

MAKE A CHANGE
Matthew 6:19-21
Mark 4:18-20
Luke 12:15
Galatians 5:16
Colossians 3:2-4
1 Timothy 6:17
Hebrews 13:5
1 John 2:15

BIBLICAL EXAMPLES
Luke 12:16-20

PRAYER
*Proverbs 30:8-9

MENTAL ISSUES
GOD'S PERSPECTIVE
*Psalm 1:1-2; 34:4-8
Romans 8:15
2 Corinthians 10:3-5

2 Timothy 1:7
1 John 4:18

GOD'S PROMISES
*Proverbs 29:25
*Isaiah 26:3

MAKE A CHANGE
Romans 12:1-2
Ephesians 4:22-24, 32
Philippians 2:5
Colossians 3:2
Hebrews 12:14-15

BIBLICAL EXAMPLES
*1 Samuel 21:12-13
*Daniel 4:30-34

MERCY
God's mercy
GOD'S PERSPECTIVE
*Exodus 34:6
*Psalm 18:25; 85:10; 89:14-15
*Lamentations 3:22-23
Luke 10:27
John 1:17
Titus 3:5
Hebrews 2:17; 8:12
James 5:11
1 Peter 1:3

GOD'S PROMISES
*Psalm 100:5; 103:8, 10-11
Matthew 5:7

MAKE A CHANGE
Hebrews 4:16

PRAYER
*Psalm 51:1-2; 86:5

We should be merciful
GOD'S PERSPECTIVE
*Proverbs 11:17
James 2:15-16
1 John 3:18

GOD'S PROMISES
Matthew 5:7

MAKE A CHANGE
Luke 6:36

BIBLICAL EXAMPLES
Matthew 18:21-35
Luke 10:25-37

MIDDLE AGE (SEE AGING)

MORMONISM
GOD'S PERSPECTIVE
*Isaiah 9:6; 43:10; 44:6, 8
Matthew 16:15-16
John 1:1; 3:16; 8:42-47
2 Corinthians 11:3-4
Galatians 1:6-9
Philippians 2:9-11
Colossians 1:19; 2:8-9
1 Timothy 1:3
Hebrews 1:4-14
2 Peter 2:1
1 John 5:20

GOD'S PROMISES
Matthew 23:12
Luke 18:14

MAKE A CHANGE
1 Peter 5:8-9

BIBLICAL EXAMPLES
*Genesis 3:13-15
*Isaiah 14:12-15

MURDER
GOD'S PERSPECTIVE
*Genesis 9:6
*Exodus 20:13; 21:14
*Leviticus 19:17
*Numbers 35:30-31
*Deuteronomy 5:17
Matthew 5:21-22;
15:18-19; 18:15
Romans 13:9
Galatians 5:19-21
James 1:14-16
Revelation 9:21

BIBLICAL EXAMPLES
*Genesis 4:8
*2 Samuel 2:9
Matthew 19:16-19

PRAYER
*Psalm 51:9-17

N

NEEDS (SPIRITUAL AND MATERIAL)
GOD'S PERSPECTIVE
*Nehemiah 9:15
Matthew 6:7-8, 31-34
John 6:35; 15:16
1 Timothy 4:8
James 1:2-4
1 Peter 1:3-7

GOD'S PROMISES
*Deuteronomy 6:3; 30:9-10
*Psalm 34:9-10; 84:11
Matthew 7:7-11
Romans 8:32
Philippians 4:19
Revelation 7:16

MAKE A CHANGE
*Psalm 37:7-9, 34
2 Corinthians 6:4-10
Hebrews 4:16
James 1:2-8

BIBLICAL EXAMPLES
John 6:31
Acts 4:24
Philippians 4:11-13

PRAYER
*Psalm 23:1; 145:15-17
2 Corinthians 1:3-4
Ephesians 3:20-21

NEIGHBORS
GOD'S PERSPECTIVE
*Leviticus 19:18; 25:14
*Psalm 101:5
*Proverbs 11:12; 25:9, 17-18
Matthew 5:43-44
Mark 12:33
Romans 13:8-10
Galatians 5:14
James 2:8-9
1 John 4:21

GOD'S PROMISES
*Psalm 15:1-3

MAKE A CHANGE
Romans 12:1-2, 10; 15:2
Ephesians 4:25
Philippians 2:3-4

BIBLICAL EXAMPLES
Matthew 19:17-19; 22:37-40
Luke 10:29-37

NEW AGE MOVEMENT

GOD'S PERSPECTIVE
*Proverbs 14:12
*Isaiah 45:21; 46:9-10
*Jeremiah 17:9-10
Matthew 7:13-14
Luke 13:24
John 14:6
Acts 4:12
Romans 6:23
Philippians 2:5-11
1 Timothy 2:5-6
2 John 1:9

GOD'S PROMISES
1 Peter 1:3-9
1 John 2:23; 5:11-12

MAKE A CHANGE
*Isaiah 45:22
Ephesians 5:5-7
Jude 1:21

BIBLICAL EXAMPLES
*Isaiah 14:14-15
*Ezekiel 14:1-11

O

OBEDIENCE
(TO AUTHORITIES)

GOD'S PERSPECTIVE
*Deuteronomy 17:12-13
*Psalm 75:6-7
*Ecclesiastes 8:3-5
Matthew 22:21
2 Peter 2:9-11

GOD'S PROMISES
Romans 13:3
Colossians 3:22-24
1 Timothy 2:1-4; 5:17

MAKE A CHANGE
*Proverbs 24:21-22
*Ecclesiastes 10:4
Romans 13:1-2
Ephesians 6:5
Philippians 2:12-15
1 Thessalonians 5:12-13
Titus 3:1-2
Hebrews 13:17
1 Peter 2:13-17

BIBLICAL EXAMPLES
Acts 23:1-5
2 Peter 2:10
Jude 1:8-9

PRAYER
*Proverbs 5:13-14

OBEDIENCE (TO GOD)

GOD'S PERSPECTIVE
*Exodus 19:5-6
*Deuteronomy 10:12-13
*Psalm 81:8-13
*Isaiah 48:18
Matthew 7:21, 24-25
Luke 8:21
John 15:10
Hebrews 12:6-11

GOD'S PROMISES
*Psalm 1:1-3; 112:1; 119:1-6,
165; 128:1
*Jeremiah 7:23
Luke 6:47-48; 11:28
John 14:21

MAKE A CHANGE
*Proverbs 3:11-12
John 14:15
James 1:22-24
1 John 2:3-6

BIBLICAL EXAMPLES
*1 Samuel 15:22
Matthew 8:24-27
Acts 5:29

PRAYER
*Psalm 119:32-35; 143:10

OBEDIENCE (TO PARENTS)

GOD'S PERSPECTIVE
*Exodus 20:12
*Deuteronomy 5:16
*Proverbs 15:5; 20:20; 28:24
Mark 10:19
Luke 18:20
Romans 1:28-32

GOD'S PROMISES
Ephesians 6:1-3
Colossians 3:20

MAKE A CHANGE
*Proverbs 1:8-9; 23:22
2 Timothy 3:1-2, 5

BIBLICAL EXAMPLES
Matthew 15:4-9
Luke 2:51; 15:11-24

OCCULT

GOD'S PERSPECTIVE
*Leviticus 19:26, 31; 20:6-7
*Deuteronomy 18:9-14
*Isaiah 8:19-22; 47:13-15
Romans 16:19
1 Timothy 4:1
1 John 4:1-4
Revelation 21:8

GOD'S PROMISES
2 Corinthians 10:4
Colossians 2:15

MAKE A CHANGE
Romans 13:12
2 Corinthians 6:14-18
Galatians 5:16-21
Ephesians 5:11-17; 6:10-12
Philippians 4:8-9

BIBLICAL EXAMPLES
*Exodus 7:11-13
*1 Samuel 28:3, 6
*2 Kings 17:17-18
*1 Chronicles 10:13-14
Acts 8:18-24; 3:6-12;
16:16-18; 19:19-20

OVERCOMING EVIL

GOD'S PERSPECTIVE
*Exodus 23:4-5
*Psalm 19:7-11
*Proverbs 24:28-29
Luke 6:27-30
1 John 5:4

GOD'S PROMISES
*Proverbs 20:22
Matthew 16:18
Luke 10:19
1 Peter 3:8-9
1 John 4:4
Revelation 21:7

MAKE A CHANGE
Romans 12:14, 17-21
Ephesians 6:11
1 Thessalonians 5:15

BIBLICAL EXAMPLES
Matthew 5:38-47; 18:15-17
Revelation 12:11

PRAYER
Luke 23:34

OVERCOMING SIN

GOD'S PERSPECTIVE
*Numbers 32:23
*Proverbs 6:23
*Isaiah 59:1-2
Romans 2:4; 8:9, 13-14
2 Corinthians 5:14-15
Galatians 6:7-8
Philippians 2:12-13
Titus 3:4-6
James 4:17
1 John 2:14; 3:6, 9

GOD'S PROMISES
*Ezekiel 36:25-27
John 1:12-13
1 Corinthians 10:13
2 Corinthians 5:17; 9:8
2 Peter 1:3

MAKE A CHANGE
*Proverbs 1:10; 4:14-15
Romans 6:1-2; 13:14
1 Corinthians 10:13; 15:58
Galatians 5:16
James 1:21-22

BIBLICAL EXAMPLES
John 8:31-36
2 Corinthians 13:2

PRAYER
*Psalm 119:9-11

P

PAIN

GOD'S PERSPECTIVE
*Psalm 119:71, 75, 165
John 14:1
2 Corinthians 4:16-18
Hebrews 4:15-16
1 Peter 4:12-13
Revelation 21:4

GOD'S PROMISES
*Isaiah 40:29
*Jeremiah 29:11
1 Corinthians 10:13

MAKE A CHANGE
*Psalm 55:22
*Proverbs 3:5-6
Romans 5:3-5
Philippians 4:6-7
Hebrews 12:11-12
1 Peter 4:12

BIBLICAL EXAMPLES
*Job 19:25-26
2 Corinthians 12:9

PRAYER
*Psalm 27:13; 119:50
*Isaiah 50:7

PATIENCE, PERSEVERANCE

GOD'S PERSPECTIVE
*Lamentations 3:25-27
Luke 18:1
Galatians 5:22
Colossians 1:11
James 1:2-4
2 Peter 1:5-9

GOD'S PROMISES
*Psalm 27:14

PEACE

MAKE A CHANGE
*Psalm 37:7
Romans 12:12
Ephesians 4:1b-2
Colossians 3:12; 4:2
1 Thessalonians 5:17
2 Timothy 3:10; 4:2

BIBLICAL EXAMPLES
*Daniel 9:3, 21
Acts 1:14
Colossians 4:12
2 Timothy 3:10
James 5:7-8

PRAYER
*Psalm 40:1; 102:2

PEACE, INNER

GOD'S PERSPECTIVE
*Psalm 119:165
*Proverbs 16:7
*Isaiah 48:18; 57:20-21
*Jeremiah 6:16
Luke 2:14
John 14:27; 16:33
Romans 5:1; 8:6
Galatians 5:22
Colossians 1:21

GOD'S PROMISES
*Psalm 29:11; 37:11
*Proverbs 3:24; 16:7
*Isaiah 26:3-4; 32:17;
54:10; 57:19
Matthew 11:28-30
Romans 14:17; 15:13

MAKE A CHANGE
*Psalm 85:8
Mark 9:50
Romans 12:18
2 Corinthians 5:18
Philippians 4:5-7
Colossians 3:15
1 Thessalonians 5:13

BIBLICAL EXAMPLES
Acts 27:21-25

PRAYER
*Psalm 4:7-8

PEACEMAKERS, PEACEKEEPERS

GOD'S PERSPECTIVE
*Psalm 37:37; 119:165
*Proverbs 15:1; 16:7; 19:11
*Isaiah 26:3, 12
1 Corinthians 3:3
Ephesians 2:13-14
James 3:18

GOD'S PROMISES
*Psalm 29:11
Matthew 5:9
John 14:27
Romans 16:20
Hebrews 6:10

MAKE A CHANGE
*Proverbs 3:30; 17:14
Romans 12:18; 14:19
Ephesians 4:32
Philippians 4:8-9
Colossians 3:13, 15
1 Thessalonians 5:15
Hebrews 12:14
1 Peter 3:11

BIBLICAL EXAMPLES
*Genesis 50:19-21
*Isaiah 52:7
*Nahum 1:15
Romans 10:15

PRAYER
Romans 15:13

PEER PRESSURE

GOD'S PERSPECTIVE
*Job 28:28
*Psalm 111:10
*Proverbs 1:7, 10; 9:10-11;
12:26; 13:20; 18:24;
19:4, 6; 29:25
*Ecclesiastes 7:18-19
Matthew 15:12-14
1 Corinthians 3:19

GOD'S PROMISES
*Psalm 1:1
1 Peter 1:21

MAKE A CHANGE
Deuteronomy 13:6-8
Proverbs 22:24
Matthew 10:28
Acts 5:29
Romans 12:2
Galatians 1:10
1 Thessalonians 4:1

BIBLICAL EXAMPLES
*Genesis 12:11-13;
20:2, 11; 26:7
*Exodus 32:22-24
*1 Samuel 15:24
*Job 16:2-5
*Daniel 3:28
Matthew 26:69-70; 27:24
John 9:22; 12:42; 19:12-13
Romans 1:11-12
Galatians 2:11-12

PRAYER
Matthew 6:13

PERSECUTION

GOD'S PERSPECTIVE
*Jeremiah 20:11
John 15:18-21
Romans 8:35-39

GOD'S PROMISES
*Jeremiah 1:8, 19; 15:20
Matthew 5:10-12; 10:22
Luke 21:18
Romans 8:31
James 1:12

MAKE A CHANGE
Romans 12:14
2 Corinthians 12:10
Hebrews 12:3
James 5:11
1 Peter 4:12-16

BIBLICAL EXAMPLES
*Daniel 3:12-15, 19-20; 6:2-5
Acts 5:18, 40-41; 7:52, 57-59;
14:19; 16:19-23; 21:12-13
2 Corinthians 11:23-25
2 Timothy 2:8-10; 3:10-12
Hebrews 10:32-35

PRAYER
*Psalm 7:1; 25:20; 31:15; 43:1;
59:1; 119:134; 142:6
John 17:15

PORNOGRAPHY

GOD'S PERSPECTIVE
*Psalm 101:2-4; 106:15; 119:9
*Proverbs 5:20
Matthew 5:28
Romans 13:14
Galatians 5:16-17, 19

James 1:14-15
1 John 2:16
Revelation 21:8

GOD'S PROMISES
*Psalm 119:1-2
Galatians 5:16
John 8:32

MAKE A CHANGE
*Job 31:1
*Proverbs 4:23; 6:25
1 Corinthians 5:9, 11
Galatians 5:24
Ephesians 2:1-6; 4:22
2 Timothy 2:22
Titus 2:11-12
James 1:14-15
1 Peter 1:13-16; 2:11

BIBLICAL EXAMPLES
*1 Kings 11:4-6, 11
2 Peter 2:14

PRAYER
*Psalm 19:13; 119:18, 33, 37

PRAISE

GOD'S PERSPECTIVE
*Deuteronomy 10:21
*Psalm 22:3; 50:23; 65:1;
96:4; 107:8
*Isaiah 42:8; 43:21
1 Peter 2:9

GOD'S PROMISES
*Isaiah 43:2
2 Corinthians 1:20
James 1:17

MAKE A CHANGE
*Psalm 100:4; 105:2
Romans 5:2
Ephesians 5:19
Hebrews 13:15

BIBLICAL EXAMPLES
*Jeremiah 33:11
Acts 2:46-47
Revelation 5:12

PRAYER
*Exodus 15:2
*Psalm 7:17; 34:1; 40:3;
51:15; 52:9; 63:3-5; 71:8;
86:12; 139:14; 145:10, 21

PRAYER

Scriptures for prayer
GOD'S PERSPECTIVE
*Psalm 91:15
*Jeremiah 29:12
1 Timothy 2:8
James 1:6-8

GOD'S PROMISES
*Psalm 86:7
*Proverbs 18:10
Philippians 4:6-7
1 John 5:14

MAKE A CHANGE
Romans 12:12
Ephesians 6:18
Colossians 4:2
1 Thessalonians 5:16-18
1 Timothy 2:1
James 5:16
Jude 1:21

BIBLICAL EXAMPLES
*Psalm 55:16-17; 66:17-20
Luke 18:1-8
Acts 12:5

PRAYER
*Psalm 86:5; 102:2

Scriptures for how to pray
GOD'S PERSPECTIVE
Matthew 6:5-13
Mark 11:24
1 Timothy 2:8
James 1:6

GOD'S PROMISES
Matthew 6:33
1 Corinthians 10:13

MAKE A CHANGE
Matthew 26:41
Mark 11:25
1 Peter 3:7

BIBLICAL EXAMPLES
Acts 4:24; 7:59-60

PRAYER
Luke 11:1-4

Scriptures for praying in the Spirit
GOD'S PERSPECTIVE
*Isaiah 28:11
John 4:24
1 Corinthians 14:13-15;
14:18, 22

GOD'S PROMISES
Romans 8:26

MAKE A CHANGE
1 Corinthians 14:1-5, 40

BIBLICAL EXAMPLES
Acts 2:4; 10:46; 19:6
Ephesians 6:18-19

PRIDE

GOD'S PERSPECTIVE
*Deuteronomy 8:17-18
*Psalm 101:5; 138:6
*Proverbs 3:34; 6:16-17;
8:13; 11:2; 16:2, 5, 18; 29:23
*Isaiah 2:11; 5:21
*Jeremiah 9:23-24
Matthew 6:1-4
Mark 7:21-23
Luke 14:11
1 Corinthians 4:7; 10:12
1 John 2:16

GOD'S PROMISES
*Proverbs 22:4
*Isaiah 57:15
Matthew 20:26-27
James 4:6

MAKE A CHANGE
*Proverbs 30:32
*Micah 6:8
James 4:10
1 Peter 5:5-6

BIBLICAL EXAMPLES
*2 Kings 19:22
*2 Chronicles 26:16
*Isaiah 14:13-14; 23:9; 47:5
*Ezekiel 16:49
*Daniel 4:30-37
Acts 20:18-19
1 Corinthians 5:2

PRAYER
*Psalm 131:1-3; 140:8

**PROGRESSIVE
SANCTIFICATION**
Growing in faith and godliness
GOD'S PERSPECTIVE
*Isaiah 52:11
*Malachi 3:3
John 17:17
1 Corinthians 6:11
1 Timothy 4:7-8
2 Timothy 3:16-17
Hebrews 5:12-14; 10:10; 12:1-2
1 John 3:3

GOD'S PROMISES
*Psalm 4:3
2 Corinthians 3:18; 6:16-18
2 Timothy 2:20-21
1 Peter 1:7

MAKE A CHANGE
*Psalm 119:9-11
*Proverbs 9:6
1 Corinthians 5:7-8
2 Corinthians 7:1
Ephesians 4:15, 21-24
Colossians 3:16
2 Timothy 2:22
Hebrews 2:1
1 Peter 2:2-3
2 Peter 1:5-8; 3:14, 18

BIBLICAL EXAMPLES
*Numbers 16:26
*Ezra 6:21; 10:11
*Jeremiah 1:5
Acts 13:2
Galatians 1:15-16

PRAYER
1 Thessalonians 5:23-24

PROPHECY
GOD'S PERSPECTIVE
*Isaiah 41:23; 46:9-10; 48:5-7
Matthew 13:14; 24:25-27
Acts 15:18
1 Corinthians 14:5, 24
2 Peter 1:20-21
Revelation 11:6; 19:10; 22:7,
10, 18-19

GOD'S PROMISES
Luke 21:13
Acts 2:17-18
1 Corinthians 12:10-11
Revelation 1:3

MAKE A CHANGE
Romans 12:6
1 Corinthians 13:2
1 Timothy 4:14

BIBLICAL EXAMPLES
John 13:19; 14:29; 16:4

PROSPERITY
Of the righteous
GOD'S PERSPECTIVE
*Deuteronomy 8:11-18; 30:5
Luke 12:15; 16:13
Romans 2:4; 9:23; 11:33

GOD'S PROMISES
*Deuteronomy 28:1; 29:9
*1 Samuel 2:7
*1 Kings 2:3
*Psalm 1:1-3
*Proverbs 10:22
Matthew 6:31-33
Philippians 4:19

MAKE A CHANGE
*Joshua 1:7-8
*Proverbs 23:17
Colossians 2:2

BIBLICAL EXAMPLES
*Genesis 14:22-23; 24:1; 26:13;
39:3, 23
*2 Chronicles 16:7
*Job 42:12
Hebrews 11:8-10

PRAYER
*1 Chronicles 29:12
Ephesians 3:16
3 John 1:2

PROSPERITY
Of the wicked
GOD'S PERSPECTIVE
*Proverbs 24:19-20; 28:6
Mark 8:36
Luke 12:20-21

GOD'S PROMISES
Romans 8:18

MAKE A CHANGE
*Psalm 37:7

BIBLICAL EXAMPLES
*Psalm 49:16; 73:2-3, 16-19

PROTECTION
GOD'S PERSPECTIVE
*Deuteronomy 1:30; 3:22; 20:4
*Job 33:18
*Proverbs 3:24-26
*Isaiah 54:17
*Jeremiah 15:20-21
John 17:1, 15
Revelation 3:10

GOD'S PROMISES
*2 Samuel 22:9; 22:3, 31
*Psalm 5:12; 7:10; 28:7; 33:20;
34:7-8; 37:23; 84:11; 91:4-7,
9-11; 112:7; 121:7-8
*Proverbs 1:33; 2:7; 18:10; 30:5
*Isaiah 43:2
*Jeremiah 1:18-19
Matthew 16:18
Luke 21:16-18

MAKE A CHANGE
*Joshua 1:9
*Psalm 62:8; 115:11

BIBLICAL EXAMPLES
*Exodus 14:13-14
*1 Samuel 14:6b
*2 Kings 6:15-17
*2 Chronicles 20:17, 22-23;
32:7-8, 21-22

PRAYER
*Psalm 3:3; 59:9; 71:3; 119:114

PROVIDENCE OF GOD
GOD'S PERSPECTIVE
*Psalm 37:23; 103:19; 136:26
*Proverbs 16:9; 19:21; 20:24
*Isaiah 14:24; 45:9-12; 46:10
*Jeremiah 18:5-6

GOD'S PROMISES
*Psalm 104:27-28; 111:9
Matthew 6:25-34
Acts 14:17
Romans 8:28
1 Corinthians 10:13
Ephesians 1:11
Hebrews 11:1

MAKE A CHANGE
*Psalm 55:22
Luke 12:22-32
Romans 8:32
1 Peter 5:7
1 John 4:18

BIBLICAL EXAMPLES
*Exodus 16:35; 17:6
*Numbers 11:31-32; 20:8
*Deuteronomy 8:15-16
*Nehemiah 9:15
*Esther 4:14-16
*Psalm 105:40
Acts 20:24

PRAYER
*Job 10:12
*Psalm 65:9; 119:116-117;
145:15-16
*Jeremiah 10:23
Luke 1:74-75
Romans 11:36

PURITY

GOD'S PERSPECTIVE
*Leviticus 19:17
*Psalm 24:3-4
*Proverbs 20:9
*Ecclesiastes 9:3
*Jeremiah 17:9
Matthew 5:8
Ephesians 5:26-27
1 Timothy 1:5
Titus 1:15
Jude 1:24

GOD'S PROMISES
*Psalm 119:9
*Proverbs 22:11; 28:26
*Ezekiel 11:19-20; 36:25-27
John 15:3
1 John 1:9

MAKE A CHANGE
*Deuteronomy 11:16
*Proverbs 4:23
*Ezekiel 18:31
Acts 8:22
2 Corinthians 6:6; 7:1
1 Timothy 4:12
2 Timothy 2:22
Hebrews 10:22
James 4:8
1 Peter 1:22
1 John 3:3

BIBLICAL EXAMPLES
*Malachi 3:2-4

PRAYER
*Psalm 19:12; 51:7, 10; 86:11

R

RAPTURE

GOD'S PERSPECTIVE
Matthew 24:36-44
Luke 17:33-36
John 14:3

GOD'S PROMISES
Romans 5:9
1 Corinthians 15:51-52
1 Thessalonians 1:10; 4:16-18
2 Timothy 4:8
Titus 2:13
Hebrews 9:28
1 John 3:2
Revelation 3:10

MAKE A CHANGE
Luke 21:36
Philippians 3:20

BIBLICAL EXAMPLES
*Genesis 5:22-24
*2 Kings 2:11-12
Hebrews 11:5

REBELLION

GOD'S PERSPECTIVE
*Numbers 15:30
*Deuteronomy 17:12
*1 Samuel 15:23
*Psalm 68:6; 78:7-8
*Proverbs 17:11
*Isaiah 30:1; 65:1-2
*Jeremiah 19:15
Luke 12:47
Romans 1:20-21; 8:7
Hebrews 10:26
James 4:17

GOD'S PROMISES
*Psalm 1:1-3; 119:1-7

MAKE A CHANGE
*2 Chronicles 30:8-19
*Psalm 51:16-17; 95:8
*Isaiah 1:19-20
1 Peter 5:5

BIBLICAL EXAMPLES
*Exodus 7:4
*Judges 2:2-4
*2 Kings 17:14
*Ezekiel 2:3-8

PRAYER
*Psalm 19:12-13

RECONCILIATION

GOD'S PERSPECTIVE
Romans 5:10
1 Corinthians 7:11
2 Corinthians 5:18-20
Ephesians 2:16
Hebrews 2:17

GOD'S PROMISES
Colossians 1:20-22

MAKE A CHANGE
Matthew 5:23-24
Luke 12:58; 17:3
Romans 12:21
2 Corinthians 5:20
Colossians 3:13
1 Peter 4:8
1 John 3:18

BIBLICAL EXAMPLES
*Genesis 45:1-5; 50:15-21
1 Peter 2:23

REINCARNATION (KARMA)

GOD'S PERSPECTIVE
*Psalm 78:39; 103:14-16
*Ecclesiastes 3:20; 9:5; 12:7
Matthew 25:45-46
John 3:5-7; 6:68; 14:6; 17:3
Romans 6:23; 14:10
Hebrews 9:27
James 4:13-14
Revelation 20:11-12

GOD'S PROMISES
John 5:28-29
2 Corinthians 5:8-10
1 John 5:11

MAKE A CHANGE
Jude 1:21

BIBLICAL EXAMPLES
2 Samuel 12:23

REJECTION

GOD'S PERSPECTIVE
John 1:11-12; 6:37

GOD'S PROMISES
*Psalm 27:10
Acts 10:35
Romans 8:18
Ephesians 1:6
Hebrews 13:5b

MAKE A CHANGE
Deuteronomy 31:6, 8

BIBLICAL EXAMPLES
*Genesis 37:17-18
*Exodus 2:13-15
*1 Samuel 18:6-10
*Isaiah 53:3-5
Acts 13:50
Hebrews 11:35-37

PRAYER
*Psalm 23:4-6
Ephesians 1:3
Jude 24-25

RELIGION

GOD'S PERSPECTIVE
*Job 15:14; 25:4
*Psalm 143:2
*Isaiah 57:12; 64:6
*Jeremiah 17:9
Matthew 10:32-33
Mark 7:8
John 3:3; 6:28-29; 10:1, 7-8
Romans 3:20, 28; 11:6
Galatians 2:16
Ephesians 2:8-9
Colossians 2:8
2 Timothy 1:9
Titus 3:5-7

GOD'S PROMISES
*Jeremiah 29:13
1 Corinthians 8:3

MAKE A CHANGE
James 1:26-27

BIBLICAL EXAMPLES
*Genesis 3:7; 11:4-5, 8

RELOCATION

GOD'S PERSPECTIVE
*Psalm 37:23-24; 16:9
*Proverbs 19:21; 20:24

GOD'S PROMISES
*Deuteronomy 7:9
*Psalm 32:8; 121:7-8; 139:5
*Proverbs 3:26
*Isaiah 40:31; 43:2
*Nahum 1:7
*Habakkuk 3:19
Romans 8:37

MAKE A CHANGE
*Proverbs 3:5-6

BIBLICAL EXAMPLES
*Genesis 12:1
*Deuteronomy 1:30-33
Hebrews 11:8

PRAYER
*Psalm 23:1-4
*Jeremiah 10:23-24

REMARRIAGE

GOD'S PERSPECTIVE
*Genesis 2:24
*Malachi 2:14-16
Matthew 19:3-9

Mark 10:6-12
Romans 7:2
1 Corinthians 6:16-20; 7:10-11,
15-16, 39-40

GOD'S PROMISES
1 Peter 3:1-7

MAKE A CHANGE
Ephesians 5:28-33
1 Timothy 5:14-15

REPENTANCE

GOD'S PERSPECTIVE
*Malachi 3:7
Matthew 4:17
Luke 5:31-32; 13:3-5; 15:7
Romans 2:4
2 Corinthians 7:10
Revelation 16:9

GOD'S PROMISES
*2 Chronicles 7:14
*Ezekiel 18:21-23

MAKE A CHANGE
*Isaiah 55:6-7
*Ezekiel 14:6
*Joel 2:12-13
Revelation 2:4-5

BIBLICAL EXAMPLES
*Exodus 10:16-20
*Jonah 3:4-10
*Zechariah 1:6
Matthew 3:2; 12:41
Luke 10:13; 11:32

RETIREMENT

GOD'S PERSPECTIVE
*Genesis 24:1
*Job 12:12; 32:7
*Proverbs 16:31
Matthew 3:10; 6:33
John 15:1-8

GOD'S PROMISES
*Psalm 1:1-3; 91:1; 92:14
*Isaiah 46:4
Philippians 1:6

MAKE A CHANGE
Ephesians 5:15-16
Colossians 4:5
1 Timothy 4:8

BIBLICAL EXAMPLES
*Joshua 14:10-14
*Ruth 4:15
*1 Chronicles 29:28

PRAYER
*Psalm 71:9, 18; 90:12; 143:10

REVENGE

GOD'S PERSPECTIVE
*Leviticus 19:18
*Deuteronomy 32:35
*Ezekiel 25:17
Matthew 5:38-39, 43-48
Luke 18:7-8
Hebrews 10:30
Revelation 6:10

GOD'S PROMISES
*Proverbs 20:22; 24:29
2 Thessalonians 1:6, 8

MAKE A CHANGE
Romans 12:17-19
1 Thessalonians 5:15

BIBLICAL EXAMPLES
*1 Samuel 24:12; 26:9-11

PRAYER
*Psalm 54:1; 94:1
*Jeremiah 20:12

RIGHTEOUSNESS

GOD'S PERSPECTIVE
*Job 25:4
*Psalm 11:7; 85:10
*Isaiah 61:10; 64:6
*Malachi 4:2
Matthew 5:20; 6:33
Luke 10:27
Romans 3:21-26; 9:30-33;
10:4, 10
2 Corinthians 5:21
Galatians 2:16, 21
Ephesians 2:8-9; 5:9
2 Timothy 3:16
Titus 3:5
1 John 2:29; 3:10

GOD'S PROMISES
*Psalm 23:3
*Isaiah 61:10
Matthew 5:6, 10
Romans 4:5-8
Revelation 19:8

MAKE A CHANGE
*Psalm 4:5
*Hosea 10:12
Ephesians 6:14
2 Timothy 2:22

BIBLICAL EXAMPLES
*Genesis 15:2-6
*Zechariah 3:4-5
Philippians 3:4-9

PRAYER
*Psalm 7:17

THE ROMANS ROAD
Romans 3:10; 3:23; 6:23; 5:8;
10:9-10; 10:13; 5:1; 8:1, 38-39

S

SABBATH

GOD'S PERSPECTIVE
*Exodus 20:8-12
*Leviticus 23:32; 24:8
*Deuteronomy 5:12-15
Mark 2:27-28

GOD'S PROMISES
*Exodus 31:13, 16
*Leviticus 26:2-12, 33-35
*Isaiah 66:23
*Ezekiel 20:12

MAKE A CHANGE
Colossians 2:16-17
Hebrews 4:3

BIBLICAL EXAMPLES
*Exodus 16:23
*Isaiah 1:13; 56:2; 58:13-14
*Jeremiah 17:19-27
Matthew 26:26-29
1 Corinthians 11:23-25

SABBATH DAY WORSHIP

GOD'S PERSPECTIVE
*Exodus 20:8-10
Acts 15:8-10
Romans 14:5-6
Colossians 2:16-17

BIBLICAL EXAMPLES
Matthew 12:1-8
Mark 3:1-6

SALVATION

GOD'S PERSPECTIVE
Matthew 9:12-13
Mark 10:26-27
Luke 2:21
John 3:16-18
Acts 4:10-12
Romans 3:21-24
Ephesians 2:8-9
Titus 3:4-7

GOD'S PROMISES
*Isaiah 51:6
Matthew 1:21
John 5:24
Romans 6:23; 8:1
2 Peter 3:9

MAKE A CHANGE
*Ezekiel 18:31-32
Romans 10:9-10
1 John 1:9

BIBLICAL EXAMPLES
Luke 19:7-10
Acts 16:26-31

PRAYER
*Psalm 9:14; 20:5; 35:9;
40:16; 56:13
*Isaiah 61:10
*Habakkuk 3:18

SANCTIFICATION

GOD'S PERSPECTIVE
*Leviticus 10:8-11
1 Corinthians 6:11
1 Thessalonians 4:3-8
1 Timothy 3:1-7
Hebrews 9:13-14;
10:10, 14-18, 29; 1:1-2
1 Peter 3:15-17; 5:2-3

GOD'S PROMISES
*Joshua 3:5
1 Thessalonians 5:23-24
2 Peter 1:5-10

MAKE A CHANGE
*Psalm 1:1-2
Romans 12:2
1 Corinthians 1:30-31; 5:6-8
2 Corinthians 6:17
Ephesians 5:25-27
1 Thessalonians 4:3
2 Thessalonians 2:13-15
2 Timothy 2:15, 20-22
Hebrews 13:12-15
1 Peter 1:13-16; 4:2

BIBLICAL EXAMPLES
*Leviticus 8:1-2, 10-15, 22-24
*Numbers 6:1-6
*Judges 13:7, 24
Revelation 18:4

PRAYER
*Psalm 119:46-48; 143:10
John 17:15-19

SATAN

GOD'S PERSPECTIVE
*Isaiah 14:12-15
*Ezekiel 28:12-19
Mark 3:26; 4:15
Luke 10:18
John 8:44
2 Corinthians 11:14
Ephesians 2:1-2
Jude 1:6, 9
Revelation 12:3-4, 7-9, 10-11, 13-
17; 20:1-3, 7-10, 14-15

MAKE A CHANGE
Ephesians 6:11-12
James 4:7
1 Peter 5:8-9

BIBLICAL EXAMPLES
*Genesis 3:1-5
*Job 1:6-12
*Zechariah 3:1-4
Luke 4:1-13

SATAN (RESISTING HIM AND HAVING VICTORY)

GOD'S PERSPECTIVE
*Zechariah 3:2
Mark 13:22-23
2 Corinthians 2:10-11;
10:3-6; 11:3-4
2 Thessalonians 2:9-10
Revelation 12:11

GOD'S PROMISES
*Isaiah 14:15-17
Romans 16:20
2 Thessalonians 3:3
James 4:7-8

MAKE A CHANGE
Romans 13:12-14
Ephesians 6:10-18
Colossians 3:1-3
1 Thessalonians 5:8
2 Timothy 2:3-4
1 Peter 5:8-9

BIBLICAL EXAMPLES
Matthew 4:1-11
Luke 22:31-32
Jude 1:9

PRAYER
Matthew 6:13

SCHOOL

GOD'S PERSPECTIVE
*Proverbs 1:7; 2:1-9; 3:19-24;
9:10; 15:33; 16:16
Ephesians 4:13-15
Colossians 2:2-3

GOD'S PROMISES
Matthew 11:29

MAKE A CHANGE
Matthew 6:33
1 Corinthians 9:24; 10:31b
2 Timothy 2:15
1 Peter 2:2
2 Peter 1:10; 3:18

PRAYER
*Psalm 119:66, 73
Colossians 1:9-10

SEEKING GOD'S WILL

GOD'S PERSPECTIVE
*Psalm 32:8; 37:23; 40:8-10;
119:105
*Proverbs 16:9; 19:21; 20:24
*Jeremiah 10:23
Matthew 7:21
Mark 3:35
Romans 8:27
Ephesians 4:11-12
1 Thessalonians 4:3; 5:16-18
1 Peter 2:15

GOD'S PROMISES
*Psalm 37:4-5
*Proverbs 3:5-6
John 7:17
1 John 2:17

MAKE A CHANGE
*Proverbs 2:3-9
Matthew 6:33
Romans 12:2
2 Timothy 2:22
James 1:5-6

BIBLICAL EXAMPLES
Matthew 26:39
John 4:34; 5:30; 6:38-40

PRAYER
*Psalm 34:4; 40:8

SELF-CENTEREDNESS

GOD'S PERSPECTIVE
*Isaiah 13:11
Matthew 16:24-26
1 Corinthians 13:4b-5
2 Corinthians 5:15
Philippians 2:21
2 Timothy 3:2-5
James 3:14-16; 4:1
3 John 1:9-10
Revelation 3:17-19

MAKE A CHANGE
*Proverbs 30:32
Romans 11:20b; 12:3, 10;
15:1-3
1 Corinthians 10:24
Philippians 2:3-5
James 2:8
3 John 1:11

BIBLICAL EXAMPLES
*Isaiah 14:13-15
Matthew 20:25-28
Luke 9:23-25
Philippians 2:6-8

PRAYER
*Psalm 139:23-24

SELF-CONTROL

GOD'S PERSPECTIVE
*Proverbs 14:29; 16:32; 18:2;
25:28; 29:11
Matthew 5:38-41
Mark 10:42-45
1 Corinthians 14:32
Galatians 5:22-23
Titus 1:7-9

GOD'S PROMISES
1 Corinthians 15:58
2 Corinthians 6:4-10
2 Timothy 1:7

MAKE A CHANGE
2 Corinthians 10:5
Colossians 3:5
2 Timothy 1:7
Titus 2:1-6
1 Peter 1:13; 2:11; 5:3, 5
2 Peter 1:5-6

BIBLICAL EXAMPLES
1 Corinthians 9:25-27

SELF-DISCIPLINE

GOD'S PERSPECTIVE
1 Corinthians 6:12; 10:23
2 Timothy 2:5
Hebrews 3:12-13; 12:1-2, 15
2 Peter 2:21
Revelation 3:2

GOD'S PROMISES
Romans 8:13
2 Corinthians 6:4-10
Philippians 1:6

MAKE A CHANGE
*Deuteronomy 4:9

Luke 13:24
Romans 12:10, 11, 13
Colossians 3:5

BIBLICAL EXAMPLES
*Job 2:9-10
*Daniel 10:3, 19
1 Corinthians 8:13; 9:24-27

SELF-ESTEEM
(See self-image)

SELF-IMAGE

GOD'S PERSPECTIVE
*Genesis 1:26-27
*Psalm 8:4-5
*Proverbs 16:18-19; 25:27;
26:12
*Isaiah 45:6
John 3:16-21
2 Corinthians 3:5; 4:7; 12:9
2 Timothy 3:1-2

GOD'S PROMISES
Ephesians 1:3-12

MAKE A CHANGE
*Proverbs 3:5-7
Luke 9:23
Romans 12:3
1 Corinthians 1:26-31; 4:6-7
Philippians 2:31
1 Peter 2:9

BIBLICAL EXAMPLES
*Exodus 3:11-12
*1 Samuel 15:17
2 Corinthians 1:9
Philippians 2:5-8

PRAYER
*Psalm 115:1
Philippians 4:13

SELF-PITY

GOD'S PERSPECTIVE
*Psalm 73:2-3, 16-17
*Proverbs 12:25; 15:13; 17:22
2 Corinthians 2:7-8, 10
Hebrews 12:12-15

GOD'S PROMISES
John 14:1

MAKE A CHANGE
*Psalm 42:5; 43:5; 73:28
1 Peter 1:13

BIBLICAL EXAMPLES
*Job 2:10; 19:25-26
*Lamentations 3:17-26
*Jonah 4:8-11

PRAYER
*Psalm 19:14; 63:4;
69:20, 29-30; 71:14

SERVING THE LORD

GOD'S PERSPECTIVE
*Deuteronomy 10:12; 13:4
Matthew 4:10; 6:24; 20:27-28
Romans 12:1-2
1 Corinthians 7:22
Galatians 1:10
Ephesians 6:6

GOD'S PROMISES
John 12:26
Ephesians 4:12-13
Colossians 3:23-24

MAKE A CHANGE
*1 Samuel 12:24
*Psalm 100:2
Romans 14:18-19

Colossians 4:17
1 Timothy 4:6
2 Timothy 4:5
1 Peter 4:11

BIBLICAL EXAMPLES
*Joshua 24:15b, 23-24
*1 Chronicles 28:8
1 Timothy 1:12

SEX LIFE

GOD'S PERSPECTIVE
*Genesis 1:27-28; 2:24-25
1 Corinthians 6:9-11; 7:2-5
Ephesians 5:5-7
Colossians 3:5-7
Hebrews 13:4
Revelation 22:14-15

GOD'S PROMISES
*Psalm 128:3
*Proverbs 18:22; 19:14
1 Corinthians 10:13

MAKE A CHANGE
*Proverbs 5:3-9, 18-20
*Ecclesiastes 9:9
*Malachi 2:15
Acts 15:28-29
Ephesians 5:28, 33

BIBLICAL EXAMPLES
*Genesis 2:22; 4:1, 17; 16:4;
29:23
*Ruth 4:13
*2 Samuel 12:24

SEXUAL IMMORALITY

GOD'S PERSPECTIVE
*Genesis 2:24
*Exodus 20:14
*Leviticus 20:10
*Deuteronomy 5:18
*Proverbs 2:16-19
Matthew 5:27-28; 15:19-20
Romans 1:18, 22, 24, 26-29, 32
1 Corinthians 6:13b, 16
Galatians 5:19-21
1 Thessalonians 4:3-8
Hebrews 13:4
James 1:13-14

MAKE A CHANGE
*Proverbs 5:1-5, 8-9, 15-23;
6:23-29; 7:1-5, 24-27
Romans 6:12-13; 12:1-2, 13:14
1 Corinthians 6:18-20
Colossians 3:5-7
2 Timothy 2:22
1 Peter 2:11
1 John 2:15-16

BIBLICAL EXAMPLES
*Genesis 39:12
1 Corinthians 6:15-17

SIN

GOD'S PERSPECTIVE
*Genesis 4:7
*Numbers 32:23
*Psalm 14:2-3; 51:5; 53:2-3
*Proverbs 20:9
*Ecclesiastes 7:20
*Isaiah 64:6
*Ezekiel 18:4
Matthew 5:17-19, 48
Romans 3:23; 5:20;
6:1-2, 23; 8:1
1 Corinthians 6:9-10
Galatians 3:10-13; 5:19-21
Hebrews 10:4, 8-10; 12:9
1 John 1:8-10; 3:4, 9
Revelation 1:5

GOD'S PROMISES
*Proverbs 28:13
*Isaiah 1:18; 43:25; 44:22
*Jeremiah 31:34
*Micah 7:18-19
Acts 13:38; 26:18
Romans 5:8
1 Corinthians 15:57
Galatians 3:22
Ephesians 1:7
Colossians 1:14
1 Peter 3:18
1 John 1:7-9; 4:10

MAKE A CHANGE
John 5:14; 8:10-12
Romans 6:13
Colossians 3:5-6

BIBLICAL EXAMPLES
*Genesis 6:5
John 1:29
1 Corinthians 15:3
Galatians 1:4

PRAYER
*Psalm 32:3-4; 51:2, 4, 7

SINGLENESS

GOD'S PERSPECTIVE
*Psalm 101:6
*Isaiah 41:10; 54:5, 10; 56:3-5

GOD'S PROMISES
*Deuteronomy 31:6
*Nehemiah 8:10b
*Psalm 37:4, 37; 46:1
*Joel 2:26
Matthew 19:12

MAKE A CHANGE
2 Corinthians 13:11
Hebrews 13:5
1 Peter 5:7

BIBLICAL EXAMPLES
1 Corinthians 7:7-9, 32-35

SLEEP

GOD'S PERSPECTIVE
*Leviticus 26:6
*Job 35:10
*Psalm 3:5
*Isaiah 26:3
Matthew 11:28-30
John 16:33
1 John 4:18-19

GOD'S PROMISES
*Psalm 121:3; 127:2
*Proverbs 3:21-24; 18:10
1 Peter 5:7

MAKE A CHANGE
*Psalm 4:4; 63:5-6; 77:6; 119:48

BIBLICAL EXAMPLES
*Genesis 2:21; 28:11, 16
*Psalm 6:6-9
*Daniel 2:1; 6:18
Mark 1:35
Luke 6:12

PRAYER
*Psalm 4:8

SMOKING

GOD'S PERSPECTIVE
*Genesis 2:7
*Exodus 20:3, 5
*Deuteronomy 5:6-7, 9-10
*Job 33:4
Romans 6:6
1 Corinthians 2:5; 3:16-17
Galatians 2:20

2 Timothy 2:26
2 Peter 2:19
1 John 2:14

GOD'S PROMISES
1 Corinthians 10:13
2 Corinthians 7:1
Galatians 6:7-8

MAKE A CHANGE
*Psalm 119:9-11
John 8:34, 36
Romans 12:1-2; 13:14
1 Corinthians 6:12, 19-20
Galatians 5:13, 24-25
2 Timothy 3:5
Hebrews 12:1
1 Peter 2:16

BIBLICAL EXAMPLES
1 Corinthians 9:24-27

PRAYER
*Psalm 119:37

SORROW

GOD'S PERSPECTIVE
*Isaiah 35:10; 53:3-4
*Lamentations 3:32-33
Matthew 5:4
John 14:1-3
2 Corinthians 1:3-4
Hebrews 4:15; 12:2

GOD'S PROMISES
*Psalm 30:5; 34:18; 126:5-6
John 16:20, 22
Revelation 21:4

MAKE A CHANGE
*Ecclesiastes 7:2-3
Matthew 11:28-29
1 Thessalonians 4:13

BIBLICAL EXAMPLES
*Job 1:13-22
Luke 19:41
John 11:32-33, 35

PRAYER
*Psalm 73:23-26; 119:49-50

SPIRITUAL DOUBTS

GOD'S PERSPECTIVE
*Job 34:10-12
*Psalm 14:1
*Proverbs 24:10
Matthew 14:31
John 1:12-13
Philippians 4:13
1 Timothy 2:8

GOD'S PROMISES
*Psalm 119:89-90
Mark 11:23
Romans 8:28, 38-39
Hebrews 11:6

MAKE A CHANGE
*Psalm 73:1-3
Mark 5:36
James 1:5-8
1 Peter 4:19

BIBLICAL EXAMPLES
*Genesis 3:1-4, 13
*Job 1:22; 2:10
*Jeremiah 12:1
Matthew 14:29-33; 28:17
Mark 9:24
John 20:27

Galatians 6:1
Philippians 4:13
1 Timothy 6:9-10
Hebrews 2:18; 4:15-16
2 Peter 2:9
1 John 2:14

GOD'S PROMISES
*Proverbs 28:13
1 Corinthians 10:12-13
James 1:12-15

MAKE A CHANGE
*Proverbs 1:10
Romans 6:11
Ephesians 6:10-18
2 Timothy 2:3-5
James 4:7
1 Peter 5:8-9

BIBLICAL EXAMPLES
*Genesis 39:10-12
Matthew 4:1-10

PRAYER
*Psalm 139:23-24
Matthew 6:13

TERMINAL ILLNESS

GOD'S PERSPECTIVE
*Psalm 116:15
*Proverbs 13:42
*Isaiah 57:1
John 11:4
1 Corinthians 15:54
2 Corinthians 5:1-2, 6, 8; 12:9
Philippians 1:21, 23; 2:27

GOD'S PROMISES
*Isaiah 26:19
*Daniel 12:2
*Hosea 13:14
John 5:28-29; 14:1-3
Acts 24:15
Romans 5:3-5; 8:38-39; 14:7-8
1 Corinthians 15:20-22, 51-54
Colossians 3:4
1 Thessalonians 4:13-14; 5:10
Hebrews 2:14-15
Revelation 14:13

MAKE A CHANGE
1 Thessalonians 5:16-18

BIBLICAL EXAMPLES
*2 Kings 13:14
*Job 19:27
John 11:21-26

PRAYER
*Psalm 23:4; 73:23-26

THANKFULNESS

GOD'S PERSPECTIVE
*Psalm 50:14; 95:2; 105:1; 106:1
Romans 1:18, 21
1 Corinthians 15:57
2 Corinthians 2:14; 9:15

GOD'S PROMISES
*1 Chronicles 16:8, 34
*Psalm 100:1-5

MAKE A CHANGE
Ephesians 5:18-21
Colossians 3:15
1 Thessalonians 5:18
Hebrews 13:15

BIBLICAL EXAMPLES
*Ezra 3:11
*Daniel 6:10
Luke 17:12-19

PRAYER
*Psalm 34:1; 79:13
Revelation 7:12; 11:17

THEFT (SEE STEALING)

THOUGHTS

GOD'S PERSPECTIVE
*Genesis 6:5
*Psalm 10:4; 94:11
*Proverbs 23:7
*Isaiah 55:8-9; 59:7; 65:2
*Jeremiah 4:14
Romans 1:21; 8:6-7
1 Corinthians 2:16
2 Corinthians 10:4-6
Titus 1:15
Hebrews 4:12

GOD'S PROMISES
*Psalm 1:1-2
*Isaiah 26:3

MAKE A CHANGE
*Psalm 104:34
*Proverbs 4:23; 16:3
*Jeremiah 4:14
Romans 7:25; 15:6
Philippians 4:8
Colossians 3:1-2
1 Peter 1:13

BIBLICAL EXAMPLES
Romans 1:28-32

PRAYER
*Psalm 19:12; 51:2; 139:23-24

TITHE/TITHING

GOD'S PERSPECTIVE
*Leviticus 27:30-32
*Numbers 18:26
*Deuteronomy 26:12-13

GOD'S PROMISES
*Proverbs 3:9-10
*Malachi 3:8, 10
2 Corinthians 9:6-8

MAKE A CHANGE
Matthew 6:1-4; 23:23
Luke 6:38
1 Corinthians 15:58-16:2

BIBLICAL EXAMPLES
*Genesis 14:18-20; 28:20-22
*2 Samuel 8:11
*2 Chronicles 31:5-6
Matthew 6:1-4; 23:23
Mark 10:17-22
Hebrews 7:1-2

TONGUES

GOD'S PERSPECTIVE
*Isaiah 28:11-12
Mark 16:15-17
1 Corinthians 12:7-11;
14:2-6, 13-15, 22-25, 39-40

GOD'S PROMISES
Mark 16:7
Jude 20-21

MAKE A CHANGE
1 Corinthians 13:1

BIBLICAL EXAMPLES
Acts 2:1-11; 10:45-46; 19:6

TRAINING CHILDREN

GOD'S PERSPECTIVE
*Genesis 18:19
*Exodus 13:8
*Deuteronomy 4:9; 6:6-7;
11:18-19

*1 Samuel 3:13
*Psalm 34:11; 78:4-6
*Proverbs 13:24; 23:15, 24-25;
29:15
*Isaiah 38:19

GOD'S PROMISES
*Proverbs 22:6; 29:17

MAKE A CHANGE
*Proverbs 1:8
Ephesians 5:1; 6:4
Colossians 3:21

BIBLICAL EXAMPLES
2 Timothy 1:5; 3:15

TRIALS, TRIBULATIONS

GOD'S PERSPECTIVE
*Deuteronomy 8:2-3; 13:3;
32:11-12
*Proverbs 17:3; 25:4
*Jeremiah 17:9-10
*Malachi 3:2b
John 2:25

GOD'S PROMISES
*Zechariah 13:9
*Malachi 3:3
John 16:33
1 Corinthians 10:13
James 1:3
1 Peter 1:3-7

MAKE A CHANGE
James 4:10
1 Peter 4:12-13

BIBLICAL EXAMPLES
*Exodus 19:4
2 Corinthians 12:7-10

PRAYER
*Psalm 26:2; 66:10

TRINITY

GOD'S PERSPECTIVE
*Genesis 1:1-2, 26
*Deuteronomy 6:4
Ephesians 4:4, 6
1 Timothy 3:16

GOD'S PROMISES
John 14:16-17; 15:26

BIBLICAL EXAMPLES
*Genesis 19:24
*Psalm 110:1
*Jeremiah 50:40
*Amos 4:11
Matthew 3:16-17
Hebrews 1:9

TRUST, FAITH IN GOD

GOD'S PERSPECTIVE
*Deuteronomy 32:4
*Psalm 91:1-2; 112:7; 119:41-42
*Proverbs 16:20

GOD'S PROMISES
*Joshua 1:9
*Psalm 27:8; 13-14; 40:4; 125:1
*Isaiah 26:3-4; 40:31; 41:10
*Lamentations 3:22-24, 32
*Nahum 1:7
Romans 8:28

MAKE A CHANGE
*Psalm 37:3-5; 50:15
*Proverbs 3:5-6
John 14:1
Hebrews 10:39
1 Peter 4:19

BIBLICAL EXAMPLES
*Isaiah 31:1
Matthew 8:23-26; 14:31
Romans 4:3
Hebrews 11:17-19, 24-27
James 2:21-26

PRAYER
*1 Chronicles 29:11-12
*Psalm 57:1
2 Corinthians 1:9

TRUTH

GOD'S PERSPECTIVE
*Deuteronomy 32:4
*Psalm 119:142, 160
Matthew 7:13-15
John 1:14; 3:33; 5:32; 8:14-16,
26, 31-32; 14:6; 16:13; 17:3;
18:37; 19:35
Romans 3:4
Hebrews 6:18
1 John 4:5-6; 5:6, 20
Revelation 3:7

GODS' PROMISES
John 8:32; 16:13

MAKE A CHANGE
Ephesians 4:25
2 Timothy 2:15
1 Peter 1:22

BIBLICAL EXAMPLES
Acts 26:25
1 John 2:20, 21

PRAYER
*Psalm 25:5; 26:3; 31:5; 33:4

TELLING THE TRUTH
(SEE LYING)

U

UNBELIEVER

GOD'S PERSPECTIVE
*Genesis 1:6-8, 14-15
*Psalm 19:1-4; 33:6; 53:1
*Proverbs 1:7; 9:10
*Isaiah 40:26
*Jeremiah 10:12
*Micah 6:8
John 15:22, 24
Acts 17:26-28
Romans 1:18-23
Colossians 1:14-18
Hebrews 11:6
2 Peter 3:3-9
Revelation 21:8

GOD'S PROMISES
*Ecclesiastes 3:11
*Jeremiah 29:13
John 20:30-31
1 John 4:9
Revelation 21:6

MAKE A CHANGE
*Isaiah 55:6-7
John 20:27
Romans 11:20
Hebrews 3:12; 4:6, 11; 11:3
Revelation 22:17

BIBLICAL EXAMPLES
Mark 16:4
Hebrews 11:27-29
1 Thessalonians 1:9

PRAYER
*Nehemiah 9:6
*Psalm 104:24

UNBELIEVING SPOUSE

GOD'S PERSPECTIVE
*Amos 3:3
1 Corinthians 7:12-16
2 Peter 3:9

GOD'S PROMISES
2 Corinthians 6:14-17
1 John 5:14

MAKE A CHANGE
1 Peter 3:1-4

UNFAITHFUL SPOUSE

GOD'S PERSPECTIVE
*Exodus 20:14
*Proverbs 5:15-20; 6:32
Matthew 5:28, 32
1 Corinthians 7:2
2 Corinthians 5:10
Galatians 5:19
Ephesians 5:5-6
1 Timothy 3:2, 12
Hebrews 13:4

GOD'S PROMISES
*Psalm 128:1-3
Revelation 22:14-15

MAKE A CHANGE
*Proverbs 6:25-29
1 Corinthians 6:18

BIBLICAL EXAMPLES
*2 Samuel 13:15
Matthew 19:4-9

UNITY

GOD'S PERSPECTIVE
*Proverbs 6:16-19
*Ecclesiastes 4:9-10
*Amos 3:3
John 13:35; 17:21-23
1 Corinthians 1:10; 12:12-27
Ephesians 4:1-6
Philippians 1:27
Colossians 3:14-17
Hebrews 13:1
1 Peter 3:8

GOD'S PROMISES
*Psalm 133:1-3
2 Corinthians 13:11

MAKE A CHANGE
*Psalm 122:8-9
Romans 12:16, 18; 14:19
Philippians 2:2, 5
1 Corinthians 1:10
Titus 3:10-11

BIBLICAL EXAMPLES
*Genesis 13:8
Philippians 4:2, 5

PRAYER
Romans 15:5-7

UNSELFISHNESS

GOD'S PERSPECTIVE
*Deuteronomy 15:7-8
*Proverbs 19:17; 21:13
*Isaiah 58:7
*Zechariah 7:9
John 3:16; 6:38
Romans 5:8
2 Corinthians 8:9
Galatians 2:20
James 4:1-3
1 John 4:9-10, 21

GOD'S PROMISES
*Psalm 41:1
*Proverbs 11:25; 22:9

*Isaiah 58:10
Hebrews 6:10

MAKE A CHANGE
*Deuteronomy 15:10
*Isaiah 1:17
Matthew 5:42
Luke 6:38
John 13:34
Romans 12:10-13; 15:1-2
Galatians 2:20; 6:2, 10
Philippians 2:3-4, 5-8
Hebrews 13:2-3
James 2:15-16
1 John 3:16; 4:21

BIBLICAL EXAMPLES
*Genesis 13:8-9
*Job 31:16-22
Matthew 20:26-28; 25:37-40
Mark 8:34; 10:45
Romans 8:32
1 John 4:9-10

V

VENGEANCE (SEE REVENGE)

W

WAITING ON THE LORD

GOD'S PERSPECTIVE
*Psalm 33:20-21; 40:1;
46:10; 62:1-2, 5; 25:9; 64:4
Romans 8:25

GOD'S PROMISES
*Psalm 27:14; 50:15; 30:18;
40:28-31; 64:4
*Lamentations 3:25-26
*Micah 7:7

MAKE A CHANGE
*Psalm 37:9, 34
*Proverbs 3:5-6; 20:22
*Hosea 12:6
Philippians 4:6-7
Hebrews 4:14-16
James 5:7-8

BIBLICAL EXAMPLES
*Psalm 52:6-9
Mark 15:43

PRAYER
*Psalm 25:1-5; 39:4-7; 130:5

WAR

GOD'S PERSPECTIVE
*Proverbs 15:1
*Isaiah 2:4
Matthew 5:9; 24:6
Luke 10:17-20
Romans 5:1; 7:14-25; 13:1-2
1 Timothy 2:1-2
James 4:1-2

GOD'S PROMISES
*Isaiah 55:6-7
Revelation 21:4

MAKE A CHANGE
*Psalm 34:14
Romans 12:18
1 Thessalonians 5:15
1 Peter 2:13-14

BIBLICAL EXAMPLES
*Genesis 4:2-8
*Isaiah 14:12-14
Revelation 12:3-9

WARNINGS

GOD'S PERSPECTIVE
*Genesis 6:3

*Proverbs 12:25
*Habakkuk 2:4; 3:17-19
Matthew 6:25-34
1 John 4:18-19

GOD'S PROMISES
*Psalm 46:1; 55:22
*Proverbs 12:25
*Jeremiah 17:7-8
John 14:27
Romans 8:28; 15:13
2 Thessalonians 3:16

MAKE A CHANGE
*Psalm 37:7; 62:1-2, 8
*Proverbs 3:5-6
John 14:1
Philippians 4:6-7
1 Peter 5:6-7

BIBLICAL EXAMPLES
Luke 10:41-42; 12:22-23, 27-31

PRAYER
*Psalm 42:5-6; 56:3
Matthew 6:11

Y

YOUTH

GOD'S PERSPECTIVE
*Exodus 20:12
*Psalm 119:9
*Proverbs 3:1-4; 20:11
*Ecclesiastes 11:9; 12:1
*Jeremiah 1:5-7
Ephesians 6:1-3
Colossians 3:20

GOD'S PROMISES
*Proverbs 1:8-9; 2:1-11

MAKE A CHANGE
*Proverbs 4:1-4
*Ecclesiastes 11:9-10
1 Timothy 4:12
2 Timothy 2:22
Titus 2:6

BIBLICAL EXAMPLES
*Genesis 39:2, 6-10
*2 Kings 22:1-2
*Psalm 27:7
*Proverbs 7:7
*Daniel 1:8-9; 3:16-18
Luke 2:40, 51-52
1 John 2:14

PRAYER
*Psalm 27:7; 71:17

Z

ZEAL

GOD'S PERSPECTIVE
*Psalm 69:9
*Jeremiah 48:10
Romans 10:2
Philippians 3:6
Colossians 3:23-25
Titus 2:14

GOD'S PROMISES
*2 Chronicles 31:21
Colossians 3:4

MAKE A CHANGE
*Psalm 119:106
*Ecclesiastes 9:10
*Hosea 14:9
Romans 12:8, 11
1 Corinthians 14:12
Philippians 3:14

2 Timothy 2:22
Revelation 3:19

BIBLICAL EXAMPLES
*Isaiah 59:17
*Jeremiah 3:10-13
Acts 5:1-11; 22:1-8, 10
2 Corinthians 7:11

PRAYER
*Psalm 119:10-12

ZERO TOLERANCE

GOD'S PERSPECTIVE
*Genesis 4:7
*Exodus 17:16
*Proverbs 25:28
Matthew 5:29-30
John 3:3-6, 16; 4:24
Romans 5:12; 6:16, 23
Galatians 5:17

GOD'S PROMISES
*Numbers 22:33
*Joshua 1:3
Romans 8:6
2 Corinthians 5:17

MAKE A CHANGE
*Exodus 23:32-33
Romans 6:6, 11-13; 8:8,
12-13; 13:14
1 Corinthians 6:19-20; 9:27
Galatians 2:20; 5:16-17, 24-25
Ephesians 4:21-24
Colossians 3:5-10
1 Peter 2:11
1 John 2:15-17

BIBLICAL EXAMPLES
*Genesis 3:6-7
*Exodus 17:13-14
*Deuteronomy 7:1-2; 25:17-19
*1 Samuel 15:13-23

PRAYER
*1 Kings 3:9
*Psalm 139:23-24
Luke 18:13
Jude 23
Revelation 3:4